BIRDS OF PREY OF THE WORLD

Halftone silhouettes and maps by Shelly Grossman
Line Drawings by Jo McManus

Bonanza Books • New York

BIRDS OF PREY OF THE WORLD

BY MARY LOUISE GROSSMAN
AND JOHN HAMLET
PHOTOGRAPHED BY SHELLY GROSSMAN

This edition is published by Bonanza Books, distributed by Crown Publishers, Inc.,
225 Park Avenue South, New York, New York 10003,
by arrangement with Clarkson N. Potter, Inc.
Printed and Bound in Spain
Designed by Shelly Grossman

Library of Congress Cataloging-in-Publication Data

Grossman, Mary Louise.
Birds of prey of the world.

Reprint. Originally published: New York : C.N. Potter, 1964.
Bibliography: p.
Includes index.
1. Birds of prey. I. Hamlet, John N. II. Title.
QL696.F3G76 1988 598'.91 87-32639
ISBN 0-517-06788-9

n m l k j i h g

Dedicated to Keith and Julie

Red-tailed Hawk.

TABLE OF CONTENTS

Part I

Part II

ACKNOWLEDGMENTS

The task of preparing the text and illustrations for a book of world-wide scope, which also encompasses some sixty million years of life on earth, has been possible only with the help of a great number of persons. We gratefully acknowledge the encouragement, interest, criticism, and invaluable information received during the four years that we have been completely immersed in this project.

We are especially indebted to the Bird Department of the American Museum of Natural History for work space, use of books and papers, and access to the collection of study skins; to the Chairman, Dean Amadon, for countless courtesies and for his willingness to discuss any problems in taxonomy which we brought to his door; to the late James P. Chapin for his incomparable knowledge of African species; to Eugene Eisenmann for his kind and thoughtful guidance and for specific information on Central American hawks; to E. Thomas Gilliard, on whose papers, field notes and photographs we depended in large part in describing and illustrating little-known New Guinea birds of prey; to Charles E. O'Brien and Allen O'Connell, our patient guides and mentors for the duration of the enormous and time-consuming job of checking through thousands of study skins; and to Charles Vaurie for making available his studies on the taxonomy of Palaearctic and Neotropical species.

Members of the Department of Anthropology who have been helpful are Junius B. Bird, from whom we obtained permission to photograph the Chavin temple rubbing of mythical birds of prey in the museum's special exhibit of the art of the Peruvian Andes; and Gordon Eckholm and Stanley Freed, who have been kind enough to read and comment on the sections in Chapter 2 which deal with North and Central American Indian cultures.

To staff members of the Library of the American Museum who have spent many hours supplying us with periodicals and books are tendered our appreciation and thanks for this service: Ruth Chapin, Hazel Gay, George H. Goodwin, Jr., Ilona Kunsagi, Florence Stewart, Leslie A. Taylor, and Mary V. Wissler. Rachel Nichols helped us with problems in paleontology in the Osborn Library of the Museum, and the cooperation of Marie Macdonald in the Photography Department is also gratefully acknowledged.

Various departments of the Metropolitan Museum of Art were helpful in preparing the text and selecting illustrations for Chapter 2. For their time and interest we wish to thank Brian Cook of the Classical Department, Henry Fisher of Egyptian Art, Vera Ostoia of Medieval Art, Alan Priest of the Far Eastern Department, Charles Wilkinson of the Department of the Ancient Near East; also Mildred McGill, Monica Miya, and Emma Papert in Photo Sales.

Our thanks also go to John Latham, Director of Publicity at the Brooklyn Museum of Art, who supplied us with photographs of art objects from the museum's fine Egyptian collection, to Carolyn Scoon, Assistant Curator of The New York Historical Society for permission to reproduce the Audubon Bald Eagle; to Gardner Osborn, Federal Hall Memorial Museum, for lending us a copy of *The History of the Seal of the United States;* to Amy Clampitt in the Library of The National Audubon Society for information on federal and state conservation laws; and to Robert J. Woodward for his help in securing additional bird photographs from the files of The National Audubon Society.

For our historical survey in Chapter 2 we have relied mainly on the following books: *Ancient Egyptian Religion,* by Jaroslav Cerný; *The Origin of Heraldry in Europe,* by Calvin Kephart; *The Gods of the Greeks,*

The Golden Eagle.

by Carl Kerenyi; Sylvanus G. Morley's *The Ancient Maya* (including a page from the *Codex Dresdensis*); Alice Parmelee's *All the Birds of the Bible;* Henry N. Paul's *The Royal Play of Macbeth;* Dorothy Margaret Stuart's *A Book of Birds and Beasts;* Florence Waterbury's *Bird Deities in China; Birds and Men* by Robert Henry Welker; William Willetts' *Chinese Art;* and the Casey A. Wood and F. Marjorie Fyfe translation of Frederick II's *The Art of Falconry.*

The section on the cultural significance of Andean birds of prey is based on information supplied by John H. Rowe, Department of Anthropology, University of California, and includes his translation of a Huarochirí myth. For information on Mexican birds of prey we are indebted to Guy Stresser-Pèan, Mission Archéologique et Ethnologique Française au Mexique.

Hawks, Owls and Wildlife, by John J. and Frank C. Craighead, a study of the year-round raptor and prey populations in Michigan and Wyoming test areas, has contributed much to our understanding of the role of raptors in the ecology of living things throughout the North Temperate Zone.

To these authors, and to others acknowledged elsewhere—in the text, captions, or Bibliography, we are indebted for the use of data and interpretive material.

For the courtesy and cooperation extended to us while photographing birds of prey at the National Zoological Park, Smithsonian Institution, we are most grateful to T. H. Reed, Director, and J. Lear Grimmer, Associate Director, long-time friends of John Hamlet. We also wish to thank Bill Widman, Senior Keeper of Birds at the National Zoo, and his assistant, Marion Barker, for their help.

We have appreciated the courtesy and interest shown by William G. Conway, Director of the New York Zoological Park, in our project, and wish to thank him for allowing us to photograph the Zoological Park's excellent collection of birds of prey over the past four years. We are also grateful for the help of James Bardsley, Joe Bell, Pat Clark, and Bob Eddington in handling the birds; and for the use of Zoological Park photographs in Part II.

We also wish to thank James Fowler for allowing us to photograph his African hawks and eagles, and for information on the Harpy Eagle in British Guiana; Eric Hosking for his photographs of European birds of prey; and Roger Tory Peterson for his enthusiasm and encouragement, for contributing photographs, and for permission to use the technique of silhouettes, which he has so successfully employed in his Field Guides, as a means of identifying the diurnal hawklike birds.

The job of drawing (often rare and little-known) birds, as they must appear in life, from study skins, and the few available photographs, fell to Jo McManus. We wish to thank her for the many fine portraits of hawks and owls in Part II which have made it possible for us to illustrate every genus of the birds of prey; for the artist's conception of diurnal and nocturnal predation in Chapter 3 of Part I; and for the line drawings included in the Geological Time Chart.

In the Chart, *Pseudosuchus* was based on the *Ornithosuchus* of Gerhard Heilmann; and *Neocathartes* on an illustration by Walter A. Weber. Other fossil birds were drawn from reconstructions by various artists.

Color samples have been reproduced photographically in the Color Key through the courtesy of Blanche R. Bellamy, Manager of The Munsell Color Company. These colors, taken from the original Munsell Charts, are intended as illustrations for color names used in our plumage descriptions throughout Part II, not as Munsell Standards for the notations represented.

We especially wish to thank those who have taken the time to review the manuscript: Pierce Brodkorb, Department of Biology, University of Florida, for his help with paleontology; George A. Clark, Jr., New York University, for careful checking of Part II and preparation of the Bibliography; Mrs. Joan Gordan, for preparation of the Index; Heinz Meng, Department of Biology, State Teachers College, New Paltz, New York, for reading Chapter 4 and sections of Part II, especially those on the accipiters and buteos, for permission to photograph his Red-tailed Hawk, Peregrine, Goshawk, and Gyrfalcon, appearing in Part II, and for contributing a number of photographs from his own file; and to Charles Wharton, Department of Biology, Georgia State College, who was more than a friend and adviser during the preparation of Chapters 3, 4, and 5.

In conclusion, thanks are also due John Bull, of the American Museum of Natural History, who read the manuscript in its entirety and also made many helpful suggestions while the work was in progress.

THE AUTHORS

NEW YORK CITY

part 1

INTRODUCTION

It could perhaps be said that this book really started with a special, and in these days, exceptional experience—with the hawk on the glove. As a boy on a South Dakota ranch, John Hamlet trained a Golden Eagle. Later, through his many years with the United States Fish and Wildlife Service, he became a skilled master falconer and a shrewd observer of birds of prey in their natural habitats. Our project is the outgrowth of my early acquaintance with John during my Midwestern childhood, and the renewal of that friendship nearly seven years ago, when I introduced my photographer husband to him.

In the spring of 1956 Shelly and I walked through the gateway of a tourist attraction near Ocala, Florida, called "Birds of Prey" where more than one hundred species of predatory birds had been assembled by John Hamlet. In this mews were vultures from Africa and South America, hawks and owls of the North Temperate Zone wood lots, and eagles of the rain forest. They were natural subjects for portraits and we came back in the next two years to add new faces to our scrapbook as John acquired more birds. We not only photographed them, but also talked about them, often far into the night. Out of these midnight sessions emerged an idea for a book. Here, with so many birds available from familiar and exotic parts of the world, was an opportunity to illustrate photographically how different species hunt, their modes of flight, and certain external features, such as the facial discs of owls and the bare faces and crops of vultures.

John and Shelly trained the birds for the hunting sequences and flight studies. Because of the number handled in relatively short periods of time, some were worked with a fine monofilament line, or creance, attached to their legs. This line did not hinder their performance and allowed Shelly complete freedom to record the action as many times as he wanted. Portraits of perching birds were made in settings approximating as closely as possible their natural habitats.

As time went on, our involvement was not only with the captive hawk, but also with birds of prey free in the world of nature . . . with a pair of Red-shouldered Hawks circling over their woodland territory and establishing boundaries in spring . . . with the "hoot" owl whose voice we could hear on a summer night, but whose form was indefinite, merging with the shadows. We could not consider one without the other, for when the hawk settles on its roost at nightfall the owl shakes its feathers and becomes alert to the same sounds that have drawn the attention of the diurnal hunter, perhaps the splash of a frog on the otherwise silent surface of a pool. The hawk and the owl belong to morphologically diverse orders, and do not see, or call, or hunt alike. Yet both have strong feet that seize and kill, and hooked beaks to dissect their food. And in the eyes of the comparatively new science of ecology, they are confederates—predators with complementary functions, both policemen of the habitat in which they live.

And so this book, which was essentially visual in concept, was expanded to the proportions of a photographic and text essay viewing the winged predators from many angles. What were their origins? How has man looked upon them through his social, religious, and economic evolution on earth? How are the life histories of birds of prey a reflection of different habitats and climates and of the "availability" and "vulnerability" of necessarily larger populations of food animals? What effect do their activities have on these populations? How do they function? Have specializations in structure and habits been disadvantageous to some and advantageous to others? And finally, what is their role in the now extensive semiwilderness that man has come to consider his domain?

In Part I we attempt to clarify these questions and many more, and to suggest some answers. If we have depended heavily upon the experience and insight of one man, especially in Chapters 3, 4, and 5, we have also made every effort to back up our viewpoint with as much evidence as we have been able to find by consulting standard works and reading literally thousands of accounts in ornithological journals. We do not claim to have read everything, or to have found solutions to all the problems that have been raised in these pages. In the five chapters of Part I there are new ideas, and old ones are frequently set in a new perspective. We caution the reader that, in a broad synthesis such as this, footnotes and, with few exceptions, in-text references must be sacrificed to continuity. Often the basis for an idea may be found in a scientific study which we have set down in more detail in the *Habits* sections of the various bird groups which comprise Part II. These are intended to be supplementary references, especially on such widespread genera as the accipiters, buteos, and falcons. It will be immediately apparent that there are many blank spaces in our knowledge of the habits of tropical species. Some rain-forest hawks and owls have only rarely been collected, and less frequently observed, in nature. We are necessarily brief in our accounts of these birds, both in Parts I and II.

As an additional aid to the scientific reader we have supplied as complete a Bibliography on the birds of prey as possible. If a reference cannot be traced to one of the standard bird guides, it may be found in an article or manuscript under the scientific name (Latinized binomial) of the species.

In regard to the many opinions expressed in Part I of this book which are of an intuitive nature, we can only say that we welcome criticism and hope, in fact, to stimulate research on problems that are far from solved. The predatory birds have been victims of much misinformation and misunderstanding in the past.

We have attempted to give the hawks and owls a "fair deal" by dispelling out-of-date notions and prejudices and encouraging thoughtful observation. So little "conservation" has been practiced to date that our consulting ecologist suggested changing the title of Chapter 5 to "Man's Relentless War on Birds of Prey." An occasional hopeful incident does occur. We recall a certain Florida farmer who refused to allow Burrowing Owls to be trapped on his property because he rightly observed that their chief prey was a tiny field mouse which dug up and devoured the watermelon seeds he had planted. However, it is unfortunate that this man is still so much in the minority. The normal reaction to any hawk or owl is to reach for the nearest firearm. There is, we feel, no greater testimony to man's misunderstanding of nature than a row of hawks impaled, along with a crow or two, on some barbed wire fence.

MARY LOUISE GROSSMAN

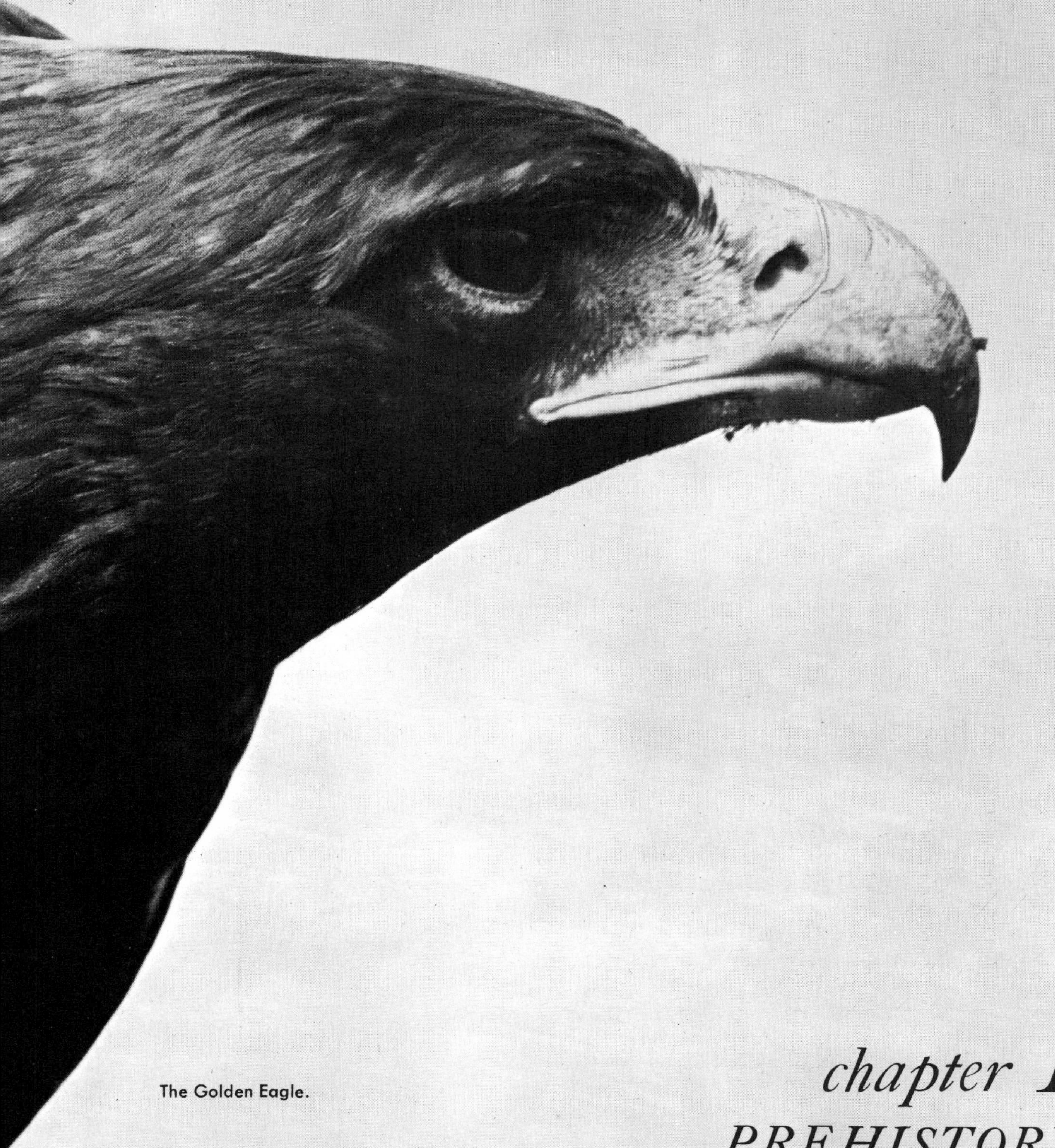

The Golden Eagle.

chapter 1
PREHISTORY

Thirty-six million years ago no man lived to recognize the now familiar "V" of vulture wings buoyant on lazy, warm air currents overhead; to trace the course of a Golden Eagle spiraling upward for the beginning of its broad-winged, straight-out glide; or to pause, listen, and perhaps wonder about the growlings and chucklings of the Great Horned Owl, concealed in daylight hours within the deep forest. Yet we know from a scattering of fossil finds that primitive types of these birds existed at the dawn of the Cenozoic era, differing only in minor points of structure and by their vast removal from us in geological time.

Only two years after the publication of *The Origin of Species* in 1859 the link between reptiles and birds was uncovered in the Solnhofen limestone of a quarry at Langenaltheim, Bavaria. Estimated to be 138 million years old, the *Archaeopteryx* imprint (*Archaeo* = ancient + *pteryx* = wing) described an agile, airborne creature with teeth and a long reptilian tail; the body and three-fingered wings and tail were feathered. Three skeletons, as well as this original imprint, which shows a single feather, are now known.

What type of reptile could the *Archaeopteryx* have come from? Certainly not the dinosaur, which developed too late to fit into the ancestral line of the birds. The first lizard-like birds lived during the Upper Jurassic period along the shores of shallow, salt-water lagoons with pterodactyls (flying lizards) and dinosaurs, small forerunners of titans which were to rule the partly submerged continents in the Cretaceous period, 30 to 70 million years later. All three of these ancient orders became extinct at the end of the Mesozoic era, the Age of Reptiles.

It is generally agreed now that both the birds and the dinosaurs evolved from primitive, carnivorous

The King Vulture, with its broad black-bordered wings and colorful head, painted in shades of red, yellow, and blue-gray, has been a part of the tropical American avifauna since the Pliocene.

lizards of the Triassic period—pseudosuchians in which the hind legs were longer than the front legs. In some forms, the fifth hind toe was somewhat reduced in length. When certain tree-climbing members of this group became warm-blooded, they were probably covered with scales and a few scattered feathers, the filaments of these feathers serving as an insulating layer and growing more abundant and longer as time progressed. Gerard Heilman (in *The Origin of Birds,* 1926) described the tree-climbing lizard which may have developed wings and learned to fly by jumping from branch to branch. To date we have no fossil evidence of his proavian creature, but the reconstruction was based on our knowledge of other pseudosuchians.

A quartet of possible ancestors from the Jurassic period had three claws on the elongated fingers of the hand, and so did the corresponding wing of the *Archaeopteryx.* Vestigial claws still appear on the wings of many modern birds, especially nestlings. Two claws are common in ducks and geese and the hoatzin (a primitive fowl-like bird of Amazonia which inhabits dense riverbank vegetation). Perhaps because of the nature of their habitats, the water birds and the hoatzin use these claws for clambering about in bushes until their wing quills grow in and they are able to fly. The usefulness of these claws as hooks depends on how large and curved they are, and this is extremely variable. None compare with those of *Archaeopteryx.* Wing claws, when they occur in birds of prey, are apparently non-functional, for these slow-maturing birds do not have any climbing tendencies when very young. A more prominent vestige of their reptilian ancestry is the alula, a feathered movable "thumb" which comes into play during soaring and other phases of flight.

In the early stages of its growth, the embryonic feather looks like a scale. There are many other close morphological and behavioral ties between lizards and birds, such as similarities in bone and muscle structure, the use of color in courtship displays, and the same general type of egg and embryological development, including, on the upper jaw, an egg tooth which drops off several days after it has been used by the embryo to break out of the eggshell.

The avian eyeball utilizes several features of the visual apparatus of the lizard; the eye muscles are

Feathers evolved from scales like these, on a South American lizard *(Crocodilurus lacertinus)*; and wings, from forelimbs, used for climbing.

The alula, a feathered "thumb," flares at the bend of the wing of this Red-tailed Hawk as it poises on the ground before attacking a Banded Water Snake. By spreading its wings, the bird also appears bigger to its intended victim.

From its position on the ground, the hawk leaps onto the snake's head and fastens its talons securely.

Completely mantling the snake, the hawk holds fast and begins to tear its prey. The cloudy appearance of the eyes is due to the protective nictitating membrane, which closes automatically as the hawk brings its head down in the last stage of the struggle.

striated fibers, designed for extremely rapid changes of focus, unlike the smooth fibers in the eyes of mammals. A ring, composed of from ten to eighteen overlapping platelike bones, like those of the primitive climbing and flying lizards and *Archaeopteryx,* strengthens the eyeball of modern birds. In owls and some hawks this sclerotic ring is actually a tube- or cone-shaped structure.

The pecten, a comblike organ in the back of the eye, supplies blood and also throws shadows on the retina, apparently sharpening a bird's perception of objects at a distance. The extent of the shadows is directly related to hunting habits. The most elaborate foldings are found in the eyes of hawks and diurnal insectivorous birds, and the simplest patterns, in those of nocturnal birds. This structure may explain why diurnal lizards and birds, which depend primarily on their sight for survival, are so quick to notice movement: how a chameleon can pick off an elusive fly with instant and deadly accuracy, and a Red-tailed Hawk flying above a field can detect the presence of a mouse or a snake by the slightest movement of its prey from cover.

The nictitating membrane, a "third eyelid" which blinks across from the inner corner of the eyes of lizards to keep out sand and dirt, also effectively shields the eyes of birds, whether in flight through trees and brush, or in a struggle with prey on the ground. Although the avian membrane is usually translucent, it is sometimes, like the Barred Owl's, opaquely reflecting light and probably serving as a defense mechanism for this completely nocturnal hunter.

*B*irds (class Aves) are differentiated into some twenty-nine living and six fossil orders, the name of each group ending in *-iformes,* as in Falconiformes (hawklike birds), Strigiformes (owls), etc. The hawklike birds and owls, popularly linked as diurnal and nocturnal birds of prey, are morphologically distinct, but have certain common external adaptations for capturing and feeding on a wide variety of living creatures. The two orders are virtually unique, among birds, in the raptorial habit of seizing or striking prey with the talons. In vultures, the carrion-feeding members of the Falconiformes order, the only predatory feature is the more or less hooked beak, which, together with large size, gives even the relatively weak-billed species a distinct advantage over the scavengers of other orders—gulls, ravens, and crows. Some of the orders appear to be closely related to each other—the auks to the plovers, the woodpeckers to songbirds, and the owls, in spite of their strongly predatory role in nature, to the completely insectivorous nightjars and owlet frogmouths. However, the majority seem to be without known close relatives. The orders of large flightless birds—penguins, emus, ostriches—are descendants of flying ancestors which independently adapted millions of years ago for a terrestrial or aquatic existence. These orders are small, containing few species.

Within each order, the birds of the various families with names all ending in *-idae* (Falconidae, Strigidae, etc.) show certain structural features in common—peculiarities of the skeleton, the musculature, the foot, etc.

The genus, the first category to appear in a bird's scientific name, further divides the family into smaller groups showing even closer relationships. However, genera are rather arbitrarily set up for the convenience of systematists.

Forming the second part of the scientific name, the most useful of the identifying units, the species, defines the breeding population of birds. Cross-breeding of two species, even within the same geographical area, rarely occurs, and when it does, usually results in sterile offspring. There are usually obvious physical differences between species, but a few differ mostly in behavior.

The races which make up the species replace one another geographically, and since they are all mutually fertile, interbreed where their ranges meet. Variations within species are largely selected by the environment. Races of humid areas tend to be darker, and those in dry places, lighter (Gloger's rule), whereas races of cold climates are usually larger and those of warm regions, smaller (Bergmann's rule). The differences become so slight at this lowest level of systematics that the racial name of a bird is often omitted from field guides if the range is clearly stated.

The fossil record is still so fragmentary for the class Aves that it can only suggest when and where certain types of birds developed on earth. Bird bones are hollow, fragile, and easily destroyed, and the conditions necessary to preserve them so special that only 1,600 species of birds living 10,000 or more years ago are known from their remains, whereas about 8,650 species exist today. We have no reason to suppose that the number of species was less in former ages. It may have been greater. But the

GEOLOGICAL

Eras	PRE-CAMBRIAN ERA 4,500,000,000 Years Ago	PALEOZOIC ERA 600,000,000 Years Ago	MESOZOIC				
Periods			TRIASSIC 230,000,000 Years Ago	JURASSIC 180,000,000 Years Ago	CRETACEOUS 135,000,000 Years Ago		
Epochs						PALEOCENE 63,000,000 Years Ago	EOCENE 58,000,000 Years Ago	OLIGOCENE 36,000,000 Years Ago

PSEUDOSUCHUS*

ICHTHYORNIS*

ARCHAEOPTERYX*

HESPERORNIS*

STILT VULTURE*
NEOCATHARTES*

DIATRYMA*

PROTOSTRIX OWLS*

CATHARTID VULTURES
EOCATHARTES*

BUTEO HAWKS
BUTEO

LONG-EARED OWL
ASIO

HORNED OWLS
BUBO

SECRETARY BIRD
SAGITTARIUS

BOOTED EAGLES
AQUILAVUS*

The **eras** of the Geological Time Chart represent climatic conditions which have allowed certain kinds of life to be paramount for **periods** of millions of years. These **periods** are further broken down into **epochs,** the newest of which encompass only a million or a few thousand years. The story of birds begins in the Mesozoic era, the Age of Reptiles, in which we find their lizard ancestors.

The first primitive birds lived in the late-Jurassic period. All those known from the Cretaceous are water birds (probably about 1,000 species in existence at any one time); and although a few land birds may have been living, their radiation must necessarily have followed that of the flowering plants in the subtropical or tropical forest habitats. By mid-Tertiary the grasslands were widespread, and the granivores, and consequently all of their predators, increased. The number of bird species existing during any given portion of the early Tertiary may have been 10,200; during late Tertiary and Pleistocene, 11,600.

The average length of life of an animal species has been no longer than 500,000 to 5,000,000 years—in bird species, less, as might be suspected from their high rate of metabolism. They never cross epochal boundaries, except in the case of the equivocal Pliocene-Pleistocene periods, where birds now living first appeared. However, some modern bird genera are known from the beginning of the Tertiary, and most of the types we know today were well established by the mid-Tertiary, 25 million years ago. The birds seem to have passed their peak of evolutionary development in the Pleistocene.

The repeated glacial invasions had profound effects on the vegetation and animal life of the globe, including numbers of extinctions—in birds, perhaps reaching 50 per cent. The present world avifauna, composed of about 8,650 species, appears to be on the decline.

All but the Recent figures, covering an epoch of 15,000 years, are very rough estimates. They are taken from Pierce Brodkorb's "How Many Species of Birds Have Existed?" published in 1960, in which we learn that the living and fossil birds which have been **described** total about one-half of 1 per cent of those potentially knowable.

This chart of **The Birds of Prey** since the beginning of the Tertiary cannot attempt to show the speciation of every genus of hawklike birds and owls—only the introduction of fossil progenitors and modern types, as far as known from the fragmentary record. Seen in relation to the development of the entire avifauna of the world, the birds of prey, too, had their heyday of great variety and abundance from the mid-Tertiary expansion of the grasslands to the Pleistocene. Evolutionary dead ends, such as the large extinct vultures and eagles of the Pleistocene (mentioned in the text), have been omitted, and it may very well be that some of the living genera as yet found only in the Pleistocene had a much earlier beginning.

***Extinct**

Ancestral types are represented by photographs of living genera.

TIME CHART

CENOZOIC

TERTIARY

MIOCENE

25,000,000 Years Ago

GREAT BLACK HAWK
BUTEOGALLUS

MILVINE KITES
PROMILIO*

SEA EAGLES
HALIAETUS

BARN OWLS
TYTO

BUZZARD EAGLE
GERANOAETUS

ACCIPITRINE VULTURES
NEOGYPS *

HAWK-EAGLES
PALAEASTUR *

BARRED OWL
STRIX

FALCONS
FALCO

PLIOCENE

12,000,000 Years Ago

CONDORS
VULTUR

TURKEY VULTURES
CATHARTES

KING VULTURE
SARCORAMPHUS

QUATERNARY

PLEISTOCENE

1,000,000 — 15,000 Years Ago

HARRIS HAWK
PARABUTEO

MARSH HAWKS
CIRCUS

SCREECH OWLS
OTUS

FOREST HAWKS
ACCIPITER

GRIFFON VULTURES
GYPS

HARRIER EAGLES
CIRCAETUS

CRESTED EAGLES
MORPHNUS

PIGMY OWLS
GLAUCIDIUM

BURROWING OWL
SPEOTYTO

CARRION HAWKS
CARACARA

LAMMERGEIER
GYPAETUS

FISH HAWK
PANDION

SOLITARY VULTURE
TORGOS

farther back we search, the fewer skeletons or fragments of skeletons can be found.

The Cretaceous, the period of 72 million years duration best known for colossal reptiles, also fostered a wide radiation of birds. We can guess about the variety of avian forms which must have existed on the North American continent from the remains of two very different birds preserved in the marine chalk-beds of Kansas—small, gull-like *Ichthyornis* and the toothed, flightless swimmer, *Hesperornis*. From deposits of the same age we have unearthed extinct members of the pelican and flamingo orders in Europe, and a Cretaceous grebe in Chile.

The Tertiary, the 63-million-year period of great marshes and generally warm temperatures, produced a number of flightless walking birds. Some of them were predators, related to the ancestral types of cranes and rails. Towering seven-foot *Diatrymas* wandered the flatlands of Wyoming, New Mexico, New Jersey, England, and France; and, as they gave way, after millions of years, to the big predatory mammals, a new evolutionary series of similar flightless birds, the Cariamae, replaced them. Several species of *Bathornis,* among the earliest members of the suborder, lived in the Lower Oligocene of Wyoming and neighboring states, but they were relatively small and probably never ruled the plains of North America to the same extent that their South American relatives dominated the pampas of the then isolated island continent. We know of four cariamas in the Lower Oligocene of South America, only one of them as small as *Bathornis,* and the succeeding epochs brought forth many more, culminating in the Pliocene with eight-foot *Onactornis,* a

You can see the sky through the Black Vulture's perforate nasal septum—a distinguishing feature of all the Cathartid, or American, vultures.

monster armed with a 15-inch beak which could easily eviscerate young ground sloths. After the Isthmus of Panama rose out of the sea in the Pliocene, and North American predatory mammals—pumas, jaguars, and giant dogs—streamed southward over the new land bridge, the day of the cariama as a predator was over. Survivors of the family in modern times (*Cariama* and *Chunga*) are weak-billed and omnivorous, feeding on lizards, snakes, insects, and berries.

The Cathartid, or American, vultures once existed in both hemispheres, with the earliest fossil records from the Middle Eocene of Europe and the Lower Oligocene of Colorado. They are not far removed from the primitive types of wading and swimming birds, and, like the marsh-dwelling cranes and rails, have a completely perforate nasal septum. This conspicuous hole through the beak is one of the obvious differences between Cathartid vultures and the generally stronger-billed Accipitrine or Old World vultures, which apparently developed 30 million years later in the Miocene of Europe and North America.

The two groups are anatomically diverse, but have certain common external adaptations, such as bare legs and heads, for eating carrion, and usually lack the well-developed grasping feet needed for killing and carrying live prey. Why the so-called American vultures vanished from Europe in the Oligocene and the Old World vultures became extinct in the New World within postglacial time is one of the unsolved mysteries of paleontology, but it is clear that vultures have been named according to their present separate distribution in the two hemispheres—at least since written history began.

The pink-faced Pondicherry Vulture, with its conspicuous lappets and heavy chopping beak, represents the stronger, heavier accipitrine vultures.

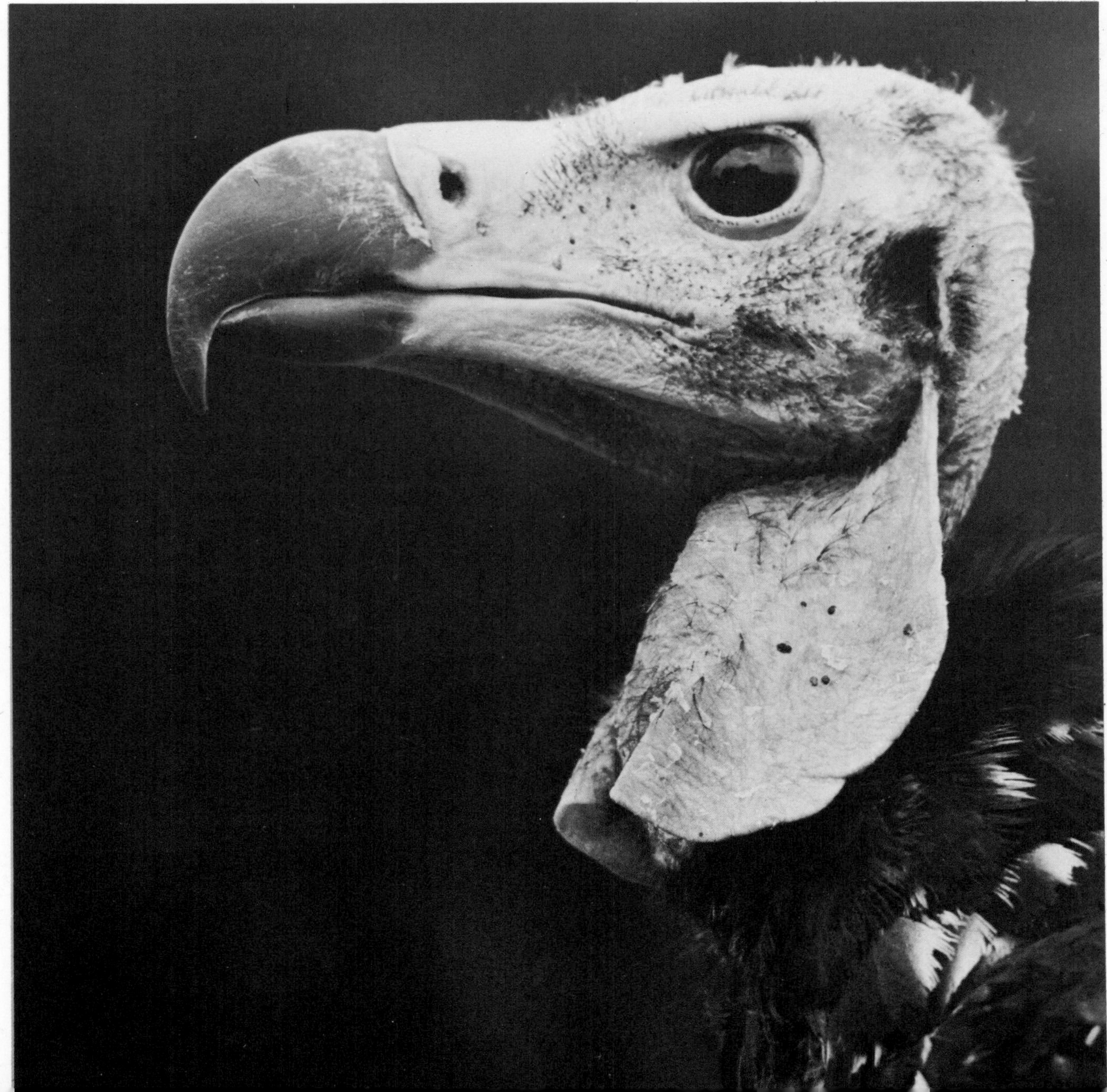

Related to the Carthartid vultures was a long-legged scavenger with relatively undeveloped wings. It could fly, but evidently lived mostly on the ground, along with other prehistoric walking birds of Wyoming. This so-called Stilt Vulture (*Neocathartes*) became extinct after the Eocene.

Protostrix owls, the precursors of typical owls (Strigidae), lived in Wyoming and probably many other places on the earth in the Eocene. Perhaps these owls, like their present-day counterparts, were equipped with special adaptations for seeing and hearing in the dark, and short fluffy feathers on which they could drift silently downward to surprise their prey. Perhaps they, too, could turn their outer toes back, so they had two talons in front and two behind, for a firmer grip on slippery objects. By Oligocene times Protostrix owls had been replaced by at least two modern genera—the eared owls, (*Asio*) and the great horned or eagle owls (*Bubo*).

Primordial eagles of the *Aquila* type, present in the Oligocene of France and North America, may not have been strong soaring birds like the modern eagles but they did have even larger feet with unusually long and powerful toes. Part of the toe of an eagle found in Kansas equals in size the corresponding element in the largest eagle of Recent times, the Monkey-eating Eagle of the Philippine Islands.

The large, slow-flying buteonine hawks or buzzards of the world, first known from the Upper Oligocene and Miocene, were probably ground-killers of small mammals, lizards, and snakes. Three fossil species of the modern *Buteo* differed from the Red-tailed, Broad-winged, and Ferruginous Rough-legged hawks of North America only in larger size.

*T*wenty plumes cascade from the head of the Secretary Bird, which is named for its imagined resemblance to a lawyer's clerk carrying bunches of quill pens behind his ears. This peculiar ground-dwelling hawk, about four feet tall, now frequents the higher and drier bush country of Africa. It lives on the open plains and near the mud huts of villages. In the Oligocene and Lower Miocene it had a wider range, at least to southern France. It hunts in pairs, or in groups of five or six, stamping snakes, rats, lizards, and locusts to death with its powerful and agile legs. The Secretary Bird resembles American carrion hawks, or caracaras, in the shape of its head and beak. These are the only birds of prey except the Cathartid vultures that have well-developed basal webs connecting three toes.

The Secretary Bird has existed, virtually unchanged, since it wandered the plains of southern Europe in the early Tertiary. Now found in Africa, it is becoming increasingly rare.—*Photographed at the National Zoological Park.*

In North America the Great Horned Owl preys on a wide variety of creatures and, in many ways, dominates the rest of the wildlife community in which it lives.

The seed-bearing plants, which are the primary food source of mice, came into prominence during the Miocene; thus mice which originally might have raised only one litter a year could easily have been raising five times that number by the end of the Miocene, 13 million years ago. With the prey multiplying at such a staggering rate, the way was prepared for the emergence of birds with more specialized hunting habits: the Common Barn Owl (*Tyto*), which can, if necessary, depend entirely on hearing to kill on the darkest nights and which specializes in hunting along the edges of the woods.

The snake-eating black hawks (*Buteogallus*) and seven kinds of buzzard-eagles ranged over the Caribbean area and North America from the Miocene to the Pleistocene. Only one of the Pleistocene Buzzard-Eagles (*Geranoaetus*) survives in South America. But three genera of large, crested eagles on this continent—*Morphnus, Harpyhaliaetus,* and *Harpia*—are other living examples of eagles which show the leg armor characteristic of the genus *Buteo* and related groups such as the black hawks, in which the front of the bare tarsus is scutellate (plated) and the back reticulate (resembling fine network).

The Great Horned Owl's method of attack is a dive, head-first, directly from a tree branch.

Proof that owls will strike any part of the target—this one finds that it's tails!—and the snake is free to battle its attacker. In this exigency both the snake and the owl could be killed.

While the owl tries to reach the snake's head, its legs become completely encoiled.

The snake rears off for another strike (above) and, buried in feathers, sinks its teeth into the owl's breast (right).

Finally the owl grabs the snake's head with its beak and proceeds to crush it.

All but dead, the snake hangs limp.

Its wings hung from exhaustion, the owl roosts on the lifeless prey like a proud hen.

Forest-dwelling hawk-eagles, found in Nebraska, and possibly many other intrepid hunters of small to medium-sized mammals, and game birds, may have ranged over all of tropical America, Africa, and Asia in the Miocene.

The early sea eagles, like the Bald Eagle of North America and Steller's Sea Eagle of northeastern Asia, frequented the seacoasts and the shores of interior rivers and lakes, wherever there were dense forests. The ancient birds were probably not ambitious predators for their apparent size and strength, living primarily on dead fish; but if this food was not available, they would take live fish, sea birds, and small mammals.

The primitive kites which left their remains in Florida and France had a weaker foot than the more predatory hawks and eagles. Modern species have a small head and a partly bare face, and the bill is nearly always narrow, but varies in shape from compressed to elongated or even sickle-shaped, as in the snail-eaters. Kites are generally high-flying birds and frequently hover or "still," apparently motionless for half a minute at a time. They often capture and eat their insect prey in mid-air. The larger Old World kites (*Milvus* and *Haliastur*) are notorious scavengers.

Miocene pigeon hawks or merlins, smaller than the modern species, must have been highly specialized aerial hunters. The members of the subfamily Falconinae are among the most efficiently designed of all the birds of the world for attaining high speeds. The Peregrine Falcon, known universally, kills by striking its victim—often a much larger game bird—out of the sky by sheer force of impact. Then, following the fall to the earth, it breaks the neck of its prey with a strong twist of its "toothed" and notched beak. Kestrels and pigmy falcons are smaller than the Peregrine and many are insectivorous. The latter belong to a separate subfamily.

The million years of the Pleistocene produced four successive glacial invasions, with intervening periods of warming during which the ice melted and retreated northward. Continents were being uplifted and world-wide heavy precipitation accompanied the formation of the ice sheets, while temperatures in the Northern Hemispheres plummeted.

An ancestor of the tropical Ornate Hawk Eagle, shown here, ranged as far north as Nebraska in the warm climate of the Miocene.

The effects of Pleistocene cold could be measured even on mountain peaks in the tropics, in the lowering of snow lines and the lengthening of glaciers. The last glaciation came to an end, according to carbon-14 dating, about 10,000 years ago. As long as the Antarctic and Greenland icecaps exist there will be some question as to whether we are living in postglacial times (the Recent Epoch) or in a fifth interglacial period which may terminate in another segment of the Ice Ages.

All modern birds of prey appear to have evolved by the Pleistocene. Large concentrations of their remains have been found in areas where conditions were unusually good for fossilizing or otherwise preserving them: in quicksand, marine sandstone, caves, and asphalt pits. Two-thirds of 114 species of birds recovered from the La Brea tar pits of Los Angeles County, California, were predators that had been drawn to the natural trap by the struggles of other creatures, only to fall prey to the bubbling pools themselves.

Some of the predatory birds that we first know from this more recent and favorable period must have had an earlier start: the snake-eating harrier-eagles; the harrier-hawks, which habitually fly very low or "quarter" the swamps, plains, and steppes like a hare hound for prey, and rest on the ground; omnivorous American caracaras which, with the exception of one tropical-forest species, are also at home on the ground; the buteo-like Harris' Hawk; the Osprey, the most common fish hawk the world over, equipped with an owl-like reversible outer toe and spiny pads on its feet; and the fast, aggressive "bird hawks"—the accipiters—whose tactics are concealment and surprise.

Extremely fragile bone structure may account for the rarity, even in Pleistocene deposits, of the small owls—pigmy owls and long-legged terrestrial owls—which, active by day and night, appear to have developed later than many other winged predators.

As relationships in geological time shorten, we also find the fossilized bones of many species that are comparatively recent evolutionary dead ends. The North American Black Vulture (*Coragyps atratus*) has outlived a larger, heavier species that ranged widely over the continent during the Pleistocene. The abundance of remains in a few places suggests that the extinct vulture *Coragyps occidentalis* was gregarious, roosting together at night and feeding together in the daytime like the Black Vulture and the Turkey Vulture of Recent times.

A galaxy of large eagles is peculiar to the Pleistocene only, among them, *Harpagornis,* a massive sea eagle of New Zealand which probably preyed on moas. The harpy-like Woodward's Eagle and Daggett's Eagle (a great black hawk) were present in numbers in the asphalt pits of California. Another huge long-legged relative of the modern black hawks may have ranged over the entire Caribbean area, and barn owls larger than our Great Horned Owl have been discovered in the Bahamas and Haiti. They may have extended over the Greater Antilles.

No one knows what process of selection was operating as, in some cases, entire genera, and in others, Pleistocene species of modern genera became extinct, except that the larger birds of prey tended to become less numerous, along with the larger mammals, towards the end of the Ice Ages, coincidental to the rise and spread of man to all the habitable places on earth.

The largest flying birds ever to exist, the teratorns, failed to survive to our times as it became increasingly difficult for them to find carcasses of a

size or quantity to satisfy their tremendous appetites. The extinct *Teratornis merriami* has been identified from west-central Florida, Nuevo León, and Rancho La Brea, where the bones of more than one hundred were recovered from the asphalt pits. The bird was vulture-like in form but had a heavy skull and a compressed, arched beak almost like an eagle's. It weighed an estimated 40 or 50 pounds and had a wing span of at least 12 feet, compared to the 20 pounds and 9½-foot wing span usual for the living *Gymnogyps* or California Condor, which also lived during the Pleistocene.

The *Teratornis* wing musculature indicates a degree of flapping flight unusual in condors, which can soar for hours in supporting air currents, and yet this huge vulture was apparently eclipsed in its own times by *Teratornis incredibilis,* an unbelievable flying bird described by Hildegarde Howard from a single bone found in Smith Creek Cave, Nevada. If the relative wing proportions are assumed to be the same in both species, the wing span of the larger teratorn (with a carpal bone nearly twice as large as that of *Teratornis merriami*) was *17 feet.*

The fossil finds, together with the widespread use of the "Thunderbird" symbol among Indians from Mexico and the southwestern United States to Alaska, and a Blackfoot legend about a huge bird that was seen from time to time up to half a century ago along the eastern foothills of the Rockies in Montana and Alberta, suggest a wide range for the big condors on the North American continent within the memory of man.

*P*ast and present condor ranges are rather transitory, since these formidable carrion-eaters move from place to place in groups, wherever food is available. California Condors (*Gymnogyps*) have been seen in the interior valleys and the foothills of the Coastal Ranges of California, with the summit of Mount Pinos (8,826 feet) probably representing the greatest height they have frequented in recent times. The larger Andean Condors (*Vultur*), with a wing span of 10 feet and weighing about 23 pounds, range from sea level to altitudes considerably above 15,000 feet in the Andes of South America.

With the decline of large Pleistocene mammals, part of the population of California Condors may have drifted from inland haunts to the seashore and as far north as the lower Columbia River region. In

The North American Marsh Hawk is a member of a worldwide group which characteristically courses very low, in a zigzag pattern, over fields and marshes, usually in search of rats and mice, frogs, small snakes, and insects.

1806 Lewis and Clark reported: "We have seen [them] feeding on the remains of a whale and other fish which have been thrown up by the waves on the seacoast. . . ." (The journals make no mention of condors eating the dead fish which lined the banks of the Columbia River in late summer and fall after the salmon run.) Other observers, up to 1861, saw them gathered about the carcasses of seals and whales near Monterey. The food supply is probably inadequate for California Condors now along the Pacific Coast, but Andean Condors still feed on the remains of whales and sea birds along the western coast of South America.

Condors lived on the carcasses of antelope and elk in the San Joaquin and Sacramento valleys in the early 1800's and vanished when these herds were depleted about 1870. During the corresponding "Mission Era," twenty-one ranchos covering great areas of California and each owning cattle, sheep, and horses in the thousands, supported large groups of condors. At mid-century, with cattle being slaughtered for hides and tallow only, the already tremendous food supply greatly increased, and condors apparently ceased drifting northward to the Columbia River region. Their population remained at a peak in California until, in the early 1900's, the better growing-lands became subdivided and converted to grain, beans, and orchards. Where ranching still prevails, though on a much smaller and more economical scale, a few condors are still to be seen, often feeding, with the Turkey Vultures, on ground squirrels and rabbits.

The difficulty in finding good foraging places, together with the fact that California Condors are five years old before they breed and produce only one young bird every other year, make it appear unlikely that these great scavengers will ever be numerous again. Their population is now less than 60 individuals, according to the Audubon Society and the University of California. They have been protected from extinction by state law since 1937 on a 1,200-acre preserve surrounding one of their last remaining roosts, near Sisquoc Falls, Santa Barbara County, and it is hoped that this group, relatively safe from collectors of birds and birds' eggs and curious, destructive humans in general, will survive.

The association of man with the winged scavengers and predators dates back at least 8,000 years to Indian campsites along The Dalles of the Columbia River and 5,000 years to Mesopotamia and the Nile Valley. Himself a predator, man assumed the eagle feathers of courage and bravery and translated into songs and dances his emulation of the powerful soaring condors. Even before he invented the crossbow, he trapped falcons and used their strength and speed to hunt the animals and birds which were his food supply. In his agrarian societies he killed the hawks and owls which stole his chickens, at first with his primitive slings and arrows, and in later times with his guns. Man became, in fact, the most efficient killer of all time. He completely destroyed the sea eagles of Britain and the caracaras of Guadalupe, yet—paradoxically—protected the vultures with his religious taboos in Egypt and India. Wildlife sanctuaries for predatory birds and legislation protecting them from unlimited slaughter are opposed by many people even today, for man is still unable to think in rational terms about their useful role in his world. It is within this dual framework of admiration and resentment, persecution and protection, that the predatory birds have coexisted with man in recent times.

With the exception of the California Condor, a dying relic of the Pleistocene, the large Cathartid Vultures are largely restricted to tropical America. The Andean Condor shown here lives either in the high valleys of the mountains or at lower altitudes along the Pacific Coast of South America.—*Photographed at the National Zoological Park.*

Vulture-goddess Nekhebt, Queen Hat-shepsut's temple, near Thebes, ca. 1485 B.C.—*Reproduction in the Metropolitan Museum of Art.*

chapter 2
BIRDS OF PREY AND MEN

Among primitive men, the simplest form of worship is the adoration of beasts. The cave artists of Altamira in Spain and Lascaux in France, and the reindeer and red-deer hunters of Germany, among others, have left us the images of their food animals, the bison, deer, and reindeer, which were almost certainly regarded as deities. A few birds, including the eagle and the owl, seem to have been less frequently used motifs of paleolithic "home" art, and may or may not have had religious significance.

But we need not go back to the oldest drawings scratched on stone to see men ascribe supernatural powers to animals. It is part of the spoken legends of many existing "low culture" peoples that the animals were the oldest inhabitants of the earth and that their descendants, endowed with divine ancestral souls, must be propitiated by man if he—the latecomer and intruder on this planet—is to survive. In North Borneo the hawk is believed to be the messenger of a god, and is in fact treated as a deity. The people implore his help before going to work in the fields and before undertaking warfare, and his wooden image stands before the houses to ward off evil spirits. The Shavanté of the Amazon and the Jivaro of the montaña of Ecuador make their arrows with Cooper's Hawk primaries so that they will go as swiftly to the mark as the woods hawk to its prey; and the Amahuaca of the Peruvian montaña smear their bodies with the juice of boiled talons of hawks before hunting the tapir, peccary, and alligator. Other tribes in Peru worship the vicuñas and fish which they eat, and also pay homage to the monkeys for their cunning and to the Sharp-shinned Hawks for their keen sight. The Ainu of Japan address the Collared Scops Owl as "Dear Little Divinity," and shamans or medicine men in many primitive tribes use the feathers of owls with those of eagles and hawks in their headdresses.

Snake worship is universal; worship of jaguars, tigers, bears, wolves, and crocodiles or alligators

nearly so; and all kinds of relatively unassuming beetles, frogs, and toads have been regarded as powerful gods by different peoples at one time or another, and are still regarded with, at the very least, superstitious awe. The worship of hardly any form of animal has been neglected, and many bizarre hybrids have been invented. However, the large or rapacious creatures and those of the water or of the night—including the vulture, the eagle, the hawk, and the owl—have been the most frequently loved or feared.

The widespread myths of the Thunderbird contrive to explain, describe, or personify thunder and lightning as a great eagle or vulture. Objects of copper and shell from the mound regions of Illinois and Georgia bear the image of an eagle, its eyes ornamented with zigzag lines of "lightning," or of an anthropomorphic creature with hooked nose, wings, tail, and clawed feet; in North American Indian legends, the realm of the winds and clouds that lay below the sun, moon, and stars was haunted by spirits and traversed by the Thunderbird which was, apparently, many things to many tribes. To the Mandan, he was the bird of Manitou or even the Great Spirit himself. The Dakota could point to the "footprints" of this mythical creature twenty-five miles apart at Thunder Tracks, near the source of St. Peter's River, and the Assiniboin too claimed to have seen him.

To the Iroquois, he was an invisible spirit, Hino the Thunderer, surrounded by assistants, the Lesser Thunderers, without whom the earth would become parched and the grass wither away. Among these, Keneu, "the Great War Eagle" of Hiawatha (the Golden Eagle), and Oshadagea, the Great Dew Eagle whose lodge was in the Western Sky and who was said to carry a lake of dew in the hollow of his back to put out the fires set by malevolent incendiary spirits, held first prominence. Iroquois eagle dances and songs were once war and peace ceremonies, but by the close of the eighteenth century, when the Indian Wars were over, the chiefs turned the eagle rites over to medicine societies, where the arts of clan joking (telling tall tales), lacrosse, and a bowl game replaced the recounting of brave deeds in battle.

In the Far North the Thunderbird is said to have created the world. One of the quainter tales comes from Vancouver Island, where the Nootka speak of him as "Tootooch," the single survivor of a group of four such birds which once fed on whales. It is said that the god Quawteaht, taking on the guise of a whale, lured one of these birds after another to strike him until three perished by drowning as he plunged to the bottom of the sea, but the last one flew away to the heights where he has remained ever since. The meaning of the story may be that thunderstorms come especially from one quarter of the heavens.

In Central America, the Bird Voc is the messenger of Hurakan, the tempest god of lightning and thunder (whose name has been accepted in European languages as *huracano, ouragan, hurricane*). And there is, among the Brazilian tribes of the Carib religion, the Cook Islanders of Australia, and the

The Lightning Snake, the Thunderbird with the Whale in its Talons, and the Wolf figure in the adventures of a mythical Nootka hero, Sin-set.—*Northwest coast housepainting; the American Museum of Natural History.*

Karen of the Burma hills, as well as the Bechuana and Basuto of Africa, the legend of a terrifying bird with flashing eyes and thunderous wings which beneficently brings rain.

Hawks, eagles, and condors are prevalent among the surviving textile and ceramic designs and stone sculptures of the ancient cultures of the Andes. These may be purely decorative, but are sometimes given religious significance—perhaps as sky gods with solar attributes. The Andean Condor is the earliest bird representation known from Peru, and recurs frequently, while hawks of various species are most commonly used in symbolic or mythological contexts, at least in the art of the Moche and Nasca, dating back to the middle of the first millennium.

Some of these peoples also worshiped a demigod —a Thunderer in human form with hooked beak and wings, whose influence extends to the time of the Incas (A.D. 1200–1438)—for at the great solar festival in Cuzco, the fetish idol of the Thunder stood next to those of the Creator and the Sun. When the beasts to be sacrificed were led around them, the priests chanted: "O Creator, and Sun, and Thunder, be forever young! Do not grow old! Let all things be at peace! Let the people multiply, and their food, and let all things continue to increase."

At the time of the Spanish conquest, the hawk seems to have been much more important in native ritual and mythology than the condor. Garcilaso de la Vega, a Peruvian chronicler of 1607, wrote at length about the Andean Condor, but he also implied that its worship, in the remote province of Chachapoyas, was as exceptional (and even bizarre) as the worship of the dog in Jauja.

The birds then dominant in sierra belief and ritual were those the Incas called *waman, qoriqenqe,* and *'anka. Waman* included all hawks, though the Sharp-shinned Hawk was specifically called *k'illi; quoriqenqe* referred to one or two species of caracaras; and *'anka* meant eagle (of indeterminate species). The hawks were held in highest regard for their courage, swiftness, and intelligence, and the caracaras were esteemed both for their pugnacious qualities and handsome black-and-white plumage, which was conspicuously displayed in the Inca imperial regalia. Very little is recorded about the eagle.

The legendary supernatural protector of the Inca emperors was a bird called *'inti* (literally, "sun"), which, according to the story, they kept in a basket and consulted in time of need. When the Spaniards asked about the *'inti,* they were told that it was "like a hawk." The Spaniards found further evidence of hawk-worship which must have had its roots far in the pre-Inca past. At the great oracle of the Creator God, the figures of an eagle and a hawk guarded the entrance; at the shrine of Yawira, also near Cuzco, there were representations of two hawks; and farther north, the hawk was worshiped at Recuay.

If the Andean Condor was a great god of antiquity in Chicama Valley, at Chavin de Huantar,

A religious cult with its center at Chavin de Huantar (900 B.C.-400 B.C.) in the Peruvian Andes focused on some species of cat and on mythical creatures such as these feline eagles or condors, each with bands of teeth, supplementary eyes, and serpents.—*Rubbings, taken from Chavin stone carvings by Fred D. Ayres, University of California, and the American Museum of Natural History.*

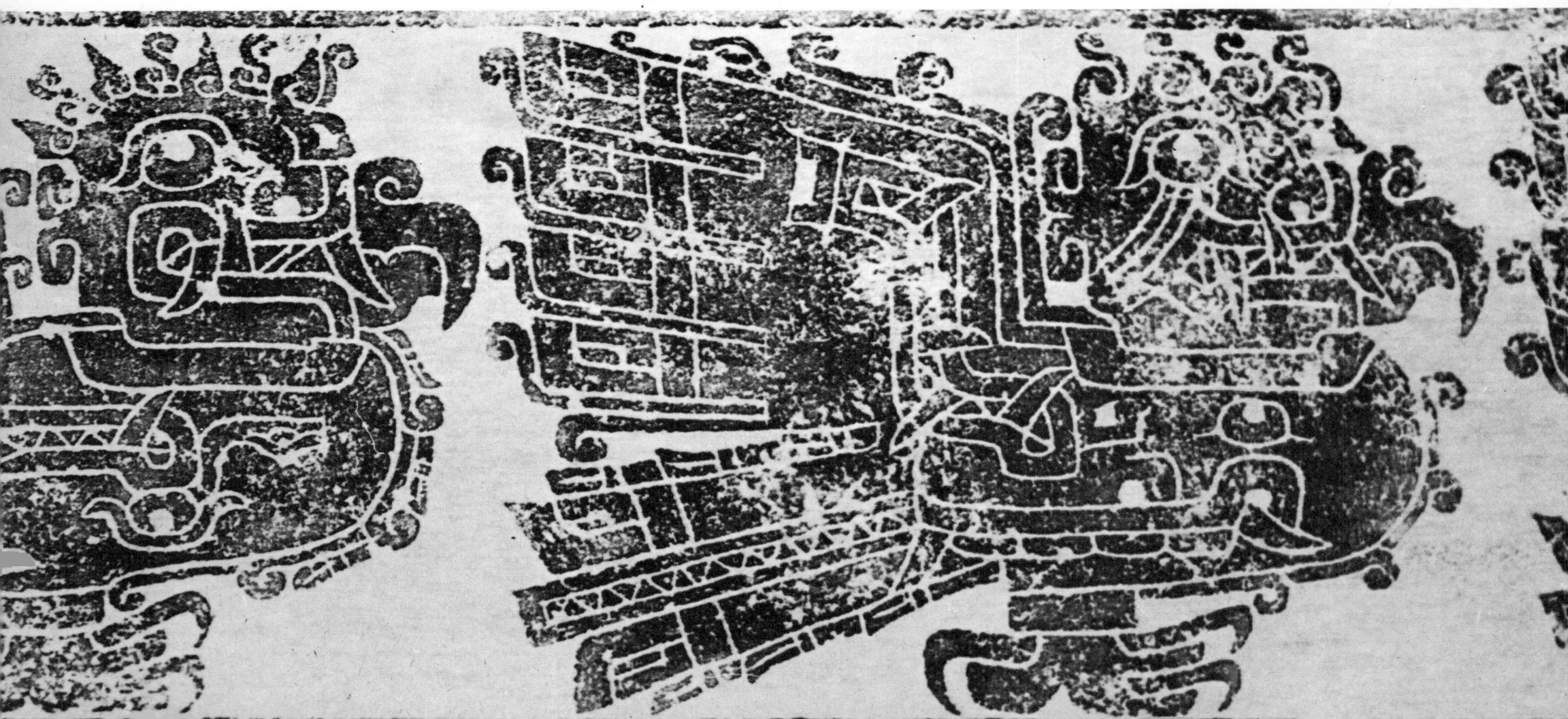

and perhaps other places, it had long since been forgotten in the legends of the peoples of the Andes.

A myth preserved in an early seventeenth-century manuscript in the Inca language treats the condor with respect, but singles out the hawk for its ritual importance.

It is said that Kuniraya, the trickster-hero of the Huarochiri in the central Peruvian sierra, forced his attentions on Qawillaqa, who fled from him. As he pursued her, he stopped to ask each animal along the road how far ahead she was. If he was pleased with the answer, Kuniraya blessed the animal, and if displeased, he cursed it. Thus he was able to make of the encounters an explanation of the habits of each of a long list of living creatures, and its fate in relation to man:

> First he met a condor.
>
> He said, "Brother, where have you met that woman of mine?" and the condor answered, "You will find her probably nearby." He said, "May you live forever and eat all the guanacos and vicuñas that die on all the punas. And may whoever kills you die himself also. . . ."
>
> So also they say he met a hawk [*waman*]. They say that the hawk said, "She is going nearby; soon you will find her," whereupon he said: "You will be very happy; in your eating you will lunch first on hummingbirds and then on other birds; and when you are killed, the man who kills you will make sacrifice with one llama, and thereupon he will place you on his head when he dances, that you may perch there being beautiful."
>
> *Translation by* JOHN H. ROWE
> *University of California*

The modern cult of the condor in Peru may not go back any further than Garcilaso for its inspiration. After Independence, the new state of Peru easily found a symbol, both native and impressive, in the Andean Condor—the same symbol which appears on the coats of arms of four neighboring countries—Colombia, Bolivia, Ecuador, and Chile.

The Inca prayer to the Thunderer finds an echo in the Navajo night chant, a supplication to the winged genius of the thunder clouds, rain, and chief of pollen, at the end of nine days of ritual:

> With your moccasins of dark cloud, come to us
> with your leggings and shirt and headdress of dark cloud, come to us,
> with your mind enveloped in dark cloud, come to us,
> with the thunder above you, come to us soaring . . .
> abundant dark clouds I desire
> an abundance of vegetation I desire,
> an abundance of pollen, abundant dew, I desire.
> Happily may fair yellow corn, fair blue corn,
> fair corn of all kinds, goods of all kinds, jewels
> of all kinds, to the end of the earth, come with you.

We know from National Geographic Society excavations that the Pueblo Indians—the Cliff Dwellers who came into the Southwest before the time of Christ—kept birds of prey in captivity for the same reason they kept parrots and macaws: to use their molted feathers as decorations and prayers. The practice continues among their latter-day descendants. The Hopi Indians of Arizona are still

Fabulous gold ornaments displayed by peoples from Mexico to the Andes of South America, greatly encouraged the Spanish conquest of the advanced Indian cultures of the New World.—*Mixtec gold Harpy Eagle and owl; American Museum of Natural History.*

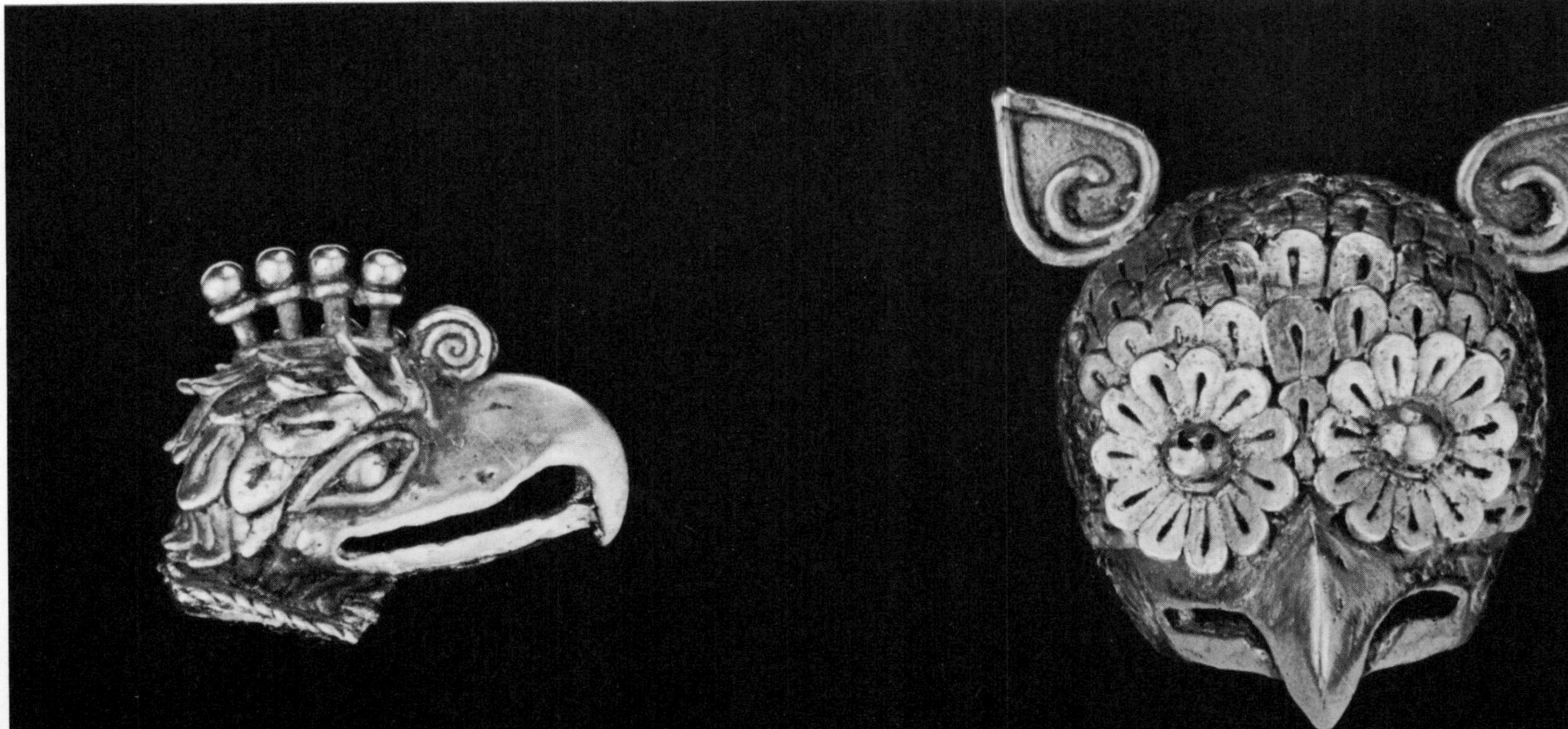

The Black Vulture, often associated by the Mayans with human sacrifice, was represented with an elongated beak and conspicuous nasal perforation.—*Sculpture, basaltic rock; Philadelphia Museum of Art.*

exercising their rights as individual owners of eyries from which they take the young of the Golden Eagle and the Bald Eagle.

Pottery found in the ancient cliff-dwellings links the Pueblo Indians with the early and highly developed agricultural civilizations of Middle America, including central Mexico: Mayan, Mixtecan, Zapotecan, and Toltec, among others.

Of these various peoples whose cultural backgrounds were similar, the Maya of Guatemala, Yucatan, southeastern Mexico, and western Honduras achieved the most elaborate nature cult. Mayan sculptured stone monuments, corbeled stone roof-vaulting, and Tzakol pottery first appeared at Uaxactún at the beginning of the Christian Era. Though the early steles were but crudely carved, the priestly class had perfected hieroglyphic writing, a system of chronology, and a permutating calendar more accurate than any used in the Neolithic societies of Egypt and Sumeria. This calendar was at once religious and secular, bound both to the sun and the agricultural economy that flourished under it.

Just as Christians through the centuries have taken the names of the saints, the Maya customarily took the name of one of the nineteen gods who were patrons of the months in their religious year. Animal- or bird-month patrons were: Pop the jaguar, Zotz the bat, and Zac the toad, as well as the Moan bird or Screech Owl, associated with the war gods and especially the god of death, Ah Puch. Still another series of deities presided over the twenty days of the month. Ah Puch's day was Cimi, often represented by a Moan bird glyph. The Mayan death god

According to the ancient Mayans, the world was destroyed by water several times. One of these great floods is depicted in the Dresden Codex, an almanac of mythology and religious events. Below two symbols of death and destruction, the Black God of War holds two javelins and a staff, pointing downward, and on his head sits the Moan bird—the Screech Owl, which was the companion of the gods of War and Death.—*After Morley, Stanford University Press, Oxford University Press.*

survives in the form of an evil spirit, Yum Cimil, who is still believed to prowl around the houses of the sick in Yucatán. Each of the months in this ancient calendar occasioned elaborate rituals in which animal, and in the later period, human, sacrifice played an important part in propitiating the deities. Hunters, farmers, priests—all had their dramas to enact on the stage of national religion.

We know very little and may never solve the mysteries of Mayan worship, but there appears to have been a close involvement with the animal world. The Moan bird, the Harpy Eagle of warriors, and the King Vulture sometimes appeared in the codices as anthropomorphic gods. A temple was dedicated to owls in Chichén Itzá; their prominence in Mayan art remains largely unexplained.

The Yucatán Horned Owl spread its great wings across door lintels and was frequently shown full-face, with shorter ears than the Screech Owl, as on the shield in the center of the Tablet of the Sun at Palenque. Vultures, used as headdresses for female figures, seem, as in Egypt, to be associated with fertility; and owls, also as headdresses for women, with stillbirth and death. Although evidently not a deity, the common and abundant Black Vulture was given the role of a bird of prey, attacking snakes, or of a scavenger, plucking out the eyes of a human sacrifice; and its relative, the King Vulture, distinguished by a caruncle, appeared in the Mayan manuscripts as the glyph for Cib, the thirteenth day of the month. In this connection, rain signs sometimes accompanied both the Black and the King vultures, but the more usual representation of rain, in Mayan as well as Pueblo cultures, was the turkey cock.

The Tenocha, whom we call Aztecs, established themselves much later in the Valley of Mexico. By A.D. 1450, most of the surrounding city-states had succumbed to Aztec raids of conquest and were paying tribute. Wealth poured in, creating a leisure for the people and a class of merchants heretofore unknown among American Indian societies. They were traders without a coinage who bartered the products of Aztec craftsmen for raw materials, including gold, turquoise, cotton, chocolate, chicle, rubber, live birds, and feathers from the hot tropical lowlands of Central America and Colombia. The imported birds were used to stock Montezuma's private aviary, and their feathers supplied Aztec weavers with the material from which they made mosaic feather shields, emblems, banners, and cloaks, in-

When the Aztec capital was founded, on the south shore of the Island of Mexico, an eagle is supposed to have perched on the *tenochtli* or "stone tuna," a cactus which bore hard fruits and appears in the Aztec manuscripts symbolically and solidly planted in a rock. The city then became known as Tenochtitlan and the first king, in legend if not in fact, was Tenocha. The eagle still persists on the flag and Coat of Arms of the modern state of Mexico.—*Mexican Eagle, from Codex Mendozo, courtesy of the American Museum of Natural History.*

cluding those of eagle feathers worn by the elite Knights of the Eagle.

Members of the soldier societies of the Eagle and the Jaguar were privileged companions of the sun god, warriors of the sky and of the earth. Their temple or meeting place was a round hall in Malinalco, near Toluca, where stone reliefs still show extended jaguar and eagle skins. The wooden drum used in ceremonials bore carvings of dances around the sun's symbol. In one legend, told to the Spanish friar Sahagún, the eagle and jaguar are said to have followed the hero Nanahuatzin when he threw himself into the fire and assumed the identity of the sun. Yet in the ritual combats between the societies, the jaguar was the darkness, and its fight with the eagle was a symbol of the sacred war between night and day. More warlike than the Maya, the Aztec saw in nature a continuous battle between light and darkness, heat and cold, north and south, so that conquest and the taking of captives followed the precepts of their religion as logically as day followed night. Members of the elite corps—the professional soldiers—were trained as rigorously in chivalry as medieval European knights. Below them, in the

The eagle is shown devouring a human heart, and thus closely associated with the sun god, as early as the tenth or eleventh century in the art of the Toltecs.—*One of a pair of terra-cotta tablets from the side of a dance platform near Tampico, Mexico; courtesy of the Metropolitan Museum of Art.*

ranks of Aztec society, every man belonged to a vast agrarian militia. Each had his own clan totem which he was prepared to carry to victory in war or to death by sacrifice on the altars of hostile gods.

The Aztecs adopted a permutating calendar system similar to that of the Maya. Their important ceremonies took place according to a solar year of eighteen months named for activities connected with the seasons or the crops; and in the sacred almanac, or *tonalpohualli,* an endless procession of gods and goddesses were patrons of the days, the weeks (of thirteen numbered days), and even hours of the day and night. Of the day signs in this ancient ceremonial year, the only birds are *Cuauhtli,* the eagle, and *Cozcaquauhtli,* the vulture.

We have noted, in passing, the role of the eagle as the badge of the Aztec noble dedicated to war. The Plains Indians of North America also bore shields marked with Thunderbirds or other tutelary genii. These, they hoped, would attract the arrows of the enemy, and the devices *did* protect them from harm by effectively deflecting *arrows* that came to the mark, but the bullets of the white men had greater magic. The Dakota, Blackfoot, Cheyenne, and other tribes had soldier societies originally organized to police the buffalo hunt; they were distinguished by feather bonnets, owl caps, coyote caps, and buffalo-mane headdresses.

In their more or less definite systems of grading war deeds, the "coup"—the touching of an enemy with the "coup stick" or point of a spear—was counted one of the highest deeds of bravery. The Blackfoot, at least, judged this act or the capture of a gun more honorable than taking an enemy's life. The Teton-Dakota stressed scalping, and nearly all of the tribes encouraged the stealing of horses from others. These deeds, which were required for office-holding in the tribes, naturally found expression in a kind of heraldry in which the Indian boasted his accomplishments on his buffalo robe or the sides of his tepee in picture writing, and by the number of eagle feathers or scalps on his "coup stick." The Dakota had special rules for wearing eagle feathers in the hair by which one could tell at a glance exactly what he had done to win them, and the Mandan, Assiniboin, and others had similar systems.

The badge of the plains Indian in war was his protecting genius—in this case, the Prairie Falcon, whose wing feathers are attached as prayers.— *Crow Indian painted shield cover, Montana; American Museum of Natural History.*

Some Indian tribes believed that the feathers of eagles and hawks were possessed of magical powers. The Plains Indian, seeking a vision which would reveal to him a personal protector or tutelary deity, fasted and prayed and often went so far as to cut off part of a finger to arouse the pity of the supernatural beings. If a hawk or eagle appeared in his vision, he was sure the feathers of this bird would thereafter stand him in good stead in his prayers.

One of the most unusual ceremonial uses of the eagle in Plains Indian societies was its role as the symbol of fertility in Pawnee Hako ritual. The turkey, which lays nine to eighteen eggs in a single clutch, had once been so honored, but the Pawnee replaced the turkey with the eagle, reasoning that the turkey's greater reproductive capacity was offset by the eagle's care in building the nest high off the ground and in nurturing the young for a long time after hatching.

Our studies of ecology tell us that any bird which nests on the ground and whose young are open to the attacks of predators and the ravages of wind and rain must produce many times more eggs in a clutch than a large bird of prey that characteristically chooses a remote rocky ledge and has few natural enemies. Furthermore, the turkey and other game birds hatch out in a fairly well-developed stage, covered with downy plumage, whereas the birds of prey are comparatively helpless and only slightly fluffy at hatching. The young of the Golden Eagle—never more than two or three—stay in the eyrie for about three months, as the Indians must have known, before taking their first flight. The Pawnee could hardly be expected to know about the forces which are continually operating to keep the populations of prey species and predators stable; it only seemed to them that the eagle had foresight and the turkey did not.

Although derived from animal worship, totemism seems to have been a development of the social rather than the religious conscience of mankind, representing a secularization of the animal (or plant) ancestors of the clan. This awakening of man to an increasing identity with his own species has been most conspicuously dramatized in modern times by the ceremonial dances of American Indian tribes of the Northwest Coast and the Southwest.

The bonnet and spear of a Mandan Chief, decorated with Golden Eagle feathers, testify to his rank and prowess in war. In many plains and northeastern tribes eagle feathers were more commonly used than scalps to tally on the "coup stick" the number of enemies vanquished in battle. "Coup" itself is a French word, and the practice of taking scalps increased as a result of bounties offered by white men during the Indian Wars.—*Painting by Charles Bodmer; American Museum of Natural History.*

By donning the Thunderbird mask, members of the totemic clan claiming this symbol assume the identity of their mythical ancestor—a large vulture or eagle.—*Kwakiutl ceremonial mask, Northwest coast of North America; American Museum of Natural History.*

In the Northwest, animal masks are worn and then laid aside to show the conversion of the animal beings of the First Age into mankind. These may be assumed only by those Indians born into or adopted by the various clans of the totemic tribes. Sometimes as many as six animal ancestors appear on the totem poles. Although these have purely social significance today, they nevertheless tell the stories of the origins of the clans. Common totems of this region are the eagle, the hawk, the raven, the killer whale, the snake, the salmon, the wolf, and the bear.

The Hopi, Zuñi, and Rio Grande tribes believe that the cycle of seasons, rain, and crops are gifts of the Kachina, a cult of supernatural beings, incarnate lesser gods, and ancestors, and that he who dances in the mask of the Kachina will lose his identity and assume that of the eagle, the owl, or any of a host of other creatures. The giant figures in the famous Zuñi Shakalo chant: "Behold us maned with buffaloes' dead manes and beaked with beaks beyond man's memory of birds." The Pueblo peoples do not discard their masks during the ritual dance, but as mud-headed and blanketed "clowns" tumble about in the guise of earth-born First Men.

Remnants of totemism are still found on every continent except Europe—in the tropical forests of South America from the Guianas to Patagonia; in Australia, where one of the principal clan totems of the aborigines is the eagle-hawk; among the Malay peoples; in India, where the hill tribes that have clans named after the eel, hawk, heron, etc., must not eat these creatures; above the Himalayas, in the Mongol tribes; and in Africa, among the Bantu.

In historic time few animal gods have survived in their original form; they have become either partly or completely human in appearance, or have been subordinated to the position of vehicle, messenger, or companion of some anthropomorphic god.

This has been the fate of a great Asiatic god of the sky, described in the Mahabharata as "the bird of life . . . destroyer of all, creator of all." As such, the Garuda was probably the original of all those mythical eagles or vultures which, from Tibet and India to Mesopotamia and the Nile Valley, have been worshiped as the wind, stars, sun, or storm. In Tibetan legend, the king of the Garudas was the immortal enemy of semidivine Nagas, or water serpents, that controlled the rain. This immense golden-winged bird would fly into a tree at the north of the Great Ocean, flap his wings to part the waves, and swoop down on Nagas which he took from their underwater kingdom and devoured. In their distress the water serpents appealed to Buddha, who appointed the god Vajrapani their special protector. Thenceforth, when he found it necessary to defend his wards, Vajrapani would turn into a Garuda himself, and in that form he had the head (or beak), wings, feet, and claws of an eagle. The real Garuda soon acquired a human body with these eagle-like attributes, and was a familiar figure in Buddhist temple sets at least as early as the thirteenth century. He remains something of a demigod, if only for those who have been bitten by snakes and embrace him in the belief that no other god can heal them.

In Brahman tradition, Vajrapani is called Indra, and has taken on the attributes of the thunder and lightning from his ancient association with the water serpents, whereas Garuda is only the steed and servant of the god Vishnu. His wings are red, and his face white, corresponding to the colors of the Brahminy Kite, which is sacred to Vishnu. Early Hindu emigrations carried the bird image to Indochina, Malaya, and Indonesia, where it was further changed to suit the native taste for the frightening, the grotesque, and the demonic, although the Garuda still stands, in the Tibetan tradition, holding a snake in each hand, at the corners of the ruined temples of Angkor.

Since the eleventh century the fabled Garuda has lit the stage on the Island of Bali for *wayang*—a unique combination of puppet theater and shadow play in which Hindu and Javanese legends are acted out.—*Brass oil lamp in the shape of Garuda; the Brooklyn Museum of Art.*

Only fragments remain of Eannatum's "Stele of the Vultures," which was the prototype of all later tableaus of victory carved in stone throughout western Asia.—*In the Louvre; photograph by Maurice Chuzeville.*

The role of the eagle, the vulture, and the hawk in the religions of the ancient civilizations of western Asia—Sumeria, Babylonia, Assyria, the Land of Hatti, and also Egypt—is evident in the inscriptions and reliefs unearthed from the dust and fragments of their cities and from their tombs sealed away from the desert sands.

No canal could be built and no war fought without the sanction of Ningursu, the Sumerian god of floods and war, whose companion was an eagle. Ningursu's temple at Lagash is dedicated in inscriptions on several bricks to "his divine bright black storm-bird," and another bears a direct invocation: "O divine black storm-bird, thy temple is raised up for thee." The god himself is addressed as "O Warrior, ravening Lion." The ruined temple lies twelve feet below pavements laid down in 3100 B.C. by Ur-nina, the first known historical ruler of Lagash, a city-state whose patesis, or prince-priests, occupied themselves endlessly with the building of irrigation ditches which their rivals in Umma to the north as persistently cut off from their source, the Euphrates River.

One of these glorified water commissioners, Eannatum, the great-grandson of Ur-nina, delivered a crushing blow against Umma and commemorated it with what is now considered to be the *chef d'oeuvre* of Sumerian relief sculpture from the early period. This was the Stele of the Vultures, which depicted the people of Umma, netted by the patesi of Lagash and devoured by vultures. However, the victory was short lived. The stone was broken and partially burned in a retaliatory raid. It remained for Eannatum's son, Entenema, to force on the city of Umma the control of a high priest friendly to Lagash and doubly insure the water supply to the extreme south by building a canal from the Tigris to the Euphrates—dedicated to Ningursu—whose course could not be interfered with by northern states.

The tradition of the victory stele was carried on by Sargon I, founder of the Semitic kingdom of Akkad, some two hundred miles northwest of the Sumerian city-states, and conqueror of Syria and perhaps all of Asia Minor. This king, an upstart cupbearer who overthrew his royal master, carved in a span of fifty-five years, starting in 2340 B.C., the first great empire in history, and left behind him the bloodiest trail yet seen. On the stone found at Susa, he and his officials have, like Eannatum, netted their enemies, and the vultures devour the dead.

*E*gypt, Neolithic from approximately 10,000 B.C. to 3100 B.C., entered historic time crowded with cults dedicated to the cow, the ibis, the vulture, the falcon, and many other animals, as well as five or six anthropomorphic deities.

Horus (Horew, in Egyptian) meant "Lofty One," an appropriate name for a falcon, a sky god, or a king. The predynastic kingdoms of Egypt knew many falcon gods; falcons were buried in predynastic tombs; and at Koptos and Aphroditopolis, pairs of falcons were worshiped in the temples. However, only Horus of Behdet, after whom the god was often called Behdety—"He of Behdet"—could lay claim to the name as surely as Horus of Hierakonpolis—possibly the original Horus—who was established in the third nome of Upper Egypt before the beginning of the historical period and identified there with the king, who was also called Horus.

Menes, the first historical ruler of Hierakonpolis, was also the first to conquer Lower Egypt and unite

Nar-mer, or Menes, King of Upper Egypt, celebrated his victory over the Papyrus Land, Lower Egypt, in a slate palette which clearly identifies him with Horus, the falcon god.—*Casting from ceremonial palette, Hierakonpolis, ca. 3200 B.C.; Metropolitan Museum of Art.*

The Middle Kingdom knew Horus as the chief god of the Sun Cult at Heliopolis; Re Harakhte, who bore a sun disk on his head. Here, he receives the adoration of the overseer of the royal harem, in the Reign of Aumun-hotpe III (1397 B.C.-1360 B.C.).—Fragment of a large Eighteenth Dynasty stele; Metropolitan Museum of Art.

the Delta with the rest of the Nile Valley. Soon afterward, he established his capital city at Memphis, a political move fated to change the character of the falcon god, for it brought the victorious Upper Egyptian kings under the influence of the nearby Heliopolitan sun cult, whose god was Re. It was not long before the god Horus was being called Harakhte, "Horus of the Horizon," and identified with the sun god, Re. From the Fourth Dynasty on, he was clearly a combination of the sky and the sun, Re Harakhte, a human figure with the sun disk on his head; and the king declared himself to be the sun, son of the sun, and chief priest of the sun cult. In reliefs and paintings, a winged solar disk replaced the symbolic falcon hovering over the king's head. Egypt's extensive trade with the Near East all through the second millennium B.C. carried this solar disk abroad, where it was adopted by Middle Assyrian, Babylonian, Iranian, and Hittite kings, and it appears in their name hieroglyphs and on their monuments.

However, in spite of the new identification with the sun, the falcon image continued to be an important motif in Egypt. Every king had a "Horus name" and a "personal name" from the First Dynasty through the reign of the last native king, Nectanebo II (359 B.C.–341 B.C.), who was in fact completely overshadowed by Horus. And, in the Late New Kingdom, the magical eye of Horus, always a popular amulet, appeared more frequently than ever.

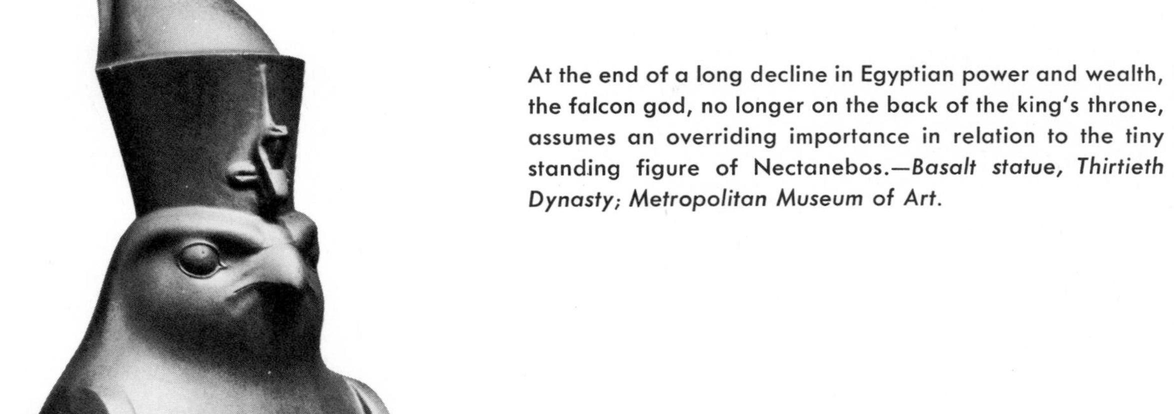

At the end of a long decline in Egyptian power and wealth, the falcon god, no longer on the back of the king's throne, assumes an overriding importance in relation to the tiny standing figure of Nectanebos.—*Basalt statue, Thirtieth Dynasty; Metropolitan Museum of Art.*

According to an ancient myth the eye of Horus, often depicted on sarcophagi and monuments, was torn to fragments by the wicked god Seth. Later the ibis-god Thoth put it back together so that the eye could again be called *wejat,* "complete" or "sound." The eye of Horus, therefore, had health-giving properties and, throughout Egyptian history, was one of the most popular amulets. Used in the corn measure, the parts of the eye represented fractions adding up to 63/64, with the missing 1/64 magically supplied by Thoth.—*Faïence, Eye of Horus, Empire Period (1580 B.C.-1150 B.C.); Metropolitan Museum of Art.*

The Griffon Vulture, the *aleph* in hieroglyphics, was commonly used as a part of speech. However, the vulture in combination with the cobra on baskets had a special meaning. This sign of the "two ladies" referred to Nekhebt and Edjo, the tutelary deities of the two kingdoms in existence before the First Dynasty. Menes, who united Egypt, was probably the first to adopt it as a title of the king.—*Limestone sculptor's model; Metropolitan Museum of Art.*

At a time roughly corresponding to the merger of the sky and the sun gods, the national religion also absorbed the (probably Mesopotamian) cult of Osiris, and it is not at all contradictory—by ancient Egyptian standards—that Horus should figure in the Osiris legend as the avenging son. Osiris may have been a human being who was deified after death. Isis, his wife and sister, probably personified his throne (for her name literally means "seat"); and another sister, Nephthys ("Lady of the House") was supposed to have been married to Osiris' brother, Setekh.

According to the myth, the wicked brother killed Osiris and cast his body into the Nile, whereupon Isis and Nephthys mourned the dead king by turning into kites. In this form, Isis bore Osiris' son, Horus, who eventually killed Setekh and succeeded to the throne. Thus every Egyptian king acquired still another identity as the son of Osiris, and in death *became* Osiris, the resurrected king.

In the burial chambers of the Valley of the Kings Osiris stands in judgment, and the falcon-headed Re-Harakhte is a protector of the dead. By the time of the Middle Kingdom, the privilege of resurrection through Osiris was accorded not only to kings and the royal family but to the common people as well. The boat in which the coffin was dragged to the tomb may have been a relict from funerals of state in which the processions crossed the Nile. In it knelt two women, relatives of the deceased, impersonating Isis and Nephthys, and called "kites."

Every Egyptian was believed to have three souls —two of them represented in bird forms. The pictograph for the most ancient of these is the Ibis. The other, Ba, a bird with a human head, dates from the second millennium B.C. This soul stays near the tomb, and, although it may go away for a time, always comes back. From its telltale habits, Ba is thought to be the Barn Owl, which commonly haunts Egyptian tombs.

Right. The owl, seldom referred to or represented, except as a hieroglyph, was the sign M. A heart-shaped face and pattern of spotting on the shoulder identify the species as the Barn Owl.—*Faïence inlay, Thirtieth Dynasty; Metropolitan Museum of Art.*

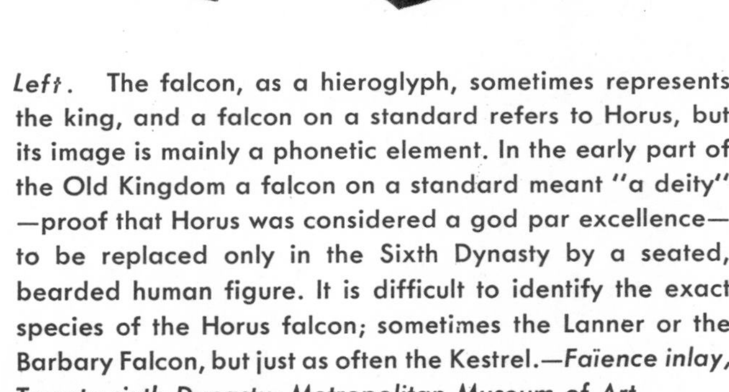

Left. The falcon, as a hieroglyph, sometimes represents the king, and a falcon on a standard refers to Horus, but its image is mainly a phonetic element. In the early part of the Old Kingdom a falcon on a standard meant "a deity" —proof that Horus was considered a god par excellence— to be replaced only in the Sixth Dynasty by a seated, bearded human figure. It is difficult to identify the exact species of the Horus falcon; sometimes the Lanner or the Barbary Falcon, but just as often the Kestrel.—*Faïence inlay, Twenty-sixth Dynasty; Metropolitan Museum of Art.*

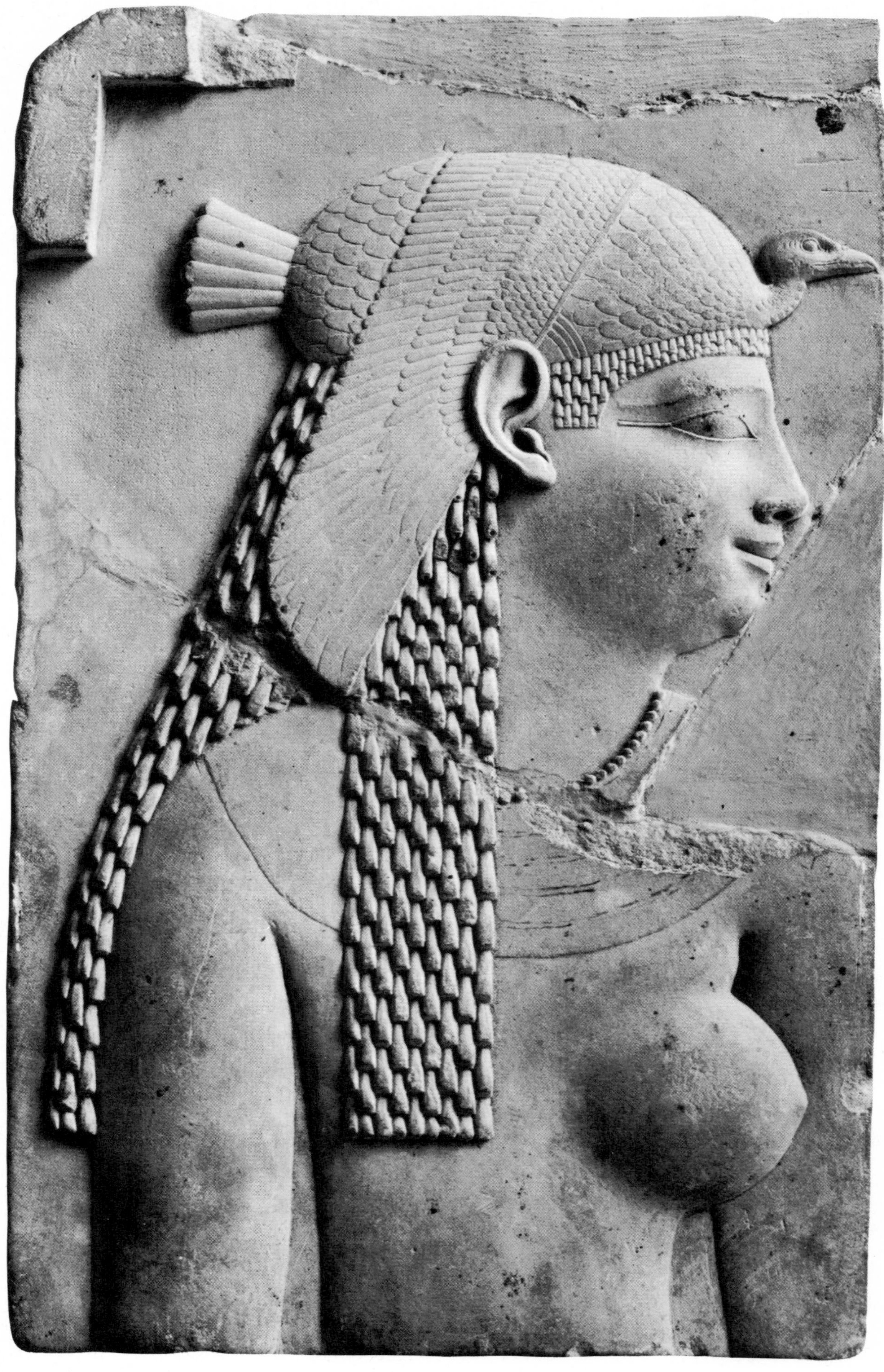

The vulture crown, the privilege of a goddess or queen, represented Nekhebt, the tutelary deity of Upper Egypt.—*Limestone sculptor's model from the Ptolemaic Period; Metropolitan Museum of Art.*

Of the two important goddesses represented as Griffon Vultures, Nekhebt, goddess of childbirth, who originated in the third nome, became the tutelary deity of Upper Egypt in the predynastic period: Her image formed the crown of that region and later part of the headdress of Isis, whose power as a mother goddess was to be perpetuated in the cult of Isis throughout the entire ancient world dominated by Greece and Rome. Mut of Ioshreu (a part of Thebes) did not come into prominence as goddess of the heavens until the Middle Kingdom.

In Egypt the ornaments of the dead were special and often bore very little relation to what they might have worn in life. In the Eighteenth Dynasty, an over-refined period of great wealth, mummies of the aristocracy were decked in fabulous treasures — gold headdresses and circlets, and broad collars of beads inlaid with gold, turquoise, obsidian, cornelian, and lapis lazuli. The sheet-gold pectoral (above) belonged to the mummy of one of Thut-mose III's wives whom he had buried with two other members of his harem in a small rock-cut tomb near Deir el Bari, Thebes. The three favorites, presumably daughters of Assyrian chieftains, were accorded every consideration due to queens *except the vulture head dress.* In later, less opulent dynasties funerary jewelry, like the pectoral of the Twenty-first Dynasty (below), was made of an alloy of lead and tin. The sacred birds were traditionally shown holding signet rings, the symbols of "countless years."—*Amulets representing the vulture-goddess Mut and the falcon-god Horus; Metropolitan Museum of Art.*

Lions guard the recently rediscovered cities of the Hittites, an Indo-European people who swept across Asia Minor, probably from the Caucasus Mountains, until they were stopped at the border fortifications of Egypt. A kind of "Thirty Years' War" of antiquity followed, ending in the first formal peace treaty of all time and a political marriage worthy of the Hapsburgs, as the great pharaoh Ramses II took a princess from the kingdom of Hatti for his queen. This was the peak of empire, for weak kings subsequently left Hatti open to new waves of migrating peoples from the west, and in 1190 B.C. Hattushash, the capital, fell to the torch. It is in the stele and inscriptions of Hattushash and the ruined city of Kartepe that these events are recorded, with an eagle-headed god or genius and winged solar disk (the signature of the king) figuring prominently.

We know that an eagle cult existed with its center at Euyuk, for the priest-king is represented with the eagle on the remnants of a sphinx jamb of the palace gateway, and its influence evidently extended locally through that part of Hatti known as Kappadochia, for at Boghaz-keui (Hattushash) there is an eagle's head in black stone, larger than life, and a cuneiform fragment there refers to the Temple of the Eagle. A headless stone eagle seven feet high, resting on lions, has been discovered at Yarmoola. Iconography at Yazilikaya describes the dominant mother goddess cult of Hatti; there, goddesses are pictured on a stone relief riding on a two-headed eagle.

The neighboring countries of Middle Assyria and Babylonia—both primarily agricultural—worshiped many genii, among them a benevolent demon with an eagle's head. On reliefs and seals he was frequently represented as transmitting life or fertility (by pollinating or watering the Sacred Tree); he bears a curious resemblance both to the Navajo Thunderbird in its capacity as chief of pollen and the eagle-headed beings found in other Indian cultures of the New World.

In Iran, about the sixth century B.C., the old Mithraic religion gave way to the worship of Ahura-Mazda, who was formless except as "the whole circle of the heaven themselves" and whose symbol was the winged sun disk from Egypt. His prophet, Zarathustra (or Zoroaster, as the Greeks called him), taught that fire, earth, water, and wind were not gods but the sacred manifestations of a supreme god; that life is a constant conflict between good and evil; and that everyone must choose between Ahura-Mazda, the Light, or Ahriman, the Living Lie. On his accession to the throne in 522 B.C. Darius I adopted the Zoroastrian faith. Some 2,000 feet above the age-old caravan trail from Ecbatana to Babylon he had graven an immense tableau of his victory over ten rivals who, with hands tied and necks roped, await his sentence of death. In Old Persian, in Babylonian, and in Elamite scripts it is repeated for all time that Ahura-Mazda gave aid to Darius because he "was not hostile, not a follower of the Lie, nor a doer of the Wrong."

Under the Sassanian kings, beginning in the third century A.D., Zoroastrianism was recognized as the official state religion. Their forebears, the Indo-Scythians (or Sace tribe) had originally migrated from the Mongol-Chinese province of Kansu in the second century B.C., and established themselves north of the Oxus River, constituting a formidable nation from the reign of King Mithridates II. They brought with them a Buddhist heritage which, when combined with the Hellenic and Iranian elements in Zoroastrianism, gave it more than just a little Oriental flavor. The Indo-Scythian religious, political, and cultural domain over Persia lasted until the introduction of Islam by the Arabs in the seventh century; then there was a large exodus of Zoroastrians to India, a natural haven for the faithful, considering that by that date their religious books echoed in many respects the Vedas. There are in India today more than 100,000 Zoroastrians (Parsees), mostly in Bombay, who subscribe to the old Iranian belief that they should not burn or bury their dead for fear of defiling the sacred elements; instead, they cast them onto "Towers of Silence" for the Pondicherry Vultures to devour. The few Zoroastrians who remained in Iran have, through all adversity, stayed true. Their center of worship is Yezd, and their "Tower of Silence" still stands on the outskirts of Teheran.

An Assyrian eagle-headed and winged genius "pollinates" a sacred tree with an object that appears to be a date spade. The demigod carries a "bag" in one hand that might contain water. *Assyrian alabaster wall panel, ninth century B.C.; Metropolitan Museum of Art.*

In Greek legend, Ganymede, the beautiful son of a Trojan king, was said to have been stolen by Zeus's eagle and made cupbearer to the gods of Olympus.—*Macedonian gold earring, from a set of funerary jewelry, last half of the fourth century B.C.; Metropolitan Museum of Art.*

A legendary history of the kings of Iran, from the earliest times to the Muhammedan conquest, finally crystallized in the tenth-century epic poem, the Shah Namah of Firdausi. Its language and morals are plainly Zoroastrian. It is highly fanciful. Kings such as Cyrus, Alexander, and the Sassanian rulers who really existed in later periods appear in it under highly supernatural circumstances; and across its rollicking pages are spread the exploits of the Iranian paladins, the mightiest of whom was Rustam.

In the Shah Namah, Rustam's father, Zal, was borne away by a large vulture or eagle called the Simurgh. The exact origin of the myth is lost in antiquity, but it gave rise to many such stories throughout the East, including that of Ganymede and the eagle.

It is related that one of the early kings, Sam, fathered a child born with white hair. Embarrassed by this surprising mutation and further intimidated by his advisers, who assured him the baby was a demon, he abandoned Zal on a mountainside near the Simurgh's nest. The great bird took what she thought to be a tender human morsel to her nestlings. However, they refused to eat him, so the Simurgh raised Zal herself, and even more, taught him the language and ways of his country. At length, Sam dreamed that his son was alive, and remorsefully went in search of him. To his inexpressible astonishment and joy, the Simurgh appeared, bearing the boy in her talons, and, after a tender speech of farewell, returned him to his sire. Zal wept, for he had not wished to leave the nest. The Simurgh presented the young prince with a feather from her breast, saying: "In day of need, cast it on the fire and I will come and aid you." Years later, when Zal's wife was giving birth and it seemed that she would die, Zal summoned the Simurgh by burning the magic feather. And so it was that the hero Rustam happened to be born by a Caesarean operation under the tender auspices of the Simurgh. Perhaps the obstetrical value of a Simurgh's feather was in some way related to the maternal aspects of such vulture goddesses as the Egyptian Nekhebt, to the very ancient belief that all vultures are female, or to the use of their feathers as charms by Greek and Roman midwives.

No less a product of the battlegrounds of Asia Minor than Ahura-Mazda was the God of Hosts revealed to Amos and Isaiah (*ca.* eighth century B.C.), who seems to have been a Thunderer established for many centuries before the ancestors of the Israelites invaded the land of Canaan (presumably from Ur in Sumeria). The Semitic tribes who adopted Him defined Him in their own likeness and gave Him the character of a war god, Yahveh, and at first He

"[The Simurgh] thus consoled [Zal's] heart, then took him up, Bore him with stately motion to the clouds, And swooping down conveyed him to his sire."—*Illustration from a sixteenth-century Persian manuscript of the Shah Namah of Firdausi; Metropolitan Museum of Art.*

One of the most common of the Palestinian birds of prey is Naumann's, or the Lesser, Kestrel, a summer resident and spring passage migrant from tropical Africa to southern Europe. More gregarious than the European Kestrel, it nests in colonies and hunts in large groups.

At least three species of vultures inhabit the land of The Bible, and in Egypt there is even greater variety. Tropical African birds such as the Lappet Faced Vultures squabbling over a carcass, in the foreground above, range as far as the Blue Nile, and Ruppell's Vulture (below), one of the griffons, reaches the Delta.

The Long-eared Owl is one of eight species of owls which the Israelites were enjoined not to eat because they were "unclean," according to a 1955 translation of the Bird List of Leviticus by Dr. C. L. Driver. In other versions, this bird had been called a "sea gull" and a "cuckoo."

The Golden Eagle nests in the brown granite mountains of Sinai, where Moses received the Covenant, and the Israelites were said to have been borne away from Egyptian bondage "on eagle's wings."

The Lanner Falcon, another species in the cliffs of Palestine, is very similar to the North American Prairie Falcon and, like it, prefers to chase birds or strike them on the ground rather than dive down upon them in mid-air as the Peregrine does.

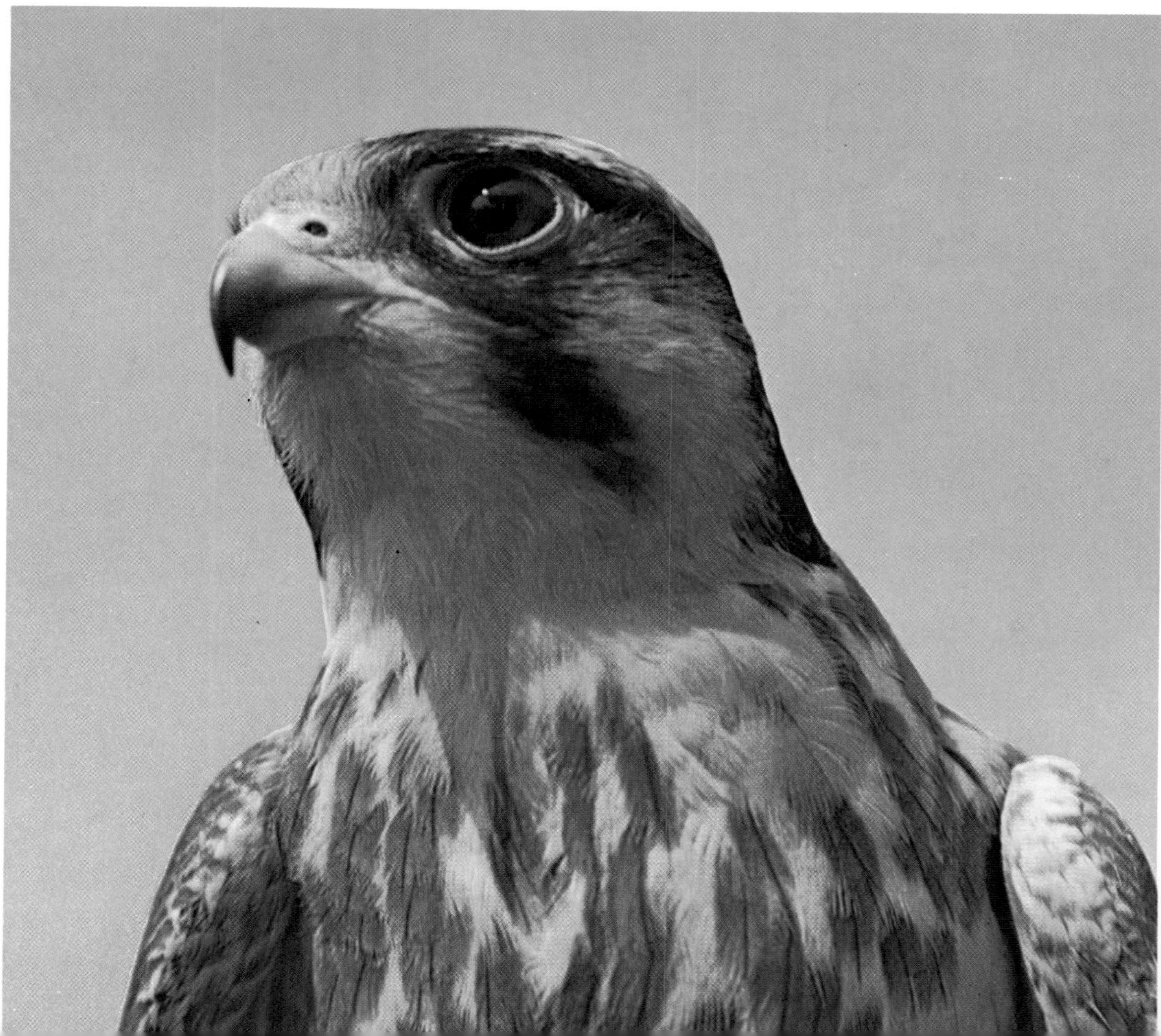

was worshiped in community with idols—Baal, Chemosh, Milcom, and Astarte. It took centuries of subjugation, exile, and slavery at the hands of the colossi of Mesopotamia on the one side and Egypt on the other before the omnipotent Hebrew God emerged in Palestine, still stern and vengeful, but also a God of Love under whose auspices the people of Israel would be led from adversity—in this life, as there could be no other until the coming of a Messiah.

It is no wonder that Biblical accounts of the trials of the people of Israel are richly laced with imagery concerning the birds of prey. More than forty species are resident in the land of the Bible, and since time immemorial, the flight of thousands of accipiters on migration from Europe across the Sinai Peninsula and the Red Sea to North African wintering grounds has been a wondrous and impressive thing to behold. To the prophets of the Old Testament it was symbolic of the mysterious ways of God which man could not divine:

> Doth the hawk fly by thy wisdom, and stretch her wings toward the south?
>
> JOB 39:26

The Hebrew word, *nesher,* translated as "eagle" in the Authorized version of the Bible, usually refers to the Griffon Vulture, the most numerous of the birds of prey in Palestine, and, occasionally, to the Golden Eagle. Whatever species was intended, however, the "eagle" symbolized the strength and protection of the Lord. It was in these terms that He offered the covenant to Moses on Mount Sinai:

> Ye have seen what I did unto the Egyptians, and how I bare you on eagles' wings, and brought you unto myself.
> Now therefore, if ye will obey my voice indeed and keep my covenant,
> then ye shall be a peculiar treasure unto me above all people:
> for all the earth is mine:
> And ye shall be unto me a kingdom of priests, and an holy nation.
>
> EXODUS 19:4–6

Later His role as a parent was emphasized in the Song of Moses:

> As an eagle stirreth up her nest, fluttereth over her young,
> spreadeth abroad her wings, taketh them, beareth them on her wings,
> so the Lord alone did lead him [Jacob] and there was no strange god with him. He made him ride on the high places of the earth, that he might eat the increase of the fields.
>
> DEUTERONOMY 32:11–13

And yet, to have one's body consumed by beasts or birds of prey was a thing of horror, for then the soul could never rest. Curses follow the blessings in Deuteronomy: "thy carcase shall be meat unto all the fowls of the air." Whenever the words were repeated, death and destruction were due to become the lot of the cursed. The prophets spoke them, Ahijah against Jeroboam, king of the Northern Kingdom of Israel, and Elijah against King Ahab, husband of Jezebel. Finally the prophet Hosea called out to warn the people of Israel, who were torn with internal strife, that there was imminent danger of conquest by the Assyrian horde:

> Set the trumpet to your lips, for a vulture is over the house of the Lord,
> because they have broken My covenant and transgressed My law.
>
> HOSEA 8:1, REVISED STANDARD VERSION

The Northern Kingdom fell, and Sennacherib's army very nearly succeeded in shutting up "Hezekiah, the Judean king who has not submitted to my yoke . . . like a caged bird in Jerusalem," according to the conqueror's own boast in his official record of the campaign. Then, in 701 B.C., the Assyrians lifted their siege—perhaps due to disease or internal pressures at home—and the faith of the prophets was justified. Israel had been saved.

But the troubles of the Chosen People had not come to an end. Less than a hundred years later, the vultures were flying again, this time at the forefront of the armies of Nebuchadnezzar of Babylon, who, like "a great eagle with great wings, longwinged, full of feathers which had divers colors, came unto Lebanon, and took the highest branch of the cedar" (Ezekiel 17:3). It was said of Egypt that this country was like a second eagle with "great wings and many feathers" (17:7) though it lacked the resplendent plumage of the Babylonian royalty.

The emperor Cyrus, carrying the vulture battle-standard of Persia, defeated Babylon in the sixth century B.C. He was seen by some nameless prophet, and quite apart from his own intents, as the instrument of God's purposes to deliver Israel from bondage and restore her to her own land: the "ravenous bird from the east, the man that executeth My [the

17.190.38

Lord's] counsel from a far country" (Isaiah 46:11, Revised Standard Version).

In New Testament times the enemy of Israel was Rome. The author of Revelation conjured up a scene of carnage in which the new forces of evil were to be destroyed in preparation for the reign of Christ: "All the fowls that fly in the midst of heaven" were to be summoned to gather at a feast of the slain and "the fowls were filled with their flesh."

An assemblage of Palestinian owls—from the rapacious Eagle Owls to the smallest insect-eating Scops Owls—and the Little Owls, whose nocturnal haunts are old ruins, always provide a doleful Biblical chorus intended for the ruins of the great capitals of the enemy. Of Edom, Isaiah wrote:

> And thorns shall come up in her palaces, nettles and brambles in the fortresses thereof,
> and it shall be an habitation of dragons and a court for owls . . .
> The screech owl also shall rest there, and find for herself a place of rest.
> There shall the great owl make her nest and lay, and hatch and gather under her shadow.
> There shall the vultures also be gathered, every one with her mate.
>
> ISAIAH 34:13–15

Isaiah and Jeremiah both predicted that Babylon would be abandoned to the wailings of these birds; the seventh-century prophet Zephaniah said that Assyria and Nineveh would suffer the same fate; and, in the New Testament, the fall of Rome was foreseen with the author of Revelation portraying the city of the Caesars as "a cage of every unclean and hateful bird."

The ancient belief that blood is "the life of all flesh" and "whosoever eateth it shall be cut off" is expressed in Leviticus. More than twenty species—mostly birds of prey that take blood with their food—are listed as "unclean," and the Israelites are enjoined both from eating these creatures and from partaking of the blood of any "clean" beast or fowl. There seems to have been no physical contact between any of the birds of prey and God's people; they did not keep hawks, as the Egyptians did, or train them to hunt, although falconry was widely practiced by their neighbors in western Asia.

A tenth-century book cover displays a familiar religious theme: *Agnus dei* on a cross between the emblems of the four Evangelists.—*Carved German or north Italian Ivory plaque; Metropolitan Museum of Art.*

Later, Christ taught that "nothing is unclean in itself," and the Muslims, who accepted him as a prophet but not as the son of God, denied themselves only carrion, running blood, and pig's meat—with no restriction on birds except those which had been profanely consecrated to gods other than Allah.

For Christians, the eagle symbolized the fulfillment of the Messianic age into which they had been born—and they hoped to escape the machinations of Rome as the people of Israel had escaped from the bondage of Egypt—on strong yet protective wings. In Revelation (12:13–14, RSV) the parable was retold on a new stage with the principal actors the dragon, which was Rome, the woman, who was the Church of Christ, and the wings of the eagle. "And when the dragon saw that he had been thrown down to the earth he pursued the woman. . . . But the woman was given the two wings of the great eagle that she might fly from the serpent into the wilderness, to the place where she is to be nourished for a time. . . ."

The bird of the Apostle John was not the vulture of doom, but the magnificent eagle of God which, in the Old Testament, protected His throne. So we see in Revelation (4:7) the very door of heaven open to John in his vision on the Island of Patmos, in which the four beings who served God with their courage, strength, wisdom, and speed appeared as a lion, an ox, a man, and a flying eagle. These, of course, are the vehicles of the four Evangelists—Matthew, Mark, Luke, and John—as familiar in religious art as the dove and the lamb of God.

In the beginning there was Ancient Night, a bird with black wings. Classical Greek mythology, as set down by Hesiod in the eighth century B.C., had already lost the quality of this song, sung by Orpheus. The ancient Creation myths were either misunderstood or unknown to the educated at the period from which the first literary documents have come down to us. In Greece, as in other parts of Asia Minor, a deity with the thunder at his right hand emerged as the paramount religious figure of historic time. He was called Zeus (by the Romans, Jove), god of the sky, and his eagle was the only bird believed to dwell on Mount Olympus.

A flying bird holding a snake in its beak may be a representation of a Short-toed Eagle.—*Sealstone intaglio from Melos, last half of the seventh century B.C.; Metropolitan Museum of Art.*

Another attendant of Zeus, and one frequently associated with the sun god, Apollo, was the griffon (in Greek, *grypos,* "hook-nosed"). There were those among the ancients to whom the bird-beast was very real, although there were some, like the elder Pliny, who were skeptical of its existence. Pliny wrote, in the first century B.C.: "I regard as fables the Pegasus, those birds with horses' heads, and the griffons [lions] with hooked beaks and long ears. . . ." The griffon, which may be Mesopotamian in origin, appears first in Egypt among the wild animals of the desert in funerary scenes painted on tombs some 5,000 years ago. A savage "crusher" or "trampler," it eventually became a protective deity and a cognizance of kings as well. Magical papyri of the late New Kingdom reveal it as an "avenger" and the "instrument of the will of the Sun God." The Greeks thought of this bird-beast as a guardian and protector, its form in the later period decorating sarcophagi and cinerary chests, and beds and other house furniture and ornaments. And the Romans associated it with Nemesis, whose proverbial wheel brought good luck or misfortune as it turned.

Certain monsters of mythology were combinations of predatory birds and women. Odysseus' shipmates had to bind him so that he would not fall prey to the enchanting songs of the Sirens, which had human heads set on birds' bodies, often a woman's breasts and arms, and powerful talon feet. The snatching creatures were, however, more properly the Harpies, which seldom appeared in birdlike form, but were winged; even when they had human fingers, these were bent like claws.

Vultures were used to punish Tityus, son of Zeus and Elara, who was struck down by lightning for attacking Leto—another spouse of Zeus—and carrying her off by force. He lay in the underworld, at his full length of nine hundred feet, and two vultures perpetually tore at his liver, which always grew again with the moon.

In Roman times the griffon became associated with Nemesis and her Wheel of Fate, and statuettes of the goddess in this form were used as offerings to ward off bad luck. Originally hawk-headed, the griffons of Roman Egypt acquired the long, curved bill of a Griffon Vulture, the long neck and standing mane of a Greek sea monster, and curly locks that may have been of Cretan inspiration.—*Blue faïence Nemesis from Egypt, Roman period; the Brooklyn Museum of Art.*

Prometheus, the vanquished Titan who had stolen the secret of fire from Zeus and given it to mankind, suffered a similar punishment. He was chained by Zeus to Mount Caucasus, with a stake driven through him. During the day an eagle tore at his immortal liver, and all that was eaten grew back at night. The punishment, laid down in anger when Zeus had just gained power and intended to last "thirty millennia," was later tempered by him when he had become a more mature and reasonable ruler. The prophecy was made in Aeschylus' *Prometheus Bound* that Prometheus would be liberated in the thirteenth generation. And so it came about, but not before a secret had been extracted from him which saved the regency of Zeus. Later on, Prometheus acquired immortality from Chiron, the wise Centaur who was incurably wounded and wanted to die and who took Prometheus' place in Hades.

The story of the god who undertook so much pain for the human race was the subject of one of the best-known literary works of the nineteenth century, Shelley's poetic drama, *Prometheus Unbound,* and later was the subject of William Vaughn Moody's *The Fire Bringer* (1904).

Of the large raptors which could have inflicted these legendary tortures, the Lammergeiers, or Bearded Vultures, most fascinated the Greeks. Pliny described their habit of breaking bones and hard-shelled turtles by dropping them on rocks from high in the air. According to him, Aeschylus was supposed to have been killed by a missile dropped by a Lammergeier who mistook his bald head for a rock.

Athene (the Roman Minerva), the winged and owl-eyed maiden goddess, was her *father's* daughter. It was said that she sprang fully armed from the head of Zeus, with a far-echoing battle cry. But her "wisdom" had been inherited from her mother, that first great wife of Zeus, Metis, or "Wise Counsel." From the little owl Athene sometimes carried on her shoulder (never a "horned" species), we can trace the growth of one of the most common clichés of modern times—the "wise old owl." This was an image that not only interested the Greek and Roman poets; it also found its way into the King Arthur legends, for Merlin, like Athene, had an owl perched upon his shoulder. In the Middle Ages of Europe this bird was everywhere considered to be the companion of seers and alchemists. The owl of *The Owl and the Nightingale,* a late twelfth- or thirteenth-century allegory, apparently represented the clergy,

Athene, the Goddess of Wisdom, gave her name to ancient Athens and her owl appeared on the coins of the city.—*Silver tetradrachm, 400 B.C.-200 B.C.; Metropolitan Museum of Art.*

Man's sinful ancestors, the Titans, dared to defy Olympus. Under the dominion of Zeus, Atlas was condemned to eternal toil at the Western edge of the earth, and Prometheus, tortured by an eagle (or vulture) at the Eastern edge, did not obtain his freedom until the thirteenth generation, when Hercules shot the tormenting bird with an arrow and Zeus unchained him.—*Greek black-figured vase; Vatican Museum.*

The poets of antiquity averred there were no owls on Crete; yet a tiny sculptured owl is one of the oldest stone seals found on the island.—*Minoan stone seal, dated between 2400 B.C. and 2200 B.C.; Ashmolean Museum.*

for it defended the church and attacked the nightingale (representing the feudal kingly estate) for its way of life.

The myth of the "wisdom" of the owl, whose eyes are large and solemn-looking and whose habits are nocturnal and mysterious, was a natural outgrowth of its primitive association with charms and magic. It certainly did not stem from any capacity for learning demonstrated to man. Owls are rather sluggish and intractable when compared to such birds of ill omen as the raven and the crow, and certainly cannot match the teachability of the Peregrine Falcon and other diurnal birds of prey that have been favorites in the pursuit of falconry.

The Bishop of Norwich, a Renaissance man, tried in vain to understand why the ancients regarded the owl as sacred, "except it be for her safe closeness and singular perspicuity . . ." and he went on to observe, that, at night, "when other domestical and airy creatures are blind, she hath inward light to discern the least objects to her own advantage."

John Gay wrote, with tongue in cheek:

> Can grave and formal pass for wise
> When men the solemn owl despise?

The nineteenth-century American poet Fitz-Green Halleck upheld the traditional viewpoint:

> The wisest of the wild fowl,
> Bird of Jove's blue-eyed maid—the owl.

And so the question has been endlessly debated, and the image of the wise old owl, often spectacled, persists to the present day in fairy tales, fables, poetry, and even advertising.

Of the bird and animal fables of classical Greece we can say, along with La Fontaine, that they seem so inspired (at least in the ways of men) as to have been the work of Socrates, the mortal most closely associated with the Divine. They were commonly ascribed to Aesop, a deformed Phrygian slave of the sixth century B.C., but many actually go back much farther, some having been discovered on Egyptian papyri of eight hundred or a thousand years earlier.

So great was the influence of Aesop that Plato gave him a place of honor in *The Republic,* hoping that the young would absorb his morals with their milk. Nurses were advised to use them as bedtime stories so that, at a tender age, children might know virtue from vice. As civilization wore on, men were rather galled by the Moral, which in medieval versions was so baldly stated, and some turned to Beast Epic of mythic origin, and not necessarily edifying nature. Nevertheless, the fanciful image of Aesop's eagle, which, finding himself fatally wounded by an arrow, mused, "And 'tis an added grief that with my own feathers I am slain," was not only repeated by Aeschylus, but also, many centuries later, appealed to Waller, Byron, and Thomas Moore.

Another of the fables concerns a sick kite whose vows were of no avail because of his temple thefts and desecrations. The bird of prey which, like the vulture, feeds on carrion, occurs in Ovid's *Metamorphosis,* hovering greedily over the entrails of a sacrifice. His hunger is as proverbial as a cook's, and humorously, he is threatened by a lawsuit for theft in the plays of Plautus.

The marriage of the kite and the dove appears in Horus as symbolic of the impossible and in any number of romantic poems of the nineteenth century. It is perhaps best illustrated by Reade's vision of "The poor white dove . . . murdered by a falcon's love." Fortunately for the kite, the moral implications of the fable did not interfere with that noble and mythical side of his character which allowed him, as Martial says, to mount to the very stars and become a constellation.

In pre-Roman Latium the spotted green woodpecker was used for divination, but in later days soothsayers turned to the less attractive birds—vul-

The Middle Ages commemorated Julius Caesar as a "pagan hero," with the two-headed eagle of the eastern and western Roman Empires on his shield.—*French tapestry, ca. 1385; Metropolitan Museum of Art.*

tures, kites, ravens, crows, and owls—for inspiration.

Owls of ill omen were supposed to gather at a certain tree in the underworld, and their hearts were eaten to obtain prophetic powers. In primitive societies owls are more often revered than feared; their association with evil comes into prominence only among the more civilized peoples, and charms invented to annul their influence persist in modern superstition and practice. Along Bayou LaFourche in Louisiana, the Cajuns, descendents of the French settlers, still get out of bed and turn their left shoes upside down to stop the calling of the Screech Owl, according to the belief, also held in Roman times, that misfortune or death attends the wailing of "the night bird."

In official, as opposed to unofficial, augury, the barnyard birds were more important than those of the open sky. The *pulli,* or sacred chickens, accompanied Roman armies into the field and Roman fleets to sea, and if they would not eat, there was nc battle. It was Julius Caesar's uncle, Caius Marius, who gave to each legion an eagle of silver or gold to be borne on a pole with a wreath of victory as the semidivine emblem of military strength, like the eagle or vulture on the battle standards of the Sumerians, the Egyptians, and the Persians. In the course of time the legionary eagle was made of less precious metal—bronze—but its importance as an idol increased. The eagle's birthday, or the day on which each permanent unit had been commissioned, never went unmarked. After every victory, field sacrifices were offered to it, and a legion which had lost its emblem in defeat might even be disbanded.

The eagle—whether one or two-headed—has been a symbol of the power of emperors at least since Belshazzar of Babylon, in the sixth century B.C. In the Christian Era, it dominates Western history as the emblem of the Caesars and of the Eastern Roman Empire, of Charlemagne and the succeeding Holy Roman emperors, of the Russian czars, and of the late Austrian emperors.

Of the birds and animals used in medieval heraldry, the German eagle was probably the oldest, dating back to twelfth-century Teutonic arms, although the imperial two-headed eagle did not appear as a fixed device upon a shield until A.D. 1414.

The practice of adopting personal arms started in Europe after the First Crusade (1096–1100) and rapidly caught on, partly because of the immense military value of heraldry in a field where armed knights looked exactly alike unless distinguished by the different colors and patterns of charges blazoned on banners, pennons, shields, and other military regalia. The use of crude emblems had been haphazard in previous times, judging from the Bayeux tapestry which records the Battle of Hastings in 1066. None of the markings on the shields can be recognized as those belonging to later generations, and the artist even represents the same individual, in various parts of the tapestry, bearing *different* arms.

However, from the beginning of the thirteenth century, all gentlemen, esquires, and knights wear-

The two-headed eagle appeared on Byzantine banners until the fall of Constantinople to the Turks in the mid-fifteenth century; then, on the marriage of Sophia, niece of the last Emperor, to Ivan III, it was added to the arms of Muscovy.—*Fourteenth-century Byzantine banner; Metropolitan Museum of Art.*

ing armor had coats of arms embroidered on the long surcoats covering their chain mail (hence, the term "coats of arms"), as well as painted on their shields or escutcheons. The more ancient or important families had crests whose proper use was limited to personal effects or to display in the pageantry of the tournament, and their servants and followers were given identifying badges which also marked their house furniture, hangings, and chairs of state.

While less widely owned than arms, the badges of the nobility were often more familiar than their coats of arms. Thus all men in fifteenth-century England understood perfectly the allusions in a popular ballad to the White Rose, the Red Rose, the Falcon, the Fetterlock, etc.

Of royal pre-eminence, besides the eagle, were the lion rampant, which first appeared on the shield of Richard I in 1189, and the griffon, the fabulous bird-beast borne rampant as a quartering on the arms of the House of Montagu at an early date—it was shown on the counterseal of Simon, Lord of Montagu, in 1301. When borne as a head only, the pointed ears and tuft under its chin distinguished the griffon from the eagle. In nearly all other cases heraldic devices played upon the bearer's name: foxes stood for Colfox, swine for Swinburne, talbots for Talbot of Cumberland, and so on, ad infinitum. The falcon or hawk borne on the escutcheon, was, as a rule, shown with closed wings, so that it might not be mistaken for an eagle.

With the accession of the Tudors, the art of blazonry declined and ceased to play an important part in military affairs. Even the tournament became a Renaissance pageant, which did not need the painted shield and armorial trappings. However, the influence of heraldry continues to the present day, not only in personal coats of arms, but in those of schools, commercial firms, cities, states, and nations.

Early in the history of the United States, the only species of eagle both native and peculiar to North America was selected as the national emblem. By act of Congress, June 20, 1782, a design for the national coat of arms displaying the Bald Eagle was adopted:

> The Escutcheon placed on the Breast of an American [the Bald] Eagle, displayed proper, holding in his Beak a Scroll, inscribed with the Motto, viz., "E pluribus Unum"—and in his dexter Talon a Palm or an Olive Branch—in the other a Bundle of 13 Arrows; all proper.

Needless to say, the "Bald Eagle" is not really bald, but merely appears to be so from a distance because of the distinctive white plumage on its head and neck. Despite the famous commentary of Benjamin Franklin, in which he regarded the Bald Eagle as "a bird of bad moral character . . . who does not get his living honestly . . ." and "like those among men who live by sharping and robbing . . . is generally poor and often very lousy," the emblem of freedom cuts as noble a figure on the Seal of the United States of America, on the President's flag and seal, on military insignia, currency, stamps, and in any number of official and semiofficial uses as any of its European counterparts.

The Frankish, or German, eagle is said to have been the badge of Charlemagne until he claimed the two-headed eagle as Holy Roman Emperor in 800. When Otto the Great succeeded to the title in 962, the imperial Frankish eagle passed over into Germany and eventually became an emblem of Teutonic heraldry.—*Fifteenth-century German shield; Metropolitan Museum of Art.*

In all of man's association with the birds of prey there has been none more intimate than that of the falconer's with his hawk. The idea of capturing falcons and training them, by reward, to hunt, for man's needs and entertainment, originated in Central Asia at about 2000 B.C. or earlier, and spread by 1700 B.C. to Asia Minor.

Although coins in circulation in the fourth century B.C. show Alexander the Great with a falcon or hawk-eagle on the fist, there is no evidence that any other European prince used falcons for hunting until the sport was introduced in Italy at about A.D. 560, or that it was widely adopted until much later. The first English hawk-fancier was the eighth-century Saxon king of Kent, Ethelbert II, and he was followed in the next century by Alfred the Great and Athelstan. After the Norman conquest (1066) new breeds like the Gyrfalcon were introduced, and falconry took hold to such an extent that by the twelfth century even the citizens of London—the merchant, the baker, and the candlestick-maker—kept sparrowhawks (accipiters) and Goshawks, the "short-

The Bald Eagle looked more like a turkey than a bird of prey on the first Seal of the United States (1782), became more predatory on the second version (1841), and finally assumed the distinctive white head and tail of the species (1902). This is the American Eagle as we know it today. However, since the design of the seal was originally adopted, its basic elements and their symbolic meaning have not changed: "The Olive branch and arrows denote the power of peace and war which is exclusively vested in Congress. The Constellation [of thirteen stars] denotes a new state taking its place and rank among other sovereign powers. The escutcheon is born on the breast of an American Eagle without any other supporters, to denote that the United States of America ought to rely on their own virtue."—*Seal of the United States of America; Federal Hall Memorial Museum.*

The first tangible records of falconry in western Asia appeared on coins and pottery.
—Persian bowl, thirteenth century; Metropolitan Museum of Art.

winged hawks." Gyrfalcons and Peregrines, the "long-winged hawks," were traditionally reserved for the pleasure of the nobility because of their greater intelligence, strength, and spectacular aerial performance. The *Boke of St. Albans* lists a bird for every rank in feudal society, a mark of "degree, priority, and place" as strictly observed as a blazon upon a shield.

The great popularity of falconry on the Continent began with the returning Crusaders, many of whom brought back trained birds and Saracen falconers from their campaigns in the East. Every man had his theories about the care, feeding, and training of hunting birds, and to own one was to value it above all other possessions. Nor was the sport confined to men. A fourteenth-century Frenchman counseled his young wife to take her hawk with her "everywhere" so that it might become accustomed to men, horses, carts, hounds, and "all other things." She was advised to take it even to church.

Nuns were particularly fond of carrying their birds into chapel, as we see from a letter of remonstrance written by William of Wykeham in 1387 to the abbesses of Romsey, Wherwell, and St. Mary's, Winchester, in which he complains that some of their sisterhood brought "birds, rabbits, hounds, and suchlike frivolous things [into chapel] with frequent hindrance to their psalmody . . . and grievous peril to their . . . souls." Later, Anne Boleyn was to choose a white falcon as her personal badge, and even the fragile Mary Queen of Scots found time during her captivity to fly a Merlin.

Almost seven centuries of addiction to this peculiar form of the chase can only be compared, in modern times, to the American enthusiasm for baseball. The English Angevins and Stuarts, the French kings from Charles VI to Louis XVI, the Holy Roman emperors, and the Russian czars all kept great falconry establishments. So intense was Emperor Frederick II of Hohenstaufen's passion for the sport that he lost an important battle for the sake of a day's hawking.

Frederick II literally inherited falconry, as he was the grandson of the famous Barbarossa who introduced the sport into Italy. He was an Orientalist to the extent of keeping his wives and concubines in seclusion and importing dancing girls from the East, and he consorted with Arab and Hebrew philosophers from Baghdad and Syria. He was learned in philosophy and all branches of medieval science. And he was more than casually acquainted with the six languages employed in his economic, political, and military dealings with the Mediterranean countries of the thirteenth century. In short, the "Sultan of Sicily," in his catholic (if also extravagant) tastes and interests, transcended the image of Medieval

Man. It is to him that we owe that vast compendium of falconry practices, *De Arte Venandi cum Avibus,* which was thirty years in preparation. Although certain sections on the anatomy of birds, on bird flight, and on migration are notable because they contain material not previously recorded by Aristotle, Pliny, or any of the medieval scholars, the bulk of the work is a detailed and fascinating picture of this Sport of Kings at its kingliest.

The hawk furniture and devices for training falcons described in *De Arte* are still in use among devoted followers of the sport in the twentieth century. The medieval falconer, like his modern counterpart, controlled his bird with *jesses,* two narrow strips of leather attached to each leg and to a short *leash; bells* of silver or brass; and a *hood,* often decoratively feathered, which served as a blinder, especially during the initial period of *manning* (getting the bird accustomed to man and its new environment). In training, he used the *lure* and the *feathered lure,* pieces of leather containing meat which served as dummy prey. The falcon was carried then, as now, on the gloved fist by holding the jesses between the fingers. In the field, when the bird was released, the jesses and bells remained on its legs.

If we go beyond the equipment to the actual practice of falconry, however, the modern falconer can become hopelessly entangled in the elaborate instructions given for "manning" newly caught birds. The medieval European hawk-fancier prolonged this process, instead of expediting it, by keeping his falcon hooded, or sealed (with eyelids sewn together) in the dark rooms for days. From time to time he stroked her feathers, beak, and feet, and plied her with bits of meat until she would deign to eat docilely from his hand.

Then, "on the night when she is granted full vision, the falconer must not wait until sunrise before taking the bird from her perch; she must be on his fist before dawn. In this way the visual images perceived at night are continuous with daylight and, as the falcon's eyes open fully and the sun rises, she gradually and with an increased sense of security, gazes on the countenance of man and other objects. It must be repeated that she should never be carried from a darkened room (or one lighted only by a lantern) into full sunlight. . . ."

The falcon had to be carried on the fist before daybreak, and to an "unfrequented wall" where the falconer stood with the bird's back to the wall so that his body would protect her on one side and the stone barrier would save her on the other from the shock of unfamiliar sights and noises.

It is apparent that medieval men took more precautions in the care of their hawks than of their own persons. In Frederick's time falconers knew no more about treating birds than doctors comprehended about the curing of human ills. They could make a splint for a broken leg, or drain the pus from an infected toe, but most of their remedies did more harm than good. Vitamin compounds and miracle drugs were, of course, centuries away, so extreme measures were observed by the emperor to prevent the illness or injury of his prized hunting birds.

Frederick enjoyed crane-hunting with Gyrfalcons and heron-hawking with Sakers and other falcons, and had many elaborate schemes for flying Peregrines at ducks. On these expeditions he was usually on horseback, accompanied by retainers and dogs. The greatest hazard, explained the monarch, was deep water. In the event that the falcon brought her duck down on the far side of an unfordable stream, the falconer had to swim to her rescue!

Legend has it that one of young Thomas à Becket's falcons disappeared into a swiftly running millstream, her talons locked in the back of a diving duck. Becket plunged to the rescue, but the strong current drew him toward the revolving mill wheel. Some chroniclers say the miller stopped the wheel, others that it stopped of its own accord, but all agree that the future saint, martyr, and Archbishop of Canterbury was miraculously saved. What, we wonder, of the falcon? And we are reminded of the Nootka story of the whale that drowned the three Thunderbird spirits by enticing them to strike him and then diving to the bottom of the sea.

If we wish to know why certain birds were preferred above others in the medieval hierarchy of the *Boke of St. Albans,* we must consider their special qualities as hunters.

The large, powerful eagles of the *Aquila* group—most commonly the Golden Eagle—were reserved for emperors. Slower than the hawks and falcons, they had to be cast off close to the quarry and were more useful for hunting mammals than birds.

The Gyrfalcon of Norway, Greenland, and Iceland, largest of the falcons, probably derives its Old Norse name, *Geirfalki*—"spear falcon"—from its strong, direct flight. It was the favorite of kings—hard to obtain, "noble" in appearance, and an extremely efficient hunter. Louis XVI was the last

According to Medieval falconry manuals, a bath invigorated a falcon before the hunt and was also an excellent means of calming a newly caught bird. A rod, used to stroke her feathers, might be employed to stir the water, and thereby tempt her to jump from the glove and bathe. Here, the lady holds a Merlin while her companion stirs the falcon's bath.—*Flemish tapestry, School of Arras, 1420-35; Metropolitan Museum of Art.*

French sovereign to whom Gyrfalcons were presented as tribute from the northern countries once a year.

Though not prized as highly as the Gyrfalcon, the Peregrine was widely used by royalty and considered the badge of the prince, the duke, the earl, and the baron. The color and marking of each bird—caused by molt (or age) and variations in "races" from different localities—were supposed to denote the degree of its "nobility" and usefulness in falconry. Frederick II had the good sense to choose his Peregrines for strength, intelligence, and build, rather than plumage alone. Nevertheless, he conformed with the style of his age when he said, in *De Arte,* that the best hunters were not only well built but dark colored and "of a superior, more exclusive and beautiful class," and "The more the color of the plumage is in accord with that of the cere and talons, the higher hope one may entertain of their superior hunting performance."

Falconers have long preferred to train Peregrines caught on their first migration—*passage birds* in brown plumage, heavily streaked on the breast. Young birds taken from the eyrie lack experience in

hunting, and wild-caught adults, or haggards, may be difficult to handle, but there is no reason to believe that the considerable variety in the coloring and marking of adult Peregrine Falcons has anything to do with their hunting capabilities. The Peregrine Falcon has, in all ages that man has pursued falconry, been considered the perfect hunter. The female is preferred, as in other species of birds of prey. She is larger and stronger than the male (the tercel). Faster than any other bird of prey—except perhaps the Gyrfalcon—the Peregrine is more versatile in the air and capable of taking a wide variety of game.

The knights of the Middle Ages were allowed another favorite of kings—the Sacred (or Saker) Falcon, one of the largest and best Eurasian hunting hawks.

Should the squire set out on a day's hawking, he carried a Lanner Falcon on his glove. Comparable in size to the Peregrine but not as powerful, this bird is a persistent hunter of quail.

The delicate but pugnacious (female) Merlin or (male) "Jack" had a special place in medieval falconry on milady's fist. The Merlin was used in England for lark-hawking for many centuries, but the sport is now prohibited under the 1954 Protection of Birds Act. Its North American equivalent is the Pigeon Hawk.

The Hobby, once the hunting bird of young squires, is now one of Britain's rarest hawks. Faster than the Merlin, on its long wings it could take young Swifts with little difficulty.

The Eurasian Sparrowhawk and the Goshawk, the birds of the yeoman and priest, must, like the Golden Eagle, be cast off at a short distance to follow and "bind to" their prey.

And last of all, at the bottom of the social ladder, reserved for knaves, servants, and children, was the pliable, brave little Old World Kestrel, whose relatives inhabit every continent and many islands on the earth. In modern times falconers use Kestrels as beginners' birds and children still keep them as pets. They live mainly on mice, shrews, and insects.

So concludes the list of favored hunting birds with which Frederick and his contemporaries were familiar. Some of the birds that man has used for hunting, such as Eleonora's Falcon, of the islands in the Mediterranean, and the Laggar Falcon of India, both trained as quail hunters, never became popular in Europe.

In North Africa, the Middle East, and various parts of Asia, falconry was—and still is—practiced by nomadic peoples primarily as a means of obtaining food. The origins of falconry are not documented, but it almost certainly started in China. There it was a favorite practice of scholars to carry a small bird on the wrist as they walked in their gardens. From the earliest times the Chinese were

The medieval hawking party was a social occasion, enhanced by splendid dress, and opportunities for making love.—*Flemish tapestry, beginning of the fourteenth century; Metropolitan Museum of Art.*

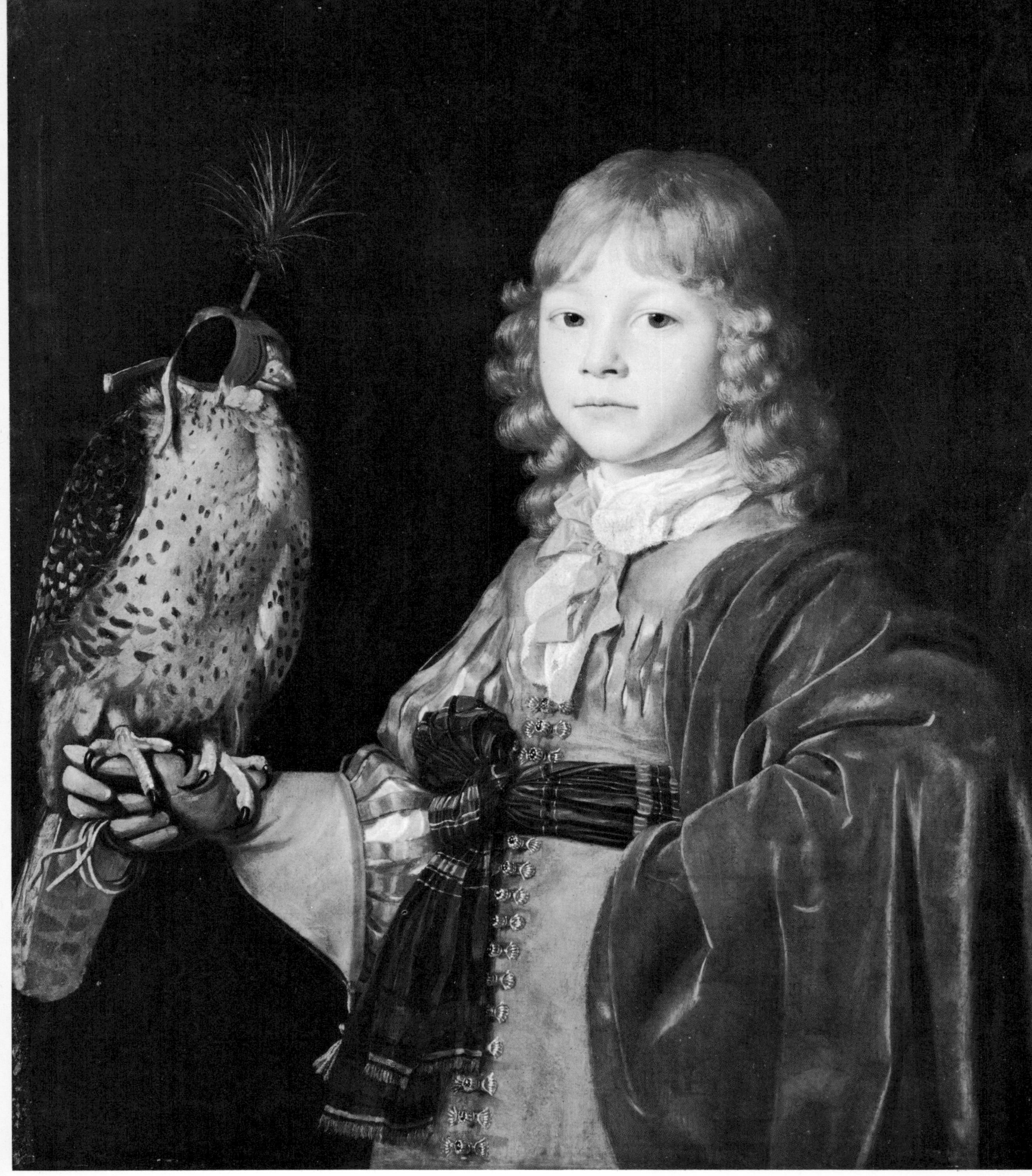

A Dutch painter of the seventeenth century shows his knowledge of the Peregrine Falcon and the details of hawk furniture—the glove, hood, jesses, and leash, expertly wound around two fingers. Falconry was to thrive in Holland for the next hundred years, when the trapping and training of birds for the nobility of all Europe became a major industry.—*Oil painting, "Boy with Falcon," by Aelbert Cuyp (1620-91); Metropolitan Museum of Art.*

constantly experimenting in new ways to capture and train birds. They employed bow nets and other traps to ensnare songbirds and game birds and had learned to use cormorants to catch fish before they thought of trapping and training falcons.

It is highly probable that the first falconer was a man who had captured a young falcon or eagle and realized that, like the cormorant, it might be useful for catching food. Thus falconry grew up in China as a method of hunting. Then, as with any of the methods of hunting devised by men, falconry also became a sport, sometimes directed against other predators. In Tartary and Mongolia, the Golden Eagle is still sent after wolves, as in the time of Genghis Khan. All the refinements of hawking, as well as the furniture, originated in the courts of the Orient. Today, Punjabi falconers are among the world's most knowledgeable, and bells made at Lahore from a secret process are sought by falconers everywhere.

In Japan, where the emperors and shoguns rode to the sport on magnificently caparisoned horses, falconry became a social distinction, as among the Indian maharajas, and even now, where its formal practice continues, falconry in the Far East is governed by tradition and ceremony as marked as any in the Middle Ages of Europe.

The invention of efficient guns and the clearing of lands for agriculture are the usual reasons cited for the decline of falconry in Europe. It lost popularity with the general citizenry as the feudal system gradually broke down, and the emperors and kings who had been its sponsors abdicated their absolute powers of government. In a word, the sport itself became archaic.

During the eighteenth century, Holland was the center of European falconry and the chief source of birds, which were trapped in elaborate bow nets during fall migrations. The art of hawking was passed from father to son to grandson in a few Dutch families which served the courts of the Continent and England. Like their Eastern counterparts, the Chinese, the Dutch had a special love for birds. They acquired the art of falconry from their experience in netting songbirds. Little by little there grew up a craft village, Valkenswaard, whose whole economy depended not only upon trapping, but on making hawk furniture and on manning and training the birds. Hawks could just as easily have been caught on the English moors, but no one believed that this could be done, and thus a monopoly established itself which was to endure until the last of the famous Mollen family of falconers died in 1937, bringing the hawk business to an absolute halt in Europe. One by one the falcons purchased from the Dutch hawk marts were lost and not replaced.

Up to the time of George III, falconry was practiced by English royalty. The Stuarts especially loved the sport, and Henry VIII may have been its greatest advocate since Frederick II. Henry fell into a dike once, when his pole vault broke during the chase, and would have drowned had he not had so many retainers to pull him out.

By ancient usage the king of England, at the time of his coronation, is presented with falcons by the Duke of Athol and Lord Derby, and the office of royal falconer, called Master of the Mews, still exists. The history of British falconry furnishes the most remarkable example of a succession of family falconers—the Flemings. An ancestor received a jeweled hawk's hood from James IV of Scotland for outflying the king's falcon with his tercel. The grandfather of the present owner of the hood was a well-known falconer, and his father kept hunting birds until his death in 1855. It is the grandfather with his falconer who is shown in the famous oil painting by Howe, done in 1811.

In France, Germany, and England, falconry clubs have kept the sport alive into the twentieth century for an ever-diminishing number of enthusiasts. In the United States and Canada, where the practice of falconry was never traditional, there are perhaps 250 falconers who actually hunt with their birds. More than half of them are members of the North American Falconers Association, with headquarters in Denver, Colorado. The exchange of information and help to beginners which this club offers should give the sport a new status on the North American continent. Conservation groups oppose falconry on the grounds that nesting populations of falcons, especially Peregrines, are dangerously low in the United States. They also fear mishandling. The birds now being used for falconry, however, are mostly trapped on their migration from northern regions—Alaska, Ungava, and Labrador—where Peregrines and Goshawks are still extremely numerous. Rather than see them black-marketed by unauthorized and sometimes unscrupulous persons, the club sensibly seeks to control the traffic in birds, and maintain standards for their training.

Undoubtedly the most impressive falconry establishment in the world today is the United States Air

Force Academy's mews in Colorado Springs, where Peregrines, Prairie Falcons, and the official mascot, a white Gyrfalcon, are trained by cadet handlers to fly at half-time celebrations of football games. Daily flights at the mews are also open to visitors.

Many of the falconry terms which have been adopted into everyday English usage are to be found in the plays of Shakespeare. In *Much Ado About Nothing,* Hero says of Beatrice:

> She is too disdainful.
> I know her spirits are as coy and wild
> As haggards of the rock.

The word for a wild-caught adult Peregrine Falcon—haggard—has become a common adjective and is used as an uncomplimentary appellation—hag, or old hag.

In the words of Sir Toby Belch:

> He's a coward and a coystril [kestrel] that will not drink to my niece. . . .
> *Twelfth Night*

A "coward" was a weak, derelict falcon that had lost her courage; and young birds shaking their wings or quivering, as evidence of obedience to the falconer, were said to be "cowering."

A broken tail feather or wing often hampered the flight of hawks, so the falconer fastened a substitute in its place, hence the familiar figurative use of "imping" by Northumberland in *Richard II:*

> If, then, we shall shake off our slavish yoke
> Imp out our drooping country's broken wing. . . .

King Duncan of *Macbeth* is described as a "falcon towering in her pride of place," the highest point in a hawk's soaring flight. To be "in a towering passion" and to "beat around the bush" are phrases once relating to birds in the field. To "truss up" referred to the hawk's seizure of its prey in the air. The falcon circling overhead as his human hunting partner flushed game birds out of cover, was said to "wait on." And "quarry" was originally game hunted with hawks, hence the object of any type of chase.

Only two of Shakespeare's plays do not mention the birds of prey and ill omen: *Henry VIII* and *Two Gentlemen of Verona.* That nearly every reference to hawks is in terms of falconry should not be surprising in view of the love the English of the Renaissance bore for these noble, well-graced, and much-valued hunting birds. The Bard's audiences well understood that

> As the ox hath his bow, sir, the horse his curb, and the falcon her bells, so man hath his desires.
> *As You Like It*

The owl that Ophelia recalls in a mad fit (in *Hamlet*) is the creature of a legend current in seventeenth-century Gloucestershire. One day, the story goes, our Savior walked into a baker's shop and asked for some bread. The baker's wife put a lump of dough in the oven but, yielding to the remonstrances of her parsimonious daughter, she broke off a piece; whereupon the dough expanded and filled the oven. The daughter cried out, "Heugh, heugh, heugh!" And was transformed into the bird whose voice is "Hoo! Hoo! Hoo!"

In *Macbeth,* the royal play calculated to please King James, who was deeply interested in Scottish witchcraft, special use is made of the owl as an evil spirit. Act I, Scene I, introduces a covin of witches planning Macbeth's destruction. Each one has a devil who is her mentor and transports her over land and sea to do evil. Two of these "spirits"—Graymalkin, the little gray cat, and Paddock, the toad—are named here, and in Act IV, the third is revealed as Harpier, a large owl. The screams of this owl are heard on the night of Duncan's murder. Lady Macbeth, awaiting her husband's return from the king's chamber, says, "Hark!—Peace! It was the owl that shrieked." Macbeth, stumbling in after the deed is done, asks, "Didst thou not hear a noise?" To which his wife replies, "I heard the owl scream."

On entering the courtyard the next morning Lennox tells that the "obscure bird," meaning the owl, "clamour'd the live-long night."

In the famous passage containing the falconry allusion to "pride of place," the Old Man also conveys a sense of the unnatural when he says that the "falcon [the king], towering in her pride of place, was by a mousing owl hawk'd at and kill'd." This is no ordinary owl in search of its usual prey, but an evil spirit, which haunts Macbeth to the end. Weary of life and his own consuming ambition, he has almost ceased to fear the Demon:

> The time has been, my senses would have cool'd
> To hear a night-shriek.

At Hampton Court and a hundred years afterward in English theaters, "A shriek like an owl" was actually heard—not only in Act II, Scene II, the night of the murder of the king, but also in Scene II of Act III, just as Banquo was about to be struck down, and in Act IV, Scene II, when the family of the Thane of Fife was seen in jeopardy.

Harpier's shrieks were banished from the stage

in later versions, probably because, in a large public theater, where the audience is unruly, the scene might be ruined by mimicry.

Less specific use of the owl's cry of ill omen occurs in other plays. An owl shrieks in concert with a host of evil birds on the birth of Richard III; and in *Titus Andronicus,* Queen Tamora laments that a lovely glen has become a place "where nothing breeds, unless the nightly owl or fatal raven"—and with good cause, for two murders, a rape, and mutilation follow directly.

Only the repulsive side of the vulture is seen in *Macbeth, King Lear, The Merry Wives of Windsor, Henry IV, The Rape of Lucrece, Venus and Adonis,* and *Titus Andronicus.*

The kite, once the most plentiful of the birds of prey in England, and sometimes called the "puttock," invokes the image of a cowardly murderer in *Henry VI, Part 2:*

> Who finds the partridge in the puttock's nest,
> But may imagine how the bird was dead,
> Although the kite soar with unbloodied beak?

While Hamlet, in a self-destructive mood, thinks of its carrion-eating habits:

> Ere this
> I should have fatted all the region's kites
> With this slave's offal.

And Antony offers insult to a friend of Caesar by addressing him as "you kite."

Hardly more to be admired were the buzzards, or buteo hawks. Petruchio teases Kate, in *The Taming of the Shrew:*

> O slow-winged turtle, shall a buzzard take thee?

Even the Osprey appears in *Coriolanus,* in one of the most apt of the Bard's bird similes:

> I think he'll be to Rome
> As is the osprey to the fish, who takes it
> By sovereignty of nature.

The Stuart period in England ushered in a considerable fad for colorful tropical birds—peacocks from Asia, blue macaws from South America, red birds from the Gold Coast, Muscovy ducks and parakeets from the West Indies—so that any bird species less brilliant than a parrot seemed hardly worth a poet's mention. We recall, however, that some had eyes and ears for owls. Thomas Vauter wrote, in *Songs of Divers Airs and Natures:*

> Sweet Suffolk owl, so trimly dight
> With feathers like a lady bright,
> Thou singst alone, sitting by night,
> Te-whit, tee-whoo!
>
> Thy note that forth so freely rolls,
> With shrill command the mouse controls,
> And sings a dirge for dying souls;
> Te-whit, tee-whoo!

The eighteenth century saw a return of Classicism, and with it the birds of the Greeks and Romans. Gray had a predilection for the owl and the eagle. In his "Elegy Written in a Country Churchyard," he carried on a traditional association of owls with ivy:

> . . . from yonder ivy-mantled tow'r
> The moping owl does to the moon complain.

He wrote to a friend: "I keep an owl in the garden as like me as he can stare, only I do not eat raw meat, nor bite people by the fingers." Passing from the elegiac to the Pindaric mood, he wrote of the eagle in Pindar's "First Pythian Ode" that was soothed by music:

> Perching on the sceptred hand
> Of Jove, thy magic lulls the feathered King
> With ruffled plumes and flagging wing;
> Quenched in dark clouds of slumber lie
> The terror of his beak and lightning of his eye.

It was a barometer of the coming Romantic age that Horace Walpole, the writer of the first Gothic novel, *The Castle of Otranto,* should develop a great passion for a marble Roman eagle. Walpole first heard of the eagle three years after it had been dug up near the Baths of Caracalla in 1742. For the next two years he suffered agonies over the arrangements to purchase the bird and have it shipped to England without mishap. But the second Jacobite Rebellion intervened, with Walpole fearful he would be left "shivering in an antechamber at Hanover," penniless, his family's fortune destroyed, and, of course, unable to pay the eagle's ransom. When the rebellion failed and the forces of Prince Charles Edward had been dispersed on Culloden Moor, he was still anxious (in February, 1746) "that the eagle may not come until the opportunity of a man-of-war; we have lost so many merchantmen lately that I should never expect to receive it that way." Suffice it to say that the precious *objet d'art* was finally delivered nearly a year later. Walpole's letter to Sir Horace Mann on June 26, 1747, reads:

> My eagle is arrived—my eagle *tout court,* for I hear nothing of the pedestal. The bird itself was sent home in a store-ship. I was happy that they did not reserve the statue and send its footstool. It is a

> glorious fowl! I admire it, and everybody admires it, as much as it deserves. There never was so much spirit and fire preserved with so much labour and finishing.

The pedestal was later found at the bottom of the store-ship; but what was Walpole's agitation to discover that the lower part of the eagle's beak had been broken and lost! Restored, it was again knocked off forty years later by a sightseer at Walpole's estate, Strawberry Hill. The sculptress daughter of his cousin, Henry Conway, replaced the missing part with wax, but as "this had not force enough to execute the command of Jove nor to crush the fingers of those who presumed to touch his royal and sacred person," a third restoration of the marble beak was soon completed. In the famous Reynolds portrait, a drawing of the "glorious fowl" depends from the table on which Walpole rests his arm.

The Romantic poets of the nineteenth century continued to write on many of the same themes as the Classical poets. In his poem "On the Death of Kirke White," Byron recreated Aesop's image of the eagle:

> So the struck eagle, stretched upon the plain,
> No more through rolling clouds to soar again,
> Viewed his own feather on the fatal dart,
> And winged the shaft that quivered in his heart;
> Keen were his pangs, but keener far to feel
> He nursed the pinion which impelled the steel,
> While the same plumage that had warmed his nest
> Drank the last life-drop of his bleeding breast.

And Keats, known for lauding the nightingale on a Grecian urn, also left a memorable impression of the owl, which, "On the Eve of Saint Agnes" "for all his feathers was a-cold."

In matters of state, in military and civil decor, the Empire period in France revived the eagle of the

Horace Walpole's "glorious fowl" has the heavy elongated beak and bare legs of a sea eagle.—*Marble eagle from the Baths of Caracalla, Italy; photograph by A. and J. Gordon, courtesy Methuen & Co., Ltd.*

Romans and Charlemagne. The Republic, the Empire, and the Directorate all affected a Classical taste, like Napoleon himself; although as a conqueror, with his star and legend, he acted the role of the most flagrant Romantic.

Then the voices of social and economic reform, set in motion by the Industrial Revolution, were heard in the lands. Browning, a Victorian poet with an almost modern power and style, had his Monk say, "G-r-r-r," and the rocks of established religion—of Mount Sinai and St. Peter—received an earthquake shock from the publication of *The Origin of Species.*

Against such a setting, the works of Alfred, Lord Tennyson, poet laureate of England from 1850 to 1892, stand in sharp contrast. His masterpiece, "The Eagle," is almost Byronic:

> He clasps the crag with hooked hands,
> Close to the sun in lonely lands;
> The wrinkled sea beneath him crawls;
> Ring'd with the azure world, he stands,
> He watches from the mountain walls,
> And like a thunderbolt he falls.

It is appalling to discover that Tennyson was also the author of an obscure play called *The Falcon* in which a stuffed "property" bird was brought in on a platter as the *pièce de résistance.* What noble of a bygone age of chivalry would sacrifice his "princess of the skies," like so many larks' tongues, to his lady love's appetite—especially when the whole affair appears to have been a misunderstanding from the beginning—and then say, as Count Federigo does, on winning the girl:

> "Why, then, the dying of my noble bird
> Hath served me better than her living."

One of the finest and best known poems about a bird of prey was written by a Victorian poet whose lyrics, dealing with nature and religion, really belonged in many respects to the age of the metaphysical poets (late sixteenth and early seventeenth centuries); in others, presaged the "difficult lonely music" of such later masters as Eliot, Pound, and Auden. Gerard Manley Hopkins describes the kestrel in "The Windhover," the common name taken from its habit of riding motionless on the wind, and addresses the subtitle "To Christ Our Lord":

> I caught this morning's minion, kingdom of daylight's dauphin, dapple-dawn-drawn Falcon, in his riding
> Of the rolling level underneath him steady air, and striding
> High there, how he Rung upon the rein of a wimpling wing
> In his ecstasy! then off, off forth on swing, as a skate's heel sweeps smooth on a bow-bend; the hurl and gliding
> Rebuffed the big wind. My heart in hiding
> Stirred for a bird,—the achieve of, the mastery of the thing!

In America, under the impetus of the expanding Western frontier, there was to be a continuing and vital release of the Romantic's desire to go back to nature. Much of the writing of this period took its inspiration from a new breed of naturalists—especially from John James Audubon, "The Woodsman," whose bird paintings and journals published in the first half of the nineteenth century breathed life into the "stuffed" science of ornithology. Both science and philosophy in the Middle Ages had been based upon the works of Aristotle, who, although he listed several hundred species of birds, was more concerned with the physiology of other creatures. With the notable exception of Frederick II's *De Arte Venandi cum Avibus,* the popular "science" concerned itself with fable and myth. The Bestiaries, the "textbooks" of the Middle Ages, designed to teach the most amazing facts about the animal kingdom, tell how the eagle renews its youth every ten years. When his limbs are stiff, his flight feeble, and his eyes dim, the aging King of Birds seeks out a spring which flows both by night and day. Having found it, he soars beyond the sixth and seventh circles of heaven and looks straight at the sun, which "maketh his eyes bright," though unfortunately "his feathers fall for the heat." Then he swoops down to the water below. His plumage is restored immediately, but his beak is still twisted. So in the next and last stage of his rejuvenation, he sharpens and straightens it on a stone. At the base of this peculiar misconception may be the purely symbolic lines from the Old Testament (Psalm 103:5 and Isaiah 40:31) which refer to the promise of the Lord to bear up his people as on the wings of the eagle and to renew their strength as the bird is renewed in Him.

It was not until the mid-1700's that the science of ornithology was established and concerned itself with describing and classifying birds according to the *Systema Naturae* (1735) of the Swedish scientist Carolus Linnaeus. The first departure from the purely academic is seen in the magnum opus of Georges Louis Leclerc de Buffon, *Histoire Naturelle des Oiseaux* (1771–86), published in ten folios with nearly a thousand full-color plates by Martinet and others. In a long series of volumes on the animal and plant kingdoms, of which this is only one, Buffon proposed many of the ideas later incorporated in Darwin's theory of evolution. Buffon was considered by many to be the ablest scientific popularizer who ever lived.

However, *Oiseaux* reveals him not so much in the character of the scientist of genius as the romanticizer of the so-called habits of birds. He called all of man's preconceived ideas about the avian kingdom to his aid and judged them by human standards. In the modern world this is the sin of anthropomorphic thinking, a legitimate device of poets, but an undesirable element in scientific investigation. Whereas the Linnaean system of Latin names had notably avoided suggesting relationships between genera and species, Buffon redesigned it to suit himself. He made the first species the eagle "which Belon, following Athene, has called the royal eagle or the king of birds." His first volume lumped the "noble" and "warlike" species together, including groups as anatomically diverse as the eagles and hawks, the owls, and the shrikes. His life histories, though readable and frequently factual, contained many absurd and emotional conclusions.

Of all the species which nature had "condemned to live by the chase," he argued, the woodpecker had the most "savage and surly nature" because it had been denied the courageous pursuit and flight of the "noble birds" and had to spend its entire existence at hard labor, piercing the bark of trees to find its subsistence.

Alexander Wilson, the first modern American ornithologist and bird artist, carried on, in *American Ornithology* (1808–14), the tradition of the bird book written in an engaging style and magnificently illustrated. His writings, too, are open to the charge of anthropomorphism, but in many ways he improved upon his predecessors by throwing out the residue of superstition and the classical hokum that was not applicable to scientific study.

One of his most eloquent passages defended the Great Horned Owl from "ignorance and superstition" engendering "fearful awe and reverential horror." He consigned to myth, where it belonged, the tale, recounted by Charlevoix and other early New World naturalists, that "the owls of Canada lay up a store of live mice for the winter; the legs of which they first break, to prevent them from running away, and then feed them carefully and fatten them, until wanted for use." And he derided Buffon for accepting ancient authority for the "noble" traits in the eagle, and showed the King of Birds in some cases to be a robber and an eater of carrion. His technical mistakes in the art work can be forgiven on the grounds of insufficient knowledge. The two color phases of the Screech Owl, for example, appear to be separate species, the "Red Owl" and the "Mottled Owl"; the juvenile of the Sharp-shinned Hawk is separated from the adult, which he calls the "Slate-colored Hawk"; and the juvenile of the Golden Eagle he assigns the name "Ring-tailed Eagle."

Whatever his shortcomings, Alexander Wilson was an innovator, and it was an accident of time and place that his work was destined to be eclipsed by *The Birds of America* in elephant folio size—as large, in fact, as the grandiose genius of John James Audubon. Wilson was to be known among ornithologists for his contributions in prose and lyric verse; and Audubon, also a prolific writer of journals, was the man who would make great art of ornithological illustration.

For various reasons, not the least of them economic, Audubon had to seek publication of *The Birds of America* in England. This work, comprising 435 plates and 1,065 figures, was begun in 1826 by Lizars of Edinburgh and shortly taken over and finished on the twentieth of June, 1838, by Havells of London. During the intervening years, Audubon labored hard and ceaselessly, collecting and drawing new birds, supervising the engraving and coloring, soliciting most of the subscriptions, and supervising the financing of the entire $100,000 project. Some idea of the enormity of the publishing venture may be gleaned from the fact that Wilson's folio, which was published in Philadelphia and sold by subscription, had encountered a good deal of sales resistance at $125 per set. Audubon's cost $1,000!

It was a magnificent gamble, and a successful one, for the appearance of *The Birds of America* (1827–38) and the accompanying *Ornithological Biography* (1831–39) caused more flurry and excitement in Europe than the current popular novels.

"Imagine," said the French critic Philarète Chasles, "a landscape wholly American, trees, flowers, grasses, even the tints of the sky and waters, quickened with a life that is real, peculiar, trans-Atlantic.

. . . It is a real and palpable vision of the New World, with its atmosphere, its imposing vegetation, and its tribes which know not the yoke of man." Recognition was quick in America, after this rousing reception, so that by 1837 the final list of subscribers showed eighty-two American, including many institutions, and seventy-nine European buyers.

The liveliness that characterized Audubon's bird paintings was the direct result of his drawing from freshly killed birds rather than from mounted specimens or from skins. European still-life artists had, of course, used such a technique. In the sixteenth and seventeenth centuries, Albrecht Dürer, Roeland Savery, Frans Snyders, Jan Fyt, and the D'Hondecoeters were noted for depicting birds, but these were often dead game birds. Audubon was not the first to use floral settings, for Mark Catesby had used them effectively in his *Natural History of Carolina* (1748), and Alexander Wilson in his work had paid careful attention to poses and details of plumage. Other artists had also worked in life-size, with a single species to a plate. So Audubon synthesized that which had been done before—often with an informed genius. We know that other artists contributed some of the backgrounds and paintings of flowers and greenery, and that Audubon plagiarized three of Wilson's birds, but these things seem totally unimportant in view of his achievement. Audubon's was the first bird art in the Western world to compare with the painting produced in the Orient.

Alexander Wilson's Peregrine Falcon is perhaps his best painting.—*From American Ornithology; American Museum of Natural History.*

In China, bird painting reached a height of excellence in the Sung Dynasty (A.D. 960–1279), or even earlier, in the work of Huang Chu'an and Hsu Hsi. It reflected the philosophy and cosmological ideas of an elite class of gentry insulated equally from the world outside of China's frontiers and from social discontent within. The Chinese artist traditionally worked from a store of memory images. The nature of his materials—black ink monochrome or color on silk or paper—left him little opportunity to correct and erase, so he projected these images, which had already been fully and precisely formed in his mind's eye, with accuracy and swiftness. His work was precise yet fully alive, highly mannered yet true to nature, so that the mynah, the magpie, the Gyrfalcon, and the hawk can be recognized as to genus or even species. The Chinese artist seemed never to involve his birds symbolically, as the classical or medieval European painter did, with the mythology or the affairs of people, nor did he consider birds inferior to men, but rather as individual inhabitants of the great natural world. A favorite subject was the hawk attacking its prey, and the influence of falconry in both China and Japan from early periods may be seen in exquisite portraits of the falcons used for hunting. The traditional subjects—landscapes, flowers and birds, and bamboos—were carried on, virtually unchanged in their manner of execution, into modern times, and transmitted, with many other features of Chinese culture, to the Japanese.

Japanese art of the Tokugawa period captures perfectly three characteristic attitudes of a Goshawk: From left to right, the bird is shown perched, plucking its prey, and preening its tail feathers.—*Paintings on silk, attributed to Kano Tsunenobu (1636-1713); Metropolitan Museum of Art.*

Audubon's paintings are often distinguished by an Oriental delicacy, as in his rendering of a Red-shouldered Hawk preying on a bullfrog, which, as we have noted, was also a classical Chinese theme. A magnificent colorist, he could change his mood and portray large dark birds in an almost monochromatic and stark setting, so that his portraits of the Black Vulture, the Great Gray Owl, and the California Condor, among others, are exceptionally dramatic. His usual method of obtaining effect is the animated pose, and here, when he misses the sublime, he sometimes falls into the most grotesque awkwardness.

Audubon's scope and genius in depicting the bird life of America were not to be duplicated until, nearly half a century later, Louis Agassiz Fuertes, in a much freer style, sketched and painted the birds of his collecting trips to Alaska, Texas, Florida, the Bahamas, the Magdalen Islands, Mexico, Colombia, and Abyssinia.

At least one of the American writers of the nineteenth century who was also a naturalist began to go beyond Romanticism toward conservation. Henry David Thoreau kept a journal in which he listed spring and fall migrants, nesting species, and occasional winter visitors. He recorded their nesting habits, how they cared for their young, their food, and their methods of acquiring it. With an eye to

identification, he noted field marks, distinctive behavior, songs, and call notes. And even more importantly, he looked at birds in relation to their habitats, often expressing concern over the growing scarcity of certain species.

As in Audubon's paintings, there are echoes of the Orient in Thoreau's writings. His was an essentially Eastern philosophy of nature, embracing men no less than birds or lichens, and he could not accept the religious postulate of the Western world that conferred upon a man a uniqueness and superiority over all living things. So, in his notes for the day, he respected the individuality of the hawk:

> The same thing which keeps the hen-hawk in the woods, away from the cities, keeps me here [at Walden Pond]. That bird settles with confidence on the white pine top and not upon your weathercock. That bird will not be poultry of yours, lays no eggs for you, forever hides its nest. Though willed, or *wild,* it is not willful in its wildness. The unsympathizing man regards the wildness of some animals, their strangeness to him, as a sin; as if all their virtue consisted in their tamableness. He has always a charge in his gun ready for their extermination. What we call wildness is a civilization other than our own.

To Thoreau the Great Horned Owl was a first settler:

> The hooting of the owl! That is a sound which my red predecessors heard here more than a thousand years ago. It rings far and wide, occupying

Audubon's Bald Eagle is a study in black-and-white plumage.—*Watercolor from* Birds of America; *New York Historical Society.*

> the spaces rightfully—grand, primeval, aboriginal sound. There is no whisper in it of the Buckleys, the Flints, the Hosmers, who recently squatted here, nor of the first parish, nor of Concord Fight, nor of the last town meeting.

Thoreau appears to have been the least anthropomorphic of the essayists concerned at that time with nature. His militantly antisocial attitude made him particularly immune to the occupational hatred of the farmer for the "chicken hawk," nor did he care for shooting, even to obtain specimens. He was strictly an observer at Walden Pond, having the prejudice neither of the farmer nor of the sportsman. In his classic tribute to a migrant Pigeon Hawk he did not feel compelled to make any judgments about this beautiful bird which he evidently accepted and appreciated for itself.

> On the 29th of April, as I was fishing from the bank of the river . . . I heard a singular rattling sound, somewhat like that of the sticks which boys play with their fingers, when, looking up, I observed a very slight and graceful hawk, like a night-hawk, alternately soaring like a ripple and tumbling a rod or two and over, showing the underside of its wings, which gleamed like a satin ribbon in the sun, or like the pearly inside of a shell. This sight reminded me of falconry and what noblesse and poetry are associated with that sport. The Merlin, it seemed to me it might be called; but I care not for its name. It was the most ethereal flight I had ever witnessed. It did not simply flutter like a butterfly, nor soar like the larger hawks, but it sported with proud reliance in the fields of air; mounting again and again with its strange chuckle, it repeated its free and beautiful fall, turning over and over like a kite, and then recovering from its lofty tumbling, as if it had never set its foot on terra firma. It appeared to have no companion in the universe—sporting there alone—and to need none but the morning and the ether with which it played. It was not lonely, but made all the earth lonely beneath it. Where was the parent which hatched it, its kindred, and its father in the heavens? The tenant of the air, it seemed related to the earth but by an egg hatched some time in the crevice of a crag;—or was its native nest made in the angle of a cloud, woven of the rainbow's trimmings and the sunset sky, and lined with some soft midsummer haze caught up from earth? Its eyrie now some cliffy cloud.
>
> *Walden*

The love of birds fostered by Thoreau was also popularized, sometimes in an overpoweringly sentimental way, by essayists like Burroughs, Trowbridge, and Torrey, and prompted by Frank Chapman's *Bird Lore,* and *The Auk* and *The Wilson Bulletin;* and by the appearance of a rash of children's books and magazines which were plainly intended to teach conservation at home and in the schools. By the end of the nineteenth century, America was the most wildlife-conscious country in the world. California passed a law for the creation of refuges in 1870; the killing of wildlife was prohibited in Yellowstone Park in 1894; and that great outdoorsman, Theodore Roosevelt, established the first federal refuge—at Pelican Island, Florida—in 1903. Local and federal governments were issuing literature on the subject, and a few states initiated bird protection laws.

From this period date the National Audubon Society, the American Ornithologists' Union, and nearly all the conservation groups that we know. Some bird species were to benefit from their efforts more than others. They were too late to save the Carolina Parakeet and the Passenger Pigeon; and their fight to save the Snowy Egret, whose nuptial plumes were coveted by the ladies' hat industry, almost failed. How much easier they found it to enlist sympathy for a robin than a crow! or a Cardinal than a Goshawk. In mid-twentieth century, poultry farmers, ranchers, owners of game farms, and sportsmen still carry on their private war with those hawks, eagles, and owls whose forays, to a lesser or a greater degree, deplete their livestock or interfere with the pleasure of their sport. No laws or societies or appeal to "love of birds" speak more cogently than man's own interests.

The Peregrine Falcon.

chapter 3
ECOLOGY AND HABITS

There is perhaps no more marvelous spectacle in nature than that of the Peregrine Falcon, coursing and searching thousands of feet above the earth for its prey. At first just a speck, but unmistakable in its silhouette, this streamlined prototype of the jet glides on long, pointed wings, looking far ahead and below. At the sight of pheasant, flushed from the brush, it performs a bank, then goes into a stoop—with its wings tight against its body, it plummets out of the flaming orb of the sun, ever downward with great speed—until, with talons clenched, it comes up sharply beneath the quarry. On the impact the sky is at once filled with feathers, for only a tremendous blow, backed by the momentum of a fast dive, is sufficient to stun a game bird which far outweighs its attacker. The pheasant falls half dead to the ground, and the falcon is close by, with its talons reaching down to administer death in the new grass of the spring meadow. The hunter bows for an almost imperceptible moment to the task, and then with wings outstretched, mantling, it looks up and about to make sure that no other predator will snatch away its hard-won game. It has all happened in seconds, and we who have been lucky enough to witness the aerial drama cannot help but pause to think upon its grace and freedom. And yet we know that the free-flying hawk, the eagle, and all they pursue are bound by natural laws which confine them within certain limits of activity which are more or less dependent on where they live and the time of the year.

The most vital of these limitations is the habitat into which birds of prey and all other creatures are born and where they must live because of their instincts and physical characteristics. The long-winged falcons are birds of the open spaces, of the wide rivers in heavily forested taiga, and of the seacoasts. In their domain live the pheasant, the quail, and the water birds, each in its turn restricted to meadows and prairies, riverbanks, dunes, or rocky shorelines. The falcon's inland habitat is shared by rodent-eaters: during the day by the Golden Eagle and Rough-legged Hawk, and at night, by the Screech Owl and Barn Owl. The falcon may also share its coastal strongholds with the Bald Eagle and the Osprey. In the woodlands the Goshawk and other accipiters keep silent vigil, waiting for an opportunity to swoop down on short rounded wings, through the lacework of branches, onto the sparrow and the warbler, and from sunset to sunup the small birds and mammals fall prey to the Barred Owl, the Saw-whet Owl, and the Boreal Owl.

The birds of prey have developed along with the food animals in the various living places on the earth —woodland and prairie, high plateau and mountain forest, desert and jungle. Some are wonderfully swift, while others are patient waiters or experts at stalking, and their qualities are not accidental, but the result of gradual adaptation for more successful living through hundreds of thousands of years.

From the earth's inception there have been constant and sometimes drastic changes in its crust and climatic conditions, producing first plant life, and then the feeders on plant life and all that subsist on them. The various habitats may be compared to living bodies whose populations of plants and animals, each having an organic function necessary for the continuing life of the habitat as a whole, eventually grew to be interrelated to a greater or lesser degree. These bodies are smoothly running assemblages of living things, reflecting the impact of soil, water, and climate. If we include these latter nonliving parts in the concept of the body, we have what modern ecologists call an "eco-system," one demanding only sun power for its perpetual operation.

By the end of the Pleistocene, the character of the world's habitats, as we know them, was well established, with the greatest variety of plants and animals, but comparatively few of each kind, in the tropics; fewer species, but more of each kind, in temperate latitudes; and still fewer species and many

The pointed wing silhouette of the Peregrine Falcon, in flight, is characteristic of all the members of the falcon group and helps to identify this bird as it courses high above the earth.

Sighting a pheasant, the falcon banks for its downward plunge. (On a dive the wings are pulled in close to the body.)

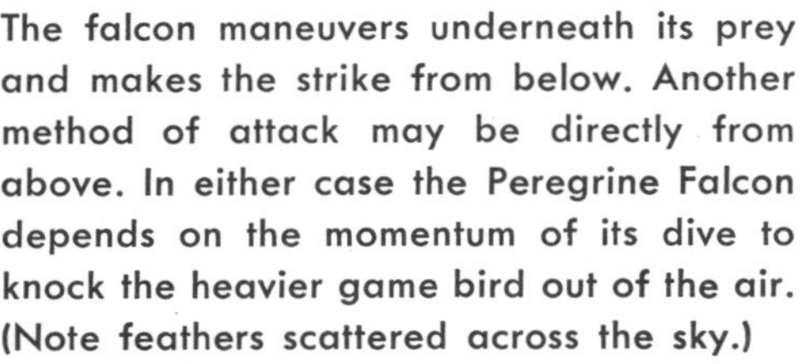

The falcon maneuvers underneath its prey and makes the strike from below. Another method of attack may be directly from above. In either case the Peregrine Falcon depends on the momentum of its dive to knock the heavier game bird out of the air. (Note feathers scattered across the sky.)

The falcon binds to the pheasant with one foot and carries it along (above), then it allows the stunned bird to fall (left) but never loses sight of it on the downward glide.

On the ground the falcon breaks the neck of the prey with its beak and mantles, or hides, it by spreading both wings. Mantling may be a holdover from the falcon's nestling days when it had to compete with other young birds for food brought to the eyrie.

After looking around and making sure that its feeding will not be interrupted, the falcon begins to pluck the pheasant. A particular eater, it may devour only the breast.

more of each kind on the Arctic tundra. This gradient operating from the Equator to the Arctic regions (and to a lesser extent to the Antarctic) will exist until geological forces deep within the earth and a changing climate work their dramatic effects upon the faces of the forest and prairie.

The oldest and most complex body in the world is the equatorial rain forest. It is the original home of the broadleaf tree, and has certainly been a focus of plant evolution for a long time. The very floristic richness which is an expression of its antiquity makes the rain forest fairly inscrutable, but we can guess that a network of mutual dependencies between plants and animals exists in it. There the periodic fruiting of many kinds of trees on which animals feed results in myriads of associations, perhaps as special as that of the wasp which fertilizes only figs; on its outer, transitional fringes, its seasonal changes are vertical, ranging up through the successive layers of the rain-forest canopy.

Drift movements of animals seeking the fruits, nuts, and seeds of plants as they become available may be particularly noticeable in the mountains of Borneo, New Guinea, Mindanao, Malaya, Madagascar, and the Kenya highlands. The "tropics" present a bewildering array of habitats that include not only hot, wet rain forests, but also jungles in which trees drop their leaves because of dryness rather than cold, montane pine forests, and even heath and tundra on the high peaks. One can camp at 5,000 feet on the Equator in Borneo—there sleeping bags and sweaters are the rule, and oak trees and squirrels are plentiful—yet, at 1,500 feet, in the same country, see orangutans sporting in the coastal plain forests, eating fruit which grows at that elevation.

In the monsoon zones of Southeast Asia, animal movement is determined by the effects of alternating wet and dry seasons, equivalent to summer and winter in the temperate zones. During dry seasons, animals may be constantly seeking the lush new grass which follows the destruction of the old by drought and fire. Or thirst may drive them to search for new waterholes, or hunger to seek fruits in the open savanna forests, when, due to the season, trees in the deep tropical forests are not producing.

The great variety of food animals available in the tropics, as well as the varied habitats, affords a picture of vast complexity. The Harpy Eagle of the Amazon rain forest may feed more heavily on monkeys when they are easiest to catch—that is, when a certain fruit comes into season—and at other times prey mostly on sloths and other tree-living mammals. But on the savannas of Kenya a number of species of eagles specialize throughout the year on a certain type of prey: snakes, small birds, game birds, or rodents. In this situation every type of prey in the tropical organism appears to have its predator, and every carcass its carrion-eaters that observe a rigid order of feeding; and species which hunt the same food animals frequently replace each other ecologically at different altitudes. Drought and fire, which originally created the savannas, also periodically leave an abundance of grasshoppers and other insects, lizards, snakes, rats, and mice exposed to predators. Many birds of prey on the world's savannas—in South America, Africa, Asia, and Australia—follow grass fires from region to region; among the most notorious drifters are grass owls, marsh owls, frog hawks, grasshopper buzzards, and kites.

The tropics produce many more specialized feeders than do northern climates. In Florida, Great Horned Owls have been known to raise their young almost exclusively on coots, while farther north the Great Horned Owls are much less discriminating—of necessity, for there, there are not only fewer species of raptors, but also fewer kinds of food animals, and these are available only at one time or another during four distinct seasons. The lives of all animals in the North Temperate Zone are rigidly governed by extreme temperature changes, especially the cold of winter. Reptiles and some mammals hibernate, and many birds migrate to escape the barren, unproductive months. The predators that feed on them must in turn adapt to conditions of food scarcity, either by taking whatever they can, or seeking more favorable hunting grounds. The farther north we go, the greater is the need for this adaptation. The Gyrfalcon, which preys almost entirely on ground squirrels during spring and summer in the Alaska Range, is able to remain through the winter because it can switch to a diet of ptarmigan; but the Peregrine, a more specialized feeder, must follow the migratory birds south or perish.

The picture of plant-animal cooperation is clearest in the North Temperate Zone, where it is dramatized by the adaptations of animals for the changing seasons. Here the habitats are sufficiently varied to have produced mutual dependencies, in some cases. Birds, deer, rabbits, and tree squirrels in the northern forests not only subsist on the surplus crop of fruits and nuts, but may aid in planting or disseminating the seeds. The crossbills pry open pine cones with their beaks, and some North American fruiting trees, such as holly, actually require that their seeds pass through the digestive tracts of birds before they can germinate. Nuts from oak trees fall off and are washed to other areas, but how would they travel uphill? Many are certainly carried by birds and mammals. Woodpeckers and jays are among the most notorious nut-hiders and cache-makers; and so, of course, are the squirrels. While these relationships are not as special as some in the rain forest, they may be just as vital to the life of the northern woodlands.

Perhaps the cache-makers really do forget those acorns which later sprout into sturdy oaks, but it is also likely that they store more than they need for the winter months. Without predators, these creatures would soon be so plentiful that they would exhaust the supply of nuts. Many would starve, and the deciduous forest itself would begin to die out in a few decades. But this seldom happens. The Goshawk and the Cooper's Hawk feed heavily on the birds and the squirrels in the spring and are undoubtedly a major influence in keeping their populations more or less within the capacity of the habitat to support them through the year. The wood hawks, then, are as essential to the forest as are the squirrels. In form and habits, they are an organ of this body. Over a million years they have evolved longer tails and shorter wings for greater maneuverability in hunting among trees, and having grown up with the forest, they are somehow necessary and cannot themselves live without it. After the breeding season, the Cooper's Hawk may also be an integral part of the winter range, not merely a "visitor," as far south as the temperate forests on the slopes of the Mexican Sierras and the mountains of Guatemala.

The mobility and food habits of the predacious birds have caused them to develop along many lines, and to accommodate themselves to all the habitats the earth affords. Among the most successful generalized feeders, the owls of the genus *Bubo* may be found in the United States in lowland forests in the East and in fairly open country in the West, at high altitudes in the Himalayas, and wherever there is an oasis or a pile of rocks in the great deserts of the world. The owls of the genus *Otus* likewise can survive everywhere except in the Far North. They nest in the trees of forests, in the mountains of the Sahara, and in the fabled valleys of the Andes at 10,000 feet with the large Condor and the buzzard eagle. Owls of the genus *Tyto,* which in temperate zones nest in holes in trees, niches in riverbanks, and even in structures made by man, become in the tropics birds not only of the deep forests and brush, but of the grasslands, where they nest on the ground. Wherever their habits and living places differ, they are recognizably different species. The Whiskered Owl of Mexico and the Screech Owl of North America, both members of the genus *Otus,* are almost identical, but the Mexican bird is more aggressive, and this may be why it is more numerous in a habitat where both birds can ostensibly live—the pine-oak woodlands (above 6,000 feet) in the mountains of northern Mexico, southern Arizona, and New Mexico.

There are 31 species of *Otus,* 45 species of *Accipiter,* and 39 species of *Falco,* showing all of these genera to be highly diverse in their habits, although every member of a single group has structural adaptations in common either for living and hunting in woods, along wood edges, or in open spaces. Many other groups—some may be comprised of only one or two species—have biological limitations that restrict them to the tropics or to the tundra of the Far North. One of the most successful and far-ranging birds, the Osprey, with special adaptations for catch-

In the tropics there is much individual variation, and the birds of prey are frequently adorned with tufted, crowned, or maned heads. This "fright wig" is worn by one of the largest predatory birds in the world—the Philippine Monkey-eating Eagle.—*Photographed by John Hamlet.*

ing fish, has never evolved into more than one species.

Predatory birds ranging in size from the minute pigmy falcons of Indonesia and Malaya to the giant forest dwellers—the fishing owls and the monkey-eating eagles—are now established in their habitats, helping to control the abundance of other living things wherever they may be found. They may dive into the ocean, crawl into holes, chase every conceivable bird through the air, or pounce on rodents, day or night; they may hawk insects in the air, or even kill full-grown deer. In these pursuits, their size and speed, the relative size of their feet and beaks, and special adaptations for hearing and seeing are directly related to the habits of the creatures they hunt.

Across the length and breadth of the habitat, birds and other animals find themselves confined, more or less securely, to territories, defined by actions that have become instinctive because they are absolutely necessary for survival within the wildlife community. Every creature must maintain such a living place, differing according to its specific physical and psychological make-up.

The Golden Eagle nests in a tall tree or on a steep cliff where his home will be safe from predators that live on the ground; and the white-footed mouse hides the entrance to his den in brush, a fallen log, or rotting stump. The home or nesting part of the Golden Eagle's territory is marked by flight and protected by combat against his own species or anything which may closely resemble other eagles, including light and heavy aircraft; and that of the white-footed mouse is determined by scent and defended vigorously against his own species with a squeak and a rush. Beyond the actual nest site, the Golden Eagle must maintain a hunting range large enough to supply food for himself, his mate, and their young in spring and summer; and the mouse must control a patch of ground covered with vegetation sufficient to feed and protect the breeding pair and their offspring during the growing season. The eagle seeks a high pinnacle on which to sit and digest his meal, preen his feathers, and observe his world; and the mouse requires a hidden room in his den where he may rest quietly within close, dark walls, in his own way invulnerable to the attacks of his enemies.

It is not strange to find that the owls, which are nocturnal and must depend on hearing for territorial demarcation, have developed the greatest variety of carrying sounds of any of the birds of prey, from the light querulous squeaks or laughing chatter of the smaller species to the great booming hoots and screams of the larger forest-dwellers. These are distinctive and clearly understood by others of the same species to say, "This place is mine."

The ornithologist Loye Miller took his students on a camping trip one summer among the yellow pines at 7,600 feet in the San Bernardino Mountains of California. Walking in the early morning near his campsite, he became adept at mimicking the Great Horned Owl. All through the territory of the owl he named "Buho," he received an answer and was closely followed; but as soon as he crossed the boundary, a different lord of the forest, "Tecolote," began calling at a slightly higher pitch. This owl would not come to meet him, but waited until Miller was some distance within his domain before he too began following, perching on the scrubby pines first on one side and then the other of the roadway, and peering about for a rival. On the way back, Tecolote followed him almost to the boundary line of Buho's territory. No amount of "hooting" would bring the two owls together. Buho came readily from the east, but stopped a hundred yards away from the little glade which appeared to be the dividing line. This no-man's-land between established territories held by Great Horned Owls allows them to live in comparative peace, instinctively, and without recourse to treaties.

The diurnal birds of prey mark their living places to a certain extent by voice, usually while on the wing, and they rely a great deal on soaring as well as sitting on exposed places to warn off any possible intruders. When a hawk or an eagle sees another of its species cross the boundary line, the home bird adopts an immediate flight-attack pattern and drives the trespasser a short distance beyond his own limit, whereupon he returns to his perch with an entirely different, and it seems, a victorious wing beat. The diurnal owls of the open spaces—the Short-eared Owl, Snowy Owl, Hawk Owl, and Burrowing Owl—also tend to use flight more than voice demarcation. Winging back from a boundary dispute, the Short-eared Owl brings his wings together under his body with a sharp cracking sound like a small flag whipped by the wind.

In nearly every instance the occupants of a well-established territory will defeat would-be intruders, the males challenging wandering immatures of their sex and their mates chasing off any other females that accidentally cross the home-nesting boundaries. It would seem that a few unmated birds are always within calling distance in spring and summer, for if one of a pair is trapped or killed, or dies of natural causes, another bird often arrives within hours and takes over the duties of the missing one. At a well-known Peregrine Falcon eyrie near Harpers Ferry, West Virginia, the female was trapped by a falconer and two days later a younger female was observed incubating the eggs belonging to the original pair.

Mammals have much less need than birds for marking their territories visually, and rely more heavily on the use of scent and sound. Some have developed special glands to put out scent messages. Mice use defecation posts at the entrances and exits of their runways. Deer mark their trails by scraping off the bark of trees and bushes with their horns. Bears give notice of their presence by rubbing against or standing up and scratching on trees. Members of the dog family—coyote, wolf, and fox—bark and howl and leave urine scent posts.

The most primitive creatures have not developed these elaborate systems of territorial demarcation. Lizards, from special sitting posts, display colors and fight others of their kind that venture close, and snakes merely patrol their living and hunting places.

As a rule, the immediate area around the nest of any bird of prey is always defended from others of the same species, though other species can and do nest close by. A hunting range is also maintained but is not always defended.

In a recent Alaskan study, Tom Cade found that Peregrines vigorously defended a circle one hundred yards in diameter around the nest, sometimes attacked intruders in a secondary defense zone, and fought with other birds only over food or favorite perches in a third zone extending two miles in diameter. Territorial behavior was further affected by the terrain, the motivation of the resident falcon, the phase of the breeding cycle, the attitude of the intruder, the weather, and the time of day.

For some years it has been thought that instinct forbade killing near the nest, and there is some basis in the observation, for prey species are frequently found nesting close to predatory birds. Thrushes and vireos may nest close to a Cooper's Hawk; a family of jackrabbits, immediately under a

The strike of the American Kestrel is a long straight swoop and flash of wings so fast as to be hardly noticed before it is over.

The Fence Lizard is firmly held in the Kestrel's talons.

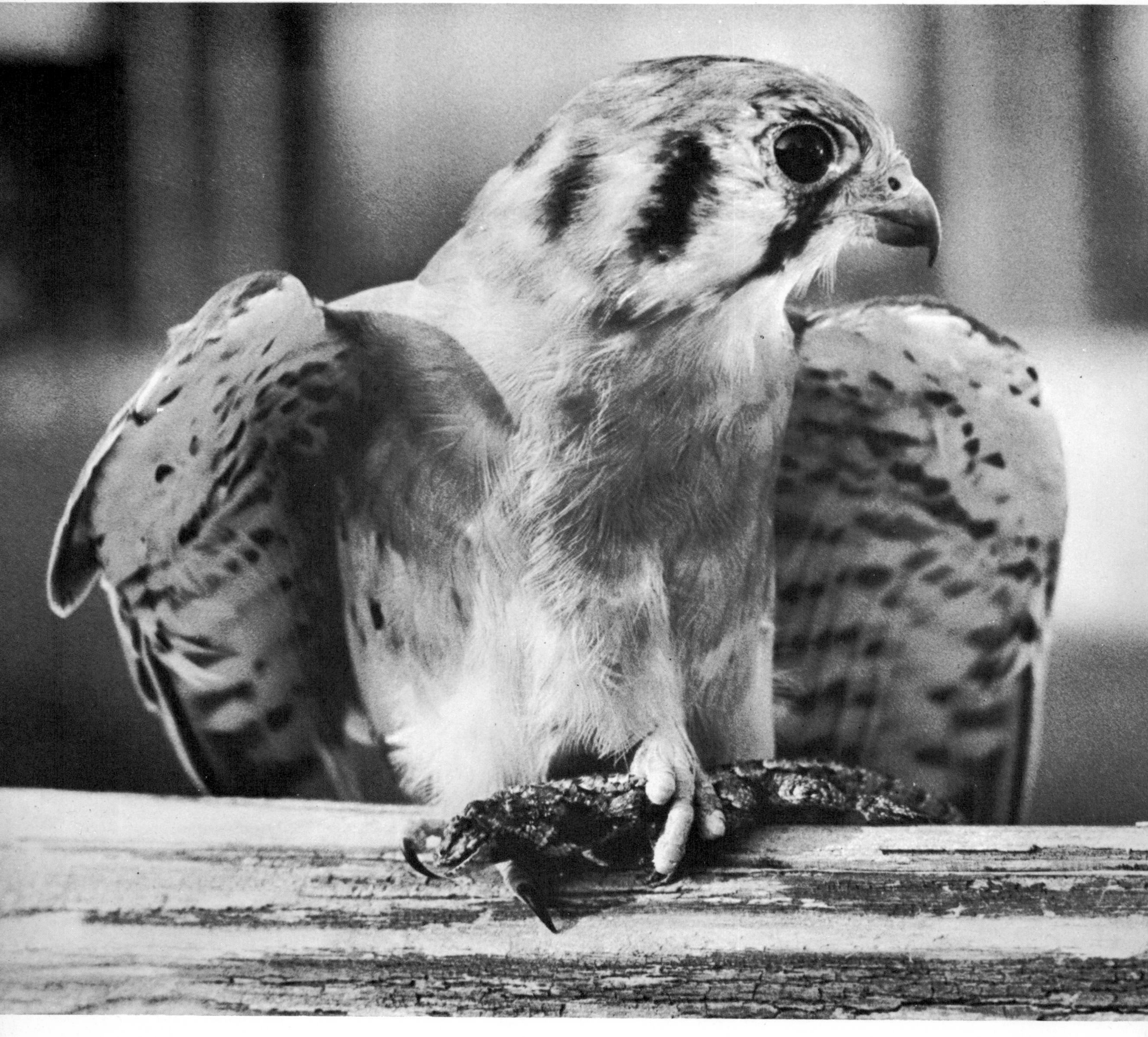

The Kestrel, like the Peregrine Falcon, kills surely and quickly. Here it uses the notched falcon beak to break the neck of its prey and hides it from other watchful eyes.

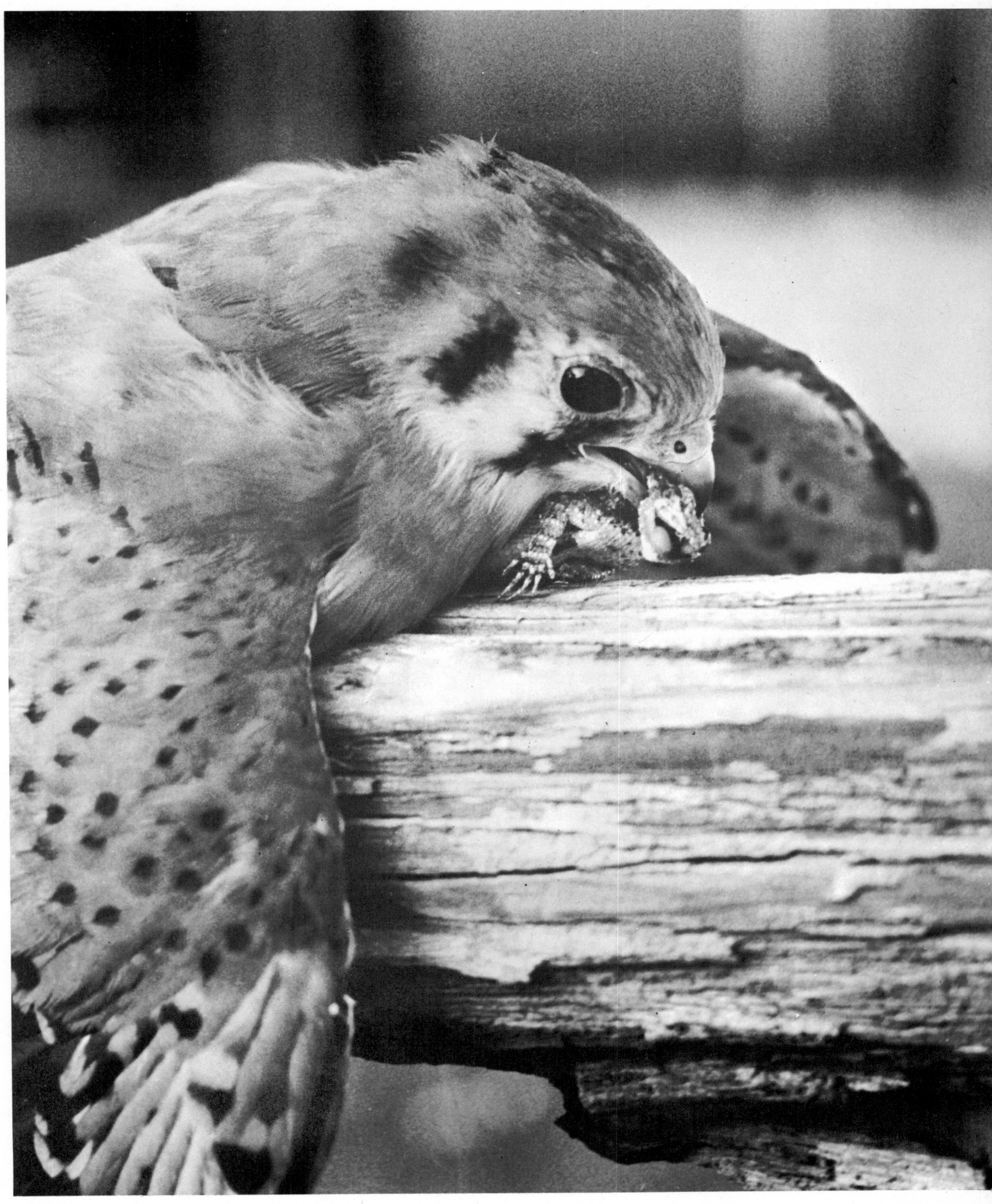

Golden Eagle's nest; ground squirrels close to the Ferruginous Rough-leg's nest; and Cliff Swallows near a Prairie Falcon's eyrie. African weavers build their colonial nests around that of the Jackal Buzzard, and lemmings raise their young under the ground nest of the Snowy Owl. Pigeons, Swifts, Kestrels, and Starlings nest near Peregrines in the Ural Mountains of Russia; and in Alaska, according to Cade, one to six pairs of geese are to be found within fifty yards of eyries. In some of these instances, the nonpredators seem to be benefiting by proximity. A pair of nesting raptors, in defending their own home, will drive away, or at least warn of the approach of other mammal, bird, or reptile predators. The prey species may also be reaping advantages from some other aspects of raptor psychology around the nest. Eagles, hawks, and owls tend to establish hunting ranges, often at some distance from the nest. When they are "at home," these birds are not usually *looking* for food, but are otherwise occupied. Every day they may be found in certain places at certain times, depending on the weather and the phase of the breeding cycle, either resting, preening, plucking, eating, attending to incubation of the eggs, or caring for their young. The individuals of the prey species that choose to be their neighbors in this situation must fit in with the more or less predictable pattern of the raptors' activities, even adopting behavior that is unusual or atypical in order to remain less conspicuous. If they do not, they may be killed.

The concept of a defended "hunting territory" may be linked not only to the amount of food available and its location, but also to the visibility of the course. In the tropics, it may be confined to birds such as the Crowned Eagle that must hunt a wide expanse of forest to find a duiker.

On the flatlands of the eastern part of the United States the nesting zone of birds of prey usually completely encloses the feeding area and is strenuously protected, but in the West, where nests are concentrated on mountains or hills, the birds hunt the region surrounding the protected nest sites, favoring certain places of abundant food supply, and these are common hunting grounds which may be shared by many species and even members of the same species without serious conflict.

Frank and John Craighead noted, in their comparative study of these regions, that Goshawks, Cooper's Hawks, Swainson's Hawks, Red-tailed Hawks, and American Kestrels defended small nesting territories on Blacktail Butte and along the Snake River bottom at Jackson Hole, Wyoming, and hunted together on the surrounding sagebrush benches. They also found that on the level farming lands of Superior Township, Michigan, hawks protected their territories vertically a thousand feet or more, whereas in the West, where nests were located on the mountainsides, a stair-step pattern of defense allowed hawks to pass over the ceilings of nest sites at various elevations without disturbing the pairs established below. These altitudinal boundaries were made very clear in the spring by the frequent high soaring of the diurnal birds of prey.

Generally, the larger the bird, the more territory is needed to provide food and shelter for a nesting pair and their young. Golden Eagle territories in Europe have been measured at 16 square miles, those of the Gyrfalcon of the northern latitudes at 14 or 15 square miles, and those of the Monkey-eating Eagle of the Philippines at 12 to 13 square miles. In Michigan the Craigsheads determined an average of 5 to 6 square miles for the Great Horned Owl, 2.5 to 2.9 square miles for the Screech Owl, 11.5 square miles for the Red-tailed Hawk, one square mile for the Marsh Hawk, three quarters of a square mile for the Cooper's Hawk, and a half square mile for the American Kestrel. In the West, Swainson's Hawk defended one square mile, the Great Horned Owl one square mile, and the Long-eared Owl, a half square mile. During one season a pair of Great Gray Owls nested near Moose, Wyoming, and their territory was measured at one square mile. Each pair of pigmy falcons in the Philippines patrols about a half square mile; the Tawny Owls of Europe, fifty acres; the tiny Flammulated Screech Owls high in the mountains of the Southwestern United States, about three acres; and the pigmy owls of Mexico, a quarter acre.

A Sharp-shinned Hawk of the northeastern woodlands illustrates how most accipters take their kill to a "butcher block" in the nesting territory, where they pluck it before feeding the young birds.—*Photographed by Heinz Meng.*

After the prey—a small bird—is plucked, the Sharp-shinned Hawk carries it to the nest in a coniferous tree.—*Photographed by Heinz Meng.*

Sharp-shinned Hawk nestlings, sitting on the edge of their large stick nest, are old enough to pick their food apart without any help from the mother. The parent bird is still in juvenile plumage. —*Photographed by Heinz Meng.*

The rule of size is somewhat modified by the specific characteristics of the birds, the nature of their habitat, and numbers and distribution of the creatures they must prey upon to survive. The far-ranging habits of the Gyrfalcon and Golden Eagle, as well as their size, result in extended territories. But species of hawks that nest close together in the woods in various places—the Red-shouldered Hawk in the East and the Red-tailed Hawk in the West—have relatively small territories. Where food is available close to the nesting site in its densely wooded habitat, the Cooper's Hawk defends an area not much larger than the kestrel's grounds. Abruptly rising terrain will cause the Great Horned Owl of the West to maintain less than half of the territory it commandeers in the eastern forests of the United States.

Most of the birds of prey will not nest within sight of another member of their own species, and the few that have a greater tolerance cannot be said to be "social" in the same sense as the weavers, for example, which gather in cooperative colonies. All of the hawklike birds and owls—even those which are notoriously gregarious—defend their boundaries against any encroachment.

The penchant of the Swallow-tailed Kite in Florida for nesting in the tops of tall pine trees, close to a cypress swamp, occasions some clustering in triangles of pairs spaced 200 or 300 yards from each other, and in the San Joaquin Delta of California, White-tailed Kites are found nesting close together on willow-covered marshy islands and foraging widely over cultivated acreage. In Germany some Ospreys nest a quarter of a mile apart, and on a small island in the Red Sea five pairs have been observed to take up housekeeping only 60 to 70 yards apart, a situation repeated on islands off the shores of Long Island, for hundreds formerly gathered during the breeding season on Gardiner's Island. Off the Gulf Coast of Florida, as many as seventeen pairs have nested on one small island. Six or seven nests are normally occupied each year on mile-long islands off Florida's Cedar Keys (Atsena-Otie and Sea Horse Key). In the Queen Charlotte Islands off British Columbia, Peale's Falcon, a race of the Peregrine, spreads out along the coasts, where the food supply is mainly ducks and sandpipers, but at the northwest corner of the main island and on the rocky shores of Langara Island, just across Parry Passage, birds clustered in thirteen eyries are living on the Ancient Murrelets, Cassin's Auklets, and Leach's Petrels which are breeding there by the thousands. On the Island of Cyprus in the Mediterranean there are several colonies of Eleonora's Falcons, over the cliffs of Cape Aspro and on the Northern Range, especially in the Kormakiti area. The Black Vulture is often gregarious in its nesting habits, a dozen or more pairs seeking shelter together under the intertwining stems of the yucca on islands off the coast of the southeastern United States. Griffon Vultures gather by the hundreds in the breeding season on the cliffs of Spain, the Sinai peninsula, and in various scattered places throughout Africa—as on a rocky hill rising several hundred feet from the surrounding plain in Sokoto Province, West Africa, or high in the cliffs near Lake Naivasha, East Africa.

The Gyrfalcon pre-empts the Peregrine's nesting sites in the far north, and its diet includes many more mammals. The juvenile shown here has the characteristic broad white feather-edging of the first year plumage.

There have been a number of records of *interspecific* gregariousness—in Alaska, Europe, Africa, and elsewhere—the most famous instance being "Eagle Hill" in Kenya.

In a four-year survey of the Kenya slopes, Leslie Brown, author of *Eagles,* covered 140 square miles of open savanna, thornbush, and rocky hills. He found two unusual concentrations of eagles in which pairs of different species were nesting within 300 yards of each other on wide expanses of otherwise untenanted savanna: Bateleurs, African Hawk-Eagles, Wahlberg's Eagles, Long-crested Hawk-Eagles, and Martial Eagles. But his most remarkable discovery was "Eagle Hill," a 1,500-foot kloof covering 4.2 square miles on which five (and in one year, six) species of eagles were living peaceably. In the immediate vicinity surrounding the hill, there were six other pairs of four different species of eagles.

None of these groups formed to take advantage of nearby food supplies or because of any scarcity of nesting places. In fact, in the case of "Eagle Hill," two other hills in the area—one apparently similar in every aspect and another even larger—were virtually ignored by eagles.

It seems hard to believe that the inhabitants of "Eagle Hill" simply liked each other's company. Such close proximity was in all probability tolerable only because food appears to have been abundant and readily available and the species nesting together had strikingly different food preferences and habits.

The Verreaux's Eagle took hyrax (small relatives of the elephant) and hunted low in fairly open rocky areas; the Martial Eagle fed on game birds and hunted high over the open plains (never close to the nest); the Crowned Eagle fed principally on duikers and a few monkeys in the forest; the African Hawk-Eagle fed on game birds such as guinea fowl, usually around vegetation about three miles from the hill itself; and Ayre's Hawk-Eagle took small birds of the treetops by aerial dives. In the surrounding terrain, Wahlberg's Eagle and the Long-crested Hawk-Eagle acted as ecological complements—Wahlberg's preying on rats and snakes in the savanna below 4,000 feet, while the Long-crested hunted the same food animals above 4,500 feet. The Brown Harrier was a snake-eater, and the Bateleur, a "vulture of small things" that robbed other birds and preyed upon snakes. Among these species there was no real competition for food.

Gregariousness in raptors could have the advantage of mutual protection. It is generally accepted that such aggregations of birds that are not competitive do have survival value. Small eagles, such as Ayre's Hawk-Eagle, might nest near the large Crowned Eagle for the protection afforded from roving bands of monkeys and other egg-stealing predators. Leslie Brown even shows that the Verreaux's Eagle and the African Hawk-Eagle chose aberrant nesting sites on "Eagle Hill," perhaps in response to the safety enjoyed by commensal nesting.

On the African savannas, the Martial Eagle, shown here with its crest flared, preys on many of the same animals which are staple food of the Crowned Eagle—but it hunts the open, rather than the wooded places. Consequently there is little competition between the two species.

There are more eagles in tropical Africa than on any other continent. One of the largest is the Martial Eagle, a savanna bird which hunts large game birds in the Embu District of Kenya but is also capable of killing other game, including small antelopes and jackals.

Similar to the Holarctic Golden Eagle in its preference for cliff nests and small mammal prey, the Verreaux Eagle (left) seldom competes with other species of eagles on the African savanna, which specialize locally on game birds, as the Martial Eagle does, or perhaps on snakes, the favorite food of the Brown Harrier Eagle (below).

The large aggressive African White-headed Vulture blushes red in excitement or anger. The angular shape of its head—flat, covered with white down—and a deeply hooked red beak distinguish it from other carrion-eaters.

The African Black-shouldered Kite (above) is among the predators of the savanna which follow grassfires, as the Marabou Stork does, to obtain an easy meal of fleeing animals and insects.

The Lizard Buzzard (left), a small African raptor, itself falls prey to eagle owls on the roost at night and is sometimes killed by eagles, too.

Coursing over a field, a North American Red-tailed Hawk depends primarily on sight to find its prey, but hearing also assists in the capture. Sometimes a Red-tail will find and dig out a nest of meadow mice without any visual clue at all.

In Scotland the Golden Eagle maintains a territory which supplies ten to thirty times the amount of small mammals necessary to feed the pair and young. Thus, even in years of low prey populations, they are well-provided.

The northern Gyrfalcon, shown here in juvenile plumage, usurps the Peregrine's nesting places. Far more generalized in its feeding habits, it hunts both birds and mammals.

Although many hawks spend relatively little time hunting on the wing, the North American Marsh Hawk has been observed in flight for half a day. Its roost may also be miles away from the hunting area.

Across the heartland of the North American continent, some Peregrines winter in their nesting territories and feed on the remaining populations of birds. Attracted by the flash pattern of a Blue Jay in flight, the falcon, opposite, snatched it from the air and now pauses, on a dead stump, before bending to the kill.

In Cade's Alaskan study, Peregrines, both in the taiga and tundra, nested close to owls, Rough-legged Hawks, Red-tailed Hawks, and Ravens, but only occasionally close to the Gyrfalcon, which, after the eagle, was the number two intruder or enemy in its domain. Some Ravens' nests were as close as 50 yards; those of the Rough-leg, within 100 yards—and if nests of other birds were any closer they *were not in view* of Peregrine eyries.

The nesting habits of the birds of prey are a fascinating study in variety. Many owls and vultures display no instinct at all for building. The condors and the Griffon Vulture lay their eggs on cliffs, and the Black and Turkey vultures seek caves, hollow stumps, and rotting trees on the ground. Some of the largest of the Old World vultures as well as the African Eagle-Owl and the Great Gray Owl of the Northern Hemisphere construct sturdy stick nests like the eagles' and hawks'. Ground-nesting birds provide for the possibility of flooding; the Marsh Hawk's nest near tidal flats along the coast of New Jersey provides a strong foundation calculated to keep its structure above the high spring tide level. And there are similar instances of nests at various heights, dependent upon the extent of spring flooding, in such areas as the marshes of North Dakota and Utah.

Where conditions allow, all have preferences. The Great Horned Owl chooses large hollows in old trees of the deep forest, or lacking these, the abandoned nests of Red-tailed Hawks, crows, and other large birds; the Sharp-shinned Hawk nearly always nests in coniferous trees, and the Long-eared Owl and Tawny Owl also have a distinct predilection for coniferous woods. Many birds of prey habitually raise their families in high places—the eagles with a great deal of preparation, and the falcon making scrapes barely sufficient to keep the eggs from rolling over the edge of the cliff. But when any or all of these birds are influenced by a plentiful supply of food to nest out of their usual habitat, they may be found in strange and wondrous places.

On the prairies of North Dakota, it is not uncommon to find a Golden Eagle's nest on the ground; at Stump Lake, North Dakota, two Cooper's Hawks' nests have been found on the flatlands; and on islands off the coast of Maine you can walk through the grasses and sedges and trip over Osprey nests. Pigeon Hawks in the Far North will occupy old nests of other birds in trees or in clumps of grass; Barn Owls are occasionally flushed from badger holes in the western United States, and Long-eared Owls from the moors of England.

Although man has most often been responsible for destroying the habitat of a bird, as he did the Bald Eagle's forest stronghold in the United States, he occasionally provides an ideal situation. The Peregrine Falcon that usually nests on high cliffs once occupied the Palisades across the Hudson River from New York City, and the man-made cliffs of Manhattan, where he was well fed on a fat larder of pigeons. So effortless and inconspicuous were the daily hunting forays of the city Peregrines that pedestrians hurrying on their various ways did not even stop to wonder what had happened when a falcon made its strike; they merely brushed a few falling pigeon feathers from their coats and kept on walking. But Peregrines became the subject of a newspaper story when the inhabitants of the St. Regis penthouse were "buzzed" day after day by a pair nesting on the roof, and the management of the hotel had to net and remove the offenders, still protesting, from their oddly but obviously well-established territory. Philadelphia, Washington, D.C., and other large cities have also had their quotas of Peregrines.

There are strong indications, from banding in the United States and India and marking in China and Japan, that many of the birds of prey are monogamous. Peregrines return year after year to nest in the same places in the eastern United States —to eyries at Taughannock Falls, New York, and Wysox, Towanda, and Laceyville, Pennsylvania. At least they did from the early 1900's to about 1945. Several Alaskan cliff sites are known to have been used consecutively for intervals of thirty to sixty years; and on the Eurasian tundra there are records of favorite nesting cliffs going back to the seventeenth century. The carefully kept records of falconers show that the cliffs of the Isle of Wight once housed Peregrines nearly every spring for a period of 350 years. Golden Eagles in Scotland hold on to their old homesites, refurbishing an old nest or building a new one close by, and Bald Eagles in America keep adding to their stick nests until the ungainly structures fall to the ground of their own weight. Near Vermilion, Ohio, a storm toppled a dead tree containing one such nest in its thirty-sixth year of occupancy—although not necessarily by the same pair of birds—and this was found to weigh about a ton; another is recorded from St. Petersburg, Florida, weighing 1,274 pounds. Hawks return from migrations to their old territories, but many species build a new nest. Other hawks, which are resident, and non-migratory owls may not stray far from their established breeding grounds for years. The stability of the breeding ranges of the adults makes it difficult for the young birds, which in their first year must wander about looking for unclaimed lands where they can live and hunt until they reach maturity.

The smaller hawks and owls may breed when they are one year old, but larger birds mature more slowly—the bubos and buteos when they are two or three years old; eagles when they are three or four; and condors at five or six years of age. Immature Goshawks, Peregrine Falcons, Gyrfalcons, harriers, Golden Eagles, and Bald Eagles do breed occasionally, but it is rare to find both sexes of a nesting pair in young plumage. The female is usually immature, and the male, adult. Tom Cade suggests, in his Alaskan study, that one- or two-year-old Peregrine females may be less prolific than three- or four-year-old females, and, that the inexperienced male, particularly, must be paired with the female for some time before he is able to make the psychological adjustments necessary for successful nesting—this includes not only fertilizing the eggs, but also sharing incubation duties and providing most of the food for the female and young during the crucial first few weeks after hatching. Thus, a pair of young falcons or Golden Eagles may be seen together at a nesting site for several years before they produce any young of their own.

Generally the length of time taken for all birds to reach adulthood is a yardstick of their life expectancy. The smaller hawks and owls have a shorter life span than the large buteos and eagles; and these birds, in turn, cannot expect to live as long as the condors, although disease, accident, and especially the predatory activities of man have proven a great equalizer. In captivity the large birds of prey may live to be fifty years or more.

It has been observed that long incubation periods developed in some orders of birds in response to their relative safety from predation. Thus, even the smaller hawks and owls incubate their eggs longer than songbirds, which have more enemies. Within the two orders of predatory birds, small and large species may have very similar incubation periods, however; the difference in their development, if any, occurs after hatching, in the length of the fledging periods. For some reason, vultures are very slow to mature compared to most hawks and eagles of comparable size. American Black Vultures are fledged and ready to fly at about fourteen weeks—or nearly four weeks later than Golden Eagles, which are larger birds. Even more striking are the prolonged fledging periods of the condors, among the largest of all birds of prey. California Condors stay in the nest fully twenty weeks—as long as any land bird—then spend ten weeks wandering about in the vicinity as flightless juveniles, and seven months learning to fly and forage for themselves. Like the elephant, they can raise young only in alternate years.

The territorial instincts needed by birds of prey that have more or less definite prey populations to depend upon are less important to the carrion-eaters, whose feeding is contingent upon accident and death. Vultures may be solitary or sociable. After the breeding season the young birds join their elders at communal roosts, the norm being a general drifting of individuals to regions where fire, disease, starvation, or hunting by man may be taking an unusual toll of wildlife or domestic stock. In the latter part of the nineteenth century, when California Condors were still numerous, a hunter saw one hundred and fifty of these birds in the vicinity of antelopes he had killed. And the Philadelphia botanist, William Bartram, wandering the Florida wilderness before the American Revolution, told of the King Vultures, now extinct in that region, which would descend on the deserts whenever there was a fire set by lightning or by the Indians for the purpose of rousing game: "gathering from every quarter . . . to gather up the roasted serpents, frogs, and lizards, filling their sacks with them."

In the streets of villages in Africa and Asia Minor the Egyptian Vultures feed on human excrement, and the Black Vultures living in the warmer climes of the New World congregate around city dumps and slaughter pens. Some of these carrion-eaters

The Bald Eagle's nest is a conspicuous part of the landscape wherever these large birds are still to be found on the North American continent; in this instance the nest tree was in the midst of a town in Florida.—*Photographed by Roger Tory Peterson.*

Unlike the Sharp-shinned Hawk, the northern Goshawk (here, in the Ithaca region of New York State) displays no preference for nesting in conifers.—*Photographed by Heinz Meng.*

show aggressive traits. The African White-headed Vulture, solitary in its habits and fearless in attitude, attacks and kills antelopes occasionally; and the Black Vulture of Florida will take piglets, lambs, and young chickens and herons. Anyone who has raised a young vulture in captivity knows that it prefers fresh meat. However, all the Old and New World vultures are predominantly scavengers, and as such have not developed a high territorial instinct.

In winter the stability demanded of the breeding range of all the birds of prey, to a greater or lesser degree, is no longer a necessity. Within their winter ranges are food lookout-stations, roosting places, and hunting areas; but the boundaries are not heavily guarded and tend to be fluid, opening up and encompassing new areas of prey abundance. For the Great Horned Owl, the Screech Owl, the Goshawk, and other birds that stay the year round, there may be only a slight shifting over a few acres in the temperate zones, or a few miles in the Far North, depending on the food supply. Other species are divided in their habits, some of the individuals being forced to migrate because the habitat cannot support the whole population during the winter. Those Red-shouldered, Red-tailed, and Rough-legged hawks, Prairie Falcons, or Peregrine Falcons which remain in the north must then enlarge their old nesting territories if they are to survive.

Many of the harrier hawks—the Marsh Hawk of North America, the European Hen and Montagu's Harriers, and the Pied Harriers of North Asia—change their behavior pattern from pair protection of territories in spring and summer to communal roosting in late fall and winter, radiating out each morning to their own individual food ranges and returning at night. In Superior Township, Michigan, the Craigsheads found that from late fall until the last week in February, forty-eight Marsh Hawks traveled, day after day, from their roosting areas at a steady measured speed of 25 miles per hour, without coursing, until they reached hunting ranges from one to five and a half miles distant. These ranges varied in size from 30 or 40 acres to a square mile. The Short-eared Owls which coursed from dusk to dawn over these same marshes and meadows also flocked together on the ground and fanned out to hunt specific areas. Their roosts were so close together at one point that owls and hawks often rested side by side as the night and day shifts overlapped. In breeding season the Short-eared Owls are the most conspicuous of the nocturnal birds of prey which forage during daylight hours to provide enough food for their young. Communal roosting is also characteristic of Long-eared Owls. They are commonly seen in groups of eight or twelve, in Europe and America, roosting in coniferous woods and hunting in open fields from late December to mid-March, when they begin to disperse and look for nesting places again.

Across their world-wide winter ranges these hawks and owls are partly migratory, and tend to gather in larger groups for several days before flying north to their breeding grounds. Meinertzhagen reported seeing Montagu's and Marsh Harriers assembled in a vast roosting area in North Africa for their passage to northern Europe and Asia in the latter part of January, 1956. Predominantly Montagu's Harriers, they were closely packed on the ground, and in the last hours of daylight, constant arrivals swelled their numbers to well over two hundred. Two and three days later, Meinertzhagen saw just as many birds using the roost. During the early part of the day he seldom saw more than two, so the hunting grounds of these harriers must have covered a vast countryside. On migration these species do not travel in a flock but follow each other in a closely spaced line of flight.

In early spring the instinct to defend a breeding range returns just as surely to those migratory birds of prey which have not yet begun their journey to northern grounds as to the non-migratory individuals which have never left home. Before they leave their southern wintering place, a change of attitude occurs and there is an increased amount of diving and harassing of birds crossing the winter range boundaries.

Much has been said, in recent years, about the effect of predators upon the prey. In the temperate zones, where there are large populations of the various prey species, the bird of prey has—through a long association—been a moderate, neutral, or even beneficial, influence. Only when animals have been reduced in numbers and exposed to predation —as a result of a sudden change in the habitat, perhaps caused by man—is the effect considerably greater.

Ordinarily, a Red-tailed Hawk, on its winter range, will take only those mice which, by pressure of numbers, are forced out of their normal shelter to find food in strange and open places; and as these excess individuals become fewer and fewer, the bird must find other, more vulnerable creatures.

The hawk, by its activities, not only helps to reduce the surplus populations of prey species, but also weeds out the weak, sick, and incautious individuals. It will kill any mouse of a color that is not advantageous for concealment against the background of grass or soil where it lives, or which acts in a manner not conforming to the habit patterns of its kind. We have striking evidence of the effectiveness of such selection, even at the low-light intensities under which nocturnal raptors can see to hunt. Laboratory tests by Lee R. Dice, in 1947, revealed that protectively colored deer-mice (*Peromyscus maniculatus*) were 20 per cent more successful in eluding capture by Long-eared and Barn Owls than those which contrasted with their background. The differences in pelage colors of the mice used were no greater than the variations which distinguish certain local races of the species. Since the oddly colored mice were most readily taken, Dice concluded that predators must be an important factor in the evolution of pelage colors. Natural selection by the hawk and the owl tends to standardize the prey species, keeping individuals alike in form, pattern, and actions most useful for the survival of the population of any given locality. Nor are the predators themselves exempt, for the young (and consequently incautious), the sick and the old, and even deviates in color or behavior among their numbers also become vulnerable to other hawks and owls.

The populations of predators cannot, however, compare in size with those of their staple food animals, the rodents, the control of which is vastly important to the life of the habitat. Meadow mice or voles in their short life span of two years may produce seventeen litters of four to nine, and sometimes as many as thirteen, young, which in their turn have been known to breed at two weeks. The bird of prey reduces this potentially vast number of individuals by applying heavy predator pressure at critical periods in the life cycle, particularly during spring, when cover is minimal and activity maximal; and at all times predation by the hawks and owls tends to maintain an equilibrium between the varied elements of prey populations.

Some biologists contend that to remove the influence of the bird of prey would be to invite a chain reaction throughout the habitat. If some hawk or owl were not present to turn its attention to the fast-breeding rabbit population, their surplus numbers would nibble away not only their usual foods, but the exotic ones of last resort—the bark of small trees and bushes—thereby destroying the cover of several creatures which would be forced to change their ways of living, becoming more vulnerable. Countless others would likewise be disrupted in their feeding habits and shelter, with the result that the habitat would sicken. They contend that it has become necessary, in this North Temperate Zone woodlot and the fields around it, that every food animal, as it becomes available, be subjected to pressure by all of its predators, day and night.

However, François Bourlière writes:

"The exact part played by predation in the dynamics of wild mammalian populations remains to be determined. Most of the older naturalists believed that predators (carnivorous mammals, birds of prey, and the like) had an essential role in holding certain populations of very prolific species at a constant level. As a matter of fact, this does not seem to be true in most cases. The common barn owl, for example, is the chief predator on the Levant vole in Palestine, and the remains of one or sometimes two individuals of this species are found in one regurgitated pellet out of two. Now, this owl exploits a hunting-terrain of more than 9 square miles on the average around its nest—that is, an area supporting at least 25,000 voles; as one hardly finds more than 600 pellets under each nest, it is highly probable that the proportion of these voles destroyed is insig-

A praying mantis backs off before the attack of an American Kestrel on a Georgia farm.

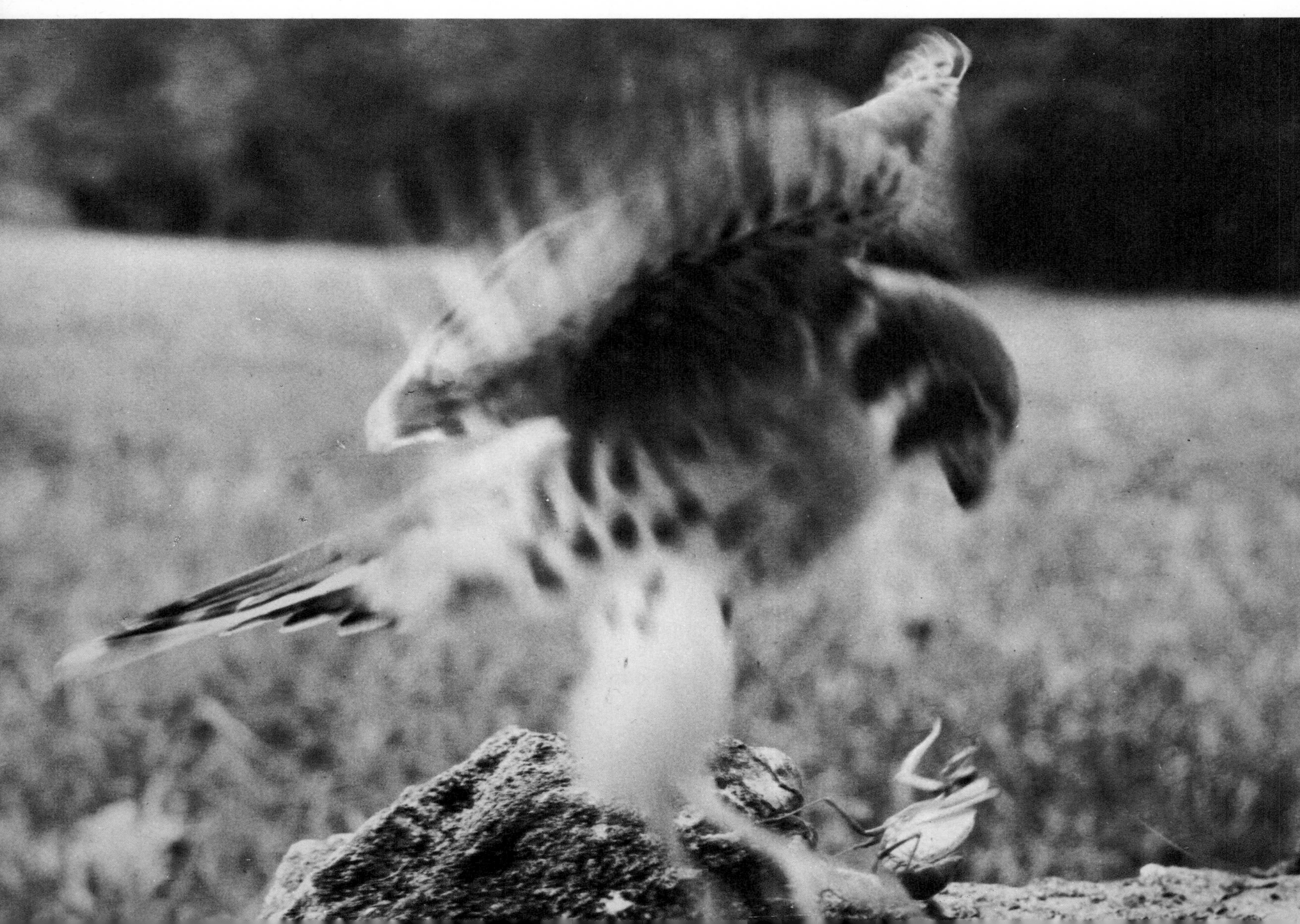

nificant." If so, why did the investigator have difficulty collecting individuals more than 100 days old in the field? And why are "practically no adults born at the beginning of winter still alive the following summer." Why is "the surviving population . . . much reduced when the period of high fertility arrives toward the end of autumn?" The fact that other predators also contribute their pressures is not mentioned—there are, for example, twelve species of hawks and eagles in Palestine which prey upon small mammals, and the activities of one or more of these diurnal hunters have been completely ignored. So has the tendency of some hawks and owls to leave their nesting territories and congregate during the winter where prey density is high.

Even though large numerical fluctuations are not necessarily explained by the absence of one or more predators in the localities where they occur, the existence of other factors should not negate predation. If there are enough predators to effectively reduce the surplus, there may not be a large enough increase in the numbers of the prey to produce shock, or disease, from overcrowding, and a sharp decrease in productivity, the so-called self-limiting factors.

The Craigheads, whose work on this subject is the most exhaustive to date, sum up their findings as follows: "The data so far presented in this book indicate that where raptor populations have not been persecuted and drastically reduced in composition and numbers by man, the effect of predation can be controlling. Certainly the published accounts of increases of prey populations following predator destruction tend to support this thought. In the winter of 1942, predation by raptors was a limiting factor [in Superior Township, Michigan] in checking the meadow mouse populations. The effect of predation in controlling a population in this instance hardly can be doubted when we consider that mammalian predation, probably equal in effect and observed to be directed primarily on meadow mice, was simultaneously operative. Had bird and mammal predation not been the limiting factor, some other force naturally would have been or have become limiting, but probably would have been less generally and

Startled, the mantis rises up in a defensive attitude which completely changes its shape and gives the Kestrel pause. (In this instance the bird was successfully bluffed.)

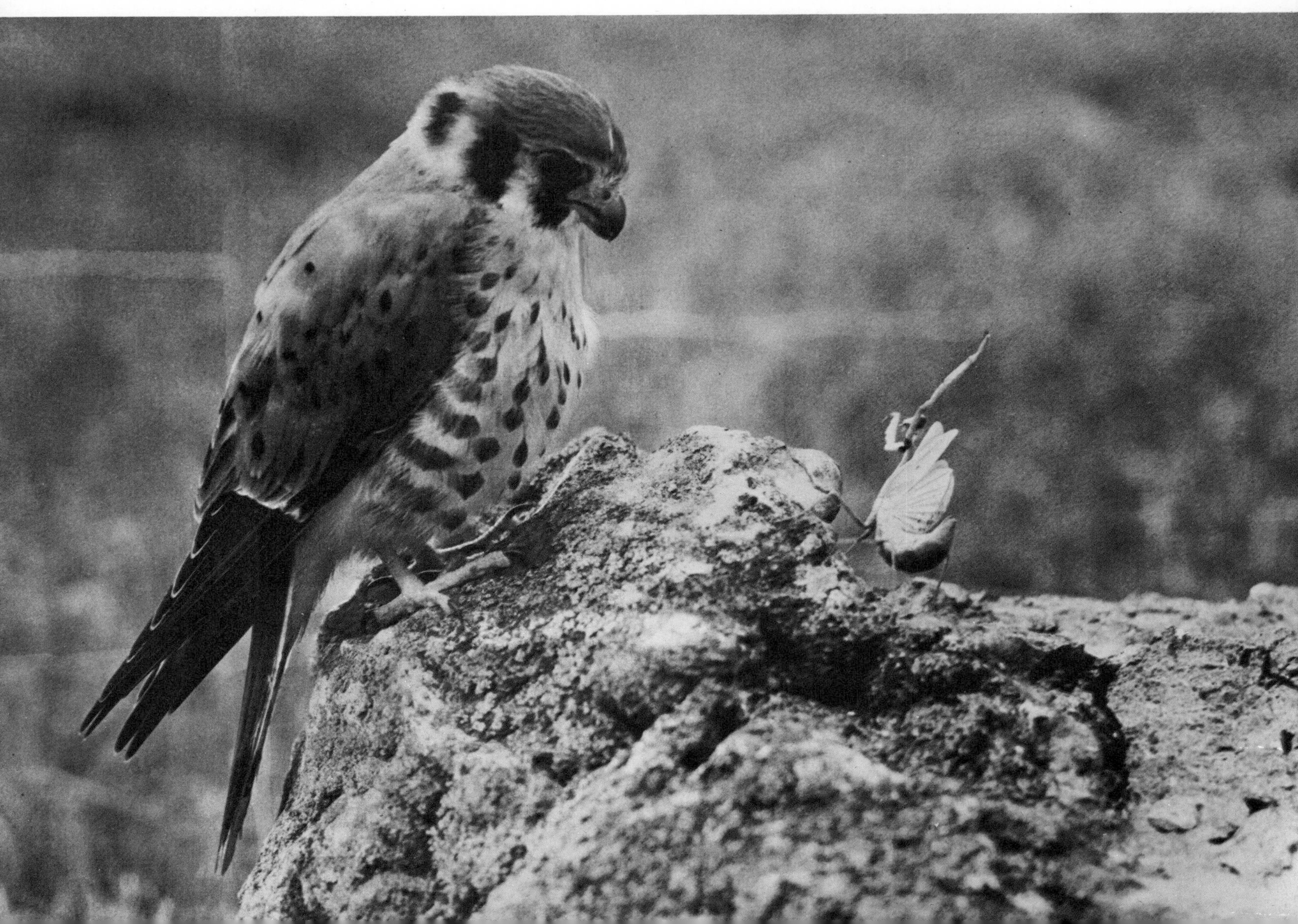

In temperate zones predator pressure, first on one species, then on another, at critical times in their life cycles, usually prevents population "explosions" of fast-breeding rodents, and is an important factor in balancing all prey populations, the

["Daylight"]
1 Song Sparrow and grasshopper
2 Peregrine Falcon
3 Teal drake
4 Cooper's Hawk and Bobwhite
5 Gray Squirrel
6 Bobwhite
7 Wood Frog
8 Red-tailed Hawk
9 Ring-necked Pheasant

["Twilight"]
1 Crow
2 Hairy Woodpecker
3 Opossum
4 Whip-poor-w
5 Marsh Hawk

year round. In this artist's conception of some of the wildlife along a woodland stream and in an adjacent open field (northeastern North America), the hawks are replaced at night by owls, their vigils overlapping somewhat in the late afternoon and twilight hours.

6 Cottontail
7 Screech Owl

8 Bullfrog
9 White-footed Mouse
10 Short-eared Owl

["Night"]
1 Nighthawk
2 Barred Owl
3 Flying Squirrel

4 Barn Owl and Wood Rat
5 Raccoon
6 Water snake

7 Great Horned Owl and Cottontail

proportionally regulatory. The point is that predation was controlling. Raptor predation operated to decrease the prey populations most in need of reduction and exercised a continuous and proportional pressure on all populations, helping to limit fluctuations." They further state that "the great mobility of raptors . . . enables them to concentrate from distant regions and thereby rapidly increase hunting pressure on dense prey populations that have increased during spring and summer," and suggest that "a dearth of winter predator pressure in the far north may have an important effect on prey fluctuations."

The insects and young rodents which are under the surveillance of the Kestrel at the edge of the woods and in the fields in the morning and afternoon are caught (in the same places) by the Screech Owl from dusk to dawn. The snakes, frogs, rats, and mice living on the banks of streams and in marshes and swamps in the interior of the forest are in the daytime under the searching eye of the Red-shouldered Hawk, while at night, the Barred Owl listens for their telltale rustling and splashes. In the highlands and semiopen country, the rabbits, snakes, rats, and mice that are preyed upon by the Red-tailed Hawk by day become a source of food at night for the Great Horned Owl. As the small passerine birds do not stir after sundown, there is no "bird owl" which specializes in their capture, but the "bird hawks"—the accipiters and falcons—watch over them in the hours of daylight.

An overlapping of these policing activities occurs when, at sunset, the diurnal and nocturnal predatory birds may be seen hunting together; during the breeding season many of the owls extend their foraging to late afternoon, especially on cloudy days, to provide themselves and their young with sufficient food during this period of increased activity. At these times, then, the songbirds and other creatures which are abroad in daylight fall prey to Long-eared, Short-eared, and Great Horned Owls. So the prey and the predators find themselves enmeshed in a dependence not only on and with each other, twenty-four hours a day, but varying according to seasonal changes which cause the populations of various food animals to become relatively vulnerable or invulnerable.

Grazing, flooding, burning, and other natural and man-made catastrophes which destroy the food and cover of animals in a habitat produce the effect of overpopulation, and the predators react to these situations in the same way as to vulnerability caused by overbreeding. Swainson's Hawks in the agricultural regions of the western United States, Chimangos in Argentina and sometimes even vultures follow the plow, which turns up the nests of meadow mice, shrews, and pocket gophers; and on the African savanna, a grass fire will draw a pair of eagles from a distance of fifteen miles, although they are amply supplied with food at a hunting area only a mile away from their nest. Even the dropping barometer preceding storms can force animals into a situation of frenzied escape, so that they become easy prey. Under winter-range conditions the speed with which predatory birds assemble from near and far for such a feast is phenomenal.

The day before the hurricane of 1938 struck New England, John Hamlet, the co-author of this book, stopped his car to watch a large number of immature Red-tailed and Red-shouldered Hawks and Kestrels diving and catching mice on a steep hillside near the Connecticut-Massachusetts border. He wondered, at the time, what was going on, as no doubt did others in three Northeastern states who saw armies of rodents crossing roadways three days in advance of the monumental disturbance which caught the human population in the area by surprise. The field mice, white-footed mice, and short-tailed shrews, possibly reacting to a falling barometer, left their native hills and valleys en masse, in an exodus fully enjoyed by the hawks.

The physical characteristics and habits of certain kinds of animals attract specific predators. L. Tinbergen has cited numerous examples of birds that are heavily preyed upon by the Sparrowhawk (*Accipiter nisus*) of the Old World. The noisiness and social habits of the English Sparrow leave it exceptionally open to attack; the Great Tit is more vulnerable than the Blue Tit because of greater size, color, and noisiness; and the Redstart, which chooses exposed places for singing and feeding, is more conspicuous than the Wren in the comparative shelter of the bushes. The Craigheads, observing the food habits of Peregrine Falcons at twenty eyries, noted that the flash pattern of Meadowlarks, Red-winged Blackbirds, and Blue Jays and the conspicuous flight of Flickers appear to increase their vulnerability to the falcons.

The nocturnal or diurnal habits of the prey species, of course, make them more vulnerable to the predators which are abroad at the same time of day or night—the white-footed mouse and cottontail rabbit

A Screech Owl descends on its prey noiselessly. Nocturnal owls have special downy filaments at the bases of their feathers which cushion the sound.

The female (left) of the Snowy Owls of the tundra has protective marking to conceal her as she incubates the eggs in the nest, which is placed on the ground among the grasses; the male (right) is nearly pure white.—*Photographed at the National Zoological Park.*

to the Screech Owl and Great Horned Owl, and the ground squirrels and tree squirrels to the hawks. All animals are highly vulnerable in the spring, as they go about establishing territories and foraging for their young. Snakes and ground squirrels, which attract predation by hawks in spring and summer, keep themselves safe in hibernation during the winter. And the white-footed mouse traveling on top of the snow in winter is far more easily caught than the meadow mouse which tunnels under drifts.

No niche in the habitat is really safe from the activities of winged predators since they have adapted to hunt nearly every species of animal. The mole and pocket gopher are heavily preyed upon when they emerge from their burrows. Even aquatic species are taken by the Osprey, Bald Eagle, and great fish owls as well as Great Horned and Barred Owls. The physical protections of scent, poison, and armor often fail to be a deterrent: Skunks are a favorite food of the Great Horned Owl and Red-tailed Hawk. The harrier-eagles and the Secretary Bird of Africa have heavy plating on their legs and use special tactics when tangling with constrictors and poisonous snakes; and in Florida we know of a Red-tailed Hawk's nest which contained three partly eaten Eastern diamondback rattlesnakes, one still alive and wiggling, which sent the human investigator shinnying quickly down the tree. At another nest close by, young Red-tails were being brought up on gopher tortoises.

Hawks and eagles extract turtle meat and leave the empty shells, contrary to the habit of the Lammergeier, which drops turtles on rocks to break them, as it does the larger bones of mammals. Porcupines, however, are well protected against birds of prey. The occasional Great Horned Owls or Golden

Eagles that enter into combat with them are found dead or dying with their faces full of quills. The fisher and the mountain lion are among the few predators that have learned to rip open the porcupine's soft belly.

Few living creatures can successfully bluff a hawk as the praying mantis does by rising up and presenting a different and menacing shape, but the offensive method of defense is common among the birds of prey. An owl which has remained motionless and thin next to a tree trunk while danger approaches will suddenly ruffle up its plumage and spread both wings to appear larger, bow its head, and clack its beak angrily. The Barred Owl has the peculiar habit of raising one wing and holding the other close to its body, an attitude which gives it the appearance of a mammal rather than a bird. And the North American Burrowing Owl in its hole gives a perfect imitation of a rattlesnake, which is extremely effective since a would-be intruder cannot see what is actually making the noise.

In their turn, the diurnal birds of prey, when threatened, spread both wings, and the occipital feathers on the heads of many eagles and hawks flare in regal array. If pressed further, they fall over on their backs with talons presented to do battle, as many a falconer will attest from his experiences in trapping hawks and taking young birds from nests or eyries.

In forest or field the prey species may escape pursuit by remaining motionless and blending with their surroundings, for birds have difficulty distinguishing form unless there is movement. Hawks and owls on their part employ the same tactic on the offensive, for they will sit quietly on a post or branch, unobserved, until something moves below.

Variations in color in birds seem to have evolved according to their needs, the greatest necessity being the protection of incubating and brooding birds and their young. The somber colors of most female songbirds and their stillness while on the nest are a protection against predators, and many birds of prey are themselves vulnerable to attack when in this defenseless position. When males and females share in incubating eggs and brooding young, and nest on the ground, both sexes are as a rule protectively colored. The male harrier-hawks throughout the world which generally do not sit on the nest have a light gray or colorful plumage, in contrast to the female's mottled brown, whereas the male of the European Marsh Harrier, which takes some part in incubating the eggs, has brown plumage similar to the female's.

Another male in a ground-nesting situation, the Arctic Snowy Owl, is almost pure white, but the female, which incubates alone, tends to be heavily barred with gray which makes her unrecognizable, at a distance, in the grasses and melting snows of the tundra. On the other hand, the brightly colored and differently marked male of the North American Kestrel has no need for somber plumage, even though he assists the female, because the eggs of this species are laid in holes in trees and not in an open nest.

The general absence of bright plumage in most hawks, owls, and eagles serves to keep them less conspicuous both to other predators and to the animals they prey upon. The juveniles almost always have a first plumage of highly protective coloring which helps them through the period of clumsiness when they are learning to fly and hunt.

The entire complex of factors causing vulnerability in the temperate zones is usually amply compensated for by the many predators which apply steady pressure and even change their feeding habits to meet potential imbalance. However, in the Far North there has never been enough predator pressure from the fox, the mink, the ermine, the weasels, the birds of prey, the skuas, and the sea birds, to keep up with the rising populations of the short-tailed mice—the meadow mice or voles, and lemmings. Every three to four years their numbers rise to such heights that they destroy their own food and cover, and entire communities of mice are so weakened that their breeding potential decreases and many may die of epizootic diseases. The Norwegians have a superstition that the lemmings, in peak years of population, come down in snowstorms out of the sky. On their great migrations in quest of food, these indomitable little animals travel great distances, crossing rivers and lakes in their path, until, finally arriving at the ocean, thousands swim to their deaths.

At these times the usual populations of birds of prey are augmented by Great Gray Owls, Snowy Owls, and Gyrfalcons from the surrounding countryside. But the feast precedes a famine, for the "explosions" of the predators occur as they breed in numbers because of the success of the previous year. But, in fact, the mice have been so weakened and reduced in numbers that it will be a year of want for the mammals and birds that prey upon them.

Corresponding with the mouse scarcity occasionally are the lows reached by other important food animals of great reproductive capacity—by the Arctic hares, every seven years, and by the snowshoe hares, every nine to ten years. The Hudson's Bay Company trappers in northern Canada reaped a rich harvest of furs at these times of famine, for not only the weak and the sick, but the prime fox, ermine, and mink could be easily trapped. The frequency of the imbalance over the vast Indian territory of Canada, which the Hudson's Bay Company controlled exclusively by charter of Charles II, helped to produce the wealthiest trading post in the British empire. From 1690 to 1800 annual profits paid on the company's capital stock reached 60 to 70 per cent on the average. And all because of a mouse.

Whereas the carnivores find themselves caught between the alternatives of starvation or the baited trap, the winged predators travel widely searching for food. So once every few years it is not surprising to find Snowy Owls stationed around the city dump in Washington, D.C., or a substantial winter population of Goshawks as far south as the mountains of Maryland. In the worst years of scarcity, when a dearth of rabbits as well as mice occurs in the Western Hemisphere, the Snowy Owls of the tundras drift southward, a few stragglers even reaching the Caribbean, and the Great Horned Owls of the northern forests range to Montana and Connecticut. In the Old World, the Hawk Owls of Scandinavia irrupt in a southeasterly direction into the Balkans.

These cyclic phenomena recur with regularity and may be found in various stages of progression throughout the high boreal and Arctic regions. When the lemmings are decreasing in numbers nearly everywhere in eastern Canada, for example, their populations are growing north and northwest of Hudson Bay, and have possibly reached a peak on the west coast of Victoria Island, and their predators, the Arctic foxes and Snowy Owls, are relatively scarce or abundant, according to the availability of these staple food animals.

In *The Natural Regulation of Animal Numbers,* David Lack rules out predators as a factor in either meadow mouse or lemming decline, and indicates that the cycles in the Far North are probably due to interaction with the few widespread plant species on which they feed. The very failure of birds of prey to exercise control at the *start* of a rodent cycle there seems inevitable, however, since "control" may depend on whether or not the hawk or owl can see to grab the mouse. Meadow mice and lemmings live under the complete protection of snow cover, and stay hidden, for the most part, until crowding and starvation force their mass emigrations. At that point it is too late for any number of hawks or owls which can assemble from far-flung regions to be of any effective *stabilizing* influence.

Raptors also respond to sporadic "explosions" of meadow mouse populations throughout the temperate zones by laying more eggs and raising two or three broods in a season instead of one; and in the fall and winter, the Rough-legs, harriers, and Short-eared Owls collect in regions afflicted with "mouse plagues." As in the Far North, there is some question as to whether their fall and winter activities are responsible for rodent declines; probably the other regulatory factors take over.

Many prey species hardly fluctuate in numbers from year to year. Among these are white-footed mice, pocket gophers, chipmunks, and in most cases the tree squirrels, songbirds, snakes, lizards, crayfish, and fish. A predator that lives in a North Temperate Zone habitat offering these standard food animals may go from one to the other in rapid succession as each becomes more vulnerable through the various seasons.

A specialized woods-dweller, the Goshawk is best trained to pursue birds and mammals in this habitat. Bells on the legs help the falconer to find hawk and quarry after a strike.—*North American Goshawk, photographed by Heinz Meng.*

Late in the winter a nocturnal predator of the temperate woods, the Great Horned Owl, changes the tone of his voice to a deep, resonant hoot. With this signal that mating time has arrived, he vigorously defends the area which has been the winter range for the pair. His calls woo the female, who replies in a higher voice. And then begins the strange and fascinating courtship ceremony which, for all its apparent similarity to the rituals of other owls in breeding season, is unique and serves to keep the species separate. The male bows his head, ruffles his feathers, and spreads his wings. At first the female watches but remains aloof. Growing impatient, he hops from branch to branch, snapping his bill. His attempts to move closer and caress her are sharply rebuked by a flurry of ruffled feathers, and he takes to the air, sailing up and down and around, now and again snapping at her to call attention to his antics. After a few moments he alights again and bows and dances as before.

The performance does not cease until the white flag of a rabbit scurrying down a bank catches his eyes. He rises and drops downward without the flap of a wing to snatch his prey from the ground, glides back to her with it, and presents it as an offering, much as the plains Indian would leave a deer at the door of the tepee of his betrothed. Together they devour the rabbit and afterwards, when he resumes the love dance, she joins in the bobbing and billing with as much enthusiasm as her mate. Because most owls do not build nests, the pair lay claim to one which has been the home of Red-tailed Hawks or crows, or they move into the large cavity of an old tree used by fox squirrels in a previous season, and busy themselves with the task of cleaning out the debris from the bottom, or perhaps plucking a few breast feathers to give it a soft lining.

Their nesting takes place in late January and February, when snow is on the ground and severe winter storms still threaten. To prevent freezing, the female must be in constant attendance on the eggs, which are laid at intervals of several days. Sometimes the nest and the incubating bird are covered with a mantle of snow, but the devoted mother generally succeeds in keeping the center of the nest warm and dry. After an incubation period of 34 to 36 days, the young owls break out from their shells, the last egg laid usually being the last to hatch. The downy white nestlings, little larger than newly hatched chicks, are for several days unable to hold up their heads; their eyes are not yet open, and their voices are feeble peeping preludes to the loud and persistent hunger cries they will utter later. At two weeks, or when the nestlings are about one-third grown, their white down will be replaced by a fluffy buff-colored and mottled covering. This second down is characteristic of most owls and many of the diurnal birds of prey. The young will be brooded in the nest four to seven weeks and cannot fly until their juvenile, or first contour, plumage has grown in (at nine to twelve weeks).

During this prolonged fledging period, and probably for some weeks longer, they are wholly or partly dependent on the adults for food. So the early nesting of the Great Horned Owls, which appears to be a disadvantage at first, is actually of great importance to their survival. The care of the young, which takes almost twice as long as the time required by the Red-tailed Hawks to raise their families, has made it imperative for them to nest first, and since they are the most versatile predators in North America, capable of taking almost any animal, they find little difficulty in feeding their charges on the schedule of seasonal vulnerability afforded.

With the coming of spring, new life begins to stir in the woods. Prompted by some ancient instinct, birds that have wintered in the south start on their journeys, often to their deaths, but nevertheless directed to places where they have bred year after year, and with their arrival dates coinciding with the beginning of the most favorable season for reproduction. Crocuses push up through the lingering patches of snow, buds burst open on the trees and bushes, and insects, grubs and caterpillars come forth. The earth warms, making it possible for the hibernating frogs, snakes, lizards, and mammals to emerge and the days become milder and longer. Throughout the winter the mice and rabbits have sustained the raptors which remained and established feeding ranges during the coldest months. Now the growing grasses and plants restore their cover and food is plentiful, giving the prey a respite and a chance to repopulate the fields and meadows. The Red-tailed Hawk, the Red-shouldered Hawk, the Screech Owl, Barred Owl, and Great Horned Owl that have preyed heavily upon them now must turn to another group of animals. So, timed with the invulnerability of the mice, is the arrival of the songbirds, which have not yet established their territories, and they—strangers in an unfriendly land, with their arboreal cover just beginning to leaf out—become vulnerable to predatory birds.

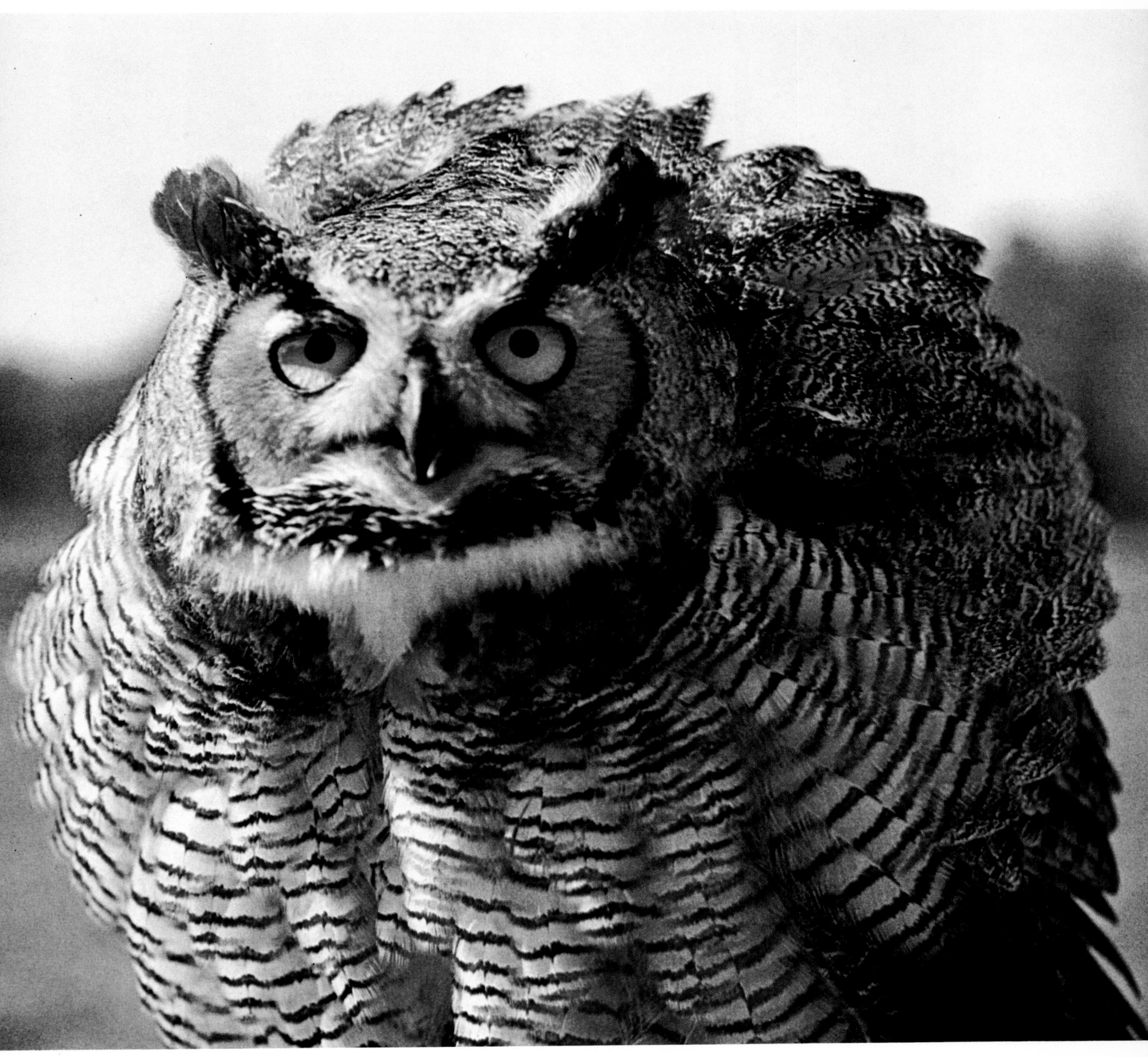

The North American Great Horned Owl clacks its beak, fluffs out its feathers, and spreads both wings in a threat attitude very similar to the courtship display.

The Screech Owl lives along the edges of the forest and hunts insects and rodents in the open places, often preferring to stay close to farms and orchards where it is usually safe from larger owls.

The Ferruginous Rough-legged Hawk, the largest of the North American hawks, nests in trees along streams or on barren, treeless badlands. As it sails above the prairies, it appears white except for the "V" of its bright ferruginous leggings.

A young Red-tailed Hawk demonstrates that the power of flight and strong, killing talons are not all that is necessary to capture a large animal. Landing close to an Opossum, it tries to maneuver into position for an attack. But the opponent is formidable, hissing and baring its teeth, and the Red-tail is extremely cautious.

A single powerful leap brings the Opossum to the ground, with the hawk's talons embedded at the base of the neck, crushing it in a vicelike grip and inflicting instant death.

Without relaxing its grip, the hawk uses its beak to tear fur from the dead prey, and then proceeds to eat.

Near streams, ponds, or swamps the Red-shouldered Hawk of North America (above) feeds on frogs, reptiles, and rodents by day. After sundown the same prey is taken by the Barred Owl (right) to feed its young. Both the hawk and the owl kill poisonous as well as non-poisonous snakes.

The raptor's grasping foot is often used for carrying prey. Having killed a Banded Water Snake, this Red-shouldered Hawk flies off to a favorite roosting tree, where it will eat undisturbed.

It is from these early arrivals and other rising populations that the Great Horned Owls feed their nestlings in early March. Then, as the foliage encloses the songbirds and they set about their family-raising, in mid-March, the game birds and rabbits become vulnerable for the duration of their mating and territory-defining activities. By the end of March or the first part of April, when the young owls need the most food, there will be newly hatched young in the nests of many crows, waiting to be served up to them. Where Great Horned Owls are nesting in a woodlot, over 60 per cent of the white nestling crows fall prey to them, although the adults, in their black plumage, are relatively safe. When the surviving crows have outgrown their vulnerability, the juvenile Horned Owls are off the nest, learning to hunt by practicing their skills on the snakes and frogs and the young of a great variety of prey animals—including the rabbits and skunks. Meanwhile, the other raptors have been far from secure from the ravages of the Great Horned Owls, for in their later nesting they have left themselves open to attack.

The Red-tailed Hawk returns from his winter range in the south late in February or early in March and, like the nocturnal raptor, begins to make sounds and movements around his nesting territory of last year, becoming, as the days progress, more belligerent in boundary disputes with other male Red-tails passing through. The female arrives soon after his ascendancy is established, and the pair join in a series of courtship flights which continue more or less all through the season. Calling in high, whiny whistles, they spiral upward and follow each other's paths closely in the ether, almost vanishing from sight, until one closes its wings and plummets earthward, only to check the fast dive at the treetops and shoot sharply to the heights again. This spectacular flight pattern, repeated again and again, has been described as a series of deep V's.

Red-tailed Hawks nest in the highest trees they can find—35 to 70 feet from the ground—and unlike the owls which appropriate their old nests, always build a new one. Both sexes test out likely sites, and sometimes there seems to be competition between the two. However, it is usually the male who makes the final decision, as he brings twigs of various sizes, which he wedges tightly into the crotch of a tree, interlacing them to make a sturdy platform. The cooperative nest-building efforts of the pair are among the most intriguing of the sights to be seen in the forest in springtime—they dive together into a treetop, grabbing and breaking off a branch with a loud snap by the force of their flight, and then wing back to the nest with their prize. As the work progresses, the female stays for longer and longer periods at the nest, placing the sticks, and testing them by walking back and forth. The pair take time out for patrolling the territory, soaring, and other courtship antics, after which they occupy themselves with nest-building again. And so the days pass.

The Red-tailed Hawks, after the habit of many diurnal birds of prey, decorate their nests with sprigs of greenery. As far as anyone knows, these bits of frippery are purely for effect and not for any utilitarian purpose; however, the practice is widespread. The Common Black Hawk and Ferruginous Rough-legged Hawk show a partiality for green willow sprigs, the Cooper's Hawk for pine sprays, the Gray Hawk for mesquite, and the Canadian Goshawk for fresh sprigs of balsam fir. Golden Eagles in Scotland come winging in to the eyrie with a bit of heather, woodrush, or fir, and Bald Eagles in Vermilion, Ohio, bring corn tassels to their enormous stick nests.

At the northern limits of the tropical Short-tailed Hawk's range, in Florida, this bird lines its nest with green cypress. And in perhaps the strangest instance, the Black Vulture habitually places pearl, bone, and china buttons as well as pieces of glass and figured china around and under the eggs. These decorative objects are supplied weeks before the eggs are laid and their frequent renewal continues during incubation and brooding, until the young are beginning to feather out.

For Red-tails, during courtship and nest-building, a rich larder of food is available. Migrating birds are passing through in tremendous numbers; the partridges and pheasants are in the open looking for nest sites of their own; the first litters of rabbits are out of their burrows; and to the great advantage of the Red-tails—inveterate mouse-eaters—the disappearing snow exposes myriads of meadow mouse tunnels. The hawks quietly incubate their eggs in March, as do hundreds of songbirds, with the male sometimes relieving his mate over an approximate period of thirty-four days, and bringing food to her when she is on the nest. In marked contrast to the aggressive Great Horned Owl, the incubating Red-tail is watchful and very shy, and will leave at the

A Red-tailed Hawk, one week old, is downy and helpless but has a distinctly hawklike appearance, even at this early age.—*Photographed by Heinz Meng.*

Five-week old Red-tails (Ithaca region, New York State) have taken to branches and are molting in their juvenile, or first contour, feathers. Their dappled appearance blends perfectly with surrounding foliage.—*Photographed by Heinz Meng.*

approach of danger, probably because of the experience learned in centuries past that the hawk which defends its nest will almost certainly be killed. And since some birds are capable of laying another clutch if the first or second is destroyed, the safety of the adult is of even greater importance to the species than "nesting success."

The young hatch at intervals of only one or two days, so they do not show the differences in size and development which are obvious in a brood of young owls. They are provided with a soft, silky down of light buff or gray which is replaced later by a whiter and woollier down.

When about half-grown, they become very lively, walking about the nest, stretching or flapping their wings, and backing up to void "whiting," in a long stream, far over the edge. Curious heads often bob up, straining for a look at passing birds or in expectation of the return of the parents, who are foraging for snakes, lizards, and turtles just out of hibernation, and for the baby raccoons and possums now wandering the fields. When one or the other of the parent birds does put in an appearance, carrying dinner in its talons, the youngsters become quite excited and abandon their usual weak peeping notes, indulging in louder screams in imitation of the adults. At seventeen days their wing quills appear, closely followed by those of the tail, and at the end of six weeks the fledglings are ready to leave the nest.

At this stage the parents bring the young birds to their hunting range—the broad, open fields and mowings of the nearby farms—where the first lessons in hunting are given. An adult will be seen to plunge down fifty or a hundred feet at a scuttling mouse, check its rush just above the ground, and turn on its back, giving a wheezy whistle of two syllables. This is the signal for one of the circling young to dive and hang clumsily in mid-air over the spot, and quite often the fledgling catches the rodent when it moves again. The parents also will occasionally drop an animal in flight so that the fledglings can try their skill at catching it in mid-air, a playful gesture rather than a serious attempt at teaching, for the Red-tailed Hawk must become skilled at binding to its prey and killing on the ground. Its training—and that of a young accipiter, which must learn the technique of stalking birds in the forest—is much less complex than that of the long-winged bird-hawks. The Peregrine's technique of killing in mid-air by high-speed dives and complicated maneuvers is probably improved through imitation of the adults.

In the quiet, lazy summertime, the new-flying juvenile hawks and owls as well as the adults are fairly inactive, for in summer they require proportionally less food for their body weight to maintain normal body temperature than in the colder months.

At this time of year the hawks and owls sit out most of their days and nights in the cool forest, shaded and concealed by dense foliage. But with the advent of fall, which the Indians called "the Crazy Months" for all creatures, the days become shorter, initiating greater activity among the various species of the habitat. For longer than man can remember, this has had the effect of producing physiological changes and instinctual responses, so that when the leaves are turning rust and gold and crimson, the squirrels begin feverishly to store the seeds of the trees; the chipmunks and ground squirrels store up layers of fat to last them through the long winter of hibernation; and the amphibians and reptiles also ready themselves, their rate of metabolism gradually slowing with the dropping temperatures, until finally, in hibernation, their systems will be geared to only one-seventh of their normal heartbeat.

The songbirds fly about, at first in small groups and then in larger flocks, as they circle, exercising their pectoral muscles and following allelomimetic instincts for turning and maneuvering in formation, like schools of fish in the sea. The predatory birds also show signs of seasonal excitement, especially the young of the year, who roam around the neighborhood making false passes at flocks of small birds, teasing and playing with one another, diving at falling leaves, and generally indulging in strange and infantile behavior for such great birds. The Peregrine Falcon finds fun in driving a flock of gulls before her, first up the beach, then turning and driving them in the opposite direction, like a border collie herding sheep. She will chase kingfishers down into the water, time after time, until the harassed birds yell at her with their rattling calls. These haphazard forays cause many reports to be written by bird watchers in praise of the grackle, the meadow lark, or some other member of the avian kingdom which outflew a Peregrine one fine fall day; but the truth is that a hungry falcon can take any of these birds.

The Red-tailed Hawk, usually a predator on mammals, now seems to feel that he can catch anything in the world, for he is seen diving clumsily at flocks of Barn Swallows whose members merely shift to the left or the right, as necessary, and allow him to pass through their ranks with great staring eyes, not knowing quite what has happened. And an inveterate mouse-eater, the Marsh Hawk, will follow and chase after a Blue-winged Teal, losing ground continually.

During all of this illogical activity, some of the smaller birds work out defense mechanisms against their natural predators and will, upon sight of the accipiters, begin to "sky," rising higher and higher in a tight flock, knowing instinctively that they can outrise the round-winged forest hawk and perhaps even confuse him with their flying maneuvers. This same flock of birds, however, upon recognizing the pointed wings of a falcon, will, if possible, immediately lose altitude, staying the while in a group for the axiomatic "safety in numbers," hoping to reach the protection of the treetops and bushes. To combat the instinctive defensive maneuvers of their prey, the hawks begin to augment their normal stalking abilities. Whereas the Cooper's Hawk normally conceals himself behind a tree and then shoots into the open with a straight glide so that one bird cannot perceive the motion or speed of his attack, he will now hide behind a hill or a ridge, swoop down low to the ground, and—meeting a flock of birds around the corner—take one by suprise before all can rise beyond his ken. The Peregrine Falcon sights a bevy of ducks landing on a gravel bar in the midst of a river, and instead of coming in high, attacks at such a low altitude that her wings disturb the pebbles before she turns and shoots straight up through the milling flock to strike her quarry.

With the advent of autumn the hawks and owls which remain through the winter begin to prepare for the months when fewer animals will be moving about in the northern forests to provide them with food and the colder weather will make it necessary for them to eat more than in the season of abundant prey. By November, the territory held by the Great Horned Owl family cannot support its four or five members, and perhaps not even the adults. So the young are driven out and forced to find winter ranges of their own, the older birds themselves drifting to find the creatures most vulnerable in winter. Now they must be satisfied with rabbits and mice and an occasional carnivore—a skunk, a wandering house cat, or a half-grown fox unschooled in the wily ways of its parents—or a pheasant caught unaware in its foraging.

During this time of travail the Great Horned Owl works very hard at his hunting. In the North Woods of Minnesota his reputation is established as the most dangerous bird of prey. Forest Service personnel wearing muskrat hats are in peril of being attacked, and in one or two instances a ranger has been blinded or killed by the sharp and deeply penetrating talons of *Bubo*. Yet in the midst of hardship, from mid-January on, the call of the Great Horned Owl again changes, and the winter range becomes in a very short time the nesting territory, with every species in the habitat contributing to the success of this bird of prey—either by its habits of migration, or hibernation, or by having its young at a propitious time.

Not all of the individuals of the various "migratory" species of birds leave their northern homelands, but those which are genetically equipped to respond to the shortening day length with fat-storing and glandular changes that enable them to fly many thousands of miles, guided by the stars and the sun arc, to far southern climes have been subjects of awe and wonderment to man since Job and Aristotle and probably earlier. The young of the season fledged to this mysterious journey cannot be following the leader, because they leave before the majority of the adults. Beginning with the nighthawks in August, the numbers of birds on the wing gradually build up through September, reaching a peak in October in the temperate zones, then dwindling off to a few stragglers by late November.

The birds of prey are day migrants, usually traveling in a broad front at widely spaced intervals and at steady rates of speed, with infrequent—if any—stops for food. Some, like the songbirds, seem to have definite migration routes; others, apparently stimulated to leave their breeding grounds because of a lack of food as well as for more obscure reasons, drift and meander. Many follow the crests of north-south ridges, riding on the updrafts which are the way of least resistance. The traffic in these lanes becomes heaviest after the passage of a cold front, when more wind is deflected upward, providing optimum flying conditions. Hawks and eagles from all over New England and above the St. Lawrence in Canada travel the ridges of the Connecticut Valley, past Mount Tom in eastern Massachusetts, across the Hudson River near Bear Mountain Bridge, and over the New Jersey countryside until, at a high and slender point in the Kittatinny Ridge near the village of Drehersville, Pennsylvania, many of these birds are funneled into a narrow lane.

For many years sportsmen gathered there to

shoot thousands of birds as they passed almost within reach, and the bodies of rotting hawks accumulated in mounds at the base of the promontory or were draped with spread wings along barbed-wire fences in grim testimony of the slaughter. In 1934, however, it ended. The ridge-top observation point was purchased at that time and turned into the world's first sanctuary for hawks. It is now owned and operated by the Hawk Mountain Sanctuary Association, whose membership includes more than three thousand persons in forty-three states, Canada, and a number of other countries. Visitors to Hawk Mountain today bring only binoculars and cameras to record the passage of the birds of prey which use this flyway from late August to late November. Maurice Broun, the ornithologist in charge during twenty-four autumn seasons, has recorded the passage of more than 372,000 migrants—Bald Eagles, Broad-winged and Red-tailed hawks, accipiters, and many others.

Elsewhere in the United States, flight lanes also become narrow crossing the bluffs on the shore of Lake Superior, overlooking Duluth, Minnesota, and on the west shore of Lake Michigan near Cedar Grove, Wisconsin. Woods hawks most commonly follow the shorelines and bunch up on peninsulas.

Sharp-shinned Hawks from Newfoundland drift to Long Island Sound, turning westward along the coast, then south, passing over Cape May, New Jersey, which is noted for flights of accipiters, falcons, Ospreys, and Turkey Vultures which breed in the northeast. The young Sharp-shins pass Fisher's Island, New York, early in September, and the adults come through later, mostly in mid-September. Some of these birds fly high up, sailing straight along and keeping up momentum by an occasional beat of their wings; others fly close to the ground, taking advantage of hollows and hillsides to get the most favorable wind currents; and still others may be seen darting through the patches of woods, hunting for small birds. Likewise, Scandinavian Honey Buzzards, on their southward flight from the northern Palaearctic region to tropical Africa, are observed to follow the wooded shoreline of the island of Als, off the coast of Denmark, where they can stop to forage.

During migration, all birds are tourists and much more susceptible to predation, accident, and trapping by man than on their home territories, where every tree, hedgerow, and clump of grass is a familiar part of the landscape, and the location of their food supply known and relatively stable.

Falconers know Assateague Island, off the coast of Maryland, Cape Hatteras, North Carolina, and Daytona Beach, Florida, as places where Peregrines will feed and can be lured with bait into a head-set or dhogazza trap. The Peregrine Falcon, a noted wanderer over lands and seas, seems to have no set plan in its migration, yet at these various observation points the first to come through, over a period of many days, are the juvenile females. Next come a majority of juvenile males, and finally—still segregated, but not to such a great extent—the adults pass over, showing that the departure of these birds, like the accipiters, is correlated with age or sex or both factors.

In North America, Swainson's Hawk, which breeds in Alaska, Canada, and the western United States, winters south of the Equator in Argentina; and the Broad-winged Hawk, nesting east of the Mississippi and from Canada to the Gulf Coast, winters from the Florida Keys and Southern Mexico to the upper Amazon. For a few days in October, enormous numbers of these hawks come together over Central America, passing in review for hours over any given point on their journey to subtropical wintering grounds in the most spectacular funneling of flight lanes occurring anywhere in the Western Hemisphere, rivaling the great autumn passage of European accipiters to Arabia and east and central Africa over the Sinai Peninsula. Although many of the temperate-zone owls tend to be entirely non-migratory, drifting only short distances to establish winter feeding-ranges near their breeding territory, the Scops Owl of Europe makes the trip to tropical Africa annually, and the tiny Flammulated Screech Owl, which breeds at high altitudes in the mountains of the southwestern United States and Mexico, spends the winter in Central America.

The smaller New World scavengers, the Black Vulture and the Turkey Vulture, are highly erratic in the extent of their wanderings, being frequently recorded farther south or north than their usual summer and winter ranges. Across the continent of North America, particularly in the Pacific and Atlantic regions, their migrations are not as conspicuous as those of the hawks, since in many areas they are resident throughout the year.

Old World vultures in the temperate zones are strongly migratory. Egyptian Vultures are rarely seen in the Mediterranean region during the winter, as all migrate to Africa just south of the Sahara;

and some of the Griffon Vultures and Lammergeiers of Central Asia desert their breeding grounds to cross the Himalayas, according to the records of one of the Everest expeditions, at altitudes of between 20,000 and 23,000 feet, to winter in Northern India.

In winter, high-elevation birds are forced to migrate to lower levels by the exigencies of weather and the descending snowline, as the higher life-zones in the mountains above 6,000 feet nearly everywhere correspond to the climate of the Far North. These movements also take place at lower heights, where conditions approximate the temperate zones with their four seasonal changes. The Kashmir race of the common Pariah Kite, breeding up to 8,000 feet in the Himalayas, comes down to the plains in winter; and the Brahminy Kite, found up to about 6,000 feet, is locally migratory. In all of these instances, the hawk, the eagle, the vulture, and the owl go generally in whichever direction will take them out of an unfavorable climate to a milder one, whether only from a cold temperate to a warm temperate zone, or far below the Equator to a tropical dry season, where September to October is springtime. Birds resident in warm temperate areas south of the Equator move northward, but rarely beyond the equatorial belt. Southern South America extends much farther towards the ice sheets of the Antarctic than the extreme southern limits of any other continent. Consequently, predatory birds such as the Red-tailed Buzzard (*Buteo ventralis*) and the Long-winged Harrier (*Circus buffoni*) are absent from their breeding grounds in Chile and Argentina in winter (July); their northward movements, as far as the Guianas, in the case of the harrier, are as regular as the southward migrations of the Red-tailed Hawk (*Buteo jamaicensis*) and the Marsh Hawk (*Circus cyaneus*) of North America. In South Africa and the South Australian region, however, annual northward migrations are rare.

Among the mysteries of migration is the annual fall exodus of Marsh Harriers from Tasmania, where the grazing paddocks and new grain of the fields are patrolled in May, June, and July only by the Brown Falcon. The number of Marsh Harriers in New Zealand exceeds their combined numbers in Australia and Tasmania, but they do not migrate generally from this region. There are odd long-distance records confined to New Zealand itself, and some of the birds are regular winter visitors to Lord Howe Island, where they prey on the young muttonbirds (petrels) which are leaving their burrows for the ocean, or to Kermadec Island, six hundred miles north of North Cape, New Zealand.

Similarly, no one knows why the young Bald Eagles fledged in spring in Florida move *northward* soon after leaving the nest. By May and June many of the banded individuals are 1,000 to 1,500 miles north of their nesting ground.

We know little of "migratory" movements in the flat rain-forests. In other tropical habitats the birds of prey begin nesting at the end of the rainy season, and raise their young in the dry season, which is most favorable, but their food supply is relatively stable the year round. They leave their nesting grounds for varying periods of time and for reasons that are individual and often obscure. In *Eagles,* Leslie Brown notes that a number of African Fishing Eagles nesting close together on a group of uninhabitated islands in Lake Victoria move each year at the close of the breeding season to the mainland; and that Verreaux's Eagles disappear from the Embu district of Kenya during March and do not return until mid-May, when they begin to work on their nests, the young birds raised by them remaining until December. Here a variety of situations produces equally varied behavior among the many species of raptors, in contrast to the more or less predictable patterns of temperate-zone life.

The Brown Falcon, native to Australia and Tasmania, is not migratory, but these birds drift in winter by the hundreds to nearby districts suffering from caterpillar "plagues."

The Red-tailed Hawks take their time and migrate over an extended period from the end of September to the close of November, or in many cases, stay in the North and establish winter ranges, just as those which have gone to Florida, Jamaica, or Mexico, will do on their arrival.

This winter hunting-range is a well-established area with boundaries not protected against other Red-tailed Hawks or, with rare exceptions, any other species. The ranges in the South as well as the North seem to spread out over great areas, even though there may be a localized superabundance of prey species in one place. The Red-tails on these winter ranges take a wide variety of food, each bird specializing in a different combination of prey. Of three hawks hunting in the same places, one may be taking a toll of cotton rats and mice, another of land tortoises, and still another of rabbits or possums or muskrats.

In the South the juveniles tend to wander from range to range, evidently unable to establish their own hunting grounds as yet. Later, when they return in spring to their northern breeding ground, they will learn to establish a range by being buffeted constantly from one nesting territory to another until they eventually find a small section of land unclaimed by any pair. Beginning their movement northward before some of the songbirds, the ducks, and the geese, they drift slowly and erratically. The adults arrive at the same nesting territory they held the previous year, and begin immediately to establish, by characteristic sounds and movements, the boundaries of home.

And so, season after season, and year after year, the Great Horned Owl and the Red-tailed Hawk raise their families in the northern forests and woodlots, in the shadows of the oaks planted by the squirrels, every one of their actions governed by instincts hundreds of thousands of years old.

A Red-tailed sails in for a landing on broad wings. When hunting, this direct approach gives open field prey no conception of the speed of attack; the hawk looms larger and larger, then suddenly grabs.

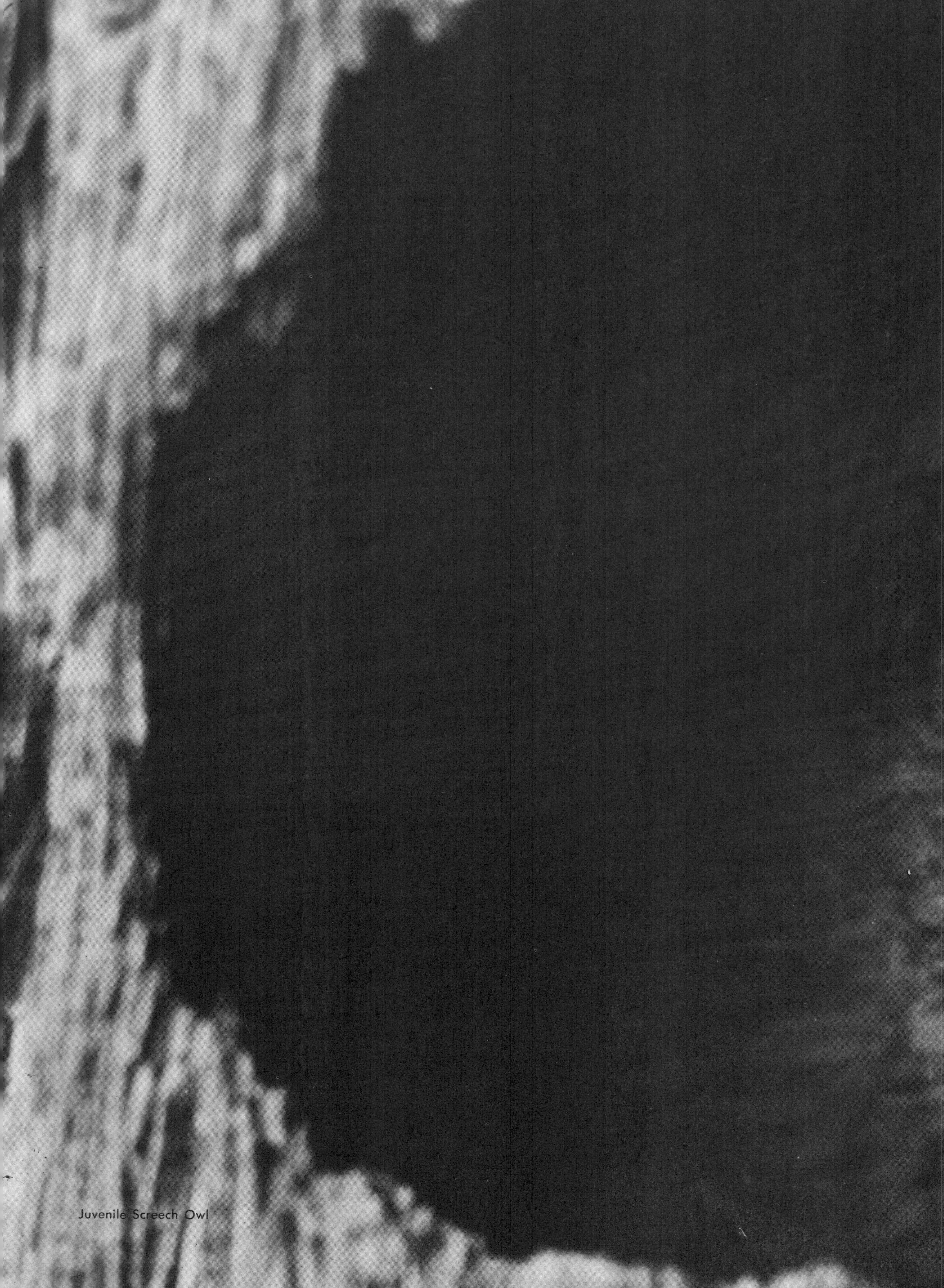

Juvenile Screech Owl

chapter 4
DESIGNS FOR SURVIVAL

In the late afternoon, when the sun is low on the horizon, one of the distended "stubs" on a tree branch suddenly fluffs itself out and, surprisingly, is seen to be a Screech Owl, with its eyelids parting to reveal great and solemn yellow eyes. How does he look at our world? we wonder. If he were to be disturbed at his time of siesta, at, say, high noon, this tiny predator could see perfectly well, but the pupils of his eyes would be reduced to pinheads to exclude the light which he cannot use because of his natural physiological affinity for low-light intensity. However, at nightfall, when he instinctively becomes active, his eyes dilate to let in all the available light.

All birds have keener sight than mammals, including man. The large size of their eyes and of the images cast on the retina partly account for this. Other factors are the high concentration of visual cells and of nerve fibers in the cells. Hawks have the highest known concentrations—about a million per square millimeter in the Common Buzzard (*Buteo buteo*)—as compared to an estimated 400,000 in the English Sparrow, and 200,000 in man. Although owls are provided with an abundance of rods—the light-sensitive cells which are necessary for night vision—they also have a good proportion of the cones which are responsible for the sharp vision of diurnal birds in bright sunlight. They differ most from the hawks in their almost total lack of monocular vision. They cannot look out of the corners of their eyes, which are fixed in the sockets, and so must move their extremely mobile necks back and forth constantly in order to see—with both eyes—to the sides. This jerking motion covers an arc of 180 degrees and is accomplished so quickly that it seems like a single reaction. Another peculiarity of owls is their farsightedness. Unable to adjust their lenses efficiently by muscular action, they will frequently tilt their heads to bring objects close up into focus. The resulting quizzical poses make them look wise. But many an owl has been grabbed by a man or shot at close range because it stayed to stare instead of taking wing—a very unwise course of action.

The eye of a hawk or eagle is set further back on the side of its head than the owl's. Although its eyes are scarcely more movable than the owl's, it does have the ability to perceive objects on its right or left; thus, it has a relatively narrower binocular field of vision straight ahead, even though its total view is wider. Muscles for focusing, increasing the curvature of the eyeball to sharpen objects close by, or flattening it for distance perception, are particularly well developed. In flight, adjustment seems to be instantaneous. In sighting its prey and diving to the kill, the hawk never seems for a moment to lose the clear image of its moving target.

Despite differences in their visual adaptations, however, the hawk and the owl are both hunters with the type of forward-directed vision that is necessary for pursuit. The songbird and the game bird which are the hunted have eyes directed much further to the side, and sometimes even to the rear, the better to avoid their pursuers. The woodcock offers the extreme example of this; its field of vision to the rear appears to be wider than its forward view.

Birds of prey which take their food from the water have made some learned or physiological adjustments to the double images caused by light refraction. To be successful, the fishing hawk, eagle or owl must strike where the fish really is, and not where it appears to be—the disparity between reality and illusion increasing with the depth of the prey. Very little is known about the owls' methods of fishing, for they are predators of the dense forests of Africa and Asia. They do, however, fish the shallow waters of coves and streams which are also favorite haunts of fishing eagles. As far as is known, only the Osprey and its cousin, the Black-collared Hawk of tropical America, habitually dive into the water to capture fish at greater depths. This habit of submerging suggests the possibility of even further specialization, similar to that of the kingfishers, for clear underwater vision.

Smell appears to be insignificant in the lives of most birds. However, its importance to vultures has been a cause for controversy for many years. Do they, or don't they, find decomposing animal matter by smell? John James Audubon thought he had settled the question. He concealed a carcass under one of his canvases, and the scavengers did not find it; but, in another experiment, they were drawn to a painting of a partly dissected dead sheep. As time went on, other observers, who noticed that Turkey Vultures could find dead mammals hidden in woodchuck holes or under boxes, came to the conclusion that they must depend on smell as well as sight to find their food. Frank Chapman found that Turkey Vultures on Barro Colorado Island in the Canal Zone would come to decomposing mammals, but not to dead fish which he had hidden. He thought this gave evidence of discriminating smell.

One suggestion is that vultures have learned to associate crawling insects and buzzing flies with

The Peregrine Falcon, a diurnal bird of prey, has eyes placed slightly to the sides of its head; it can see straight ahead, to the sides, or below as it pursues, strikes and follows prey to the ground. The successful hunter shown here, a bird of the year, is bending to kill a pigeon it has knocked out of the air.

carrion, and may be able to detect this activity in the neighborhood of a carcass even if they can't see it. Or perhaps the King and Turkey vultures, which are associated with forests, where their food would be more difficult to find, *do* have a better developed sense of smell than the Black Vultures and Condors of tropical America. Kenneth Stager, Curator of Birds at the Los Angeles County Museum, has shown that the area of the brain which controls the sense of smell is three times larger in the Turkey Vulture than in the Black Vulture. Since none of the Old World vultures is found in deep tropical forests, it would seem unlikely that any of these birds would need a good sense of smell.

Birds that forage during the day become conditioned to eat certain foods and avoid others, according to their colors. Granivorous birds, for example, normally feed on white seeds and will not eat poisoned grain stained blue or purple; but rats and mice, which find their food to a great extent by smell, will eat grain no matter what color it is. Among the predatory birds there are those that will not tangle with poisonous snakes and lizards, which are marked with bright warning colors; but bright coloration makes these creatures even more vulnerable to the occasional specialist. One of the most spectacular sights of the tropical forests in Central and South America is the White Hawk, winging back to its nest with a coral snake, a brilliantly marked poisonous reptile on which this bird, as well as the Laughing Falcon, commonly feeds.

Unpleasant experience warns birds away from bees, stinging insects, and even tree hoppers with spines on their backs, and when they are bitten, stung, or made ill by these foods, some tactile sense in the bill, mouth, skin, or bases of the feather bristles may be involved. The owls, nightjars, and other nocturnal species have highly specialized feathers around their beaks. These may have something to do with touch, as the birds come into close contact with their prey in darkness; or perhaps they are a protective camouflage covering the beak and giving the bird a mammal-like appearance, especially when it strikes a defensive pose with one wing outstretched, such as the Barred Owl adopts.

Recently a formidable amount of physiological and experimental evidence has been collected concerning the complicated ear structure and extremely acute hearing of owls. Generally, a diurnal bird best hears sounds corresponding to the middle range of tones in all of its various songs and calls, but the owls are sensitive to about the same wide tonal range that is heard by man. Owls respond most readily, in fact, to frequencies high above the middle range of their own voices. The squeaking of mice and certain high-pitched sounds which are produced by their movements through grass, leaves, and brush give owls a cue not only to the presence of prey, but to its exact location in partial or even complete darkness.

The ear structure of owls differs from that of mammals and diurnal birds. Internal modifications allow owls to pick up slight sounds that other creatures cannot hear, and may also give them the ability to analyze complex combinations of vibrations. Their heads are large and wide, and their ear openings are so far apart that in the case of the larger owls there is a distinct time lag between the arrival of sounds at one ear and the other which may be sufficient to indicate direction. In addition, they have either asymmetrical ear holes or flaps, so that vibrations are received differently by each ear. Such differential reception seems, in theory, to be necessary for determining distance to a sound source. The Common Barn Owl, for example, has evenly placed ear openings, but the highly developed flaps of skin in front of the ears are not symmetrical.

It is not surprising, then, to find that owls depend more on their hearing, at times, than on their ability to see under extremely low-light intensities. In 1945 Lee R. Dice tested Barred, Long-eared, and Barn owls in different light intensities, using *dead* mice, and found that they could see and approach their prey under an illumination of 0.000,000,73 foot-candle—equivalent to that produced by a standard candle 1,170 feet away, or between 1/100 and 1/10 of the light intensity required by man to see an object. All three of these owls experienced difficulty in seeing below an intensity of 0.000,000,53 foot-candle. Two years later, when Dice used Barn and Long-eared owls to determine the value of protective coloration in mice, he coincidentally discovered that both species could strike *live* prey accurately in total darkness. Obviously sounds were being utilized by the birds to find the general location of their moving targets, but was some other factor also involved that enabled the birds to see at close range?

It remained for Roger Payne and William Drury, researchers at the Hathaway School of Conserva-

A specialized feeder of the tropical American rain forest, the Laughing Falcon preys mainly on snakes and lizards.

The eyes of the North American Bald Eagle, a diurnal fishing bird, are set farther back than those of fishing owls.

Two parabolas of filo-feathers which may be "sound-sensitive" completely cover the face of this North American Barn Owl. This species has hearing so keen that it can, if necessary, strike its prey with accuracy in total darkness. Bristles around the beak, common to all owls and some diurnal birds of prey, may be sensitive to touch.

The European Tawny Owl, ordinarily one of the most nocturnal birds, may be seen abroad in daylight during the breeding season, but under cloudy, low light conditions.

Luminous yellow eyes and a partial facial disc are characteristics of the Screech Owl, most active at dusk and dawn.

The Barred Owl, one of the most nocturnal of the typical owl family, has a facial disc forming nearly a complete circle. This species, like the Barn Owl, may be able to "home in" on its prey by sound alone.

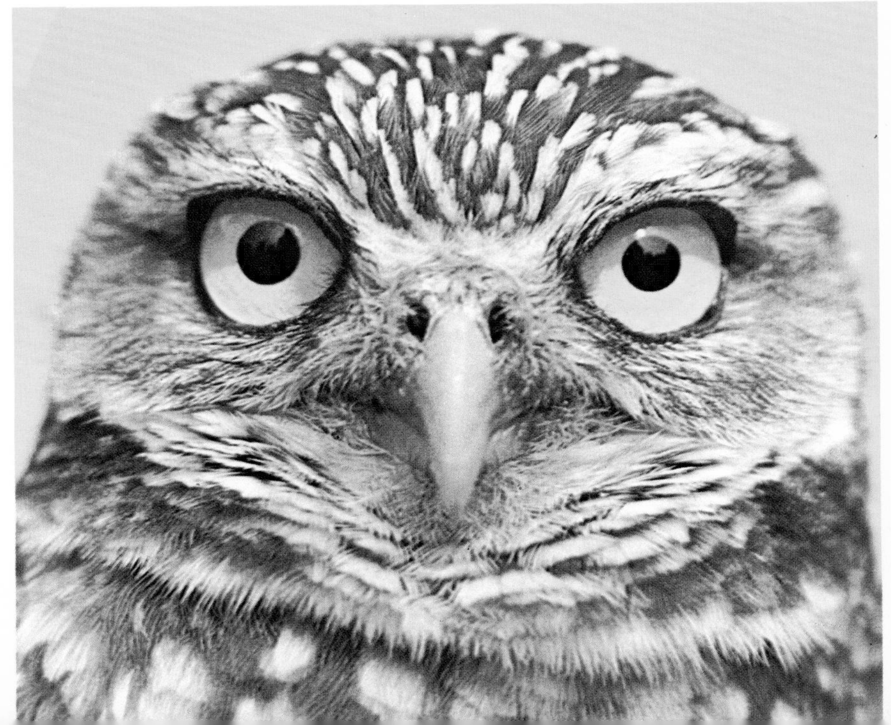

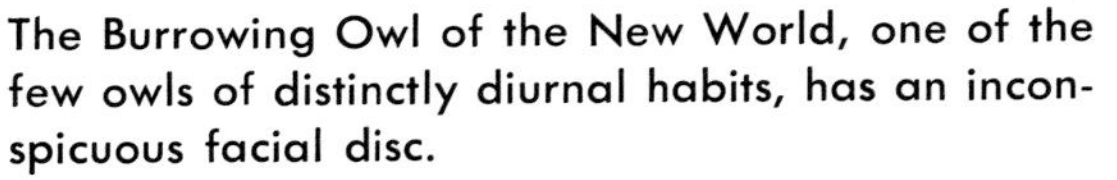

The Burrowing Owl of the New World, one of the few owls of distinctly diurnal habits, has an inconspicuous facial disc.

The Saw-whet Owls (above) are common throughout northeastern, central, and western North America, but so nocturnal and shy that they are seldom seen and almost never heard, except in the mating season. They have extremely full facial discs, compared to the diurnal Ferruginous Pigmy Owl of the Southwest (right).

The Malay Fishing Owl, which is abroad in daylight, has a rudimentary facial disc. Thick tufts of feathers over its unusually deep-set eyes probably help to eliminate the glare of the sun.

Specialized filo-feathers on the face of the Marsh Hawk may indicate its partial dependence on hearing. It hunts rodents in the same habitat as the Short-eared Owl which quarters the fields and swamps by day as well as by night, especially in the breeding season.

White eyebrows and lores give the Spectacled Owl its name; a deep tropical forest-dweller of the New World, it shares the habitat of the Laughing Falcon, also beautifully colored, but masked with black.

tion, in 1956, to test whether owls could, in fact, find their prey by hearing alone. They introduced Wol, a young Barn Owl, to a nearby empty room, 25 by 20 feet, where he was taught by his human instructors how to hunt. Raised by a research associate who had taken him from a nest, Wol had never learned the fine art of capturing mice, and would at first chase them all over the room, but before long he was flying from his perch and striking his prey directly in true owl fashion.

The preliminary training over, the investigators boarded up the windows and, with the lights off, exposed hypersensitive film for an hour, to make sure that the room was light-tight. Wol was then given five weeks to fly about and memorize his surroundings, at first with the aid of a small night light, then with increasingly less light, until, during the last week before the experiments, he was left in complete darkness. Finally, Payne and Drury spread leaves on the floor and set a mouse loose in the totally dark room. Rustlings were heard, and when the mouse stopped and was silent, they could hear Wol leave his perch, fly down, and strike the leaves. A little light revealed the owl sitting motionless on the floor, holding the mouse in his talons.

The researchers repeated the experiment seventeen times, and in all but four instances (when it was a near miss) Wol hit the target. The investigators ruled out any possibility that he could have, like a bat, been making his own sounds and using the echoes to guide him, for it has been proven that Barn Owls cannot echo-locate. It remained only to test whether he was seeing by infrared heat waves given off by the body of the mouse or was locating his prey by odor, or—as they had thought—was homing in on sound.

On the next trial, they pulled a wad of paper along the floor on a string, and Wol found this fake mouse, which had neither body warmth nor odor, making it absolutely certain that he was relying only on his hearing. Wol needed both ears to pounce with accuracy, for when his right or left ear opening was plugged with cotton, he consistently landed short of the target on the right or the left line from his perch, respectively.

On a cloudy night hearing must be extremely important to owls, for in forest shadow the available light may be no more than a 500th to a 3,200th of the normal intensity in the open on a clear night. It has often been suggested that owls use their ears to locate prey, then switch over to their eyes for the final strike. However, in view of Payne's experiment, proving Wol's ability to strike mice "by ear," so to speak, the owl's eyes would seem to be used to avoid obstacles such as branches and twigs, while its ears would lead it to the final strike. Under various conditions in nature, the Barn Owl probably uses either eyes or ears, but owing to its keen hearing it can strike accurately on the darkest night.

Payne has suggested that the specialized bristle-like feathers, or filo-plumes, on the facial discs of owls may be sensitive conductors of sound to the ears, although there is no experimental evidence to prove this.

The Barn Owl, which is strictly nocturnal in its habits, has parabolas composed of these feathers forming the most complete facial disc of any of the owls. That the facial disc is in some way connected with hearing is strongly suggested by the high degree of its development in other species which are strictly nocturnal, by its modification in those birds of partly diurnal habits, and by its almost total absence in the pigmy owls, Burrowing Owl, and fishing owls of strongly diurnal habits which presumably are not as dependent upon hearing to find their prey. These diurnal owls are also not as well equipped to see in the dark as their nocturnal relatives. The Burrowing Owl, tested by Dice in his 1945 experiments, could not find dead prey at a light level that was more than adequate for Barred, Barn, and Long-eared owls, and seemed to have about the same dim-light vision as man.

Among the diurnal birds of prey, the harriers also have facial ruffs with specialized contour feathers that may be conductors of sound, indicating that they probably use their ears to some extent, as well as their keen eyesight, as they course over the marshes and meadows, looking for mice and other small rodents.

Among morphological adaptations for seeing or hearing, the former are best developed in the diurnal birds of prey, and the latter, in the owls. But some of the most nocturnal owls may be conspicuously diurnal in their habits, when the days are longer, in spring and summer, and it is necessary to provide food for their young. Then the Short-eared Owl, the Tawny Owl, the Barred Owl and the Great Horned Owl forage in the daytime. However, when they are seen on the wing in the early afternoon, it is usually under cloudy skies.

The development of flight has given birds a fantastic advantage over all other creatures except man, and has given the predatory birds a mandate to hunt nearly every aquatic, terrestrial, and arboreal species —even other birds. Having located their prey by sight and hearing, the owls, with their soft feather-covering, seem to float down to the kill, utilizing to the full the tactic of surprise in darkness; the diurnal woods hawks, kites and falcons, respectively, have evolved stalking, complex aerial maneuvers, and speed; and the buteos, eagles, and vultures have the ability to soar for hours, supported on wide wings by the warm air currents or thermals rising from the earth, while over a vast range they observe the quick or wait for the dead.

The rigid single plane wing of an airplane with its two or three movable features is very simple compared to the flexible jointed avian wing. In flapping flight the bird creates its own wind, and it climbs on these air columns. In soaring, or gliding, the "arm," the "hand," and the alula which comprise the wing may act simply as supporting surfaces, or may sometimes be divided into two working units, with the "hand" functioning as a propeller. The inclination of the various planes can change momentarily, and the camber (or convexity) can be altered at will. The hawk stoops at its prey with the wing tips pulled back, an action which reduces lift, and the reverse technique is utilized in steep and perhaps even in slight climbs. The tail acts as a rudder as the bird banks, climbs, or dives. The longer the tail, the more control—as demonstrated by the long, rounded tails of the woods hawks.

As the Tawny Owl launches into the air, its "wrists" touch, producing a butterfly-like configuration. The wing and feather structure is more flexible than in the hawklike birds and accounts for the "silent" wavering flight of owls.

Slotting of the wing and tail feathers is an important factor in flight, for the air pressure under the supporting surface must be greater than on the upper surface, and this creates pockets of whirling air, or turbulence, along the edges, especially at the wing tips. By separating the primaries and rectrices, and bringing out the alula, spaces are created for the smooth release of air onto the upper surface, thus minimizing dragging and stalling effects. Falcons and kites, with relatively narrow or pointed wings, experience less turbulence at the wing tips than large soaring birds with long, wide and, therefore, square-tipped wings; so, in the eagles, vultures, and buteos that depend almost entirely on riding air currents, the alula is prominent and the primaries are deeply emarginated, or narrowed, for greater speed and forward lift.

Take-off of large soaring birds, such as the Red-tailed Hawk, from a tree branch is a powerful jump into the wind with wings raised; the outermost primaries are slotted deeply to allow some of the first scoop of air to slip over onto the upper surface. Full-out, the hawk takes advantage of its jump to remain airborne; wings, slanted in the direction of take-off, provide added lift. On the downbeat, the wings are folded to release air pressure, and with a slight drop in altitude the hawk is well on its way with enough flying speed. Seen from the side, this looks like a parachute maneuver.

Wrists are raised and tips of wings are held close to the body to give least resistance to the wind just before the upbeat. Now gliding, the Red-tail presents a long and wide supporting wing surface, flattened for greater speed. By tilting the body and maneuvering the slotted wing tips and tail, the bird will gradually gain height and soar with stability and control for long periods of time.

The Red-tailed Hawk maneuvers tail and wings in the final plunge toward the startled pheasant.

At the moment of impact, the hawk's legs are stretched to the fullest, the head is tucked into the breast, and the tail and wings are brought into play as a brake. Falconers call this action "binding to" the prey. The kill is made by the hawk's powerful talons.

Among the diurnal birds of prey, wing structure and mode of flight are extremely varied, and behavior in the air is affected more by wind conditions, temperature, stimulus, and condition of the bird than any rigid morphological design.

However, we associate the relatively long, wide wings of vultures, buteos, and eagles with soaring; the shorter rounded wings of the accipiters with alternate fast wing beats and glides; and long, pointed wings with falcons, which, with their streamlined bodies, are built for rapid flapping flight and high-speed dives. Some of the kites are buoyant gliders having long narrow wings. Their normal flapping flight is slow. The Black-shouldered and White-tailed Kites often pause, and with or without a wind, "still" with very fast wingbeats over the ground before sighting their prey and descending for the kill. "Stilling" is a common tactic of Kestrels and Rough-legged Hawks, as well. Most hawks, however, do not "still," but hover by taking advantage of heavy wind, or updrafts along ridges, to soar against the wind in such a way as to remain in the same spot long enough to look for prey.

For the large soaring hawks, condors, and eagles, flapping is an auxiliary device used in gliding or circling when there are no updrafts, in crossing low over ridges and passes, for picking up speed in escape and pursuit, in turning in calm air or where space is restricted, or in gaining stability in rough air. When condors are ascending in calm air, they more commonly utilize flapping in turns than in straight flight, for, like airplanes, they apparently lose lift on a bank. All of these birds must flap to rise for the take-off, unless they are gliding directly into the wind at high altitudes from the eyrie or some high promontory.

The Harris' Hawk, a New World soaring bird, displays, on its take-off, the longer primaries and increased use of slotting typical of the larger buteo hawks, eagles, and vultures.

Strong legs are undoubtedly of great assistance in flying. Condors, for example, have difficulty in getting off the ground after they have eaten. Heavy and gorged with carrion, they must run twenty-five to forty feet and then jump and flap into the air, a practice which enabled the South American and California Indian tribes to trap them readily in small baited pens, open on top, which they could enter easily enough to feed, but could not leave. Once it has gained the air, the condor, with a supporting surface of 497 square centimeters per pound, is more stable in a good wind than the Turkey Vulture, which has a supporting surface of 1,125 square centimeters per pound of body weight. On several occasions Carl Koford has seen a California Condor scratch its head with its foot without a waver in the vertical and horizontal lines of flight. In the Turkey Vulture, the high ratio of supporting surface to its slight body weight contributes to instability, since air currents have a relatively greater surface on which to act. In quiet air, however, lighter wing-loading becomes an advantage. When the Condor is becalmed, the Turkey Vulture has good control. Differences in the soaring ability of these two vultures are apparently related to the time of take-off and the air currents. Observing them in the same canyon in California, Koford noted that the Turkey Vultures started soaring at least twenty minutes earlier in the morning and continued later in the day. The Condors needed more wind or a warmer day with rising currents for successful soaring.

The flight of the American Black Vulture is unique among large soaring birds, for it has a comparatively short wing and must flap frequently to take advantage of the wind.

In landing, the wing and tail feathers are used full out to counter the pull of gravity and provide the greatest measure of control. Since World War II, a man-made safety device patterned after the deep wing-slotting of heavily loaded soaring birds has made it possible for heavy aircraft to land at slow speeds without crashing.

The King Vulture, coming in for a landing, presents a wide, tilted braking surface and balances by slipping more air through the primaries on one side than the other. Then, with the vulture's tail still braking, but with the wings going back as in flapping flight, the landing gear is in position. Finally the tail goes back, slipping air, and the wings fold in toward the body.

In a familiar kite maneuver, the African Black-shouldered Kite turns into the wind with a peculiar tast vibration of the wings of about half a minute's duration. The spread wings, seemingly perfectly "still," give it the appearance of some forms of paper kites used for fishing by the Japanese, Chinese, and the peoples of the South Seas.

The kite's wings are then raised in a V-shape for several seconds betore the bird loses altitude and, with outstretched talons, drops swiftly down on its prey.

Characteristic wing configurations of the soaring and gliding birds aid in their identification. Straight wings are typical of the eagles and buteos; the Turkey Vulture and some harriers have a marked dihedral; and the deep V formed by the outstretched wings of a "stilling" kite, resembles the outstretched wings of the *Victory of Samothrace*. The Osprey exhibits a distinctive crooked-wing shape.

Under certain stimuli, the normal flight-patterns of the birds of prey vary considerably. While they are hunting, the falcons utilize thermals to gain altitude before going into their high-speed dives, and many birds that do not have a broad soaring wing can assume the silhouette of a buteo hawk by increasing the slotting of their wings and tail.

During courtship, the Marsh Hawk goes through great dives and loop-the-loops, the Golden Eagle does a fluttering dance high in the sky, ending in a gigantic dive toward the eyrie, and the sea eagles soar in ever-tightening circles together, going higher and higher, finally grasping each other's feet and pinwheeling toward the earth. The Black Kite takes a zigzag course downward to the female with half-closed wings, and the pair grasp claws and remain upright with wings beating for several seconds before beginning their spinning fall. The owls that are abroad in daylight at this time indulge in soaring—the Short-eared Owl joining the Marsh Hawk over the meadow in short slanting dives and upward swoops, punctuated by clapping sounds of the long primaries meeting under its body. And the Black Vulture plummets downward from great heights and comes out of its dive with a loud booming sound.

The narrow crooked wing of the Osprey is adapted for soaring over water, which does not throw up warm supporting air currents (or thermals) as effectively as the plowed field, the highway, and other areas on land.

From the earliest practice of falconry, men who knew their hawks believed they could tell whether they had a slow or fast bird by the simple or complex structure of the nostril. The Peregrine Falcon's round, ridged nostril contains a slender rod with a swelling on the end. Behind this are two rising fins. When the falcon dives, air streams over the ridges into the nostril, is broken up by the rod, and whirls. The whirl is further broken up by the fins, so that it takes only a quarter-ounce of pull to bring air from the outside to the lungs. Without this adaptation the bird could not breathe normally while traveling at its extremely high rates of speed. The less complex the structure of the nostril, the slower the bird, so that in the sea eagles, caracaras, vultures, and owls the opening is not ridged at all and contains no inner rod.

The members of the diurnal genus *Falco* are the swiftest of the birds of prey, hunters of open country or fairly open woods. Many of them wear black patches under the eyes which absorb light. Man has also discovered that black reduces glare, for we find football players, skiers, and Eskimos using the same technique.

Deeply hooked beaks characterize the birds of prey; the most compressed are possessed by the owl family, and the largest and heaviest belong to the northern sea eagles and the monkey-eating eagles of the South American and Philippine jungles. Correlations between the shape or size of the bill and feeding habits are often difficult to make, for birds acquire preferences for strange foods. Along the coast of Burma, small hawk owls, generally insectivorous, specialize in stalk-eyed crabs, and in Africa, the Palm-nut Vulture has developed a taste for the nuts of the oil and raffia palms. There are a number of kites which have notched beaks like the falcons, although not all of these birds use them as the Peregrine does to break the neck of its prey. The Double-toothed Kites of Central and South America and their close relatives, the crested cuckoo falcons of Africa and Asia, are tropical species which have two large serrations or "teeth" on each side of the upper mandible. Whether this peculiarity is related to feeding habits is not known.

Possibly the strangest beak is that possessed by the tropical Bat Hawk of Africa and Asia. This bird comes out at dusk to pursue small birds and

The Eurasian White-tailed Sea Eagle, now common only in the Balkans and southern Russia, is known for its omnivorous feeding habits. It has a large oval "slow" nostril, lacking external ridge and inner rod. Like other sea eagles and the large vultures, it is a comparatively slow soaring and gliding bird.

Sleek falcons, the speediest fliers among birds of prey, often have moustachial stripes under their eyes that absorb light and reduce glare. These markings range from the black cap of a Peregrine (above) to the pencil-thin line across the face of an Australian Brown Falcon (below). The former also has a complicated nostril structure that facilitates breathing in a fast aerial dive.

The American Kestrel (above), a small, fast bird which also hunts in open country, has black stripes below and behind the eyes and a black spot on the back of the neck. At a distance, it seems to have a face on the back of its head. It is not known if this is a protective marking. Collars of spots across the nape are common in small owls, but some larger ones, presumably not under the same amount of predator pressure, also have them.

Dickinson's Kestrel of tropical Africa lacks the brilliant coloring of the temperate zone kestrels. The male, shown at right, has no eye stripe; the female, only a faint marking.

Three tropical American relatives of the falcons are omnivorous feeders with strong killing and dissecting bills. The Common Caracara (top right), a ground-dweller, is larger and more aggressive than the Yellow-headed Caracara (center) and the Red-throated Caracara (bottom) which prefer insects.

The coppery plumage of the South American Savanna Hawk blends into the drying grasses of its habitat, where it patrols the ground, hunting snakes, lizards, and insects.

The Crane Hawk (left), an agile South American species capable of catching birds, is one of the few that has an odor—strong and musky—which grows even stronger when it is frightened or angry.

The beak of a rodent killer, the Ferruginous Rough-legged Hawk of North America (below), is slight compared to those eagles, but just as strongly hooked.

Vultures tend to have bare crop regions, heads, necks, legs, and feet; being featherless, these areas are likely to be kept dry and relatively free of bacterial growth. The King Vulture's bare crop is usually hidden under the feathers of the breast, but protrudes after a meal.

Bare ceres on the faces of some of the diurnal hunters indicate that they feed to a greater or lesser degree on carrion. The topical African Bateleur Eagle kills snakes and may tackle game as large as small antelopes, but it is also a scavenger.

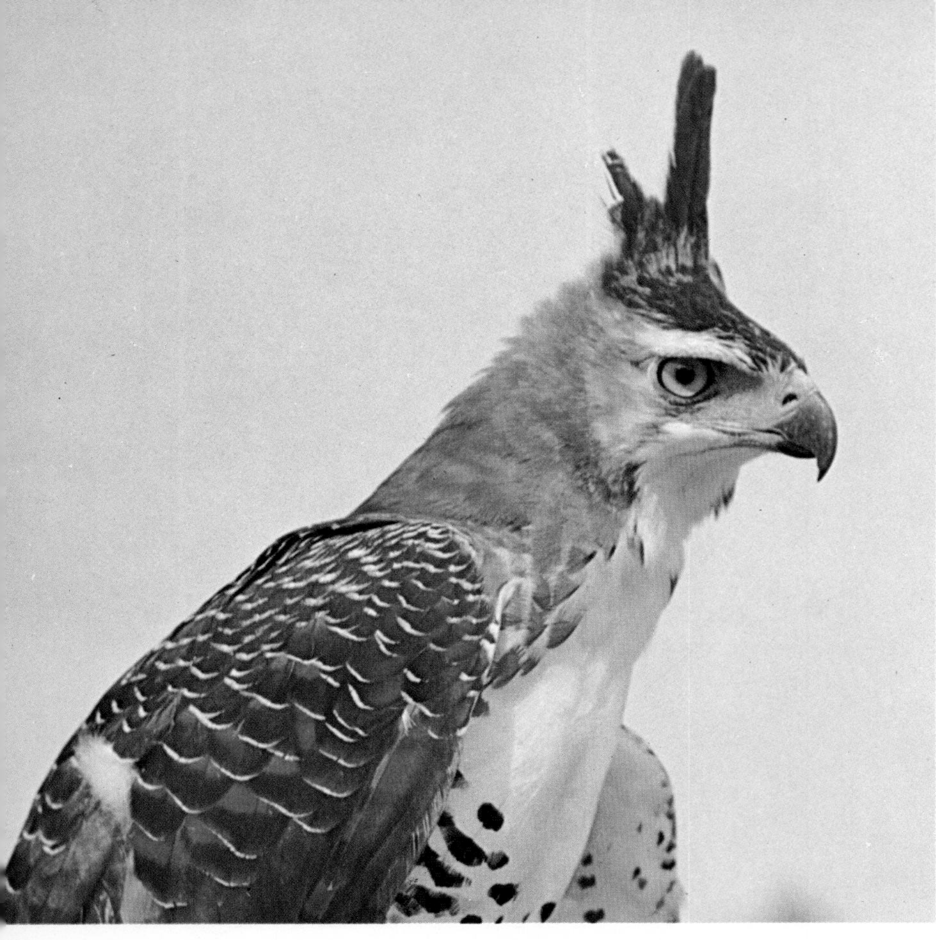

Species in warmer climates need relatively smaller amounts of food to maintain their body metabolism than those in cold climates; the Ornate Hawk-Eagle of South America (shown at left) is equipped with a crop which holds less than that of a Goshawk, although the former is the larger bird.

The double-toothed bill of the tropical American Plumbeous Kite may be used to kill its prey, as are the notched bills of falcons and kestrels.

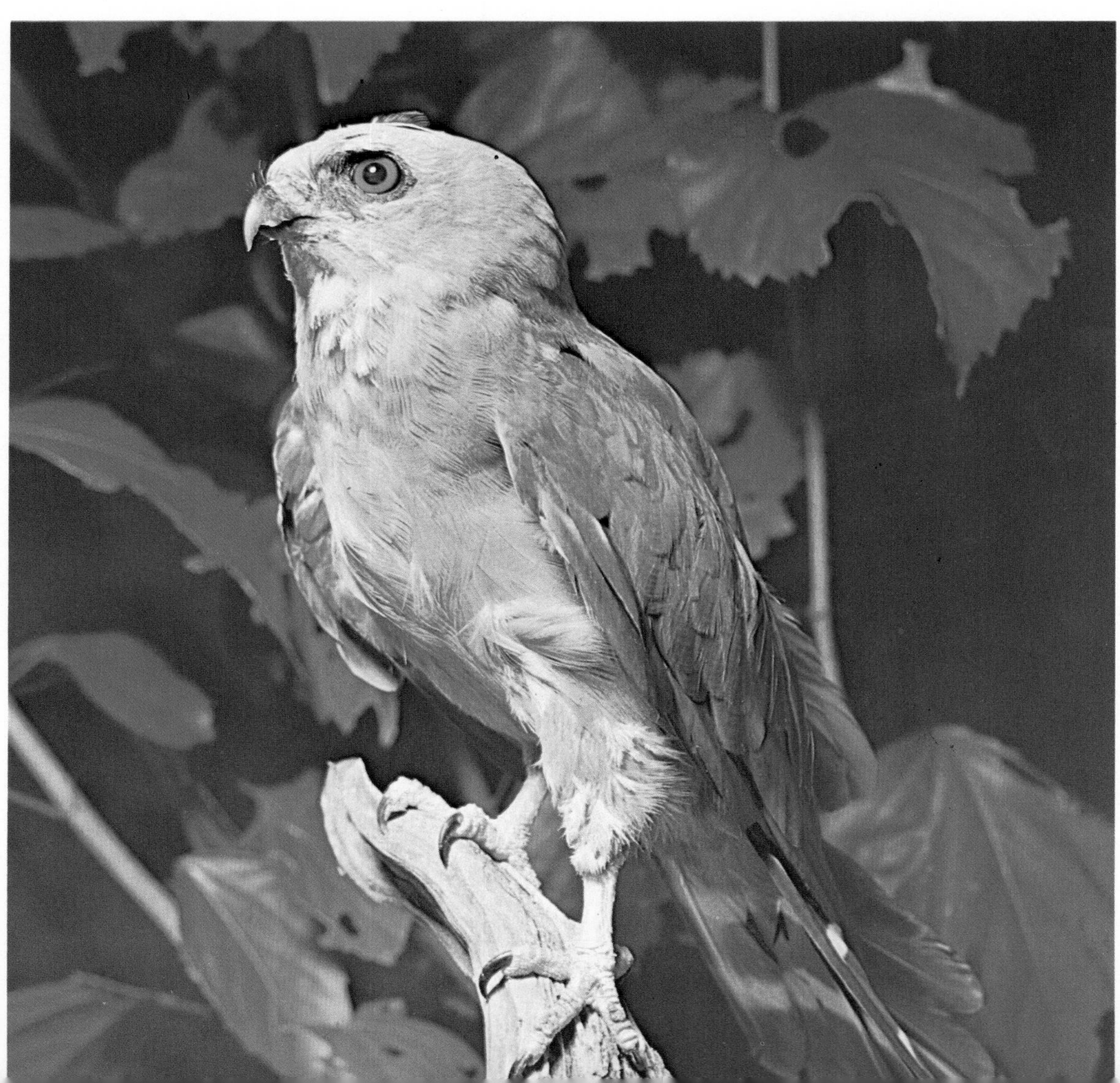

The tropical American Harpy Eagle, which preys on deer, macaws, sloths, and monkeys, has one of the largest of the hooked cutting beaks characteristic of the diurnal raptors.

bats, and swallows them whole on the wing. The Hook-billed Kite of Cuba specializes in feeding on an arboreal snail. The preference of the Everglade Kite, which has a long, slender, sickle-shaped beak, for a fresh-water snail has nearly resulted in its extinction in Florida, for in reclaiming vast tracts of swampland for agriculture, man has concentrated these snails in drainage ditches in many places, and this has increased the incidence of the lung fluke carried by the snails. John Hamlet has found a number of dead kites, infested with flukes—the apparent cause of their decline. Only seven or eight remain to be counted by the National Audubon Society.

Among the vultures, the largest condors and Old World scavengers have formidable beaks, indicating that they may kill to some extent, or at least are capable of tearing fresh meat. The Egyptian, the Hooded (*Necrosyrtes*), the Black (*Coragyps*) and the Turkey vultures have the weakest carrion-feeding bills, and generally must wait until the others have ripped open a carcass or it has decayed and softened. Everywhere that various species of vultures, large and small, feed together, a rigid order of peck is observed at the feast, strictly according to the hook and size of the beak. On the African veld, the more numerous White-backed Vultures are scouts for all the scavengers. When they find a carcass, they stand on it, trample it, and tear at it until the Lappet-faced and White-headed vultures sail in. Then it is clear that these are the dominant ones, for the others back off and let them feed. When they have been feeding for some time, the most aggressive of the Whitebacks reassert their claims, followed by the more timid of their kind. During the hissing and clawing fights between the larger vultures, the Hooded Vultures—least in the order of peck—sneak in and grab a cropful here and there.

(above) The deeply hooked bill of this immature Florida Everglade Kite comes into play only after the prey—a large fresh-water snail—begins to extrude. It clamps down on the snail between the operculum and the shell. A muscular contraction apparently detaches the body, which is promptly swallowed, together with the operculum, and the shell is discarded.

(left) Long tearing beaks of the smaller American vultures are well suited for dissecting ripe carrion. The Turkey Vulture removes the eyeballs of a carcass first, then nips through the skin and, by tearing or pulling it back, lays bare the muscles underneath. From beginning to end, the meal is a clinical affair.

The walking foot of vultures, used for holding down carrion while the beak pulls and tears, is illustrated by an Andean Condor feeding on a dead rat. Vultures stand on larger carcasses.—*Photographed at the National Zoological Park.*

One of the marvels of nature is the digestive system of the scavenger, which destroys the most virulent strains of bacteria. Of necessity, the vulture is the most "antiseptic" of the birds of prey, inside and out. Its ejecta may also kill germs, for a vulture habitually directs streams of "whiting" down its bare legs, instead of throwing them clear, as a hawk or an eagle does. Its more or less bare head, neck, and crop, exposed to the ultraviolet rays of the sun, may be kept relatively free from microscopic parasites, infectious bacteria, and Protozoa; it is certain that hot, dry skin surfaces do not encourage the growth of cultures as matted feathers would. Generally, those parts of its body that come into contact with carrion during feeding are partly or wholly bare. The head of the Griffon Vulture and the White-backed Vulture—and the long neck, which is an adaptation for reaching far into carcasses—are featherless or sparsely covered with clumps of down. The White-headed Vulture and the Cinereous Vulture, which are somewhat predatory, have a thick downy covering on much of the head and neck, and a very high collar of longer, fluffier feathers. And the various hunters which feed partly on carrion—the Common Caracara and the Bateleur Eagle, for example—tend to have bare faces. The vulture has a "walking" rather than a "raptor" foot, and this it plants firmly on the body of the animal as it pulls away at the flesh with its beak.

On the plains of Barotseland, Northern Rhodesia, a two- or three-day-old hyena carcass draws many of the sociable White-backed Vultures, an occasional Hooded Vulture, and one or two of the solitary White-headed and Lappet-faced Vultures. The large proportions and massive tearing beak of the Lappet-faced Vulture (landing) discourage all would-be challengers at the feast. The various species can be easily distinguished by size. In the center foreground group another Lappet-faced Vulture towers over a White-backed Vulture and the Hooded Vulture is the smallest. The conspicuous white head identifies the White-headed Vulture at the carcass (left).

Among raptors, the toes of the mammal-eaters tend to be short and powerful, and those of the bird-eaters long and slender, and many have bumps or pads on the undersurface for grasping. The more powerful the bird, the greater the size of the foot in proportion to the body. The feet and talons of the predatory birds are their tools for killing, as their beaks are for tearing; of two species of eagle owls in Africa which are the same size, the one with the weakest bill and feet (*Bubo leucostictus*) feeds almost entirely on orthoptera, especially cockroaches, which it catches on the wing, and the other (*Bubo poensis*) with larger feet and a heavier beak, eats not only orthoptera and locusts, but also tree hyraxes, squirrels, rodents, frogs, and small birds. The automatic locking of the talons secures the prey so effectively, once the bird binds to it, that the predator sometimes has difficulty in relaxing its grip. The skeletons of Ospreys have been found in fishermen's nets still attached to the fish that apparently drowned them.

The Osprey, the fishing owls of Africa, and Asia, the Black-collared (or Fishing) Hawk of tropical America, and all fish eagles as well as the snake-eating harrier-eagles are equipped with spicules on the bottoms of their feet, an adaptation for grasping slippery prey. The oddest case of foot specialization is that of the Black Eagle of India, the only bird of prey having a long, straight talon like an ice pick on the hind toe, supposedly for use in piercing eggs. This unusual predatory bird, which has a predilection for the eggs and young of pheasants and jungle fowl, may fly off with a nest in its talons, examining the contents as it sails lazily along. However, its year-round diet consists mainly of frogs, lizards, and large insects.

The African Hawk-Eagle has a powerful bird-eater's foot, with long slender toes and bumps at the middle joints for grasping. It normally hunts at low altitudes and surprises prey in the open like an accipiter. Small game, including birds, snakes, squirrels, and rodents comprise its diet with the addition, in some localities, of poultry. Like all the hawklike raptors (except the Osprey), its foot is constructed for perching and grasping with three toes forward and one opposed.

The Black-collared, or Fishing, Hawk of tropical America has thorny spicules on the soles of its powerful feet, similar to the Osprey.

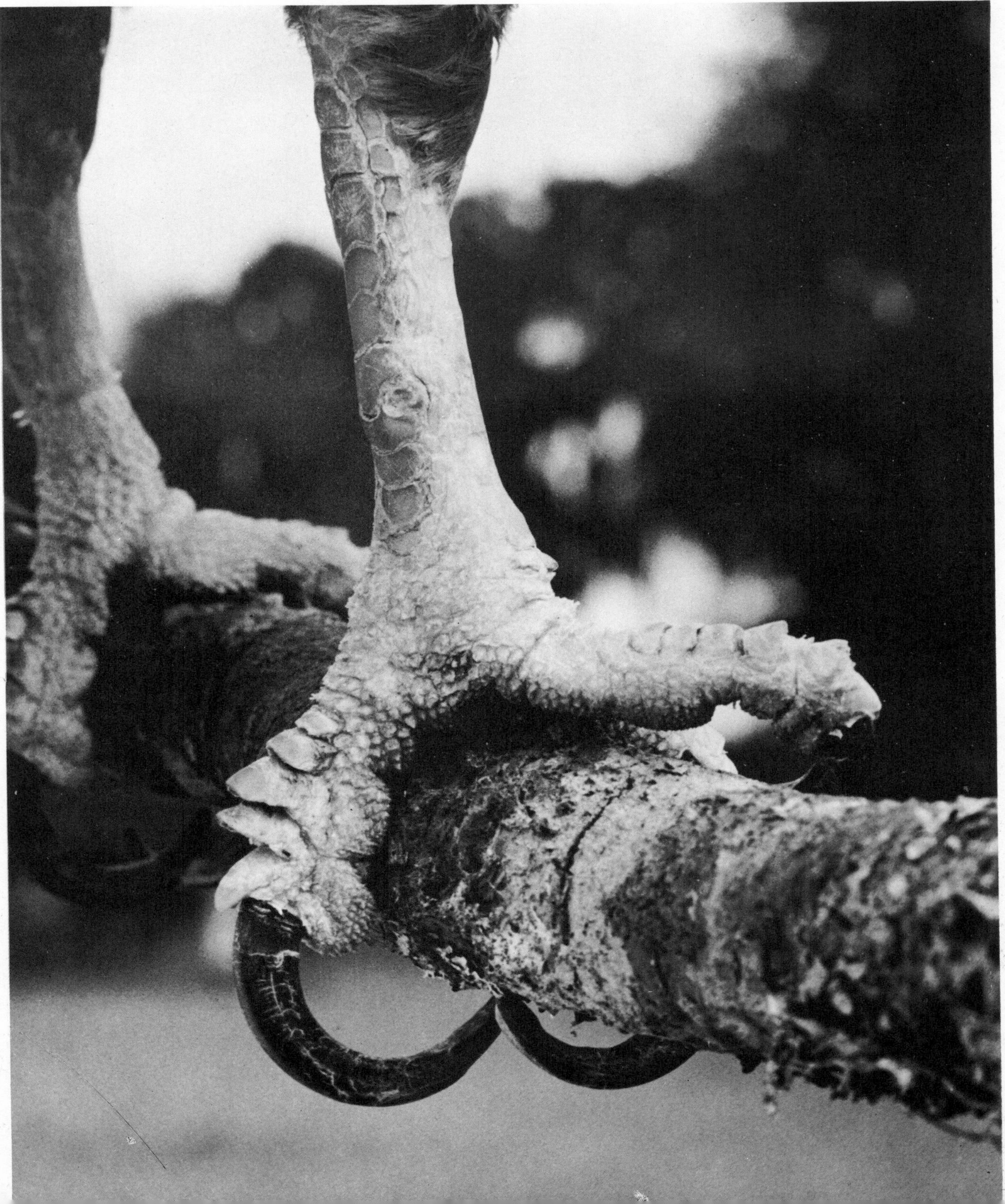

*L*ength of legs relates to the ground-dwelling or arboreal habits of the birds—the Secretary Bird, the Savanna Hawk, and the Marsh Hawk being examples of long-legged terrestrial birds that kill and spend a good deal of time walking on the ground. The kestrels and the kites are among the short-legged species that are strongly arboreal.

A soaring bird, the African Black-shouldered Kite is short-legged (left) in contrast to the South American Savanna Hawk (below) which has long legs and is primarily a ground-dweller.

The snake-eaters do not have a feathered tarsus, and the harrier-eagles, which take a heavy toll of large poisonous snakes and constrictors, are particularly well protected against bites by a heavy armor of reticulated scales. The harrier-eagles, the Savanna Hawk, and even the Red-tailed Hawk, which is not a specialized feeder, may fly directly at and grasp a small snake, but will settle on the ground near a large one and perform a "ritual dance" around it, with wings outstretched, causing the snake to strike until it is tired and can be easily grabbed by the neck.

Only one bird of prey—the Honey Buzzard—has facial armor; its lores (space between eye and bill) and forehead are covered with small scale-like feathers without any bristles. Like a buteo hawk, it captures small vertebrates on the ground, but it is better known for its habit of digging out wasps' and bumblebees' nests from hollow trees, sometimes penetrating so far into a hole that only its tail protrudes.

The African Brown Harrier-Eagle has heavy reticulated scales on the tarsi and is thickly padded with feathers on the chest; both physical features that serve as protections against the bites of poisonous or nonpoisonous snakes. Here it attacks a Hog-nosed Snake near the head, using its powerful feet and sharp talons.

Opposite, above. With talons of both feet planted firmly in the snake, the Harrier-Eagle applies a deadly squeezè and waits for movement to stop.

With a sharp cutting beak, eagle chops the dead snake in half.

Opposite, A little more than bite-size is this morsel which the stalwart predator swallows whole.

As the birds of prey evolved to meet the changing conditions in the environments and habitats of the world, they took on physical characteristics which are often used to separate them generically and specifically—the shape of the wing, the cast of the eye, the length of the talons, size and length of the legs—in a vast and varied array of designs for survival. Their speciation seems to have kept pace with the radiations of birds and mammals, and their populations with the increasing productivity of these food animals, although, like other predators, birds of prey have always been at the top of the "pyramid" of numbers—that is, far fewer in terms of populations than their prey.

Over the course of geological time, the unspecialized types of feeders have endured longest, practically without change, and the others, with their specializations, may or may not do as well, for an adaptation that is advantageous under one set of conditions can, when climate, topography, or food supply is altered, prove to be a handicap, or even a cause of extinction.

Man-made changes in the environment have now become the key to the success or failure of specialists in many parts of the earth. It is man who drains the swamps, indirectly causing a snail-feeder, the Everglade Kite, to disappear; but conversely, man is also a provider of lush habitats for rodent species on which the Common Barn Owl, the Short-eared Owl, and a host of other currently successful specialists prey.

Large vultures which specialize in feeding on the carcasses of large mammals have been on the decline since the end of the Pleistocene. In regions where game has been shot out and sanitary animal husbandry is practiced, they can no longer subsist. Smaller vultures flourished while there were still kitchen middens, and have always attended battlefields. These species, and the scavengers among the hawks and eagles, continue to find local abundance in the refuse provided by man—especially in the least sanitary farm, town, and village districts.

We shall take a long-range view now of that field called conservation, in which man in recent times began to control, encourage, or merely tolerate the birds of prey.

Standing on the remaining half of the snake, the Harrier-Eagle pauses to rest in the middle of its two-course meal.

chapter 5
CONSERVATION

The Golden Eagle.

Somewhere in West Texas a rancher looks into the sky and, as he watches, a Golden Eagle soars into view. He quickly telephones the nearest Eagle and Coyote Club and soon a light plane rises off the ground in pursuit. Within minutes the pilot has gained altitude, and putting his plane into a dive, maneuvers alongside the great bird at an altitude of about 300 feet. Then, allowing the aircraft to fly pilotless for a moment, he pours a charge from a 12-gauge sawed-off shotgun into his target at close range.

No more dramatic picture could be painted of man as a predator upon the birds of prey, for in his enthusiasm to control their abundance in any locality, he has resorted to every annihilative device born of his inventive brain. From a variety of traps and subtle poisons to high-powered rifles and shotguns, he has now equipped himself with machines that outdistance all he pursues across land and water—he even ascends into the air, himself, to hunt like a bird of prey.

Golden Eagles attacked in this manner at first gave battle to the enemy. J. O. Casparis, the pilot hired by the Eagle and Coyote Club in Brewster County to fly out of Alpine, had a few bad moments on one foray when one of his intended victims dived at his plane and hit it with an impact that ripped off several feet of fuselage, tore through the window, and showered him with glass. Most birds, however, are no match for aircraft, and no other method has proven to be as effective in destroying Golden Eagles on the sheep and goat ranges of West Texas.

Darwin Ivy, for many years a U.S. Fish and Wildlife employee (now supervisor) in the Trans-Pecos District, recalls that during the fall and winter of 1940 a total of only sixty eagles was taken from the Davis Mountain foothills with strychnine-treated jackrabbits, whereas during the spring of 1958, one plane, on a single flight, took twenty-three eagles from this same vicinity *during six hours' flying time.*

Casparis, in Brewster County, claims to have shot down more than 8,000 eagles between 1945 and 1952. The toll has been heavy, especially during the years mentioned, when eagle populations were high, but Ivy considers it doubtful that all the planes operating in the Trans-Pecos region ever took as many as a thousand eagles in any one year. "Old Cass" hired one gunner who reported fourteen eagles downed during two months' work with the seasoned eagle hunter.

For the most part, the numbers of eagles killed have been birds that drifted in from distant northern regions and remained to prey upon the heavy concentration of livestock and the abundance of small mammals in this marginal area of grassy slopes and luxuriant valleys—the only good wintering grounds within miles of arid mountains. Prior to the advent of the plane clubs, in the mid-'30's (in emulation of a much less extensive operation in California), ranchers say they were losing nearly all of their new lambs and kid goats each spring to eagles, coyotes, bobcats, and mountain lions.

In 1938, Casparis, at Alpine, and another pilot based at Stockton, in Pecos County, were mainly exterminating coyotes. There was very little emphasis on control of eagles until the increase of their numbers from 1940 to 1950. It was during this decade that two more clubs were formed: one at Kent, in Culberson County, and another in Brewster County, at Marathon. The ranchers were still concerned about coyotes, but were hunting eagles more rigorously before, during, and after the lambing season. There is no question about the vulnerability of young livestock (also fawns of antelope and deer) at this time of year in comparison to the elusive, fleet-footed jackrabbits in the bush which are otherwise staple fare for the Golden Eagles.

The eagle-hunters cost their sponsors eight dollars per hour flying time, so it is no wonder that in the last eight or ten years only the two original clubs have been active. Then, in 1952, a drought caused a reduction in the size of the herds and a consequent decline in populations of predators; and, too, the Fish and Wildlife Service has, since World War II, developed better and less expensive methods of dealing with coyotes in the field. Meanwhile, with their natural enemies restrained, the black-tailed jackrabbits have multiplied, and the hard-pressed Texans must, from time to time, initiate campaigns against *them,* for which planes are of little use.

Ivy admits that there have been moments when those responsible for wildlife in the area wondered if the eagles were not "under control"—or worse, on their way to extinction—"only to have the mountains fill up with them after the first few northers in the fall."

Unlikely, at least within the next few years, is the complete cessation of the war against the eagles. On October 24, 1962, the Congress of the United States passed the Golden Eagle Act, placing the species under federal protection. But the governors of Texas and several Southwestern states, which are strongholds of the Golden Eagle, have requested exceptions to the law during subsequent hearings. They are waging a long-term battle for an amendment, allowing eagles to be destroyed in the localities where they are "doing damage."

Fortunately, not all of man's problems with the birds of prey are as complicated as the situation in West Texas. An understanding of the direct and indirect relationship every predator has to all the species in the various habitats, including Homo sapiens, will do much to alleviate them.

In past centuries man has altered the world he lives in by cutting down trees, by planting fields with strange and exotic plants, and then by tearing up the earth and sowing the seeds of still other plants. He has dammed up rivers and flooded valleys, diverted streams from their normal courses, and drained swamps. He has dynamited mountains and pushed up new hills with his bulldozers. The natural effect of all this activity has been to destroy some of the animals in a habitat and greatly increase the populations of others for which man has provided optimum living conditions. He brings in large animals in such numbers that he often overgrazes the land and disperses the normal inhabitants of the range; he imports chickens, ducks, and game birds from foreign countries; and he experiments with grasses from Africa, India, and other far-off climes. In the temperate climate of North America, the British Isles, and the continent of Europe the new grasses provide excellent food and cover for meadow mice, rabbits, and other species whose numbers are likely to multiply, sometimes assuming the proportions of a population "explosion."

Needless to say, these changes man has wrought create problems in his relationship with other predators. Having established game birds, he wants to conserve them for himself, protecting his hunting range not only from his own species with "No Hunting" signs, but from all the predatory birds and mammals which instinctively hunt them. He wants to keep or sell the grain which he has harvested, and despairs of the rodents which breed heavily to take advantage of his granaries. When he realizes that hawks and owls eat quantities of mice, rats, and rabbits, man is happy to have them around. However, when he sees a hawk catch one of his planted and "fed in" game birds, he goes all-out to kill him. At this point the bird of prey becomes "vermin," a term which, with the support of the major gun and munitions manufacturers, has become a convenient excuse to justify man's love of the hunt. Sportsmen who have no direct ties with the farm or the game areas go out regularly with specialized guns, sights, and other equipment to kill "vermin" and systematically teach their children to do the same.

Meanwhile, unaware that they are "vermin," the birds of prey continue to follow the same natural laws which governed them for the millennia before man arrived. They kill whatever is available or vulnerable, shifting and drifting to keep a pressure on population explosions that in many cases are man made. As they come close to man's home territory to prey instinctively on the concentrations of birds, mice, rats, and rabbits in his fields and open woodlots, they also come within range of his guns. So man has now become the chief predator on hawks and owls. On their winter ranges and nesting territories, he has killed off a large percentage of the most curious, the most active, and the boldest individuals, until now, around most heavily civilized areas, those birds of prey which remain to breed are quiet and nervous and given to scooting away at man's approach. Thus he has gradually changed the disposition and psychology of the raptor population, and finds it increasingly difficult to trap or shoot its members on familiar grounds. These birds are by far most vulnerable during their migrations. When the falcons are flying over strange lands and the woods hawks are coursing over plains and mountains and stretches of water foreign to them, they must catch and eat their food on the run.

This situation makes it possible for man to station himself at certain points along these migratory routes and literally slaughter thousands of birds. It is said that a farmer sitting in his front yard one autumn afternoon on Point Pelee, Ontario, shot fifty-six Sharp-shinned Hawks without leaving his chair, and the general carnage is repeated wherever the flight lanes of fall migration narrow, on the high ridges and across peninsulas, except on one pinnacle of sanctuary, "Hawk Mountain," Pennsylvania. The practice of shooting birds of prey on migration with anything but a camera serves no real or imagined purpose, for a large proportion of the birds are from the tundras and northern forests and have little or no effect on man and his enter-

prises. In order to reduce this slaughter, and partly to compensate for their unprotected status under the Migratory Bird Treaties between Mexico, the United States, and Canada, some conservationists have proposed that all hawks be protected during migrations (September 1 to November 30 and March 1 to April 30) by an act of Congress.

In years past, the Cooper's Hawk of North America earned a reputation as a "chicken hawk" for its impudent boldness in pursuit of barnyard quarry. This bird has been known to fly into a barn after a chicken or come back into a yard time after time, in spite of being yelled at and shooed away, until it has triumphantly carried off a pullet. The only effective discouragement has been a *well-aimed* bullet, for the Cooper's Hawk, like the smaller Sharp-shinned Hawk, is shifty and adept at dodging. The farmer's solution was to shoot the birds which were nesting in the area, but of course, as soon as one pair was eliminated, another would soon move in to take over the newly available territory. Nowadays, however, the problem is not as pressing as it was ten years ago, for in the United States, at least, poultry-raising has become big business. Chickens raised in wire bins and multi-story houses not only get fatter and produce more eggs than those which were allowed to range free in the early 1900's, but are also protected from birds of prey.

The chief difficulty encountered by the game farms, on the other hand, is one that can be solved by a little more knowledge of practical ecology. The owner who plants a hundred pheasants on a hundred acres of land notices the featherings on the ground where two of these birds have been killed by hawks or owls during the season and, in the fall, when he reaps a slim harvest of only twenty or twenty-five pheasants, naturally blames predation for his lack of success. True, he may have given his pheasants sufficient cover, but not of the right kind to provide them with enough seeds, berries, or other food. So, in spreading out to forage, some have wandered away, and in doing so, two have been killed, quite naturally and normally, by the predatory pressure in that area. This man could plant on the same land, under identical conditions, a thousand pheasants, and even if there were no predators about, he would still harvest only twenty-five. On the other hand, if he were to create a habitat rich enough to hold them, he could afford to lose two, for he would harvest about seventy-five out of a hundred on his range.

In the southern part of the United States, where for many years game farms were trying unsuccessfully to raise Bobwhite Quail, bounties were paid on every winged predator that happened by, in the hope that this would save a few of the quail. The farmers, impressed with the showy predation of the hawk, failed to recognize that they had to deal with a sneak thief. The principal villains in this story were cotton rats, which were varying their normal diet during quail-nesting time by eating thousands of quail eggs. Following closely on their heels were the red fire ants, which were killing baby quail soon after they emerged from their eggs. By exterminating the hawks nesting in the region, man succeeded only in increasing the numbers of cotton rats. In this instance the hawks were doubly beset, for not only were they under extreme hunting pressure, but they themselves suffered the ravages of fire ants which destroyed their young as readily as those of the quail.

Recently, chemical warfare on the ants has ended in disaster. Dieldrin and heptachlor killed not only ants, but also several millions of birds, and cost about twenty million dollars in federal and local funds.

It has been learned through sad experience that predation by hawks and owls makes little if any difference on the game farm. If man wants super-populations of game birds to hunt, he must fertilize the soil on his ranges, provide exotic plants to support them, and allow the predators to exercise their natural control measures over the entire region. For man to tamper any further with nature is to invite disastrous consequences in unwanted chain reactions of population explosions affecting all the members of the habitat. During fall migration, a relatively few weeks out of the year, concentrations of vulnerable game birds in the path of hundreds and thousands of buteos, accipiters, and harriers are inevitably irresistible. But nesting pairs of these birds cannot substantially affect the breeding populations of pheasant or quail which have been well provided for, in spite of the traditional prejudices against them.

The Cooper's Hawk may acquire the chicken-stealing habit, especially if the farmer's yard is within its nesting territory. However, it feeds its young mostly on the common wild birds, especially Starlings, and on small mammals such as chipmunks and Red Squirrels.

It is unfortunate that man tends to pass judgment on other predators by the direct effect which they have—or he believes that they have—upon him, and never upon their less obvious activities. In the early 1900's, when the science of conservation emerged, hawks and owls were labeled neatly and placed in two categories. In the old way of thinking, "good" birds of prey were those which, according to analysis of pellets and stomach contents, ate a preponderance of insects, mice, and rats; and the "bad" ones, those which preyed heavily on game birds, chickens, and songbirds. Therefore, the buteo hawks, the Screech Owl, and the Barn Owl were "good," and the accipiters and the Great Horned Owl "bad," although the wide range of prey that could be taken by *Bubo* gave rise to confusion among the scientists about his moral character. Not so, however, among the farmers. Some of the specimens of this bird in the collections of the American Museum of Natural History have, added to their labels, bits of heartfelt invective along with the places and dates of their demise.

The first conservation laws adopted in the United States protected "good" hawks and owls, and declared open warfare on the others, offering bounties for them. Many of these laws still stand as they were written. Actually, even as far as man and his strange practices are concerned, there are no "bad" hawks except for particular individuals who within their nesting territories have developed the habit of taking some vulnerable prey that man wishes to protect. So we hear of a pair of sheep-killing Golden Eagles in the Hebrides which would work together, one deliberately attracting the attention of the ewe, which would charge and rear and strike at its attacker while the other bore off the lamb. In this case, and in many others, there are special reasons involved. The chief food animals taken by eagles on the mainland are rabbits, and these are not found in the Hebrides, so here the eagles must find a substitute food. In the light of experimentation and research it is now recognized that any species of hawk can be "good" or "bad" at various times of the year and under different circumstances. More knowledge and a greater tolerance are needed. Every habitat needs to be policed by its winged predators, and the more man investigates what he must have to live successfully on the earth, the greater is his awareness of their importance.

As a result, eleven of the states in the United States have to date passed model laws protecting *all hawks and owls* "except when they do damage to either poultry or livestock" or "unspecified property." Neither the old nor the new versions of the conservation laws add up to more than a deterrent, for offenders are seldom fined or prosecuted. However, the adoption of model laws has helped to discourage the notion that a few species are "vermin," to be exterminated en masse, and the removal of bounties has taken away any possibility of economic gain from the wholesale shooting of birds of prey. For this reason the National Audubon Society and other local and state conservation groups hope that all of the states will follow with new legislation. In the meantime they are attempting to fill the need for information by distributing circulars which discuss food habits and ecology, and also show the flight silhouettes of the hawks. Wherever the old laws are in effect, they are virtually useless in protecting any of the birds of prey, for most people cannot distinguish between a buteo hawk and an accipiter. Since the former are much more numerous than the latter in their normal distribution over the United States, great numbers of the "useful" hawks are mistakenly shot in these states and turned in for bounties.

Since the beginning of conservation in the United States, only two federal laws have been passed to protect birds of prey, and both have encountered strong opposition. The National Emblem Law, which banned the killing of the Bald Eagle, preceded the currently controversial Golden Eagle Act by more than twenty years. When the former bill was enacted in 1940, its enforcement was not extended to Alaska. And herein lies the story of a magnificent bird—concentrated in great numbers along the coast of Alaska and on the outlying islands—whose persecution over four decades by the fishing and fur industries has finally been abandoned, to the satisfaction of all. The staff of life of this eagle is fish—much of it already *dead*. However, the real cause of the fishing industry's aversion to Bald Eagles was due not to the fact that they ate fish but to their habit of perching on the poles of the big outland fish traps, causing the salmon to panic and beat against the nets until they were unfit for canning. The fox farmers also had troubles because

The Screech Owl, which feeds on many species that man does not like—rats, mice, grasshoppers, locusts, scorpions, beetles, cutworms, and House Sparrows—was considered "good" by early conservation standards. However, this species will also kill small insectivorous birds, such as juncos and Song Sparrows, during the nesting season. In the 1938 *Life Histories of North American Birds of Prey,* A. C. Bent considered their economic status "doubtful," depending on the season and the available food supply—an appraisal closer to the Screech Owl's actual relationship to the various prey species under its domain. We would no longer think of labeling this pair of Florida Screech Owls as either "good" or "bad," but as merely necessary to their part of the forest.

The North American Barn Owl belongs to a worldwide group of rodent specialists. The foot of this bird is much weaker in proportion to body size than that of the Great Horned Owl.

The Great Horned Owl's short, heavy toes are capable of killing mammals as large as skunks and reptiles as formidable as a full-grown Coachwhip.

Traditionally protected in India, the Pondicherry Vulture, a shy bird for such a large and powerful scavenger, is the official undertaker of the Parsees, who cast their dead onto Towers of Silence near Bombay for the vultures, rather than defile the sacred elements of fire, earth, or water.

The Bald Eagle, persecuted for many years in Alaska, now enjoys complete protection by federal law in all of the United States of America. In 1961 the National Audubon Society initiated a census, to be undertaken annually for five years. At the end of the study the Society expects to have the basis for a program to stop their steady decline. The total across the continent, excluding Alaska, is now reduced to some 5,000 individuals, but the northern population has probably become re-established, in large measure, since the termination of bounty hunting in 1952.—*Photographed at the National Zoological Park.*

they allowed their stock to roam free on small islands which the eagles could easily raid. Therefore legislation by the Territory of Alaska was always connected with the enactment or repeal of bounties for the destruction of the species.

The initial bounty law of 1917 provided fifty cents payment for each pair of eagle feet. In that year and succeeding ones through 1922, bounties were paid on 15,745 eagles. In 1923 the amount was increased to $1, and from then until 1940 available records show that an additional 79,746 eagles were killed. (The computation does not account for those which may have been killed or wounded and not retrieved.) Although the law remained in force in subsequent years, no money was appropriated for biennial periods either in 1941 or 1943. The bounty law was repealed in 1945, only to be re-enacted in 1949 with an increase to $2 for a pair of eagle feet. As of February 11, 1951, payments were made on 7,455 eagles under the revised statute. In all, over 100,000 eagles died before man's predator pressure ceased.

It was the United States Fish and Wildlife Service which eventually came to the rescue with an amazingly simple device—a spike set on the poles of the fish traps which prevented the eagles from perching on them. Meanwhile, the problem of protection of the blue fox had been alleviated not only by the declining market, which forced many fur farmers out of business, but also by more progressive methods of confining the animals under screens. On July 1, 1962, the fish and fur industries of Alaska bowed to the National Emblem Law, and eight months later the territorial eagle-bounty law was repealed. With the termination of bounty hunting, the Bald Eagle might be expected to replenish its numbers in Alaska. However, residual hydrocarbons in their food may reverse the trend.

Elsewhere on the continent Bald Eagles are becoming increasingly rare, even under the protection of federal law. Industrialization, lumbering, and the growth of cities and housing developments have destroyed their wilderness nesting sites, and pesticides have contaminated the rivers and estuaries that supply them with fish. Formerly found in virtually every state, they concentrate today in significant numbers only in Florida. The Floridians are exceptionally tolerant of their colonies. They have set aside 1,678,550 acres as sanctuaries for the national bird. The tale is told of one lady bird-watcher who, after surveying the situation on the Kissimmee flats, decided that there weren't enough Bald Eagle nests. She was seriously considering building some, like so many giant wren houses, to attract more of the great birds! But preserves are not enough. The populations of Kissimmee flats and the Everglades, where the water is unpolluted, are holding well compared to those in polluted areas, such as Tampa Bay. Recent biological investigation strongly suggests that there is a link between DDT, DDE, and other derivatives which become highly concentrated in fish and the Bald Eagle's lack of nesting success in certain places. The same is true of the Osprey, which may disappear entirely from the Connecticut River in a decade, and of many other fishing birds, such as the Brown Pelican, which no longer breeds in Louisiana, possibly due to the contamination of the Mississippi.

Laws regulating the killing of birds of prey anywhere in the world are only as effective as the attitudes of men toward them. The vultures that are fed on the steps of Indian temples are, through long association with religious custom, safer than they would be under the protection of any legislation by local or national governments.

From about 1918 on, the Black and the Turkey Vultures in the southwestern United States were suspected of spreading anthrax and other livestock diseases by pathogenic bacteria dropped from their feet and plumage or by their dejecta after they had fed on animals dead of a virus. In Texas, on the Laureles Ranch alone, 3,500 Turkey Vultures were trapped during the winter of 1918–19. After the door of the wire enclosure would shut on a group of them, a Mexican was sent in with a club to beat the birds to death and burn their bodies. However, by 1932 the Biological Survey was discouraging such practices, for it had been found that the virus of charbon, or anthrax, is destroyed in passing through the digestive tract of the Turkey Vulture and there were on record similar data regarding hog cholera. Experiments by the Bureau of Animal Industry also indicated that the transmission of hog cholera on the feet or feathers of birds was by no means so likely to occur as generally supposed.

In Florida the Black Vulture is still being exterminated for its habit of preying on newborn calves and even on weakened cows that have just given birth. In 1953 Charles Wharton found several huge walk-in funnel-type vulture traps on the Kissimmee prairie near Lake Okeechobee. These traps were baited with hundreds of pounds of rough fish or the entrails and heads of catfish. As soon as enough birds had been trapped, they were herded into what appeared to be an inverted metal watering trough about 12 feet long, into which was inserted the exhaust pipe of a truck, and they were promptly asphyxiated by carbon monoxide fumes.

Although vultures are protected in Mexico, the Golden Eagle, the national emblem of that country, is as little appreciated there as in West Texas. In Canada, all but four provinces have followed the United States in enacting laws protecting birds of prey, but only one—Ontario—has a model law: ten provinces permit the destruction of Snowy and Great Horned Owls, and Alberta specifically does not protect the Golden Eagle. In Sweden and most of Finland the Golden Eagle may not legally be hunted, but the Lapps kill the bird, seeing in its habits a threat to the populations of hares and reindeer which are staple foods for men and eagles alike on the frozen tundra. The Norwegians, perhaps in the tradition of the Griffon myth, still half believe that the Sea Eagle and the Golden Eagle carry off babies—one folktale centers around an old man called Neil Eagle because he was carried off as a baby by one of these great birds of prey.

Because Black Vultures occasionally kill newborn calves, they are trapped and killed en masse by ranchers in Florida, and other southeastern states.

The eagles are gone from the deer forests of Germany, and even in the Swiss cantons where the Golden Eagle finds protection under the law, hunters shoot the bird because it competes with them for hares and marmots. In Italy all species of eagle are classed as "vermin." The Golden Eagle is destroyed even in the national parks, where it is said to prey on young goats and chamoix. And in Spain, state and private hunters are the inveterate enemies of all birds of prey. In Japan the Golden Eagle has no protection; it is killed for its tail feathers, which are used in making arrows, as they once were in the Highlands of Scotland.

The Golden Eagles of Great Britain became extinct a century ago in England and Wales, but still hold out in the west of Scotland, the South and Southeast Highlands and the Outer Hebrides, where sheepherders frequently set fire to their eyries. One pair has bred in Ireland several times recently. The 1954 Protection of Birds Act, not yet effectively enforced, is a belated effort to save the estimated 190 pairs of eagles remaining. It levies a £ 25 penalty for every eagle or eagle's egg destroyed or taken, with imprisonment as an alternative. The tenant of a grouse moor in Scotland dislikes the Golden Eagle because of the disturbance it creates during shooting season. Although it will sometimes take grouse on the wing, it more often kills on the ground, so when an eagle appears, the grouse automatically fly away, leaving the hunters without any game.

Even more serious than persecution is the recent threat posed by the use of pesticides, which appear to have caused a sudden decline in the nesting success of Golden Eagles in Scotland. In a survey taken over a wide area of the Western Highlands from 1961 to 1963, the number of pairs rearing young was found to be only 29 percent, compared to 72 percent from 1937 to 1960. Analysis of infertile eggs from seven eyries revealed significant amounts of dieldrin, gamma-BHC and DDE—all chemicals which are present in sheep dips and could be absorbed by sheep. The eagles, in turn, probably acquire them by feeding on sheep carrion. One of the eggs also contained a trace of heptachlor, which could be picked up from feathered prey that has been eating treated seeds.

The persecution of the Common Buzzard (*Buteo*) in England is closely linked with the history of game preservation, for all across England and Scotland estate owners employ keepers whose sole responsibility is to rid the moors of predatory birds, mammals, and poachers. In this they were aided by royal decree as early as 1457, when James II of Scotland forbade egg-stealing on the moors, excepting "the foulys of reif," the crows, Choughs, ravens, and Buzzards. During the seventeenth century the churchwarden of Tenterden in Kent paid a penny or tuppence for every Buzzard head brought to him; and in the eighteenth century, ways of catching "winged vermin" were being suggested in order to protect pheasantries and warrens. In 1853 the breechloader was in the hands of farmers and hunters, and the vogue for collecting birds' eggs reached its zenith. The logical consequence of the heavy shooting was the virtual extinction of the Buzzard in the Eastern and Midland counties of England, and in 1880 this vanishing species was finally protected under the first conservation act to include any bird of prey other than the falcons.

From 1916 to 1954 collectors of eggs largely became superseded by bird watchers, collecting sight records. Economic recessions caused the break-up of some of the largest estates, and as a result, there was correspondingly less gamekeeping. The Buzzards regained much of their old range during this time. However, the attitudes of men were to change toward them. In 1954 the rabbit population on which these birds depended heavily for food began to die off from myxomatosis, so the Buzzards were forced to feed more heavily on game birds and domestic poultry. Still nominally under the protection of the 1880 law, they were being shot in 1955 by gamekeepers from North Scotland to Devon. Today, in England, they are numerous only in the sheep walks of the western counties although there are quite a few in Scotland.

The most interesting saga concerning the birds of prey in England is that of the falcons. From the earliest times the Peregrine Falcon and Merlin used by the nobility in falconry have been protected from the common man by law. In the reign of Edward III, to "take" falcons was a felony punishable by imprisonment for a year and a day. Elizabeth I reduced the penalty to three months, but some trace of a jail sentence or fine remains today, under the 1954 Protection of Birds Act.

Unprotected by royal decree, as it was in England for many centuries, the Peregrine in the northeastern United States suffered the depredations of egg collectors until the birds began to disappear from their cliff eyries in the early 1930's and most states passed protection laws. Today nesting Peregrines are almost non-existent in the region. It has been suggested that indiscriminate use of insecticides after World War II may be at least partly responsible for their failure to recover. They feed heavily on songbirds, which may in turn have eaten poisoned insects in cultivated fields and gardens.

At the beginning of World War II, the Royal Air Force trained Peregrine Falcons to intercept Nazi carrier pigeons, in the time-honored tradition of Caesar, King Richard I, and Bismarck. Subsequently, falcons fell into ill repute for their depredations on Allied pigeons carrying intelligence messages. From 1940 to 1945 the Air Ministry destroyed six hundred young and adult birds on the south and east coasts of England and parts of Scotland and Northern Ireland. However, the Peregrine was not considered the hardiest of the English hunting hawks without reason. At the cessation of hostilities, the Peregrine made a quick comeback, recovering most of its former numbers. Then, during the last decade, a decline was noted. By 1964, there were only about four pairs on the south coast of England and perhaps less than two hundred in all Britain. This is apparently because of toxic chemicals in their food.

How chemicals build up in a food chain was recently explained to a senate subcommittee in Washington, D C., by Roger Tory Peterson: "Hydrocarbon pesticides . . . accumulate in soil and water, and in the bodies of all members of the animal pyramid based upon the earthworms, plankton, insects and other invertebrates of the soil and water. One of the classic cases . . . occurred at Clear Lake in California. DDT was applied, with several treatments within eight years in very dilute quantities—one part of insecticide to 50 million parts of water—to kill gnats. It did. It was also eaten and concentrated 250 times by the water plankton, the tiny invertebrate animals. It was found in 500 times concentration in the small fishes that ate the plankton. It killed most of the western grebes that ate the fishes—a thousand pairs—and they died with an 80,000 times concentration. Those birds at the top of the pyramid are particularly vulnerable, for they take poison biologically concentrated by their prey and their prey's prey." The birds of prey which are apparently in most danger are the bird-eaters and fish-eaters; some may disappear in our generation.

In conclusion, it may be seen that the role of hawks and owls in nature—including the cultivated and semiwilderness world of man—must be understood before there can be any thought of conservation. Especially in the temperate zones, where there are large populations of a few prey species, the predators figure importantly, and to apply a highly selective annihilative pressure against any of them without regard for the consequences is to invite unwanted surpluses of the animals they normally prey upon. In his control measures, man must consider not only his short-range economic interests, but his position in the habitat as a predator. How much can he destroy without ultimately willing a far

The actual prey which any one bird will tackle depends on what is available and vulnerable, and also on how hungry the hawk is (as falconers have always known). In Florida the American Kestrel feeds largely on insects and would not ordinarily attempt to kill an opponent as large and full of fight as a young wood rat.

Roused to fury, the Kestrel grabs for the rat's head and ends the struggle.

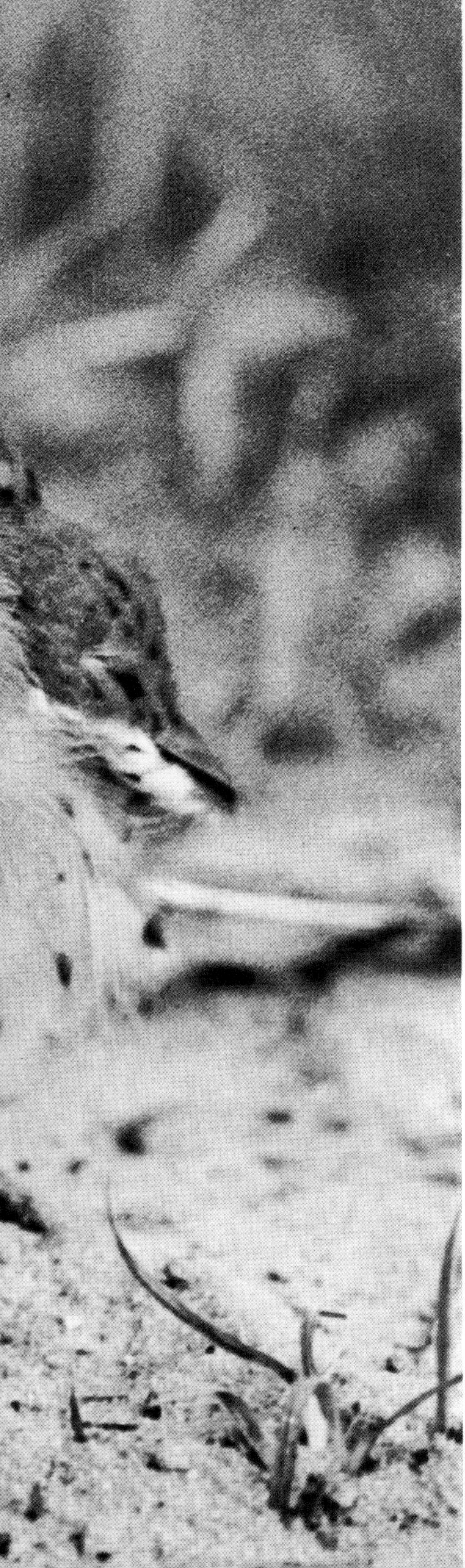

greater and more expensive legacy of further destruction to his children? How many hawks and owls can he exterminate without spending millions on poisons to curb the ever-rising numbers of rats, mice, and rabbits? The reproductive capacity of these little animals has for many millennia been geared to the feeding habits of the predators—not just a few which "specialize" in hunting them, but every existing species which at one season or another, day or night, keeps constant vigil.

All of the animal predators share in the responsibility which they have gradually taken on locally in the various habitats, but it is now realized that the birds of prey have the mobility needed to concentrate quickly from distant regions into areas of high prey density. Of all the predators they are the most effective, keeping a constant flowing pressure on the populations of amphibians, reptiles, mammals, and birds of other orders—even on themselves.

The easiest road to conservation is tolerance. We may enjoy, like Thoreau, the graceful flight of a Merlin, or make an accounting of the number of grasshoppers a Swainson's Hawk will eat during a summer, but the issue is not a sentimental, or even a practical one, as most people understand the word. For no bird of prey can be our enemy or our friend, abstracted from the great natural context in which all of us live, in one world, one universe, of unlimited diversity. We have the ability to kill to extinction, but we also have knowledge, and with it, responsibility.

With its talons firmly implanted in the rat's neck, the Kestrel sinks into a fluffed-out, brooding attitude—too exhausted to mantle the prey. During the winter, in northern latitudes, the slightly larger eastern Kestrel takes birds and small mammals exclusively—more commonly white-footed mice than rats, however.

part 2

INTRODUCTION

In this section, compiled as a supplement to our point of view on ecology and conservation, the 289 species of hawklike birds and 133 species of owls are systematically illustrated and described. Maps define their approximate breeding ranges. On the subspecies level we have attempted only a general survey of the regional variations in size, color, and plumage pattern.

Hawks and owls are downy as nestlings. Unless otherwise noted, they are white at first. Some have a second growth of down which is creamy or pale gray. In a few weeks the first contour feathers start to grow in, still carrying tufts of down on their tips. This dress is sometimes followed by one or more intermediate plumages. The adult plumage usually corresponds to full sexual maturity. (Individuals of some species nest in the "immature" plumage, especially the females, but this has been rarely observed in large eagles and vultures that mature slowly over three, four, or even five years. These birds pair, but seem to require long periods of adjustment before they raise the first brood.) To avoid the technical problems of defining plumages, which are frequently in a state of change, our terms refer to birds of various ages. In the following descriptions, a "juvenile" is a bird of the first year. An "immature" is a bird of the second year, or perhaps older. Although slight changes continue past the "normal" breeding age, the appearance of the adult bird is not substantially altered.

On a worldwide basis it is impossible to summarize the plumage cycles for all hawks and owls. Adults usually have one complete annual molt, lasting weeks, months, or even the entire year. The body feathers may be molted before the wing and tail feathers, but a complete molt commonly begins with the loss of the innermost primaries on both wings. In the hawklike birds, only the family Falconidae (falcons and caracaras) varies this procedure by losing the fourth primary from within on each wing first. The tail feathers, like the wing feathers, are usually molted in pairs—the innermost first—although the reverse is true of the cathartid vultures. Thus flight is not totally impaired at any time during the molt. Among the striking exceptions are the small owls—*Speotyto, Athene, Glaucidium, Otus,* and some species of *Ninox*—which have been found to molt all of their tail feathers at once. These birds must be able to secure their food and elude their enemies for weeks without strong powers of flight. Larger owls, which characteristically pursue larger and speedier prey, molt their wing and tail feathers gradually and serially.

We have primarily described perching birds, although the important field marks in flight—such as light underwing coverts—are also included. Plumage colors, keyed to our Color Chart (page 196) by name, represent average hues (light, medium, and dark) determined in daylight from the bird skins in the collection of the American Museum of Natural History. We have used several hundred to describe the most common species, but only one or two specimens of some rare and local species may have been available, and in one instance (the Taita Falcon) we had to work from a transparency of a skin. Occasionally it was necessary to borrow color names from other authors, and these appear in quotes. However, for most of the work the Museum's vast collection was more than adequate. The majority of the colors fell within the *Munsell Book of Color*'s Red, Orange, and Yellow chromas or the neutrals, Gray, Black, and White; a few within the Blue chroma. They are arranged on the chart to display the differences in hue (color) and value (lightness or darkness), and should be used as a guide, not as an exact scientific standard.

In the field, color patterns may seem lighter or darker than described, depending on the distance and lighting conditions. Finely mottled plumage may not be perceptible as a pattern, and, when a bird is in motion, spots tend to look like streaks. A bird which has just molted into fresh, new plumage will have a different appearance than the same species in worn, old plumage. In some vultures, kites, hawks, and eagles, a "bloom" or iridescence is produced by "powder-down" feathers which, instead of forming barbs, "give off" a fine waxy substance. The resulting purple, green, blue, or silvery-gray effects are mentioned, but they are not keyed to the color chart. They are most noticeable in adult birds that have just renewed their plumage. Such markings as white tips on tails and light-colored feather-edging quickly wear off, and the underparts of ground-dwelling birds, especially, may become stained. Unusually red or orange shading is also common in captive birds, due to new environmental conditions (higher or lower temperature or humidity) as well as changes in diet. For this reason we have not included any zoo specimen in a series studied.

Colors of the soft parts—eyes, beak, cere, bare skin of the face, crop region, legs, and feet—are not keyed to our chart. These fade quickly after death, and the color names are based on our own observation of living birds, or have been taken from museum labels and the literature.

Measurements were made from the crown to the tip of the tail, compensating for stretched or compressed study skins—in other words, as the bird would normally perch. This differs from the usual practice of measuring from the tip of the bill to the tip of the tail. Our figures may, therefore, not correspond exactly to those in other sources. In the species which show sexual dimorphism, the size range given is from the smallest males to the largest females.

Sexual dimorphism, with the female larger than the male, is most notable in the accipiters and falcons. In the Falconiformes, at least, it seems to be correlated with predatory habits. There is hardly any difference in size between the sexes in the scavengers—kites, caracaras, vultures, and the Secretary Bird.

Silhouettes show the diurnal birds of prey in flight, their markings, and characteristic shapes during some phase of gliding or soaring. The full wingspread represents an adult, and the half wings illustrate sexual dimorphism in pattern, color phases, geographical variations, and the young (immatures and juveniles). Some were adapted from the existing work of Roger Tory Peterson, who so successfully used this method of identification in his guides. The remaining silhouettes, some 550, were created from photographs or study skins. For the proportions, we measured the primaries in relation to the length of the body and the tail. Then, since we were unable to open the wings of many of the skins, we applied our observation of similar species in order to arrive at a reasonably accurate wing shape.

The Regional Guides (page 467) provide a key to the various species of Falconiformes in North America and Europe. In identifying a bird, certain "rules of thumb" are useful. The forest hawks and eagles usually have relatively short, rounded wings and long tails; buteos, broad rounded wings and tails of moderate length; vultures, long broad wings and moderate or very short fan-shaped tails; most kites, narrow wings; falcons, pointed wings; harriers, narrow wings and tightly folded tails; the Osprey, long, angled wings. These distinctions hold regardless of differences in plumage pattern due to age, sex, or color phases.

Since we show the adult (and in some cases only the adult male) of each species in the Guides, the reader may find it necessary to refer to the full series of flight silhouettes in the text to complete an identification.

Young birds are sometimes more numerous and more conspicuous than adults. Juveniles are almost universally feather-edged above (and frequently heavily streaked below), and display a distinctive tail pattern. If the adult tail is barred, the juvenile tail generally has many more (narrower) bars.

These common juvenile characters make closely related species very difficult to identify, especially the buteos in the western United States, the European aquilas, and the tropical accipiters. However, some marking of the underwing coverts, wings, or tail usually appears in the silhouettes to mark each species off from all the others.

Other important clues to the identification of the diurnal birds of prey are their characteristic habitat, manner of flight, calls, feeding, and migratory habits. Unfortunately the calls should be heard, not read. Even translating a sound that one knows well into type is not a satisfactory substitute for the real thing. For the majority of the notes on voice we have had to depend on the literature, and the ear of the particular listener who set down a phonetic record.

We have supplied no silhouettes for the owls, which are mostly nocturnal in their habits. Attitudes in perching, tail-flicking habits, terrestrial or arboreal mode of living, and voice distinguish the various species. The few diurnal owls and those which are active during daylight in the nesting season usually cannot be confused with hawks. Their flight is characteristically wavering, rather than direct, and they appear "neckless." All have relatively large round heads and facial discs, often bordered with a conspicuous dark ruff. Predominately hole-nesters, their eggs are, without exception, round and white, without the markings characteristic of most hawks' eggs.

TOPOGRAPHY OF THE BIRDS OF PREY

COLOR KEY

ivory
light tan
sandy
pale yellow-orange
buff-yellow
pale cinnamon
pale cinna-mon-buff
vinaceous buff
pale orange-buff
pale ivory-gray
buff-white
yellow-ochre
light yellow-ochre
buff
medium buff
cinnamon-buff
vinaceous
light vinaceous
light olive-gray
medium ivory-gray
dark yellow-ochre
yellow-orange
light cinnamon
light yellow-brown
medium vinaceous
medium vina-ceous-buff
pale yellow-brown
medium olive-gray
light tawny-olive
light ochre-brown
dark yellow-orange
cinnamon
yellow-brown
medium sienna-orange
sienna-orange
light sienna-orange
olive-gray
tawny-olive
ochre-brown
amber-brown
light amber-brown
medium yellow-brown
orange-buff
chrome-orange
light orange
olive-drab
olive-brown
cinnamon-brown
light rufous-brown
medium sienna
dark orange
medium orange
orange
pale gray-brown
medium olive-brown
dark amber-brown
rufous-brown
sienna
dark tawny
tawny
light tawny
gray-brown
dark olive-brown
chestnut
maroon
sienna-brown
medium ferruginous
ferruginous
dark gray-brown
dark brown
brown
chocolate
sepia
dark gray
dark slate-gray
slate-gray
medium gray
dove-gray
light gray
silver-gray
slate-blue
light blue-gray

ORDER FALCONIFORMES

FAMILY CATHARTIDAE

(*Cathartid, or American, Vultures*)

The Andean Condor *(Vultur gryphus)*, reaching far greater altitudes than the California Condor, ordinarily breeds from 10,000 to 15,000 feet above sea level in the valleys of the Andes from Chile to Ecuador, Colombia, and western Venezuela.—*Photographed at the National Zoological Park.*

GENUS *VULTUR*

The pinkish head, neck and crop region, as well as the tarsi and feet of this large New World vulture, are bare, and a white ruff adorns the lower part of the neck. The strongly arched beak is an extremely effective tearing and cutting instrument, but the feet, though large, are the least prehensile of any of those in the vultures which characteristically have walking, rather than grasping, toes. The heavy tarsi and most of the toes are covered with small, nearly circular scales; the claws are short and blunt. Wingspan, about ten feet, exceeds that of any other New World vulture. Males have a prominent caruncle on the head and are sometimes larger than the females.

Andean Condor (*Vultur gryphus*)

DESCRIPTION
(SOUTH AMERICA)

Male—glossy black; wing coverts, pale ivory-gray with a black median band; secondaries and inner primaries, also light, tipped in black, and rest of wings, black. Around the neck, a ruff of soft white down; head and neck, wattled, with a large fleshy caruncle, and sparsely bristled; crop area, bare. *Female*—no caruncle.

VULTUR GRYPHUS

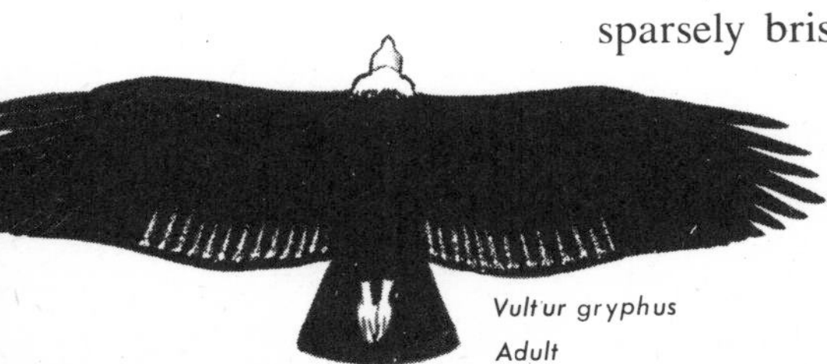

Vultur gryphus
Adult

Juvenile—medium olive-gray; secondaries, sepia; primaries and tail, black; ruff, brown.

Beak, mostly ivory; eyes, red (male) or pale brown (female); legs and feet, gray. Size, about 43–50 inches.

HABITS

An habitué of open country, the Andean Condor is a carrion-eater but may occasionally kill young and wounded llamas, goats, and lambs. Along the sea coast it is known to feed on dead fish, whales, seals, and molluscs.

Two eggs are generally laid in hollows of mountain cliffs or on remote ledges. Incubation (said to be about 55 days) and fledging periods are prolonged. The young are dependent on the adults for months, like the young of the California Condor, and mature slowly over a period of years. A South American condor, hatched in the San Diego Zoo, was nearly adult in the spring of 1948 when it was six years old.

Both males and females take an active part in the courtship dance, with their wings held straight out. The displaying bird inflates its neck, hisses, and makes a guttural clucking sound, while the skin of the head and neck turns bright red.

In *The Voyage of the Beagle* Darwin noted that "the old birds generally live in pairs; but among the inland basaltic cliffs of the Santa Cruz, I found a spot where scores most usually haunt. On coming suddenly to the brow of the precipice, it was a grand spectacle to see between 20 and 30 of these great birds start heavily from their resting-place and wheel away in majestic circles."

Throughout tropical-forested America the "King of the Vultures" (*Sarcoramphus papa*) eats from the carcass first, while the smaller, weaker-billed Turkey Vultures wait. Bare colorful head and vinaceous buff plumage make the adults of this species unmistakable. In soaring flight even the immatures show a white under surface, but the juveniles could be confused with Turkey Vultures.

GENUS *SARCORAMPHUS*

Bizarre is the only appropriate description for the face of *Sarcoramphus,* which is wrinkled and corrugated. The cere is surmounted by a caruncle in the adults of both sexes. The eyes are white, ringed with red. The bill appears strongly arched and curved at the tip. The King Vulture's chunky build, very broad wings (spanning 4–5½ feet), and short tail are those of a small condor, and like the Andean and California condors, it has a bare head and neck (except for black bristles), trimmed with a furry ruff, as well as bare crop area, tarsi, and feet.

King Vulture (*Sarcoramphus papa*)

DESCRIPTION (NEOTROPICAL REGION)

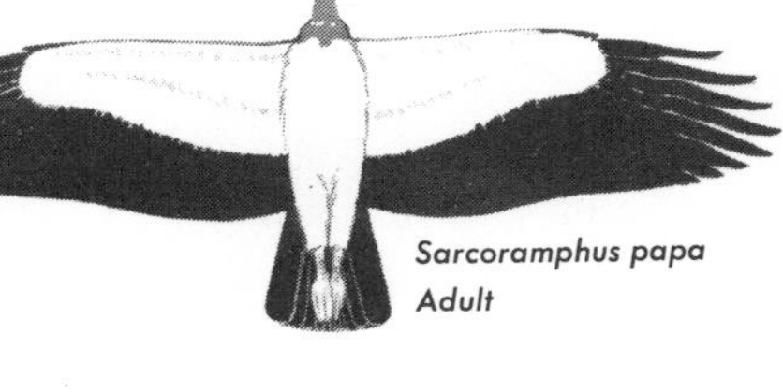

Above, vinaceous-buff with a medium-gray ruff; wings and tail, black. Head and neck, bare; underparts, including underwing coverts, white.

Immature—black above, with white underparts.

Juvenile—entirely black.

Beak, red (lighter in young); caruncle, head, and neck painted with shades of red, yellow, and blue-gray (entirely blackish and covered with gray down in young, which also lack caruncle); eyes, white, circled in red (yellow-gray in young); legs and feet, grayish-white (blackish in young). Size, about 27 inches (male and female).

SARCORAMPHUS PAPA

HABITS

This species is a scavenger of the deep tropical forests, not of the rocky promontories and open ridges frequented by the larger condors. The King Vulture habitually roosts high in the tops of trees. On its foraging expeditions it scans the ground below for dead animals and fish and also may kill small reptiles and newly dropped calves. Large flocks of these birds will gather around a carcass for the feast, but they do not breed in communities.

Nothing is known of the courtship of the King Vulture in the wild, but John Hamlet's captive bird frequently "displayed" by bending its head down to the crop, filling it with air, and bowing down with a couple of guttural grunts. Then it would rise up, move backward and forward in "bumps and grinds," and tremble its wings with a ruffling sound —all the while breathing fast and heavily.

Two or three white eggs are laid, supposedly in the interiors of hollow trees.

Juvenile King Vulture (*Sarcoramphus papa*).

Attitude of waiting, on a fence post or log, is very characteristic of the patient Black Vulture *(Coragyps atratus)*, which may allow a carcass to decompose for a day or two before eating.

GENUS *CORAGYPS*

The Black Vulture is a chunky bird with broad wings (spanning about five feet) and a short square tail. Its head and neck (except for the feathered hindneck), tarsi, and feet are bare. The young are feathered to the face, not transversely corrugated on the head and neck like the adults. The cere of *Coragyps* is long; its beak is long, slender, and very weak compared to the condor's. In many parts of its range this scavenger may be found with the Turkey Vulture, but its mode of flight—soaring *with frequent flapping*—and the light patches on the primaries are distinctive. *Cathartes* also has longer wings and a long rounded tail.

Black Vulture (*Coragyps atratus*)

CORAGYPS ATRATUS

DESCRIPTION
(NORTH, CENTRAL, AND SOUTH AMERICA)

Coragyps atratus
Adult

Glossy black, partly feathered on the back of the neck, but otherwise with bare head and neck.

Juvenile—like adult, with downy instead of corrugated neck.

Beak, bluish-gray with light tip (young, entirely gray); eyes, dark brown; legs and feet, gray. Size, 24 inches.

HABITS

At daybreak Black Vultures leave their roosts and move over the open country to begin their tireless vigil for carcasses. *Coragyps* often soars so high as to be nearly invisible, until it detects a dead animal or even a piece of garbage on the ground and dives down upon it with great speed, checking its fall by suddenly opening the wings just before landing.

The Black Vultures feed with Turkey Vultures wherever their ranges correspond and always get the better of them in a quarrel. However, they are no match for eagles or caracaras. Like the Turkey Vultures they may kill young birds or maim young animals by plucking out the eyes. In South America they also take small reptiles; and where food is difficult to find in the dense forests, they even feed on palm fruits.

At the beginning of the breeding season one might see, as Audubon did, a procession of males strutting like turkey cocks and approaching a female with open wings, lowered heads, and puffing sounds. This behavior is followed by the courtship flight of pairs over their nesting places—spiraling and chasing each other. A male performing for his mate, perched high on a dead tree overlooking a chasm, may indulge in fast dives downward in the midst of his circling.

Black Vultures may nest in available hollow stumps and standing trees, but the ground will do. They sometimes nest communally in dense thickets of palmetto, yucca, tall saw grass, or small trees. Holes in limestone bluffs and nests of other birds high off the ground have also been used. The North American birds often make no attempt to build a nest or hollow out a place for the eggs in the ground. However, in Peru and Colombia a few small sticks are brought to the nesting place, either on the ground or in willow trees.

One to three (usually two) eggs are bluish-green in color, more or less spotted with brown. Both parents incubate the eggs for 39 to 41 days. Bare-faced nestlings, covered with creamy down, develop their juvenile dress and are able to fly in about 14 weeks.

Ordinarily hissing, grunting, and blowing compose the entire vocabulary of *Coragyps,* and these sounds are rarely heard unless the birds are feeding or fighting. If the young are disturbed at the nest, they hiss and utter a blowing note very similar to that of a rattlesnake.

The Turkey Vulture *(Cathartes aura),* shown here, has a close relative in the warmer parts of the Western Hemisphere—the Yellow-headed Vulture of South America.—*Photographed at the New York Zoological Society.*

GENUS *CATHARTES*

Cathartes has a cere as long as the Black Vulture's with a much more conspicuous perforate nostril and a shorter, stronger beak. The corrugated back of the head and wrinkled face and neck are bright-colored in the adults of the two species; bare, except for sparse hairlike bristles. White papillae ("pimples") are especially thick in front of the eyes. Tarsi and feet are also bare, but not colorful. In flight a long narrow wingspan (about 5½ feet) and long tail, very little extended, give the bird a more slender appearance than either the Black Vulture or the much heavier King Vulture. Wings and tail appear light underneath.

Turkey Vulture (*Cathartes aura*)

CATHARTES AURA

DESCRIPTION (SOUTHEASTERN U.S.)

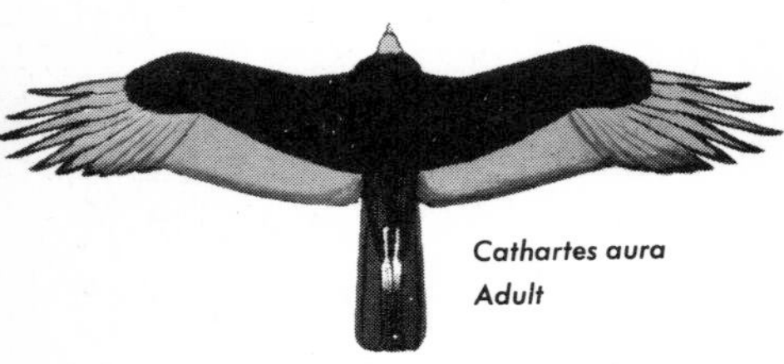

Cathartes aura Adult

Above, dark brown with a blue, green, and purple iridescence, the feathers scalloped in medium olive-gray; underparts, sepia; head and neck, sparsely bristled.

Juvenile—downy black head.

Beak, white (young, black); cere and face, vermilion; corrugated nape, dull yellow (young, blackish); eyes, grayish-brown; legs and feet, yellowish-white. Size, 29 inches.

VARIATIONS

Most do not vary noticeably from the bird described, but populations in the Amazon rain forest are darker—completely dark brown with a green, blue, and purple iridescence; green- and bronze-glossed plumage occurs in those of the Falkland Islands.

OTHER SPECIES

The Yellow-headed Vulture of South America (*C. burrovianus*) has a predominately green gloss on its black plumage; dull red eyes. According to Foster D. Smith this bird can be identified in flight by indistinct pale areas on the upper surface of the wings (at the base of the primaries). Its name is somewhat of a misnomer, for the head is not actually yellow, but a composite of many colors. The corrugated nape is light orange; crown, dark blue-gray; sides of the head, dull dark orange surrounded by an area of light blue with a greenish cast (above the eyes and on the throat and lores). The cere is red; beak, white. The young bird also has a colorful head, but its eyes are blackish-gray. Recently a larger Amazonian bird with longer, broader tail feathers has been recognized by Alexander Wetmore as a new species, the Greater Yellow-headed Turkey Vulture (*C. melambrotus*).

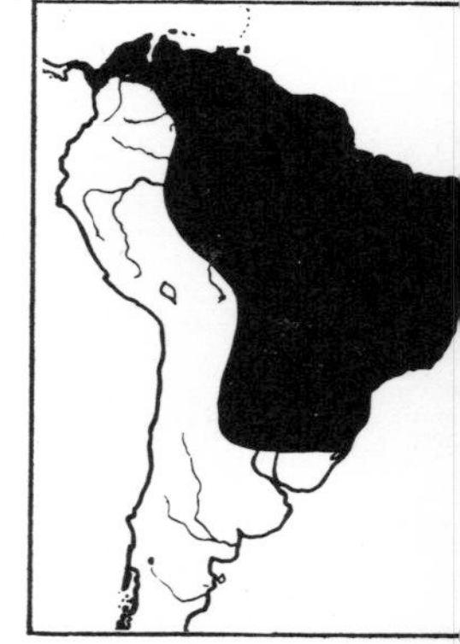

CATHARTES BURROVIANU[S]

HABITS

The Turkey Vultures usually are not as gregarious as the Black Vultures, although several dozen of these birds will sometimes collect in the sky and wheel about over a carcass. At night they gather in roosts, usually located in the tall trees of swampy lowlands or deep forests. Carrion comprises most of their diet, although they will kill newborn pigs and young herons and ibises, and they have been seen feeding on grasshoppers, fish, and even pumpkins.

The nesting place may be on a cliff, in a cave, hollow stump, or on the ground in the midst of dense shrubbery with only a narrow entrance. One to three white eggs, covered with splotches of bright brown, are laid directly on the ground or on a bed of dry leaves and decayed wood. The female makes very little attempt to build a nest, and the male, apparently none at all. Both sexes incubate the eggs for a period probably between five and six weeks, and the young spend eight or ten weeks in or around the nest before they are able to fly.

Nearly voiceless, the Turkey Vulture can only hiss or snarl as it asserts its right to a coveted carcass.

Northern Turkey Vultures are, to a certain extent, migratory. Flocks of several hundred make the long journey northward from tropical wintering grounds each spring, passing over Barro Colorado Island, Panama, in February and March. They show an attachment to old nesting sites, to which they seem to return for many years.

Red, naked skin at the base of the throat of this captive California Condor *(Gymnogyps californianus)* bulges out when the bird is perched. In its habitat the bird merely lowers its heels and rump in order to sit on a branch with the bulbous throat protruding over the perch. *Gymnogyps,* now rare, is protected in its native haunts by California law.—*New York Zoological Society Photograph.*

GENUS *GYMNOGYPS*

This large member of the American vulture family, with a wingspan of about 9–9½ feet, ranged eastward to Florida in the Pleistocene; in more recent times, to the Chisos Mountains of Texas and north to the Columbia River. It has no caruncles or well-defined corrugation on the naked skin of the head and neck. The crop region, as well as the tarsi and feet, are bare. The feathers of the ruff and underparts are lanceolate, like those of the Old World Griffon Vulture. The elongated head and cere terminate in a short, heavy beak which establishes its first right, after the Golden Eagle, to feed on a fresh carcass. Its large feet are made for standing and walking, not grasping, and the outer toe may not touch the perch at all when the bird sits on a stub branch. A strong soaring bird, the California Condor displays a long and broad flying surface with conspicuously slotted wing tips and fan-shaped tail. Sexes cannot be distinguished by their size or external features in the field, although males tend to be slightly larger than females.

California Condor (*Gymnogyps californianus*)

DESCRIPTION
(COASTAL RANGES OF SOUTH-CENTRAL CALIFORNIA)

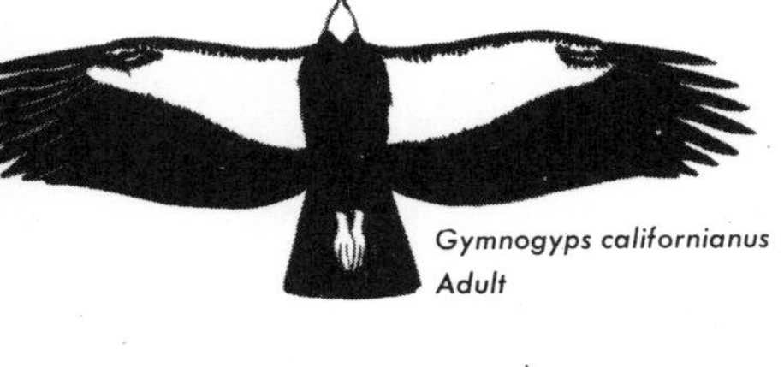

Gymnogyps californianus Adult

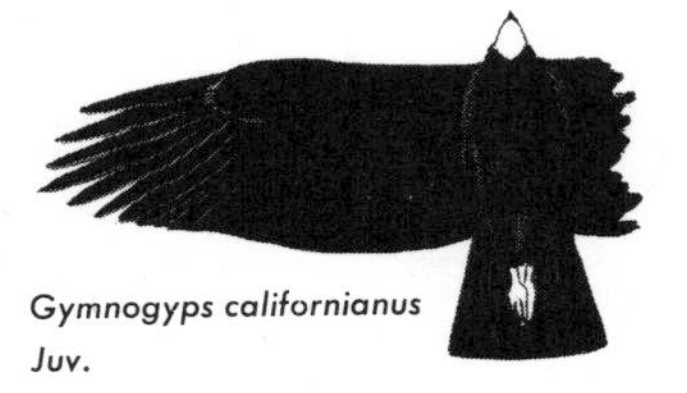

Gymnogyps californianus Juv.

Dark gray-brown, with innerwing coverts tipped in white, and lanceolate feathers of the ruff and underparts streaked with light olive-gray. Underwing coverts, white. Entire head, neck, and crop area, bare except for a few bristles on the forehead, base of beak, and in front of the eyes.

Juvenile and Immature—(until fourth year) have downy brown heads and conspicuous light feather-edging on their backs; no white on the wing coverts.

Hindneck, grayish-blue, otherwise entire head and cere, yellow; base of neck and crop area, red (dark bluish-gray in young); and beak, as well as tarsi and toes, flesh color or white (in young, very dark orange); eyes, bright red. Size, 43–50 inches.

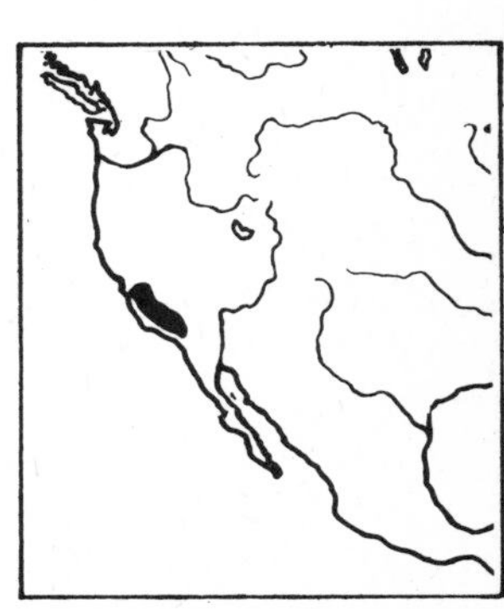

GYMNOGYPS CALIFORNIANUS

HABITS

The decline of large mammals has undoubtedly helped to bring about the drastic and apparently permanent reduction in the population of this large North American scavenger whose reproductive rate is so low.

Condors breed every other year. They deposit their eggs—only one or two—on the bare floor of a cave or among boulders, easily accessible from the air. Large hollows in old trees high off the ground (i.e., in giant redwoods) are rarely used. Near every nest, however, there are large trees which provide roosting places for the adults, and some of the nest sites have an outer ledge where the young may perch and be fed.

At least 42 days, and probably more (see Andean Condor), are required for incubation, by both sexes. Young are wholly dependent on the adults for at least seven months and partly dependent for another seven months. The color of the neck and crop region changes from gray to orange between the fourth and fifth year, and the bright red neck and full adult plumage are not attained until the fifth or sixth year.

In a courtship dance similar to that of *Vultur,* the displaying *Gymnogyps* walks back and forth and turns slowly in a circle with spread wings. Crowding by the "male" and pecking by the "female" frequently end in one or the other being forced off the edge of a cliff, and aerial pursuit and play ensue.

Pecking may also be related to social dominance, for California Condors roost in company in the fall, winter, and early spring and gather in large groups at carcasses. Adults chase other adults and the young, especially those that are obviously juveniles. Wholesale scrambles are not usual, but do occur when an eagle or coyote has kept a group of condors from a carcass for an hour or more.

The Turkey Vultures and Ravens are lowest in the peck order, although they are allowed to feed within three to five feet of the condors.

Wherever small groups of condors remain in California, they may be seen feeding in the open grasslands, especially along high ridges where it is easier for them to land and take off. They forage at any time from 8 A.M. to 5 P.M. but seem to be most numerous at any given feeding place around noon. Since they do not have to wait until the hide decays to rip a recently dead animal apart, only their more voracious competitors—the Golden Eagles and mammalian predators—can keep them waiting. On the other hand they will eat from a carcass in any state of decomposition. Most of the viscera may be eaten. However, U.S. Fish and Wildlife Service reports indicate that the stomachs and intestines of poisoned squirrels are commonly not eaten either by Turkey Vultures or Condors in California. Over a century ago mussels were found in the stomach of a condor killed at Monterey. Shells of marine molluscs found at sites of old condor nests may be at least sixty years old, for there have been no records of California Condors near the seashore during the last half century.

Condors are extremely clean scavengers. They are very fond of bathing in the clear cold waters of mountain pools and streams, and frequently stretch their wings to sun them in the manner of all the large vultures.

FAMILY SAGITTARIIDAE

(*Secretary Birds*)

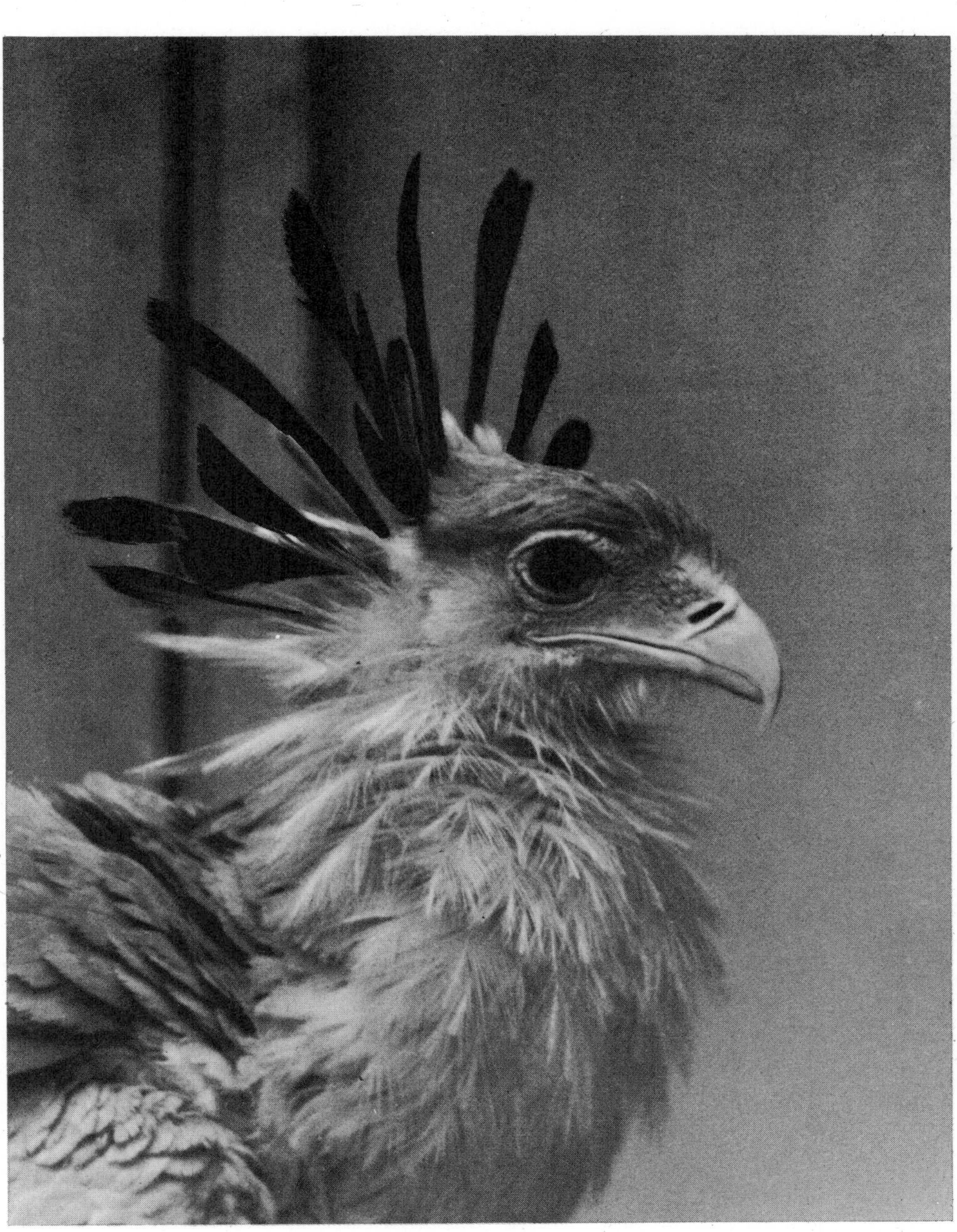

The Secretary Bird *(Sagittarius serpentarius)*, with its long crest of twenty feathers, is named for its fanciful resemblance to an old-time lawyer's clerk with a bunch of quill pens stuck behind the ear.—*Photographed at the New York Zoological Society.*

GENUS *SAGITTARIUS*

In some ways this curious bird of prey resembles the American carrion hawks (see Chapter 1), but is most distinguished by a long crest and two elongated central tail feathers that trail far beyond the others. It stands about four feet tall on long and powerful legs, heavily armored against snake bites. The toes are very short for the size of the body; the claws are short and blunt. The wingspan, seven feet, compares favorably with large vultures, although the Secretary Bird spends most of its time on the ground and does not soar. The female is slightly smaller than the male.

Secretary Bird (*Sagittarius serpentarius*)

DESCRIPTION
(AFRICA)

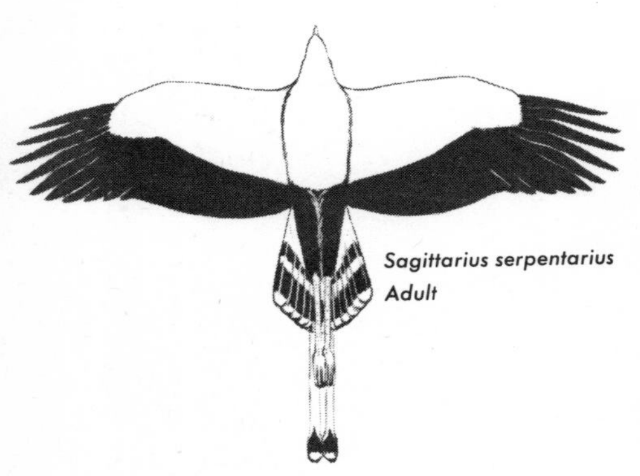
Sagittarius serpentarius
Adult

Dove-gray, with black crest feathers, wings, and thighs; tail, medium olive-gray banded with black and tipped in white. (Underwing and undertail coverts, white.)

Juvenile—similar to adult but darker and has black barring on the shoulders, underwing and undertail coverts; white barring on the thighs.

Beak and cere, yellow; eyes, hazel (young, gray) and ringed with a patch of red-orange skin; legs and feet, dull flesh color; claws, black. Size, about 33 inches from the crown to the tips of the outer tail feathers—the central ones trailing 11 inches beyond.

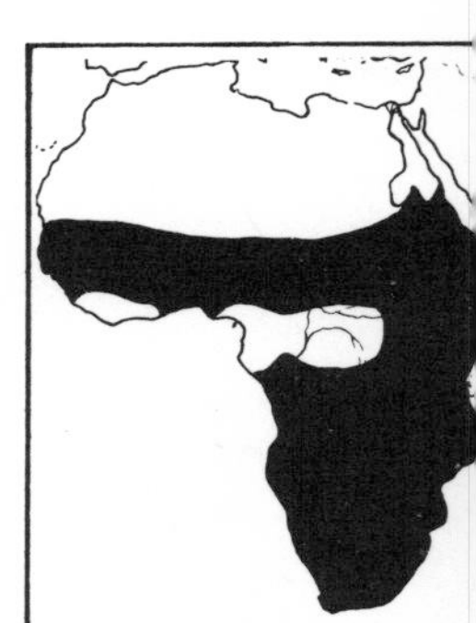
SAGITTARIUS SERPENTAR

HABITS

The Secretary Bird prefers to live on open plains or in light bush country and enters the forest in western Africa to settle only temporarily in large clearings, such as Kumasi. Usually they are seen in pairs, walking the plains perhaps half a mile apart, or just within sight of each other, but a grass fire or a large influx of migrating quail attracts parties of four or five, walking a few yards apart and always keeping that distance. In breeding season they may be looking for young birds or eggs. However, their staple foods are snakes, scorpions, lizards, rats, and grasshoppers. In South Africa they are occasionally kept in domestication to clear a farm of vermin. Increasingly rare in recent years, they are now protected by law in nearly every part of Africa.

A bird on the hunt runs at its prey and beats its wings on the ground to distract its intended victim, then it pins the victim under a heavy foot, and seizes and batters its head against the ground. If an exceptionally large snake proves difficult to kill, it is carried and dropped from a considerable height to the ground; then tackled and beaten again until it can be maneuvered into the mouth and swallowed whole. Dropping the snake in this manner is risky, for other winged predators are quick to intervene and rob the Secretary Bird of its prey, even before it hits the ground. Van Someren, in *Days with Birds,* records a noisy fight over a puff adder between a Secretary Bird and a Tawny Eagle.

Running comes more easily to a Secretary Bird than flight, but it is rather graceful in the air for such a large bird. The head and neck stretch forward and the long legs are tucked under the tail, not dangling like a crane. To become airborne it is necessary for this oversized hawk to "taxi" along the ground with wings spread. Then it will swing around and jump into the wind, flying in a wide sweep to the nest or roosting place in a bush or tree. Van Someren says that an established "take-off point" is almost invariably used for these short flights.

The huge flattened stick nest, lined with fresh grass and felted fur, is usually in the heart of a large spreading thorn tree about 10 to 24 feet above the ground. It may be used for many seasons and added to year after year. Some old nests measure six feet across.

Two white eggs (occasionally three) are rough-textured and may be streaked with reddish brown. Both sexes feed the young by regurgitation. This process may occupy a parent for 15 or 20 minutes, followed by cleaning up the nest and brooding for about half an hour before the patrol for food commences again.

Secretary Birds may occasionally be heard calling to each other, while hunting widely separated parts of their range, with a full-throated "o͞o-ōk-koc" or "ōu-ōr-kok." Annoyance or defiance is expressed by a drawn-out "u͞uu-o͞oorr"; surprise or fear by a more rapid "ou-ook ou-ook."

FAMILY ACCIPITRIDAE

(Kites, Hawks, and Eagles)

SUBFAMILY ELANINAE

(White-tailed Kites, Pearl Kites, and African Swallow-tailed Kites)

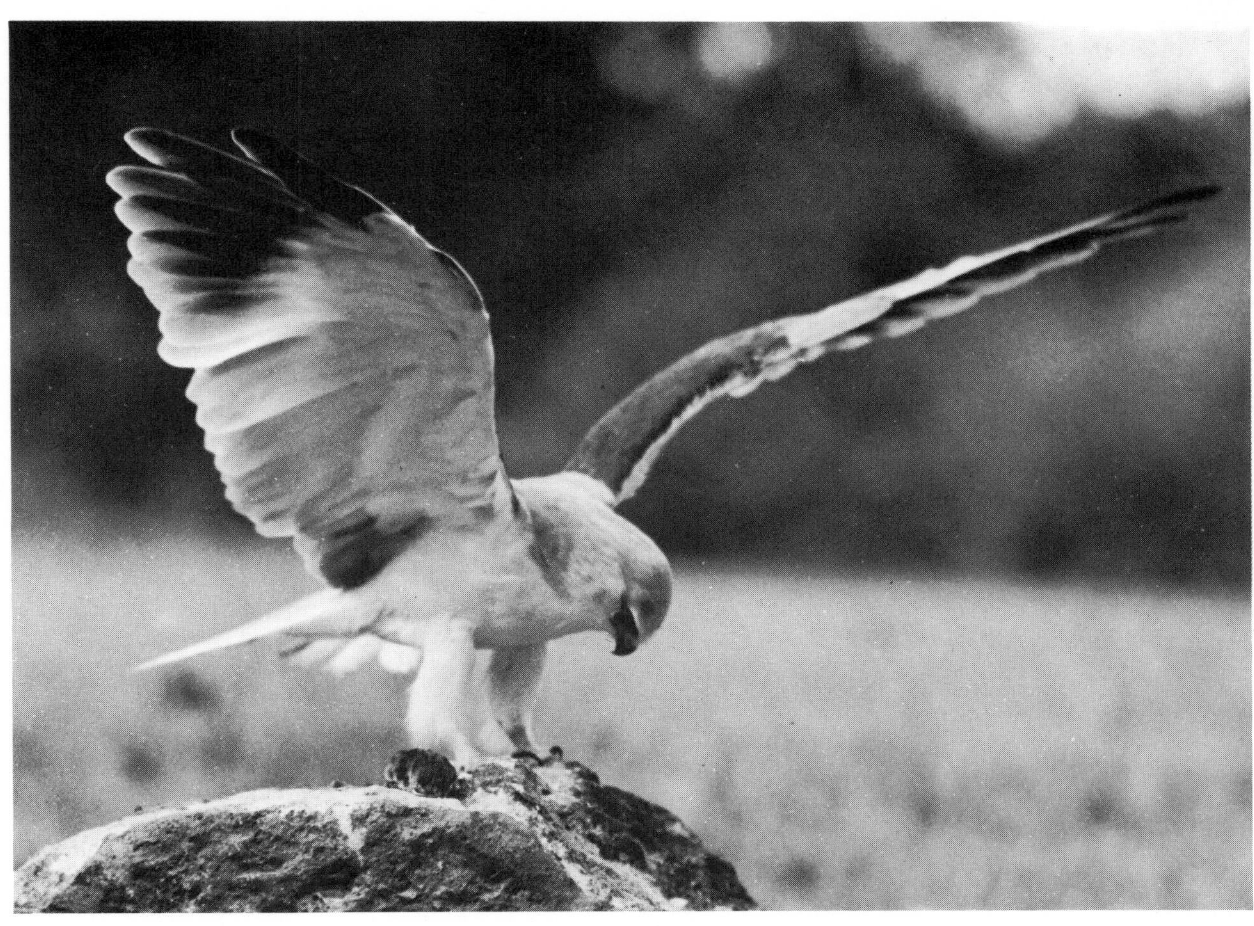

Slow and graceful flight is characteristic of the Black-shouldered Kite *(Elanus caeruleus)* of Africa and tropical Asia. It glides with outstretched wings held slightly above the horizontal and is completely white underneath, like a sea gull, except for the dark gray primaries.

GENUS *ELANUS*

The "black shoulder" is the common marking of this group, which is widely but erratically distributed throughout the warmer parts of the globe in steppe, desert, savanna, and tropical forest. Four species are very similar, except for the slight variations in the underwing pattern. Three of them are considered by some ornithologists to be geographical representatives of a single species. Australia alone, of all the major land masses, has more than one endemic species—the Australian Black-shouldered Kite (*E. notatus*) and the Letter-winged Kite (*E. scriptus*). These are probably the result of a double invasion of the continent in the far distant past.

These small kites have a diminutive beak, wide at the base and compressed at the tip; very short tarsi, feathered three-quarters; and short, bare toes. The wings are long and pointed, and the tail is only slightly notched, not forked. Sexes cannot generally be distinguished by size, but the male of the Letter-winged Kite is noticeably smaller than the female.

Black-shouldered Kite (*Elanus caeruleus*)

ELANUS CAERULEUS

DESCRIPTION (AFRICA)

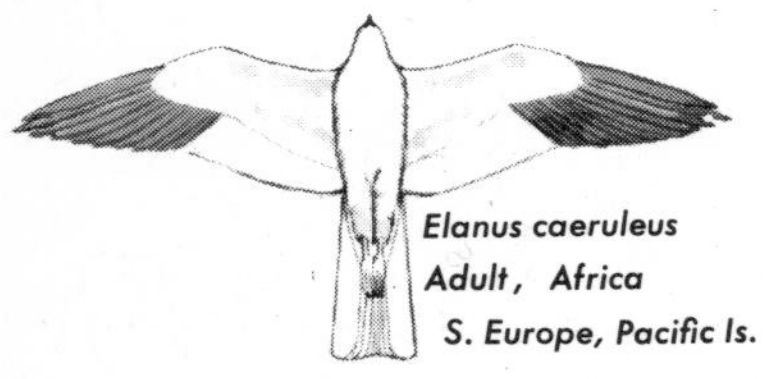
Elanus caeruleus
Adult, Africa
S. Europe, Pacific Is.

Above, including wings, dove-gray; wing coverts, black; tail, white with two dove-gray center feathers. Sides of neck and face, white; eyes, ringed with black. Below, white, sometimes tinged with light gray. In flight, underwing coverts and secondaries, pure white; primaries, dark gray.

Juvenile—black-shouldered as adult but gray-brown above with white feather-edging on the back; below, washed with light cinnamon and finely streaked with gray-brown.

Beak, black; cere, yellow; eyes, red (young, light brown); feet, dull yellow. Size, 11–14 inches.

ELANUS LEUCURUS

VARIATIONS

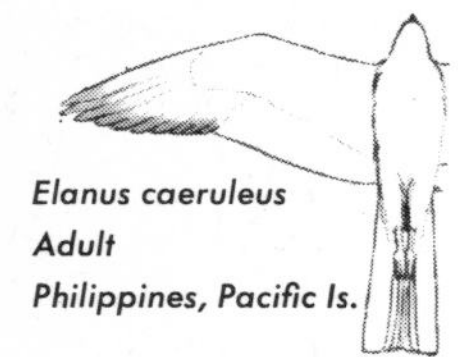
Elanus caeruleus
Adult
Philippines, Pacific Is.

Eurasian kites of this species are much like the African bird in size and coloring, but in Malaysia, the Celebes, and the Philippines a pale variant, light gray above with an almost wholly white underwing surface, outnumbers the phase which has dark gray primaries. These "white-winged" and "black-winged" phases are not generally correlated with sex, age, or geographical distribution. There were no records of the genus from New Guinea until, in 1954, Mayr and Gilliard reported finding birds of the "black-winged" variety breeding in the central highlands.

ELANUS NOTATUS

OTHER SPECIES

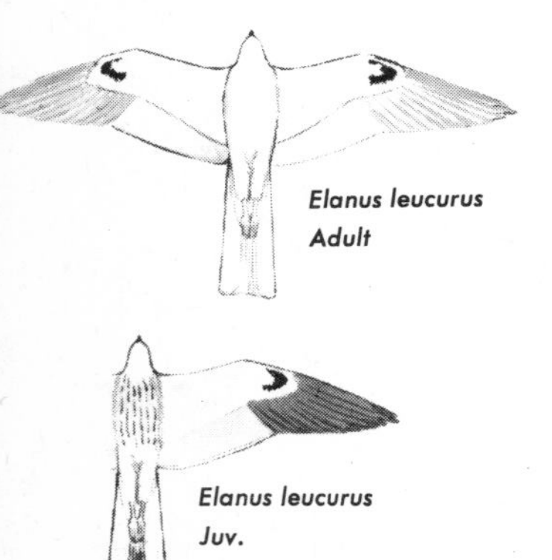
Elanus leucurus
Adult

Elanus leucurus
Juv.

The White-tailed Kite (*E. leucurus*) of the New World is larger (16 inches), has a longer tail than *E. caeruleus,* and often shows conspicuous black patches on the underwing coverts. This marking is also characteristic of the lighter, warmer-toned Australian species—the Australian Black-shouldered Kite (*E. notatus*), which is silver-gray above, and the Letter-winged Kite (*E. scriptus*), which is medium olive-gray above. The Australian Black-shouldered Kite is nomadic, whereas the Letter-winged Kite stays in the dry interior, only occasionally reaching the coastal districts of New South Wales, Victoria, South, and Western Australia. In size (13–14 inches) and color pattern they are virtually identical when perched, but the latter takes its name from the much more extensive black patches on its underwing coverts which are conspicuous in flight.

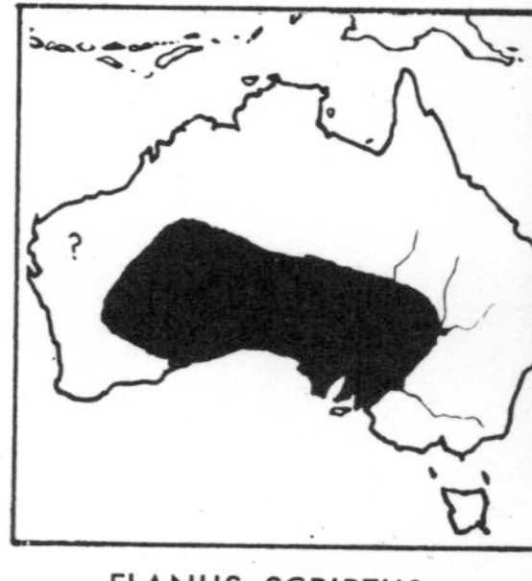
ELANUS SCRIPTUS

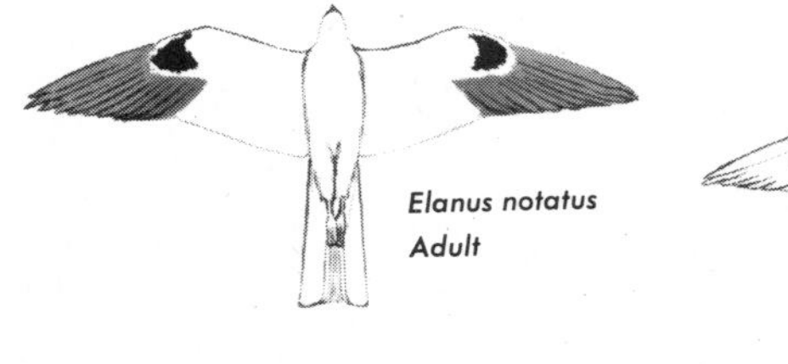
Elanus notatus
Adult

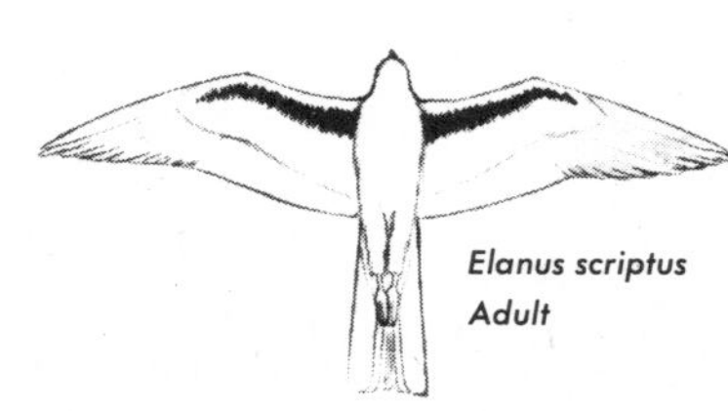
Elanus scriptus
Adult

HABITS

The Black-shouldered Kites inhabit fairly open country with scattered clumps of trees and are frequently seen hunting the plains with Marsh Harriers and buteos.

The African Black-shouldered Kite (*E. caeruleus*) does not soar to any height. While hunting it quarters the ground, maneuvering with great dexterity and hovering like a kestrel but with a slower wing beat. At other times it will hide in foliage and dart out quickly to seize its prey. This bird has a peculiar habit of cocking its tail and jerking it up and down between the drooping wings. Somewhat crepuscular, it is most active in the early morning and just before dusk.

It nests fairly low, either using old nests of other birds or constructing a bulky, loose structure of sticks with a shallow grass-lined cup in the center. Both sexes build. The female does most of the incubating (about 28 days), and the male is the chief provider of food. The young are hatched toward the end of the rainy season, and in about seven weeks, when the grass is dry or burned off and the prey vulnerable, they forage for themselves. Food is chiefly (80 per cent) various species of rats; also lizards, small snakes, frogs, mice, and other small vertebrates (occasionally birds); and insects and crabs. Nesting and foraging habits of the Asiatic populations are similar.

Strange adaptations to unusual situations occasionally occur. The Black-shouldered Kite is virtually the only raptor on the small desert island of Masira in the Arabian Sea. There are no rodents on Masira's low-lying sandy plains or in the central uplands, which are mostly jagged lava crags, and no suitable nesting trees. Nevertheless, a small population of these birds survives by scavenging along with the gulls in the Arab fishing villages. Nests are on lava crags, and—with food limited to scraps of fish and a few lizards—they usually contain only one nestling.

The Australian Black-shouldered Kite (*E. notatus*) builds a cup-shaped nest of leafy twigs at a more lofty height, 60 to 80 feet from the ground, or may use old nests of crows and magpies. It is a wanderer, although in many districts one or more birds will remain for weeks or even months before moving on.

The Letter-winged Kite (*E. scriptus*) in the interior breeds in colonies. In western Queensland groups of 12 to 18 pairs are scattered three to five miles apart, always rather close to the ground (11–19 feet) in clumps of coolibah trees on the edges of long, narrow waterholes which are filled in flood time (February) by the Diamantina River. They are nocturnal, often on the wing from dusk to early morning, hunting several species of large rats and mice. (The Black Kite, *Milvus migrans,* which may be found breeding in company with the Letter-winged Kite in this region, feeds on rats during the day.)

In the New World the White-tailed Kite (*E. leucurus*) often soars at a height of 60 or 70 feet while looking for prey on the ground. Remaining poised for half a minute at a time the bird then drops downward in an extended parachute maneuver to make the kill. Often it indulges in a pretty fluttering flight with quick wing beats. The display flight used in the nesting territory is a slow beating of the air with short strokes, the wings held at a sharp angle above the back, and the legs dangling.

The North American population has not been numerous in historic times and long ago disappeared from the southern part of the United States, except in Texas and California, west of the desert from the upper Sacramento Valley to the San Diego area. By 1900 the White-tailed Kite was considered rare in California and was protected by state law. Its beautifully marked eggs, some with a cap of brown coloring at one end, are prized by oölogists. Part of the survival problem of this evidently dying species, like that of the Swallow-tailed Kite, has been interference by humans.

The White-tailed Kite builds a bulky nest of small fine twigs, deeply hollowed, and about 18 to 59 feet high in the top of an oak, willow, eucalyptus, or other deciduous tree. Both sexes take part in building, incubating eggs (about 30 days), and raising young, and the more aggressive individuals defend the nest. In southern California these kites group together in communities. They do not object to pairs of the same species building within 200 yards of their own nest, but the territorial boundaries are strictly observed. Food, as in other species of *Elanus,* includes small mammals (field mice, wood rats, pocket gophers, ground squirrels, shrews), reptiles, amphibians, and insects. They show a decided preference for living in the vicinity of fresh-water marshes and streams where food is readily available all through the year, and probably do not wander far, even in winter.

The normal egg clutch for *Elanus* is four, but varies from three to six.

The call of the African bird is described as a clear piping whistle, "pii-uu pii-uu" or "pleu-wit," also harsher notes of alarm; of the Malay form, a clean melodious whistle. The North American bird frequently utters a spasmodic short whistle on the wing: "kēēp, kēēp, kēēp" which changes to a high-pitched and longer "krēēk" or "krēē-ēēk" with alarm. In Australia the Letter-winged Kite is noisy all night. The male cries "kack-kack-kack" as he brings food to the nest, and he is answered by the female's "kar-kar-kar-kar." Both sexes also make a chicken-like noise—"chirp-chirp-chirp-chirp-chirp" (characteristic of the male at night and of the female during the day).

The Pearl Kite *(Gampsonyx swainsonii),* although closely related to *Elanus,* is much smaller and as brightly colored as the pigmy falcons *(subfamily Polihieracinae)* of the Old World.

GENUS *GAMPSONYX*

This small kite was thought for a time to be related to the Falconidae, but its wing molt—from first (innermost) to tenth (outermost) primary—conforms to that of the hawks, eagles, and Old World Vultures, included in the Accipitridae, and the New World Vultures, or Cathartidae. Only the falcons and caracaras depart from this pattern by dropping the fourth primary from within at the beginning of a molt (see Introduction to Part II). In regard to the shape and proportions of the beak and nostril and the scutellation of the short tarsi (feathered about half) and toes, *Gampsonyx* is nearest to *Elanus.*

Pearl Kite (*Gampsonyx swainsonii*)

DESCRIPTION (CENTRAL AMERICA; NORTHERN AND WESTERN SOUTH AMERICA)

Above, dark brown more or less intermixed with dark gray and collared with a rather broad V of amber-brown; flight feathers and rectrices, flashing white on the inner webs and tipped white. Forehead and face, buff-yellow. Underparts, white with patches of black at the sides and center of neck; sides of body, amber-brown; thighs, light amber-brown.

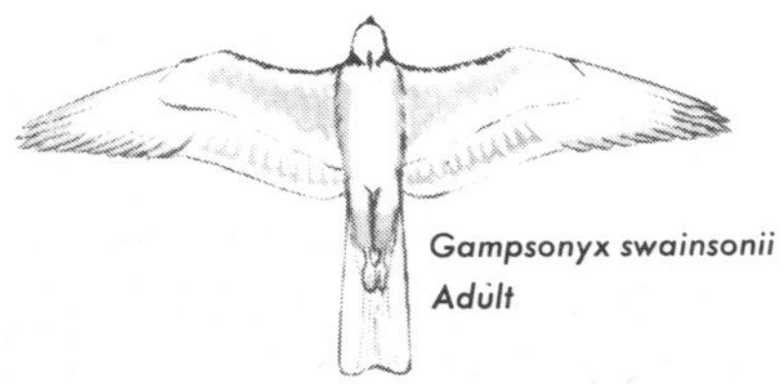

Gampsonyx swainsonii
Adult

Juvenile—similar to adult, but collared in white; the feathers of the upperparts, usually edged with amber-brown.

Beak, black; cere, dull blue-gray; eyes, red; legs and feet, bright yellow; claws, black. Size, 7½–8 inches; largest in western Ecuador and western Peru.

GAMPSONYX SWAINSONII

VARIATIONS

From the south bank of the Amazon to Paraguay, northwestern Argentina, and eastern Peru, birds average paler on the flanks, sides, and thighs and are somewhat smaller.

HABITS

The Pearl Kite is most commonly found in the seasonal forest edge and lightly wooded savanna of western Nicaragua and South America. Its food consists of insects—probably taken in the air and on the ground—and small lizards. In the same tall tree several nests may be occupied. Three nearly elliptical white eggs, blotched with brown, comprise a clutch. No call is recorded for the species.

Ternlike in its slender appearance, with an unmistakable long forked tail, the African Swallow-tailed Kite (*Chelictinia riocourii*) is much like the American Swallow-tailed Kite.

GENUS *CHELICTINIA*

Chelictinia is one of the smallest of the African kites—a powerful glider on long pointed wings and deeply forked tail, with relatively small beak and feet. Black patches along the underwing coverts are conspicuous in flight.

African Swallow-tailed Kite (*Chelictinia riocourii*)

DESCRIPTION
(AFRICA)

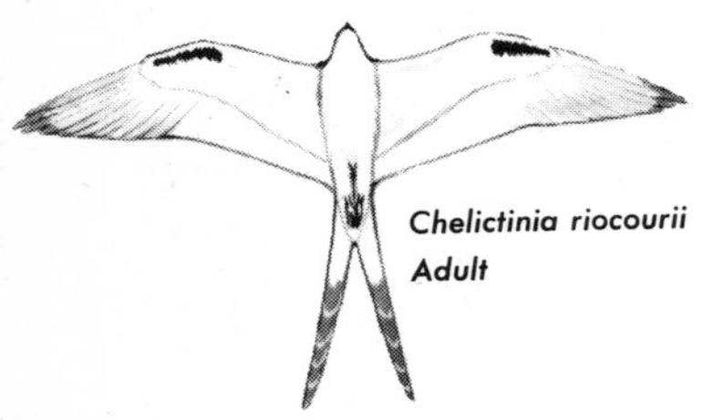
Chelictinia riocourii Adult

Above, dove-gray to medium gray; wings, lighter—light gray to medium olive-gray, tipped in white. Face, white, with a black ring around the eyes; underparts, white.

Juvenile—similar to adult, but with amber-brown feather-edging above; underparts, white, tinged amber-brown, and finely streaked with black.

Beak, dark gray; eyes, red; feet, yellow. Size, about 14½ inches.

CHELICTINIA RIOCOURII

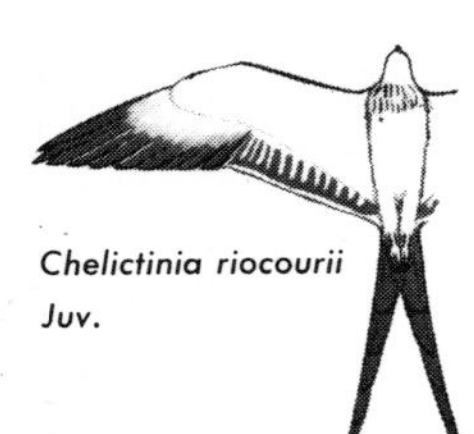
Chelictinia riocourii Juv.

HABITS

The African Swallow-tailed Kite may be seen only in the semiarid region extending from Senegal and Nigeria through the Sudan to Ethiopia and Somaliland. There, in the open bush and on the grass prairies, it quarters the ground for insects (mostly orthoptera and hymenoptera) as well as lizards and mice.

The method of hunting is by hovering over and pouncing on the prey, or hawking insects in mid-air like a kestrel. In the breeding season as well as at other times of the year, a dozen or more of these kites may be congregated in one place and move about together. Parties of 150 are not uncommon. They will sometimes congregate around nests of larger birds of prey. In Kenya, half a dozen were reported sitting on the rim of an occupied Brown Harrier Eagle's nest, and forty perched one day on a nest with a young White-headed Vulture in it.

The nest of the African Swallow-tailed Kite is a small twig structure in thorny acacias, about 12 or 15 feet from the ground. Three to four sandy-colored eggs are finely speckled with brown.

The call is a "little mewing cry."

SUBFAMILY PERNINAE

(Swallow-tailed Kites, Bat Hawks, Cuckoo-Falcons, Honey Buzzards, Gray-headed Kites, and Hook-billed Kites)

In 1840 Audubon wrote that the American Swallow-tailed Kite *(Elanoides forficatus)* was common in Louisiana and Mississippi. As late as 1900 this graceful black-and-white kite, with a grapelike bloom on its back, occurred locally east of the Rockies and casually north to Canada. Now it breeds in numbers only in parts of southern Florida, Mexico, Central America, and South America.

GENUS *ELANOIDES*

Certain osteological features of the head, neck, and backbone are common to both the Swallow-tailed Kite and the Osprey and, like the owls, *Elanoides* has no crop. This kite flies fairly high on very long pointed wings and the tail, which is long and deeply forked, is a good field mark. The legs and feet are short and stout, feathered about half in front, and reticulate.

Swallow-tailed Kite (*Elanoides forficatus*)

DESCRIPTION (FLORIDA, GULF STATES, MEXICO, AND SOUTH TO ARGENTINA)

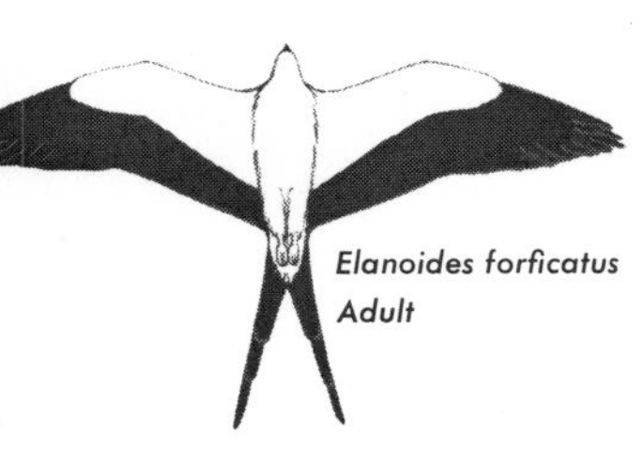

Elanoides forficatus
Adult

Head, neck, and entire underparts, white; rest of upperparts, wings, and long forked tail, black. The lower back has a distinct green-and-purple sheen (dark green in South America). White rump patch may show if a bird is in molt.

Juvenile—similar to adult, but duller, without the grapelike bloom. The head, neck, and upper breast, finely streaked with black; wing and tail feathers, narrowly edged with white.

Beak, black; cere and feet, light blue; eyes, reddish-brown or dark brown. Size, about 21 inches.

ELANOIDES FORFICATUS

HABITS

The Swallow-tailed Kites (or Scissor-tailed Kites, as they are sometimes called in South America) circle and soar a great deal, particularly in the nesting season. They quarter the ground and swoop down on prey with incredible swiftness, bearing it off to be eaten in mid-air. Many of the insects on which they feed are also taken in mid-air. They have some reputation, in the southeastern United States, for picking off water snakes that are sunbathing near the edges of marshes and streams. Other food includes lizards, frogs, tree toads, grasshoppers, locusts, cicadas, beetles, wasps, grubs, worms, and dragonflies.

The species has been virtually exterminated from most of its old range in North America by collectors of its beautifully marked eggs; and the habit of defending the nest, rather than slipping quietly away, as many raptors do, has made the adult birds exceptionally vulnerable to men with guns.

In Florida the favorite nesting places of Swallow-tailed Kites are tall slender Cuban pines—rarely far from cypress swamps—and sometimes the tops of cypresses. Two to four eggs rest on a platform of small twigs and bark mixed with Spanish moss, seldom less than 60 feet and usually from 100 to 150 feet from the ground. They repair and use old nests. Male and female share in the duties of nest building, incubation, and brooding of young.

Their call is a high-pitched "kii-ki-ki," which may be heard at a great distance, and another note, heard when several are flying together overhead, is softer—"peat, peat, peat."

Formerly the North American population migrated southward in large flocks, some at least to Ecuador; and there are records of stragglers appearing in Great Britain. Birds in the tropical zone are not migratory, but drift locally in flocks (as many as fifty have been recorded over the lowland seasonal forest at Caicara, Venezuela, and numbers also have been seen in Trinidad).

The strange, crested Bat Hawk *(Machaerhamphus alcinus)* of Africa is rarely seen, probably because of its crepuscular habits. During the day it sits quietly in the deep shade of the forest, sometimes hunched up with feathers ruffled like an owl, but in an inclined position.

GENUS *MACHAERHAMPHUS*

No other bird of prey has a keeled beak—the upper mandible ridged like the bottom of a boat. Very wide gape, large eyes, and thickly feathered lores are characteristics in common with the nocturnal nightjars and owlet-frogmouths. The long slender toes with bumps for grasping are falcon-like, and in flight the wings are long and pointed, but the tail is very short and square.

Bat Hawk (*Machaerhamphus alcinus*)

DESCRIPTION (CONGO)

Dark brown with a white patch showing at the nape when the slight occipital crest is raised; white streaking and a median black stripe at the throat; mottled white undertail coverts. Thick white feathering around the eyes marks the otherwise dark face.

Juvenile—gray-brown; underparts, coarsely mottled with white; wings and tail, barred.

Beak, dark gray; cere and skin around gape, light blue-gray; eyes, yellow; feet, white with a blue tint. Size, about 16 inches.

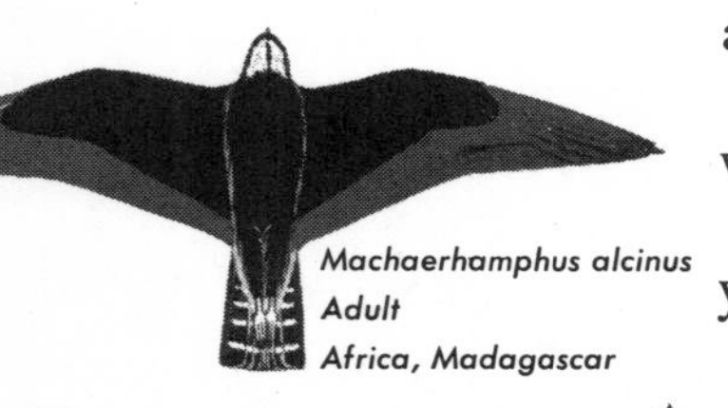

Machaerhamphus alcinus
Adult
Africa, Madagascar

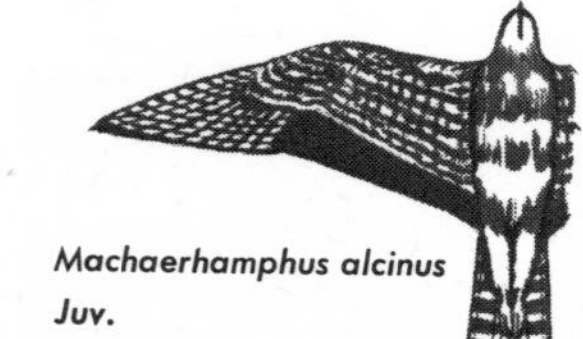

Machaerhamphus alcinus
Juv.

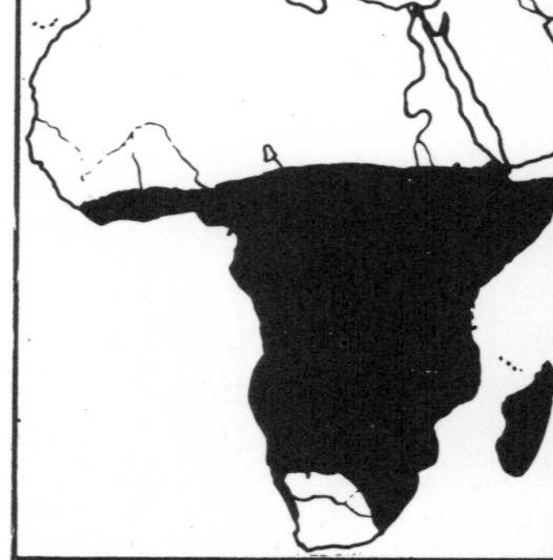

MACHAERHAMPHUS ALCINUS

VARIATIONS

The Asiatic birds, also known as Perns, are darker above, with an expanded white locket on the throat and chest; no visible white markings at the nape or on the undertail coverts. Sizes vary from 16 to 19 inches.

Machaerhamphus alcinus
Adult
S.E. Asia, Pacific Is.

MACHAERHAMPHUS ALCINUS

HABITS

These crepuscular birds emerge from their forest retreats to hunt at dawn or dusk, usually in the vicinity of limestone cliffs, roofs of houses, or other places inhabited by bats. The very wide gape gives them the appearance of huge nightjars, but their flight is falcon-like—rapid and powerful. Bats, large insects, and occasionally small birds (such as weaver birds) are captured with the talons, transferred to the mouth, and swallowed whole on the wing.

The nest of sticks, lined with green leaves, is constructed in the fork of a tall tree about 30 to 40 feet from the ground and sometimes used for several years. As far as is known, only two eggs are laid, of a pale bluish-green color, either plain or flecked with brown.

The call is recorded as a shrill falcon-like "kwik-kwik-kwik-kwik-kwik" (Africa) or "kliek-kliek-kliek" (Sumatra).

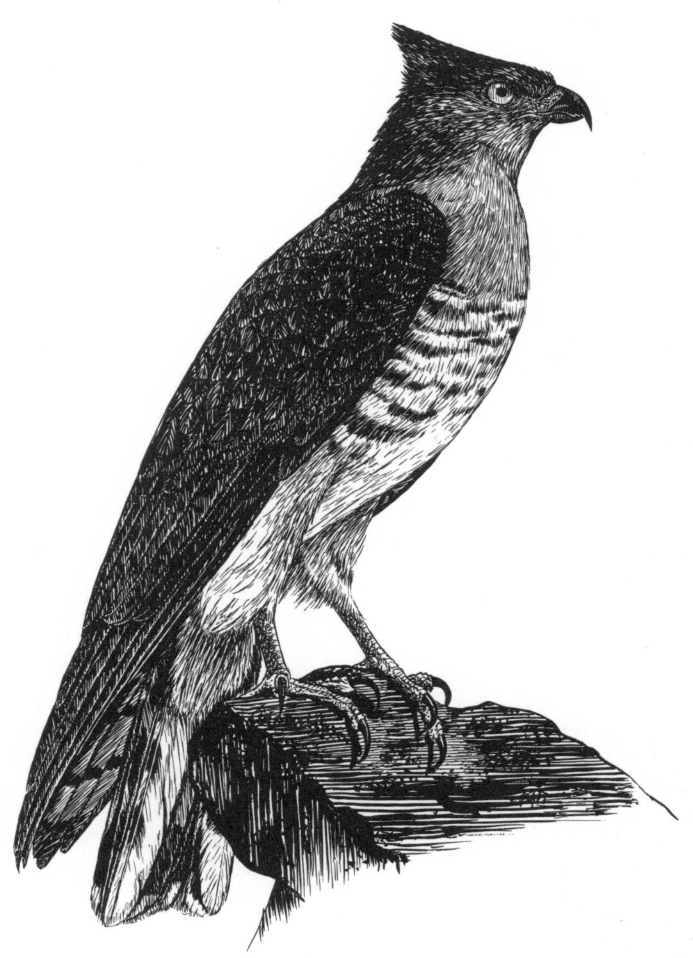

The Cuckoo-Falcon *(Aviceda cuculoides)* of West Africa occurs in dense bush, brushy savanna, and even in the depths of the Congo rain forest. It is a shy species which hides during the day in the foliage, often along forest roads or river banks.

GENUS *AVICEDA*

The cuckoo-falcons or bazas have double-toothed upper mandibles. The partly feathered tarsi are scutellate in front and reticulate in back; the feet, relatively weak. A long tail accounts for about half the length of these forest birds. Occipital crests are characteristic. These flare straight up, when they are perched, as in Spizaetus, the crested hawk-eagles. Sexual dimorphism, with females browner than males, is noticeable in *A. cuculoides* of Africa; slight in *A. jerdoni* of Asia and in *A. subcristata* of the East Indies, southwest Pacific, and Australian region. Males and females of *A. leuphotes* in India, Burma, Indochina, and Ceylon are alike; and there also appears to be no sexual dimorphism in color in the Madagascar species *A. madagascariensis.*

African Cuckoo-Falcon (*Aviceda cuculoides*)

DESCRIPTION (WEST AFRICA AND THE CONGO)

Male—dark gray above, including short crest. When the crest is raised, a patch of white feathers tipped with sienna flares at the nape. Wings are barred dark brown and two broad bands of light olive-gray show on the dark brown tail. Throat and chest, light olive-gray; rest of underparts, white, either partly or completely barred in gray-brown. In flight the underwing coverts are solid medium yellow-brown. *Female*—browner—rump and flight feathers, sienna (wings more distinctly barred than in male); throat and chest, ivory tinged with cinnamon; rest of underparts, white barred with cinnamon-brown.

Juvenile—dark brown above, collared and feather-edged in medium sienna; face, amber brown; underparts, ivory, the breast and belly heavily blobbed with dark brown. Underwing coverts, ivory, spotted dark brown.

Beak, black; eyes, yellow (juvenile, gray); feet, yellow; claws, black. Size, about 16 inches.

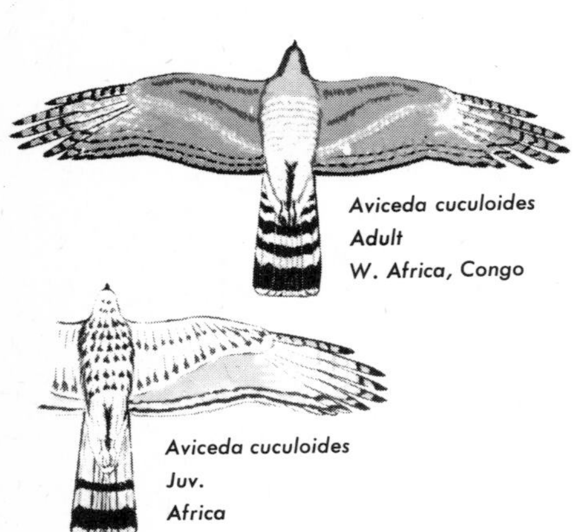

Aviceda cuculoides Adult W. Africa, Congo

Aviceda cuculoides Juv. Africa

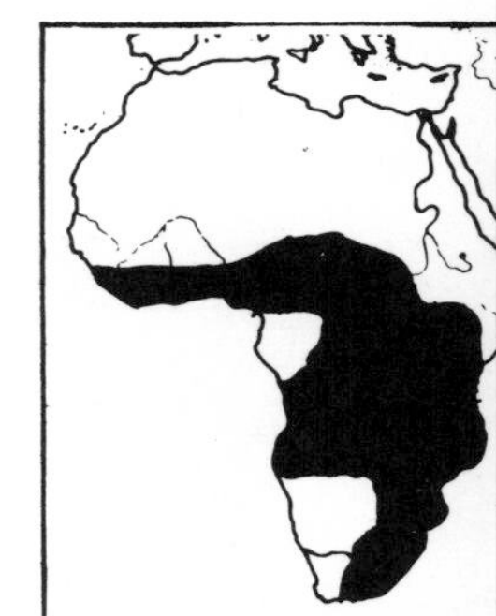

AVICEDA CUCULOIDE

VARIATIONS

Underwing coverts, barred yellow-brown and white, distinguish adult cuckoo-falcons in eastern and southern Africa, but the young are similarly spotted.

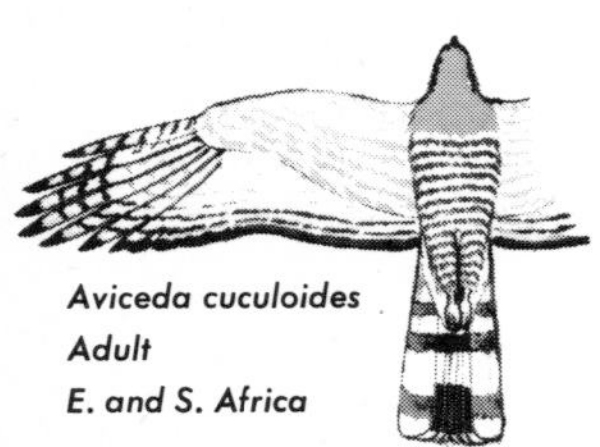

Aviceda cuculoides Adult E. and S. Africa

OTHER SPECIES

The Madagascar Cuckoo-Falcon (*A. madagascariensis*), about 15 inches, is brown above (male or female); the head, neck, and throat, as well as short crest, streaked with dark brown and white; breast, white; belly and flanks, brown.

In the East Indies, Australian region, and the southwest Pacific islands, the Pacific Cuckoo-Falcon or Baza (*A. subcristata*), 13–16 inches, is extremely variable in the intensity of its color patterns. *Male,* from Queensland, has black crest feathers and crown darker than dove-gray mantle and throat; back, gray-brown to chocolate; wing coverts and wings, slate-gray to dark gray; tail, slate-gray, broadly banded near the tip with black. The chest is amber-brown; rest of underparts, white or tinged amber-brown and barred gray-brown to chocolate. In flight, underwing and tail coverts are clear light amber-brown. *Female,* browner, with entire back, wings, and tail inclining to gray-brown; chest, light olive-gray; rest of underparts, white with a similar amber-brown tint, but barred dark yellow-orange to cinnamon-brown.

The palest birds, with the least amount of amber-brown coloring below and on the underwing and tail coverts, are restricted to the

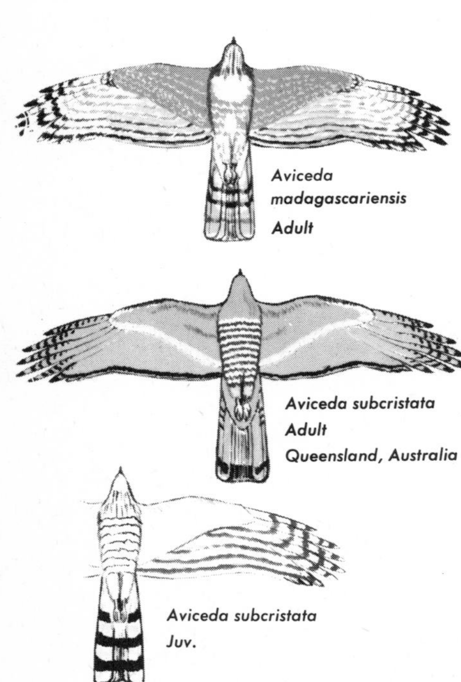

Aviceda madagascariensis Adult

Aviceda subcristata Adult Queensland, Australia

Aviceda subcristata Juv.

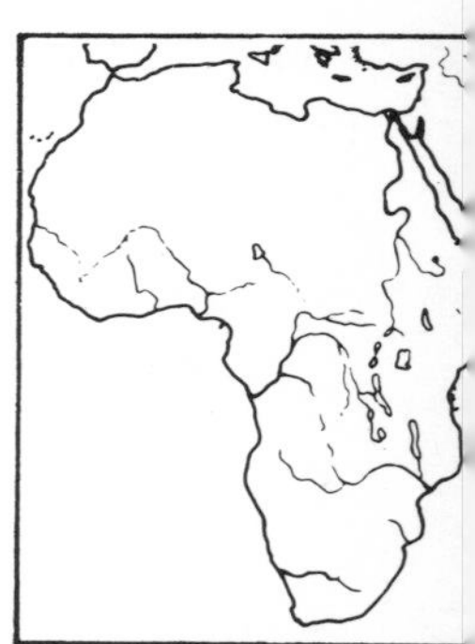

AVICEDA MADAGASCARIE

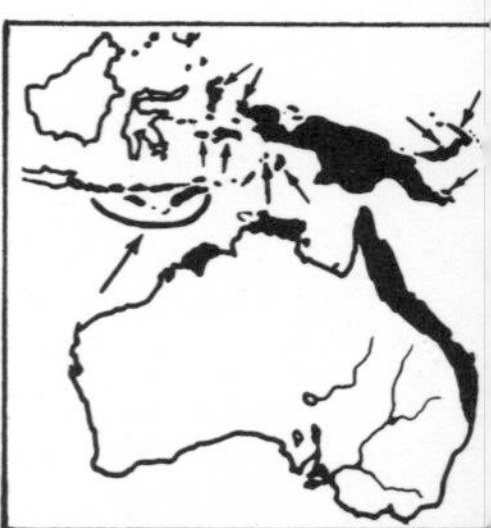

AVICEDA SUBCRISTAT

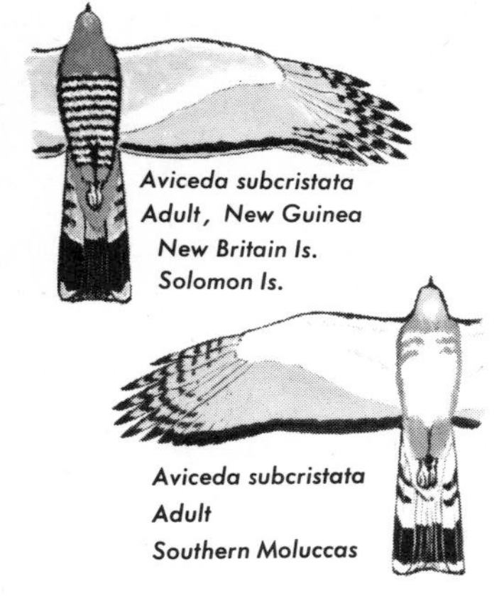

southern Moluccas (Kai Islands); the reddest, to the northern Moluccas; and the darkest, barred black and white below, occur in west Australia, New Guinea, and the Solomon Islands. These and other island populations are smaller in size than those described from northeast Australia.

The young, also variable, have brown to amber-brown streaking or a clear amber-brown suffusion on the chest, depending on the locality, and are more finely barred below than adults.

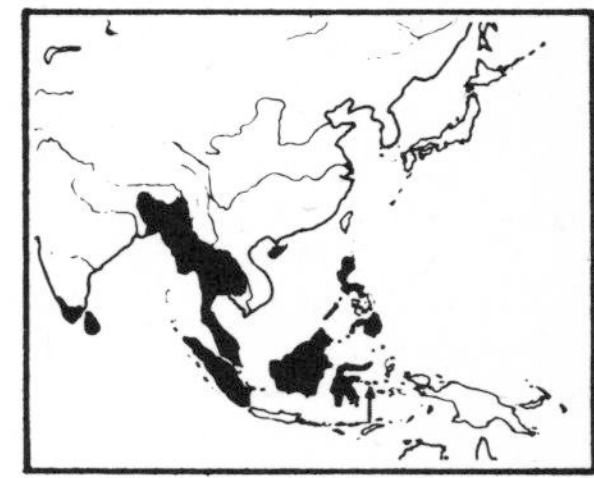

AVICEDA JERDONI

In tropical southeastern Asia and the Philippines the Crested Cuckoo-Falcon or Baza (*A. jerdoni*), 15½–17 inches, has a long black crest, tipped with white, and is also dimorphic. *Male,* ranging from light cinnamon (Hainan) to dark tawny (Celebes) on the head and mantle, heavily streaked with dark brown; back, wing coverts, wings, and tail, predominately dark gray-brown, the latter crossed with three black bands. Throat (with median black stripe) and chest, white to light olive-gray; rest of underparts, barred white and cinnamon-brown.

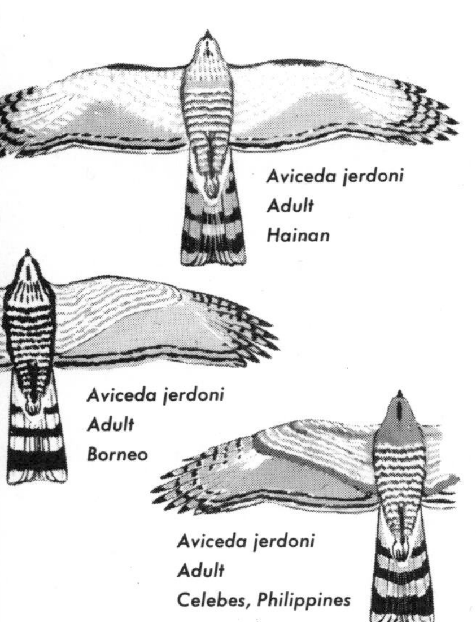

Female, paler; throat stripe, narrow and broken; chest, streaked; rest of underparts, barred light amber-brown. Young of both sexes resemble the female but are feather-edged in white above and have a four- to five-banded tail.

The Black-crested Cuckoo-Falcon or Baza (*A. leuphotes*), 11–12 inches, common between 2,000 to 3,000 feet in evergreen biotope of the hill country from Assam to Indochina, in Travancore, and Ceylon, may be recognized by its glossy black plumage and very long solid black crest. White and maroon patches show on the wings and scapulars; chest, white; breast, banded with black; rest of underparts, ivory, barred maroon across the belly. (Eyes, purple- or crimson-brown; cere and feet, dull gray or blue-gray; claws, brown.) In the young, black breast band is narrower; crest, shorter; wings, more maroon-colored.

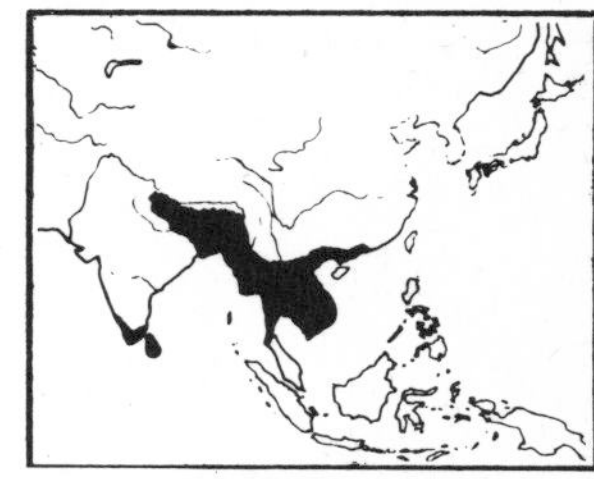

AVICEDA LEUPHOTES

Black-Crested Cuckoo-Falcon (*Aviceda leuphotes*).

HABITS

The various species of *Aviceda* are somewhat crepuscular, often hunting wood edges, open glades, and borders of streams and lakes. Cuckoo-falcons soar infrequently compared to the true falcons at sunrise or twilight and one may go unnoticed on the leafy branch of a tall tree until suddenly taking wing to hawk a flying insect or pick a caterpillar from some nearby tree or bush. These are taken immediately to a perch to be eaten. In the savanna country of east and central Africa they sometimes quarter the ground like kestrels.

Although mainly insectivorous in many localities, they also show preferences for frogs, crabs, lizards, bats, mice, shrews, and (rarely) birds or birds' eggs. The Madagascar Cuckoo-Falcon, for example, favors chameleons, even when other reptiles and locusts are abundant; and the main food of the Crested Cuckoo-Falcon on Ceylon is lizards, also frogs and birds' eggs. One observer saw a Pacific Cuckoo-Falcon on Buru hunting large doves.

A sturdy platform of sticks is constructed and may be only 25 feet up in a sapling or as high as 100 feet from the ground in a tall tree. This is lined with grass and roots and constantly renovated with fresh green leaves. In Africa one or two eggs are greenish-white, spotted and streaked with rich brown colors. One to three (commonly three) eggs are recorded for the Crested Cuckoo-Falcon and Black-crested Cuckoo-Falcon in Asia, and these are either plain grayish-white or marked with coarse specks and splotches of red at the broad end. The only difference between the eggs of the two species is in size. The female incubates (thirty-two days, Crested Cuckoo-Falcon); and the male is the main food provider.

The cry of the Black-crested Cuckoo-Falcon is a sharp or plaintive kitelike squeal, uttered either while perched or flying. A whistling noise precedes take-off and pursuit of prey. The Crested Cuckoo-Falcon's note has been described as "kee-ow kee-ow."

Wing and tail feathers from the Long-tailed Honey Buzzard *(Henicopernis longicauda)* adorn the headdresses of Wahgi Valley tribesmen in central New Guinea.

GENUS *HENICOPERNIS*

Henicopernis is a large, long-winged and long-tailed honey buzzard. The head is slightly crested; the lores are nearly bare; and the tarsi are about half-feathered in front.

Long-tailed Honey Buzzard (*Henicopernis longicauda*)

DESCRIPTION (NEW GUINEA)

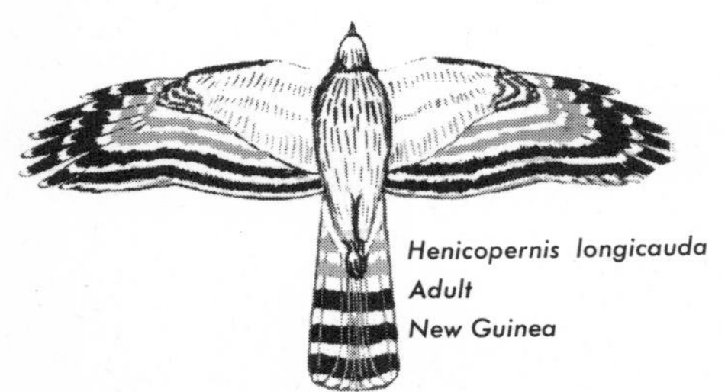

Henicopernis longicauda
Adult
New Guinea

Above, dark brown, broadly streaked on crown and nape; barred on back, wing coverts and wings in medium olive-gray; tail, medium olive-gray with three or four visible dark brown bands; face and throat, white; underparts, white tinged sandy and striped dark brown.

Juvenile—paler; tail with four to five dark brown bands.

Beak, light gray, darker at the tip; eyes, golden yellow; legs and feet, pale bluish-white. Size, about 21 inches.

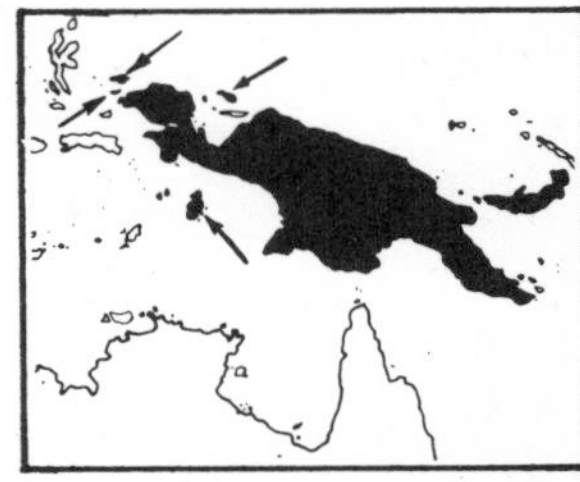

HENICOPERNIS LONGICAUDA

VARIATIONS

Henicopernis longicauda
adult
New Britain Is.

On the surrounding islands birds are smaller with a relatively shorter tail, especially in the Aru Islands and on Misol. A dark variant on New Britain has only traces of white streaking on the crown, nape, throat, and thighs. It is considered by some to be a separate species (*H. infuscata*).

HABITS

The Long-tailed Honey Buzzard on New Guinea is a forest-dweller that hunts low over cultivated areas. Its food, other than insects and grubs, is unrecorded. The altitudinal range of this bird in central New Guinea seldom exceeds 5,000 feet but one was seen at 5,800 feet in the Kubor Mountains sailing through a canyon and coursing in harrier-like fashion within two or three feet of steeply graded sweet-potato beds. Only one young bird has been found in a nest.

The small dark phase on New Britain reportedly ranges among the treetops in heavy forest and feeds on arboreal lizards.

Although it soars freely, the Eurasian Honey Buzzard (*Pernis apivorus*) spends less time in the air than the Common Buzzard (*Buteo buteo*). The wings and tail are longer, and the closely feathered lores are distinctive. Unlike the buteo it walks or runs along the ground with the ease of a corvine or gallinaceous bird.

GENUS *PERNIS*

Lores and forehead of *Pernis* are covered with small scalelike feathers, without any bristles, and the cere is nearly as long as the rest of the bill. The wings are long and the tail is slightly rounded. Short, heavy tarsi are feathered about half in front; otherwise, entirely scutellate. The toes and claws are long and slender, the latter very sharply pointed but not very much curved except in the larger east Siberian individuals. Eye color ranges from yellow in the temperate zones to orange-red in the tropics. The adult plumages everywhere are extremely variable, and there is sexual dimorphism in the tail pattern of the Crested Honey Buzzard (*P. ptilorhynchus*) in north and central Asia. Scalelike feathers of the head can be raised to give northern birds a slightly crested appearance, and distinct short or long crests are present in south Asian ones.

Honey Buzzard (*Pernis apivorus*)

DESCRIPTION (EUROPE AND WESTERN SIBERIA)

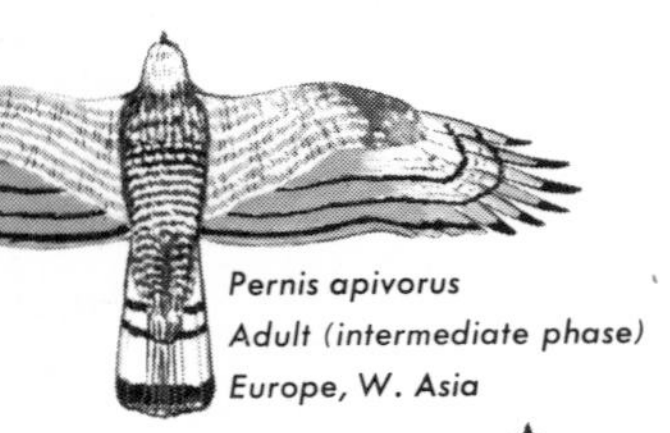

Pernis apivorus
Adult (intermediate phase)
Europe, W. Asia

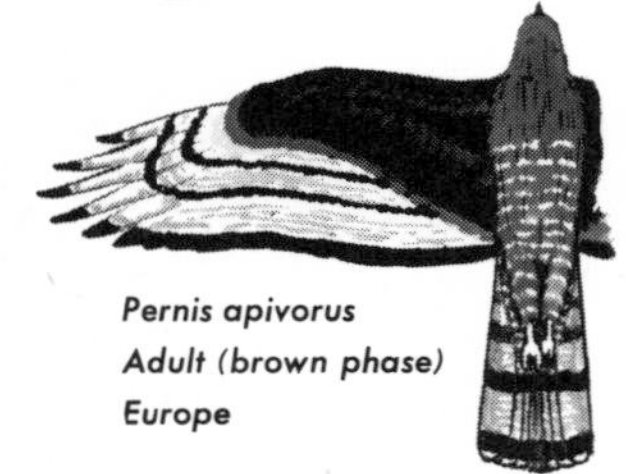

Pernis apivorus
Adult (brown phase)
Europe

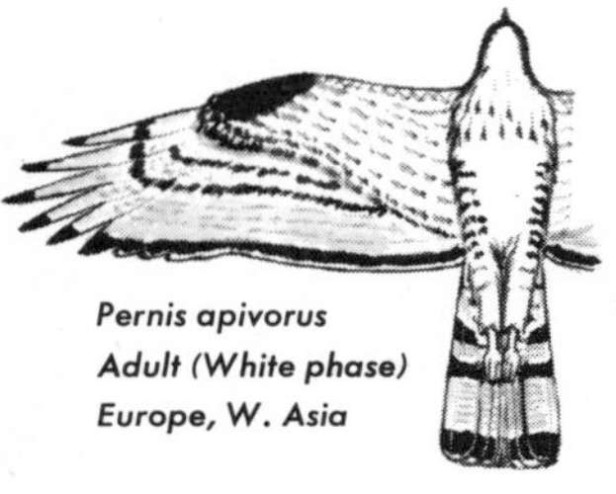

Pernis apivorus
Adult (White phase)
Europe, W. Asia

Pernis apivorus
Juv.
Europe, W. Asia

Variable. *Brown phase*—above, dark gray-brown, the feathers of the crown and nape edged with cinnamon; wings and tail, broadly barred and mottled with pale cinnamon; face, tinged dark gray-brown; sides of face, throat, and rest of underparts, varying from medium yellow-brown to sepia, finely streaked dark brown and slightly mottled with white.

Intermediate—head, light cinnamon, finely streaked dark gray-brown; underparts, mottled on the breast and barred on the belly and flanks with cinnamon and white.

White phase—dark brown above, forehead and nape, streaked with white; underparts, white, streaked on breast and blotched on belly and flanks with dark brown.

Juvenile—similar to adult, but lighter from crown to mantle; underparts, varying from almost uniform dark color in brown phase to white with dark brown streaking on the breast and mottled belly and flanks in white phase. Tail, not as distinctly marked as adults'.

Beak, black; eyes, yellow (sometimes dark gray-brown in young); feet, yellow. Size, 19–21 inches.

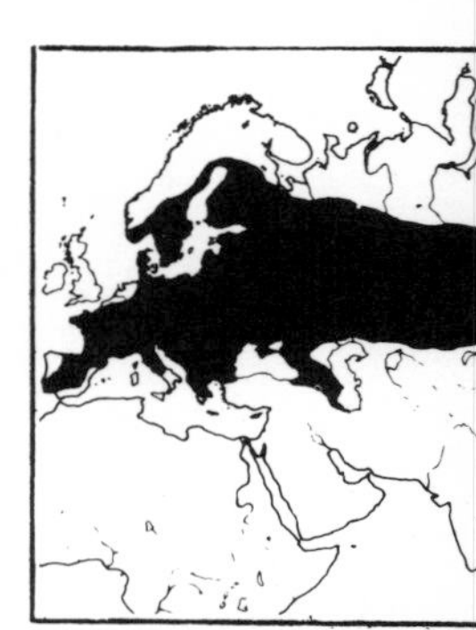

PERNIS APIVORUS

OTHER SPECIES

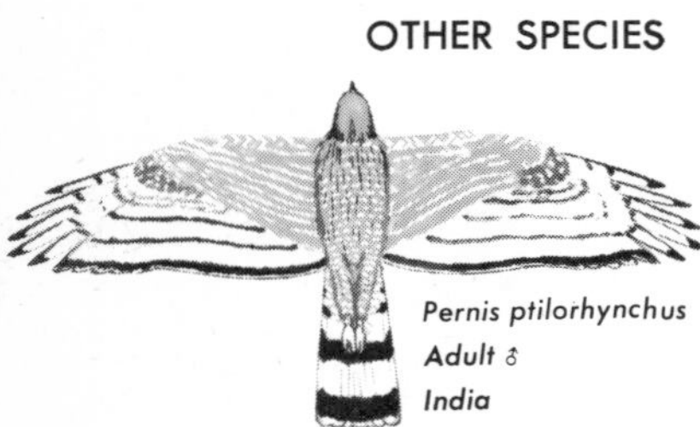

Pernis ptilorhynchus
Adult ♂
India

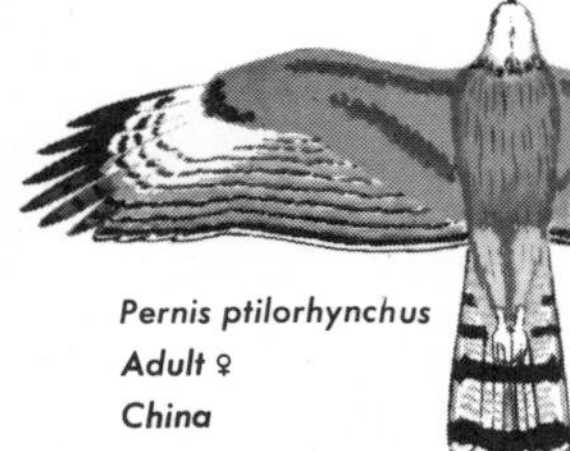

Pernis ptilorhynchus
Adult ♀
China

In northern India, China, eastern Siberia, and Japan, the Crested Honey Buzzard (*P. ptilorhynchus*), 19–24 inches, is similar to the brown and white phases of the European and western Siberian birds described, but grayer in coloring; the Chinese individuals have white throats and necklaces of dark brown streaking. Sexes are alike except for the tail pattern. Males have three visible black bands on the tail, and females show four, with fine irregular barring in the interspaces. Juveniles of both sexes have tails resembling the female's, but the pattern is less pronounced.

Malaysian birds, which are not sexually dimorphic in body or tail pattern, may constitute another species. Three color phases occur on Borneo: (1) Almost completely black, with some buff-yellow on throat and traces of barring on belly; (2) dark gray-brown above,

PERNIS PTILORHYNCHUS

Pernis ptilorhynchus
Adult
N. Borneo

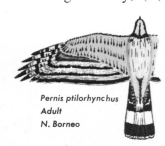

Pernis ptilorhynchus
Adult
N. Borneo

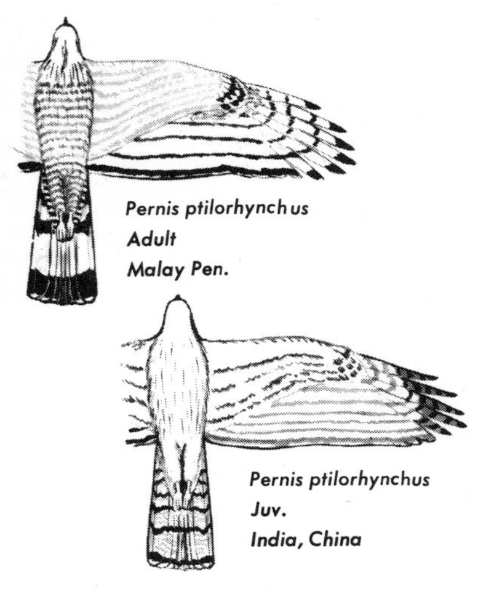

with gray face and sandy throat accented by a broad dark brown cravat; rest of underparts, pale cinnamon, with breast finely streaked dark brown and belly and flanks barred white; (3) crown to mantle, amber-brown with dark brown crest; back and wings, dark brown, edged with amber-brown; underparts, amber-brown with traces of a dark brown necklace and fine streaking. Another variation of (2), on the Malay Peninsula, lacks a necklace or cravat and is very heavily streaked and barred below. The Philippine population compares to (3) but is light amber-brown, lacks a necklace, and has much heavier streaking on the underparts. And on the island of Palawan we find a black bird like (1), but with traces of white, rather than buff-yellow. The crests of the northern birds are much shorter than those of the Malayan and Indonesian populations.

In the Celebes, another species, the Barred Honey Buzzard, (*P. celebensis*), 20–23 inches, with a short crest, is uniformly dark gray-brown above, with a gray face, white patch at throat streaked with dark brown, light amber-brown breast heavily striped, and dark gray-brown and white barring on belly. The Philippine version of *P. celebensis* becomes lighter—yellow-brown on the underparts.

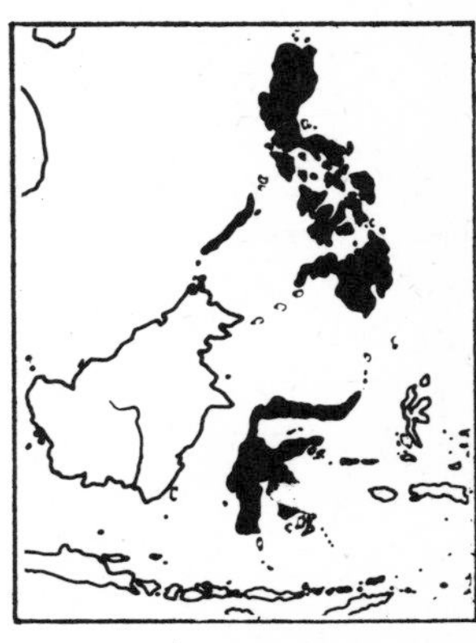

PERNIS CELEBENSIS

Pernis celebensis
Adult

Pernis celebensis
Imm.

HABITS

Pernis lives in forest where the trees are of good size, and frequents glades, clearings, roadsides, and borders of streams. The Honey Buzzard (*P. apivorus*) and its relatives throughout the temperate zone and south Asia have similar food habits—chiefly larvae and pupae of wasps, bees, and ants which they dig out of the ground from holes in trees and from nests hanging from trees and buildings, etc., as well as some adult wasps, hornets, wild bees, bumblebees, and other insects; also small mammals, reptiles, snails, eggs and young of other birds, fruit, and berries.

The breeding season is relatively late: end of May to end of June in Europe and northern Asia; mid-March to mid-July on the Indian peninsula, except in southern India where more birds lay in February than later.

Display flight is buteo-like. The Honey Buzzard indulges in repeated high dives and upward sweeps, striking the wings together above the back as it hovers for a few seconds at the peak of the ascent, and a pair will soar together high over the nesting place.

The nest is generally a renovation of an old crow, buzzard, or goshawk nest high in a tree, or, when built by the birds themselves, is not very large (one nest, 18 inches wide and 9 inches deep in Ceylon). One to three eggs are slightly ovoid in shape, the buff ground color sometimes completely obscured by deep, rich purplish-red or chocolate. These are laid at three-, four-, or even five-day intervals. Incubation, by both sexes, starts with the first egg—or occasionally with the second, the period estimated at about 30 to 35 days. The male supplies food to the female, and she feeds the young in the early stages of their development by regurgitation from her crop. Later both parents bring food. It is difficult to know exactly when the nestlings are fledged since they return to the nest to roost after leaving it. However, between six and seven weeks of age the young are fed at very long intervals and begin to forage for themselves.

The northern birds migrate in flocks from Europe and northern Asia into tropical and southern Africa, northern India, Burma, and Java.

The Honey Buzzard (*P. apivorus*) is a much more silent bird than the Common Buzzard (*Buteo buteo*). Its ordinary note, on the wing, is disyllabic (female) or trisyllabic and higher pitched (male), rendered respectively "pihā" and "püihü" with variants. Spitting, owl-like screaming, and scolding that sounds like a distant motorcycle are also recorded. In Ceylon, the Crested Honey Buzzard may be the true "Devil Bird," or "Ulama" of Sinhalese legend and folklore, whose cries are a far-sounding "hōō."

In tropical America the Gray-headed Kite *(Leptodon cayanensis)* may be seen soaring over the humid lowland forests. Its altitudinal limit in Costa Rica is said to be 3,000 feet. *Photographed at the New York Zoological Society.*

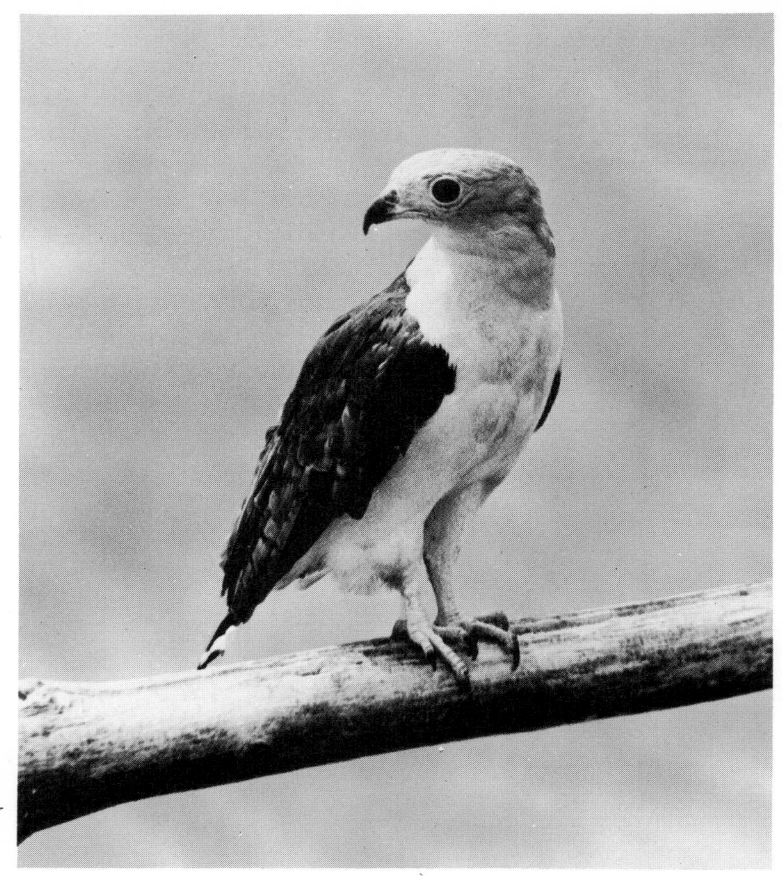

GENUS *LEPTODON*

This medium-sized tropical kite has large dark eyes, sparsely feathered lores and a rather small beak that is distinctly toothed and notched and only moderately hooked. The wings and tail are long, broad, and rounded; tarsi, very short and stout, feathered one-third to one-half and otherwise covered with hexagonal scales; toes also stout, with sharp but only moderately curved claws. The plumage of the adults is variable, and there are apparently two color-phases in the young.

Gray-headed Kite (*Leptodon cayanensis*)

DESCRIPTION
(TROPICAL AMERICA)

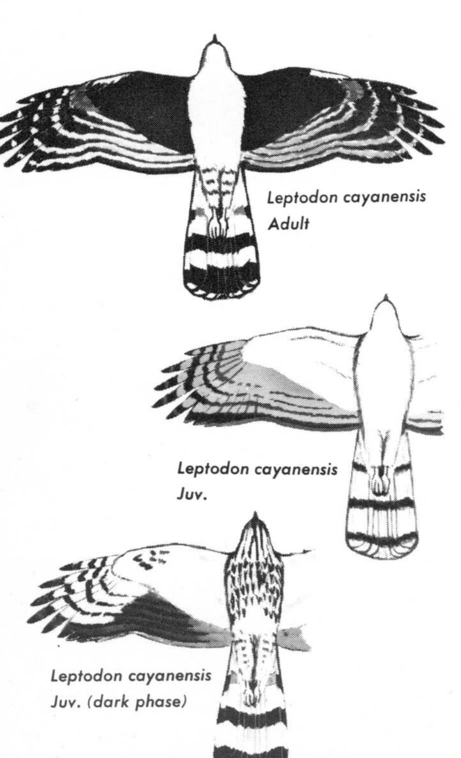

Leptodon cayanensis Adult

Leptodon cayanensis Juv.

Leptodon cayanensis Juv. (dark phase)

Head and sides of neck, either dove-gray or darker; back and wing coverts, slate-gray; wings, dark gray, barred black; tail, barred black and silver-gray. Throat and rest of underparts, white, tinged with light gray, except thighs, which are lightly to heavily marbled with dark gray. (Underwing coverts, dark.)

Light-phase juvenile has pure white head and underparts, except for a large dark brown patch on the crown; back, wing coverts, and wings, dark gray-brown barred black and feather-edged amber-brown; tail barred, dark brown and medium olive-gray, tipped with amber-brown.

Dark-phase juvenile is similar but dark-headed and heavily streaked on the white underparts with dark brown (barred or mottled on the thighs). Some birds (southern South America) have a nuchal collar of amber-brown and the crown, cheeks, and sides of neck are heavily tinged with this coloring.

In both phases underwing coverts of juveniles are white.

Beak, black; eyes, dark blue to blue-black; feet, blue-gray; claws, black. (Young, with orange-brown or hazel eyes and yellow feet.) Size, 17–20 inches.

LEPTODON CAYANENSI

HABITS

The Gray-headed Kite haunts areas of virgin forest, principally along the borders of streams and marshes, where its habits are difficult to observe. At least part of its fare is reportedly other birds and wasps.

The plumage of the Hook-billed Kite *(Chondrohierax uncinatus)* is so variable that, in flight, any medium-size broad-winged hawk with one or more conspicuous tail bands and heavily barred under parts might be this species.

GENUS *CHONDROHIERAX*

A very large, deeply hooked bill and short cere, mostly feathered on top, are distinctive features of *Chondrohierax*. Color and size of the bill are extremely variable throughout tropical America. The wings are long and broad. The short tarsi are half-feathered and longitudinally scaled; the small feet are furnished with long, moderately curved claws. There is sexual color dimorphism in both species, and dark phases also occur.

Hook-billed Kite (*Chondrohierax uncinatus*)

DESCRIPTION
(TROPICAL AMERICA)

Male—uniformly dark slate above, including face; wings, barred in black; tail, black with two white or light olive-gray bands and white-tipped. Below, medium gray, narrowly barred white, sandy; or entirely gray. *Female*—dark head, collared in amber-brown; rest of upperparts, dark gray-brown; wings, barred dark brown; tail, black with two pale gray-brown bands, tipped in white. Below, sandy, coarsely barred in shades varying from dark amber-brown to dark brown.

CHONDROHIERAX UNCINATUS

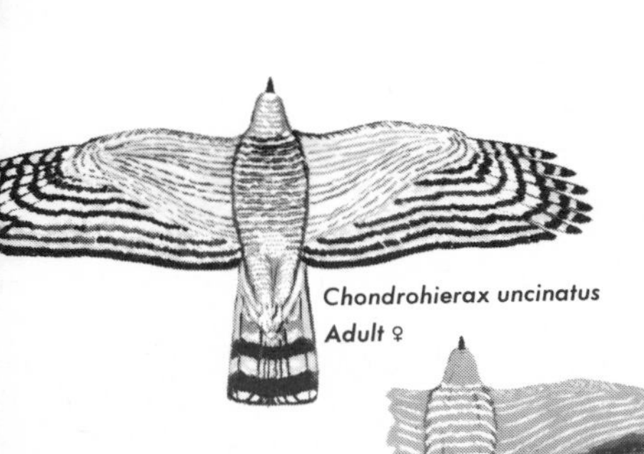

Chondrohierax uncinatus
Adult ♀

Chondrohierax uncinatus
Adult ♂ (gray phase)

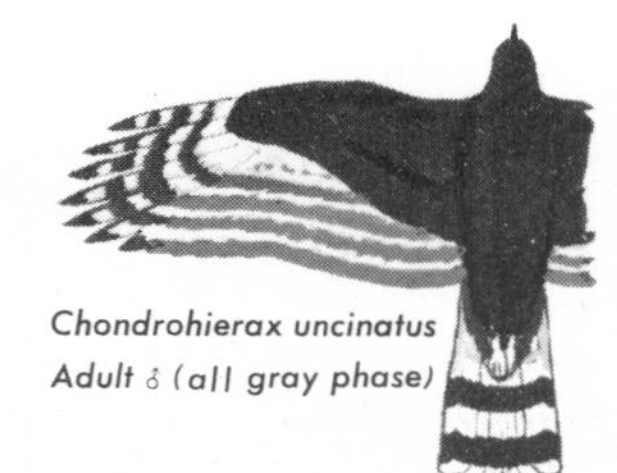

Chondrohierax uncinatus
Adult ♂ (all gray phase)

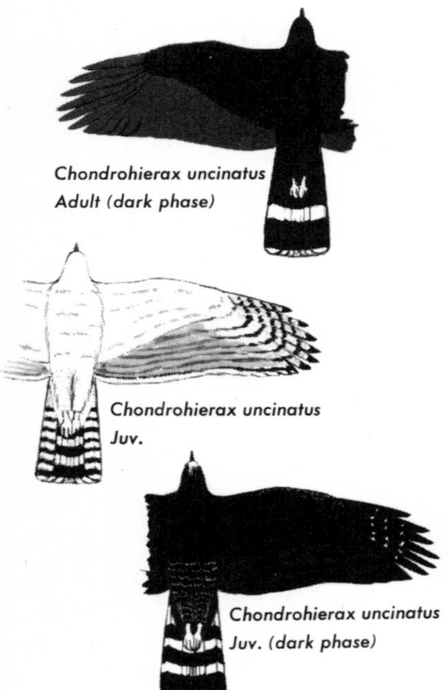
Chondrohierax uncinatus Adult (dark phase)

Chondrohierax uncinatus Juv.

Chondrohierax uncinatus Juv. (dark phase)

Dark phase (*male or female*)—dark gray above and below with a greenish-bronze gloss on the back, the tail crossed by one wide white band.

Juvenile (*sexes alike*)—dark brown from crown to mantle with a wide collar of white at the nape, continuing around to the completely white underparts; back and barred wings, edged in amber-brown. Tail, dark brown with three narrow bands of pale gray-brown, tipped in white.

Dark phase juvenile (sexes alike)—completely dark above and below with fine white barring on belly and thighs; tail, two pale bands.

Beak, black upper and yellowish-white lower mandible; bare parts of face a blend of yellow, orange, and green; eyes, white; legs and feet, orange-yellow (male) or yellow-green (female); claws, black. In *dark phase* adults the bare parts of the face as well as the legs and feet, yellow-green; beak, black (juvenile, yellow); eyes, white, as in normal phase (juvenile, brown). Size, 14½–16 inches.

VARIATIONS

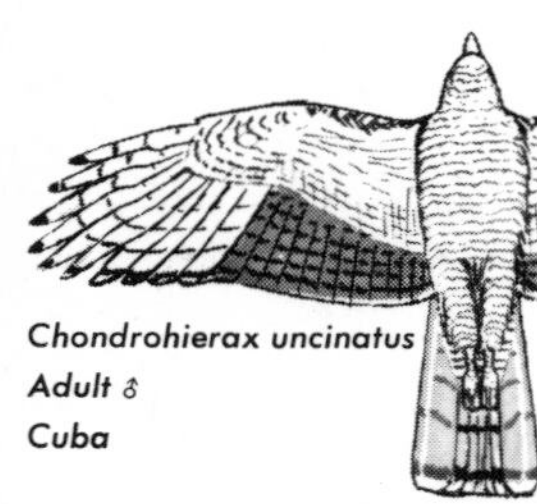
Chondrohierax uncinatus Adult ♂ Cuba

On the island of Grenada in the West Indies, birds are smaller, 11½–14 inches, with similar sexual dimorphism and corresponding juvenile plumages, but no known dark phase. (Eyes, pale green in adult male.)

The very heavy-billed form "Wilson's Kite" of eastern Cuba, 14–15 inches, appears to be lighter in the male and female plumages, the latter with finer barring below; white collar at the nape finely barred in the ground color, amber-brown. (Beak, almost entirely yellowish-white; eyes, yellow-green; feet, yellow in adults.)

HABITS

The Neotropical Hook-billed Kite lives in secluded forests, usually in the interior. It is said to feed on reptiles, birds, and insects, and probably nests in trees—although no information on nesting is available. The Cuban bird, now so rare that it is seldom seen outside of Oriente Province, subsists chiefly on arboreal snails (*Polymita*).

SUBFAMILY MILVINAE

(Double-toothed Kites, Plumbeous Kites, Snail Kites, and true Kites)

Barred underparts and white throat with a single median black stripe distinguish the Double-toothed Kite *(Harpagus bidentatus)*, from southern Mexico to northern South America.

GENUS *HARPAGUS*

These small forest hawks with large orange-red eyes are the only birds of prey in the Western Hemisphere with double-toothed beaks. The cere is relatively short in *Harpagus* and the lores are sparsely bristled. Rather long wings and tail are slightly rounded. The short tarsi, feathered about one-third and scutellate in front, are bare and reticulate in back; toes, short; claws, slightly curved. The most widely distributed species (*H. bidentatus*) is sexually dimorphic in color.

Double-toothed Kite (*Harpagus bidentatus*)

DESCRIPTION
(TROPICAL AMERICA)

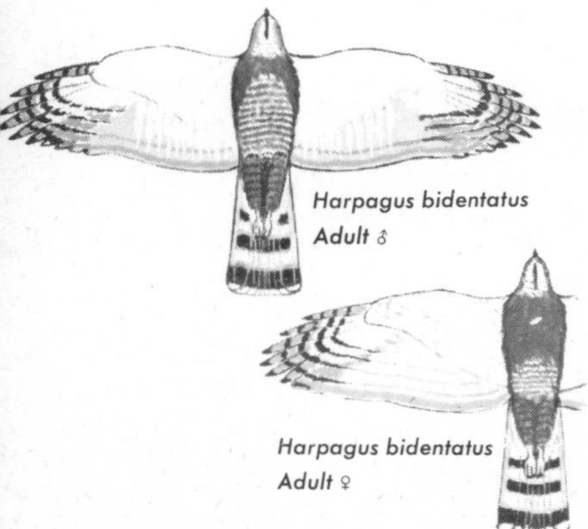

Male—head, dark slate; otherwise dark brown above; wings, indistinctly barred medium olive-brown; tail, with three narrow irregular bands of light olive-gray or white. Face and sides of throat, dark slate; throat, white with a dark median stripe; underparts, uniformly barred in olive-gray and white, and tinged (most heavily on the breast) with dark amber-brown. *Female*—upperparts and throat, same as male; below, amber-brown with white barring restricted to belly.

Juvenile—nearly uniform sepia above, the back and wings finely

HARPAGUS BIDENTATUS

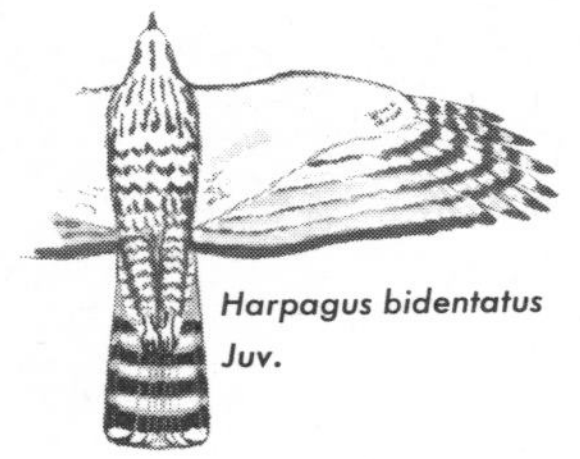

feather-edged in amber-brown; tail similar to adult's; sides of face, sepia streaked with amber-brown; throat, white with a dark stripe, as in adult; underparts, white to light cinnamon, streaked and blobbed with sepia.

Beak, dull black; cere, light olive-green; eyes, dull orange-red; legs and feet, orange-yellow; claws, black. Size, 12–14 inches.

HARPAGUS DIODON

OTHER SPECIES

The Rufous-thighed Kite (*H. diodon*) of tropical eastern South America, which is comparable in size but not sexually dimorphic, has light gray underparts and amber-brown thighs. (The juvenile resembles that of *H. bidentatus,* streaked and blobbed below, but with amber-brown thighs.)

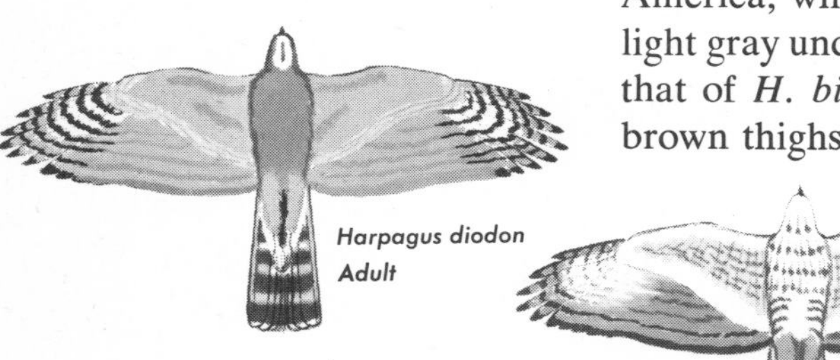

Harpagus diodon
Juv.

HABITS

The habitat of the Double-toothed Kite is the heavy rain forest of tropical America. A pair of these birds will use a tree branch as a lookout post and occasionally one or the other flies off to capture a lizard in a nearby tree. The chase is carried on in a strange way—the kite hopping after the lizard along a slanting branch with wings spread to maintain its balance. Food is almost exclusively small reptiles and insects. Its flight, while crossing clearings, has been described as an accipiter-like glide with occasional quick flaps.

The nest is a shallow saucer of twigs in the crotch of a thickly foliaged tree. Three to four white eggs are spotted with brown.

Next to nothing is known about the habits of *H. diodon.*

Fiery eyes and sienna markings on the under surface of the wings are outward manifestations of the bold and playful personality of the Plumbeous Kite *(Ictinia plumbea)* throughout tropical America.

GENUS *ICTINIA*

The small, short-legged, long-winged, and somewhat falcon-like kites of *Ictinia* inhabit the warmer parts of the Western Hemisphere from the southeastern United States to Argentina and Paraguay.

The bill is short, deep, and strongly arched and resembles that of a falcon, but the cutting edge of the upper mandible is lobed, not distinctly toothed. Pointed wings reach beyond the end of the squared-off tail, which is slightly notched in tropical birds and in some northern ones. The stout tarsi are feathered nearly halfway down and otherwise scutellate in front; feet, larger in proportion to body size than in many kites, with toes neither stubby nor compressed.

Plumbeous Kite (*Ictinia plumbea*)

DESCRIPTION (TROPICAL AMERICA)

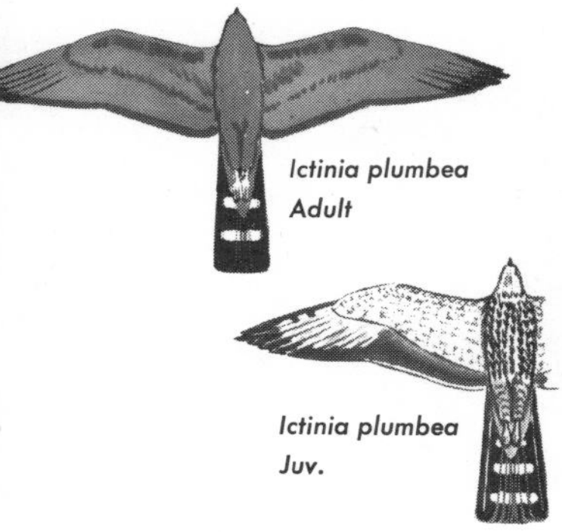

Head, neck, and entire underparts, dove-gray except for feathered black lores; back, wing coverts, and wings, dark gray, the primaries flashing sienna markings in flight. Tail, dark gray with two or three spots of white on the inner or outer webs of all but the center pair of rectrices.

Juvenile—dark gray above with white streaking on the head; back, narrowly, and wings, broadly, tipped in white; tail as in adult; underparts, white heavily blobbed with dark gray. In flight heavy sienna markings on the wings not visible.

Beak, black; eyes, red (young, paler than adult); legs and feet, deep reddish-orange or reddish-yellow; claws, black. Size, 13–15 inches.

ICTINIA PLUMBEA

OTHER SPECIES

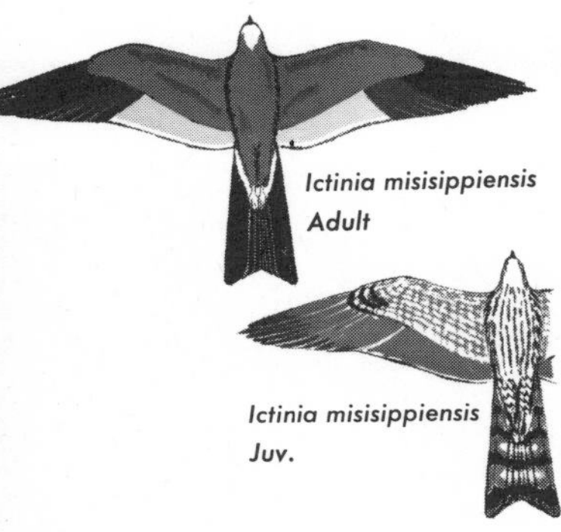

The Mississippi Kite (*I. misisippiensis*), 14–16 inches, native to the southeastern United States, has barely noticeable sienna markings on the wings and a longer forked tail, with no white bars or spots. (Head, neck, and underparts of juvenile, white, streaked with black; tail, barred.)

ICTINIA MISISIPPIENSIS

HABITS

A certain ebullience of spirit and social behavior, even in breeding season, are characteristic of both the Plumbeous and Mississippi kites.

The flight of these birds is graceful, vigorous, and sustained for long periods, often at a considerable height, where they may mingle with Black Vultures, Turkey Vultures, and Swallow-tailed Kites. In sunny weather, they catch and devour most of their insect food while soaring in ascending currents of air, but, when wind conditions are unfavorable, they are seen hawking insects from a perch and returning there to eat at their leisure. Their habit of carrying half-eaten prey for long distances in the talons, tucked under the tail, results in a permanent discolored sticky spot on the undertail coverts. They sometimes take small snakes, lizards, and frogs, but attacks on other birds and mammals are nearly always playful or in defense of the nest.

Stands of tall trees, like those found in parks and on plantations, are the most suitable habitat for *Ictinia*. The nest is a bulky shallow saucer of coarse sticks, built as high as the size of the trees in the area will allow. This can vary from 30 to 135 feet from the ground; or sometimes, as in certain parts of Texas and Oklahoma, the only nesting places available are four, five, or six feet up in mesquite or shinnery oak.

Both sexes take part in nest-building, incubation

(29 to 31 days), and care of the young. One to three eggs are plain white or pale bluish-white, usually unmarked. The young are fledged in about a month.

Although widely distributed throughout the warmer parts of the hemisphere, these kites seem to be localized in thickly populated breeding communities and may be hard to find in the intervening territory. In the nonbreeding season they also gather in large numbers wherever food is most plentiful (occasionally, in South America, in company with the Swallow-tailed Kite). In North and Central America many drift southward for the winter and return in the spring, often to the same nest for many years in succession.

Their usual cry is a shrill whistle—"phee-phew"—whether it is heard in Tamaulipas or Oklahoma; the alarm note, a loud repeated "kee-e-e." Chippering between members of a pair has also been recorded.

John Hamlet's juvenile Everglade Kite *(Rostrhamus sociabilis)*, although fed fresh meat, in its natural habitat would have lived mainly on fresh-water snails. The blunt-edged but deeply hooked bill clamps down between the operculum and the shell, and the snail's body is apparently detached by its own muscular contractions.

GENUS *ROSTRHAMUS*

The narrow, sickle-shaped beak of two species of *Rostrhamus* in tropical and subtropical America is distinctive. In the field these kites can be easily recognized by their dark color; by their long, broad, and rounded wings; by their square (slightly notched) tail; and by their slow flight. The short tarsi are one-third sparsely feathered (otherwise scutellate); toes and claws, long and slender and only slightly curved. The adult male Everglade, or Snail, Kite (*R. sociabilis*) is slate-gray to dark slate-gray, and the female, dark brown—both with extensive white areas at the base of the tail conspicuous in flight. However, male and female of the Slender-billed Kite (*R. hamatus*) are completely dark slate-gray in adult plumage.

Everglade, or Snail, Kite (*Rostrhamus sociabilis*)

DESCRIPTION (SOUTHERN FLORIDA)

Male—slate-gray to dark slate; wings, black; tail coverts, white; tail, white with a very broad subterminal band of black. *Female*—dark brown above with narrow amber-brown feather-edging on back, wing coverts, and wings; forehead and throat, streaked; breast, mottled white and light amber-brown; thighs, amber-brown barred black; the tail, including tail coverts, white as in the male, but banded more

Rostrhamus sociabilis Adult ♂

Rostrhamus sociabilis Adult ♀

narrowly with dark brown. In flight both sexes show white on underwing and tail coverts.

Immature (male)—like adult male but slightly browner, with light amber-brown streaking on chin and throat, becoming dark amber-brown below. *Female*—like adult female above but entire head and neck streaked black and white; underparts (including underwing and undertail coverts), white to light amber-brown, heavily striped black.

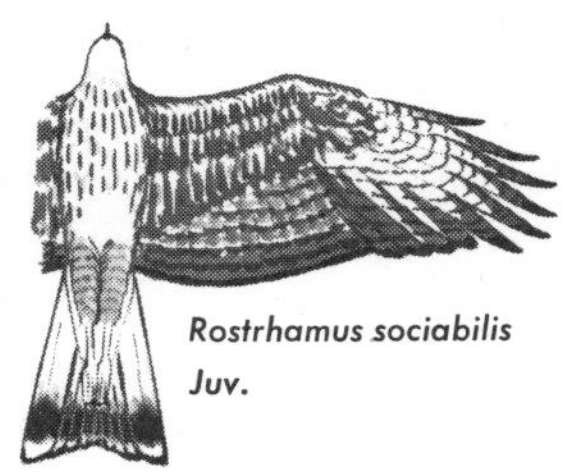

Rostrhamus sociabilis
Juv.

ROSTRHAMUS SOCIABILIS

Juveniles (sexes alike)—similar to immature female but broadly feather-edged in light amber-brown above; head and neck, darker—amber-brown streaked with black. Tail, as in adult female and immatures, white subterminally banded with dark brown.

Beak, black; bare parts of face and cere, bright orange (male) or paler (female and young); eyes, red (young, brown); legs and feet, yellow-orange (male) or dull yellow (female and young); claws, black. Size, 15½ to 16½ inches.

VARIATIONS

Other populations are similar in plumage pattern but relatively shorter-winged from Nicaragua to Argentina; larger and longer-winged in Mexico, Cuba, and the Isle of Pines.

ROSTRHAMUS HAMATUS

OTHER SPECIES

The Slender-billed Kite (*R. hamatus*), sometimes placed in its own genus *Helicolestes,* 14½–16 inches, has stouter legs and feet and a longer upper mandible, curved in an even more pronounced sickle shape. The adult male and female may be distinguished from *R. sociabilis* in widely scattered localities in northern South America by uniformly dark slate-gray plumage, smaller size, shorter wings, and shorter square tail. Juveniles are barred or flecked with white on the wings and thighs, and have white-banded tails.

Rostrhamus hamatus
Adult

Rostrhamus hamatus
Juv.

HABITS

In the early 1900's Everglade Kites were breeding all through southern Florida, but drainage of the Everglades has since resulted, indirectly, in their near extinction. The freshwater snails (*Pomacea*), on which these birds feed, have been confined over large areas to drainage ditches, and the incidence of lung flukes carried by them and transferred to the kites has greatly increased. Only a few birds are left in the permanent wet marshes such as still exist in the Lake Okeechobee region.

It is not known whether disease has played a part in the gradual decline in numbers of Snail Kites in Cuba, where marshes have also been drained for agricultural purposes. These peculiar birds of prey are still abundant in many parts of South America, their presence announced by the pearly egg clusters of the snails on the marsh vegetation and by the piles of empty shells (sometimes two or three hundred) at their feeding stations.

Everglade, or Snail, Kites nest only a few yards apart in colonies (20 to 100 in Argentina). The male does the nest-building and interrupts this activity only to feed himself and bring snails to the female. The finished product is a platform of sticks on clumps of sawgrass or dead tree stumps (Florida) or supported by rushes (Argentina) from three to seven and a half feet above the water. In Florida the cup-shaped hollow may be lined with vine and willow leaves; in South America, with grass and water rush. Two to four eggs are white, profusely patterned in varying shades of brown.

Both sexes incubate and care for the young,

which are fledged in less than a month's time after hatching.

These birds soar a great deal and seem to stand still for long intervals in one place with exaggerated tail-twisting motions. Circling, chasing, and diving from a considerable height have been observed during breeding season and may be connected with courtship.

The snails on which they feed remain submerged in the water during the hotter part of the day, but creep about on the marsh vegetation during the early morning and late afternoon. It is then that Snail Kites may be seen coursing back and forth with a slow wing beat like Marsh Hawks, frequently hovering before plunging down to pick up a snail. The snail contracts as it is borne off, so the kite's strategy is to carry its prey to a feeding post and wait quietly with one leg raised, holding the snail until the soft body is extruded and can be grasped with the peculiarly adapted beak and swallowed. The Slender-billed Kite (*R. hamatus*) secures and eats snails in exactly the same manner.

Migrating in flocks is noted from the southern part of the South American range of *R. sociabilis,* and the North and Central American birds probably drift southward in winter from the northern limits of their range.

Snail Kites are rather noisy, emitting a cry that is variously described as a rasping, chattering sound or the "shrill neighing of a horse."

The Black, or Yellow-billed, Kite *(Milvus migrans)* of tropical Africa feeds on carrion, offal, and garbage; but it also fishes and takes small mammals, poultry, water birds, frogs, and locusts and other insects. In winter it may be seen commonly scavenging along the coastal harbors and in the native villages of the interior, but it is never numerous under the canopy of the rain forest.—*Photographed at the National Zoological Park.*

GENUS *MILVUS*

Characteristics common to both species of *Milvus* are relatively large size; long, slender, and angled wings; strong beak, broad at the base with upper mandible much compressed, and tip sharply pointed; tarsal feathering about one-half, and rest of legs and feet scutellate in front.

The widespread Black Kite (*M. migrans*) is smaller and darker, with a much less deeply forked tail than that of its close relative, the Red Kite (*M. milvus*). Distribution of the latter is mainly the southwestern Palaearctic region. However, since the Red Kite is migratory to the Mediterranean and the Black Kite reaches Arabia and South Africa in winter, these birds may be confused with each other and with local populations of the Black Kite in southern Arabia and various parts of Africa. A white underwing patch is helpful in distinguishing *M. milvus;* European individuals of the Black Kite have black bills in adults, in contrast to African populations of *M. migrans* in which the bill is yellow in the adult and black in the young (except for gray-billed adults in Sudan and southern Arabia).

Sexes are virtually alike, even in size.

Black Kite (*Milvus migrans*)

DESCRIPTION (CENTRAL AND SOUTH AFRICA)

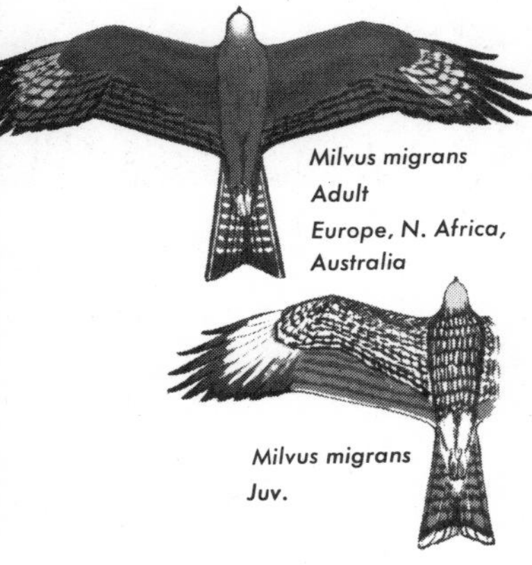
Milvus migrans Adult Europe, N. Africa, Australia

Milvus migrans Juv.

Above, crown to mantle light amber-brown, finely streaked in dark gray-brown; back, wing coverts, and secondaries, sepia, edged in light amber-brown; primaries, dark brown; slightly forked tail, dark amber-brown, narrowly barred with sepia. Face and throat, white, finely streaked with sepia; rest of underparts, dark amber-brown, streaked with black (the heaviest markings on the chest).

Juvenile—sepia, heavily streaked on the crown and underparts with ivory; feathers on other parts of the body and wings, all edged in ivory; a pale patch on the undersurface of the wing is smaller than that present in the adult or young Red Kite.

Beak, yellow (juvenile, black); cere, legs, and feet, yellow; eyes, pale grayish-yellow, surrounded by a black line. Size, 19–21 inches.

VARIATIONS

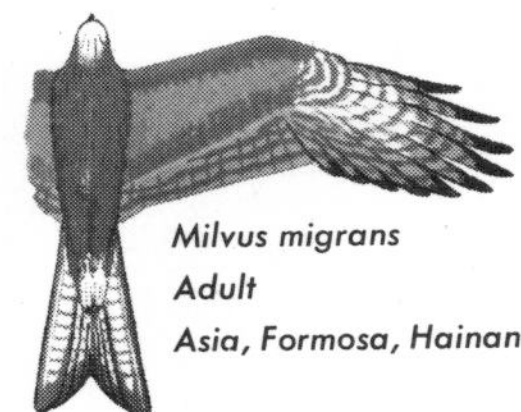
Milvus migrans Adult Asia, Formosa, Hainan

The central European, west Siberian, and north African desert birds are paler brown; the northern Asiatic individuals are generally without light amber-brown coloring, and marked on the crown and breast with white (except in Mongolia). Himalayan birds, ranging to an altitude of 8,000 feet, have a dark undersurface in flight, but those restricted to the plains of northern India and Kashmir are marked like the others with a conspicuous white patch on the wing. Moroccan and Chinese birds have darker amber-brown to rufous-brown heads; and in the rain forests of Malaysia, New Guinea, and tropical northern Australia, these kites are yellow-brown above and much darker (rufous-brown) on the underparts. Everywhere the pattern of streaking corresponds to the Black Kite described, but with differences already noted in the color of the beak. Tails are more deeply forked in individuals from Asia and Africa than in Europe. Size varies from 16–23 inches, the largest in Mongolia and the smallest in the rain forest of New Guinea.

OTHER SPECIES

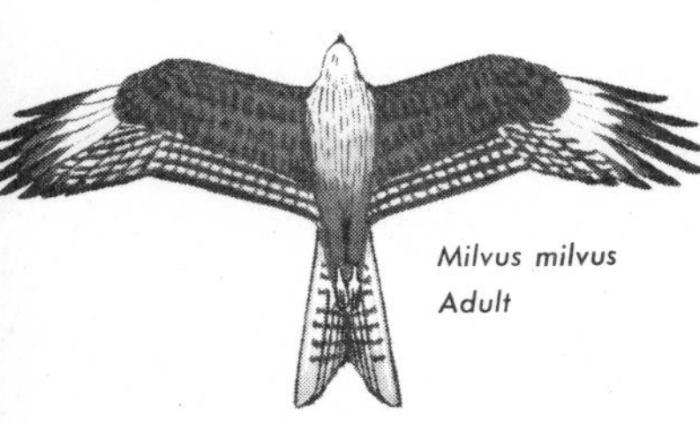
Milvus milvus Adult

The Red Kite (*M. milvus*), 22½–24 inches, of Europe, northern Africa, and Asia Minor, is as brightly colored as the rain-forest population of *M. migrans;* mantle and underparts, amber-brown heavily streaked with black and long, deeply forked, light cinnamon tail without barring on the inner rectrices. In flight, large white patches show on the underside of the wings. The Cape Verde Islands population, which is smaller, with a darker tail indistinctly barred throughout, appears to be intermediate in color between the two species of *Milvus.* (Juveniles of *M. milvus* are paler and with browner heads than adults'.)

Pair of Red Kites *(Milvus milvus)*, Europe, with downy young.—*Photograph by Eric Hosking.*

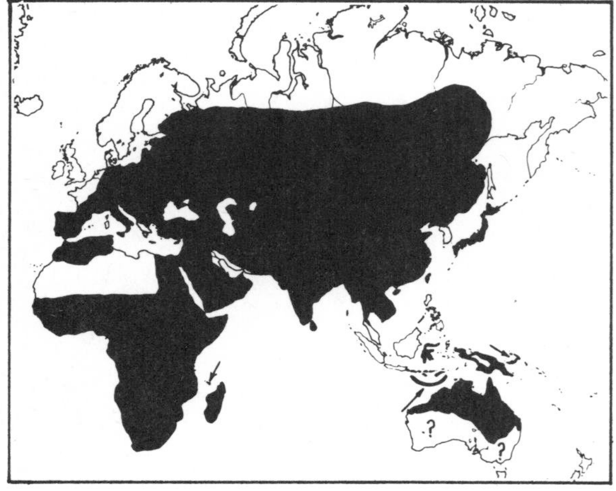

MILVUS MIGRANS

MILVUS MILVUS

HABITS

There may once have been considerable interspecific competition between the Red Kite and the Black Kite in Europe. Into historic times the Red Kite was numerous throughout western Europe in open wooded country but a tendency to become a specialized poultry-feeder caused this species to be persecuted nearly to extinction. A remnant (less than ten pairs) breeds in Wales. They have disappeared from Norway since 1900, and from Denmark, except for their reappearance on the Island of Laaland, in 1949, and only forty to sixty pairs remain in wooded parts of southern Sweden. In central Spain eight to ten pairs have been found in close association with the Black Kite. The densest population survives around ports and towns of the Cape Verde Islands and Canaries and, to a lesser extent, in the Balearic Islands. In Europe the Black Kite is more closely associated with fresh water than the Red Kite and catches more live fish.

Both species are omnivorous and will feed on any creature which is vulnerable—young birds, poultry, mammals (weasels, rabbits, mice, etc.), reptiles, amphibians, insects. (In west Africa the Black Kite also feeds on the fruit of the oil palm, like the Palm-nut Vulture.) They are second only to the vultures in carrion-eating habits and in consumption of offal and garbage. Throughout Africa, the Middle East, and Asia *M. migrans* is a common and familiar scavenger around towns, ports, and cultivated country. The Black Kites (sometimes known as Yellow-billed Kites or Pariah Kites) follow plagues of mice and insects and are also quick to gather at a grass fire, hovering in large groups over the advancing flames to pick up escaping and wounded prey.

The flight of *Milvus* is light and buoyant with long glides, slow wing beats, and frequent fluttering or twisting of the tail. Individuals hover momentarily while looking for prey. Neither Red nor Black Kite is quick enough to capture many adult birds on the wing, but hawking for insects is common. Vertebrate prey is eaten on the ground or taken to a tree branch. In display flight male and female (*M. milvus*) circle and ring around each other and hover like huge kestrels. Dives, zigzag pursuit, and tumbling with clasped claws have been observed in courtship of pairs of *M. migrans.*

Except during the breeding season, both species roost in numbers in woods or copses, and they range out to hunt in the surrounding country, often in parties, from sunup to shortly after sundown.

The Black Kite shows a stronger tendency towards sociable breeding, although solitary nests also occur, and members of a "colony" are distinctly spaced out. Old nests of ravens, crows, herons, storks, or cormorants often form the foundation, or a small structure of sticks, twigs, earth, dung, moss, and paper is built, nearly always lined with rags. The usual site is a tall tree—sometimes, in southern Europe, on the face of a cliff or, in Africa, on a rocky kloof or even a building. Both sexes share in building the nest, incubating eggs (not less than four weeks), and caring for young (42 to 43 days). The clutch size may be from one to five, but is usually three (single-brooded). White eggs are marked with a few blotches, spots, streaks, or hair-lines of sepia or reddish-brown.

Nests of the Red Kite are situated in tall deciduous trees or in pines, where available, and constructed much as those of the Black Kite. One to four (usually three) eggs are white, often faintly marked with brown but sometimes blotched or spotted reddish- to purplish-brown. The female takes the major part in nest-building, incubates alone (starting with the first egg for perhaps 28 to 30 days or longer), and broods the young, leaving the nest to hunt (male infrequently brings food). Two weeks after the eggs have hatched, both sexes bring a quantity of food to the nest. This species is also single-brooded.

Red and Black kites are both migratory from the northern parts of their Palaearctic range, as described. The tropical populations of the Black Kite, in Africa, and the Red Kite, in India, are subject to regular seasonal movements, and the Black Kite, in the interior and northern parts of Australia, to occasional drifting.

These are relatively silent birds, except in the breeding season, when the Black Kite gives a peculiar half-whinnying, half-squealing cry similar to a curlew or the young of one of the larger gulls; also "queeū-kiki-kiki-kik" and variations in alarm or anger. A display note, a soft hoarse rattle, is also recorded. The Red Kite, even less vociferous, calls to its mate in a higher-pitched mewing voice interpolated between a buteo-like "weeoo-weeoo-weeoo." A single scream serves to sound an alarm.

The Square-tailed Kite *(Lophoictinia isura)* is a rare species, widely but locally distributed throughout Australia. Most records in Western Australia are from the midlands to the southeast coast where this bird may be seen coursing low over the sand-plain scrub on long wings, like a Marsh Hawk.

GENUS *LOPHOICTINIA*

The single member of this endemic Australian genus bears a strong physical resemblance to the Red Kite (*Milvus milvus*) of Europe, but the tarsi are reticulate, not scutellate, and the tail is only slightly notched. It is rare in South Australia.

Square-tailed Kite (*Lophoictinia isura*)

DESCRIPTION (AUSTRALIA)

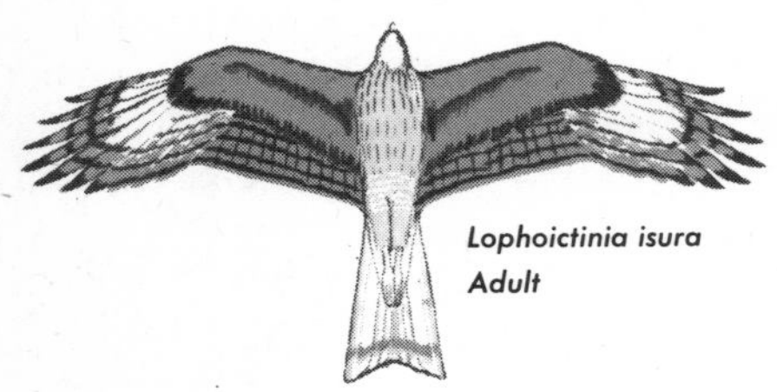

Similar to the Red Kite, but with black streaking heaviest on the chest; tail unbarred except for indistinct subterminal band.

Juvenile—paler ("more golden") than adult, without heavy black streaking on head and underparts; rump patch, "whitish." May be confused with the Marsh Harrier (*Circus aeruginosus*) in the field.

Beak, blue-gray; cere, yellow (young, flesh color); eyes, yellow (juvenile, gray-brown); legs and feet, yellow (young, grayish-white); claws, black. Size, about 20 inches.

LOPHOICTINIA ISURA

HABITS

The actions of the Square-tailed Kite are harrier-like as it quarters open country for prey, but the kite soars at a greater height and with more speed and grace than a Marsh Harrier. The Square-tailed Kite, usually seen in pairs or flocks, has a marked preference for smaller watercourses, where it breeds in adjoining belts of timber. It is a persistent hunter of young birds, also caterpillars and reptiles.

Old nests of other hawks may be used, or the usual kite stick nest is constructed in a high tree and ordinarily lined with leaves and the inner bark of gum trees. Two or three buff-white eggs are freckled or blotched reddish-brown, sometimes with underlying lavender markings.

In shape and behavior, the Australian Black-breasted Buzzard Kite *(Hamirostra melanosternon)* is unlike any other medium-sized hawk in Australia. This kite has an almost buteonine shape, soars in wide circles, often to great heights, and binds to its prey on the ground in true buzzard fashion.

GENUS *HAMIROSTRA*

The "only" buteo-like bird of prey in Australia, where there are no true buteos, is the Black-breasted Buzzard, so named for the adult of the dark phase. Light phase adults are very similar to the Australian Square-tailed Kite in color pattern.

In *Hamirostra,* however, the legs and feet are stouter with a single row of somewhat larger reticulate scales in front. The wings are shorter and more rounded; the body, heavier; and the tail, much shorter and fan-shaped (not slightly forked).

Black-breasted Buzzard Kite (*Hamirostra melanosternon*)

DESCRIPTION (AUSTRALIA)

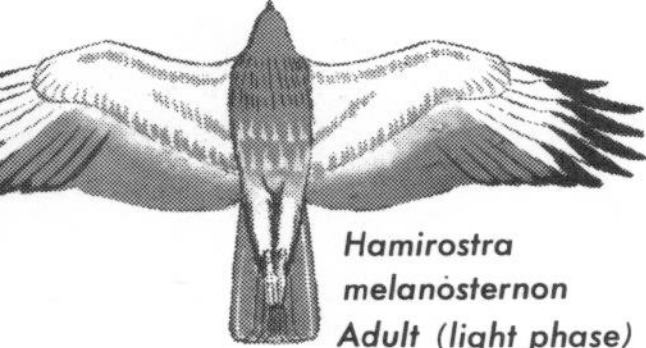
Hamirostra melanosternon Adult (light phase)

Light phase—similar to Square-tailed Kite but easily distinguished by its chunky silhouette with broad, deeply "fingered" wingtips and shorter unmarked tail.

Dark phase—head and underparts (and sometimes entire upperparts), black.

Juvenile—like adult of light phase; tail, white-tipped. (Dark phase not known in young.)

Beak, gray-brown; cere, greenish-white; eyes, hazel; legs and feet, pinkish; claws, black. Size, 20–24 inches.

HAMIROSTRA MELANOSTERNON

HABITS

This strange buteo-like kite preys mainly on lizards and rabbits, robs emus and bustards of their eggs, and occasionally eats carrion. Some observers have reported that the bird cracks the shells of emu eggs with a stone held in the beak, corroborating, at least in part, the old aboriginal story that it would drop a stone on the eggs from the air. When not soaring high, it may be seen sitting on the ground—seldom in trees, unless visiting the nest. It breeds in belts of timber on plains or along watercourses.

A typical kite nest of sticks is constructed in a tall tree, its shallow cavity lined with fresh green leaves. Two eggs are similar to those of the Wedge-tailed Eagle—white with blotches of dark chocolate and light purple.

The Brahminy Kite *(Haliastur indus)* is sacred to the god Vishnu. Near cities and towns on the Indian peninsula it is tame and fearless, and may be seen catching fish thrown up to it by pious Hindus. The bird in the photograph is in immature plumage; brown-backed, with head and under parts mottled and striped.

GENUS *HALIASTUR*

These scavenger kites of Asia and Australasia bear some physical resemblance to *Milvus*. *H. indus* extends from India to the Solomon Islands; *H. sphenurus* breeds mainly on the inland waterways of Australia, but also occurs along the coast. Both species are chunkier, with a shorter and broader wing than *Milvus*. The tail is nearly square in *H. indus* and slightly wedge-shaped in *H. sphenurus*, not notched nor forked. The beak is elongated, and the nostrils are round with a bony margin; the tarsi and feet are completely bare. Females are only slightly larger than males.

Brahminy Kite (*Haliastur indus*)

DESCRIPTION (ASIA)

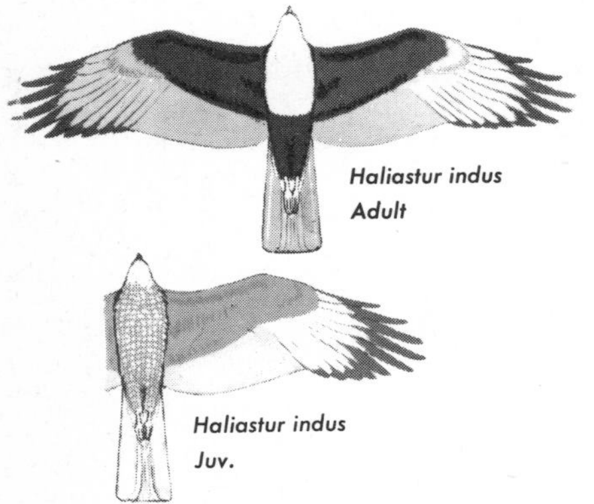

Head, neck, breast, and upper belly, pure white with fine black streaking (less noticeable in older birds); back, wings, lower belly, and thighs, uniform chestnut.

Immature—similar to adult, but head, breast, and upper belly, mottled and striped gray-brown.

Juvenile—head, neck, and entire underparts, cinnamon-brown, distinctly barred and striped black; back, wings, and tail, sepia, feather-edged with light amber-brown.

Beak, ivory-gray with yellow tip; eyes, brown; legs and feet, dull yellow. Size, 17–20 inches.

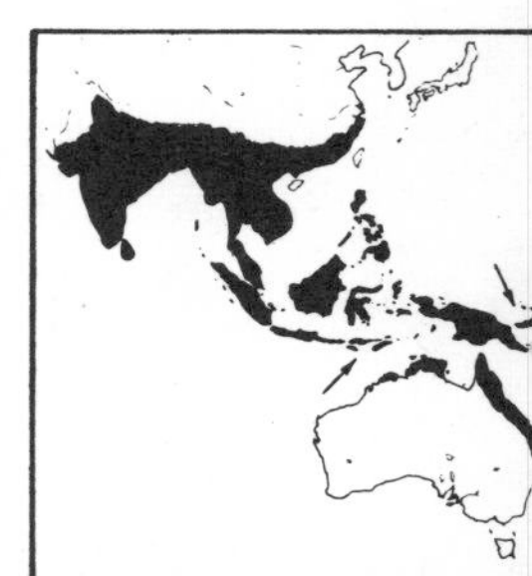
HALIASTUR INDUS

VARIATIONS

In the Australian region it is popularly named the White-headed, or Red-backed, Sea Eagle for its eagle-like silhouette. The white plumage of its head, neck, and breast is unmarked. (Solomon Islands birds have very large beaks, entirely yellow, like the sea eagles'.)

OTHER SPECIES

The Whistling Kite (*H. sphenurus*), 20–22 inches, is sandy-colored, mottled and streaked dark brown and light amber-brown above; sandy below with dark brown feather-edging on breast and belly; wings, dark brown; tail, medium olive-brown, tipped in sandy. (The juveniles are similar, but lighter, and have barred tails.)

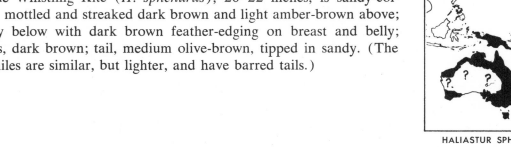

HALIASTUR SPHENURUS

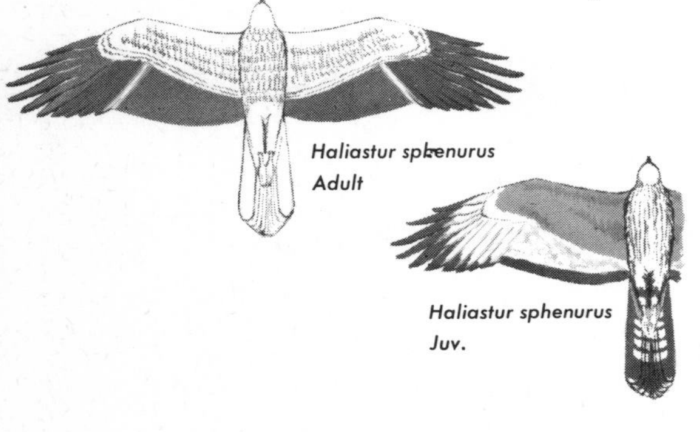

HABITS

The favorite haunts of the Brahminy Kite on the Indian peninsula are harbors, riverbanks, mangrove swamps, and marshy paddy fields where it may be observed singly, in pairs, or parties (sometimes hundreds), seated on the bunds and crossbunds. In the Himalayas, the species ranges up to 6,000 feet.

This bird feeds on offal or garbage (which it prefers to pick off the surface of the water), on young or wounded birds and poultry, and on dead fish and live fish either stolen from fishermen's nets or captured near the shore.

A shrill wheezy squeal announces the presence of the Brahminy Kite as it sails high, turning its head from side to side searching for prey. When it sights something of interest, the kite performs several circular maneuvers and descends "like a whirlwind" to snatch away the tidbit—then sits on a neighboring tree to devour it. Chicks, frogs, crabs, lizards, small snakes, insects, mice, and shrews are taken in this manner, either from the water or the ground. During the monsoons, land crabs in inundated country become staple fare, along with winged termites, which are hawked as they emerge from the rain-sodden ground.

Other populations throughout Asia and Australasia have a similar preference for scavenging and hunting the coastal bays and inland waterways (to 5,200 feet in the highlands of New Guinea). The Australian representative is normally a bird of the northern mangrove-bordered coast, but frequently drifts far inland along the margins of rivers.

The Indian kites nest in December and have a second brood in June. A loose structure of sticks and twigs is built high in the fork of a tree and is sometimes lined with rags, paper, leaves, dried mud, or cow dung. Large trees, near water, are preferred —casuarinas, banyans, pipals, mangoes—and especially palms (near the coasts). Sometimes the nest tree stands in water, a castle surrounded by a protective moat against the intrusion of men or monkeys, which are the chief enemies of this bird. Two (perhaps three) eggs are laid, which are grayish-white, scantily speckled reddish-brown. Both sexes share in nest building, incubation (about four weeks), and feeding the young. The female, however, does most of the incubating.

Local drifting movements of *H. indus* are probably connected with seasonal rains and consequent vulnerability of certain kinds of prey.

The Whistling Kite (*H. sphenurus*) is popularly named for its loud call "chew-ew-ew" while soaring high overhead. It is a species of the inland waterways and coast of Australia. Although called an "eagle," it flocks in the manner of kites, and its choice of nesting place, nest and eggs, and eating habits does not appear to differ much from that of *H. indus.* This kite will, however, occasionally take over an old hawk or crow's nest rather than build its own. It seems to be more predatory in Western Australia, where it is referred to as the "main rabbit-eating hawk," but also eats carrion and gathers in abundance wherever there is a locust or caterpillar plague.

Adult Brahminy Kite *(Haliastur indus).—Photographed at the National Zoological Park.*

SUBFAMILY ACCIPITRINAE

(Short-winged and Related Woods Hawks, Long-tailed Hawks, and Savanna Hawks)

Large size distinguishes the Goshawk *(Accipiter gentilis)* from other North American accipiters. It also has a distinct white eyebrow, in adult and juvenile plumage. The bird shown here is a juvenile.

GENUS *ACCIPITER*

The forest hawks belong to the largest and one of the most widely distributed of all the Falconiform genera. The comparatively sedentary tropical species are many compared to only a few in temperate climates.

There are only three accipiters in North America, but Middle America, the Caribbean, and South America together have six species—including the white-breasted and red-thighed variations of the North American Sharp-shinned Hawk (*A. striatus*). Similarly, there are only three species in north temperate Eurasia, but Africa has seven or eight—including populations of the Middle Eastern and Asiatic Shikra (*A. badius*); Madagascar, three; and South Asia, six species in the region from India, Ceylon, Car Nicobar, the Indochina peninsula, and southern China through Malaysia, Hainan, Formosa, and the Philippines. Of the four or five species in the Celebes and Moluccas, only one, the Crested Goshawk (*A. griseiceps*), also belongs to this south Asiatic grouping. Three accipiters found on the Australian mainland and Tasmania have close relatives on New Guinea and the surrounding islands, which are heavily populated with eight endemic species. Five of the seven species in the southwestern Pacific show close ties to New Guinea.

Similarity of young, and sometimes even of adult, plumages of the accipiters in these various regions makes it extremely difficult to identify them, especially in tropical and subtropical regions where the confusion is compounded by the arrival of migratory birds from the north.

Common accipiter characteristics are the relatively short, deep bill (without distinct tooth or notch); sparsely bristled lores; long tarsi (usually scutellate, but sometimes partly feathered in front); and long slender toes with conspicuous bumps underneath for grasping. Variations in the length of tarsi and toes may be correlated with preferences for different kinds of foods and ways of hunting. The Spot-tailed Sparrowhawk of the Celebes (*A. trinotatus*), which feeds mostly on lizards and other reptiles that it takes from the ground, has very long tarsi and short toes.

Short rounded wings and a long tail afford greater control as the forest hawk threads its way swiftly through tree branches and bushes to secure its prey. Some accipiters have a slightly longer wing or longer tail than others. The shape of the tail is usually square or notched when folded and slightly rounded in flight. The exceptions are important field marks. In North America the Cooper's Hawk (*A. cooperii*) and the Goshawk (*A. gentilis*) have distinctly rounded tails, even when folded; the Eurasian Sparrowhawk (*A. nisus*) has an almost forked tail; and Bürger's Goshawk of New Guinea (*A. bürgersi*) has a sharply squared-off tail.

Females are generally browner above than males, but, as will be seen, sexual differences in the coloring of the underparts are extremely varied. The female of the Eurasian Sparrowhawk has somber dark brown barring below in contrast to the bright amber-brown barring of the male. In the Cooper's Hawk and the Sharp-shinned Hawk, the difference is only one of paler barring in the female; but in the Shikra and related species, the female is more heavily and brightly barred below. In other instances (*A. francesii* of Madagascar and *A. novaehollandiae* in New Guinea, for example), the males tend to be plain-breasted and the females, barred below. Aside from these sexual differences, there are many color phases: two or more are prevalent in the same localities in the Neotropical region, Australasia, and the southwest Pacific islands.

The greatest difference between the sexes in most species of accipiters is size, with females so much larger than males that the biggest females of a small species are often comparable in size to the smallest males of a larger one. The female North American Goshawk averages 37 ounces, nearly one-third heavier than the male. Storer suggests that this may have been the result of intraspecific competition. Much larger size in one member of a pair increases the size range of food animals which can be taken by them. The female Sharp-shinned Hawk is able to take the same prey as the male Cooper's Hawk, and the female Cooper's Hawk, prey as large as the male Goshawk.

The smaller accipiters appear to mature sooner than the Goshawks. Cooper's Hawks, Sharp-shins, and Eurasian Sparrowhawks begin to take on their adult dress and may breed in the spring of their second year. Even though Northern Goshawks occasionally breed in their second year, they are not fully adult until the spring of the third year. There are, of course, exceptions to this correlation of smaller size with earlier maturity. At least three Asiatic sparrowhawks (*A. gularis, A. virgatus,* and *A. soloensis*) evidently have distinct juvenile, immature, and adult plumages.

There are more changes in eye color in the larger accipiters than in any other large birds of prey. In captive North American Goshawks, John Hamlet noticed the following changes in eye color over five years: gray to blue-gray to yellow in the juvenile; orange-yellow in the immature of the second year; orange in the adult of the third year; red-orange in its fourth year; and scarlet in its fifth year. Eye color in European Goshawks evidently changes from yellow, in the juvenile, to yellow-orange in the second year, and orange-red in the third year, but never becomes bright red. Yellow-eyed juvenile Cooper's Hawks become, in three to five years, orange- to red-eyed adults, and in a number of other accipiters there is a change from yellow to orange, orange-red, or red, although there is not enough information to tell us how long it takes. However, many of the small bird hawks— the Sparrowhawks and Sharp-shinned Hawks and their kin in appearance and habits—start life as nestlings with gray or pale bluish-gray eyes which quickly change to greenish-yellow and turn, as adulthood is reached, to bright chrome yellow.

We have attempted to compare birds of similar size. Many tropical accipiters were once placed in a separate genus (*Astur*) with the Goshawks on the basis of similarities in toe structure that have since proven too variable to justify associating these small hawks that prey mainly on insects, small reptiles, and small birds with the large and powerful Northern Goshawks. Consequently we refer to them as other species of sparrowhawks (not goshawks).

Northern Goshawk (*Accipiter gentilis*)

DESCRIPTION (NORTH AMERICA)

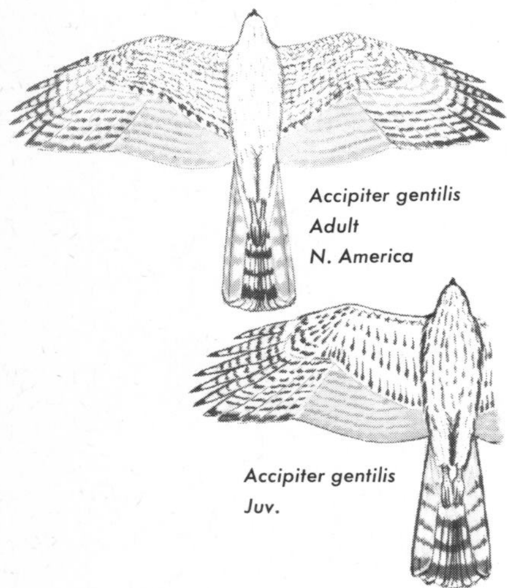

Accipiter gentilis Adult N. America

Accipiter gentilis Juv.

Above, capped in dark brown or black with conspicuous white eyebrows and white mottling at the nape; back and wing coverts, gray-brown, heavily washed with slate-gray; wings and tail, gray-brown, barred darker, the latter tipped in white. Forehead, cheeks, and throat, as well as entire underparts, white, faintly mottled gray-brown and finely streaked dark brown.

Immature—like adult, but with heavier mottling and broader streaking below.

Juvenile—also eyebrowed; brown above, streaked on the head and feather-edged on the back and wing coverts with white or light cinnamon; wings and tail, more distinctly barred than older birds' and white-tipped; below, white to light cinnamon, heavily blobbed with dark brown.

Beak, blue-black; eyes, red (juvenile, yellow); feet, yellow; claws, blue-black. Size, 20–24 inches.

VARIATIONS

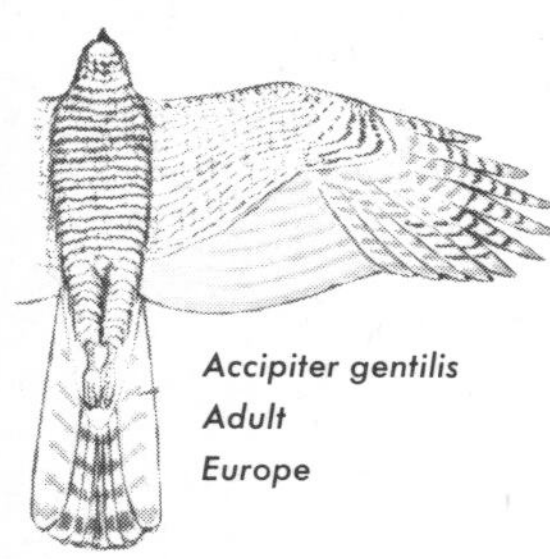

Accipiter gentilis Adult Europe

Old World Goshawks in the temperate zone are slightly smaller and range from yellow-brown (Germany, Sweden, Poland, middle Russia) to dark brown above (Italy). The underparts appear heavily barred, not mottled. Northern individuals are considerably whiter—marked only with medium ivory-gray patches on the head and back, and faintly streaked and barred below (eastern Siberia). Size, 18–20 inches, the northern populations slightly larger than those at the southern limits of the range.

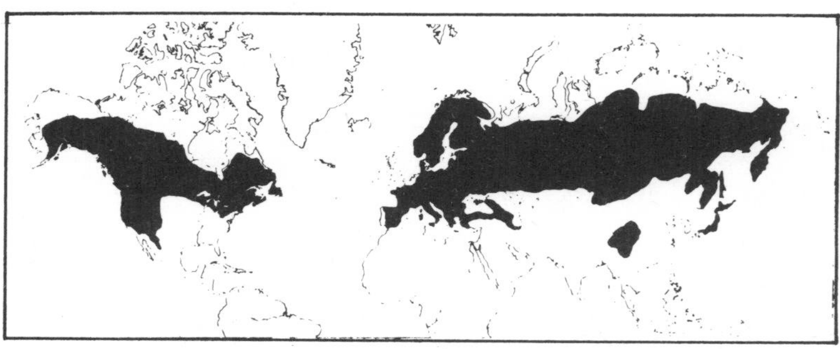

ACCIPITER GENTILIS

OTHER SPECIES OF GOSHAWKS

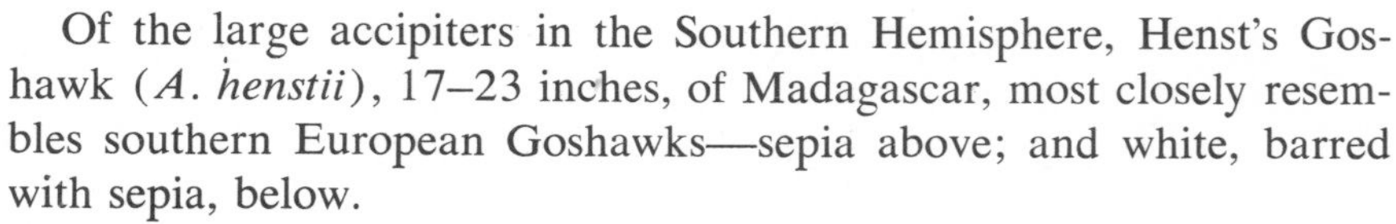

Of the large accipiters in the Southern Hemisphere, Henst's Goshawk (*A. henstii*), 17–23 inches, of Madagascar, most closely resembles southern European Goshawks—sepia above; and white, barred with sepia, below.

On the African continent the Black Goshawk (*A. melanoleucus*), 16–20 inches, is of slighter build and the black upperparts contrast with mostly white underparts, barred black only on the sides of the breast and flanks; thighs, black. A black phase also occurs.

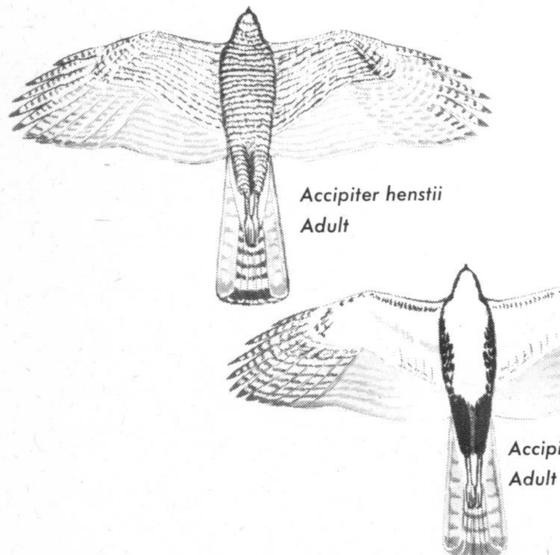

Accipiter henstii Adult

Accipiter melanoleucus Adult

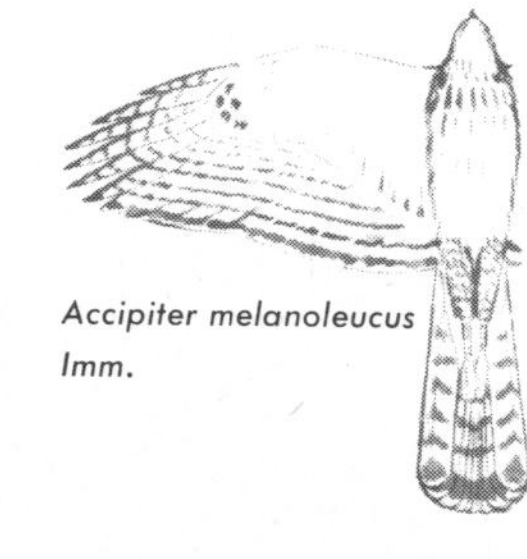

Accipiter melanoleucus Imm.

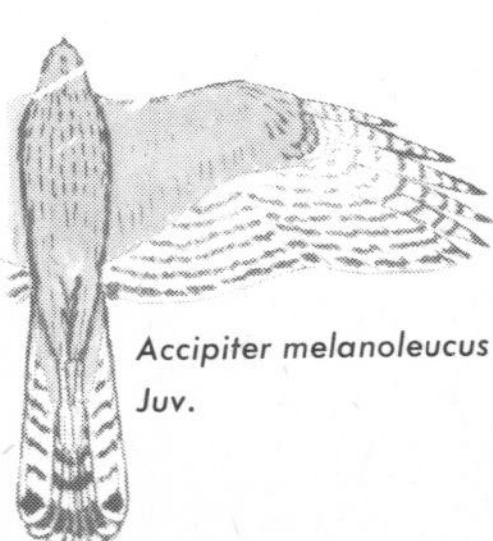

Accipiter melanoleucus Juv.

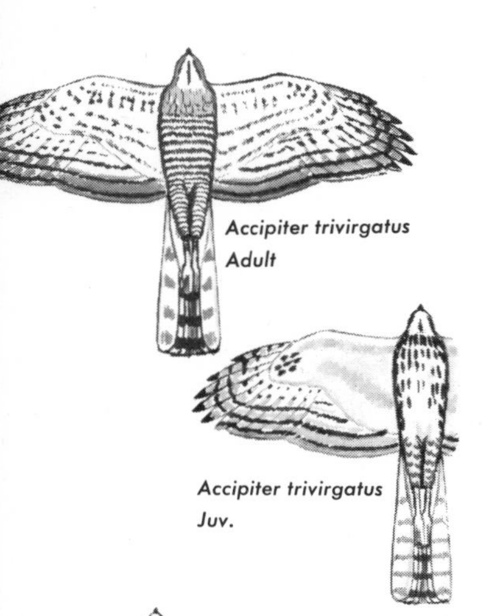
Accipiter trivirgatus Adult

Accipiter trivirgatus Juv.

ACCIPITER TRIVIRGATUS

The Crested Goshawk (*A. trivirgatus*), 12–16 inches, resembles the Crested Cuckoo-Falcon (*Aviceda jerdoni*), which is found throughout its range. The *male* Crested Goshawk has a grayer mantle than the female and may also have a nearly plain cinnamon or cinnamon-brown chest. *Female,* brown above, tends to be more distinctly streaked amber-brown to dark brown on the chest. In both sexes the white throat patch is divided by a median black streak and the lower breast, belly, and thighs are white, coarsely barred with cinnamon, to dark brown. The largest individuals may be found at the northern edge of the range from northern India to Formosa; the smallest, in the Philippines.

The closely related Celebes Crested Goshawk (*A. griseiceps*) is comparable in size to the Crested Goshawk (*A. trivirgatus*) in the Philippines but is differently marked in the adult plumage with slate-blue head and pure white underparts, heavily striped dark brown. (Juveniles—brown above, with light heads streaked dark brown, and light underparts, the streaking fine and sparse, and the thighs brown-barred.)

Meyer's Goshawk (*A. meyerianus*), 19–21 inches, found in the mountain forests of Jobi, Gilolo, New Britain, Ceram, and the Solomon Islands is very similar to Bürger's Goshawk (*A. bürgersi*) of the mountains of eastern New Guinea. Both are large powerful accipiters resembling the Northern Goshawk; black above in the adult plumage and white below, finely streaked with black (sides and flanks streaked and barred). An adult (possibly immature) male of *A. bürgersi,* described by H. Kirke Swann, retained some of the "chestnut-rufous" feather-edging characteristic of the juvenile on the upperparts, especially on the upperwing coverts, and the undertail coverts and thighs were barred with black and "chestnut-rufous." Black phases occur in the two species.

Accipiter griseiceps Adult

ACCIPITER GRISEICEPS

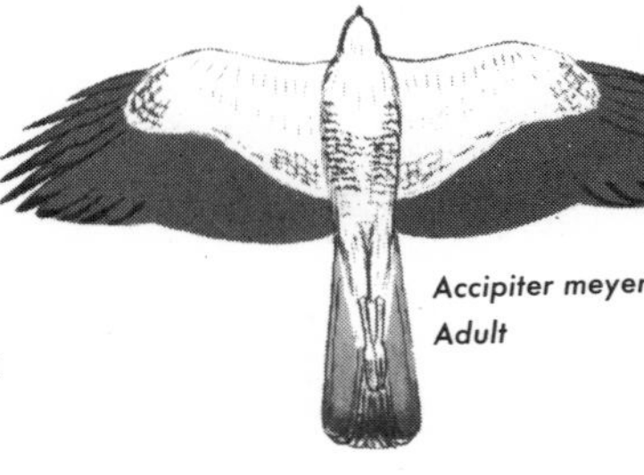
Accipiter meyerianus Adult

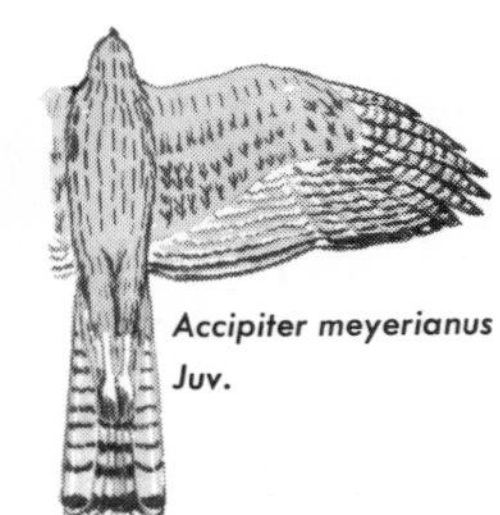
Accipiter meyerianus Juv.

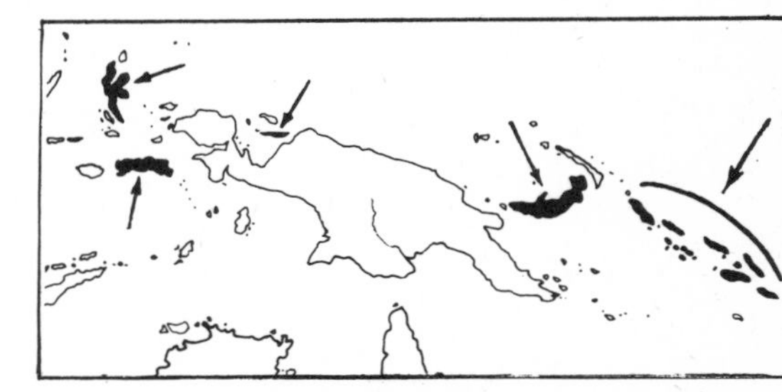
ACCIPITER MEYERIANUS

Accipiter bürgersi Juv.

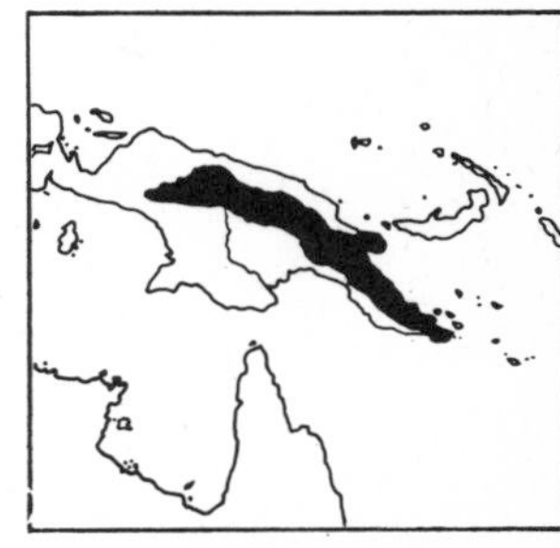
ACCIPITER BURGERSI

The smaller Gray-headed Goshawk (*A. princeps*), 15–17 inches, of New Britain is medium gray above and white below, faintly barred on the breast with silver-gray.

Accipiter princeps Adult

ACCIPITER PRINCEPS

The Brown Goshawk (*A. fasciatus*), 12½–18 inches, collared and barred below with amber-brown, breeds in Tasmania and all parts of Australia and is widely distributed in the tropics from Christmas Island in the Indian Ocean through the Lesser Sundas and Timor to New Guinea, New Caledonia, Lifu, Loyalty Islands, and Fiji eastwards. In different localities the flanks and thighs are either predominantly white or light amber-brown, finely barred with white.

Accipiter fasciatus Adult

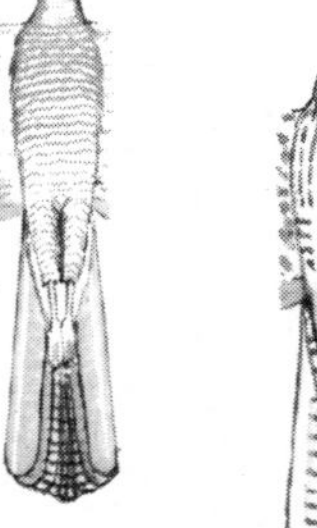
Accipiter fasciatus Adult

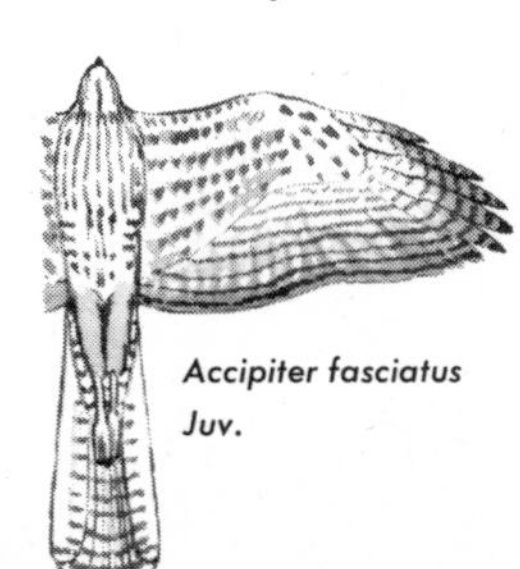
Accipiter fasciatus Juv.

ACCIPITER FASCIATUS

Its coloring is strikingly dissimilar to that of the Variable Goshawk, also called the White Goshawk of Australia and Tasmania, 16½–20 inches (two distinct color phases of *A. novaehollandiae*): white phase, pure white above and below, and gray phase, medium gray above and pure white or faintly barred with light gray below. The breeding population of Tasmania is entirely of the white phase, but on the continent white and gray phase birds are equally widespread.

North of Australia the hawks of this species are much smaller (from 11 inches in the southwestern Pacific islands to 16 inches in New Guinea). The New Guinea white phase is immaculate, but the gray phase differs—dark gray above and medium vinaceous to dark amber-brown below. Melanistic (all gray) individuals also occur in Netherlands New Guinea. It is in this area also (Snow Mountains) that the females of the gray phase are somewhat barred below, and the juveniles vary in the coloring of the underparts—some "red-breasted" and others "white-breasted." Throughout the Sundas, the Bismarck Archipelago, and northern Melanesia, upperparts range from dove-gray to slate-gray, the birds being frequently "red-collared"; and underparts, from medium vinaceous to medium sienna—sometimes with indistinct white barring on the belly. This barring may be a regional variation (as on Great Banda Island), but in some localities there is sexual dimorphism; males are plain-breasted, and females, barred. The Moluccan population is sometimes considered to be a distinct species (*A. griseogularis*). The juveniles of most of these tropical and subtropical Goshawks follow the *A. gentilis* pattern with certain modifications in southern Asia and the southwest Pacific islands, where they are usually darker above, feathered-edged in tones of amber-brown, and either white with contrasting ferruginous thighs or entirely ferruginous below but characteristically streaked on the chest and barred on the flanks and thighs in dark brown.

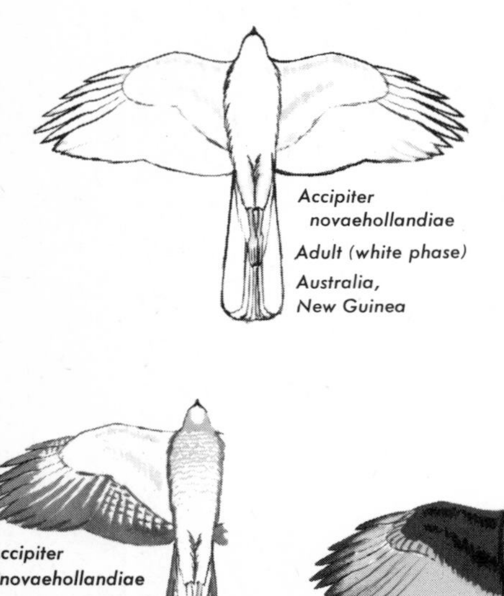

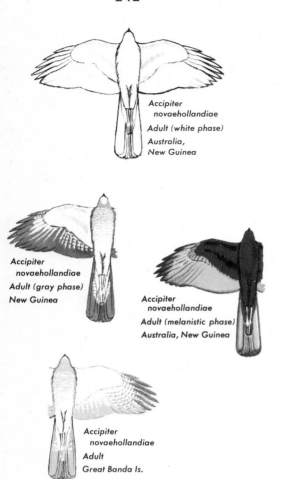

Accipiter novaehollandiae
Adult (melanistic phase)
Australia, New Guinea

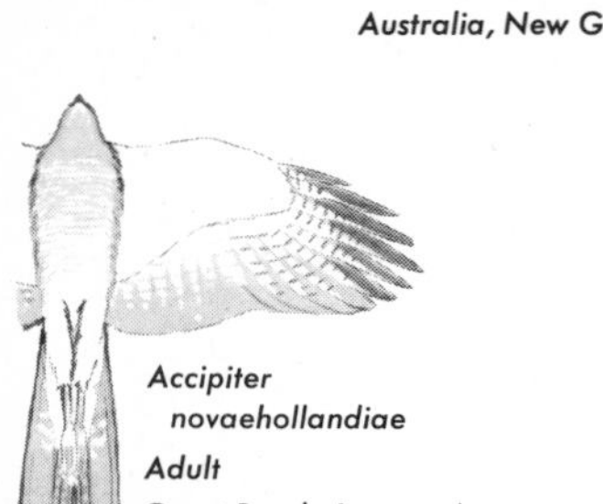

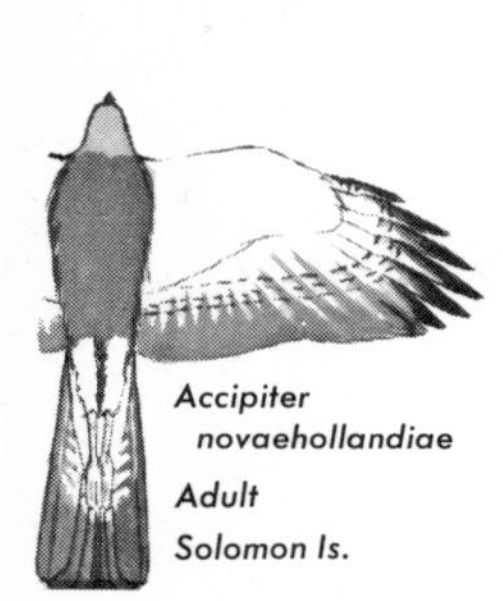

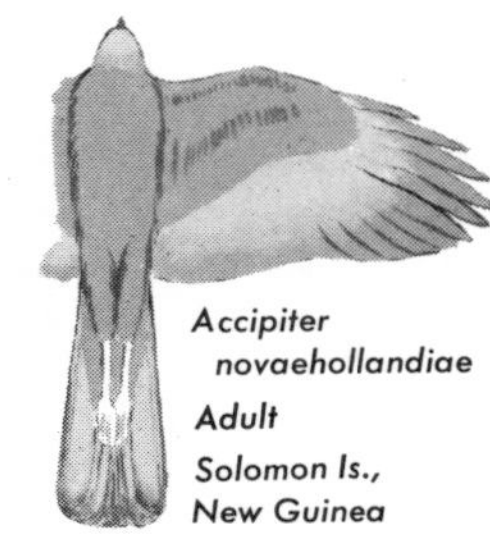

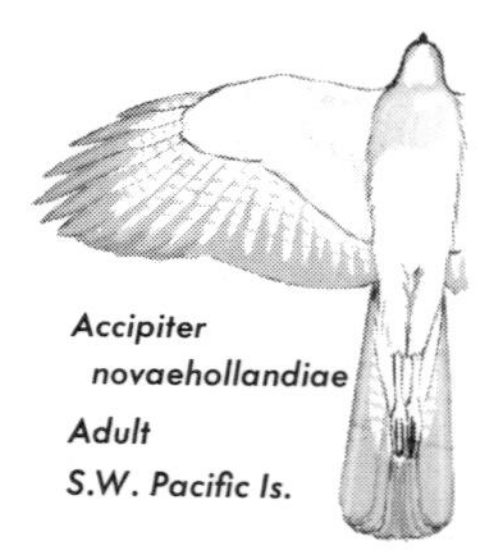

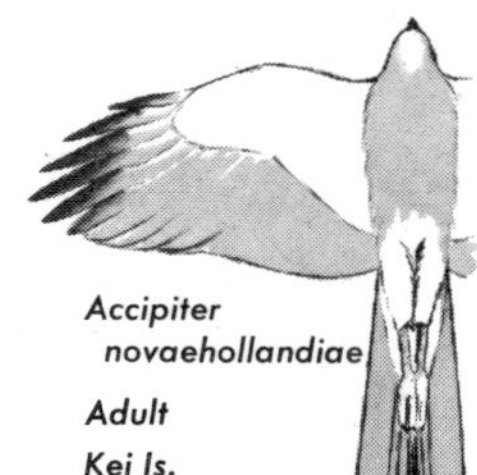

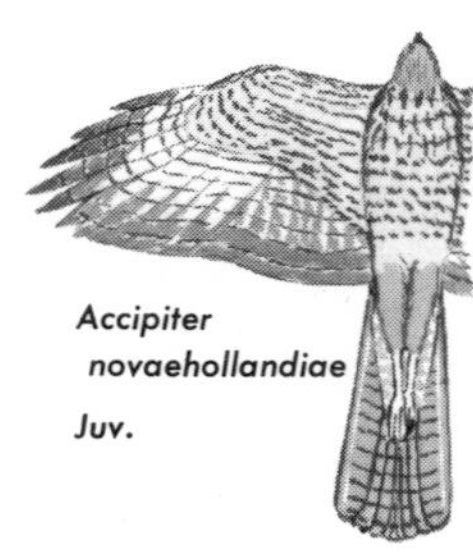

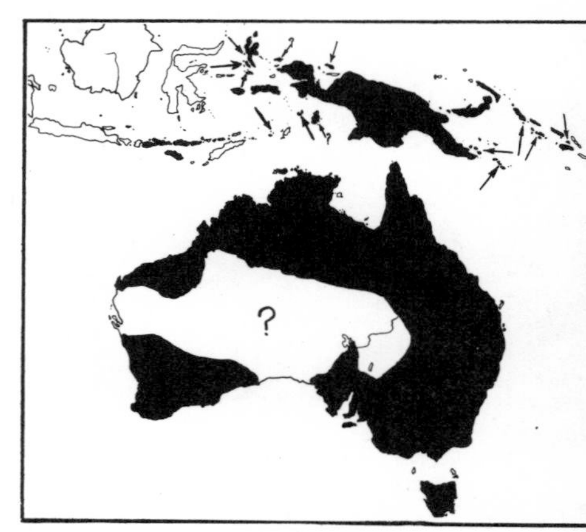

ACCIPITER NOVAEHOLLANDIAE

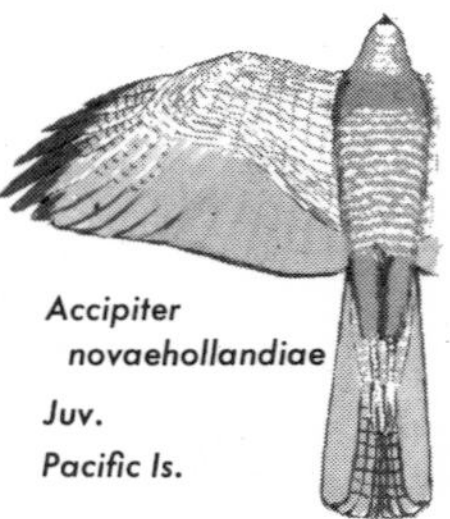

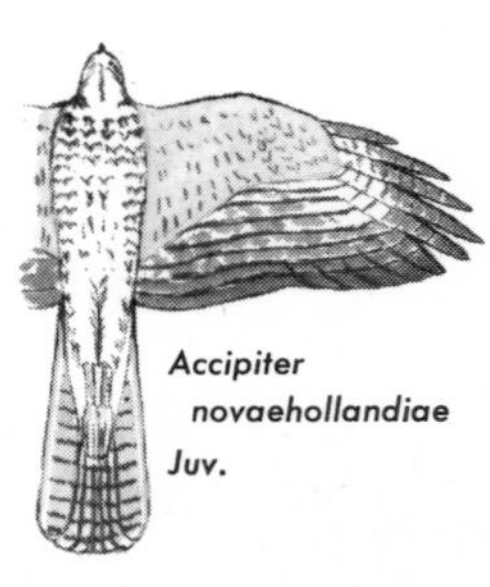

Adult Cooper's Hawk (*Accipiter cooperii*).

Cooper's Hawk (*Accipiter cooperii*)

DESCRIPTION (NORTH AMERICA)

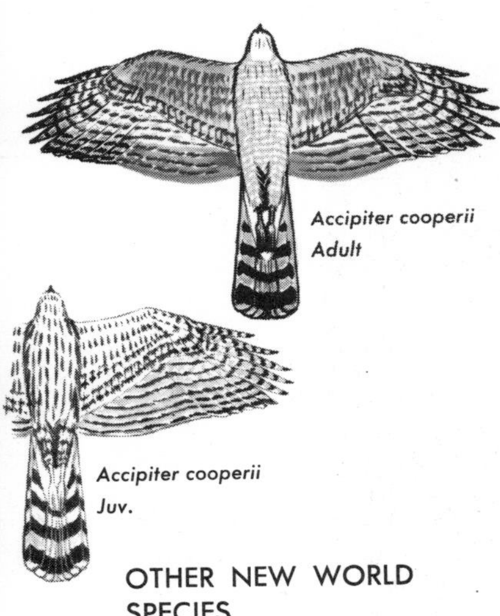

Accipiter cooperii Adult

Accipiter cooperii Juv.

Smaller than North American Goshawk, *without white eyebrows;* white spots or faint tawny collar at the nape variable and sometimes not present; underparts barred yellow-brown to tawny. (Females are browner above and tend to be paler below than males.)

Juvenile—brown above, with amber-brown, streaked head and mantle, also white spots at the nape; back, feather-edged amber-brown and spotted white; below, white, streaked and blobbed rufous-brown to chocolate, the breast often suffused with light amber-brown.

Beak, black; eyes, orange-red (juvenile, yellow); tarsi and toes, deep lemon-yellow. Size, 15–18 inches.

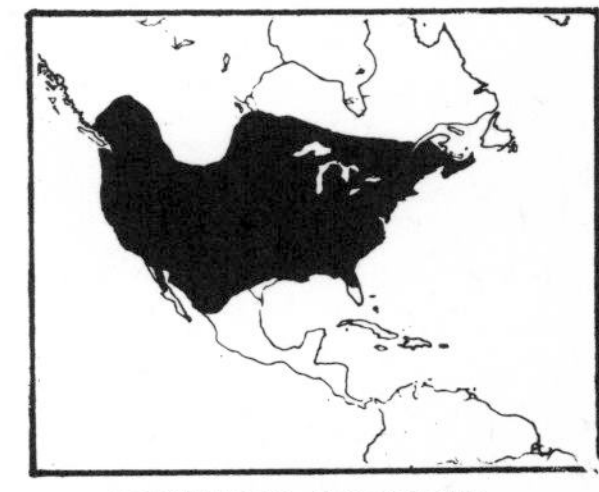

ACCIPITER COOPERII

OTHER NEW WORLD SPECIES

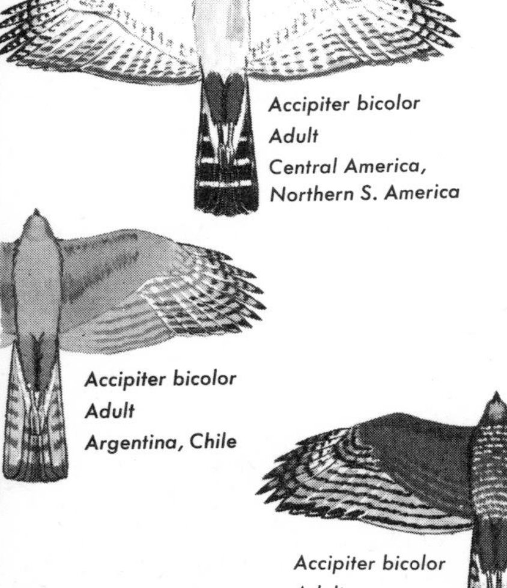

Accipiter bicolor Adult Central America, Northern S. America

Accipiter bicolor Adult Argentina, Chile

The small Neotropical version of the Cooper's Hawk is the yellow-eyed Bicolored Hawk (*A. bicolor*), 13–15 inches, generally varying from silver-gray to medium gray below with bright ferruginous thighs. In temperate Chile and Argentina, however, a barred variety occurs; underparts, barred amber-brown and white with overtones of gray. All others in this region have patches of amber-brown coloring that blend with the medium gray of the underparts. Both phases are always ferruginous-thighed.

From Mexico to the Matto Grosso, Brazil, bicolored juveniles may be either immaculate amber-brown below or white to sandy below with amber-brown thighs; in southern South America, the young of the barred variety have darkly streaked breasts and the sides of the body and thighs are barred.

ACCIPITER BICOLOR

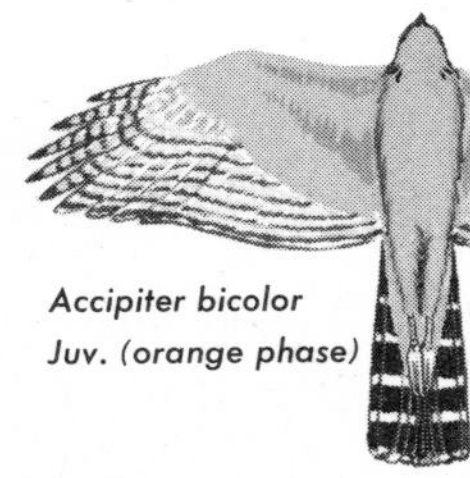

Accipiter bicolor Adult Argentina, Chile

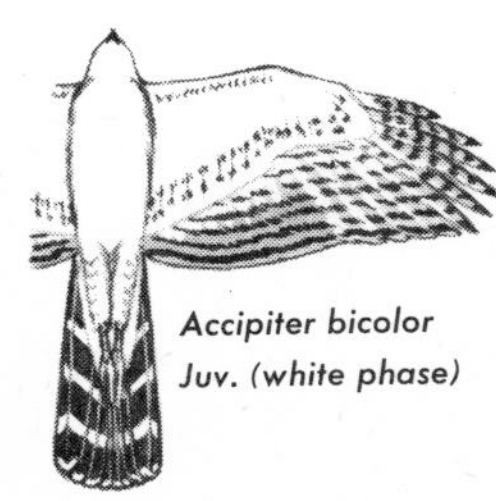

Accipiter bicolor Juv. (orange phase)

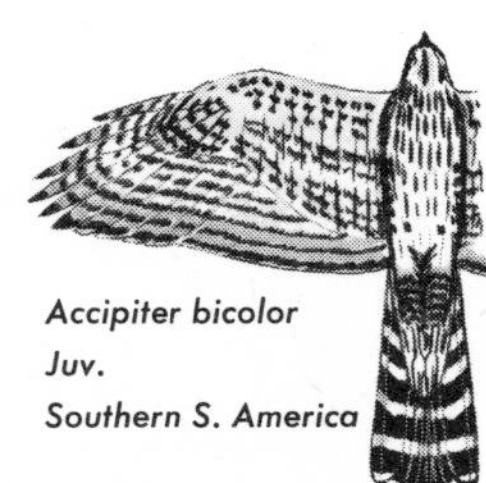

Accipiter bicolor Juv. (white phase)

Accipiter bicolor Juv. Southern S. America

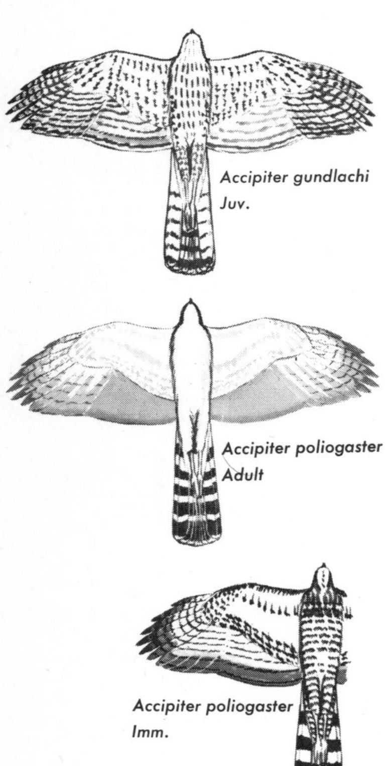

ACCIPITER GUNDLACH

Now rare in the wooded lowlands of Cuba, Gundlach's Hawk (*A. gundlachi*), 16–19 inches, has a rounded tail and is barred below like the Cooper's Hawk, but its legs and feet are much heavier.

The Gray-bellied Hawk (*A. poliogaster*), 17–19 inches, an uncommon hawk ranging locally from Colombia and the Guianas to southeastern Brazil, Paraguay, and northeastern Argentina, is entirely white or light gray below in adult plumage. A nearly unbarred underwing surface is distinctive; both the white-breasted juveniles of the Bicolored Hawk and the white-breasted variety of the smaller Sharp-shinned Hawk in South America have barred wings.

The young of *A. poliogaster* are so strikingly different that, until recently, they were considered a distinct species, *A. pectoralis.* Marked with a ferruginous collar at the nape (extending to the sides of the face), a brilliantly streaked chest, and heavy dark brown barring below, the immatures seem to be mimicking *Spizaetus ornatus,* the Ornate Hawk-Eagle.

ACCIPITER POLIOGAST

North American Sharp-shinned Hawk (*Accipiter striatus*).—*Photograph by Heinz Meng.*

Sharp-shinned Hawk (*Accipiter striatus*)

DESCRIPTION (NORTH AMERICA)

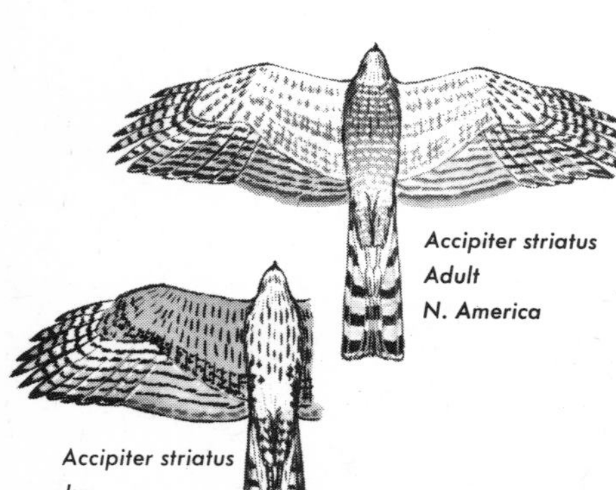

Similar to Cooper's Hawk, but smaller; has a *square* (not rounded) tail. The females are also browner above and paler below than males.

Juvenile—less conspicuously feather-edged and spotted above than young Cooper's Hawk (sometimes immaculate); underparts white to sandy, streaked and barred cinnamon-brown to chocolate.

Beak, black; eyes, bright yellow; (juveniles, greenish-yellow); tarsi and toes, yellow. Size, 10–14 inches.

ACCIPITER STRIATUS

VARIATIONS

In northern Mexico and the Caribbean, Sharp-shinned Hawks have solid bright ferruginous thighs (except barred, in Hispaniolan and Cuban populations) and are white below, barred with light amber-brown to gray-brown, some with a definite amber-brown suffusion on the breast. From Chiapas, Mexico, southward through Central America, they are white below and sandy-thighed; in the Andes of Colombia and Venezuela, they may be of this white-breasted variety or barred below with bright amber-brown thighs; continuing through the Andes to southern South America, they are completely light amber-brown below, very faintly barred medium gray and white. In Bolivia, Brazil, and Argentina the Sharp-shinned Hawk assumes a white-breasted plumage, barred and finely streaked below as in North America, but with patches of sienna coloring on the sides of the body and sienna thighs. These forest hawks range well up into the mountains and are comparable in size to the northern Sharp-shins.

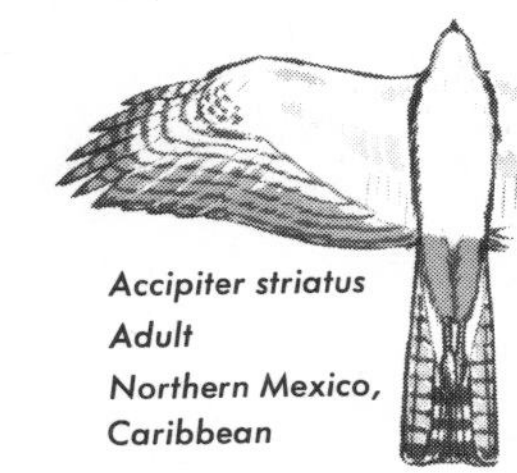
Accipiter striatus Adult Northern Mexico, Caribbean

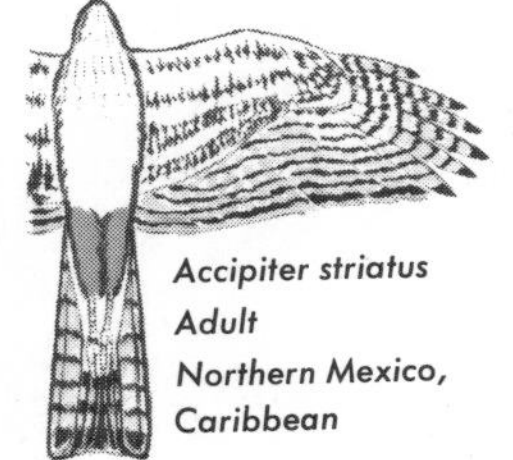
Accipiter striatus Adult Northern Mexico, Caribbean

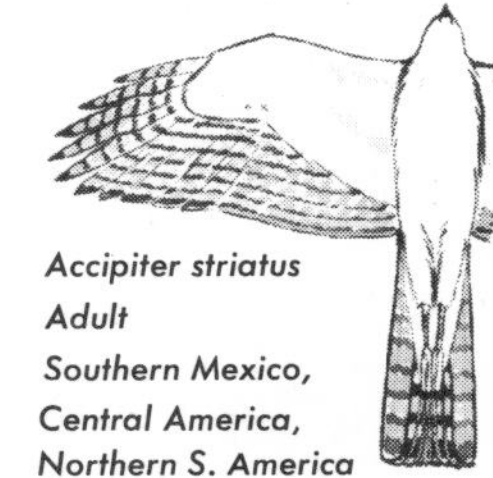
Accipiter striatus Adult Southern Mexico, Central America, Northern S. America

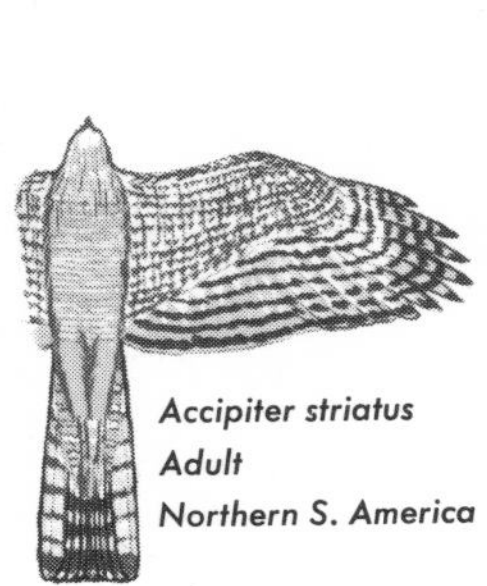
Accipiter striatus Adult Northern S. America

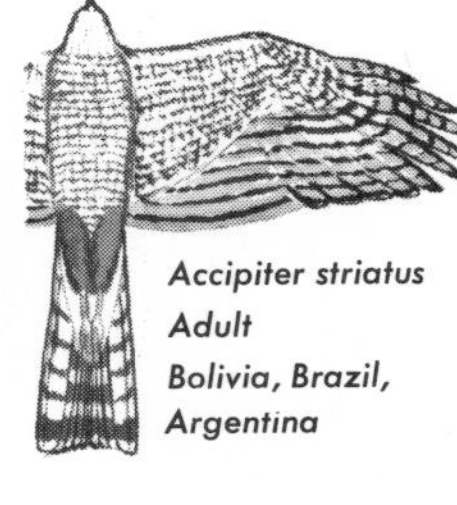
Accipiter striatus Adult Bolivia, Brazil, Argentina

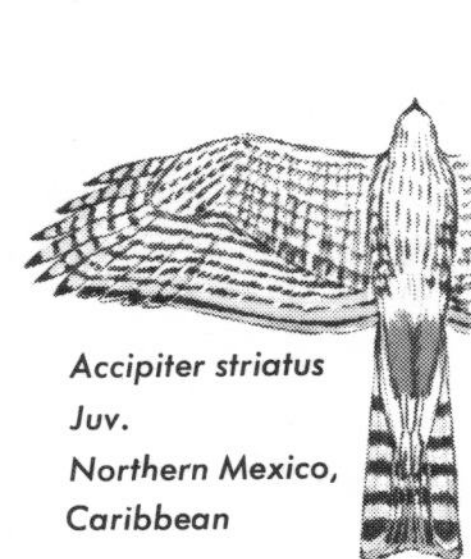
Accipiter striatus Juv. Northern Mexico, Caribbean

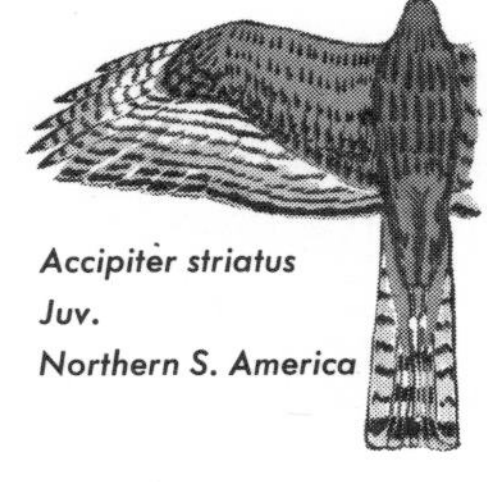
Accipiter striatus Juv. Northern S. America

OTHER NEW WORLD SPECIES

The Tiny Hawk (*A. superciliosus*), 8½–10 inches, ranging from Nicaragua south through northern South America and Brazil to Paraguay and northern Argentina, has orange feet and orange-red eyes; underparts, white, finely and uniformly barred dark olive-brown. (Juvenile, browner above and sandy below, barred amber-brown.) The Semicollared Hawk (*A. collaris*), about 12 inches, of Ecuador, Colombia, and Venezuela, appears white, barred with amber-brown below. (Young, black-capped and sienna-backed with black spotting like a kestrel, the sienna tail barred black; below, sandy, barred amber-brown.)

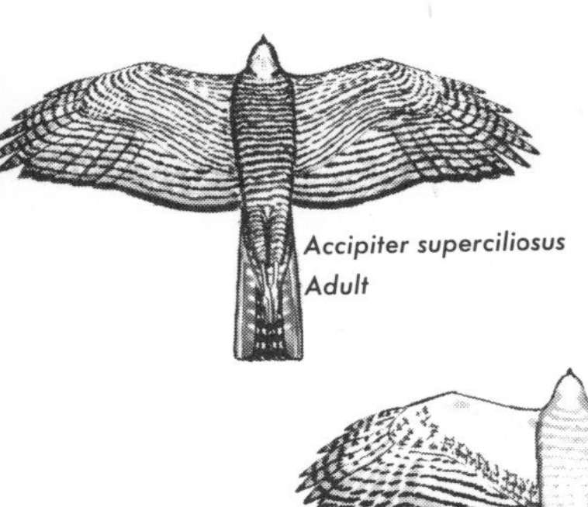
Accipiter superciliosus Adult

Accipiter superciliosus Juv.

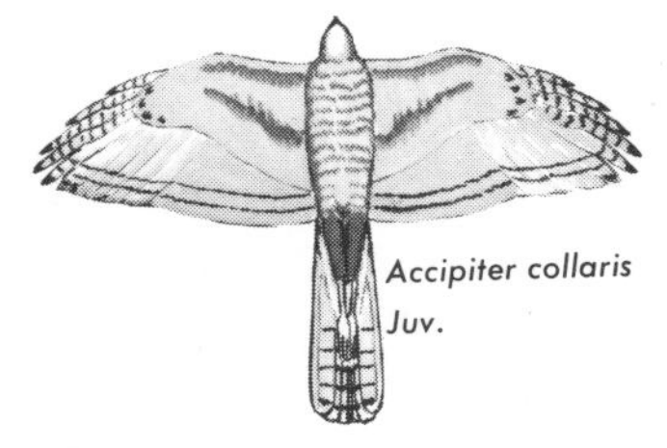
Accipiter collaris Juv.

ACCIPITER SUPERCILIOSUS

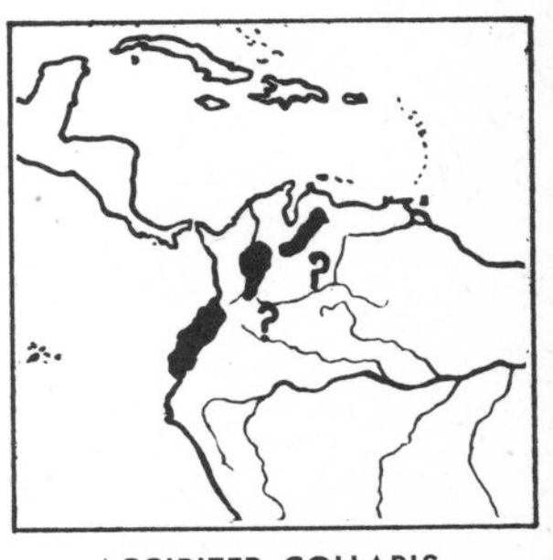
ACCIPITER COLLARIS

Female Eurasian Sparrowhawk *(Accipiter nisus)* at the nest with downy young—*Photograph by Eric Hosking.*

Eurasian Sparrowhawk (*Accipiter nisus*)

ACCIPITER NISUS

DESCRIPTION (EUROPE)

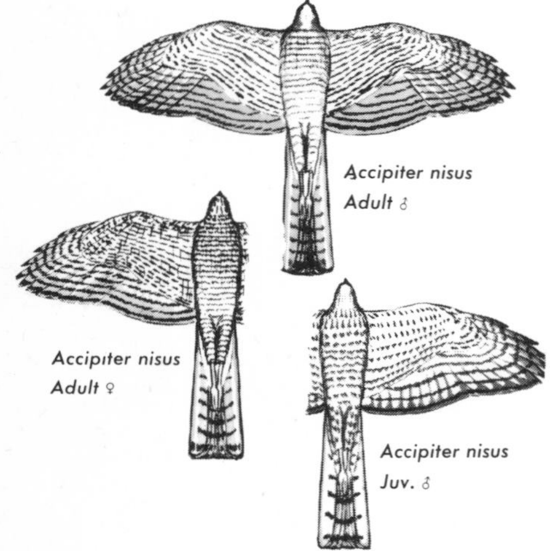

A miniature version of the Northern Goshawk, but the *male* is brighter; sides of face, amber-brown; throat, light cinnamon, streaked dark gray-brown; rest of underparts, white barred amber-brown and dark gray-brown. *Female*—browner above; face, throat, and eyebrows, white; underparts, white, more noticeably barred dark gray-brown to dark brown.

Juvenile—similar to young goshawk above, but flanks and thighs, and sometimes breast also, marked with a distinct barring.

Beak, dark gray; eyes, yellow; tarsi and toes, yellow. Size comparable to the Sharp-shinned Hawk, 10½–13 inches.

VARIATIONS

Follows the pattern of the Old World Goshawks; darker in southern Europe, temperate north Africa, the Mediterranean and Atlantic islands—the largest birds are found in northern and central Asia; and the smallest, in the Canary Islands. Size, 10½–15 inches.

OTHER OLD WORLD SPECIES

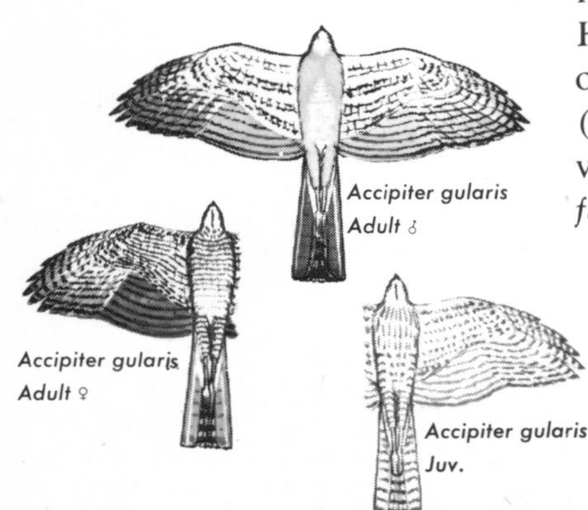

In some regions the Eurasian Sparrowhawk (*A. nisus*), which ordinarily ranges high into the mountain forests like the Sharp-shinned Hawk of the New World, is ecologically replaced at lower altitudes by other species: in eastern China and Japan, by Lesser Sparrowhawk (*A. gularis*), 9–11 inches, in which the adults are darker above but very pale below. The *males* tend to have light amber-brown breasts; *females* are barred white and rufous-brown. This species is a close

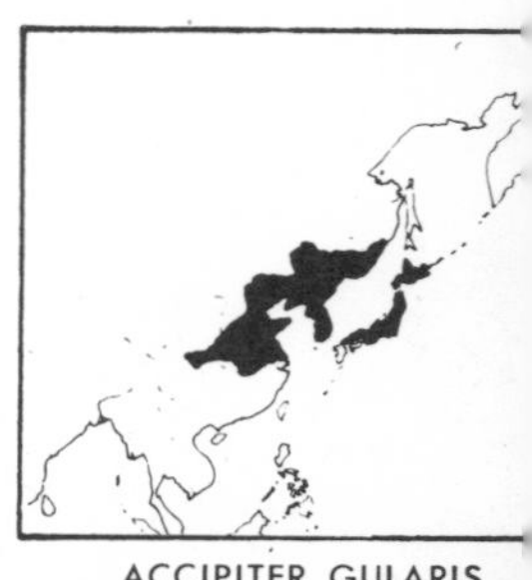

ACCIPITER GULARIS

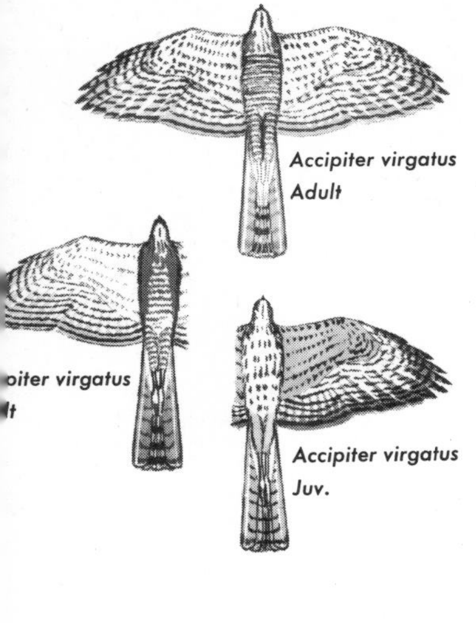
Accipiter virgatus Adult

Accipiter virgatus Adult

Accipiter virgatus Juv.

ACCIPITER VIRGATUS

relative of the brightly-colored and variable Besra Sparrowhawk (*A. virgatus*), 9½–11 inches, in southeast Asia; *male,* dark brown above, streaked and barred below; *female,* distinguished by an amber-brown suffusion on the breast and sides. In southeastern Europe, *A. nisus* is replaced below 3,000 feet by the Levant Sparrowhawk (*A. brevipes*), 12½–15 inches, which also ranges through Asia Minor. Although its slate-gray and amber-brown dress appears at first glance to be very much like that of the male Eurasian Sparrowhawk, heavier amber-brown barring on the underparts, longer unbarred wings, and red eyes are distinctive. The Levant Sparrowhawk is supposed to be a comparatively recent offshoot of the Shikra (*A. badius*), 9½–11 inches, in India, Africa, and Turkistan. In the south Caspian region, where their ranges meet, there is some interbreeding. Both species prefer dry open districts and parklands to the forest patches which are the haunts of *A. nisus* in the Palaearctic. The Shikra varies from dove-gray to dark gray above and often has an amber-brown collar at the nape in Asia: *males,* white below, barred light amber-brown or uniformly light amber-brown; *females,* white below, barred rufous-brown. In both sexes the outer tail feathers are dove-gray, either plain or barred.

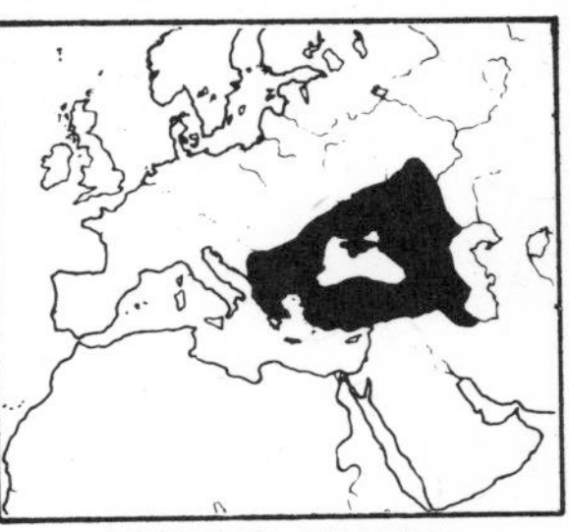
ACCIPITER BREVIPES

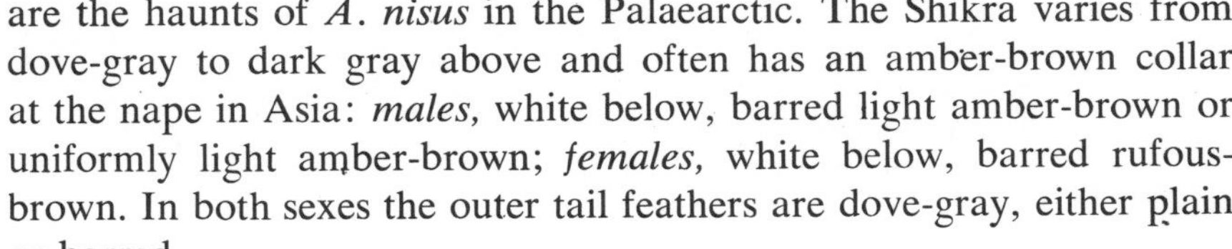
Accipiter brevipes Adult

Accipiter brevipes Juv.

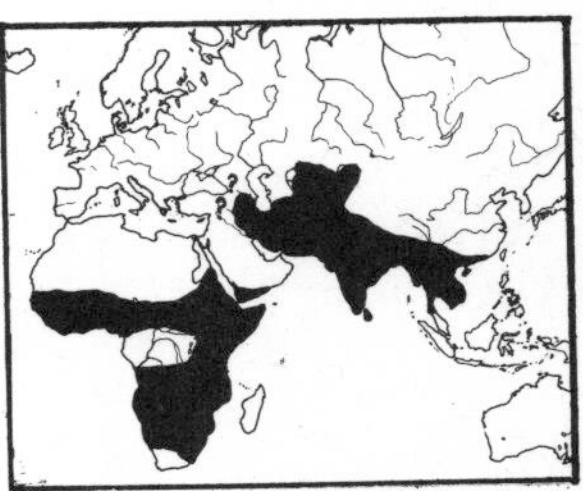
ACCIPITER BADIUS

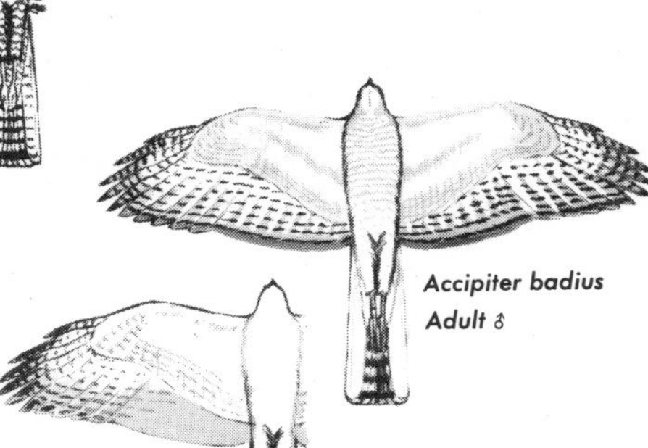
Accipiter badius Adult ♂

Accipiter badius Adult ♂

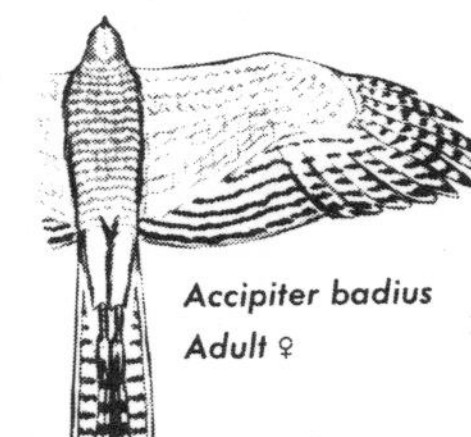
Accipiter badius Adult ♀

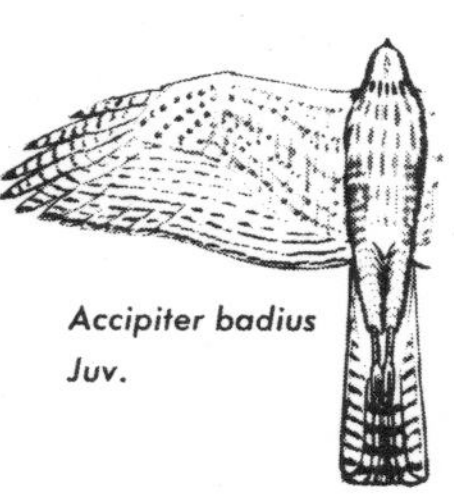
Accipiter badius Juv.

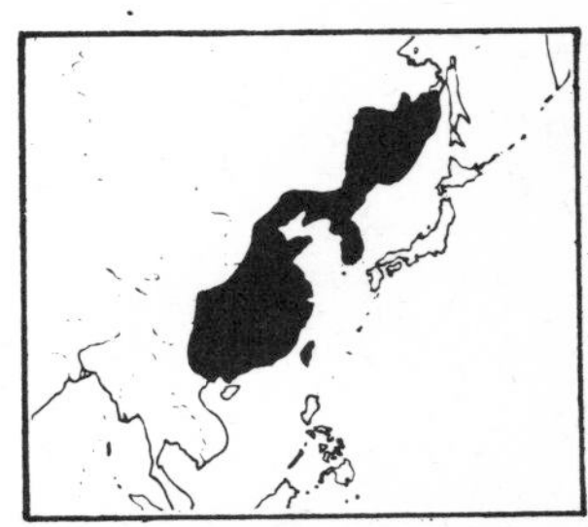
ACCIPITER SOLOENSIS

The relationship of the Asiatic Little Sparrowhawk (*A. soloensis*), 10–11 inches, of the open woodlands and pine forests in the south China foothills, to the Shikra and Levant Sparrowhawk is not clear, but this long-winged, slate-gray hawk with white or vinaceous underparts tinged silver-gray, occupies a similar ecological niche.

Another gray sparrowhawk, the Nicobar Shikra (*A. butleri*), 10½–13 inches, restricted to Car Nicobar in the Bay of Bengal, has dove-gray upperparts and light vinaceous underparts faintly barred white. (Juvenile—chestnut above, streaked and spotted black; underparts white, heavily streaked and blobbed with chestnut.) Throughout the northern part of its range—Upper Guinea, Fernando Po (in the Gulf of Guinea), and northeastern Africa—the African Sparrowhawk (*A. tachiro*), 13–16 inches, has bright ferruginous sides and flanks, paling to amber-brown in east and south Africa, and is barred below in similar colors. In the deep rain forest the patterned underparts tend to disappear, shifting to light cinnamon with traces of white barring in Gabon and southern Cameroon, and plain cinnamon in the lower Congo. At the eastern edges of the Congo forest, barred and immaculate birds may be seen in the same clearings.

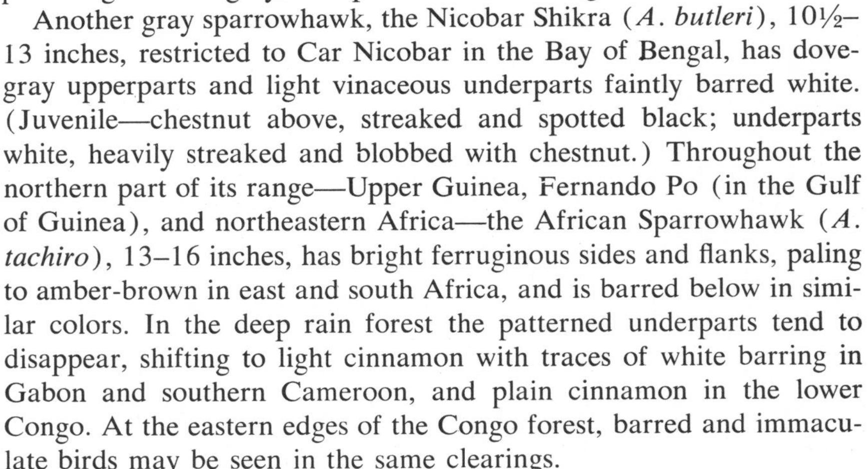
Accipiter soloensis Adult

Accipiter soloensis Adult

Accipiter soloensis Juv.

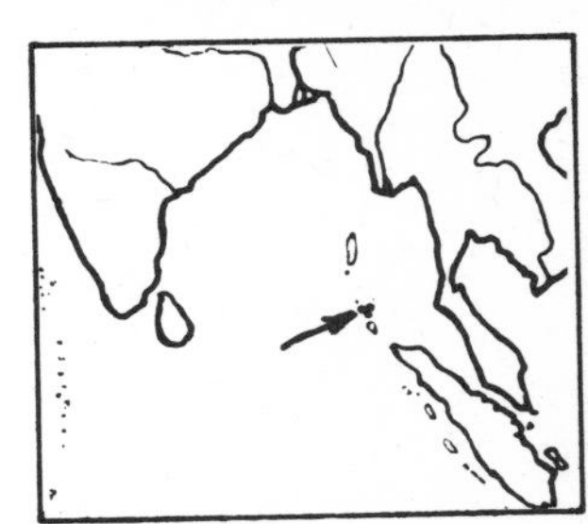
ACCIPITER BUTLERI

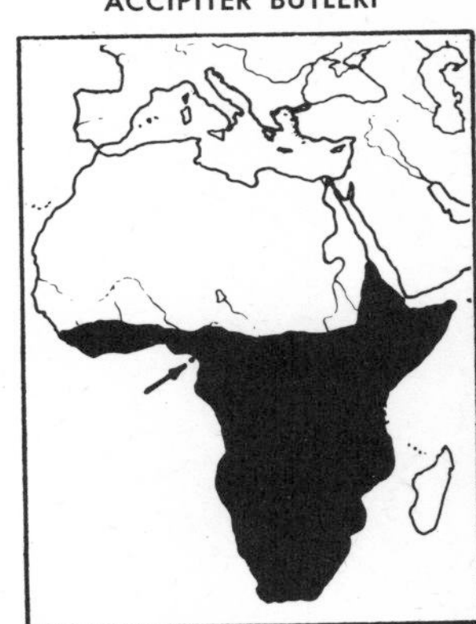
ACCIPITER TACHIRO

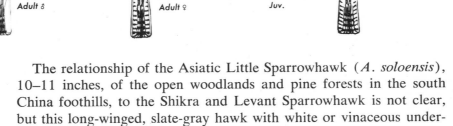

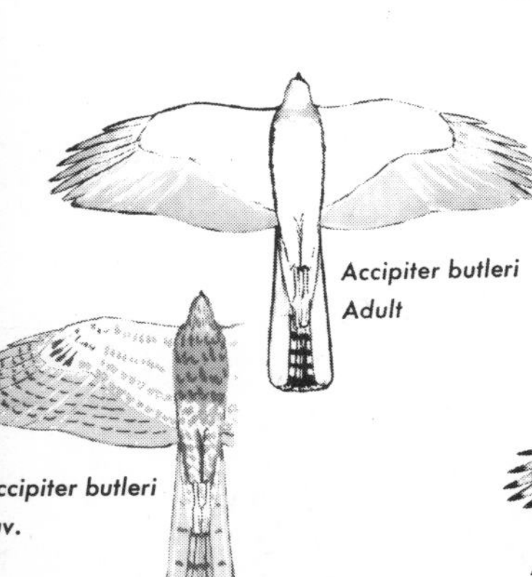
Accipiter butleri Adult

Accipiter butleri Juv.

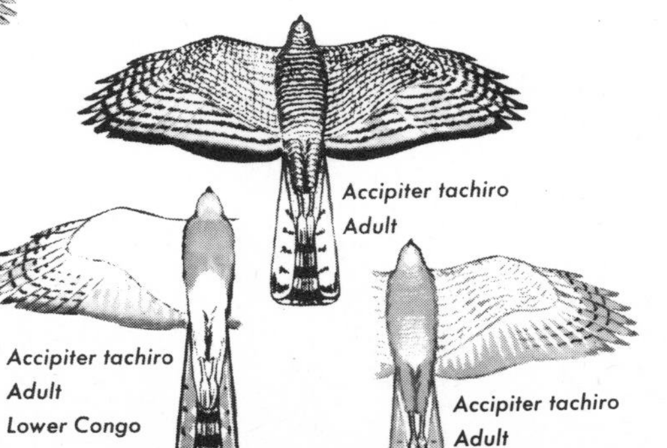
Accipiter tachiro Adult

Accipiter tachiro Adult Lower Congo

Accipiter tachiro Adult Gabon, S. Cameroon

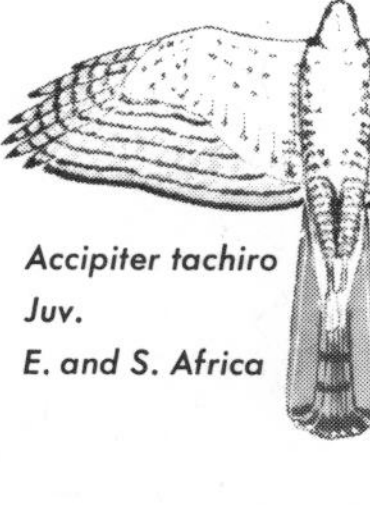
Accipiter tachiro Juv. E. and S. Africa

Accipiter tachiro Juv. N.E. Africa

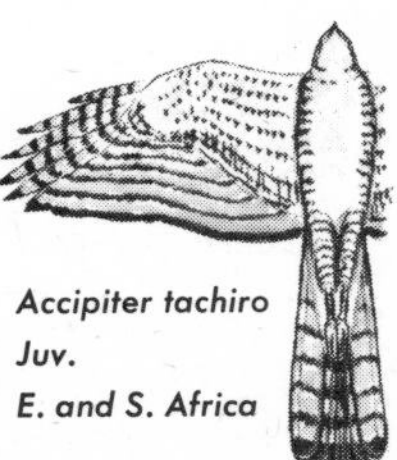
Accipiter tachiro Juv. E. and S. Africa

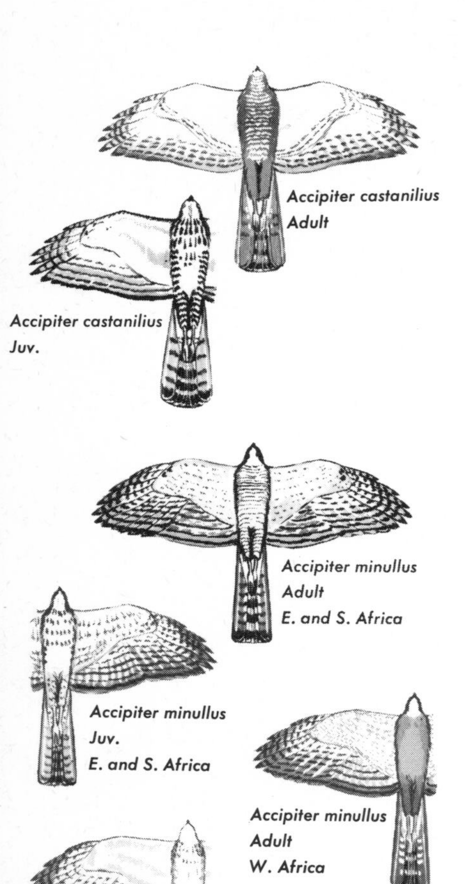

A slate-gray species, the Chestnut-bellied Sparrowhawk (*A. castanilius*), also found in the forests of Upper and Lower Guinea, 12–16 inches, has relatively shorter wings and tail; underparts, heavily banded white and sepia with ferruginous coloring on the sides of the breast and flanks. This species retains its barred pattern, even in the Congo forest.

The African Little Sparrowhawk (*A. minullus*), in east and south Africa, 8–9 inches, is a tiny version of *A. tachiro* without ferruginous or amber-brown coloring on the sides and flanks. The most extreme variant of this pattern occurs in west Africa, where the population is black above with a black face, white throat, and medium vinaceous underparts faintly barred silver-gray on the belly. It is sometimes treated as a separate species (*A. erythropus*). The very long-winged Ovampo Sparrowhawk (*A. ovampensis*), 8½–11 inches, a savanna bird, is medium gray above and faintly barred with white and medium gray below (or dark phase—dark brown, with barred wings and tail). Its habitat in south Africa is the acacia veld, especially trees along streams and rivers.

Far less common than the others within its range, the Rufous-breasted Sparrowhawk (*A. rufiventris*), of central and south Africa, 11–13 inches, is dark gray-brown to slate-gray above, and has light cinnamon underparts sometimes faintly barred or blotched white; white undertail coverts.

ACCIPITER CASTANILIUS

ACCIPITER MINULLUS

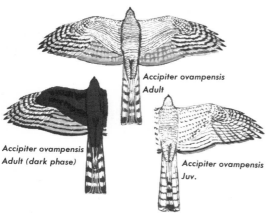

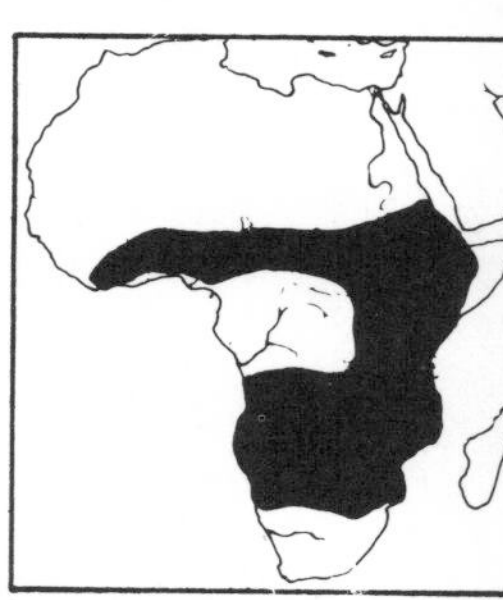
ACCIPITER OVAMPENSIS

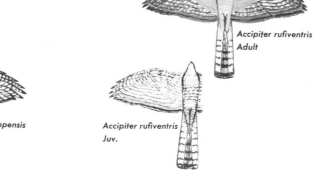

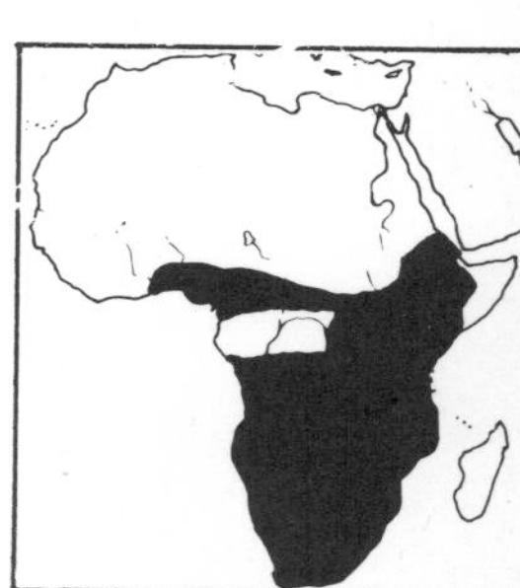
ACCIPITER RUFIVENTRIS

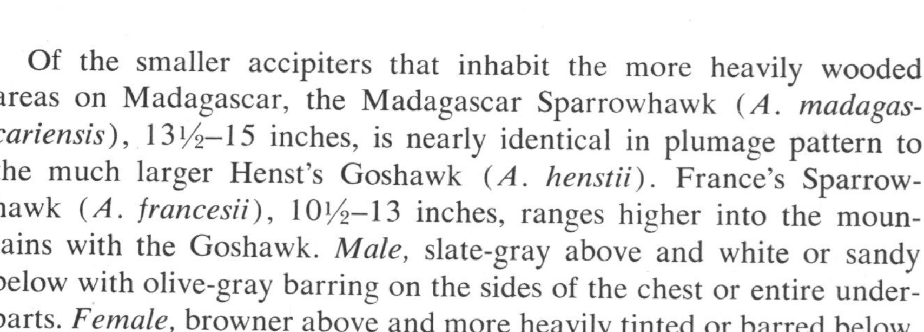

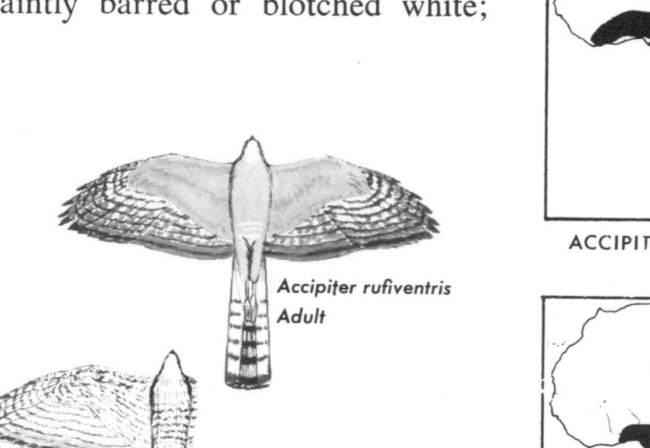

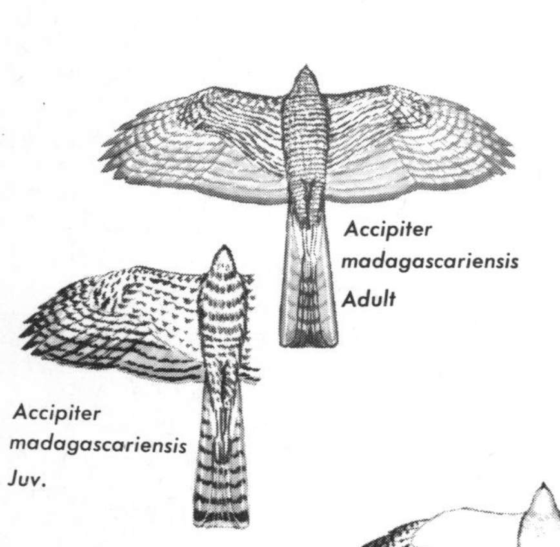

Of the smaller accipiters that inhabit the more heavily wooded areas on Madagascar, the Madagascar Sparrowhawk (*A. madagascariensis*), 13½–15 inches, is nearly identical in plumage pattern to the much larger Henst's Goshawk (*A. henstii*). France's Sparrowhawk (*A. francesii*), 10½–13 inches, ranges higher into the mountains with the Goshawk. *Male,* slate-gray above and white or sandy below with olive-gray barring on the sides of the chest or entire underparts. *Female,* browner above and more heavily tinted or barred below.

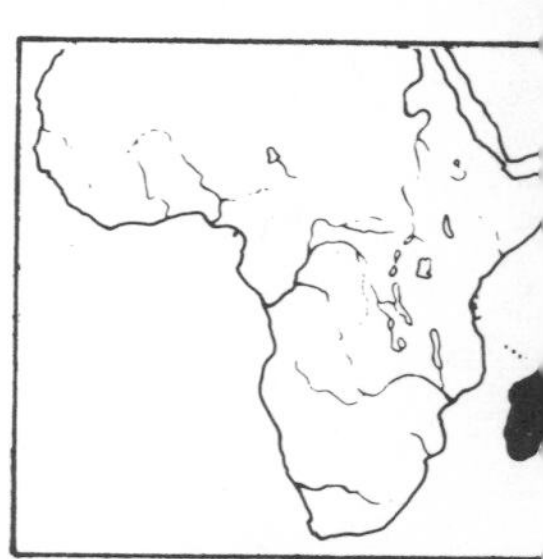
ACCIPITER MADAGASCARIEN

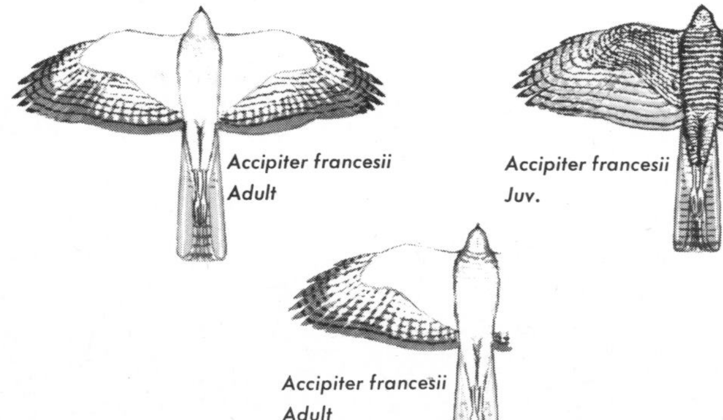

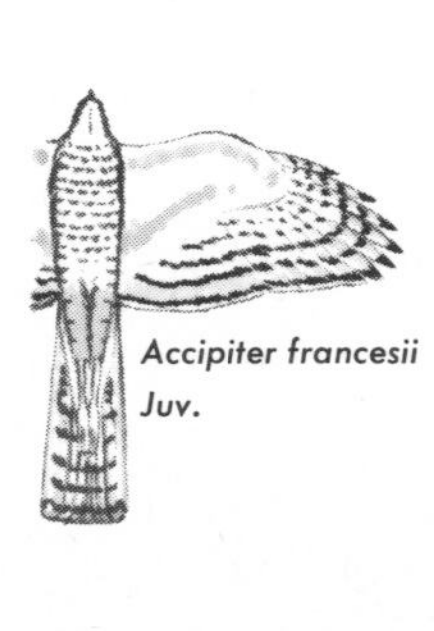

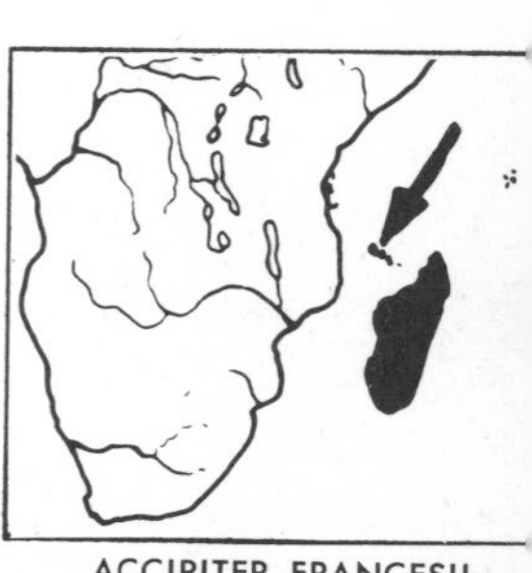
ACCIPITER FRANCESII

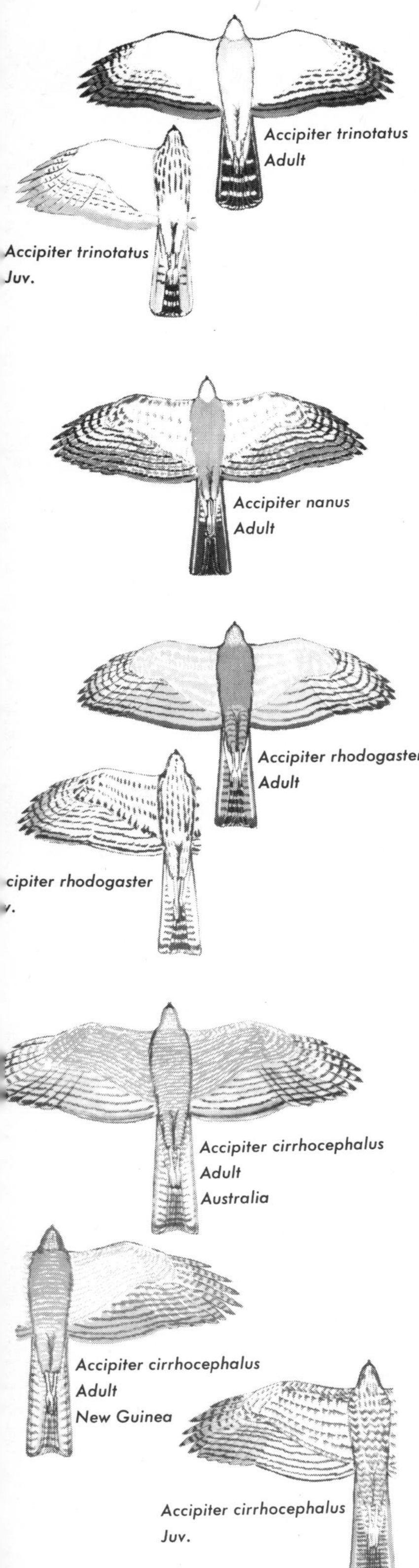

ACCIPITER TRINOTATUS

ACCIPITER NANUS

Three endemic sparrowhawks of Celebes, the Spot-tailed Sparrowhawk (*A. trinotatus*), 10–11 inches, the Celebes Little Sparrowhawk (*A. nanus*), 9–10½ inches, and the Vinous-breasted Sparrowhawk (*A. rhodogaster*), 10½–13 inches, appear virtually identical when perched: slate-blue above and light to medium vinaceous below; the last mentioned, faintly barred dove-gray to medium gray on the throat and thighs. *A. trinotatus* has a striking tail, which is black, with white spots. The dark brown tail feathers of *A. nanus* appear banded basally with white on the undersurface, and those of *A. rhodogaster* are entirely banded light gray beneath. The underwing coverts also differ. However, habits and calls of these sparrowhawks as well as a knowledge of the frequency of their occurrence at various altitudes are better guides to recognition than such minor field marks. They are all virgin forest species, but *A. trinotatus* is a reptile-eater of the dark mangrove forests (Tanahwangko), the Mahawoe Mountains, and Goenoeng Sopoetan, from sea level to about 4,500 feet—less frequently higher. *A. rhodogaster,* comparatively rare at any altitude in these coastal and mountain forests is the least known. And *A. nanus,* a typical bird hawk, primarily inhabits the higher mountain zones between 3,000 and 6,000 feet.

ACCIPITER RHODOGASTER

Juveniles of these species are sienna-backed and more or less spotted or barred with black; white, spotted and barred black, below. Like the adult, the young *A. trinotatus* has a black tail with three or four white spots, but the tail feathers of young *A. rhodogaster* and *A. nanus* are sienna, barred with dark brown.

ACCIPITER CIRRHOCEPHALUS

Many of the small accipiters in the Australian region and southwest Pacific are so closely related as to be considered in species groups:

CIRRHOCEPHALUS GROUP. In Australia the Collared Sparrowhawk (*A. cirrhocephalus*), 10–13 inches, barred below, is a smaller version of the Brown Goshawk (*A. fasciatus*), but in New Guinea it may be either barred or plain medium sienna below. The Red-collared, or New Britain, Sparrowhawk (*A. brachyurus*), 10½–13½ inches, is light gray below or entirely dark slate, in dark phase; and the Gray-throated, or Moluccan, Sparrowhawk (*A. erythrauchen*), 11–13½ inches, is similarly marked above and medium vinaceous below, faintly barred light gray (or, in another variation, light gray below, tinged with vinaceous). These small- to medium-sized accipiters replace each other geographically and perhaps ecologically in the region north of Australia and east of New Guinea.

ACCIPITER BRACHYURUS

The large Blue-and-Gray Sparrowhawk (*A. luteoschistaceus*), of New Britain, 12–15 inches, is dark slate above and white to sandy below, with fine dark barring on the sides sometimes crossing the breast. (Juvenile, barred black and light amber-brown above; underparts coarsely barred sandy and sienna-brown.)

ACCIPITER ERYTHRAUCHEN

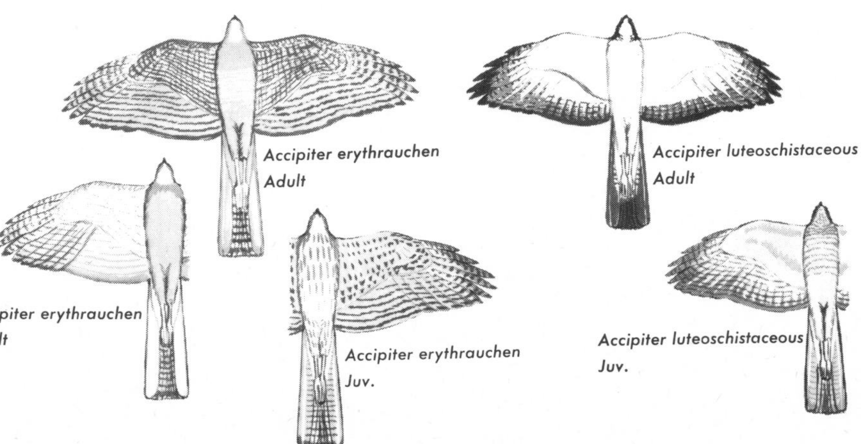

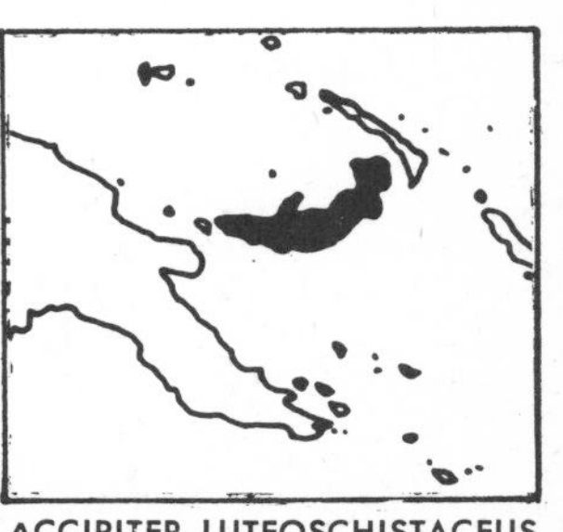

ACCIPITER LUTEOSCHISTACEUS

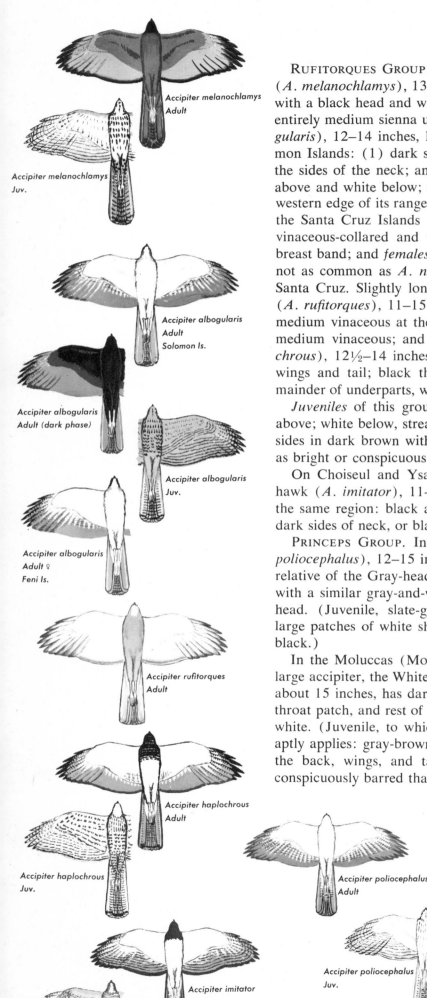

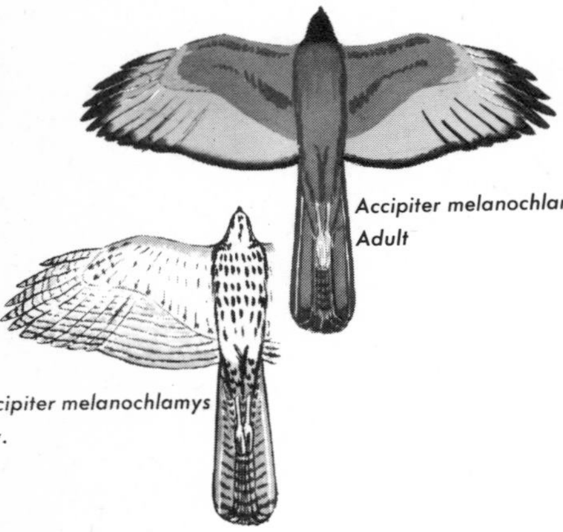

Accipiter melanochlamys
Adult

Accipiter melanochlamys
Juv.

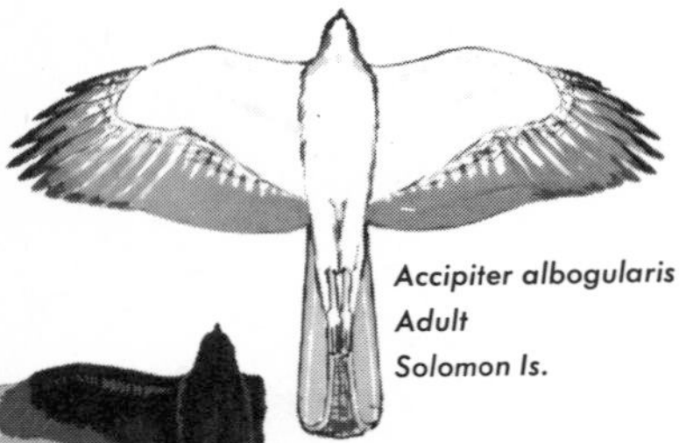

Accipiter albogularis
Adult
Solomon Is.

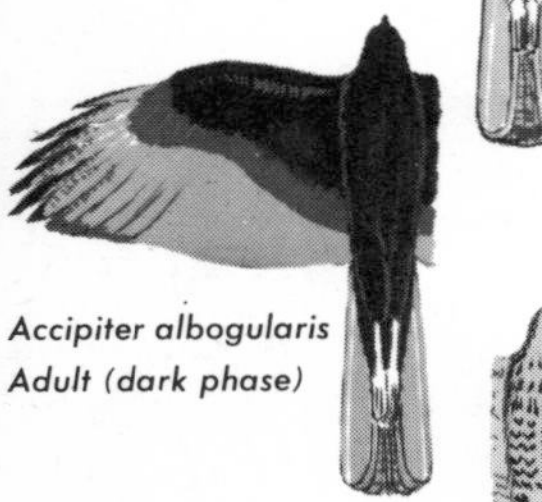

Accipiter albogularis
Adult (dark phase)

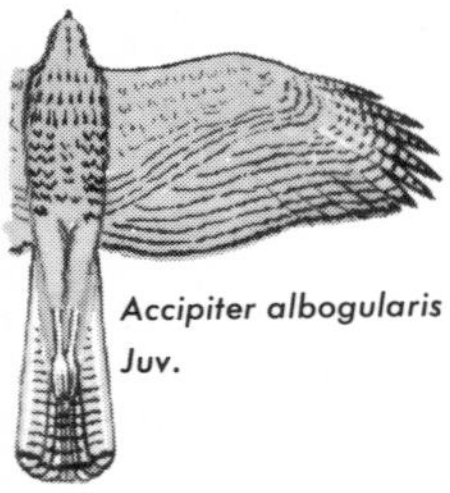

Accipiter albogularis
Juv.

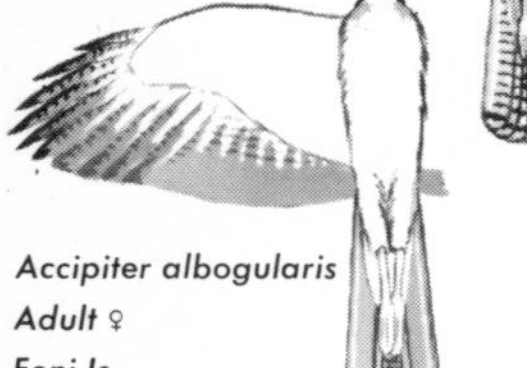

Accipiter albogularis
Adult ♀
Feni Is.

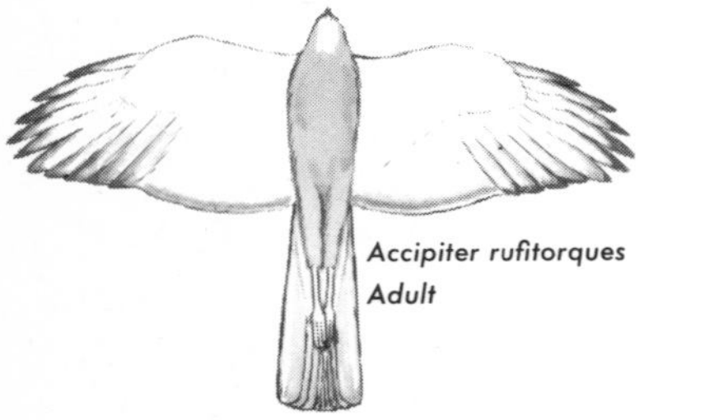

Accipiter rufitorques
Adult

Accipiter haplochrous
Adult

Accipiter haplochrous
Juv.

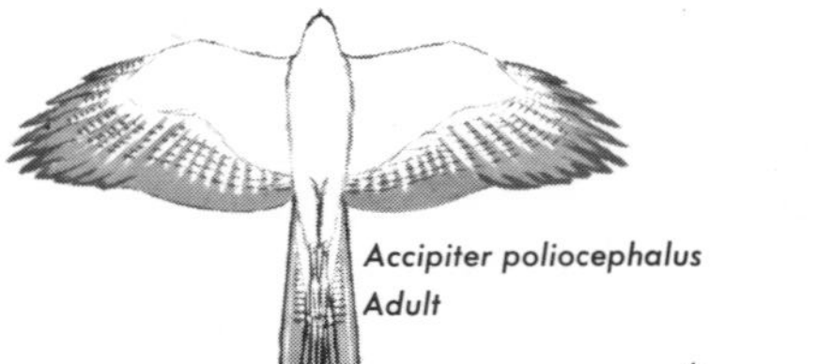

RUFITORQUES GROUP. Including the Black-mantled Sparrowhawk (*A. melanochlamys*), 13–15 inches, of New Guinea and New Britain, with a black head and wide collar of medium sienna extending to the entirely medium sienna underparts. The Pied Sparrowhawk (*A. albogularis*), 12–14 inches, known in at least three variants in the Solomon Islands: (1) dark slate above with a sienna collar extending to the sides of the neck; and underparts, white; (2) entirely dark slate above and white below; and (3) dark slate above and below. At the western edge of its range, Feni Island (Bismarck Archipelago) and in the Santa Cruz Islands (Vanikoro and Utupua), the Pied Hawk is vinaceous-collared and white below; *males,* with a faint vinaceous breast band; and *females,* faintly barred on the breast. This species is not as common as *A. novaehollandiae* except on San Cristobal and Santa Cruz. Slightly longer-winged relatives: The Fiji Sparrowhawk (*A. rufitorques*), 11–15 inches, medium gray above with a collar of medium vinaceous at the nape; wings and tail, unbarred; underparts medium vinaceous; and the White-bellied Sparrowhawk (*A. haplochrous*), 12½–14 inches, of New Caledonia, black above including wings and tail; black throat, and chest black or barred black; remainder of underparts, white.

Juveniles of this group are barred black and light amber-brown above; white below, streaked on the chest and belly and barred at the sides in dark brown with sienna-barred thighs characteristic, but not as bright or conspicuous as in the young of *A. novaehollandiae.*

On Choiseul and Ysabel in the Solomons the Imitator Sparrowhawk (*A. imitator*), 11–13 inches, is smaller than *A. albogularis* of the same region: black above, and either all-white below, except for dark sides of neck, or black throat and chest.

PRINCEPS GROUP. Including the Gray-headed Sparrowhawk (*A. poliocephalus*), 12–15 inches, of the islands off New Guinea; a small relative of the Gray-headed Goshawk (*A. princeps*) of New Britain, with a similar gray-and-white plumage pattern, but lighter dove-gray head. (Juvenile, slate-gray head and gray-brown upperparts with large patches of white showing on the mantle; white below, streaked black.)

In the Moluccas (Morty Island, Batjan, and Halmahera) another large accipiter, the White-headed Sparrowhawk (*A. henicogrammus*), about 15 inches, has dark slate upperparts, a mottled gray and white throat patch, and rest of underparts dark amber-brown, faintly barred white. (Juvenile, to which the vernacular name of the species more aptly applies: gray-brown above with white-spotted head and mantle; the back, wings, and tail barred amber-brown. Underparts, more conspicuously barred than adult's, with white and sienna.)

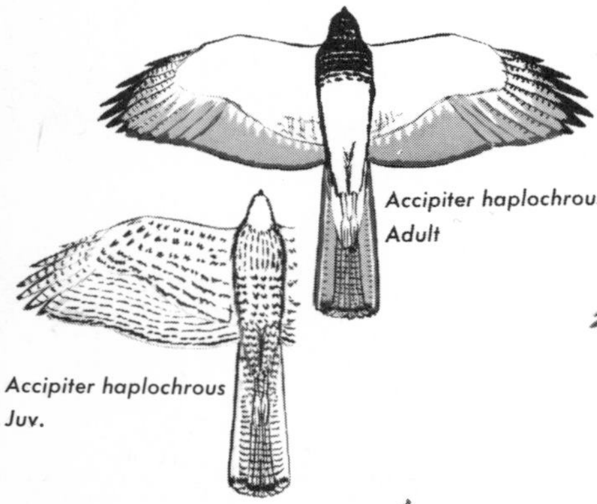

Accipiter poliocephalus
Adult

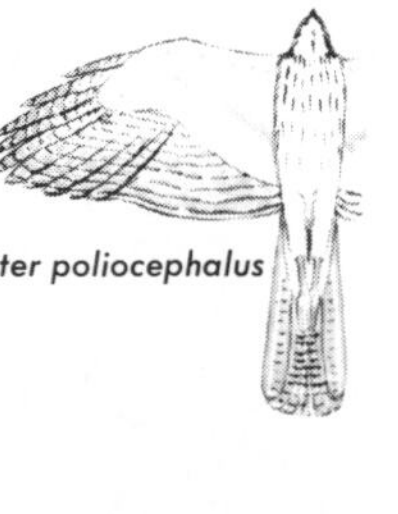

Accipiter poliocephalus
Juv.

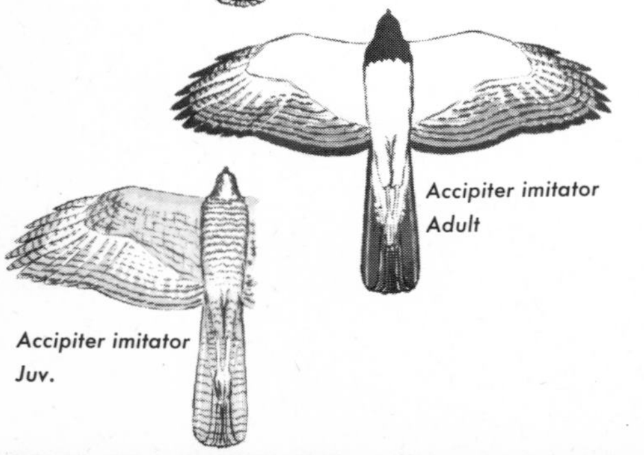

Accipiter imitator
Adult

Accipiter imitator
Juv.

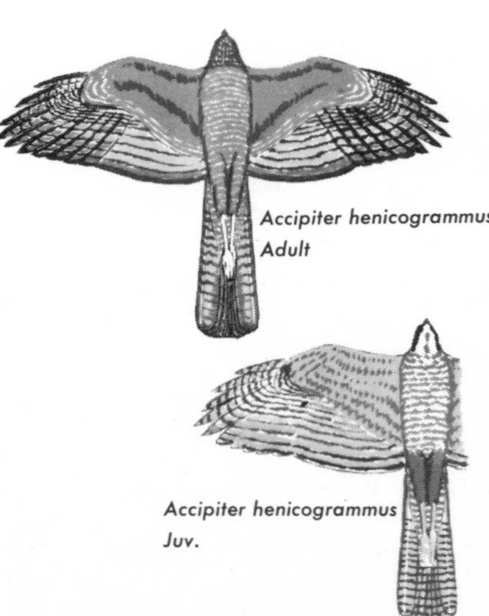

Accipiter henicogrammus
Adult

Accipiter henicogrammus
Juv.

ACCIPITER MELANOCHLA

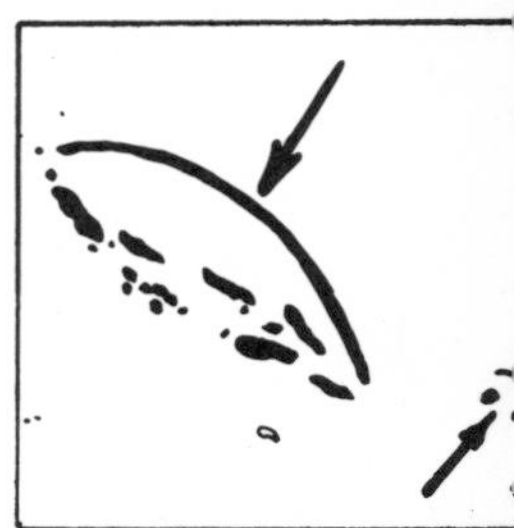

ACCIPITER ALBOGULARI

ACCIPITER RUFITORQUE

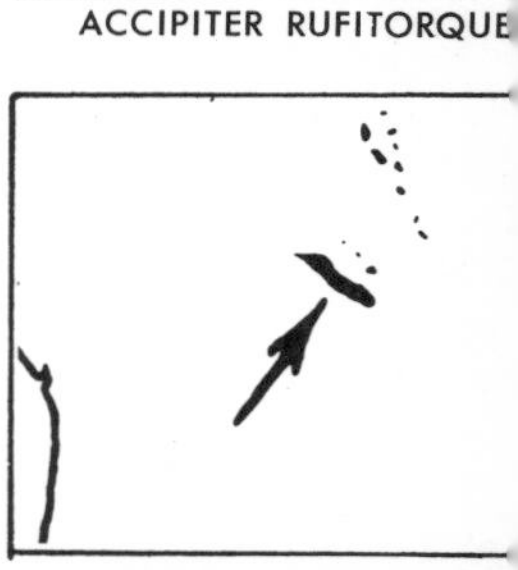

ACCIPITER HAPLOCHROU

ACCIPITER IMITATOR

ACCIPITER POLIOCEPHAL

ACCIPITER HENICOGRAMM

HABITS

The accipiters "prospect" for concentrations of prey by circling high or flapping low over the woods —the characteristic pattern, a succession of glides interrupted by fast wing beats. Their success in hunting, however, depends on more secretive tactics. Quiet waiting, either on an exposed branch (typical of the Goshawk, Shikra, some other species of sparrowhawks) or behind screening foliage, is rewarded by the appearance of prey. Then, either in a swift dash or a downward plunge through the trees, with wings partly folded, they secure their food. If the foliage is very thick, the woods hawks may run on their long legs along branches. Goshawks have been known to chase rabbits on foot through brush.

Northern Goshawks and Cooper's Hawks and their allies take a larger proportion of small mammals and medium-sized birds than do the smaller accipiters. Lemmings are the staple food of Goshawks along the northern fringe of the boreal forests in Alaska and northern Canada and the Siberian taiga; and southward not only birds but all kinds of small mammals are fair game, including the young of fox and wildcat; also lizards, snails, grasshoppers, and insect larvae. Some individuals acquire the poultry-stealing habit, but most of these large accipiters—like other birds of prey—tend to specialize in the common wild birds or mammals that are more or less vulnerable throughout the year.

According to a 1948–53 study by Heinz Meng in the Ithaca region of New York State, the diet of Northern Goshawks in the nesting season consisted mainly of red squirrels and Common Crows, besides comparatively small numbers of gray squirrels, cottontails, chipmunks, and grouse. Cooper's Hawks took 82 per cent birds—mainly Starlings, and less frequently Yellow-shafted Flickers, Eastern Meadowlarks, Robins, and Common Grackles. The mammals most heavily preyed upon were chipmunks and red squirrels.

The Sharp-shinned Hawk, the Eurasian Sparrowhawk, the African Sparrowhawk (*A. tachiro*), and the Collared Sparrowhawk (*A. cirrhocephalus*), among others, are typical "bird hawks," and a number of small accipiters, especially those of more open woodland and savanna country—the Shikras, for example, have the goshawk habit of sitting on exposed branches and preying heavily on grasshoppers, small lizards, and rodents on the ground.

The accipiters usually require large trees for nesting, although there are records in Europe of Goshawks building on the ground in open country and the breeding ranges of Cooper's Hawks and Sharp-shinned Hawks include regions where patches of forest or shrubbery afford the only nesting places.

Northern Goshawks (*A. gentilis*) build a bulky nest of large branches, sometimes improving on an old base of their own or another hawk's nest of a previous year. A lining of bark flakes and a few pine sprigs is usual. Unlike the Sharp-shinned Hawk, the Northern Goshawk displays no preference for conifers, but a pair usually selects the largest trees in deep woods, nesting on the average of 30 to 40 feet up, but nests as high as 75 feet from the ground have been found. Three to four pale blue eggs, laid three or four days apart, are usually unmarked. Incubation (36–38 days), almost entirely by the hen, begins with the second or third egg. The male at first brings all the food to the nest and the female divides it among the young birds. Later both sexes provide food. After 41 to 43 days the fledglings take to branches and soon learn to fly.

The nest of the Cooper's Hawk (*A. cooperii*), either placed in an upright crotch of a deciduous tree (or next to the trunk on several horizontal branches in a conifer) is similar in shape to that of the Northern Goshawk, but smaller. Made of dead branches, it has a shallow egg cup lined with bark flakes. Bits of down are more often seen on this hawk's nest than on the "Sharp-shin's," and it is never as heavily decorated with fresh sprigs as is a buteo's. The location is often 30 feet or higher, with some records in the plains states of nesting on the ground. In his study of the pine-oak woodlands of southeastern Arizona and northern Mexico, Marshall states that of all the birds observed in this mountain habitat the Cooper's Hawk was the most faithful in returning to the same spot to nest. Small birds nesting in close association with the Cooper's Hawk in the Ajos Mountains—Black-chinned Hummingbird and Solitary Vireo—seemed to do so through a similar preference for sycamores.

Three to six white or bluish-white eggs are laid one or two days apart. Incubation, mainly by the female, may not start until the clutch is complete, and lasts 36 days, according to Heinz Meng's studies in the Ithaca region of New York State. Young males leave the nest for the first time when 31 days old, and females when 34 days old.

The Sharp-shinned Hawk (*A. striatus*) prefers coniferous trees; also nests in deciduous trees in some localities (alders and sycamores in the Ajos Mountains). The core of the breeding population in North America is concentrated in eastern Canada.

The Sharp-shin's nest, usually a rather flat platform of "clean" sticks, is built on horizontal branches against the trunk of a tree. (Small accipiters may build a fairly large nest for their size, so that even the incubating bird's tail cannot be seen over the edge.) Four to five is the usual clutch size and the eggs are highly prized by collectors since they show an almost endless variety of colorful patterns on a bluish-white ground. Incubation, which usually does not begin until the set is complete, lasts 35 days (according to Meng) and is done mostly by the female. The young take to branches from the twenty-first to the twenty-fifth day—males leaving before females.

The "equivalent" of this species in the Old World, the Eurasian Sparrowhawk (*A. nisus*), also usually builds in evergreens, but may sometimes nest in deciduous woods, and as low as seven feet from the ground. Four to five eggs are either plain bluish-white or marked only on the larger end. Clutch sizes of eight, nine, and ten probably can be explained by "bigamy," as the presence of more than one female has been recorded several times. Incubation, mainly by the female, begins with the second, third and occasionally the last egg (exactly 35 days for each egg in many cases). The male is chief provider and feeds the female during this period, but not at the nest. Later he brings food to her at a nearby "butcher block" or (already plucked) to the nest, where she will divide it among the fledglings. Sometimes prey is transferred while the parent birds are in flight. At the end of 21 to 30 days the young are ready to fly.

Scattered feathers at the feeding stations or "butcher blocks" announce the presence of the woods hawks universally.

Northern accipiters are single-brooded, but this may not be the case with other species in tropical and subtropical climates. African Sparrowhawks (*A. tachiro*) may start another brood two months after the young have achieved independence.

Although present to some extent throughout their range in winter, the northern-breeding accipiters have definite migrations, especially the Sharp-shinned Hawks and Eurasian Sparrowhawks. Large numbers of Northern Goshawks leave the far north in some years, probably because of food shortages.

The accipiters are ordinarily silent birds, except at the nest. Warning notes of species in the Northern Hemisphere are similar—a shrill "kek, kek, kek," or "gek, gek, gek—" but those of the larger species are louder and harsher. (This is also an ordinary note of the females.) The female Northern Goshawk like the Red-shouldered Hawk or Common Buzzard, calls "kee-a-ah" or "whaaaa" to the male as he brings food, with emphasis on the first syllable, and may be answered by a higher, thinner, and less powerful rendition. (There are also other notes in the breeding season.)

The calls of the Black Goshawk (*A. melanoleucus*)—"ku-ku"—and of the African Sparrowhawk (*A. tachiro*)—"wut-wut"—are distinctive. The Shikra (*A. badius*) in open country, as well as the denser brush near the coastal belt of tropical west Africa, calls "ki-ek-ki-ek-kik—ki-ki-ki" in alarm and a softer "choo-chee-choo" at the nest, which is akin to the Shikra's double note—"ti-tiu,"—in Asia. And the common sparrowhawk of the east African savanna and the south African acacia veld (*A. ovampensis*) cries "coo-coo-coo-coo-coo-cook."

In the Celebes, *A. nanus* makes its presence known by a fiercely pronounced "klee-klee-klee-klee-klee"; the call of *A. trinotatus* is more deliberate and slow-measured; and the Crested Goshawk of the mountain forests (*A. trivirgatus*) has a high faint voice.

These differences in voice—in pitch, number of syllables, and tempo—are often the best clue to the identity of forest hawks, which are usually vociferous when their nesting territory is invaded. However, some individuals slip away quietly, and the male may not come back until he is sure that no one is watching.

Adult North American Goshawk (*Accipiter gentilis*).—Photograph by Heinz Meng.

One of the least common birds of prey, the Red Goshawk *(Erythrotriorchis radiatus)* now is restricted mainly to northern and eastern Australia.

GENUS *ERYTHROTRIORCHIS*

This large woods hawk has longer wings and a somewhat shorter tail than a Northern Goshawk; tarsi partly feathered and scutellate in front. The powerful "bird-eater" foot, with a very long middle toe, is characteristic of the accipiters—which also have prominent bumps on the undersurface of the toes and long curved talons.

Red Goshawk (*Erythrotriorchis radiatus*)

DESCRIPTION (AUSTRALIA)

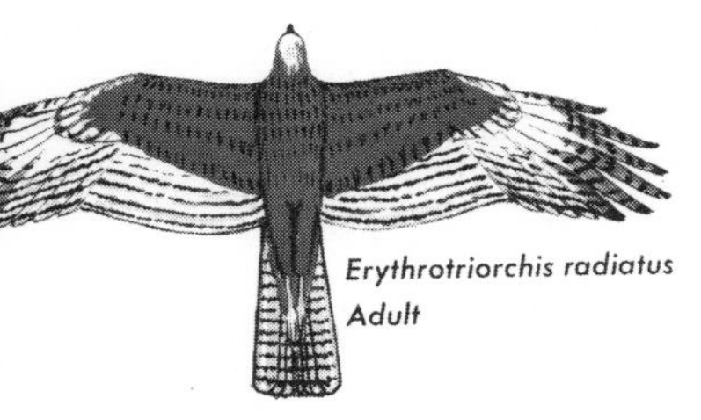

Erythrotriorchis radiatus *Adult*

Dark brown above, the head streaked white and amber-brown; back and wing, as well as tail coverts, broadly scalloped amber-brown; rump, wings, and tail barred medium olive-gray and tipped light olive-gray. Face, light amber-brown, finely streaked. Below, amber-brown varied with a patch of white on the throat and heavily streaked dark brown (thighs, either amber-brown or dark amber-brown).

Immature and *juvenile*—similar. An incompletely barred tail is a subadult characteristic.

Beak, blue-gray with black tip; cere, pale blue; eyes, golden; legs and feet, yellow. Size, 19–22 inches.

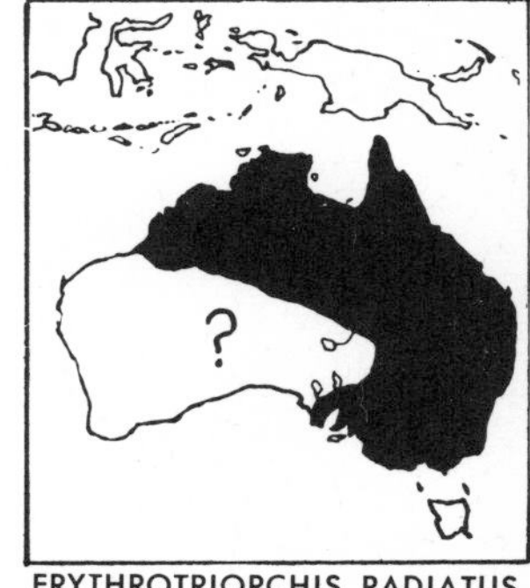

ERYTHROTRIORCHIS RADIATUS

HABITS

The Red Goshawk has sometimes been given the common name of "Buzzard" because it frequently looks for its prey while circling high above the ground, and can be drawn from great distances by a freshly killed wallaby or kangaroo rat. It raids birds' nests and attacks smaller birds (even the Black-shouldered Kite, which can usually outmaneuver its relatively clumsy pursuer); it also feeds on snakes.

In Queensland old crows' nests often provide the foundation for their large nests of sticks, lined with eucalyptus leaves. These are most likely to be found in dense foliage at the top of lemon-scented gum or ash trees, 50 to 70 feet from the ground. Two dull bluish-white eggs, nearly globular in shape, may be uniform in color or brown-blotched. The nesting behavior of this rare and extremely shy species apparently has never been recorded.

Doria's Goshawk *(Megatriorchis doriae)* closely resembles the young of Bürger's Goshawk of New Guinea, but is larger and has a much longer tail. A small crest of pointed plumes may show when the bird is perched.

GENUS *MEGATRIORCHIS*

The single member of this genus is a modified goshawk with very short wings and extremely long twelve-banded tail, rounded at the tip. The tarsi are partly feathered and scutellate in front; toes, long and slender.

Doria's Goshawk (*Megatriorchis doriae*)

DESCRIPTION (NEW GUINEA)

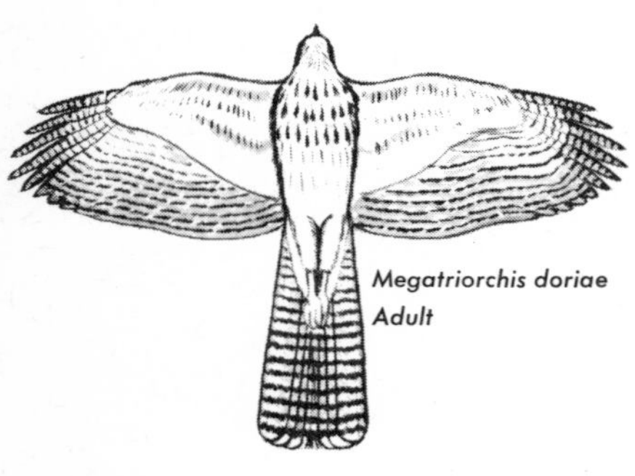

Megatriorchis doriae Adult

Dark brown above, including short crest; streaked dark tawny and white on the head, with a dark patch behind the eye, and a short white eyebrow; otherwise, upperparts, barred in tones ranging from dark tawny to light yellow-brown or pale gray-brown. Sides of face, throat, and underparts, white to sandy, with chocolate streaking usually broadest on the chest and upper belly.

Immature—like adult above; broadly streaked amber-brown below.

Juvenile—paler and not as distinctly barred above; underparts appearing mottled light amber-brown and white with fine dark streaking.

Beak, black; cere, ash color; eyes, chestnut-brown; feet, light gray. Size, about 20 inches.

MEGATRIORCHIS DORIAE

HABITS None recorded, to our knowledge.

A 13- to 15-inch tail with light-tipped graduated quills gives the African Long-tailed Hawk *(Urotriorchis macrourus)* its name and somewhat cuckoo-like appearance.

GENUS *UROTRIORCHIS*

Urotriorchis compares in body size to the Black Goshawk (*Accipiter melanoleucus*), but it has shorter wings and an extremely long wedge-shaped tail. The tarsi are feathered about halfway down in front.

Long-tailed Hawk (*Urotriorchis macrourus*)

DESCRIPTION (EQUATORIAL AFRICA)

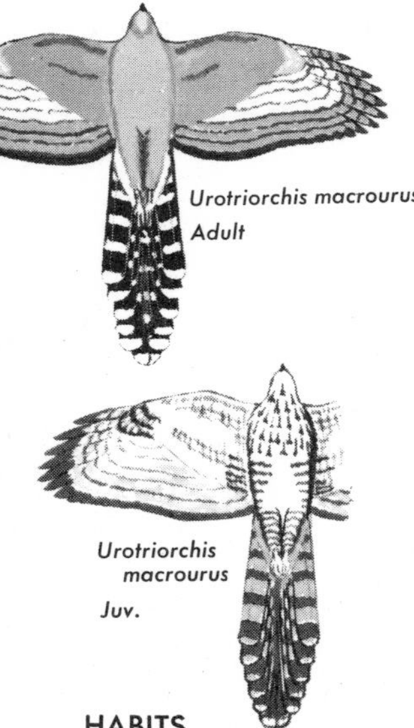

Above, dark slate with a white rump patch; wings, dark brown, barred with black; rectrices, dark brown with four white spots at the centers of the shafts and broadly tipped white. Face and neck, dove gray; entire underparts, chestnut, except pure white undertail coverts. Dark phase—slate-gray below, but otherwise similarly marked.

Juvenile—browner, with a conspicuous long tail, barred buff and dark brown like the back. Face, buff; underparts white with dark brown blobs on the chest and heavy barring on the flanks and thighs.

Beak, black; cere, yellow; eyes, red (juvenile, brown); tarsi and toes, yellow (juvenile, grayish-green). Size, about 22–23 inches.

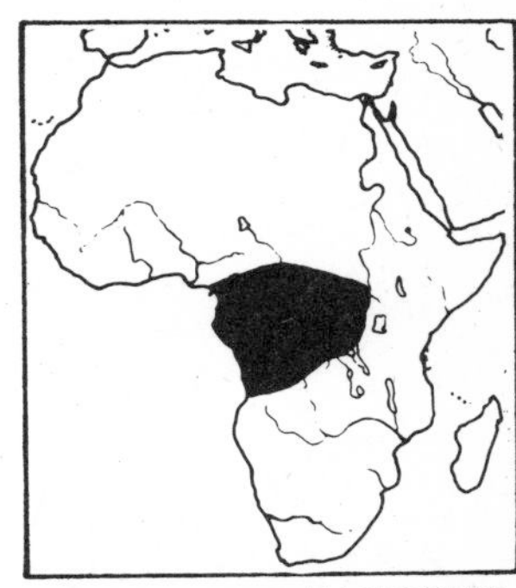

UROTRIORCHIS MACROURUS

HABITS

The Long-tailed Hawk has been seen in deep and second-growth forests throughout equatorial west Africa, but only rarely. The Bulu people of Cameroon call it "Leopard of the Air," for it hunts in the treetops, preying on birds and scale-tailed squirrels—rodents that rarely or never come to the ground. Occasionally, however, this bird leaves the forest and walks around in the poultry yards of villages until it finds an opportunity to seize and make off with an unwary chicken. This kind of sneak attack is not at all accipiter-like. It also has been known to eat vegetable matter.

The nest of the Long-tailed Hawk has not been recorded.

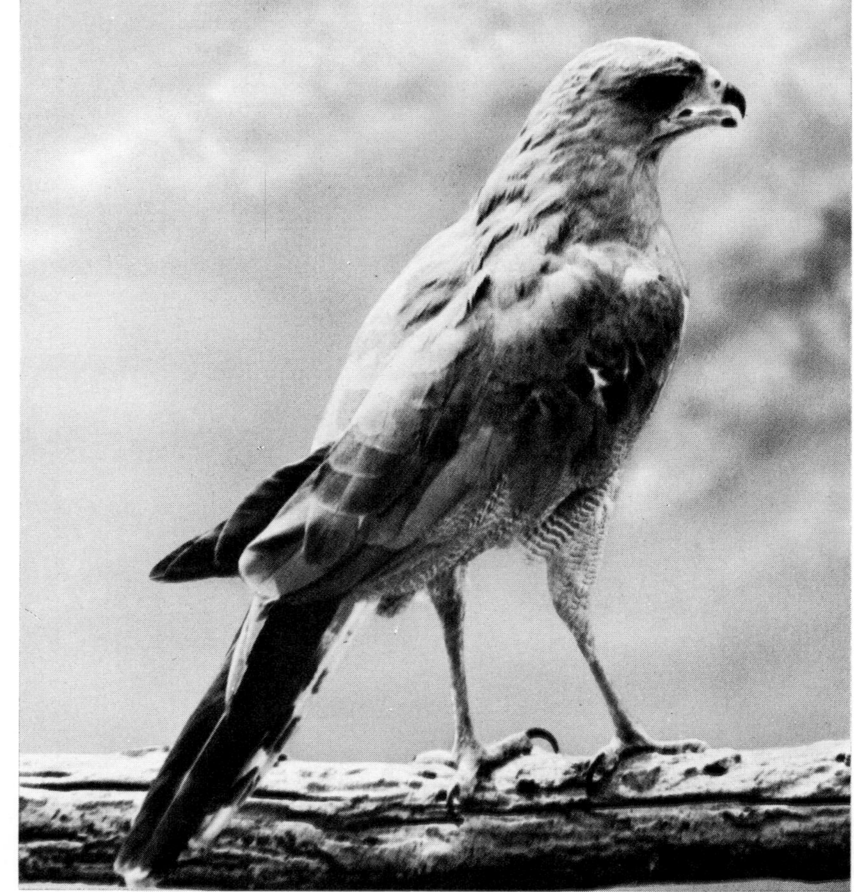

The Pale Chanting Goshawk *(Melierax musicus)* is the common large gray hawk of the east African savanna, rather slender-looking while perched and accipiter-like in flight. *—Photographed at the New York Zoological Society.*

GENUS *MELIERAX*

The larger hawks of this widespread African genus are long-winged, long-legged goshawks with relatively short toes, which live exclusively in open country, even encroaching on the Sahara, the Kalahari, and the Arabian deserts. Their diminutive cousin, the Gabar Goshawk, compares with the small accipiters of the savanna and brush. Bright orange-red cere and legs and pure white or black-and-white barred uppertail coverts are usually distinctive field marks, although the black phase of the Gabar Goshawk has no marking on the rump.

Pale Chanting Goshawk (*Melierax musicus*)

DESCRIPTION (EASTERN AFRICA)

Above, slate-gray; wing coverts and secondaries, light gray, the latter tipped in white; primaries and tail, dark brown. A white patch shows on the rump, the outer rectrices are barred, and all the tail feathers are tipped in white. Face and sides of neck, dark gray; rest of underparts white, barred slate-gray.

Juvenile—olive-brown above, the feathers generally edged lighter; wings and tail, barred; face, eyebrows, and throat, white, streaked with light cinnamon; chest, light cinnamon, finely streaked with gray-brown; rest of underparts, irregularly barred white and light cinnamon.

Beak, black; cere, orange-vermilion; eyes, red-orange (juvenile, yellow); legs and feet, red-orange. Size, 17–20 inches.

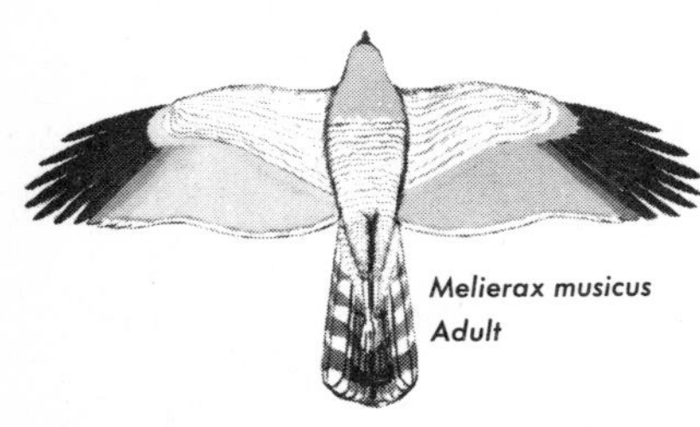

Melierax musicus Adult

MELIERAX MUSICUS

VARIATIONS

In the Karoo regions of Cape Province the Pale Chanting Goshawk is much darker with heavier barring below; in southwestern Africa, Bechuanaland, and northwestern Transvaal, it is paler with a silvery appearance—the secondaries and wing coverts white, finely mottled light gray, and the barring on the underparts much finer.

MELIERAX METABATES

OTHER SPECIES

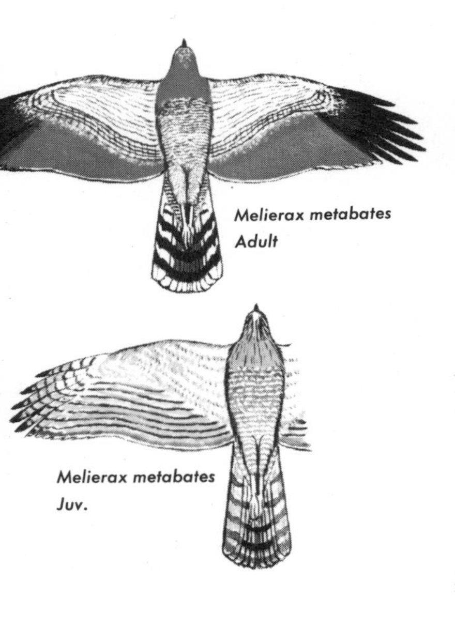

Melierax metabates *Adult*

Melierax metabates *Juv.*

The Dark Chanting Goshawk (*M. metabates*), slightly smaller, and darker above and below, has a barred rump patch and barring on the underparts gray-brown and white (Congo) or predominantly dark gray and white (Angola)—frequently darker on the coastal plains of Arabia. Even the comparatively pale Sahara Desert population, barred brown and white below, is not as silvery-white in appearance as the Pale Chanting Goshawk of the Kalahari Desert.

Juvenile—similar to young of the Pale Chanting Goshawk. The most common phase of the small Gabar Goshawk (*M. gabar*), 11–14 inches, "mimics" the Pale Chanting Goshawk except for a completely barred undersurface in flight. In the dark phase, it could be confused with the dark variant of the long-winged Ovampo Sparrowhawk *(A. ovampensis),* also a savanna bird, but one without distinctive white "windows" in the barred wings.

MELIERAX GABAR

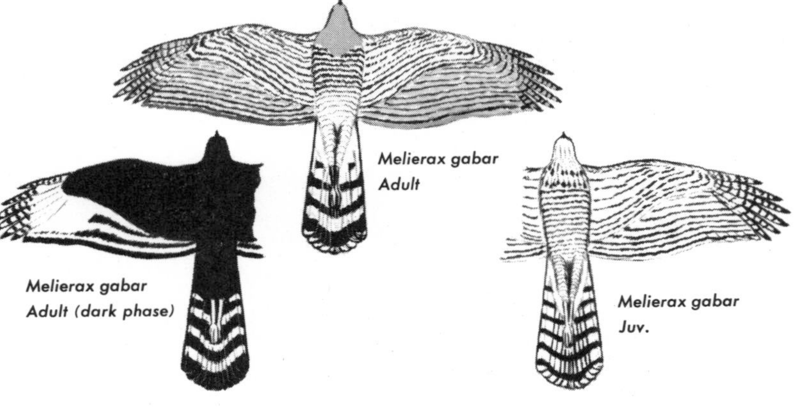

Melierax gabar *Adult*

Melierax gabar *Adult (dark phase)*

Melierax gabar *Juv.*

HABITS

The chanting goshawks are more often seen perched on some exposed branch, telephone pole, rock pile, or ant hill than on the wing. Their food is mainly lizards; also frogs, small snakes, grasshoppers and other insects, and occasionally mice or small birds. The larger species, the Pale Chanting Goshawk, can take game up to the size of hares. In the early morning these goshawks course very low over the plains. However, their ground foraging habits are so pronounced that their underparts, which are silvery to darkly metallic in fresh plumage, quickly become soil-stained and their claws blunted and worn.

Their large shallow stick nests are built 25 to 30 feet from the ground in various kinds of bushes and trees. These are used year after year, or new ones may be built close by. The Dark Chanting Goshawk provides a lining of feathers, mud, rags, or camel dung, and its nest is often covered with cobwebs. The eggs, one or occasionally two, are white, greenish-white, or pale bluish-green.

The Gabar Goshawk does not sit about in the open, and its behavior and food are much like the "typical" bird hawks'. In east Africa it preys heavily on weaver finches.

It nests high (50 to 60 feet from the ground) on the flat fork of a large tree. Camouflage of web, spider cocoons, and acacia bark similar to that of the Dark Chanting Goshawk have been recorded. The Gabar Goshawk transports spiders along with their webs, and the spiders continue to weave gossamer around the small structure of sticks and twigs. Two to three white or greenish-white eggs are laid at two- or three-day intervals. The hen sits close, because at nesting time the acacias and other trees are leafless.

Like the accipiters, the hawks of this genus are ordinarily silent except in the breeding season. The musical piping note of the chanting goshawks is varied by shrill whistles, wailings, and an occasional loud "kek." The Gabar Goshawk gives a series of thinner chittering notes; also an alarm note much like that of a sparrowhawk.

The Savanna Hawk *(Heterospizias meridionalis)*, occurring from Panama to Argentina, may be recognized by its conspicuous coppery-colored head and wings.

GENUS *HETEROSPIZIAS*

Heterospizias is a common South American hawk with long, slender, and scutellate tarsi and proportionally short toes. In flight, the red wings appear rather long, narrow, and darkly bordered. The slate-blue bloom on the plumage of the back is not a characteristic of the species until the bird is fully adult in its fourth year.

Savanna or Red-winged,Hawk (*Heterospizias meridionalis*)

DESCRIPTION (PANAMA AND SOUTH AMERICA)

Heterospizias meridionalis Adult

Heterospizias meridionalis Imm.

Heterospizias meridionalis Juv.

Head and nape, light amber-brown, finely streaked with light blue-gray; back and greater wing coverts, medium olive-gray with a slate-blue cast, shading to brown on the rump and tail coverts; lesser wing coverts and wings, light amber-brown to amber-brown, the latter finely barred with dark gray-brown; tail, dark brown with a wide median band of white, also white-tipped. Face, light blue-gray streaked with brown; underparts, white to light amber-brown, finely barred dark gray-brown; thighs, dark amber-brown.

Immature (third year)—similar to adult, but entirely brown above without any slate-blue cast on the back.

Immature (second year)—dark brown above, a white patch on the forehead and white eyebrows; face and throat, white, finely streaked; underparts, streaked to lower breast, which is feather-edged (or irregularly barred) dark brown. Wings are paler than in the adult, but more completely barred; tail, mixed white and light amber-brown, narrowly barred at the base and subterminally banded black.

Juvenile—like immature, but darker below, with pale feather-edging; wings and tail, whiter.

Beak, black; cere, pale yellow; eyes, golden-brown; tarsi and feet, pale yellow. Size, 18–20 inches.

HETEROSPIZIAS MERIDION

HABITS

As suggested by its name, the Savanna Hawk frequents grasslands and fields, especially around swamps and streams. It is not restricted to lowlands, and may be found in open valleys at higher altitudes in southeastern Brazil; also in tropical savanna and occasionally along the edge of the deciduous seasonal forest in Venezuela.

When not sailing low over the ground looking for reptiles and rodents, these brightly colored hawks may be seen perched on some small prominence such as a grass hummock, tree stump, or low fence post. In the Argentine Chaco they frequently follow grass fires. An observer records their aerial display during the nesting season in British Guiana, during which two or three birds will play for hours at a great height, circling and uttering sharp screams, and repeatedly descend on motionless wings, with their long legs hanging downward.

The nest of twigs, lined with fresh branches, is built high in the crotch of a tree in the interior of the forest. One or two white or bluish-white eggs are sometimes marked with reddish-brown spots.

The call note, given in flight, is a high-pitched "kree-ee-ee-er"; and in courtship is a snarling, grunting "kweh, kweh, kweh-h kweh kweh."

Immature Savanna Hawk *(Heterospizias meridionalis)*.

SUBFAMILY BUTEONINAE

(*Broad-winged Hawks, White Hawks, Lizard and Grass-hopper Buzzards, Black Hawks, Fishing Hawks, Giant Forest Eagles, Crested Eagles, True Eagles, and Sea Eagles*)

In its habits the Patagonian Buzzard-Eagle *(Geranoaetus melanoleucus)* is a "true" eagle, capable of taking small to medium-sized mammals, and at the carcass of a sheep or horse all other scavengers—the Carancho, Chimango, and gulls—wait until its appetite is satisfied before they will approach.—*Photographed at the National Zoological Park.*

GENUS *GERANOAETUS*

These medium to very large-sized buteo-like hawks have a substantial and rather compressed, deeply hooked beak; wide gape; and sparsely feathered lores. The feathers of the head and neck are lanceolate as in the genus *Aquila* and some of the large vultures. Feathering covers the tarsi about one-third down, with the stout legs and toes otherwise scutellate. In flight the wings are long and broad, and the tail appears short and wedge-shaped or strongly rounded. The young birds do not molt into their fully adult plumage, with pure white or faintly barred underparts—depending on the locality—until the fourth year.

Buzzard Eagle (*Geranoaetus melanoleucus*)

DESCRIPTION
(CHILE; NORTHWESTERN ARGENTINA TO PATAGONIA AND THE STRAITS OF MAGELLAN)

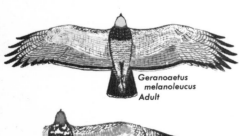

Geranoaetus melanoleucus Adult

Above, dark slate-gray; wing coverts, light olive-gray, barred and finely streaked with slate-gray; wings and tail, dark slate-gray, the former barred and the latter tipped with light olive-gray; face and throat, light olive-gray; chest, dark slate-gray; rest of underparts, white, barred with medium olive-gray.

Immatures—begin to molt into white, heavily barred underparts at two and one-half years, and the succeeding year they become adult with paler, finer barring.

Juvenile—dark brown from crown to mantle, streaked with light amber-brown; rest of upperparts brown, the wing coverts heavily mottled and edged in pale yellow-orange and white; wings and tail, finely barred light olive-gray; face, throat, and underparts, light amber-brown, with dark brown streaking and barring.

Beak, black; eyes, dull red-orange; legs and feet, yellow. Size, 25–27 inches.

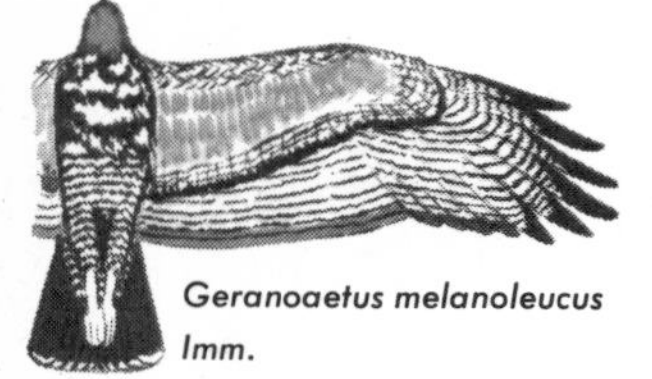

Geranoaetus melanoleucus Imm.

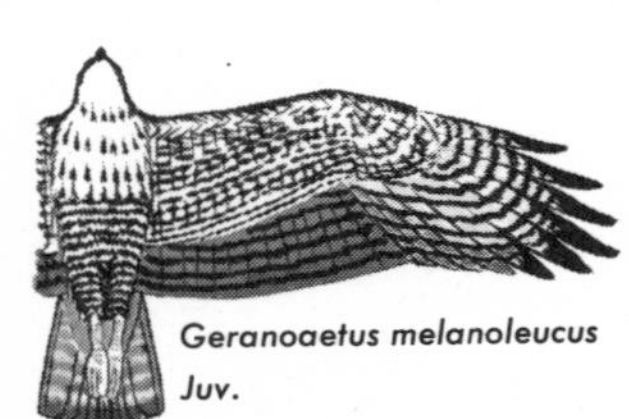

Geranoaetus melanoleucus Juv.

GERANOAETUS MELANO LEU

VARIATIONS

In Paraguay, southern Brazil, Uruguay, and eastern Argentina, the Buzzard Eagle has a pure white lower breast and belly, immatures only retaining the heavy barring like those in extreme southern South America. However, the smaller northern Buzzard Eagle (22 inches) that ranges through Colombia, Ecuador, Venezuela, and Peru differs little from the barred Patagonian population except in size.

HABITS

Buzzard Eagles are birds of the mountains and plains. Their broad soaring wings carry them high above the earth as they circle and search for their prey. If no obstacles are in the way, they will bear off a cavy, rat, or opossum without touching the ground. Single birds may be seen at carrion on the plains, or frequently stationed on a rock for an hour or more watching over the dens of rats or a chicken yard. They also hunt in pairs. In breeding season the young are fed with small mammals and birds up to the size of ducks, pigeons, and poultry.

Their nests, built of large sticks nearly the thickness of a man's wrist, are over three feet in diameter; the older ones that have been built on year after year are at least five feet high, and the egg cups are lined with dry grass. Very large trees or high cliffs are preferred as nest sites, but some birds may build in stunted trees or bushes only six feet from the ground. Two to three white eggs show either no markings or a varying profusion of red, gray, purplish, or yellowish-brown blotches. The female incubates alone (probably longer than the 30 days recorded) while the male guards, circling in the air or perching on a rock or branch at some distance from the nest. He varies this routine by hunting and bringing his catch to her. Young are fledged in about four weeks.

Buzzard Eagles are very shy at the nest, and desert if disturbed. When eggs were taken from a pair in Chile, they did not nest again for two years. If wounded, however, shyness turns to ferocity (in self-protection), as one Chilean soldier found, shot an individual and received a pair of talons in his eyes.

Only rarely does the Buzzard Eagle cry out, in a voice that is partly a wild human laugh, partly a clear note like a curlew's. This happens in the vicinity of the nest and nearly always while the bird is on the wing.

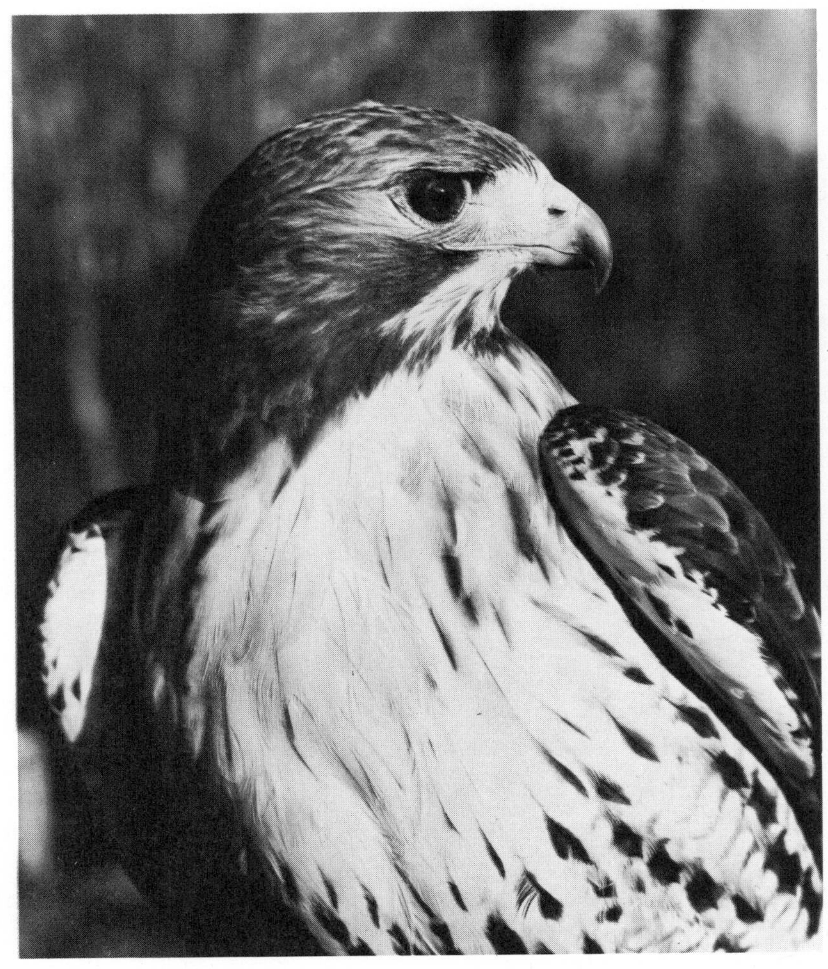

Broad wingspan and bright flared tail immediately identify the formidable Red-tailed Hawk *(Buteo jamaicensis)* in eastern North America. Individuals of Krider's Hawk, the Great Plains version, may have a white tail, but in the west even the Dark Phase is red-tailed.

GENUS *BUTEO*

The Red-tailed Hawk, Common Buzzard, and their allies inhabit wooded temperate and mountain zones of the Northern Hemisphere; also plains, savannas, steppes, and deserts with little tree growth. In boreal and tundra climate zones they are replaced by the Northern Rough-legged Hawk (*B. lagopus*). Although nearly cosmopolitan in distribution, including many species, the genus *Buteo* is not represented in the Indo-Malayan and Australian regions or in the southwest Pacific.

The beak and feet of a buteo hawk are generally moderate to large-sized; legs and feet scutellate in front, relatively short and stout with short toes (very slight in proportion to body size in the large rough-legged hawks, *B. lagopus* and *B. regalis*). Most buteos have partly feathered tarsi, but those of the Long-legged Buzzard (*B. rufinus*) are mostly bare, and the Mountain Buzzard (*B. hemilasius*) and rough-legged hawks have "leggings" or heavy thigh and tarsal feathering to the base of the toes. A broad supporting wing surface with from three to five outer primaries deeply notched enables buteos to soar more easily and for longer periods of time than accipiters and most kites, and wings of exclusively open-country species are proportionally longer. The buteo tail is short, and slightly to distinctly fan-shaped in flight.

Differences in size between males and females are not as striking among the buteos as in the genera *Accipiter* and *Falco,* and sexual differences in marking seem to occur only in the Northern Rough-legged Hawk and South American Red-backed Buzzard (*B. polyosoma*). Many species are individually variable in their plumage patterns—the Red-tailed Hawk in the western United States, for example, ranging from almost black (except wings and red tail) to red phase and a richly colored light phase. At their points of geographical contact, eastern, middle-western and western Red-tailed Hawks, and also Swainson's Hawks, breeding together, produce birds in which the strains are mixed and "mongrelized," perhaps with the characteristic underparts of one, back of another, and tail of still another.

Albinism is not infrequent in Red-tailed and Red-shouldered Hawks of the eastern United States. The Northern Rough-legged Hawks are polymorphic rather than dimorphic in their color phases, the lightest grading in an unbroken series to the darkest extremes with pale variants predominating in the cold and dry regions of Siberia and dark forms most frequently found in the cold and wet parts of northern North America.

Buteos undoubtedly do breed in young plumages even though they may not be fully mature until the second, third, or fourth year. The process of molting is extremely—and sometimes individually—variable. Some buteos keep their juvenile plumage for a year or longer—the Red-shouldered Hawk, up to eighteen months, at which time the feather-edging is so well-worn that the young bird closely resembles the adult. Since the molt commences with the breast feathers, however, it will be late winter before this bird has its adult wings and tail. Individuals of other species may begin their molts very early in the breeding season, starting with the wing and tail feathers. The juvenile Red-tailed Hawk of eastern North America may be seen with new red feathers in its tail in February, and most will have molted in the adult plumage by the fall of the second year. In certain light-phase birds—Swainson's Hawks, White-tailed Hawks, and the two Rough-legged—differences in plumage (lighter heads, underparts, or tails) continue to be noticeable over a period of three to four years. In these instances we are really noticing the light color phase as it develops from a dark juvenile to a light adult through a series of annual molts; while the development of the dark phase is not as conspicuous.

Red-tailed Hawk (*Buteo jamaicensis*)

DESCRIPTION (EASTERN NORTH AMERICA)

Brown above, crown and nape streaked with light amber-brown and white; lower back streaked with these colors; wings, barred dark brown; tail, dark amber-brown with a narrow subterminal black band and white-tipped. Face, light amber-brown, heavily streaked with brown. Chin and entire underparts, white or sandy-tinged with patches at the sides of the neck, spots across the belly, and fine barring of cinnamon-brown on the thighs.

Juvenile—appears more white than amber-brown streaked above, and instead of being brightly colored, the tail feathers are medium olive-gray entirely banded with brown. The face is white, and the underparts are white, broadly streaked (and barred on the thighs and lower belly) with brown.

Beak, blue-black; eyes, brown (juvenile, dull yellow); legs and feet, yellow; claws, black. Size, 19½–22 inches.

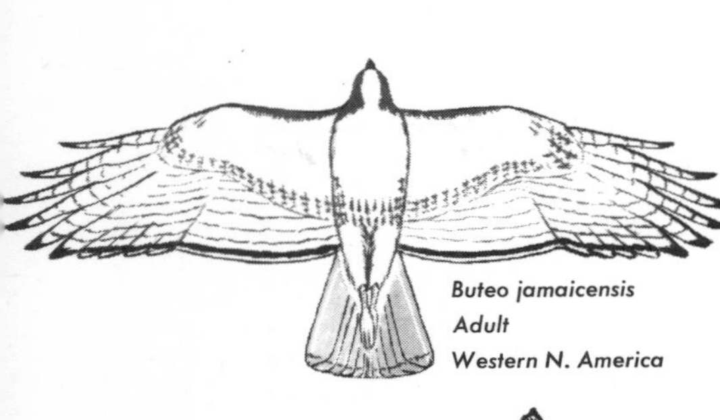

Buteo jamaicensis
Adult
Western N. America

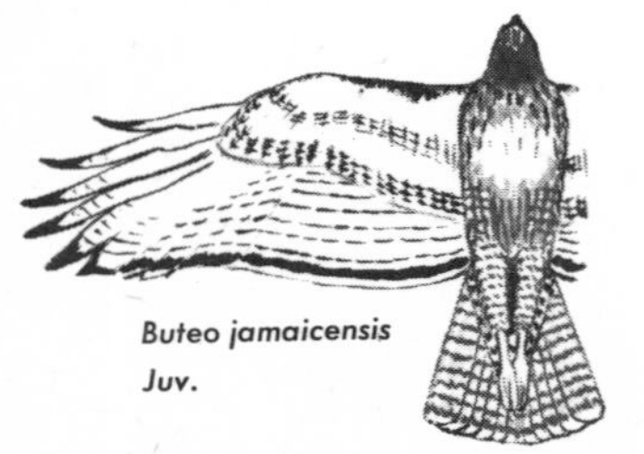

Buteo jamaicensis
Juv.

BUTEO JAMAICENSIS

VARIATIONS

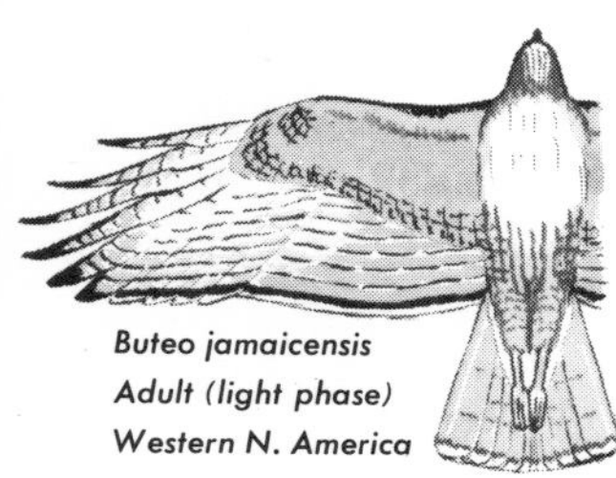
Buteo jamaicensis
Adult (light phase)
Western N. America

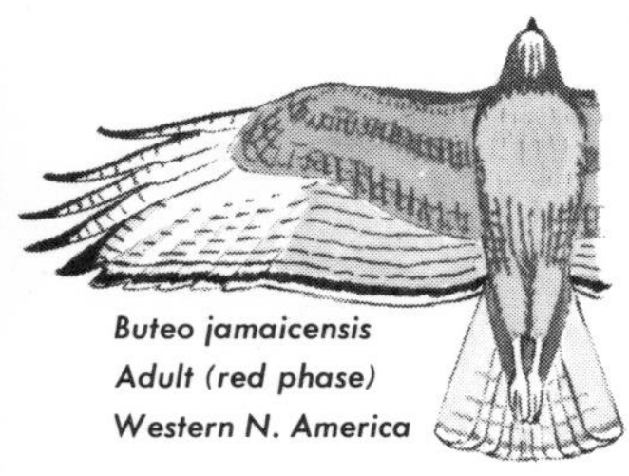
Buteo jamaicensis
Adult (red phase)
Western N. America

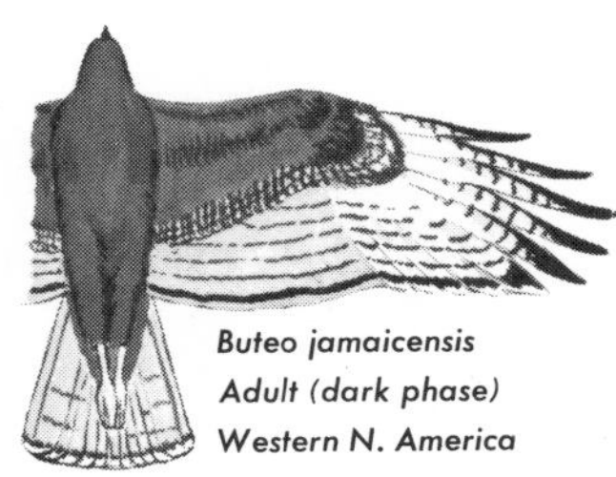
Buteo jamaicensis
Adult (dark phase)
Western N. America

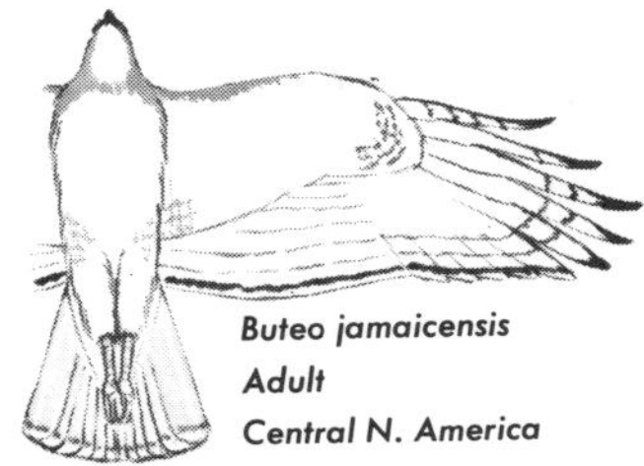
Buteo jamaicensis
Adult
Central N. America

Three phases occur through the interior of western North America from the Yukon to southern Baja California and northern Mexico in the west, and from the prairie provinces of Canada through the central plains to northwest Texas and Oklahoma: (1) Light phase similar to that of the Red-tail of the eastern United States, but darker above and more sandy-colored below, belly and thighs distinctly streaked and barred with amber-brown; (2) red phase, dark brown above and dark amber-brown below, streaked and barred on the belly and thighs and heavily tinged with sepia; (3) dark phase, dark brown above and below. Unlike other dark buteos in the west, red and dark phase birds have "red tails" irregularly or completely barred. In contrast, the pale variant on the Great Plains is nearly white below, sometimes with a white tail, subterminally banded black. Any one of these and many intermediates may be seen in the plains states. Along the Mississippi River, which roughly separates the Red-tailed Hawk populations of the eastern and western United States, there is much interbreeding which results in a mixture of racial types.

The relatively isolated Big Bend and south Texas population is paler on the underparts and underwing coverts than the western light phase, and the Tres Marías and Socorro Island birds in the Pacific Ocean, west of Mexico and south of Lower California, appear more uniformly sandy—not as distinctly streaked and barred below.

Several coastal, and island populations— including southeastern Alaska through the Queen Charlotte Islands, Florida and the Bahamas, Cuba and the Isle of Pines—resemble the eastern Red-tailed Hawks, but the tails may be marked with several narrow black bands. Other Caribbean birds—on Jamaica, Haiti, and the neighboring islets, Puerto Rico, and the Virgin Islands—are heavily marked with black across the belly; tails, with a single subterminal black band. In the highlands of Central America the Red-tailed Hawks are more cinnamon-colored below than in eastern North America, and in the northern part of their range (southern Mexico), tend to be like the western hawks.

Sizes range from 17 to 25 inches, the smallest in Jamaica and Alaska and the largest in Texas and northern Mexico.

OTHER NEW WORLD SPECIES

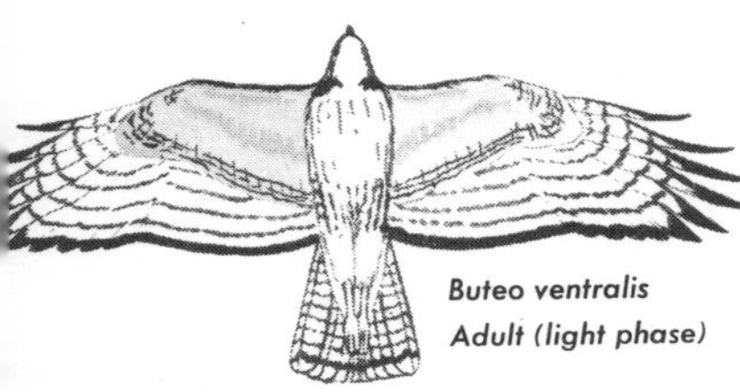
Buteo ventralis
Adult (light phase)

Several New World species are comparable in size or plumage pattern to *B. jamaicensis.*

The South American Rufous-tailed Hawk (*B. ventralis*), about 18–20 inches, nests in Chile from Ñuble to the Strait of Magellan and in the Santa Cruz area of Argentina. This bird resembles the light phase Red-tailed Hawk of western North America, but is darker, having brighter ferruginous streaking on the face and sides of neck and a ferruginous tail narrowly banded black and white-tipped. (Juvenile is like the northern Red-tailed Hawk, but lacks the bright tail.) The dark phase appears dark brown, except for the white-barred undersurface of the wings and tail.

BUTEO VENTRALIS

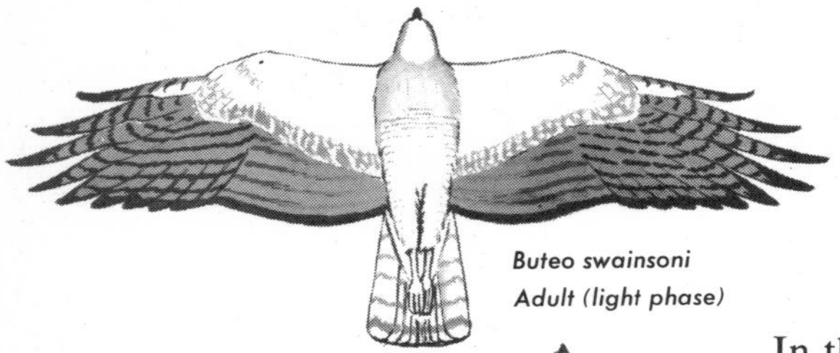

Buteo swainsoni
Adult (light phase)

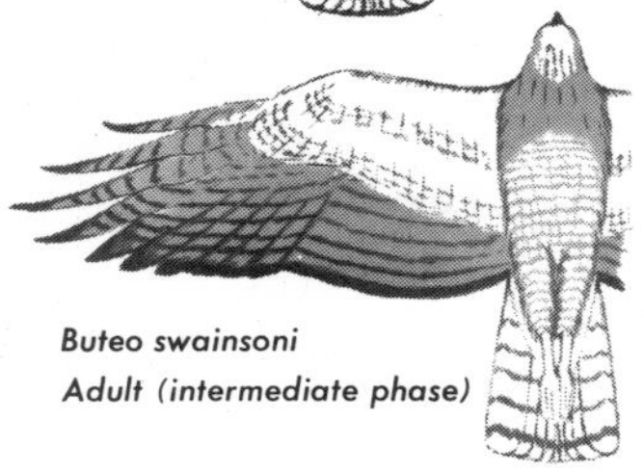

Buteo swainsoni
Adult (intermediate phase)

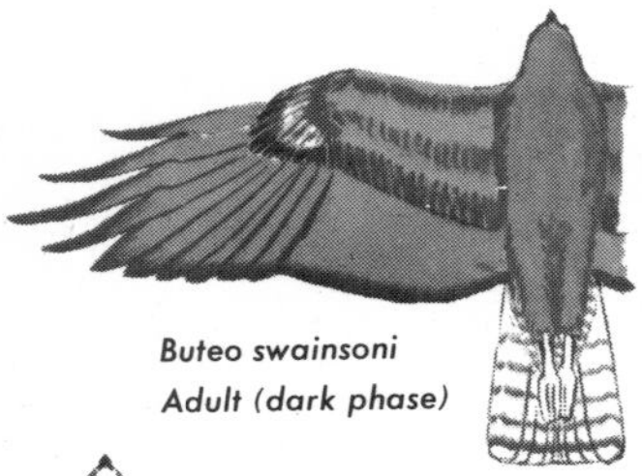

Buteo swainsoni
Adult (dark phase)

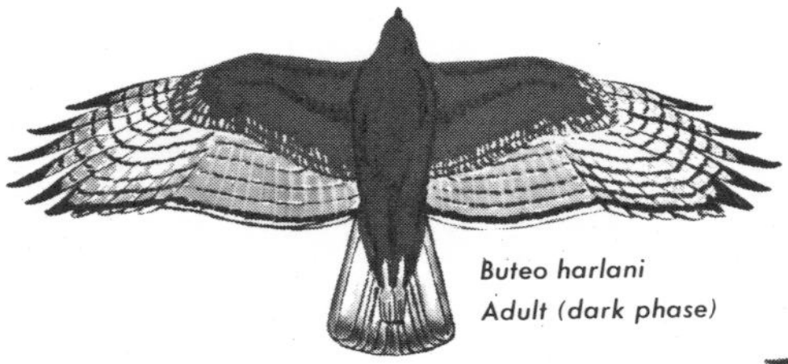

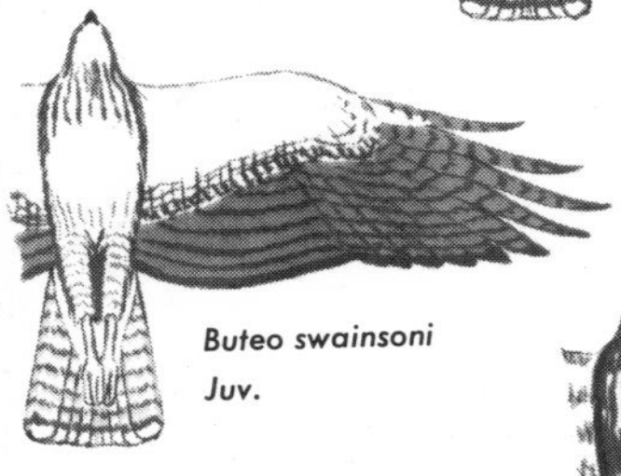

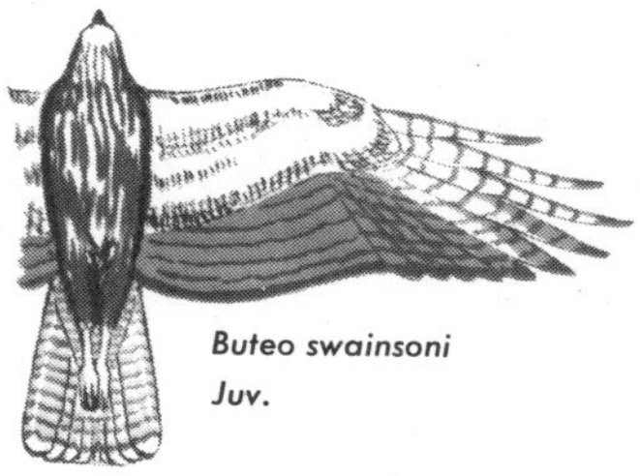

Buteo swainsoni
Juv.

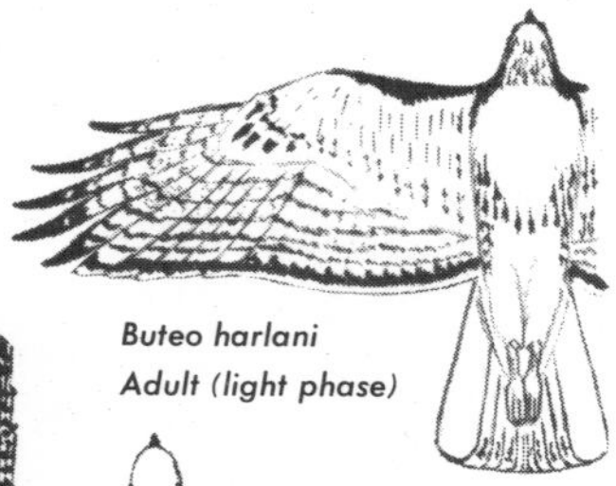

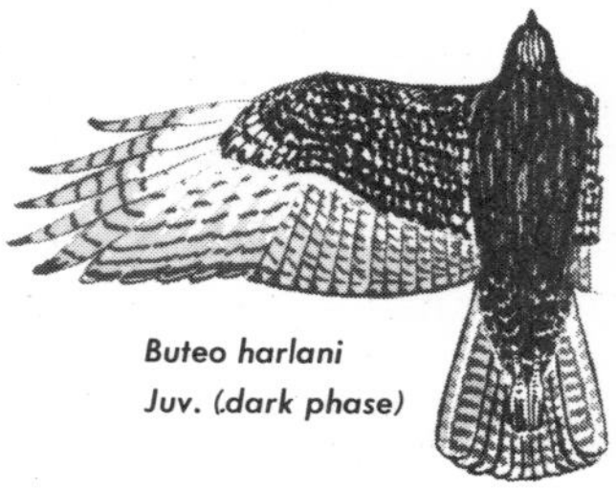

Buteo swainsoni
Juv.

In the western part of North America, Swainson's Hawk (*B. swainsoni*), 17½–20 inches, has a light cinnamon to cinnamon-brown breast in the light phase and the rest of the underparts barred. This bird is also commonly seen in a dark phase, but in either plumage, may be distinguished by its medium olive-gray tail, finely barred brown. Also in the northwest, Harlan's Hawk (*B. harlani*), 17½–20 inches, has a light phase with underparts, white, heavily streaked and barred with dark brown on the sides of the breast and upper belly, but it is most commonly known in the dark phase; the tail is white to amber-brown and is finely marbled in a darker color with a fragmentary subterminal band.

BUTEO SWAINSONI

BUTEO HARLANI

Buteo harlani
Adult (dark phase)

Buteo harlani
Adult (light phase)

Buteo harlani
Juv. (dark phase)

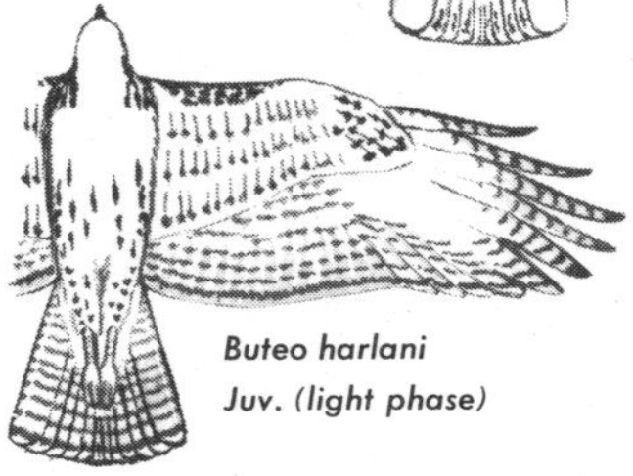

Buteo harlani
Juv. (light phase)

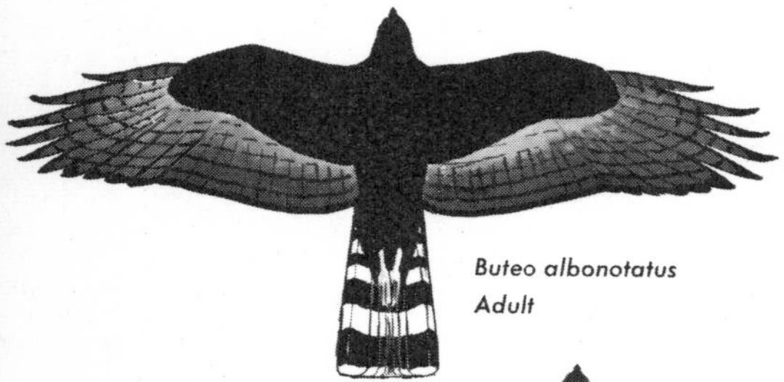

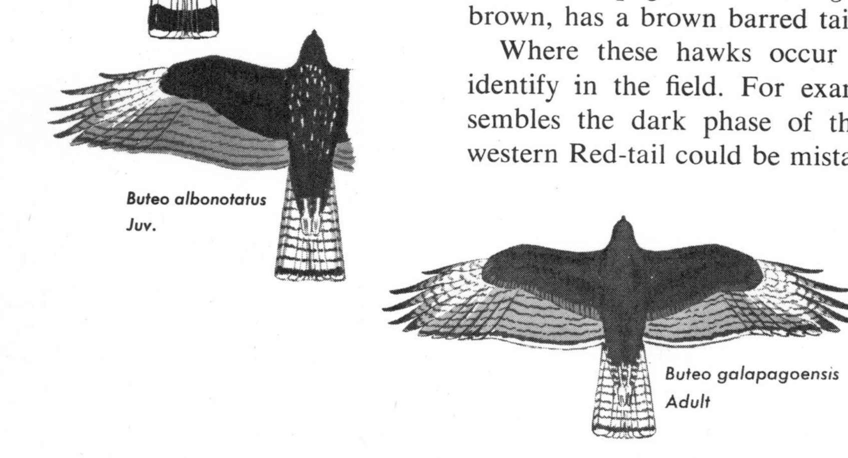
Buteo albonotatus
Adult

Buteo albonotatus
Juv.

Buteo galapagoensis
Adult

The Zone-tailed Hawk (*B. albonotatus*), 17½–20 inches, ranging from the mountains of the southwestern United States and Mexico to Paraguay and Bolivia, is dark brown to black with the tail barred black and white and an underwing pattern like that of the Turkey Vulture, which it sometimes resembles in flight.

The Galapagos Hawk (*B. galapagoensis*), 18–21 inches, also dark brown, has a brown barred tail like Swainson's Hawk.

Where these hawks occur together, many are very difficult to identify in the field. For example, the juvenile Harlan's Hawk resembles the dark phase of the western Red-tail, and the juvenile western Red-tail could be mistaken for an adult Swainson's Hawk.

BUTEO ALBONOTATUS

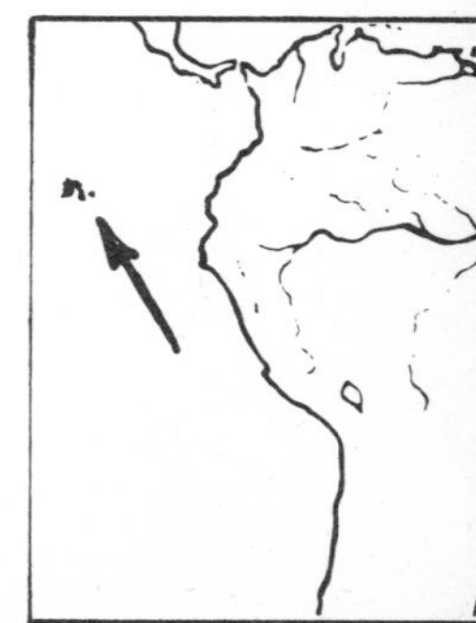
BUTEO GALAPAGOENSIS

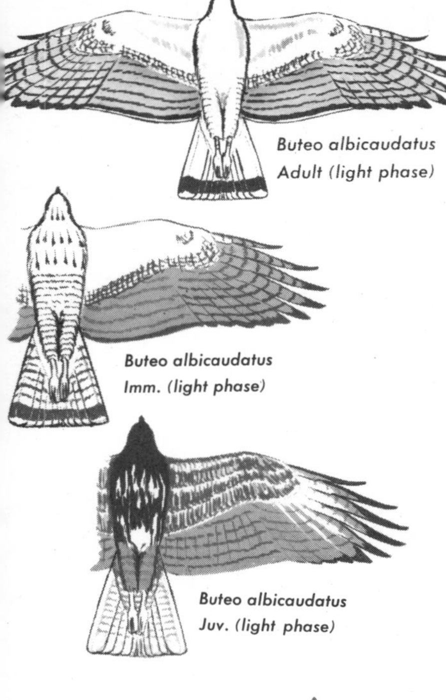

The White-tailed Hawk (*B. albicaudatus*), 23–24 inches, is a large, long-winged species, ranging locally from southern Texas through Central America and northern South America, and also southern South America. The light-phase birds in Texas have dove-gray heads and upperparts with amber-brown shoulders, and are distinguished in flight by white underparts (thighs and sides of belly sometimes faintly barred) and white tails, broadly and subterminally banded black. Some individuals have gray throats and/or gray patches on the sides of the chest also. In Central America and southward, light-phase individuals are slightly darker above—slate-gray, with amber-brown shoulders. The uncommon gray phase, in northern South America, is slate-gray above and below, sometimes without the amber-brown shoulder markings, and occasionally suffused with amber-brown on the thighs and flanks. A dark phase (dark brown above and below) occurs in southern South America. (Juveniles of all phases are darker than adults and have dark tails.)

BUTEO ALBICAUDATUS

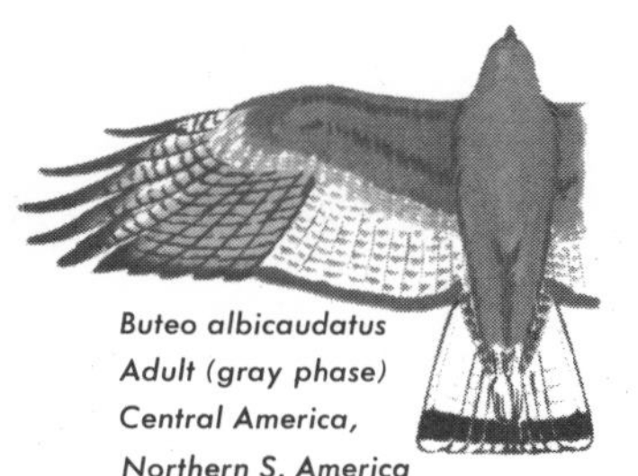

Common Buzzard *(Buteo buteo)*, with young. —*Photograph by Eric Hosking.*

Common Buzzard (*Buteo buteo*)

DESCRIPTION (EUROPE)

European "version" of Swainson's Hawk. Brown above with varying amounts of amber-brown and white streaking and feather-edging; wings, barred; tail, either brown or amber-brown, barred with dark brown; underparts, variable, even in light phase, and there is a dark phase like that of the North American species.

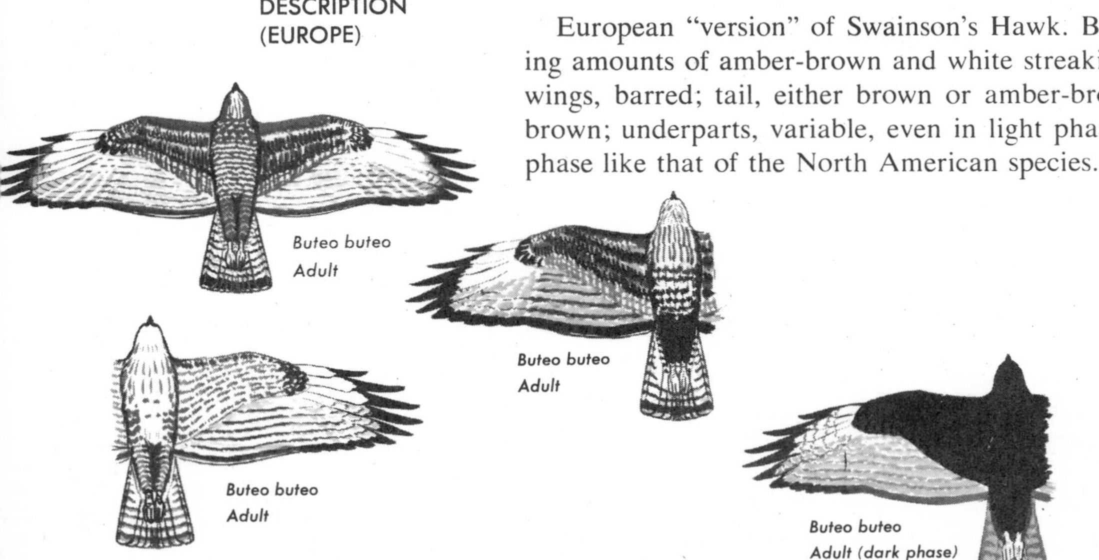

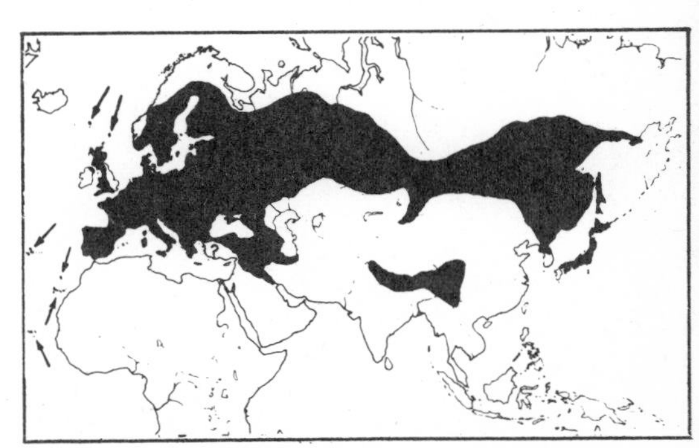

BUTEO BUTEO

Juvenile—somewhat similar to buteos previously described and variable according to light and dark phases; feathers of the upperparts edged pale ivory-gray or brighter (amber-brown); underparts within this range of color, streaked with sepia or gray-brown (lower belly and thighs sometimes barred); wings, as in adult; tail, occasionally tinged with amber-brown.

Beak, blue-black; eyes, brown (juvenile, gray); legs and feet, yellow; claws, black. Size, 18–21 inches.

VARIATIONS

The Cape Verde birds are much smaller and paler than *B. buteo* of Europe. On Corsica and Sardinia the population has stripes below, never coarse barring. Steppe populations of eastern Europe and western Asia, strongly tinged with amber-brown to cinnamon-brown, show "reddish thighs" which are especially conspicuous in the light phase but otherwise generally follow the color pattern of western European individuals. Dark variants in the Caucasus, described as a separate race, are (1) dark brown above, streaked with chestnut, and nearly solid chestnut below, shaft-streaked with dark brown—the tail amber-brown with or without a dark subterminal bar; (2) uniformly brown with dark shaft-streaking above and below—the tail barred with light olive-brown. In central and eastern Asia, buzzards of this species are similar above in coloring and marking to the steppe birds but less variable below in the light phase, having chestnut breasts, darkly shaft-streaked, with barring on the belly, and almost uniformly cinnamon-brown flanks and thighs. A dark phase has been noted (Swann). (The juveniles are very much lighter than any other population of *B. buteo* with white streaking and feather-edging above and nearly uniform white below, lightly streaked with cinnamon-brown.) Sizes vary from 17–21 inches.

OTHER OLD WORLD SPECIES

Adult Jackal or Augur Buzzard (Buteo rufofuscus) of tropical Africa.—Photographed at the New York Zoological Society.

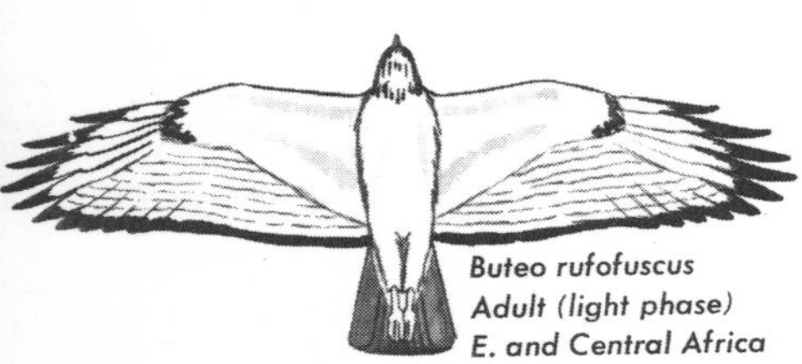

Buteo rufofuscus
Adult (light phase)
E. and Central Africa

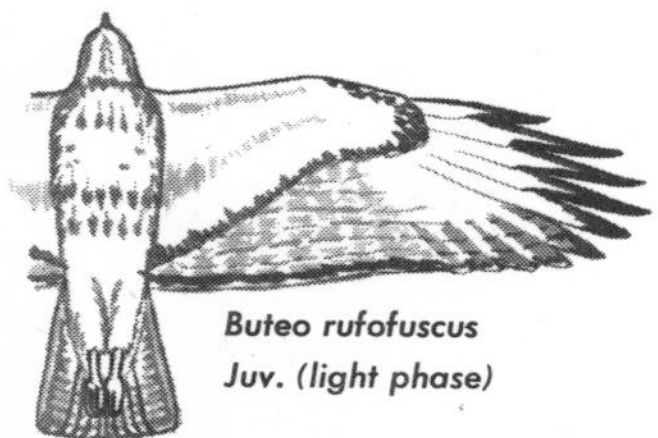

Buteo rufofuscus
Juv. (light phase)

The Jackal, or Augur, Buzzard (*B. rufofuscus*), 18–21 inches, throughout east and central Africa, is black above, with white barring on the secondaries and white underparts; tail, amber-brown, some-

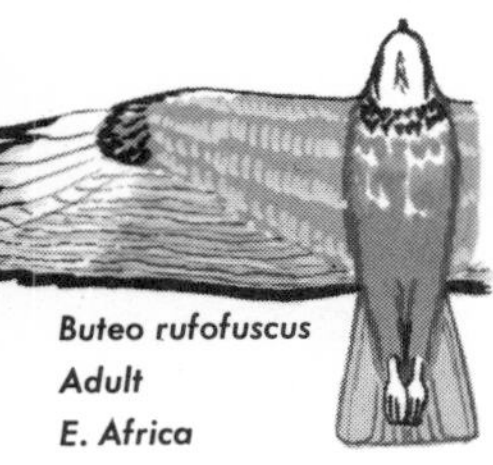
Buteo rufofuscus
Adult
E. Africa

times with a subterminal black bar. However, in British Somaliland (northeast Africa) it is richly streaked amber-brown above and nearly solid amber-brown below, except for fine dark streakings on the upper breast. The markings of the south African birds are quite different—the breast, black; upper belly, amber-brown; and lower belly, flanks, and thighs, black, barred in white (females slightly brighter than males). Everywhere a dark phase also occurs, distinguished from other dark-phase buteos by the unbarred white undersurface of the wings in flight and an amber-brown tail broadly and subterminally banded.

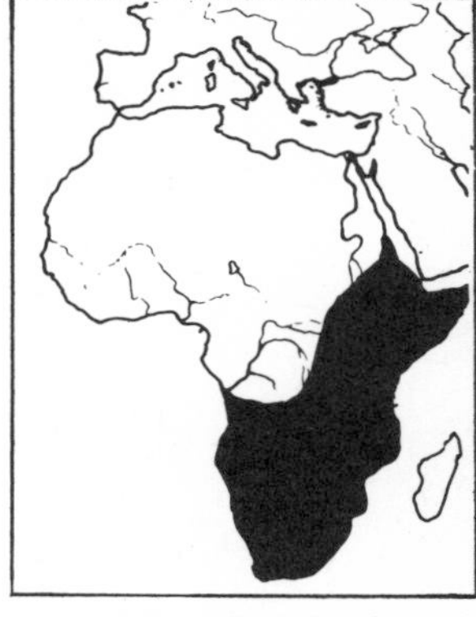
BUTEO RUFOFUSCUS

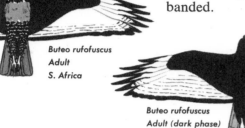

Buteo rufofuscus
Adult
S. Africa

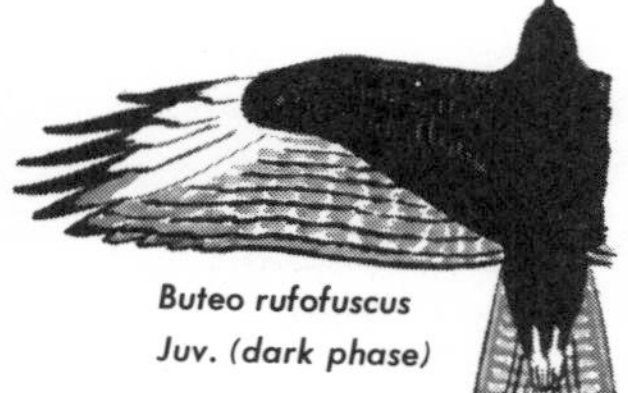
Buteo rufofuscus
Adult (dark phase)

Buteo rufofuscus
Juv. (dark phase)

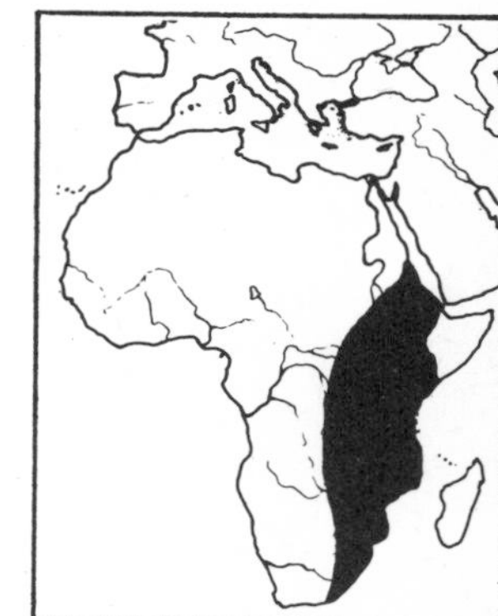
BUTEO OREOPHILUS

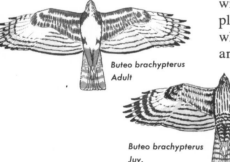

The Mountain Buzzard (*B. oreophilus*), 15–17 inches, indigenous to altitudes between 6,000 and 15,000 feet in east, central, and south Africa, has dark upperparts, except for some light streaking on the head and medium olive-gray barring on the wings. The light tail (which is seven-banded with a wider subterminal black bar) has ferruginous center rectrices in southern Africa. Underparts are white, heavily spotted or streaked with dark brown except for a ferruginous-barred lower belly, flanks, and thighs. (Juvenile—whiter below and not as heavily barred on the thighs.)

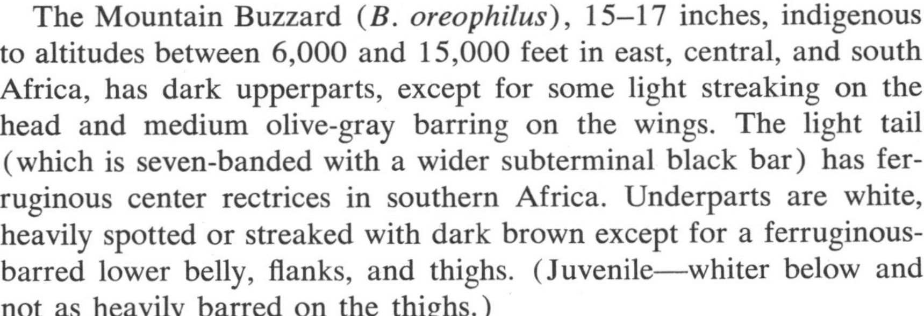
Buteo oreophilus
Adult

The Madagascar Buzzard (*B. brachypterus*), 15–17 inches, with wings proportionally much shorter than the tail, is very similar in plumage pattern to the Mountain Buzzard but has more extensive white areas below. (Young birds are heavily streaked on the belly and lightly barred on the thighs.)

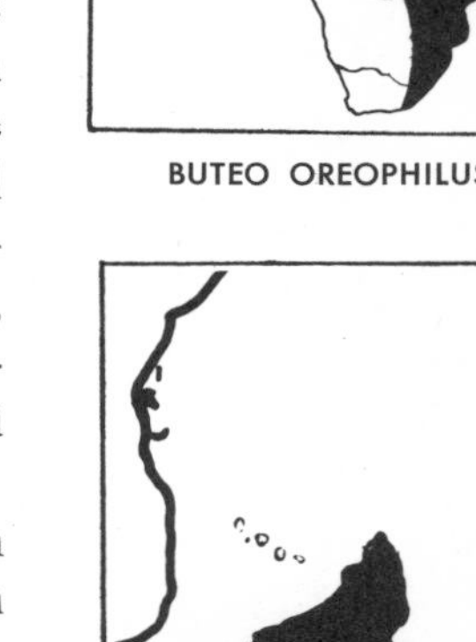
BUTEO BRACHYPTERUS

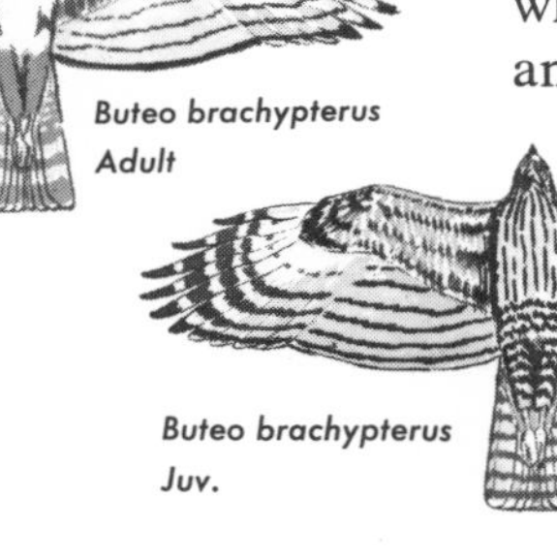
Buteo brachypterus
Adult

Buteo brachypterus
Juv.

African Red-tailed Buzzard *(Buteo auguralis)* in juvenile plumage.

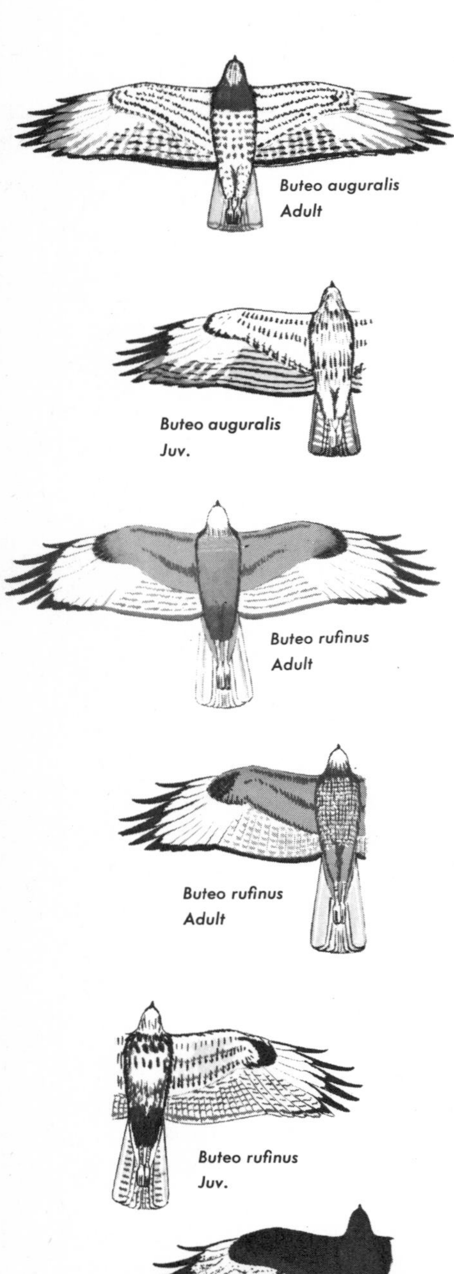

The African Red-tailed Buzzard (*B. auguralis*), 15½–17 inches, common in tropical west Africa, also occurs in northeast Africa (Sudan and Ethiopia) where it is known as the Red-necked Buzzard. Smaller than other African buteos, it has a distinctive amber-brown streaked head, neck, and mantle, the color of the chest sometimes in striking contrast to the white, sparsely spotted underparts. (Juvenile—dark brown above, feather-edged amber-brown; light amber-brown below, with a variable amount of dark streaking.)

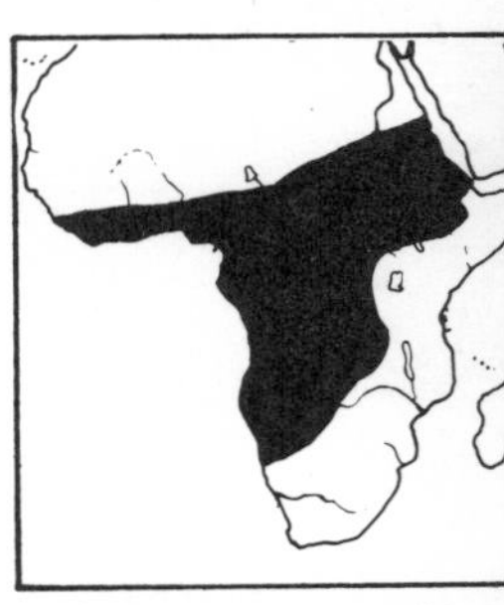
BUTEO AUGURALIS

Built like a small eagle with heavy beak, legs, and feet, the Long-legged Buzzard (*B. rufinus*), 23–26 inches, breeds along with the smaller Common Buzzards (*B. buteo*) on the arid steppes and plains of southeastern Europe and Asia Minor, extending beyond their ranges to western Mongolia and the western Himalayas. Liberally streaked with amber-brown and dark brown above, the Long-legged Buzzards vary from white below with amber-brown sides of breast, flanks, and thighs, or solid amber-brown below, to amber-brown, finely barred with dark brown. The unbarred amber-brown tail distinguishes this species from *B. buteo.* (Juveniles—tail is dark brown with indistinct barring.)

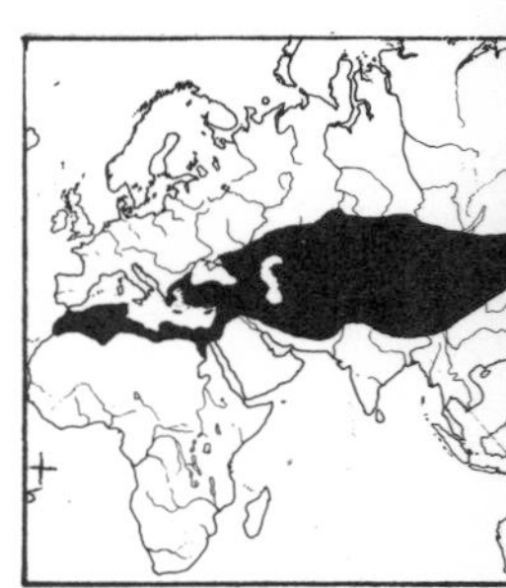
BUTEO RUFINUS

The dark phase in the Caucasus has a medium olive-gray tail broadly tipped with dark brown. The generally paler north African desert birds are much smaller (about 18 inches). In winter the European birds may be found chiefly from northern Sudan to the valleys of the White and Blue Nile, and the Asiatic buzzards reach northwestern India.

The Upland Buzzard (*B. hemilasius*), 23–26 inches, breeds at altitudes between 12,000 and 15,000 feet in Tibet. This species is a close relative of the Long-legged Buzzard, which it resembles except for heavy tarsal feathering to the base of the toes, darker thighs, and a faintly barred or marbled tail, tinged with amber-brown, especially at the tip. (Juveniles show white streaking on the head and patches of white on the underparts, with only a light amber-brown tint, and the tail is completely barred.)

BUTEO HEMILASIUS

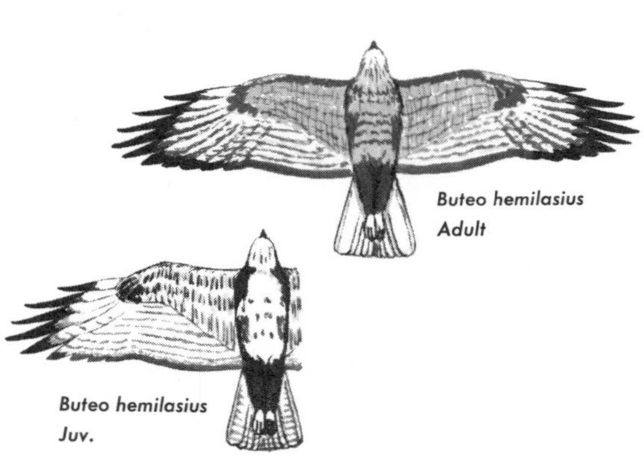

Ferruginous Rough-legged Hawk *(Buteo regalis)*.

Ferruginous Rough-legged Hawk (*Buteo regalis*)

DESCRIPTION (ARID WESTERN AND CENTRAL NORTH AMERICA)

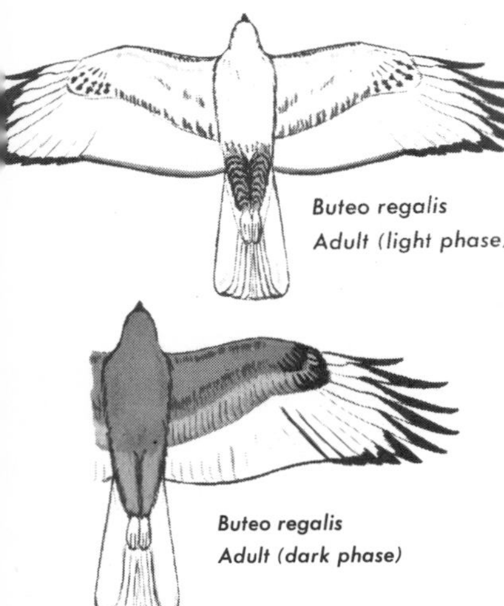

Buteo regalis
Juv. (light phase)

Light Phase—Above, sepia, variably streaked with white and amber-brown; wing coverts with extensive amber-brown; wings light olive-gray, barred with sepia; tail, light tan (marbled with sepia and tinged amber-brown above). Face and underparts, including underwing surface, white; lower belly streaked and barred with sepia, and "leggings" amber-brown, barred with dark brown. As in other western buteos, there is a dark phase. In flight the unbarred wings and tail distinguish this dark variant from the dark-phase Northern Rough-legged Hawk (*B. lagopus*), which has barred wings and a dark-tipped tail.

Immatures—like adults, but darker above in the light phase, with mostly white streaking; underparts, entirely white except for brown-spotted "leggings"; tail, family barred and tipped in white. (Juveniles, heavily barred with a broader white tip.) Dark-phase young are probably similar to adults, except for tail markings.

Beak, blue-black; eyes, brown (young, yellow); feet, yellow. Size, 23–25 inches.

BUTEO REGALIS

OTHER SPECIES

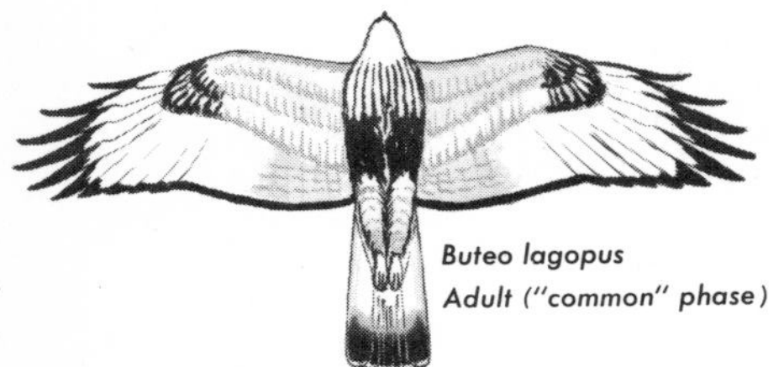
Buteo lagopus
Adult ("common" phase)

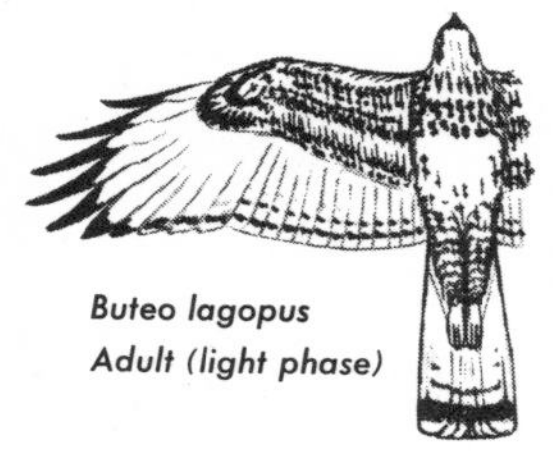
Buteo lagopus
Adult (light phase)

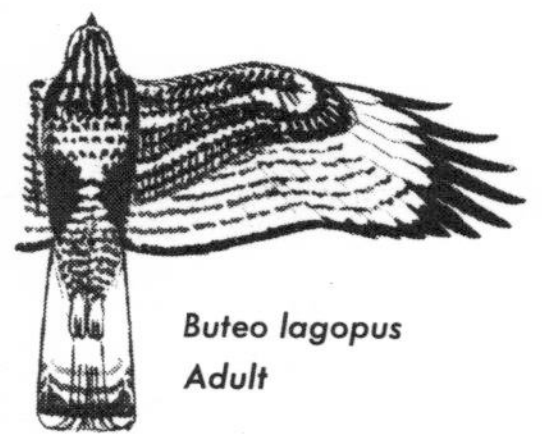
Buteo lagopus
Adult

Buteo lagopus
Adult (dark phase)

The circumpolar Northern Rough-legged Hawk (*B. lagopus*), 20–23 inches, is extremely variable. North American *light phase,* white below, is lightly streaked on the breast and heavily barred with dark gray-brown on the sides, flanks, and "leggings." The banded tail distinguishes it from the light phase Ferruginous Rough-legged Hawk, which has immaculate white wings and tail. The common phase is much darker—predominantly dark gray-brown, with the head, neck, and breast sandy streaked with dark gray-brown, and so heavily barred on the sides that a dark patch or "shield" often covers the belly. The tail appears more or less broadly and subterminally banded with dark gray-brown.

Variations in the "shield" and tail pattern are to some degree sexual differences. The *female* tends to have the dark belly; also, the basal half of her tail is white and the subterminal part broadly banded with brown and dark gray-brown. The *male* may have a white tail narrowly barred near the tip with dark gray-brown.

Sexual dimorphism in tail pattern, as well as in size, breaks down in an east to west direction (except for the pronounced difference between males and females in the Aleutians and southwestern Alaska), but the solid belly pattern becomes more constant in females westward.

Young resemble adults, but they are usually less heavily marked dark brown and are tinged yellow-orange on the chest.

The dark phase, with a white underwing surface and white tail subterminally banded black, is most abundant in the Aleutians, southwestern Alaska, Ungava, and Labrador. Within their northern breeding range, size and more slender shape distinguish dark Northern Rough-legged Hawks from the dark phases of the larger western Red-tailed Hawk and the smaller Harlan's Hawk; and the white undersurface of the wings and tail, from the darker Swainson's Hawk. (Juveniles resemble the adults, but are lighter—sepia above and below, and have barred tails.)

The individuals of *B. lagopus* of the tundras of northern Scandinavia and Russia (to the Yenisei) do not differ much from the American birds in their light and dark plumage. The east Siberian population tends to be much whiter in the "normal" phase, but dark variants also occur, and in the Bering Sea region, the population freely interbreeds with North American individuals resulting in a variety of intergrades.

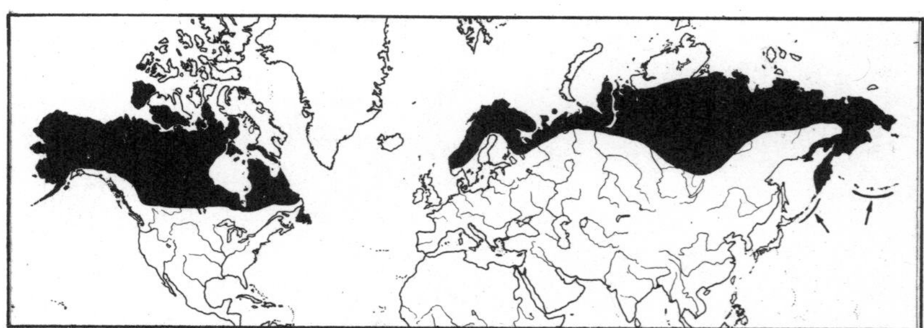
BUTEO LAGOPUS

Red-shouldered Hawk *(Buteo lineatus)* of Florida.

Red-shouldered Hawk (*Buteo lineatus*)

DESCRIPTION (EASTERN U.S. AND CANADA)

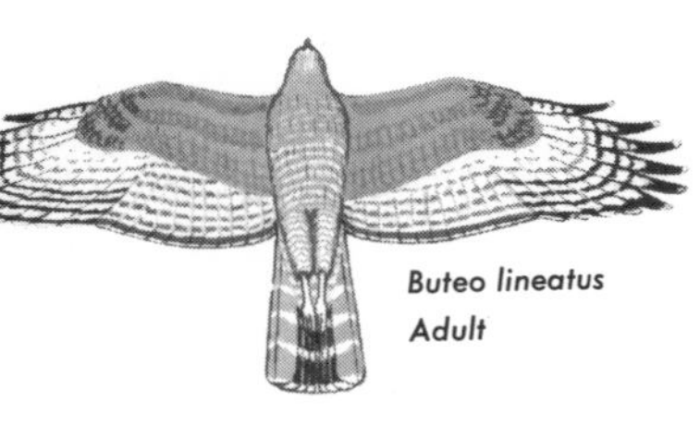

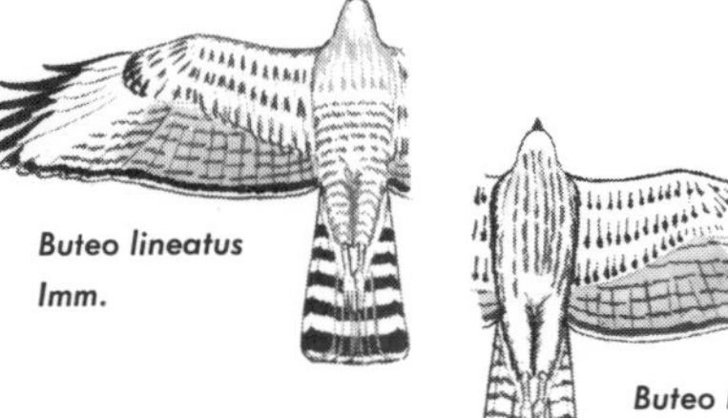

Buteo lineatus
Juv.

Brown above, with broad ferruginous streaking; wing coverts, ferruginous, tipped in white; wings, brown, barred white to medium olive-gray and tinged ferruginous as well as white-tipped; tail, dark brown, with four to five white bands and white-tipped. Face and throat, light tan, streaked with dark brown. Underparts, light amber-brown, shaft-streaked with dark brown, becoming conspicuously barred buff-white on the lower breast, belly, and flanks.

Juvenile—darker above, with less ferruginous streaking; wings and tail, indistinctly barred; below, white, streaked with dark brown.

Beak, blue-black; eyes, brown; legs and feet, yellow. Size, 18½–20 inches.

BUTEO LINEATUS

VARIATIONS

The Florida population is smaller (16–18 inches) and paler above and below, with bright ferruginous coloring only on the shoulder, but its wings and tail are darkly barred. The western population, restricted mostly to the humid Pacific coastal valleys and lowlands, compares in size to the eastern bird, but it may average slightly darker (amber-brown) below.

Short-tailed Hawk (*Buteo brachyurus*)

DESCRIPTION
(CENTRAL AMERICA, SOUTHERN AND EASTERN MEXICO [TO 6,500 FEET IN MICHOACÁN] AND PENINSULAR FLORIDA)

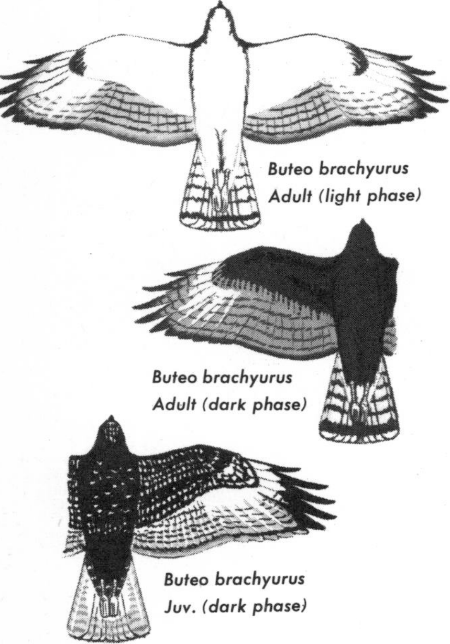

Buteo brachyurus Adult (light phase)

Buteo brachyurus Adult (dark phase)

Buteo brachyurus Juv. (dark phase)

Light phase—Dark brown above, sometimes collared in cinnamon-brown or cinnamon; wings flashing white, with dark mottling underneath; tail olive-brown barred with dark brown (but lighter below with bands sometimes absent, unlike Florida Red-shouldered Hawk). Black cap contrasts with white forehead and throat, and white underparts, marked with patches of cinnamon-brown or cinnamon only at the sides of the neck. *Dark phase*—dark brown to black, sometimes with a white patch on the forehead; tail dark brown barred with medium olive-gray (lighter below, frequently with only one subterminal band showing).

Juvenile (*light phase*)—like adult above, but with much white from bases of feathers showing at the nape and hindneck and buff feather-edging on the upperwing coverts and scapulars; sides of head and neck mixed with black and buff; underparts buff with a few black streaks across the upper breast (occasionally also on the belly or flanks). *Dark phase*—heavily mottled or streaked with dark brown and white and washed with buff below and on the underwing coverts.

Beak, black; cere, yellow; eyes, brown; legs and feet, yellow. Size, 14½–16 inches (largest in Florida).

BUTEO BRACHYURUS

VARIATIONS

The South American birds, found at altitudes up to 7,000 feet in the Andes, are black above, in the light phase, and marked on the sides of the neck with black (rarely amber-brown). The young birds in this phase are very much like the older ones, conforming to the juvenile previously described, but are darker above and usually lack any spotting on the underparts. A dark phase is known in Colombia.

RELATED SOUTH AMERICAN SPECIES

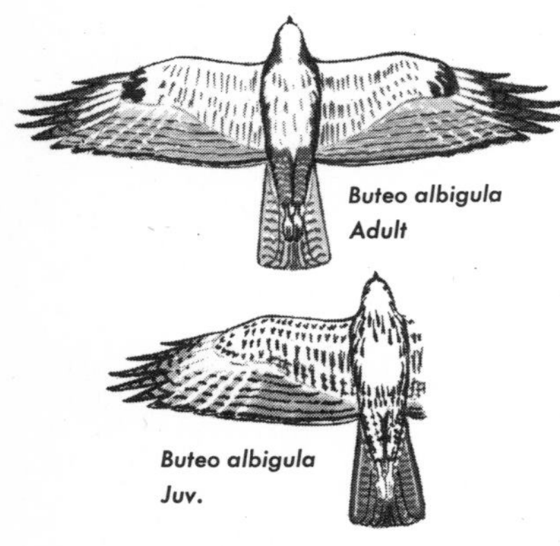

Buteo albigula Adult

Buteo albigula Juv.

The White-throated Hawk (*B. albigula*), which is comparable in size, replaces *B. brachyurus* generally in the Andes of South America above 7,000 feet. However, in Chile, where the Short-tailed Hawk does not occur, *B. albigula* lives at low altitudes, from sea level to 1,300 feet. The two species somewhat resemble each other and have been treated as conspecific, but amber-brown streaking at the sides of the neck, amber-brown or dark brown spotting on the underparts, and the thighs distinctly barred with amber-brown are good field marks for identifying the White-throated Hawk. (Juvenile—white or buff-colored below; more heavily spotted than the adult, with sepia-barred "flags.") No dark phase is recorded.

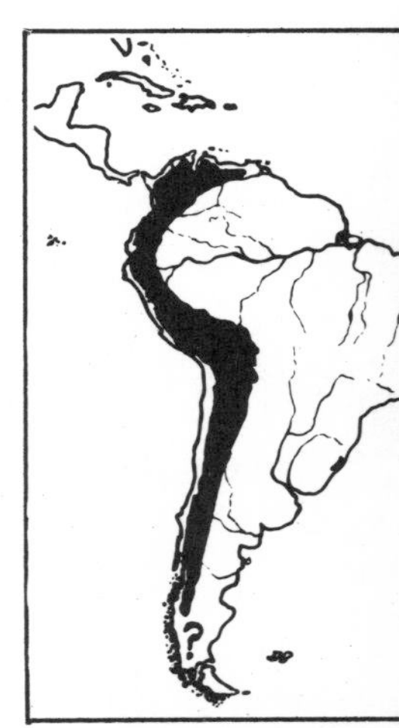

BUTEO ALBIGULA

White-rumped Hawk (*Buteo leucorrhous*)

DESCRIPTION
(ANDES MTS.)

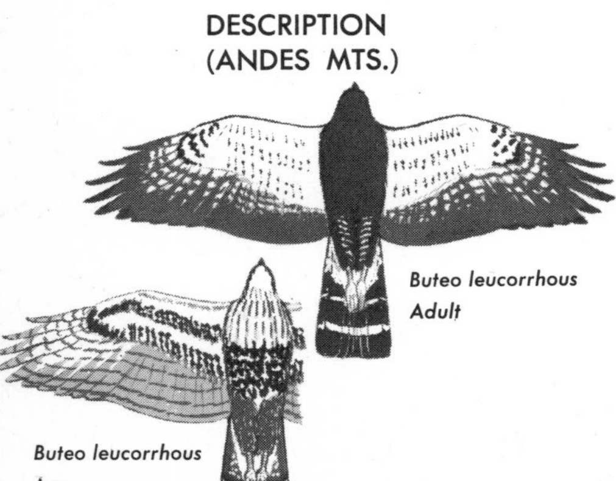

Buteo leucorrhous Adult

Buteo leucorrhous Juv.

Black, with a gray sheen; uppertail coverts, white; tail, crossed by a single subterminal band of medium olive-gray; thighs, amber-brown, barred with black. (In flight the undersurface of the wings appears dark except for white underwing coverts, spotted with black; tail shows two white bars.)

Juvenile—lighter, with sandy streaking on the head and feather-edging on the back; pale yellow-orange below, streaked on the breast

BUTEO LEUCORRHOUS

and barred on the belly with black; thighs, sienna brown, barred with black and white. (Wings appear barred in flight.)

Beak, orange-yellow, with a black tip; eyes, yellow; legs and feet, orange-yellow. Size, 13½–15 inches.

Black and Normal Phase of the Hawaiian Hawk *(Buteo solitarius)*.—*Photograph by R. Van Nostrand, from National Audubon Society.*

Hawaiian Hawk (*Buteo solitarius*)

DESCRIPTION (HAWAII)

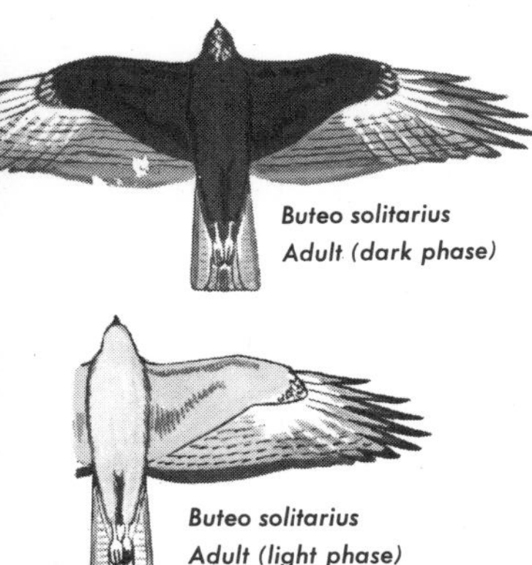

Buteo solitarius
Adult (dark phase)

Buteo solitarius
Adult (light phase)

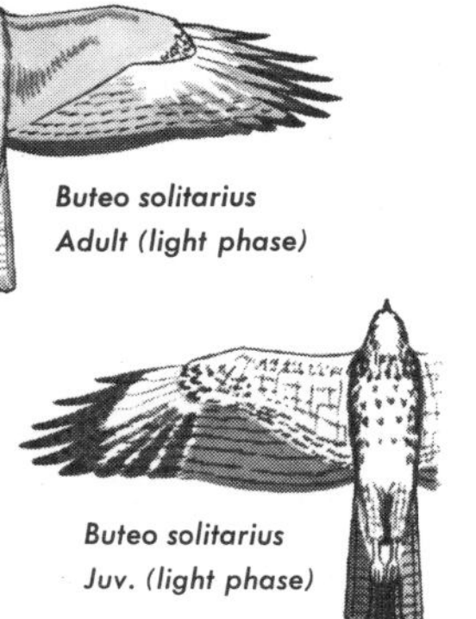

Buteo solitarius
Juv. (light phase)

Light phase—white head, neck, and underparts, heavily suffused with sandy and sometimes lightly streaked or spotted with dark brown; rest of upperparts, dark gray-brown, with white or light amber-brown barring and feather-edging; tail, medium olive-gray, irregularly barred with dark gray-brown. *Dark phase*—entirely dark brown, with some light streaking on the throat; tail, same as in light phase.

Juvenile (*light phase*)—lacks white head and has dark spotting on the underparts and a more distinctly barred tail. *Dark phase*—has sandy underparts deepening to pale yellow-orange, with dark spotting.

Beak, blue-black; eyes, dark hazel; legs and feet, greenish-yellow. Size, 14½–16 inches.

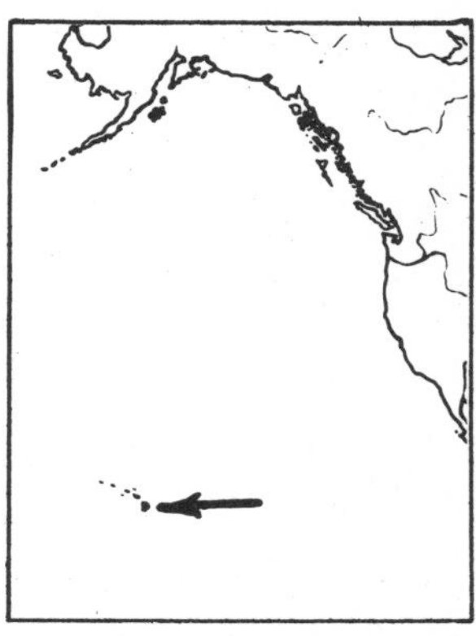

BUTEO SOLITARIUS

Broad-winged Hawk *(Buteo platypterus).*

Broad-winged Hawk (*Buteo platypterus*)

BUTEO PLATYPTERUS

DESCRIPTION (EASTERN NORTH AMERICA)

Small and chunky. Gray-brown to dark brown above, streaked on the head and feather-edged on the back with amber-brown; wings, dark (white underneath); tail coverts, barred white; tail, dark brown, barred white to light olive-gray; underparts, olive-gray or dark amber-brown, completely spotted or barred with white. *Dark phase* (rare) is virtually indistinguishable in the field from the dark phase of the Short-tailed Hawk in tropical climates.

Juvenile (*light phase*)—has dark spots or streaks on light underparts; tail, barred narrowly. *Dark phase*—similar to light phase but dark amber-brown below with dark spotting.

Beak, blue-black; cere, yellow; eyes, light reddish-hazel (juvenile, pale brown); legs and feet, light yellow; claws, black. Size, 14–18 inches, smallest in Florida.

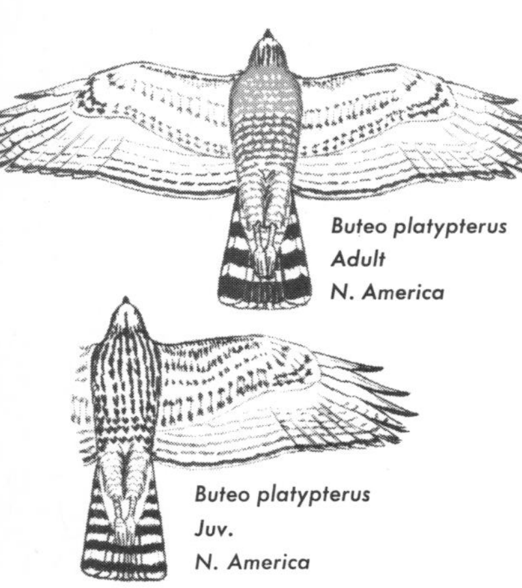

Buteo platypterus
Adult
N. America

Buteo platypterus
Juv.
N. America

VARIATIONS

In the Caribbean, Broad-winged Hawks are generally smaller and redder than most amber-brown-breasted individuals known throughout most of eastern North America, with the exception of the Antigua population, which is paler than the lightest of the gray-breasted North American birds. The dark phase has not been recorded in the Lesser Antilles. Sizes vary from 13–16 inches.

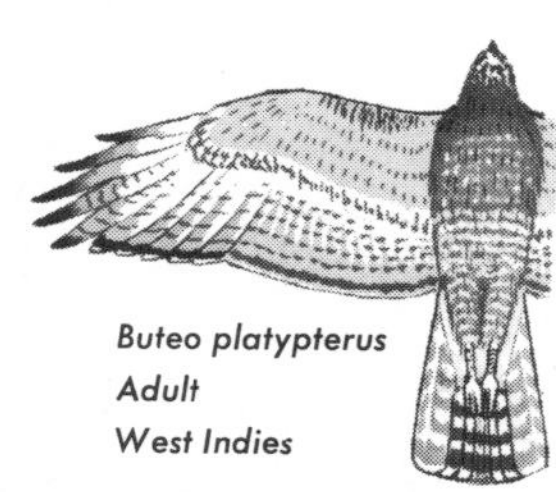

Buteo platypterus
Adult
West Indies

Roadside Hawk (*Buteo magnirostris*).

Roadside Hawk (*Buteo magnirostris*)

DESCRIPTION (NORTHERN SOUTH AMERICA, EAST OF THE COLOMBIAN ANDES)

Head, neck, chest, and back, medium olive-gray; secondaries, brown; primaries, sienna, barred with dark brown; tail, medium olive-gray, with three broad, dark brown bands; lower breast, belly, and thighs, barred white and yellow-brown, with a gray tinge.

Juvenile—sepia above with sandy streaking from crown to mantle; the feathers of the back, edged amber-brown. Face, also sandy-streaked; underparts, sandy to pale yellow-orange, streaked on the breast and V-spotted or barred with sepia on the belly and thighs.

Beak, black; cere, yellow; eyes, bright yellow; legs and feet, yellow; claws, black. Size, 11–13 inches.

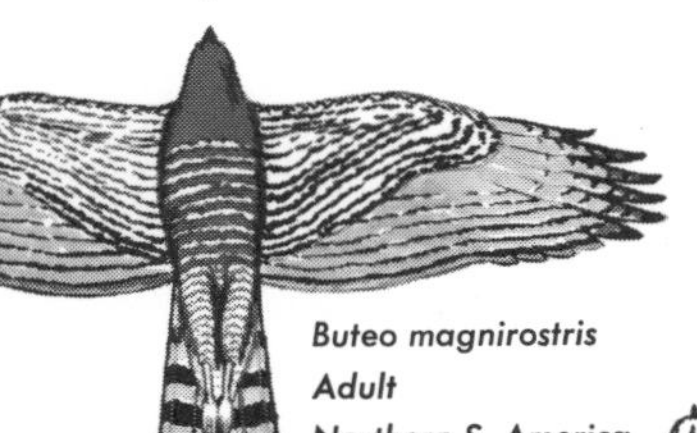

Buteo magnirostris
Adult
Northern S. America

Buteo magnirostris
Juv.

BUTEO MAGNIROSTRIS

VARIATIONS

The Roadside Hawks from Mexico to northern Argentina vary considerably in size and coloring according to locality, with much intergrading of local populations where ranges meet. In Venezuela and along the Amazon River they closely resemble the gray savanna bird described, but in many tropical forested regions they tend to be browner above, with gray chests and sienna and white or buff barring below (Mexico), or with sienna chests and sienna barring on the remainder of the white underparts (southeastern and central Brazil). In these redder individuals the wings are more extensively sienna-

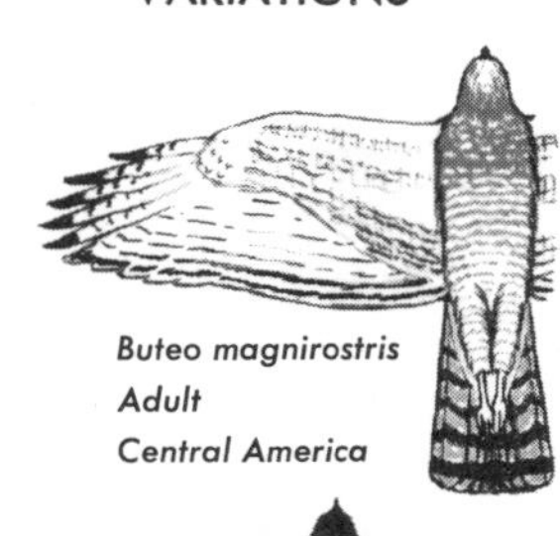

Buteo magnirostris
Adult
Central America

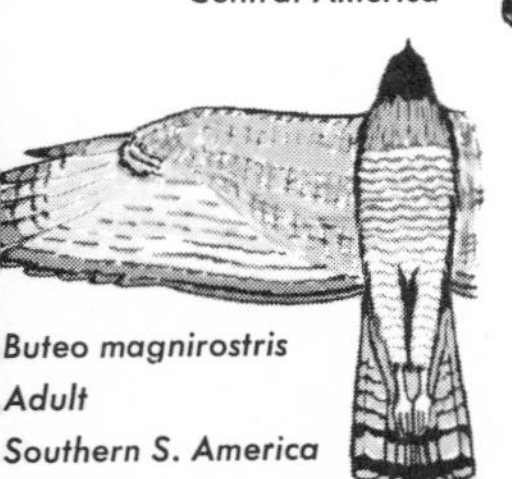

Buteo magnirostris
Adult
Southern S. America

colored in flight, and the tails tinged with sienna (most noticeable in Panama and Costa Rica). Other variations have pale yellow-orange chests and more or less distinct sienna barring below but their most distinctive field mark is a bright sienna tail, barred dark brown (Argentina, Paraguay, and Bolivia). A dark-phase hawk with a gray chest and white belly barred dark brown seems to occur only in Ecuador (to 3,000 feet above sea level).

Eye color in Central America is bright yellow, but the Mexican bird has orange-red eyes.

Juveniles appear streaked and spotted above and below like those of the South American population described.

Size, 13–15 inches, the largest in Mexico and the southern part of South America.

RELATED CARIBBEAN SPECIES

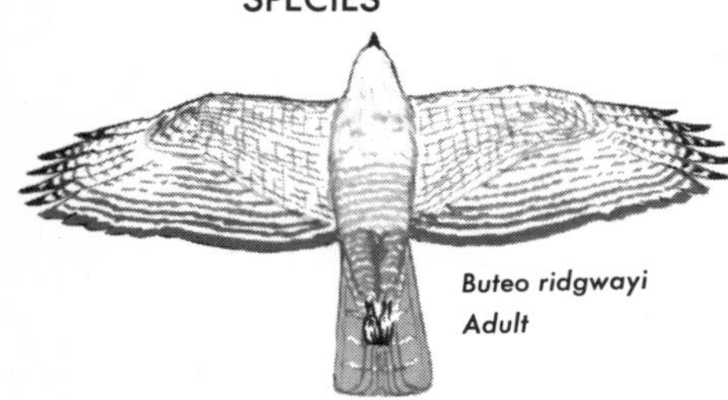

Buteo ridgwayi
Adult

Ridgway's Hawk (*B. ridgwayi*), of Hispaniola, somewhat resembles Mexican individuals of the Roadside Hawk but is slightly smaller and paler with brown-and-white barred wings, narrowly barred tail, and amber-brown patches on the wing coverts as well as dark tawny thighs finely barred with white. (Juvenile—darker above and streaked dark gray-brown below on a white background; wings, barred amber-brown.) The eyes in mature birds are brown or brownish-yellow; cere and tarsi, yellow-green.

BUTEO RIDGWAYI

Gray Hawk (*Buteo nitidus*)

DESCRIPTION (SOUTHWESTERN U.S. AND MEXICO)

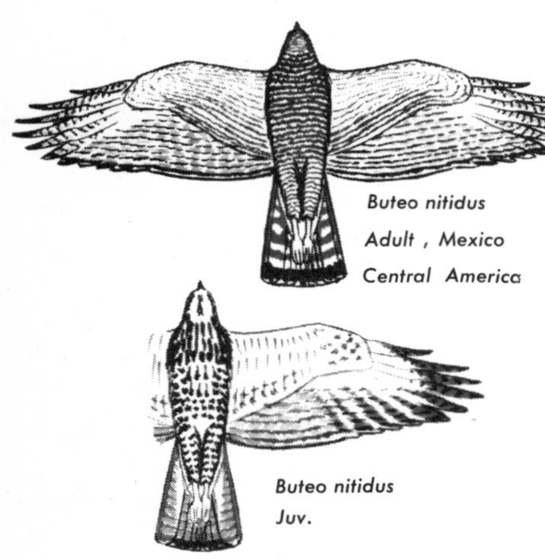

Buteo nitidus
Adult, Mexico
Central America

Buteo nitidus
Juv.

At a distance it appears entirely medium gray; closer, shows a faint pattern of lighter streaking and barring on the head, neck, and shoulders; back and secondaries, white-tipped in fresh plumage; primaries, dark brown; upper- and undertail coverts, pure white; tail, dark brown, with one or two complete white bands and broadly white-tipped; below, evenly barred slate-gray and white. No other hawk of buteo proportions in Middle America is completely barred below, and the Northern Goshawk, an accipiter which has this type of marking, is much larger and is found to the north.

Juvenile—dark gray-brown above, streaked with amber-brown and white; wings and tail ochre-brown, barred with dark brown; face and underparts white or buff streaked with brown (except barred thighs).

Beak, blue-black; eyes, dark brown; cere, legs, and feet, yellow; claws, black. Size, 15–17 inches.

BUTEO NITIDUS

VARIATIONS

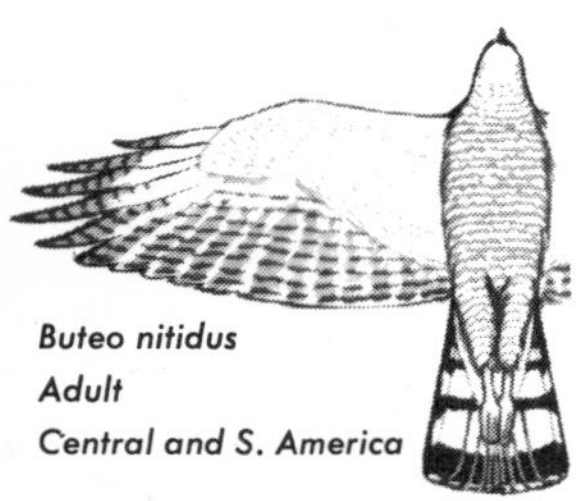

Buteo nitidus
Adult
Central and S. America

In tropical America from southwestern Costa Rica to northern Argentina, the Gray Hawks are distinctly barred with white on the head and neck and have lighter gray feathering on the back, the palest being found in southern South America. Size, 14–16 inches.

Red-backed Hawk (*Buteo polyosoma*)

DESCRIPTION (WESTERN SOUTH AMERICA, TO 15,000 FEET IN THE NORTHERN ANDES; ALSO TIERRA DEL FUEGO AND THE FALKLAND ISLANDS)

White-breasted phase (*Female*)—slate-gray above with a large amber-brown patch on the back; wings, medium gray, barred darker; uppertail coverts, barred, and undertail coverts, pure white; tail, pure white or finely barred at the base, but always subterminally banded black; face, slate-gray with white lores; underparts, white, sometimes marked with patches of amber-brown and slate-gray on the sides of breast and belly; or belly, flanks, and thighs, finely barred amber-brown. *Male* may have an amber-brown back, but it usually has only scattered spots of this coloring or plain slate-gray upperparts; otherwise, like female.

Gray phase (Female)—amber-brown back; throat, breast, and thighs, slate-gray; belly, dark amber-brown; underwing coverts, dark slate; axillaries, dark amber-brown. A rare variety with underwing coverts and axillaries boldly barred with slate and white may have a median band of dark amber-brown across the breast and a white-barred belly and thighs; only traces of a band or barring; or virtually concolorous and with dark underparts. *Male*—slate-gray to black above and below, with some amber-brown spotting or feather-edging on the mantle, as well as narrow white barring on the underwing coverts and axillaries.

Juvenile (*white-breasted phase*)—sepia to dark brown above, often with amber-brown feather-edging; underparts, white to pale yellow-orange, heavily and darkly streaked and barred; tail, white or light gray, narrowly barred with dark gray-brown to the tip. *Gray phase*—either completely dark brown or streaked and spotted with pale yellow-orange below; tail, light olive-gray, narrowly barred with dark brown.

Beak, bluish; eyes, brown; legs and feet, yellow. Size, 19–21 inches.

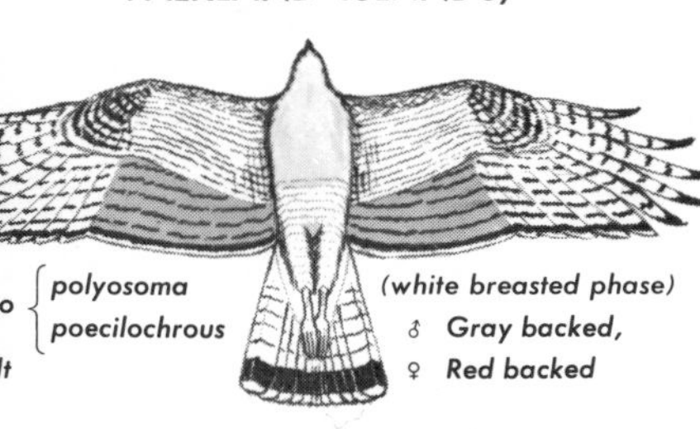

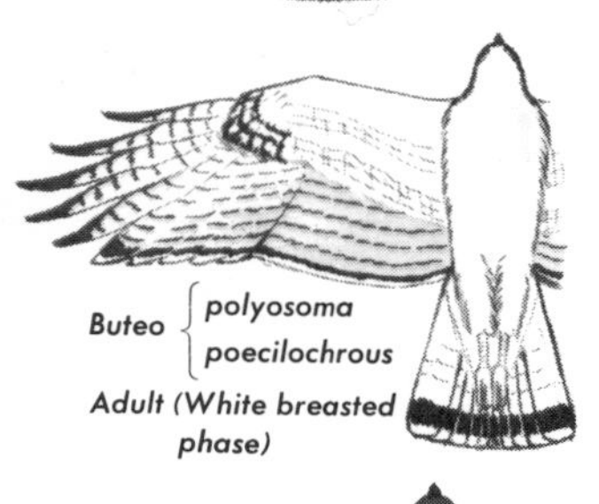

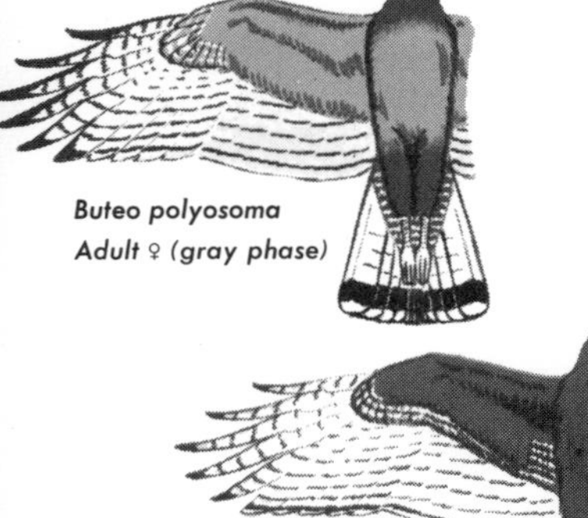

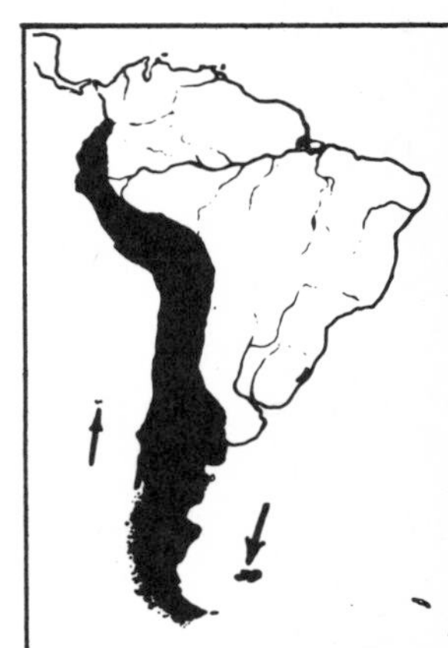

BUTEO POLYOSOMA

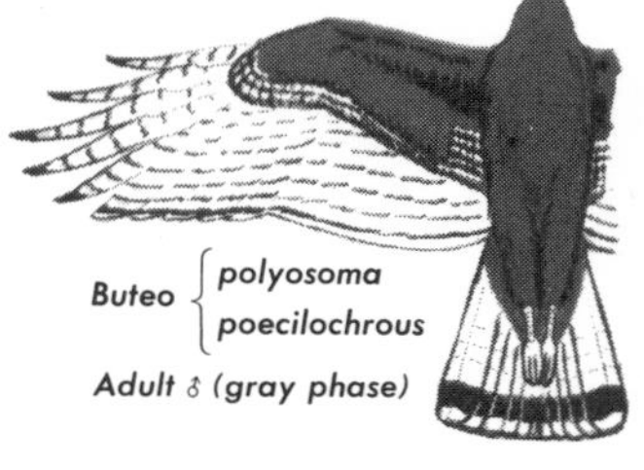

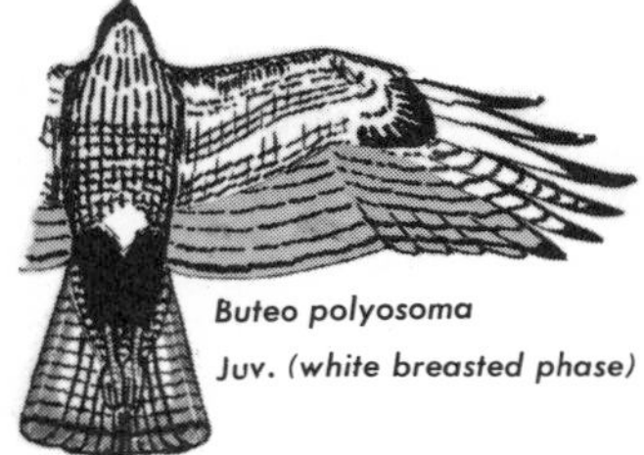

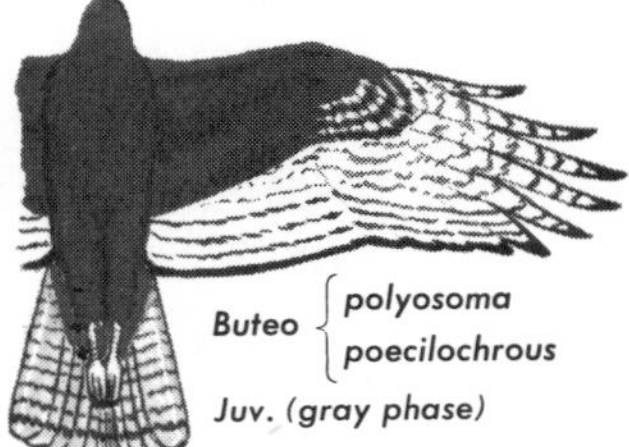

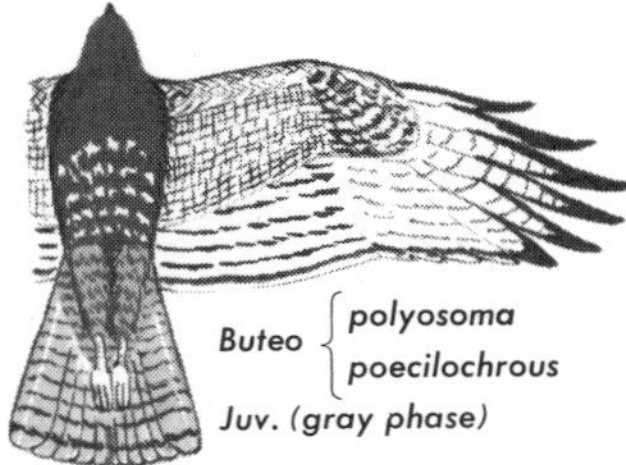

VARIATIONS

On the Juan Fernandez Islands, off the coast of Chile, the adults of both sexes are dark slate above and white below with traces of barring on the belly. Young birds, however, have amber-brown feather-edging on their backs.

RELATED SPECIES

Gurney's, or Variable, Hawk (*B. poecilochrous*), 19½–22 inches, is a larger bird with wings averaging slightly longer. The range of this species is completely overlapped by that of *B. polyosoma* although it reaches considerably higher altitudes in the Peruvian Andes (18,000 feet). The color phases correspond exactly, except for the apparent lack of any red-backed and red-breasted females in the gray phase. The variety of gray phase female, rare in *B. polyosoma,* which has the white-barred underwing coverts, is common in *B. poecilochrous.*

(Juveniles of *B. poecilochrous* are usually darker than those of *B. polyosoma,* both in the white-breasted and gray phases.)

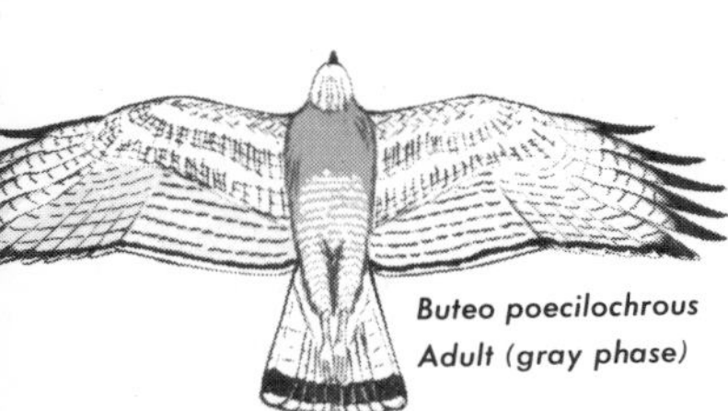

BUTEO POECILOCHROUS

HABITS

The large buteos and buzzards are noted for their marvelous soaring ability. While prospecting for prey they ride the thermals in wide circles to great heights with apparently minimal adjustment of the primaries and tail. The Red-tailed Hawk frequently hovers on the windward side of a mountain ridge—wings straight out and tail spread, remaining fixed and motionless for several minutes at a time. The Zone-tailed Hawk characteristically soars with wings raised, and slight side-to-side tipping like a Turkey Vulture, but in a strong wind the resemblance is lost. This species, the African Red-tailed Buzzard, and some others are more active in flight, indulging in rolls and elaborate aerial maneuvers.

In the breeding season, display flight is spectacular. A pair of Common Buzzards circle around each other, always facing, and with the male above the female. The tails are wide-spread and the wings are held stiffly and at a steeper angle than in ordinary flight. In a diving display, or "loop-the-loop," similar to American Red-tail courtship, one bird may have prey in its claws.

At rest, the buteo chooses a barren treetop or a rocky ledge commanding a view of the countryside. In barren or treeless plains the Rough-legs beat low over the ground. The Ferruginous Rough-leg of the Great Plains may stand on the ground, patiently waiting for a prairie dog or ground squirrel to come out of its hole. However, the buteos of lightly wooded country exhibit the best-known mode of attack. When prey is sighted during an extended patrol or from a lookout post, both the North American Red-tail or the Common Buzzard of Europe will come in low with talons outstretched and bind to it on the ground.

Red-tailed Hawk *(Buteo jamaicensis)*, eastern United States.

Many large buteos have the predatory habits of eagles, but North American and European species supplement their diet of rodents (up to the size of hares) with whatever is seasonally available—insects (especially grasshoppers), insect larvae, reptiles, amphibians, and birds; also worms, carrion, minnows, and dead fish. Some hawks may even develop a preference for one of these supplementary foods. Different kinds of habitats influence species to specialize. Smaller American buteos that live in swamps or in deep woods—Red-shouldered and Broad-winged hawks—take a wide range of prey but often seem to chose the items on the list that are easiest to catch—toads, minnows, larvae, squirrels, and wood mice. The mountain buteos of Tibet and the Andes of South America live mostly on small mammals, but other mountain buteos in Africa and Madagascar prey mainly on chameleons and other lizards. Insects are important to the subsistence of the Gray Hawk and Roadside Hawk, small tropical species in dry open country. The habits of the Short-tailed Hawk and White-throated Hawk, tropical and mountain-zone species of Central and South America, are not very well known, but they have heavier feet and longer claws than any other small buteos, and may specialize in hunting birds.

Rough-legs are rodent specialists with very small feet for their size. The Northern Rough-leg is particularly dependent on meadow mice. Its populations fluctuate drastically, following the cyclic abundance or scarcity of lemmings (and hares) in the Arctic.

The large buteos may nest on ledges in barren mountains or high up in trees, but have also been recorded nesting in shrubs close to the ground. Competition with smaller buteos for nest sites occurs in woods interspersed with open bogs, swamps, woods, cleared fields, and pastures. In southeastern Massachusetts, Red-tails took over a nest on a ridge between an open bog and a maple swamp that had been previously used by Broad-winged and Red-shouldered hawks.

Nests of Red-tailed Hawks average somewhat larger than those of Red-shouldered Hawks. The sticks and twigs form a compact V, neatly lined with strips of inner bark and a few sprigs of pine, cedar, or hemlock, or fresh green foliage. Both sexes build, and old nests are sometimes repaired in the autumn. The height of the nest gives the birds a good lookout, and it is usually placed in a tree at the edge of a patch of heavy timber for this purpose. The same nest may be used four to five years, or another built, and the previous one returned to in another year. The Red-tailed Hawk lays one to three (usually two) eggs at intervals of one or two days; these are dull white or bluish-white and not as heavily marked as the Red-shoulder's. Incubation, by both sexes (but mainly the female) lasts 34 days. After the young are hatched they remain in the nest about six weeks, at first fed by the male, who leaves food near the nest to be picked up by the female, and later by both parents.

Breeding behavior in Swainson's, Harlan's, and Zone-tailed hawks, the Common Buzzard, and some tropical species is similar to that of the Red-tail. Young of the South American Red-backed Hawk are fledged in 40 to 50 days and those of the Jackal Buzzard in South Africa, in 46 to 51 days. However, young of the African Red-tailed Buzzard, which are fully-feathered at eight weeks, may not leave the nest until nine weeks old.

The nest of the White-tailed Hawk in the top of yucca on open prairies and coastal sand ridges of Texas, Mexico, and Central America looks like the Red-tail's, and is sometimes lined with grasses. Two to three eggs are dull white, generally spotted with pale brown. Mouse-colored (brownish-gray) nestlings differ from the white nestlings of most hawks, and may also be recognized by a unique mask of bare black skin around the eyes.

The Red-shoulder's nest, built in whatever large tree is available, becomes well decorated with bits of white down from the hawk's breast as incubation progresses. The egg cup, about two to three inches deep and eight inches in diameter, has a soft lining of mosses, lichens, inner bark, spruce, or other green twigs. Two to four eggs (rarely five or six) are dull white or bluish-white, usually boldly and irregularly marked in a variety of browns, yellow-browns, and red-browns. Incubation (about 27 days) and fledging periods are shorter than those of the Red-tailed Hawk. If undisturbed, the Red-shoulder will come back to two or three nests in the same tree or adjoining trees, alternately, through the years. The unused nests often serve as feeding stations. Pairs nesting close together (four in one-half mile in Texas) seem to be influenced by lack of other nesting trees and concentration of food supply.

The nest of the Broad-winged Hawk is usually small and rather poorly built, and this species is not as attached to the same patch of woods over several seasons as the Red-shoulder. The eggs are very similar in size and marking. Both sexes incubate, and care for the young, which are fledged in about a month.

The Short-tailed Hawk is tropical and subtropical in its distribution. Breeding birds are rare in Florida and most individuals seen in the mangroves, pinelands, and cypress swamps in winter are probably visitors from the south. The nest, usually in the topmost branches of a large cypress or magnolia tree, resembles the Red-shoulder's, and one to three white to pale bluish-white eggs are either immaculate or heavily spotted and blotched.

The Northern Rough-leg builds on ledges, cliffs, or among rocks—but also on the ground in open tundra. Its large buteo nest is lined with heather stalks where available, as well as earth, dead

Juvenile Broad-winged Hawk *(Buteo platypterus).—Photograph by Heinz Meng.*

grasses, and fresh shoots of pine. The number of eggs, three to four, increases in lemming years to five, six, and even seven. Some are white; others, very sparsely marked. Incubation is done chiefly by the female with the male guarding nearby. After the young birds are hatched, the male brings food and drops it near the nest for the female, who then takes and divides it among the nestlings. They are fledged in about 41 days.

A plains-dweller, the Ferruginous Rough-leg nests in trees, but frequently not far from the ground. Three to four eggs (rarely five or six) are white, handsomely blotched in various shades of brown, amber-brown, tawny, etc. Incubation is shared by both sexes. Young remain in the nest until two months old.

The migrations of northern buteos are spectacular; Harlan's Hawks, Ferruginous Rough-legs, and Red-tails migrate to the southern parts of the United States and Swainson's and Broad-winged hawks to South America. Eurasian, or Common, Buzzards travel to tropical Africa, Arabia, and western India in winter. And the Northern Rough-legged Hawk in the Western Hemisphere winters from the northern United States to California, Texas, and rarely to North Carolina; in Europe, south to the Pyrennees, Alps, and Balkans; in Asia, south to Transcaspia, Turkestan, northern China, and northern Japan.

A long drawn-out rasping squeal, "kree-e-e-e-e" is typical of the Red-tail, Zone-tail, and Harlan's Hawk. Swainson's Hawk calls "kreeeeer" in a shrill, plaintive whistle, and the Broad-winged Hawk's voice, "pweeee," is weaker and higher-pitched than that of the Red-tail. During the breeding season the Red-shoulder is one of the noisiest of the North American hawks; its call, "kee-aah" or "kee-oow," is repeated three or four times, the first syllable higher-pitched, the second lower and drawn-out. Notes of the tropical Short-tailed Hawk are similar. The White-tailed Hawk repeats "ke-ke-ke-ke-ke-ke," also "cut-a cut-a." The Northern Rough-leg delivers squalling or "miaowing" whistles, much like the "mewing" note of the Common Buzzard. The Ferruginous Rough-leg cries "kree-a, ke-a-ah," or a harsh "kaah kaaah" compared to one of the notes of the Herring Gull.

The mewing note of the African Red-tailed Buzzard is distinct from the Jackal Buzzard's cry—"aung-aung-aung." The Mountain Buzzard of the Congo and Mount Ruwanzori has a shrill and far-echoing "keer-keer-keer" or "kee-you kee-you."

The high hoarse whistle, "seeu," of the Roadside Hawk is one of the typical sounds of the dry woods and wood edges in tropical America; and the voice of the Gray Hawk is similar, but not as harsh (a loud, plaintive "cree-eer").

One of a number of "black hawks" that can be easily confused with each other in the arid southwestern United States and Mexico is Harris's, or Bay-winged, Hawk (*Parabuteo unicinctus*). It has a conspicuous white rump and undertail coverts and broadly white-tipped tail. In spite of sienna markings on the shoulders and thighs, this hawk often appears solid black in the field, except for these identifying white areas.

GENUS *PARABUTEO*

Parabuteo is a small, heavy-set, buteo-like bird with long and broad wings, deeply emarginated at the tips. The sturdy scutellate tarsi are feathered about halfway down, and the toes and claws are rather long and powerful for the body size. Lores appear conspicuously bare.

Harris', or Bay-winged, Hawk (*Parabuteo unicinctus*)

DESCRIPTION (SOUTHWESTERN U.S., THROUGH NORTHERN SOUTH AMERICA)

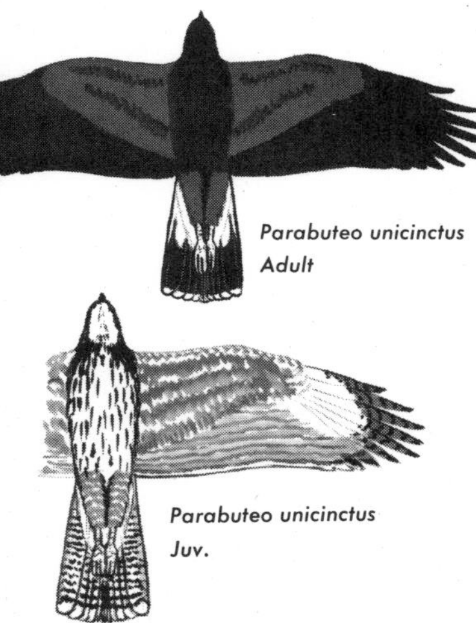

Parabuteo unicinctus Adult

Parabuteo unicinctus Juv.

Above, sepia with sienna patches on the shoulders; wings, dark brown; uppertail coverts, white; tail, dark brown, banded near the base and broadly tipped in white; below, sepia with sienna thighs.

Juvenile—feather-edged sienna and sandy above; wings, showing white on the inner webs; tail, sepia, narrowly (and sometimes indistinctly) barred with dark brown as well as white-tipped; face and throat, white streaked with sepia and pale yellow-orange; underparts, white to pale yellow-orange with blobs of sepia (and fine dark barring on the thighs).

Beak, light blue-gray (darker at the tip); cere, lores, and orbit, yellow; eyes, red-brown; legs and feet, orange-yellow; claws, black. Size, 18–22 inches.

PARABUTEO UNICINCTUS

VARIATIONS

The South American bird, sometimes called the One-banded Hawk, is usually found only in the savanna country of central and southern South America. It is dark brown with the characteristic white markings and sienna shoulders, and the sienna thighs are barred dark brown and sandy.

HABITS

Described as having a dual personality, Harris' Hawk combines the characteristic modes of hunting and flight of the buteos and goshawks. In scrub countryside it may be seen perched in a low tree; dashing through thorny bushes in search of the creatures that inhabit these dwarf forests; or, in the early morning, circling high above the still misty resacas. It is also common along wooded streams, and in Mexico, Sutton saw it perched on the tall flower stalks in sisal-growing districts, watching the ground for lizards. Food consists of various mammals, reptiles, and birds (including cottontails, wood rats, gophers, lizards, small snakes, Common Gallinule, Sora Rail, night herons, Green-winged Teal, and Gilded Flicker); possibly carrion, also.

In the southwestern United States, both the Redtail and Ferruginous Rough-leg are said to give this small aggressive hawk a wide berth. The principal enemies of the Harris' Hawk are the coyote and bobcat, which pull down any nest they can reach. Some nests are only eight, nine, or ten feet from the ground—others, as high as 30 feet in the top of Spanish bayonet, yucca, mesquite, cactus, hackberry, and in other low trees. The compactly made platform of sticks, twigs, weeds, and roots is lined with grass, bark, elm shoots, Spanish moss, and green mesquite. Three to four (sometimes five) eggs are dull white and are usually unmarked. The eggs are laid at intervals of several days. Incubation, by both sexes, commences with the first egg and lasts about four weeks. The male and female share in raising the young.

In the fall, large flocks of Harris' Hawks gather and wander about at the extreme northern and southern part of the range, where they may withdraw respectively southward or northward for a short distance in winter, depending on the weather.

The voice is a harsh "karrr."

The tropical American White Hawk *(Leucopternis albicollis)* is unmistakable—the only deep-tropical forest bird with white plumage except for black shoulders, black subterminal tail band, and black wings.

GENUS *LEUCOPTERNIS*

The neotropical genus *Leucopternis* includes small to rather large hawks similar in structure to the black hawks (*Buteogallus*), but with shorter legs and wings not as broad. Thigh feathers are short, not forming "flags," except in the White Hawk (*L. albicollis*) and the extremely rare Barred Hawk (*L. princeps*). Plumage varies from nearly pure white to striking combinations of black and white and solid slate-gray. The young birds look remarkably like the adults.

White Hawk (*Leucopternis albicollis*)

DESCRIPTION (TROPICAL LOWLANDS OF CENTRAL AMERICA)

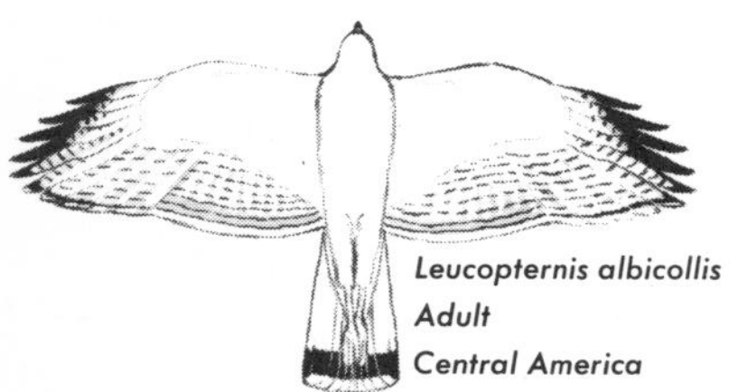

Leucopternis albicollis
Adult
Central America

Completely white, above and below, except for black shaft-streaking behind the eyes and at the sides of the neck; black shoulders; much black in the wings; black subterminal tail band.

Immature—very similar to adult, has black-and-white barred wing coverts and scapulars.

Juvenile—barred like immature but heavily marked with black streaks behind the eyes and on the back of the head.

Beak and cere, blue-gray; eyes, dark brown; legs and feet, reddish-yellow; claws, blue-black. Size, 18–20½ inches.

LEUCOPTERNIS ALBICOLL

VARIATIONS

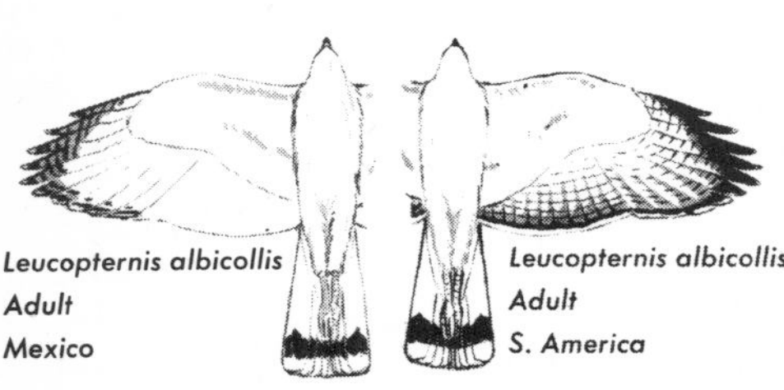

Leucopternis albicollis
Adult
Mexico

Leucopternis albicollis
Adult
S. America

Mexican White Hawks resemble the Central American birds described but have yellow eyes and are whiter—with pure white wing coverts in adult plumage and outer webs of flight feathers barred black and white rather than solidly black. (*Young,* white with black-barred wing coverts and wings.)

However, across most of northern and central South America, the same species is called the White-collared Hawk because it has a white head and mantle, and black back with irregular white barring and feather-edging. The tail coverts are white, and the tail, so broadly

LEUCOPTERNIS OCCIDENTALIS

banded black on the upper surface that only the base and tip are white. Underneath the tail appears white banded black. (Young, heavily streaked on the head and spotted on the mantle.) Sizes vary from 16½ inches, in northern South America, to 20½ inches in Mexico.

OTHER SPECIES

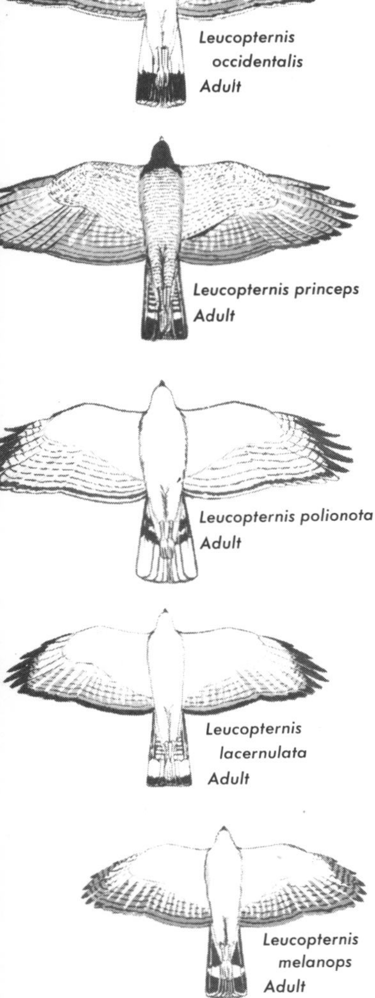

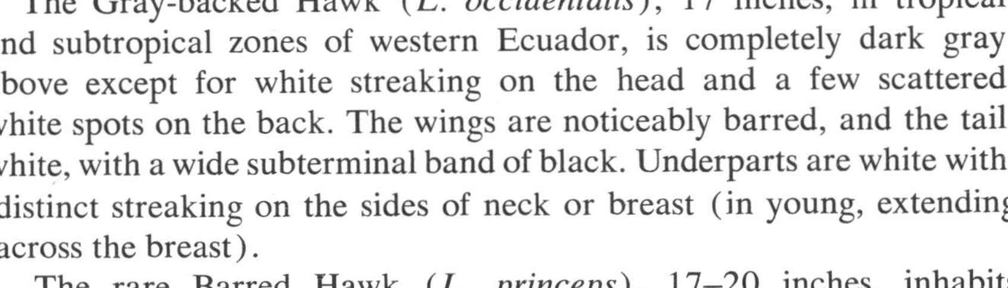

The Gray-backed Hawk (*L. occidentalis*), 17 inches, in tropical and subtropical zones of western Ecuador, is completely dark gray above except for white streaking on the head and a few scattered white spots on the back. The wings are noticeably barred, and the tail white, with a wide subterminal band of black. Underparts are white with distinct streaking on the sides of neck or breast (in young, extending across the breast).

LEUCOPTERNIS PRINCEPS

The rare Barred Hawk (*L. princeps*), 17–20 inches, inhabits mountain forests between 4,000 and 5,000 feet in Central America and higher in northern South America. The head, chest, and back are completely black with a purple iridescent sheen; the underparts, undertail, and underwing coverts are white barred black. The uppertail coverts are also barred, and the tail is black with a narrow white median band. (Cere, orange; eyes, dark blue.)

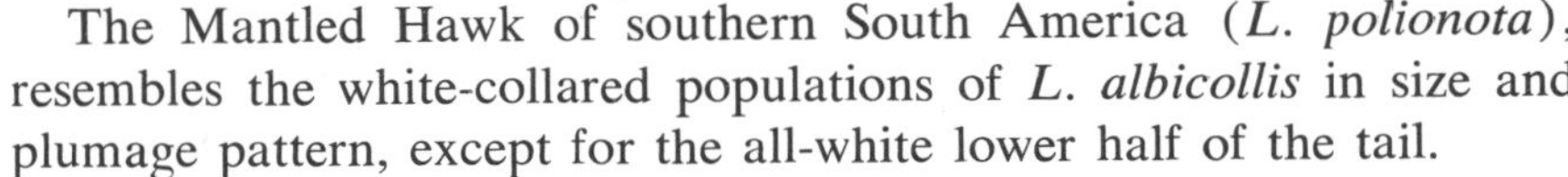

The Mantled Hawk of southern South America (*L. polionota*), resembles the white-collared populations of *L. albicollis* in size and plumage pattern, except for the all-white lower half of the tail.

LEUCOPTERNIS POLIONOTA

The White-necked Hawk (*L. lacernulata*), about 14 inches, native to the wooded regions of southeastern Brazil, has the face, head, and neck washed with light gray and may be distinguished from *L. polionota* by its white tail, narrowly barred at the base and subterminally banded with black (in young, evenly barred black and white-tipped).

A savanna species, the Black-faced Hawk (*L. melanops*), about 14 inches, which has never been found south of the Amazon River, has an orange cere and striking black mask across the eyes; black tail with a median band of white.

LEUCOPTERNIS LACERNULATA

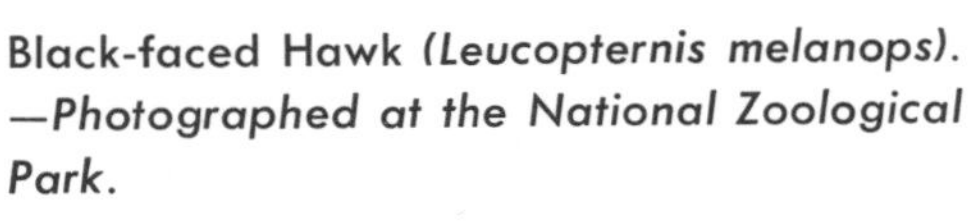
Black-faced Hawk (*Leucopternis melanops*). —Photographed at the National Zoological Park.

LEUCOPTERNIS MELANOPS

LEUCOPTERNIS KUHLI

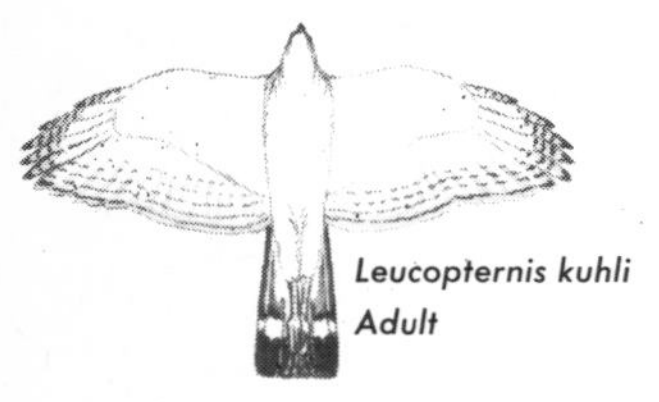

The White-browed Hawk (*L. kuhli*), 13–14 inches, an Amazonian bird, is completely dark above except for conspicuous white eyebrows, white streaking at the sides of face, and white spotting on the nape and mantle. The tail shows a median band of white like *L. melanops.* Also included in this group is the Semiplumbeous Hawk (*L. semiplumbea*), about 13½ inches, whose range extends from northern South America into Central America. Face, sides of neck, and entire upperparts are slate-gray; the tail is black with a narrow median band of white; the underparts are white.

LEUCOPTERNIS SEMIPLUM

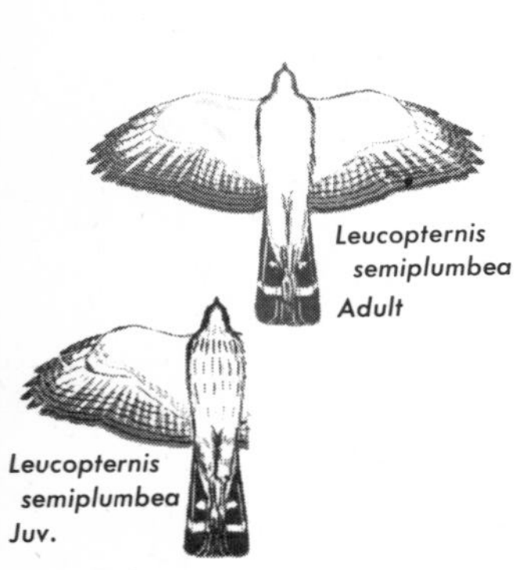

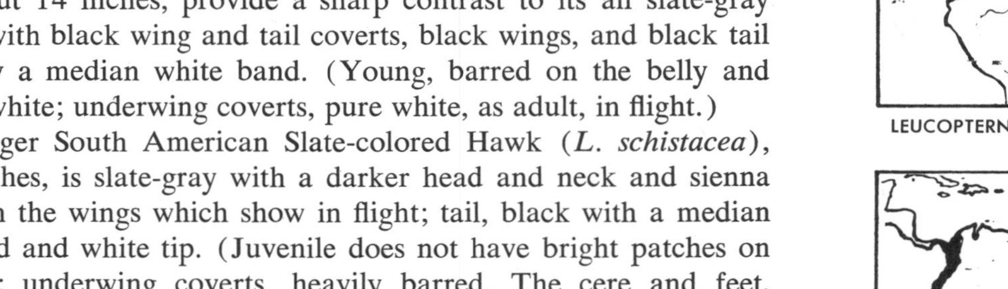

Orange cere and bright red eyes of the Plumbeous Hawk (*L. plumbea*), about 14 inches, provide a sharp contrast to its all slate-gray plumage with black wing and tail coverts, black wings, and black tail crossed by a median white band. (Young, barred on the belly and thighs in white; underwing coverts, pure white, as adult, in flight.)

The larger South American Slate-colored Hawk (*L. schistacea*), 16–17 inches, is slate-gray with a darker head and neck and sienna patches on the wings which show in flight; tail, black with a median white band and white tip. (Juvenile does not have bright patches on the wings; underwing coverts, heavily barred. The cere and feet, orange; the eyes, yellow.)

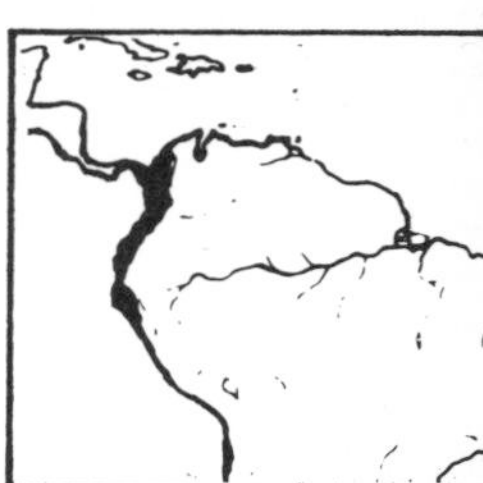
LEUCOPTERNIS PLUMBEA

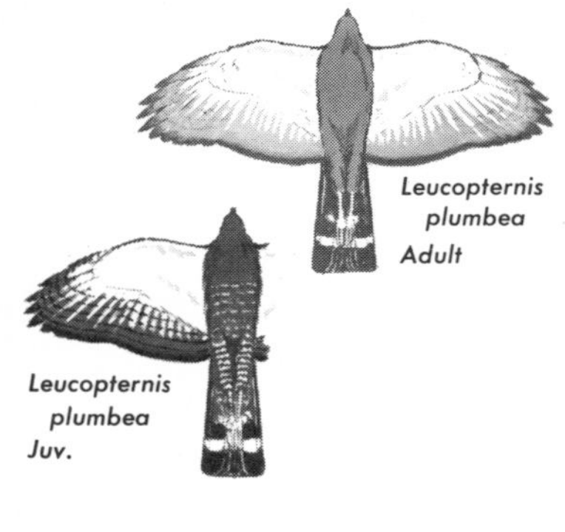

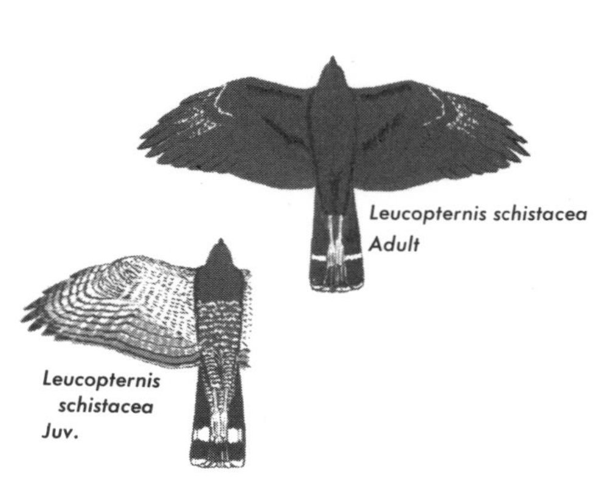

LEUCOPTERNIS SCHISTAC

HABITS

Most of these hawks are rather sluggish forest-dwellers whose flapping flight is slow, interspersed with sailing. Like the black hawks, they perch, virtually immobile, for long periods of time near water holes, swamps, or streams, waiting to pounce on their prey. The White Hawks (*L. albicollis*) in the Guianas and the Amazon region also hunt by hopping about from branch to branch under forest canopy. Black-faced Hawks (*L. melanops*) are more often seen than their rain forest relatives for these birds haunt the water holes of the savannas. Both species are reptile-eaters, and small mammals, insects, and some birds (including Cocks-of-the-Rock) are also captured by the White Hawks.

Hawks of the genus *Leucopternis* usually nest in dense forest, and their characteristic call (*L. albicollis*) is a "shrill prolonged screech, repeated several times."

Juvenile Plumbeous Hawk (*Leucopternis plumbea*).

The Lizard Buzzard *(Kaupifalco monogrammicus)*, a spunky little bird of prey, breeds throughout the African savanna but shuns the deep forest, the treeless grasslands, and deserts.

GENUS *KAUPIFALCO*

A small but compact body and longer, rather rounded, wings distinguish this genus from the trim, lightweight African Sparrowhawk and Gabar Goshawk, which it otherwise resembles because of its white rump patch and bright orange cere and legs. The rather short scutellate tarsi are feathered about halfway down in front. The juveniles are practically like the adults, without the bright eyes, cere, and legs.

Lizard Buzzard (*Kaupifalco monogrammicus*)

DESCRIPTION (TROPICAL AFRICA)

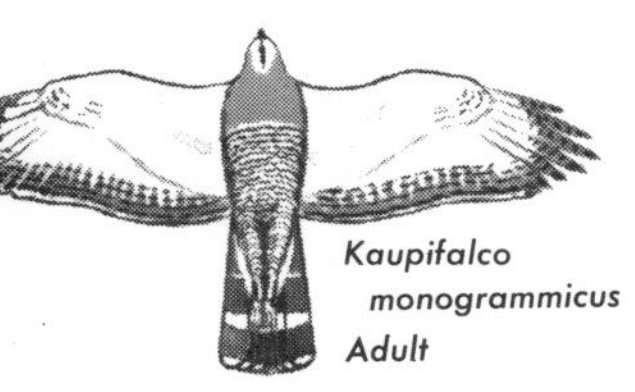

Kaupifalco monogrammicus Adult

Head, neck, chest, and back, dove-gray to slate-gray with a white patch and black median stripe at throat. Wings, dark brown. Tail coverts, white; tail, dark brown with a single broad white subterminal band, also tipped in white. Lower breast and belly, white, finely barred with sepia to dark brown.

Juvenile—similar, with a two-banded tail.

Beak, black; cere, red-orange (young, chrome-yellow); eyes, red (juvenile, grayish-brown); legs and feet, orange (young, yellow); claws, black. Size, 11½–13½ inches.

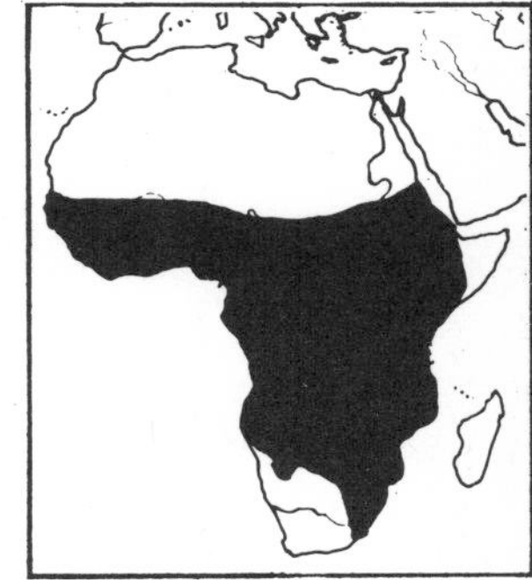

KAUPIFALCO MONOGRAMMICUS

HABITS

The flight of this little hawk is slow but graceful, and it hunts by gliding from one tree to another, then swooping down on its prey. It also soars a good deal, like a small buteo. Food is mainly grasshoppers and other insects taken from the ground; also lizards, frogs, rats, mice, small snakes, and, to some extent, small birds and young chickens. In west Africa it has a reputation for harrying weaver birds.

The nest, often in the fork of an isolated tree, is a small flat platform of sticks, sometimes lined with moss or leaves. One to three greenish-white or pale blue eggs are unmarked or show a few rusty spots and blotches.

The Lizard Buzzards are comparatively sedentary over most of their range.

A repeated ascending and descending musical note described as "unhawklike" is varied by long whistles and whines, and a falcon-like "kek-kek-kek-kek."

Thousands of Gray-faced Buzzards *(Butastur indicus)* fill the skies for several days each fall in their southward journey from Honshu past Kagoshima and Yaku Shima, Japan, to the Kuriles and south China. Their spectacular migration is known as the "taka-kudari" (descent of hawks).

GENUS *BUTASTUR*

Long, broad, and slightly rounded wings, rather long scutellate legs, and weak bill and feet characterize four species of *Butastur*. These are the smaller buzzards of Japan, northern China, and the drier parts of Burma, the Indian peninsula, Malaysia, and the Celebes; also of the thinly wooded plains and grasslands above the equator in Africa.

Gray-faced Buzzard, or Frog, Hawk (*Butastur indicus*)

DESCRIPTION (JAPAN AND NORTHERN CHINA)

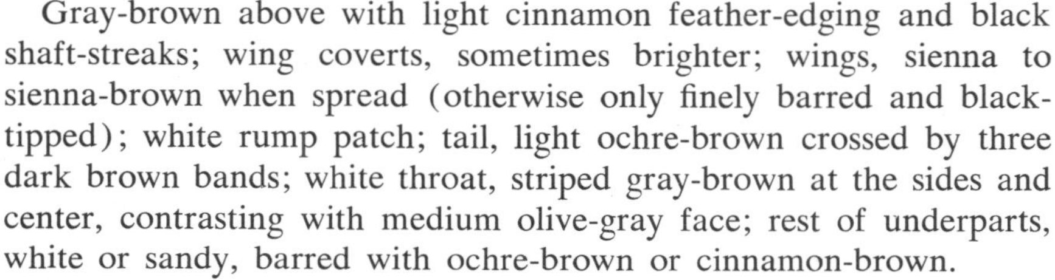

Gray-brown above with light cinnamon feather-edging and black shaft-streaks; wing coverts, sometimes brighter; wings, sienna to sienna-brown when spread (otherwise only finely barred and black-tipped); white rump patch; tail, light ochre-brown crossed by three dark brown bands; white throat, striped gray-brown at the sides and center, contrasting with medium olive-gray face; rest of underparts, white or sandy, barred with ochre-brown or cinnamon-brown.

Immature—darker above with heavy streaking on the head and brighter sienna feather-edging on the back; breast, sienna with gray-brown streaking; rest of underparts, like adult's; wings, with sienna marking as in mature plumage.

Juvenile—white or sandy head and neck, darkly streaked; underparts, white or sandy, lightly streaked throughout in gray-brown; wings, without sienna coloring.

Beak, black; cere, yellow; eyes, yellow; legs and feet, yellow; claws, black. Size, 15½–17 inches.

BUTASTUR INDICUS

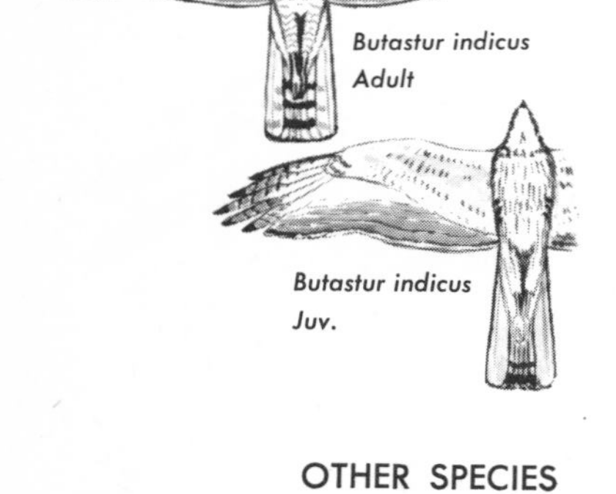

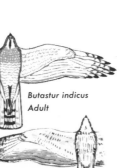

Butastur indicus Adult

Butastur indicus Juv.

OTHER SPECIES

The White-eyed Buzzard (*B. teesa*), 13–15 inches, is paler (cinnamon-brown above); wings, tinged with amber-brown; tail, amber-brown, very indistinctly barred except for the dark subterminal band; underparts, cinnamon-brown, barred with white on the belly; thighs, white, narrowly barred.

The Rufous-winged Buzzard (*B. liventer*), 12–13½ inches, resembles this bird (*B. teesa*) in coloring above, but has paler—almost unmarked—underparts and much brighter sienna wings and tail. (Young of both *B. teesa* and *B. liventer* follow the same color pattern as *B. indicus,* but are more finely marked.)

BUTASTUR TEESA

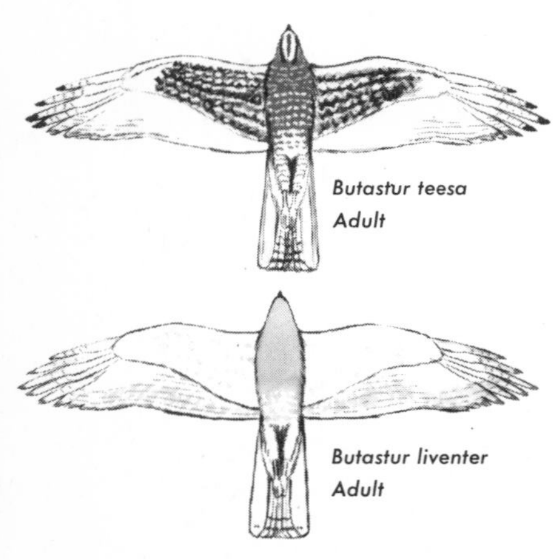

Butastur teesa Adult

Butastur liventer Adult

BUTASTUR LIVENTER

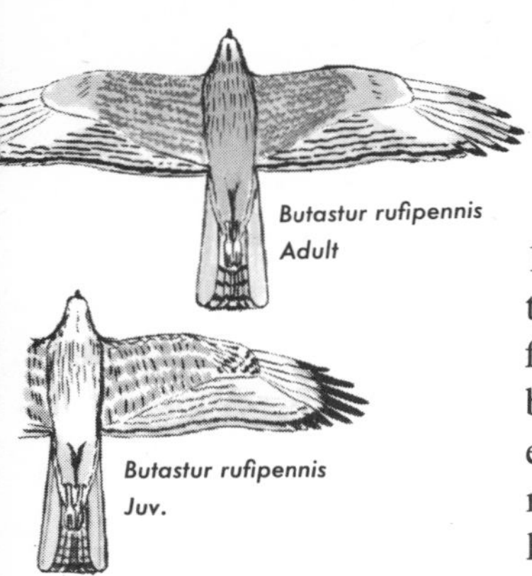

The Grasshopper Buzzard (*B. rufipennis*), of central Africa, 13½–15 inches, is the darkest above—dark gray-brown, the feathers of the back and wing coverts, edged in amber-brown; wings, dark orange, finely barred and broadly tipped with dark brown; tail, ochre-brown, barred a number of times in dark brown (the subterminal band broadest); the face is dark and the throat white or buff with black streaking; rest of underparts amber-brown, finely streaked with black. (Juvenile has an amber-brown head, neck, and chest streaked with black; throat and belly, white, also streaked.

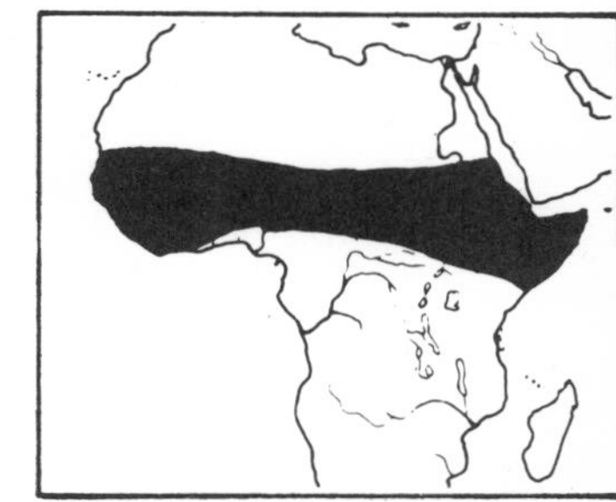

BUTASTUR RUFIPENNIS

HABITS

The hawks of this genus inhabit thin deciduous woods, cultivated land, and bare open plains to about 2,700 feet above sea level; also low jungle of the hot, dry hard-leaf or leafless type. Although sluggish, compared to the savanna sparrowhawks, their flight is rather swift and buoyant for buzzard-like birds. In the breeding season they soar in circles high in the air, often with larger birds of prey. However, they are usually seen perched on a favorite stump, post, or telephone pole, from which they swoop down to pick up their prey. Occasionally they walk about on the ground, foraging for grasshoppers and other insects, also field rats, mice, lizards, and young, sick, or wounded birds. The Malaysian species (*B. liventer*) is usually found along rivers, and feeds mostly on crabs and reptiles.

In Japan the Gray-faced Buzzard ordinarily nests in an evergreen, 15 to 40 feet up, and lays two to four eggs. The White-eyed Buzzard's nest is a loose, unlined structure of twigs fairly high up in the fork of a thickly foliaged tree, such as a mango (preferably one of a clump). Three eggs are unspotted greenish-white. The female alone incubates, but both sexes share in nest-building and caring for the young. The nest of the Grasshopper Buzzard, placed in the tops of low trees, is lined with leaves, and two to three bluish-white eggs may be speckled red or brown with pale lilac undermarkings.

In the nonbreeding season these hawks may be seen in parties, and are attracted from long distances to grass fires. *B. indicus* is the most migratory species, but *B. teesa* and *B. rufipennis* are subject to local migrations, the latter as far south as Tanganyika.

The White-eyed Buzzard is a noisy bird, especially in the breeding season. The female's mewing cry, frequently repeated the day after the eggs are laid, gives away the location of the nest. No calls have been recorded for the other species, and the African bird is believed to be "mute."

In the Pleistocene the Great Black Hawk *(Buteogallus urubitinga)* had many relatives throughout the warmer parts of the Western Hemisphere which are now extinct. The size of the bird shown and its wide black tail band are identifying marks of the Brazilian population.

GENUS *BUTEOGALLUS*

These buteo-like neotropical hawks have long tarsi, extremely broad wings with five notched primaries, and short, square tails.

The black hawks hardly differ, except in size. The Common Black Hawk is smaller than the Great Black Hawk, has weaker feet, a less powerful bill, and a more extensive bare area on the face (lores, orbital space, and forehead). In flight, unlike the Great Black Hawk, whose underwing surface appears entirely black, the Common Black Hawk has distinct white patches on the primaries. The similar mottled and striped plumages of young black hawks are also easily confused in the field.

The brightly colored Rufous Crab Hawk is slight in build, has narrower wings, and a shorter tail. The soles of its feet are very smooth, considering that it hunts slippery amphibians and reptiles, but its beak is distinctly toothed and notched.

Great Black Hawk (*Buteogallus urubitinga*)

DESCRIPTION (CONTINENTAL TROPICAL AMERICA)

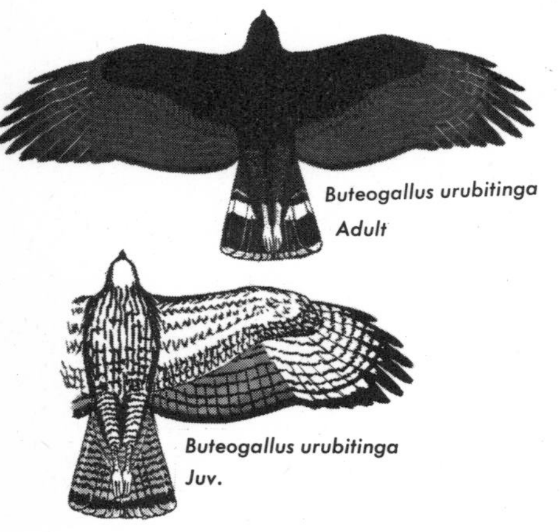

Almost entirely black; wings, barred slate-gray; underwing coverts and thighs, finely barred or spotted with white (indistinct or missing in birds of four years and older); uppertail coverts, white; undertail coverts and tail, black with only one or two white bands showing underneath, narrowly tipped in white.

Immature—dark brown with sandy to pale yellow-orange streaking on the head, neck, and underparts; wings with flashing amber-brown mottling; tail, white to sandy with dark brown barring or marbling at the base, a broad dark subterminal band, and a white tip.

Juvenile—white to sandy head, neck, and underparts, darkly streaked; rest of upperparts, sepia to dark gray-brown, barred and scalloped with amber-brown; tail, crossed by 10–14 narrow dark brown bars and a wider subterminal band.

Beak, blue-black (black at tip); cere, lores, tarsi, and feet, orange-yellow; claws, black; eyes, dark brown. Size, 19½–21½ inches.

BUTEOGALLUS URUBITIN

VARIATIONS

From Panama to Bolivia individuals compare in size to middle American birds. There are no white spots on the underwing coverts or thighs; both the upper- and undertail coverts are black; and the upper surface of the tail appears white at the base with a single broad subterminal band of black. Underneath, however, the tail is black with a white median band and is white-tipped. (Beak, pale yellow at base and black at tip; eyes, deep red; feet, greenish-yellow.) In Brazil, Paraguay, and Bolivia they are larger (22–24 inches), but otherwise like the population in northern South America.

OTHER SPECIES

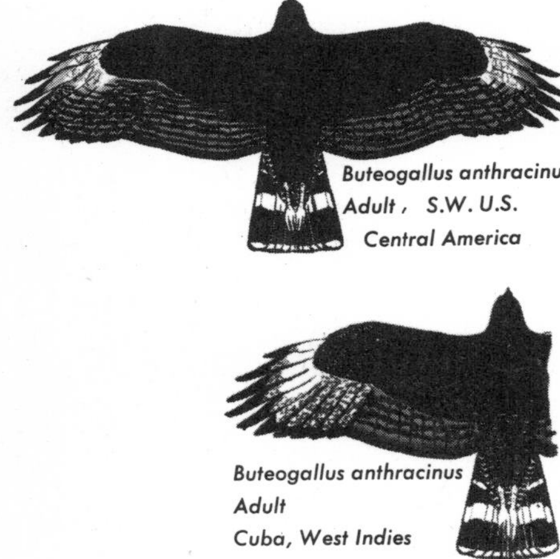

The Common Black Hawk (*B. anthracinus*), 17½–19 inches, has traces of amber-brown mottling and white patches on the undersurface of the wings. White or sandy coloring (on light bases of feathers) often shows at the back of the head, nape, and mantle when the bird is perched. The black tail coverts (upper and under) are white-tipped; tail, black, crossed by a single white median band (or a wide band and a narrow one) and white-tipped. This species may be found from southern Arizona and Texas through Central America and the West Indies to Colombia and southern Ecuador. Populations in the West Indies have more extensive white patches on the underwing surface and two distinct white bars on the black tail. The birds in the mangrove swamps of the Pacific slope from El Salvador to southern Ecuador show not only white primaries, but also entirely amber-brown secondaries. They have a single band on the tail, which is shorter, like that of the Rufous Crab Hawk. There is no definite immature plumage, such as described for the Great Black Hawk. The Common Black Hawk seems to molt directly into adult plumage from a juvenile one similar to the Great Black Hawk's (but with conspicuous

BUTEOGALLUS ANTHRA

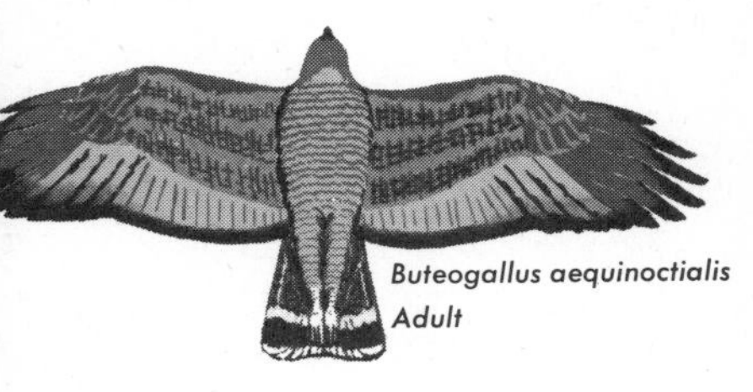

amber-brown on the wings in the mangrove swamps); tail, white and narrowly barred in black.

In the swampy forests of the Atlantic coast of South America, the Rufous Crab Hawk (*B. aequinoctialis*), 15–17 inches, has the general coloring of the Savanna Hawk (*Heterospizias meridionalis*). Its head and throat are slate-gray with a blue sheen; feathers of the back and wing coverts, iridescent slate-gray, scalloped with amber-brown; wings, dark brown crossed by a wide amber-brown bar; tail, also slate-gray, mottled amber-brown with an indistinct white median band, and white-tipped; underparts, amber-brown, very finely barred with slate-gray. Like the Common Black Hawk, this bird has no distinct immature plumage. The juvenile is plain dark gray-brown above except for its sandy nape; lighter below than other species of *Buteogallus,* with fewer dark spots on the chest and fainter barring on the thighs.

BUTEOGALLUS AEQUINOCTIALIS

HABITS

These large buteo-like hawks of sluggish disposition are usually seen perched on the lower branches of trees waiting for prey, or engaged in fishing, like the Black-collared Hawk (*Busarellus nigricollis*), along swamps, woodland streams, and pools. Food consists mainly of frogs, lizards, and fish. The largest form of the Great Black Hawk (Brazil) also takes small mammals and birds, but the northern birds seem to have habits similar to the smaller Common Black Hawks and the Rufous Crab Hawk.

The Great Black Hawks nest high in tall trees; Common Black Hawks, about 35 feet up in mesquite (Central America). These structures are platforms of sticks, sometimes lined with green leafy twigs and shredded bark. One to two eggs (both species) are pure white, finely speckled with red or blotched with brown. The Rufous Crab Hawk builds its nest—a heap of dry sticks lined with a few green leaves—in the forked branches of the courida trees in the savannas of Guiana and also in the forests along the seacoast. As far as is known, only one white egg, blotched with brown, is laid.

The call of the Great Black Hawk is a shrill "ker-r-re-ee," like a policeman's whistle; of the Common Black Hawk, a weak quavering scream (in middle America) or a piercing "ba-tis-ta-ooo" (in Cuba, where it is locally called *gavilán batista*). Pairs of Rufous Crab Hawks, playing in the air and swooping at each other, utter a loud musical, laughlike six or seven notes—at first rapid, then slower and descending in scale.

Immature Great Black Hawk *(Buteogallus urubitinga).*

The Black-collared Hawk *(Busarellus nigricollis)* frequents coastal lagoons, marshes, lakes, and inundated plains from southern Mexico to Paraguay and Peru.

GENUS *BUSARELLUS*

Busarellus is a wide-winged, short-tailed, and extremely heavy-footed bird of prey. The thigh feathers are short (not plumed); tarsi, mostly bare and scutellate; feet, furnished with spicules like those of the Osprey (*Pandion*), the Fish Hawk of worldwide distribution. The large beak is rather narrow, compressed, and strongly curved.

Black-collared Hawk (*Busarellus nigricollis*)

DESCRIPTION
(TROPICAL AMERICA)

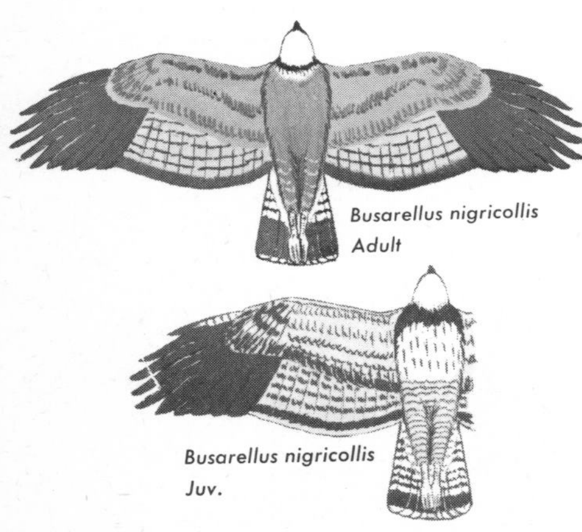

Heads, entirely white to sandy, finely streaked on the crown and nape in black; otherwise, sienna above with black-bordered wings and tail. Below, sienna, with a conspicuous black collar across a light mottled throat.

Juvenile—similar to adult but back, wing coverts, and secondaries are dark gray-brown, barred and feather-edged with sienna; tail, barred and broadly tipped black; chest appears darker and breast, lighter—sandy, streaked dark gray-brown and pale yellow-orange; belly, dark gray-brown tinged with sienna, the feathers also sandy-edged; thighs, amber-brown, narrowly barred with dark gray-brown.

Beak and cere, black; bare part of face, bluish-slate; eyes, bright reddish-brown; legs and feet, light blue-gray. Size, 17½–19½ inches.

BUSARELLUS NIGRICOL

VARIATIONS

In northern Argentina and Paraguay the Black-collared Hawk is slightly larger and paler than in the warmer parts of South America.

HABITS

This hawk is sedentary and does not soar frequently or very high except in the nesting season. Its favorite perch, where available, is a telegraph pole. Otherwise it sits and watches for prey on the branches of bushes or trees. Rice fields provide good hunting grounds in floodtime (British Guiana). Rats, mice, lizards, snails, large insects, worms, small birds, and fish are all taken, but the Black-collared Hawk is mainly a fisher. It swoops down on the water, picks up a fish, and rises to another perch in one continuous movement, with scarcely a stroke of the wings. In British Guiana one of the fish species commonly preyed upon is the Armored Hasser (*Hoplosternum*).

The Black-collared Hawk's nest of twigs is constructed in the tallest trees available. The clutch consists of one or two eggs.

The Solitary Eagle *(Harpyhaliaetus solitarius)*, a formidable raptor of the mountains of Central and South America, is apparently rare or difficult to find.

GENUS *HARPYHALIAETUS*

It is not known whether the ranges of the two species of *Harpyhaliaetus* overlap. The Crowned Eagle occurs in Brazil, Bolivia, Paraguay, and northern Argentina, and the Solitary Eagle, which has only a short nuchal crest, breeds from Peru north, very locally, to Sonora, Mexico. These are larger, heavier relatives of the black hawks (*Buteogallus*), with longer, aquiline beaks, broad wings, and short, squared-off tails. The Crowned Eagle has longer legs than the Solitary Eagle, but both species have an irregular pattern of plating, not a continuous series of transverse scutes, like the black hawks, on the tarsi.

Solitary Eagle (*Harpyhaliaetus solitarius*)

HARPYHALIAETUS SOLITARIUS

DESCRIPTION (HIGHLANDS OF MEXICO, AND SOUTH AMERICA)

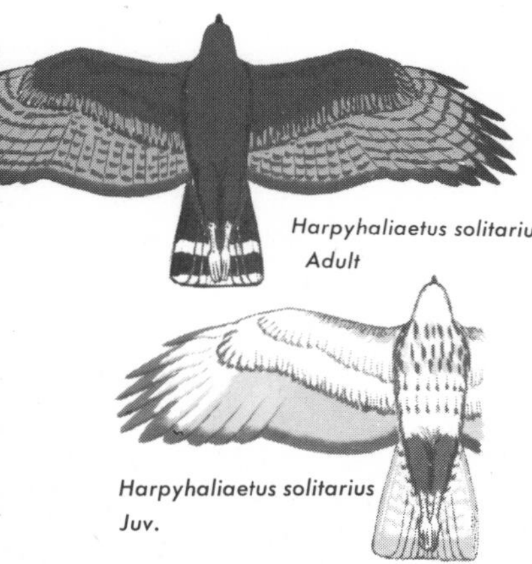

Almost entirely dark olive-brown above and below, including the short occipital crest; wings, slate-gray (primaries, black below the notch); tail coverts, black, tipped in white; tail, also black, crossed by a median white band and tipped in white.

Immature—similar to adult.

Juvenile—dark brown to black above, streaked on the crown and collared at the nape in buff-yellow; wing coverts and lower back, mottled as well as narrowly edged with light cinnamon; tail, white to medium olive-brown, finely and darkly vermiculated in a pattern of broken barring; face and throat, white, streaked with black and tinged buff-yellow; lower breast and belly, white, heavily streaked black and tinged buff-yellow; thighs, finely barred in cinnamon.

Beak, dark blue-gray; eyes, dark brown (juvenile, light yellow); legs and feet, yellow (juvenile, greenish). Size, 24–26 inches.

VARIATIONS

The population known only from the mountains of extreme southeastern Sonora, Mexico, averages larger, with heavier feet and toes. The over-all color is black, rather than slate-gray; the undertail coverts, distinctly barred and mottled in white.

OTHER SPECIES

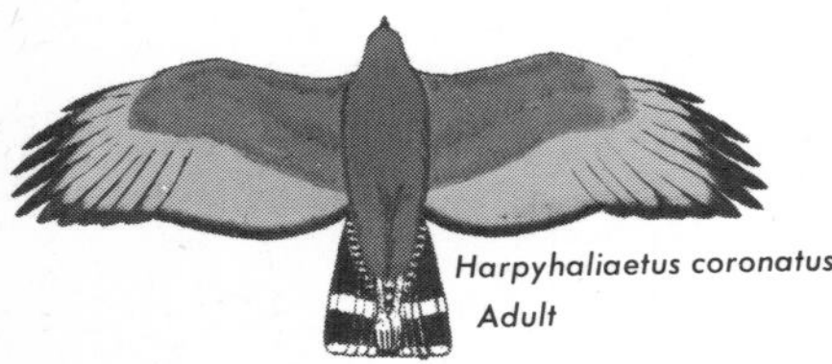

In central South America, the Crowned Eagle (*H. coronatus*), 25–27 inches; has pale gray-brown crown, face, and underparts; the long occipital crest feathers and the back, darker; wings, pale gray-brown, barred and broadly tipped with dark brown or black. In flight, however, the undersurface of the wings appears unbarred. The tail coverts are dark brown, tipped in white; the tail, also dark brown, is crossed by a median white band and tipped in white. Eye color, reddish-brown. (Immatures probably resemble adults, and juveniles follow the same plumage pattern as those of the Solitary Eagle, but are paler—dark gray-brown, sandy, and white in coloration.)

HARPYHALIAETUS CORON

HABITS

Although related to the black hawks, these eagles are far more powerful and apparently more predacious in their habits. The Solitary Eagle attacks fawns, and the Crowned Eagle preys on skunks, among other mammals. We have no information on nesting.

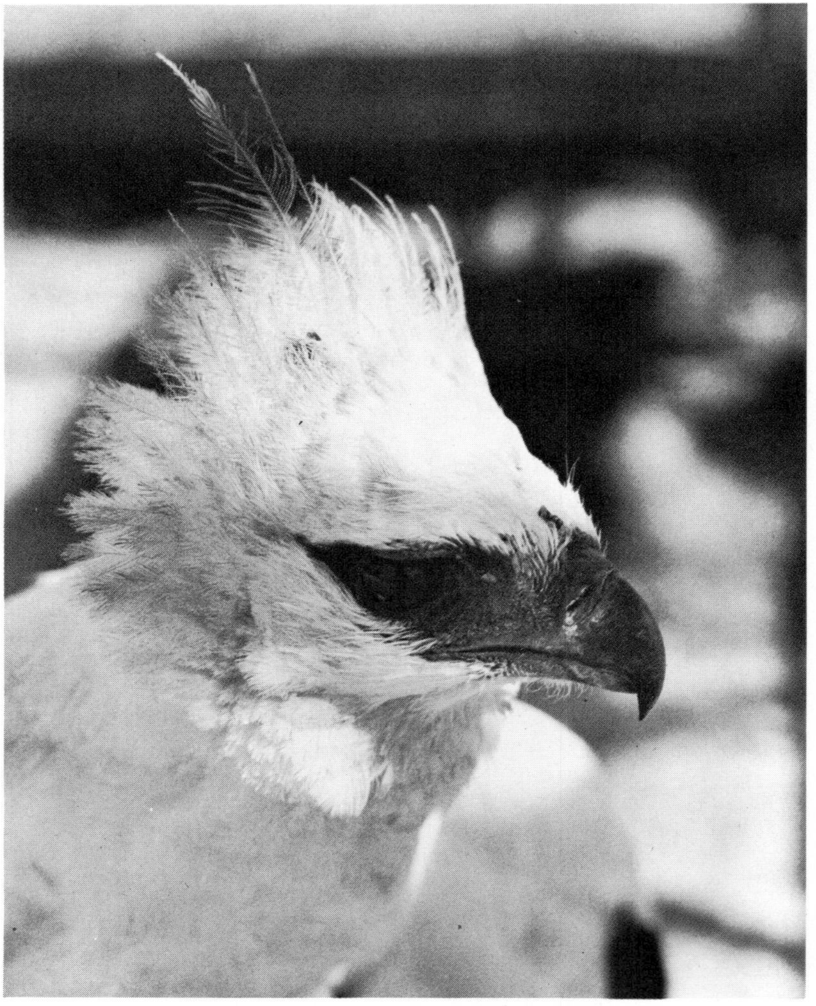

From a distance, the Crested Eagle *(Morphnus guianensis)* looks much like the Harpy Eagle *(Harpia harpyja)* of tropical-forested America but falls far short of that huge monkey-eater in size. The juvenile, shown here, is white.—*Photographed at the Tarpon Zoo.*

GENUS *MORPHNUS*

These are large eagles with short, full crests, broad wings, and nearly bare scutellate tarsi. They are not as large nor as heavy as *Harpia,* nor equipped with as formidable legs, feet, and beak in proportion to their body size. The tail in *Morphnus* is very much longer. Both light and dark variants and intermediates occur throughout the tropical American range.

Crested Eagle (*Morphnus guianensis*)

DESCRIPTION
(TROPICAL AMERICA)

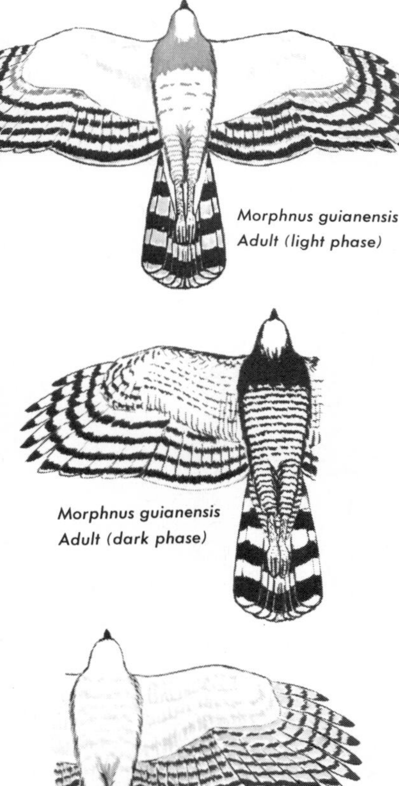

Morphnus guianensis
Adult (light phase)

Morphnus guianensis
Adult (dark phase)

Morphnus guianensis
Juv.

MORPHNUS GUIANENSIS

Light phase—head and neck, medium olive-gray to black; the crest, sandy-tipped, and the long occipital feathers, solid black; rest of upperparts, black, the lesser wing coverts narrowly scalloped in white; wings, dark brown, narrowly tipped in white; uppertail coverts, black, tipped in white; tail, light olive-gray, mottled and broadly banded with black; chin, white; chest, medium gray to tawny-olive; rest of underparts, white, with fine barring of sandy or more distinct pale yellow-orange coloring.

Dark phase—head and neck, black with white feather-edging; chin, white; chest, black; rest of underparts, heavily barred black and white; in flight the greater part of the undersurface, including the underwing and tail coverts, barred.

Immature (third year?)—similar to adult, but lesser wings coverts, more conspicuously edged with light olive-gray or tawny-olive (in light phase); greater wing coverts and wings, entirely mottled in the same range of colors (both phases) so that wings appear freckled when folded, not solid black as in adult plumage; chest feathers of dark phase immature, also broadly tipped in light olive-gray, not solid black, as in adult.

Immature (second year?)—head, neck, and crest, buffy-white (light phase) to dove-gray (dark phase), tinged with sandy coloring; the long occipital crest feathers, spotted with dark brown at the tips or all the crest feathers heavily spotted; upperparts, dark brown, more or less mottled buff-white; wing coverts, also finely mottled buff-white; wings, very heavily mottled as compared to older birds, the tail bands, narrower and more numerous (seven or eight), the subterminal band, wider and most conspicuous below; underparts, entirely white, tinged sandy (light phase), or irregularly banded with dark brown, except for the dove-gray chest band, which is spotted with dark brown (dark phase).

Juvenile—white above, tinged sandy to pale ivory-gray with indistinct dark vermiculations (light phase) or heavily mottled on the back and wing coverts (dark phase); wings similar to immatures, (second year), except for pure white or mottled tips, especially conspicuous on the secondaries; tail, white, finely mottled and very narrowly barred (eight or nine bars); underparts, white, tinged sandy (light phase) or freckled with pale ivory-gray (dark phase).

Beak, black; cere, slate-colored; eyes, pale gray (juvenile, brown); legs and feet, yellow; claws, black. Size, 26–30 inches.

HABITS

The Crested Eagle ranges over most of tropical America from Honduras south to southern Brazil and Paraguay, but is most numerous in the selvas, or rain forests. These eagles habitually perch on the branches of high trees along river banks, or may be seen circling high over the treetops. Their food consists of opossums, monkeys of the genus *Lagothrix* (*churucos*), young llamas, and reptiles.

Little is known of their nesting habits, except that they build in the largest trees, like other forest-dwelling crested eagles of the genera *Spizaetus, Harpyhaliaetus,* and *Harpia.*

Their calls are similar to those of the black hawks, but louder and more varied.

The gray mottled color of the tropical American Harpy Eagle *(Harpia harpyja)* blends into the bark of the huge silk-cotton trees where it prefers to nest, and its crest blends in with the foliage.

GENUS *HARPIA*

The tropical American Harpy Eagle is crowned with long and very broad plumes, adding an awesome touch to an otherwise impressive appearance. The powerful beak is short, very deep, and relatively narrow. The lores and orbits are only sparsely bristled. The short, stout tarsi are half-feathered—otherwise, scutellate in front and the feet are as large as a man's hand. Females weigh about twenty pounds and have extremely big feet and claws. Like its almost exact counterpart, the Philippine Monkey-eating Eagle, the Harpy Eagle has very broad wings and a rather long, squared-off tail. According to Jim Fowler's observations of captive Harpy Eagles, the young birds go through two distinct subadult molts after the juvenile plumage. They are fully adult at the end of their fourth year—with black crest, black chest band, and tail broadly banded black.

Harpy Eagle (*Harpia harpyja*)

DESCRIPTION (TROPICAL AMERICA)

Head and neck, entirely pale ivory-gray to dove-gray, with long occipital crest darker—slate-gray to black, faintly edged in white; otherwise, black above, with some narrow white feather-edging on the lower back, wings, and tail coverts; tail, olive-gray to olive-brown, with three broad black bands. Chest, black; rest of underparts, white; thighs, finely barred black.

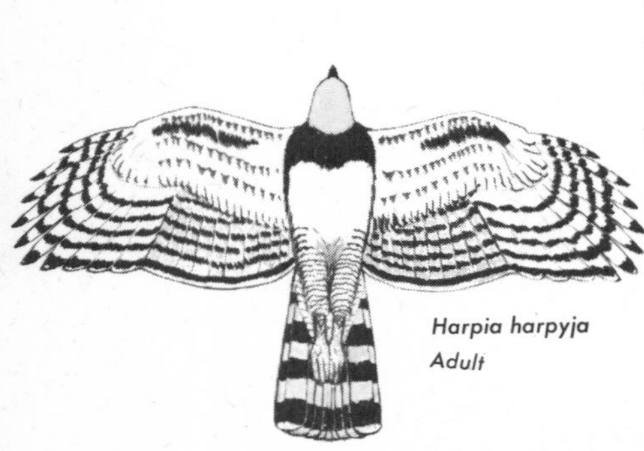

Harpia harpyja
Adult

HARPIA HARPYJA

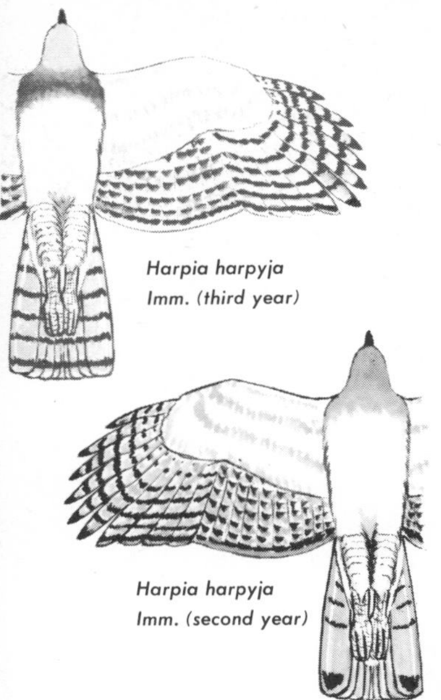

Harpia harpyja
Imm. (third year)

Harpia harpyja
Imm. (second year)

Immature (third year)—pure white head and nape, except for a black occipital crest, heavily mottled with dove-gray and white-tipped; rest of upperparts, medium gray, mottled or barred with black; tail, lighter than adult's, with five narrow, widely spaced, black bands; throat, pale ivory-gray; chest marking, spotty; thighs, indistinctly barred.

Immature (second year)—has pure white head, nape, and occipital crest; rest of upperparts, including wing coverts, pale ivory-gray; tail, light olive-gray, with broken bars near the base and a narrow black subterminal band; throat and upper chest, pale ivory-gray; rest of underparts, white, except for barred thighs.

Juvenile—lighter than (second year) immature, above and below; tail, mottled and marked with ten or eleven dark bands.

Beak and cere, blue-black; eyes, dark brown or black; tarsi and toes, pale yellow; claws, black. Size, 32–36 inches.

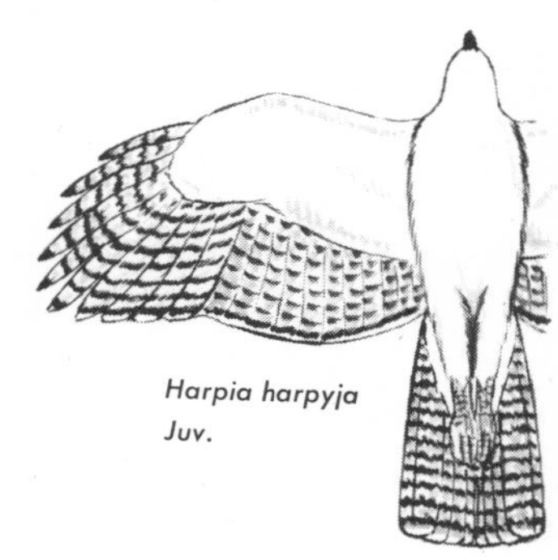

Harpia harpyja
Juv.

Adult Harpy Eagle (*Harpia harpyja*).—*Photographed at the National Zoological Park.*

HABITS

The Harpy Eagle lives entirely in the rain forests of tropical America. Until recently practically nothing was known of its life history. Although the bird is legendary in the regions in which it is found, few people have actually seen one. Jim Fowler and Jim Cope discovered two families of Harpy Eagles in British Guiana and observed them on their nesting territories from December, 1959, to May, 1960. Eventually one adult female and two juveniles were trapped and trained and have been successfully kept in captivity for two and one-half years. Their behavior has been studied both in the wild and under controlled conditions, and an accurate record kept of food requirements and molts.

The short, broad wing of the Harpy Eagle affords almost vertical movement through the trees. This bird is seldom seen soaring high above the treetops and habitually enters its nest, high in the tallest trees, from below. Its flight—a few fast wing beats and a glide—resembles that of an accipiter, albeit an enormous one. While hunting, the Harpy Eagle covers short distances, from tree to tree, paying close attention to movements and sounds, especially the noises made by monkeys. Its mottled gray plumage and raised crest feathers blend into the pattern of the foliage in its forest habitat, where it preys primarily on Capuchin monkeys and sloths; also other mammals—agouti, tree porcupine, coatimundi, and opossum, as well as macaws and probably parrots, although birds were not recorded during the nesting season in British Guiana. In pursuit of prey through the trees, this huge raptor is remarkably fast and agile.

The Harpy's nest tree often borders on a creek, its location marked by an accumulation of bones, most of them at the base of the trunk, but a few also under the main branches. In the Amazon region a nest was once found in a large old mahogany tree, but in British Guiana the silk-cotton tree, which towers above the rain forest to a total height of 200 feet or more, is preferred. There, on limbs which fork almost at right angles from the trunk, at a point just above the other trees (or 70 to 135 feet above the ground), a platform of large sticks is constructed, about four feet across and two feet thick. The structure is added to considerably another year—to five feet in diameter and four feet thick. In the shallow cup there is a lining of green leaves, seed pods, organic matter, and bones. As far as is known, the Harpy lays only one egg.

The nests found by Fowler and Cope were twelve miles apart at Nappi and Moco-moco in a valley in the Kanaku Mountains of southwestern British Guiana. The juveniles, between eight and ten months old, were already in their first immature molt and had well-developed powers of flight. However, they were still entirely dependent on the adults for food. A single adult—in the case of the eagle that was trapped, a female—attended each young bird. The young stayed in their respective nesting territories, that is, within a radius of 100 yards of the nest tree which was used for perching. Occasionally a juvenile would sit either on the edge of the nest or on one of several perches in neighboring trees. At midday, especially on hot days of 85 degrees or more, it would seek shade in the dense bushy tops of mora trees, well below the lower limbs of the silk-cotton trees, or on the tops of dead snags nearby. Its pale gray plumage proved to be an effective camouflage, blending into both the gray bark of the nest tree and the usual white or gray cloud background of the sky.

At night, especially if the juvenile eagle had not eaten the day before, it would roost in the top of the nest tree. About half an hour after sunrise, it would begin calling. If especially hungry, the juvenile would perch on one of the higher exposed branches and flap its wings, perhaps "signaling" the parent by the flashing of the white underwing coverts. Food calls became more and more frequent with increasing hunger. At this stage the parents at the two nests had obviously lost interest in supporting the young and were encouraging them to become independent. Even though screaming sessions (of ten to twenty successive calls) averaged ten per hour at the Nappi nest site, food was brought only once in five days. After ten days without eating, the Moco-moco juvenile's food-begging call changed to a combination "scream" and pathetic "whine"; this bird was fed only once in 14 days.

When the parent finally arrived with prey, it was grabbed away by the juvenile, which mantled the food and screamed until the adult left, and then tried to "kill" the offering with its talons several times before starting to eat. The young bird would carry its food around or leave it in the nest for as long as three days, eating it piecemeal.

With its hunger satisfied, the juvenile would settle down for long periods, usually in the shade of a treetop, and appear to be keenly interested in every movement or sound in the vicinity. Every bird or insect was viewed from all angles by cocking and twisting the head and neck.

John Hamlet's captive Harpy Eagle (the adult in our photograph) also had the habit of turning its head completely upside down and scrutinizing its human visitors.

The Nappi and Moco-moco juveniles were very reluctant to go to new perches—and even more so to land on the ground. When the observers attempted to feed one of them on the ground, it would not take the offering, even if obviously hungry, but when a chicken was placed in the nest tree, flew to it immediately.

Although both birds were excited by sounds such as those of a tribe of monkeys calling in the distance or a flock of parrots chattering, they showed no ability to kill for themselves.

In September, 1961, there was a young eagle in the Moco-moco nest again, indicating that the adult (at the nest site where only a juvenile had been trapped) had laid the egg in April, May, or June of that year.

The extremely long dependence of the juveniles on their parents and the alternate-year nesting record at Moco-moco suggest that the Harpy may nest every other year in British Guiana.

The adult Harpy Eagle gives voice to high-pitched screams, "whee-e-e-e-ee whe-e-e-e-e," repeated ten to twelve times at regular intervals. Besides the food-begging call, the juveniles have at least three other vocal notes, including croaking noises (when a parent is near) and various conversational "quacks" and whistles. The female also has a scream similar to the juvenile's, but lower pitched. Her reply to the food-begging cry of the young bird is a scream preceded by a croak.

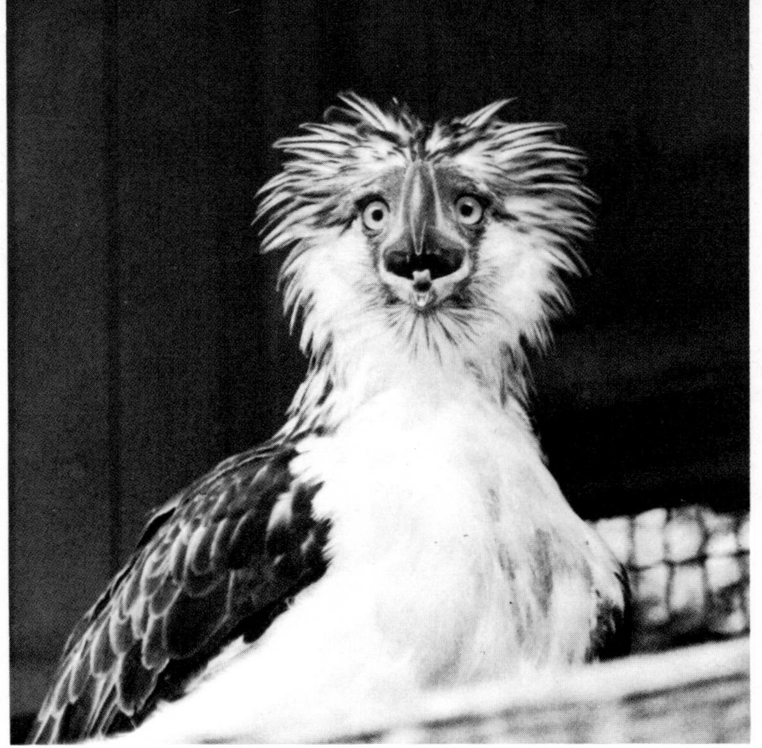

Monkey-eating Eagle (Pithecophaga jefferyi).—Photographed at the National Zoological Park.

GENUS *PITHECOPHAGA*

Pithecophaga, with its full crest of long, narrow lanceolate feathers, is the ecological equivalent of the South American Harpy Eagle (*Harpia*). Its sturdy legs are partly feathered, otherwise transversely plated in front, and the feet and claws are enormous. Its short, broad wingspan and long square tail are also adapted to forest living. The Monkey-eating Eagle is not quite as heavy as the Harpy, but its powerful bill is much narrower, deeper, and more highly arched.

Monkey-eating Eagle (*Pithecophaga jefferyi*)

DESCRIPTION (PHILIPPINES)

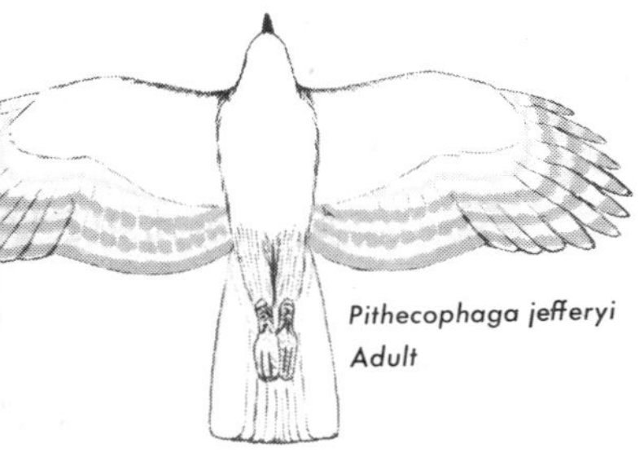

Pithecophaga jefferyi Adult

Crown and long occipital crest, white, heavily tinged with cinnamon and shaft-streaked with dark brown; rest of upperparts, including wings, sepia, the feathers edged with cinnamon and white. Tail, dark brown with very indistinct narrow brown bands and white-tipped (but paler and unmarked on the undersurface). Sides of face and throat, white with fine black shaft-streaking; underparts, white except for cinnamon-striped thighs and long flank feathers. Some darkly striped lanceolate feathers may decorate the upper chest as well as the crown.

Juvenile—similar to adult.

Beak and cere, blue-black; eyes, pale blue; legs and feet, yellow; claws, black. Size, about 36 inches.

PITHECOPHAGA JEFFERYI

HABITS

The Monkey-eating Eagle inhabits the least accessible rain forest and mountain areas of the eastern Philippine Islands. Flapping flight, with little soaring, is characteristic of this raptor, which looks like a gigantic goshawk and utters "strange wailing" cries on the wing. It feeds on monkeys (*Cynamolgos*), as well as hornbills, and also preys on small dogs, pigs, and poultry in native villages. Pairs may specialize and bring up their young on an almost exclusive diet of any one of these items, depending on the location of the nest and whatever is most available and vulnerable.

As might be expected, they build in the tallest trees on mountainsides or above the canopy in the giant kapoks of the rain forest—trees very similar to the silk-cottons preferred by the Harpy Eagle in tropical America. At the base of these kapoks are accumulations of bones three or four layers thick, evidence of as many years' occupation, and food remains can also be seen hanging from the nests. Although as a rule only one eaglet seems to survive in each nest, there may be two eggs, and occasionally (in at least one known instance) two young birds. The adults at several nest sites have produced young every year.

The feathers of the New Guinea Harpy Eagle *(Harpyopsis novaeguineae)* are probably as highly treasured by the natives of the central highlands as those of the male Greater Bird of Paradise. High-ranking tribesmen usually wear one or more primaries or tail feathers on ceremonial occasions.

GENUS *HARPYOPSIS*

The New Guinea Harpy Eagle is a smaller version of the immense Philippine Monkey-eating Eagle with some modifications. It has a short, full crest, an extremely long rounded tail, longer tarsi (scutellate front and back), and long, thin toes.

New Guinea Harpy Eagle (*Harpyopsis novaeguineae*)

DESCRIPTION (NEW GUINEA)

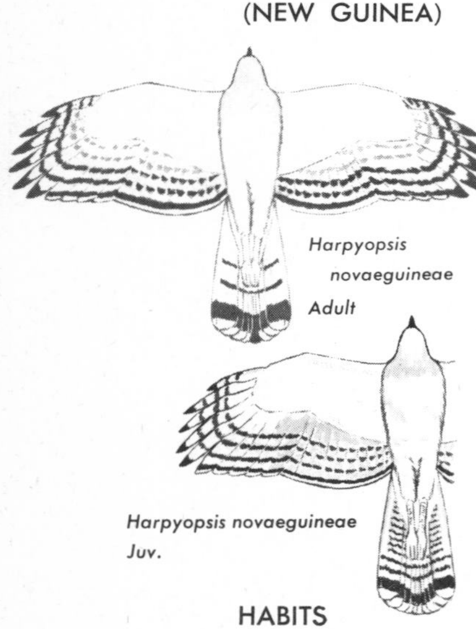

Above, gray-brown, the feathers of the crown, crest, and sides of neck scalloped in buff, and those of the back, wing coverts, and flight feathers, barred darker and scalloped in white; tail, gray-brown, mottled and barred dark brown; face, gray-brown, streaked with buff; underparts, white, heavily tinged with buff and marked on the sides of the body and sometimes across the breast with patches of medium ivory-gray.

Juvenile—similar but paler; tail, with more numerous mottled bands.

Beak, black with a bone-colored tip; feet, brownish-gray. Size, 31 inches.

HARPYOPSIS NOVAEGUIN

HABITS

Thomas Gilliard encountered the Harpy Eagle in the beech forest of the central highlands of New Guinea between 7,500 and 9,500 feet, where it is common but thinly distributed. This species feeds on mammals such as the kapul (a marsupial) and is said to kill small pigs in open farming areas, like the Monkey-eating Eagle of the Philippines. Its huge nest is placed high in the largest trees of the cloud forest.

Isidor's Crested, or Black-and-Chestnut, Eagle *(Oroaetus isidori)*, a beautiful glossy black and sienna-colored raptor, lives at high altitudes in the Andes of South America.

GENUS *OROAETUS*

Oroaetus, feathered to the toes and displaying a regal, long pointed crest, closely resembles the Ornate Hawk-Eagle (*Spizaetus ornatus*). However, it is a larger bird with proportionally heavier feet, longer wings, and a shorter tail.

Black-and-Chestnut Eagle (*Oroaetus isidori*)

DESCRIPTION (ANDES OF SOUTH AMERICA)

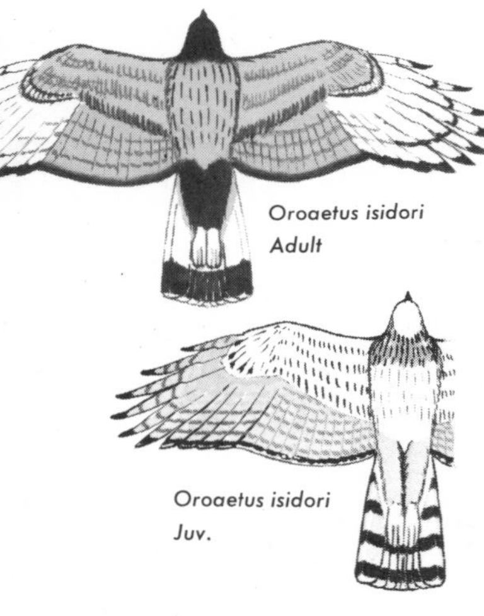

Above, glossy black; the head, ornamented by a long black crest; wings, pale gray-brown, spotted darker (black at the tips); tail coverts, black; tail, pale gray-brown with some white mottling and a broad terminal band of black; face, throat, and thighs, black; rest of underparts, sienna-brown, striped black.

Immature—also black, has yellow-brown streaking and feather-edging on the crest, face, and sides of neck; patches of light olive-gray on the wing coverts; narrow white edging on the wings; white throat; underparts, as in the adult, but lighter, since the feathers are edged in white; tail, more distinctly mottled in white than adult's, with three black bands—the subterminal one usually wider and white-tipped.

Juvenile—lighter and conspicuously feather-edged in white above; face, head, and neck as well as chest, light tan with dark streaking and long crest feathers solid dark brown; band across the wing coverts and upper back, pale gray-brown; rest of upperparts, gray-brown to dark gray-brown; wings, barred dark brown; tail, as in immature; underparts, mostly white with a few black stripes; tarsi, barred. Size, 25–29 inches.

OROAETUS ISIDORI

HABITS

Like other large forest eagles, the Black-and-Chestnut Eagle is thinly distributed throughout its wide range. Although this species has been sighted at altitudes from 1,800 to 9,000 feet in Colombia, it appears to nest most often between 6,000 and 7,000 feet—not higher on the brush and barren heath of the mountaintops, or lower in the valleys. At this altitude the steep ravines and river gorges are covered with dense vegetation—principally oak trees and silver-leaved Cecropias. The eastern side of the cordillera is preferred because it receives the morning sun. In the afternoon the mountainsides are generally covered by dense fog, or drenched by heavy rains. Therefore, the western slopes receive little or no direct sunlight. The adults may be seen hunting on either side, usually at the same or higher altitudes. As they fly low over the forest, covering a considerable territory, monkeys scream and run for cover on the lowest branches. The Indians say that they feed on *Churucos,* the monkeys (*Lagothrix lugens*) of the mountains; tree-living mammals—squirrels, sloths, pottos, porcupines, and nasuas (South American raccoons); also game birds and poultry. Thus they appear to replace ecologically the Harpy (*Harpia*) and the Crested Eagle (*Morphnus*) of the flat rain forests in the paramos (high mountain zones). Where all three species occur at lower altitudes in the Putumayo region of Colombia, they are called *Grulla,* the Indian word for "eagle," and no distinction is made between them.

According to F. C. Lehmann's observations of several pairs of Black-and-Chestnut Eagles in Colombia, the young are fed primarily on squirrels until eight weeks old. Immatures are more likely to steal poultry from farm yards in the valleys than the adults, but some individuals may acquire the chicken-stealing habit.

The nest, made of sticks (oak), is usually at least 60 feet up in the fork of a large tree which projects to a total height of about 200 feet from the side of a ravine or gorge. The single egg is white, washed and spotted with chocolate-brown. In one instance recorded by Lehmann, an egg laid in April was hatched in May; and in July the young bird was still in the nest—not fully fledged. The fledgling lives six months or longer in the vicinity of the nest. Fresh leaves and twigs in the nest cavity are renewed periodically from the time of hatching until the young bird is between six and seven weeks old.

The male provides most, if not all, of the food for the family. Coming in swiftly, with partly closed wings, he cries "pee-ee-eéo," then drops the prey in the nest and retires to a nearby perch. When the nestling is small, the female stays at the nest, and the male remains at his roost for regular periods each day; i.e., between 9 and 11:30 A.M. and 1:30 to 4:00 P.M. During the remaining daylight hours they are either hunting or effectively concealed among the branches of neighboring trees by their dark coloration. Ordinarily silent on the nesting territory, they, nevertheless, have certain notes that seem to be used for communicating with each other —"chee-chee-chee" and "pee-pee-pee," while "kee-kee-kee" warns the young of danger. Later in the season they spend longer periods away from the nest.

The Black-and-White Hawk-Eagle (*Spizastur melanoleucus*) is a smaller, chunkier relative of the tropical American species of *Spizaetus*.

GENUS *SPIZASTUR*

A small eagle with feathered tarsi and a short crest, *Spizastur* has a very large beak and big feet for its size, as well as longer wings and a shorter tail than the Ornate Hawk-Eagle.

Black-and-White Hawk-Eagle (*Spizastur melanoleucus*)

DESCRIPTION (CONTINENTAL TROPICAL AMERICA)

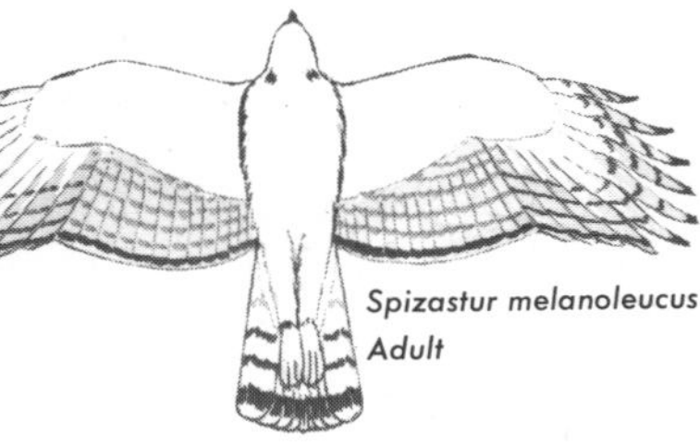

Head, neck, and underparts white, except for black lores, orbital region, and streaking on back of crown; rest of upperparts, glossy black with a chocolate cast wherever light bases of feathers show; wings, pale gray-brown or darker, banded black; tail, pale gray-brown, banded with dark brown and white-tipped.

Young birds, similar to adults, but browner above, with white-tipped wing coverts; beak, black; cere and basal part of mandible, reddish-orange; eyes, yellow; legs and feet, yellow; claws, black. Size, 19–20 inches.

HABITS

This eagle inhabits hot lowland rain forests from Oaxaca, Chiapas, and Veracruz, through Central and South America. It preys on small mammals, birds, and reptiles.

Bright amber-brown feathering on the head and sides of the chest distinguish the Ornate Hawk-Eagle *(Spizaetus ornatus)* from its close relative, the Black Hawk-Eagle *(S. tyrannus)*, in the forests of tropical America.

GENUS *SPIZAETUS*

The members of the genus *Spizaetus* (whose legs are completely feathered) are not as large as the crowned eagles and the harpies, but their comparatively slight build is offset by strong, deeply hooked beaks and exceptionally powerful feet. The heaviest Asiatic birds are capable of taking large game. Japanese falconers of the royal household trained hawk-eagles for the hunt, and the Himalayan birds were favorites of Genghis Khan.

In *Spizaetus* the wings are short and extremely wide, and the tail is long and rounded. The face is copiously bristled, and the feathering on the legs stops just short of the base of the toes or, in some cases, extends down between the bases of the toes. Some kind of head ornamentation is always characteristic. The populations of *S. cirrhatus,* ranging from the Himalayas to Indochina, Malaysia, and the Philippines, have short full crests like *S. lanceolatus* of the Celebes and *S. africanus* of western Africa, and *S. cirrhatus,* of peninsular India and Ceylon, and other species all display two or three long, black erectile crest feathers.

There may be some difficulty in identifying the various hawk-eagles in the field in Asia, for at both the northern and southern limits of its range, *S. cirrhatus* overlaps breeding ranges of other species. Also, Cassin's Hawk-Eagle, in West Africa, might be confused with Ayre's Eagle or the African Hawk-Eagle (*see Hieraetus*).

Ornate Hawk-Eagle (*Spizaetus ornatus*)

DESCRIPTION (TROPICAL AMERICA)

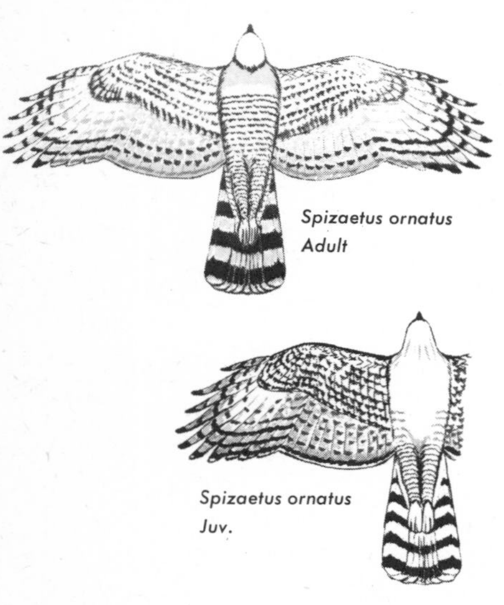
Spizaetus ornatus Adult

Spizaetus ornatus Juv.

Forehead and long occipital crest, black; back of head and nape, amber-brown; rest of upperparts, including wings, barred black and chocolate with narrow white feather-edging on wing coverts; tail, ochre-brown with four black bands; throat, lores, and eyebrows, white, with contrasting black mustachial stripes and amber-brown cheeks; patches of amber-brown at the sides of neck and sometimes entirely across the white chest; rest of underparts, white spotted and barred black (evenly barred in older birds).

Immature—not as distinctly barred on back; head and sides of chest, white or sandy, rather than amber-brown, and finely shaft-streaked; underparts, spotted; tail, with five narrow bands.

Juvenile—gray-brown above with dark barring only on wings and fine white barring on wing coverts; head and neck, entirely white except for black occipital crest; underparts, white, with barring restricted to flanks and thighs; tail, as in immature.

Beak, black; cere and bare part of face, grayish-yellow; eyes, orange-yellow (young, yellowish-white); feet, yellow; claws, black. Size, 21–25 inches.

SPIZAETUS ORNATUS

OTHER TROPICAL AMERICAN SPECIES

The Tyrant, or Black, Hawk-Eagle (*S. tyrannus*), 23–26 inches, a somewhat shorter-winged and longer-tailed species, is black with a chocolate cast, except for white spots on the crest feathers; tail, barred black and olive-gray; some white spotting on the lower belly; black-and white-barred thighs. The young are more chocolate-colored, with a white or sandy head; throat and breast, heavily streaked black; rufous-brown suffusion at sides of neck and breast; belly, flanks, and thighs, conspicuously spotted or barred dark brown to black; the tail, more narrowly barred than in adult.

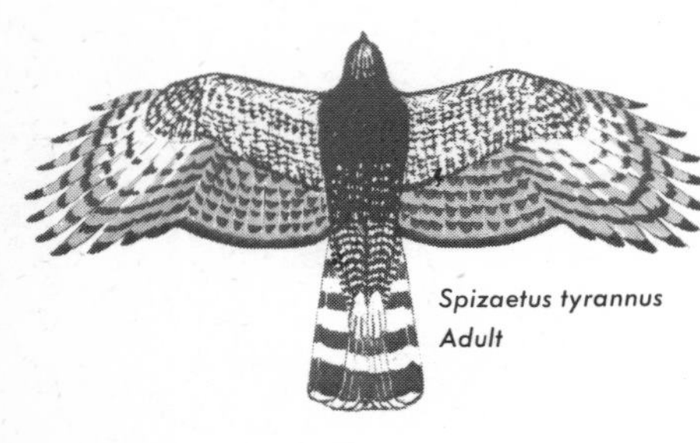
Spizaetus tyrannus Adult

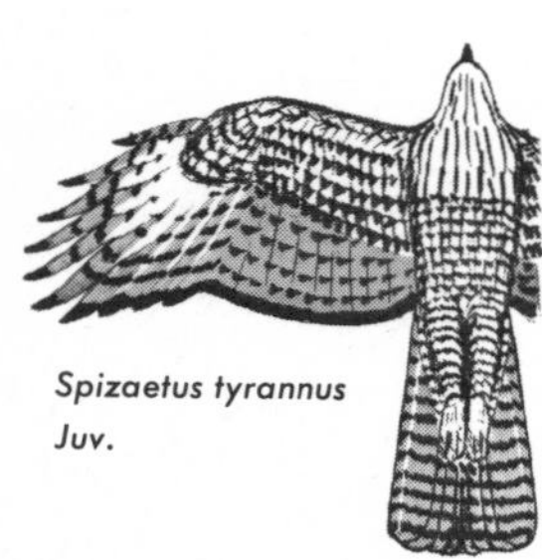
Spizaetus tyrannus Juv.

SPIZAETUS TYRANNUS

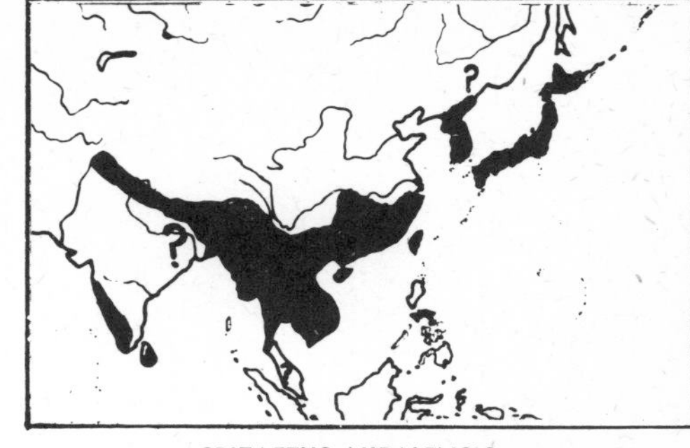
SPIZAETUS NIPALENSIS

Mountain Hawk-Eagle (*Spizaetus nipalensis*)

DESCRIPTION (BETWEEN 2,000 AND 7,000 FEET IN THE HIMALAYAS AND LICHIANG RANGE, YUNNAN)

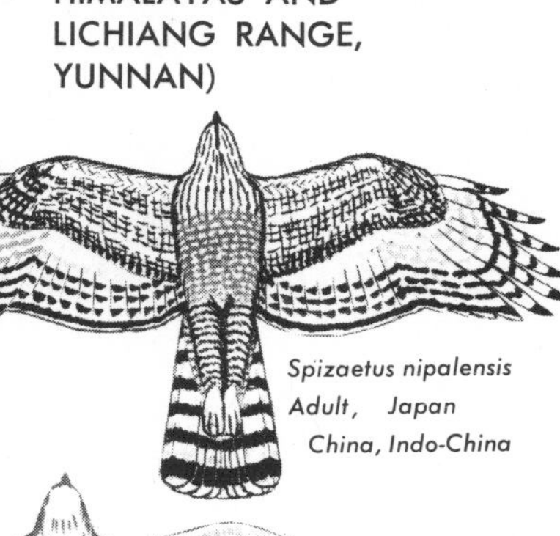
Spizaetus nipalensis Adult, Japan China, Indo-China

Spizaetus nipalensis Juv. Japan, China, Indo-China

Head, dark brown, striped with light cinnamon (on feather edges); long occipital crest, tipped in white; otherwise chocolate above, with wings barred darker; tail coverts, barred white; tail, light olive-gray with dark brown barring; face, dark brown, streaked in light cinnamon; breast, light cinnamon, streaked dark brown; rest of underparts, cinnamon-brown, with broken white barring.

Juvenile—much paler, the feathers of the upperparts edged in white; head and neck, white, with dark brown streaking; underparts, white, very faintly barred with light cinnamon; tail, with narrower and more numerous bars.

Beak, black; eyes, yellow; toes, yellowish-white; claws, black. Size, 24½–28 inches.

VARIATIONS

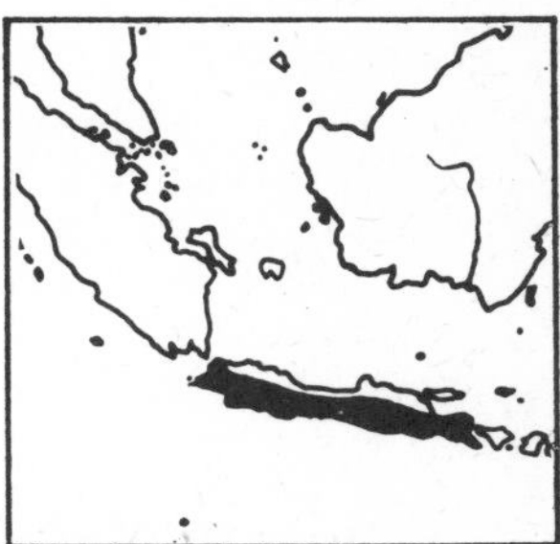
SPIZAETUS BARTELSI

Japanese individuals are by far the largest (28–31 inches) and much lighter than the Himalayan birds described, although their pattern of coloration is similar; the Hainan birds are smaller and lighter; and the smallest, in southern India and Ceylon, have fainter streaking on the throat and chest, as well as unbarred underwing coverts and thighs.

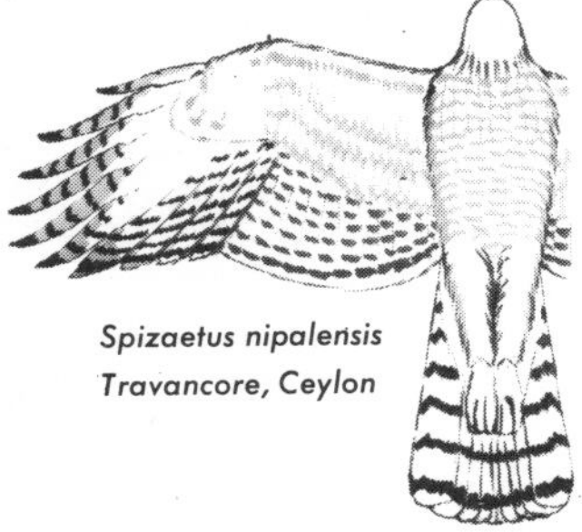
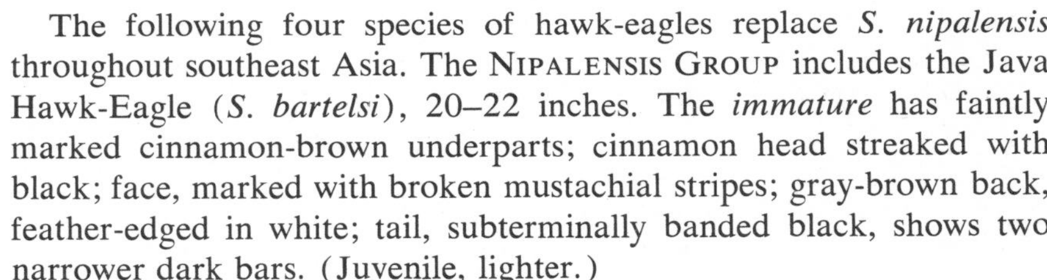
Spizaetus nipalensis Travancore, Ceylon

OTHER SPECIES

The following four species of hawk-eagles replace *S. nipalensis* throughout southeast Asia. The NIPALENSIS GROUP includes the Java Hawk-Eagle (*S. bartelsi*), 20–22 inches. The *immature* has faintly marked cinnamon-brown underparts; cinnamon head streaked with black; face, marked with broken mustachial stripes; gray-brown back, feather-edged in white; tail, subterminally banded black, shows two narrower dark bars. (Juvenile, lighter.)

From Thailand and the Malay peninsula to Borneo, the Asiatic Black-and-White Hawk-Eagle (*S. alboniger*), 19–21 inches, is very dark above; breast, white, heavily streaked with black; belly, thighs, and tarsi, barred black and white; tail, white, basally and subterminally banded black. (Juvenile, unmarked buff head and underparts.)

The rare Philippine Hawk-Eagle (*S. philippensis*), about 24 inches or larger, recorded from Luzon to Basilan and Palawan, has chocolate and black upperparts, with cinnamon streaking on the head and face; chest, cinnamon, heavily striped in black; rest of underparts, uniformly sepia, except for white-barred tarsi. (Immature, similar to adult but lighter.)

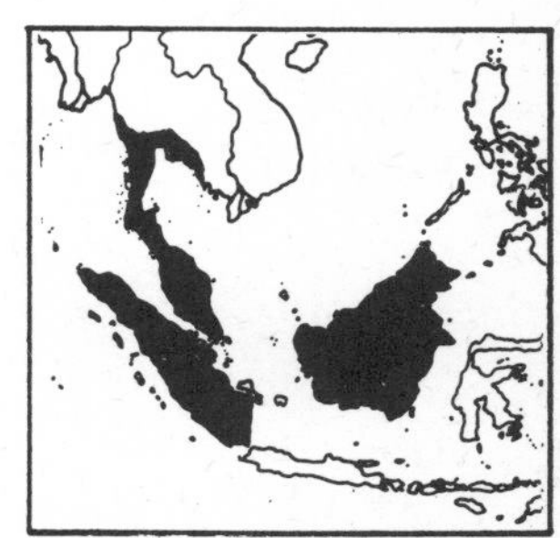
SPIZAETUS ALBONIGER

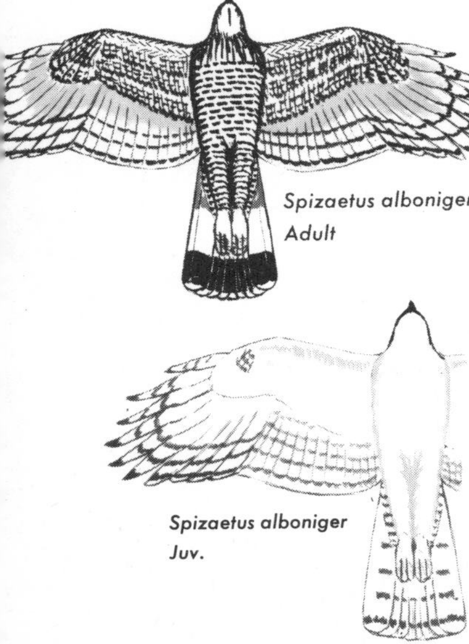
Spizaetus alboniger Adult

Spizaetus alboniger Juv.

SPIZAETUS PHILIPPENSIS

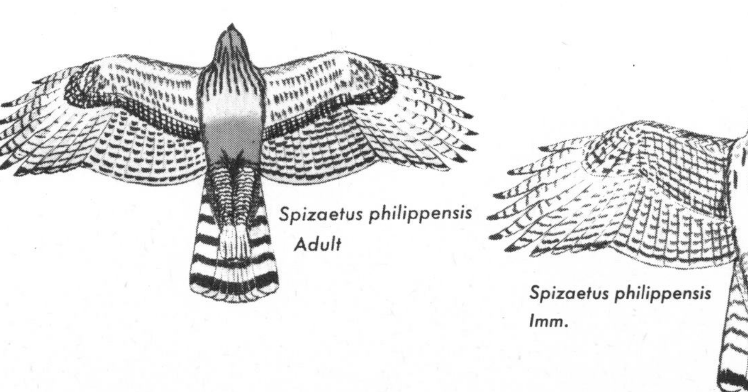
Spizaetus philippensis Adult

Spizaetus philippensis Imm.

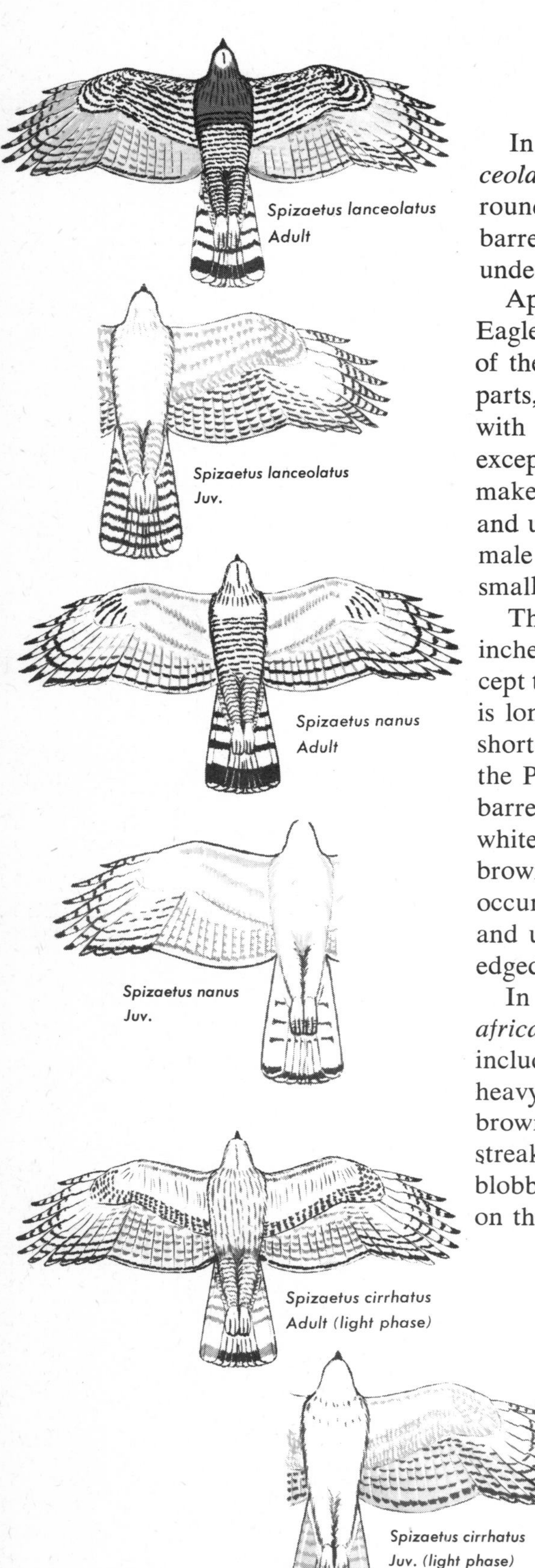

Spizaetus lanceolatus
Adult

Spizaetus lanceolatus
Juv.

Spizaetus nanus
Adult

Spizaetus nanus
Juv.

Spizaetus cirrhatus
Adult (light phase)

In the Celebes, the Short-crested, or Celebes, Hawk-Eagle (*S. lanceolatus*), about 22 inches (but slightly smaller in the islands surrounding Celebes), is similarly colored, but the belly and thighs are barred with chocolate and white. (Juvenile, light underparts and underwing coverts.)

Apparently not closely related to this group is Wallace's Hawk-Eagle (*S. nanus*), about 18 inches, which breeds throughout the range of the Asiatic Black-and-White Hawk-Eagle. Light cinnamon underparts, streaked and barred black, are distinctive. The tail is marked with three dark bands. (Juveniles of the two species are identical except for size, and the "normal" sexual dimorphism in size tends to make even this difference insignificant. A small bird with buff head and underparts and long black occipital crest could be either a young male of the larger species, *S. alboniger,* or a young female of the smaller one, *S. nanus.*)

The range of the Changeable Hawk-Eagle (*S. cirrhatus*), 20–24 inches, overlaps the ranges of all other Asiatic species of *Spizaetus,* except the Celebes Hawk-Eagle. The tan head, streaked with dark brown, is long-crested in individuals from peninsular India and Ceylon, and short-crested in birds from the Himalayas, Indochina, Malaysia, and the Philippines. The rest of the upperparts are dark gray-brown; tail, barred with dark brown, the subterminal band broadest; underparts, white, streaked with dark gray-brown; flanks and thighs, barred ochre-brown; tarsi, white and finely barred. A Melanistic (black) Phase occurs in the short-crested birds. (Juveniles have white or buff heads and underparts, the former indistinctly streaked; upperparts, feather-edged in white.)

In Africa, a rarely seen Congo species, Cassin's Hawk-Eagle (*S. africanus*), 21 inches, is entirely black and chocolate-colored above, including the face; throat and rest of underparts, white, except for heavy black patches at the sides of the body and legs; tail, ochre-brown, barred dark brown, with a broad subterminal band. (Juvenile, streaked white and amber-brown on head, crest, and cheeks; heavily blobbed with black and tinged light amber-brown below, especially on the breast.)

SPIZAETUS LANCEOLAT

SPIZAETUS NANUS

SPIZAETUS CIRRHATUS

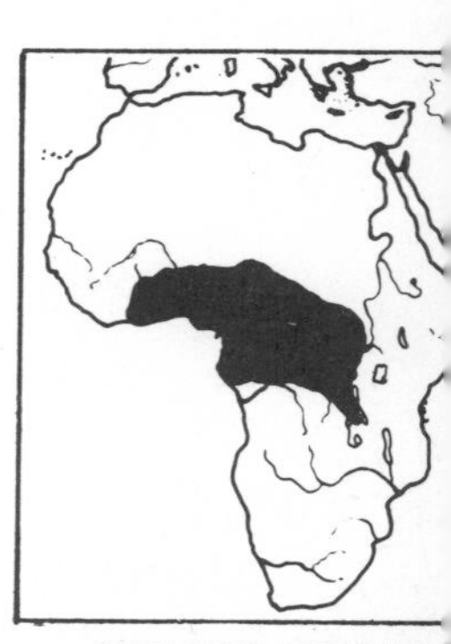

SPIZAETUS AFRICANU

Spizaetus cirrhatus
Juv. (light phase)

Spizaetus africanus
Adult

Spizaetus cirrhatus
Adult (dark phase)

Spizaetus africanus
Juv.

HABITS

The Mountain Hawk-Eagle is found mostly at higher altitudes in the mountain forests, except in winter. The hawk-eagles of peninsular India and Ceylon frequent wooded low country and hills up to 4,000 feet; also cultivated fields. In Malaysia, Celebes, and Philippines, as well as Central America and South America, other hawk-eagles keep to the humid, tropical-forested lowlands.

Among the most voracious raptors, the hawk-eagles of this group kill small- to medium-sized mammals from the size of rats, mice, and squirrels up to hares; sizable birds, such as ptarmigan, peacocks, quail, parrots, and herons; also lizards, snakes, and bats. The Changeable Hawk-Eagle is most closely associated with man, sometimes even nesting in large trees in the midst of villages, and may occasionally steal from chicken yards.

Most of these birds watch for their ground-living quarry from a concealed perch in a high tree; then descend to a lower branch, from which they can make a short, fast swoop. The hawk-eagles of the deep forest may also be seen soaring high above the treetops. The Ornate Hawk-Eagle is not as much in evidence on Barro Colorado Island and elsewhere in the forested parts of central Panama as the Black Hawk-Eagle, which, according to Eugene Eisenmann, often flies over open country, though not far from forest—calling, as it passes overhead, "whee wheeea," or with a more liquid quality in its voice, "ooeeeoo." Cassin's Hawk-Eagle, in the rain forest of the Congo and Gabon, preys mainly on birds living above the canopy—also on squirrels—in the domain of the Long-tailed Hawk (*Urotriorchis*) and the Crowned Eagle (*Stephanoaetus*).

With rare exceptions, the nests are in deep forest. A hawk-eagle usually constructs a large platform of sticks in the crotch of a tall, old tree, at a height of 30 feet or more where the smaller limbs are spaced far enough apart to permit the adults to enter easily from below, and the young to scramble about when they are large enough to take to branches. The nest tree is often near or overhanging a stream in the deciduous and evergreen forests of the Japanese Alps and the Himalayas, and in the hill forests of Burma and Ceylon. The Mountain Hawk-Eagle keeps two nests in use—the extra one serving as a roost and feeding post. Mangoes and other large trees are favored in western and central India. In the rain forests of Central and South America, the Ornate Hawk-Eagles are among the large birds of prey that build just above the canopy, between 70 and 135 feet above the ground, in silk-cotton trees that reach a total height of 200 feet. In 1960 Jim Fowler found two such nests in British Guiana. Another nest in a tall tree rising at the side of a ravine in heavy forest on Barro Colorado Island, Panama, was shown to Eugene Eisenmann by E. O. Willis in April, 1961. It was placed about 90 feet up, in a crotch where a main branch left the trunk. Displaying concern over the invasion of the nesting territory, one of the adults flew down and perched over their heads, calling "wheéoo, whéepeepee." A young bird was last seen peering over the edge of the nest on May 27.

Most hawk-eagles appear to lay only one egg—in Asia either plain white or grayish-white and sometimes densely freckled or heavily blotched and spotted red. The Mountain Hawk-Eagle, which ordinarily lays three eggs, may be the single exception.

These birds are noisy, especially during the breeding season. The Ornate Hawk-Eagle, in tropical America, and the Mountain Hawk-Eagle will defend the eggs or young. However, the Changeable Hawk-Eagle, which breeds in great numbers in many parts of western and central India, does not, as a rule.

The hawk-eagles' calls are very much alike, either a long shrill scream, or with variations. (An ascending "quick, quick, quick, quick, quick, quick kweeee" is also recorded for the Changeable Hawk-Eagle.)

Fierce in appearance but often tame in spirit, the Long-crested Eagle *(Lophaetus occipitalis)* commonly inhabits forest strips and well-watered, parklike country throughout tropical and south Africa.—*Photographed at the New York Zoological Society.*

GENUS *LOPHOAETUS*

One of the smaller eagles with fully feathered tarsi, *Lophaetus,* displays a long unruly crest. A bird that shuns the deep forest, it is long-winged and relatively short-tailed; its rather weak bill and small feet are those of a mouse-eater.

Long-crested Eagle (*Lophoaetus occipitalis*)

DESCRIPTION (TROPICAL AFRICA)

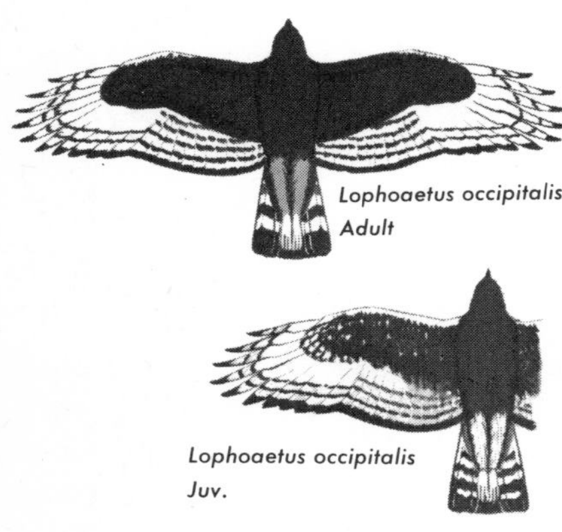

Entirely dark brown or black except for white-streaked feathering on the tarsi; dark brown tail with three light bars on the uppersurface and two that can be seen from below; white patches show on the undersurface of the wings in flight.

Juvenile—similar to adult but browner, with white spotting on the tips of the crown and crest feathers; white tarsi; tail, with one more light band above and below; the white bar on the leading edge of the underwing surface is distinctive in flight.

Beak, blue-black; cere, pale yellow; eyes, bright yellow; feet, light yellow; claws, black. Size, 18½–21 inches.

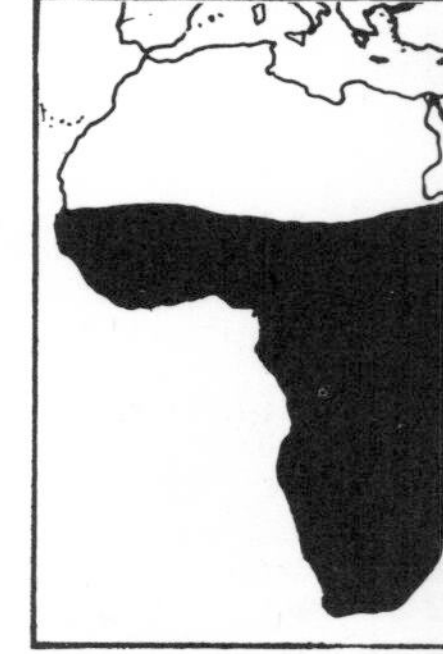

LOPHOAETUS OCCI

HABITS

The Long-crested Eagle customarily perches on some dead bough or vantage point. It preys on small rodents, snakes, lizards, frogs, and insects in the forest clearings as well as in the brush and tree savannas of western Africa; and in eastern Africa (Kenya, at least) it replaces Wahlberg's Eagle (*Aquila wahlbergi*) at altitudes above 4,500 feet. In certain areas this species has a predilection for swamps; in others, for farmland, where its food is easily obtainable. Occasionally the Long-crested Eagle will steal a young chicken, but its main interests in the haunts of man are rats and mice. This bird ordinarily hunts alone or with its mate, but several individuals may follow grass fires.

Long-crested Eagles build their stick nest, lined with green leaves, in the topmost branches of any large tree (in one instance, about 70 feet from the ground). One or two eggs are white, spotted and blotched with brown and rufous. The male and female both incubate, and the young are fledged in about 65 to 70 days.

A shrill goatlike bleating or screaming uttered while flying, often at great heights, announces the presence of the Long-crested Eagle. Like most other African eagles, it is silent on its perch.

The feathers of the African Crowned Eagle *(Stephanoaetus coronatus)* are prized by west Africans. Among the Mangbettus their use as ornaments is restricted to the chiefs and their relatives, along with those of Pel's Fishing Owl *(Scotopelia peli)*, the red wing quills of the plantain-eaters, and the long white tail feathers of the Paradise Fly-catcher.—*Photographed at the New York Zoological Park.*

GENUS *STEPHANOAETUS*

This African monkey-eating eagle is the only one of its kind in the world with heavy legs feathered to the toes. Its crest flares regally like the Harpy's; the broad rounded wings and long tail also compare to those of its forest-dwelling counterparts in South America, New Guinea, and the Philippines; and the feet and claws are very large and powerful.

African Crowned Eagle (*Stephanoaetus coronatus*)

DESCRIPTION
(TROPICAL AFRICA)

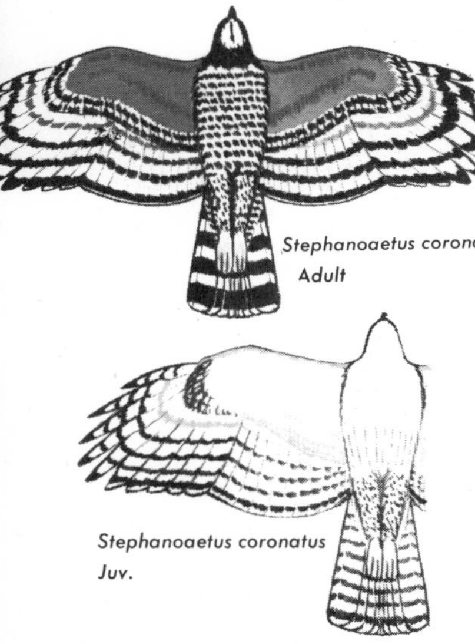

Head and neck, medium olive-gray, the crest feathers, black with white tips; rest of upperparts, including wing coverts, black with a bluish or grapelike bloom. Wings, barred olive-brown and black. Tail coverts, black, edged with white; tail, broadly (three-) banded light olive-gray and black; face, medium olive-gray, streaked in black; throat, white with some streaking; underparts, white to light cinnamon, spotted and barred with black. In flight the underwing coverts are light cinnamon, and the undersurface of the flight feathers is conspicuously barred with black and white.

Immature—like adult above, but lighter on the back, with dark barring; wing coverts and back feathers, edged with white; below, almost entirely white with touches of light cinnamon and black spots; thighs and tarsi, barred as in adult.

Juvenile—has a white head tinged sandy and faintly spotted with olive-gray; back and wing coverts, light olive-gray with dark shaft-stripes and conspicuous white feather-edging; wings, as in adult, but tail narrowly (six-) banded; underparts, white, lightly tinged sandy with indistinct light cinnamon spots on the breast, and traces of black spotting on the thighs and tarsi.

Beak, blue-gray; eyes, pale yellow; feet, pale yellow; claws, black. Size, 27–30 inches.

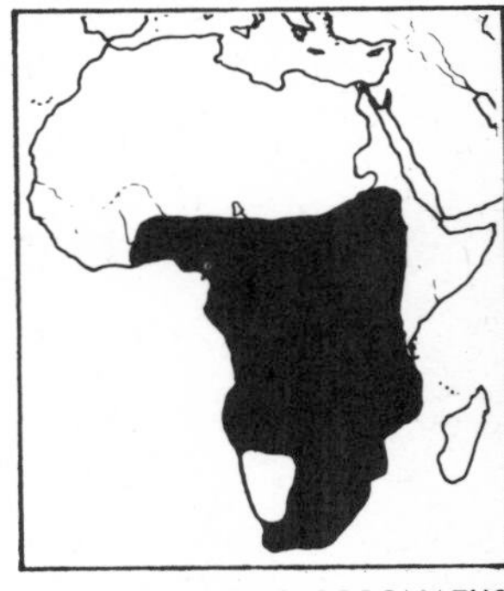

STEPHANOAETUS CORONATUS

HABITS

The African Crowned Eagle's short broad wings allow it to rise, like the Harpy Eagle, almost straight up; it is a remarkably agile and fast arboreal raptor. In the tropical rain forest, it is one of the chief predators on monkeys, aside from leopards and African tribesmen who hunt them for food. Malaria research brought A. J. Haddow into the deep forest of Uganda in 1952 to study monkeys. There, from an 82-foot platform, he was able to watch a pair of Crowned Eagles nesting above the forest canopy in a tree only a half mile away. They were observed to spend much of their time in slow and silent flight, slipping over and around the treetops like harriers quartering a stretch of bushy ground. Occasionally they were seen soaring together above the forest screaming repeatedly. However, the birds did not perch in a commanding position on the tops of dead trees or rocks, but in dense foliage. Not infrequently one would descend to hunt well below the canopy, and prey also was taken from the ground in a short, rapid swoop. There is some evidence that large monkeys are carried from the trees to the ground to be dismembered and eaten.

In the savanna forests of Kenya and the south African bush, Crowned Eagles feed mainly on mammals captured on the ground; small antelopes, hyrax, and, to some extent, mongoose and the young of large mammals such as the reedbuck; also game birds, and comparatively few monkeys.

Like the large monkey-eating eagles in other parts of the world, they are rather thinly distributed over their breeding range. Haddow noted that over a six-year period, three pairs were regularly present in a twenty-mile stretch of the Semliki Forest edge, each requiring a large hunting territory. This would be considered an unusually dense population.

The male Crowned Eagle courts his mate with loud calling during an undulating flight which Leslie Brown has watched at "Eagle Hill" in Kenya, and on other African hillsides. The bird plunges downward for one hundred feet or so, then turns upward and, as his momentum decreases, gives a few flaps of his wings. At the top of this rising flight his head is thrown back, and he seems to pause for a split second before plunging down. Up and down he goes, and circles, so that at one moment the blue-gray of the back and, at another, the cinnamon color of the underwing coverts is visible.

There is nearly always a litter of skulls and other bones on the ground beneath the sizable stick nest of the Crowned Eagle. In heavy forest it may be built just above the canopy, 60 to 70 feet or more from the ground, or in one of the large forks of a tall tree set off from the others, where, although visible from below, the nest is protected from arboreal mammals. When constructed in isolated trees, in this way, or in relatively open bush, it is often conspicuous from a distance. After many years of habitation, such a nest may be built up to enormous proportions. One, near Cape Province, has been in use for over 75 years.

Two eggs are usually laid: either plain white or marked with a few rusty streaks. During incubation, about 49 to 50 days, the nest is lined with green leaves; and after the eaglets have hatched, with leafy branches. The larger and stronger fledgling usually kills the smaller and weaker one. The surviving eaglet is practically full-grown and able to fly at 95 to 110 days, but shows no ability to hunt for itself. James Chapin tells of a Congo eagle, about five months old, that was still being fed in the nest tree. It would fly only occasionally to neighboring trees and called frequently. An adult arrived once or twice a day to leave food on the edge of the nest and quickly slipped away.

The adults actively defend their eggs and young against intruders, but at other times of the year they are extremely shy of man.

Their call, uttered on the wing, is described as a shrill musical sound of two or three syllables, rising and falling in pitch: "kee-u-ik—kee-u-ik—kee-u-ik." The notes of the young bird are strung out nearly to a trill, when they do not sound more like "ki-ki-ki-ki-ki" or "kwe-kwe-kwe-kwe."

This female Martial Eagle *(Polemaetus bellicosus)*, trapped on the plains of Barotseland in Northern Rhodesia by Jim Fowler, now resides at Mud Creek Plantation in Georgia. It can be trained to hunt wild turkeys, for game birds rank high on the list of its normal prey in tropical Africa.

GENUS *POLEMAETUS*

Among African eagles, *Polemaetus* is second only to the Crowned Eagle (*Stephanoaetus*) in size and strength. Its strong tarsi are feathered down to rather long, powerful toes. The beak is strong and sharply curved to match the "defiant" attitude of the short full crest and the fierce expression in its notably large, bright yellow eyes. A bird of the open country, the Martial Eagle has a much more impressive wingspan than does the Crowned Eagle.

Martial Eagle (*Polemaetus bellicosus*)

DESCRIPTION
(TROPICAL AFRICA)

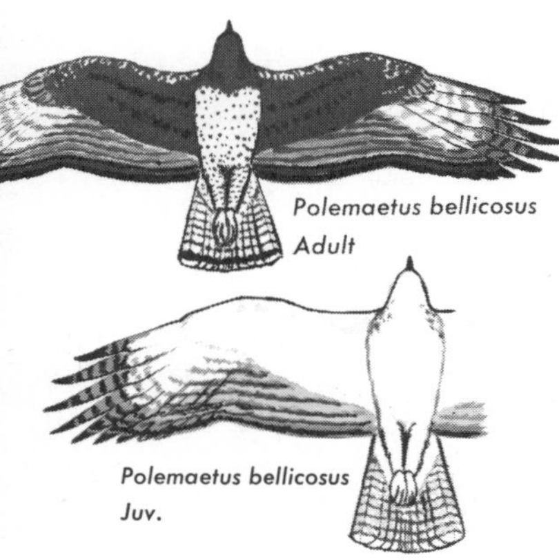

Above, including crest and wing coverts, sepia, the feathers edged in tan; wings and tail, barred with sepia and light olive-gray; face, throat, and breast, also sepia; rest of underparts, pure white, spotted with sepia (more finely on the tarsi).

Juvenile—has a white head and neck, spotted with gray-brown; upperparts, pale gray-brown, the feathers edged in white; flight feathers and tail, similar to adult's; underparts and underwing coverts, pure white.

Beak, black; cere, bluish; eyes, bright yellow; toes, pale yellow; claws, black. Size, 26–30 inches.

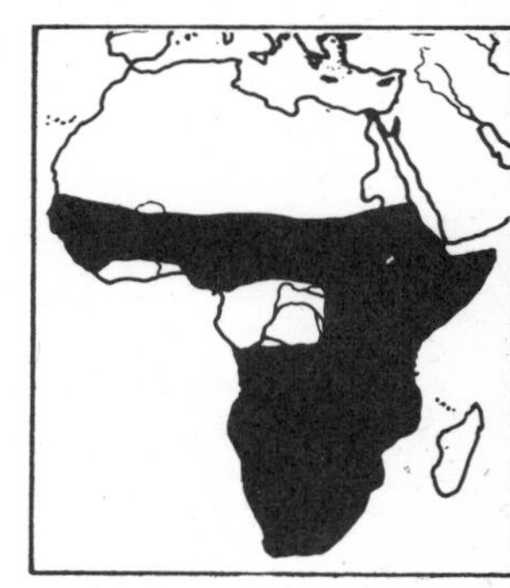

POLEMAETUS BELLICOSUS

In Georgia, Jim Fowler's trained Martial Eagle *(Polemaetus bellicosus)* strikes a Wild Turkey. The victim's head is visible over a flurry of wings.

HABITS

The Martial Eagle prefers scrub woodland or savanna that is sparsely dotted with trees. This bird ordinarily soars high as it searches out its prey. Or it may be seen resting on one of the topmost branches of a tree—frequently near a hyrax colony, where it can drop and glide quickly down on these small hooved mammals when they appear in the open. Occasionally the Martial Eagle hovers while hunting, like a huge kestrel. Food varies according to locality. In Kenya its diet consists mainly of game birds (francolin, partridge, and guinea fowl) and hyrax and other mammals up to the size of an impala calf or duiker. More partial to domestic livestock than other large African eagles, the Martial Eagle is persecuted by Europeans and resented (and sometimes killed) by Africans. Leslie Brown mentions in *Eagles* that it steals chickens from the Wambere tribesmen and also kids—a serious offense, for goats are the measure of their wealth. In Kenya this far-ranging hunter seems never to kill close to its eyrie.

The large stick nest of the Martial Eagle, lined with green leaves, is usually placed in a high tree, and it is frequently rebuilt and used year after year. Only one large white egg is laid—rough-textured and generally marked with pale blotches. The female does most of the incubating and brooding; the young bird is fledged in 95 to 110 days.

The Martial Eagle is one of the few African Eagles that calls habitually from its perch, "kloo-ee, kloeee-kloee ku-leee."

After the struggle, the Martial Eagle stands in a "victory" attitude, with wings raised. She claimed part of the breast of the turkey, now held firmly in the talons, as her reward.

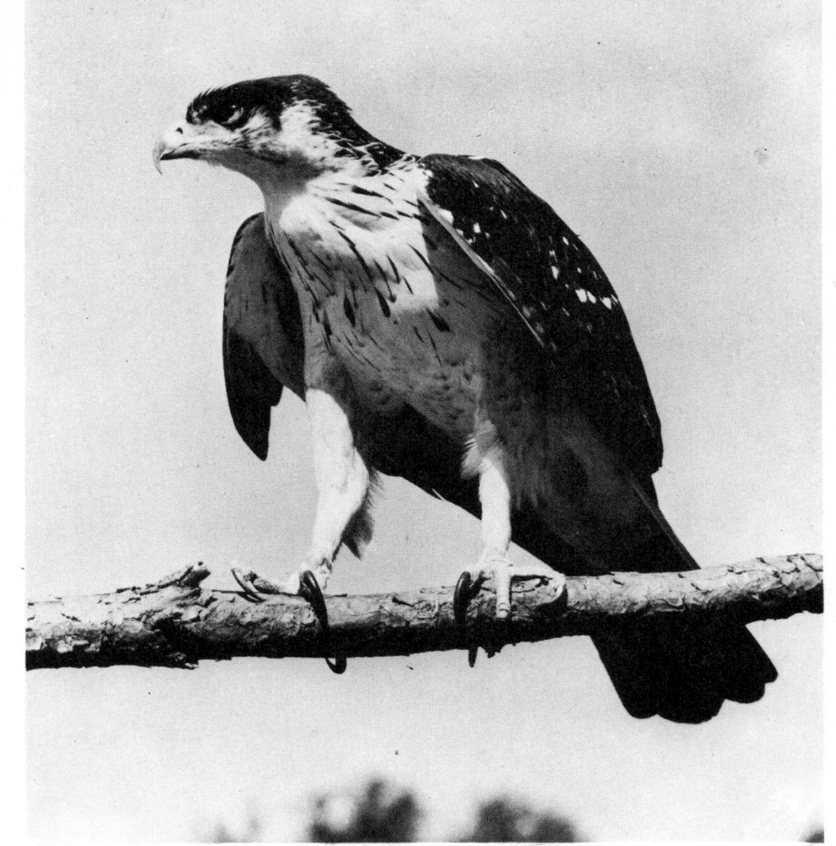

The African Hawk-Eagle *(Hieraetus fasciatus)* frequently waits on an exposed perch and then captures its prey with a fast swoop either from the ground or in mid-air.

GENUS *HIERAETUS*

These small- to medium-sized "booted" eagles appear more slender than those of the genus *Aquila,* and are furnished with a heavy, long-toed, and strong-clawed accipiter-type foot. Most are forest or forest-edge species, although the African Hawk-Eagle which is called "Bonelli's Eagle" in Eurasia and North Africa, inhabits a great variety of more sparsely wooded regions, preferably savannas, and scrub steppes in areas with hills or low mountains. *Hieraetus* seems to be essentially a tropical, rather than a Palaearctic group. The birds of Indian, African, and Australian distribution are crested, and color phases occur only in the Booted Eagle, and in the Little Eagle of Australia—a light phase with head, neck, and underparts predominantly white, and a dark phase in which these areas are entirely amber-brown or rufous-brown.

African Hawk-Eagle
(*Hieraetus fasciatus*)

DESCRIPTION
(TROPICAL AFRICA)

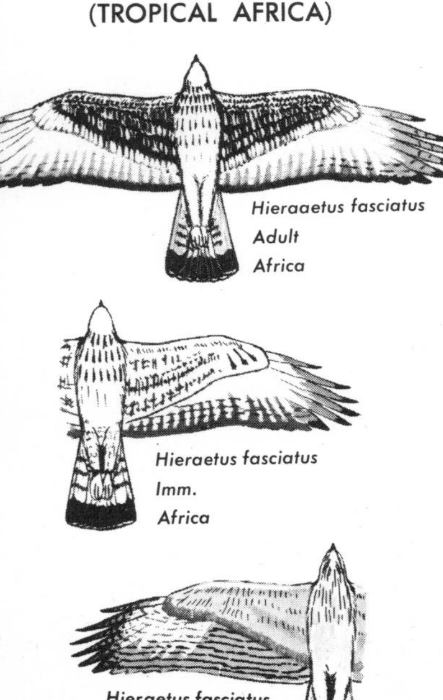

Above, including very short crest and wing coverts, dark brown, with some white streaking on the mantle and mottling on the lower back; wings and tail, pale ivory-gray or white, mottled and subterminally banded with dark brown; face, dark brown, streaked in white; rest of underparts, white, with large dark brown blobs appearing heavier on the breast and flanks; thighs and tarsal feathering pure white. Very similar to a smaller species, Ayre's Eagle, also of Africa, but the underside of the wings appears white (unbarred) and the underwing coverts are black.

Immature—head, neck, and underparts, mixed light amber-brown and white, striped with dark brown; wings and tail, similar to adult's.

Juvenile—head, neck, and underparts, solidly amber-brown, with very fine dark brown striping; back and tail, sepia, mottled and more narrowly barred six or eight times.

Beak, blue-gray; cere, yellow; eyes, yellow; feet, yellow; claws, black. Size, 21–24 inches.

HIERAETUS FASCIATUS

VARIATIONS

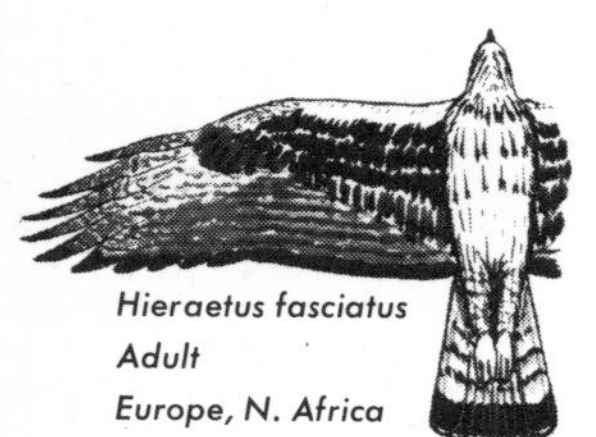
Hieraetus fasciatus
Adult
Europe, N. Africa

"Bonelli's Eagles" ranging from the Mediterranean to India and China are slightly larger, with finer dark markings on the chest, and brown tarsal feathering and undertail coverts.

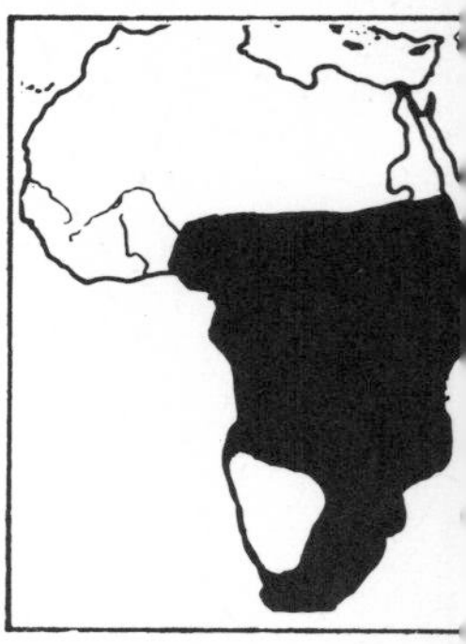
HIERAETUS AYRESII

OTHER SPECIES

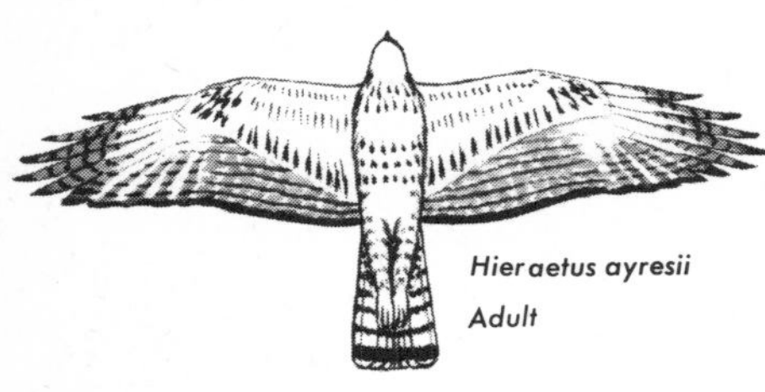
Hieraetus ayresii
Adult

Ayre's Eagle (*H. ayresii*), 16½–19 inches, a comparatively rare tropical African bird, resembles *H. fasciatus,* but is much smaller, has more white on the forehead and face, and has a longer crest; underparts, heavily mottled; and undersurface of the wings and tail, barred. Young birds have pale, but distinctly striped breasts, more like miniature adult Tawny Eagles than the young of Bonelli's Eagle, which are less distinctly striped and heavily tinted with amber-brown below.

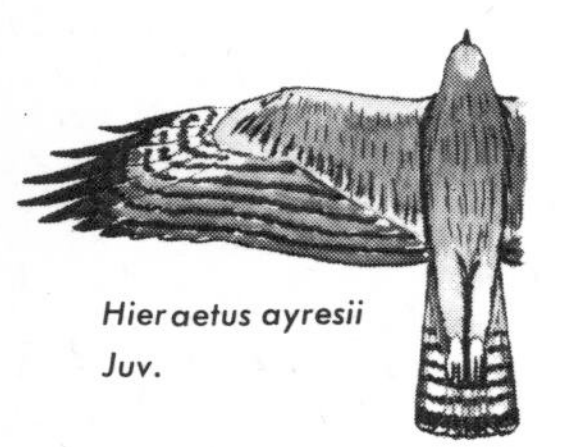
Hieraetus ayresii
Juv.

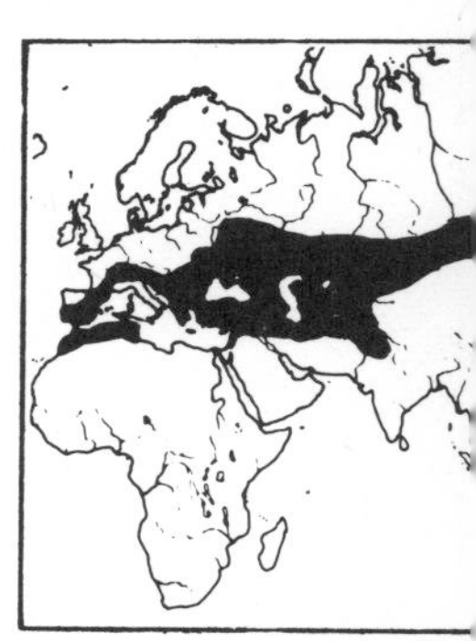
HIERAETUS PENNATU

The Booted Eagle (*H. pennatus*), 17½–21 inches, a Turkistanean-Mediterranean species, has two distinct color phases. *Light phase*—head, buff, finely streaked with dark brown; rest of upperparts, dark with a band of buff across the wing coverts and lower back; wings and tail, dark brown; underparts, white, tinged with light cinnamon-brown, with fine dark brown streaking on the chest and indistinct barring on the thighs. *Dark phase*—entirely dark above; underparts, rufous-brown, streaked with dark brown. (*Young birds in light phase* are similar to adults, but have brown—not yellow—eyes. *Dark phase juvenile* is spotted and barred with white below.)

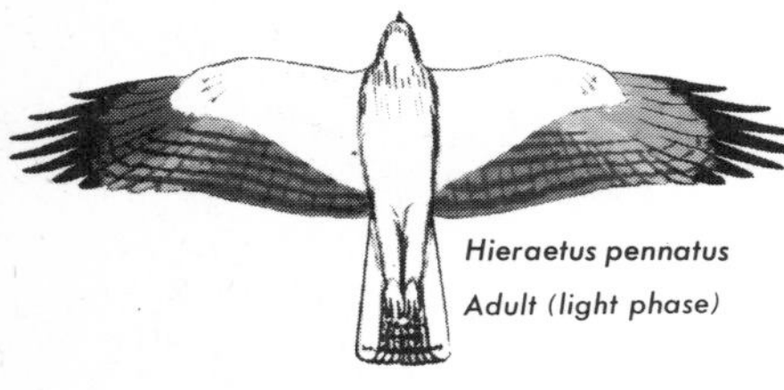
Hieraetus pennatus
Adult (light phase)

Hieraetus pennatus
Adult (dark phase)

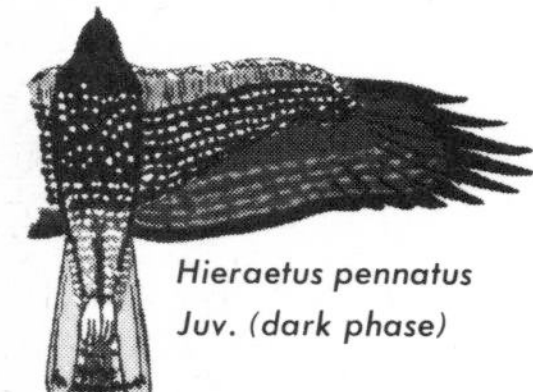
Hieraetus pennatus
Juv. (dark phase)

The Rufous-bellied Eagle of southern Asia (*H. kienerii*), 17–20 inches, has black plumage above mixed with chocolate; also a long crest; face, black; throat and breast, white or sandy; rest of underparts, medium sienna, with black streaking throughout. (*Juvenile,* generally lighter than adult—sepia to black above, with fine white feather-edging; face and forehead, white with a black line around the eyes; underparts, white.)

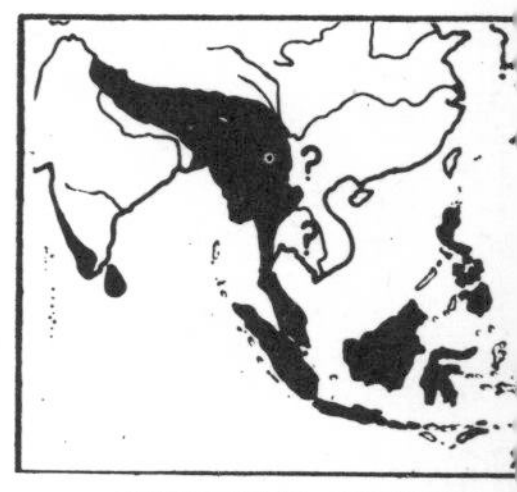
HIERAETUS KIENERII

In the Australian region the Little Eagle (*H. morphnoides*), 16–19 inches, in the *light phase* has a sienna-colored crown, nape, and a short occipital crest streaked with black; otherwise sepia above with a band of light ochre-brown across the wing coverts and lower back; wings, dark brown; tail, medium olive-gray, narrowly barred with sepia; face and throat, white, darkly streaked; rest of underparts, white to light amber-brown, finely striped black. *Dark phase* appears more uniformly amber-brown to dark amber-brown below, heavily striped in black. The birds of New Guinea are the smallest and most heavily marked below. (*Juveniles*—resemble dark phase adults, but have white faces; otherwise, uniformly dark brown head, neck, and back.)

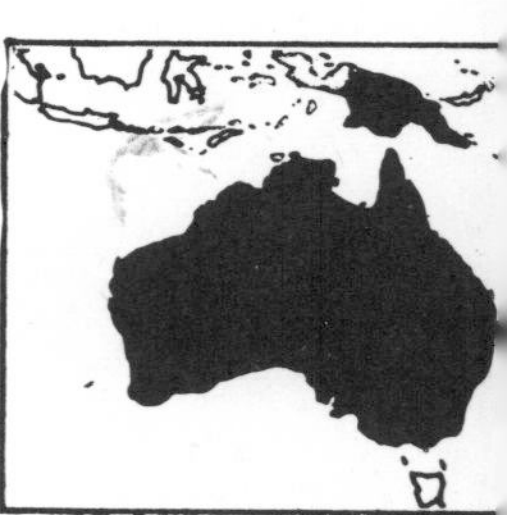
HIERAETUS MORPHNOID

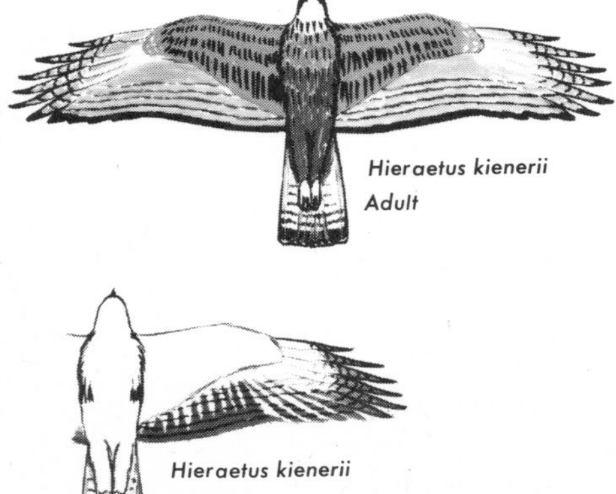

Hieraetus kienerii
Adult

Hieraetus kienerii
Juv.

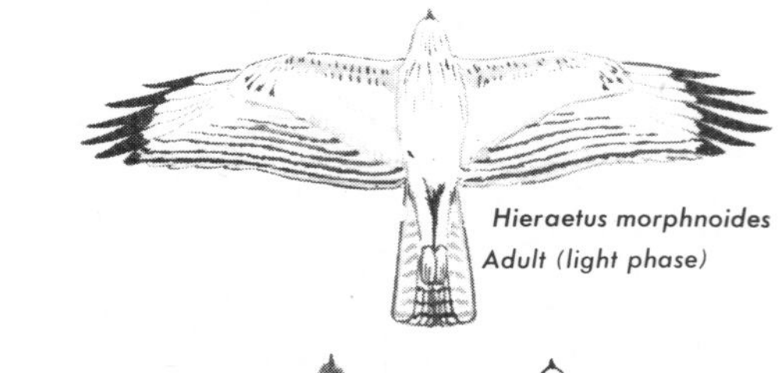
Hieraetus morphnoides
Adult (light phase)

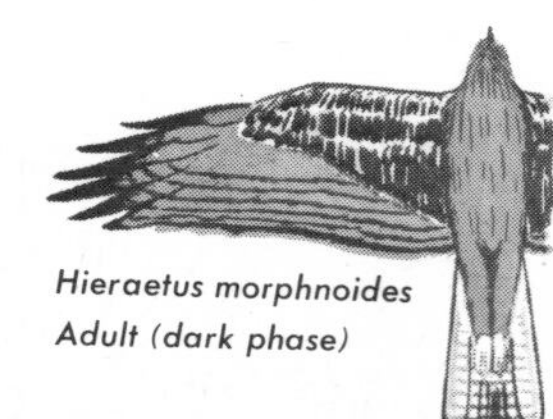
Hieraetus morphnoides
Adult (dark phase)

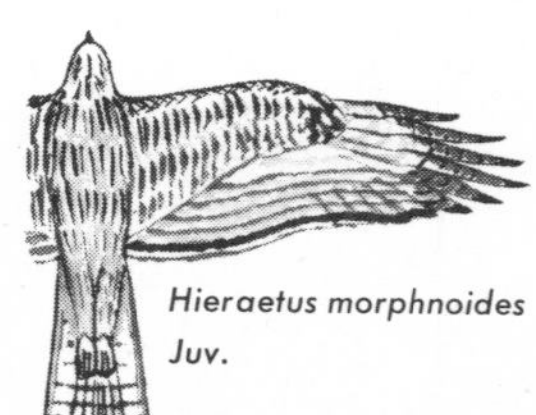
Hieraetus morphnoides
Juv.

HABITS

These trim, graceful eagles of rocky ravines, deep woods, or wooded savannas are not typical soaring birds. They spend much of their time perching on the tops of trees and on other exposed places, and ordinarily soar and circle at a low altitude, then drop almost straight down to secure their prey.

The African Hawk-Eagle and Bonelli's Eagle have a definite predilection for game birds and the reputation of chicken thief. Their regular fare consists of small- to medium-sized animals and birds, taken either from the ground or in accipiter-like pursuit, in and out of trees. Ayre's Eagle of Africa is an agile treetop hunter of small birds and squirrels, and we suspect that the little-known Rufous-bellied Eagle of tropical Asia is accipiter-like and specialized in its feeding habits, for it is very long-toed.

However, the Booted Eagle and the Little Eagle of Australia and eastern New Guinea are more like medium-sized buteos. They feed their nestlings almost exclusively on young rabbits which are coming out of their burrows during the eagles' breeding season; this staple food is supplemented by whatever is available to them seasonally—rats and mice, snakes, lizards, and insects. As a rule, they do not eat carrion, although an Australian observer says that the Little Eagle will do so if the weather is unfavorable for hunting. A comparatively shy raptor, this eagle is constantly mobbed by Little Falcons, plovers, magpies, and ravens, and often forced by White-bellied Sea Eagles and Wedge-tailed Eagles to give up its prey.

A display flight not unlike that of buteos is recorded for the Booted Eagle and the Little Eagle. An undulating aerial maneuver is varied by climbing with rapid wing beats, then plummeting downward at the same steep angle. This is repeated over and over. Sometimes the wings and tail tremble violently when opened at the bottom of the dive, and the birds call loudly and often. An Australian pair may also bow to each other from neighboring branches or from perches in different trees.

Bonelli's Eagle nests on cliffs, and where these are not available, in the crowns of tall trees (pines, in Spain; pipal, in India). The tropical African representative of the same species always builds in trees; and the Booted Eagles and Little Eagles are tree-nesters—the latter keeping to the tallest creekside manna gums and casuarinas.

These nests are large—four to six feet in diameter and lined with fine green twigs or leaves. The Booted Eagle may enlarge an old nest of the Black Kite. The same sites are used repeatedly. A clutch of one or two eggs is common for species of the genus *Hieraetus* (sometimes as many as three in Europe); the eggs have pale yellowish-brown or reddish brown blotches and, frequently, pale violet undermarkings. Ayre's Eagle seems to lay only one egg, and the male does not incubate; in other species, with the possible exception of the Rufous-bellied Eagle, both sexes take part in incubation and brooding. Leslie Brown gives the incubation period of *H. ayresii* as 45 days and the fledging period of this and other small African eagles as 65 to 70 days —figures which probably apply more or less to others in the genus *Hieraetus*.

The Eurasian Booted Eagle migrates in winter to Nyasaland, and perhaps as far south as Natal; also to the Indian peninsula. Other species are sedentary.

The call of the Booted Eagle is a thin high "keee"; also a sharp "bee-bee-bee-bee" (courtship) and other notes. The Rufous-bellied Eagle calls "chirrup." The Little Eagle's two or three-syllabled note "choo-oo" or "choo-oo-oo" in Australia is "not as loud, hearty, or cheerful" as the Whistling Kite's (*Haliastur*). And the notes of the African Hawk-Eagle or Bonelli's Eagle are described as "mellow and fluting." These birds call a great deal during the nesting season, especially when the male brings food to the female at the nest.

Large size, powerful build, and golden hackles at the nape distinguish the Golden Eagle *(Aquila chrysaetos)* in North America from buteos; longer, broader, and squarer tail, from the dark young of the only other North American eagle, the Bald Eagle *(Haliaetus leucocephalus)*.

GENUS *AQUILA*

The "true" eagles are represented throughout the Holarctic region by the Golden Eagle (*A. chrysaetos*). In forested parts of Eurasia and Africa this species is replaced by the Imperial Eagle; in scrub desert and steppes, by the Steppe and Tawny eagles —the Golden Eagle keeping in these instances to the higher mountains. These other aquilas are comparatively slow fliers which rarely attack sizable prey, habitually steal from other winged predators and vultures, and more often feed on carrion. Verreaux's Eagle of Africa and the Wedge-tailed Eagle of Australia, bold hunters with very large feet and a marked preference for remote and rocky country, are more nearly the ecological equivalents of the Golden Eagle. The Wedge-tailed eagle is as large, if not quite as heavy, as the Berkut (a Siberian Golden Eagle) of the Tartars which, when trained in falconry, brings the price of two camels in the hawk mart, for it can kill antelope, foxes, and wolves.

The larger aquilas which breed in Eurasia are not only difficult to distinguish from each other, but may also be confused with the Greater Spotted Eagle—a sluggish bird associated with open forest edges bordering on lowland swamps, rivers, and lakes. The Lesser Spotted Eagle is often, but not as frequently, found near water in the same kind of remote lowland or hilly forested country interspersed with meadows. Only the young of these smaller species are spotted.

The Lesser Spotted Eagle appears to be closely related to Wahlberg's Eagle, although this small aquila, found generally throughout tropical Africa, is closely associated with cultivated fields.

All but the Golden Eagle may be seen south of the equator in winter.

The aquilas have stronger legs and feet and deeper, more highly arched beaks than buteos; ceres with free, "ear-shaped" nostrils (except the Spotted Eagles, which have large round perforations); and more or less sparsely bristled lores. The appearance of a bare face is pronounced in Verreaux's Eagle and the Wedge-tailed Eagle. Wings are long and rounded with deeply emarginated tips; tails, long and broad, appearing either rounded or squarish. (The Australian bird literally has a wedge-shaped tail.) Paler, lanceolate feathers, or "hackles," may decorate the back of the head, nape, and mantle. The tarsal feathering extends down to the toes, and the flanks appear extremely long and fluffy.

Streaky or dark juveniles, with broad white areas at the bases of the feathers and mostly white tails, acquire successively darker plumages until they reach adulthood at about four and one-half years. Golden Eagles in Europe may show considerable white marking even in adult dress. The somewhat closely related Wedge-tailed Eagle from Australia is six or seven years old before it becomes entirely black.

Golden Eagle (*Aquila chrysaetos*)

DESCRIPTION (NORTH AMERICA)

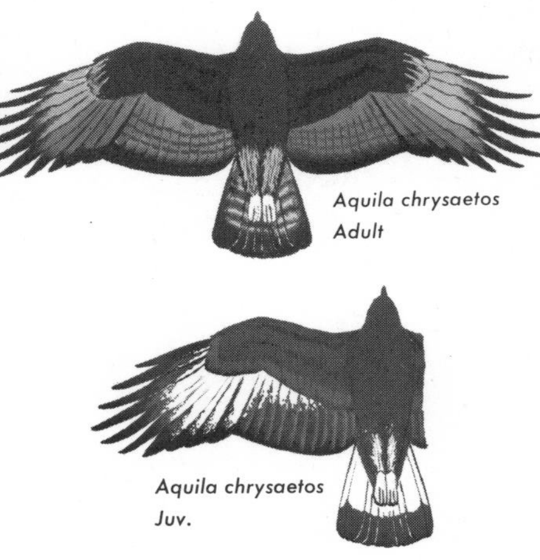

Over-all coloring, sepia to dark brown; the "hackles," or lanceolate feathers of the head and hindneck, suffused with amber-brown and tipped light tan; wings, mottled buff-white; tail, marked with narrow irregular bars at the base, but dark-tipped; feathering on tarsi is slightly paler.

Immature (second and third year)—has white bases of the body plumage showing occasionally; tail, broadly banded white basally; tarsi, much lighter than adult's.

Juvenile—body plumage, nearly all-black, but lanceolate feathers, lighter, and extensive white on bases of feathers, more conspicuous than in immatures; tail, with more extensive white portion basally and subterminal dark brown band (in fresh plumage, white-tipped); tarsi, dull white; in flight white patches also show on undersurface of the wings.

Beak, black; cere, dull yellow; eyes, brown; toes, yellow; claws, black. Size, 30–36 inches.

VARIATIONS

Although very much alike, North American and Palearctic populations differ in size and in generally paler, redder, or darker plumage. The continental Golden Eagles—ranging from northern Europe to the Pyrenees, Caucasus, and Asia Minor—are smaller than those in North America and paler, with tarsal plumes distinctly mottled in white. Individuals breeding in the British Isles are also smaller and redder—tinged with amber-brown on the underparts, and the tarsal feathering, amber-brown with some white mottling. Mediterranean birds, the smallest of the Palearctic populations, have darker underparts than their northern relatives; the juveniles show much more extensive white markings on the wings and tail. Siberian birds average as large as North American individuals and are darker, with black tibial plumes covering the toes. In western Asia and the Himalayas individuals are large, but tend to be redder, with amber-brown tarsal feathering. In Japan, Korea, and northeastern China they are also redder, but smaller. Sizes, 26 inches (Mediterranean) to 36 inches (Siberia).

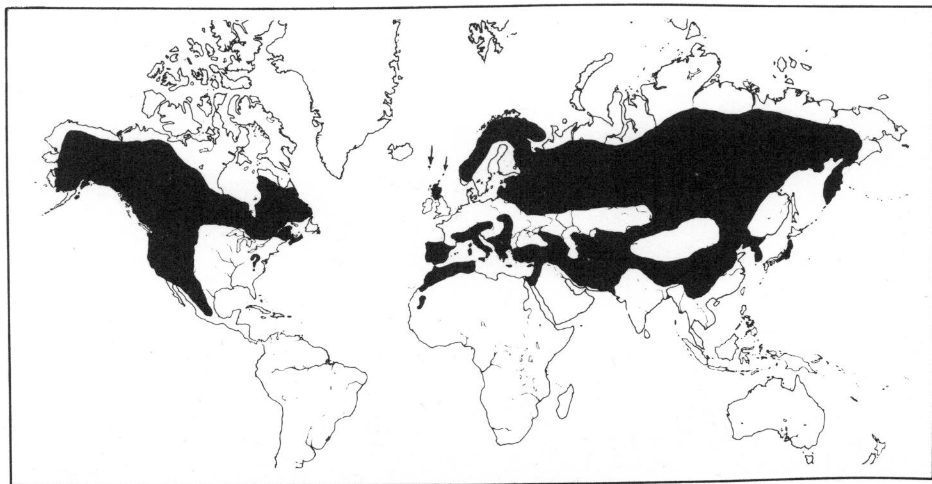

AQUILA CHRYSAETOS

Imperial Eagle *(Aquila heliaca)*, Spain.—*Photograph by Eric Hosking.*

Imperial Eagle (*Aquila heliaca*)

DESCRIPTION (ASIA MINOR, NORTHERN INDIA, AND CHINA)

Forehead and crown, dark brown; lanceolate feathers of the head and hindneck, sandy mixed with buff, shading to cinnamon-brown on the mantle; rest of upperparts dark brown to sepia with white patches on the shoulders; wing coverts, edged, and scapulars, mottled in sandy; wings, mottled light olive-gray; tail coverts, tipped in sandy; tail, medium ivory-gray, indistinctly mottled and barred, with a wide, dark brown subterminal band and sandy tip; throat and breast, chocolate; rest of underparts, dark brown; tarsal feathering, sandy-streaked.

Juvenile—paler with distinct dark brown streaking above and below; wings, dark as adult's but white-tipped; tail, solid brown, also white-tipped.

Beak, blue-gray; cere, pale yellow; eyes, brownish-yellow; feet, pale yellow; claws, black. Size, 28–33 inches.

VARIATIONS

The Imperial Eagle population in Spain and North Africa is slightly smaller but similar in the adult plumage. (Juvenile—redder than Turkistanean young and more uniformly colored; light amber-brown above and below, lacking the heavy dark streaking.)

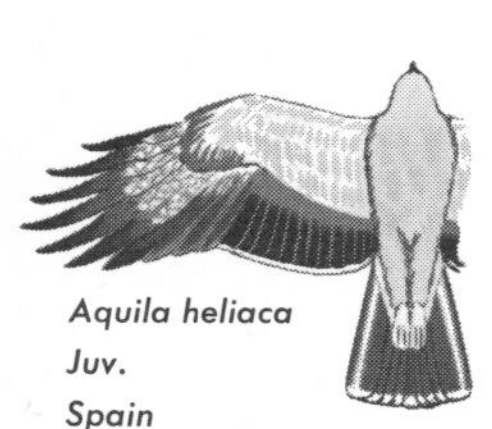

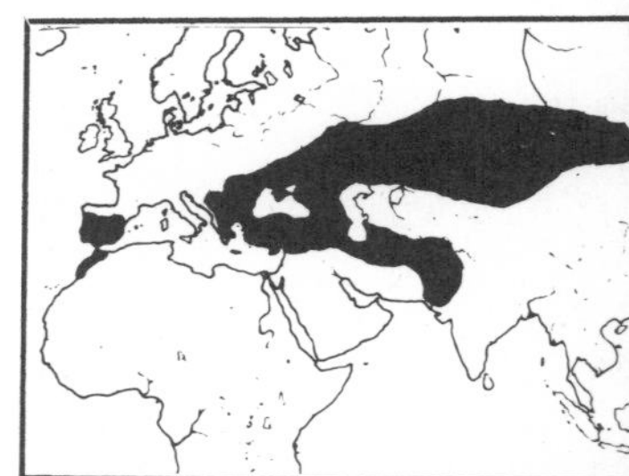

AQUILA HELIACA

Immature Imperial Eagle *(Aquila heliaca)*.—*Photographed at the New York Zoological Society.*

Steppe Eagle (*Aquila nipalensis*)

DESCRIPTION
(CENTRAL ASIA)

Aquila nipalensis
Adult

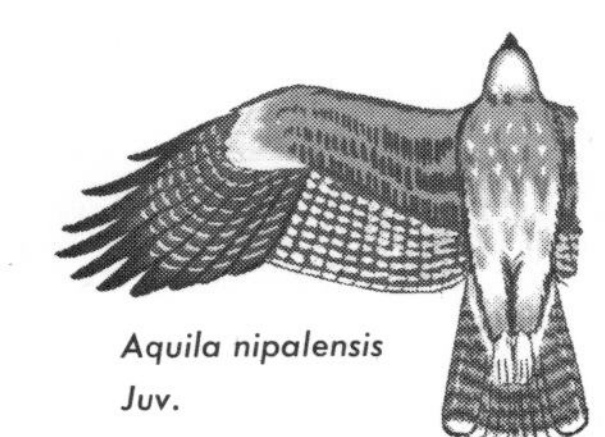

Aquila nipalensis
Juv.

Dark brown and chocolate above; crown, marked with black; rest of head and hindneck, streaked with light cinnamon; wings, dark brown, indistinctly barred; tail, also dark with faint traces of barring; underparts, chocolate.

Immature—completely cinnamon-brown above and below; greater wing coverts, wings, and tail, dark brown tipped with light ochre.

Juvenile—like immature, but feathers of the head, neck, and back, also edged with light ochre and underparts mottled light ochre. Upper- and undertail coverts, light buff, with the tail more distinctly barred.

Beak, black; cere, yellow; eyes, yellow; feet, yellow; claws, black. Size, 25–28 inches.

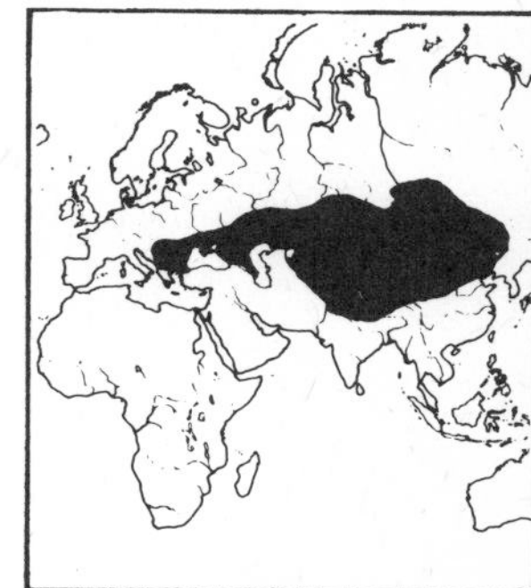

AQUILA NIPALENSIS

VARIATIONS

The Steppe Eagles in western Asia and southeastern Europe are slightly smaller and darker. (Juveniles have ochraceous coloring replaced by light amber-brown, and extending to the underparts, but immatures are more uniformly dark.)

Greater Spotted Eagle (*Aquila clanga*)

DESCRIPTION
(EUROPE AND ASIA)

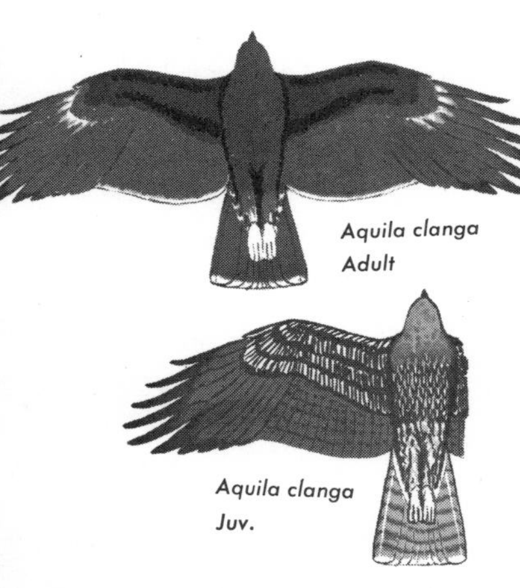

Aquila clanga
Adult

Aquila clanga
Juv.

Dark brown above and below; light points of head and neck feathers barely visible; secondaries and upper- and undertail coverts, tipped in white; tail, uniformly dark, tipped in white; lower tarsi, mottled with white.

Immature—more distinctly streaked on head, hindneck, and mantle with medium buff; spotted on wing coverts, scapulars, and secondaries in white; upper- and undertail coverts, white; tail, indistinctly barred and tipped white; underparts, uniformly streaked throughout with light buff.

Juvenile—similar to immature.

Beak, blue-black; cere, yellow; eyes, brown; feet, yellow; claws, black. Size, 24–27 inches.

AQUILA CLANGA

RELATED SPECIES

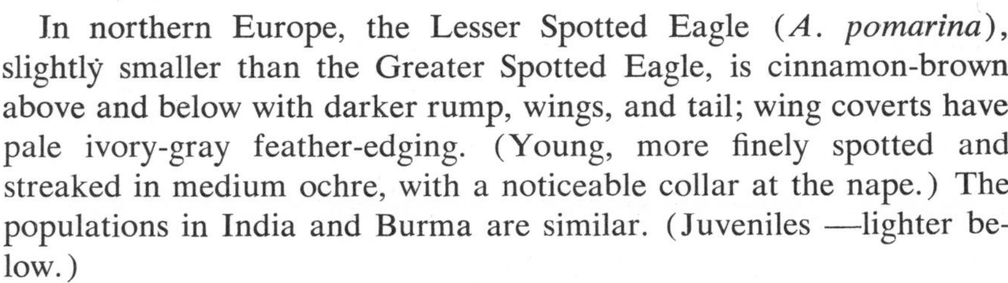

In northern Europe, the Lesser Spotted Eagle (*A. pomarina*), slightly smaller than the Greater Spotted Eagle, is cinnamon-brown above and below with darker rump, wings, and tail; wing coverts have pale ivory-gray feather-edging. (Young, more finely spotted and streaked in medium ochre, with a noticeable collar at the nape.) The populations in India and Burma are similar. (Juveniles —lighter below.)

AQUILA POMARINA

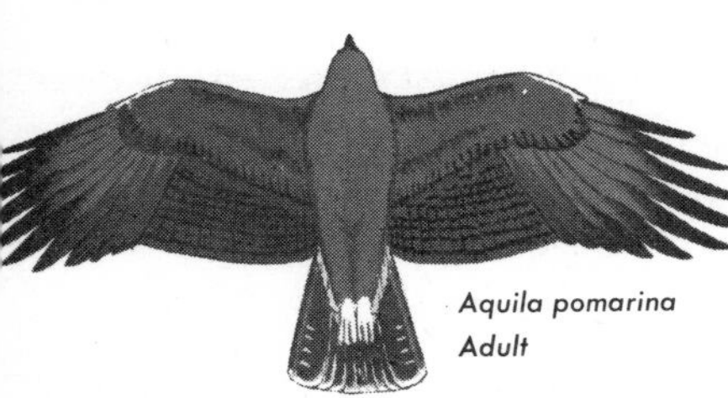

Aquila pomarina
Adult

Aquila pomarina
Juv.

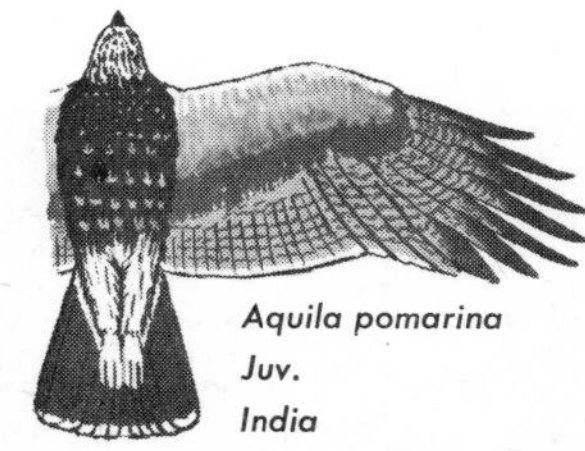

Aquila pomarina
Juv.
India

Tawny Eagle (*Aquila rapax*)

DESCRIPTION
(TROPICAL AFRICA)

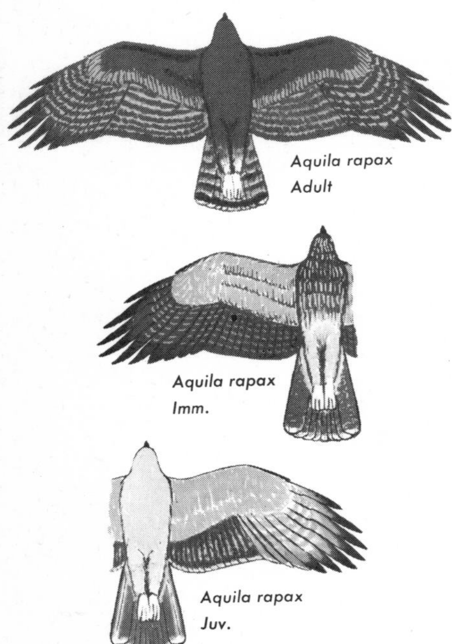

Almost entirely chocolate to dark brown, with some tan streaking on the lanceolate feathers of the head and hindneck; wing coverts, narrowly edged in tan; wings and tail barred.

Immature—head and neck, amber-brown; rest of upperparts, chocolate, with cinnamon edgings; wings, as in adult, and uppersurface of the light tail unbarred; underparts, cinnamon, lightly (second year) to heavily (third year) streaked on the breast and belly in rufous-brown.

Juvenile—light cinnamon; wing coverts and lower back, marked with rufous-brown; wings, as in adult and immature; tail, unbarred.

Beak, black; cere, yellow; eyes, yellow; toes, yellow; claws, black. Size, 24–26 inches.

AQUILA RAPAX

VARIATIONS

The slightly smaller birds of northeastern Africa, southwestern Arabia, Palestine, and Syria are darker above but paler on the head and neck; throat, white, streaked with rufous-brown; underparts, entirely rufous-brown. (Young are paler than birds from tropical Africa; immatures vary from rufous-brown to cinnamon-brown, streaked with light olive-gray; juveniles have wing coverts and entire underparts in light olive-gray.) The Tawny Eagles from India and Burma are smaller and are very dark above and below. (Young resemble north African immatures and juveniles.) Size, 23–25 inches.

Wahlberg's Eagle (*Aquila wahlbergi*)

DESCRIPTION
(TROPICAL AFRICA)

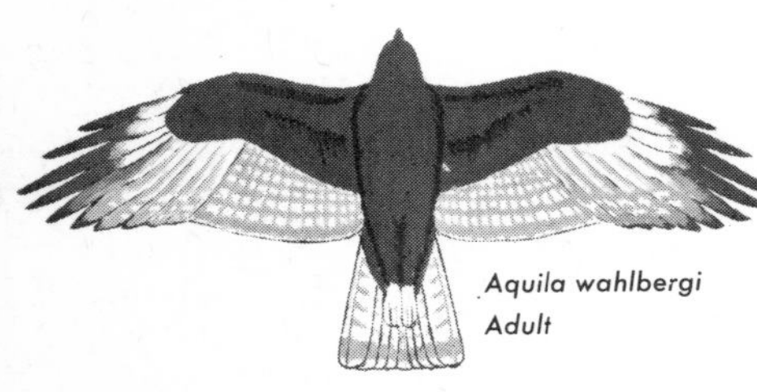

Slightly crested at the nape. Entirely chocolate and dark brown; hindneck, amber-brown; crest, wings, and tail, dark brown to black. (A light phase occurs rarely; in Kenya, almost pure white.)

Juvenile—medium olive-gray above with dark brown crest; wings, similar to adult's; tail, also dark, but tipped with pale ivory-gray; throat (and sometimes breast also), dark brown; rest of underparts, medium olive-gray, tinged with amber-brown.

Beak, black; cere, yellow; eyes, brown; feet, yellow; claws, black. Size, 19–21½ inches.

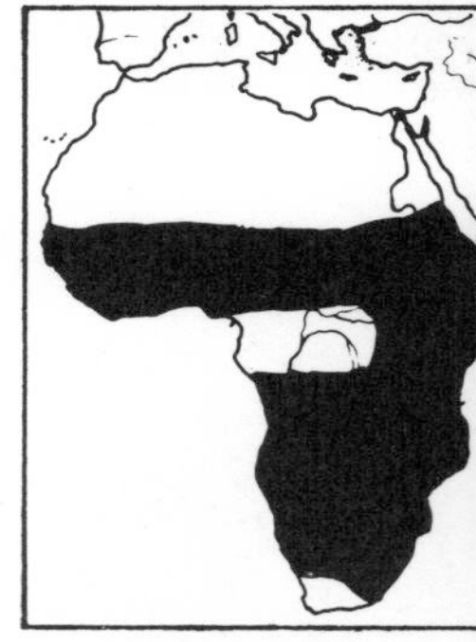
AQUILA WAHLBERGI

Verreaux's Eagle (*Aquila verreauxii*).

Verreaux's Eagle (*Aquila verreauxii*)

DESCRIPTION
(TROPICAL AFRICA)

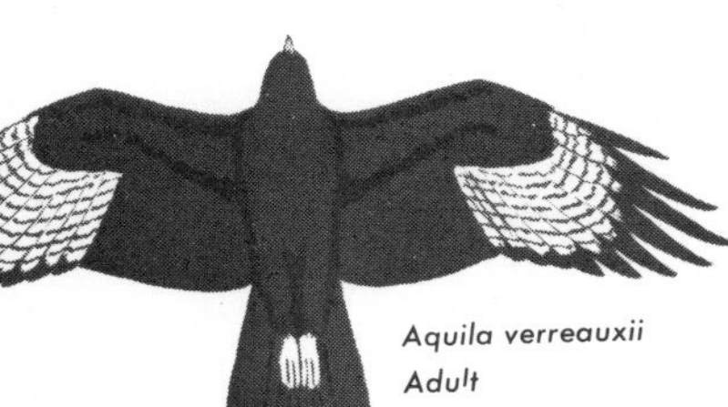

Entirely black, except for white center of back, rump, and barred inner webs of flight feathers, all concealed while perching.

Immature—black above and below with broad amber-brown tips to the feathers.

Juvenile—plain light amber-brown head, neck, back, and underparts; similar to the juvenile Tawny Eagle, but paler.

Beak, blue-gray; cere and bare skin around the eyes, bright orange-yellow; eyes, brown; feet, yellow; claws, black. Size, 28–32 inches.

AQUILA VERREAUXII

Wedge-tailed Eagle (*Aquila audax*)

DESCRIPTION
(AUSTRALIA)

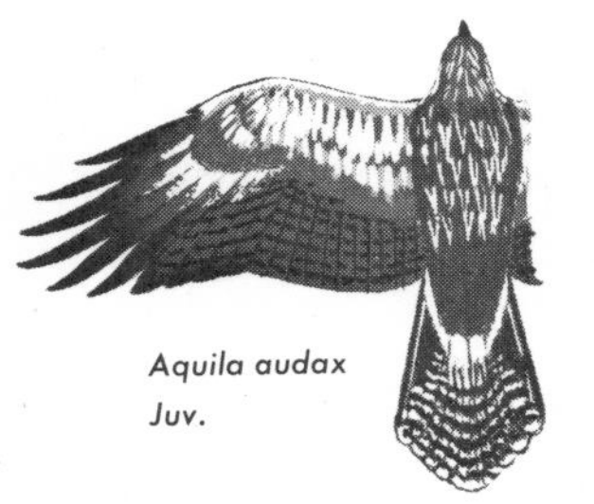

Black and chocolate; lanceolate feathers of hindneck and mantle, tawny, streaked with black; wing coverts, edged with light ochre-brown (disappearing with age); undertail coverts, paler. In flight, white patches on undersurface of the wings and wedge-shaped tail are distinctive.

Immature—black with rufous-brown head and neck; otherwise, like adult.

Juvenile—black, tawny, and chestnut—the chestnut predominating on the nape, mantle, upper- and undertail coverts, median wing coverts, and breast; tail, black, mottled and tipped with pale ivory-gray.

Beak, bluish-yellow; cere and bare skin around eyes, yellowish-white; eyes, hazel; feet, light yellow; claws, black. Size, 30–36 inches.

AQUILA AUDAX

Wedge-tailed Eagle (*Aquila audax*).—Photographed at the New York Zoological Society.

Gurney's Eagle (*Aquila gurneyi*)

DESCRIPTION
(NORTHERN MOLUCCAS
AND WESTERN NEW GUINEA)

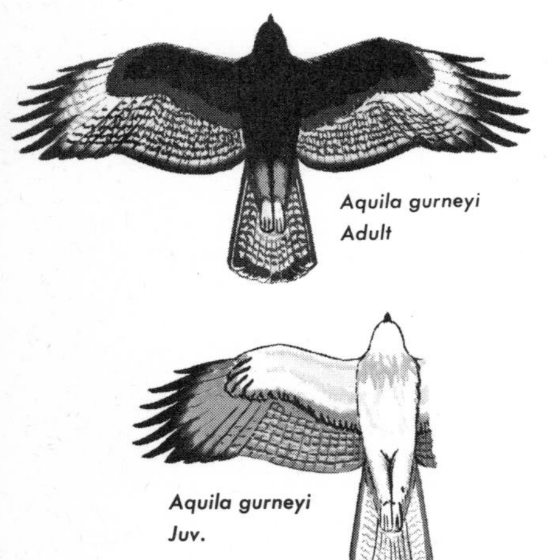
Aquila gurneyi
Adult

Aquila gurneyi
Juv.

Entirely dark with black predominating above and chocolate below; undersurface of wings and tail lighter, with narrow dark barring; long, rounded tail resembles that of the New Guinea Harpy Eagle.

Juvenile—cinnamon head, neck, mantle, and underparts, shaded with gray-brown and sharply tipped with sandy coloring; rest of upperparts, including wing coverts, light to dark gray-brown, scalloped or barred with white. Ochre-brown wings, narrowly barred with dark brown (primaries black-tipped); tail, dark brown to black with a suggestion of ochre-brown barring (lighter underneath and more noticeably barred).

In the young, beak is recorded as bluish-white with darker tip; cere, bluish-white; eyes, yellowish-olive; feet, yellowish-white.

Size, about 30 inches.

AQUILA GURNEYI

HABITS

Aquilas require open country to hunt and are therefore, of necessity, edge-of-forest birds—ranging also across scrub, steppe, and low calcareous mountains; inhabiting canyons (and formerly sea cliffs in the British Isles); and ascending to the most remote mountain heaths and tundras.

The Golden Eagle has been exterminated as a breeding species in most of the eastern portions of the United States and throughout much of Europe. In the Western Hemisphere it breeds in numbers only in Alaska, Canada, and the western part of the United States, south to Baja California and central Mexico. In Europe it may be found principally in the Scottish highlands, northern Ireland, Scandinavia, and the Bavarian, Swiss, and Austrian Alps. Elsewhere its range extends to remote parts of Algeria, Asia Minor, Siberia, the Himalayas, Korea, and Japan.

The most "distinguished" of the northern soaring birds, the Golden Eagle flies a direct course with leisurely wing beats that suggest its power—far exceeding the buteo's—and its long glides are now and again interspersed with a single strong downstroke. In the breeding season it gives marvelous demonstrations of aerial agility, mounting in spirals into the sky, rolling, and diving at its mate. Headlong dives, from a height, with half-closed wings, and an upward sweep, at the end of each plunge, resemble the repeated dives of buteos during courtship. However, the Golden Eagle has greater mastery of the air. It often indulges in playful harassing of other large birds, such as ducks and Great Blue Herons. One American observer tells, in Bent's *Life Histories,* of a Golden Eagle's headlong plunge after a heron, vertical as a stone might fall, yet all the time revolving like a spinning rifle bullet. Diving displays are also recorded for the Greater Spotted and Lesser Spotted eagles.

While hunting, the Golden Eagle beats over hillsides at a relatively low altitude and flies down to seize its quarry in a fast swoop from above, a typical aquila tactic. It preys mainly on hares, rabbits, or ground squirrels—depending on the locality; also a variety of other small- to medium-sized mammals, including the young of antelope and deer; snakes (even rattlesnakes, in the western United States); and many kinds of birds, especially in the higher latitudes and on mountain heath and tundra (pheasants, grouse, ptarmigan—even crows, in some parts of the Himalayas); and such unlikely prey as grasshoppers and fish. During the winter in the north or at other times in any place which does not provide easier prey, this eagle will attack animals larger than itself—full-grown deer, reindeer, antelope, and mountain goats. It should be mentioned that a certain amount of this larger prey is already carrion when it is eaten. However, hunting in pairs is more frequent in winter, and groups of three eagles may cooperate in flying down an animal and inflicting lethal head or back injuries.

Attacks on humans are purely defensive or accidental. Men who were themselves stalking game, and appeared in their actions like animals (perhaps with the added attraction of a fur cap) have been attacked by Golden Eagles. However, the persistent tales of baby-snatching eagles must be relegated to legend. In most cases even the occasional human intruder at the eyrie finds himself alone with an eaglet or two in the great stick nest, for the parents have slipped away and will not return until he leaves.

The Golden Eagle has been persecuted in America and Europe because of livestock depredations by individuals in certain localities. The Wedge-tailed Eagle of Australia, whose habits are similar, also has been intensively killed by man in sheep-raising country, most recently in aerial campaigns similar to those carried on against the Golden Eagle in western Texas and California (see Chapter 5). The main food of Verreaux's Eagle is hyraxes, as well as smaller species of antelope, francolin, and guinea fowl; and in some districts individuals prey on lambs and poultry. The damage which the large aquilas and sea eagles do to livestock has been, however, vastly exaggerated in relation to their activities over a wide range. Even in regions where man's agricultural or ranching enterprises are concerned, the staple foods supplied to young eagles in the eyrie are usually small mammals, supplemented by whatever the versatile adults can catch. Their much-disputed lifting power cannot be much more than their own weight—a female Golden Eagle, weighing nine and one-half to thirteen pounds; a male, seven and one-half to eleven pounds. Under unusually favorable conditions, as in a take-off from a ridge with a strong updraft, a large eagle may be able to carry to its eyrie an animal weighing up to eighteen pounds.

The weaker-footed Steppe and Tawny eagles of the dry plains are habitual carrion-eaters, but also prey on small mammals. The Greater Spotted Eagle, which lives and hunts near water, feeds on small mammals (hedgehogs, moles, shrews, hamsters, rats); moderate-sized water and marsh birds; amphibians, reptiles, insects, and molluscs; also carrion. The smaller aquilas of the lowlands live primarily on rats, mice, small snakes, frogs, lizards, insects, and worms. Wahlberg's Eagle of tropical Africa hunts these prey species in cultivated fields, but the Lesser Spotted Eagle prefers remote woodland meadows.

In forested regions, aquilas nest in isolated trees, not always very far from the ground. Eyries may be in low bushes and trees (*A. rapax*) and even on the ground in plains, steppes, and scrub desert (*A. chrysaetos* and *A. nipalensis*). But in rock deserts, canyons, heath-covered highlands and high mountains the Golden Eagle characteristically chooses an inaccessible site in an old tree overhanging a river or in caverns on steep faces of rock where it commands a view of the surrounding territory. So does the Verreaux's Eagle and the Wedge-tailed Eagle. New nests may be quite small—two and one-half to three feet in diameter and eighteen inches high, but as they grow, year after year, with use, become bulky—perhaps five, six, or even eight feet across, and very deep. The largest known eyrie of a Golden Eagle in British Columbia was nearly twenty feet from the base to the crown. These large aquilas often alternate between two or more nests in the same locality for many years. These are typically constructed of large dry sticks, the shallow cup lined with dry grass and twigs. Fresh leaves, leafy twigs, or sprigs from coniferous trees are renewed continually, and these are sometimes brought to the eyrie from considerable distances.

In Australia and Africa the usual clutch is one or two eggs (Wahlberg's Eagle, just one egg); in North America, Europe, and Asia rarely one, normally two, and sometimes three or four. The color of the eggs is extremely variable, even in the same clutch—pure white; irregularly spotted or blotched with pale purple, brown, reddish-brown, or yellow-brown; or a combination of underlying purple and reddish-brown. The markings are sometimes concentrated at the smaller or the larger end. Eggs of the smaller eagles can sometimes be identified by size alone; for example, the eggs of the Lesser Spotted Eagle are much smaller than those of the Greater Spotted Eagle, as well as generally more richly colored.

According to Seton Gordon's observations of the Golden Eagle in the Scottish Highlands and a record in captivity (Vökle), both sexes—but mostly female—incubate the eggs 44 to 45 days, and Robert Mitchell records an approximate period of 41 days in Texas. The male assumes a more equal share in brooding the young and is the chief provider, although it is the female that usually feeds carefully selected tender morsels to the nestlings. A young eagle is not able to tear food apart itself until nearly six or eight weeks old, and takes its first flight at about eleven weeks.

It is generally true of aquilas that only one of two eggs may hatch, and if two eaglets hatch, only one survives the fledging period. Since the eggs are laid at two- or three-day intervals, and incubation begins with the first egg, the older eaglet is the larger in the eyrie. It gets the lion's share of the food, and usually succeeds in pecking the smaller one, which is also getting progressively weaker from lack of food, to death. Thus, of two fledglings, only one generally survives, and of an occasional three or four in northern latitudes, only two or three live to take their first flight.

The incubation periods of other aquilas scarcely differ from those of the Golden Eagle (Verreaux's Eagle, 44 days; Wahlberg's Eagle, 45 days; Lesser Spotted Eagle, 40 days), but the young of smaller species are fledged two or three weeks sooner.

In winter the Imperial and Greater Spotted eagles

migrate south into Ethiopia, Arabia, and India; and the Lesser Spotted Eagle and Steppe Eagle may reach eastern and southern Africa. The Holarctic Golden Eagle usually winters in the north. Some are seen passing over Hawk Mountain, Pennsylvania, every fall, possibly to winter in the southeastern United States. The birds in western North America may drift as far south as Mexico. They are especially affected by the periodic shortages of hares. Most tropical aquilas are sedentary, but Wahlberg's Eagle is one of the savanna birds of Africa which drifts northward in the nonbreeding season to take advantage of the brush fires during the dry period above the equator.

Aquilas ordinarily are silent birds. The Golden Eagle has three distinct cries which are typical: a thin, shrill "cheop" unbecoming to its size, and rarely heard near the nest; a buteo-like mewing uttered in courtship flights; and barking sounds of alarm. Wahlberg's Eagle is said to have a "clear, plaintive whistle of two notes."

On the wing, the bright yellow toes of the Black Eagle *(Ictinaetus malayensis)* are set off by the dark underparts; none of the other crested eagles within its range appears almost entirely black. The yellow cere and white patch under the eye are clearly visible at close range.

GENUS *ICTINAETUS*

This kitelike eagle, with a round crested head, large cere, and comparatively small beak, has a longer tail than the Tawny Eagle and most other eagles. Like the Golden Eagle, it soars on broad wings, ending in upturned "splayed fingers." The tarsi are not heavy, but are completely feathered; the inner toe and claw are much longer and straighter than the middle ones—all only moderately curved.

Black Eagle (*Ictinaetus malayensis*)

DESCRIPTION (SOUTHERN ASIA)

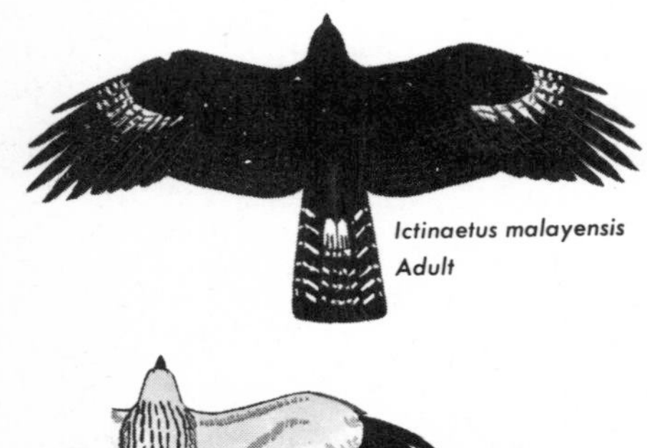

Ictinaetus malayensis Adult

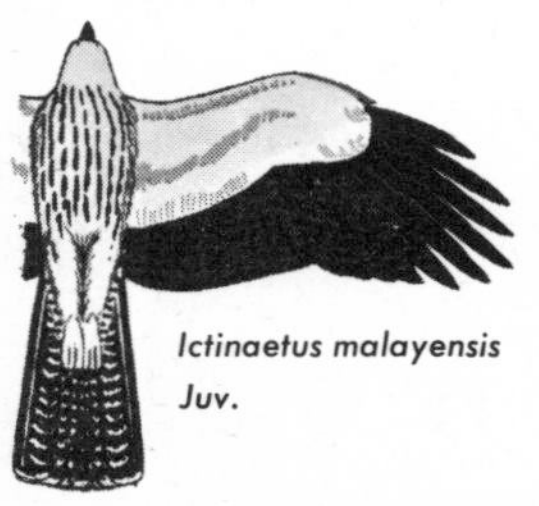

Ictinaetus malayensis Juv.

Entirely black except for white patches under the eyes; uppertail coverts, medium olive-gray, barred in white; black tail, barred medium olive-gray.

Immature—chocolate to dark brown above, with touches of pale yellow-orange and buff on the crown, nape, and sides of neck; underparts, buff to pale yellow-orange, entirely streaked with black.

Juvenile—head, neck, and underparts, pale yellow-orange (back of head, black with white and pale yellow-orange feather-edging; sides of neck and breast, heavily streaked in black); wing coverts and back, dark, but liberally spotted in white and pale yellow-orange; tail coverts, very broadly barred and edged in white.

Beak, bluish-green; cere, yellow; eyes, dark brown; feet, yellow; claws, black. Size, 23–28 inches; the largest individuals occur in India, Ceylon, Burma, and the Malay Peninsula.

ICTINAETUS MALAYENSIS

HABITS

The Black Eagle is partial to hilly or evergreen country, sailing gracefully on outstretched wings, circling above the treetops in forested ravines and quartering the brushy slopes for frogs, lizards, and large insects, also young or wounded birds up to the size of pheasants and jungle fowl. It is a confirmed robber of birds' nests, taking both eggs and young,

The nest of the Black Eagle is a neat and compact platform of sticks, built high in evergreens and usually hidden by the foliage. One or two eggs vary from white to pinkish, densely and finely stippled with pale brick-red. The parents are bold in defense of the eggs and young.

No regular call has been recorded.

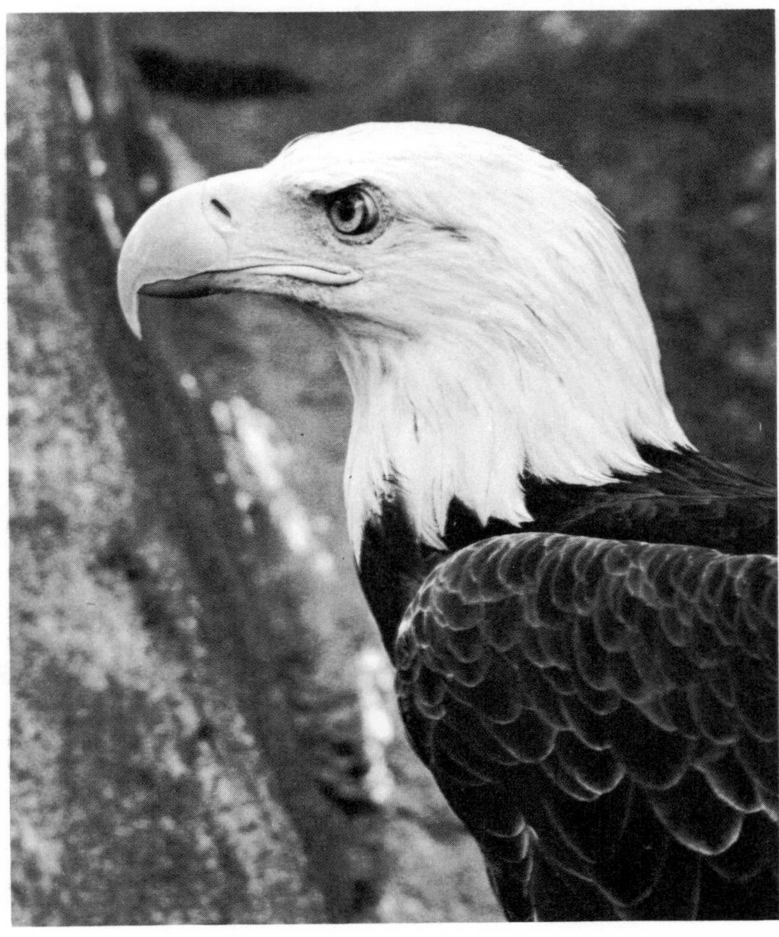

The Bald Eagle *(Haliaetus leucocephalus)*, the only eagle restricted to America, is the emblem of the United States. In recent years its snowy-white head and tail as well as its querulous or loud harsh cries have become less and less familiar sights and sounds across the continent, except in a few scattered breeding communities, and in Alaska, where Bald Eagles may always have been most numerous.

GENUS *HALIAETUS*

Most fish eagles are included in this nearly cosmopolitan group, absent only from South America. The Bald Eagle, White-tailed Sea Eagle, and Steller's Sea Eagle together have a Holarctic distribution along wide rivers, lakes, and pools as well as sea coasts and estuaries, but generally not in mountains. Pallas' Sea Eagle is an inland species of the lowland and highland steppes of central Asia (to 14,500 feet, in Tibet). It also may be found near lakes and in regions made swampy by meandering rivers, and it ranges as far as the northern Indian plains, which are drained by the great Indus, Ganges, and Brahmaputra rivers, as well as the river system of the Irawaddy, but seldom to the sea coast. This species is most nearly the ecological replacement of the Steppe and Tawny eagles (*Aquila*) that live in drier parts of the same regions.

The White-bellied Sea Eagle is a common bird along the coastline of India, from about the latitude of Bombay southward, through Malaysia to the Philippines and the Australian region, and lives on the coast or on the banks of large rivers and lakes near the sea. Sanford's Sea Eagle ranges upland to 3,000 feet above sea level in the mountains of the Solomon Islands. The African bird (*H. vocifer*) is called the "Sea Eagle" in Cape Province, but in central and eastern Africa it becomes the "River Eagle" associated with large rivers and lakes and sometimes with drier country that has only shallow ponds, where its food must be almost exclusively wading birds. On Madagascar, the Sea Eagle (*H. vociferoides*) is particularly common on muddy mangrove-bordered bays, where shallow water and numerous fish make feeding easy.

These sea or river eagles are seldom found in the same places, although their ranges may overlap, and both adults and young of one species are nearly always distinct from those of another in plumage pattern and shape of the tail. In southern Asia and the Australian region the young are most often confused with juvenile and immature Brahminy Kites and Whistling Kites (*Haliastur*), due to their similar coloration and scavenging habits, although their larger size alone, and vulturine silhouette, with very broad wings, head projecting far beyond the shoulders, and short, broad tail should be sufficient to distinguish sea eagles from these two kites. The change from juvenile to adult plumage takes about four years in most species, but Steller's Sea Eagle is not fully adult until the fifth year.

The larger fish eagles have much heavier and more highly arched beaks than the Golden Eagle (*Aquila*); ceres with prominent, obliquely vertical nostrils; long lanceolate feathers on the head and neck; flanks heavily feathered and tarsi about half-covered—the bare parts are reticulate except for a series of scutes in front, continuing down onto the toes. The rough, almost spiculate, soles of the feet and strong claws, grooved underneath, are adaptations for catching fish. The long wings are very broad, and the tail is slightly rounded in some species and wedge-shaped in others. A Goliath among giants, Steller's Sea Eagle, of northeastern Asia, has a more powerful beak than any other bird of prey—even larger than those of the great fishing owls and the monkey-eating eagles. It also has a broad tail of fourteen rectrices, rather than twelve, the usual number in large hawks and eagles. In the smaller species—the fish eagles of Africa and Madagascar and the White-bellied Sea Eagle of southern Asia and the Australian region—the bills are much weaker and shallower; the head, neck, and flanks are not as thickly feathered or plumed; and the tarsi appear mostly bare.

Bald Eagle (*Haliaetus leucocephalus*)

DESCRIPTION
(NORTH AMERICA)

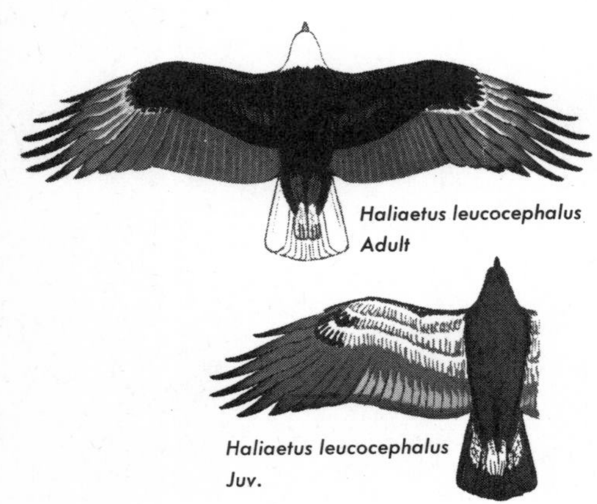

Head, neck, and tail, white; rest of plumage, dark brown, nearly all the feathers edged in pale olive-gray.

Immature—dark head and neck; pointed tips of the feathers, buff; otherwise, mottled buff, most conspicuously on the underparts; tail, buff, mottled and subterminally banded in dark brown.

Juvenile—entirely black, except underwing coverts and tail, which are mottled and banded like the immature's.

Beak, cere, and bare skin around eyes, dull yellow; eyes, light yellow; feet, dull yellow; claws, black. Size, 27–30 inches, the largest individuals in Alaska.

HALIAETUS LEUCOCEPH

White-tailed Sea Eagle (*Haliaetus albicilla*)

DESCRIPTION
(NORTHERN ASIA, EUROPE, ICELAND, GREENLAND)

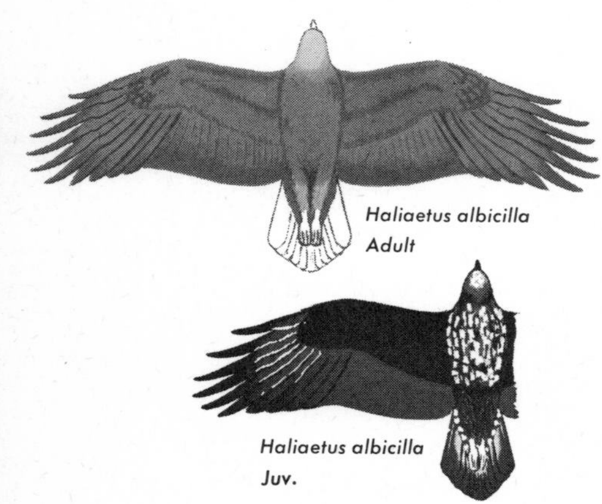

Head and neck, tan to buff-white, narrowly shaft-streaked in sepia; mantle and wing coverts, sepia, broadly edged in white; lower back, as well as wings, sepia; underparts, brown, the feathers of the breast tipped with buff-white; tail, white.

Immature—lighter, showing much white above and below; tail, white, mottled with sepia; birds gradually acquire generally darker back and underparts, but a whiter tail.

Juvenile—darker than immature, with broad cinnamon-brown streaking and feather-edging; tail, dark brown, mottled with buff.

Beak and cere, yellow; eyes, yellow; legs and feet, yellow; claws, black. Size, 27–37 inches. The largest are in Greenland.

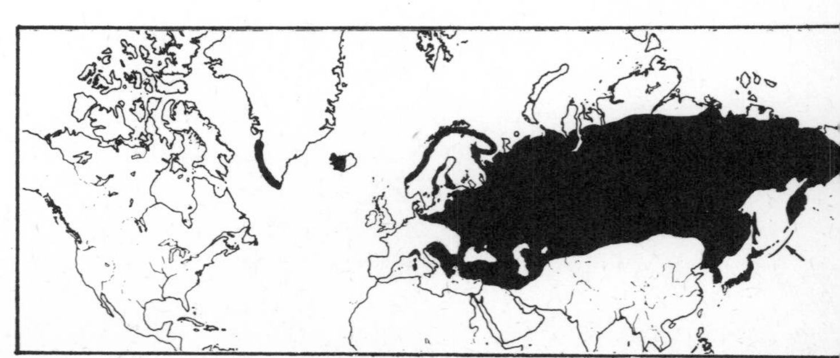

HALIAETUS ALBICILLA

White-tailed Sea Eagle *(Haliaetus albicilla).* —*Photographed at the New York Zoological Society.*

OTHER SPECIES

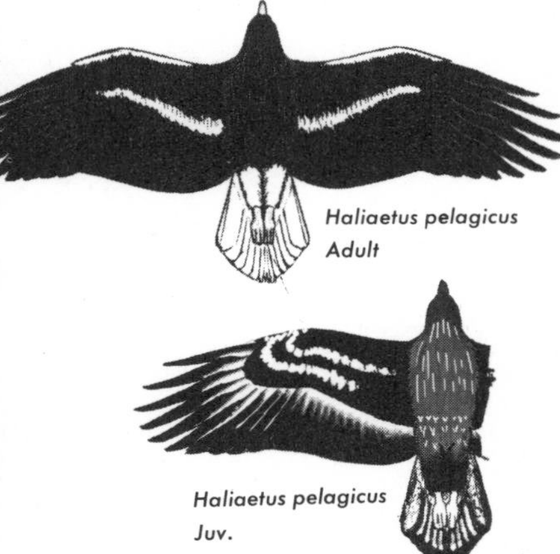

Steller's Sea Eagle (*H. pelagicus*), of northeastern Asia, 35–40 inches, has by far the heaviest beak of the sea eagles. This bird is black, with pale ivory-gray streaking on the head and neck, and may be easily identified in adult plumage throughout most of its range by snowy-white shoulder bands; white bars on the underwing coverts; also white thighs, and tail. (In the immature these white parts are mottled, and the dark brown juvenile has mottled underparts and narrow white bars on the underwing coverts. The shoulder bands are very faint.) Cere and beak, which are slate-gray in the juvenile, turn bright yellow in immatures and adults; dark brown legs and feet become deep yellow. A dark phase—completely black except for the characteristic streaking on the head, white undertail coverts, and tail —occurs in Korea.

HALIAETUS PELAGICUS

Juvenile Steller's Sea Eagle *(Haliaetus pelagicus).*—*Photograph by John Hamlet.*

Steller's Sea Eagle *(Haliaetus pelagicus).*—*Photograph by R. Van Nostrand, from National Audubon Society.*

White-bellied Sea Eagle *(Haliaetus leucogaster)*.

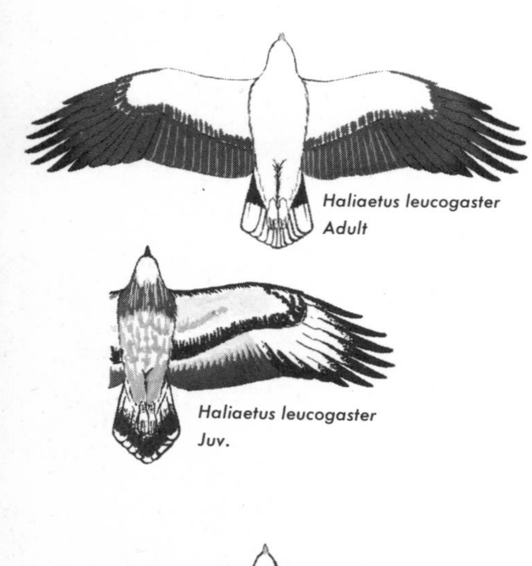

The White-bellied Sea Eagle (*H. leucogaster*), 25–27 inches, reaches the Celebes and the Australian region. Its dove-gray to olive-gray back and contrasting white head, neck, and underparts set this species apart from the predominantly brown-and-gray Fishing Eagles (*Icthyophaga*). The primaries are black, and the black tail shows a very broad terminal band of white. (Juvenile—sepia, noticeably streaked on the head, neck, and underparts and generally feather-edged with buff or sandy. The mottled white tail of the young bird is subterminally banded with sepia.)

HALIAETUS LEUCOGASTE

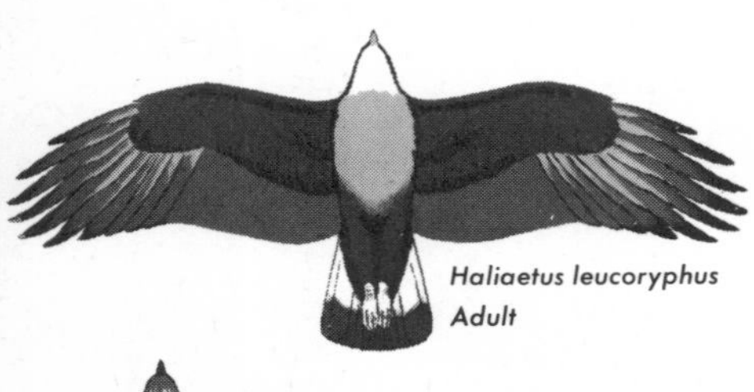

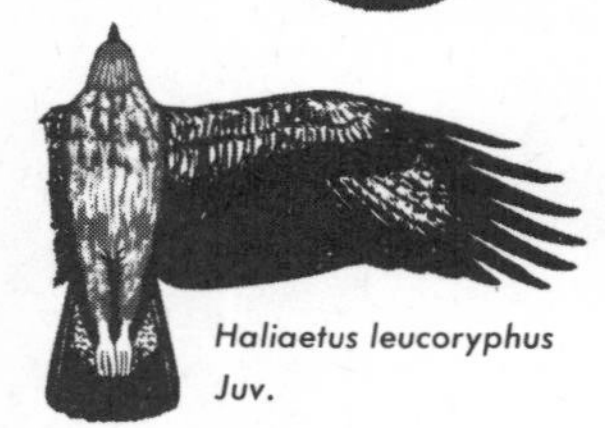

Pallas' Sea Eagle (*H. leucoryphus*), of central Asia, 27–30 inches, is sepia above with a white or buff face and throat; crown, mantle, and underparts, yellow-orange (with darker sides and flanks); tail, sepia, with a very broad median white band (juvenile lacks light head and tail band and appears generally mottled above and below); beak, gray; feet, grayish white; eye, pale brownish-yellow.

HALIAETUS LEUCORYPHU

The only large eagle in the Solomon Islands is Sanford's Sea Eagle (*H. sanfordi*), 25–28 inches. Its head and neck are buff to sandy, streaked with ferruginous; back, wing coverts, and secondaries, brown; primaries and tail, brown; underparts, ferruginous. (Immature—darker and less ferruginous, with more pronounced sandy streaking. Juvenile—black above but sandy below, with heavy black streaking on chest, belly, and thighs; tail, dark brown, with a white subterminal band.)

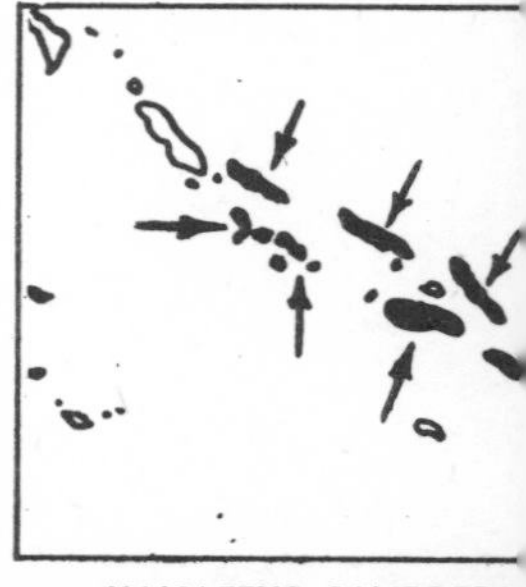

HALIAETUS SANFORDI

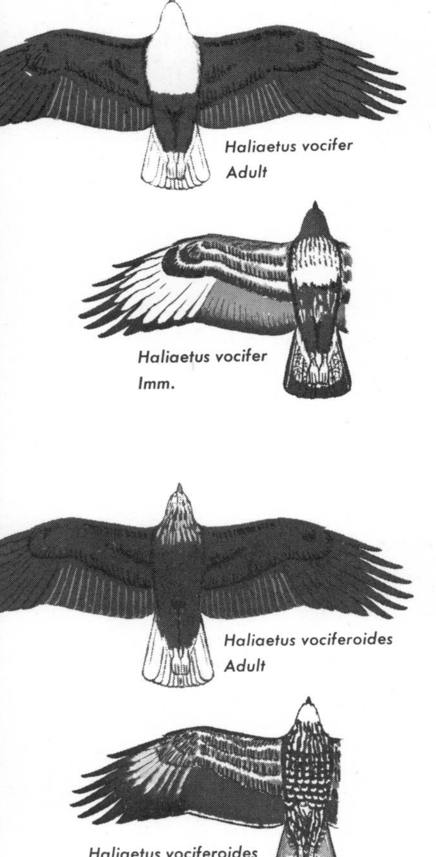

The African Sea,or River,Eagle (*H. vocifer*), 23–26 inches, is distinctively marked on the shoulders, belly, and thighs with medium ferruginous; head, neck, mantle, chest, and tail, white; back, greater wing coverts, and flight feathers, black. (Immature—completely sepia to dark brown above with streaking on head and neck; feather-edging on mantle and shoulders, ferruginous; underparts are tri-colored with a dark vest streaked with ferruginous, a white breast band, and dark brown belly barred with light amber-brown. (Juvenile—light head, neck, and underparts, heavily streaked or mottled with dark brown; back and wings, sepia to dark brown with white mottling, especially on shoulders. Tails of young at any age are mottled white and have a dark subterminal band on the undersurface.)

HALIAETUS VOCIFER

The Madagascar Sea Eagle (*H. vociferoides*), 23–25 inches, is almost entirely sepia to dark brown, with medium ferruginous streaking on crown, chest, and underwing coverts; pure white cheeks and tail. (Juvenile—streaked on head, underparts, and underwing coverts and generally feather-edged above with light amber-brown and buff; tail, white, heavily mottled and subterminally banded with sepia—indistinctly on the undersurface. Tails of young birds apparently become whiter and less mottled with successive molts, until the pure white rectrices of the adult plumage appear.)

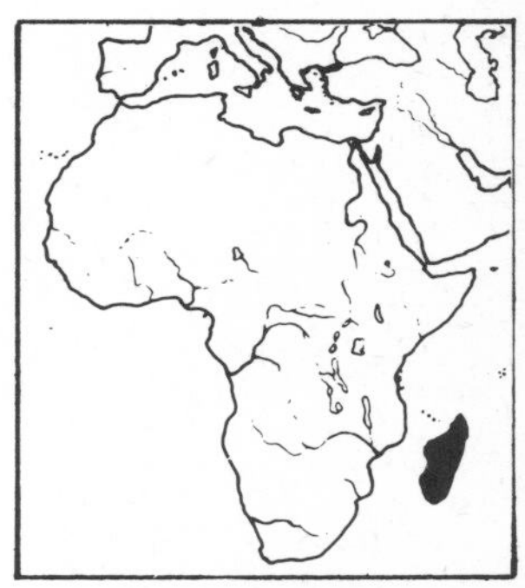
HALIAETUS VOCIFEROIDES

HABITS

In slow flapping flight, with angled wings, the Bald Eagle and the White-tailed Sea Eagle appear heron-like, but they also circle and soar a great deal with broad wings held perfectly horizontal. This wing configuration is not necessarily typical of the smaller species of *Haliaetus,* however, for the White-bellied Sea Eagle soars with its wings slightly upturned in a shallow V.

A sea eagle may sit for hours on some dead bough or other vantage point over shallow water waiting for fish to rise, then swoop to capture one from the surface, barely getting its feet wet. Although it may dive into the water occasionally, this is a tactic more commonly used by the Osprey. Other modes of hunting are coursing low over a stretch of water, and hovering with very slow wing beats. Since a sea eagle is not exceptionally fast, it frequently depends on surprise—swooping into or at right angles to the sun, so that its shadow will not frighten fish and cause them to dive out of reach.

Few birds are such expert opportunists as the Bald Eagle, which locates schools of fish by following sea birds and systematically robs Ospreys. Other sea eagles also have the habit of lying in wait for

Immature African Sea Eagle (*Haliaetus vocifer*).

Ospreys—as do kites, buteos, and gulls—and may even chase vultures and force them to disgorge their carrion.

Whenever or wherever fish are not readily available, a sea eagle may attack diving birds, its maneuvers directed towards isolating one or two from a flock. Then it will stoop until the victim is exhausted from diving and becomes easy prey. Sea birds, wading birds (and penguins on islands off Tasmania) are particularly vulnerable during the breeding season—the eagle simply alighting in the midst of a colony and seizing one of the incubating adults or newly hatched young.

Large fish or birds that are too heavy to lift are towed to the shore over the surface of the water; other prey may be eaten in the air or carried in both talons to a feeding place. Live-caught prey is immediately decapitated in the manner of all hawks and eagles.

Other prey species which are taken include (locally) marine and freshwater snakes, crabs, turtles, molluscs, and small to medium-sized mammals. A large part of the food of most sea eagles is undoubtedly carrion—dead water mammals and fish washed up on the shores of rivers, lakes, and seas. In Alaska dying and dead salmon and herring are piled along the river banks at the end of their spawning season—late spring and summer—providing a feast not only for Bald Eagles but also for wolverines, bears, and other predators. The sea eagles of the Holarctic region are large, powerful birds which, in spite of their penchant for feeding on carrion, may be no less predatory than the Golden Eagle, especially in winter. They have been known to prey on ptarmigan and water birds up to the size of Canada geese, as well as rabbits, hares, foxes, and the young of antelope and reindeer. Their livestock and game depredations, like those of the aquilas, have been local in nature and much exaggerated. However, the White-tailed Sea Eagle has aroused such resentment among sheepmen and gamekeepers in past centuries that the species has been exterminated from many parts of Europe where it formerly bred. It was numerous in England until the end of the eighteenth century and widely distributed in Ireland and Scotland up to the middle of the nineteenth century, but is now a rare migrant to these regions. Its scattered occurrence in central Europe may indicate a formerly wider range on the continent.

Numbers of Bald Eagles have declined in the southern part of the North American breeding range for other reasons, perhaps a combination of the following causes that have been suggested: disappearance of wilderness nesting sites, industrial contamination of rivers, and the use of DDT and other poisons to kill insects that are in turn eaten by fish and consequently affect fish-eaters. For the story of the persecution of Bald Eagles in Alaska, see Chapter 5.

One large tropical species—Sanford's Sea Eagle of the Solomon Islands—appears to be the insular equivalent of the more predatory continental sea eagles.

Like Ospreys, sea eagles are frequently sociable. Pairs associate during the breeding season, and they generally nest in close proximity for such large predatory birds (in Florida as many as three pairs of Bald Eagles nest within a mile of each other). They breed in the most favorable seasons—in the north, in spring and summer; in tropical and subtropical climates, in the cooler dry season, when water levels are low and fish, snakes, turtles, etc., are more concentrated and easier to see from the air. Bald Eagles in Florida begin nesting in October, a month or two before most other birds—partly, it has been suggested, because their young must be fledged before the heat of the summer, but also in anticipation of a plentiful supply of coots, which will be most vulnerable in their breeding colonies when the eagles have fledglings to feed.

The sea eagles prefer to build their large stick nests high in inaccessible places. These are commonly placed in the tops of tall trees, either isolated or standing in water. In the tropical rain forests they may be 120 feet from the ground, above the canopy. In treeless regions cliffs are preferred, but where these are not available, the ground is used.

Remoteness, however, is not always a requirement. In Florida, where Bald Eagles are seldom disturbed by people, eyries are constructed in trees in the midst of towns or on golf courses.

These structures are used for many years and become either as large as, or larger than, the most massive Golden Eagle eyries. The soft lining of the nest may be very thick. The Bald Eagle, according to various accounts in A. C. Bent's *Life Histories,* carefully covers the eggs with this material before each absence from the nest. All sea eagles bring fresh sprigs of greenery during incubation and fledging periods. Most, like the aquilas, slip away rather than attack intruders at the eyrie, but the White-bellied Sea Eagle stays to defend its eggs or young.

Almost invariably two white eggs are laid (rarely one, three, or four in the Holarctic region), but Pallas' Sea Eagle in central Asia and India usually lays three and sometimes four eggs.

During incubation (by both sexes, but female mostly) the male sea eagle feeds the female. Both sexes care for the young, but the female generally divides the food among them. The Bald Eagle and White-tailed Sea Eagle probably incubate the eggs as long as the Golden Eagle does. Fledglings leave the nest when ten to thirteen weeks old and stay near the eyrie, to be fed by their parents for the remainder of the summer. The young of Pallas' and the White-bellied Sea eagles are ready to leave the eyrie at least a week or two before those of their larger relatives take their first flight.

As in the aquilas and other large eagles, the young birds hatch at intervals of a few days, and the first eaglet often feeds at the expense of the second (or third) one, which, weakened by hunger and constant attacks by its nestmate, may not survive.

In some years a pair of sea eagles may repair the eyrie and remain in the vicinity all during the season without breeding.

In the nonbreeding season, most sea eagles are resident within the range of the species, but drift away from the vicinity of their nesting sites in search of new feeding grounds, where they may be seen singly, in pairs, or—if the food supply is plentiful—in larger groups. Northern birds may leave the interiors of continents to winter on the sea coasts where they can find open water, or travel south for some distance to warmer climates. White-tailed Sea Eagles in northern Europe and Asia reach the shores of countries bordering the North Sea and are occasionally seen southward, to the Mediterranean and its islands, the Canaries, Egypt, southern Baluchistan, and India.

Steller's Sea Eagle, an inhabitant of the interior and coast of Kamchatka, winters in Japan, northern China, and Korea. A peculiar migration pattern occurs in North America, where Bald Eagles fledged in Florida in June travel as far as 1,600 miles to "summer" in northeastern North America. Thus peak numbers of Bald Eagles passing over Hawk Mountain, Pennsylvania, in September are probably members of the southern population returning from Canada to breed along the Gulf coast of Florida. Some individuals raised in the far north come down into the United States on this flyway, but at a later date; others follow a more central course, concentrating along the Mississippi and other large rivers in Illinois, Iowa, and Missouri, and even westward in Oklahoma.

Calls are the chief form of display among sea eagles. The Bald Eagle's "ke-ke-ke-ke-ker" or "kweek-kik-ik-ik-ik-ik-ik" (near the nest) is almost a squeal, rather than a scream, but a loud, low-keyed "kak-kak-kak" may also be heard. The White-tailed Sea Eagle has a similar shrill cry, "krikrikrikri," and deeper, gull-like "gah, gah, gah, gah" of alarm. The creaking raucous scream of Pallas' Sea Eagle seems to need oiling and carries for great distances. The White-bellied Sea Eagle has a loud, nasal cackling call, "kenk, kenk, kenk, kenk." The truly "vociferous" African Sea Eagle delivers a mewing screech, "whee-oh-hyo-hyo-hyo," and a low cluck, and is best known for its loud, weird, and far-sounding scream of four notes, "wah, wah, wah-wah," with the head flung far back, nearly resting on the back, and slowly brought forward.

Gray head and neck and brown-patterned underparts distinguish the Gray-headed Fishing Eagle *(Icthyophaga ichthyaetus)* from the White-bellied Sea Eagle throughout southern Asia.

GENUS *ICTHYOPHAGA*

The Gray-headed Fishing Eagle, found in forests along seashores, large lakes, and rivers, is smaller than the White-bellied Sea Eagle (*Haliaetus*), but otherwise somewhat similar. The tail is rounded, not wedge-shaped. The heavy tarsi are scutellate in front and behind; and the powerful toes are scutellate above and covered with tiny spicules underneath, as in *Haliaetus,* but the claws are not grooved. The outer toe is almost as reversible as the Osprey's.

Gray-headed Fishing Eagle (*Icthyophaga ichthyaetus*)

DESCRIPTION (INDIA, CEYLON, BURMA, MALAYSIA, PHILIPPINES)

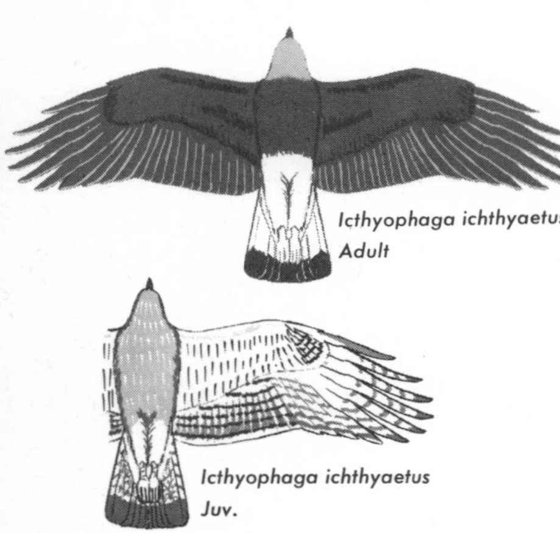

Icthyophaga ichthyaetus Adult

Icthyophaga ichthyaetus Juv.

Head and neck, dove-gray (darker on crown); entire back and wings, sepia; tail, white, with a terminal band of dark brown; below, brown, with white flanks and thighs.

Juvenile—completely dark above, with buff and light amber-brown streaking on head and neck; buff edging on back and wing coverts; tail, dark brown, with mottled white or light cinnamon-brown barring; underparts, mixed light amber-brown and brown, narrowly streaked with white, including flanks and thighs, which are also heavily mottled with white.

Beak, gray shading to blue-black at the tip (young, grayish); eyes, yellow (juvenile, dark brown); legs and feet, pale yellow (juvenile, white). Size, 22–24 inches.

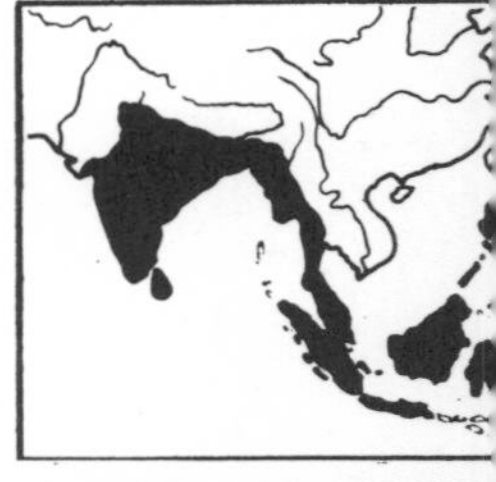

ICTHYOPHAGA ICHTHYA

OTHER SPECIES

The Lesser Fishing Eagle (*I. nana*), 20–23 inches, also resident through Burma and Malaysia, but of more northern distribution in India (up to 5,000 feet in the Himalayas), is similar in coloration, but has a solid dark brown tail. Malaysian individuals are the smallest. (Juvenile—similar to *I. ichthyaetus,* but lighter below.)

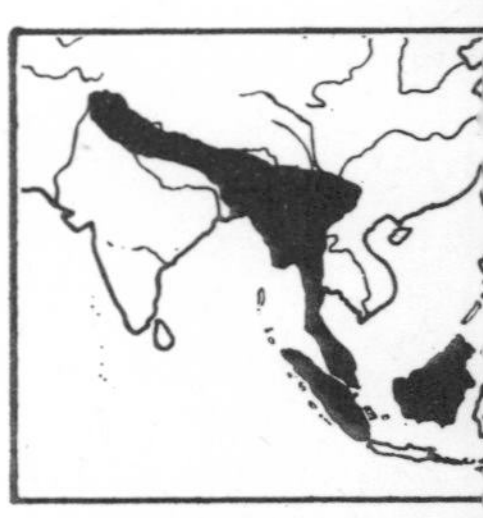

ICTHYOPHAGA NANA

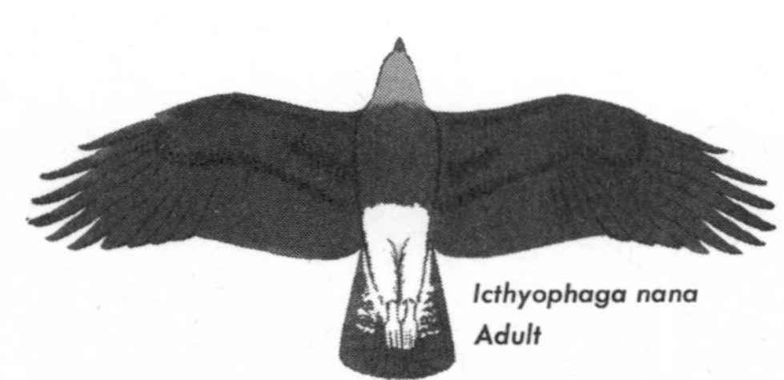

Icthyophaga nana Adult

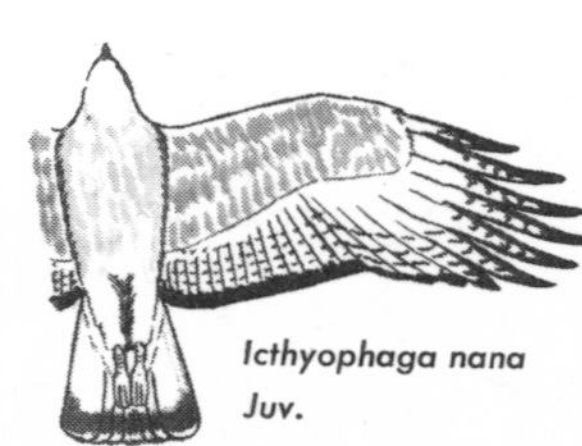

Icthyophaga nana Juv.

HABITS

These fishing eagles are found not only in the lowland coastal parts of India, Malaysia, the Celebes, and Philippines, but also in the hills up to about 5,000 feet (Himalayas and Ceylon). Forest-dwellers, they may spend entire days perched upright, motionless, and inconspicuous on the leafy boughs of trees, watching for fish to come up to the surface of the water. Their mode of hunting, as with *Haliaetus,* is a pounce on the quarry when it comes within striking distance. Food consists mainly of fish, sometimes large species; also reptiles, ground birds such as jungle fowl, and small mammals.

The nest, a large bulky platform of sticks lined with green leaves, is placed high in a tall tree growing near the seashore, the lakeshore, or along the bank of a large river. One (of *I. ichthyaetus*) has been recorded in the midst of a village near Calcutta in a mango, which towered over the houses. Surrounding palm trees were well below the level of the structure. Nests are used year after year. Normally two white eggs are laid.

Calls of the larger species of more southern distribution have been described as an owlish sound— "ooo-wok, ooo-wok, ooo-wok," and a high-pitched scream, not particularly loud.

SUBFAMILY AEGYPIINAE

(Old World Vultures, Palm-nut Vultures, and Bearded Vultures)

In lightly wooded or cultivated open country, the Indian Black Vulture *(Sarcogyps calvus)* may be seen perched in the top of a bare tree or sailing high on outstretched wings held well above the body in a wide V.

GENUS *SARCOGYPS*

Huge lappets hang from the sides of the neck of this very large bareheaded Asiatic vulture, which is sparsely bristled on these parts, as well as wrinkled on the back of the head. The pinkish skin of the face and neck "blushes" redder, as in its close counterpart the African *Torgos.* The tarsi and feet, too, are dull red, as are the bare inner thighs. The yellow-orange crop may be almost concealed by a loose covering of dark fluffy feathers. In flight the white chest feathers contrast with its otherwise dark silhouette.

Pondicherry, or Indian Black, Vulture (*Sarcogyps calvus*)

DESCRIPTION
(SOUTH-CENTRAL ASIA)

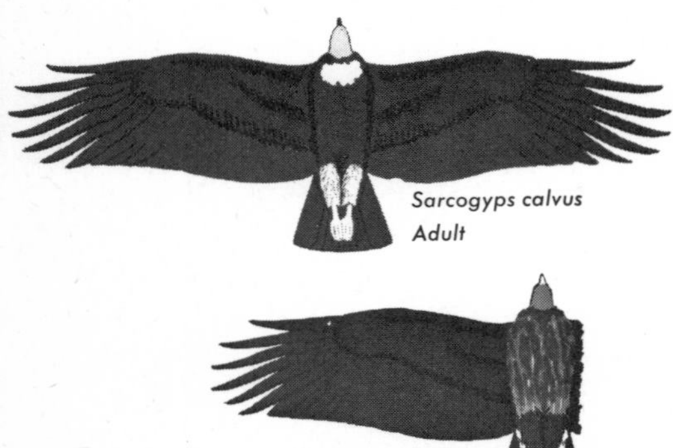

General coloring, glossy black, shading to chocolate on the lower back, wings, and tail. Head and neck have scattered black hairlike feathers, and lappets at the sides of the neck are bare. The ruff at the back of the neck is black; the crop patch, chocolate and black. The chest has an extended patch of white downy feathers.

Young birds—head, covered with light down; above, brown, darkening to black on the wings and tail; they lack the conspicuous white patch on the breast. Underparts, dark brown, heavily streaked and mottled with light cinnamon-brown; undertail coverts, white.

Beak, horn-black; bare skin of head, neck, lappets, and crop, yellow-orange; eyes, reddish-brown; thighs, tarsi, and feet, dull red. Size, 29–31 inches.

SARCOGYPS CALVUS

HABITS

Like other extremely large carrion-feeders, the Indian Black Vulture is rather solitary in its habits. Seldom are more than two seen in a group of smaller vultures. They often stand aloof of the squabble, now and then surreptitiously squeezing in amongst the press of Griffons, White-backed Vultures, and Long-billed Vultures, seemingly no more aggressive than the smallest scavengers, the Egyptian Vultures.

However, no other vulture of the low country and hills (up to about 5,000 feet in the Himalayas) equals *Sarcogyps* in size and strength of bill. The Cinereous Vulture (*Aegypius*) is not common in its domain and might be considered its ecological replacement on the barren steppes of Turkistan, on the upland plateaus of Tibet, and at high altitudes in the Himalayas, the hills of Burma and northern China.

The Black Vulture is the only one of all the carrion-eaters characteristic of the Indian peninsula and Burma which can tear open fresh carcasses of the larger mammals, and for all its apparent timidity, is the "King Vulture," as it is often called.

It avoids both dense forest and dry barren country and comes closer to human habitations than does either *Aegypius* of the more northern regions of Asia or *Torgos* of the African plains.

The nest, a substantial platform of sticks lined with straw, toddy palm, pipal, banyan, or neem leaves, may be constructed in a high tree or, where this is unavailable, even in a low bush (seldom on a cliff). The same site may be used year after year. Only one pure white or faintly marked egg is laid. Both sexes incubate (about 45 days) and feed the young.

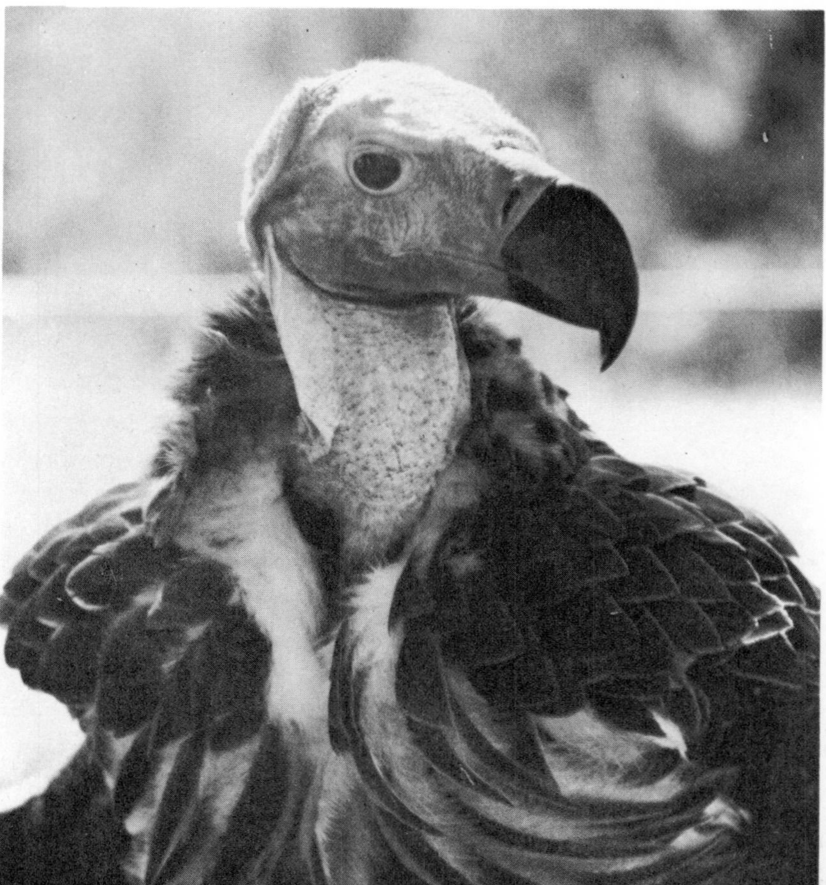

The ear-lappets of the Lappet-faced Vulture (*Torgos tracheliotus*) of southern Africa are much more conspicuous than those of individuals north of the equator.

GENUS *TORGOS*

In a group of African vultures, *Torgos* stands, symbolically and literally, far above the others; its bare pinkish head and neck are brilliant in contrast to a mass of dark brown and downy white plumage. (This vulture has a bluish-gray face, but often "blushes.") The bill is deep and very large, and the heavy tarsi are slightly feathered, but otherwise bare. The feet of this Old World carrion-eater have little grasping ability. In flight the darkly feathered crop patch contrasts with the striped underparts; the wings show narrow areas of white, and the short tail is wedge-shaped. The wingspan is about nine feet.

Lappet-faced Vulture (*Torgos tracheliotus*)

DESCRIPTION (AFRICA, SOUTH OF THE ZAMBEZI)

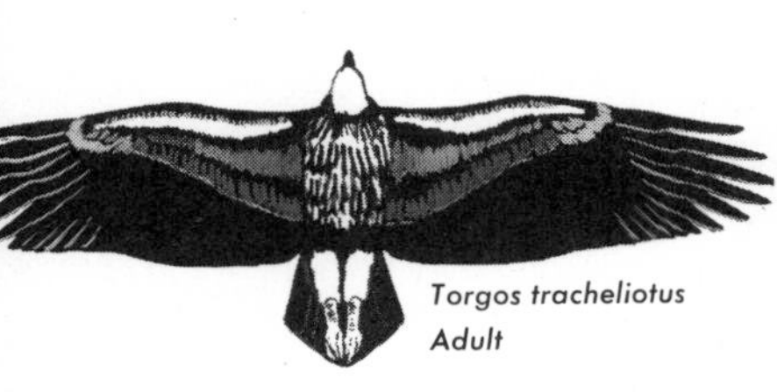
Torgos tracheliotus
Adult

Dark brown and chocolate above, including the ruff, with feathers more or less edged in light cinnamon-brown; wings and wedge-shaped tail, black; head and neck have little or no down, but a few black bristles under the chin, around the ear orifice, and above the eyes; the lappets, bare; crop, covered with a patch of short dark brown down; rest of underparts, thickly clothed in white down, with dark brown lanceolate feathers intermixed, giving the appearance of striping throughout.

Young birds—closely resemble adults but are more downy on the head and hindneck; lanceolate feathers of the chest have pale edgings; undertail coverts and tail are also tipped lighter.

Beak, black with a yellow-orange tip; cere, blue-gray; skin of head and neck, yellow-orange; eyes, deep brown; legs and feet, blue-gray; claws, black. Size, 37–40 inches.

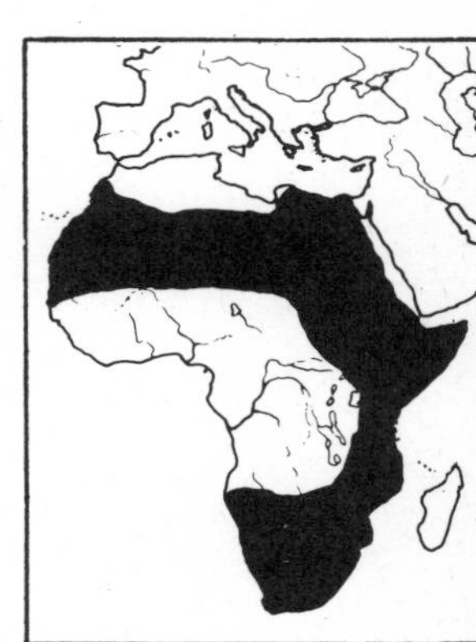
TORGOS TRACHELIOTUS

VARIATIONS

The slightly smaller Northern population is lighter—cinnamon-brown to ochre-brown and white, and has distinct cinnamon-brown to ochre-brown shading on the thighs.

HABITS

Torgos may be found only in the driest parts of Africa, where one or two at a time, sometimes as many as four individuals, will appear with a large number of Griffon Vultures, White-backed Vultures, and a few small Hooded Vultures. The northern population is concentrated mostly in the mountains of northeastern Africa (to 12,000 feet), and below the equator pairs are scattered from Kreuger Park and the Transvaal up through the Kalahari. The Lappet-faced Vulture is frequently solitary in the nonbreeding season, and may roost alone in the top of a tree or on a cliff far from its feeding grounds.

All vultures, including the aggressive White-headed Vulture (*Trigonoceps*), allow *Torgos* to feed at its whim, for none come anywhere near its massive size; the weight of the female is thirty pounds, and the beak is enormous, capable of tearing open the hides of the largest game animals in Africa—hippo, elephant, and rhino.

The nest, in the top of a table-topped mimosa or other thorn tree, is a huge platform lined with dry grass and hair. During incubation, brooding, and fledging, it is reconditioned with fresh green branches. One white egg sometimes has reddish or brown markings.

In the nonbreeding season *Torgos* appears in regions where it does not breed (drifting from Somaliland into Kenya, in time for the dry season below the equator).

This bird is apparently silent except for the hissing and spitting characteristic of all vultures as they fight over a carcass.

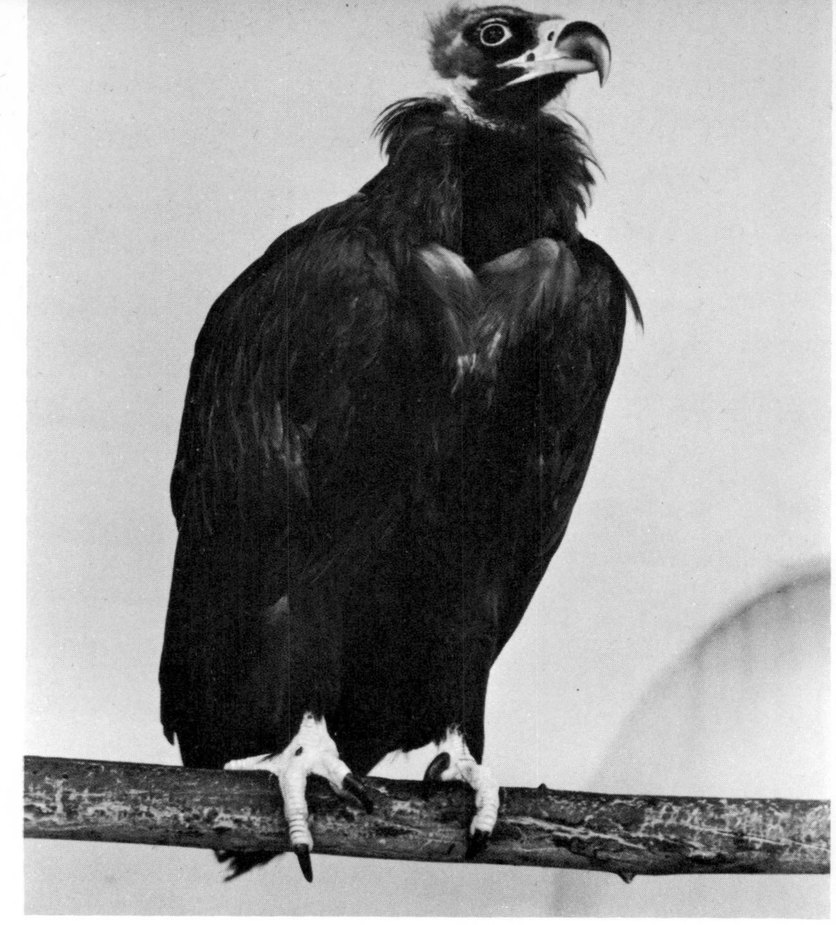

The Cinereous Vulture *(Aegypius monachus)* has more feathering on its head than any other Old World vulture, and long, fluffy feathers nearly covering the otherwise scutellate lower legs and toes.—*Photographed at the New York Zoological Society.*

GENUS *AEGYPIUS*

Aegypius is probably the most northern Palearctic vulture. It has bred in the past in many of the temperate parts of southern Europe and in northern Africa, but now it is confined principally to southern Russia and the great pine woods of Spain.

Perhaps the dense black "furlike" feathers on its head and neck and the long tarsal plumes are an adaptation to the cold of the steppes and the high mountain fastnesses of the Himalayas. In these climes the Cinereous Vulture—with its heavy raptorial beak and large, rather prehensile, feet—is "king," just as *Torgos* is "king" on the continent of Africa and *Sarcogyps* is the "first" vulture of India. In flight it appears entirely black with a wedge-shaped tail.

Cinereous Vulture (*Aegypius monachus*)

DESCRIPTION (MONGOLIA AND TIBET TO THE MEDITERRANEAN)

General coloring dark brown and chocolate; head and neck (except back and sides) covered with down; crop with short downy feathers; ruff, continuous from back of neck around edge of crop. Older birds are paler and have more scanty down on head and neck.

Young birds—darker than the adults; downy portions of head, neck, and crop, black.

Beak, dark horn-colored; cere, pale mauve; eyes, brown; legs and feet, white. Size, 36–39 inches.

AEGYPIUS MONACHUS

HABITS

The Cinereous Vulture lives in open, arid regions and is most numerous on the central Asiatic steppes and in the Himalayas, where it is the most powerful of the many species of accipitrine vultures which populate the region (to 10,000 or 11,000 feet above sea level).

Its food is almost exclusively carrion (large animals), including the bones, but occasionally it may catch steppe marmots, lambs, and tortoises.

The bulky stick nest, lined with small twigs and wool, is usually built in an isolated large tree, but where this is not available, in a smaller tree (rarely on a cliff). One or two eggs are white, richly marked with dark brown, red, and underlying purple.

The species is mostly sedentary. The Himalayan birds winter at high altitudes, with some drifting down into central China.

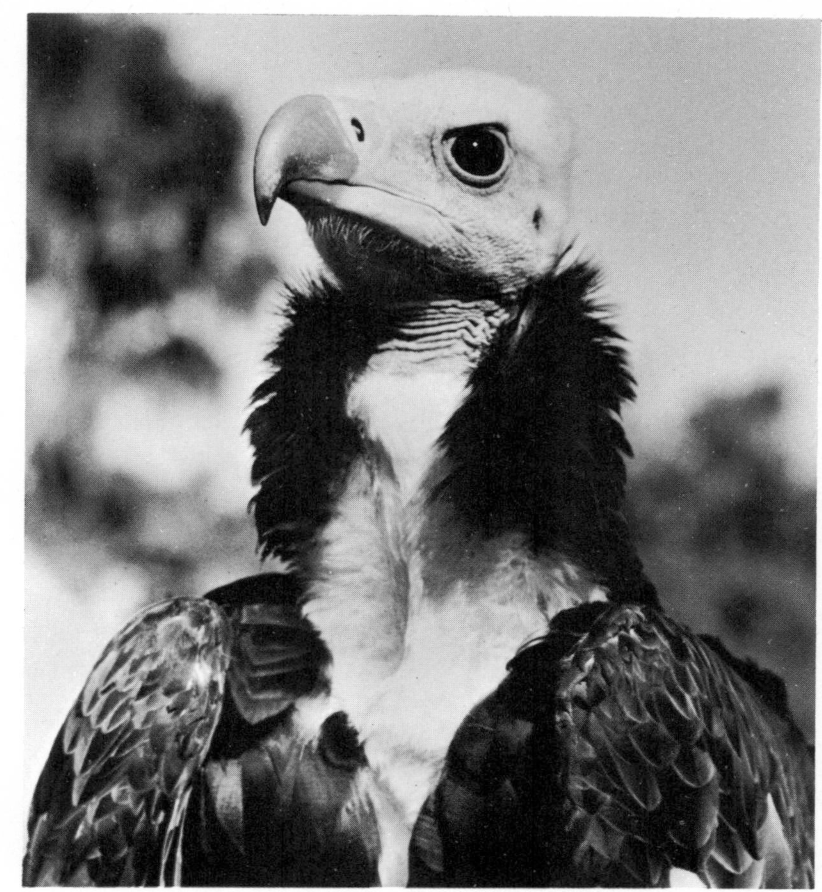

The White-headed Vulture (*Trigonoceps occipitalis*) of Africa is an aggressive, alert, and strong-footed carrion-feeder which occasionally attacks and kills birds and small antelopes.

GENUS *TRIGONOCEPS*

Due to its uniquely angular skull structure, *Trigonoceps* appears to have a slight occipital crest of white down. The bare skin of the face and neck are normally pale, but this bird, like the small Hooded Vulture, "blushes" red in excitement or anger. The red color of the large raptorial beak is also a distinctive feature, even of the juvenile. The bare legs are partly clothed in white down, and the large feet are more prehensile than those of any other vulture of the New or Old World. It is high up on the peck order—a raptorial vulture of large proportions, weighing fifteen to twenty pounds, and with a wingspan of about six feet, as large as any eagle of the dry African savannas. In flight, this bird shows a distinctive pattern of dark and light patches on the undersurface of the body and wings.

White-headed Vulture (*Trigonoceps occipitalis*)

DESCRIPTION
(TROPICAL AFRICA)

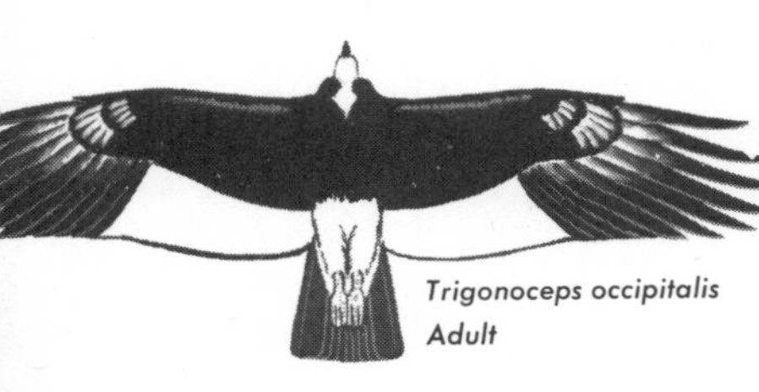

Trigonoceps occipitalis
Adult

Trigonoceps occipitalis
Juv.

Black and chocolate above, including ruff, with a band of white across wing coverts; secondaries and undertail coverts, white; primaries and tail, black; crown, heavily capped in fluffy white down, forming a short crest on the occiput; sides of face and chin, scantily bristled in white; crop, covered with short white down; below crop, a patch of fluffier down; chest, feathered chocolate and black; rest of underparts, white.

Immature—sepia or chocolate-colored down on head, neck, and crop; lacks the white band on the wing coverts characteristic of the adult; secondaries, white; thighs, mottled darker.

Juvenile—completely dark above and below, except for white bases of flight feathers and white mottling on undertail coverts.

Beak, red (black at tip); cere, blue-gray; skin of head and neck, pale yellow-orange; eyes, dark brown; legs and feet, pale yellow-orange; claws, black. Size, 27–30 inches.

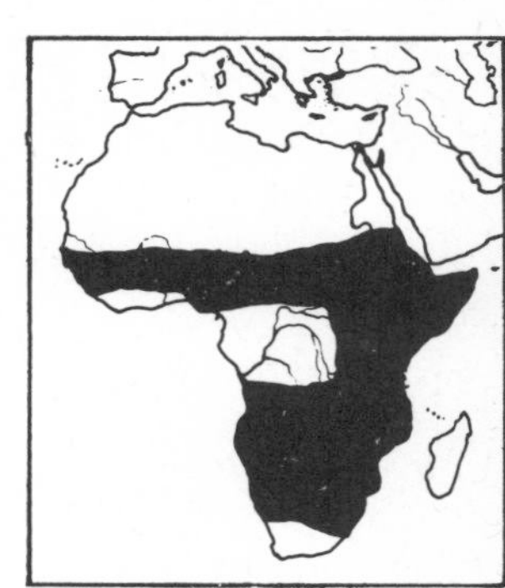

TRIGONOCEPS OCCIPITALIS

White-headed Vulture *(Trigonoceps occipitalis).*

HABITS

White-headed vultures may be seen in pairs throughout eastern and central Africa, soaring high like other vultures, but capable of stronger, faster wing beats.

They feed on carcasses of large mammals and are reported to kill birds and small antelopes—the young, and individuals that show signs of being wounded or sick. They have also been seen picking up ants and locusts.

If *Trigonoceps* is the first to find a fresh carcass, it rips open the hide, thus coincidentally preparing the way for other vultures with weaker bills to come in after it has fed. Only *Torgos,* the great Lappet-faced Vulture, takes precedence in this function or in feeding. If it is a late arrival, the White-headed Vulture may stay around the outskirts of a crowd of White-backed Vultures or other scavengers and still be there when they have gone. However, there is no question that it can, if it wants, drive all but *Torgos* away.

The large stick nest, built in the flat top of a thorn tree, may be used year after year. One occupied for six years on a game reserve in east Africa was woven of thorn twigs, bits of reed, coarse grass stems, sprays of acacia, and seed pods, and measured three feet by three feet. Only one egg is laid, either white or blotched faintly with brown. Incubation lasts about 43 days.

The White-headed Vulture has several call notes which are seldom heard, as well as an assortment of grunts, screams, and other noises used in a contest over carrion.

Griffon Vultures *(Gyps fulvus),* in Spain, quarreling over a carcass.—*Photograph by Eric Hosking.*

GENUS *GYPS*

The disappearance of game animals, the introduction of sanitary livestock raising, and poison bait set out for predators have all contributed to the demise of the Griffon Vulture (*G. fulvus*) in western and central Europe, and the reduction of its numbers in southern Europe and southern Africa; but in the mountains of Spain, northern Africa, the Near East, central Asia, and the Himalayas it is still a common species. Two other griffons inhabit central Asia and the Himalayas at about the same altitudes (2,500 to 7,000 feet above sea level)—the Long-billed Vulture (*G. indicus*) and the large Himalayan Griffon (*G. himalayensis*). There the similar brown young, not only of these birds, but also of the somewhat closely related White-backed Vulture (*Pseudogyps*), are extremely difficult to identify. Both adults and young of Rüppell's Griffon (*G. rüppellii*), which breeds in northern and eastern Africa, are distinctively feather-edged and have a more spotted appearance, even in flight, than the dark young and indistinctly striped adults of the European and north African populations which drift south of the Sahara in the nonbreeding season.

All griffons appear very broad-winged in flight, with long, deeply emarginated primaries; their tails are short and square; and their extremely long necks may protrude far beyond their ruffs. On the ground, this snakelike neck, sparsely covered with patches of light down, is their most conspicuous feature. The face is bare; the crown, sparsely to thickly clothed with filamentous (threadlike) or downy feathers. The crop patch and a small part of the otherwise naked tarsi are closely feathered.

Griffon Vulture (*Gyps fulvus*)

DESCRIPTION (MEDITERRANEAN AND CENTRAL ASIA)

Gyps fulvus
Adult

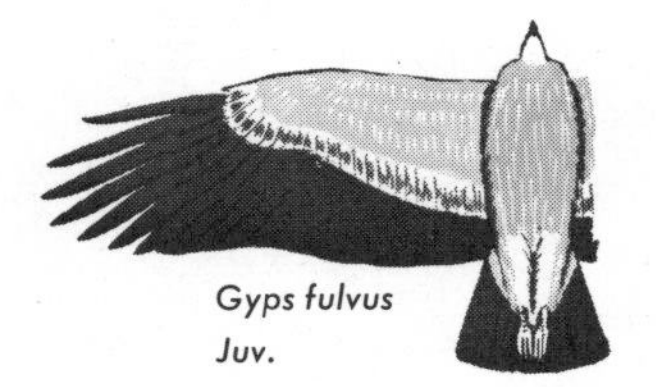
Gyps fulvus
Juv.

Loosely constructed feathers of ruff, sandy to white; above, medium olive-gray, becoming light tan on the wing coverts and lower back; secondaries, darker than back; primaries, as well as tail, black; head, covered with filamentous white feathers, and the long neck, with clumps of short white down; crop patch and rest of underparts, mixed with light cinnamon and light ochre-brown, shaft-streaked in white.

Immature (*third year*)—like adult, but feathers of ruff edged with cinnamon.

Juvenile (*and second year*)—completely feather-edged above in cinnamon; underparts cinnamon, striped in white. (Down on the head of juvenile is gradually replaced with age by filamentous feathers, and the very long lanceolate feathers of the neck are succeeded by the adult type of ruff.)

Beak, yellowish-white; cere, bluish-black; eyes, reddish-orange; legs, feet, and claws, dark gray. Size, about 40 inches.

GYPS FULVUS

VARIATIONS

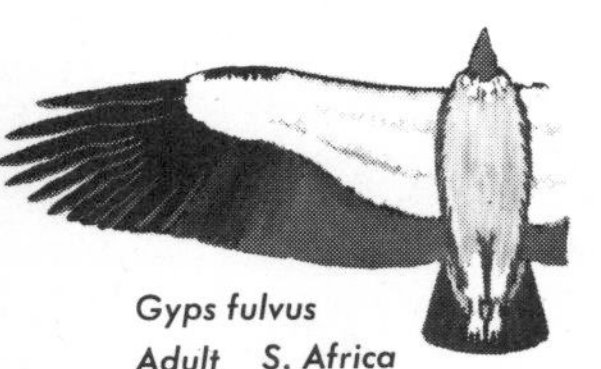
Gyps fulvus
Adult S. Africa

The Indian bird is cinnamon-colored on the lighter parts of its plumage, and has thick white or buff-tinged down on the crown and a dark crop patch. From South Africa, north to the Zambezi River, the Griffon Vulture (often considered a distinct species, *G. coprotheres*) is paler—light tan or buff-white, lacking the striping on the underparts in young and adult plumage. Adults have very little down on the head; juveniles even less.

OTHER SPECIES

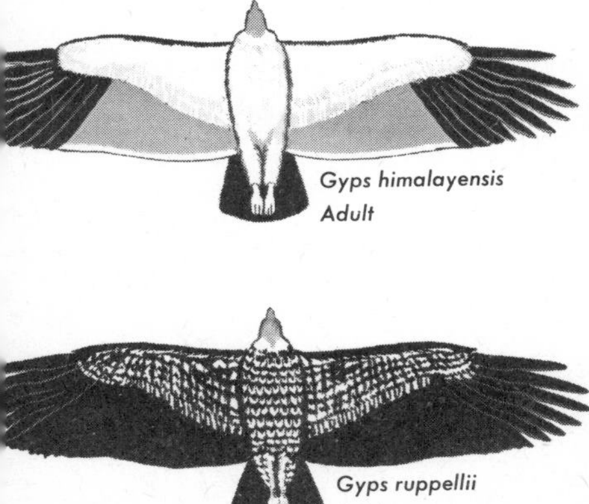
Gyps himalayensis
Adult

Gyps ruppellii
Adult

The Himalayan Griffon (*G. himalayensis*), about 40 inches, resembles the South African population, but it is as large as the individuals of that species in the Mediterranean. The filamentous white feathers on the head and the down on the neck are longer than in any other griffon; bare legs, feet, and cere, paler; beak, grayish-green. (Young—darker than adult, with distinct light striping below.)

Rüppell's Griffon (*G. rüppellii*), about 34–36 inches, has short buff-colored down on the head and neck and a distinct buff or white collar. The tropical African population is entirely sepia with a cinnamon tinge and feather-edged white to tan; crop patch, wings, and tail, dark brown. In these regions the adult Rüppell's Griffon, with its spotted appearance above and below, is very similar to the juvenile

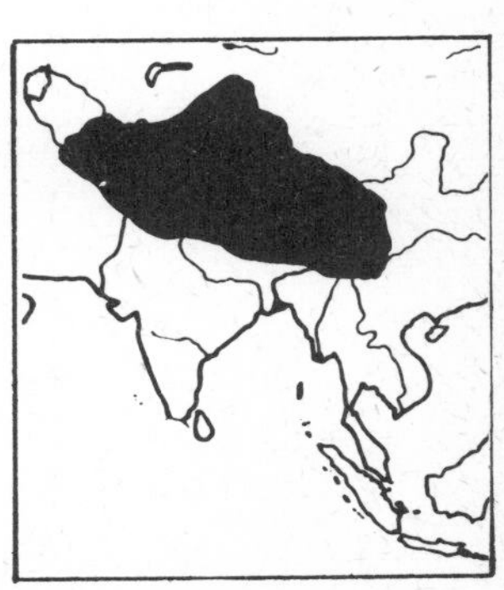
GYPS HIMALAYENSIS

of the White-backed Vulture (*Pseudogyps*), but the latter has a plain brown back. In Eritrea, highlands of Ethiopia, and British Somaliland, however, the underparts are more uniformly light, without any distinct feather-edging. The yellowish-orange beak is a conspicuous feature of the nearly mature and adult Rüppell's Griffon. Cere and bare skin of face and neck, greenish-gray or black; eyes, dark brown, legs and feet, black. (Young—variable throughout the species range, show very broad white to buff feather-edging above; dark underparts with light streaking, or the reverse, as well as feather-edging.)

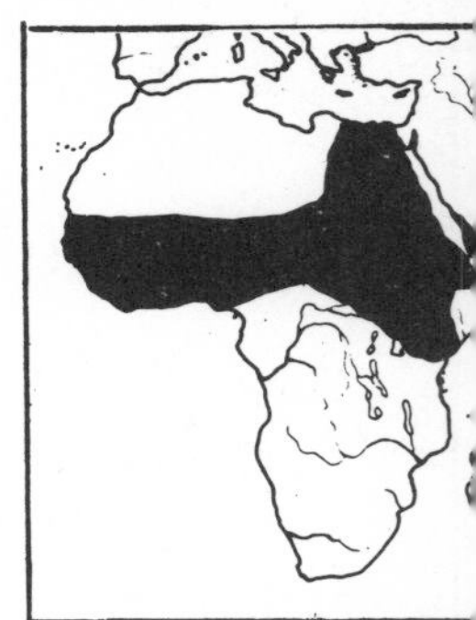

GYPS RUPPELLII

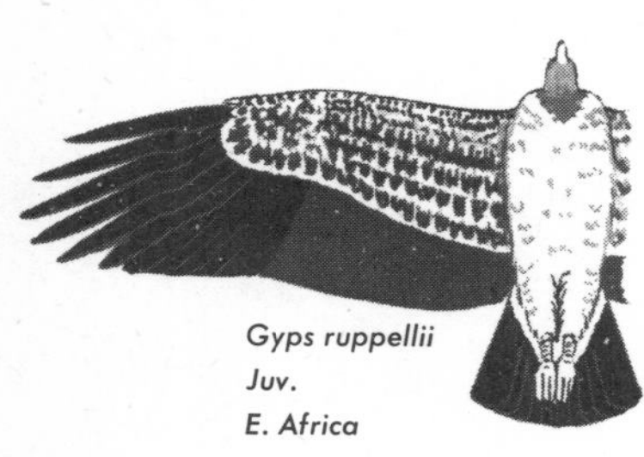

Rüppell's Griffon *(Gyps rüppellii)*, one of the larger African vultures, compares in size to the White-headed Vulture *(Trigonoceps)*, but does not have its strong, deeply hooked beak and more prehensile toes. This bird feeds strictly on large dead mammals in open plains, avoiding the villages and cultivated regions where small omnivorous vultures congregate.—*Photographed at the National Zoological Park.*

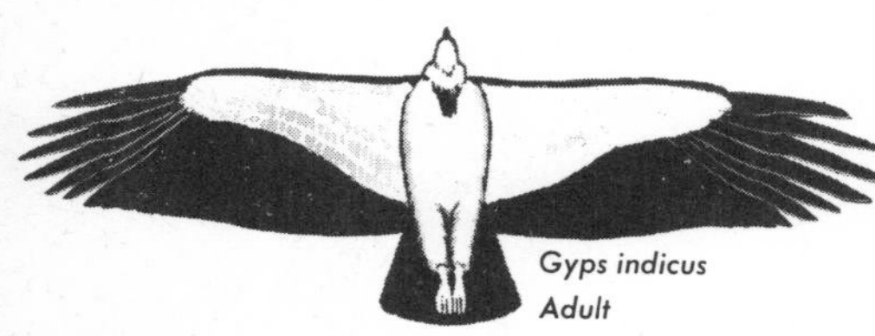

The Long-billed Vulture (*G. indicus*), about 31 inches, with a sparsely feathered or bare head and neck, is medium olive-gray and buff above; wings and tail, sepia to dark-brown; crop patch, cinnamon-brown; ruff and underparts, mixed with buff and sandy. (Young—entirely dark below, streaked conspicuously with buff.)

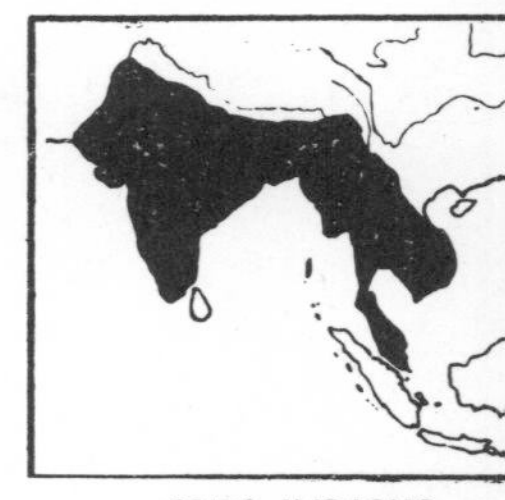

GYPS INDICUS

HABITS

These are the most sociable of the Old World vultures, nesting together in scattered communities, usually on cliffs or rocky outcrops (but occasionally in trees); feeding together and roosting in large groups.

On the wing, griffons are magnificent soaring birds. Their hunched-up appearance, while roosting on a rock ledge or waiting on the ground, and other attitudes, such as "sunning" with wings outstretched, are characteristic of all large vultures. However, their long necks make it possible for them to assume bizarre shapes which others cannot, except the very similar White-backed Vultures (*Pseudogyps*). Like the small scavenger vultures they walk clumsily, tipping from side to side; often take large ungainly hops, using their wings; and can be surprisingly fast when it is expedient to run.

Aside from their relationship to smaller and larger (or more aggressive) species, in the feeding order of peck, they may also display an order of social dominance within groups of individuals of their own species that ordinarily associate and fight over carcasses of large mammals. Among hungry Griffon Vultures (*G. fulvus*) there are the dominant ones who assert and get their rights first, the runners-up who give them a continual fight until they have displaced the inner circle, and on the outer periphery, the greater number of submissive individuals who simply wait until the others have gorged themselves. In threat actions, the attitude of the feet appears to be most important, but biting, hissing, and screaming are also part of the ritual.

Since the Griffon Vultures and the White-backed Vultures (*Pseudogyps*) do not have beaks large or sharp enough to tear open the hides of fresh carcasses, they must either wait for decay to set in or for one of the more powerful vultures to arrive and do the dissecting. In central Africa the White-backed Vultures are usually the first to find a carcass, but not to eat. Their presence attracts one or two of the less numerous solitary vultures, the White-headed Vulture (*Trigonoceps*) or the Lappet-faced Vulture (*Torgos*), which sail in, do the cutting, and eat first. Then the big vultures stand on the sidelines while the White-backed Vultures fight it out, their long necks seemingly well-adapted for reaching into the carcass. Their aloofness is often mistaken for shyness. Actually the large vultures, "kings" by virtue of their strong, raptorial beaks, may lumber in at any time and scatter the smaller ones.

This relationship of griffons to the larger vultures with heavy beaks repeats itself in Europe, central Asia, and the Himalayas, where the Cinereous Vulture (*Aegypius*) is at the top of the social order, and in tropical India, where the Indian Black Vulture (*Sarcogyps*) is "King of the Vultures." There is no contest over their supremacy, which seems to be mutually beneficial to large and small. Most of the fighting occurs between members of the same or various species of griffons or White-backed Vultures which are in direct competition, in larger numbers, for food. The very weak-billed scavengers (*Neophron* and *Necrosyrtes*) are at the very bottom of the order of peck. However, the mammalian predators take precedence over all vultures. On the high steppes and in the mountains, during the cold winter, and when food is especially scarce, wolves will keep the Cinereous Vulture and its cohorts, the griffons, waiting on the sidelines for hours.

Griffons eat only the flesh and internal viscera of a carcass, and leave the bones for the Lammergeier, that strange eagle-like vulture, for other large vultures that are bone-swallowers, and for mammalian predators, both large and small.

Cliff nests are scanty, consisting of a few feathers and small sticks on an earth base, but nests in the tops of trees are much like those of White-backed Vultures. Some of the largest vulture nests may have originally been built by hawks. One (or two) eggs are white, rarely spotted or smeared with dark red. Incubation, chiefly by the female, is estimated to last about 48 to 50 days in the wild. Records in aviaries have been 51 or 52 days (longer in cold weather). During brooding the male brings food in his crop for his mate and the female feeds the young by regurgitation, a little at a time, so that bits of carrion are not left around the nest. Young are said to remain in the nest three months. In about four months fledglings raised in aviaries are able to vie for themselves.

In tropical eastern Africa the breeding season of Rüppell's Griffon is so irregular that eggs can be found at any time of the year (but mostly in July and August) and fully fledged young in April, September, or December. Large numbers of nonbreeding immatures live with the adults and juveniles in the colonies and feed with them. However, the mountain birds of the temperate zone have a more definite spring and summer breeding season and in winter some may drift down into the low hills and plains, or to lower latitudes (not usually south of the equator) in search of new feeding grounds.

Griffons are often noisy at their nesting places as well as while feeding. Hissing noises and a "harsh croak" (*G. fulvus*) are also used as warning sounds when the eggs or young are in danger.

Immature African White-backed Vultures *(Pseudogyps africanus)* rest after feeding on the carcass of a hyena on the plains of Barotseland, Northern Rhodesia. The bird in the foreground, is "sunning" its wings, a habit common to all large vultures.

GENUS *PSEUDOGYPS*

Bristles and clumps of down are the only feathering on the head and long neck of *Pseudogyps,* except for a rather small ruff at the base of the neck. The crop patch is closely feathered, and down appears on a small part of the otherwise bare tarsi, just below the thigh feathering. Feet and beak are of moderate size. In most features, except the "concealed" white back, the African and Indian White-backed Vultures resemble the griffons (*Gyps*). In flight, however, no other large vultures have their characteristic white underwing coverts and dark tail and wings. The dark young become progressively lighter over a period of four years (see immatures in photograph above).

African White-backed Vulture (*Pseudogyps africanus*)

DESCRIPTION

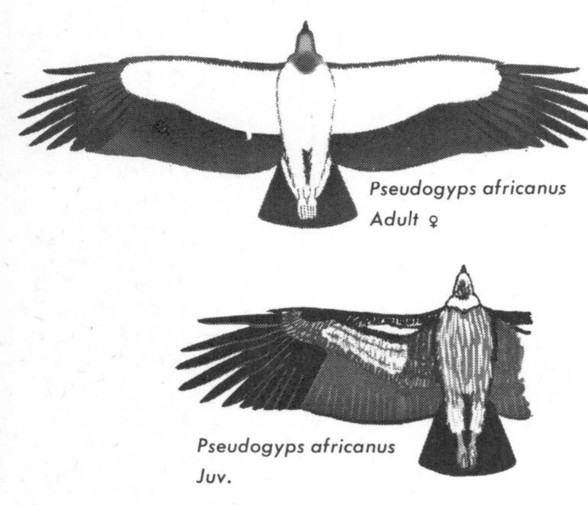

Pseudogyps africanus Adult ♀

Pseudogyps africanus Juv.

Male—Ruff, upper back, and wing coverts, tan, becoming olive-brown on the lower back and secondaries; primaries and tail, dark brown; underparts, uniformly tan with an olive-brown crop patch; forehead, throat, and cheeks, covered with tan bristles; back of head and entire neck, clothed in white down. The "concealed" white back of this vulture is visible as it takes off from the ground and in some extremely slumped-over attitudes—reaching, pulling, etc. In flight it has small areas of white on the underwing coverts. *Female*—paler, with entirely white underwing coverts.

Immature—over-all coloring of mottled sepia and tan; the underparts, striped in white; downy feathers of the ruff and thighs, white; wings and tail, dark; concealed part of the back, white, as in the adult.

Juvenile—much darker, lacking the white back; lanceolate ruff as well as the back, wing coverts, and underparts, vividly shaft-striped in white.

Beak, black; bare skin of head and neck, black; eyes, dark brown; legs and feet, dark gray; claws, black. Size, about 30 inches.

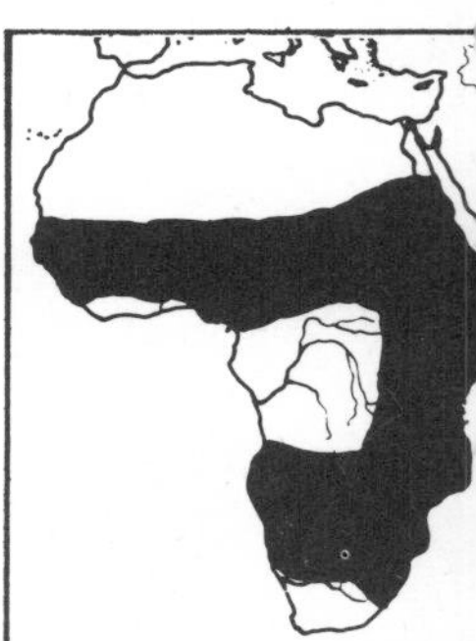

PSEUDOGYPS AFRICAN

OTHER SPECIES

Pseudogyps bengalensis Adult

The Indian White-backed Vulture (*P. bengalensis*), 30 inches, is darker—chocolate and black, has a much scantier white ruff and downy circlet, and a smaller concealed white patch on the back. The underparts are narrowly streaked with white. (Young—chocolate-colored above and paler below with similar streaking; head and neck, covered with stubby white down; lanceolate ruff of white feathers, edged in chocolate.)

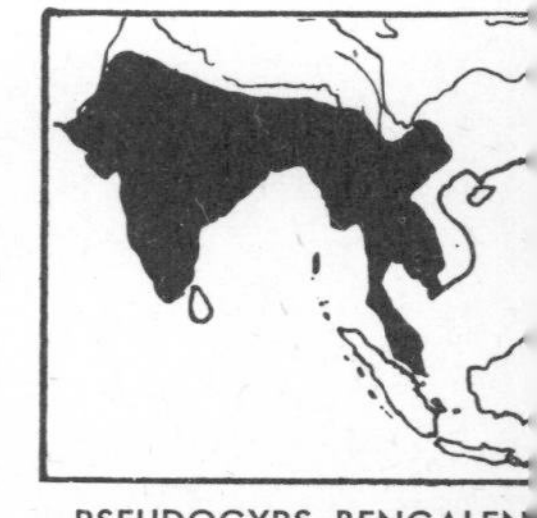

PSEUDOGYPS BENGALEN

HABITS

White-backed Vultures replace griffons (*Gyps*) in parts of tropical Africa and India and also inhabit many of the same regions—northern and eastern Africa and northern India (to about 4,000 feet in the Himalayas). Although similar in their habits, they are more likely to be seen in the neighborhood of villages than is *Gyps,* and they always nest in trees.

Either solitary or sociable, they may gather in loose, straggling colonies, perhaps a hundred in a single stretch of woods along a river, but many of these individuals, as in *G. rüppellii,* are nonbreeding immatures. The nest, a platform of twigs or palm fibers in the top of a tree, is decorated with leafy green branches, and may be reused for many years. One, in a woods of borassus palms (eastern Africa), was occupied for eleven years by vultures and another year by a pair of buteos. Usually only one egg is laid—white and granular in texture, sometimes blotched with rufous or grayish-yellow. The nesting season is so irregular that eggs may be found in eastern Africa from July and August (mostly) to the following January. Both sexes incubate (45 days), and the young bird, which is fed by regurgitation, is fledged in about four months.

Like griffons, these vultures are noisy at a carcass, screeching and hissing at each other as they spread their wings and dance about, either in an attempt to push out the birds that are feeding, or to keep their places in the inner circle.

On the plains of Barotseland, Northern Rhodesia, the carcass of a hyena draws vultures—here, one can observe the predetermined order of feeding. As the large aggressive White-headed Vulture *(Trigonoceps occipitalis),* left, walks away, the African White-backed Vulture *(Pseudogyps africanus)* takes over. The small Hooded Vultures *(Necrosyrtes monachus)* will be the last to eat.

GENUS *NECROSYRTES*

Necrosyrtes is a small brown vulture with bare legs and face, light down on the back of the head and neck, and a darker wedge-shaped tail. Throughout its east African range this bird breeds more commonly and in greater numbers than the Egyptian Vulture, of comparable size, weak bill and feet, and omnivorous habits. The color of the bare parts of the head and neck varies according to the stimulus affecting the circulation of the blood, as in some other birds of prey. The female, on the nest, ordinarily has a purplish-white appearance; but she "blushes" red at the approach of the male, and turns greenish-white when frightened.

Hooded Vulture (*Necrosyrtes monachus*)

DESCRIPTION (TROPICAL AFRICA)

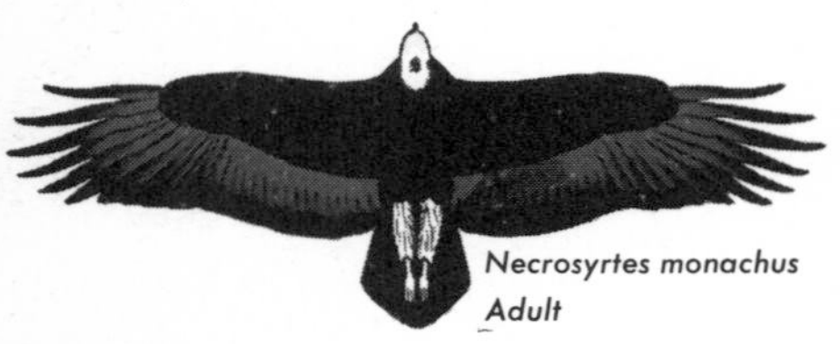

Short ruff and entire plumage, sepia to dark brown, except for white down on back of the head and long neck; white crop patch, bordered with a circlet of fluffy white down; thighs, mottled white. Bare parts of head and neck are scantily bristled and base of neck is marked with a contrasting clump of short, dark brown feathers.

Young birds—similar, but may be distinguished by dark-colored down on head, neck, crop, and thighs.

Beak, gray-brown (juvenile, pale flesh-color); bare skin of head and neck, variable—sometimes red or purple; eyes, brown (juvenile, black); legs and feet, blue-green (juvenile, brown); claws, black. Size 23–25 inches, the north and east African birds largest.

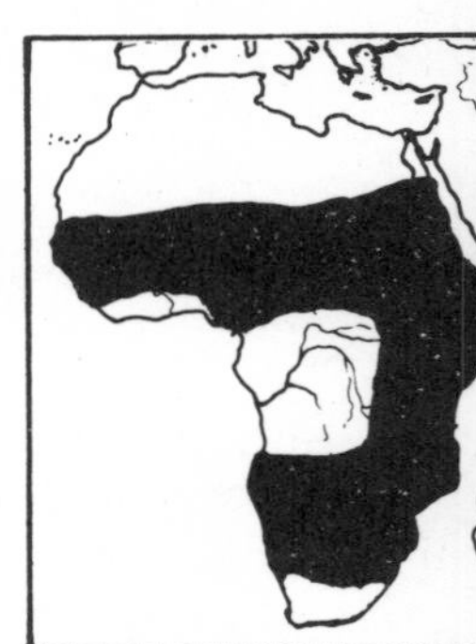

HABITS

The feeding habits of the Hooded Vulture are virtually the same as those of the Egyptian Vulture (*Neophron*). This bird is completely omnivorous; eats garbage, offal, and carrion; picks up fish and crustaceans on the seashore; and will eat lizards and other reptiles.

However, it is more sociable than *Neophron,* nesting closer together in colonies, either in the tops of high trees or on cliffs. One egg is either plain white or blotched with pale to reddish-brown, sometimes with lilac undermarkings as well.

During a period of 46 days the female (mostly) incubates and is fed twice a day by the male, who relieves her for about an hour at midday. Only the female broods the young bird, which is fed by regurgitation, a little at a time, also by the female only. After about four months in the nest the fledgling takes its first flight.

The female Hooded Vulture is as meticulous as a hawk or eagle in furnishing her stick nest with fresh green foliage each day. In one east African nest, watched by G. L. Van Someren, mistletoe was the favorite decoration. He notes that the Sykes Monkeys, which take the eggs, are the chief enemies of this bird.

No call note is recorded for the adults, but the young have a "chic chic" note or a chirping greeting for their mother.

The Egyptian Vulture (*Neophron percnopterus*) is the constant companion of the raven, the kite, and the crow. The ancient Egyptians carved its image on their monuments, but it was never worshiped like the Griffon Vulture.—*Photograph by Eric Hosking.*

GENUS *NEOPHRON*

An untidy mane of lanceolate feathers cascades from the head and neck of this creamy-white vulture, which has the weakest feet and beak of any Old World scavenger except the Hooded Vulture (*Necrosyrtes*)—its ecological replacement in the tropical parts of Africa. This mane, present to a lesser extent in the brown immatures, and a different shape in flight (long narrow wings and much longer wedge-shaped tail) help to distinguish young Egyptian Vultures from young Hooded Vultures. The crop, face, and legs are bare.

Egyptian Vulture (*Neophron percnopterus*)

DESCRIPTION
(EUROPE, AFRICA,
ASIA TO NORTHWESTERN
INDIA; CANARY AND
CAPE VERDE ISLANDS)

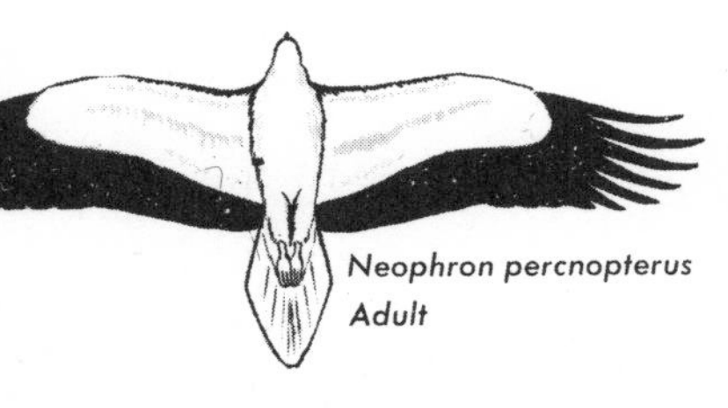

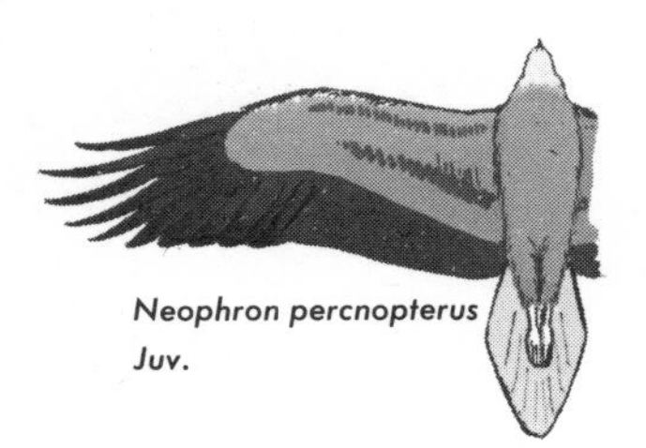

Lanceolate feathers at the ruff, tan or orange-buff; otherwise white above, tinged with varying amounts of light gray and tan; secondaries, dark brown, edged with light olive-gray; primaries, black; tail, white; below, including underwing coverts, white, tinged with tan or orange-buff; head and throat, bare, except for fine white bristles; crop, completely bare.

Immature (third year)—ruff and primaries, sepia; otherwise ochre-brown, with white feather-edging and spotting.

Juvenile (and second year)—sepia or dark brown, feather-edged and spotted with buff. (Young birds have short tufts of black bristles on the head and throat, a mixture of white and black down on the back of the head and throat, as well as a thicker, less extended ruff which, through various molts, is replaced entirely by bristles and an adult type of ruff.)

Beak, brown or yellow (juvenile, paler); cere and bare skin of face, yellow; eyes, brown to dark orange; legs and feet, grayish-white to pale yellow. Size, 22–25 inches.

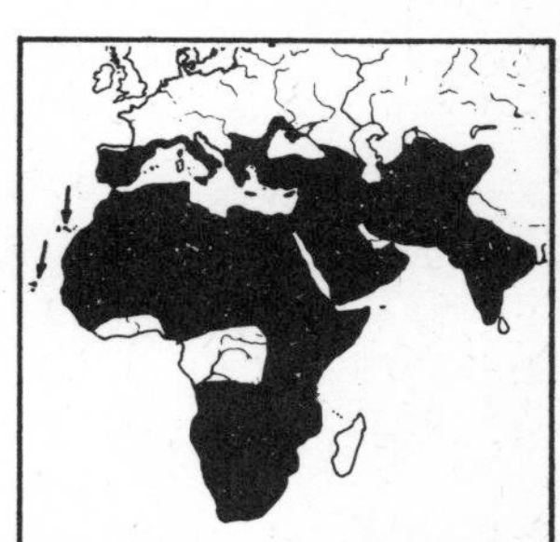
NEOPHRON PERCNOPTERUS

HABITS

Egyptian Vultures soar as high and effortlessly as the griffons of the Mediterranean, Africa, and Asia, and may—like these large scavengers—roost on rocks, also on trees, buildings, etc. On the ground they stride about, their bodies tilting from side to side, and even run with ease. They inhabit desert, steppes, savannas, and tropical regions, especially on the Indian peninsula. Together with the Hooded Vultures, they are the least discriminating of the Old World scavengers, feeding on all kinds of animal and vegetable matter, including dates, human excrement, garbage, and carrion; also rats and other small mammals, which are probably picked up alive by these scavengers as they follow the plow; and live crustaceans taken from the water. They are attracted in numbers to the streets of towns and villages in northern Africa, Asia Minor, and India, and in tropical Africa they patrol the grasslands that have recently been burned off, looking for scorched animals. Less sociable than griffons, they are seen singly or in pairs at times.

Egyptian Vultures nest in rock clefts and crevices and on narrow ledges that provide a view of the surrounding territory; or, if cliffs are not available (as in India), in old ruins or date palms and other trees. In the untidy pile of sticks may be found remains of their food as well as hair and skin that may have been brought to the nest as lining. Both sexes take part in nest-building, incubating the eggs (about 42 days), and feeding the young by regurgitation. Generally two eggs are laid, either creamy-white or tinted pink and mottled with pale to deep reddish-brown, the markings sometimes concentrated on the larger end.

They apparently wander in search of new feeding grounds after the breeding season is over.

A very silent species, the Egyptian Vulture has never been heard to utter any sounds other than the usual vulture grunts and hisses of anger while asserting its claim to food—except a "disagreeable whining mew" (in India).

More vulturine than eagle-like in appearance, because of its long neck and bare face, the Palm-nut Vulture *(Gypohierax angolensis)* is primarily a vegetarian and scavenger.—*Photographed at the New York Zoological Society.*

GENUS *GYPOHIERAX*

Gypohierax of Africa has the very long neck and small head of a vulture and the large, deep beak of a sea eagle. The flesh of the region around the eyes, lores, and at the sides of the throat is bare. The legs are covered in front with large hexagonal scales; the long toes are reticulate; and the claws, also long, sharply curved, and grooved underneath, are similar to *Haliaetus'*. The sexes are alike in size and coloring of the plumage. In flight, the black-and-white markings of the adults are distinctive, and the young can be easily separated from young Egyptian Vultures (of similar size and coloring) by their shape—broad rounded wings and short square tail.

Palm-nut Vulture (*Gypohierax angolensis*)

DESCRIPTION (AFRICA)

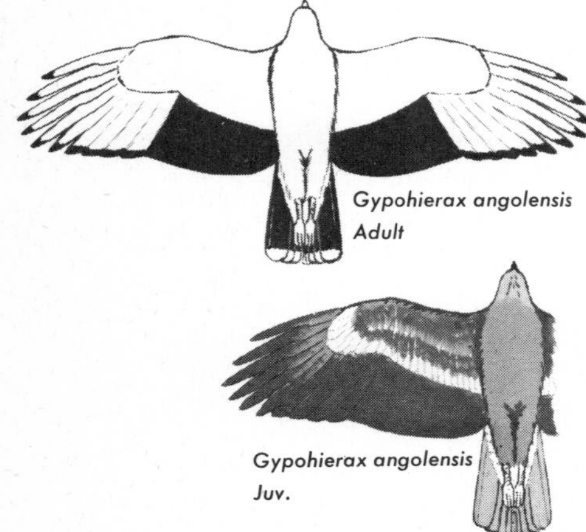

Head, neck, lesser and median wing coverts, and entire underparts, white; back, greater wing coverts, and secondaries, black; primaries, white, tipped in black; tail, black, with a white terminal band.

Immature—over-all sepia, with fine sandy spotting on head and wing coverts; wings and tail, dark brown to black.

Juvenile—light tawny-olive, with lower back and flight feathers darkening to sepia; tail, sepia-mottled and terminally banded in buff.

Beak, yellow (juvenile, black); cere, greenish-gray; bare skin of face, orange (juvenile, dull yellow); eyes, yellow; legs and feet, pinkish-yellow; claws, black. Size 20–23 inches.

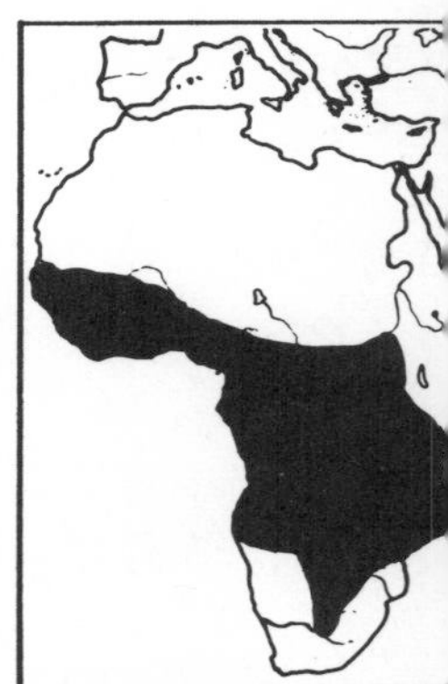

GYPOHIERAX ANGOLEN

HABITS

The Palm-nut Vulture lives along the coast, estuaries, and rivers, but especially where oil and raffia palms grow. It eats the pericarp or fleshy covering of the nuts of these trees and has been seen boring holes in the stems looking for insect larvae. It also picks up fish that have been stranded along river banks and bays; takes freshwater crabs and crayfish from mangrove swamps; and feeds on carrion. Only rarely does it attack mammals or birds on the ground.

During the nesting season (the middle of the dry season in western Africa) the birds indulge in aerial dives from high up, like sea eagles. Both sexes take part in building the bulky stick nest, which is placed in a silk-cotton or ironwood tree above the canopy in the gallery forest. Where oil palms or raffia palms occur throughout the savanna belt, pairs build in these trees and, according to one account, may even use the large old nut clusters of the raffia palm, three feet in diameter and five feet deep, which are hollow inside and provide shelter for the young. The single egg is white, heavily blotched with dark brown and chocolate and clouded with lilac or pale brown. A young bird in a raffia palm nest at Mtunzini, Zululand, was fed—exclusively, at first—with bits of pericarp from the fruit of the tree (by the female), then, after about a month, gathered nuts for itself. However, according to other sources, the fledging period lasts more than 90 days. The old birds use nearby roosts.

The nestling cries incessantly and plaintively, but the adults are usually silent near the nest. Coughing, barking, or growling sounds accompany threat actions, and a "mewing" call recorded may be part of their courtship display.

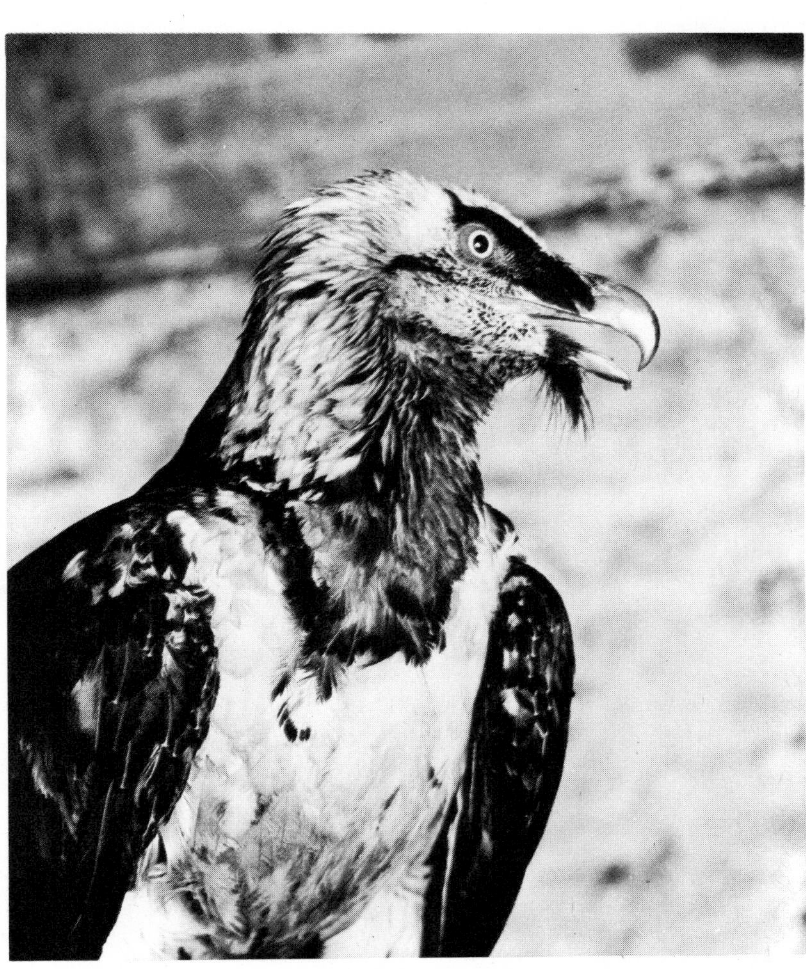

White feathering on the head and chest of a young Lammergeier *(Gypaetus barbatus)* from Tibet, is common in central Asia.—*Photographed at the New York Zoological Society.*

GENUS *GYPAETUS*

No one can decide whether the Lammergeier is a vulture or an eagle. Its face is not only feathered, but bearded, and the mane of long feathers on the back of the head and neck stands out in wild array. The legs have full pantaloons. Complementing the large hooked beak, the feet are as prehensile as any hawk's or eagle's, and the claws are long and sharply curved. In flight the immense wings (spanning eight or nine feet) are pointed like a falcon's and the long tail is wedge shaped.

Lammergeier, or Bearded, Vulture
(*Gypaetus barbatus*)

DESCRIPTION (MOUNTAINS OF SOUTHERN EUROPE, ISLANDS OF THE MEDITERRANEAN, AND ASIA MINOR)

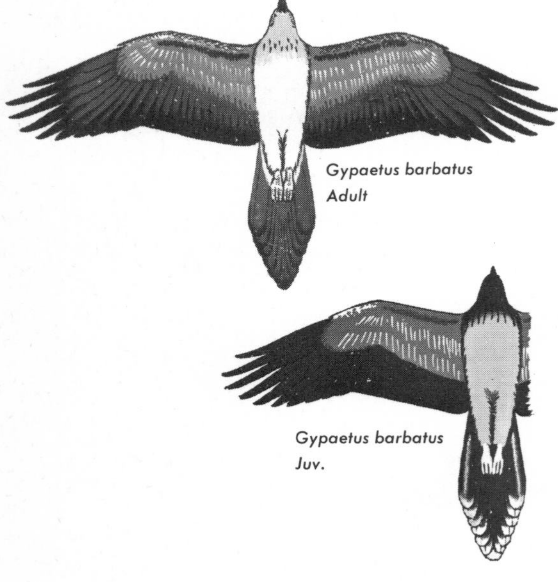

Head and neck, white to sandy, with black streaking; broad black patch extending from above the eye to the "beard" of black bristles on the chin; rest of upperparts, dark brown, with light olive-gray centers of the feathers becoming broader and more conspicuous on greater wing coverts, wings, lower back, and tail—and entirely shaft-streaked in white; underparts, sandy to yellow-orange with an amber-brown tinge, especially on the throat and breast. Dark-brown spotting on the chest is variable, sometimes absent.

Immature—has an entirely black head and neck; rest of upperparts, ochre-brown, becoming dark brown on greater wing coverts, wings, lower back, and tail—not distinctly shaft-striped, but conspicuously spotted with white throughout; underparts, mixed light amber-brown and yellow-orange.

Juvenile—shows some buff streaking on the dark head and neck, especially the throat; above, spotted like immature; underparts, uniformly ochre-brown.

Beak, blue-gray (young bird, bare bluish-gray face and greenish beak); eyes, yellow-orange (juvenile, hazel-brown, with the "white" of the eye vivid orange); feet, gray (young, yellowish-white); claws, brown (juvenile, black). Size, 39–42 inches.

VARIATIONS

The largest of the Lammergeiers (46 inches) found in northern and central Asia are nearly white below, except for a completely spotted chest. The Himalayan birds, however, are heavily tinged with dark orange on the throat and chest, and variably spotted, like smaller (35–38 inches) African birds. (Young, similar to European immatures and juveniles.)

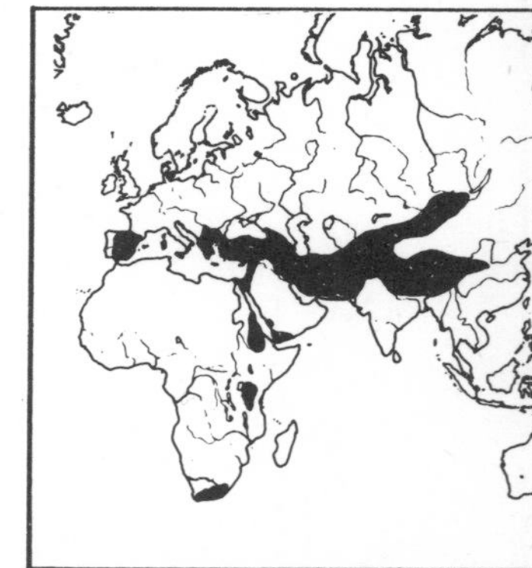

GYPAETUS BARBATUS

In its remote mountain stronghold, the Lammergeier *(Gypaetus barbatus)* frequently waits—either by preference or through shyness—for vultures to clean off the bones of a carcass.—*Adult, photographed in Spain by Eric Hosking.*

HABITS

In the ancient world this bird was named the "lamb vulture," and in the Himalayas today some Lammergeiers feed their young on dead lambs. Their present-day distribution is confined to the high steppes of central Asia, the Himalayas (to at least 25,500 feet), and the rugged mountains of Corsica, Sardinia, Sicily, Spain, and eastern Africa.

The Lammergeier is often seen on garbage heaps at hill stations in the Himalayas, and until recently frequented railroad yards in eastern Europe. In this region it has been exterminated by man—not breeding in Bavaria since 1855, in the Swiss Alps since 1886, or in the Carpathian Mountains since about 1935.

On its long wings the Lammergeier courses over wide stretches of countryside seeking wounded, sick, or dead mammals and birds and even tortoises, which it smashes on the rocks as it does the larger bones of mammals. It may, however, swallow whole bones up to the size of a femur of a lamb. Large animals may be taken by surprise as this immense bird swoops down into steep valleys from the tops of precipices, in the manner of an eagle.

The nest of the Lammergeier is placed in a cave on the side of a cliff or on a ledge protected by an overhang; sometimes also on low rocks rising from arid plains. In Spain one structure was entirely made of branches of pine, oak, and juniper, between 16 and 30 feet long, with a thick lining about a yard across of pure sheep's wool. There were only a few sticks by the wall of the cave, but branches had been piled high on the outside edge. In the Himalayas grass, skins, bones or rags, pieces of sacking, and even bits of green bottles have been added to nests.

In Europe and Africa the Lammergeier lays one or two eggs, either plain dull white or with orange or reddish-brown blotches and speckling; in Asia, two and, rarely, three eggs. But no more than one young bird is usually reared. Eight weeks' incubation is followed by three months or more in the nest. The fledgling is fed at first (four to six weeks) by regurgitation, like a vulture, and in the later stages of development the adults bring food to the nest in their feet. At two months the young bird is probably ready to stand and walk as well as eat by itself.

The call is a ringing, whistling sound.

SUBFAMILY CIRCINAE

(Harriers or Marsh Hawks and Crane Hawks)

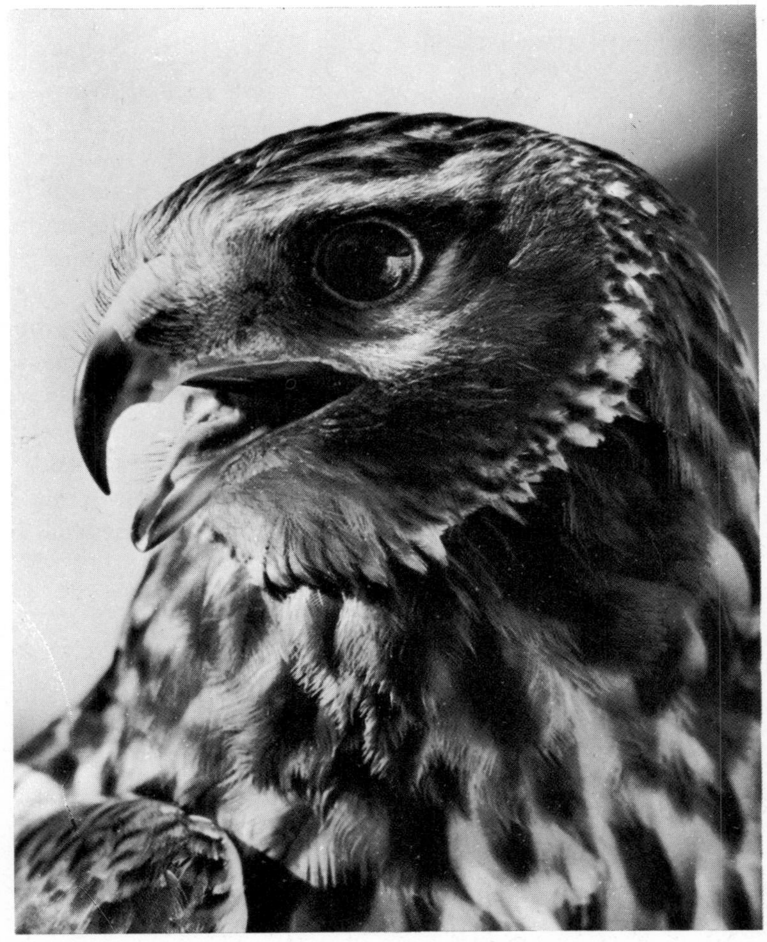

This adult female Marsh Hawk (*Circus cyaneus*) belongs to a Holarctic species that is perhaps the least specialized of the many harriers of worldwide distribution. The facial disc and distinct ruff are characteristic of *Circus*.

GENUS *CIRCUS*

Ten species of harriers (*Circus*) are the diurnal counterparts of the short-eared owls (*Asio*), for they hunt the same marshes and dry open country the world over and may even share the same roosts on the ground (see Chapter 3). They may be found nearly everywhere at one season or another except on the most barren tundras and polar ice caps, the islands of the southwest Pacific, and the Galapagos Archipelago. Since they are, almost without exception, ground-nesting hawks, the open spaces are their major ecological requirement.

The Holarctic Marsh Hawk (or Hen Harrier, as *C. cyaneus* is known in Europe), the African Marsh Harrier (*C. ranivorus*), and the Cinereous Harrier (*C. cinereus*) of western and southern South America seem to be most adaptable to a great variety of open grassy districts in boreal, temperate, or steppe climates. The Cinereous Harrier breeds from lowlands in Chile up to 12,000 feet in Ecuador. Two smaller species, the Pallid Harrier (*C. macrourus*) in the dry climate zone of Turkistan and the western Palearctic Montagu's Harrier (*C. pygargus*), may be somewhat competitive where their ranges meet in the central Palearctic region. The Pied Harrier (*C. melanoleucus*) of northeastern Asia and the Black Harrier (*C. maurus*) of southern Africa may be descendants of a more widely ranging Montagu's Harrier of ancient times.

The Marsh Harriers (*C. aeruginosus*) of Palearctic and tropical distribution are much more restricted to low marshy regions with open reeds or slowly running water and to river deltas. Ranging through the tropical eastern half of South America, the Long-winged Harrier (*C. buffoni*) is most numerous on the pampas of Argentina, Uruguay, and Chile. The Spotted Harrier (*C. assimilis*) of Australia is the only tree-nesting bird of the group, but it hunts low over the ground and is as much at home perching on a knoll or a fence post as any of its relatives.

The harrier is a slender, long-legged hawk with an owl-like facial ruff, long cere, large nostrils covered with loral bristles, and a small compressed beak. The tarsi are mostly bare with a single row of transverse scutes down the front and on the long toes; the claws are sharply curved. In flight the wings appear long, narrow, and pointed, and the tail is also long. The most important field mark of many of these low-coursing hawks is a conspicuous white rump patch.

In most species there is distinct sexual dimorphism; females tend to be brown and white or entirely brown, contrasting with the gray and white plumage of the males. Immature males and females (of those species which have a distinct second-year plumage) usually resemble the adult female; juveniles are darker below. Dark phases are common.

Marsh Hawk or Hen Harrier (*Circus cyaneus*)

DESCRIPTION (NORTH AMERICA)

Female—dark gray-brown above, streaked on the head in dark tawny and spotted with white and buff on the mantle, sides of neck, and wing coverts; white rump patch is distinctive in flight, wings have some gray coloring but at rest or from above appear dark gray-brown, barred with dark brown; tail, medium olive-gray, barred with dark gray-brown; forehead, patch around eyes, chin, white; face, dark tawny, streaked and bordered with a dark gray-brown ruff; underparts, white, most heavily streaked with dark gray-brown and tinted buff on the chest; thighs, buff. *Male*—dove-gray above, with an olive-brown cast and fine black shaft-striping; like the female it has a conspicuous white rump patch which shows in flight; tail is barred with dark brown, the subterminal band broadest; forehead and chin, touches of white; face and chest, dove-gray; rest of underparts, white, spotted with amber-brown (entire undersurface of wings, except for dark tips of primaries and barred secondaries, is white in flight.)

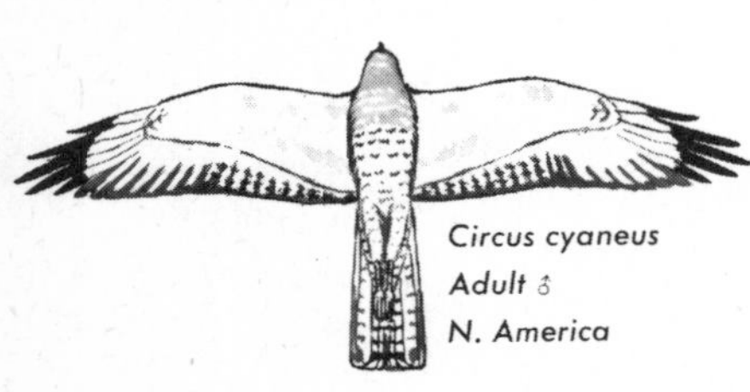
Circus cyaneus Adult ♂ N. America

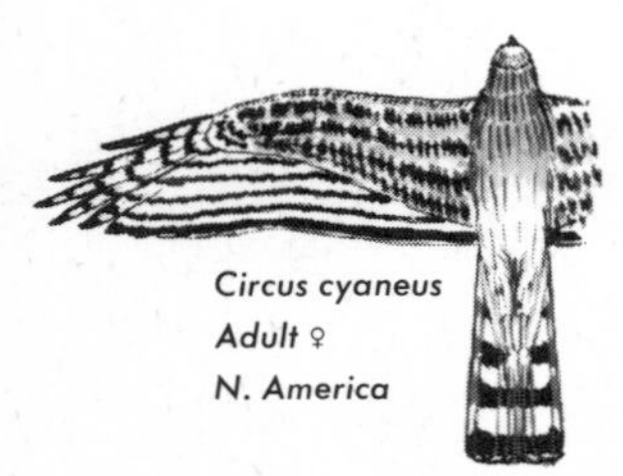
Circus cyaneus Adult ♀ N. America

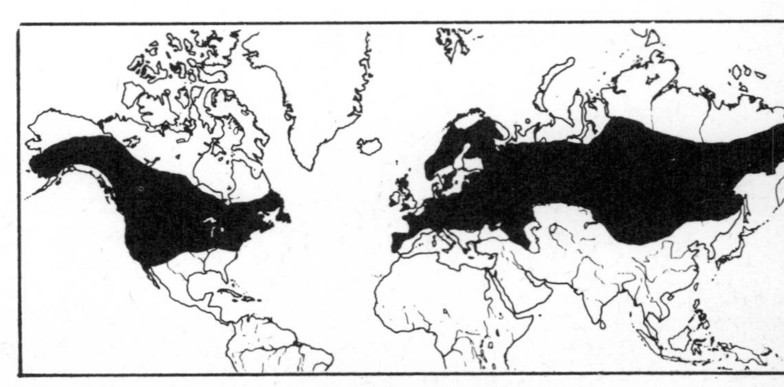
CIRCUS CYANEUS

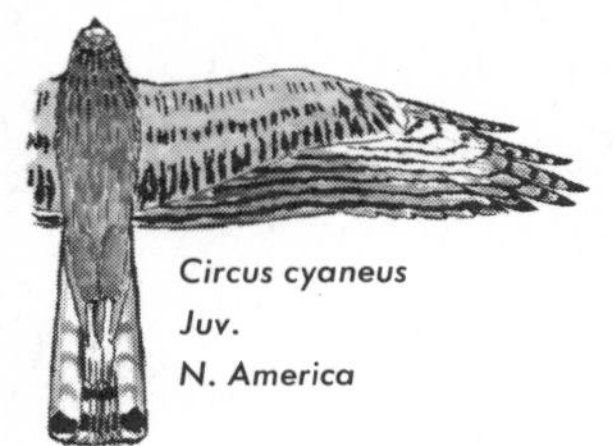

Juvenile (*sexes alike*)—similar to adult female but completely light cinnamon to cinnamon-colored below, and streaked on the chest and belly. Young also have a white rump.

Beak, black; cere, greenish-yellow; eyes (*female*), pale gray-brown to dark brown, or (*male*), yellow; legs and feet (*female and young*), orange, (*male*), pale yellow; claws, black. Size, 18–22 inches.

VARIATIONS

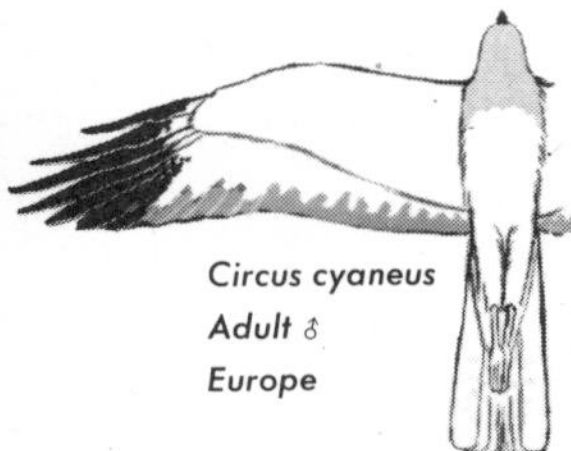

Hen Harriers in Europe are similar to North American birds in size and coloring. The *female and the juveniles of both sexes,* however, are more heavily and completely striped below. The *immature male* resembles the adult North American male. The *adult male* Hen Harrier in Europe is lighter above and has a pure white belly and an unbarred tail.

Male Hen Harrier (*Circus cyaneus*), Europe.—*Photograph by Eric Hosking.*

OTHER OLD WORLD SPECIES

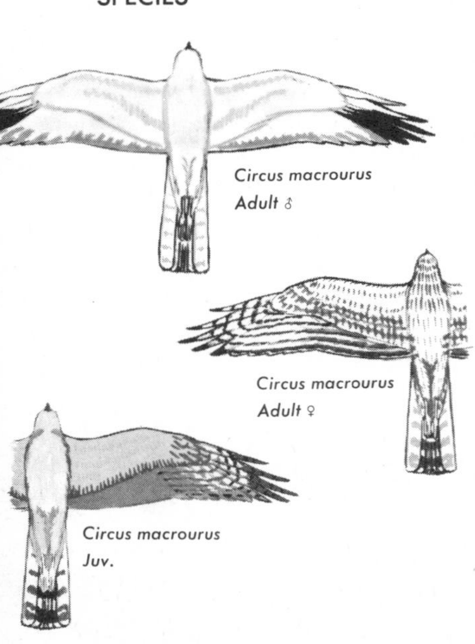

The females, immatures, and juveniles of two smaller Eurasian harriers—the Pallid Harrier (*C. macrourus*), 17–19 inches, and Montagu's Harrier (*C. pygargus*), 16–18 inches—all have white rump patches, are confusingly like those of the Hen Harrier, and are practically indistinguishable from each other. The males of these three species, however, are not alike; the *male* Pallid Harrier has nearly white face and sides of neck and chest, but the pure white rump patch is absent. (Juveniles of both sexes have solid, light amber-brown underparts.)

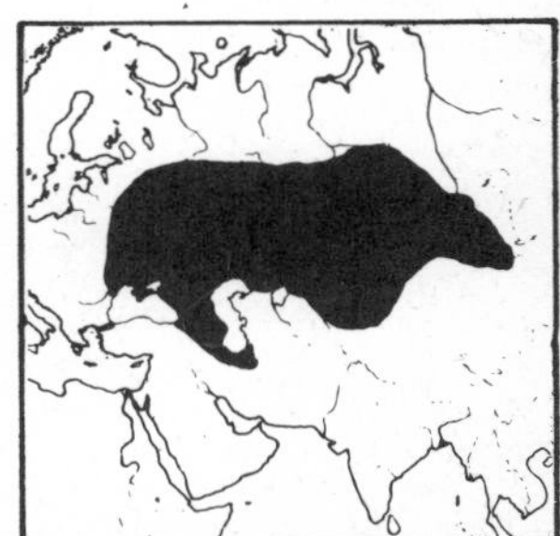

CIRCUS MACROURUS

Montagu's Harrier has narrower wings than either the Hen Harrier or Pallid Harrier. The *male* is darker above—medium- to slate-gray, with no white rump patch; has a narrow black band on the wing coverts; and also more black primaries; the breast is dove-gray and the belly white, striped with medium yellow-brown. Dark-phase birds also occur, with the *females* presumably dark brown with barred tails, and the *males* grayer, with unbarred tails.

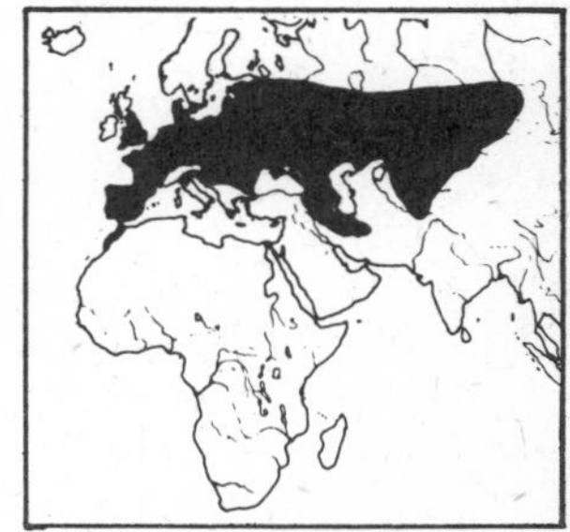

CIRCUS PYGARGUS

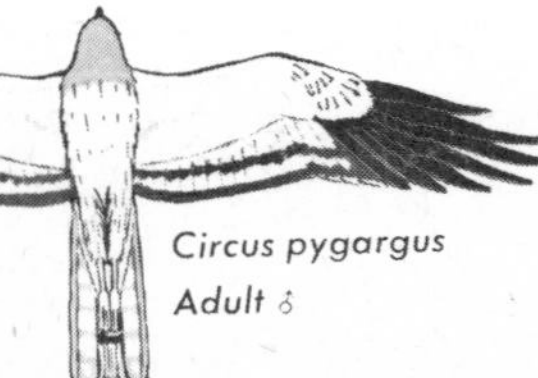

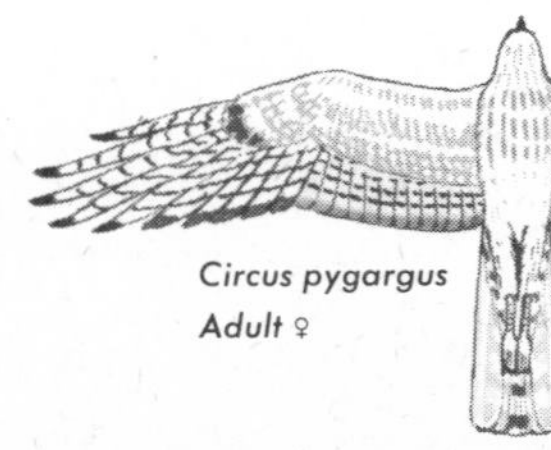

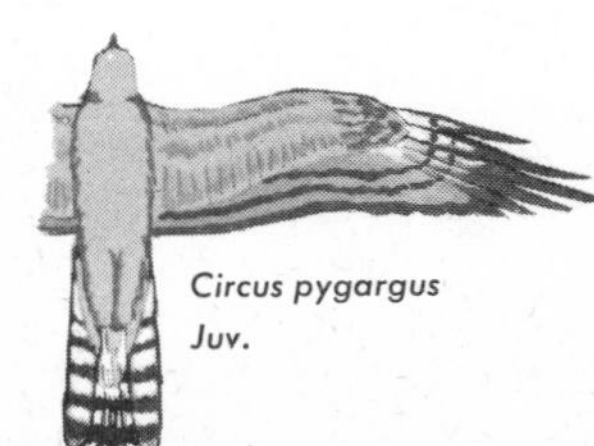

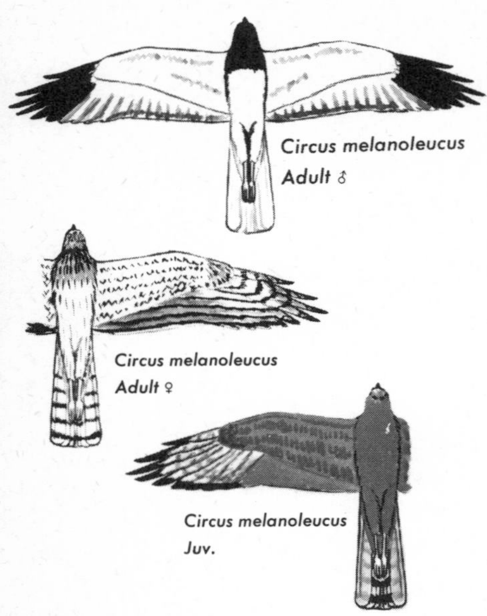

The Pied Harrier of northern Asia (*C. melanoleucus*), 15–18 inches, has silver-gray wings and tail, similar to the Marsh Harrier (*C. aeruginosus*). Adult *male,* glossy black, except for conspicuous white rump patch and shoulder patches; lower breast, belly and thighs, white. *Female*—sepia to dark brown except for white rump patch and striped belly. There is a slight gray cast to the wing coverts, wings, and tail.

CIRCUS MELANOLEUCUS

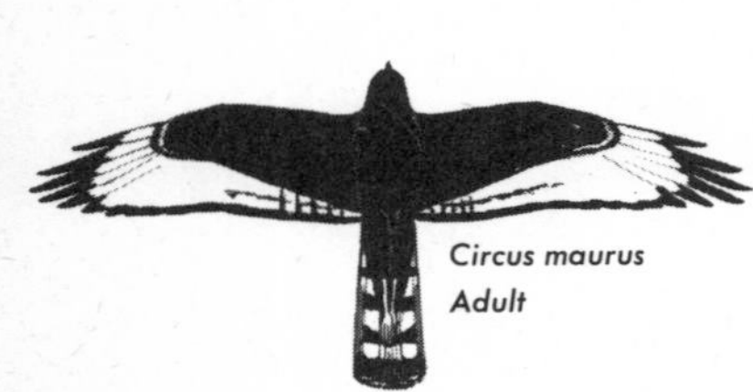

The Black Harrier (*C. maurus*) of South Africa, about 17 inches, is completely dark brown to black (male and female) except for the white rump patch and gray-banded tail; in flight, it has extensive white on primaries and white-banded undersurface of tail. (Juvenile—chocolate-colored above, streaked on head and neck in buff or white, and feather-edged in amber-brown; like the adult, it has a white rump patch and banded tail. Below, ochre-brown, spotted on chest and striped on flanks in dark brown.)

CIRCUS MAURUS

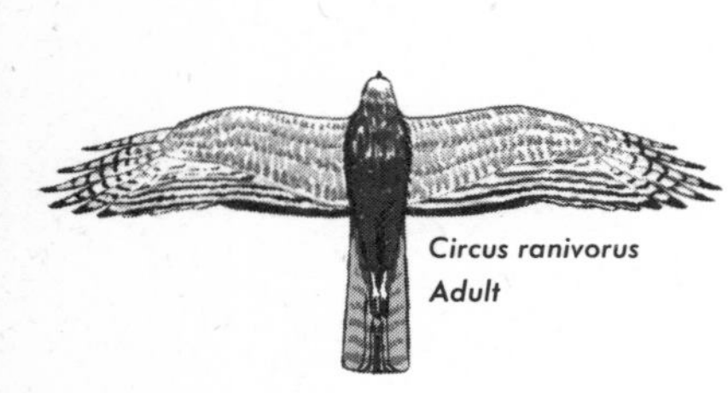

The African Marsh Harrier (*C. ranivorus*), 16–18½ inches, in southern and eastern Africa, is also very dark, with the sexes hardly differing. *Male* has silver-gray secondaries, greater wing coverts, and tail distinctly barred in dark brown; head, darkly streaked; chest, dark brown striped in buff; lower belly and thighs, nearly solid sienna-brown. *Female* is similar, but lacks silver coloring on the wings and tail. (Juveniles resemble adult females, but have a light patch on back of head.) A dark phase occurs.

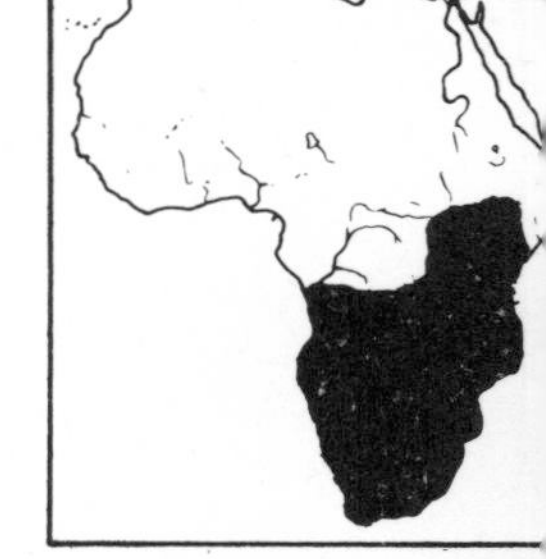
CIRCUS RANIVORUS

OTHER NEW WORLD SPECIES

The Cinereous Harrier (*C. cinereus*) of South America is slightly smaller than the North American Marsh Hawk. The *male* is very similar in color, but barred below. The *female,* broadly barred below in amber-brown and white, has gray secondaries, wing coverts, and tail, like the male. (Young, lighter below than North American juveniles, have a dark throat patch.)

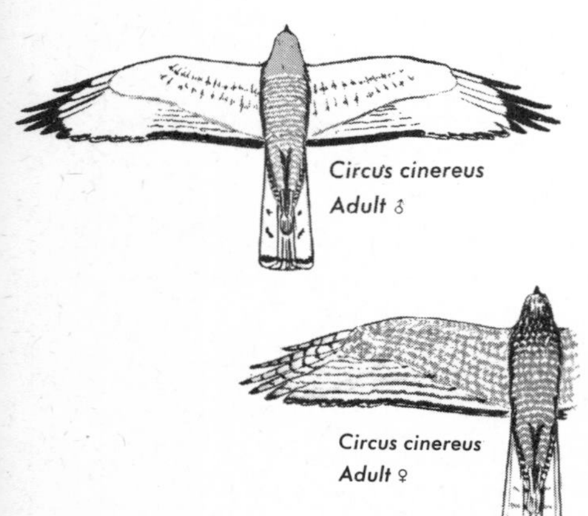

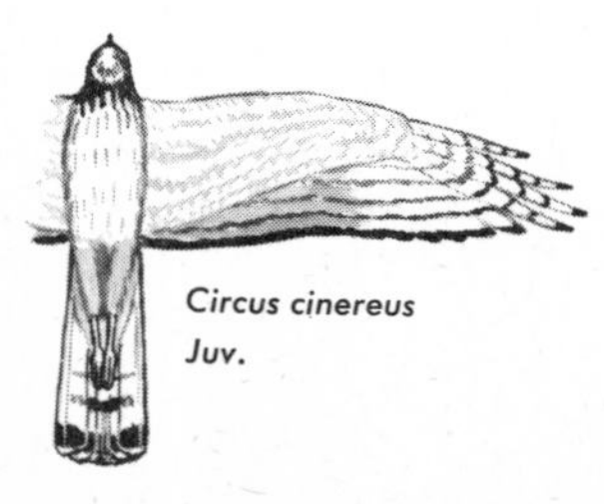

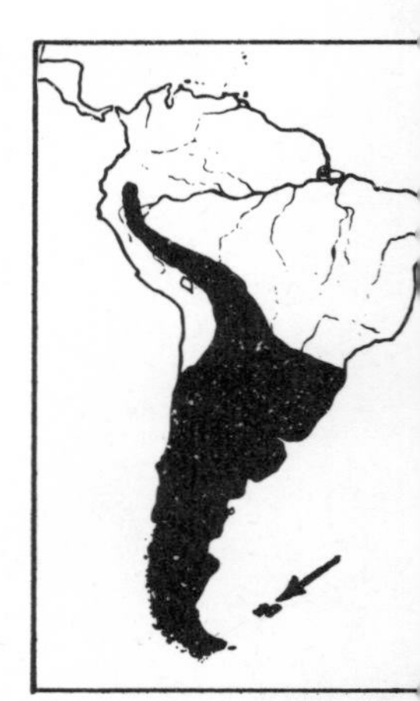
CIRCUS CINEREUS

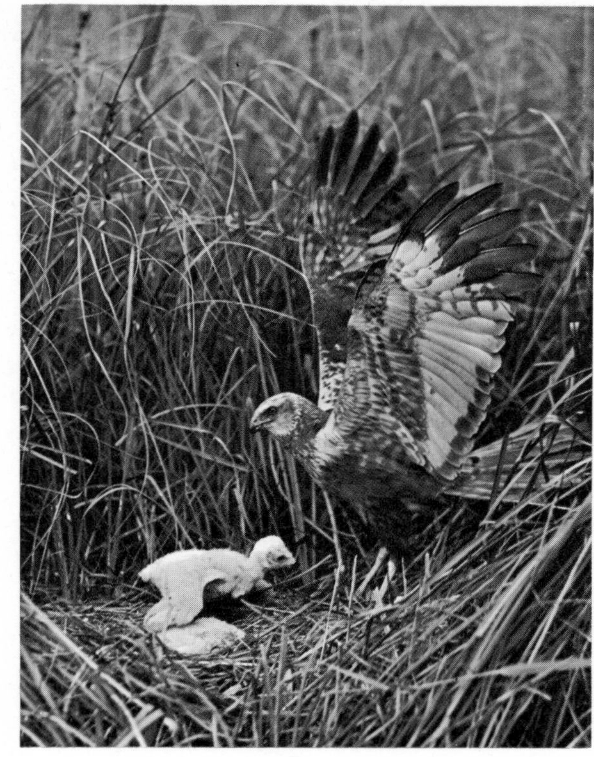

Marsh Harrier *(Circus aeruginosus)* and young.—*Photographed by Eric Hosking.*

Marsh Harrier (*Circus aeruginosus*)

DESCRIPTION (EUROPE, ASIA MINOR, AND WESTERN ASIA)

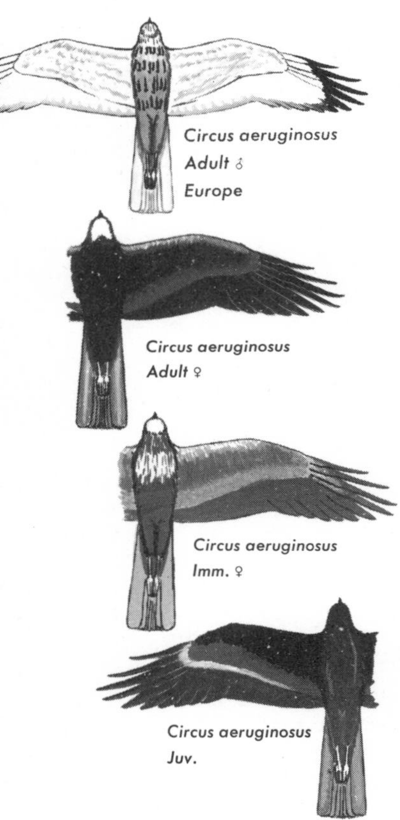

Female—crown, nape, and sometimes part of mantle, buff to yellow-orange, streaked in chocolate; rest of upperparts, chocolate, feather-edged on wing and tail coverts with buff to light amber-brown; distinct light patches on the shoulders reach the bend of the wing in some individuals; wings and tail, chocolate, tipped in buff or white; face, sides of neck, and underparts, brown with buff patches on throat and, often, also on breast. *Male*—face, entire neck, mantle, and underparts, amber-brown, streaked with black or chocolate; upperparts, chocolate to dark brown, feather-edged in buff like female, but greater wing coverts, secondaries, and tail, silver-gray; primaries, dark brown; no white shows on rump.

Immature female (second summer)—similar to adult, but with light patch on upper belly; *immature male,* like female, second summer, but wings and tail have a silvery cast; belly and thighs may be more uniformly dark; outer tail feathers buff to yellow-orange and may or may not be barred dark brown. *Juveniles* (*both sexes*), much like adult female—solidly dark with light head, chin, and feather-edging.

Some juvenile and immature females may have completely dark heads.

Dark-phase birds occur in Russia and are dark brown with only a small buff or light amber-brown patch at back of neck, streaked in black. Young seem to be paler.

Beak, black; eyes, yellow (*male*), or brown (*female* and *young*), but a very old female's eyes turn yellow, like male's; cere, greenish-yellow; legs and feet, yellow; claws, black. Size, 18–21 inches.

VARIATIONS

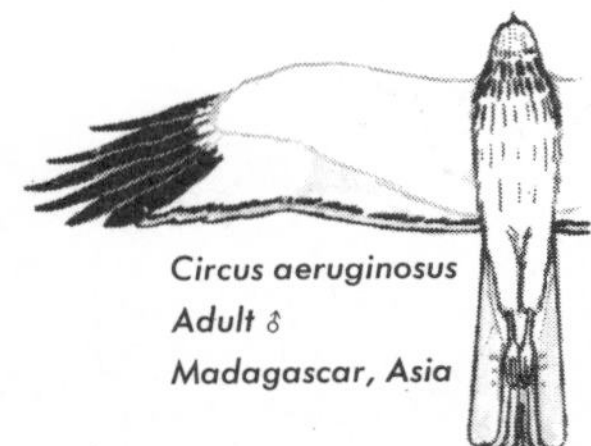

The *male* of the Mediterranean population in southern Spain and northern Africa is much darker above; head and neck black, streaked with white or buff. Throughout Siberia and northern Asia and on Reunion Island and Madagascar, *males* are black above; head, neck, and most of underparts, white, streaked in black; lower belly and thighs, pure white. The *females* are sepia above and buff-colored below, entirely streaked in chocolate; have banded wings and tail. (Adults and immatures of both sexes have conspicuous white rump patches, but juveniles lack them.)

In the Australian region and southwest Pacific, the *males* are black, streaked on the head in buff to light amber-brown and having the characteristic gray wing and tail characters and white tail coverts; underparts white, finely streaked in sepia; thighs, white. *Females* appear more chocolate-colored above, have dark wings and barred tail; underparts, mixed amber-brown and chocolate, becoming almost clear amber-brown on thighs, and finely shaft-streaked throughout in black. The young are light amber-brown below, darkly striped (*male,* with grayer wings and tail).

Size, 18–21 inches, the smallest on Reunion Island and the largest in Australia and northern Asia.

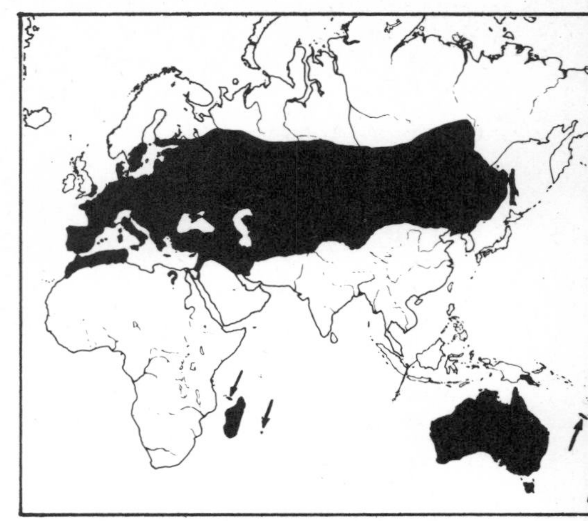
CIRCUS AERUGINOSUS

OTHER OLD WORLD SPECIES

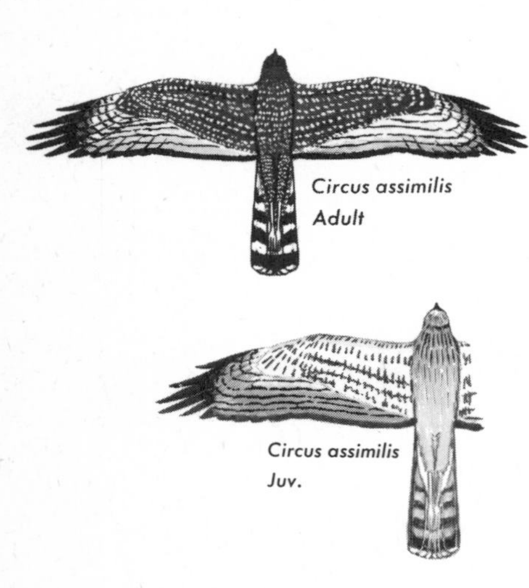

Fantastically polka-dotted plumage distinguishes the Spotted Harrier of the Australian region (*C. assimilis*), 18 inches in the islands north of Australia to 22 inches on the continent. Sexes are alike—in temperate Australia, olive-brown above; head, sides of face, and throat streaked, and shoulders marked with patches of sienna; rest of wing coverts, spotted with white or buff; secondaries, lower back, and tail, dove-gray, barred darker; rump, spotted in white; below on neck, band of olive-brown; rest of underparts, including underwing coverts, yellow-brown, spotted in white. (Juveniles—sepia above, with streaking on crown and shoulder patches; broad feather-edging on wing coverts and back, amber-brown and buff; tail, darker than adults', is not as distinctly barred; underparts, light amber-brown to white, streaked in sepia.) In northwestern Australia, Northern Territory, Sumba Island, and Celebes the coloring is brighter, upperparts of adults medium gray with a blue cast, underparts deepening to rich sienna-brown. (The young are dark brown above with amber-brown markings; underparts, amber-brown to buff.)

CIRCUS ASSIMILIS

OTHER NEW WORLD SPECIES

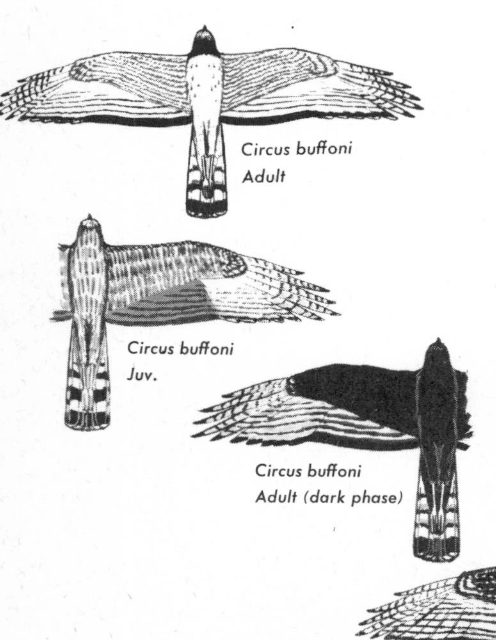

Light and dark phases have been noted in the Long-winged Harrier (*C. buffoni*), 18–21 inches, of South America. Light phase: *male*—black with a chocolate cast above, except for a white rump patch; secondaries and tail, light to medium gray, barred with dark brown. Black head and neck show distinct white eyebrows, forehead, and chin, as well as some light spotting on the ruff; throat, black; rest of underparts, white, with a few dark brown spots; flanks, indistinctly barred with cinnamon-brown; thighs, white. *Female*—browner above and more heavily spotted below. (Immature male resembles adult female; immature female is sienna-brown below. Juveniles—entirely and heavily streaked on underparts with sepia; thighs, sienna-brown.) The dark-phase adults (both sexes) have light markings on the head and a white-barred rump patch; wings and tail, barred black and white. (Young—entirely sepia to dark brown or with a white-spotted chest.)

CIRCUS BUFFONI

HABITS

The harriers may be recognized by their flight—cruising only a few feet from the ground, with leisurely wing beats and swift glides. This systematic coursing or beating of the bush may flush a bird or startle a small mammal or reptile into revealing its presence. Then the harrier drops suddenly and seizes its prey.

In the breeding season the males circle and soar high in the air, calling and performing spectacular dives and somersaults. The displays vary in the different species. The Marsh Harrier male ascends to a great height and plunges downward for as much as 200 feet, with an upward sweep at the end. For half an hour at a time the bird will completely "loop the loop," or in another version, tilt over sidewise and spiral downward, then rise and repeat the act again and again. Sometimes he carries prey in his talons for the female, who joins him in the air. The cock builds a second nest, on which the pair alight after circling flights, and he may bring offerings of food to her there.

The males of the Marsh Hawks, or Hen Harriers, and their relatives, vary steep diving with tumbling, in which they are joined by the females. Occasionally they will flip over and drift momentarily on their backs in mid-air.

The display of Montagu's Harrier hardly differs from that of the Hen Harrier, but the ascents and descents are shorter and less strenuous, often omitting the somersaults and acrobatics. No exact comparison has been made of the habits of the Pallid Harrier.

The food of these harriers is very similar: amphibians and small reptiles; mammals (especially hamsters, rats, mice, and young rabbits); small- to medium-sized marsh-breeding birds and their nestlings as well as eggs; some small land birds (larks, and song thrushes); also fish and, in nearly all species, large insects. The prey characteristically taken depends entirely on the locality and the season. Both the Pallid and Montagu's harriers feed heavily on migratory locusts on their wintering grounds in southwestern Asia and tropical Africa. Until disease recently wiped out much of the rabbit populations of Australia and New Zealand, they were the main year-round prey of Marsh Harriers, and their breeding cycles consequently affected the numbers of harriers.

In the Palearctic region the male Marsh Harrier appears to take more part in nest-building and incubation of the eggs than either his tropical or subtropical counterparts, and he also builds a second nest which is used during courtship for perching and ritual feeding. Nests, usually in swamps, are bulkier than those of other harriers. They are elaborate affairs, built just above the high tide or flood level of dead reed stems, sedges, water plants, with thorns or branches of alder and willow worked in. The linings are of finer marsh grasses. In several species three to eight (but usually four to five) white eggs are rarely marked. The eggs are laid at intervals of two to three or even four to five days, and each requires about 36 days' incubation before hatching. During this period both sexes (but mostly the female) sit very close. The male either brings food to the nest or calls his mate off, with a rather high-pitched mewing sound, to a "feeding table" (which may be the alternate nest) some yards distant.

In Australia, at least, when a clutch of five eggs is laid, the hen usually ceases to incubate after the third egg has hatched, so that there are seldom as many as four or five young raised. When the oldest nestling is about four days, and the youngest 24 hours old, the hen is away hunting, or perched on a fence post or knoll nearby, while the male hunts and brings in the food. The hen does all the feeding of the young, until at two weeks they can tear a carcass apart by themselves. At a month they are nearly grown, and at six weeks they are fully fledged and wandering about in the vicinity of the nest. For two or three weeks after the young can fly, the parents continue to hunt for them, and the nest or some part of the nesting territory serves as a roosting place for the brood at night.

The Marsh Hawk or Hen Harrier of North

Female Marsh Hawk (*Circus cyaneus*)

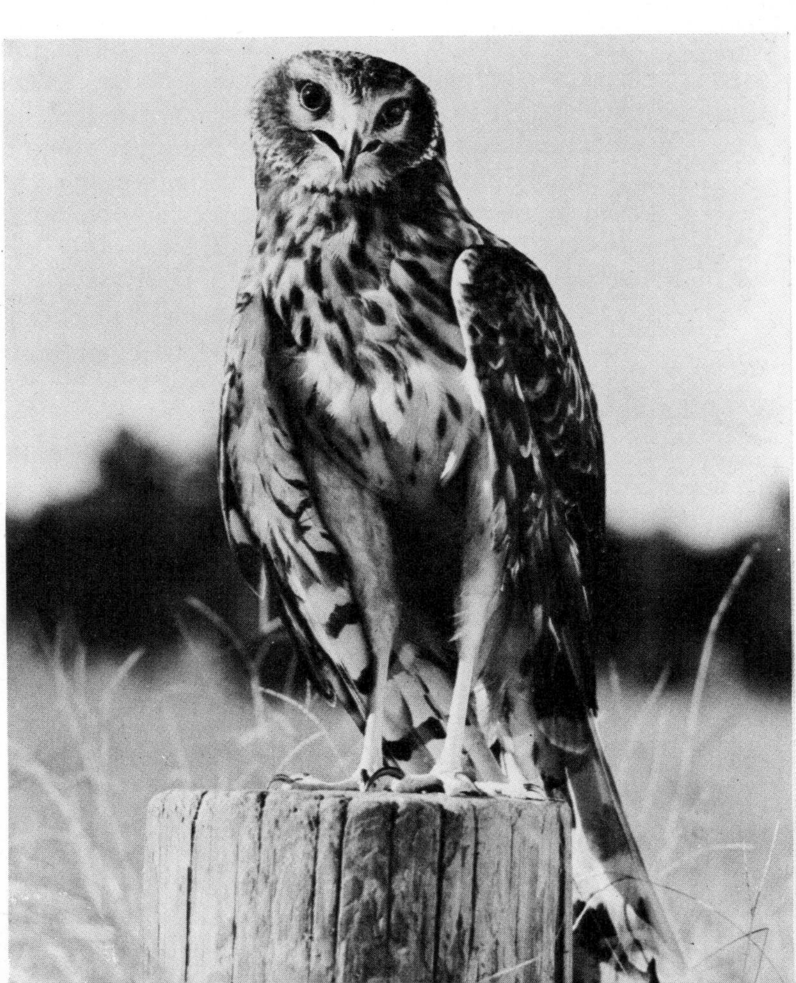

America and the Palearctic region, the Cinereous Harrier of South America, and the African Marsh Harrier build smaller nests above the water, in swamps, but also commonly line hollows in the ground—in cornfields, moorlands, and meadows. Around a thick pad of dead rushes or grasses, the female (mostly) arranges dry stalks of plants, such as heather and small twigs. The white eggs are seldom marked. In the north, three to eight eggs are laid but the tropical and subtropical species usually lay only three to four eggs. Incubation, mostly by the female, lasts 29 to 30 days for each of the eggs, which are laid at three- to four-day intervals. At first the male brings all the food to the nest. Later both parents hunt. The development of the young is similar to that of the Marsh Harrier (*C. aeruginosus*).

The nesting habits of the Pallid and Montagu's harriers are much the same as that of the Hen Harrier; but the males do all the hunting for their families until the young are able to fly. In 1952 unusual weather conditions brought the Pallid Harrier to northern Germany and Scandinavia, far north of its normal breeding limit in Europe (55° N). This circumstance gave ornithologists in western Europe a chance to observe Pallid and Montagu's harriers breeding in the same region. The latter tends to be sociable on the continent—many pairs nesting close together in one marsh. One instance was noted in Sweden of "cooperation" between a Pallid Harrier male (with young in the nest but no mate), and a female Montagu's Harrier (still paired), which had evidently lost her young. Both males were feeding the female, who in turn fed the Pallid Harrier's young, but the male Montagu's Harrier somewhat neglected his hunting responsibilities. Such "joint feeding" of one female by two males of different species is unknown in any other group of predatory birds, but does occur among song thrushes and house sparrows, song sparrows and American robins, nuthatches and starlings, and other passerines.

Nesting habits of the Pied Harrier, which lays four to five eggs, and the Black Harrier, for which three to four eggs are recorded, may be similar to those of Montagu's Harrier.

The Long-winged Harrier nests among vegetation in pasturelands and lays three uniformly white eggs.

The only member of the group which differs greatly from all the other harriers in its breeding behavior is the Spotted Harrier of the Australian region.

The nest of this species is a loose, almost flat, structure of small sticks placed among the dense branches of some small tree—usually 20 to 30 feet from the ground, but sometimes lower or on the ground. Two to four white eggs are laid. The birds provide a lining of green eucalyptus leaves.

The harriers are extremely nervous about their nesting territory. They may desert or even smash the eggs during incubation if disturbed. Once the eggs have hatched, however, they are not so easily discouraged and can be extremely aggressive in defense of the young. The fledglings can be moved from one side of a field to the other, and the parents will find and feed them.

At the end of the summer, harriers either disappear from their breeding grounds to nearby winter ranges, where they roost in communities (see Chapter 3), or travel considerable distances. The Palearctic species reach eastern and southern Africa, the steppes of central Asia, India, Burma, China, Japan, Malaya, and the Philippines. In North America there is a general withdrawal from the extreme northern part of the range. A few individuals remain during mild winters on the coastal marshes of southern New England, and in other localities throughout the northern part of the United States, but the majority follow the migrations of the small birds and spend the winter from the southern states to Baja California, Central America, and the Caribbean.

The harriers are generally silent birds, except for mewing calls during their courtship antics and a varied assortment of sounds in the immediate vicinity of the nest.

The spring note of the male Marsh Harrier is a plaintive "kweeoo," or variations including "kooa," "kooack," "kooih," "kwih," etc., uttered once or twice. The female has a more plaintive whistling note: "beeyuh," "bee," etc., often repeated several times. The female may also whine uneasily on the nest. Her alarm note is "chink-*a*-chink-*a*"; that of the male, "chuck-a-ra, chuck-a-ra." A shrill, feeble "kyik" has also been heard while the birds were playing together in autumn.

The usual cry of the Hen Harrier or Marsh Hawk, *male,* is "ke-ke-ke-ke—"; *female,* weaker, the notes running together, "pepepepe." In alarm: the *male* has a shrill scream, "cha-cha-cha-cha-cha-cha"; *female,* "kee, kee, kee, kee, kee, kee, kee, kee." Both also have many other notes. A "kak-kak-kak" call is recorded for the South American species.

The chattering note of Montagu's Harrier near the nest, "yick-yick-yick," is softer and higher pitched than the Hen Harrier's call, and other notes are very similar to Hen Harrier sounds, as are those of the Pallid Harrier.

A slender, lightweight predator, the Crane Hawk *(Geranospiza caerulescens)* appears much larger than it really is because of its fluffy gray plumage, which, when unworn, has a bluish or purplish bloom. The browner juvenile plumage is worn until the second fall season.

GENUS *GERANOSPIZA*

The Crane Hawk of tropical America corresponds in general build and habits to *Gymnogenys* of Africa and Madagascar, although not as powerful, and shares with these harrier hawks the adaptive feature of the double-jointed leg, which enables it to reach into holes in trees and into the subterranean burrows of frogs, crayfish, etc. The wings, however, are modified, more nearly the shape of the Cooper's Hawk, and the rounded tail is very long. The face is completely feathered.

Crane Hawk (*Geranospiza caerulescens*)

DESCRIPTION (NORTHERN SOUTH AMERICA AND TROPICAL ZONE OF EASTERN PANAMA)

Medium to slate-gray above and below; wings, dark gray to black; tail, black, with wide white bands on the central rectrices, and the outer ones yellow-orange; all the tail feathers are tipped in white. In flight the white median band on the undersurface of the primaries is distinctive.

Juvenile—olive-brown and medium gray with white face, forehead, and throat; underparts, mostly barred finely in white and tinged with sandy coloring; undertail coverts, barred sandy; sandy-colored tail also barred.

Beak, blue-black; cere, dull gray; eyes, yellow-orange; legs and feet, orange-red; claws, black. Size, 16½–18 inches.

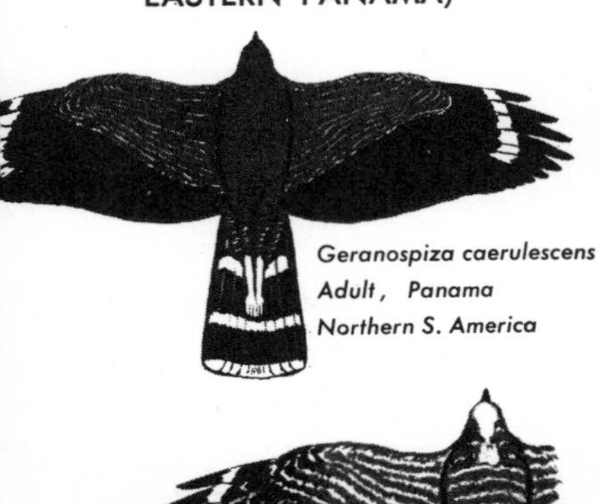

Geranospiza caerulescens
Adult, *Panama*
Northern S. America

Geranospiza caerulescens
Juv.

GERANOSPIZA CAERULESCENS

VARIATIONS

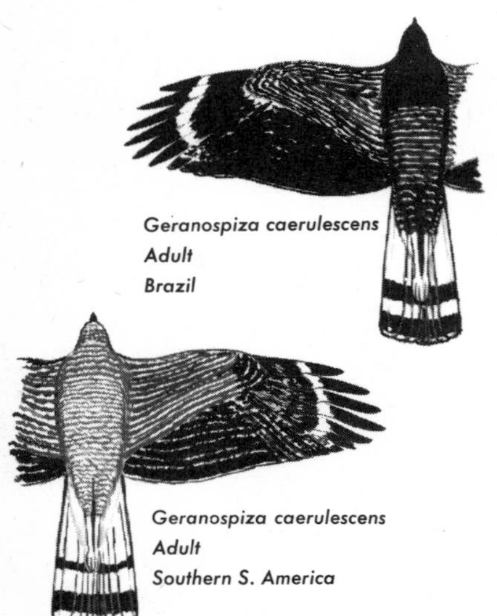

In Mexico and Central America the Crane Hawk is darker—slate-gray to dark gray, except in arid northern Mexico (Sonora)—and has orange-red eyes. The yellow-eyed birds inhabiting South America from the southern bank of the Amazon to northern Argentina, Paraguay, and Bolivia are either very dark above and below, with a solid gray chest and barring on the belly and thighs; or considerably paler—dove-gray to medium gray, and usually completely barred with white below, as well as mottled with white on wing coverts, wings, and lower back. The head may be solid gray or finely barred on the throat and lores in white; the plumage of the underparts is also white-tipped. (Juveniles—dark brown with broad, almost blotchy, feather-edging below; forehead, eyebrows, sides of face, and throat, more or less streaked with buff-white; coloring of eyes and feet, paler.)

HABITS

Although commonly found along streams and near water, the Crane Hawk is also resident in arid regions and seems, in Central America, at least, to be a lowland species (between 1,500 and 2,000 feet). Its usual wont is to scramble about in the branches and up and down the trunks of trees, sticking its head into holes, perhaps to feed on bee larvae, ants, or eggs and young of birds (although small birds have not been seen mobbing this predator, as they do *Gymnogenys* in Africa). It is known to feed on small snakes, including coral snakes, and lizards. The northern population keeps to the woods in spring and summer, but during the winter George M. Sutton has seen it coursing over rocky, lizard-infested ground, like a harrier. It is one of the birds which follow a grass fire. Food is apparently not always swallowed whole. Lizards are neatly dissected down the back, and the soft parts are removed.

According to Sutton, a nest—in a cypress about 50 feet from the ground—resembles that of the Cooper's Hawk but is made of smaller sticks, vine stalks, and weeds and lined with branches and leaves of the wild fig. One or two white eggs are laid, and the young, at about five weeks, are still in the nest.

The call is "whaow," in a drawn-out nasal tone.

The African Harrier Hawk *(Gymnogenys typicus)* haunts parkland, secondary forest, brush, and swamps. In the Uelle district of the Congo its Amadi name, "Nobwa-pungu," the beater of hollows, refers to its unusual mode of hunting in trees.

GENUS *GYMNOGENYS*

Naked faces and fleshy ceres of bright yellow give the large harrier hawks of Africa and Madagascar a unique and startling appearance. As in some other birds of prey, the color of the facial skin changes under different conditions to deep orange or dull purplish-red, but the bare legs and feet do not. Their black bills are rather short, deep, and sharply hooked, and their small heads and extremely wide wings give them a distinctly vulturine appearance on the wing, although their tails are not as abbreviated as most vultures'. Like the somewhat similar Crane Hawk of South America (*Geranospiza*), these long-limbed birds are double-jointed, an adaptation which allows them to reach into holes in trees or on the ground. Their plumage is fluffy and both the crest and frill at the nape can be raised at will.

African Harrier Hawk (*Gymnogenys typicus*)

DESCRIPTION (AFRICA)

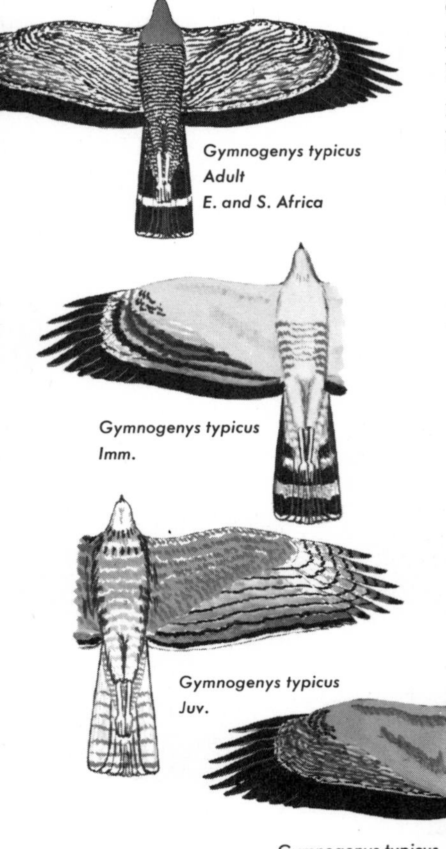

Crested head, neck, and chest, dove-gray; feathers of back and wing coverts, dove-gray, very finely mottled with light olive-brown and narrowly tipped in black and white; scapulars, marked with conspicuous black spots; secondaries, gray, subterminally banded black and narrowly tipped in white; primaries, black; upper tail coverts, barred black and white; tail, black, with a single mottled white band, and white-tipped; face, bare; throat, gray; rest of underparts, barred black-and-white (sometimes entirely gray except for barred thighs).

Immature (third year)—like adult, but head, spotted with rufous-brown; chest, rufous-brown, shaft-streaked in black and tinged with yellow-orange. *Second year*—head, neck, and breast, sandy to buff, the crest and frill spotted in sepia; back, sepia, the feathers finely edged with sandy; wings and tail, black, barred several times in sepia (lighter on undersurface) and tipped in white; belly and thighs, sandy, barred in sepia.

Juvenile—entirely rufous-brown with black streaking on head; wings and tail, more mottled and less distinctly barred than immature's.

Beak, black; cere and orbital ring, light yellow; eyes, dark brown; legs and feet, bright yellow. Size, 20–21 inches.

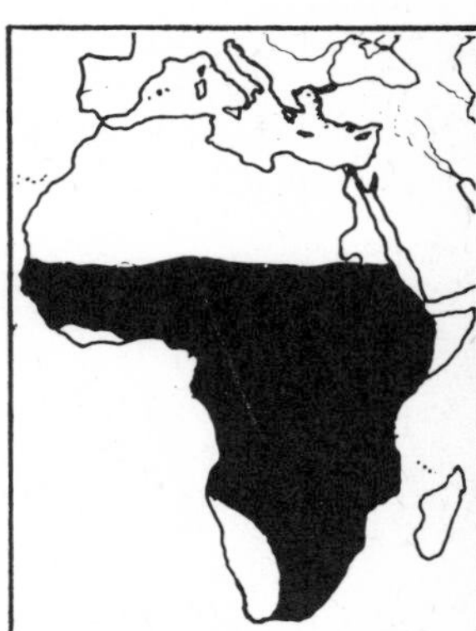

GYMNOGENYS TYPICUS

OTHER SPECIES

The Madagascar Harrier Hawk (*G. radiatus*), about the same size, resembles the African species but has nearly pure silver-gray head, neck, back, and chest, lacking the black spotting and feather-edging above. The young have a similar succession of molts.

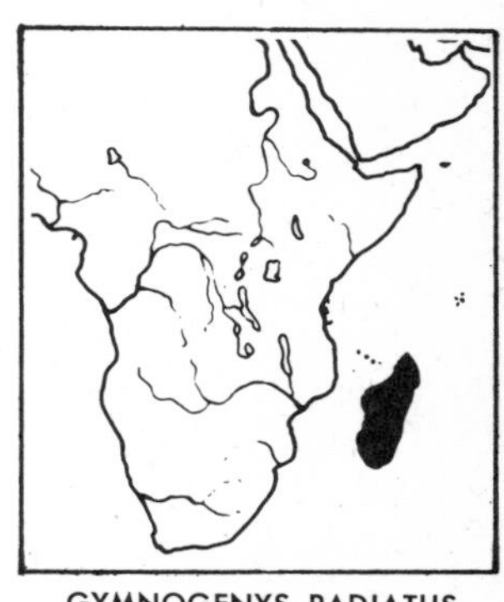

GYMNOGENYS RADIATUS

HABITS

The harrier hawks are more characteristic of the African savannas than of the forest clearings, being present from sea level to about 6,000 feet. They may be seen in leisurely flapping or sailing flight, coursing low over the ground, or hopping about in the foliage of trees, clinging to the bark and even hanging on the inner side of some rotten stub in search of insects, lizards, bats, and the eggs and young of birds. It is not uncommon to see them hanging also from the eaves of houses. On the ground they may be looking for ants, locusts, termites, frogs, and snakes, as well as small rodents The food of these hawks is extremely varied, depending on the season and the place. In some districts of Africa they favor palm nuts and in others they are certainly specialists in robbing weaver birds' nests. In the Uele District of the Congo, *Gymnogenys* breeds during the rainy season to take advantage of colonies of weaver birds nesting at the same time. There many small birds, and even kites, delight in mobbing the gray marauder. The Madagascar Harrier Hawk appears to be a heavy feeder on locusts, reptiles, and amphibians and is especially attracted, in the northeast, to banana plantations, where it takes numbers of the little green lizards that feed on the insects around the banana flowers.

On the continent, nests have been found 100 feet or more from the ground on the horizontal limbs or in the forks of trees—either appropriated from the Black Kite or built by the birds themselves; in Madagascar they both nest in trees and on the ground in the long grass of the marshes. One to three (generally two) eggs are almost completely covered with reddish-brown mottling.

The cry has been described as a "feeble scream."

SUBFAMILY CIRCAETINAE

(Bateleur, Harrier Eagles, and Serpent Eagles)

A captive female Bateleur *(Terathopius ecaudatus)*, belonging to Jim Fowler, displays the gray secondaries which distinguish her from the entirely black-winged male of the species.

GENUS *TERATHOPIUS*

Although not a large eagle, the Bateleur is chunky and provided with powerful, heavily scaled legs and feet. The bare, colorful face and cere, and the long wing, with as many as 26 secondaries, suggest an affinity to the vultures; and the heavy mane of feathers on the head and neck, to the harrier eagles. The downy young develop head, neck, and wing feathers before the flanks and tail, as in *Circaetus*. Its half-moon shape, with the feet projecting just beyond the ridiculously short tail, is probably more familiar than that of any other bird in the African skies, as the Bateleur is almost always on the wing. A pale phase occurs throughout its range, and Africans noticed the sexual differences in the coloring of the wings long before they were recorded by Europeans. This strange eagle does not appear to be fully adult until nearly six years old.

Bateleur (*Terathopius ecaudatus*)

DESCRIPTION
(TROPICAL AFRICA)

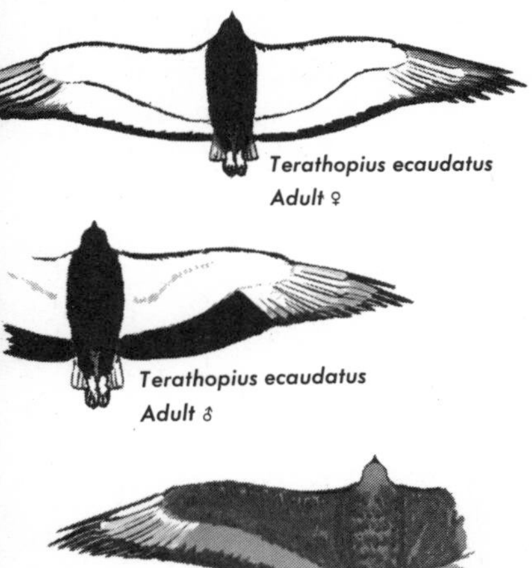

Male—head, with short full crest, neck, and entire underparts, glossy black; back, chestnut, fading to cinnamon-brown on the concealed part of the rump and tail; scapulars and wings, black (underwing coverts, white); shoulders, pale ivory-gray to ochre-brown, tinged with black. *Female*—similar, but has pale ivory-gray secondaries, tipped in black.

Pale phase—with same wing characters, differs in having very much lighter back and tail—white or buff, tinged with light amber-brown.

Immature (from about three to six years)—wing characters of the adults, but spotty in appearance; head, light streaking; back, variable amount of chestnut or cinnamon-brown (white or light buff, in pale phase); underparts, more or less feather-edged or intermixed with cinnamon-brown or gray-brown.

Juvenile (and immature up to two and one-half or three years)—gray-brown above; head and underparts, lighter, tan to amber-brown, indistinctly spotted in white.

Black-tipped beak; cere and facial skin, bright red-orange (young, black or greenish, changing between the third and sixth year); eyes, dark brown; legs and feet, red-orange (young, bluish-white, gradually turning pink); claws, black. Size, 22–25 inches.

TERATHOPIUS ECAUDATUS

HABITS

Some African tribes believe that the Bateleur never comes to the ground. Its name is derived from its resemblance to a circus performer. It engages in side-rolls, somersaults, and other aerial acrobatics. In display flight during the nesting season the noise of the Bateleur's flapping or wing-clapping may be audible for a considerable distance. Behavior in flight seems to vary a great deal in eastern, southern, and western Africa. When it descends from the sky its dive is fast and noisy—"like a six-inch shell." It avoids deep forest, and during its extensive survey of the open countryside, concentrates particularly on snakes; kills lizards and other reptiles as well as rats, mice, and shrews; may attack larger mammals, up to the size of small antelopes; and also picks up tortoises, birds' eggs, grasshoppers, and bits of carrion.

Leslie Brown describes how this bird stoops repeatedly at a snake, causing it to strike until it becomes exhausted and then becomes easy prey. Even puff adders are believed to be taken in this manner. The carrion that provides most of the remainder of its diet in many areas may be stolen from other predators, either on the ground or in the air. The Bateleur attacks Tawny Eagles, Lammergeiers, and vultures—forcing them to drop or disgorge their food.

The nest, about 30 feet from the ground in an acacia or other spreading tree, is roughly constructed of sticks and lined with green leaves. It is of modest size, for an eagle—one recorded was 30 inches across and a foot deep. One large white, rough-textured egg is rarely stained or spotted with rufous and occasionally may also have lilac undermarkings. Incubation (by the female) lasts at least 43 days; the fledging period, about 95 to 130 days —a very long time for a small eagle. In eastern Africa Bateleurs frequently raise their young in trees overhanging roads, native paths, or hard-beaten elephant paths. They are relatively "sociable" with

Juvenile Bateleur (*Terathopius ecaudatus*).

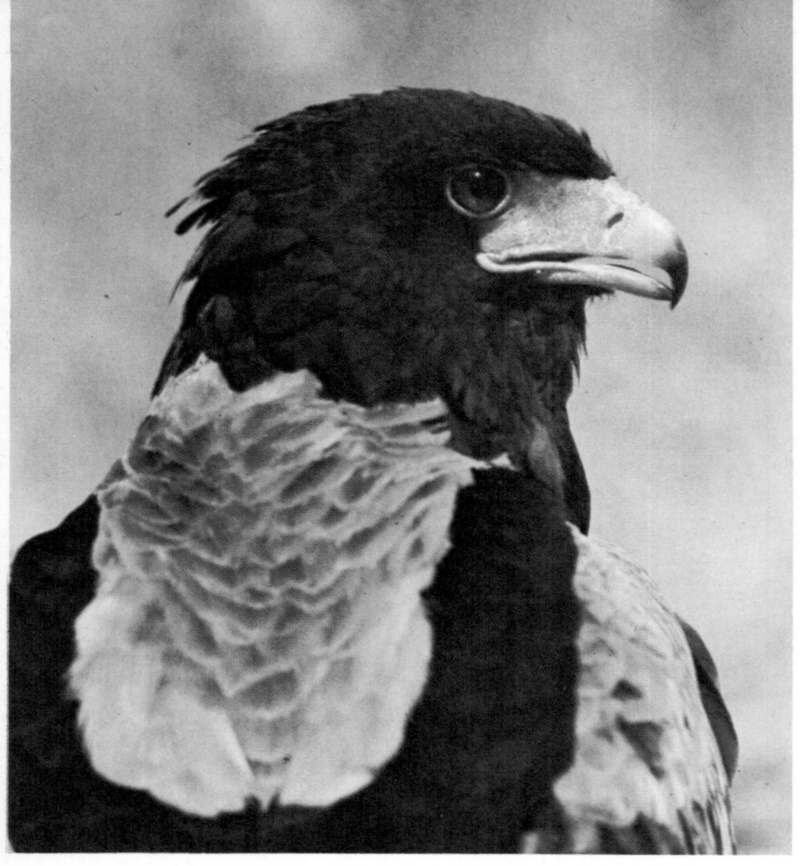

other adult birds of their own or other species, and tolerate sub-adults. Leslie Brown records two instances of a *ménage à trois* (two males and one female). In the first, one of the males disappeared after the egg was laid; in the second, the extra male remained in the vicinity but did not feed either the incubating female or the nestling after it hatched.

The characteristic call is a "caw," at intervals but this—described as a "bark," "yelp," "scream"—seems to be as variable locally as its behavior in the air. The jackal-like "schaor," also recorded, is similar to that of the Jackal Buzzard, but deeper and more powerful, and may be a mating call. In captivity, the usual sound made by a Bateleur is a soft "qua-qua"; rarely, a louder "kach, kach," or a shrill "kau."

Female Bateleur *(Terathopius ecaudatus)*; back view, showing the patch characteristic of both sexes.

The Brown Harrier Eagle *(Circaetus cinereus)* is one of the commonest eagles in tropical Africa. The bird in the photograph was trapped in Barotseland, Northern Rhodesia, by Jim Fowler. Its snake-eating habits in captivity are recorded in a series of photographs in Chapter 4.

GENUS *CIRCAETUS*

Circaetus may once have been entirely of Indian-African distribution. In the Mediterranean region, the Short-toed Eagle (*C. gallicus*) is becoming more and more sporadic, possibly due to the disappearance of its principal food, snakes. This eagle, virtually the only migratory bird of the group, joins its close relatives, the Black-chested Harrier Eagle and Beaudouin's Harrier Eagle, in tropical Africa in winter. Throughout its Asiatic range, the Short-toed Eagle is mostly sedentary, although some individuals winter in the Lesser Sunda Islands. Their breeding range, still unknown, may be somewhere in eastern Asia. Of the three other African species, only two—the Brown Harrier Eagle and the Banded

Harrier Eagle—are widely distributed, and these are comparatively rare. The Southern Banded Harrier Eagle may be found only from Tanganyika to Natal.

The harrier eagles are heavily feathered on the head and neck and have short, powerful, irregularly plated tarsi and toes, and rough-soled feet—all adaptive features for hunting and killing reptiles. They are birds of the forest edges or open spaces with impressive wingspans (about five feet) but stockier than the "booted" eagles of their size and furnished with much weaker beaks.

CIRCAETUS CINEREUS

Brown Harrier Eagle (*Circaetus cinereus*)

DESCRIPTION (AFRICA)

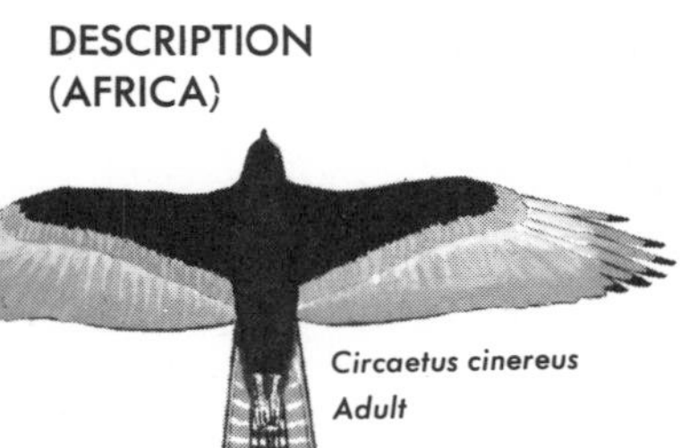

Entirely chocolate with fine feather-edging of pale ivory-gray, and often with a purple iridescent sheen; primaries, darker; tail, dark brown, banded and tipped in ochre-brown.

Immature—similar to adult (several molts).

Juvenile—like adult but with varying amounts of white on lower breast and belly.

Beak, black; cere, gray; eyes, bright yellow; legs and feet, greenish-white. Size, about 25 inches.

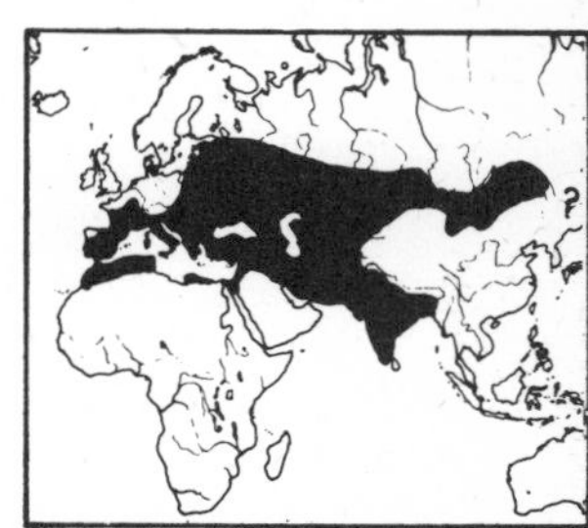

CIRCAETUS GALLICUS

OTHER SPECIES

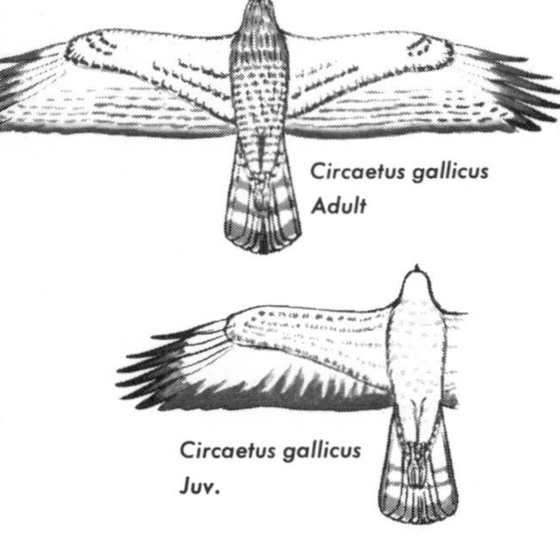

Circaetus pectoralis
Adult

Circaetus pectoralis
Imm.

The Eurasian Short-toed Eagle (*C. gallicus*), 26 inches, is entirely dark gray-brown above with the characteristic light feather-edging, except for white forehead, lores, and orbital region; throat and breast, gray-brown streaked with white and black; lower breast, belly, and thighs, white, coarsely barred with gray-brown; secondaries and tail, light olive-gray, barred with dark brown and white-tipped; primaries, darker.

In eastern and southern Africa the Black-chested Harrier Eagle (*C. pectoralis*), 25 inches, differs in having a pure white belly and thighs; and from Senegal to the Sudan. Beaudouin's Harrier Eagle (*C. beaudouini*), 24 inches, has very fine barring below and a squared-off tail.

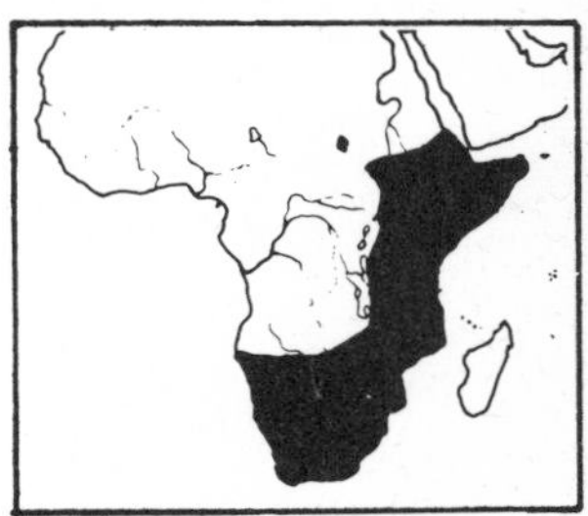

CIRCAETUS PECTORALIS

The young of the Short-toed Eagle in all stages are paler and show more white than adults. The *immature* has dark streaking on the chest and barring on the belly; and the *juvenile*, a nearly pure white head, neck, and underparts. The Black-chested Harrier Eagle has the remainder of the underparts white, in *immature* plumage, barred with dark gray-brown like the adult of the Short-toed Eagle; and in *juvenile* plumage, cinnamon-brown underparts with patches of white showing.

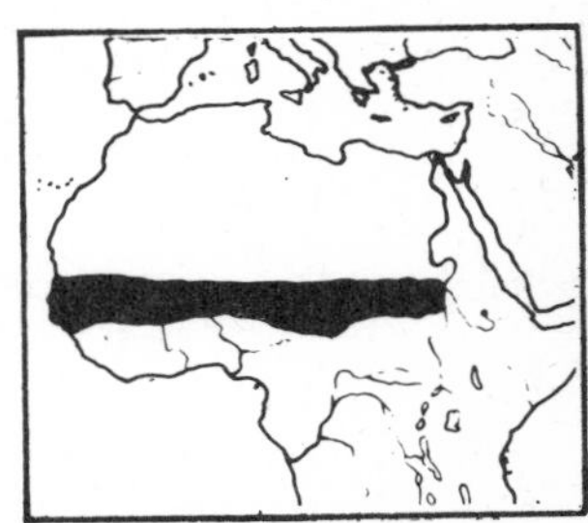

CIRCAETUS BEAUDOUINI

The immature of Beaudouin's Harrier Eagle looks whiter below than the adult, but the juvenile is entirely dark except for barring on the wings, which helps to distinguish it from the young of the Brown Harrier Eagle (*C. cinereus*), a larger bird with heavier legs, feet, and beak.

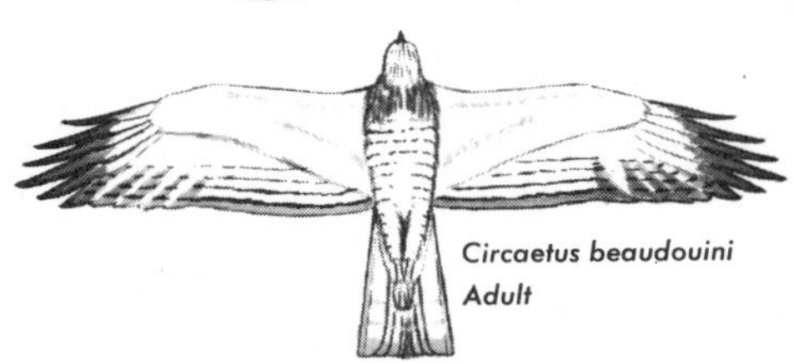

Short-toed Eagle (*Circaetus gallicus*), holding a water snake for young.—*Photograph by Eric Hosking.*

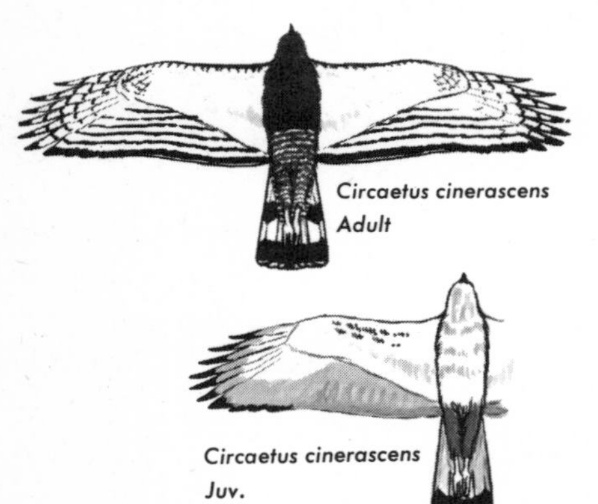
Circaetus cinerascens Adult

Circaetus cinerascens Juv.

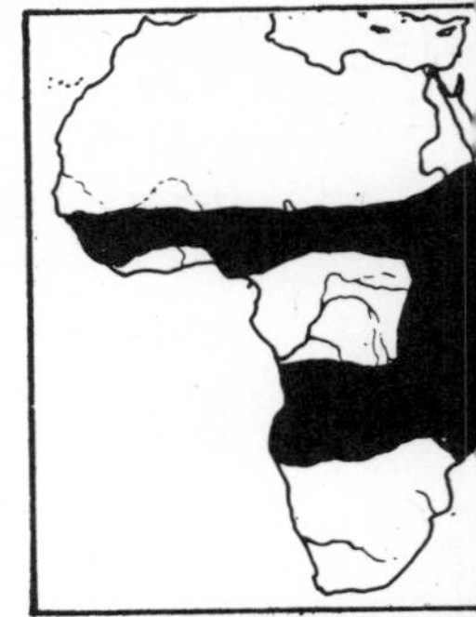
CIRCAETUS CINERASCE

Across tropical Africa the somewhat smaller Banded Harrier Eagle (*C. cinerascens*), 20–22 inches, varies from dark gray-brown to dark olive-brown above; underparts, sepia to cinnamon-brown with white barring on thighs, and sometimes the belly as well. A distinctive field mark to look for is the tail—mostly black, with a white median band, and tipped in white. (The juvenile is paler, especially on the head, neck, and underparts, and the tail shows a wider white band.)

The Southern Banded Harrier Eagle (*C. fasciolatus*), restricted to southeastern Africa, is similar in size and general coloration, but has a light-colored breast and belly barred with brown; tail, evenly banded black. (The young are paler, like those of *C. cinerascens,* with nearly white head, neck, and underparts, but the breast and belly are darkly spotted.)

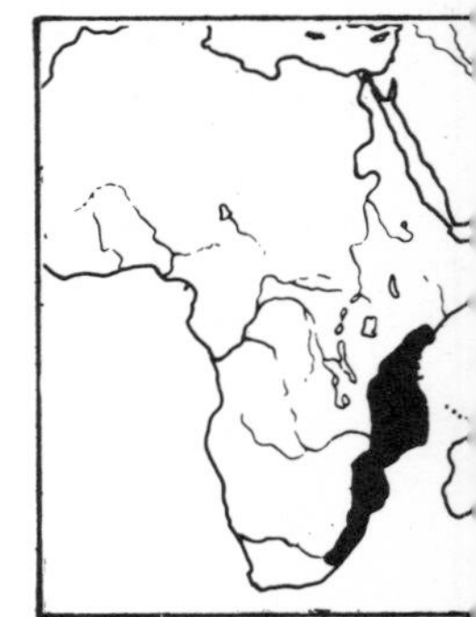
CIRCAETUS FASCIOLAT

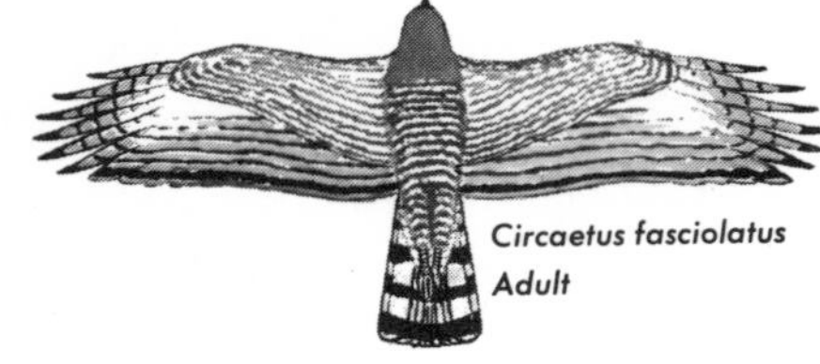
Circaetus fasciolatus Adult

HABITS

Harrier eagles inhabit forest edges and open country, their preferences differing regionally; old deciduous forests, near bogs and heathlands, as well as dry steppes, and rocky regions with low scrub (Europe); dry plains, foothills, and scrub jungle (Asia); savanna and scrub, but not equatorial rain forest (tropical Africa). Where more than one species may be found breeding "together," they prefer different kinds of countryside. In Kenya, the Black-breasted Harrier Eagle lives on open plains with ant-gall acacias or whistling thorn, but the Brown Harrier Eagle keeps to the dense thornbush of Mbere and Ukamba. A harrier eagle may be seen sitting on a branch or flying high, and while hunting, sometimes hovers gracefully like a huge Kestrel. G. L. Van Someren describes how the Brown Harrier Eagle performs its dance on the ground with wings uplifted to distract the prey so it can be grabbed at the neck, its head torn off, and the body swallowed whole. This procedure may be varied, in the case of a large snake, by chopping it in half and swallowing the pieces. Frequently the victim is borne off and devoured in the air. Poisonous and nonpoisonous snakes and a variety of other terrestrial reptiles undoubtedly form a large part of the diet of all harrier eagles. In the breeding season the female and young are fed primarily on snakes, regurgitated by the male at the nest. Other foods include frogs, crabs, small mammals, and birds living on the ground which happen to be especially vulnerable, also large insects, and even an occasional fish is reported in India.

Nests of harrier eagles are generally small, shallow, and untidy for such large birds, and they are not necessarily used again. These are built in the tops of trees. Occasionally old nests of other birds are appropriated. In Kenya both the Black-chested and Brown harrier eagles have nested in the tops of euphorbias (cactus-like trees) and flat-topped acacias, where their eggs and young were especially vulnerable to other predators—Augur Buzzards and kites. Perhaps because of this precarious situation, the Brown harrier eagle female is a very close sitter. Only one or two rough-textured white eggs are laid (sometimes marked with a few brown or rusty red spots, in the Black-chested and Southern Banded harrier eagles).

In *Eagles,* Leslie Brown gives us an amusing portrait of a young Brown Harrier Eagle eagerly pulling and tugging to get the snake out of the crop of the male, which has just arrived with a meal. This fledgling on its first flight (110 days old) was more fully feathered than an aquila at the same stage.

Hoarse cries, uttered on the wing (often when the birds are too high to identify with accuracy otherwise), are characteristic of the African birds. The Brown Harrier Eagle cries "kok-kok-kok-kaaaow"; the Banded Harrier Eagle delivers a series of loud mournful notes (and a subdued "caw"); and the Southern Banded Harrier Eagle's call is "ko-ko-ho-ho-ho." The Short-toed Eagle of the Mediterranean and Asia has a plaintive mewing cry like a buzzard, heard chiefly in the breeding season during tumbling and darting displays in the air. Leslie Brown believes the Black-chested Harrier Eagle to be mute, but the *African Handbook of Birds* records "an occasional loud shriek, uttered while soaring."

The Crested Serpent Eagle *(Spilornis cheela)* in peninsular India is more closely associated with well-watered jungles, forest clearings, and cultivation than is the Short-toed Eagle.

GENUS *SPILORNIS*

Spilornis of India, Ceylon, Burma, China, Malaysia, Celebes, and the Philippines could hardly be more varied in its coloring and plumage patterns, although in adults of the various species only a single wide light median band shows on the black tail, and the wings are conspicuously barred. The Crested Serpent Eagle (*S. cheela*) is most widely distributed and several island serpent eagles in the Bay of Bengal and southern Asia probably represent former populations of this bird which have become distinct species with time and isolation. The Andamans in the Bay of Bengal may have been invaded by this group twice in past ages—first by the indigenous Andaman Serpent Eagle (*S. elgini*), of more inland habits, and much later by *S. cheela,* which is usually seen along the coastal mangrove creeks feeding on crabs. Borneo, too, may have been the focal point of a double invasion, originally of the Celebes Serpent Eagle (*S. rufipectus*), native to that island and Celebes, and then of various populations of *S. cheela* which settled in the lowlands and mountains as well as the islands north of Borneo. The young of *S. cheela* are dimorphic regionally, either white-breasted, or dark below, like the adults, but they always have a light tail with three or more narrow dark bands. Those of other species resemble the white-breasted variety.

In structure, the serpent eagles are very similar to *Circaetus,* but have shorter wings, bare faces with only a few short bristles, and conspicuous fan-shaped crests.

Crested Serpent Eagle (*Spilornis cheela*)

DESCRIPTION (INDIA, SOUTH OF THE HIMALAYAS)

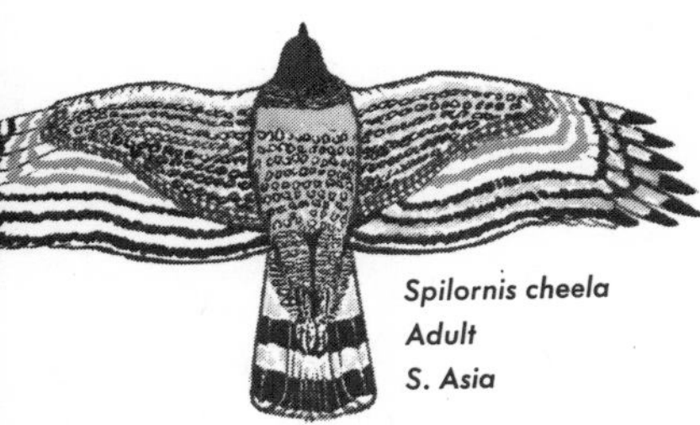
Spilornis cheela
Adult
S. Asia

Head and fanlike crest, black, the feathers spotted and barred with white; generally sepia to dark brown above with fine light feather-edging on back, white spots and light edging on wing coverts, and wings banded with black; tail, black, with wide median band of pale buff (white in older birds), and white-tipped; sides of face and throat, dark brown, tinged with slate-gray; breast, sepia, finely barred buff (becoming solid sepia in older birds); rest of underparts, cinnamon, spotted on belly and barred on thighs in white—these markings circled or bordered with black.

Immature—has a buff to light amber-brown head and buff throat, with dark crown, crest, and mantle broadly feather-edged, giving the bird a much more barred appearance than the adult; wing coverts, more conspicuously spotted as well as edged in white; tail, mottled light olive-brown with three dark brown bands.

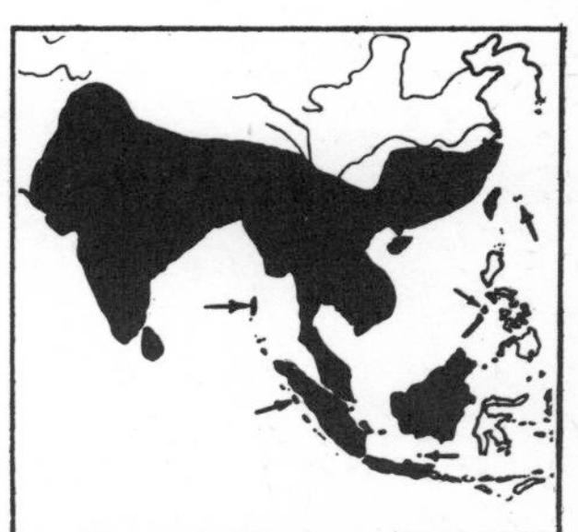
SPILORNIS CHEELA

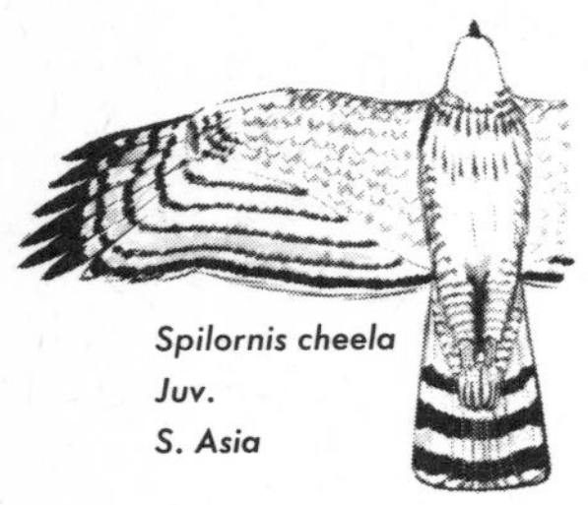
Spilornis cheela
Juv.
S. Asia

Juvenile—head, crest, and throat, much lighter than in immature; underparts, white tinged light cinnamon-brown, with fine striping throughout, and ochre-brown barring and mottling on thighs and flanks.

Beak, gray with black tip; cere and bare skin of face, bright yellow; eyes, deep yellow; legs and feet, pale yellow; claws, black. Size, about 24 inches.

VARIATIONS

The species is common and widespread from the Himalayas east to China, Formosa, and the Ryukyu Islands and south to Indonesia and Palawan. The temperate zone birds are paler, and the tropical and equatorial rain forest populations generally—although not always—more chocolate-colored above and rufous-brown below, the white spotting often replaced by broken barring on the underparts, with or without dark borders. One light band shows on the tail. The southern populations ordinarily have a solid chest at maturity, but the paler northern birds (in the Himalayas and northern China, for example) may either retain a finely mottled chest or darken with age. The character of medium gray on the cheeks and chin seems to be individually variable with darker coloring. The comparatively dark, gray-cheeked serpent eagles of Ceylon and the lowlands of Borneo and the pale variants on the islands north of Borneo are grayer over-all than the others. The Palawan birds resemble the peninsular Indian serpent eagles described, but are more conspicuously barred on the chest, with this marking extending to the chin, sides of face, and back of neck below the black ruff. The birds confined to the mountains of Borneo are darkest of all, and have no fine white spotting on the wing coverts.

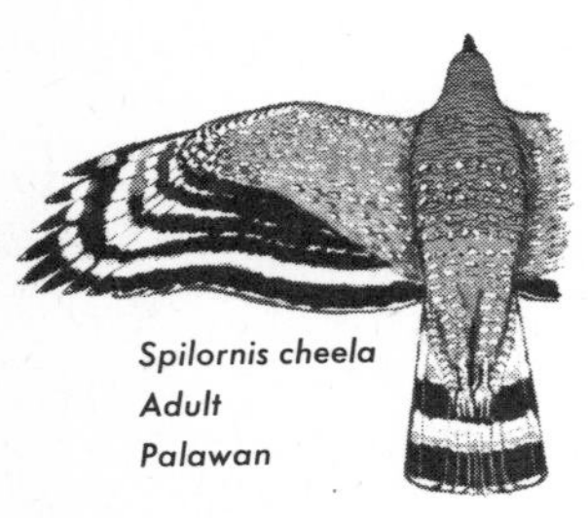
Spilornis cheela
Adult
Palawan

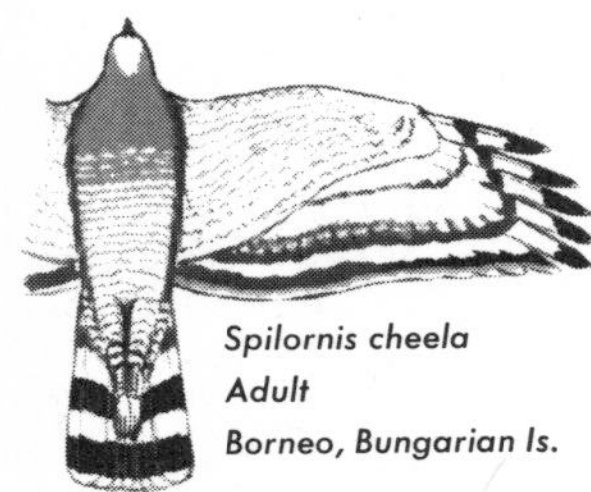
Spilornis cheela
Adult
Borneo, Bungarian Is.

Juveniles—white-breasted on the Asiatic continent, Hainan, Formosa, and the Andamans; but dark-breasted like the adults in Malaya, Sumatra, and generally north of Sumatra. Both light and dark phase young evidently occur in the islands north of Borneo, in Java, and Ceylon. Sizes, 14 inches (islands north of Borneo) to 26 inches (northern China and the Himalayas).

OTHER SPECIES

The very dark Celebes Serpent Eagle (*S. rufipectus*), 19 inches, of northwest Borneo (Sarawak) and the Celebes has a completely black head and neck, except for gray cheeks; also solid dark amber-brown chest. The Sula Besi Island population is smaller (16 inches) and paler, with gray extending to the throat and a light amber-brown chest. In these various regions white spotting below assumes the character of broken barring, as in the southern Asiatic populations of *S. cheela*. (Juvenile—white-breasted.)

The Philippine Serpent Eagle (*S. holospilus*), 18–21½ inches, is sepia above with large white spots, and buff or sienna feather-edging across the mantle; underparts, medium ferruginous, with a gray cast and entirely spotted in white. (Juvenile—white-breasted.)

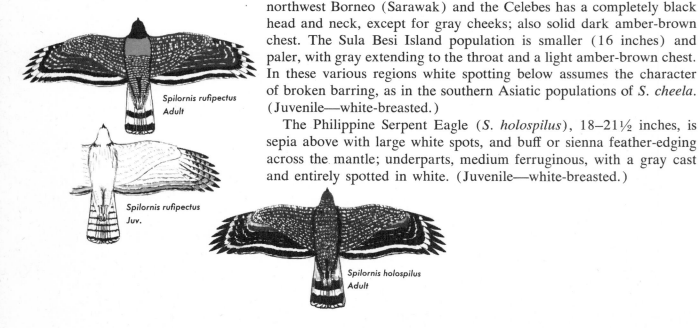

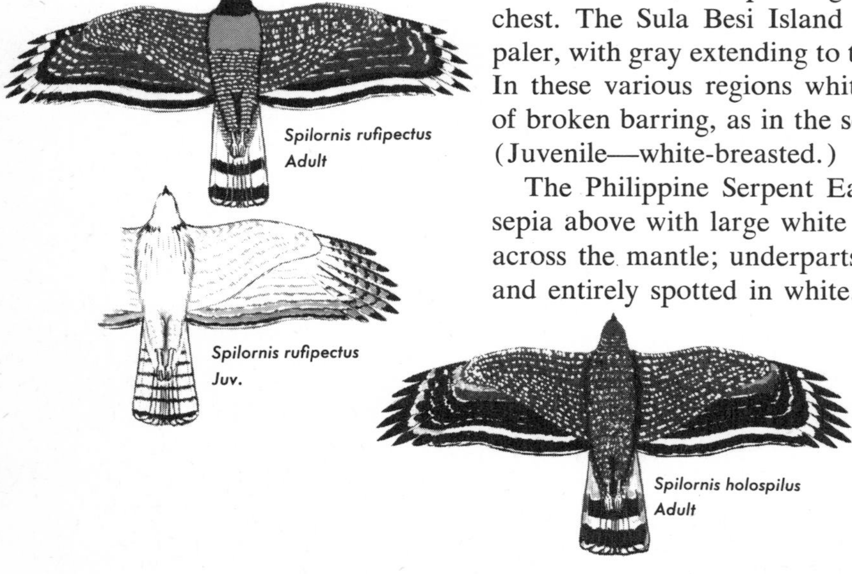
Spilornis rufipectus
Adult

Spilornis rufipectus
Juv.

Spilornis holospilus
Adult

SPILORNIS RUFIPECTU

SPILORNIS HOLOSPIL

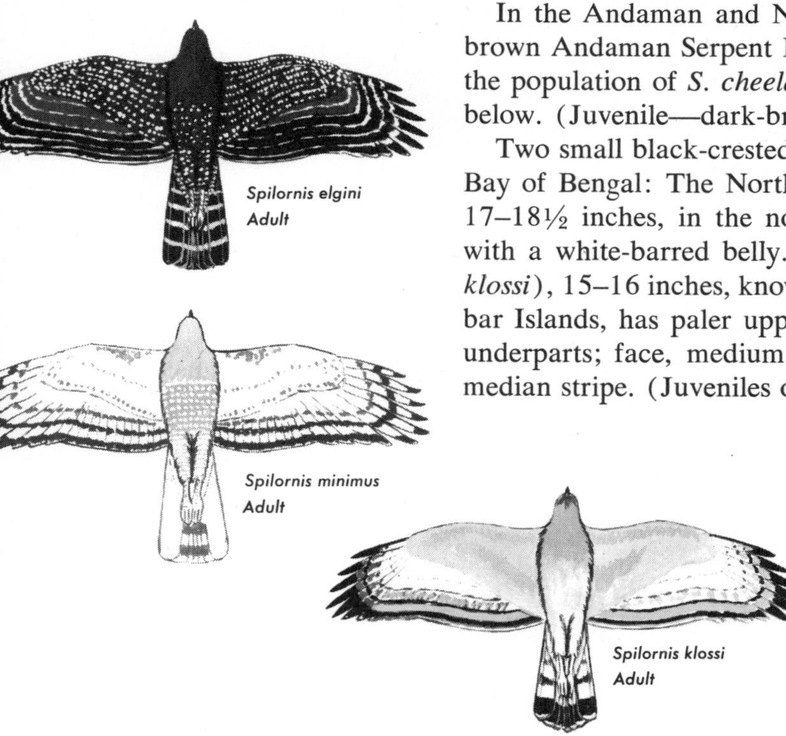

Spilornis elgini
Adult

Spilornis minimus
Adult

Spilornis klossi
Adult

In the Andaman and Nicobar islands, Bay of Bengal, the rufous-brown Andaman Serpent Eagle (*S. elgini*), 22 inches, is darker than the population of *S. cheela,* also found there, and completely spotted below. (Juvenile—dark-breasted.)

Two small black-crested serpent eagles inhabit the Nicobar Islands, Bay of Bengal: The Northern Nicobar Serpent Eagle (*S. minimus*), 17–18½ inches, in the northern Nicobars, is light cinnamon below with a white-barred belly. The Southern Nicobar Serpent Eagle (*S. klossi*), 15–16 inches, known only from Great Nicobar, southern Nicobar Islands, has paler upperparts and light cinnamon to buff-colored underparts; face, medium gray; throat, faintly marked with a gray median stripe. (Juveniles of both species are similar to adults.)

SPILORNIS ELGINI

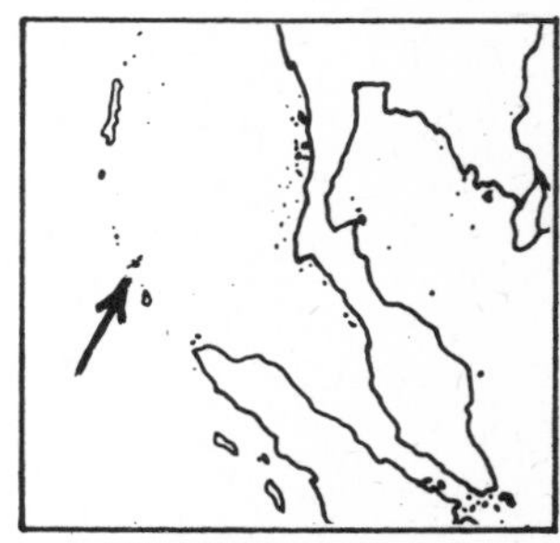

SPILORNIS MINIMUS

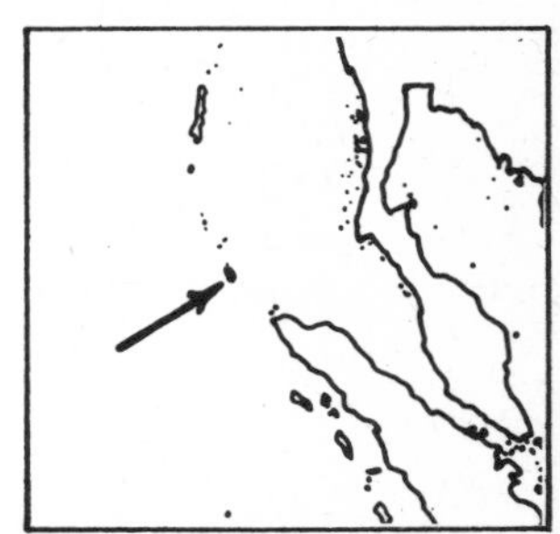

SPILORNIS KLOSSI

HABITS

The haunts of *Spilornis* are forested tracts on the plains as well as in hills—usually near water—to 7,000 feet. High in a lofty tree, the serpent eagle may be concealed, but commands a view of the surrounding countryside, and it is often seen soaring in wide circles, at considerable heights. Food is principally snakes, including large poisonous species, and its diet otherwise corresponds to that of *Circaetus,* depending on the locality and the time of the year. The Indian birds are said to be capable of catching ducks, jungle fowl, and even peafowl.

The nest is placed about halfway up (35 to 40 feet) in the fork of a tree, generally on the edge of a wooded stream, or near a swampy field. Like that of *Circaetus,* it may not be very large. It is nearly always made of fresh twigs and lined with leaves, and the nest hollow appears deeper. One or two eggs are heavily freckled, blotched or streaked on the white background with brown or reddish-brown, sometimes with underlying purple spots and a solid brown cap on either the large or small end; or the only markings may be the brown cap and purple spotting.

The serpent eagle's call (India) is a high-pitched, screaming whistle of three or four notes, "kek-kek-kek-kee," uttered while soaring, and clearly audible from great heights, like that of *Circaetus.* Pairs are particularly noisy during the breeding season.

The forests of equatorial Africa are the home of the African Serpent Eagle *(Dryotriorchis spectabilis),* otherwise known as the "Beautiful Wood Hawk."

GENUS *DRYOTRIORCHIS*

This bird of the deep forest is shaped like a large goshawk with short wings and a long tail, but it has heavy feathering on the head and neck, and bare, scaled legs like *Circaetus.* The male and female, as well as the juvenile, have eyes of different colors.

African Serpent Eagle (*Dryotriorchis spectabilis*)

DESCRIPTION
(EQUATORIAL AFRICA)

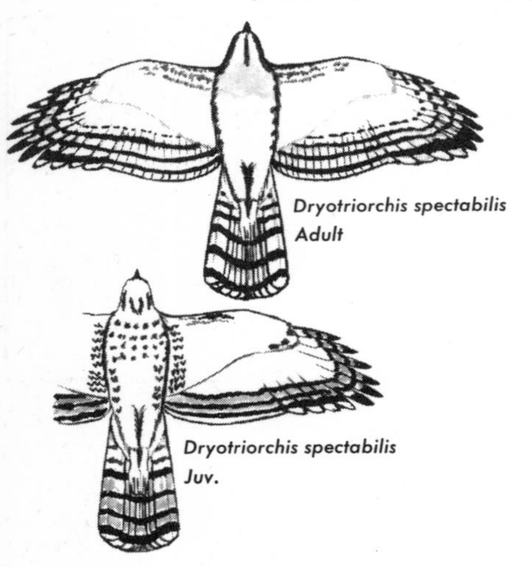

Dark brown above with varying amounts of white showing on bases of the lanceolate feathers at the back of head and nape; shoulders, always dark with narrow white edgings—but upperparts, including wings, otherwise entirely rufous-brown, barred with dark brown; tail, also rufous-brown with six dark brown bands; face and sides of neck, light ochre-brown with dark moustachial streaks; throat, paler, showing a single heavy median black stripe; underparts, white, tinged with light ochre-brown and more or less spotted and barred dark brown.

Juvenile—light head, streaked and spotted with dark brown; light edges on feathers of back, making it appear scalloped above; throat, spotted rather than distinctly striped; chest and sides of body, tinged with light amber-brown and blobbed with dark brown.

Beak, blue-black (juvenile, horn-brown); cere, orange-yellow; eyes, dull yellow (male), dark brown (female), or brown (juvenile, both sexes); legs and feet, yellow; claws, black. Size, 21½–23 inches.

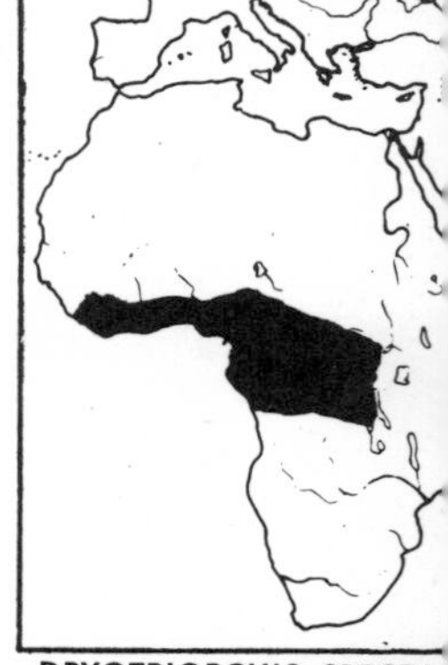

DRYOTRIORCHIS SPECTA

HABITS

Dryotriorchis perches on the larger branches of great trees in deep rain forest and, like *Circaetus,* feeds mostly on snakes; also toads, lizards, small mammals, and insects. It is almost never seen about clearings or open watercourses. Presumably this bird nests above the forest canopy. In the Ituri (Congo) its loud, nasal, and mournful cries—"cow" repeated at intervals, and all in one key—may be heard from June to October or November. They are expressed by "lo" in the native name of the species, "Nalolo."

The rare Madagascar Serpent Eagle *(Eutriorchis astur)* is a close relative of the *Dryotriorchis* of the west African forests.

GENUS *EUTRIORCHIS*

Like *Dryotriorchis,* this serpent eagle has short wings and an elongated tail, but it displays a full, rounded crest. The lores are feathered, and black hairlike bristles overhang the nostrils.

Madagascar Serpent Eagle
(*Eutriorchis astur*)

DESCRIPTION (MADAGASCAR)

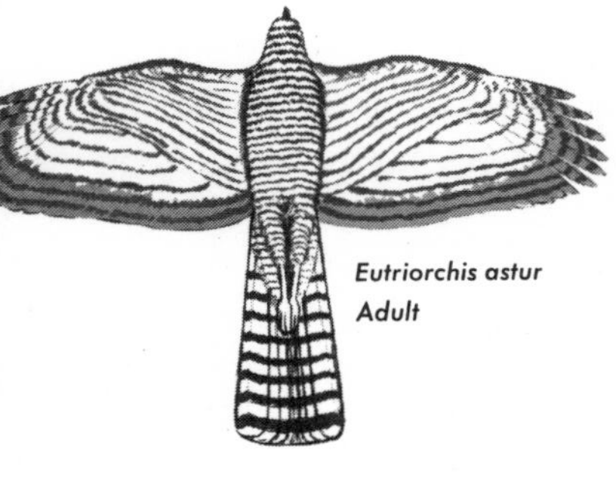

Above, sepia, narrowly barred on head, short crest, and neck with light amber-brown and white; back, wing coverts, and wings, barred more broadly but less distinctly with dark brown; very long tail, sepia, with six to eight dark brown bands; face, feathered, except for bare orbital region, sepia faintly barred with white; chin and underparts, barred with white and sepia.

Beak, yellow at base and black at tip; eyes, yellow; legs and feet, yellow; claws, black. Size, males, about 22½ inches.

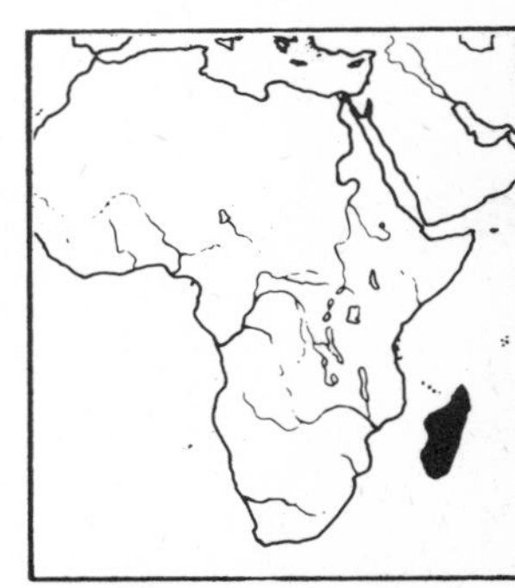

EUTRIORCHIS ASTUR

HABITS

A. L. Rand found the Madagascar Serpent Eagle only in the northern part of the forests of the humid eastern portions of the island to about 1,800 feet. It is probably confined to large trees of the rain forest, feeding, like *Dryotriorchis* of western Africa, on snakes, lizards, and insects.

SUBFAMILY PANDIONINAE

(*Ospreys*)

North American Osprey *(Pandion haliaetus)* at the nest.—*Photograph by Roger Tory Peterson.*

GENUS *PANDION*

Pandion breeds in almost every kind of habitat except tundra—in the Holarctic, Oriental, Australasian, and African regions—requiring, for the most part, only water and fish for its livelihood.

Certain anatomical features link the Osprey or Fish Hawk with the falcons; others, with the accipitrine family of hawks, eagles, and Old World vultures; and still others, with the more primitive Cathartid vultures. In many ways, too, it differs from all other Falconiformes. Therefore, it has generally been regarded as an isolated type—a subfamily composed of only one widespread species.

The Osprey's head is kitelike and small in relation to the large, slightly arched beak, and the elongated feathers of the head and nape can be raised in a short crest. The plumage is hard and close, and the feathers of the thighs are extremely short, dense, and compact, not elongated. The short, strong tarsi are entirely covered with projecting scales. An owl-like reversible outer toe, spicules on the soles of the feet, and claws which are long, very much curved, and of equal length, aid in capturing fish. The wings appear long, narrow, and distinctly angled in flight, and the tail is also rather narrow.

The eggs of *Pandion* are more elongate-ovoid than those of most raptors and are not greenish- or yellowish-tinted on the inside of the shell. The nestlings do not develop a second down before the first contour feathers, as many eagles and hawks do, and are protectively patterned, not plain white or grayish.

Osprey or Fish Hawk (*Pandion haliaetus*)

DESCRIPTION (NORTH AMERICA)

Male—head and neck, white, with black patches on crown and nape and a heavy black band through cheeks; rest of upperparts, dark brown; wings and tail, barred; underparts, plain white or with a few dark brown streaks.

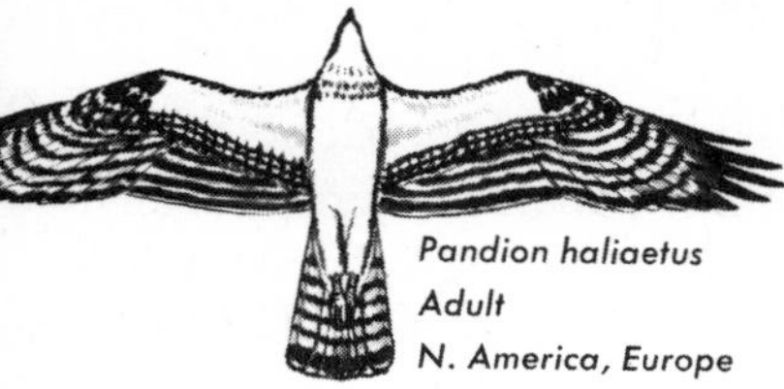

Female—similar, but with distinctly spotted chest.

Immature—like adult, but showing some white feather-edging above.

Juvenile—head is darker and distinct white feather-edging on rest of upperparts.

Beak, black; cere, bluish-gray; eyes, yellow (juvenile, orange-red to brownish-yellow); tarsi and toes, pale bluish-yellow; claws, black. Size, 20–23 inches.

VARIATIONS

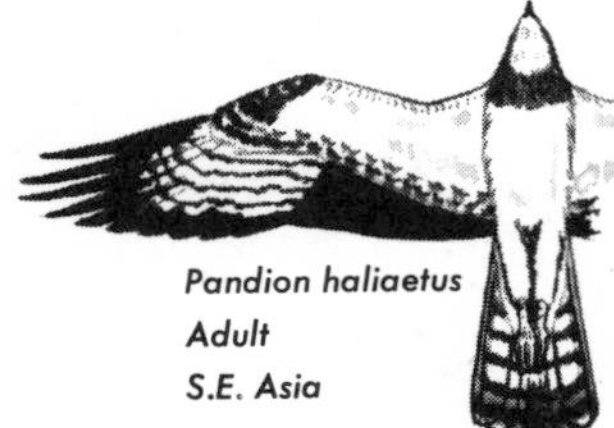

Smaller and paler individuals in the Bahamas have almost entirely white heads and immaculate white underparts (both sexes). Throughout the Palearctic region the lower throat and breast of males and females are broadly banded or streaked with cinnamon-brown; Malaysian and Australian birds are similarly marked, but have whiter heads. Tails of Old World Ospreys are not as distinctly barred as in New World individuals. Size, 19 inches (Buru, New Caledonia) to 22 inches (Europe, northern Asia).

HABITS

In temperate zones the Osprey frequents seacoasts, lakes, ponds, or slowly flowing rivers, both in open and wooded regions; in the tropics, usually seacoasts with rocky shores, reef walls, or mangrove swamps.

Like the sea eagles, it takes fish from the surface of the water, but more frequently submerges. The Fish Hawk generally flies 30 to 100 feet above the water, alternately flapping and gliding. Perhaps it may hover for a moment with drooping legs and wings. Then it goes into a falcon-like dive, throwing up a shower of spray and vanishing for a second or two. Rising, the Osprey shakes the water from its plumage. It has a firm hold on its catch (with both talons, in the case of a large fish) and carries it head foremost—just as it was caught—to the feeding place or nest, on a bare tree or cliff. Although it subsists mainly on fish, up to about four pounds in weight, the Osprey has been known to take small mammals, small ducks, sandpipers, and other birds, crustaceans, turtles, frogs, sea snakes (in the tropics), and large sea snails (Australia) whose shells are smashed on the rocks. An industrious hunter, the Fish Hawk also helps to support a number of birds which systematically rob it of its catch—fish eagles, man-of-war birds, and terns.

In courtship the male Osprey may indulge in a series of short aerial dives (of about 30 feet) for as long as nine minutes without a pause; and pairs may be seen soaring and chasing each other.

The nest, often of considerable size and added to year after year, is placed in the tops of large isolated trees, giant cactus (Baja California), on rocky pinnacles (Grand Canyon of Yellowstone Park and islands off California), on telephone poles along roadways, on bridges, towers, and windmills. Height, sufficient for security, is desirable, but in various localities Ospreys attempt—not always successfully, it seems—to nest on the ground; on duck hunters' blinds, in boxes, on old tires, on the roots of fallen trees, or even in a cup hollowed into the mud of a marsh. In these low situations there is more danger of predation and, although the female sits close in such concealment as is afforded and can be overlooked by a potential predator, a sudden distraction—for example, the noise of a passing motorboat—can cause her to take flight so awkwardly and hastily that she accidentally smashes the eggs with her feet. In addition, the nest may be flooded by high tides or extra-heavy rains, or a combination of both.

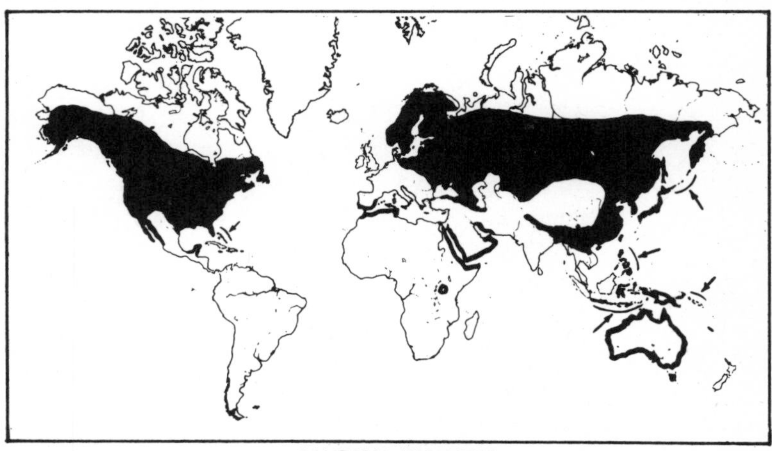
PANDION HALIAETUS

Nesting materials vary locally. Branches of trees, heather stems, seaweed, dead vegetable matter, bones, moss, or driftwood are used with a lining of grasses and finer material. Two to four eggs are boldly blotched and spotted brown or red-brown on a white or buff-tinted ground. Incubation (35 days) is mainly by the female; the male provides for the family; and the fledglings are fed from the female's beak for about six weeks. In the last stages both parents bring fish, which they throw down into the nest, and at about eight to ten weeks the young are ready to fly.

Ospreys in North America breed in rather dense colonies in certain favorable places, mainly along the Atlantic coast and the Gulf coast of Florida. Many of the more inland colonies in the northeast had already disappeared by the end of the nineteenth century. Their members apparently drifted to the coast, but, even there, numbers have dwindled yearly, and have declined sharply over at least the past ten years, in spite of the fact that Ospreys are tolerated more than other hawks and eagles in North America. Farmers often put up poles and supports to encourage their nesting, either as a picturesque feature of the landscape or in the belief that they will drive away other hawks. In Saybrook, Connecticut, Ospreys nest in red oaks and other trees close to houses, and interested homeowners put up nest poles.

A possible answer to the lack of nesting success in the Connecticut River region is the residual effect of DDT, which the birds obtain by eating fish in contaminated waters. Roger Tory Peterson, who has been involved with DDT research since 1945, recently informed a Senate subcommittee of the decline of a colony of Ospreys near his home at Old Lyme, Connecticut:

"In 1954 there were about 150 nests in the general area . . . two or three years later I investigated the concentration of nests on Great Island [when] there should have been full-grown young. Most of the nests were empty. The next year was also a failure. Some of the birds sat on unhatched eggs for 60 to 70 days.

"At about that time Peter Ames, a graduate student in ornithology at Yale University, started his studies of our local Ospreys, and we became deeply involved. There were about 20 nests in one concentration on Great Island. One season they produced six young, one year three, and one year only one. Normal success should have been between one and two young per nest—perhaps thirty birds out of twenty nests. Twenty-one raccoon-proof poles with platforms were erected to rule out predation by raccoons and other disturbances, but even after the birds adopted these sites the survival percentages remained the same, about 10 per cent of the norm. Finally several eggs were analyzed. They contained significant amounts of DDT, DDE, and other derivatives of DDT. Thirty samples of fish taken from the nests all contained these poisons. We could only come to one conclusion.

"Without proper replacement of young birds the colony has been shrinking. Here are some of the statistics: In 1954 there were approximately 150 nests in the area. In 1960, there were 71; in 1963, 24; this year, 15. They are dropping out at a rate of more than 30 per cent yearly. Projecting this decline, we should see our last nest on the Connecticut in 1970 or 1971—in only five or six years.

"There is not much spraying at Old Lyme, but half a dozen towns upriver spray. There is undoubtedly air-drift and runoff. You cannot confine these poisons as long as wind blows, water flows, or fishes swim. Where we are likely to get the magnification effect is in the estuarine waters at the mouth of the river. Traces of poisons ingested by little fish upriver—either in the runoff or through poisoned insects—make them easier prey for larger fish. Numbers of affected fingerlings compound their poison in their predators, and it is the large fish that is wobbly, swimming near the surface, that is most likely to be caught by the Osprey which transfers the accumulated poisons to its own tissues. Natural selection has become unnatural selection.

"Nor are the Ospreys the only birds that are disappearing on the Connecticut. We no longer hear the bitterns booming and the colonies of night herons have disappeared. We have not seen a single kingfisher this year. It is a sad thing to see a beautiful river becoming devoid of life.

"Ospreys in Massachusetts and Rhode Island and on the coast of New Jersey are also dropping fast, apparently for the same reasons. At Gardiner's Island, off the end of Long Island, where there were formerly 200 nests, there are now only a few and these produce very few young."

In localities where the young birds hatch but do not survive to fledging age, parasites may be the cause. John Hamlet found this to be true of one island population in the Cedar Keys off the Gulf Coast of Florida some years ago.

Undoubtedly disturbances in populated areas have contributed to the problem. Motorboats passing, campers or fishermen eating their lunch under an Osprey's nest, can keep the incubating bird off the eggs until they grow cold, and egg-stealing small boys can do more damage than raccoons and Great Horned Owls.

In Europe Ospreys may have been exterminated from many areas (France, Holland, Belgium). They were breeding in Scotland until the latter part of the nineteenth century, and have disappeared from Denmark only in this century. Sociable tendencies in Germany and along the Red Sea are recorded in Chapter 3.

Their breeding seasons the world over are governed by climate and food supply like the sea eagles', but northern Ospreys migrate into the tropics. The winter range in North America may be roughly described as from California, Arizona, Texas, Louisiana, and Florida southward to the Brazilian states of Amazonas, Matto Grosso, Bahia, and Rio de Janeiro (rarely Argentina and Chile). Florida birds are also partially migratory. Ospreys from northern Europe, regularly seen on passage in the British Isles, winter in the Mediterranean and tropical Africa; and from northern Asia, reach India and Ceylon. Vagrants are reported from time to time in Ireland, Iceland, Faeroes, Madeira, and the Azores.

When carrying fish, the Osprey calls "kyeek, kyeek, kyeek," "*zü*ik, *zü*ik-*zü*ick," or "*pü*lick, *pü*-lick, *pü*lick." There are also various whistles and cluckings of alarm and soft greeting notes.

FAMILY FALCONIDAE

(Forest Falcons, Caracaras, Pigmy Falcons, and Falcons)

SUBFAMILY HERPETOTHERINAE

(Laughing Falcons and Forest Falcons)

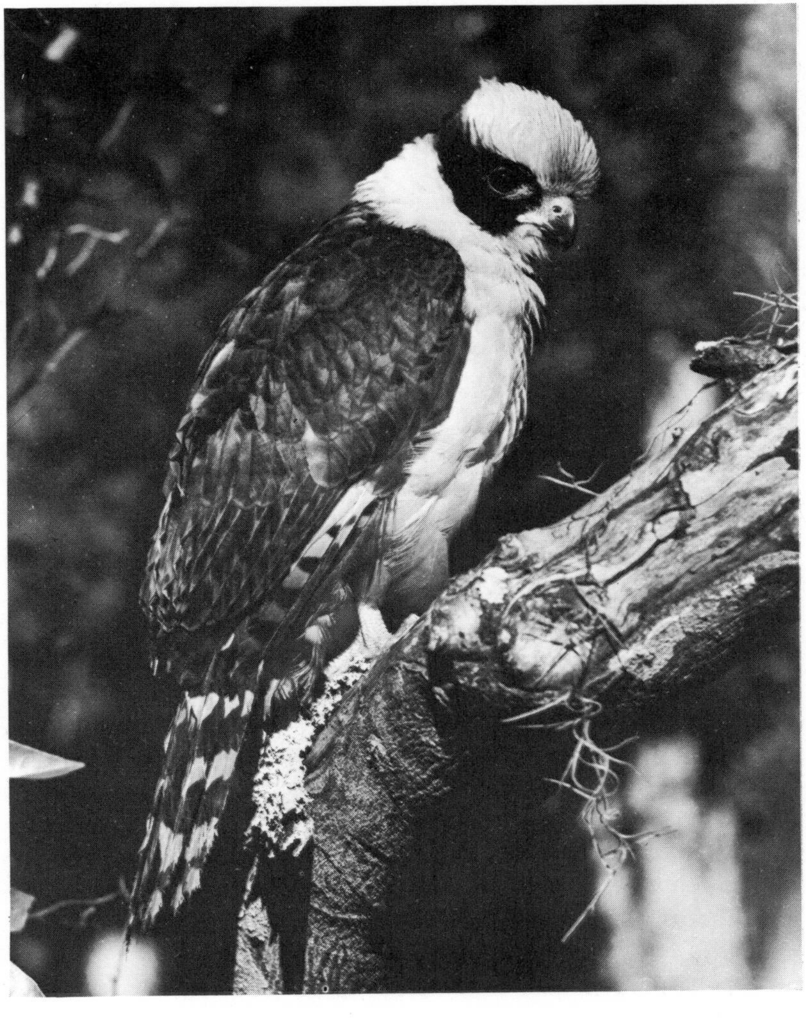

The Laughing Falcon (*Herpetotheres cachinnans*) is one of the most renowned snake-eating hawks in Mexico and Central America.

GENUS *HERPETOTHERES*

Herpetotheres has a chunky body and the short wings of a forest dweller as well as a long, fan-shaped tail of twelve rectrices. The large head is slightly crested. This bird has a falcon-like bare orbital patch, densely bristled lores, and eyelids furnished with strong bristle-like lashes. A conspicuous field mark is the black mask across the face. The beak, legs, and feet are comparatively weak. The tarsi and toes are covered with small hexagonal scales; the undersurface of the toes is rough, or spiculate; and the claws are unusually sharp.

Laughing Falcon (*Herpetotheres cachinnans*)

DESCRIPTION
(MEXICO TO HONDURAS)

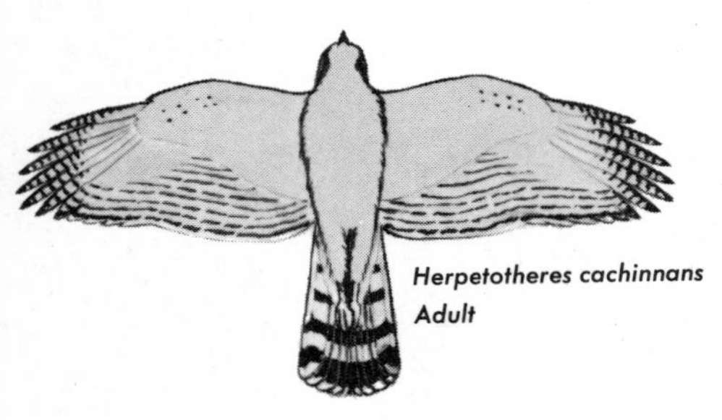

Herpetotheres cachinnans
Adult

Crown and nape, sandy, streaked with black; collared in black; rest of upperparts, chocolate, finely feather-edged in amber-brown; tail, black, barred and tipped with sandy; face, masked in black; underparts, white to sandy, sometimes spotted on the thighs.

Juvenile—broadly feather-edged above, and with fewer bands on the tail.

Beak, black; cere, yellow to orange-yellow; bare skin around eyes, dark gray; eyes, reddish-brown to dark brown; tarsi and toes, dull yellowish-white; claws, black. Size, 17–19 inches.

HERPETOTHERES CACHIN

VARIATIONS

From Amazonia to Argentina, Laughing Falcons closely resemble the birds described, but the head and underparts of the population native to the region from Nicaragua to Ecuador are usually darker—pale cinnamon-buff. Size, 16½–18 inches.

HABITS

The Laughing Falcon may be found in the humid regions of tropical America, which are covered with heavy rain forest; or amid cacti and thorny scrub of the arid districts; and in Argentina, Paraguay, Uruguay, and Chile it inhabits the taller growths of heavy forest. Nearly always a lowland species, it is absent from the Andes. Most often seen perched on some high tree, it circles above the forest infrequently and comes out into the open only to hunt snakes.

The Laughing Falcon drops down upon its prey and carries it off beneath and parallel to its body, the serpent's tail often trailing through the air behind the bird's long fan-shaped tail. Like the White Hawk (*Leucopternis*), it frequently feeds on the poisonous coral snake as well as its colorful imitator, the false coral snake. The heads of snakes are removed before they are brought to the nest.

This snake-eater breeds in hollows of tall trees or holes in cliffs; and where these are unavailable, as in southwestern Ecuador, in old nests of other birds—the Red-backed Hawk (*Buteo polyosoma*) and caracaras. The nest hole recorded by Alexander Skutch in Costa Rica was 100 feet above the ground facing a steep wooded slope, where only the tayra, a forest-dwelling member of the weasel family, might reach it to take the single egg or young. The egg is entirely covered with a wash of dark chocolate-brown, splashes of darker brown, and streaks of yellowish-brown, like some eggs of *Caracara plancus,* and the buff-colored nestling has the characteristic black band of the adult on its downy head. The female either stays all day at the nest site or perches on a branch nearby, and the male feeds his mate and young in the early morning and near dusk. Skutch found that the female either made little effort to defend the young against the tayra or was unable to do so.

The pair engage in a duet early in the morning or late in the evening, crying "wah-co, wah-co, wah-co." The appellation "Laughing Falcon" refers to its loud, shrill "ha ha ha," repeated up to fourteen times.

The Collared Forest Falcon *(Micrastur semitorquatus)* is one of the least-known tropical American hawks.—*Photographed at the National Zoological Park.*

GENUS *MICRASTUR*

In tropical America three species of forest falcons possess a facial ruff similar to, but not as conspicuous as, those of the harriers (*Circus*). The wings are relatively short and rounded, and the tail is very long and rounded. Lores and orbital space are bare except for bristles, and the beak is short, deep, and compressed, the tip of the mandible presenting, in front view, a V-shaped notch. The long tarsi and toes are like those of an accipiter, but they are covered in front with irregular scutes.

Collared Forest Falcon (*Micrastur semitorquatus*)

DESCRIPTION
(TROPICAL AMERICA)

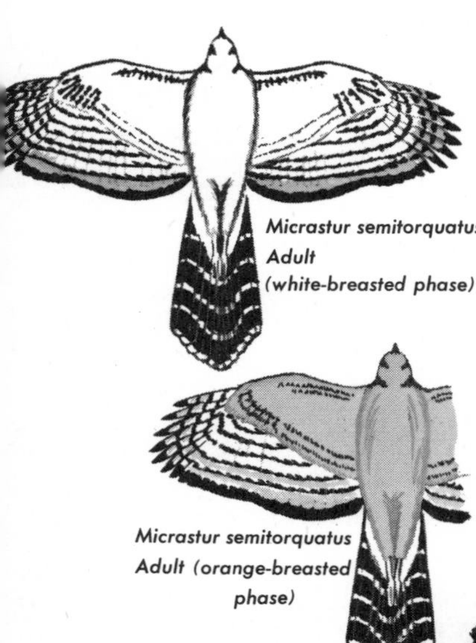

White-breasted phase—black-capped; collared in white; rest of upperparts, chocolate to black; tail, barred black and white and tipped with white; face, white, finely barred and bordered with black ruff; underparts, pure white or tinged with buff, sometimes finely streaked with black.

Orange-breasted phase—similar, but face, collar, and entire underparts, amber-brown.

Dark phase—dark brown, above and below.

Juvenile—barred amber-brown on back as well as on tail; underparts, correspond to color phases of adult plumages: *white-breasted phase,* white, tinged with buff, and barred dark brown; *orange-breasted phase,* buff to amber-brown, barred dark brown; *dark phase,* dark gray-brown, indistinctly barred with amber-brown.

Beak, black (young, greenish); cere and bare part of face, greenish; eyes, brown or orange-brown; legs and feet, yellow; claws, black. Size, 18–21 inches, smallest in eastern Ecuador.

MICRASTUR SEMITORQUATUS

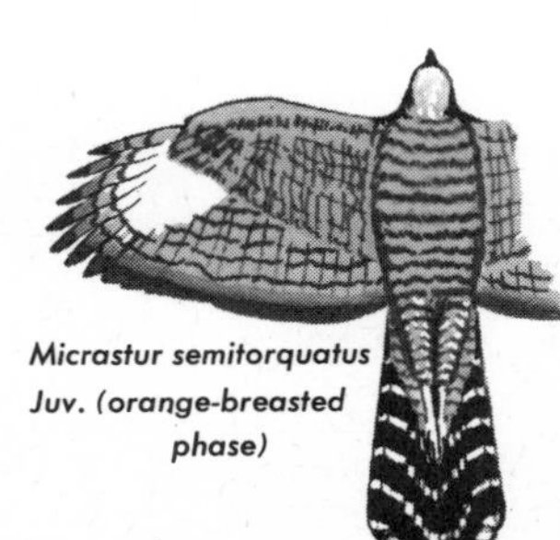

Micrastur semitorquatus
Juv. (orange-breasted phase)

OTHER SPECIES

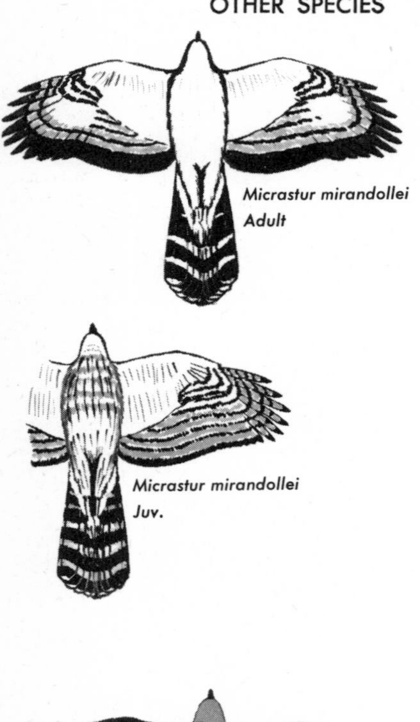

Micrastur mirandollei
Adult

Micrastur mirandollei
Juv.

MICRASTUR MIRANDOL

Another tropical American species, the Slaty-backed Forest Falcon (*M. mirandollei*), 16½–18 inches, is a smaller version of the species previously described, but it lacks a collar and has a slate-gray back. (The young birds are streaked and faintly barred below.)

The black-and-white Barred Forest Falcon (*M. ruficollis*) of Central and South America, 12–15 inches, is generally variable from chestnut (*female*) to slate- or dove-gray above (*male*), the browner birds with distinctly slate-gray caps and the grayer individuals with olive-brown (Mexico) or chocolate-colored wings (Bolivia). The females are more coarsely barred on the underparts and seem to show three white tail bands above; the males, two. In the tropical zone of eastern Venezuela and Colombia, where some of the birds show the brightest backs, the sides of face and throat are tinged with chestnut; and in Matto Grosso (Brazil), Paraguay, Bolivia, and northern Argentina there is considerable variation. Some individuals have a dark head and a sienna-brown cast to the back and tail; underparts, barred and suffused (on the upper chest) in sienna-brown. Others have slightly darker crown, wing, and tail feathers and a more conspicuous sienna-orange suffusion below. The only species which has one visible tail band is the Plumbeous Forest Falcon (*M. plumbeus*) —female, 12 inches, which breeds in the tropical zone of the Cauca Valley, Colombia, and northwestern Ecuador. It is otherwise like the Barred Forest Falcon (*M. ruficollis*). (The juveniles of *M. ruficollis* and *M. plumbeus* vary from white to light amber-brown below, with or without fine dark brown barring. The forest falcons seem to molt directly from the plain or barred juvenile plumage into the adult plumage. If the underparts of the young bird are barred, the backs will often show spotting or barring also.)

MICRASTUR RUFICOLLIS

Micrastur ruficollis
Adult
Central and S. America

Micrastur ruficollis
Juv.

Micrastur ruficollis
Juv.

MICRASTUR PLUMBEUS

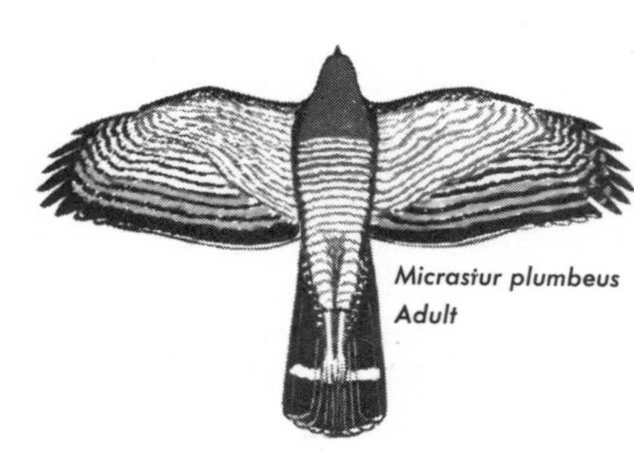

Micrastur plumbeus
Adult

Micrastur ruficollis
Adult
Brazil, Paraguay

HABITS

In thickly wooded country, the forest falcons glide through tangled branches and undergrowth with the ease of the Sharp-shinned Hawk. They can run very fast along the ground; also spring from branch to branch in the trees without opening their wings. In flight the wing strokes are rapid and short, covering only short distances. They prey upon various species of woodland birds, the largest of these hawks (*M. semitorquatus*) favoring chachalacas, arboreal gallinaceous birds.

Practically nothing is known of the breeding habits of the forest falcons. They are said to nest in tall trees.

SUBFAMILY POLYBORINAE

(*Caracaras*)

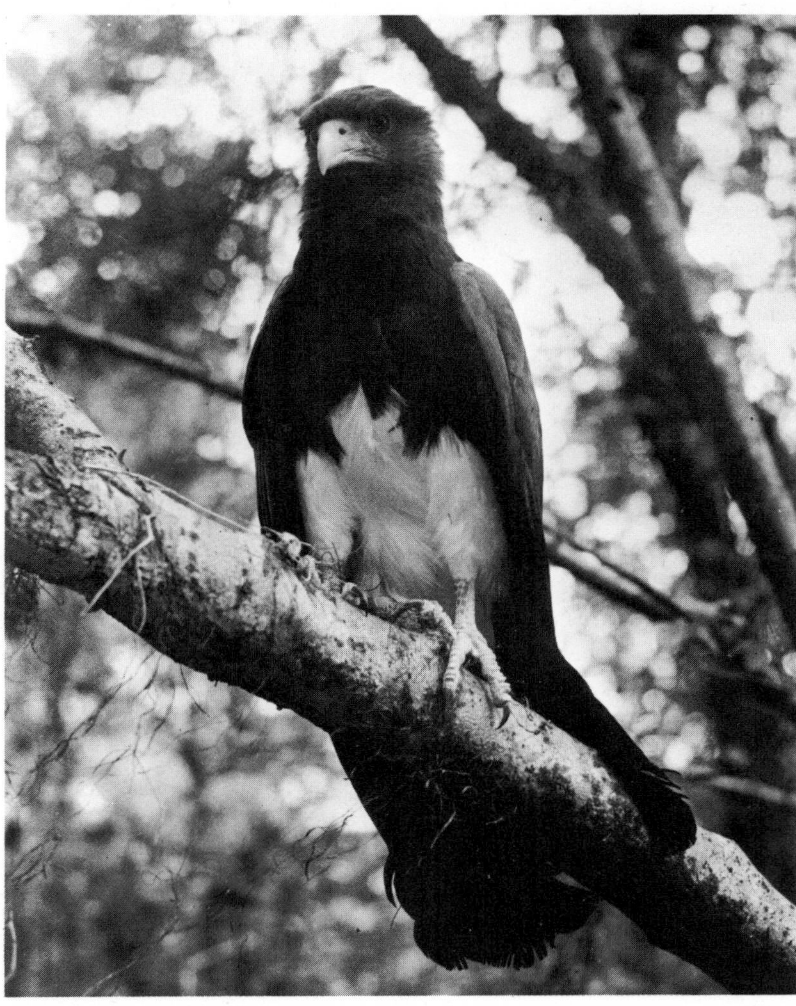

In southern Costa Rica the Red-throated Caracara *(Daptrius americanus)* is called the Cacáo, in imitation of its loud call.

GENUS *DAPTRIUS*

These are the deep tropical forest caracaras with mostly bare faces, naked crops, concealed by feathers unless distended; long ceres and rather highly arched beaks in which the upper mandibles are festooned; and short tarsi, slightly feathered and otherwise covered with irregular hexagonal scales down to the scutellate toes; claws are long and rather acute. In flight, their wide wings and very long rounded tails are conspicuous features.

Red-throated Caracara (*Daptrius americanus*)

DESCRIPTION (CONTINENTAL TROPICAL AMERICA)

Glossy black; belly, flanks and thighs, white; streaking at base of colorful bare throat, light gray.

Juvenile—like adult.

Beak, yellow; cere, gray; bare skin on face and throat, red; eyes, deep red; legs and feet, red; claws, black. Size, 19–21 inches.

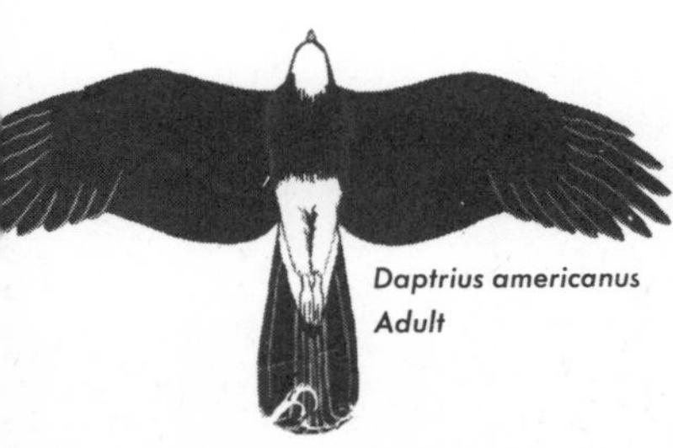

Daptrius americanus Adult

DAPTRIUS AMERICANUS

OTHER SPECIES

The Yellow-throated Caracara (*D. ater*) of the Amazon is about 16 inches; entirely glossy black except for a white band at base of shorter tail. Soft parts differ from *D. americanus;* cere and bare skin of face, bright yellow in contrast to black beak; eyes, brown; feet, yellow. The juvenile is similar, but it has white barring at base of tail.

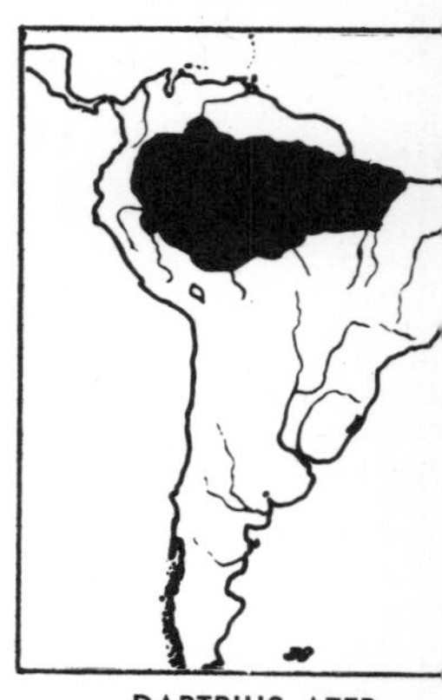
DAPTRIUS ATER

HABITS

The two species of *Daptrius* that live in the deep tropical forests of Central and South America are very specialized arboreal birds.

They have been known to prey on small birds, lizards, and small snakes, but they are mainly insect- and fruit-eating hawks. The Indians of Peru say that the Red-throated Caracara eats wasps, and in Costa Rica, according to Alexander Skutch, it tears open the hives of large blackish wasps (a species of *Synoeca*) and eats the tender white larvae and pupae. Hanging upside down, the "Cacáo" keeps a toehold on the edges of the perforations in the side of the nest's envelope and buries its head in the interior, consuming the entire contents of the vespiary in one meal, while the wasps fly about aimlessly and helplessly. None of the smaller insectivorous birds prey upon this formidable species of wasp.

The Red-throated Caracaras are always conspicuous, flying high over the valleys from forested ridge to forested ridge, and calling, often three together but not in large flocks.

The stick nests of *Daptrius* are built high in the great trees of the tropical forest. Two to three eggs are buff, spotted with chocolate and reddish-brown.

These hawks are noisiest in the breeding season (dry season). The Red-throated Caracara calls "cacáo ca-ca-ca-ca-cacáo," and indulges in loud, harsh laughter—"ha-ha-ha"—over and over.

The Red-throated Caracara (*Daptrius americanus*).

The Yellow-headed Caracara *(Milvago chimachima)* is one of the more common diurnal birds of prey from Panama to the northern Chaco of Argentina.

GENUS *MILVAGO*

The small caracaras have distinctly toothed and notched beaks, short ceres, bare orbital rings, and sparsely feathered faces and throats. A double series of longitudinal scutes on the front of the tarsi joins a single row on the tops of the toes. The claws are strongly curved and sharp. In flight the wings appear rather long and narrow and the underparts and underwing coverts are either very light or much more finely barred than those of the Crested Caracara (*Polyborus plancus*). In the northern species, barring distinguishes juveniles or immatures, but in eastern and southern South America, juveniles of the Chimango Caracara are streaked and spotted below, and the adults are barred. There is little difference in size between the sexes, but in the Chimango Caracara the color of the feet differs.

Yellow-headed Caracara (*Milvago chimachima*)

DESCRIPTION (CONTINENTAL TROPICAL AMERICA)

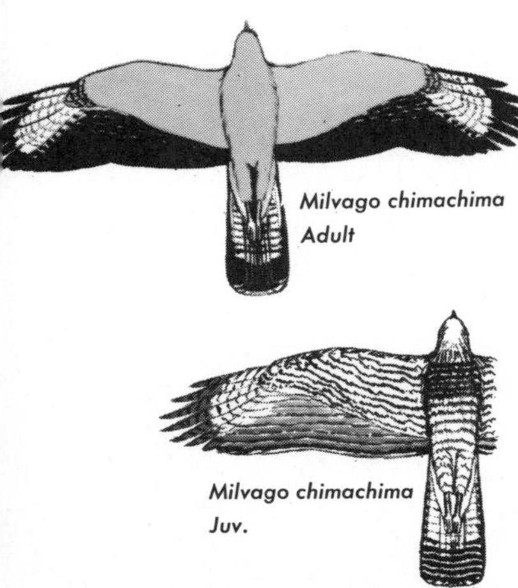

Head, neck, and entire underparts, buff-white to sandy, with heavy black lines behind the eyes; back and wings, dark brown with sandy feather-edging; tail, sandy, barred and broadly banded at the tip with dark brown.

Immature—darker sandy to buff-yellow head, neck, underparts, and tail.

Juvenile—chocolate above; head, dark, streaked with buff-white or buff-yellow; completely barred wing and tail feathers, tinged amber-brown without any broad terminal band; underparts sandy, or buff-yellow, mottled and irregularly barred in chocolate.

Beak, pale blue; cere and bare skin about eyes, deep yellow; eyes, dark brown (young, paler); legs and feet, pea green (feet, black in young); claws, brown. Size, 15–17 inches.

MILVAGO CHIMACHIMA

OTHER SPECIES

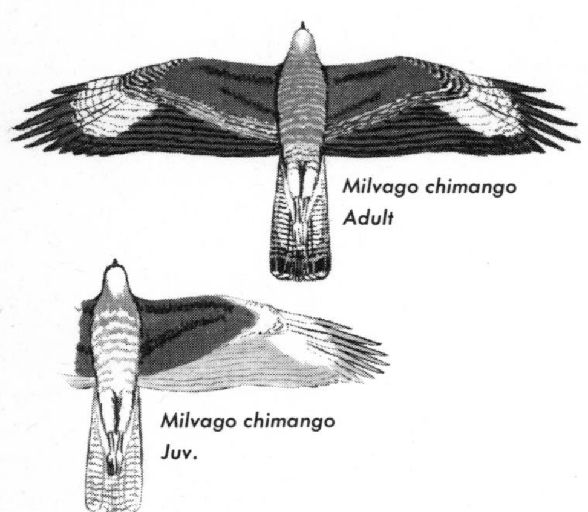

The Chimango Caracara (*Milvago chimango*), 14–16 inches, is cinnamon-brown in eastern South America (from the Falkland Islands to Rio de Janeiro, Brazil) and rufous-brown in southern Chile, streaked on the crown and nape with dark brown; rest of upperparts show pale feather-edging; tail, buff-white, finely barred or mottled in dark brown, broadly banded, and tipped in white; underparts, pale cinnamon with fine light barring and buff-white spotting; the male has bluish-gray legs and feet, the female, yellow. (Juvenile—irregularly barred below, lacking a distinct tail band.)

MILVAGO CHIMANGO

HABITS

The Yellow-headed Caracara, as the northern species is called, and the Chimango Caracara, in the eastern and southern parts of South America, frequent partly wooded pasturelands and pampas.

These small hawks are completely omnivorous, feeding on carrion, insects, larvae, eggs, nestling birds, etc., even vegetable matter. Both species have the habit of riding on the backs of cattle and removing ticks. Their picking is a great annoyance to the animals, for it also opens up old and partly healed sores. However, in regions where they are simply replacing the crows of the Northern Hemisphere as general scavengers, and following the plow, they are tolerated and even encouraged.

Although not as large or aggressive as *Polyborus plancus,* they will occasionally hunt small reptiles and rodents, their mode of attack more like that of a small falcon than the terrestrial Crested Caracara, which runs about on the ground.

The bulky nest of *Milvago*—an assortment of twigs from the nesting tree, and vines or whatever plants are locally available—is built in high trees (woodlands) or in the tops of low trees, bushes, in rushes, or on the ground among grasses (pampas). In the Falkland Islands a lining of wool or hair is provided. Two to four, but usually three, eggs are heavily blotched and spotted with reddish-brown, or almost uniformly colored like those of Old World kestrels.

On the open pampas, Chimango Caracaras are said to nest only in the swamps, several pairs close together. They are extremely gregarious, congregating in companies of thirty or forty, squabbling like vultures, and robbing one another of food. In the nonbreeding season they roost together in trees at night.

The call of the Chimango Caracara is a loud, prolonged "whe-ew," followed by "chaw-chaw-chaw."

The slender, long-legged Mountain Caracara *(Phalcoboenus megalopterus)* lives chiefly in the desolate, remote parts of the Andes between 2,000 and 6,000 feet above sea level.—*Photographed at the National Zoological Park.*

GENUS *PHALCOBOENUS*

The small upland caracaras of South America are slender and display short curly crests, but otherwise they have the bare face and throat as well as the long-necked and long-legged appearance of *Polyborus.* The Carunculated Caracara, in the mountains of Ecuador and Colombia, with its wattled throat and more elongated beak, differs somewhat from its close relatives both in appearance and more sociable habits. Three species replace each other geographically throughout the Andes, and one occurs in the Falkland Islands. Although the adult plumages are strikingly different, the juveniles are practically identical.

Mountain Caracara (*Phalcoboenus megalopterus*)

DESCRIPTION (ANDES OF ECUADOR, PERU, BOLIVIA, AND ARGENTINA)

Glossy black; shoulders, belly, flanks, and long tail coverts, white; wing and tail feathers, white-tipped.

Juvenile—sienna-brown, with fine black streaking above and below; wing coverts, spotted in white; flanks and long tail coverts, pale orange-buff; wing and tail feathers, also sienna-brown, marked with broad central streaks of pale orange-buff and spotted at the tips in white.

Beak, light bluish; cere and bare skin of face, reddish-orange; eyes, brown; legs and feet, orange. Size, about 19 inches.

Phalcoboenus megalopterus Adult

PHALCOBOENUS MEGALOPTERUS

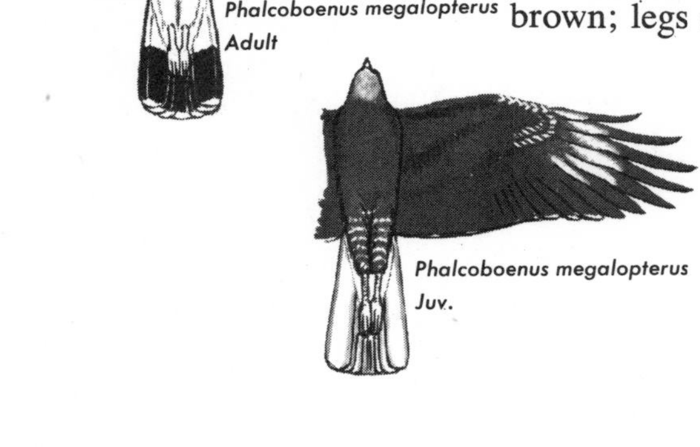

Phalcoboenus megalopterus Juv.

OTHER SPECIES

Almost identical juvenile plumage suggests that two other species of comparable size, occurring in different parts of southern and northwestern South America, are closely related to the bird described. In adult dress the White-throated Caracara (*P. albogularis*) of Patagonia has throat and entire underparts white. The Carunculated Caracara (*P. carunculatus*), in the Paramo zone of southwestern Colombia and Ecuador, looks like the Mountain Caracara, but has broad white streaking on the dark underparts. The Striated Caracara (*P. australis*) in the Falkland Islands, 21–23 inches, is much larger. The upperparts are dark brown with a broad collar of buff-white streaking; tail, black, broadly tipped in white; breast, dark brown, streaked with buff-white; belly and flanks, darker; thighs, amber-brown. (Immature—less conspicuously buff- or sienna-barred on thighs; a sienna suffusion on the tail, without the white tip. Juvenile—chocolate, collared above in sienna and unmarked below, with a plain sienna tail.)

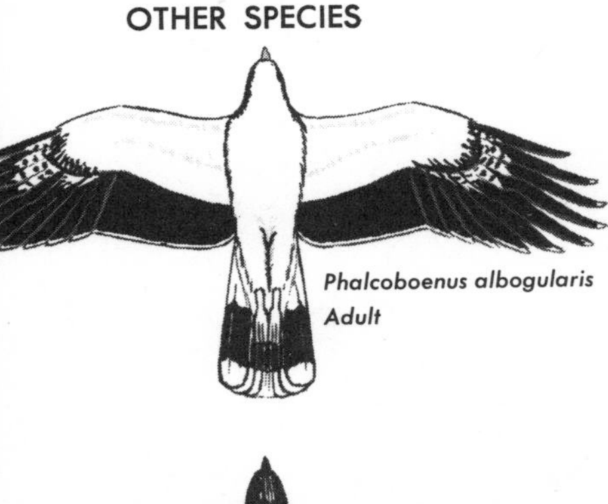

Phalcoboenus albogularis Adult

PHALCOBOENUS ALBOGULARIS

Phalcoboenus carunculatus Adult

PHALCOBOENUS CARUNCULATUS

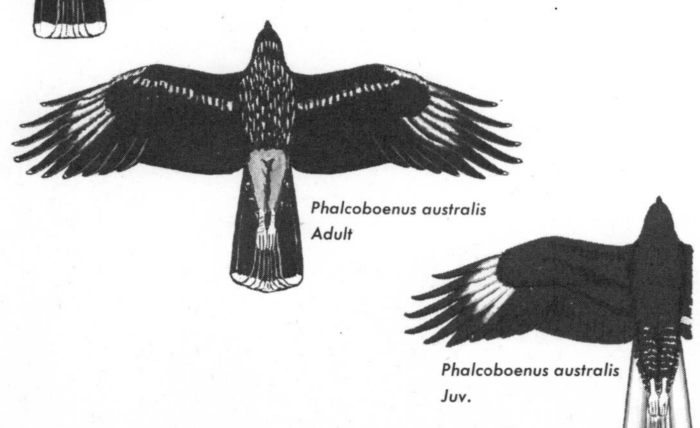

Phalcoboenus australis Adult

Phalcoboenus australis Juv.

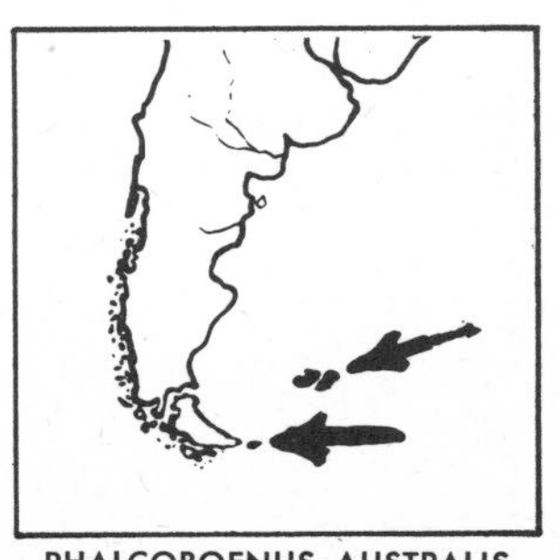

PHALCOBOENUS AUSTRALIS

HABITS

These small upland scavengers are not seen as frequently or in such large numbers as *Milvago* and *Polyborus,* even at high altitudes. Perhaps a few White-throated Caracaras will attend a carcass in the Cordillera, the high "backbone" of the Andes, along with many condors. In Chacalluta and Arica, Chile, the Mountain Caracara, ordinarily a solitary bird of the remote mountain areas, may be found near the sea, and the Striated Caracara inhabits the rocky shores of the Falkland Islands, the Diego Ramirez Rocks, the Il Defonso Islands, and some others, including the Woodcock Islands in the Beagle Channel, but not the mainland of Tierra del Fuego.

On rocky coastlines and islands devoid of vegetation, they feed almost entirely on marine life, steal from gulls, and take garbage and offal from the vicinity of houses.

The Carunculated Caracara is the most gregarious member of the group, and it may once have been more numerous. A century ago forty or fifty of these birds would gather in one field on the plains of northwestern Ecuador, wherever there were herds of cattle, but the Indians are said to have killed many for food. In the eastern Andes, where there are more flatlands, they have always been more widely distributed. Accounts from the early 1900's tell of groups of seven or eight foraging together and, in some places, even roosting on the roofs of houses.

The various species of *Phalcoboenus* are the "crows" of the Andes and Falkland Islands; their food is principally carrion, worms, larvae, garbage, offal, etc., depending on the locality. Occasionally the Mountain Caracara, and perhaps some of the others, will attack animals.

They nest on cliffs, using only a few twigs, dry grass, or sheep's wool, or simply laying the eggs in a depression in a rock. The usual clutch of the Mountain Caracara is composed of three to four cream-colored eggs, spotted and capped at the broad end with brown. The Striated Caracara lays two to three eggs, and the nestlings are covered with light yellow down. Nothing is known about the eggs or young of the other species.

John James Audubon, in whose honor the most northern of the ground-dwelling American carrion hawks *(Polyborus plancus)* is often called Audubon's Caracara, first saw these birds near St. Augustine, Florida, in 1831. On the Florida prairies they almost invariably nest in the tops of cabbage palmettos.

GENUS *POLYBORUS*

Polyborus is a specialized carrion-feeding hawk of warmer but not humid or heavily forested parts of the New World. It is morphologically related to the falcons and its deep, much compressed beak shows a slight indication of the falcon's tooth on the upper mandible. The long fleshy cere and bare skin of the face are bright red. At the back of the head a short crest flares. The bare tarsi are very long and are scutellate on the lower portion, and transverse scutes continue down the short toes, which are furnished with long, but only moderately curved talons. In flight the wings are long and narrow, and the tail appears either rounded or squared off.

Crested, or Common, Caracara (*Polyborus plancus*)

DESCRIPTION (SOUTHERN UNITED STATES, MEXICO, CENTRAL AMERICA, WESTERN PANAMA, GREATER ANTILLES)

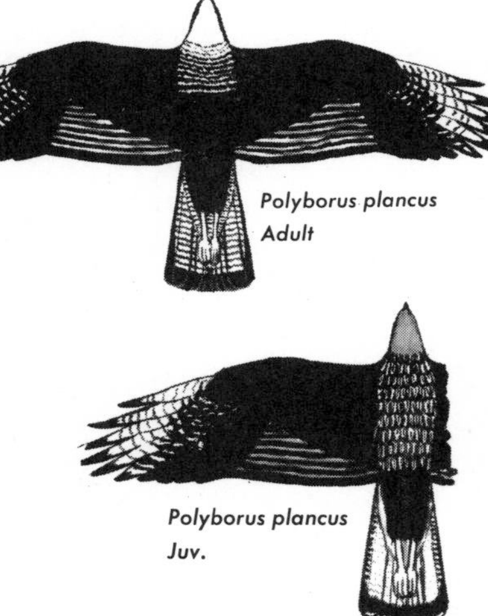
Polyborus plancus Adult

Polyborus plancus Juv.

Capped from crown to crested nape in dark brown; collared white or sandy, with light barring on upper part of the dark brown back; wing coverts and wings, dark brown except for patches of white barring on primaries; tail, white, narrowly barred and broadly banded at the tip in dark brown; face, bare; throat, sides of face and neck, and upper breast, ivory; breast, otherwise barred with ivory and dark brown or with V-spots of dark brown on light background; rest of underparts, dark brown.

Immature—rufous-brown, with light amber-brown head and neck; collar and breast, broadly streaked with sandy and narrowly striped in black.

Juvenile—similar, but has light cinnamon cheeks and throat; white or sandy streaking above and below, without black shaft-stripes; lacks distinct collar on nape.

Beak, bluish-white; cere and bare skin of face, red; eyes, reddish-brown; legs and feet, bright to very pale yellow; claws, black. Size, 20–22 inches.

POLYBORUS PLANCUS

VARIATIONS

From eastern Panama through northern South America, the markings do not differ, but the Crested Caracara is darker; and in temperate southern South America the Carancho—as it is called there—has a chocolate-colored back and more extensive barring above and below. Sizes, 19½–22 inches; the smallest birds are in the Tres Marías Islands, off Lower California and western Mexico, and the largest are in the Argentine.

HABITS

On prairies, savannas, and pampas from Florida to the Argentine, Crested Caracaras commonly gather in groups of two, three, or four. At times they may be seen sailing above the ground in circles, prospecting for food; or alternately sailing and flapping like Black Vultures (*Coragyps*). Their usual flapping flight is crowlike—direct, and very rapid, with noisy wing beats. During the day they often perch in the tops of tall trees which command a view of the surrounding region; and in the nonbreeding season, as many as ten of these birds may return from foraging to roost together at night in one of the occasional groves of trees that are scattered through open country. However, even though they roost high in trees, they are just as much at home on the ground—perhaps sitting on their haunches in the dust with the tail spread flat and the body and head upright, as casually as an eagle would "sun" on a remote rocky ledge.

While hunting, Crested Caracaras fly low over the ground or actually run about in the grass, picking up insects, grubs, worms, lizards, and mice. In some localities (Tres Marías Islands) iguanas are said to be their main food. At carrion, with other scavengers, they have been observed to eat more of the insect larvae than of the rotting flesh itself. However, Crested Caracaras, or Caranchos, as they are called on the Argentine and Paraguayan pampas, are omnivorous—feeding on live or dead fish or mammals, eggs, young or wounded birds, and (on the seashore) live shellfish. They frequent newly plowed fields, clean up the roadways and the slaughter pens, and pick up floating carrion from the rivers. In most of these pursuits Crested Caracaras do not interfere with man and are tolerated. But from the northern Chaco to Tierra del Fuego, where they have acquired the habit of attacking young livestock, they are persecuted.

The Guadalupe Caracara (*Polyborus lutosus*) is one of the few bird species which has been deliberately destroyed by man in modern times. Goatherders, tormented by the caracaras, initiated a campaign of extermination, which, perhaps aided by a plague of feral house cats, succeeded in wiping out the entire population in a few years. Although "abundant on every part of the island" in 1876, according to the Bulletin of the U.S. Geological Survey of that year, not one Guadalupe Caracara was to be found in 1906 when a collecting expedition scoured the island from one end to the other, nor have any been seen since. Meanwhile, man with his herds was also destroying the natural habitat.

The Crested Caracara customarily holds down carrion with one foot, in vulture fashion, and tears it to pieces with its heavy bill; but, as it is also a raptor, it can seize and carry prey with its feet.

This bird shares with the scavenger aquilas and the sea eagles the habit of attacking other raptors, gulls, and vultures and either robbing them of their prey or forcing them to disgorge. The White-tailed Hawk (*Buteo albicaudatus*) has been seen to drop a lizard, without a fight, when assailed by a Crested Caracara; and birds as large as the White Ibis, the Brown Pelican, and the Bald Eagle have also been victimized.

Caracaras may raise two broods a year in South America, but in Florida, where eggs are found from December to April, they are usually single-brooded.

Nests may be built in single isolated trees, in small groves, or in swamps; rarely on the ground. The large tree nests, used year after year, are constructed of dry sticks; the deeply cupped interior is lined with either felted dry grass or pellets of wool or hair ejected by the parents. On the Argentine pampas they may also contain cowhide, sheepskin, lariats, bones, and food remains. Two to three eggs have a creamy or pinkish ground nearly obscured by blotches and mottlings of brown or reddish-brown. Both sexes take part in incubation. At about five weeks (Florida) the young are still in the nest, and they may be fledged when two or three months old. They are given bits of meat or fish from the parents' beaks, like falcons—they are not fed by regurgitation, as the nestlings of vultures are fed.

The name caracara is of Guaraní Indian origin and onomatopoeic, for the cry of this bird is a harsh, grating sound, like two pieces of wood being rubbed against each other. It is sometimes written "traro, traro." Another common sound is "eh-eh-eh," as though someone were clearing his throat.

Crested Caracara *(Polyborus plancus)* in Florida.

SUBFAMILY POLIHIERACINAE

(Pigmy Falcons)

The Spot-winged Falconet *(Spiziapteryx circumcinctus)* is called "Rey de los Pajaros," or King of the Birds, by Argentine natives, who admire its courage and strength.

GENUS *SPIZIAPTERYX*

This kestrel-sized genus, which inhabits only certain parts of northern Argentina, has a moderately notched bill, a round nostril with a central tubercle, and bare orbital spaces. It is a forest-dweller with wings much shorter than a kestrel's. The scaled tarsi are feathered about one-fourth in front, and the middle toes are very short. The white rump patch is a prominent identification mark.

Spot-winged Falconet (*Spiziapteryx circumcinctus*)

DESCRIPTION
(ARGENTINA)

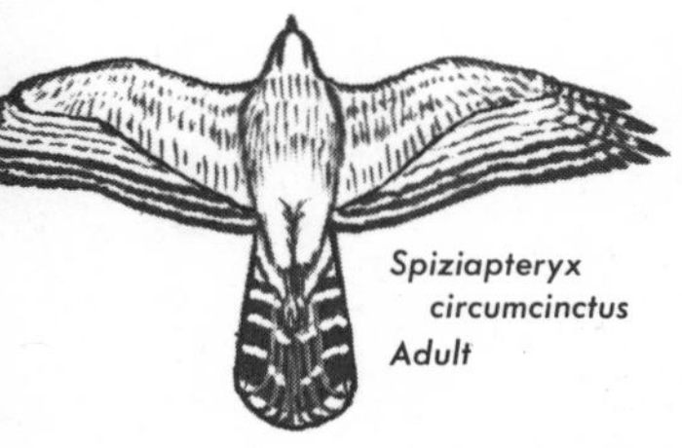

Spiziapteryx circumcinctus Adult

Olive-brown above, streaked with dark brown (especially on head); wing coverts, finely dotted; darker flight feathers, conspicuously spotted with white; rump patch, pure white; tail, dark brown, spotted (except for plain center feathers) and tipped in white; face, dark with distinct white eyebrows and loral streaks, sometimes extending to back of neck; chin, white; underparts, white, with dark brown streaking on breast.

Beak, gray, with black tip; cere and bare skin around eyes, yellow; eyes, orange-yellow; legs and feet, buff; claws, black. Size, 10½–11½ inches.

SPIZIAPTERYX CIRCUMCINCTUS

HABITS

The Spot-winged Falconet frequents woodlands on the pampas of northern Argentina, where heavy-limbed stocky trees are fairly open. On cooler days this bird sits on exposed branches, but when the weather is hot, it perches and hops agilely about in shaded trees, such as calden, in which the foliage is confined to the tips of the branches and serves as a protective screen. Its flight is direct, with a distinctive "violent" wing beat.

This falconet presumably preys on birds. Whenever it comes out into the open it is pursued by passerines—the Fork-tailed Flycatcher and other species.

Its querulous whining calls are similar to one of the call notes of the Catbird, but much louder.

The habitat of the African Pigmy Falcon *(Polihierax semitorquatus)*, the only tiny falcon in Africa, is dry watercourses with doom palms, acacias, and thorn scrub.

GENUS *POLIHIERAX*

This pigmy falcon has a small, single-notched beak. The tarsi are feathered only one-fourth, otherwise covered with round scales, large in front and smaller behind. The wings are kestrel-like and the tail is short and square. There are sexual differences in coloring; males, gray-backed, and females, red-backed.

African Pigmy Falcon (*Polihierax semitorquatus*)

DESCRIPTION (EAST AND SOUTH AFRICA)

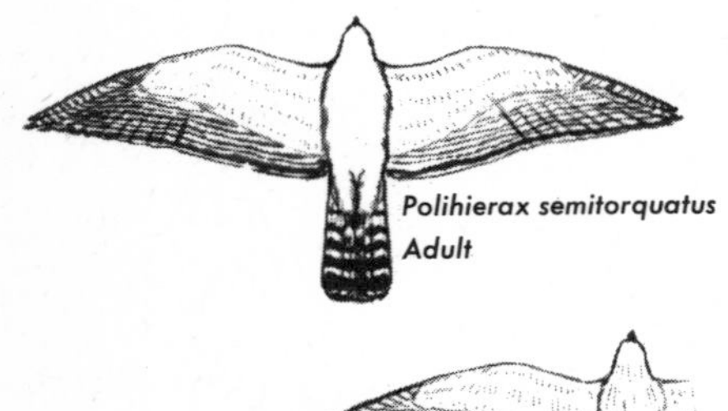

Polihierax semitorquatus Adult

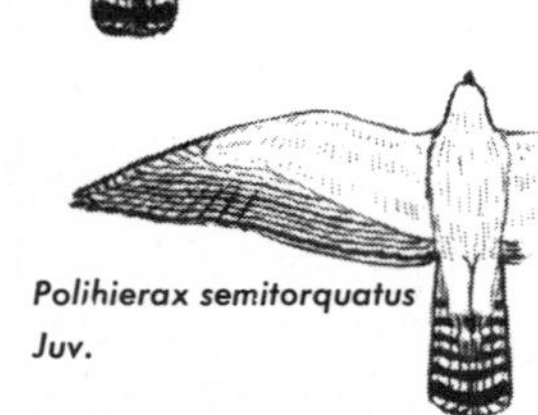

Polihierax semitorquatus Juv.

Male—dove-gray to slate-gray above, with white collar and rump patch; wings and tail, dark brown, spotted and tipped in white; forehead, eyebrows, face, throat, and entire underparts, white or tinged with buff. *Female*—large sienna-brown patch on back.

Juvenile (*both sexes*)—faint sienna-brown feather-edging above and buff underparts finely streaked (but female soon acquires a distinct sienna-brown patch.)

Beak, gray, with black tip; cere and bare skin around eyes, red; eyes, brown; legs and feet, red; claws, brown. Size, 6–7 inches.

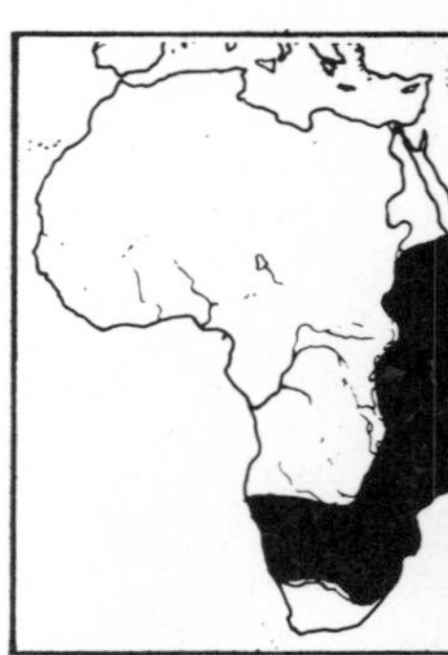

POLIHIERAX SEMITORQU

HABITS

This tiny falcon of the dry brush country of Africa could be mistaken for a large shrike, because its food habits and actions are very similar. It flies from its perch with a few quick flaps, then glides up to settle on another tree. Pairs sit conspicuously on the branches of dead trees, low thorn trees, or bushes, from which they usually drop to the ground to capture their prey—mostly beetles and other insects, but also small birds, mice, and lizards.

A pair of African Pigmy Falcons apparently always appropriates an old nest of the White-headed Buffalo Weaver or other weavers (often in the midst of a colony) or the deserted nest of a Wedge-tailed Glossy Starling. In the colonies they are said not to molest their neighbors. Two to three white eggs are laid.

The call is a shrill "tu-tu-tu-tu-tu" crescendo.

The Burmese Pigmy Falcon (*Neohierax insignis*) was first thought to be an Asian representative of the African genus *Polihierax*. In the *Monograph of the Birds of Prey,* however, Kirke Swann noted several unique characteristics, including the strikingly different shape of the tail, and renamed it *Neohierax*.

GENUS *NEOHIERAX*

The bill of Indomalayan *Neohierax* is single-toothed; the tarsi are mostly bare with round scales; the toes are weak. Rounded wings and a long graduated tail (outer feathers extremely short) distinguish the species from the Asiatic Pigmy Falcons of the genus *Microhierax,* which are smaller. The male is gray-headed; the female, red-headed.

Burmese Pigmy Falcon (*Neohierax insignis*)

DESCRIPTION (BURMA TO INDOCHINA)

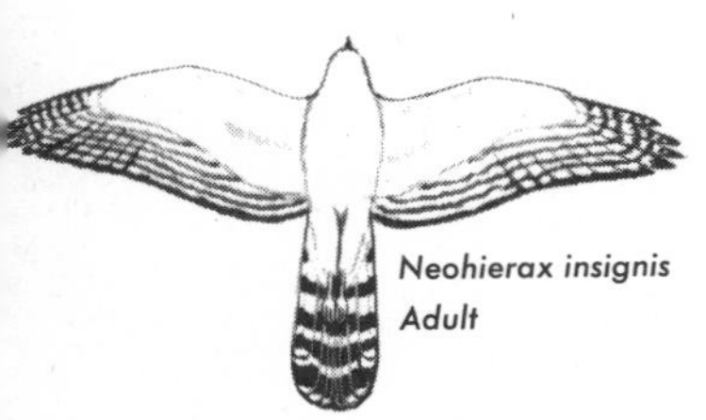

Neohierax insignis Adult

Male—head and mantle, light gray, finely striped with dark slate; back, dove-gray to slate-gray, with white rump patch; wings, black, spotted white; tail, also black with spots on the outer rectrices, underparts, white or tinted with buff; flanks, light gray. *Female*—bright sienna head and mantle, striped black; otherwise, similar.

Juvenile (*both sexes*)—like adult male, but more heavily streaked on crown; collar of gray or white spotting at hindneck; underparts, heavily tinged with buff.

Beak, black; eyes, dark brown; cere, bare skin around eyes, legs, and feet, yellow. Size, 8½–9½ inches.

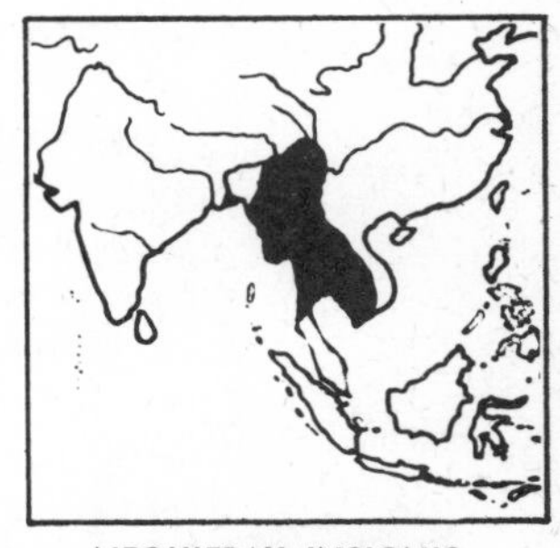

NEOHIERAX INSIGNIS

HABITS

Clearings in the dry forests of Burma, Siam, and Indochina, are the habitat of this small falcon. Its flight is undulating—much like that of a magpie. From its perch on the high bare branch of a tree, the Burmese Pigmy Falcon pounces on locusts, grasshoppers, and various other insects on the ground.

Like other pigmy falcons, it nests in holes or structures built by other birds. The gray-white eggs resemble those of the Shikra (*Accipiter badius*), except in size.

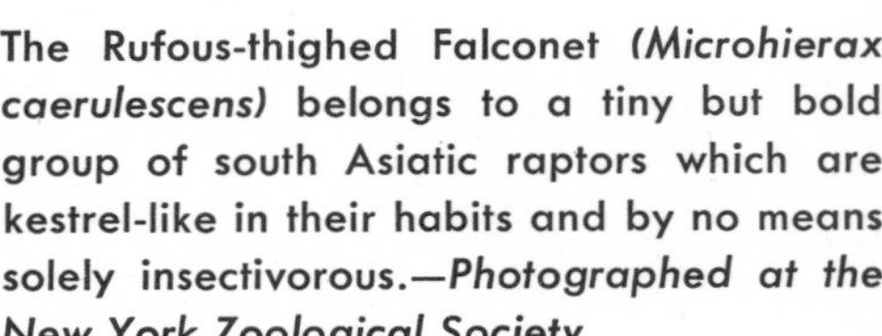

The Rufous-thighed Falconet *(Microhierax caerulescens)* belongs to a tiny but bold group of south Asiatic raptors which are kestrel-like in their habits and by no means solely insectivorous.—*Photographed at the New York Zoological Society.*

GENUS *MICROHIERAX*

In the five species of *Microhierax* the bill is large, slightly compressed, and distinctly double-toothed. The nostril has no central tubercle. The legs and feet are large and powerful in relation to body size; the tarsi are half-feathered and scutellate down the front and on the toes. The wings are long and rather rounded; and the tail is long and nearly square. Red patches on the crown or cheeks (or both) and pale lower belly (and thighs) generally distinguish juveniles from adults, which have the reverse coloring.

Rufous-thighed Falconet (*Microhierax caerulescens*)

DESCRIPTION
(LOWER SLOPES OF THE HIMALAYAS IN ASSAM, HILLS OF BURMA, AND INDOCHINA)

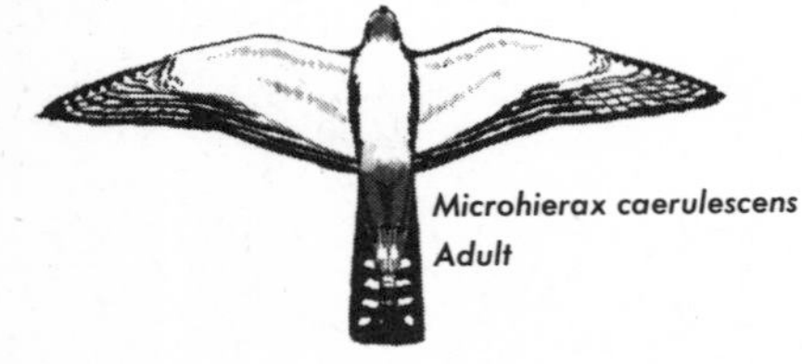

Above, glossy black, with white collar at nape; wings and tail, spotted with white; tail also spotted on outer rectrices; forehead and face, white, with a black line behind each eye; throat, lower belly, and thighs, dark tawny; breast, white, tinged with buff.

Juvenile—dark tawny coloring on forehead, eyebrows, and cheeks; white throat; otherwise, like adult.

Beak, blue-black (juvenile, paler); eyes, brown; legs and feet, dark slate; claws, black. Size, 5½–6½ inches (largest between 2,500 and 9,000 feet in the Himalayas).

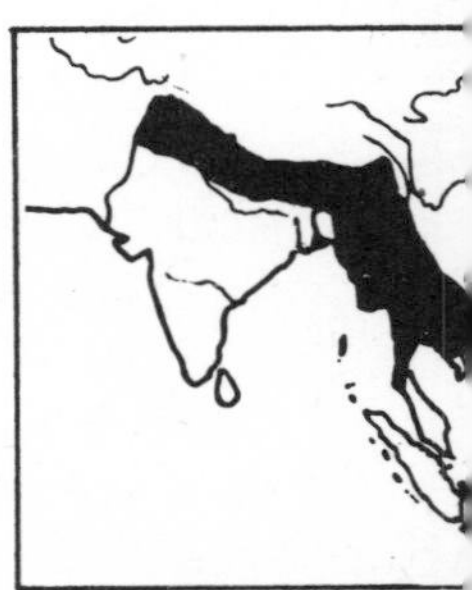

MICROHIERAX CAERULE

OTHER SPECIES

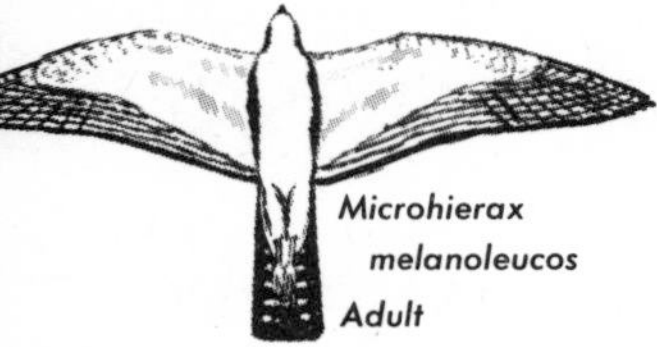

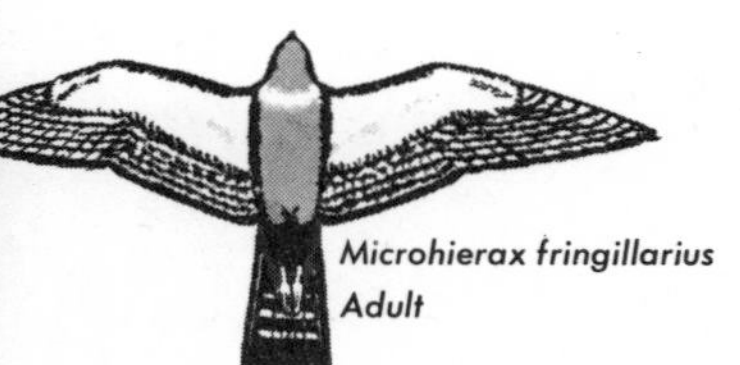

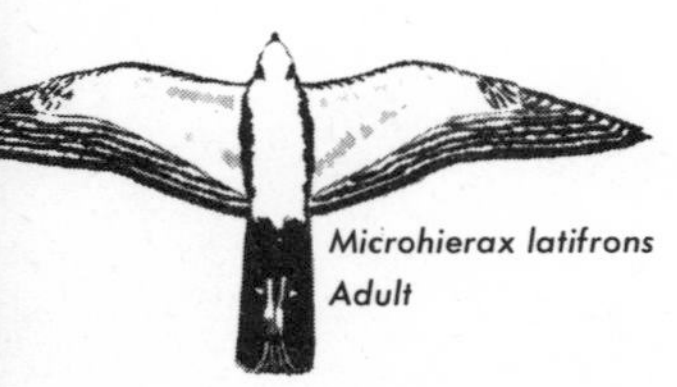

The Pied Falconet (*M. melanoleucus*) of Assam and southeastern China, 5½–7 inches, is common below 3,000 feet, but may range up to 5,000 feet, has white eyebrows, cheeks, and underparts; black patches on neck, sides, and flanks; sometimes an irregular white nape band (southern China); barred tail.

In the Malay peninsula, Sumatra, Java, and southwestern Borneo, the Black-legged Falconet (*M. fringillarius*), 5½–6 inches, lacks the white collar and white eyebrows that mark the other falconets, but it has white lines behind the eyes and heavy black patches at the sides of the neck. The belly is tawny, contrasting with glossy black feathering on the sides, flanks, and thighs. (The juvenile has tawny coloring on the forehead and cheeks, as well as tawny lines behind the eyes and paler underparts; otherwise, like adult.)

The Bornean Falconet (*M. latifrons*), about 6 inches, has a white patch which covers the forehead and greater part of the crown; white cheeks; black feathering around the eyes; black patches at sides of neck; black sides, flanks, and thighs, like *M. fringillarius,* but much paler below; tail, not spotted or barred. (The juvenile has a tawny crown patch and cheeks; otherwise, resembles the adult.)

On Luzon, Mindoro, Negros, Cebu, Bohol, Samar, and Mindanao, the Philippine Falconet (*M. erythrogonys*), 6½–7 inches, is entirely glossy greenish-black, except for white throat, breast, and belly. A bright tinge of light tawny at the sides of the face marks the juvenile.

MICROHIERAX MELANOLEUCOS

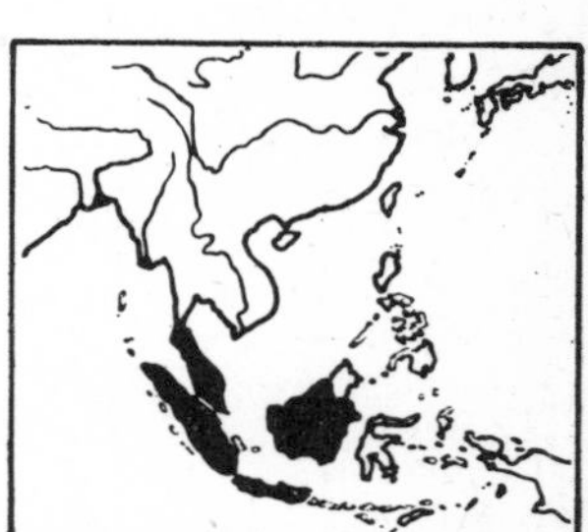
MICROHIERAX FRINGILLARIUS

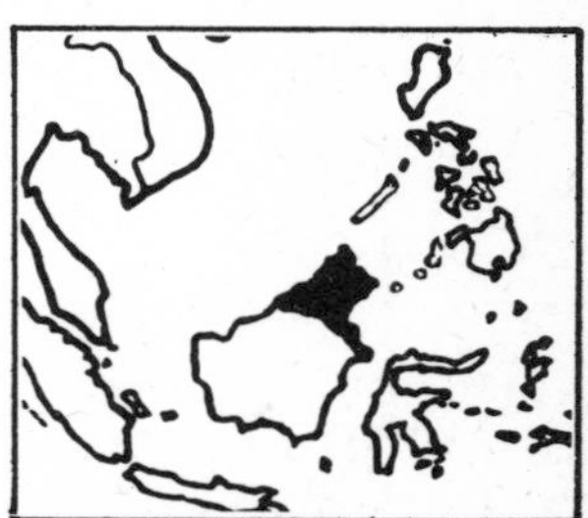
MICROHIERAX LATIFRONS

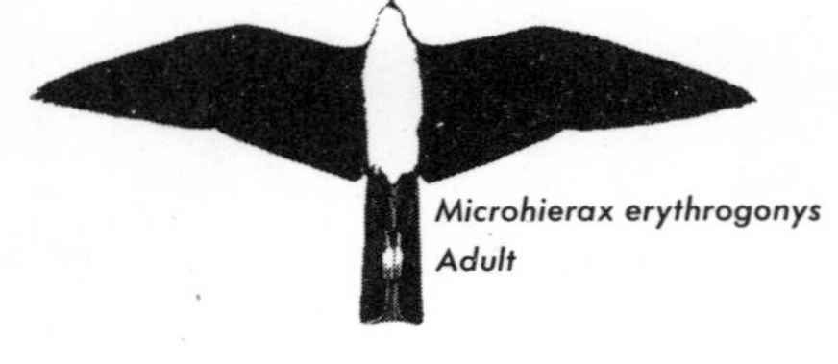

MICROHIERAX ERYTHROGONYS

HABITS

The Asiatic falconets prefer open lowlands and hill country, but they are occasionally seen along rivers or near clearings in dense forest. Their habitats are similar to those of the genus *Falco.* Although mainly insectivorous, they are capable of fast swoops, capturing in this manner birds much larger than themselves—scimitars and other babblers, thrushes, etc.

They habitually sit in pairs on exposed branches of dead trees, and occasionally fly out to snatch an insect or a small bird from the air. These tiny falcons also sail in circles, hawking insects, which they eat on the wing. Small birds and mammals are carried to a perch, and larger ones are eaten on the ground.

Falconets nest in holes in trees, often at a great height from the ground. They prefer the deserted nest holes of barbets and woodpeckers, and the Black-legged Falconet has been known to nest in the roofs of houses. Three to four white eggs are laid directly on insect debris.

The Rufous-thighed Falconet migrates out of the Himalayas in winter, but the other species are sedentary.

The cry as given by the Pied Falconet is a shrill scream. A chattering call and warning sound—a prolonged hiss—are also recorded.

SUBFAMILY FALCONINAE

(Gyrfalcons, Falcons, and Kestrels)

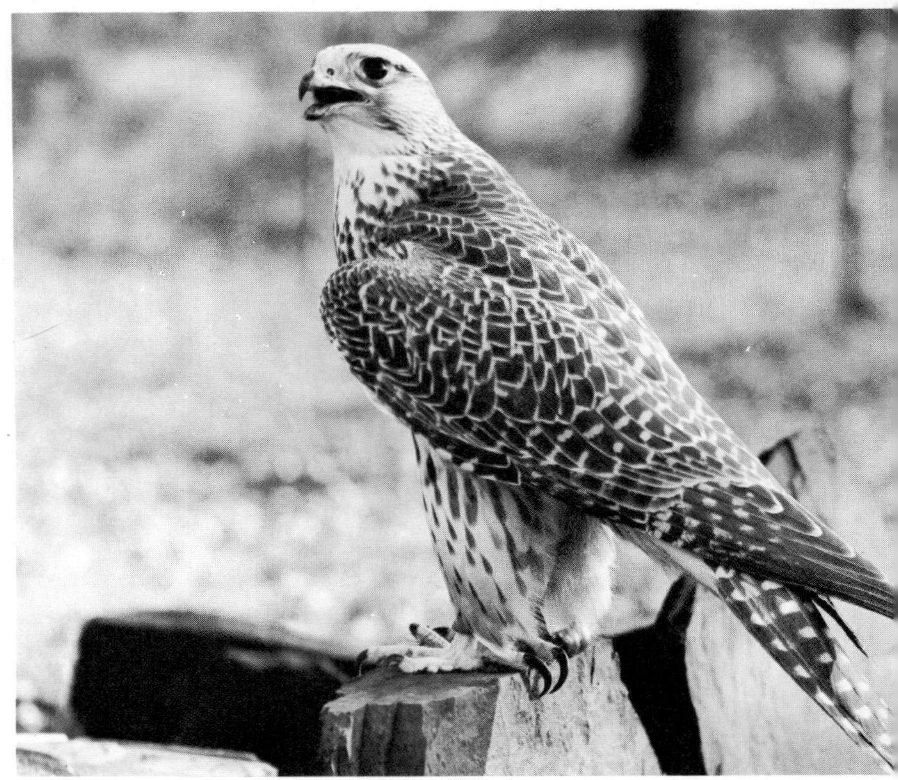

This juvenile Gyrfalcon *(Falco rusticolus)*, a Gray Phase bird from Alaska, belongs to Heinz Meng. In the interior of Alaska the Gyrfalcon and the Peregrine Falcon are competitive species, but the Gyrfalcon ranges farther north into the tundra and to higher altitudes in the mountains (above the Peregrine's 2,200-foot limit).

GENUS *FALCO*

Falcons are the most trimly designed of all the predatory birds; both in body structure and plumage, they are exceptionally well-adapted for pursuit in the open. The genus *Falco* includes thirty-nine species, ranging in size from the smallest falcons and kestrels weighing six or seven ounces to the largest Gyrfalcons, weighing about three pounds. These may be broken down, roughly, into groups, according to their habitat preferences and particular modes of hunting.

The northern Gyrfalcon and its relatives (including, among others, the Saker, the Lanner, and the Laggar of Palearctic, African, and Indian distribution) and the North American Prairie Falcon inhabit tundra, barren mountain plateaus, deserts, plains, and steppes, and they capture some prey on the ground.

The Peregrine Falcon occurs in semi-forested country in all climate zones (less frequently in the tundras and deserts) and preys almost exclusively on birds which it strikes in flight.

The more diminutive Hobbies and other falcons that thrive on small birds and insects inhabit lightly wooded hills or mountains and forest edges close to open tundras, deserts, meadows, or parklands. Included in this group are the Red-footed Falcon, Eleonora's Falcon, and the Sooty Falcon, which are sociable, nesting close together in colonies and hunting together on their winter ranges.

The Palearctic and North American Merlin, an extremely versatile hunter for its size, claims only the Red-headed Falcon of India and Africa as a close relative. Both species are adaptable to open forest situations (palm groves in the tropics); also plains, heaths, steppes, and tundras, and although they hunt mostly birds by a low direct aerial pursuit, they take a certain amount of their prey from the ground.

There are also a number of small- to medium-sized tropical and subtropical falcons, such as the Australasian Brown Falcon and its close relatives in that region, and the American Aplomado Falcon, which are more sluggish and spend a good deal of time perching on some exposed place, from which they dash out to seize small birds or insect prey.

From these various types it is only a step to the myriad species of Old and New World kestrels—primarily small rodent- and insect-eaters, often sociable, and closely associated with towns, villages, meadows, and cultivated fields. Birds are rarely captured in full flight, and the Common Kestrel, hawking insects, shows much less adroitness than does the Hobby. Many of these birds characteristically hover and pounce on their prey on the ground; others are less active fence-post sitters. The Common Kestrel and the Lesser Kestrel are sibling species which live in the same region and show only minor differences in structure and details of plumage pattern, and in parts of eastern and southern Africa the Greater Kestrel has a similar relationship to the Common Kestrel.

Probably no genus of raptorial birds having the same general characteristics is more varied in its specific morphological traits and habits, and only the accipiters, which show an even greater degree of speciation, are as widespread. Any subgeneric groups are bound to overlap, and it is not at all certain that some birds which we have compared are related. They may be geographically separate species, which, for example, in arid parts of Australia, have developed along lines parallel to those in similar habitats in the Northern Hemisphere.

The falcon traits are a small head marked with dark moustachial stripes; short, strong, deeply hooked bill, conspicuously toothed and notched; a bare orbital region, usually brightly colored like the bare part of the legs, and lores with bristle-like feathers arranged more or less in a whorl. The body is streamlined and the feathers are hard and compact. The tarsi never show a single series of transverse scutes, but they are often covered with small, round scales. The Gyrfalcon leg is about half-feathered with long fluffy pantaloons; the Peregrine Falcon has feathering about one-third down; and smaller falcons have very little feathering in front. All have fluffy thigh feathering to some degree. However, the Australasian Brown Falcon's tarsi are slender for its size, very long, and covered with large, round scales. The toes, especially the middle one, are very long, as in the accipiters, which are also bird hawks, and the claws are strongly curved, their undersurface broadly grooved or concave.

The wings of falcons are long and pointed, and the tail feathers are tapered at the tips, except in the Brown Falcon, which has a very full, rounded tail. In some species the wings and tail are longer, reaching an extreme in the Fox Kestrel of Africa.

Females are much larger than males, especially in the large aggressive species, such as the Gyrfalcon and the Peregrine Falcon. Female dominance appears to be an important factor in successful pairing, and the size differential between the sexes also enables the pair to take a greater range of prey. Tom Cade has shown that in Alaska the Peregrine tercel (or male) takes passerines and shore birds in the 30- to 150-gram categories (less commonly birds up to the size of teal and ptarmigan weighing 400 to 600 grams). The falcon (or female) takes larger passerines, shore birds, and small waterfowl in the 200- to 600-gram categories, and is capable of striking down waterfowl up to 1,500 grams. This gives her the same advantage which the male Gyrfalcon has, although the female Gyrfalcon exceeds his capabilities. On the other hand, the males and females of the smaller falcons and kestrels are more evenly matched in size and show a distinct sexual dimorphism in the coloring of the plumage.

Cade has suggested that the great difference in size between, for example, the falcon weighing 750 to 1,200 grams and the tercel weighing 500 to 800 grams, has very largely replaced an ancestral sexual dimorphism in plumage that is still conspicuous in the kestrels. In the large species there is a very slight tendency towards color dimorphism, with females generally, but not always, darker than the males. The Holarctic Gyrfalcon, in addition, is polymorphic, its color (male or female) ranging from almost pure arctic whiteness in northern Greenland to many degrees of gray or dark gray in the low arctic regions.

Gyrfalcon (*Falco rusticolus*)

DESCRIPTION (CIRCUMPOLAR-LOW ARCTIC)

Gray phase—above, gray-brown, barred and narrowly feather-edged from the collar downward in white; wings and tail, also barred; forehead, throat, and sides of neck, white, streaked with gray-brown and often marked with a distinct mustachial stripe; underparts, white, with streaking on the chest becoming conspicuous blobs of dark gray-brown on the belly; sides and flanks, heavily barred.

Dark gray phase—similar in pattern, but dark gray-brown above and heavily streaked and barred below; black underwing coverts and slate-gray wings and tail are indistinctly mottled in white.

Juvenile (*gray phase*)—like adult, but it has a white head and broad white feather-edging on the back; underparts, white, heavily streaked with gray-brown; *dark gray phase* has a dark head and coloring of the underparts reversed—dark with white streaking.

Beak, bluish-horn; cere, legs, and feet, bright yellow (bluish to greenish-gray in young); eyes, dark brown. Size, 21–24 inches.

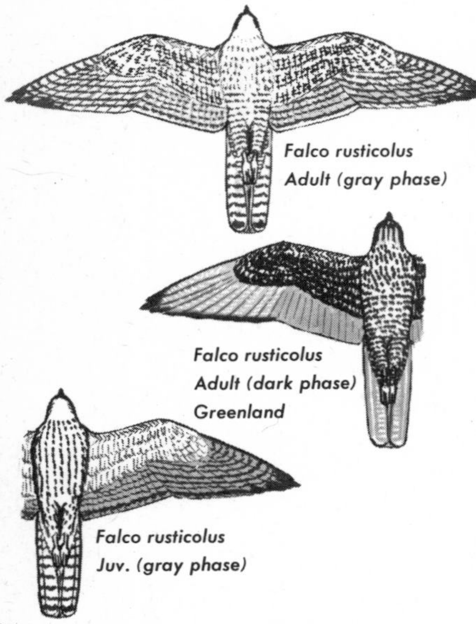

Falco rusticolus Adult (gray phase)

Falco rusticolus Adult (dark phase) Greenland

Falco rusticolus Juv. (gray phase)

VARIATIONS

Occurring with the gray phase in the high arctic is a white phase: white above, finely streaked on the crown and heavily marked on the back with blobs or spotty barring of cinnamon-brown; wings and tail, either barred or unbarred; face and neck, white, without any distinct stripe; underparts, pure white or lightly spotted with brown. (The juvenile has broad dark V-markings above and a darker undersurface.) A yellow bill is also characteristic of the white phase.

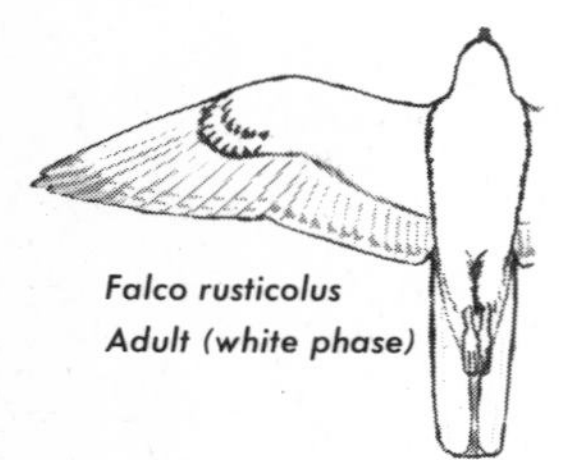

Falco rusticolus Adult (white phase)

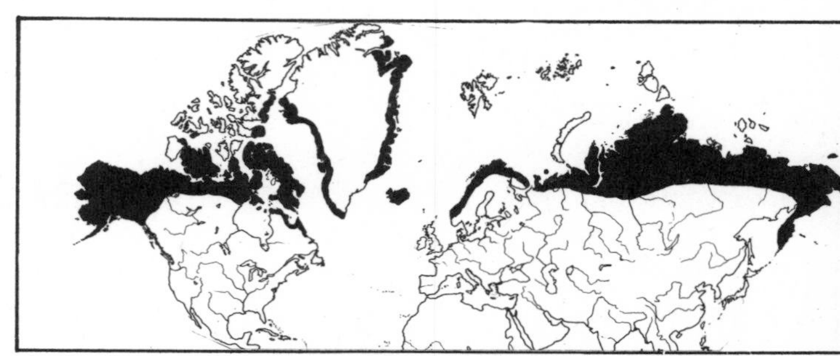

FALCO RUSTICOLUS

OTHER SPECIES

The Altai Falcon (*F. altaicus*), 17½–19 inches, is a little-known inhabitant of the mountain ranges of central Asia. It has been described as "slate-blue to reddish-brown" above, either barred or unbarred in the adult plumage; underparts, lightly to heavily streaked and spotted in a pattern similar to that of the gray phase Gyrfalcon, but tinted with "ochraceous." Light head and underparts, more or less streaked or spotted with brown, distinguishes the Saker Falcon (*F. cherrug*), 17–20 inches. The plumage is otherwise pale gray-brown, broadly feather-edged in amber-brown. This falcon has no distinct moustachial stripe, except possibly in the region from Tibet and Mongolia to Korea, where the head is darker and the plumage of the upperparts is more rufous.

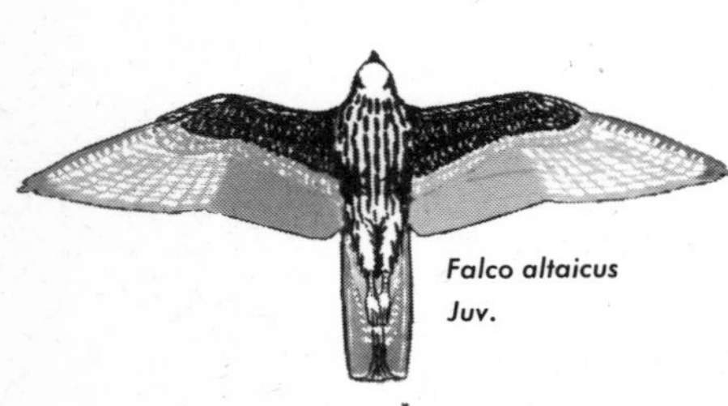

Falco altaicus Juv.

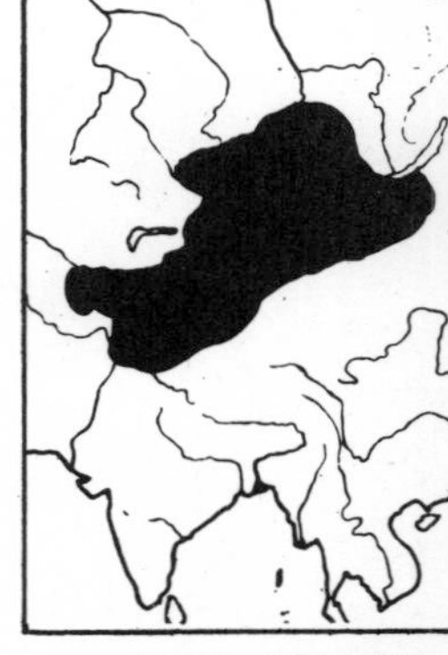

FALCO ALTAICUS

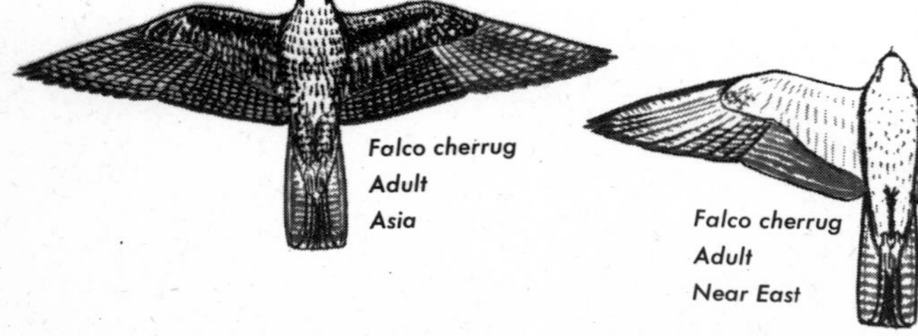

Falco cherrug Adult Asia

Falco cherrug Adult Near East

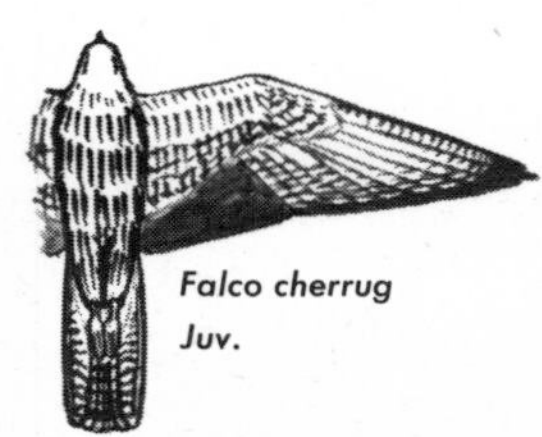

Falco cherrug Juv.

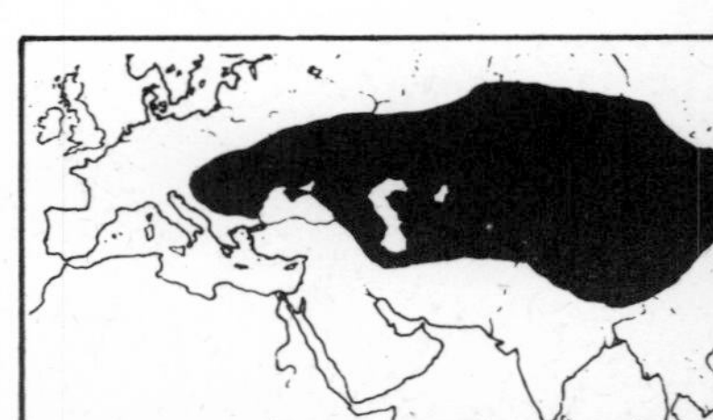

FALCO CHERRUG

Juvenile Lanner Falcon (*Falco biarmicus*), central Africa.

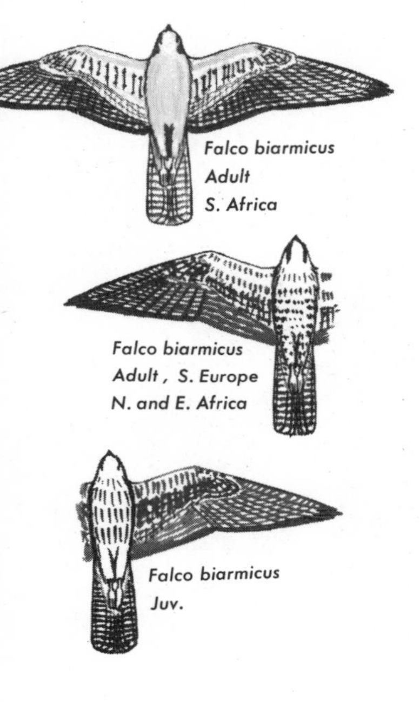

FALCO BIARMICUS

The Lanner Falcon (*F. biarmicus*), 15 inches in Africa, to 17 inches in southern Europe, may be distinguished from the more chunky Peregrine Falcon in southern Europe by its medium ferruginous head, streaked in black; and in Africa, from Gambia and the Sudan to South Africa, not only by this character but also by its larger size and different streaked or spotted underparts. Old birds in the southernmost part of the species' range become almost plain vinaceous below. The desert Lanners of Egypt and northern Africa are generally paler above, with barring on the back less distinct; underparts, more spotted than barred. (Young of European Lanner look exactly like dark-headed juveniles of the Peregrine Falcon, but any one of the African Lanners will have a yellow-brown head, streaked on the crown; underparts, white to pale yellow-brown, heavily streaked or blobbed.)

Amber-brown or ferruginous cap, streaked with black, marks the Laggar Falcon (*F. jugger*), 14–16 inches, of India, otherwise gray-brown above; tail, barred white only on outer rectrices; white face and neck show distinct brown moustachial stripe; below, white, spotted on belly with brown; flanks and thighs, almost solid brown. (Young—similar to adults above, but have streaked faces, solid brown underparts; tail, unbarred on uppersurface, tipped in buff.)

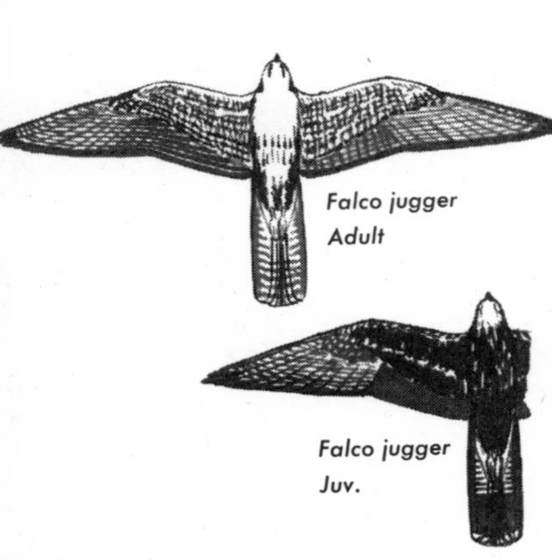

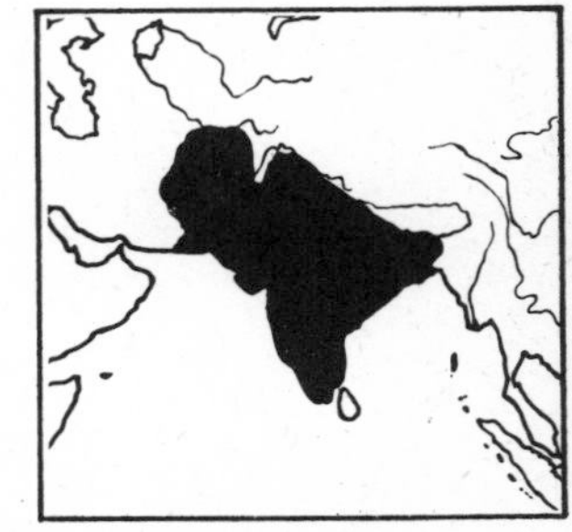

FALCO JUGGER

The Black Falcon (*F. subniger*), 17–19½ inches, endemic to the more open country of the mainland of Australia, is entirely dark brown except for white streaking on forehead, cheeks, and throat. The black moustachial stripe is not always well-defined. (Young—very similar but lighter, with more white on face; some white spotting on breast.)

FALCO SUBNIGER

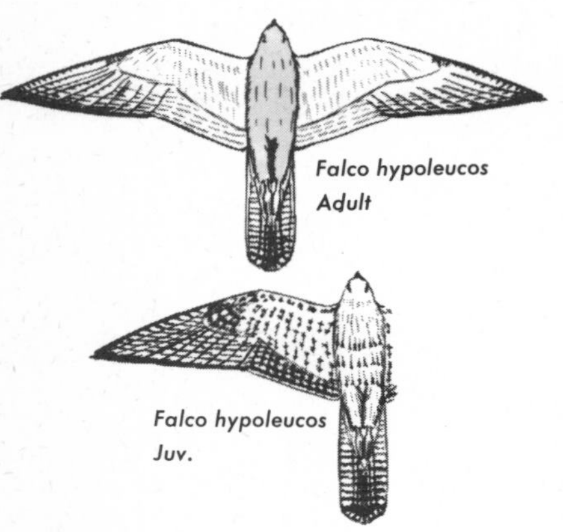

The Gray Falcon (*F. hypoleucos*), 14–16½ inches, of the semi-arid regions in the interior of Australia, is light gray above, finely streaked on the head and wing coverts with black; primaries, dark brown; tail, gray with dark barring; silver-gray underparts, finely striped. (Young—darker above; more heavily striped and washed underneath with buff-yellow.)

FALCO HYPOLEUCOS

Prairie Falcon (*Falco mexicanus*).

Prairie Falcon (*Falco mexicanus*)

DESCRIPTION
(WESTERN NORTH AMERICA)

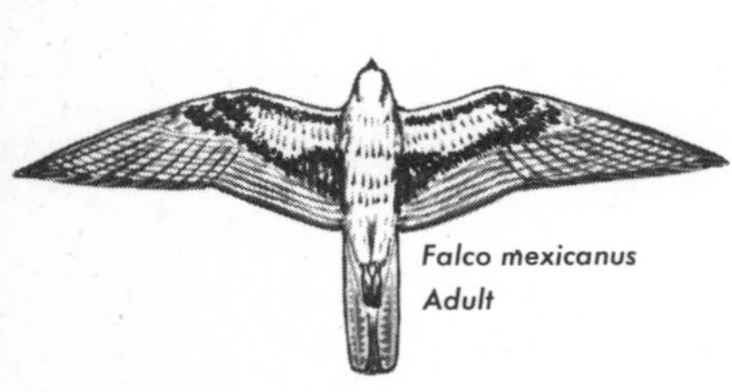

Cinnamon-brown or sepia above, collared in white and finely streaked with black; feathers of the back, wing coverts, and wings, all edged light amber-brown to buff-white; tail, cinnamon-brown, plain, outer ones spotted or partly barred on the outer rectrices; forehead, eyebrows, cheeks, and throat, white, showing brown moustachial stripe; underparts, white, streaked and blobbed with brown, most heavily on sides and flanks.

Immature—similar to adult.

Juvenile—darker above with light streaking on the head; face, throat, and underparts, washed with buff-yellow.

Beak, yellow, with blue-gray tip; cere, tarsi, and toes, yellow; claws, black; eyes, brown. Size, 15–18 inches.

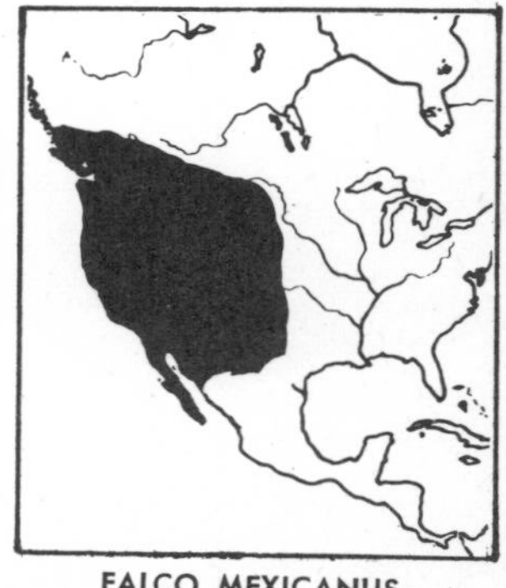
FALCO MEXICANUS

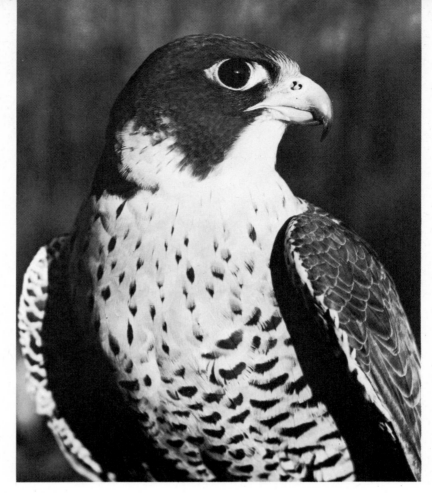

Female Peregrine Falcon *(Falco peregrinus)*, eastern North America.

Peregrine Falcon (*Falco peregrinus*)

DESCRIPTION (WORLDWIDE, EXCEPT EXTREMES IN RAIN FOREST AND COLD DRY ARCTIC CLIMATES)

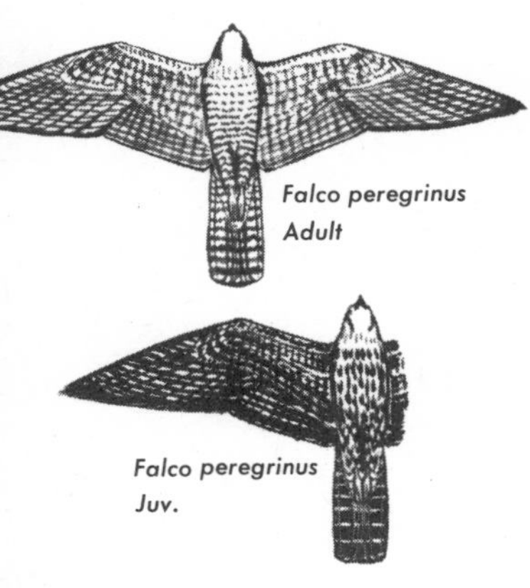

Head, black with heavy moustachial stripes; rest of upperparts, slate-blue, barred dark brown; primaries, dark brown; tail, barred like back and tipped in light yellow-brown; throat and entire underparts, white to sienna-orange, narrowly striped on chest and barred (heavily in females) on belly and flanks with dark brown.

Juvenile—head and neck, dark brown, with sandy streaking; rest of upperparts, dark brown, with light amber-brown feather-edging; tail, gray-brown, with ferruginous spots; face, sandy, with black ring around eyes and narrower dark mustachial stripe; below, white to sandy, entirely striped (heavily in females) with dark brown.

Beak, slate-blue; cere, yellow (juvenile, bluish-gray); eyes, dark brown; legs and feet, bright yellow (juvenile, bluish-gray to greenish-yellow); claws, blue-black. Size, 13 inches (male) to 19 inches (female); the smallest birds are in South America, Madagascar, and the Mediterranean region; the largest, in North America.

VARIATIONS

In northern Asia, the Peregrines are paler above, narrowly barred below; those in the arctic region in North America, much smaller and paler with indistinct moustachial stripes.

The darker falcons are completely black-headed. "Peale's Falcon," which breeds on islands off the coast of North America, from the Aleutians to the Queen Charlotte Islands, compares in size to continental birds but is darker above and below. In India individuals are dark below with heavy black barring. On New Guinea, New Britain, New Caledonia, New Hebrides, and Fiji, the Peregrines are intermediate in size and entirely black above; underparts, heavily tinged with sandy or ferruginous; breast, sides, and flanks, sometimes light blue-gray.

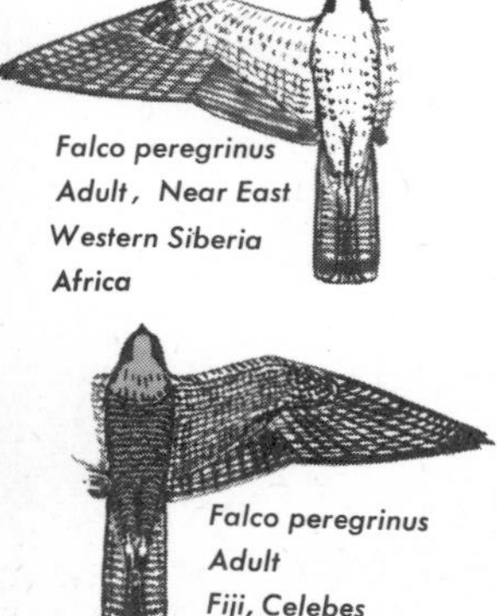

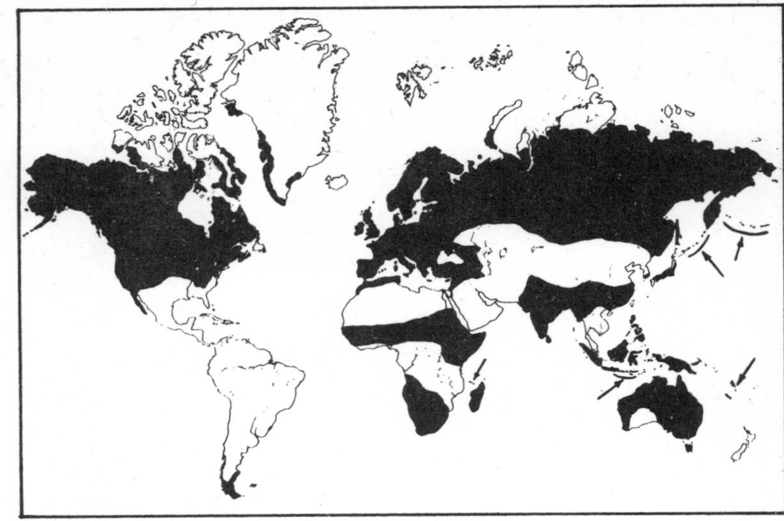

FALCO PEREGRINUS

OTHER SPECIES

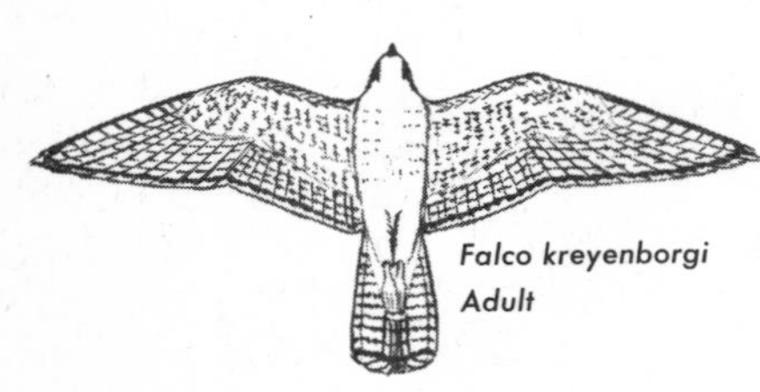

Falco kreyenborgi
Adult

The Pallid or Tierra del Fuego Falcon (*F. kreyenborgi*), 14–16½ inches, has proportionally longer wings and a shorter tail than the Peregrine Falcon. Its head is lighter (predominantly buff-colored with black moustachial stripes); underparts, nearly pure white; undersurface of wings and tail, light-colored, the narrow black bars widely spaced. (Juvenile—light head; dark brown back and wings, barred and feather-edged with light amber-brown; tail, white, barred black.)

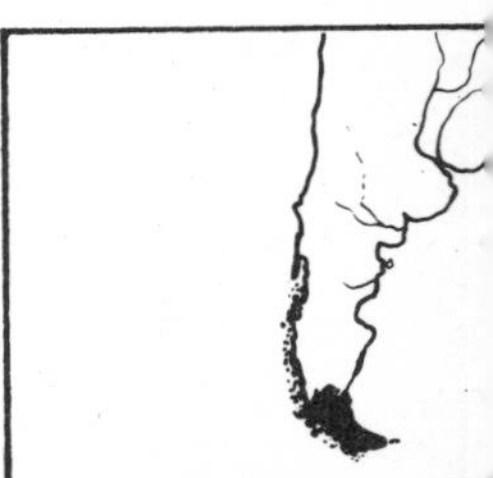

FALCO KREYENBORGI

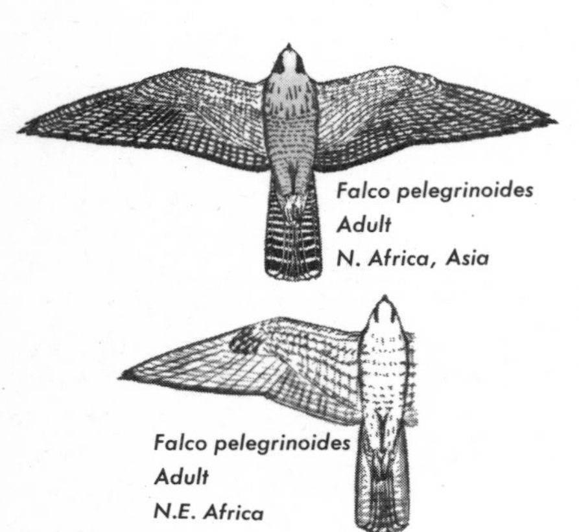

Falco pelegrinoides
Adult
N. Africa, Asia

Falco pelegrinoides
Adult
N.E. Africa

The Barbary Falcon or Shaheen (*F. pelegrinoides*), 15–17 inches, has the general coloration of the Peregrine Falcon, but it is paler in the deserts with only traces of barring on the underparts. The north African and Arabian Barbary Falcons have amber-brown collars only, but in central Asia the dark Shaheen Falcon's distinguishing marks are a ferruginous crown and collar. These Turkistanean-Mediterranean individuals rarely breed with Peregrines where their ranges coincide, and they appear to have different ecological requirements. In northern Africa the Barbary Falcon usually inhabits arid, rocky sites; the Peregrine, more wooded places.

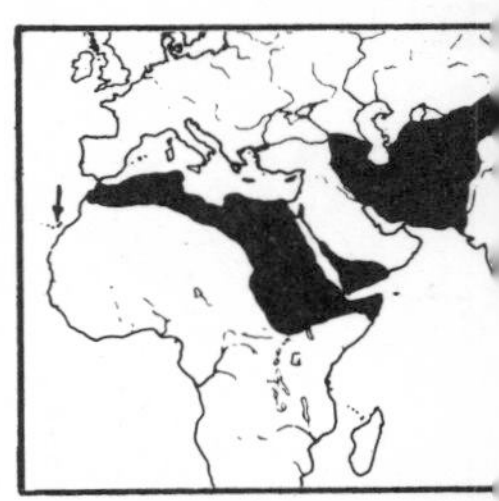

FALCO PELEGRINOIDES

In eastern and central Africa, the small and very rare Taita Falcon (*F. fasciinucha*) is dark above and has an amber-brown collar at the nape like the Barbary Falcon. However, the white throat contrasts with much darker amber-brown underparts, finely striped with black.

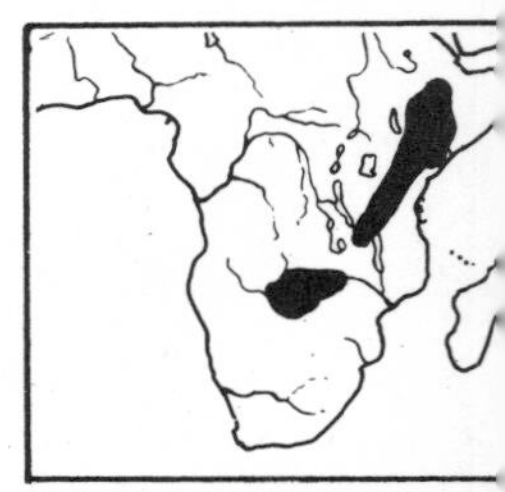

FALCO FASCIINUCHA

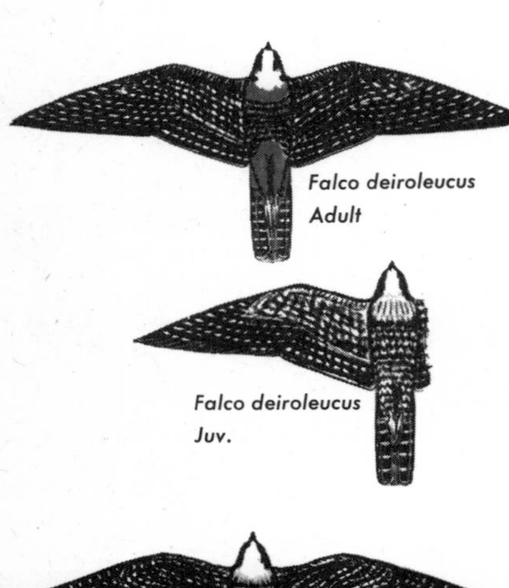

Falco deiroleucus
Adult

Falco deiroleucus
Juv.

The Orange-breasted Falcon (*F. deiroleucus*), 14½–16 inches, of Central and South America, is slate-blue above like the Peregrine Falcon, with similar dark-brown barring. Feet and beak are also comparable in size, but the tail is much shorter. The throat is white, and the underparts are dark orange with broad bands of black across the breast. (Young—resemble adults, but dark brown above, and black striped on the chest; thighs and flanks, pale yellow-orange; barred with black.)

FALCO DEIROLEUCUS

Falco albigularis
Adult

A smaller falcon of almost identical build and coloration, the Bat Falcon (*F. albigularis*), 10–11½ inches, has a black-and-white barred breast. This species breeds in southern Mexico and throughout the range of the Orange-breasted Falcon, but it is much more numerous than the latter.

FALCO ALBIGULARIS

Hobby *(Falco subbuteo)*, Europe, with downy young.—*Photograph by Eric Hosking.*

Hobby (*Falco subbuteo*)

DESCRIPTION (EUROPE, ASIA, NORTHWESTERN AFRICA)

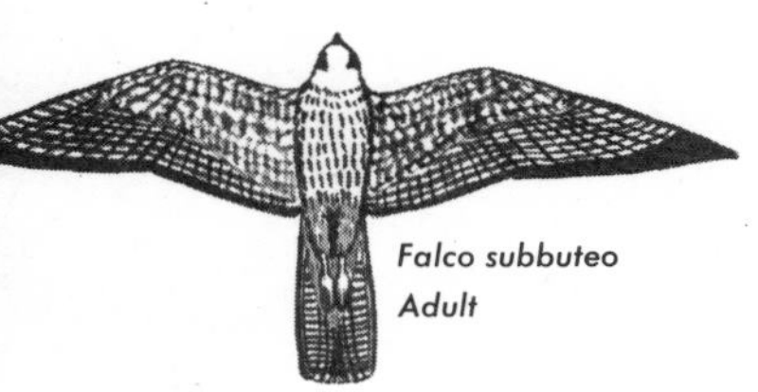

Above, dark brown, collared in buff; blue cast to back and tail, which is barred on outer rectrices; sides of face and throat, white, with heavy black moustachial stripe; underparts, white, broadly streaked with dark brown, except thighs and undertail coverts, which are light amber-brown with fine dark streaking.

Juvenile—similar to adult, but it has fine light feather-edging on back; pale sandy thighs and undertail coverts.

Beak, blue-black; cere, bright yellow (juvenile, blue-black); eyes, dark brown; legs and feet, bright yellow (juvenile, paler). Size, 10½–13 inches; the smallest individuals are in China.

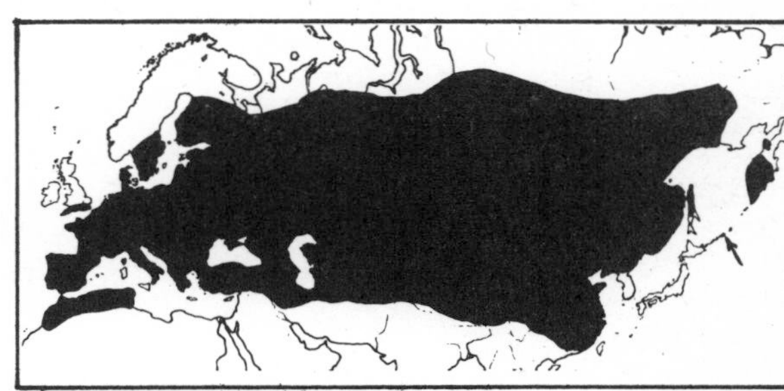

FALCO SUBBUTEO

OTHER SPECIES

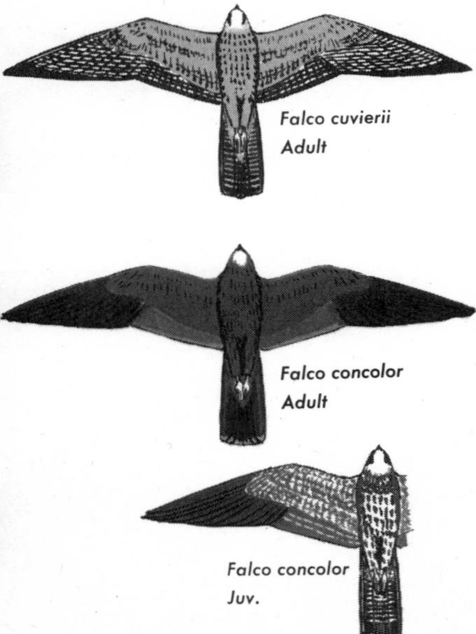

The African Hobby (*F. cuvierii*), 9½–11 inches, can be distinguished easily from paler European migrants of *F. subbuteo* by its richly colored ferruginous underparts, broadly streaked with black. (Young—browner above, but otherwise exactly like adult. Older birds tend to have narrower, less conspicuous striping on the breast.)

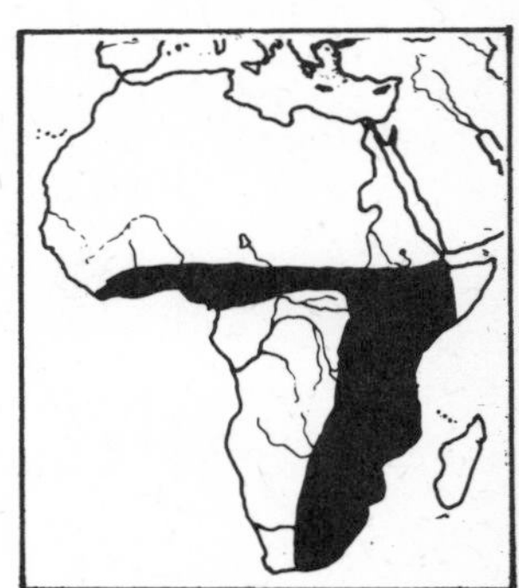

FALCO CUVIERII

Breeding grounds of the Sooty Falcon (*F. concolor*), about 13 inches, are in northern and eastern Africa. The North African individuals also migrate down the coast in winter. Some stop off in Madagascar on their passage south in November, and again on their way home, in early April. The moustachial stripe is not very noticeable; plumage, completely dove-gray to medium gray, except for dark brown wings. A dark phase occurs. (Young—darker above, collared and feather-edged in white to buff; tail, barred on outer rectrices and broadly tipped in buff; underparts, buff, streaked and spotted with slate-gray.)

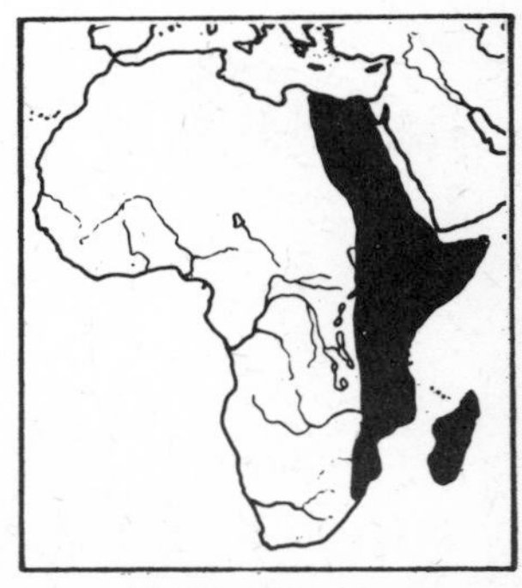

FALCO CONCOLOR

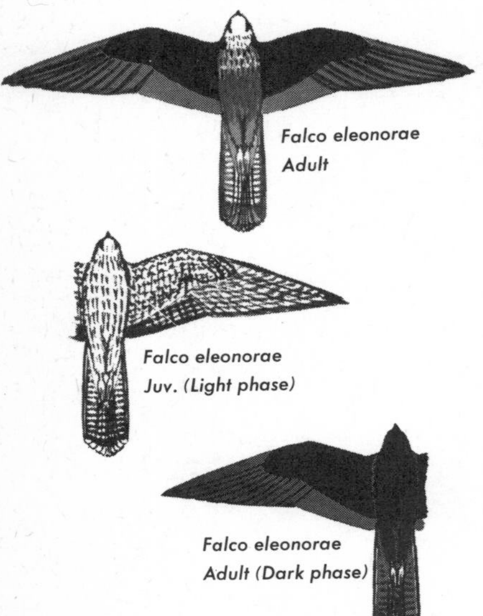

A Mediterranean species, Eleonora's Falcon (*F. eleonorae*), 13½–15 inches, is dark brown above; sides of face and throat, white, with "falcon" stripe; underparts, light amber-brown, heavily streaked with dark brown or black; thighs and undertail coverts, amber-brown. The common dark phase is dark brown. (Young—dark brown or black above in both phases with wide amber-brown feather-edging; tail, more distinctly barred; face shows stripe; underparts, buff to light amber-brown, heavily streaked with dark brown or black—without darker thighs. This falcon is only a visitor to East Africa and Madagascar.

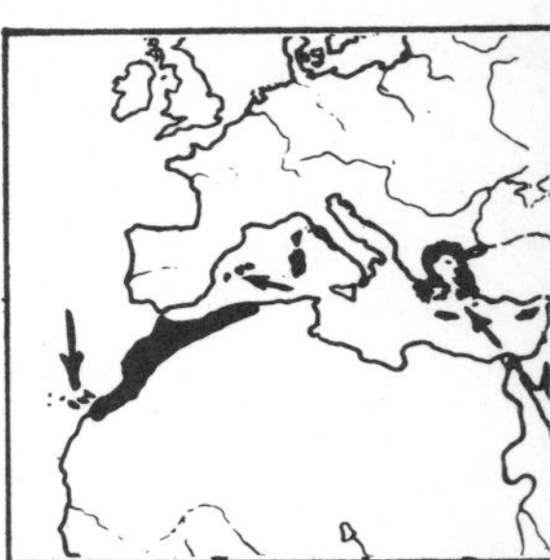
FALCO ELEONORAE

The Oriental Hobby (*F. severus*), 10 inches, is black above, with a bluish cast to the back and tail; face, solid black; throat, buff-yellow; rest of underparts, rich chestnut. (Young—like adults, but heavily spotted with black below.)

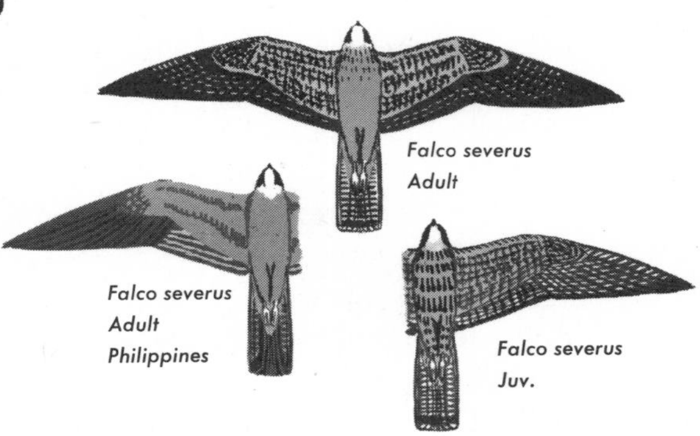

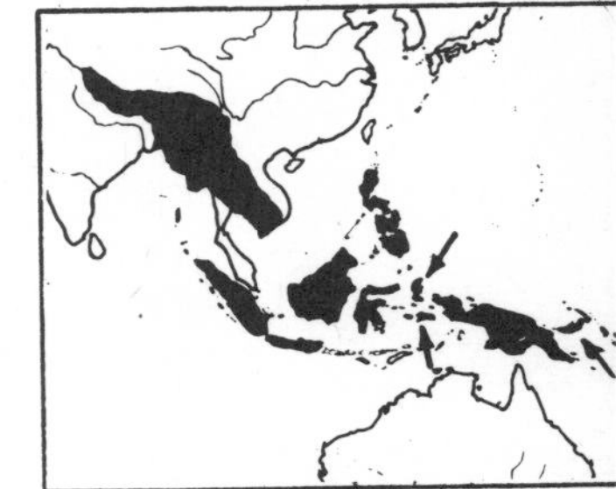
FALCO SEVERUS

Aplomado Falcon (*Falco femoralis*)

DESCRIPTION (SOUTHWESTERN UNITED STATES AND MEXICO)

Head, slate-gray; collar, yellow-orange; back, medium gray; wings and tail, black, barred in white; eyebrows, forehead, and sides of neck, white to pale yellow-orange, with narrow black mustachial stripes; throat and breast, vary from white to pale yellow-orange, but patches of black finely barred with white always show on sides of breast and flanks, narrowing to a thin band across belly; rest of underparts, yellow-orange.

Juvenile—similar to adult, but brown above; breast, heavily streaked with brown.

Beak, light yellow, darkening to slate-gray at tip; cere, light yellow; eyes, yellow-brown to dark hazel; tarsi and toes, light yellow; claws, black. Size, about 15 inches.

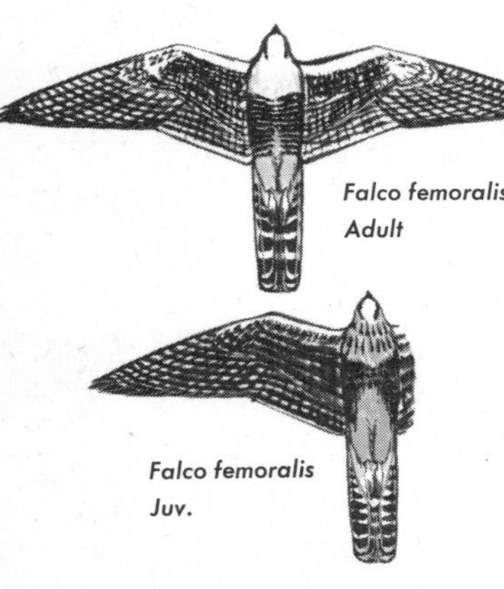

FALCO FEMORALIS

VARIATIONS

South American birds are slightly smaller, except in the Andes, where the population compares in size with northern birds, and adults are usually finely streaked on the breast.

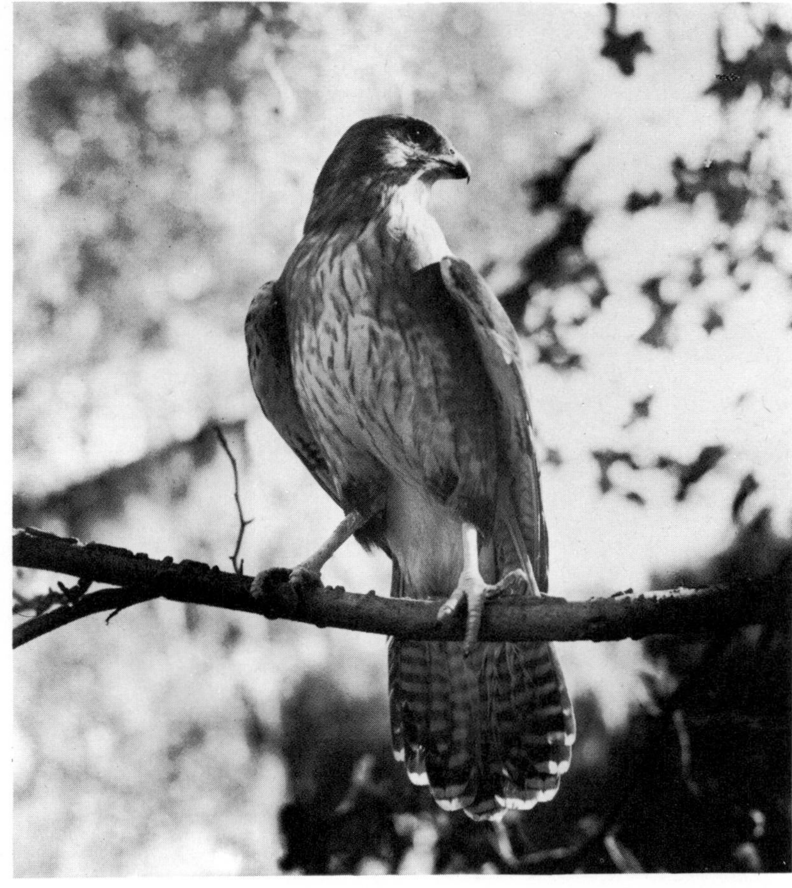

Australian Brown Falcon *(Falco berigora)*.

Brown Falcon (*Falco berigora*)

DESCRIPTION (AUSTRALIAN REGION)

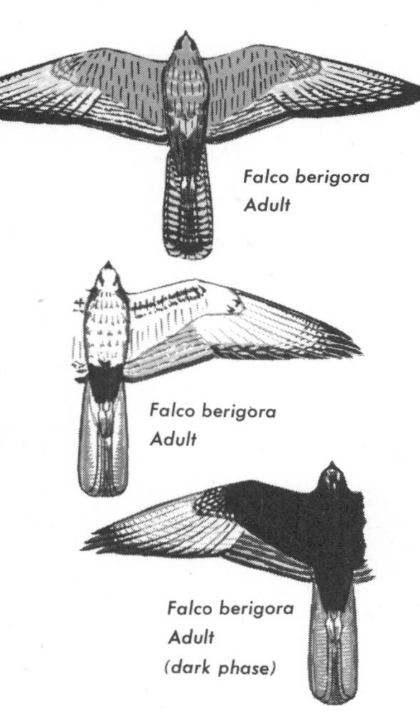

In two color phases, extremely variable, and with intermediates. *Light phase*—sienna-orange to cinnamon-brown above, striped in black; wing coverts and scapulars gray-brown; wings, dark-brown; tail, gray-brown, barred or spotted with sienna-orange to ferruginous; face and throat, white or buff, with dark brown moustachial stripes; underparts, same as ground color of back, intermixed with white, and finely striped black. (Some individuals are entirely white, striped with black below, except for dark amber-brown thighs.)

Dark phase—rufous-brown to dark gray-brown above; back streaked black as in the light phase, but feather-edged and occasionally spotted with light amber-brown or sandy; tail, barred or spotted as in light phase; face and throat, sandy to buff, heavily marked with patches of dark gray-brown and conspicuous mustachial stripes; underparts, either entirely as above or with varying amounts of white, sandy, or buff; thighs, always dark gray-brown. (Juvenile—similar to adult, but darker below in corresponding color pnases from medium buff in light phase to almost black in dark phase).

Beak, blue-gray (juvenile, white); cere, variable (pale blue-gray, sometimes yellow); eyes, hazel, brown, or yellow (juvenile, dark blue); orbital patch, bluish-white; legs and feet, yellowish-gray. Size, 15½–18 inches.

FALCO BERIGORA

VARIATIONS

Light phase birds are more common in the arid parts and less so (even rare) in the scattered wet regions of Australia and Tasmania. However, the darkest extremes of both phases are numerous in New Guinea.

RELATED SPECIES

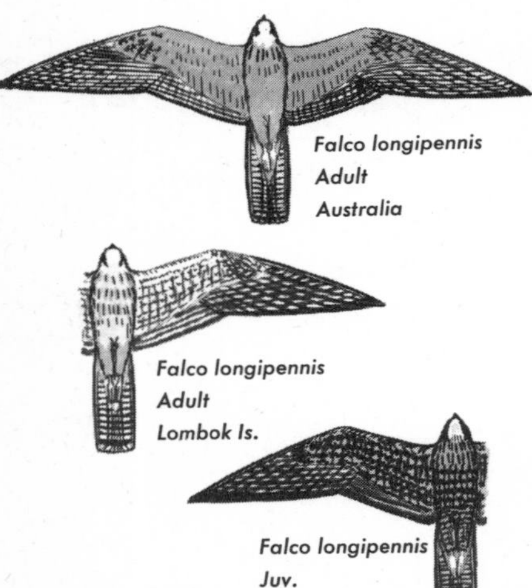

In its plumage pattern the Little Falcon (*F. longipennis*), 10–12 inches, of Australia, is a pale version of the Oriental Hobby; slate-blue above, collared and barred on the outer tail feathers with amber-brown; underparts, instead of pure chestnut, are amber-brown finely streaked and somewhat clouded with black. (Young—darker above and more definitely streaked and blotched below. The smallest birds inhabit Timor, Lombok, and other outlying islands.)

FALCO LONGIPENNIS

The New Zealand Falcon (*F. novaeseelandiae*), 13–16 inches, has black crown, cheeks, and upperparts; sides of neck spotted with ferruginous and showing the black moustachial stripe; buff throat patch; underparts, rufous-brown, occasionally spotted with buff and lightly to heavily streaked or suffused with black; some narrow and indistinct white barring appears on tail. (Young—barred with amber-brown above; underparts, buff-colored, streaked on breast and spotted or barred on belly with dark brown; thighs, ferruginous.)

FALCO NOVAESEELAND

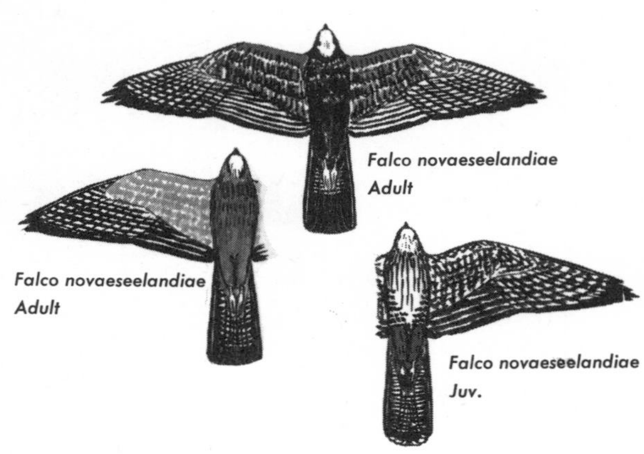

North American Merlin, or Pigeon Hawk (*Falco columbarius*).—Photograph by Heinz Meng.

Merlin or Pigeon Hawk (*Falco columbarius*)

DESCRIPTION (NORTH AMERICA)

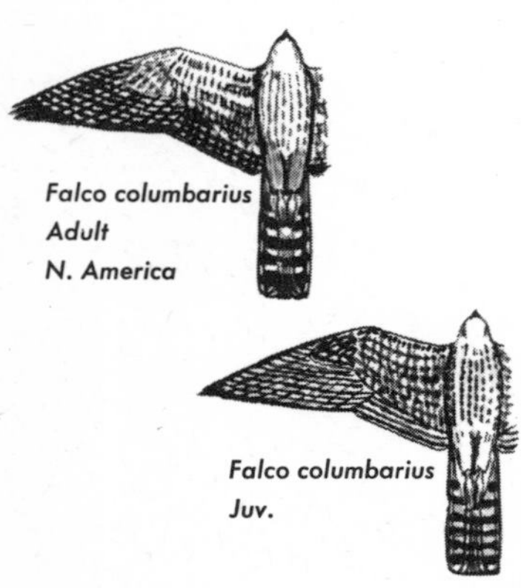

Male—head, slate-gray streaked in black; collared with white and light amber-brown spots; wing coverts and back, slate-blue, entirely black-streaked secondaries, slate-blue barred dark brown; and primaries, dark brown; tail, slate-blue, barred and subterminally banded with dark brown; forehead, eyebrows, and cheeks, white, finely streaked with black (no distinct "falcon" stripe); underparts, white to light amber-brown, broadly streaked with dark brown or black.

Female—dark gray-brown above, collared like male; tail, barred white to pale yellow-orange; underparts, same as in male.

Juvenile (*both sexes*)—like adult female, but brown above without any trace of gray.

Beak, blue-gray; cere, greenish-yellow; eyes, very dark brown; tarsi and toes, yellow; claws, black. Size, 9–11½ inches.

VARIATIONS

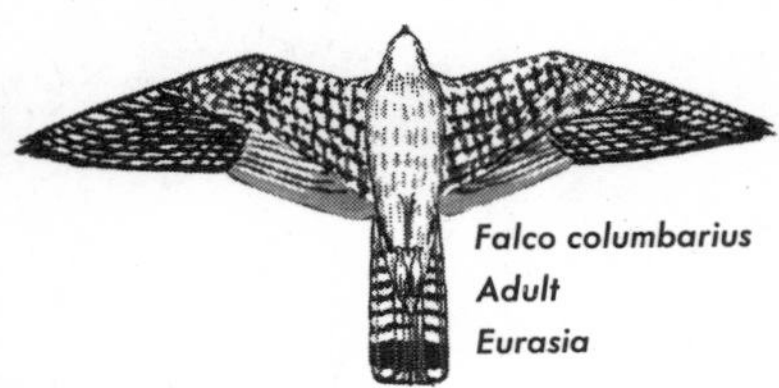

Falco columbarius
Adult
Eurasia

The populations of interior and western North America are lighter; in Vancouver, British Columbia, however, they are so dark that they are called "Black Pigeon Hawks."

The Old World Merlins are generally comparable in coloring to the Pigeon Hawks of the central and western parts of North America, varying from light gray (*male*) and light cinnamon (*female*), in arid regions, to medium gray (*male*) and gray-brown (*female*), in northern Europe. Only in the dark Icelandic population are they as heavily striped below; in southern Russia and northern Asia, they are very finely striped below. Tails of Old World *males* are not as distinctly barred as their New World counterparts, but they show the characteristic broad subterminal band. (Young Merlins resemble adult females, but have broad feather-edging on the back and wing coverts.)

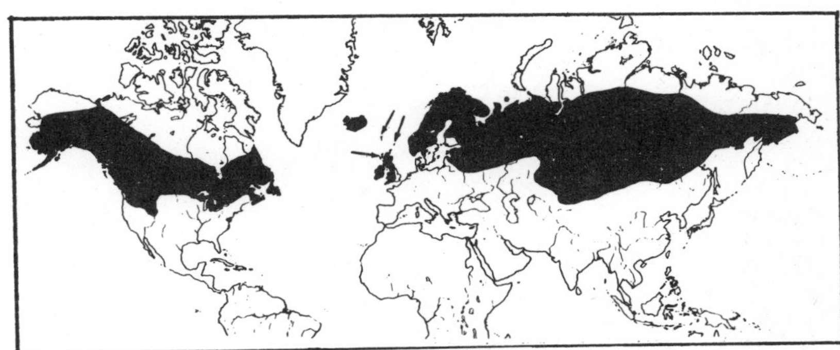

FALCO COLUMBARIUS

OTHER SPECIES

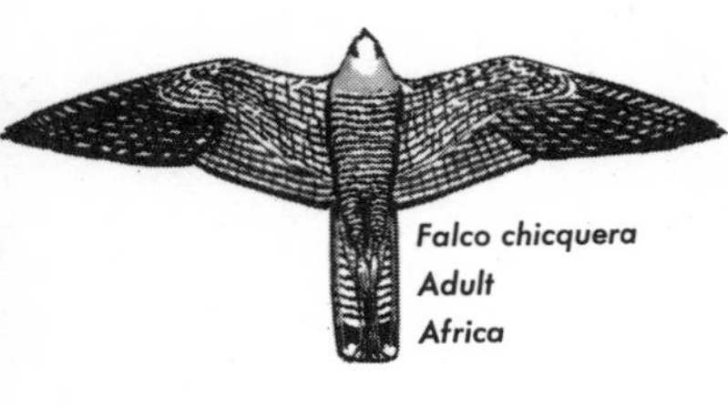

Falco chicquera
Adult
Africa

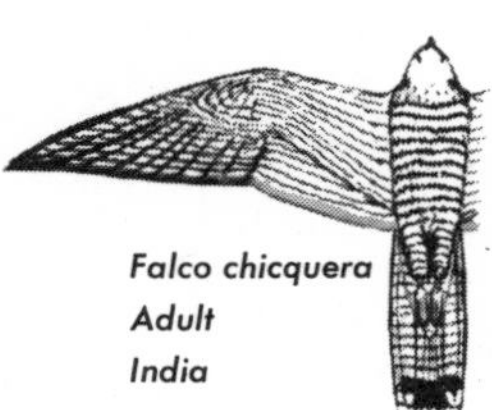

Falco chicquera
Adult
India

The Red-headed Falcon of India and Africa (*F. chicquera*), 11–13 inches, is, throughout its range, brightly capped with chestnut, but on the other parts of the body the plumage is variable from region to region. The Asiatic birds are nearly plain slate-gray above and lightly barred below; populations in the drier areas of western and southern Africa are barred above and below, but not heavily; and the darkest individuals, heavily barred with black, are found throughout eastern and northeastern Africa. The largest birds are the extremely pale individuals from South Africa. (The young are like adults above, but heavy black streaking makes the head appear darker; otherwise a collar at the nape and indistinct feather-edging on the back are variable in pale or dark individuals from buff to chestnut; underparts, buff to yellow-orange, streaked and barred as in adult with dark brown.)

FALCO CHICQUERA

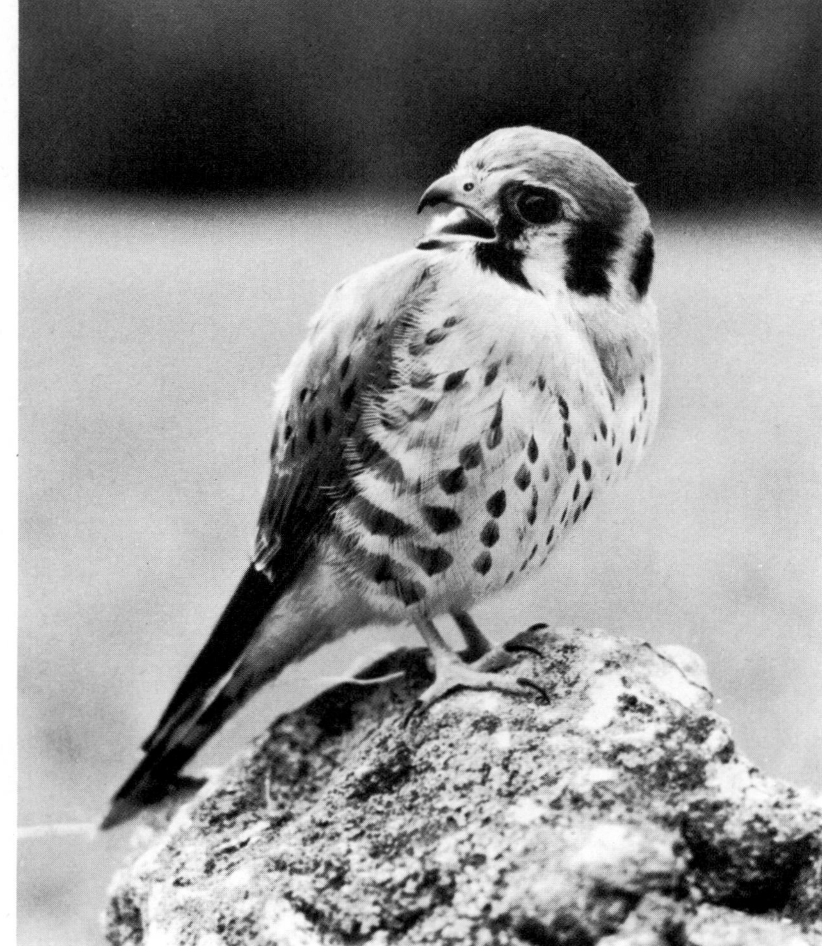

Juvenile male American Kestrel, or Sparrow Hawk *(Falco sparverius),* eastern North America.

American Kestrel or Sparrow Hawk (*Falco sparverius*)

DESCRIPTION (NORTH AMERICA)

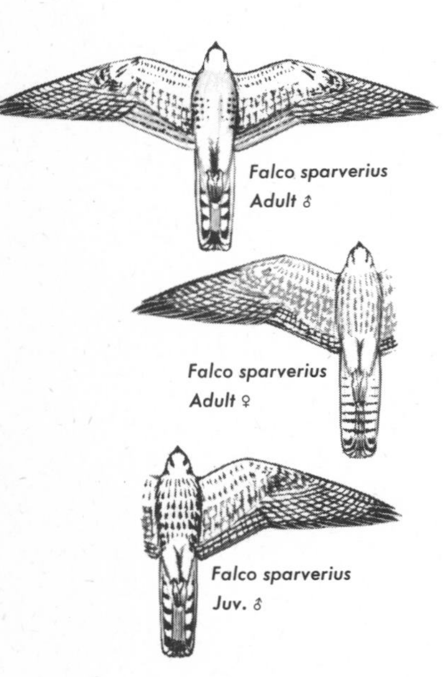

Male—slate-blue above, with spots or distinct patch of ferruginous coloring on head; back, almost completely ferruginous; nape, collared with black spots; wing coverts, spotted with black; secondaries, slate-blue, and primaries, dark brown; tail, ferruginous, with a black subterminal band and white tip (outer rectrices mostly white, barred in black). Face and throat, white, with heavy black stripes below and behind eyes; rest of underparts, white, suffused with light amber-brown on breast and spotted on sides and flanks with black.

Female—back, wing coverts, and tail, broadly barred with ferruginous and dark brown; underparts, white, streaked (and barred on the flanks) in cinnamon.

FALCO SPARVERIUS

Juvenile (*male*)—similar to *adult male,* but slightly darker ferruginous back is completely barred; tail, tipped with ferruginous (not white); underparts, streaked and spotted throughout. *Juvenile* (*female*)—like *adult female,* but with less conspicuous ferruginous streaking on head; back, darker, with heavier black barring. American Kestrels keep the juvenile wings, tail, and part of the body plumage through an incomplete molt starting in September or October of the first year; they do not lose these feathers until their second annual molt. At two years (or by spring of the third year), the immatures are indistinguishable from the adults.

Beak, blue-black; cere, legs, and feet, yellow to yellow-orange (paler in female and young); eyes, dark brown. Size, 9–11 inches.

VARIATIONS

The smaller kestrels of the southeastern United States are slightly darker. (*Males*—usually not barred on the back or spotted on wing coverts below.) The tropical populations of the Caribbean islands and Central and South America (8–9½ inches) are generally much darker and more vividly colored, either with entirely slate-blue heads or less conspicuous ferruginous patches. (*Adult males*—as in the southeastern United States, are frequently unbarred above and plainer below, less commonly have a barred tail like adult females.) On Cuba and the Isle of Pines both males and females may be seen in distinct white or ferruginous-chested phases. The *adult male* of the dark variant has plain slate-gray head and back; *juvenile male,* red patches on head and back. All *females* are barred above and streaked below according to the usual patterns. Individuals in southern South America are similar in size and coloring to the larger North American kestrels.

Old World Kestrel (*Falco tinnunculus*)

DESCRIPTION (EUROPE AND WESTERN ASIA)

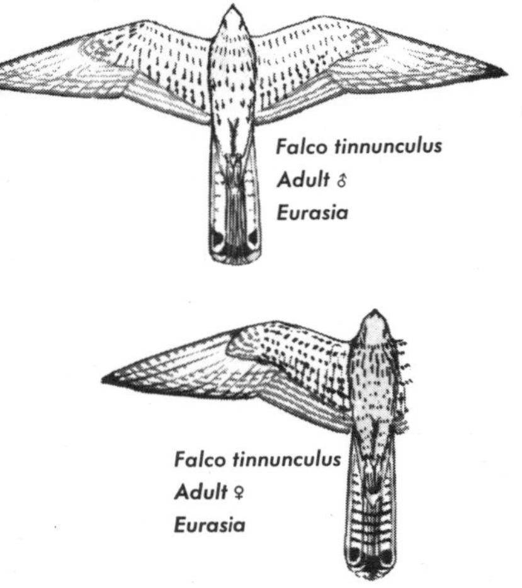

Male—head and nape, dove-gray to slate-blue, streaked with black; back and wing coverts, medium sienna-orange to sienna, V-spotted with dark brown; primaries, dark brown; tail, dove-gray to slate-blue, subterminally marked with a broad band of black; sides of face, dove-gray, with indistinct black moustachial stripes; underparts, pale yellow-brown, finely streaked and V-spotted with dark brown. *Female*—head and nape, light amber-brown to sienna, streaked with black and sometimes tinged dove-gray to slate-blue; upper back, more heavily V-marked, and wing coverts and lower back, barred dark brown; tail, light amber-brown to sienna, barred and subterminally banded with black and tinged dove-gray; underparts, light amber-brown, more heavily marked than male's.

Immature (August of second, to April of third year) resemble adult, but *males* have gray tails tinged with sienna coloring; *females* have heavily barred tails, not gray-tinged like adults'. *Younger birds* (August of first, to April of second year) have a "mixed" appearance due to incomplete molt of juvenile body feathers and wing coverts; wing and most tail feathers are not molted until the end of the second year; new gray-tinged feathers at this period come in on the head and nape. *Males* are heavily spotted; *females,* broadly streaked on the underparts.

Old World Kestrel *(Falco tinnunculus)* at nest hole with young.—*Photograph by Eric Hosking.*

Juvenile (*sexes alike*)—shows no gray coloring; light amber-brown to sienna above, streaked on head and nape and very broadly barred on back and wing coverts with dark brown; tail, light amber-brown, barred and subterminally banded; below, light amber-brown, with wide streaking; heavy spotting or barring on sides of body. Beak, blue-black; cere, legs, and feet, yellow; claws, black; eyes, brown. Size, about 13 inches.

VARIATIONS

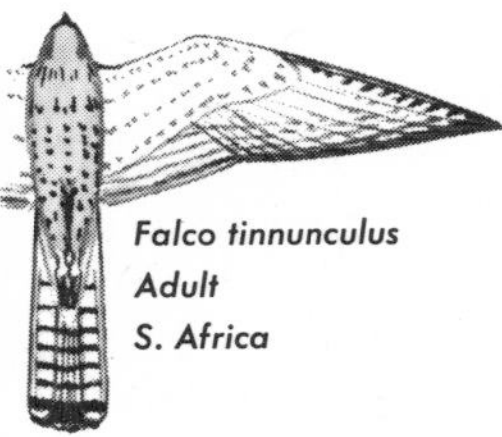
Falco tinnunculus
Adult
S. Africa

Kestrels breeding in south temperate climates—Mediterranean, Cape Verde Islands, Canary Islands, Indian peninsula—become darker-breasted, and subtropical populations are very much darker (sienna below.) Thus, migrant European birds are always lighter-breasted than those resident in Africa. In western, central, and southern Africa, sexual dimorphism disappears, and the sub-adult and adult females have slate-blue heads and tails like males of the same age. Sizes, 11–13½ inches; the smallest birds are on islands; the largest, in eastern Siberia.

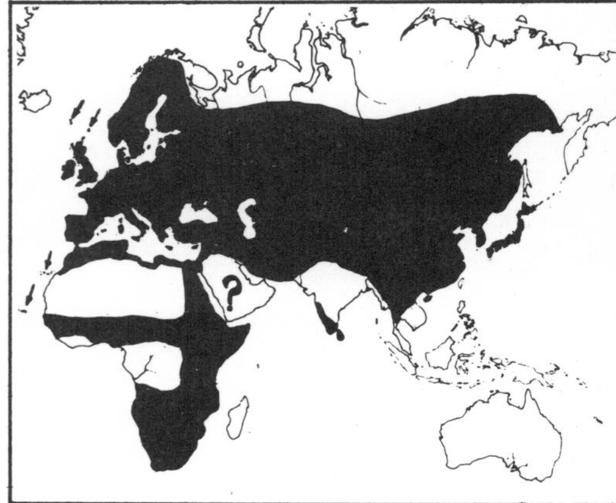
FALCO TINNUNCULUS

OTHER SPECIES

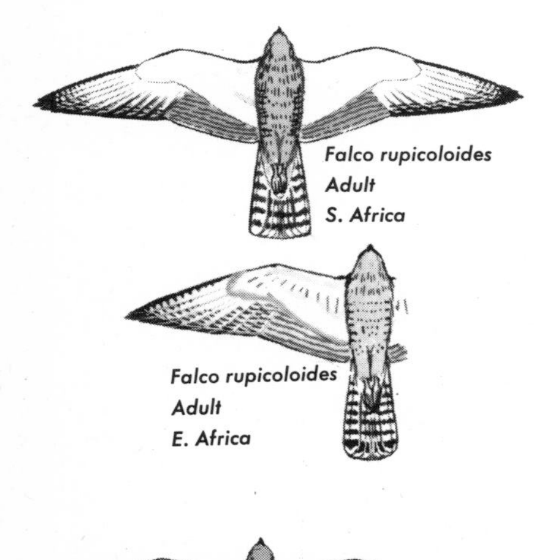
Falco rupicoloides
Adult
S. Africa

Falco rupicoloides
Adult
E. Africa

The Greater Kestrel (*F. rupicoloides*), 11–13 inches, resembles heavily barred juveniles of the Old World Kestrel, but without distinct moustachial stripes; tail coverts and tail, light gray to slate-blue, barred and subterminally banded with black and broadly tipped in white; ground color of head and neck, back, wing coverts, and underparts varies from buff to amber-brown. The Somaliland population averages smaller, paler, and more finely marked than in South Africa; that of Kenya, smaller and darker, with narrower barring on the back; but underparts, heavily streaked and spotted. (Young—similar to adults; wings, tipped with amber-brown.)

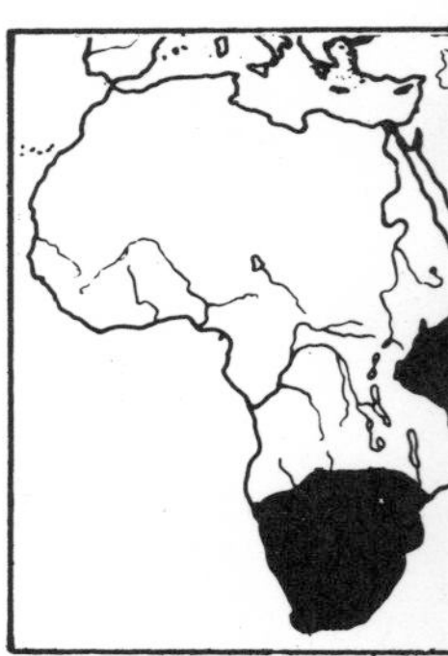
FALCO RUPICOLOIDES

Very distinctive, with long wings and long graduated tail, more than half the length of its body, the Fox Kestrel (*F. alopex*), 13½–15 inches, cannot be confused with any other bird of prey except, perhaps, the Grasshopper Buzzard (*Butastur*). *Male*—amber-brown, striped with black above and below; primaries, dark brown; tail, amber-brown, with varying amounts of narrow broken barring. (Adult females and juvenile—more heavily streaked, with distinctly barred tails.)

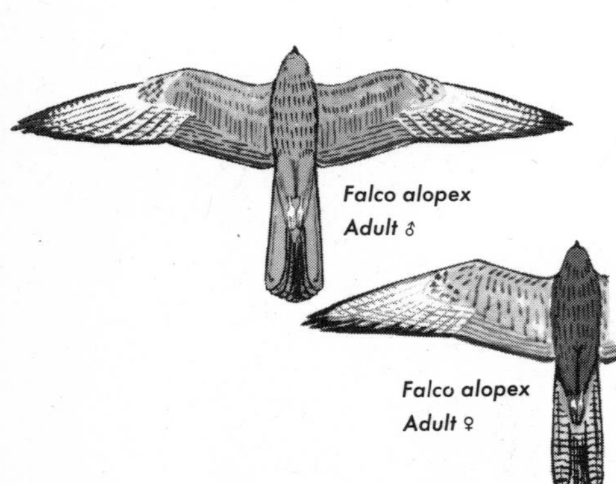
Falco alopex
Adult ♂

Falco alopex
Adult ♀

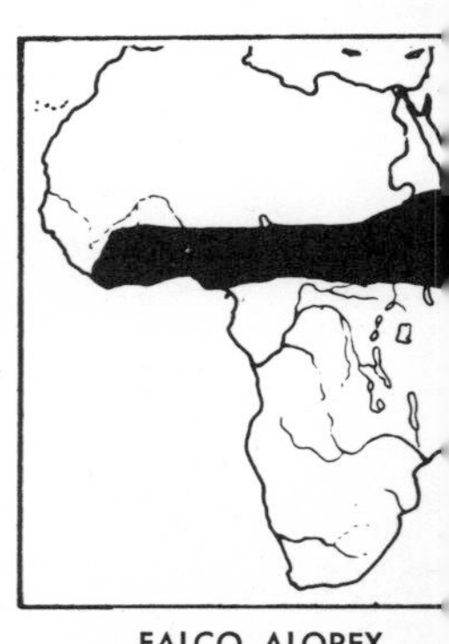
FALCO ALOPEX

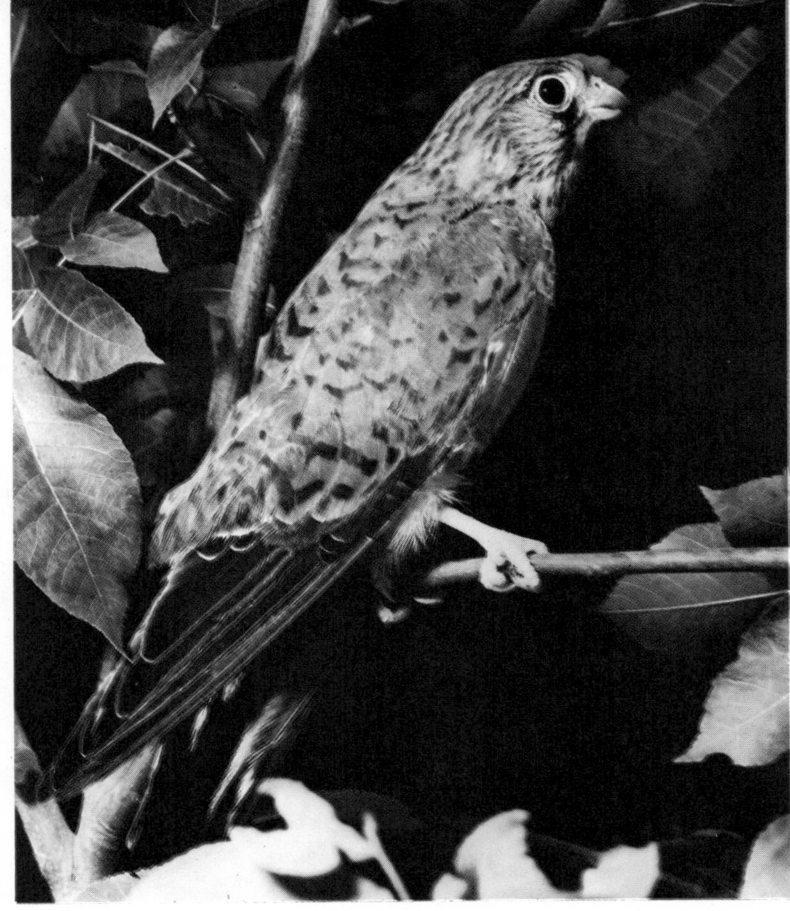

Lesser Kestrel (*Falco naumanni*), Europe.

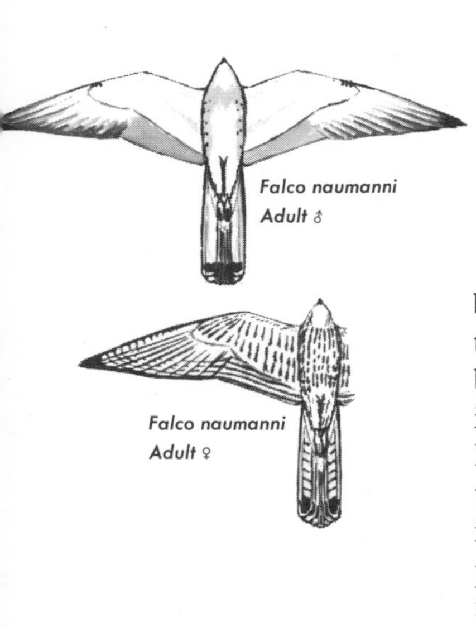

The Lesser Kestrel (*F. naumanni*), 10–12 inches, is a smaller, brightly colored version of the Old World Kestrel with white claws; the adult *male* has plain head; plain sienna back and wing coverts; below, either plain sienna or lightly spotted with black. Adult *female* is hard to distinguish except by size from adult female of Old World Kestrel; it has narrower and more widely spaced barring on back than the latter and a barred tail. (Juveniles of both sexes resemble the adult female, but tails are sienna, with slate-blue tinge; moustachial stripe, present only in adult female and young, is broken and is not very noticeable. The annual molt is gradual, November or December through March. Like the Old World Kestrel, the Lesser Kestrel does not lose any wing feathers for about a year and a half, but its body and tail molt is more complete. By spring of the third year immatures are indistinguishable from adults.)

FALCO NAUMANNI

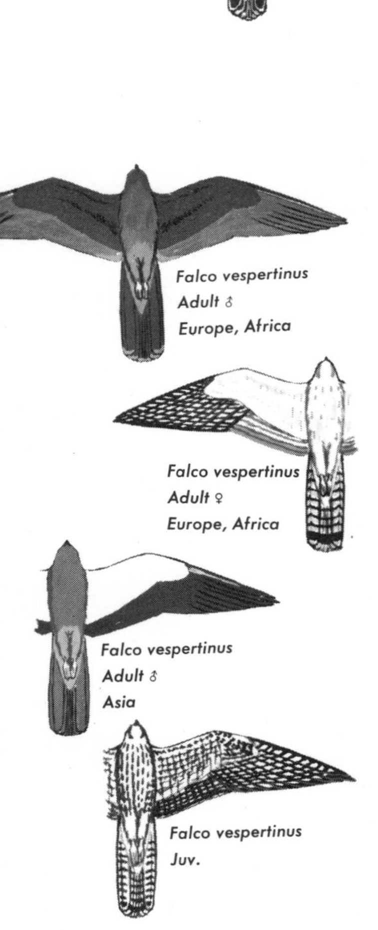

A very different pattern of sexual dimorphism distinguishes the Red-footed Kestrel (*F. vespertinus*), 10–11 inches. Throughout central Europe, Asia Minor, and western Asia the adult *male* is slate-gray with slightly paler wings and underparts; thighs and undertail coverts, sienna; feet, legs, cere, and orbital spaces, orange-red; eyes, dark brown. The *female* has a bright sienna cap; rest of upperparts, including tail, slate-blue, barred with dark brown; wings, dark brown; amber-brown underparts, finely streaked with dark brown. (Juveniles of both sexes resemble the adult female, but are streaked on the head and nape in black; rest of upperparts, broadly feather-edged with amber-brown; underparts, buff, heavily streaked with dark brown. In young, legs are yellow.) *Adult male* of eastern Siberia and northern China differs in having white (not black) underwing coverts in flight; *female* has paler underparts with heavier black streaking. (Head and mantle of juvenile male and female, appear dark brown or black and may be collared with buff spots; back and tail, slate-blue, barred with black and edged with brown; below, buff, heavily spotted and barred; thighs, clear, light amber-brown.) The adult females and young in all regions have black patches under the eyes and distinct moustachial stripes, sienna in female, black in juveniles.

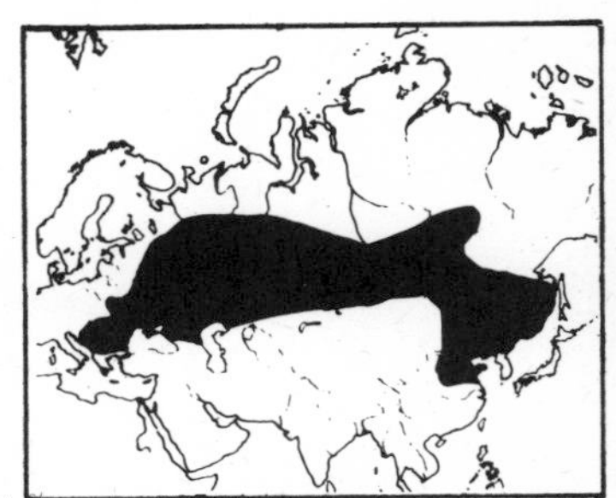

FALCO VESPERTINUS

Dickinson's Kestrel (*Falco dickinsoni*), central Africa.

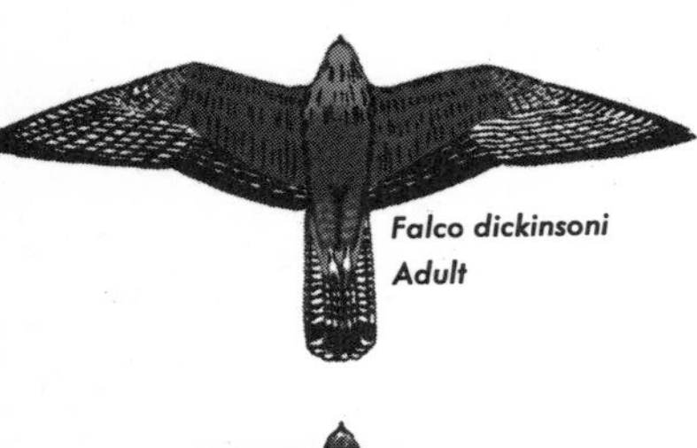

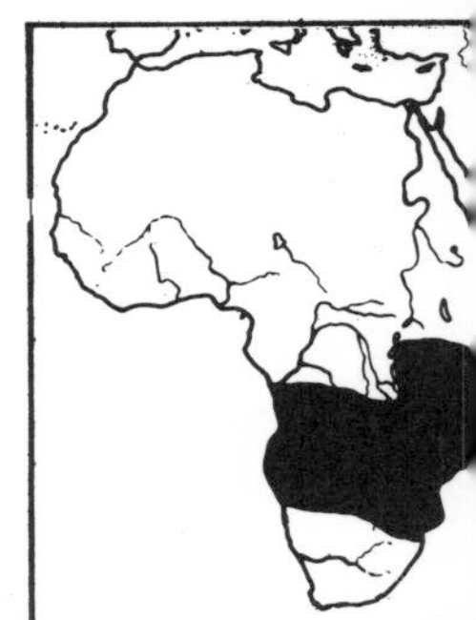

FALCO DICKINSONI

Two tropical African species are gray, and not sexually dimorphic. Light gray head and medium olive-gray underparts, finely striped in black, contrast with the slate-gray back and wings of Dickinson's Kestrel (*F. dickinsoni*), about 11 inches. The tail is barred black and white. (Young—browner than adults.)

Falco ardosiaceus Adult

Falco ardosiaceus Juv.

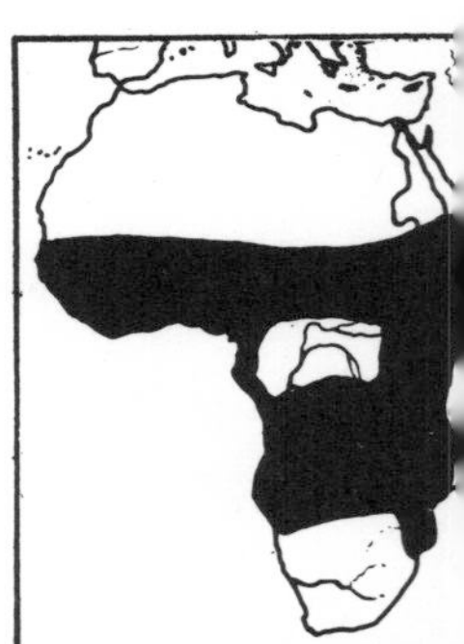

FALCO ARDOSIACEUS

The Gray Kestrel (*F. ardosiaceus*), 11–13 inches, is entirely slate-gray with a blue cast; head and underparts, narrowly striped with black; tail indistinctly barred. This species may be distinguished from the Sooty Falcon (*F. concolor*) in eastern Africa by faintly barred, rather than solid gray, undersurface of wings. (In the *young* the feathers are all edged with sandy, especially on the lighter underparts.)

Falco zoniventris Adult

Falco zoniventris Juv.

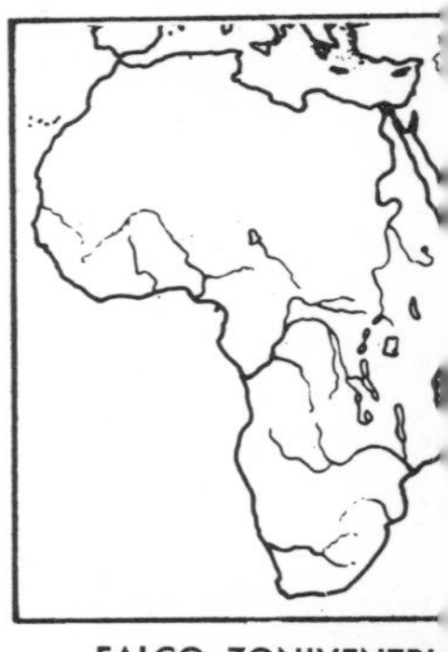

FALCO ZONIVENTRIS

On Madagascar the Barred Kestrel (*F. zoniventris*), 10½–12 inches, is medium gray to dark slate, faintly barred and streaked with black above; primaries, black; tail, black, with outer feathers narrowly barred in white; face and breast, medium gray, streaked in black; rest of underparts, heavily barred black and white. (Young—white below, not as finely barred.)

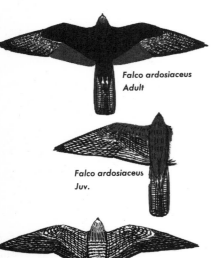

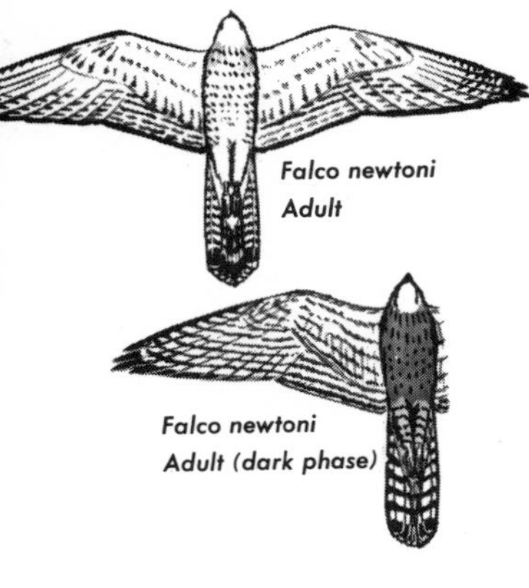

In Madagascar, Newton's Kestrel (*F. newtoni*), 10–11½ inches, has a gray-tinged and black-striped cap; rest of upperparts, richly colored chestnut, relatively unspotted in light phase with white breast, to heavily streaked and spotted in dark phase with chestnut breast; tail, slate-blue, barred black. (Juvenile resembles those of the Old World Kestrel—chestnut above, streaked and barred with black; tail, chestnut with a blue cast, barred and banded black; underparts, probably both phases, amber-brown, heavily streaked and barred.)

FALCO NEWTONI

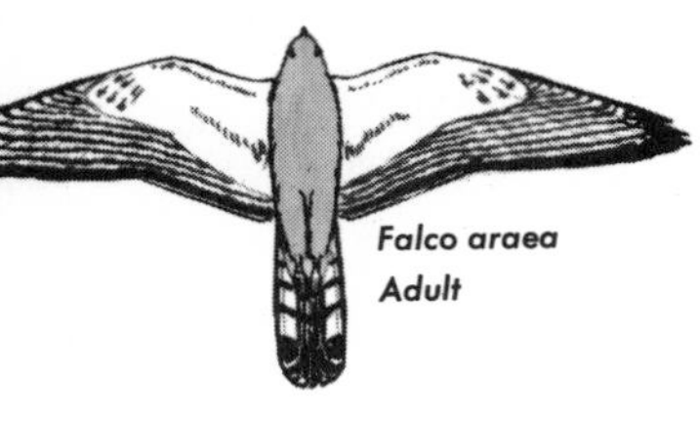

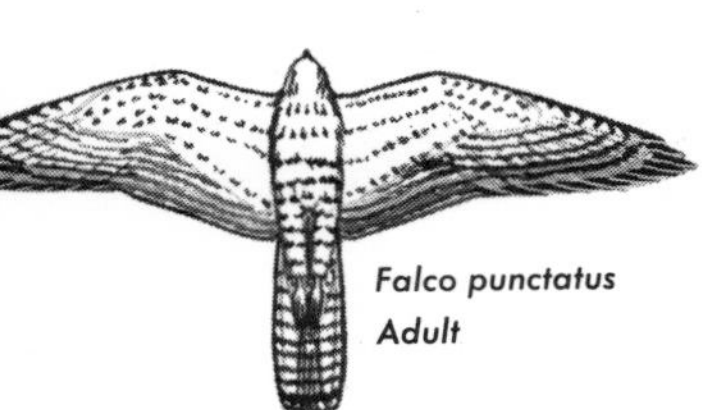

In the Indian Ocean the tiny Seychelles Kestrel (*F. araea*), 8–9 inches, resembles the light phase of Newton's Kestrel, but is vinaceous below. (Juvenile—banded above and spotted below like those of *F. newtoni.*) The few remaining adults of the almost extinct Mauritius Kestrel (*F. punctatus*), 9–10 inches, look like the adult female of the Old World Kestrel, but they are without any distinct moustachial stripe; white below, with blobs or V-spots of rufous-brown or black; barred tail, not as broadly banded near the tip. (Young—probably much like the adults.)

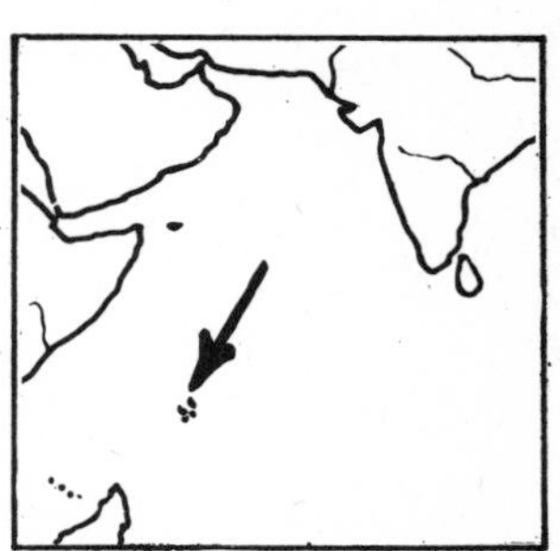
FALCO ARAEA

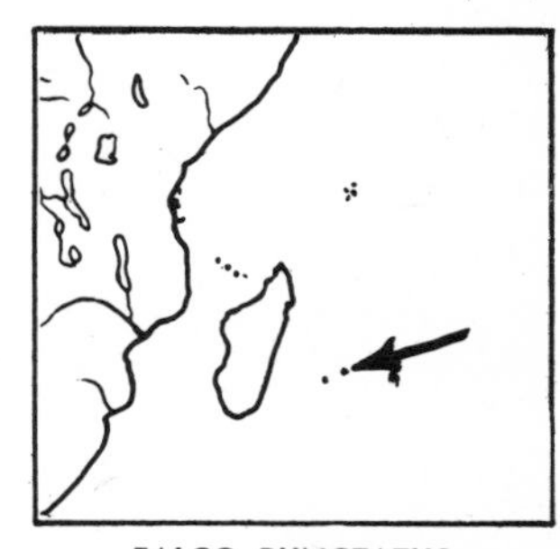
FALCO PUNCTATUS

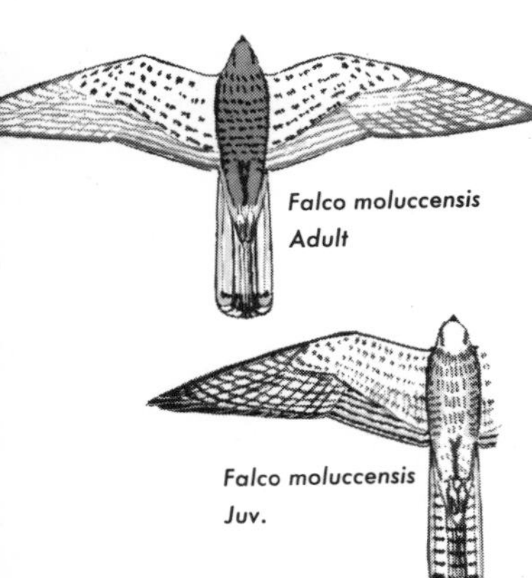

Its bright sienna plumage spotted or barred completely, the Spotted Kestrel (*F. moluccensis*), 11–12 inches, is resident from Java to the Moluccas and Celebes. Slight sexual dimorphism is apparent in the slate-blue tail, subterminally banded in males, and barred, as well as broadly banded, in females. (Young—very much like the adults; tails, light amber-brown distinctly barred with dark brown.)

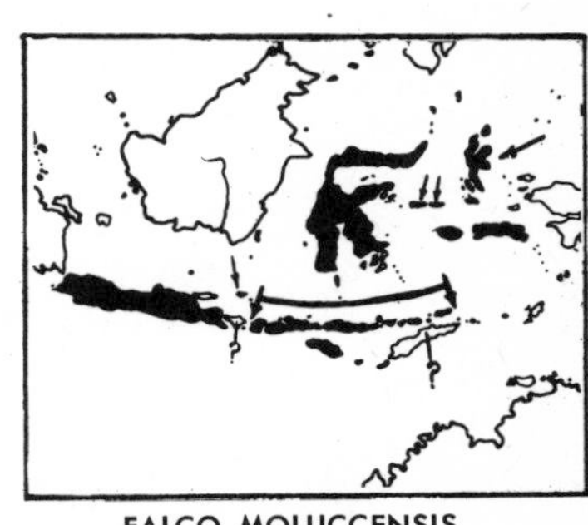
FALCO MOLUCCENSIS

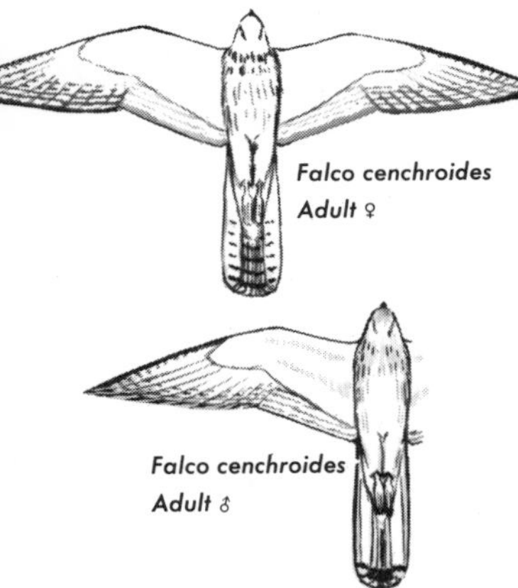

The Nankeen Kestrel (*F. cenchroides*), 12–13 inches, is more noticeably dimorphic in Australia than in New Guinea, where both sexes are like the adult Australian male, but darker. In Australia, the *male* has a dove-gray head; amber-brown back, lightly V-spotted with black; dark brown primaries; dove-gray rump patch, and tail, usually dove-gray with a black subterminal band; below, white, tinted throughout with light amber-brown and finely streaked in sienna. In the *female* the entire upperparts are amber-brown, more heavily spotted; rump patch, sienna; tail, usually sienna, indistinctly barred on the outer feathers and subterminally banded black; underparts, darker and more heavily streaked. (Juveniles of both sexes resemble adult female, having bright sienna rump patches and sienna tails, distinctly barred and subterminally banded black.)

FALCO CENCHROIDES

North American Peregrine Falcon *(Falco peregrinus)*, passage bird in juvenile plumage.—*Photograph by Heinz Meng.*

HABITS

Gyrfalcons and Peregrines are particular feeders and exhibit very complex behavior; these characteristics are less marked in their smaller relatives and more or less disappear in the somewhat "sociable" kestrels.

We have already discussed the hunting tactics of the larger falcons, in relation to the habitat in which they live. The terrain influences these specialized aerial hunters to earn their living in different ways. The Gyrfalcon flies low and fast across flat lava desert, or tundra intersected by crevasses and gorges. By following the contours closely, it can suddenly surprise and grab its quarry, often a ptarmigan sitting on a slab of rock in the bottom of a gorge. In this sustained, low flight, it is much faster than the Peregrine, but does not have the habit of "waiting on," which requires mountainous country with steep cliffs. Greater agility close to the ground is also characteristic of the Saker, the Lanner, and others of the Gyrfalcon type that hunt in deserts and treeless plains. The Peregrine Falcon is much more the master of the aerial chase, as are, in slightly different ways, the Hobby and the Merlin.

Rapid wing beats, interspersed with long glides on extended wings, are characteristic of the Peregrine, and its speed in a dive is seldom exceeded by any other bird. In a chase the Peregrine attempts to keep its quarry from going too far up or down, for if a bird can make the treetops it is safe, and similarly, if it can "ring up" considerably above its pursuer, it can probably get away.

Therein also lies the fascination of lark-hawking, in falconry, for the Hobby and the Merlin have developed pursuit strategies to counter the escape patterns of their prey. The Hobby, the expert in this kind of chase, has learned to double back and intercept the fast turns of the lark.

Once above its prey at a reasonable height, the Peregrine can stoop and knock it to the ground. Even this very fast bird utilizes the strategy of surprise, for it may often stoop out of the sun or sail from behind a cliff to strike its quarry. It is most frequently found along sea cliffs, or wide river gorges cut through forests, where many forest birds can be taken as they cross the rivers.

In arctic regions, during good ptarmigan years, the Gyrfalcon and the Peregrine both subsist on Willow Grouse and ptarmigan (*Lagopus*). However, the Gyrfalcon is a year-round resident in the arctic, restricted primarily to the tundra and the colder coastlines uninhabited by the Peregrine. Where they coinhabit the interior, the species are competitive, and have frequently developed different food preferences.

In his Alaskan study, Tom Cade recorded the prey species taken by coastal and insular Gyrfalcons as alcids (auks, puffins, murres), larids (gulls), and anatids (ducks). The birds in the interior preyed on ptarmigan and other tetraonids (such as grouse). In addition, Gyrfalcons may specialize locally on ground squirrels, lemmings, and even such unlikely prey as Short-eared Owls—but these specializations are always on nonmigratory species. Therefore the Gyrfalcon populations may be locally affected, in Greenland, by the rise and decline of lemmings. The Peregrine, on the other hand, feeds on a wide variety of migratory waterfowl, shore birds, and passerines, and follows these species out of the arctic in winter. Even though it may eat many lemmings in the years of their abundance, its own populations are unaffected by rodent cycles. This was probably true also in Australia in years of rabbit abundance, when the Peregrine fed, along with other hawks and falcons, on young rabbits in the spring.

Pairs of Peregrines may hunt together, one "waiting on" while the other chases the quarry into a vulnerable position. In falconry, the man hunting with a Peregrine is merely taking the place of the avian hunting partner as he (and perhaps his dogs) flush game birds for the falcon.

Strange parasitic relationships sometimes exist between species of predatory birds. In Australia, more than one observer has noticed the Black Falcon "waiting on" while the Marsh Harrier beats the brush, even urging its "partner" back to work when it alights on a fence post. The Brown Falcon occasionally takes over from the Black Falcon. Either would benefit if the Marsh Harrier were to flush a bird.

It should be mentioned that a pair of Peregrines will occasionally develop a preference for a certain bird species and may virtually eliminate the breeding population within their hunting range.

Gyrfalcons and Peregrines are also much more particular in their eating than most other birds of prey, feeding, after a bird is caught and plucked, only on the choice parts.

Unlike the falcons that follow the migratory birds, Eleonora's Falcon breeds later than any other European bird—in July and August—to take advantage of the southward migrations of small birds over the islands and shores of the Mediterranean. All during the month of September, it feeds on sandpipers, Little Crakes, Kentish Plovers, Black Terns, Turtle Doves, shrikes, swifts, larks, warblers, Nightingales, Buntings, and other species, up to the size of the Hoopoe, which are coming through, and as soon as their young are able to fly, the falcons themselves migrate, by way of the Red Sea, to Somaliland, Madagascar, and Reunion Island.

Young falcons in northern climates are fed on whatever is available. Gyrfalcons, in the High Fjeld of Norway, in Iceland, and in northern Alaska, nest early (a month before the Peregrines return) and must feed their nestlings on adult ptarmigan. It is usually the males that are taken, since they are more conspicuous in their white plumage than the females when the snows have melted. The young of the ptarmigan become available when the Gyrfalcon young are fledged and learning to hunt, and also fall prey to the Peregrines which are hunting for their nestlings. In temperate zones, most falcons, even the most insectivorous types, feed their nestlings on the young of other birds during the early part of the fledging period. An exception is the late-nesting Prairie Falcon that switches from a diet of birds to mostly thirteen-lined ground squirrels, which are abundant and conspicuous on the prairies of western North America in May and June, because they too are raising families.

The least fastidious feeders in the genus *Falco*, and the most numerous, are the kestrels. Those in northern climates shift from a summer diet of small rodents, insects, amphibians, and reptiles, to almost exclusively rodents, on their winter ranges; in Europe, they feed on field voles or long-tailed field mice, depending on the locality. Most kestrels are extremely active birds, and in England are called "windhovers" for their habit of riding against the wind while looking for their prey. Some tropical species, such as Dickinson's Kestrel and the Greater Kestrel, in Africa, are less active birds that characteristically perch on low trees or bushes, and drop directly down on their ground-dwelling prey.

Peregrines go through a complicated courtship. They use the rituals that are to be found among other hawks and even owl-like bowing and posturing, but their behavior is extremely variable. Food may be offered or dropped to the female on a ledge, or transferred to her in the air. The pair indulge in billing at the cliff nest, one sometimes turning its head upside down to bill; in nibbling toes; and in mutual preening of feathers. They chase each other, and stage mock attacks. The birds "loop the loop" occasionally. And the female has a "flutter-glide," a kind of food-begging flight, which is also characteristic of Prairie Falcons and American Kestrels. Grappling of feet as well as billing may take place in flight.

The courtship of the Hobby is very similar, but with even more elaborate aerial evolutions. Food may be transferred by the male to the female at the end of a dive, at full speed. Long soaring flights, also seen at other times during the year, in which a pair will circle to a considerable height, are more frequent in the spring.

Merlins circle above the nest site and the male feeds the female there. The male has been known to soar upward from a mound close to the nest site and hover at a relatively low altitude, then descend to the mound and repeat this action several times. However, there are no spectacular antics.

The display of the kestrels, also, is not as conspicuous as in some species of falcons.

Among the sociable Red-footed Falcons, there are remarkable aerial displays by entire flocks. Beginning high up in the morning and gradually descending by nightfall, they course back and forth over the same beat, turning sharply at fixed points.

According to Tom Cade, the Gyrfalcon is much more restricted in its nesting sites than the Peregrine. In Alaska, at least, there are no records of Gyrfalcons nesting in trees, although some have been found in isolated trees of the Eurasian tundra. This bird nests on narrow ledges and in clefts of steep, rocky cliffs preferably under an overhang, like the Prairie Falcon. The Peregrine, on the other hand, will more often accept ledges, potholes, scrapes at the brink of a cliff, high buildings in cities, occasionally trees, and sometimes also sandy ground (in tundra and on islands). However, as is common in *Falco,* both these species may use the old nests of other birds, such as that of the Northern Rough-legged Hawk and Raven.

Peregrines seem to have a more persistent attachment to their cliff sites than the Gyrfalcons, which ordinarily alternate between two nests. The Lanner, the only falcon of the Gyrfalcon "group" that goes into deep forest and forest clearings to any extent, and the Laggar Falcon, occasionally build their own nests. The Australian Brown Falcon may construct a small nest of sticks, twigs, and bark, placed in a tall eucalyptus, but also lays its eggs in the hollows of large gum trees and at the broken tops of termite hills, where it supplies only a few twigs and leaves.

In their Mediterranean colonies, varying from two to a dozen, or several hundred pairs, Eleonora's Falcons are restricted to sites in cliffs, about thirty yards from the sea. And in the flood-woods on the plains of Hungary, the Red-footed Falcons are totally dependent on the old nests of Rooks, preferably the higher ones in the oak trees containing rookeries. The Hobby annexes the unoccupied tree nests of Rooks, Magpies, Jays, Sparrowhawks, Herons, Wood Pigeons or squirrels. The Merlin, when it is not found using these, in cliffs or trees, habitually nests on the ground among tall herbs or low bushes. The American Kestrels are primarily hole nesters, preferring deep natural cavities in cliffs, walls of deserted buildings, giant cactus (in desert), and large trees. The Old World Kestrel lays its eggs in a scrape on the ledge of a cliff, often sheltered by ivy, as well as in hollows in rock; less frequently in places mentioned as characteristic of the American species, and rarely on the ground. Its African relatives, the Fox Kestrel, and the Lesser Kestrel, have a predilection for cliffs which is not shared by the Gray Kestrel, a tree-nesting species. Dickinson's Kestrel prefers the crowns of coconut and borassus palms, or the tops of decayed stumps.

An average clutch of three to five eggs is usual for most falcons and kestrels; only three in some of the less numerous tropical and subtropical species. Following a year of food scarcity the Gyrfalcon may not breed at all. The eggs are seldom unmarked, but more or less heavily spotted with reddish-brown on a whitish, buff, or light brown ground.

Incubation, mostly by the female, lasts about thirty days for all species, and eggs are laid at two- or three-day intervals. The fledging periods differ, however. In the small falcons and kestrels, the young are fledged at four or five weeks; Peregrines, at five or six weeks; and Gyrfalcons in about seven weeks (or two to three weeks longer than the Peregrines). In the early stages, the male supplies all the food. The length of time required for development depends somewhat on how often and how much the young are fed. They remain with their parents in the vicinity of the nest for two weeks to a month. In many species social hunting groups of juveniles are formed. These are broken up either by fall migration or the invasion of aggressive territory-seeking adults.

The Gyrfalcon "group" is mainly sedentary, with some drifting out of the northern part of the Gyrfalcon's range in Eurasia. The Saker is somewhat migratory, to northeastern Africa. The northern Peregrines migrate far below the Equator in the Old World, and reach northern South America in the New World. Merlins reach the tropics in the New World. Northern individuals of the American Kestrel rarely travel farther south than Mexico and Central America, and many spend the winter in the southern states. The Old World Kestrel, however, goes to tropical Africa in winter, where it is joined by Red-footed Falcons, Hobbies, and Lesser Kestrels, these species often associating in large mixed flocks, hunting migratory locusts. Eleonora's Falcon, as we have mentioned, reaches Madagascar. Most falcons resident in the Southern Hemisphere are sedentary, although the Black Falcon of the Australian interior occasionally visits the coastal districts, and some individuals of the Little Falcon drift to southern New Guinea and the islands north of the continent.

The "typical" falcon scream is a shrill "kek-kek-kek-kek," with variations. Pairs are often very noisy when the nesting territory is invaded (American Kestrel cries "killy, killy"), have special courtship notes and sounds they make when bringing food to the nest for the young. At other times during the year they are relatively silent birds.

ORDER STRIGIFORMES

FAMILY TYTONIDAE

SUBFAMILY TYTONINAE

(*Barn and Grass Owls*)

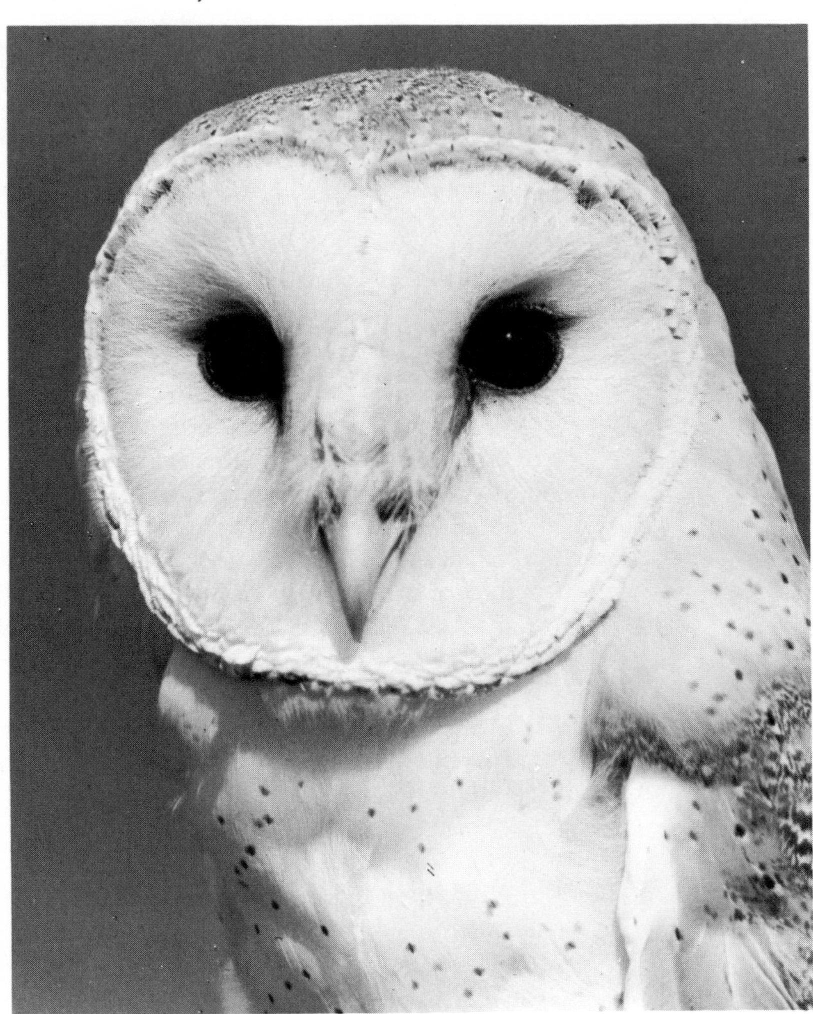

The Common Barn Owl of the Western Hemisphere *(Tyto alba)* also extends over large parts of the desert, temperate, and tropical areas of the Old World, where its range supplements and overlaps those of grass, brush, swamp, and forest-dwelling species.

GENUS *TYTO*

The many faces of *Tyto* wear the same eye spots or mask, encircled by a heart-shaped disc and more or less conspicuous dark ruff. More than ornamentation, the disc is composed of two parabolas, presumably for picking up sound, and marks the Barn and Grass owls as night hunters that depend largely on hearing to locate their prey. The small dark eyes and elongated beak are distinctive. There are no ear tufts. Wings are long, measuring almost twice the length of the tail. The tarsi are long and are partly or completely covered with short, soft feathers; the remaining parts of the legs and feet are bristled; the talons also are very long and sharp—middle claws expanded and serrated distally.

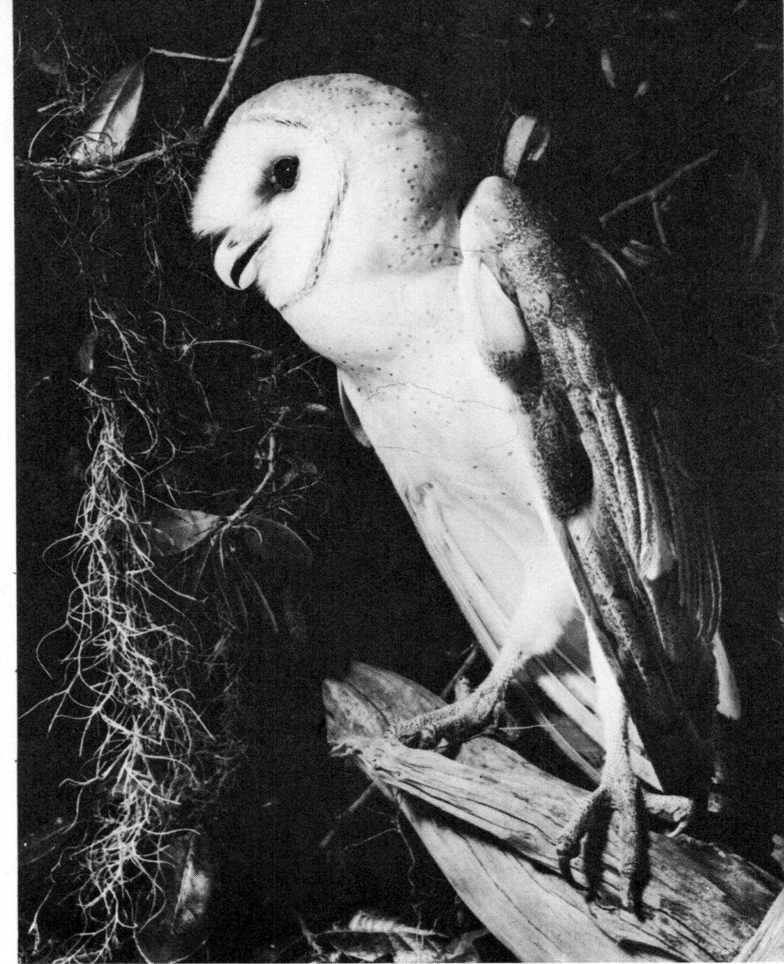

Common Barn Owl *(Tyto alba),* North America.

Common Barn Owl (*Tyto alba*)

DESCRIPTION (NORTH AMERICA)

Light or dark variants. White-breasted phase—above, pale yellow-orange, mottled and spotted with dark gray-brown and white; wings, tawny, almost completely mottled or faintly barred; tail, medium orange, or occasionally white with mottled dark gray-brown barring; facial disc, white, encircled by a dark brown ruff and marked only with brown patches in front of the eyes; underparts, white, spotted or V-marked lightly to heavily with dark brown and sometimes sandy-tinged. Orange-breasted phase—above, darker; facial disc, medium sienna; underparts, pale yellow-orange, spotted or V-marked in brown; tail, tawny, with mottled dark gray-brown barring.

Juvenile—similar to adult. Beak, very pale yellow; eyes, black; feet and talons, black. Size, 15–17 inches.

VARIATIONS

White-breasted and orange-breasted color phases are common throughout North, Central, and South America; the Caribbean islands; the Galapagos Islands; Africa; the Comoro Islands and Madagascar; Ceylon, India, northern Burma, and Malaysia.

The southern and western European population of *T. alba,* in two color phases, is replaced by an invariably dark and sometimes gray-faced population in northern and eastern Europe, the two intergrading in eastern France, Belgium, and western Germany. Gray facial discs are also a characteristic of some dark phase island birds—those from Tortuga and Hispaniola and the Canary Islands. The former, as well as the Barn Owls from Central America and the Galapagos Islands (among the smallest in the world), are barred, rather than spotted, below.

The light variant tends to predominate in the Australian region; on most of the South Sea Islands; in Arabia, Iraq, and the desert regions of Palestine; and on the islands of Corsica and Sardinia in the Mediterranean, where some individuals are almost pure white above and below. Size varies from 11 to 17 inches; the smallest are prevalent near the Equator, and the largest occur at the northernmost and southernmost limits of the range of *T. alba*.

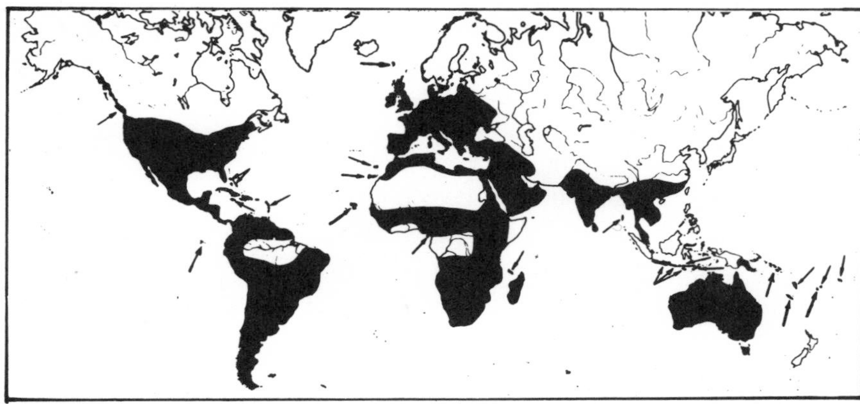

TYTO ALBA

TYTO NOVAEHOLLANDIAE

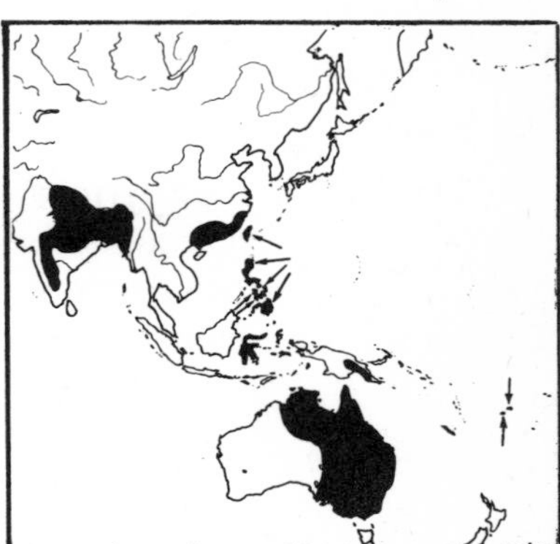

TYTO CAPENSIS

OTHER SPECIES

As in *T. alba,* two color variants have been recorded for the large Masked Owl (*T. novaehollandiae*), 14–20 inches, in the forests of the Australian region, and the Common Grass Owl (*T. capensis*), 13–17 inches. The coloring of the latter is similar in Africa and Asia—brown above but with expanded pale yellow-orange patchwork on the back characteristic of tropical rain-forest birds ranging from India to the Philippines and New Guinea. Other rain-forest species are dark phase only, including the Celebes Barn Owl (*T. rosenbergii*), 16–20 inches, and the Madagascar Grass Owl (*T. soumagnei*), about 10½ inches. A prominent yellow-orange patchwork shows on the backs of the dark brown New Britain Barn Owl (*T. aurantia*) on New Britain Island, and the Minahassa Barn Owl (*T. inexspectata*) in northern Celebes, both 11–13 inches.

The only species of *Tyto* completely lacking yellow-orange coloring is the Sooty Barn Owl (*T. tenebricosa*), 13–15 inches. Individuals vary from nearly solid dark brown in the rain forests of New Guinea, to white below, spotted with dark brown, in the temperate moist forests of Australia.

TYTO SOUMAGNEI

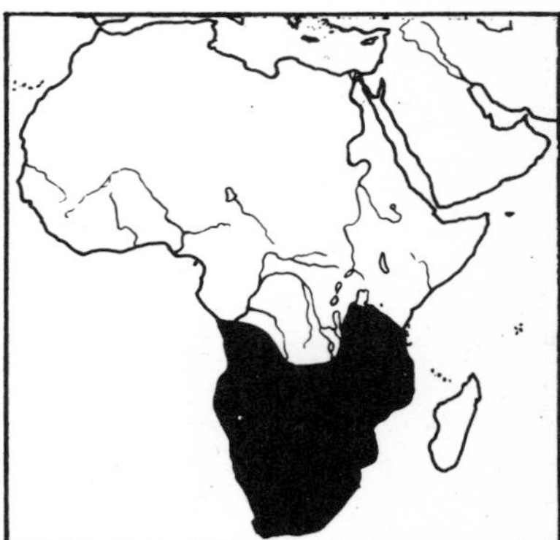

TYTO CAPENSIS

TYTO TENEBRICOSA

TYTO INEXSPECTATA

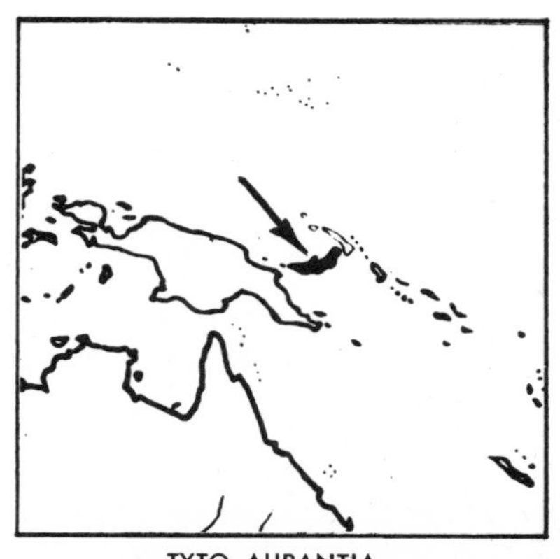

TYTO AURANTIA

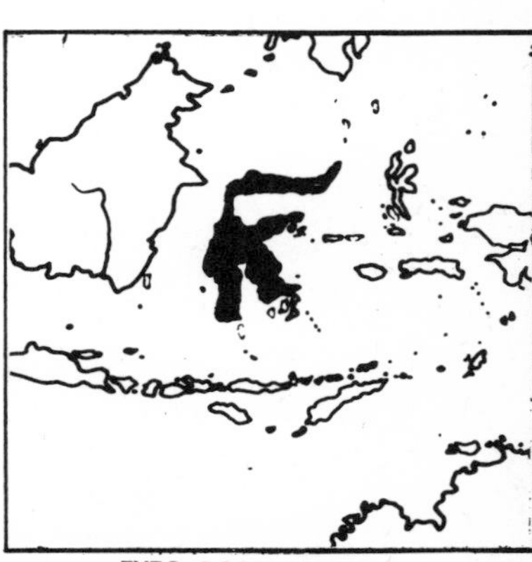

TYTO ROSENBERGII

HABITS

During daylight hours Common Barn Owls (*T. alba*) stay close to the man-made edifices where they prefer to nest—or, if barns, church steeples, water towers, and dilapidated buildings are not available, in hollow trees, hollows in river banks, among boulders, caves, or other secluded places. Usually four to seven, and sometimes as many as nine to eleven, eggs, ovate and more pointed than those of other owls, are laid on a scattering of rubbish that gathers a mattress of down and pellets from the growing family. Barn Owls have been tenants in old eagle nests in Africa and have frequented deserted crow nests and badger burrows in California and Texas. Wing-clapping by males in the breeding season has been recorded, and accumulations of food at the nest site for some time before the eggs are laid may be presentations to the female.

In *T. alba,* eggs are laid at times in pairs at intervals of 48 hours and then a pause of about a week, or else regularly, at about two-day intervals. The female incubates alone (about 32 to 34 days) and is fed during this period by the male. Both sexes bring food to the nestlings, whose short white down is replaced by creamy down at ten to fourteen days. Young are feathered at about 60 to 64 days, and flying at 64 to 86 days. Barn Owls often have two broods a year.

At night Barn Owls find their best food supplies along woods edges, where they take a high percentage of woodland rodents, and around barns, granaries, and other buildings that attract rats and mice. They have come to depend on man, indirectly, for food. But unlike most creatures that are ever-present with civilization (the House Sparrow, for example) they cohabit unobtrusively and are barely noticed—a disembodied screech uttered day or night, a gray shadow passing after sundown. Their defensive attitude—crouching or lying flat on the ground with wings spread horizontally—is different from that of other owls. Warning is expressed by lowering the head and swinging it to and fro close to the ground or stretching it forward, hissing, and snapping the bill and drooping the wings.

Other species appear to be almost exclusively wilderness birds. The Common Grass Owl (*T. capensis*) is terrestrial and lays eggs on a pad of shredded grass in high jungle, savanna, or open veld. Those restricted to rain forest may be "grass owls" as well, but little or nothing is known of their habits. People seldom encounter these owls, unless they are accidentally flushed on safari—so they are considered even more of a rarity than the numerous, but little-noticed, Barn Owls that inhabit our belfries. Their call is purported to be indistinguishable from the "sksch-sksch-sksch" scream of *T. alba.*

SUBFAMILY PHODILINAE

(Bay Owls)

A colorful predator of the temperate and tropical forests of Asia, the Bay Owl *(Phodilus badius)* is linked by structural similarities to both of the recognized families of owls.

GENUS *PHODILUS*

Phodilus has a broad head and large, dark eyes, like *Strix*—the Barred, Tawny, and Spotted owls. However, the heart-shaped facial disc resembles the Barn Owl's; the beak is weak and compressed; the tail, short. Wings are short and rounded; legs, short; the tarsi, always feathered to the toes. The talons are proportionally very large and the middle claw is serrated on the inner edge, as in *Tyto.*

Bay Owl (*Phodilus badius*)

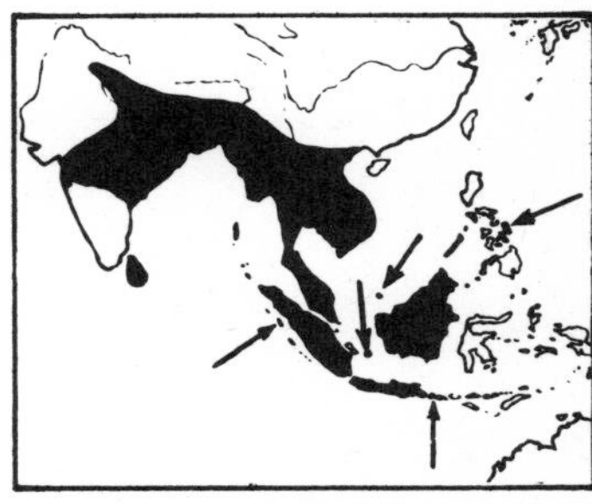

PHODILUS BADIUS

DESCRIPTION (KANDY, CEYLON)

Above, sienna-brown, irregularly marked and collared at the nape with yellow-orange, as well as mottled and spotted like the Barn Owl; wings and tail, ferruginous with irregular dark brown barring; forehead, facial disc, and underparts, vinaceous; eye mask, sienna-brown; ruff surrounding face, dark brown; locket at throat, white. Patches of buff-yellow and dark brown spotting mark the breast and extend down to, and including, the fully feathered tarsi.

Beak, creamy yellow; eyes, black; feet, yellow-brown; talons, paler. Size, 9–11 inches.

VARIATIONS

The bird of the high-altitude rain forest described is vividly marked compared to other Asiatic populations of *Phodilus,* which have lighter (sienna) upperparts and are only occasionally streaked or spotted. Bay Owls of the sub-Himalayas and northern mountains of the Indo-chinese Peninsula are larger (11–13 inches) than those of the Malay Peninsula and Indonesia (9–11 inches).

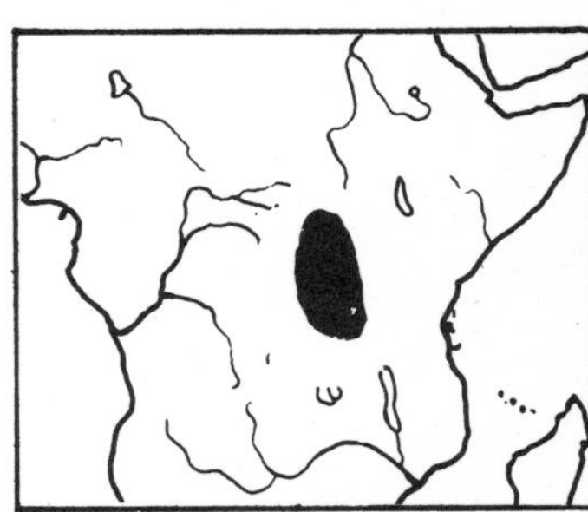

PHODILUS PRIGOGINEI

OTHER SPECIES

A Bay Owl collected at 7,500 feet in the highlands northwest of Lake Tanganyika (in the Congo) in March, 1951, known as the Congo Bay Owl (*P. prigoginei*), suggests an unknown range for the genus in eastern Africa. The single specimen is darker than *P. badius,* according to Chapin; the forehead, colored like the crown (rather than the facial disc); the beak more compressed; and the feet and claws, smaller.

HABITS

The Bay Owls are forest birds, entirely nocturnal, and feed on small mammals, birds, lizards, frogs, insects, and possibly fish, for they are often found near pools or rivers at night. They lay their eggs (no more than three to four, white and oval) in large natural hollows in trees, where the adults also rest during the day. Their call is a single, soft hoot, except in the breeding season, when they become much more vociferous. A pair of Bay Owls can sound "like half a dozen cats fighting."

FAMILY STRIGIDAE

SUBFAMILY BUBONINAE

(*Typical Owls*)

Screech Owls *(Otus asio)* in the eastern United States are of two color phases: this Florida pair is mixed—gray phase (left) and red phase (right). The offspring may be all gray, all red, or of both phases. (A gray phase pair apparently produces only gray young.)

GENUS *OTUS*

The genus *Otus* spreads in a wide dichromatic array across the world, unbroken until it reaches the Australian region and the southwest Pacific islands. It is composed of a large number of species occupying many different habitats, often within a relatively small geographical area. Although New World birds are commonly called Screech Owls and the Old World forms Scops Owls, recent studiés have shown that certain Asiatic species, *Otus bakkamoena,* for example, are more closely related to the boldly marked North American Screech Owls, *O. asio,* than to the smaller, more finely mottled Old World *O. scops;* and conversely, the tiny Flammulated Owl (*O. flammeolus*) of the Western Hemisphere may be a form of *O. scops,* which it resembles in appearance and habits. Only one species has become extinct in modern times: the Seychelles Owl (*O. insularis*), a "dark red" relative of the Asiatic *O. bakkamoena.*

Otus may be distinguished from other small nocturnal owls of the world by generally conspicuous ear tufts and a partly developed facial disc. The cere is inflated and the beak short and highly arched. Eye color is variable, ranging from bright yellow, as in *O. asio* and *O. scops,* to hazel or brown, as in *O. flammeolus* and some of the populations of *O. bakkamoena.* The wings are long, especially in the migratory *O. scops* and *O. flammeolus.* The tail is usually short and slightly rounded at the tip; the tarsi are short; the feet and talons are of average size. While most of the Screech and Scops owls of the world are partly to fully feathered on the tarsi and are bare-toed, northern and montane individuals of *O. asio* and *O. bakkamoena,* as well as *O. leucotis,* the White-faced Scops Owl of the Central Sahara and the dry hot African scrub, may be provided with fully booted toes. Other close relatives of *O. asio,* such as *O. trichopsis,* and *O. cooperi,* found along the arid Pacific slope of Central America, have bristle-like feathers on the toes. *O. nudipes,* the Caribbean bird, derives its scientific name from the nakedness of its legs and feet.

Common Screech Owl (*Otus asio*)

OTUS ASIO

DESCRIPTION (EASTERN NORTH AMERICA)

In two color variants. Gray phase—above olive-gray, including ear tufts, finely mottled and streaked with dark brown and white; hindneck and wing coverts spotted in white; wings and tail barred; facial disc, white, finely barred in dark brown; ruff, also dark brown;

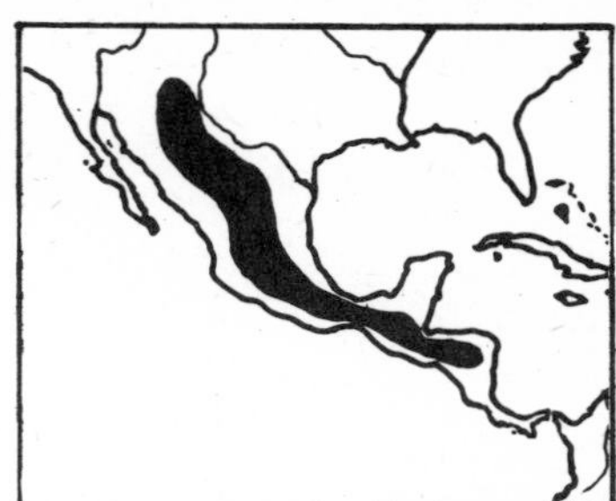
OTUS TRICHOPSIS

below white, boldly streaked and finely barred with dark brown, a "protective design" like tree bark. (Intermediate—same as gray phase, but washed heavily above and slightly on facial disc and underparts with medium sienna-orange.) Red phase: ferruginous above with fine black streaking; wing coverts spotted prominently in white; facial disc, orange-buff; lores and eyebrows, white; ruff, dark brown; below, white, with heavier black streaking and patches of dark orange barring.

Juveniles—correspond to adult phases but are lighter and completely barred. Beak, pale blue with yellow tip; eyes, bright yellow; toes, dull yellow; claws, dusky.

Size, 7–9 inches.

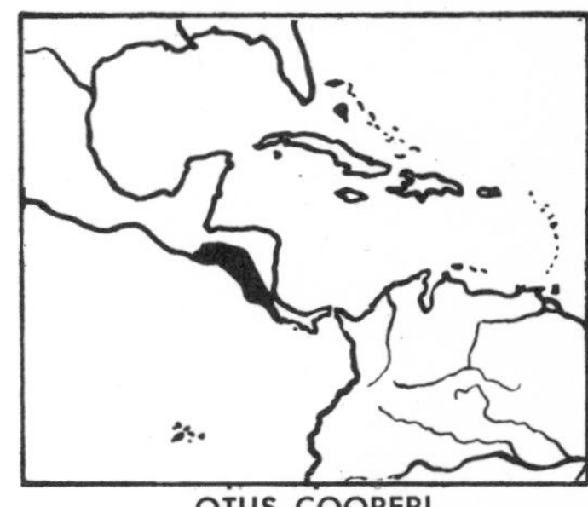
OTUS COOPERI

VARIATIONS

Screech owls of the western United States show only the gray phase and a brown phase (like intermediates in the East). The desert birds of the Great Basin are still further limited by hot arid conditions to a pale gray-brown variant very sparsely streaked with dark brown. From southeastern and extreme southern Texas to central Nuevo León and south-central Tamaulipas, Mexico, *O. asio* follows the color-phase pattern of eastern North America.

Sizes correspond to Bergmann's Rule. The largest are in the north or at high altitudes in the western coastal ranges; the smallest, in hot desert lowlands.

OTUS BARBARUS

OTHER NEW WORLD SPECIES

OTUS CHOLIBA

Gray and red phases, comparable to eastern Screech Owls (*O. asio*), occur throughout the range of the Whiskered, or Spotted, Screech Owl (*O. trichopsis*), from the mountains of southeastern Arizona to the southern limits of the arid tropical Sierra Madres, as well as throughout the range of the Tropical Screech Owl (*O. choliba*), from the arid Pacific slope of southern Central America to the Argentine Chaco.

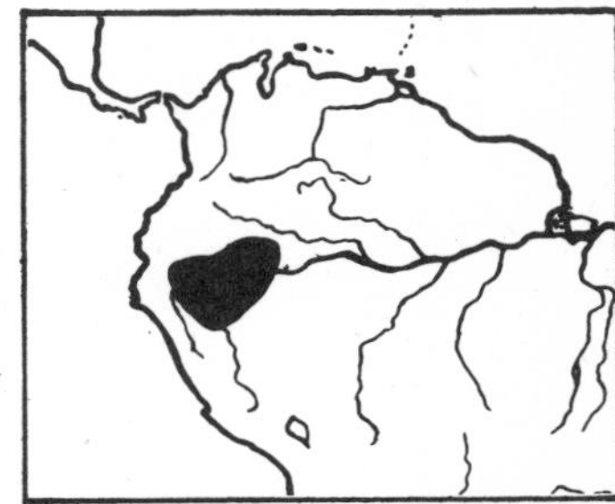
OTUS ROBORATUS

The Pacific Screech Owl (*O. cooperi*), in arid parts of Central America, is a pale gray-brown, boldly marked with black streaks and a few white spots above, and very finely streaked and mottled below.

The Bearded Screech Owl (*O. barbarus*) and the Dark-crowned Screech Owl (*O. roboratus*) are examples of species from humid zones or high altitudes in Central and South America which, in the red phase, are sienna above, streaked with brown and conspicuously collared in white. The Puerto Rican Screech Owl (*O. nudipes*) is plain sienna above in the red phase.

OTUS NUDIPES

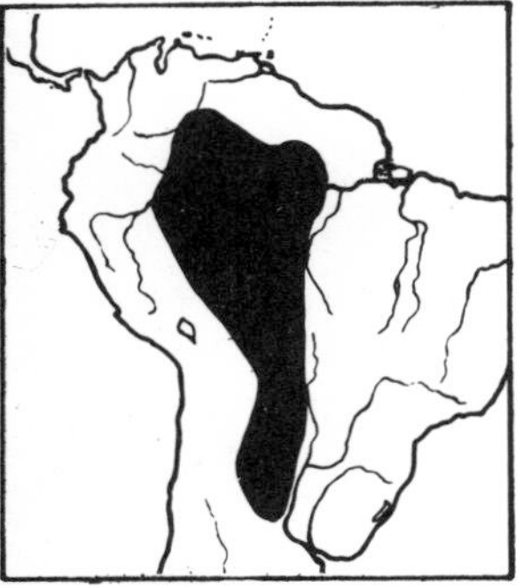
OTUS WATSONII

Following the pattern of North American *O. asio* and most populations of Mexican *O. trichopsis,* the underparts of all these birds are white, with dark streaking and barring.

Extreme dark variants, common in the Andes and the mountains of Venezuela, but also found in wet, tropical forests from the Caribbean to northern Argentina (Túcúmán), are: the Tawny-bellied Screech Owl (*O. watsonii*) in two color phases, the Black-capped Screech Owl (*O. atricapillus*), the Vermiculated Screech Owl (*O. guatemalae*), the Rufescent Screech Owl (*O. ingens*), the White-throated Screech Owl (*O. albogularis*), and the Bare-shanked Screech Owl (*O. clarkii*).

OTUS CLARKII

OTUS ALBOGULARIS

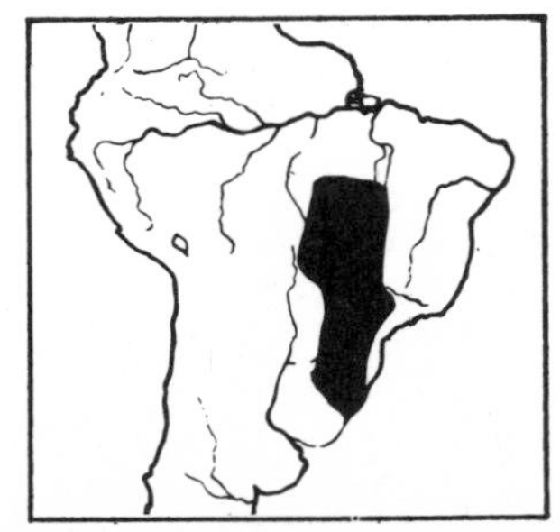
OTUS ATRICAPILLUS

OTUS GUATEMALAE

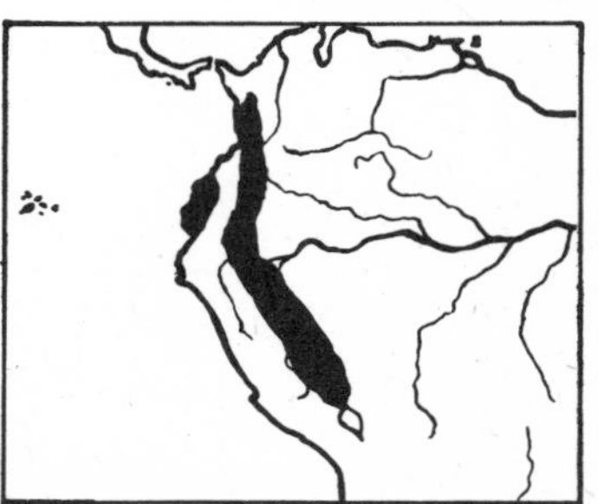
OTUS INGENS

Sizes of the Mexican, Central American, and South American owls approximate North American *O. asio,* but they are consistently a little larger, especially away from low rain-forest areas, and reach 10½ inches in the Andes of northern South America.

OTUS FLAMMEOLUS

The Flammulated Owl (*O. flammeolus*), both gray and brown phases, in the mountains of western North America, always seeks the higher altitudes (to 6,000 feet). It is much smaller (6 inches) than *O. asio* and has naked toes and rudimentary ear tufts, like the Scops Owl of the Old World. In the southern Mexican highlands this tiny predator occurs either in the brown or red phase.

Common Scops Owl (*Otus scops*)

DESCRIPTION (SOUTHERN EUROPE)

Brown phase (intermediate)—as in North American *O. asio,* but more finely marked above; collared very indistinctly; wing coverts, marked with sandy spotting; facial disc, white, very finely barred and bordered by a dark ruff; below, whiter than upperparts, with broader streaking.

Juvenile—mottled like adult, but paler.

Beak, blue-black; eyes, bright yellow; feet, gray.

Size, about 7½ inches.

OTUS SCOPS

Brown (intermediate) *O. scops* and a red phase, almost identical to that of *O. asio,* may be found on the four main islands of Japan in heavy forests with large, old trees (to 4,500 feet in the Japanese alps), in southeastern China, and the Indian peninsula—the red phase is darker (sienna, with varying amounts of dark brown mottling above) in the eastern Himalayas, the heavy rainfall districts of Japan, the Philippines, and the outlying islands of Indonesia. The brown phase birds in Africa, south of the Sahara (perhaps a separate species, *O. senegalensis*), the central provinces of India, and Cyprus are heavily mottled with dark brown and have large white spots on the upperparts. A pale gray-brown phase ranging across the arid plateaus and steppes of Asia Minor, southern Siberia, and Mongolia is sometimes considered a separate species, the Pallid, or Striated, Scops Owl (*O. brucei*). Some Japanese birds, as well as variants from China, the central provinces of India, and Africa, below the Sahara, are smaller (6½ inches).

OTHER OLD WORLD SPECIES

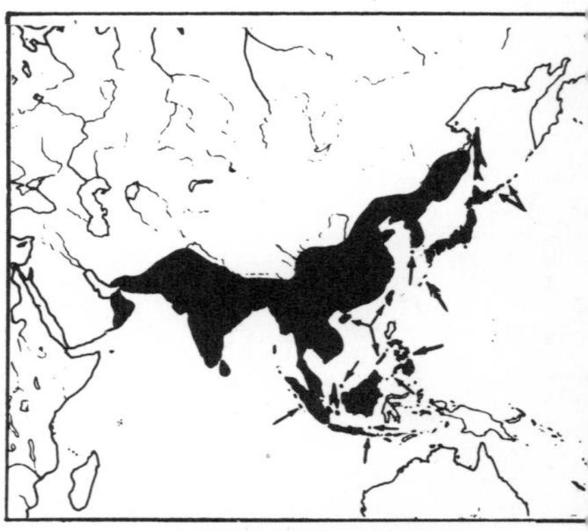
OTUS BAKKAMOENA

Throughout the temperate forests of the Himalayas, northern China, and Japan the coloring of the Collared Scops Owl (*O. bakkamoena*) corresponds to the brown intermediate phase of *O. asio* of northwestern North America, but the Asiatic bird is slightly larger (10 inches) and less heavily streaked. Only in southeastern China, and on Hainan, Formosa, and northern Luzon, do these birds approach the gray phase of *O. asio*. Throughout southern Asia, from central India, Malaya, Indonesia, and the Philippines to Okinawa, they tend to be smaller (some, 7½ inches) and heavily saturated on the underparts with yellow-orange, and in especially heavy rainfall areas (Ceylon and the eastern Himalayas, for example) are also darker above—more heavily mottled or streaked with dark brown.

OTUS SPILOCEPHALUS

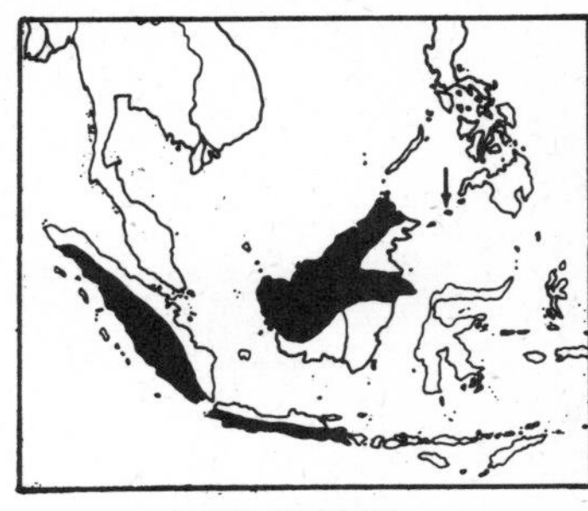
OTUS BROOKII

The Spotted Scops Owl (*O. spilocephalus*), which has a spotted back but is barred below, shows definite geographical separation of color phases; brown phase in the western Himalayas and red phase (sienna) in the eastern Himalayas, Sumatra, Java, and Borneo. It is smaller (6½–8 inches) and much less common than the Collared Scops Owl.

Found in the highlands of Sumatra, Java, and Borneo, the Rajah Scops Owl (*O. brookii*), 9½ inches, is larger than the Collared Scops Owl and has dark orange coloring and a distinct white collar. Replacing other Asiatic species in the East Indies, the Celebes Scops Owl (*O. manadensis*), 7½–9 inches, lacks a collar and shows both a brown phase and a red phase (dark orange) with markings similar to *O. scops*.

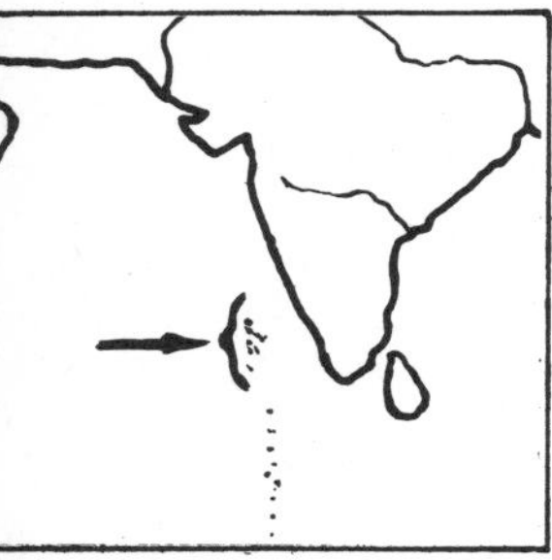
OTUS BALLI

OTUS MANADENSIS

The Andaman Scops Owl (*O. balli*), about 8 inches, has the uppersurface "deep rufous brown," faintly mottled black and with a few "rufous-buff" spots; tail, barred in a paler color and with very narrow bands of black; underparts, "rusty buff," finely mottled and spotted with black and white.

The Lesser Sunda Scops Owl (*O. silvicola*), 10 inches, found in shore jungle on both Flores and Sumbawa, is a brown phase owl comparable to the Collared Scops Owl (*O. bakkamoena*) in size and color pattern, but it has much larger beak, feet, and claws (with strong toes completely bare). There is scarcely, if any, trace of a nuchal collar.

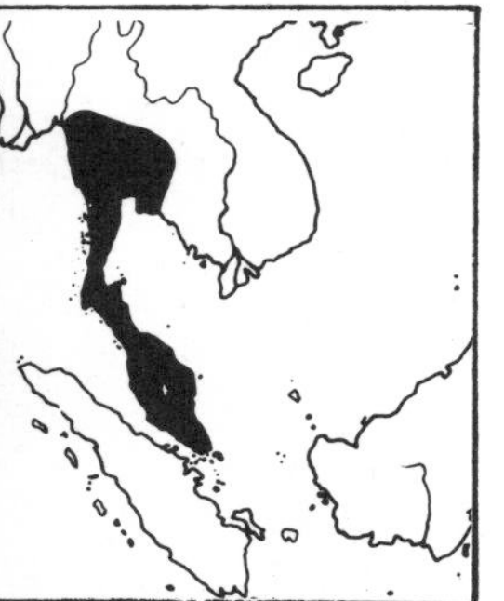
OTUS SAGITTATUS

OTUS SILVICOLA

The Flores Scops Owl (*O. alfredi*), 7½ inches, a mountain species, above 3,000 feet, on Flores, appears entirely medium ferruginous with white-spotted scapulars and wings; mottled white forehead and underparts. The Mentawi Scops Owl (*O. umbra*), found on the Mentawi Islands of Simalur and Engano, off Sumatra in the Indian Ocean, is similar to *O. alfredi,* but it is smaller, with the tail distinctly barred.

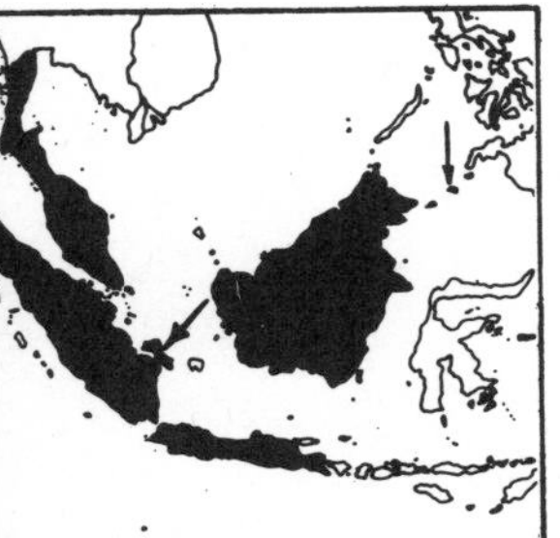
OTUS RUFESCENS

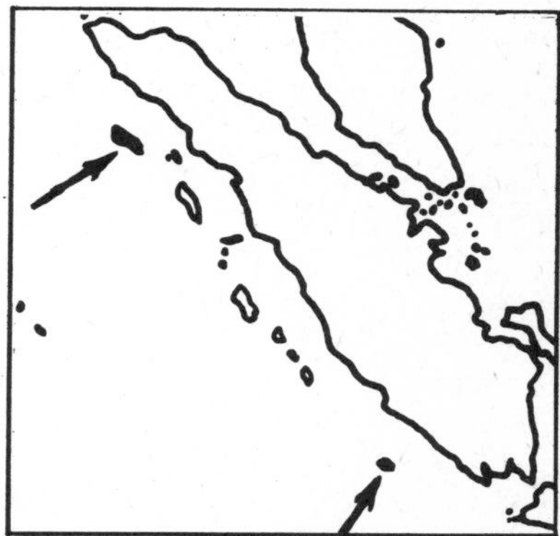
OTUS UMBRA

Other Asiatic species are mostly red phase—sienna to sienna-brown above spotted with yellow-orange; the underparts white to pale yellow-orange, barred or spotted with dark brown. The small Reddish Scops Owl (*O. rufescens*), 6–7 inches, in the dense interior submontane jungle of Malaysia and Indonesia, has distinctive pale yellow-orange or white eyebrows and forehead; the larger White-fronted Scops Owl (*O. sagittatus*), 10–11 inches, peculiar to the foothill forests of Malaya, is conspicuously marked with white on the eyebrows, forehead, crown, and sides of throat. Two barred species of Melanesia, the Palau Scops Owl (*O. podarginus*), 8½ inches, and the Biak Scops Owl (*O. beccarii*), represent the farthest dispersal points of the genus *Otus* to the fringes of the southwest Pacific.

OTUS BECCARII

OTUS PODARGINUS

OTUS ALFREDI

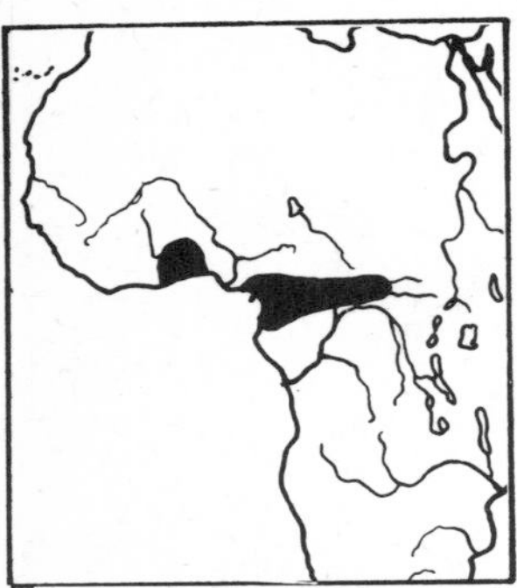
OTUS ICTERORHYNCHUS

OTUS GURNEYI

The largest member of the genus in the world, and very rare, is the Giant Scops Owl (*O. gurneyi*), 12 inches, a red-phase species boldly streaked with dark brown, which has been found only on the islands of Mindanao and Marinduque in the Philippines. The Cinnamon Scops Owl (*O. icterorhynchus*) 7–8 inches, of the west African rain forest, is the single red-phase species of *Otus* on the African continent.

The Madagascar Scops Owl (*O. rutilus*), 7½–9 inches, found on Madagascar, the Comoros, and Pemba Island, plays a mysterious role in native witchcraft. In two phases—gray phase: pale gray-brown above with white or light amber-brown underparts, characteristically streaked and barred; or red phase: sienna above, with a dark orange breast, similarly marked.

White-faced Scops Owl (*Otus leucotis*).—*New York Zoological Society Photograph.*

OTUS RUTILUS

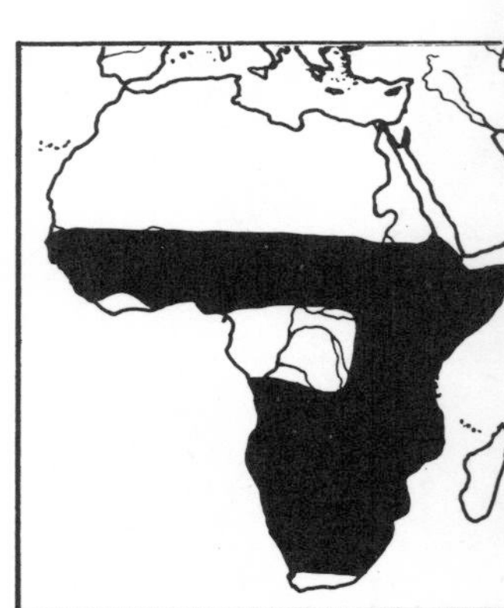
OTUS LEUCOTIS

The White-faced Scops Owl (*O. leucotis*), 7–9½ inches, common in the African bush, penetrates far into the scrub desert of the Sahara and the arid southwestern coastal region which is avoided by other members of *Otus*. This pale gray-brown bird is heavily streaked in black and very finely mottled with gray-brown above, and shows the same pattern intermixed with white below. Black patches or heavy streaks appear on the crown. The facial disc is white, the ruff, black; and the ear tufts, black-tipped. Unlike other African scops owls, *O. leucotis* has heavily booted and finely striped tarsi and feet. The young resemble the adults, but they are lighter.

HABITS

The small owls of the genus *Otus* hide in hollow trees or dense foliage during the day. When alerted to possible danger, they stretch out as tall as possible, hold their wings close to the body, and utilize their protective tree-bark coloration to simulate dead stubs on the branches of trees. In late afternoon and after dark they move from secluded to open perches, ready to fly at the slightest flicker of insect wings or rustle of small rodents in brush or leaves on the ground.

The larger species, including *O. asio* in North America, feed heavily on mice and other small mammals, birds, and insects; also bats, lizards, frogs, fish, crayfish, and worms. Smaller species—such as *O. scops,* in Europe, and related small owls, in Africa and Asia—are almost exclusively insect-eaters. Grasshoppers and other insects on the ground or tree branches are snatched with the feet, but moths and beetles may be caught in mid-air with the beak in the manner of a flycatcher or nightjar.

Usually four to five eggs are laid in holes in walls, natural hollows in trees, and the deserted nests of other birds anywhere from five to forty feet above the ground. No attempt is made to build a nest, but the Collared Scops Owl (*O. bakkamoena*) of India "renovates" the borrowed nests of woodpeckers and barbets by lining them with grass. In Arizona the desert screech owls raise their families in abandoned Gila Woodpecker holes in the giant cactus plants, also favored nesting places of Elf Owls, Wied's Crested and Ash-throated flycatchers, American Kestrels, and Purple Martins.

North American Screech Owls lay their eggs at intervals of two or three days, and sometimes at longer intervals. Incubation, by the female, may begin after the first, second, or third egg, and lasts about 26 days. The male provides all the food for the female and nestlings, which are fledged and leave the nest in about four weeks. Probably the young are then watched over and fed, more or less, by the parents for an additional five or six weeks. Incubation periods, in smaller owls, are one or two days shorter, and they evidently have a much shorter fledging period. The young of *O. scops* in Europe leave the nest at 21 days, before they are full-grown.

The soft juvenile plumage, which takes the place of a second down, in owls of this group is generally pale and distinctly barred or mottled. In the first winter the immatures also have a more mottled appearance than adults.

Most Screech Owls are resident the year round in the areas in which they breed, although there may be some movement out of the northern regions in cold weather. The tiny Flammulated Owl, however, is migratory and winters chiefly south of the United States through the highlands of Guatemala. The Common Scops Owl of Europe and northern Africa winters in tropical Africa from Timbuktu to Ethiopia and south to Uganda; the same species of northern Asia, to the Upper Nile, southwestern Asia, northwestern India, southeastern China, and Formosa.

The eerie whistling and wailing calls of some *Otus* have prompted men to all manner of superstitious belief and poetic fancy about them—recorded in Western literature, from classical antiquity to modern times, and in the religious lore of the Orient, from the days of Buddha. The characteristic call of *O. asio* is a tremulous wail, rarely a screech, but it is for this startling sound that the bird is named. *O. scops* has a low, short musical song—"kiu," repeated with monotonous persistence. Beak-snapping and trilling are also recorded for many species of *Otus.*

The Maned Owl (*Jubula lettii*) is one of the least common predators of equatorial Africa.

GENUS *JUBULA*

The rare Maned Owl of tropical west Africa is a forest-dweller, with relatively short wings and a long tail. The head is distinguished by very long ear tufts and crest and facial discs bordered by a pronounced ruff. It is not a very ambitious hunter, as may be seen by its very small feet. The tarsi are feathered; the eyes, yellow.

Maned Owl (*Jubula lettii*)

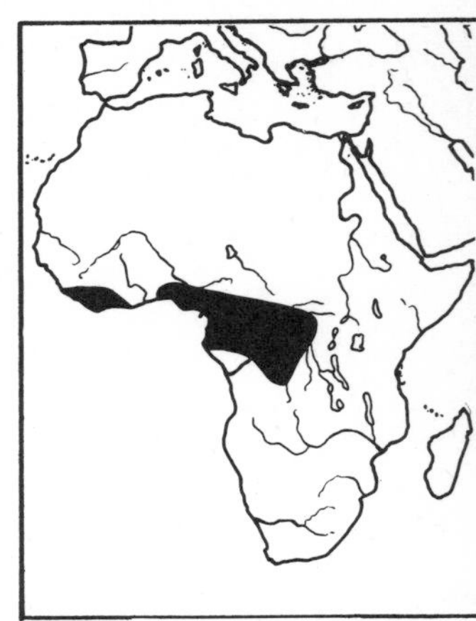
JUBULA LETTII

DESCRIPTION (CONGO)

Above, sienna-brown from crown to mantle, with fine fragments of dark brown and white barring on the forehead, long crest, and ear tufts; back, darker—dark brown, barred in sienna-brown; wings and tail, ferruginous, barred and mottled in dark brown; facial disc, sienna, with dark brown eye patches and ruff; below, ferruginous to pale yellow-orange, finely barred in chestnut and streaked only on the belly with dark brown.

Juvenile—crown, throat, and face, white; lighter above and below.

Beak, pale yellow; eyes, yellow; feet, white, tinted with yellow. Size, about 11 inches.

HABITS

The Maned Owl of equatorial Africa has never been seen outside the rain forest, gallery forest, or forest clearings. It feeds principally on insects, but vegetable matter resembling squashed green peas has also been found in the stomach. Breeding habits and calls are unrecorded.

The Crested Owl *(Lophostrix cristata)* of tropical America has conspicuous light eyebrows and ear tufts and very fine mottling on the underparts.

GENUS *LOPHOSTRIX*

The tropical American Genus *Lophostrix* is conspicuously sandy or white-tufted, with a bright sienna face. Wings and tail are long; tarsi are densely feathered to the toes, which are naked.

Crested Owl (*Lophostrix cristata*)

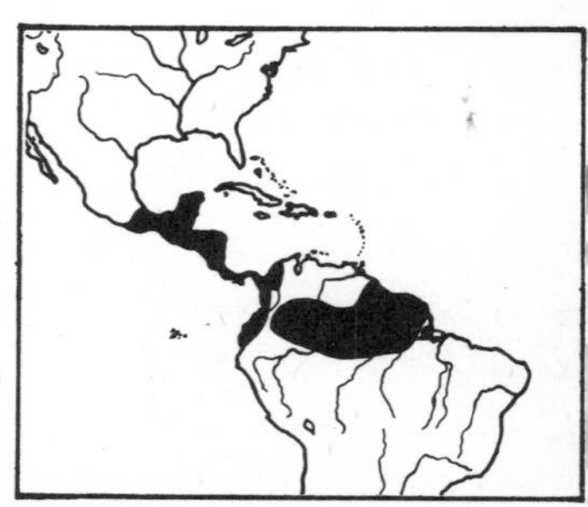
LOPHOSTRIX CRISTATA

DESCRIPTION (BOGOTÁ, COLOMBIA)

Crown, dark brown with sandy ear tufts; rest of upperparts, chocolate, with very fine dark brown barring; wings, barred buff; tail, finely mottled with dark brown; face, sienna to dark brown at the sides with long sandy eyebrows; breast, chocolate, finely barred with dark brown, fading to tawny; belly, finely barred with chocolate. Beak, horn color (light yellow at tip); eyes, yellow. Size, 17 inches.

VARIATIONS

In Central America most of the individuals in the Atlantic coast region (Veracruz to eastern Costa Rica) resemble the Colombian bird described. Paler cinnamon-brown birds, with nearly white ear tufts, eyebrows, and breast, are found mainly, if not entirely, on the Pacific side (Chiapas, Mexico, to Panama). Very light amber-brown-colored birds from the headwaters of the Rio Napo near Archidona, eastern Ecuador, have no dark patches at sides of face, which is clear sienna; they have pure white eyebrows and ear tufts.

HABITS

The habits of this owl, which occurs in heavy lowland forest, are unrecorded.

Diurnal, as well as nocturnal in their habits, and extremely voracious killers, the Great Horned Owls *(Bubo virginianus)* reign undisputed kings of most of the New World forests, from Alaska to the Strait of Magellan.

GENUS *BUBO*

Ferocity shines from the great yellow eyes as the feathers of the head fluff in anger and the heavy compressed beak clacks a warning. Above its partly developed facial discs, conspicuous ear tufts are set wide apart. This is the portrait of *Bubo,* with the exception of species which have dark eyes—hazel or dark brown to blackish in four African eagle-owls (*B. lacteus, B. poensis, B. shelleyi,* and the west African *B. africanus*) and in two Asiatic species (*B. sumatrana* and *B. nipalensis*). The Eagle-Owl (*B. bubo*) of Eurasia and northern Africa, and Shelley's Eagle-Owl (*B. shelleyi*) of the Congo forest, rival, in size and strength, the fishing owls of Africa and Asia (*Scotopelia* and *Ketupa*) but may be easily distinguished where their ranges correspond by differences in habitat and habits, and by their densely feathered tarsi and toes. Their wings are wide and long, spanning four to five feet in the largest birds, making it possible for them to soar with all the grace and power of an eagle or a large buteo hawk. Nearly cosmopolitan, the owls of the genus *Bubo* may be found everywhere except in the forests of the Australian region and on the southwest Pacific islands, where they are ecologically replaced by boobook owls (*Ninox*).

Great Horned Owl (*Bubo virginianus*)

DESCRIPTION (EASTERN AND PACIFIC COASTAL NORTH AMERICA; MEXICO)

In two variants. *White-breasted phase*—above, including ear tufts, dark brown, mottled in white and tinted with buff-yellow; wings, darker; tail, white to light yellow-ochre, barred and mottled; face, white to buff-yellow; ruff at sides, dark brown; locket at throat, white; rest of underparts, white, barred with dark brown and tinted as above with buff-yellow; feathering on tarsi and toes, white, sometimes barred or mottled. *Orange-breasted phase*—facial disc tawny; above and below, similar to white phase, but heavily marked with tawny, including tarsi and toes; tail, light amber-brown, barred and mottled.

Juvenile—lighter, barred above and below in sepia.

Beak, black; eyes, deep yellow; claws, black. Size, about 19 inches.

VARIATIONS

New World bubos sometimes show only one of the color variants regionally. Great Horned Owls of the Great Basin of western North America are very pale; on the wooded plains of North and South America, white-breasted phase; and in the cold, dry regions of Alaska and central Canada (to Hudson Bay), much whiter. Andes birds, living at altitudes up to 10,000 feet in western Ecuador, are almost solid brown or dark olive-brown above, with a few buff-yellow spots; underparts, either white or buff-yellow below, barred in dark olive-brown.

Sizes vary from 17 to 18 inches in the lowlands of Mexico and Lower California to 20 inches in Alaska and northern Canada and 21 inches in the Andes of Ecuador.

BUBO VIRGINIANUS

Great Horned Owl (*Bubo virginianus*), Florida.

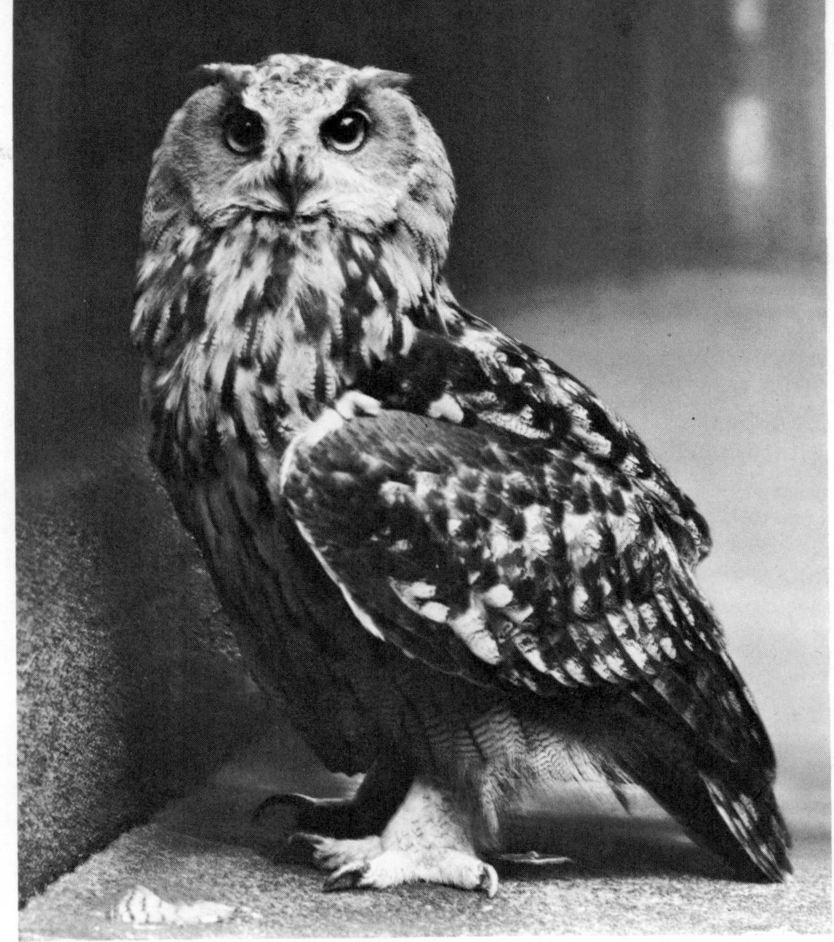

The Eagle Owl *(Bubo bubo)* of the Old World.— *Photographed at the New York Zoological Society.*

Eagle-Owl (*Bubo bubo*)

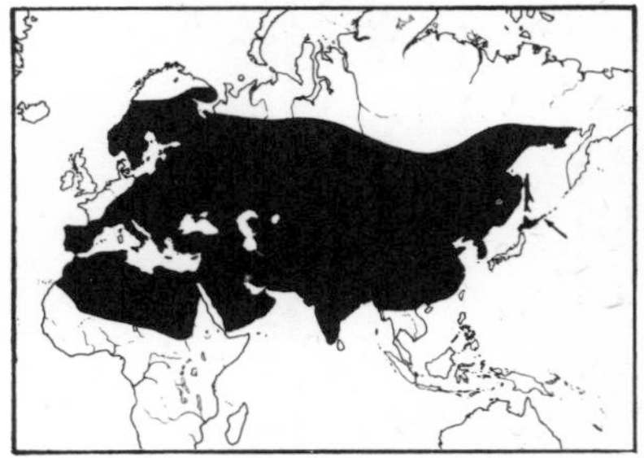

BUBO BUBO

DESCRIPTION (EUROPE)

Above, including ear tufts, pale yellow-orange with dark brown streaking and white mottling; wings and tail, darker, barred and mottled; facial disc, pale ivory-gray, with very fine dark brown barring and dark ruff at sides; locket at throat, white; breast, white; belly, as well as the feathering on tarsi and toes, pale yellow-orange, boldly striped and finely barred with dark brown.

Juvenile—lighter, barred above and below.

Beak, black; eyes, orange; claws, black. Size, about 27 inches.

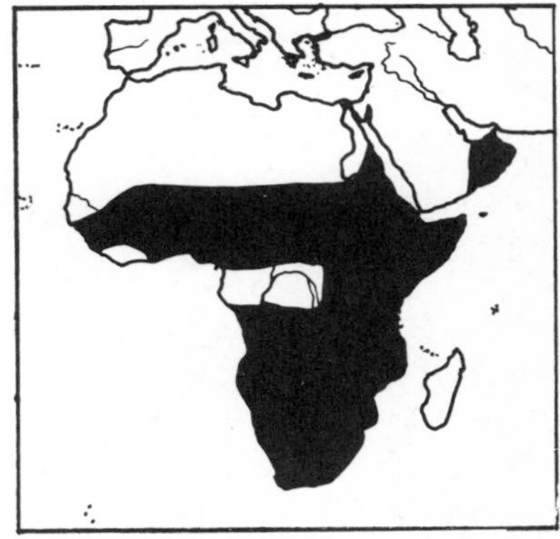

BUBO AFRICANUS

VARIATIONS

The eagle-owls of Scandinavia and Siberia, as far north as the tree limit, and their smaller relatives, on the dry steppes of the Near East and southern Siberia, are lighter. The smallest birds (18 inches), found in semi-desert regions of northern Africa and Palestine and in the Syrian desert, are uniquely orange-buff, with very much reduced areas of dark brown and almost no white, except on the belly and face.

OTHER OLD WORLD SPECIES

Two smaller species of eagle-owls, found in tropical forest and savanna of Africa, resemble *B. bubo* in coloring and marking. The Spotted Eagle-Owl (*B. africanus*), 12–16 inches, shows two distinct color phases throughout Africa, south of the Sahara. From the Cape to Uganda and Kenya these eagle-owls are spotted boldly with white or light orange on the back of the head and wing coverts; heavily barred below, and always tinted vinaceous-buff or light orange. Throughout the dry bush country from Sierra Leone, west Africa, to coastal Somaliland and southern Arabia, birds lack conspicuous spots and appear paler above but are similarly marked below. The Cape Eagle-Owl (*B. capensis*), 19 inches, is much larger and darker above than the Spotted Eagle-Owl, which shares its range; underparts, white below, spotted on the breast and barred on the belly with dark brown.

BUBO CAPENSIS

Milky Eagle Owl *(Bubo lacteus)*, central Africa.—*Photographed at the New York Zoological Society.*

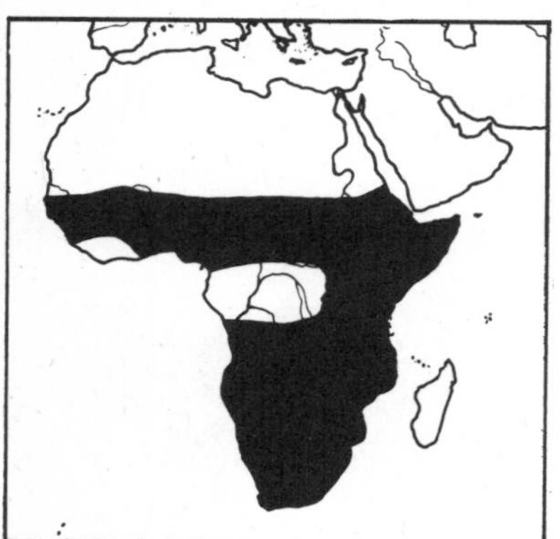

BUBO LACTEUS

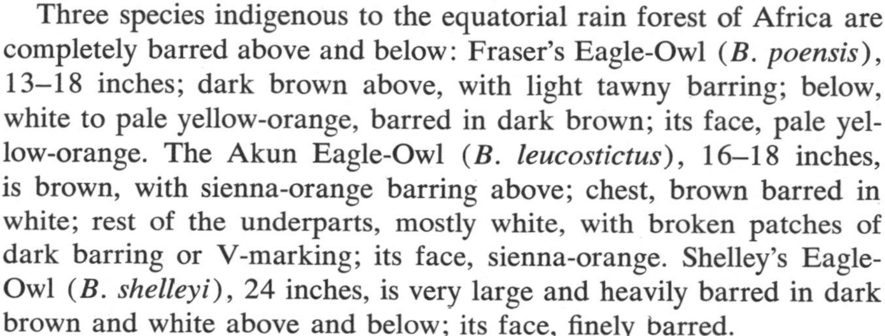

The Milky Eagle-Owl (*B. lacteus*), 21 inches, found in both dry and heavier rainfall areas of tropical Africa (excluding the equatorial forests), varies regionally from light to dark. In the central African bush, this species is gray-brown, very finely mottled in white above and the reverse below. In eastern and southern Africa the bird called "Verreaux's Eagle-Owl" is dark gray-brown. Large size and lack of heavy barring on the underparts distinguish this species from all others in its range.

Three species indigenous to the equatorial rain forest of Africa are completely barred above and below: Fraser's Eagle-Owl (*B. poensis*), 13–18 inches; dark brown above, with light tawny barring; below, white to pale yellow-orange, barred in dark brown; its face, pale yellow-orange. The Akun Eagle-Owl (*B. leucostictus*), 16–18 inches, is brown, with sienna-orange barring above; chest, brown barred in white; rest of the underparts, mostly white, with broken patches of dark barring or V-marking; its face, sienna-orange. Shelley's Eagle-Owl (*B. shelleyi*), 24 inches, is very large and heavily barred in dark brown and white above and below; its face, finely barred.

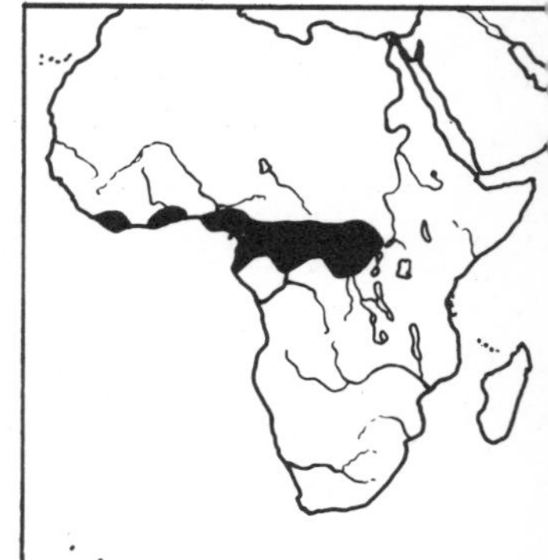

BUBO SHELLEYI

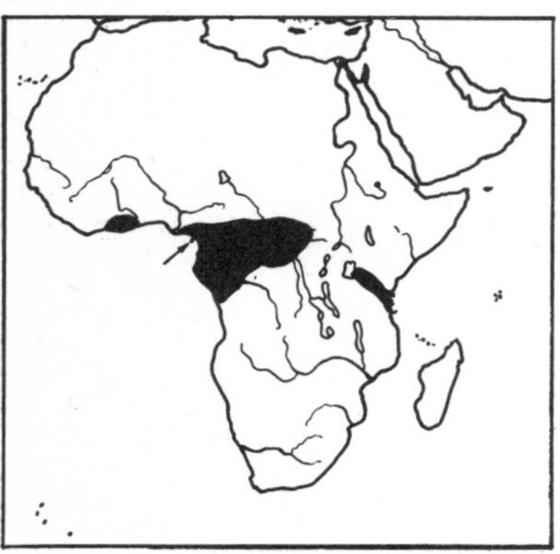

BUBO POENSIS

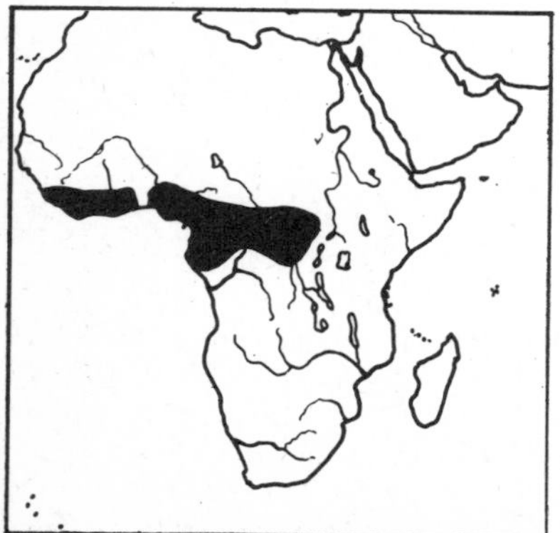

BUBO LEUCOSTICTUS

Shelley's Eagle Owl *(Bubo shelleyi)*, western Africa.—*Photographed at the New York Zoological Soc*

BUBO SUMATRANA

BUBO PHILIPPENSIS

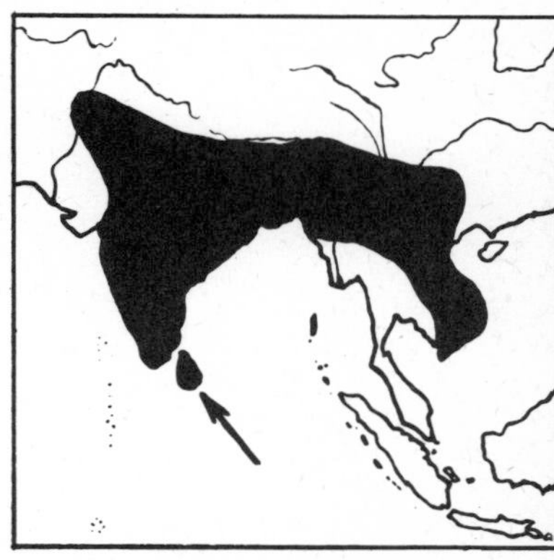
BUBO NIPALENSIS

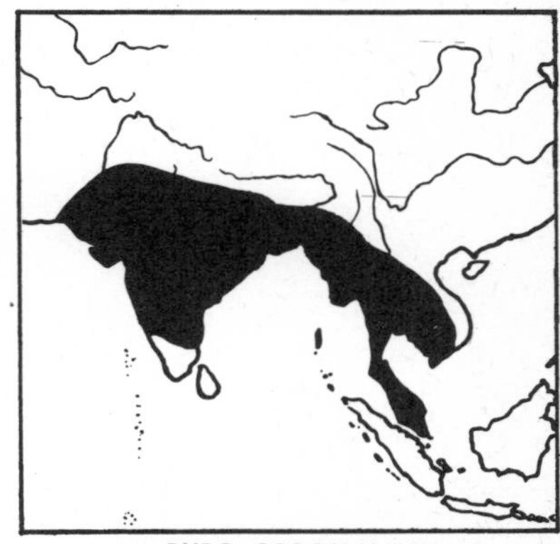
BUBO COROMANDUS

No one could mistake the big Forest Eagle-Owl (*Bubo nipalensis*), 20–24 inches, of the Himalayas and Indian peninsula, which is dark brown from crown to mantle, the feathers distinctively scalloped around the tips in pale orange-buff; rest of the upperparts, pale yellow-orange, irregularly barred with dark brown. The underparts, white to pale orange-buff, are boldly V-marked in dark brown. The smaller Dusky Eagle-Owl (*B. coromandus*), 18 inches, of peninsular India, is dark gray-brown, finely mottled in white above, and the reverse below, like the Milky Eagle-Owl of tropical Africa, but distinctly striped.

The Malay Eagle-Owl (*B. sumatrana*), 16–18 inches, resembles the African *B. poensis,* but its ear tufts, patches at sides of neck, and chest are finely and evenly barred in white and brown; belly, white, coarsely barred in brown. Both of these rain-forest species have dark eyes and yellow beaks and toes.

Unique among the species inhabiting heavy rainfall areas, the Philippine Eagle-Owl (*B. philippensis*), 16 inches, has vivid dark orange plumage, closely streaked with dark brown above; underparts, white to medium orange, also streaked.

All of the eagle-owls of the Orient have pale ivory-gray facial discs, except *B. philippensis,* in which the lores are white; the facial disc, dark orange.

The white locket at the throat, characteristic of most of the temperate and tropical species of *Bubo* throughout the Americas, Europe, northern Asia, and Africa, is absent from the Indian eagle-owls, as well as from the deep rain-forest birds of Malaysia, the Philippines, and equatorial Africa.

HABITS

The Great Horned Owl and eagle-owls of the world are predators of the deep temperate and tropical forests, with the capacity to adapt to more open country, especially semi-desert. They breed as far as the tree limits in the dry, cold regions of the north; in the heart of the hot, dry Sahara and the Arabian Desert, wherever there may be a pyramid, a pile of rocks, or a water hole with an occasional date palm; and in the primeval jungles of the Amazon Valley and equatorial Africa.

Most are diurnal as well as nocturnal hunters, and they are frequently mobbed by crows, jays, and smaller birds during daylight hours. Their effective enemies, however, number only man and occasionally another bird of prey. They usually win when attacked by large hawks in contests over nests. Great variety is shown in nesting sites—the eggs (usually one to three) are laid in old hawks' or eagles' nests, on the floor of rocky caves, in hollow trees, or even on the ground. The Milky Eagle-Owl (*B. lacteus*) of Africa and the Dusky Eagle-Owl (*B. coromandus*) of India occasionally put together platforms of sticks or line tree hollows with twigs. The females do most of the incubating in the Great Horned Owl and Eagle-Owl, from the first egg (34 to 36 days). Males provide food in the early stages of development. Young leave the nest at five weeks, but they do not fly until nine or ten weeks old. For details of courtship and family-raising, see Chapter 3.

Rodents and smaller mammals provide staple fare, wherever they are abundant; they are supplemented by a long list of bird species, snakes, frogs, fish, crawfish, and orthoptera. The larger bubos are undiscouraged by such formidable quarry as porcupines, foxes, minks, weasels and civets. The Dusky Eagle-Owl of India will attack anything but prefers crows, and during other birds' breeding seasons it is a notorious egg thief; and the Forest Eagle-Owl (*B. nipalensis*), which preys constantly on large birds and mammals, has also been observed eating carrion —the remains of tigers and goats. Only the Akun Eagle-Owl (*B. leucostictus*), a weak cousin of equatorial Africa with comparatively small beak and feet, feeds almost entirely on cockroaches and other insects, which it catches on the wing.

The common call of these owls is a deep-toned hooting "whoo-hu-hoo" and variations, accompanied by many softer notes, growls, hisses, and coughs.

The Malay Fish Owl *(Ketupa ketupu)* haunts jungle and brush, emerging in late afternoon to fish the rice fields of the Malay Peninsula and some of the Indonesian islands.—*Photographed at the National Zoological Park.*

GENUS *KETUPA*

The owls of the Asiatic genus *Ketupa* are monsters in the size range of *Bubo,* with long and pointed ear tufts, powerful and strong beaks, bright yellow eyes, and rudimentary facial discs. The wings, suited to heavy forest and lightly wooded country, are comparatively short and rounded. Feathering on the tarsi varies—the two tropical species, completely naked; the Himalayan, Indochinese, and Chinese mountain birds, feathered in back and three-quarters down the front; and the largest species, in northeastern Asia, completely feathered to the toes. The bottoms of the feet, in all species, are covered with sharp-edged scales, and the claws are large and well-curved, each with a sharp cutting edge beneath, the middle claw with a sharp keel on the inside also.

Malay Fish Owl (*Ketupa ketupu*)

DESCRIPTION
(SOUTHEASTERN ASIA)

KETUPA KETUPU

Above, including ear tufts, light amber-brown, streaked in dark brown with white or sandy spots on the back; wings and tail, dark brown, with sandy barring; face, light amber-brown; locket, white; underparts, light amber-brown, heavily streaked with dark brown.

Juvenile—paler, buff; streaked in gray-brown above and below.

Beak, black; cere, light yellow; eyes, yellow; tarsi and feet, horn color. Size, 15–17 inches.

KETUPA FLAVIPES

OTHER ASIATIC SPECIES The Tawny Fish Owl (*K. flavipes*), 19–20 inches, ranges across Asia from the Himalayas to Indochina, southeastern China, and Formosa; it resembles *K. ketupu,* but it is lighter—striped in gray-brown rather than dark brown. Blakiston's Fish Owl (*K. blakistoni*), 17–22 inches, of northeastern Asia, the largest of the fish owls, completely lacks amber-brown coloring. Amur Bay birds are white to pale orange-buff above, barred in cinnamon-brown and heavily streaked in sepia; underparts, buff, completely barred and streaked as above. Japanese individuals have a lighter over-all appearance, the breasts white instead of buff. The Brown Fish Owl (*K. zeylonensis*), 19–20 inches, variable from buff in desert areas of Palestine to yellow-brown in forested portions of Indochina, is heavily streaked above and noticeably barred and streaked below.

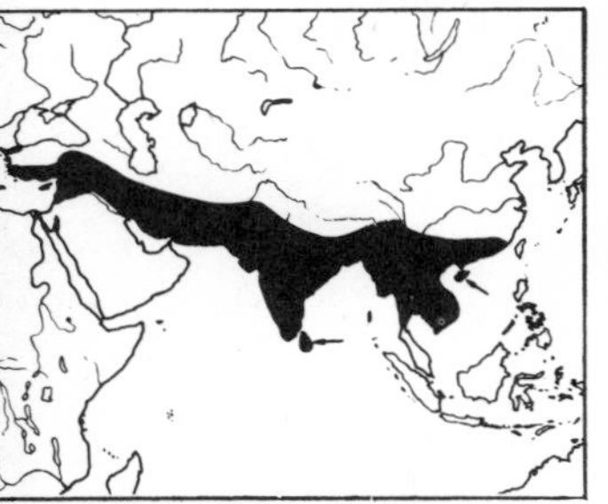
KETUPA ZEYLONENSIS

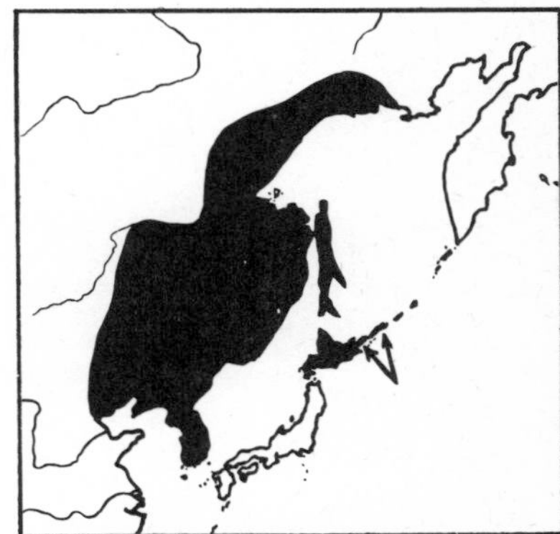
KETUPA BLAKISTONI

HABITS

These owls prefer to live in wooded country near water, as their food consists primarily of fish. They will also kill and eat small mammals, birds as large as pheasants, snakes, lizards, frogs, all kinds of insects, and occasionally settle for carrion. They are diurnal birds of prey, but seem sluggish, indulging in the common owl habit of sitting motionless on a tree branch until late afternoon. On their hunting forays they are often mobbed by small birds.

One to three (usually two) eggs are laid either on ledges of cliffs, holes in banks or trees, in hollows formed by the branching of two or more boughs, or in the abandoned nests of eagles and other birds.

The call of *K. zeylonensis* and *K. flavipes* has been described as a deep and guttural "who-hoo"; and of *K. ketupu,* as a soft, musical "to-wee to-wee," but all the owls of this genus are supposed to have another voice, much like the mewing of a cat.

Pel's Fishing Owl (*Scotopelia peli*), which stands two feet high and has a considerable wingspan, haunts both the larger rivers in forested country and tree-lined streams on the savannas from Senegal and Eritrea to South Africa.

GENUS *SCOTOPELIA*

Large round-headed owls without ear tufts comprise the African genus *Scotopelia* which, like the Asiatic genus *Ketupa,* have bare, roughly scaled tarsi and toes of impressive size, and strong claws. The feet are also spiny on the bottom, an adaptation common to the fish owls, the Osprey, and the Black-collared Hawk of tropical America. Eye color varies from dark brown or black for the two sienna-colored birds (*S. peli* and *S. bouvieri*) to yellow for the "bright rufous" rain-forest species (*S. ussheri*).

Pel's Fishing Owl (*Scotopelia peli*)

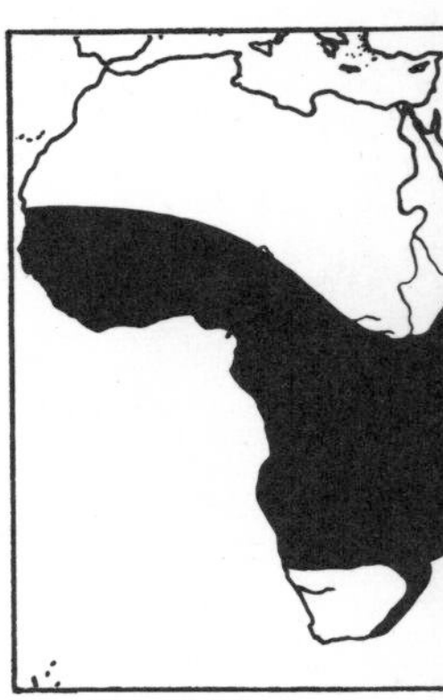

SCOTOPELIA PELI

DESCRIPTION (TROPICAL AFRICA)

Above, sienna, barred with dark brown; wings and tail, amber-brown, barred in dark brown; face, light amber-brown, circled indistinctly with a dark brown ruff; below, light cinnamon with fine streaks and blobs of dark brown, tinged medium orange.

Juvenile—paler, light cinnamon above and below.

Beak, black; eyes, dark brown; legs and feet, light pink with a tinge of yellow. Size, 20–24 inches.

OTHER SPECIES

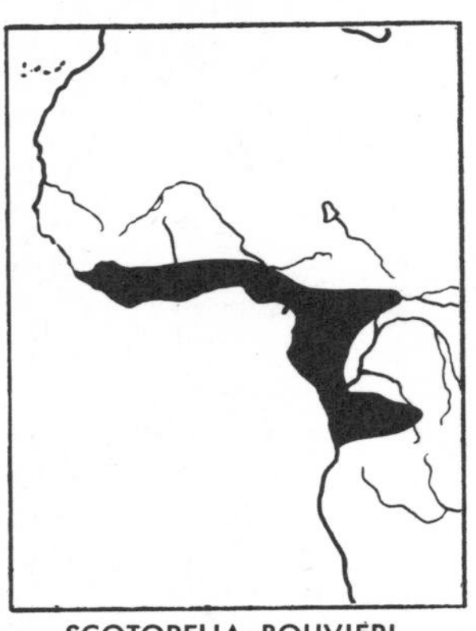

SCOTOPELIA BOUVIERI

The two species restricted to equatorial Africa are smaller than Pel's Fishing Owl, which is found not only in the rain forests but throughout most of wooded tropical Africa. The Rufous Fishing Owl (*S. ussheri*), 20 inches, may be distinguished by the "bright rufous color" (Bannerman) of the upperparts, which are neither barred, as in *S. peli,* nor finely mottled, as in the other strictly rain-forest species. The Vermiculated Fishing Owl (*S. bouvieri*), 14–16 inches, sienna-brown, with dark gray-brown mottling above, is the only one of the group that is *white,* heavily striped below.

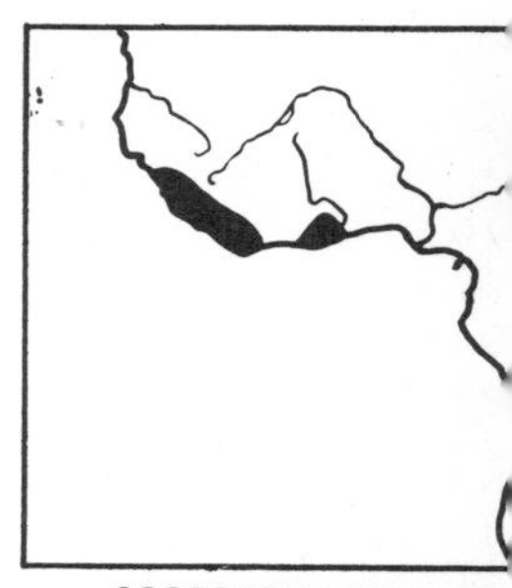

SCOTOPELIA USSHERI

HABITS

Scotopelia inhabits dense riverside trees and feeds on fish. Pel's Fishing Owl (*S. peli*) and perhaps the other two species, as well, are both diurnal and nocturnal. A pair in Kenya were observed to hunt a certain swamp at four o'clock every afternoon. Their appearance in flight is similar to the large eagle-owls'. There has been no record of foods other than fish for Pel's Fishing Owl, although it is as capable of taking a variety of prey, including small mammals, as are the large Asiatic fish owls of the genus *Ketupa.* The smaller African fishing owls, which have weaker feet, may be less voracious, as they are known to feed on small fish, prawns, and small birds.

The African fishing owls have never been seen building nests, but they use large stick nests, like the eagles', high in riverside trees, and apparently line them with small twigs and feathers to receive four eggs.

Their voices resound from the tropical forests as a deep and resonant "hmmmm" or "hu-hu-hu-hu," etc., or a long, protracted "hoot."

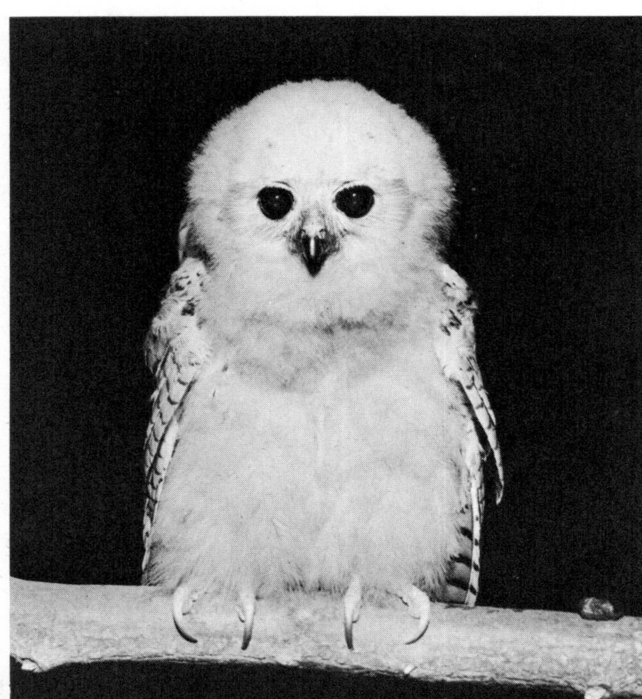

Juvenile Pel's Fishing Owl (*Scotopelia peli*).
—*New York Zoological Society Photograph.*

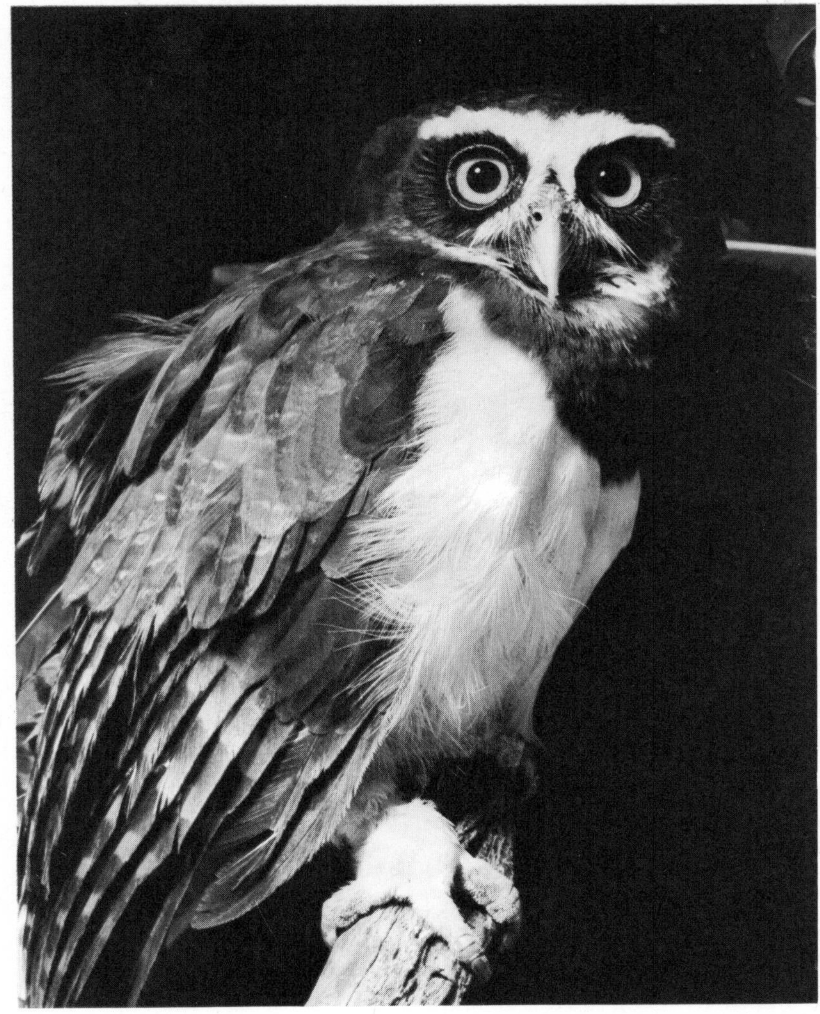

Although a chronicler of New Spain, Sahagun, first described the unusual appearance and call notes of the Spectacled Owl *(Pulsatrix perspicillata)* in 1530, the succeeding centuries have added little to our knowledge of its comings and goings, nesting, or the prey species it hunts in the nearly impenetrable depths of rain forests.

GENUS *PULSATRIX*

The hornless owls of the genus *Pulsatrix* are somewhat closely related to *Ciccaba* of tropical America, but they are larger and heavier, with stouter beaks and feet and more colorful plumage, all have dark faces outlined by light "spectacles." The legs and feet of the Spectacled Owl are heavily feathered almost to the talons, but the two remaining South American species, which are relatively rare, have naked toes.

Spectacled Owl (*Pulsatrix perspicillata*)

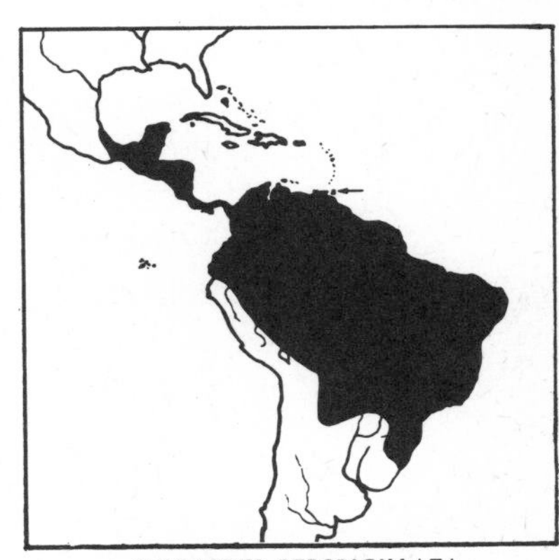

PULSATRIX PERSPICILLATA

DESCRIPTION (PERU)

Above, dark brown, becoming chocolate on back; wings, as well as tail, brown with pale cinnamon barring; facial disc, brown with distinctive white markings; a crescent-shaped patch of white covers the lower throat and foreneck; chest, chocolate, sometimes partly barred; rest of underparts, light yellow-ochre in males and a slightly deeper color in females.

Immature—like adult, but changes in a series of molts from mostly white on crown, hindneck, and sides of neck to a dark-headed bird with white lores and eyebrows, and sometimes a collar of pale cinnamon barring; underparts, darker than adult's.

Juvenile—completely white, tinged with pale orange-buff; face, dark, without white markings.

Beak, pale yellow-green; eyes, yellow-orange; claws, black. Size, 16–19 inches.

VARIATIONS The size range is approximately the same. Birds increase in size with distance from the equator or lower mean annual temperature. In certain areas where the humidity and precipitation are greater (for example, the tropical zone west of the Andes of Colombia and Ecuador), their colors are more intense.

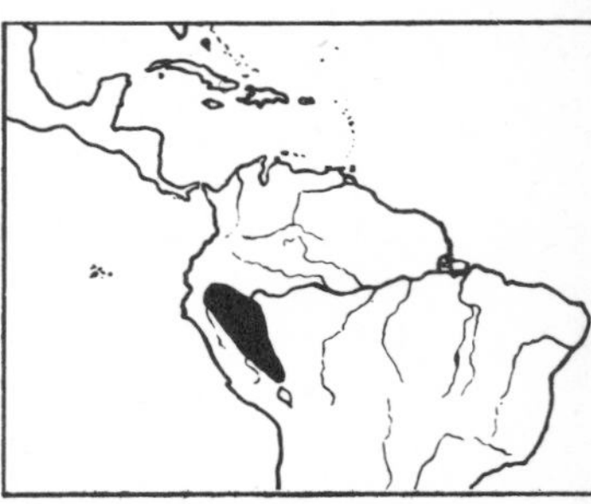

PULSATRIX MELANOTA

OTHER SPECIES At the southern limits of the range the White-chinned Owl (*P. koeniswaldiana*), about 17 inches, has pale yellow-orange eyebrows and belly; tail, barred thinly in white. However, in eastern Ecuador and eastern Peru, the Rusty-barred Owl (*P. melanota*), about 19 inches, has white eyebrows and white tail bars and is white below, completely barred in chocolate.

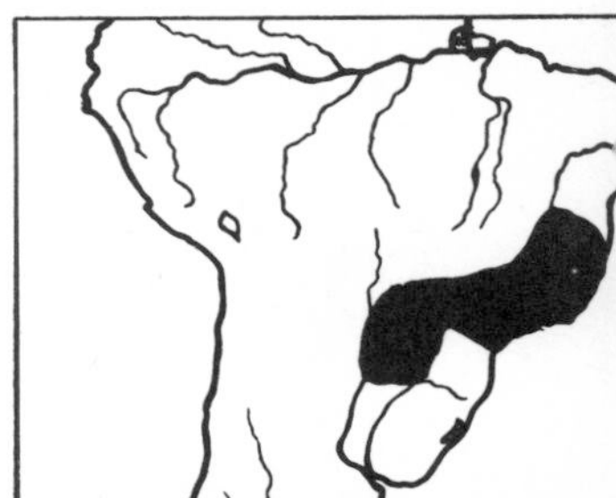

PULSATRIX KOENISWALDIANA

HABITS

Almost nothing is known of the habits of these owls, except that they are nocturnal and prefer to stay near water. Insects found in the gizzard of a Spectacled Owl and the fact that one of its vernacular names is "Crab Owl" are clues to its eating habits. Spectacled Owls may be seen in dry open woods, but characteristically they nest in the jungle, where trees 25 to 75 feet high look down on the intertwined epiphyte society, consisting of plants which rest on trunks, branches, and leaves of other plants: large arums, orchids (*Dichaea, Oncidium*), filmy fern, and strangling fig. In Brazil they are sometimes known as "Knocking Owls" because their call sounds like the continuous tapping of woodpeckers. To the early Spanish historian, Sahagun, the noise seemed more like tiles or plates being struck together. It is something like "titiriji."

Many striking plumage changes mark the growth of these owls from white nestlings with dark masks to dark birds with white or bright ochre eyebrows. The juveniles are called "White Owl," "Downy Owl," or "Masked Owl" locally, as though they were completely different birds. The Spectacled Owl in captivity at John Hamlet's "Birds of Prey" in Ocala, Florida, attained its adult plumage in five years.

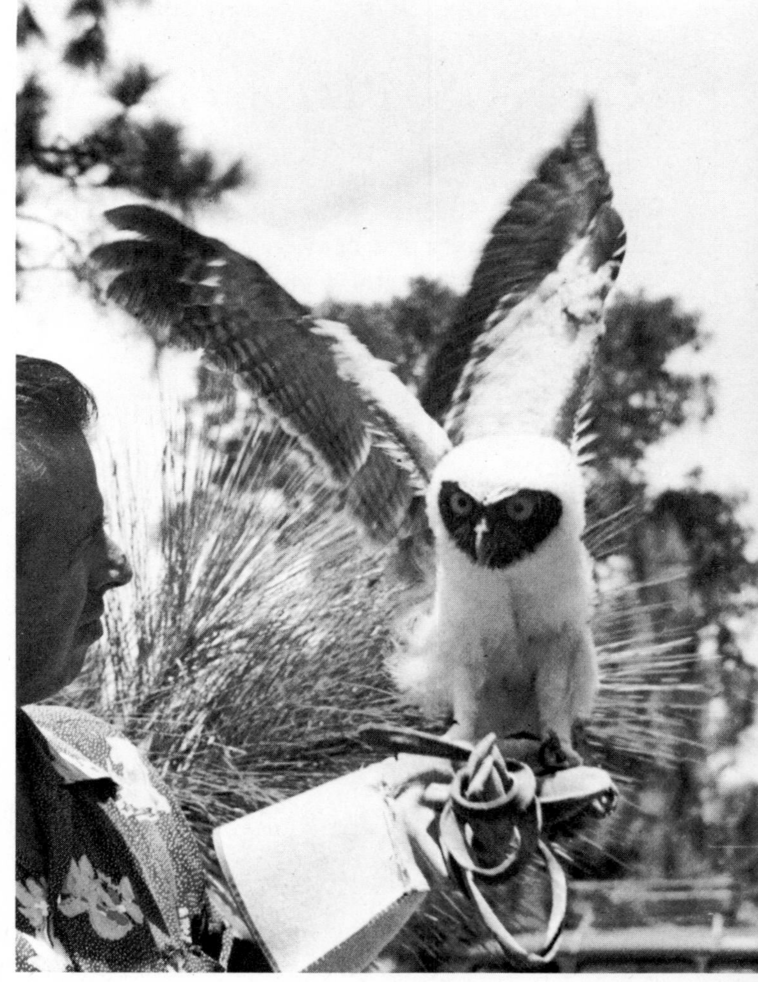

Juvenile Spectacled Owl *(Pulsatrix perspicillata)*, landing on the gloved fist of its owner, John Hamlet.

The voracious Arctic Snowy Owls *(Nyctea scandiaca),* of circumpolar distribution, are themselves killed and their nests robbed of eggs by the Eskimos, who call them "Ookpik-juak" and depend on them for a part of their food supply on the desolate tundra, where men and animals alike are hard-pressed for survival.—*Photographed at the National Zoological Park.*

GENUS *NYCTEA*

Classed among the most powerful in the world, the owls of the genus *Nyctea* have the Gyrfalcon's color pattern, but no other large white bird in the arctic is so heavily built, with great rounded head and broad wings. Feathers on the lores nearly conceal the beak; and yellow eyes, widely separated and narrow vertically, peer out from a slightly, rather than very distinctly, owlish flattened face. Tarsi and toes are heavily booted, some of the feathers covering the claws. There is some sexual dimorphism among the Snowy Owls. The darkest males and lightest females do not differ radically, but the whitest birds, sometimes almost pure white, are always males; the most heavily barred ones, females.

Snowy Owl (*Nyctea scandiaca*)

DESCRIPTION (CIRCUMPOLAR)

Above, almost pure white (males) or white with varying amounts of wide barring from sepia to gray-brown in color (females); flight feathers and tail, white, very lightly spotted to heavily barred; face, white; below, pure white (males) to heavily barred (females).

Immature—white, much more heavily barred everywhere than adults.

Juvenile—completely dark gray (somewhat paler on legs and feet).

Beak, black; eyes, yellow; claws, black. Size, 20–24 inches.

HABITS

Nyctea breeds north of the limits of trees on the tundras as far north as explorers have found land not covered with perpetual ice and snow. Because man has been the traditional enemy of these owls and their habitat is an open one, they have been known to take flight at the approach of an intruder between 100 and 200 yards away. Hillocks on the plains are apparently essential to their existence, for they serve both as roosting and nesting places.

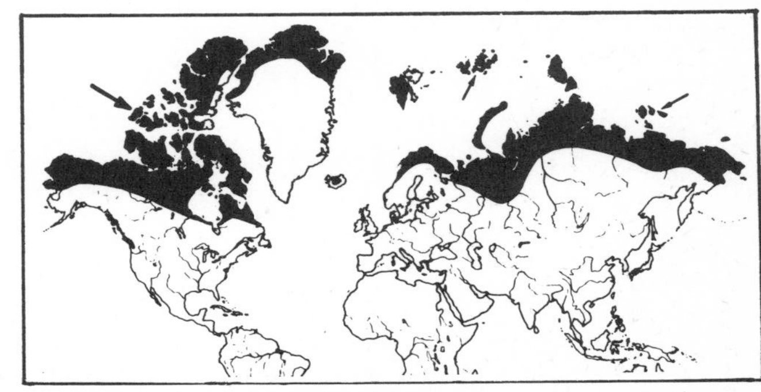

NYCTEA SCANDIACA

In Alaska nests are located on tidal flats or on slopes near small lakes or marshy tracts, also on salt marshes partly enclosed by mountains. The number of eggs varies greatly—ordinarily five to eight, sometimes as few as three or four, or as many as thirteen, depending on the cycles of prey abundance. In a brood of seven or eight only four or five may survive. The eggs and young of these ground-nesting owls are subjected not only to heavy rains but also to the foraging of arctic fox, jaegers, Skuas, and huskies, besides the regular spring egg-collecting by the Eskimos. The female alone incubates (between 32 and 34 days). Eggs are laid over an extended period of time and at irregular intervals, and incubation begins with the first egg, so that in large clutches there is a considerable size difference between the oldest and the youngest nestlings. The male provides the food, and the female feeds the young at first; later both sexes bring prey to the nest. Young are apparently fledged at 51 to 57 days. Adults may not breed following a year of low food supply (Greenland).

The Snowy Owl has a defensive posture much like the Great Horned Owl and Eagle-Owl. It has been seen to thrust the wings forward and flap them in front in defense against Skuas.

In addition to their staple diet of lemmings and various species of mice, Snowy Owls kill hares, rabbits, ground squirrels, rats, moles, and shrews; and depending on their location and the season, varying numbers of sea birds, shore birds, game birds, and small passerine birds. When really pressed for food they also fish, steal poultry, attack animals and birds in traps, and devour any bit of carrion or meat they can find about human habitations.

Spectacular "invasions" by large numbers of Snowy Owls occur considerably south of their limited winter ranges—sometimes every four or five years (or multiples thereof), coinciding with the periodic scarcity of lemmings and hares. In the Western Hemisphere they have drifted as far south as California, Texas, Georgia, and Bermuda; in Europe, to England, France, Austria, and the Balkans; and in Asia, to Turkistan, northwestern India, northern China, and Honshu, Japan.

The deep, angry voice of the Snowy Owl in the arctic solitude sounds almost like a raven's, but not as hoarse. The warning cry is a loud rattle or a very shrill human kind of whistle.

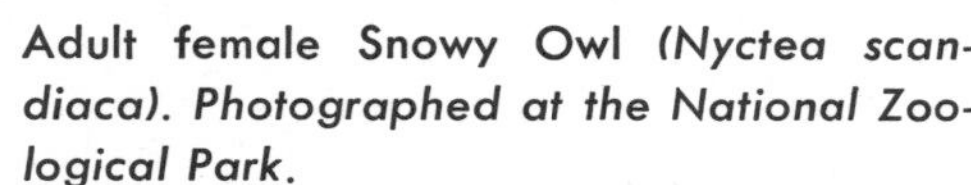

Adult female Snowy Owl ***(Nyctea scandiaca). Photographed at the National Zoological Park.***

Unlike the Snowy Owl *(Nyctea)* of the tundra, which is extremely shy, the Holarctic Hawk Owl *(Surnia ulula)*, whose range is bounded on the north by wooded tundra, and, generally, on the south by wooded plains or steppes, seems fearless of man's approach. Both species frequently hunt by day.—*New York Zoological Society Photograph.*

GENUS *SURNIA*

The Hawk Owl perches in an inclined hawklike position and, due to its short, pointed wings and long, rounded tail, could be mistaken for an accipiter in flight. The head of *Surnia* is rounded, without ear tufts, and the facial disc, incomplete, not extending above the relatively small yellow eyes. The strong beak has a very distinct terminal notch on the lower mandible. Tarsi and toes are densely covered with long, hairlike feathers.

Hawk Owl (*Surnia ulula*)

DESCRIPTION (CANADA)

Above, dark brown, fading to gray-brown and spotted and barred in white; wings, spotted; tail, barred in white; face, white, with a dark brown ruff, locket, and heavy bands at sides of chest, gray-brown. Below, white, barred in gray-brown down to the talons.

Juvenile—lighter, and indistinctly barred above and below.

Beak, yellow; eyes, yellow. Size, 14–16 inches.

VARIATIONS

The amount of white spotting increases in the Scandinavian countries and northern Siberia.

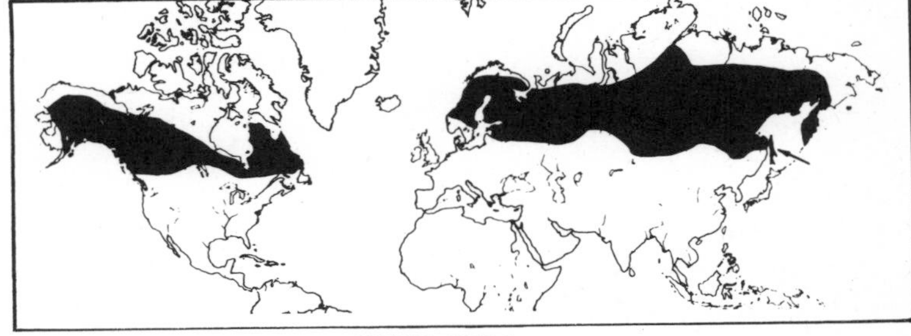

SURNIA ULULA

HABITS

These diurnal birds hunt in open woods, park lands, and plains or barrens which are covered with low bushes and occasional scattered trees. Like the Sharp-shinned Hawk, they skim noiselessly close to the ground in search of prey, frequently alighting on some low bush; but they have also been observed to rise high in the air and hover over the ground in the manner of the Old World Kestrel. Their staple diet consists of smaller mammals, such as mice, lemmings, and ground squirrels, as well as insects of various kinds. In winter, when the deep snows hide these creatures, Hawk Owls follow flocks of ptarmigan and willow-grouse and feed on them. Occasionally they drift as far south as the northern part of the United States; or in Europe, to northern France, Belgium, Holland, Switzerland, and the Balkans.

Their usual nesting sites are cavities in trees, but three to seven, and sometimes as many as nine, eggs are laid on the decayed tops of stumps, among the limbs of thick conifers, and in the deserted nests of raptors or crows.

They chatter and scream like hawks and indulge in a variety of "melodious" songs, at least one very similar to that of the Long-eared Owls.

The Ferruginous Pigmy Owl *(Glaucidium brasilianum)* is a tropical species which ranges north into the lower Rio Grande Valley in Texas and southern Arizona.

GENUS *GLAUCIDIUM*

New World pigmy owls stand pugnaciously, but insignificantly, 5¾ to 6½ inches tall; Old World species, 6 to 10 inches. Facial features to look for are the relatively small rounded head, bulbous cere and beak. The wings are short and rounded, and the tail is roughly two-thirds as long as the wings. Tarsi and feet are feathered (heavily in mountain regions), and the toes are covered with white bristles. Eurasian Pigmy Owls (*G. passerinum*), although nesting at no higher altitudes than their Rocky Mountain counterparts (*G. gnoma*) or Ferruginous Pigmy Owls (*G. brasilianum*) in the Andes, are heavily feathered to the talons. The feet are enormous in relation to body size, a good yardstick for estimating the ability of the pigmy owls to kill prey almost as large as themselves.

Ferruginous Pigmy Owl (*Glaucidium brasilianum*)

DESCRIPTION
(RIO GRANDE VALLEY, TEXAS)

In two color phases and a distinct intermediate plumage. Gray phase—olive-brown above, streaked from crown to mantle; collared in white, with two large black spots on either side of the neck; rest of upperparts, more or less spotted in white; tail, dark brown, marked with pairs of white dots; face, eyebrows, and locket, white; banded throat, olive-brown; underparts, white, streaked with olive-brown. (Intermediate, same as gray phase, except for dark orange tail barred with dark brown.) Red phase—rufous-brown above, streaked from crown to mantle and spotted on wing coverts in buff; below, white, streaked in rufous-brown; tail, dark orange, barred with dark brown.

Juvenile—similar to adult but less distinctly streaked (if at all) on head and neck.

Beak, yellow; eyes, yellow; talons, dark brown. Size, about 6½ inches.

GLAUCIDIUM BRASILIANUM

VARIATIONS

Two color phases may be found throughout tropical lowlands and at altitudes under 5,000 feet in the mountains of Mexico, Central and South America. A particularly bright red phase (sienna) and brown phase, either spotted or streaked on the crown, occur on both slopes of tropical Central America to the Canal Zone and along the eastern base of the Andes, from southeastern Colombia to Peru; also on the island of Trinidad.

Breasts of the red phase owls vary from white to pale yellow-orange, streaked with sienna; tails, plain sienna, faintly barred or distinctly barred, as in those of the Rio Grande Valley. Sizes approximate the Texas bird described.

OTHER NEW WORLD SPECIES

The Northern Pigmy Owl (*G. gnoma*), 5¾–6 inches, of western North America, is gray-brown or cinnamon-brown above, and white below, streaked in dark brown. It is spotted on the crown, unlike the streaked Ferruginous Pigmy Owl. Birds are larger in British Columbia and smaller in the mountains of Arizona and Mexico.

GLAUCIDIUM GNOMA

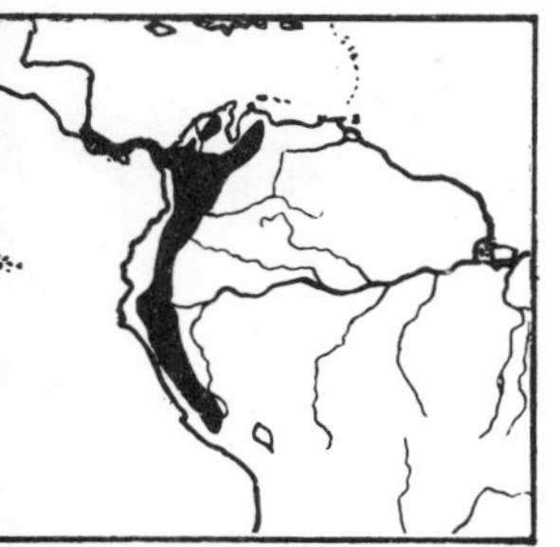

GLAUCIDIUM JARDINII

The Andean Pigmy Owl (*G. jardinii*) is smaller, about 5–5½ inches, in the mountains of Costa Rica and Panama, and larger, 6½ inches, at high altitudes (up to 9,000 feet) in Colombia, Ecuador, Peru, and Venezuela; it geographically replaces *G. gnoma*. It is richly colored in brown phase (chocolate), intermediate phase (dark amber-brown), and red phase (amber-brown). The brown phase may be conspicuously spotted white to light amber-brown above and on the sides of the body.

GLAUCIDIUM SIJU

The Cuban Pigmy Owl (*G. siju*), 6½ inches, is both brown phase (gray-brown) and red phase (cinnamon-brown); tawny collared; and appears spotted rather than streaked below in tawny; face, white, marked with tawny barring; tail, gray-brown, barred straight across, in tawny or white.

The Least Pigmy Owl (*G. minutissimum*), 4½–5 inches, of Mexico, Central America, and the Amazon Valley, is gray-brown from crown to mantle, streaked in white and collared in white dots; back, chocolate; underparts, white, streaked in medium yellow-brown.

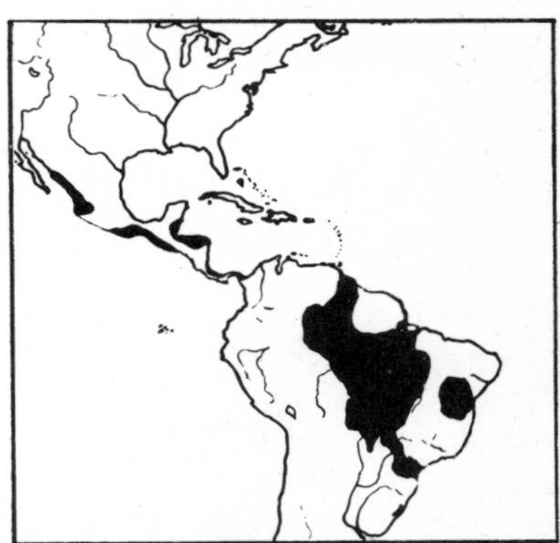

GLAUCIDIUM MINUTISSIMUM

OLD WORLD SPECIES

The Eurasian Pigmy Owl (*G. passerinum*), 6½ inches, is comparable in size to the largest of the New World birds; olive-brown, spotted on crown and back, and collared in white; face, white, distinctly barred in dark brown; breast, white, barred in olive-brown; belly, streaked in olive-brown; tail, olive-brown, barred straight across in white.

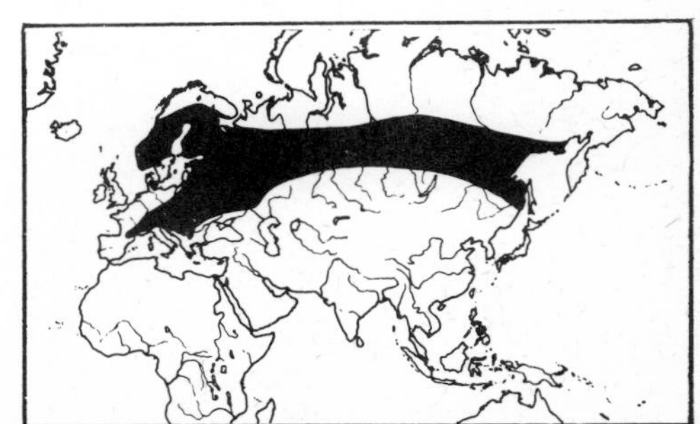

GLAUCIDIUM PASSERINUM

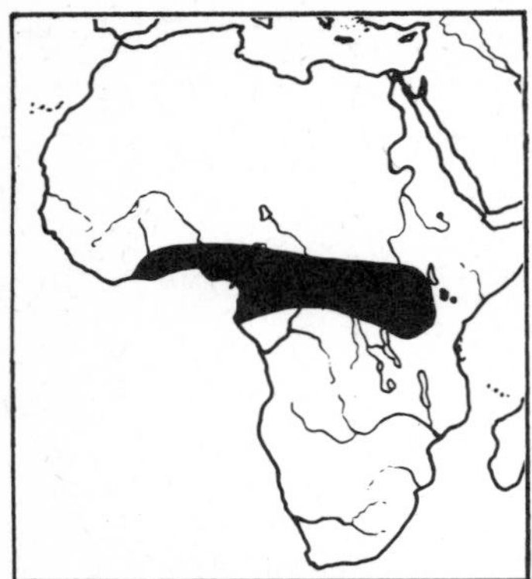

GLAUCIDIUM TEPHRONOTUM

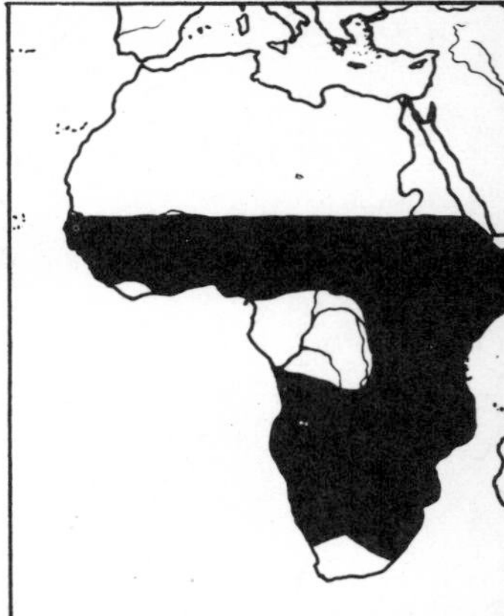

GLAUCIDIUM PERLATUM

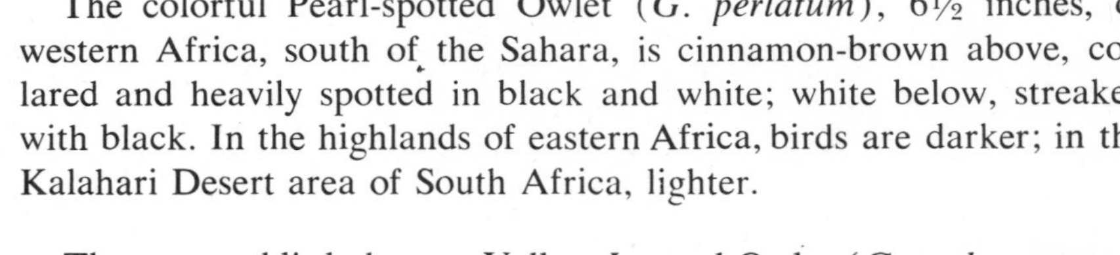

The colorful Pearl-spotted Owlet (*G. perlatum*), 6½ inches, of western Africa, south of the Sahara, is cinnamon-brown above, collared and heavily spotted in black and white; white below, streaked with black. In the highlands of eastern Africa, birds are darker; in the Kalahari Desert area of South Africa, lighter.

The rare and little-known Yellow-Legged Owlet (*G. tephronotum*), 6¾ inches, of equatorial Africa, is dark olive-brown above, with a white spotted collar; sides of chest and flanks, ferruginous; breast, white, with dark brown spots; face, dark. The tail has large white spots on inner webs of rectrices only.

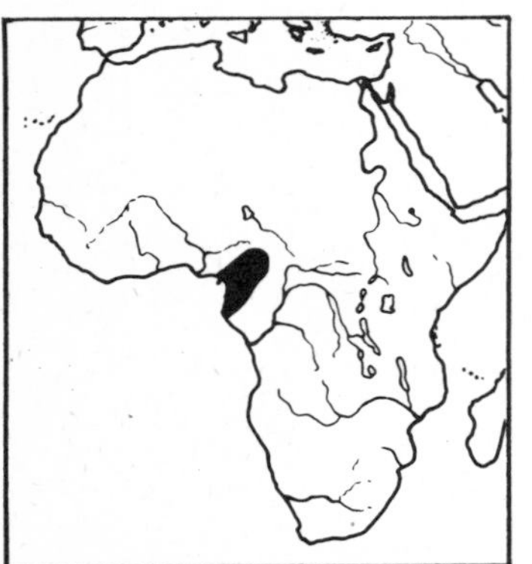

GLAUCIDIUM SJOSTEDTI

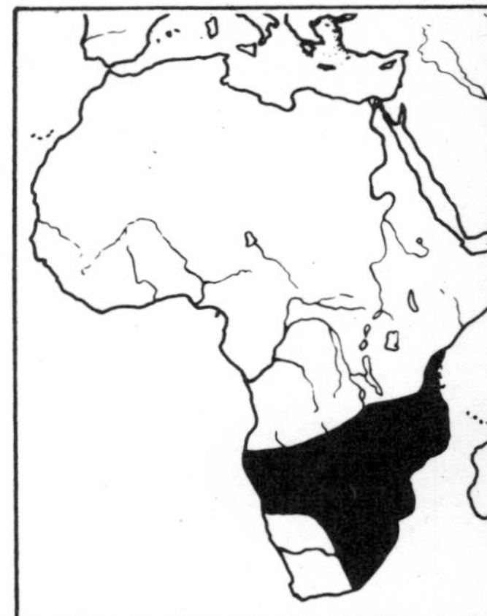

GLAUCIDIUM CAPENSE

The Barred Owlet (*G. capense*), 8 inches, is sepia above; crown and mantle, finely barred in white; back, wings, and tail, coarsely barred with pale yellow-orange; barring on face and sides of neck extends across upper breast; rest of underparts, appear white, V-spotted in brown; tarsi, barred. The largest of the African species, and most dramatically marked, is restricted to tropical rain forest, with a preference for rattan or vine palm. The Chestnut-backed Owlet (*G. sjöstedti*), 10 inches, is dark brown, finely barred in white on head, sides of neck, and upper breast; coarsely barred on flight feathers and tail; face, barred like *G. capense;* lower back, sienna; unlike *G. capense,* however, the underparts are yellow-orange, with dark amber-brown barring on sides of breast and belly.

The Collared Owlet (*G. brodiei*), 5¾–6½ inches, in brown or red phase from India to southeastern China, is either dark brown or dark tawny above; head, spotted in white or dark gray-brown, respectively; back, primaries, and tail, coarsely barred in pale yellow-orange or dark gray-brown; underparts, white, crossed by an almost complete vest of brown; streaked on the belly and barred on the sides and flanks, as above.

GLAUCIDIUM BRODIEI

GLAUCIDIUM RADIATUM

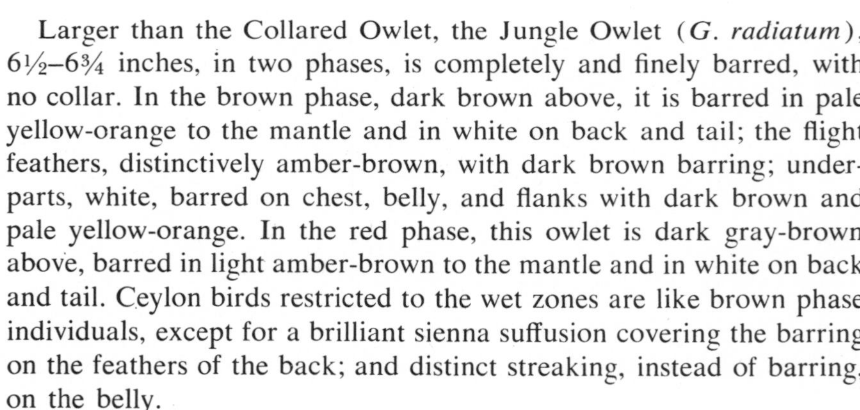

Larger than the Collared Owlet, the Jungle Owlet (*G. radiatum*), 6½–6¾ inches, in two phases, is completely and finely barred, with no collar. In the brown phase, dark brown above, it is barred in pale yellow-orange to the mantle and in white on back and tail; the flight feathers, distinctively amber-brown, with dark brown barring; underparts, white, barred on chest, belly, and flanks with dark brown and pale yellow-orange. In the red phase, this owlet is dark gray-brown above, barred in light amber-brown to the mantle and in white on back and tail. Ceylon birds restricted to the wet zones are like brown phase individuals, except for a brilliant sienna suffusion covering the barring on the feathers of the back; and distinct streaking, instead of barring, on the belly.

The Cuckoo Owlet (*G. cuculoides*), 8–10 inches, the largest of the Asiatic members of the genus *Glaucidium,* lives above 4,000 feet in the Himalayas but in the temperate forests of southern China and the jungles of Malaysia, it replaces the Jungle Owlet at lower altitudes. Like *G. radiatum,* it is barred above and below, with no collar, but it does not show a difference in coloring between crown and back or brightly hued wings. The dark olive-brown (Punjab) birds are barred in pale cinnamon. In the red phase (upper Assam), it is chocolate, barred with light amber-brown. The Cuckoo Owlet of

GLAUCIDIUM CUCULOIDES

Java and Bali is dark brown above, barred in pale yellow-orange, and streaked with sienna on the belly, and shows a sienna-brown suffusion on the back, as in *G. radiatum* from the wet zones of Ceylon.

HABITS

Diurnal as well as nocturnal hunters the world over, pigmy owls or owlets favor early morning and sundown, the hours when few people notice an owl the approximate size and coloring of a sparrow. Their tail-flicking habit is unique among small owls and their flight, rather than soundless and owl-like, resembles that of shrikes. All but the strikingly barred owlets of the Old World have collars which presumably give the protective illusion of a face on the back of the head. Juveniles are not generally as distinctly marked with spots, streaks, or stripes as are adults.

Look for pigmy owls at the fringe of the forest or the scrub desert, close to the open places where they hunt small mammals, lizards, and small snakes; also insects and small birds.

They are not nest-builders, laying three or four—or more—eggs directly in hollow trees and old woodpecker or barbet holes. The young of *G. gnoma* remain in the nest three to four weeks or longer. Although the male may occasionally bring food, the young are tended and fed by the female mostly during the nestling period. When almost fully fledged they are coaxed out onto a limb of the nest tree and are fed there. In a few days they begin to try short flights. Dependence on the adults does not last long, for the juveniles soon learn to catch insects—then larger prey.

Although not generally migratory at lower altitudes, pigmy owls that summer in the mountains drift down to foothills and plains in winter.

The many species of *Glaucidium* make their presence known by a variety of sounds. The Northern Pigmy Owl of western North America coos like a mourning dove, but each note is sharper and more distinct: "too-too-too-too-too-too-too-too—toot—toot—toot," with a long pause between each of the last three notes. As in many of these owls, there is also a ventriloquistic quality to the voice, so that the least turn of the bird's head apparently changes the location of the sound. The male's rendition is more high-pitched and staccato than the female's, which is soft and liquid. The call of the Ferruginous Pigmy Owl is a single, high-pitched, clear, and mellow note continuously repeated with an occasional ten-second pause. The Cuban Pigmy Owl calls loudly "ku-ku-ku-se-se-si-si-si," and other more owl-like notes. The Eurasian Pigmy Owl is known for its whistling notes, "keeoo," "kitchick," etc., or its song, a bull-finch-like "whee, whee, whee."

In Africa one can hear the Pearl-spotted Owlet's series of flutelike whistles, ascending and descending abruptly in scale; also a long drawn-out "pee-uh." Another African species, the Barred Owlet, has a low, penetrating "kroo-kroo," and another call recorded is a series of clear whistles accelerating and breaking into a number of soft "kroos." Its alarm call is a croaking purr.

The musical call of the Jungle Owlet is one of the most common night sounds in India. Starting softly and slowly, the notes are gradually accelerated and increase in volume until suddenly stopped: "turtuck, turtuck, turtuck, turtuck, turtuck, turtuck, turkatu, chatackatuckatuck." From the Himalayas eastward to southern China and Hainan, the Collared Owlet has a similar accelerated whistle that sounds miles away at first and becomes louder. It is a musical four-note call with a distinct interval between the first and second as well as the third and fourth notes, but none between the second and third.

Ferruginous Pigmy Owl *(Glaucidium brasilianum).—Photographed at the New York Zoological Park.*

The Elf Owl *(Micrathene whitneyi)* is very numerous in the saguaro cactus belt of southern Arizona, where it is also one of the most common bird species.—*Photograph by Roger Tory Peterson, from National Audubon Society.*

GENUS *MICRATHENE*

At hatching, an Elf Owl is said to be no larger than a man's thumbnail, and grows, at most, to no more than 5½ inches. One of the smallest owls in the world, it fails to measure up to the tiniest of the screech owls (*Otus flammeolus*) and the pigmy owls (*G. gnoma* and *G. brasilianum*) found within the range of *Micrathene*. Bright yellow eyes peer with a startled expression from the round elfin head, which, like the pigmy owl's, is without ear tufts. The beak is bulbous, but relatively small and weak, as are the feet. Wings are rounded, and the tail, shorter than in *Glaucidium,* is composed of only ten rectrices, instead of the usual twelve. The Elf Owl often takes a knock-kneed stance while perching and feeding, a quirk of behavior especially evident because the long, slender tarsi lack feathering, for the most part, but they are bristled, like the feet and toes.

Elf Owl (*Micrathene whitneyi*)

DESCRIPTION (SOUTHERN ARIZONA)

Above, olive-gray to gray-brown; collared in white and dark brown and spotted over-all in buff and white, mottled with dark brown; face, white to buff; short eyebrows and locket at throat, white, edged with dark brown; underparts, white, irregularly marked with buff or light tawny patches containing fine dark brown mottling.

Juvenile—similar to adult.

Beak, pale brown; eyes, lemon yellow. Size, about 5–5½ inches.

VARIATIONS

The Elf Owls of comparatively heavy rainfall savanna, from the lower Rio Grande Valley through central Mexico, generally lack buff or light tawny coloring. In the Cape region of Baja California gray phase individuals, with and without buff coloring, differ only slightly from those in Mexico and Arizona; more vivid, tawny birds are apparently restricted to Socorro Island.

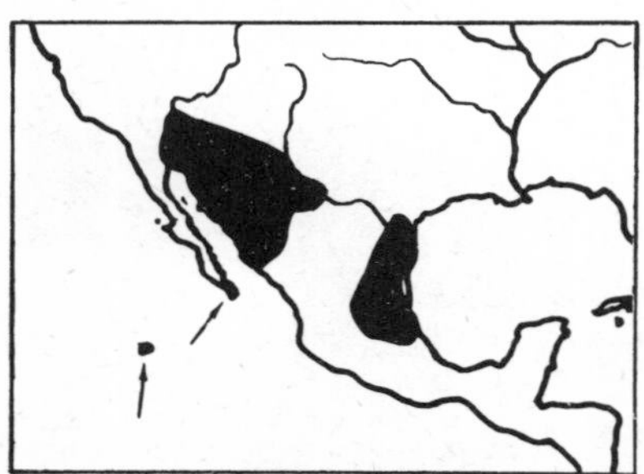

MICRATHENE WHITNEYI

HABITS

The tiny Elf Owls, their otherwise drab plumage painted with various tints of orange, seem peculiarly suited to the saguaro deserts of southwestern North America. In late May the towering candelabra of the giant cactus, or saguaro, in which they nest, are crowned with white blossoms; the paloverdes and prickly pears add bouquets of yellow; the ocotillos are tipped with vermilion; and rainbow cactus plants along desert trails become masses of dark crimson and magenta flowers, with white and yellow centers. Perhaps this is their best-known habitat—so much so that for many years no one looked for them elsewhere. Actually the Elf Owls populate, in undiminished numbers, every type of forest which occurs, in the dry river bottoms and tablelands, and on mountain slopes of the saguaro cactus belt, reaching their altitudinal limit within pine-oak woodland at 7,000 feet. On the dry, grassy plains which wander through the saguaro desert, or in the wetter savanna from the lower Rio Grande Valley through central Mexico, they inhabit scattered clumps of oaks, cottonwoods, or sycamores.

Any suitable cavity in a large cactus plant or tree —usually a hole abandoned by a woodpecker or flicker—serves to house a pair of these owls and two to five (commonly three) eggs. The nests in the saguaro cactus are fifteen, twenty, and sometimes thirty feet from the ground. So many bird species use these holes that they are occasionally forced to double up: woodpeckers with Elf Owls, screech owls with Elf Owls, and so forth. Consequently there is a great clamoring and mutual protest at nightfall when these nocturnal owls are emerging and the woodpeckers are retiring.

While the diurnal pigmy owls are on the wing, Elf Owls sit motionless in their holes or thickets and adopt a rigid defensive pose if startled—face partly shielded with one wing. In active hunting after sundown they move rapidly from one low observation perch to another, intermittently skimming the grass for arthropods or capturing large moths and other insects in mid-air.

The Elf Owls are fairly vocal; the most common elements of their song are a "churp" and a "tw-jur-r-r-r."

The New Guinea Hawk-owl *(Uroglaux dimorpha)* is indigenous to New Guinea and the island of Jobi (or Japen).

GENUS *UROGLAUX*

Indigenous only to New Guinea and the Island of Jobi (or Japen), this medium-sized hawk owl has the rudimentary facial disc, the swollen cere, and weak feet characteristic of the smaller Sooty-backed Hawk Owl (*Ninox theomacha*), but has a more rounded wing and an even longer tail. Heavy feathering covers the tarsi and toes almost to the talons. Bases of feathers of the crown are white, as is the face, and the pattern of coloration—barred on the upperparts and striped below—differs from any of the species of *Ninox*.

New Guinea Hawk Owl (*Uroglaux dimorpha*)

DESCRIPTION Dark brown above, streaked on the head and barred on the neck with white or vinaceous-buff; flight feathers and tail, also dark brown, with medium sienna barring; face, white, with a heavy concentration of black bristles around beak; underparts, white, striped in dark brown and suffused with vinaceous-buff.

Juvenile—paler; crown, mantle, and face, as well as underparts, pure white.

Beak, dark slate; eyes, bright golden yellow; feet, lemon chrome. Size, 10–12 inches.

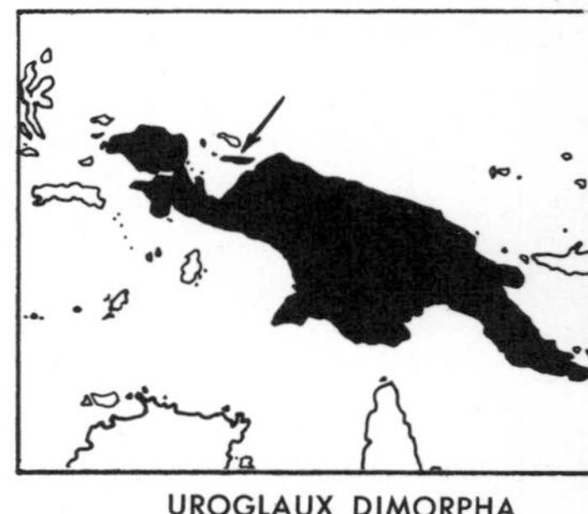

UROGLAUX DIMORPHA

HABITS

Like other hawk owls of the genus *Ninox* within its range, the New Guinea Hawk Owl probably hawks insects and may occasionally feed on mice, small birds, etc. Its habitat is lowland and hill forest.

The Barking Owl *(Ninox connivens)* (left), and the largest member of this genus, the Great Hawk-owl *(Ninox strenua)* of Australia (right).

GENUS *NINOX*

The owls of the genus *Ninox* are called hawk owls throughout Asia, from India to Japan and the Philippines, and in the Australian region and southwest Pacific islands. Color variants are common regionally, but two phases occur together only in the peculiarly isolated species restricted to western Madagascar. Despite great differences in size, all of the sixteen species resemble *surnia*, having only a rudimentary facial disc, long pointed wings and long tail, rounded at the tip. The cere is swollen, and the beak is distinctly notched. The larger species of *Ninox* also have shorter, stronger legs and toes. Tarsi are feathered to the feet and bristled on the toes, except in rain-forest species, which have mostly bristled tarsi and bare toes.

Barking Owl (*Ninox connivens*)

DESCRIPTION (NEW GUINEA)

Above, sepia, with white spotting on the flight feathers and lower back; tail, sepia, barred in white or pale buff; face, white, with black lines around the eyes and black bristles; below, white, streaked with dark amber-brown.

Juvenile—lighter, with almost complete white collar.

Beak, black; eyes, yellow; feet, yellow. Size, 12–15 inches.

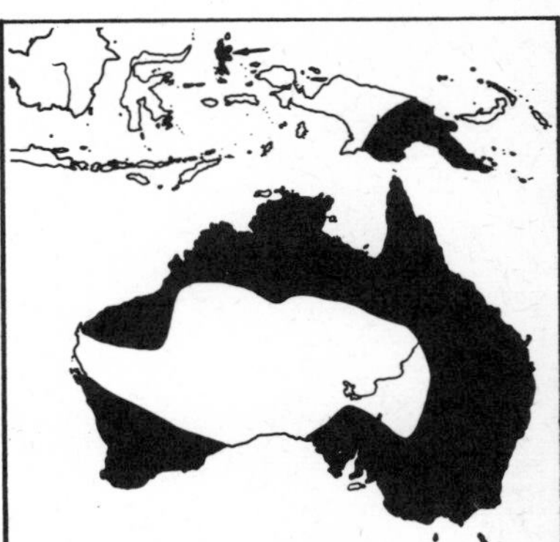
NINOX CONNIVENS

VARIATIONS

Moluccan birds are smaller; the underparts are barred with dark amber-brown (instead of streaked). Australian individuals are gray-brown above with some white spotting at the nape and lower back; underparts, white, streaked in cinnamon. Sizes range from 10 to 18 inches, the largest in Australia.

OTHER SPECIES IN THE AUSTRALIAN REGION AND SOUTHWEST PACIFIC

In the temperate forests of southern Australia, the Boobook Owl or Spotted Hawk Owl (*N. novaeseelandiae*), 10–14 inches, is brown above, streaked on crown and mantle in pale yellow-orange; spotted and streaked in chocolate on white underparts. Darker owls on North Island, New Zealand, have most of the white on breast replaced by yellow-orange. However, in the tropical and equatorial forests of New Guinea, northern Australia, and Melville Island a much lighter phase is found—gray-brown with a definite buff tinge above; the underparts, white, streaked in light cinnamon. Variations on this light phase appear on Babar Island in the Moluccas, and on Lord Howe Island off eastern Australia in the Tasman Sea. Babar Island birds are dark tawny, streaked in gray-brown above; underparts, light tawny, spotted in white and finely streaked with gray-brown. On Lord Howe Island they are cinnamon-brown above, and below, spotted in white.

NINOX NOVAESEELANDIAE

NINOX RUFA

A rarity in tropical northern Australia and New Guinea is a very large long-tailed species called the Rufous Hawk Owl (*N. rufa*), 17–18 inches, chocolate, completely and finely barred in buff, above; white below, coarsely barred with cinnamon-brown; face, also barred, is heavily bristled; eyes, outlined in dark brown. It may be some years before this plumage is reached, the younger birds appearing lighter—cinnamon-brown above; cinnamon below, not as broadly barred as adults.

The Great Hawk Owl (*N. strenua*), 20 inches, of southeastern Australia, is, with the exception of two eagles, the most impressive raptorial bird on that continent. This species is sepia above, barred in buff and white; underparts, white, barred or V-marked in sepia; the face, darkly bristled. Like the Rufous Hawk Owl, the Great Hawk Owl has an exceptionally long tail, but it is larger, with a proportionately heavier beak and enormous claws.

NINOX STRENUA

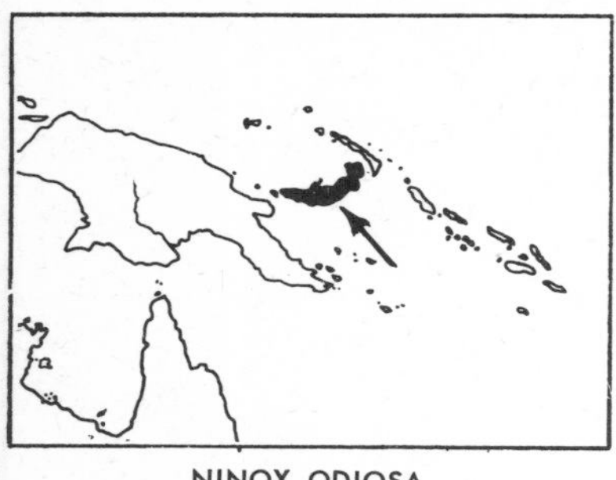
NINOX ODIOSA

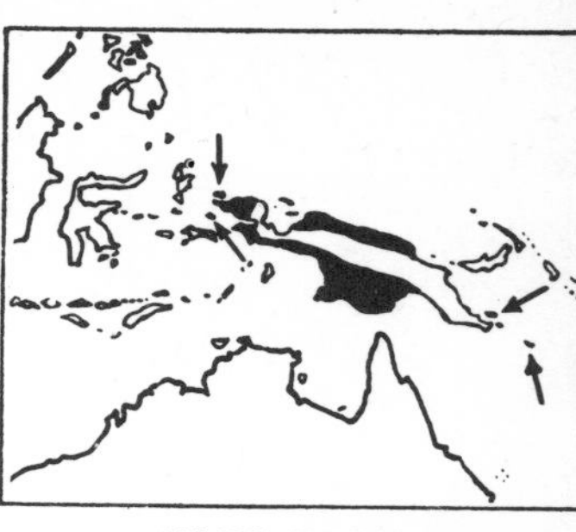
NINOX THEOMACHA

A small New Guinea species, the Sooty-backed Hawk Owl (*N. theomacha*), 8–10 inches, has a dark face, is solid brown above, with some white spotting on the wings, usually visible only in flight, and sienna-brown below. On the outlying islands the coloring appears similar above and either rufous-brown below, spotted in white (D'Entrecasteaux Archipelago), or white below, streaked with rufous-brown (Louisiade Archipelago). White spotting is prominent on a chestnut-backed species, the New Britain Hawk Owl (*N. odiosa*), 8½ inches, especially on the crown; face, light tawny, barred with chestnut; chin and short eyebrows, pure white; belly, white, barred and streaked with chestnut.

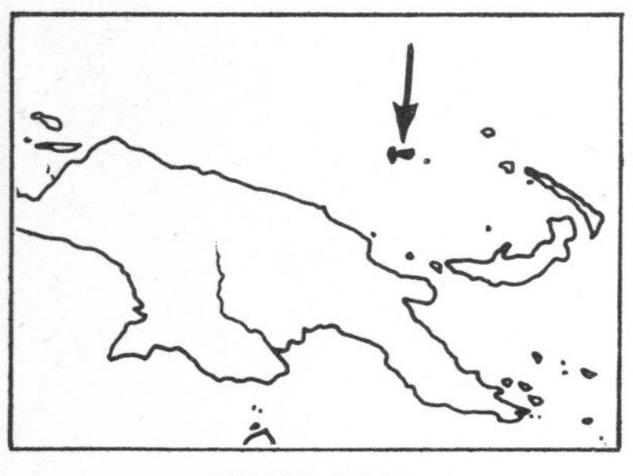
NINOX MEEKI

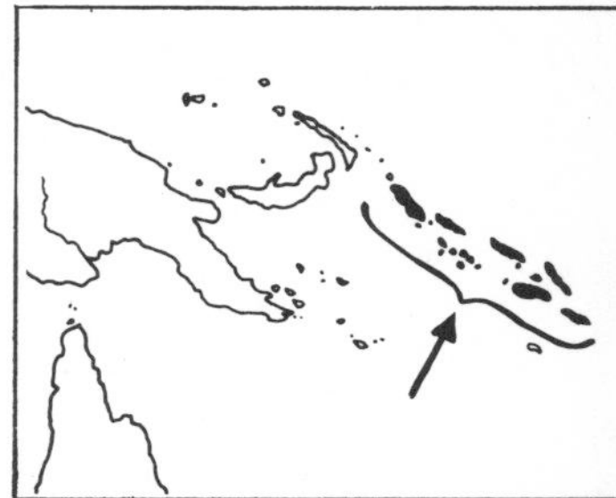
NINOX JACQUINOTI

The Admiralty Islands Hawk Owl (*N. meeki*) 8–10 inches, is medium yellow-brown above, with irregular white barring; underparts streaked. The Solomon Islands Hawk Owl (*N. jacquinoti*), 8–12 inches, and the New Ireland Hawk Owl (*N. solomonis*), 9–12 inches, are completely barred below. Some of the southwest Pacific birds are white-breasted (Guadalcanal), brown-breasted (Malaita), or tawny-breasted (San Cristobal) and completely barred; others are sandy, with a vest of dark barring (Choiseul). These are not difficult to recognize because each island is inhabited by only one hawk owl of this genus.

NINOX PUNCTULATA

NINOX SOLOMONIS

Two very small species, the Speckled Hawk Owl (*N. punctulata*), 8–10 inches, and the Ochre-bellied Hawk Owl (*N. perversa*), 8–10 inches, are confined to the Celebes. The former is dark brown, very finely spotted in white above, barred on the sides and flanks in yellow-brown. *N. perversa,* nearly solid chocolate above, may be distinguished in the field by a few large white spots on the wing coverts, and it has a dark vest and yellow-orange underparts, streaked in chocolate.

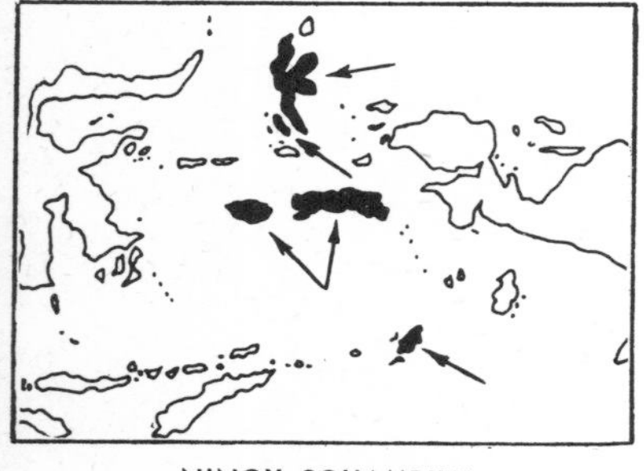
NINOX SQUAMPILIA

NINOX PERVERSA

In the nearby archipelagoes are many variants of the Moluccan Hawk Owl (*N. squampilia*), 10–14 inches. Individuals are brown above (northern Moluccas), or range from amber-brown above (Tenimber Island) to sienna-brown above (Ceram and Buru), with very little spotting. The underparts are white, coarsely to finely barred in dark amber-brown, except in the Buru bird, which alone is amber-brown below, barred in medium yellow-brown.

ASIATIC SPECIES

NINOX SCUTULATA

One species, the Oriental Hawk Owl, (*N. scutulata*), 8–10 inches, reaches northern Asia and these hawk owls also breed throughout southern Asia, where the coloring of their upperparts—nearly solid sepia—and their white underparts, with prominent sepia streaking or spotting, generally distinguish them from other owls of the genus *Ninox* where ranges overlap or migrating hawk owls join the resident birds in the Celebes and the Philippines. The populations of the Andaman and Nicobar islands are darker; brown above and chocolate on the breast with nearly distinguishable sandy barring. The smaller

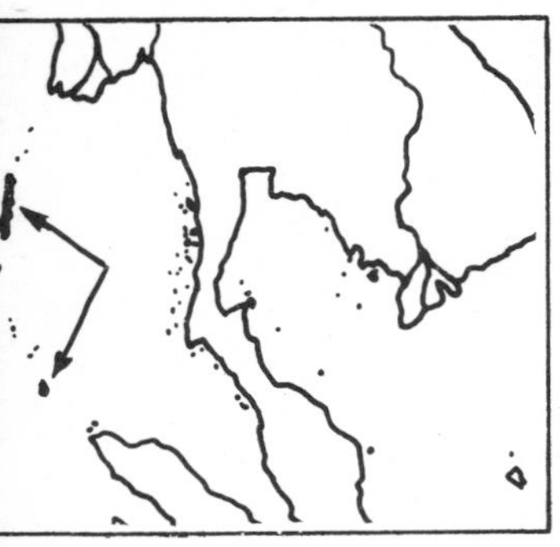
NINOX AFFINIS

Andaman Hawk Owl (*N. affinis*), 8½–9 inches also of these two islands, is gray-brown above and sienna below.

The small Philippine Hawk Owl (*N. philippensis*), 6–8 inches, falls into three geographical groups—birds which are (1) plain medium yellow-brown above; underparts white, streaked with medium yellow-brown (Luzon, Marinduque, Samar, Leyte, Tico, Masbate, Siquijor, Panay, Quimaras, and Negros); (2) varying only in buff spotting or barring from crown to mantle (Mindanao, Basilan, Sulu, Tawitawi, Bongao, and Siasi); and (3) spotted or barred from crown to mantle in buff; underparts, light amber-brown with fine gray-brown barring (Mindoro, Tablas, Sibuyan).

NINOX PHILIPPENSIS

MADAGASCAR SPECIES

One species, the Madagascar Hawk Owl (*N. superciliaris*), 9–11 inches, in two color phases, is known in western Madagascar: Gray phase—gray-brown above, conspicuously spotted on the wing coverts in white; underparts, white, heavily barred in gray-brown. Brown phase—chocolate, similarly marked above; underparts, pale yellow-orange, barred in chocolate. The eyebrows and face of the gray-phase birds are white, and of the brown-phase birds, light tawny.

NINOX SUPERCILIARIS

HABITS

The smaller owls of the genus *Ninox* frequent the forest or jungle edges and hunt in the clearings; they are nearly as plentiful near human habitations as in the wild. Both diurnal and nocturnal, they are often seen hawking insects in mid-air like nightjars, but occasionally feed on mice, small birds, bats, frogs, lizards, and snakes. On the coastal mud flats of Burma, the Oriental Hawk Owls (*N. scutulata*) have developed a taste for the small crimson stalk-eyed crabs that are common along the tide line. Small mammals and birds are favored by the Barking Owl (*N. connivens*) and the Rufous Hawk Owl (*N. rufa*). The Great Hawk Owl (*N. strenua*) is an eagle-owl in size and feeding habits, restricted to dense brush and woodland gullies. In Australia it preys on magpies, rabbits, rats, and ring-tailed possums.

Holes in trees are utilized for nests, the smaller species placing their eggs (three to four and rarely two or five) closer to the ground than the larger owls (averaging two eggs) which nest as high as eighty feet in the giant manna and gum trees of the deep forest.

Like the Great Horned Owl (*Bubo*) of the New World, the Great Hawk Owl is the undisputed king of the forest. It nests three months ahead of the Boobook Owl and two months before the Barking Owl—both more often found in open watercourse timber. Paradoxically, the Great Hawk Owl is said to be very shy and will not defend its nest, unlike the smaller, but very aggressive Barking Owl. Probably only the female incubates the eggs.

The common call of *Ninox* is a musical double hoot, "whoo-hoot" or "whoo-woop," which has been easily converted into the name "boobook" in the Australian region and southwest Pacific. There are, of course, more slight variations in the two-syllable sound than can be presently catalogued. The Boobook Owl (*N. novaeseelandiae*) calls "mopoke," which sounded like "boobook" to the aboriginal ear and became "cuckoo" to European emigrants, after one of their favorite birds in a distant homeland. This species not only replies to imitations of the call but will also respond exactly to "morepork," "cuckoo," "buckbuck," and "boobook."

The Oriental Hawk Owls resident in the north migrate in winter to Malaysia, the Celebes, and the Philippine Islands. The Barking Owl not only barks and growls like a dog but also occasionally—and disconcertingly—screams like a woman.

The Bare-legged Owl (*Gymoglaux lawrencii*) is a common species on Cuba and the Isle of Pines.

GENUS *GYMNOGLAUX*

The genus *Gymnoglaux* occupies an ecological niche on Cuba and the Island of Pines similar to that of *Otus nudipes* on Puerto Rico, Savana Island, St. Thomas, St. John, and St. Croix. The two bare-legged Caribbean species look somewhat alike, but the Cuban bird is smaller and has no ear tufts. Males average larger than females.

Bare-legged Owl (*Gymnoglaux lawrencii*)

DESCRIPTION (CUBA)

Sienna, streaked with brown from crown to nape; otherwise, brown above, with large white spots on the back and wings; tail, faintly barred; face, brown or sienna, marked with broad white lores and eyebrows; below, white or light yellow-ochre, barred and streaked with brown.

Juvenile—solid sienna above and on breast, shading to lighter on belly, which is regularly and broadly barred in sienna; face, sienna, with white eyebrows and lores.

Beak, yellow; eyes, brown; bare legs and toes, yellow; claws, horn color. Size, 8–9 inches.

GYMNOGLAUX LAWRENCII

HABITS

Common in limestone country, the Bare-legged Owl remains concealed in densely foliaged trees, thickets, or caves during the day and emerges at dusk to feed on insects or, rarely, small birds. Two eggs are laid in cavities in trees or caves. The wavering trill of this owl resembles the common cry of some screech owls, and its love call is the mellow, sonorous "coo-coo," also peculiar to the Puerto Rican Screech Owl (*Otus nudipes*) and Burrowing Owl (*Speotyto cunicularia*). All three species are known locally in the Caribbean as "Cuckoo Birds."

Since the mid-1800's, the New Zealand Laughing Owl *(Sceloglaux albifacies)* has become increasingly rare, probably due to the rapid increase in the numbers of European settlers and accompanying cats and rats. The owls disappeared at first from the vicinity of the growing towns and, by the turn of the century, were gone from many of the outlying districts.

GENUS *SCELOGLAUX*

The Laughing Owl inhabited open country on North Island, New Zealand, until about 1889; it disappeared from the vicinity of Canterbury and Otago on South Island about 1900, but may still be found in small numbers in the southern Alps. These birds have reduced facial discs and are not tufted. Feathering on the tarsi extends to the toes, which are bristled.

Laughing Owl (*Sceloglaux albifacies*)

SCELOGLAUX ALBIFACIES

DESCRIPTION (SOUTH ISLAND, NEW ZEALAND)

Pale yellow-orange to tawny above and below, broadly striped brown; wings and tail, barred; facial disc, white, finely striped brown; tarsal covering, pale yellow-orange; toes with light bristles.

Beak, black, with horn-colored tip; eyes, brownish-yellow. Size, 14–16 inches.

HABITS

These owls nest in open or brushy country, usually in crevices or small caves in limestone cliffs. They feed on rats, mice, lizards, and insects. Whatever the cause, or causes, of their near extinction, the ground-nesting habit has made them particularly vulnerable not only to weasels but also to introduced cats and rats. Their staple food, the Maori Rat, is supposed to have been killed off by the imported rats.

Three eggs are laid. Incubation, by the female (mostly), is said to last 25 days. At least part of the diet of the nestlings is worms. A second brood may be raised.

The Laughing Owl lives up to its name by uttering many and varied sounds; the common note is a loud "coo-e-e-e." In captivity it has been known to "chuckle like a turkey, mew like a cat, yelp like a puppy, and whistle tunelessly."

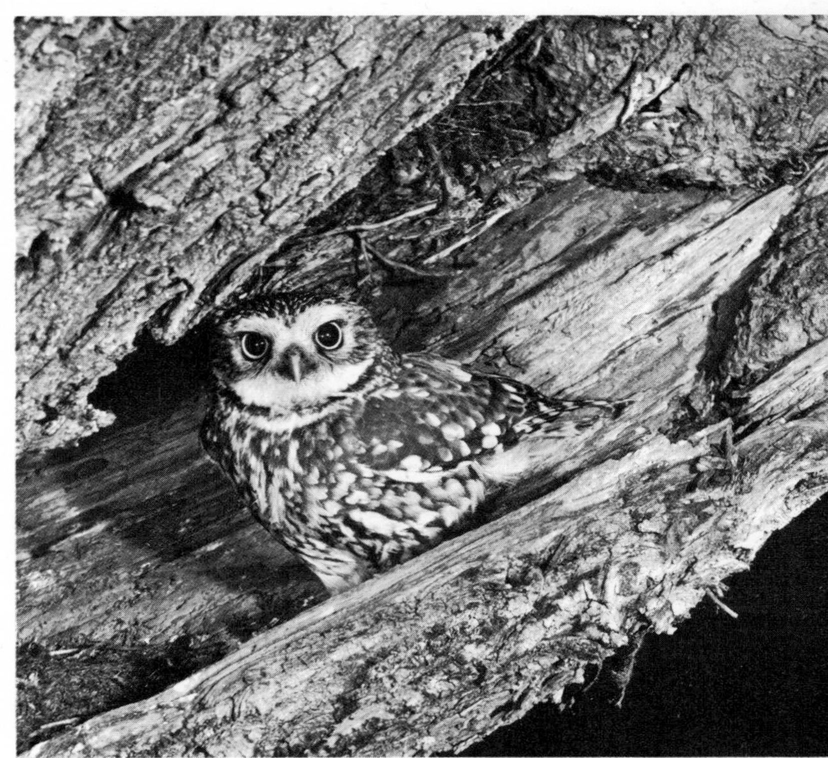

Little Owls *(Athene noctua)* have been introduced from continental Europe into England and New Zealand in this century.—*Photograph of New Zealand Little Owl by M. F. Soper from National Audubon Society.*

GENUS *ATHENE*

Old World *Athene* is a "frowning" owl with the facial disc depressed above a short, bulbous beak and large eyes. The body is compact and plump; the tail, short; and the wings, slightly rounded. The long tarsi are feathered; the feet, scantily feathered or bristled (the northern birds, only, are heavily feathered to the talons). This genus lacks the ear tufts of the various Scops Owls (*Otus*) found throughout its range in Europe, northern Africa, central and southern Asia, and New Zealand. Complete facial disc, slightly large size, and more slender form distinguish *Aegolius* from the Little Owl in Central Europe.

Little Owl (*Athene noctua*)

DESCRIPTION (ENGLAND AND WESTERN EUROPE)

Above, gray-brown, heavily streaked and spotted in white; mantle, crossed by a broad V-shaped collar; flight feathers, barred in white to buff; tail, barred buff; face, eyebrows, and chin, white; bands at sides of neck, dark brown; locket below, white; underparts, white to buff, heavily spotted and streaked with dark brown.

Juvenile—paler than adult.

Beak, yellow; eyes, yellow; claws, dark horn color. Size, 8½ inches.

VARIATIONS

In the temperate forests and grasslands of central Europe, the Balkans, southern Russia, the Atlas Mountains of northwestern Africa, and the mountain savanna country of Somaliland, these owls are lighter—tawny-olive to cinnamon, and a light cinnamon variant occurs throughout the deserts of Palestine and Iraq and the northern fringes of the Sahara. Pale and darker (probably ochre-brown) birds breed together in the Syrian and Arabian deserts, resulting in many intermediates; and on the dry steppes of central Asia, Mongolia, and northern China the ochre-brown variant prevails. Sizes range from 7 inches, in the mountains of Somaliland, and 7½ inches, in the desert regions of the Near East and northern Africa, to 8 inches, in Morocco and central Europe, and 9 inches, in central Asia.

ATHENE NOCTUA

OTHER SPECIES OF *ATHENE*

The relatively small Spotted Owlet (*A. brama*), 7½ inches, of southern Asia, from hot desert in Sind to rain forest in Assam, is spotted, instead of streaked, like the Little Owl, from crown to collar; underparts, barred on breast and V-spotted, rather than streaked, down the belly. Coloring varies from ochre-brown in the hot deserts of Baluchistan and rufous-brown in the savannas of the Punjab in northwestern India to gray-brown throughout tropical forested southern India and central Burma. The tropical Forest Spotted Owlet of central India (*A. blewitti*), 9 inches, is as large as the Mongolian race of *A. noctua;* gray-brown above, very indistinctly and finely spotted; underparts, white, barred heavily in dark brown.

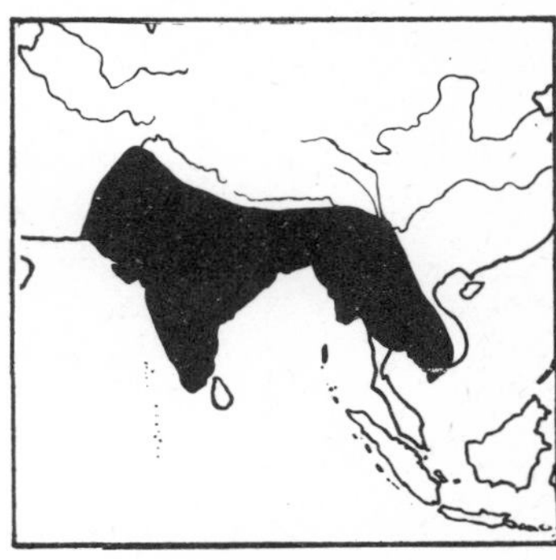

ATHENE BRAMA

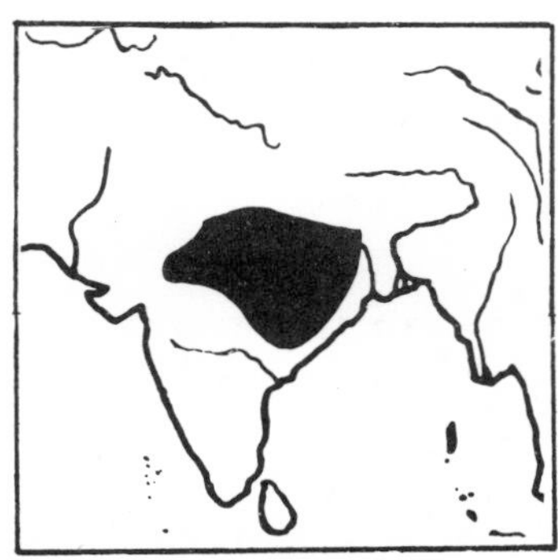

ATHENE BLEWITTI

HABITS

Aside from the comparatively rare deep-forest species (*A. blewitti*) in central India, the members of this genus prefer open—usually agricultural—country or small towns with buildings and scattered stands of trees which provide nesting places. They occasionally take over the deserted nests of other birds, but more commonly they lay three to five eggs on a loose bed of rubbish (or nothing) in burrows or holes in rocks, walls, and trees. In Europe the female does most of the incubating (28 or 29 days), leaving the nest briefly in the morning and evening. Nestlings are at first fed by the male; later by both sexes. The fledging period lasts about 26 days. Occasionally two broods may be raised in a season.

Little Owls (*A. noctua*) are diurnal fence-post sitters like the Burrowing Owls with the same bobbing habit, and in the deserts they may be seen perching on heaps of stones, walls, or in palm trees. Their flight, from one perch to another, is usually low and bounding like a woodpecker's, but while hunting at dusk it is swift and direct, more nearly resembling the pigmy owls'. On the whole, Little Owls are bolder and more voracious throughout their range than the almost entirely insectivorous Spotted Owlets (*A. brama*). In Europe, *A. noctua* takes insects and mammals in varying proportions, and to a lesser extent will eat bats, lizards, frogs, fish, snails, slugs, earthworms, and even some vegetable matter. During the nesting season they kill many small birds (mostly starlings, sparrows, blackbirds and other thrushes, in that order). In desert areas this species feeds mainly on insects, as well as on lizards, frogs, and small snakes—rarely on rodents or birds. However, in northern China, as in other dry temperate portions of their range, these owls may depend on sparrows and other small birds that stay through cold weather for their food in winter. The species is apparently not migratory.

The owls of the genus *Athene* are not only in evidence during the day, but they are extremely noisy then. The ordinary note of the Little Owl in Europe is a monotonous, rather plaintive "kiew, kiew," with variations. Hurried yelping and chattering cries, sometimes interspersed with a barking "wherrow," are heard chiefly at the nest or when the young are fledged, and faint "snoring" and heavy breathing sounds are distinctive. Short hysterical "laughter," trilling notes (when disturbed), and soft whistles are also recorded, as well as bill-snapping as in other owls. The Spotted Owlet of the Indian peninsula becomes vociferous long before the sun has set, uttering a hurried, breathless torrent of squeaks, chatter, and "gibberish": "kucha, kwachee, kwachee, kwachee, kwachee," etc.

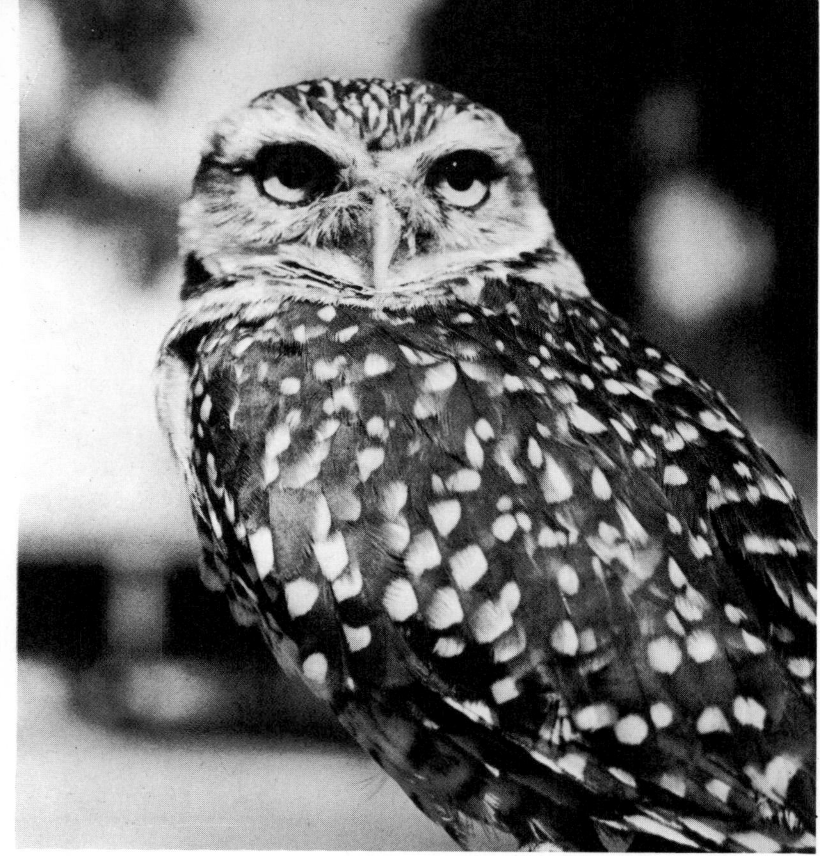

Like their relatives in the western part of the United States, Burrowing Owls *(Speotyto cunicularia)* of Florida nest in burrows abandoned by various mammals or by the gopher tortoises which abound in their favored habitat—the higher, drier grazing lands. If housing is scarce, they dig their own.

GENUS *SPEOTYTO*

The only small ground-dwelling owl on the prairies throughout the Western Hemisphere, *Speotyto* is hornless and round-headed with a short, bulbous beak and yellow eyes. The wings are large; the tail, short; and the long slender tarsi, clothed in short hairlike feathers, terminating in sparse bristles on the feet (or more heavily feathered in Haiti and along the western coast of South America, from Ecuador to Tierra del Fuego).

Burrowing Owl (*Speotyto cunicularia*)

DESCRIPTION (FLORIDA) Above, chocolate, streaked and conspicuously spotted in white; wings and tail, barred with white; face and eyebrows, white; throat, banded at the sides with chocolate; below, locket, white; breast, chocolate, spotted in white; rest of underparts, white to buff, barred with chocolate.

Juvenile—like adult, but not as heavily spotted above; sandy and only faintly barred below.

Beak, horn color; eyes, yellow; feet, gray. Size, about 8 inches.

VARIATIONS Other New World populations of *Speotyto* vary only slightly in coloring, from chocolate in southern South America and Haiti to sienna-brown in arid regions—on the plains of western North America, along the coast of northern South America, and in the interior of Brazil. In other light birds, found in the Guiana highlands, the Andes of northwestern South America, Margarita Island (off Venezuela), and tropical-forested areas of coastal Venezuela, as well as certain Pacific islands off the coast of Mexico and southern California, white markings are replaced in varying degrees by sienna-orange above and below. Sizes range from 7 to 8 inches (from sea level to 9,000 feet) in the highlands of northern South America; to 9–10 inches (from 1,400 to 13,000 feet) throughout the Andes.

SPEOTYTO CUNICULARIA

HABITS

On the dry, open prairie, a small owl sitting on a fence post, bobbing up and down, and then flying off a short distance to another perch, could be nothing else but a Burrowing Owl. Active during the day as well as in the early evening and at night, they hover in mid-air like kestrels, "hawk" insects, or catch them on the ground. Other prey consists mostly of mice, rats, ground squirrels, young prairie dogs, young cottontails, pocket gophers, chipmunks, and shrews. They also eat lizards, snakes, crayfish, frogs, toads, salamanders, fish, scorpions, and myriapods—and during the breeding season take a number of small birds.

Before 1900 there were large settlements of Burrowing Owls in the western part of the United States. Even now, where the terrain is suitable and the food abundant, they sometimes tend to gather in colonies—ten or a dozen pairs in two or three acres. However, they are more frequently found in isolated pairs. Piles of rubbish mark the entrances to their burrows, which have been taken over from prairie dogs, woodchucks, viscachas (South America), wolves, foxes, skunks, armadillos, and gopher tortoises. If no ready-made holes are available, they may dig their own. In any event these owls enlarge burrows for their use and line the nesting chamber with grass, weed stalks, feathers, and other materials. The eggs are more glossy than most owl eggs and the number laid varies from six to eleven (on the average, six to nine). Both parents assist in incubation, probably 28 or 29 days. When the young owls are large enough to leave the burrow, they usually roost on the top of the mound in front of the entrance and are guarded and fed by the adults, which have separate perches on fence posts or other lookout stations. Only one brood is raised in a season.

Like other ground-nesting owls, Burrowing Owls are especially vulnerable to predation. In North America skunks, opposums, and rattlesnakes destroy many of the eggs and young. But man, by destroying the prairie dog colonies and in his campaigns to poison ground squirrels, has taken a far greater toll.

Burrowing Owls of several islands in the West Indies (Marie Galante, Antigua, Nevis, and St. Kitts) disappeared at the end of the nineteenth century, shortly after the introduction of the mongoose.

In winter some individuals migrate from the region north of Oregon and Kansas southward. Florida Burrowing Owls also disappear for a time from their usual haunts when the breeding season is over.

The "cack-cack-cack-cack" alarm call is given as the owl flies away or into its hole, and the cooing notes heard only during the mating season have resulted in its being called "cuckoo bird" in various parts of the Caribbean and South American range. When disturbed in its home, the Burrowing Owl's best defense is a rattling kind of hiss in almost perfect imitation of its enemy, the rattlesnake.

The Black-and-White Owl *(Ciccaba nigrolineata)* (left) occurs with the more widespread Mottled Owl *(Ciccaba virgata)* (right) in very heavy rainfall sections of tropical America—southern Mexico, the Caribbean slope of Central America.

GENUS *CICCABA*

Ciccaba largely replaces temperate zone *Strix* in the tropical forests of America and Africa, south of the Sahara. Where the ranges of the two genera of "wood owls" overlap, as in Mexico and southern South America, the tropical owls occupy lower altitudes.

The face of *Ciccaba* is round, hornless, and marked with almost fully developed facial discs and conspicuous eyebrows. The color of the eyes varies from yellow, or yellow-brown, to dark brown. Wings and tail are long. Tarsi are feathered; the toes, naked throughout tropical America and partly feathered in Africa.

Mottled Owl (*Ciccaba virgata*)

DESCRIPTION (JALISCO, MEXICO)

Above, brown, with white spotting and fine light tawny mottling; wings and tail, barred white; face, brown, spotted and streaked in white; underparts, white, finely barred across breast; broadly streaked on belly in brown and tinted throughout with light tawny.

Juvenile—pale yellow-orange, with a white face.

Beak and feet, yellow; eyes, dark brown. Size, about 14 inches.

CICCABA VIRGATA

VARIATIONS

Two color variants prevail in the other tropical American populations of *C. virgata*—a white-breasted and a light tawny-breasted phase. The latter appears to be the dominant one from Central America southward. Birds in the southern part of Tamaulipas as well as southern Mexico, Central America, and northern South America are smaller and much more finely (and distinctly) barred above, with no white spotting except on the wing coverts. Those restricted to Venezuela, northern Colombia, and the extreme eastern end of the isthmus of Panama are brown with fine light tawny barring, and those in the Amazon Valley, also finely barred, are larger and "redder," brown with chrome-orange.

Size, from 11–14 inches.

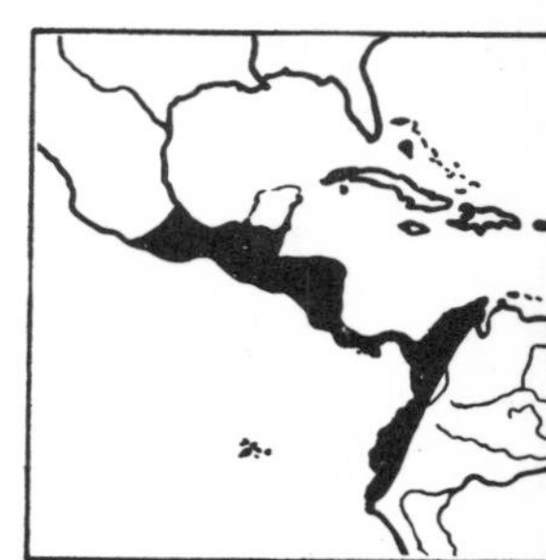

CICCABA NIGROLINEATA

OTHER NEW WORLD SPECIES

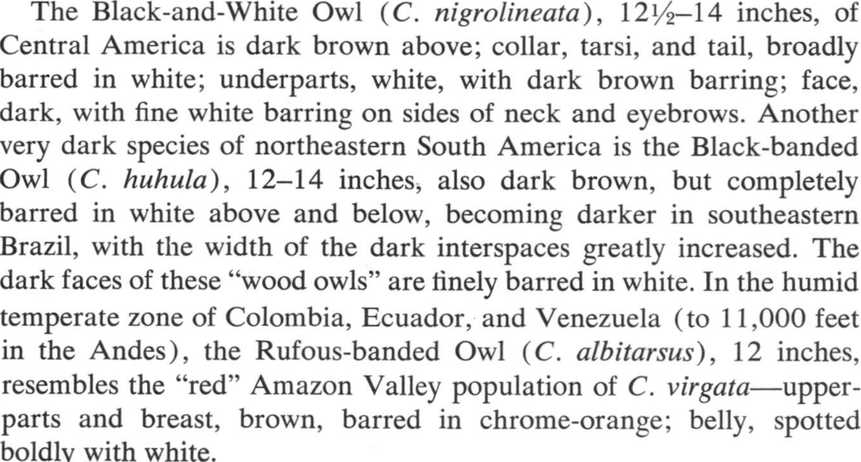

The Black-and-White Owl (*C. nigrolineata*), 12½–14 inches, of Central America is dark brown above; collar, tarsi, and tail, broadly barred in white; underparts, white, with dark brown barring; face, dark, with fine white barring on sides of neck and eyebrows. Another very dark species of northeastern South America is the Black-banded Owl (*C. huhula*), 12–14 inches, also dark brown, but completely barred in white above and below, becoming darker in southeastern Brazil, with the width of the dark interspaces greatly increased. The dark faces of these "wood owls" are finely barred in white. In the humid temperate zone of Colombia, Ecuador, and Venezuela (to 11,000 feet in the Andes), the Rufous-banded Owl (*C. albitarsus*), 12 inches, resembles the "red" Amazon Valley population of *C. virgata*—upperparts and breast, brown, barred in chrome-orange; belly, spotted boldly with white.

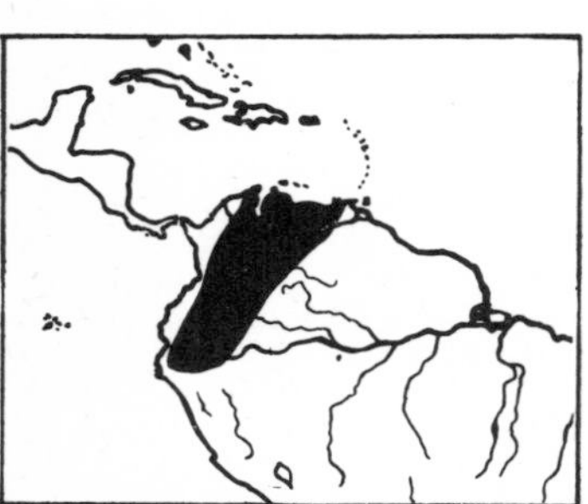

CICCABA ALBITARSUS

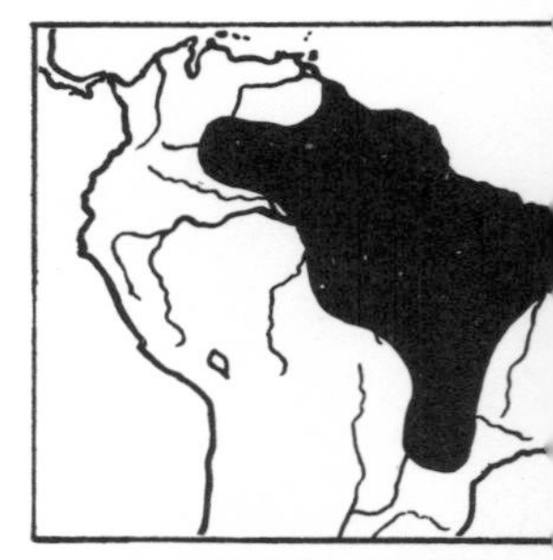

CICCABA HUHULA

OLD WORLD SPECIES

The tropical populations of the African Wood Owl (*C. woodfordii*), 12–14 inches, are chocolate above, spotted and finely mottled like the Jalisco, Mexico, bird described. Their faces are dark, marked with conspicuous white lores and eyebrows; underparts, broadly barred white and dark brown and tinted with yellow-brown or sandy coloring. African Wood Owls, confined to the highlands of Kenya and Tanganyika, have slightly more feathering on the toes than others, and those in the rain forest are "redder"—from sienna to sienna-brown.

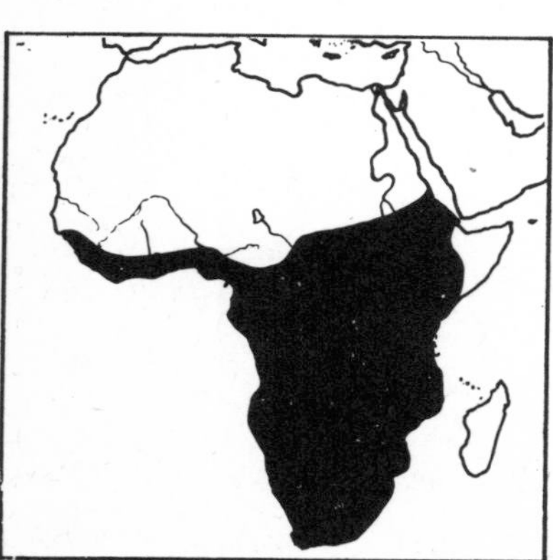

CICCABA WOODFORDII

(Juveniles in the Medji district of the Congo are tawny above, barred with white, and the reverse on the breast.)

The African Wood Owls are comparable in size to the New World species of this genus.

HABITS

The "wood owls" of the genus *Ciccaba* are largely nocturnal, subsisting on a diet of beetles, cockroaches, grasshoppers, rodents, reptiles, and small birds. By day they sit motionless on tree branches and are not easily disturbed. In Africa they stay in especially dense bush along the banks of streams or forest belts and outskirts. The African Wood Owl is probably the commonest owl of the upper Guinea forest region and southern Cameroon, where it comes close to the native villages, attracted by mice. The tropical American species are sometimes abundant in banana and coffee plantations.

One or two eggs are laid, ordinarily in the open hollow of a tree in deep forest, in Africa sometimes as high as 100 feet from the ground.

The call of the African Wood Owls has been described as either a single loud and rather high-pitched hoot or a lower "hu-hu, t'hu-u, t'hu." The two cries are dissimilar and believed to be female and male, respectively.

Like *Pulsatrix,* these owls go through an involved series of plumage changes which are not, however, well enough known to be described.

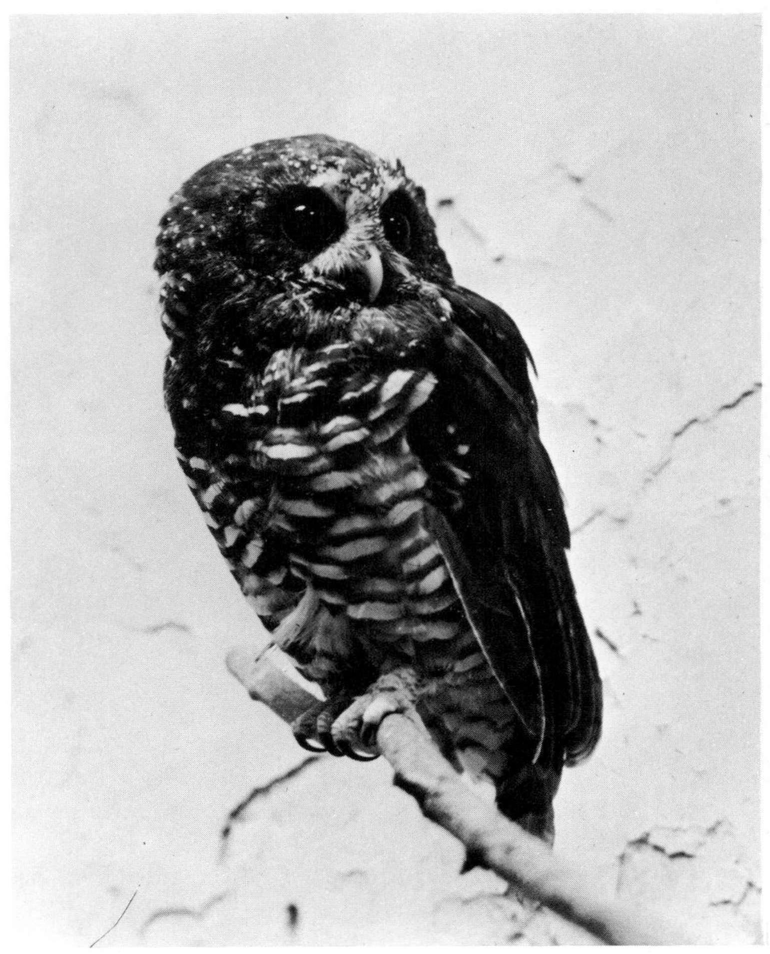

Wood Owl (Ciccaba woodfordii), western Africa.—Photographed at the New York Zoological Park.

SUBFAMILY STRIGINAE

Like most of its relatives, the Barred Owl *(Strix varia)* of the eastern United States is a "mild-mannered" raptor which ordinarily takes a very "complacent" view of mankind. It depends chiefly on mice and other small mammals for food, but can also subsist on insects, crayfish, and amphibians for long periods of time.

GENUS *STRIX*

The eleven species of *Strix* are hornless with disproportionately large, rounded heads, well-developed facial discs (usually bordered by a distinct dark ruff), and characteristically have "spectral" black eyes of great magnitude. The Great Gray Owl, however, has small yellow eyes. Beaks are strong and much compressed; the claws are long, curved, tapering, and very sharp. Wings are wide and rounded; tails, moderate to long, also rounded. Tarsi and feet are fully feathered. Only the Barred Owl (*S. varia*) in the South Atlantic and Gulf states and the Brown Wood Owl (*S. leptogrammica*) of southern India, Ceylon, and Malayasia have completely bare toes.

Something of an anomaly in *Strix*, the Great Gray Owl (*S. nebulosa*) has the largest and most perfectly circular facial disc to be found among all the owls. It exceeds *Bubo* and *Ketupa* in over-all dimensions —the wings, very large; the tail, extremely long; however, the deceptively loose, fluffy plumage conceals a body not much heavier than the Barred Owl's. The beak and claws seem small in relation to the apparent size of the bird and are nearly eclipsed by feather plumes.

Barred Owl (*Strix varia*)

DESCRIPTION (EASTERN NORTH AMERICA)

Crown to nape, dark brown, uniformly barred in pale yellow-orange and white; back, sienna-brown to cinnamon-brown, similarly barred; wing coverts, spotted; wings and tail, barred in white; facial disc, white or buff, barred in dark gray-brown and bordered in dark

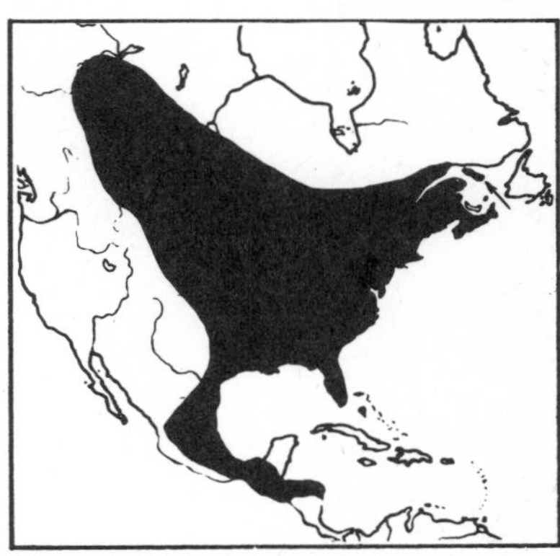
STRIX VARIA

brown; breast, white, barred in sienna-brown to cinnamon-brown; belly, streaked, with an over-all sandy tint.

Juvenile—sienna-brown to cinnamon-brown, barred above and below with pale yellow-orange and white.

Beak, dull yellow; eyes, black; toes, dull yellow-gray; claws, dark horn color, becoming black at tips. Size, 16–18 inches.

VARIATIONS

Throughout the mountains of central Mexico these owls are larger (18½ inches) and darker—barred in dark brown and white, only slightly tinted; while the smaller Guatemalan birds (about 14 inches), also darker, are heavily tinted with medium yellow-orange.

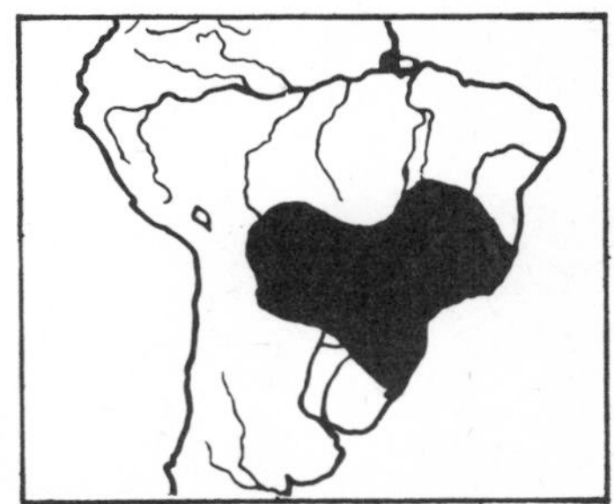
STRIX HYLOPHILA

OTHER NEW WORLD SPECIES

The Spotted Owl (*S. occidentalis*), 16–18 inches, of western North America, is comparable in size and coloring to *S. varia,* but it is spotted above in white and completely barred below.

STRIX OCCIDENTALIS

In South America, the Brazilian Owl (*S. hylophila*), 14 inches, is smaller and dark brown above, barred with medium yellow-orange; locket, white; underparts, barred in dark brown and white; the breast, heavily tinged in medium yellow-orange. The Rufous-legged Owl (*S. rufipes*), 13–15 inches, is sepia above, with thin white barring and patches of yellow-orange throughout; locket, white; underparts, evenly barred. In northern Chile the facial discs appear to be strongly barred in dark brown and white; in southern Chile, suffused with dark orange.

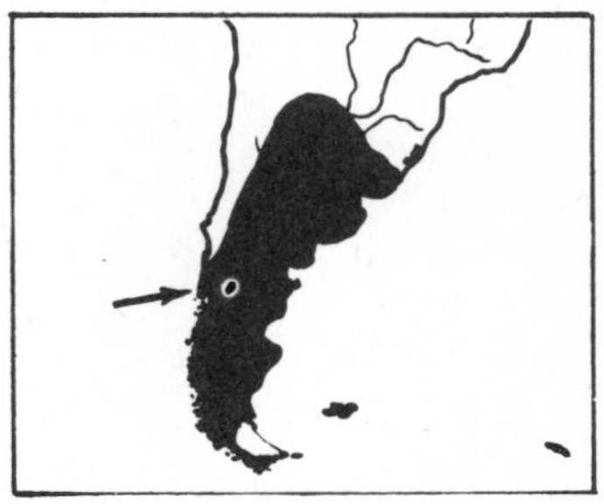
STRIX RUFIPES

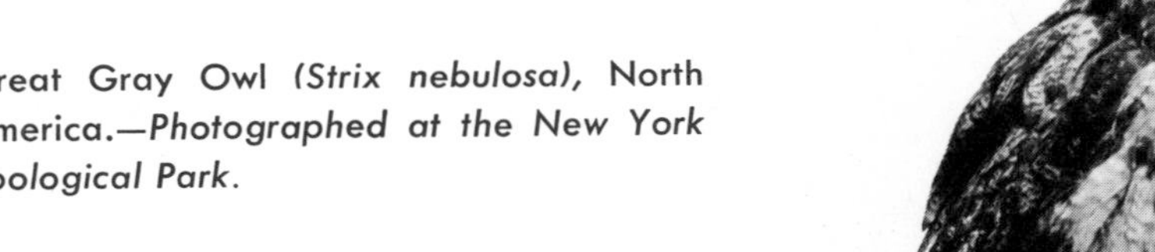
Great Gray Owl *(Strix nebulosa),* North America.—*Photographed at the New York Zoological Park.*

Great Gray Owl (*Strix nebulosa*)

DESCRIPTION (NORTHERN NORTH AMERICA)

Above, sepia, irregularly spotted from crown to nape and mottled on back in white, occasionally tinged with pale yellow-orange; wings and tail, as above, with mottled white barring; facial disc, barred in white and brown; below, white, broadly streaked on breast, becoming barred on belly in sepia.

Juvenile—olive-brown, barred darker, as well as spotted with white above; completely barred below.

Beak, light dull yellow; eyes, yellow. Size, 24–30 inches.

VARIATIONS

The Great Gray Owls of northern Europe and Asia are comparable to North American individuals in size, but they are lighter and finely (rather than coarsely and heavily) barred on the belly, with the appearance of being completely streaked below.

STRIX NEBULOSA

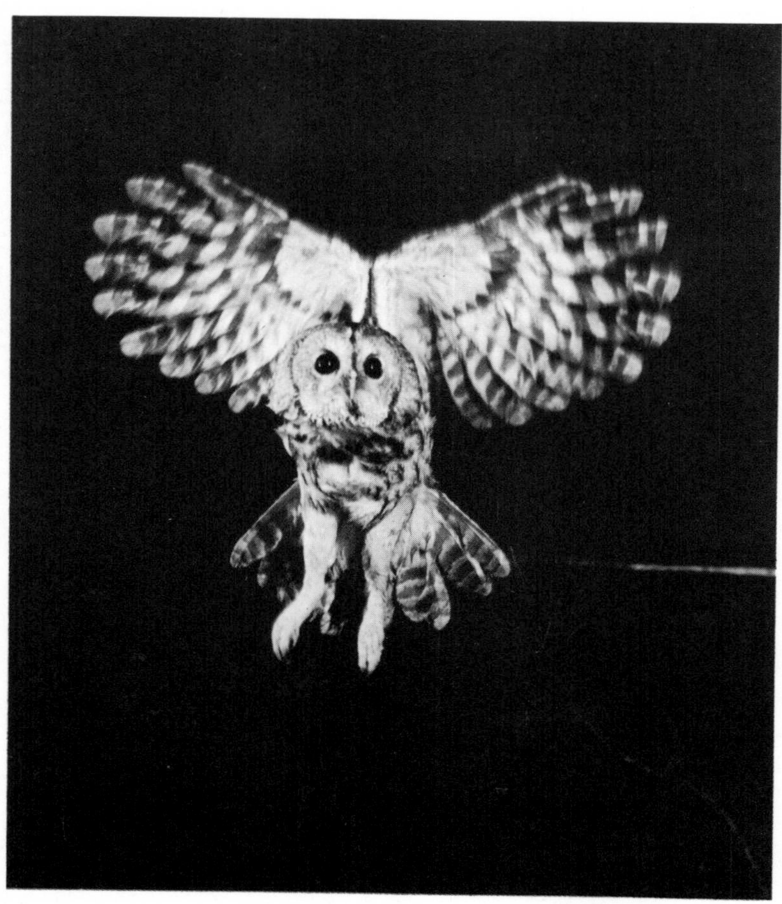

Tawny Owl (*Strix aluco*) leaves a tree branch with wings coming together over its head forming a peculiar pattern not often seen.

Tawny Owl (*Strix aluco*)

DESCRIPTION
(BLACK FOREST, GERMANY)

In two color variants: Common brown phase—crown to mantle, sepia, spotted in white; back, cinnamon-brown, mottled in dark brown and white and washed with tawny; scapulars, spotted with white; wings and tail, as above, with mottled white or dark brown barring; facial disc, white, barred in cinnamon-brown; lores, white; facial ruff, dark brown and dark tawny; below, white, streaked and barred in dark brown and suffused with yellow-brown. Tawny phase (less frequent) —above, dark tawny, streaked and mottled with dark brown; large white spots on wing coverts; wings, as above, barred in sepia; tail, ferruginous, with mottled dark brown barring; facial disc, white, suffused at sides with dark tawny; ruff, brown; underparts, white, streaked and barred in dark brown and washed throughout with sandy.

Juvenile—similar in coloring, but barred above and below.

Beak, pale yellow; eyes, black; claws, white at base and black at tips. Size, 14–15 inches.

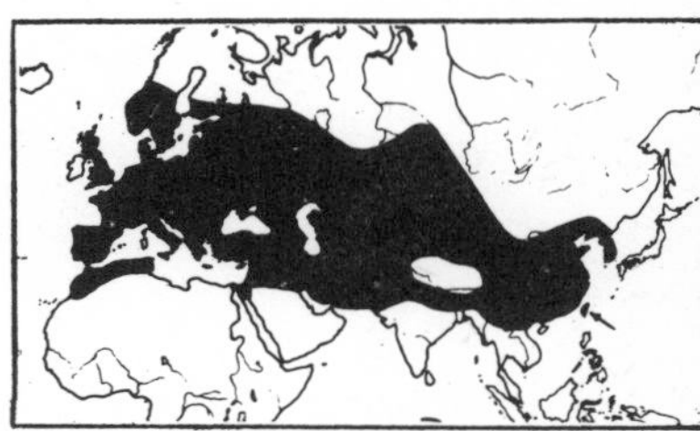
STRIX ALUCO

VARIATIONS

Reversing the trend on the Continent, *S. aluco* is more commonly of the tawny, than of the brown, phase in the British Isles. The large brown-phase owls of northern Siberia are more generously spotted and mottled with white, as are the smallest of the species, the ochre-brown steppe birds of Asia Minor. In northern Africa they are darker than the European brown phase (dark brown on the crown and nape); and in the Caucasus, apparently in three phases—brown, tawny, and a distinctive dark phase (cinnamon-brown, streaked and finely mottled with dark brown above and below, and the facial disc dark brown striped in white). Two color phases in the Himalayas, also darker (heavily mottled but without streaking on the back), are geographically separate: the larger birds in northwestern India, dark brown and white only; and smaller birds, usually dark brown and yellow-ochre, from Nepal through Assam, the hills of Burma, and in southeastern China. Sizes vary from 13½ inches to 16 inches.

OTHER OLD WORLD SPECIES

Throughout its range, the large Ural Owl (*S. uralensis*), 17–20 inches, is white, streaked in dark amber-brown to dark brown, and has a very long tail. The east European population also has a dark phase similar to the Caucasus form of *S. aluco;* a brown phase with white underparts darkly streaked has been described from western Szechwan; and another dark variant, found in Japan, is strongly marked above with yellow-orange and white spotting, the underparts white—streaked and barred like the European Tawny Owl.

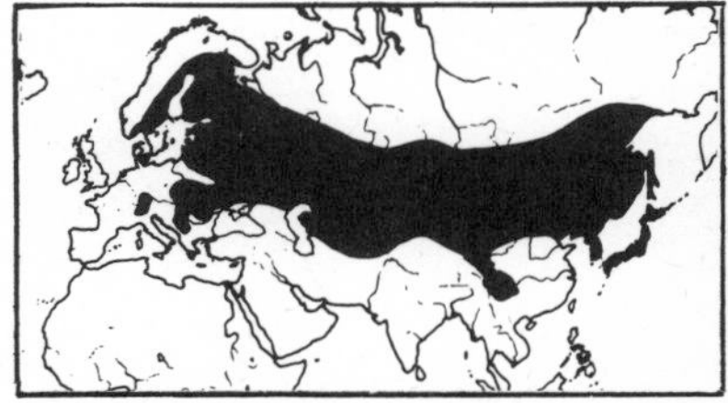
STRIX URALENSIS

In arid southwestern Asia the small Hume's Tawny Owl (*S. butleri*), 12 inches, shows lighter coloring than *S. aluco* of the same region—light rufous-brown and orange-buff, streaked with brown above; chin and locket at throat, white; feathers of underparts, also white, with fine brown streaking and orange-buff tips; wings and tail, very distinctly barred, rather than mottled in brown.

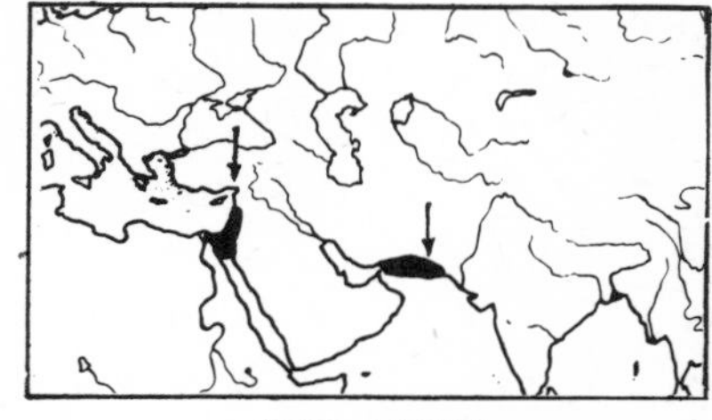
STRIX BUTLERI

Patches of dark orange and white spotting on the head and mantle, as well as on the upper breast, are peculiar to the Mottled Wood Owl (*S. ocellata*), 15 inches, of the mango groves in central India. Its back, wings, and tail are mottled brown and white; facial disc, strongly barred; locket, white; underparts, barred.

The Brown Wood Owl (*S. leptogrammica*), 18–21 inches, is almost solidly dark above—chestnut, in the western Himalayas (commonly between 2,500 and 8,000 feet), Burma, and southern China, with white barring at sides of neck and on wing coverts; face, barred; black mask and white eyebrows; underparts, finely and closely barred in white and chestnut. Smaller Indonesian birds, 13–17 inches, vary from brown (southern Borneo) to sienna (Nias) on the crown and nape,

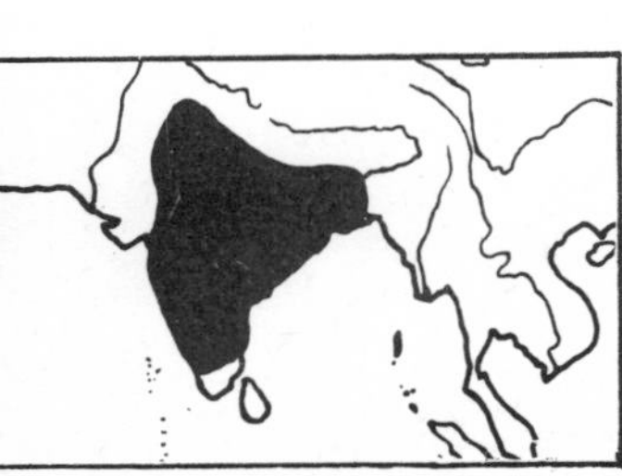
STRIX OCELLATA

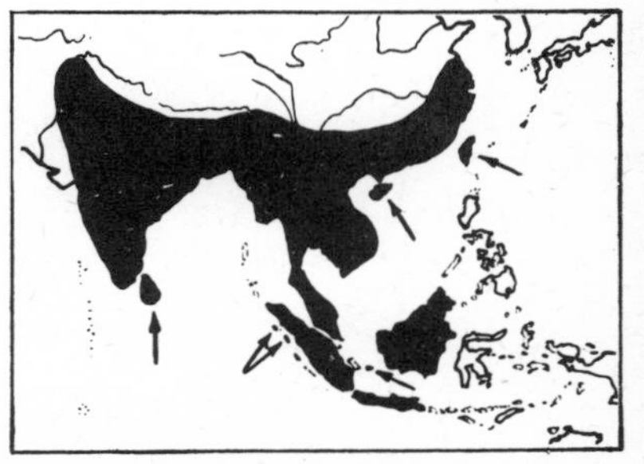
STRIX LEPTOGRAMMICA

collared in dark orange; back, wings, and tail, barred in white and brown, and heavily suffused with sienna (southern Borneo) or sienna-brown (Nias); faces and chests, dark orange; underparts, otherwise finely and closely barred in light tawny and dark brown. (Juveniles of this species show more barring and have almost completely white heads.)

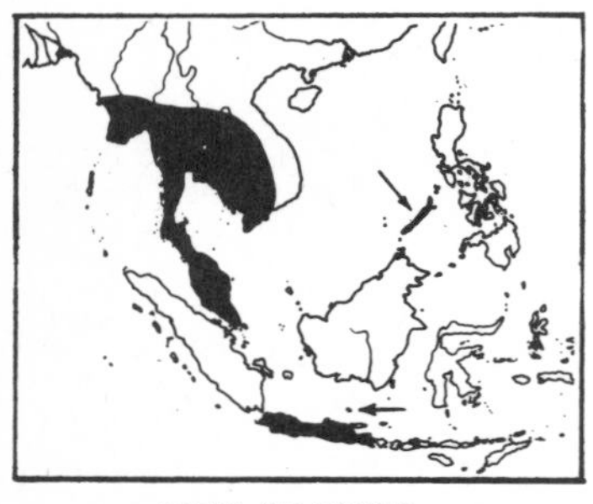
STRIX SELOPUTO

The Spotted Wood Owl (*S. seloputo*), 15 inches, of Malaysia, may be distinguished from the Brown Wood Owl by its dark gray-brown coloring, with white spots on the forehead, crown, and mantle and very sparse broken white barring on the back. Distinct white patches on the wing coverts are barred in gray-brown. There is a white locket at the throat; the underparts vary from white to tawny, with brown barring widely spaced. The face is tawny.

HABITS

The owls of the genus *Strix* are nearly all nocturnal hunters of woods edges and open glades in deep coniferous and temperate mixed forests, their flight buoyant and noiseless with a rather slow wing beat effective for gliding among tree branches. The Barred Owl (*S. varia*) ventures into open farm country and villages and, during the breeding season, is often seen flying about in daylight, especially in cloudy weather. The Tawny Owl (*S. aluco*) occasionally hunts by day in the subdued light of the woods, especially when feeding young, but is rarely noticed in the open. Prey species—chiefly small mammals—are captured on the ground and these owls often drive birds from their roosting places by beating the bushes with their wings. The more voracious Brown Wood Owls (*S. leptogrammica*) prey not only on the smaller mammals and birds but also on pheasants, jungle fowl, larger squirrels, and small monitor lizards. Bats, fish, amphibians, mollusks, worms, arthropods, insects and their larvae supplement their staple diet, depending on the locality. In the southern United States, where the favored habitat of the Barred Owl (*S. varia*) is the mixed hammock or swampy woods, crayfish, frogs, and various kinds of fish are primary foods, and the semidiurnal Brown Wood Owls of Ceylon (a southern variant of *S. leptogrammica*) are also partial to fish. The strictly nocturnal Spotted Wood Owls in Malaysia (*S. seloputo*) feed heavily on large beetles. The Great Gray Owls (*S. nebulosa*), which hunt in the perpetual daylight of the arctic summer, are the only truly diurnal members of the genus *Strix* and become more nocturnal at the southern limits of their range. All the species have nocturnal feeding stations, sometimes the same roosts used during the day.

Eggs are commonly laid in tree hollows and old nests of large hawks, 20 feet from the ground and higher. In Florida the Barred Owl may nest in the broken tops of cypress trees; the Tawny Owl occasionally forsakes woodlands for buildings or rabbit burrows; and the desert birds, as well as the mountain birds that live in rocky forests broken by ravines, also lay their eggs in caves, under large rocks, or between boulders. No nesting material is used on the ground, but existing nests may be scooped out and casually relined with sprays of pine needles or other materials. Only the Great Gray Owls build nests—and these are constructed of

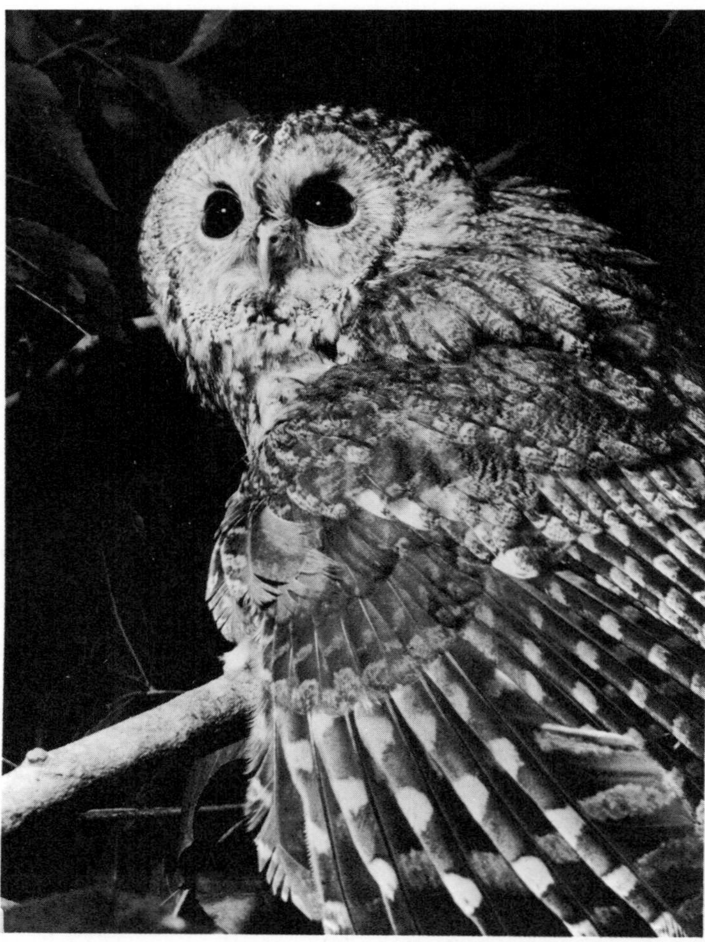
Tawny Owl (*Strix aluco*), Germany.

sticks, lined with feathers, deer hair, pine needles, and bark, high in an evergreen, or aspen of the northern forests.

A clutch of two or three eggs is common for the Barred Owl and Spotted Owl in North America, as well as for the Tawny Owl (*S. aluco*) in India; one or two for other species of wood owls; two to four (sometimes only one, and five to seven, also recorded) for the Tawny Owl in Europe; and three (less often four or five) for the circumpolar Great Gray Owl.

Incubation, by the female mostly, lasts about 28 to 30 days (*S. varia, S. aluco,* and *S. leptogrammica*). The interval between eggs may be 48 hours to a week (*S. aluco*), incubation starting with the first egg. The young are brooded for about three weeks (*S. varia* and *S. aluco*), the male providing food. They take to branches at about five or six weeks, and remain with the parents (and are perhaps fed by them) for the rest of the summer.

These owls are mostly sedentary, with some "drifting" out of the northern regions. In seasons of deep snow, when mice can keep under cover, and especially when hares are scarce, great flights of Barred Owls come from the north into New England and farther south. Food scarcity probably also causes the Great Gray Owls to go south (and east, in North America), although irruptions far south of their range are rare.

Strix is the "hoot" owl of the world, its common calls a two-, three-, four- or five-syllable "who-hoo-to-hoo-ooo" and prolonged, tremulous "who-oo-oo" like that of the Screech Owl (*Otus*), but louder. In the breeding season the woods echo with laughing, cackling, and whooping. The Barred Owl also spits like a bobcat and bays like a dog.

The Striped Owl (*Rhinoptynx clamator*) has rarely been seen north of Panama; however, a few individuals breed in the lowland forests as far north as southern Veracruz and Chiapas, Mexico.

GENUS *RHINOPTYNX*

Striped underparts and white face and throat, as well as larger, stouter beak and feet, distinguish the tufted owls of the genus *Rhinoptynx* from other long-eared owls (*Asio*) in tropical America. The wings are short; the tail is long. Tarsi and toes are densely feathered, almost to the talons.

Striped Owl (*Rhinoptynx clamator*)

DESCRIPTION (TROPICAL AMERICA)

Above, including ear tufts, yellow-orange, heavily streaked and mottled with dark brown; wings and tail, mottled and barred; facial disc and throat, white, bordered on the sides in dark brown; underparts, white or tinged with yellow-orange and heavily streaked with dark brown.

Beak, gray; eyes, brown. Size, 12–14 inches.

RHINOPTYNX CLAMATOR

VARIATIONS Larger birds occur on the island of Tobago.

HABITS

The Striped Owls, found in deciduous seasonal forest and lowland seasonal forest, are known to eat small mammals. They roost in groups of at least fifteen and apparently nest on the ground. At one nest site in a Panama citrus orchard—merely a beaten place in the grass—there were two unfledged young.

Different as night and day—the Long-eared Owl *(Asio otus)*, shown here, is essentially nocturnal and arboreal, while its cousin, the Short-eared Owl *(Asio flammeus)*, might be mistaken for a Marsh Hawk *(Circus)* as it skims over open country, hunting in broad daylight.

GENUS *ASIO*

The owls of the genus *Asio* fall into two widespread, but usually ecologically distinct, groups: the Long-eared Owls, distributed throughout the temperate zones of the Northern Hemisphere, in tropical America, and locally in Africa and Madagascar; and the Short-eared Owls, found at one season or another nearly everywhere in cold and temperate regions (absent only from Australia and New Zealand and most Pacific islands, except the Hawaiian group, where the Short-eared Owl is the only native owl, and probably came originally from North America).

The Long-eared Owl is intermediate in size between the Great Horned Owl and the Screech Owl and has long ear tufts set closer to the center of the head than these horned owls; bright golden-orange eyes; a long, distinctly arched cere that brings the feathering of the facial disc downward into a deeper V; and relatively small beak and feet. The body is slimmer, and the legs, as well as the wings and tail, are relatively longer than in most other woodland owls (the wings with a brown spot on the underside). Tarsi and feet are thickly feathered almost to the talons, except for the tropical American Stygian Owl (*A. stygius*), which is barefooted.

The Short-eared Owl has scarcely visible ear tufts and a better defined facial disc, which is small compared to its stocky body. It leans forward on long legs while perching (usually on the ground), in marked contrast to the Long-eared Owl's upright, elongated posture on a branch. Its generally light coloring, with dark streaking above and below, is quite different from the darker Long-eared Owl's, which is mottled above and streaked and barred below. In flight the Short-eared's wings are longer, thinner, and not as rounded as those of the forest-dwelling species of *Asio*. Tarsi and feet are densely feathered, almost to the talons in the northern populations, but are sparsely feathered or bare in the tropics. Its African counterpart is the Marsh Owl (*A. capensis*).

In some parts of the world, during the breeding season and often during migration, the Long-eared Owl may be found in the Short-eared Owl's habitat; but diurnal habits, longer wings, and regular occurrence in open country place the latter closer to the hawks in its general appearance and ecological function than any other owl. The diurnal bird of prey most likely to be confused with this bird is the Marsh Hawk (*Circus*), but the Short-eared Owl has no white on the rump, and its wavering flight, round head, and short tail are distinctive.

Long-eared Owl (*Asio otus*)

DESCRIPTION (NORTHERN EUROPE)

Above, yellow-orange to medium yellow-orange, mottled and streaked in chocolate or olive-brown and spotted with white; ear tufts, dark with light borders; wings and tail, tawny, barred and mottled; facial disc, yellow-orange to medium yellow-orange, with crescent-shaped black patches partly encircling the eyes; lores and short eyebrows, white; ruff, speckled brown and white; below, white, heavily streaked and faintly barred with brown and entirely washed with tawny, including unmarked feathered legs and feet.

Juvenile—barred above and below, except on the belly, which is yellow-orange, without streaking or barring.

Beak, black (lighter at tip); eyes, bright golden-orange; claws, black. Size, 13–14 inches.

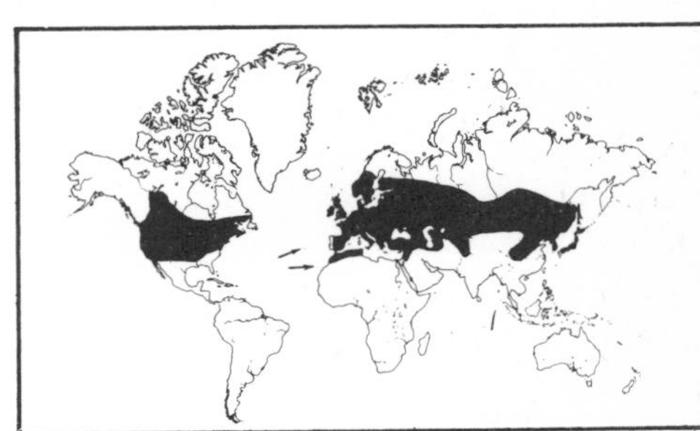

ASIO OTUS

VARIATIONS

In eastern North America the Long-eared Owl is dark olive-brown with light areas much reduced above. Westward across the Great Plains into the southwestern United States it becomes lighter and slightly smaller, but throughout the continent it has heavier streaking on the breast than the Old World population and broad and prominent streaking and barring on the underparts. The very small Canary Islands population follows the eastern North American color pattern. Sizes vary from 11 to 14 inches.

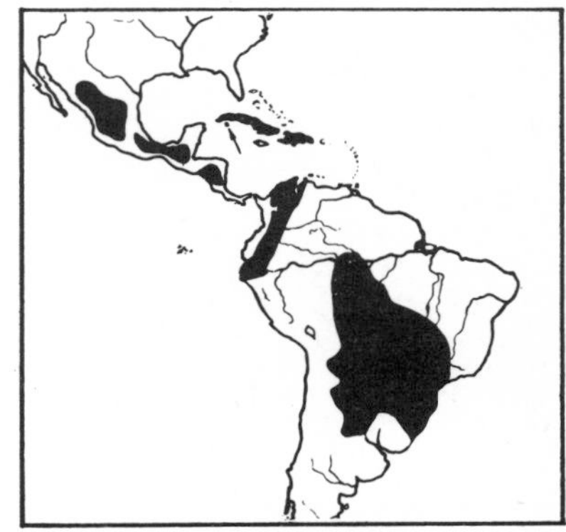

ASIO STYGIUS

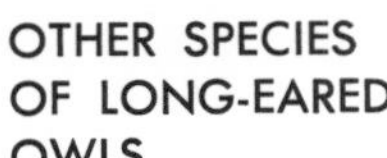

OTHER SPECIES OF LONG-EARED OWLS

Together with the owls of the genus *Ciccaba,* the formidable Stygian Owl (*A. stygius*) is the "blackest" of the nocturnal avian predators in tropical America. This owl is nearly solid sepia above with some yellow-orange spotting on crown and mantle; underparts, very heavily streaked and barred. Bare feet and larger size (15–16 inches) also distinguish this species from the Long-eared Owl that winters in the mountains of Mexico.

In the high mountain country of northeastern Africa the Abyssinian Long-eared Owl (*A. abyssinicus*) is uniformly mottled and spotted above; heavily streaked and barred below. A smaller, darker variety is known from the forest northwest of Lake Tanganyika and on Mt. Kenya.

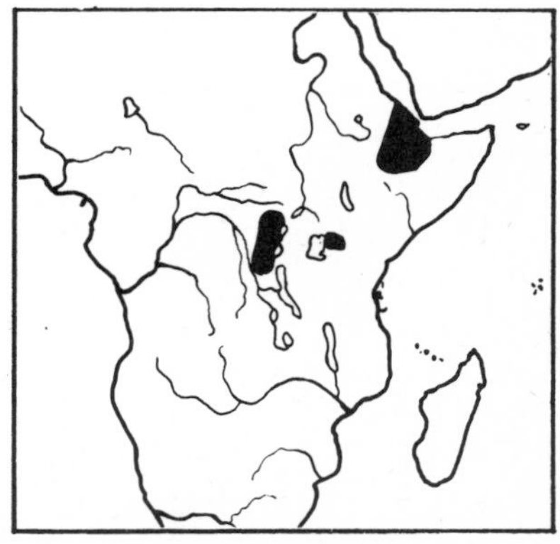

ASIO ABYSSINICUS

The Madagascar Long-eared Owl (*A. madagascariensis*), apparently confined to the forests of the humid east and around Sambirano, is also smaller (13 inches) and darker; brown, spotted on crown and mantle and mottled on back with pale yellow-orange; underparts, white, heavily streaked and barred, and suffused with pale yellow-orange. Barring on the tarsi and toes is unique among the long-eared owls.

ASIO MADAGASCARIENSIS

Short-eared Owl *(Asio flammeus)*, North America.—*Photograph by Hal H. Harrison, from National Audubon Society.*

Short-eared Owl (*Asio flammeus*)

DESCRIPTION (NORTH AMERICA)

Above, including rudimentary ear tufts, uniformly streaked in yellow-orange and sepia without the heavy dark mottling characteristic of the American Long-eared Owl; wings and tail, barred; facial disc, sandy, striped above the eyes, which are masked in black and completely encircled by a dark ruff; underparts, white to pale yellow-orange, streaked heavily on breast and slightly on belly with sepia. (Long-eared Owl is streaked and barred.)

Juvenile—face and upperparts, darker; underparts, plain yellow-orange.

Beak, black; eyes, bright lemon-yellow; talons, black. Size, about 15 inches.

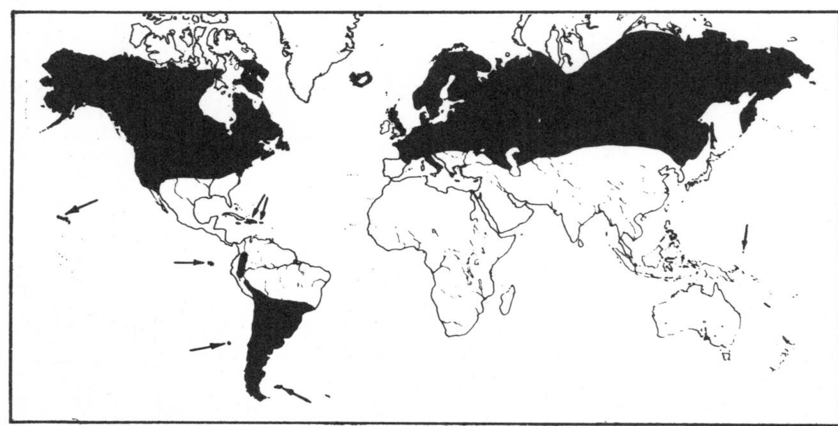

ASIO FLAMMEUS

VARIATIONS

The short-eared owls are remarkably similar everywhere, but the South American and island birds of the Western Hemisphere are darker. The Galapagos bird, an extreme dark variant, is sepia to dark brown above, with only traces of white and yellow-orange; and, providing the single exception to the rule, it is streaked and barred below. Sizes range from 13 to 15 inches.

OTHER OLD WORLD SPECIES OF SHORT EARED OWLS

The African Marsh Owl (*A. capensis*), 12–16 inches, south of the Sahara, is cinnamon-brown, very finely mottled above and across breast, becoming barred in white on belly; face, white, barred in cinnamon-brown, with brown circles around eyes and brown ruff. The eye color is blue-black. (Southern Ethiopian and Madagascar individuals show only a remnant of the finely mottled breast. The latter are nearly solid sepia above, with spotting on head and faint mottling on sides and lower back.)

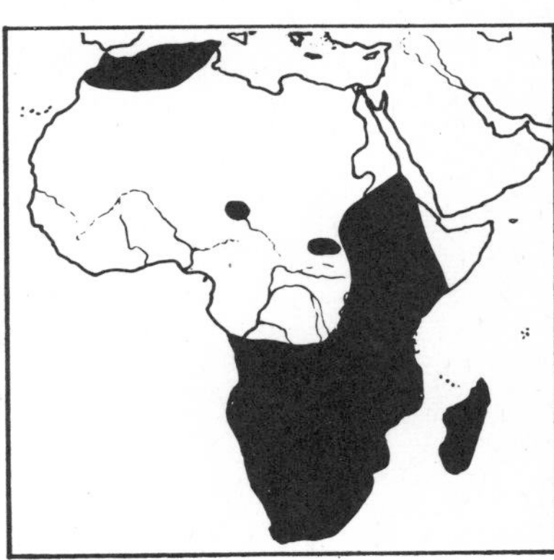

ASIO CAPENSIS

HABITS

Small copses and belts of timber (especially near rivers and lakes) on plains, steppes, and even in temperate desert provide enough cover for the Long-eared Owls (*A. otus*), which are nocturnal but not deep-forest dwellers. They show a decided preference for evergreen stands or dense coniferous thickets, but they are also commonly found in mixed woodlands; the mountain birds frequent grasslands and bushy ravines; and completely open country is recorded as the less frequent habitat of these owls in the British Isles.

The Short-eared Owl (*A. flammeus*) is more diurnal than other owls during the breeding season, and also hunts freely at dusk, early dawn, and all during the night. In the lands of the midnight sun this owl must, like the Hawk Owl, Snowy Owl, and Tawny Owl, hunt exclusively by daylight in summer. The African Marsh Owl (*A. capensis*) is occasionally seen by day, but it seems to be more nocturnal in its habits.

The Short-eared Owl and its relative, the African Marsh Owl, will sit on an observation post and wait for their prey; but more frequently they quarter the ground, their flight wavering, but low and rolling, with frequent periods of gliding. Occasionally the Short-eared Owls fly very high, and in springtime they engage in spectacular courtship displays of wing-clapping high over meadow and marsh.

The Long-eared Owl and Short-eared Owl are among our most effective mousers, with meadow mice, gophers, and other small rodents topping the list of prey species taken, supplemented by birds (in the breeding season), beetles, and other insects (said to be a major food of the African Marsh Owl), frogs, and occasionally small snakes and fish.

The Short-eared Owls are particularly noted for congregating in areas overpopulated by mice. In England during the sixteenth century and in South America in 1872–73, they are said to have been important agents in stopping plagues of mice (see Chapter 3, on rodent cycles). They also patrol grain fields at threshing time.

The owls of the genus *Asio* are often gregarious, roosting together in winter and even nesting in colonies. Old nests of squirrels, hawks, crows, magpies—and in England, rooks, herons, and Wood Pigeons—are extensively used by Long-eared Owls, sometimes close to the ground in brush or as high as 40 feet up in tall conifers. The North American Long-eared Owl may, like the Great Gray Owl, build a nest of sticks, rubbish, and bark and line it with bark and feathers. Mountain birds (Kashmir, Ethiopia, Mexico) frequently nest on the ground, and in England some rugged individualists not only hunt open country but even breed on heaths, dunes, or marshes. Generally four or five eggs are laid, but there is considerable variation in numbers.

The Short-eared Owl and African Marsh Owl always nest in a slight hollow on the ground near a clump of vegetation in marsh or meadow, generally laying two to four eggs in Africa, and four to seven in other parts of the world, typically on a sparse lining of weed stalks and feathers. During rodent plagues the number increases, with nine, thirteen and even fourteen eggs recorded in a single clutch.

Incubation by the female mostly (in *A. otus*) begins with the first egg (the eggs are laid on alternate days) and probably lasts about 28 days. The young leave the nest when 23 or 24 days old. The female Short-eared Owl (*A. flammeus*) incubates for a corresponding period. Eggs are laid normally at about 48-hour intervals, but sometimes with a pause of up to a week, and in some cases apparently in pairs. Eggs that are laid earlier take longer than later ones, possibly because of partial incubation at first. Food is provided for the young by the male, and the female feeds them. They leave the nest at about 12 to 17 days (sometimes earlier), but are unable to fly until the 24th or 25th day. In both Long- and Short-eared Owls one brood is normally raised; two broods, in response to a plentiful supply of food (high rodent populations).

The call of the Long-eared Owl is more like the cooing of a pigeon or dove than a hoot, but this versatile vocalist can produce an "oo-ack, oo-ack" alarm call, a slurred whistle, and many other sounds. The female voice is higher-pitched. Out of breeding season the Short-eared Owl is one of the most silent of birds; its courtship ditty, a "toot-toot-toot," higher than that of the Great Horned Owl, is accompanied by barking sounds. Only a harsh screech or grating croak is recorded for the African Marsh Owl.

The Jamaican Owl *(Pseudoscops grammicus)* is a nocturnal species seldom encountered during the daytime. Its local name is the Brown Owl, or Potoo.

GENUS *PSEUDOSCOPS*

There are apparently only two owls on the island of Jamaica in the Caribbean—the Barn Owl (*Tyto*) and the indigenous Jamaican Owl (*Pseudoscops*), which is closely related to the genus *Asio*. The Jamaican Owl is medium-sized and has short tufts, but the general body shape, fullness of facial disc, comparatively short wings and tail, and naked toes are characteristic of the big tufted Stygian Owl (*Asio stygius*), a Neotropical species that inhabits Cuba, the Isle of Pines, Hispaniola, and Gonave Island as well as Central and South America, but is absent from Jamaica.

Jamaican Owl (*Pseudoscops grammicus*)

DESCRIPTION (JAMAICA)

Above, including short ear tufts, dark amber-brown; streaked and barred dark brown from crown to nape and mottled on back; wings and tail, mottled and barred; facial disc, dark amber-brown to white on the sides, tinged around the eyes and bordered with brown; underparts, tawny, mottled and streaked dark brown.

Juvenile—lighter above and below.

Beak, dull yellow deepening to horn color; eyes, brown; toes, dull lead color. Size, 11–12½ inches.

PSEUDOSCOPS GRAMMICUS

HABITS

The Jamaican Owls are completely nocturnal, arboreal birds of the woodlands. Two eggs are laid in the cavity of a tree.

Their call has been described as a curious "wow" or a prolonged, quavering "whoooo."

A powerful relative of *Asio,* the Fearful Owl *(Nesasio solomonensis)* may be found only on the islands of Bougainville, Choiseul, and Ysabel in the southwest Pacific.

GENUS *NESASIO*

This rare owl of the southwest Pacific has beak and feet as powerful as those of the Great Horned Owl (*Bubo virginianus*), which stands half a foot taller. The tarsi are completely feathered to the feet, and the toes are sparsely bristled.

Fearful Owl (*Nesasio solomonensis*)

DESCRIPTION (SOLOMON ISLANDS)

Above, dark tawny, streaked with dark brown from crown to mantle; irregularly barred as well as streaked on back; wings and tail, brown; facial disc, tawny; ruff, brown, black mask around eyes, and contrasting white eyebrows, lores, and chin; below, tawny, with brown streaking.

Beak, black; eyes, yellow; feet, gray. Size, 11–15 inches.

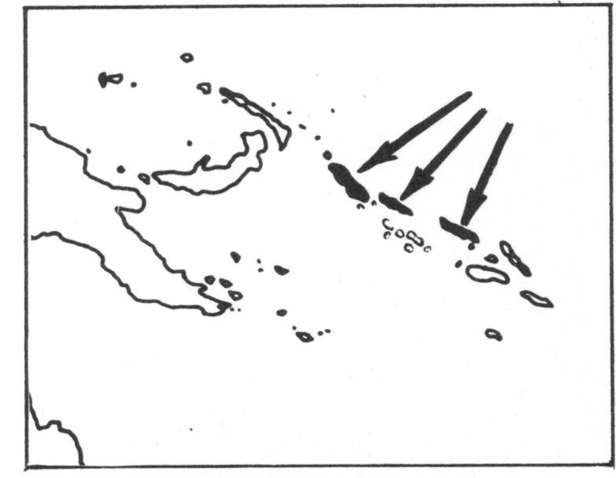

NESASIO SOLOMONENSIS

HABITS

A bird of the lowland and hill forest, the Fearful Owl probably lives on opossums and birds.

Bird or grasshopper? It takes a keen ear to recognize the call in the mating season of the Saw-whet Owl *(Aegolius acadicus)*, hidden in daylight hours in pine forests and swamps.

GENUS *AEGOLIUS*

Aegolius could be characterized as a miniature edition of the Tawny Owl in shape, having no ear tufts, a more complete facial disc than any other small owl, and an even larger head, in proportion to its body, than *Strix*. Small eyes and a comparatively weak bill complete the "portrait" of the face. The wings are long and wide, and the tail is short. The tarsi and rather large feet are heavily feathered in the Holarctic species *A. funereus;* the toes are partly feathered in *A. acadicus* of temperate North America, and completely bare in the tropical Central and South American species. Where the ranges of the two North American birds overlap, the Boreal Owl (*A. funereus*) may be distinguished by its larger size, yellow (not black) beak, dark rim around the facial disc, and spotted, rather than streaked crown. The Palearctic *A. funereus,* known as Tengmalm's Owl in Europe, breeds from the far north to the more southerly mountain ranges.

Saw-whet Owl (*Aegolius acadicus*)

DESCRIPTION (NORTH AMERICA)

Above, sepia, streaked with white on crown and collared in a distinct white V; wing coverts, spotted with white; wings and darker tail, marked with spots of white barring; facial disc, pale yellow-orange, striped in dark brown with conspicuous white eyebrows forming a broad V between the eyes; dark ruff; locket at throat, white; underparts, white, streaked with sienna; feathering on legs and feet, pale yellow-orange.

Juvenile—solid sepia above; face, dark brown, with a more conspicuous white V; chest, sepia; rest of underparts, medium yellow-orange.

Beak, black; eyes, lemon-yellow; naked part of toes, dull yellow; claws, black. Size, 6½–7½ inches.

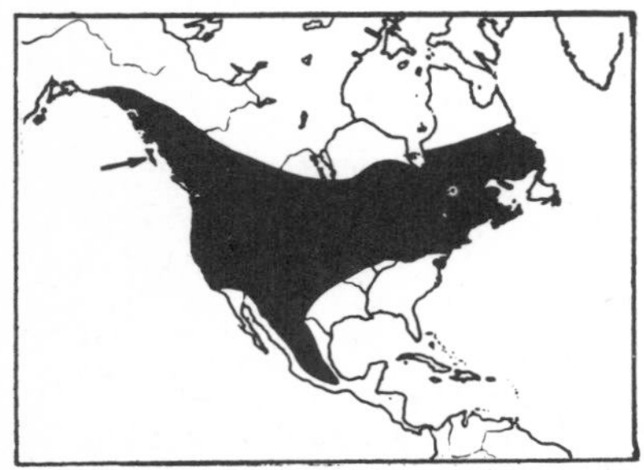

AEGOLIUS ACADICUS

VARIATIONS

Saw-whet Owls resident in the Queen Charlotte Islands off British Columbia are somewhat darker.

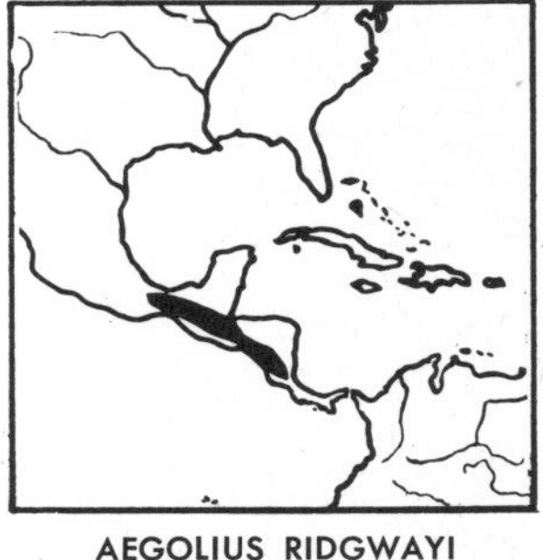
AEGOLIUS RIDGWAYI

OTHER SPECIES

The Unspotted Saw-whet Owl (*A. ridgwayi*), 7 inches, distributed locally from southern Mexico to the highlands of Costa Rica, lacks white spotting on the wings and tail. It is closely related to the northern Saw-whet Owl, however. It has the same general coloring and streaking on the crown and underparts.

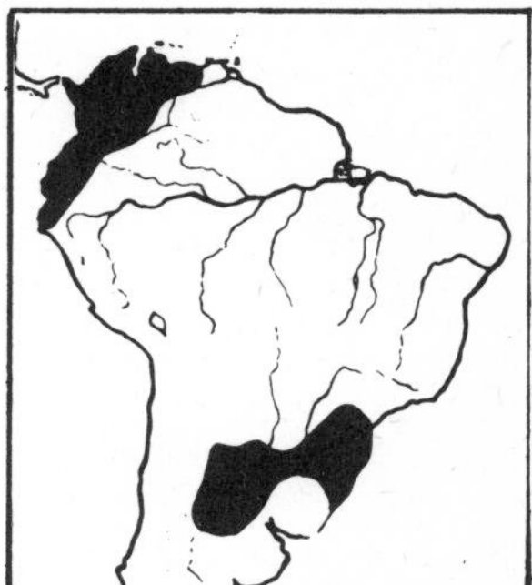
AEGOLIUS HARRISII

The little-known Buff-fronted Owl (*A. harrisii*), 7 inches (Venezuela) to 8½ inches (southern South America), has white-spotted coverts and wings. The tail is also spotted or barred white. Birds originally described from Venezuela and Argentina appear to be juveniles or at least not fully adult. A Tucuman individual, with face, collar, and underparts of "reddish-tawny," is said to be darker over-all than the others. Two specimens in the collection of the American Museum of Natural History from northern South America have a yellow-orange crown, cheeks, sides of neck, and underparts; a black patch on the head and nape; brown ruff and throat; upperparts, chocolate; coverts, wings, and tail, spotted white.

Boreal or Tengmalm's Owl (*Aegolius funereus*)

DESCRIPTION (NORWAY)

Above, sepia, spotted with white; collared in white; wings and tail marked with spots of white; facial disc, white, heavily bordered with brown; locket, white; underparts, white, streaked with sepia down to the toes, which are thickly feathered in white.

Juvenile—almost entirely chocolate, with patches of white on the lores and a few white spots on the flight feathers and tail.

Beak, yellow; eyes, yellow; claws, black. Size, 9 inches.

VARIATIONS

Boreal Owls of northern and central Europe are almost identical in size and coloring to North American individuals. Central Asiatic and northern Siberian birds are larger and lighter—cinnamon-brown, with much more white spotting on underparts. Sizes range from 9 to 10 inches.

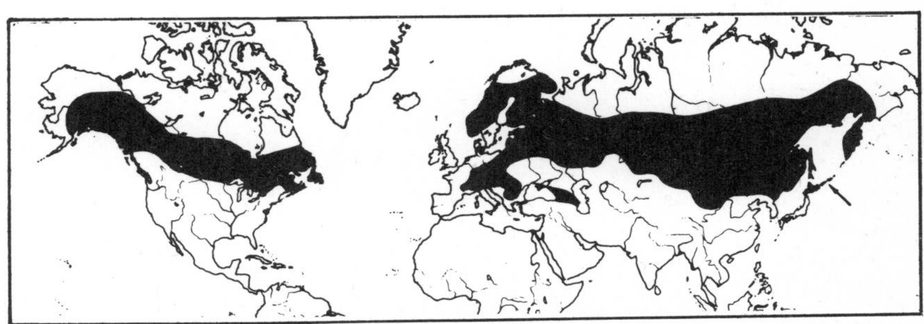
AEGOLIUS FUNEREUS

HABITS

The owls of the Genus *Aegolius* ordinarily live in deep forest—coniferous or predominately pine woodland and tropical rain forests. In northern regions, at least, they are relatively tame and unafraid of man. Their chief enemies seem to be larger owls.

They are diurnal, of necessity, at the northernmost limits of their breeding range (in Alaska, Lapland, and eastern Siberia, where daylight lasts through the summer), and nocturnal elsewhere, with sundown and sunrise the hours of greatest activity. The Saw-whet Owl (*A. acadicus*) spends most of the day napping on a thickly foliaged tree branch close to the ground; or, when prompted by hunger, it flies off like a small woodpecker or a woodcock, with a faster wing beat than most owls, to a more open perch where it will wait patiently for the sight or sound of prey on the ground.

Everywhere the staple food of *Aegolius* is woodland mice, supplemented by other small rodents, small birds, bats, occasionally frogs, and (rarely) insects. Like the pigmy owls (*Glaucidium*), these deceptively small, but sometimes voracious predators, are capable of taking birds and mammals larger than themselves (i.e., pigeons and flying squirrels). These owls nest in holes in trees, especially deserted woodpecker holes, usually in dense damp forests or near water. Typically five or six eggs are laid (*A. acadicus* and *A. funereus*), but the number is extremely variable—as few as three in North America, and as many as eight or ten in Europe. Incubation, by the female, is not less than 25 days long. The eggs are laid at intervals of from one to three days, and as incubation begins with the first egg, the young hatch at various intervals. Newly hatched and nearly grown young are sometimes found in the same nest. The fledglings leave the nest at 28 to 36 days, often before they can fly. Ordinarily one brood is raised; probably two occasionally.

A circling display flight above the treetops is recorded for *A. funereus* in North America and Europe, during which the male utters a "song"; also wing-clapping is recorded as the birds fly among the tree trunks.

Boreal Owls (*A. funereus*) occasionally drift long distances in winter, occurring as rare vagrants in the United States as far south as Pennsylvania, Illinois, Idaho, and Oregon; and in Scotland, the Shetlands, England, southern France, northern Spain, Belgium, Denmark, and Poland; also in Asia Minor.

The call of *A. funereus* in the mating season is a single, soft, liquid, and rather musical note, repeated for two to three seconds at a time, together with a trill—like the tolling of a high-pitched bell or water dripping. (One of the Indian names for the Boreal Owl is "pillip-pile-tschish," which means "water-dripping bird.") The Saw-whet Owls, best known for their soft "sa-a-ay t-sch-whet-t" and other "saw-filing" notes, almost as suggestive of a grasshopper as a bird, also have a springtime vocabulary (especially males) of bell-like notes, whistles, and gasping sounds. In other seasons they are seldom heard.

REGIONAL GUIDES

On the following pages, all the species of Falconiformes in North America and Europe are represented by at least one adult silhouette, showing the differences in their shapes. They have also been grouped according to the particular areas where they are found on the North American and European continents. In the North American Guide, birds which are restricted to the southeast, northwest, and southwest have been separated by a solid line from the more generally distributed ones. In the European Guide, more overlapping of ranges occurs, and the birds have been more or less grouped, from top to bottom, as they inhabit the continent from north to south. For exact identification of birds (females, juveniles, and color phases) and their specific ranges, refer to the text.

GUIDE TO THE FALCONIFORMES OF NORTH AMERICA

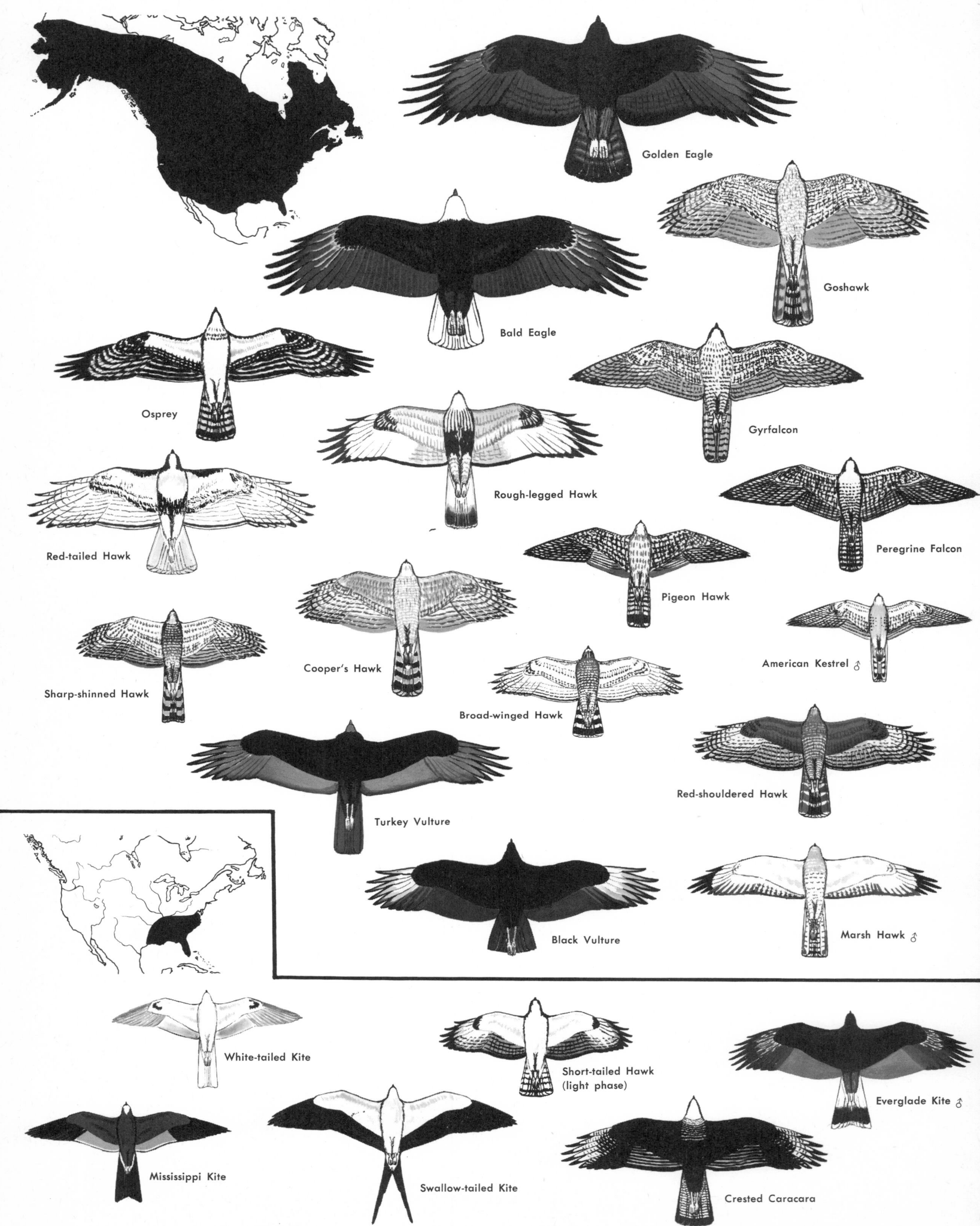

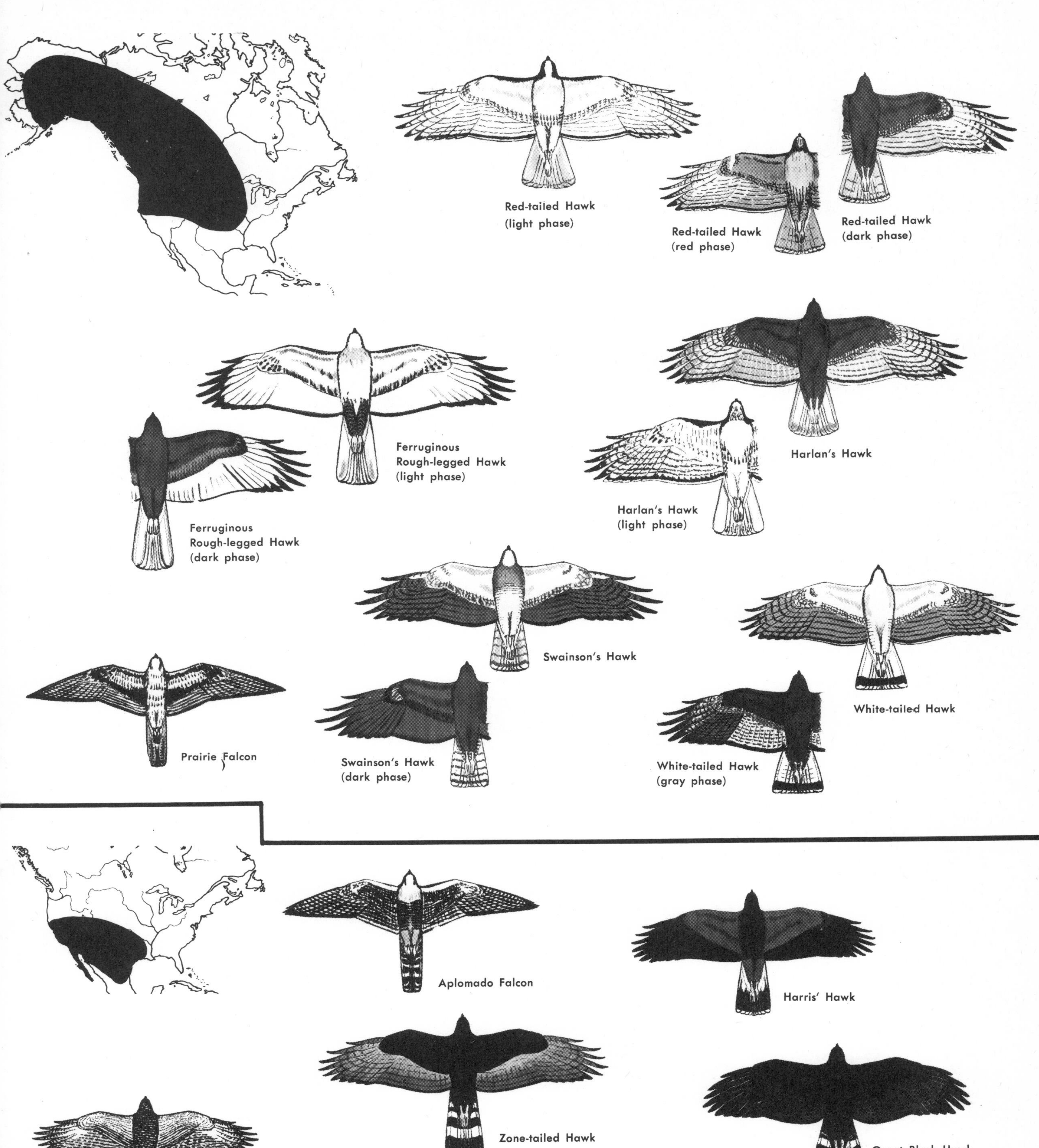

Red-tailed Hawk
(light phase)
Red-tailed Hawk
(red phase)
Red-tailed Hawk
(dark phase)
Ferruginous
Rough-legged Hawk
(light phase)
Ferruginous
Rough-legged Hawk
(dark phase)
Harlan's Hawk
Harlan's Hawk
(light phase)
Swainson's Hawk
Prairie Falcon
Swainson's Hawk
(dark phase)
White-tailed Hawk
White-tailed Hawk
(gray phase)
Aplomado Falcon
Harris' Hawk
Zone-tailed Hawk
Great Black Hawk
Gray Hawk
Common Black Hawk
California Condor

GUIDE TO THE FALCONIFORMES OF EUROPE

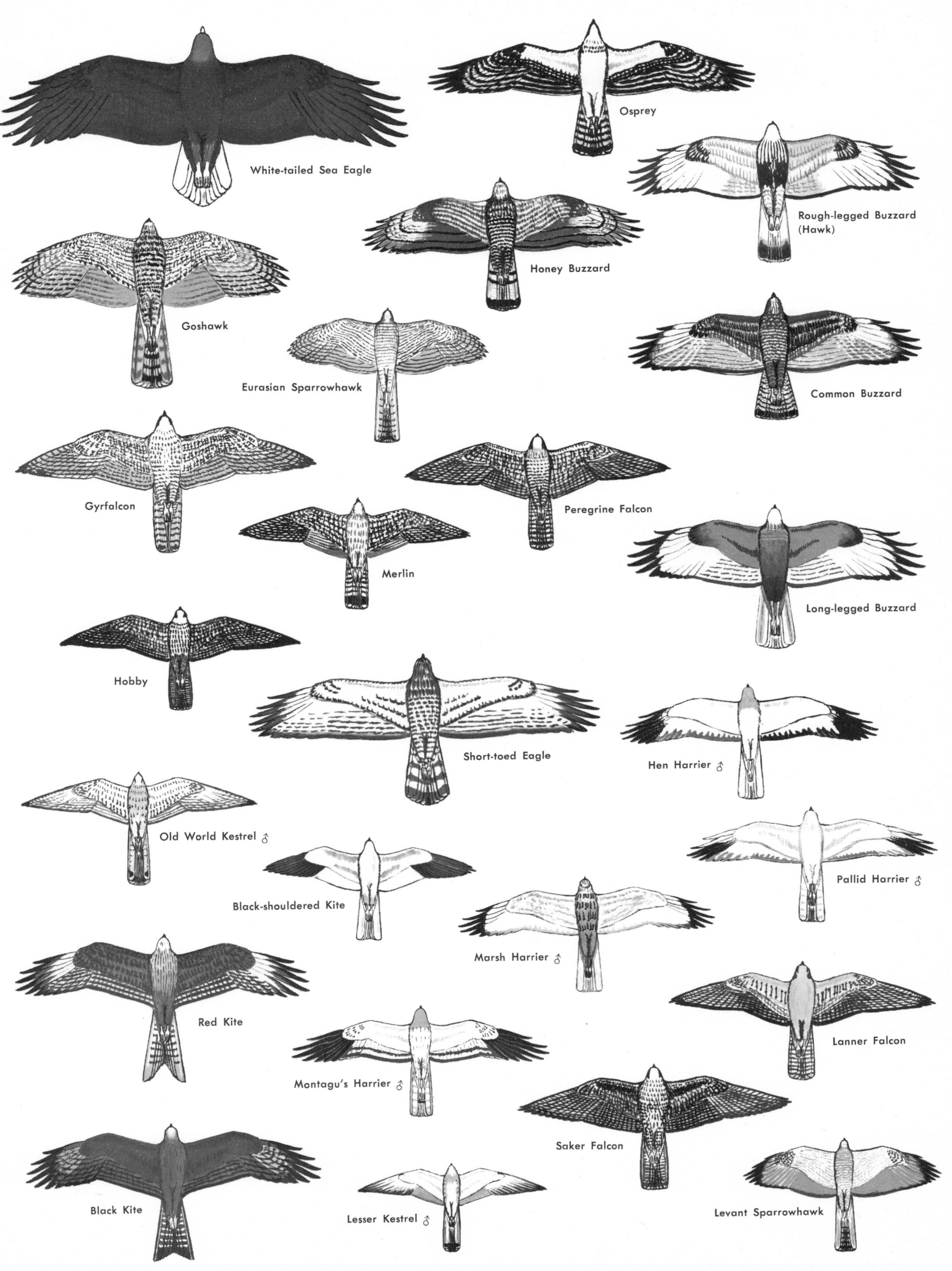
White-tailed Sea Eagle
Osprey
Rough-legged Buzzard
(Hawk)
Honey Buzzard
Goshawk
Eurasian Sparrowhawk
Common Buzzard
Gyrfalcon
Peregrine Falcon
Merlin
Long-legged Buzzard
Hobby
Short-toed Eagle
Hen Harrier ♂
Old World Kestrel ♂
Pallid Harrier ♂
Black-shouldered Kite
Marsh Harrier ♂
Red Kite
Lanner Falcon
Montagu's Harrier ♂
Saker Falcon
Black Kite
Lesser Kestrel ♂
Levant Sparrowhawk

BIBLIOGRAPHY

General Reference

AMADON, DEAN. "Specialization and Evolution," *Amer. Nat.,* 77 (1943):133–41.

———. "Taxonomic Notes on Birds of Prey," *Amer. Mus. Nov.,* 2166 (1964), 1–24.

BROUN, MAURICE. *Hawks Aloft, The Story of Hawk Mountain.* New York: Dodd, Mead & Co., 1949.

COTT, HUGH B. *Adaptive Coloration in Animals.* London: Methuen & Co., London, 1940.

DARLINGTON, PHILIP J., JR. *Zoogeography.* New York: John Wiley & Sons, 1958.

FISHER, HARVEY I. "The Occurrence of Vestigial Claws on the Wings of Birds," *Amer. Mid. Nat.,* Vol. 23, No. I (1940):234–43.

———. "Adaptations and Comparative Anatomy of the Locomotor Apparatus of New World Vultures," *Amer. Mid. Nat.,* 35 (1946):545–727.

FISHER, JAMES and PETERSON, ROGER TORY. *The World of Birds.* New York: Doubleday, 1964.

GREENWAY, JAMES C., JR. *Extinct and Vanishing Birds of the World.* New York: The Amer. Committee for Inter. Wildlife Protection, Special Pub. No. 13, 1958.

HILL, N. P. "Sexual Dimorphism in the Falconiformes," *Auk,* 61 (1944):228–34.

HUMPHREY, PHILIP S., and PARKES, KENNETH C. "An Approach to the Study of Molts and Plumages," *Auk,* 76 (1959):1–31.

LINCOLN, F. C. *Migration of Birds.* New York: Doubleday & Co., 1952.

MAYR, E., and MAYR, M. "The Tail Molt of Small Owls," *Auk,* 71 (1954):172–78.

MEINERTZHAGEN, R. "Desert Coloration," *Proc. 10th Internatl. Ornith. Congr.,* Vol. X (1951):155–62.

NICE, M. M. "Incubation Periods of Birds of Prey," *Die Vogelwarte,* 16 (1953):154–57.

———. "The Problem of Incubation Periods in North American Birds," *Condor,* 56 (1954):173–97.

PETERS, J. L. *Check-list of Birds of the World.* Vols. I and IV. Cambridge, Mass.: Harvard University Press, 1931.

PETERSON, ROGER TORY. "Statement on Pesticide Hazards" to Subcommittee on Reorganization and International Organization, Senate Committee on Government Operations. Washington, D.C.: The Congressional Record, April 22, 1964.

PETTINGILL, OLIN S., JR. *A Laboratory and Field Manual of Ornithology.* Minneapolis: Burgess Pub. Co., 1958.

RICHARDS, P. W. *The Tropical Rain Forest,* Cambridge, Eng.: Cambridge University Press, 1952.

STORER, ROBERT W. "Weight, Wing Area, and Skeletal Proportions in Three Accipiters," *Int. Orn. Congr.,* 11 (1956):287–90.

STRONG, R. M. "A Bibliography of Birds," *Field Mus. Zool. Ser.,* Vol. XXV, Parts 1, 2, 3, (1939–46).

SWANN, H. KIRKE, and WETMORE, ALEXANDER. *Monograph of the Birds of Prey.* Parts 1-16. London: Wheldon and Wesley, Ltd., 1924–45.

VAN TYNE, JOSSELYN, and BERGER, ANDREW J. *Fundamentals of Ornithology.* New York: John Wiley & Sons, 1959.

WALLS, G. L. *The Vertebrate Eye and Its Adaptive Radiation.* Bloomfield Hills, Mich.: Cranbrook Institute of Science, 1942.

WELTY, JOEL C. *The Life of Birds.* Philadelphia: W. B. Saunders Co., 1962.

WOLFSON, A. (Ed.) *Recent Studies in Avian Biology.* Urbana: University of Illinois Press, 1955.

Ecology

BAUMGARTNER, A. M. and F. M. "Hawks and Owls in Oklahoma 1939–1942: Food Habits and Population Changes," *Wils. Bull.,* 56 (1944):209–15.

BOURLIÈRE, FRANÇOIS. *The Natural History of Mammals,* 2nd ed. New York: Alfred A. Knopf, 1962.

CRAIGHEAD, J. J. and F. C., JR. *Hawks, Owls and Wildlife.* Harrisburg, Pa.: Stackpole, 1956.

ELTON, C. *Voles, Mice and Lemmings.* London: Oxford University Press, 1942.

ERRINGTON, PAUL L. "Predation and Vertebrate Populations," *Quart. Rev. Biol.* (Baltimore), 21 (1946): 147–77, 221–45.

ERRINGTON, PAUL L., and HAMERSTROM, FRANCES and F. N., JR., "The Great Horned Owl and Its Prey in North-Central United States," *Agric. Exp. Station, Iowa State College of Agriculture and Mechanic Arts, Research Bull.* 277 (September, 1940):759–850.

FITCH, H. S. "Predation by Owls in the Sierran Foothills of California," *Condor,* 49 (1947):137–51.

LACK, D. "Competition for Food by Birds of Prey," *J. Animal Ecol.,* 15 (1946):123–29.

———. "Significance of Clutch Size," *Ibis,* 89 (1947): 302–52.

LESLIE, P. H., and RANSON, R. M. "The Mortality, Fertility, and Rate of Natural Increase of the Vole (*Microtus agrestis*) as observed in the Laboratory," *J. Animal Ecol.,* 9 (1940):27–52.

MARSHALL, JOE T., JR. *Birds of Pine-Oak Woodland*. Berkeley, Calif.: Cooper Ornithological Society, 1957.

MEBS, T. "Zur Biologie und Populationsdynamik des Mausebussards (*Buteo buteo*)," *J. für Orn.*, 103 (1964): 248–303.

MEINERTZHAGEN, R. "Roost of Wintering Harriers," *Ibis*, 98 (1956):535.

ODUM, EUGENE P. *Fundamentals of Ecology*. Philadelphia: W. B. Saunders Co., 1953.

RANDLE, W., and AUSTING, R. "Ecological Notes on Long-eared and Saw-whet Owls in Southwestern Ohio," *Ecology*, 33 (1952):422–26.

RUDEBECK, G. "The choice of prey and modes of hunting of predatory birds with special reference to their selective effect," *Oikos*, 21 (1950):65–88.

SCHMAUS, M. "Der Einfluss der Mausejahr auf das Brutgeschaft unser Raubvogel und Eulen," *Beitr. Fortpfl.-biol. Vog.*, 14 (1938):181-84.

SPRUNT, ALEXANDER, JR. "Hawk Predation at the Bat Caves of Texas," *Texas J. Sci.*, 2 (1950):462–70.

WILSON, K. A. "Owl Studies at Ann Arbor, Mich.," *Auk*, 55 (1938):187–97.

TINBERGEN, L. "The Sparrow-hawk (Accipiter nisus L.) as a Predator of Passerine Birds." Ardea, 34 (1946): 1–213.

Paleontology

BRODKORB, PIERCE. "Two New Birds from the Miocene of Florida," *Condor*, 58 (1956):367–70.

———. "How Many Species of Birds Have Existed?" *Bull. Florida State Museum*, 5 (1960):41–53.

HAAST, J. "Notes on Harpagornis," *Trans. New Zeal. Inst.*, 4 (1872):192–96.

———. "On Harpagornis," *Trans. New Zeal. Inst.*, 13 (1880):232–34.

HEILMAN, G. *The Origin of Birds*. London: H. F. and G. Witherby, 1926.

HOWARD, HILDEGARDE. "Eagles and Eagle-like Vultures of the Pleistocene of Rancho La Brea," *Carnegie Inst. of Washington*, 346 (1932).

———. "Fossil Birds," *Mus. of the County of Los Angeles Sci. Ser.*, No. 17 (1955).

———. "The Prehistoric Avifauna of Smith Creek Cave, Nevada, with a Description of a New Gigantic Raptor (*Teratornis incredibilis*)," *Bull. So. Calif. Academy of Sciences*, 51 (1952):50–54.

———. "A Review of the Pleistocene Birds of Fossil Lake, Oregon," *Carnegie Inst. Washington*, 551 (1946):141–95.

LAMBRECHT, K. *Handbuch der Palaeornithologie*. Parts 1–2, Berlin: Verlag von Gebruder Borntragger, 1933, 391–424, 611–18.

SHUFELDT, R. W. "On the Affinities of Harpagornis," *Trans. New Zeal. Inst.*, 28 (1896):665.

WETMORE, ALEXANDER. "Additional Specimens of Fossil Birds from the Upper Tertiary Deposits of Nebraska," *Amer. Mus. Nov.*, 302 (1928):1–5.

———. "Ancient Records of Birds from the Island of St. Croix with Observations on Extinct and Living Birds of Puerto Rico," *J. of Agric., U. of Puerto Rico*, 21 (1937):5–16.

———. "Another Fossil Owl from the Eocene of Wyoming," *Proc. of U.S. Nat. Mus.*, 85 (1938):27–29.

———. "The Avifauna of the Pleistocene in Florida," *Smithson. Misc. Coll.*, 85, No. 2 (1931):1–46.

———. "Birds of the Pleistocene in North America," *Smithson. Misc. Coll.*, 138, No. 4 (1959):1–24.

———. "Bird Remains from Cave Deposits on Great Exuma Island in the Bahamas," *Bull. Mus. Comp. Zool., Harvard University*, 80 (1937):427–41.

———. "Bird Remains from the Oligocene Deposits of Torrington, Wyoming," *Bull. Mus. of Comp. Zool., Harvard University*, 75 (1933):297–311.

———. "Description of a Fossil Hawk from the Miocene of Nebraska," *Ann. of the Carn. Mus.*, 16 (1926): 462–68.

———. "Footprint from Miocene of Louisiana," *Condor*, 58 (1956):389–90.

———. "Fossil Birds from Mongolia and China," *Amer. Mus. Nov.*, 711 (1934):1–15.

———. "Fossil Birds from the Oligocene of Colorado," *Proc. of the Colorado Mus. of Nat. Hist.*, 7 (1927):3–9.

———. "Miscellaneous Notes on Fossil Birds," *Smithson. Misc. Coll.*, 135, No. 8 (1958):1–11.

———. "A New Terrestrial Vulture from the Upper Eocene Deposits of Wyoming," *Ann. Carnegie Mus.*, 30 (1944):57–69.

———. "An Oligocene Eagle from Wyoming," *Smithson. Misc. Coll.*, 87, No. 19 (1933):1–9.

———. "The Pleistocene Avifauna of Florida," *Proc. 7th Int. Orn. Congr.*, Amsterdam (1930):479–83.

———. "Remains of Birds from the Rexwood Fauna of the Upper Pliocene of Kansas," *U. of Kansas Sci. Bull.*, 30 (1944):89–105.

———. "The Status of *Minerva antiqua, Aquila ferox* and *Aquila lydekkeri* as Fossil Birds," *Amer. Mus. Nov.*, 680 (1933):1–4.

———. "The Tibeo-tarsus of Buteo Typhoius," *Condor*, 30 (1928):149–50.

———. "Two More Fossil Hawks from the Miocene of Nebraska," *Condor*, 45 (1943):229–31.

———. "Two New Species of Hawks from the Miocene of Nebraska," *U.S. Nat. Mus.*, 84 (1936):73–78.

WETMORE, ALEXANDER, and CASE, E. C. "A New Fossil Hawk from Oligocene Beds of South Dakota," *Contr. Mus. Paleont. U. Mich.*, 4 (1934):129–32.

Historical

ALEXANDER, H. B., *Mythology of All Races*. Boston: Marshall Jones, 1916.

CERAM, C. W. *The Secrets of the Hittites*. New York: Knopf, 1956.

CERNY, J. *Ancient Egyptian Religion*. London: Hutchinson House, 1952.

CHRISTENSEN, A. *L'Iran sous les Sassanides*. Copenhagen: Ejnar Munksgaard, 1944.

CURTIS, E. S. *North American Indians*. Cambridge, Mass.: The University Press, Vol. I–XX, 1907–1930.

DEMENTIEV, G. P. "La Fauconnerie en Russie," *Oiseau,* Paris, 15 (1945):10–35.

EMBURY, L. "The Odyssey of Uncle Sam's Eagle," *Nat. Hist.* N.Y., 45 (1940):276–79.

EPSTEIN, H. J. "The Origin and Earliest History of Falconry," *Isis,* 34 (1944):497-509.

FENTON, W. N. "Iroquois Eagle Dance and Songs," *Bull. Amer. Ethnol.,* 156 (1953):1–222.

GARDINER, A. *Egyptian Grammar*. London: Oxford University Press, 1957.

GAYRE, R. *Heraldic Standards and other Ensigns*. London: Oliver and Boyd, 1959.

GETTY, A. *The Gods of Northern Buddhism*. London: Oxford University Press, 1927.

HAYES, W. C. *The Scepter of Egypt*. Cambridge, Mass.: Harvard University Press, 1959.

JAMES, E. O. *The Cult of the Mother-Goddess*. New York: Barnes and Noble, 1959.

KEPHART, C. *Origin of Heraldry in Europe*. Virginia: Shenandoah Publishing House, 1953.

LUM, P. *Fabulous Beasts*. New York: Pantheon Books, 1951.

MORLEY, S. G. *The Ancient Maya*. Berkeley, Calif.: Stanford University Press, 1947.

MURDOCK, G. P. *Ethnographic Bibliography of North America,* 3rd Ed. New Haven: Human Relations Area File, 1960.

PARMELEE, ALICE. *All the Birds of the Bible*. New York: Harper & Bros., 1959.

PAUL, HENRY N. *The Royal Play of Macbeth*. New York: The Macmillan Co., 1950.

SELTMAN, C. T. *The Cambridge Ancient History*. Cambridge, Eng.: Cambridge University Press, Vol. I, 1927.

SPECK, F. "The Iroquois," *Bull. Cranbrook Inst. of Sci.* No. 23 (1945).

SPINDEN, H. *Maya Art and Civilization*. Colorado: The Falcon's Wing Press, 1957.

STUART, DOROTHY M. *A Book of Birds and Beasts*. London: Methuen & Co., 1957.

TOZZER, A. and ALLEN, G. M. "Animal Figures in Maya Codices." *Pap. Peabody Mus. Am. Arch. and Ethn., Harvard University,* Vol. IV, No. 3 (1910).

WATERBURY, F. *Bird Deities in China*. Asconia, Switz.: Artibus Asiae, 1952.

WELKER, R. H. *Birds and Men*. Cambridge, Mass.: Belknap Press of Harvard University, 1955.

WILLETS, WILLIAM. *Chinese Art*. New York: George Braziller, 1958.

WOOD, A. W. and FYFE, F. M. *The Art of Falconry (De Arte Venandi Cum Avibus)*. Stanford, Calif.: Stanford University Press, 1943.

Regional References

North America

AMERICAN ORNITHOLOGISTS' UNION, *Check-List of North American Birds,* 5th ed. Baltimore: Port City Press, 1961.

CORY, C. B. "Catalog of the Birds of the Americas," *Field Mus. Nat. Hist., Zool. Serv.,* Vol. XIII, Part II, No. 1 (1917):17–50.

FRIEDMANN, H., GRISCOM, L., and MOORE, R. T. *Distributional Check-List of the Birds of Mexico,* Part I, Berkeley, Calif.: *Cooper Ornithological Society,* 1950.

HELLMAYR, C. E., and CONOVER, B. "Catalog of the Birds of the Americas," *Field Mus. Nat. Hist. Zool. Ser.,* Vol. XIII, Part I, No. 4 (1949).

PETERSON, ROGER TORY. *A Field Guide to the Birds*. Boston: Houghton-Mifflin Co., 1960.

———. *A Field Guide to Western Birds*. Boston: Houghton Mifflin Co., 1961.

RIDGWAY, R. and FRIEDMANN, H. "Birds of North and Middle America," *U.S. Natl. Museum, Bull.* 50, Part XI (1950).

SUTTON, G. M. *Mexican Birds, First Impressions*. Norman, Okla.: U. of Oklahoma Press, 1951.

WOLFE, L. R. "A Synopsis of North American Birds of Prey and Their Related Forms in Other Countries," *Bull. Chicago Acad. Sci.,* 5, No. 8 (1938).

Central and South America

BOND, J. *Field Guide of Birds of the West Indies*. New York: The Macmillan Co., 1960.

CONOVER, B. "Notes on Some Neotropical Hawks." *Fieldiana Chicago Zool.,* 31 (1946):39–45.

DE SCHAUENSEE, R. M. *Birds of Colombia*. Philadelphia: Livingston Press, 1964.

DUGAND, A. "Clave Analitica Artificial de las Rapaces (Accipitridae y Falconidae) Colombianas," *Rev. Acad. Colombiana Cienc. Bogota,* 4 (1941):394–404.

EISENMANN, E. "The Species of Middle American Birds." *Trans Linn. Soc. N.Y.,* 7 (1955). See also *Proc. Linn. Soc. N.Y.* 66–70 (1958) Corrigenda, unpaged.

FRIEDMANN, H. "Birds Collected by the National Geographic Society's Expeditions to Northern Brazil and

Southern Venezuela," *Proc. U.S. Natl. Mus.*, 97 (1948):373–569.

FRIEDMANN, H. and SMITH, FOSTER D., JR. "A Contribution to the Ornithology of Northeastern Venezuela," *Proc. U.S. Natl. Mus.*, 100 (1950):411–538.

GOODALL, J. D., JOHNSON, A. W., and PHILIPPI, R. A. *Las Aves de Chile*. Buenos Aires: Platt Establecimientos Gráficos S.A., 1951.

HOUSSE, E. "Les Oiseaux de Proie du Chili," *Ann. Sci. Nat. Paris*, 3 (1941):1–161.

JUNGE, G. C. A. and MEES, G. F. "The Avifauna of Trinidad and Tobago," *Zool. Verhandl.*, 37 (1958):1–172.

MARSHALL, JOE T. "Additional Information Concerning the Birds of El Salvador," *Condor*, 45 (1943):23–26.

MITCHELL, M. H. *Observations on the Birds of Southeastern Brazil*. Toronto: University of Toronto Press, 1957.

SKUTCH, ALEXANDER F. *Life Histories of Central American Birds*. Part I—Berkeley, Calif.: Cooper Ornithological Society, 1954, 1960.

WETMORE, ALEXANDER. "Observations on the Birds of Argentina, Paraguay, Uruguay, and Chile," *Bull. U.S. Natl. Mus.*, 133 (1926).

———. "Observations on the Birds of Northern Venezuela," *Proc. U.S. Natl. Mus.*, 87 (1939).

Eurasia

AUSTIN, OLIVER L., JR. "The Birds of Korea," *Bull. Mus. Comp. Zool.*, 101, No. 1 (1948).

AUSTIN, OLIVER L., JR. and KURODA, N. "The Birds of Japan, Their Status and Distribution," *Bull. Mus. Comp. Zool.*, 109 (1953):277–639.

BANNERMAN, DAVID A. and W. MARY. *Birds of Cyprus*. London: Oliver and Boyd, 1958.

BEHRENDS, O. "The Routes of Birds of Prey on Their Spring Migration Over the Island of Als (Denmark)," *Dansk. Orn. Foren. Tidsskr.*, 42 (1949):11–24.

CALDWELL, HARRY R. and JOHN C. *South China Birds*. Shanghai: Hester May Vanderburgh, 1931.

DEMENTIEV, G. P., and GLADKOV, N. A. *The Birds of the Soviet Union*. Moscow: Sovietskaya Nauka, 1951–1954.

GOETHE, F. and KUHK, R. "Beringungs-Ergebnisse in deutschen Adlern, Weihen, Milanen und Wespenbussarden," *Vogelwarte*, 16 (1951):69–76.

———. "Beringungs-Ergebnisse in deutschen Wanderfalken (*F. peregrinus*) und Baumfalken (*F. subbuteo*)," *Vogelwarte*, 16 (1952):104–108.

GOODWIN, D. "Notes on the Migration of Birds of Prey Over Suez," *Ibis*, 91 (1949):59–63.

HARTERT, E. *Die Vogel der paläarktischen Fauna*, Vol. 2. Berlin: R. Friedländer & Sohn, 1912–1921.

HEINROTH, O. and M. *Die Vögel Mitteleuropas*. 3 Vols. Berlin: H. Bermühler, 1924–28.

HOLSTEIN, V. "The Autumn Migration of the Birds of Prey at Jaegerspris (Zealand) during twelve years, 1934–1945," *Dansk. Orn. Foren. Tidsskr.*, 40 (1946): 161–188.

LATOUCHE, J. D. D. *A Handbook of the Birds of Eastern China*, Vol. 2. London: Taylor and Francis, 1931–1934.

MEINERTZHAGEN, R. *Birds of Arabia*. London: Oliver and Boyd. 1954.

OSMOLOVSKAYA, V. I., and FORMOZOV, A. N. "Methods of Calculating the Number and Geographical Distribution of Diurnal and Nocturnal Birds of Prey," *St. Peters. Acad. Imp. Sci. Inst. Geogr.* (1952):68–96.

PARKER, E. *Predatory Birds of Great Britain*. London: Br. Field Sports Soc., Vol. 8, 1949.

PETERSON, R. T., MOUNTFORT, G. and HOLLOM, P. A. D. *A Field Guide to the Birds of Britain and Europe*. Boston: Houghton Mifflin, 1954.

POULDING, R. H. "Migration Automnale de Rapaces en Auvergne," *Oiseau*, 20 (1950):152.

PYMAN, G. A. "Autumn Raptor Migration in the Eastern Mediterranean," *Ibis*, 95 (1953):550.

SCHÄFER, E. "Ornithologische Ergebnisse Zweier Forschungsreisen nach Tibet," *J. für Orn.* (1938):146–66, 169–72.

VAURIE, CHARLES. "Systematic Notes on Palearctic Birds No. 43, Strigidae: The Genera *Otus, Aegolius, Ninox and Tyto*," *Amer. Mus. Nov.*, 2021 (1960).

———. *The Birds of the Palearctic Fauna, Non Passeriformes*. London: H. F. and G. Witherby, Ltd., 1964.

VOOUS, K. H. *Atlas of European Birds*. London: Nelson (1960).

WITHERBY, H. F. *et al.*, *Handbook of British Birds*, Vols. II, III. London: H. F. & G. Witherby, Ltd., 1947.

Africa

AMADON, DEAN and BASILIO, A. "Notes on the Birds of Fernando Po Island, Spanish Equatorial Africa," *Amer. Mus. Nov.*, 1846 (1957):1–8.

BANNERMAN, DAVID A. *The Birds of West and Equatorial Africa*, Vol. I. London: Oliver and Boyd, 1953.

BROWN, LESLIE H. *Eagles*. London: Michael-Joseph, 1955.

CHAPIN, JAMES P. "The Birds of the Belgian Congo," *Bull. Amer. Mus. Nat. Hist.*, Part I, Vol. 65 (1932) and Part II, Vol. 75 (1939).

MACKWORTH-PRAED, C. W. and GRANT, C. H. B. *African Handbook of Birds, Birds of Eastern and Northeastern Africa*, Vol. I, 2nd Ed. London: Longmans, Green & Co., 1957.

———. *African Handbook of Birds, Southern Third of Africa*, Vol. I. London: Longmans, Green and Co., 1962.

MARCHANT, S. "Some Birds of the Owerri Province, S. Nigeria," *Ibis*, Fourteenth Ser., Vol. 6 (1942):143–47.

MEINERTZHAGEN, R. *Nicoll's Birds of Egypt*, Vol. I. London: Hugh Rees, Ltd., 1930.

———. *Pirates and Predators.* London: Oliver and Boyd, 1959.

NORTH, M. E. W. "Field Notes on Certain Raptorials and Water Birds in Kenya Colony," *Ibis,* Fourteenth Ser., 3 (1939):487–507.

PAKENHAM, R. H. W. "Field Notes on the Birds of Zanzibar and Pemba," *Ibis,* 85 (1943):171–72.

RAND, A. L. "The Distribution and Habits of Madagascar Birds," *Bull. Amer. Mus. Nat. Hist.* 72, Art. 5 (1936).

ROBERTS, AUSTIN. *The Birds of South Africa,* 2nd Ed. London: Witherby, Ltd., 1957.

SERLE, W. "Field Observations on Some Northern Nigerian Birds," *Ibis,* Fourteenth Ser., Vol. III (1939): 659–64.

VAN SOMEREN, G. L. "Days with Birds," *Fieldiana: Zool.,* 38 (1956):25–112, 200.

WILLIAMS, J. G. "The Identification of Kenya Birds of Prey in Flight, Part I, Vultures," *J.E. Afr. Ug. Nat. Hist. Soc.,* 22–3 (1954):78–79.

South-East Asia and Australian Region

ALI, SÁLIM. *The Book of Indian Birds,* 4th Ed. Bombay: Bombay Nat. Hist. Soc., 1946.

———. *Indian Hill Birds.* Oxford, England: Oxford University Press, 1949.

———. *The Birds of Travancore and Cochin.* Oxford, England: Oxford University Press, 1953.

BAKER, E. C. S. *Fauna of British India: Birds,* Vols. 5, 7. London: Taylor and Francis, 1928, 1930.

———. *The Nidification of Birds of the Indian Empire,* Vol. 3. London: Taylor and Francis, 1932–35.

BERULDSEN, G. "Hawks of York Peninsula," *S. Aust. Orn.,* 22 (1956):23–5.

CONDON, H. T., and AMADON, DEAN. "Taxonomic Notes on Australian Hawks," *Rec. Australian Mus.,* 11, No. 2 (1954).

DELACOUR, J. and MAYR, E. *Birds of the Philippines.* New York: The Macmillan Co., 1946.

———. *Birds of Malaysia.* New York: The Macmillan Co., 1947.

DEWAR, DOUGLAS. *Glimpses of Indian Birds.* London: John Lane, 1913.

LOWTHER, E. H. N. "Notes on Some Indian Birds: Eagles, Owls and Vultures," *J. Bombay Nat. Hist. Soc.,* 45 (1944):5–16.

MAYR, E. *Birds of the Southwest Pacific.* The Macmillan Co., 1945.

MAYR, E., and GILLIARD, E. T. "Birds of Central New Guinea," *Bull. Amer. Mus. Nat. Hist.,* 103 (1954): 311–74.

MUNRO, G. C. *Birds of Hawaii.* Honolulu: Tongg Pub. Co., 1944.

OLIVER, W. R. B. *New Zealand Birds,* 2nd ed. New Zealand: A. H. and A. W. Reed, 1955.

RIPLEY, S. D., II. *A Synopsis of the Birds of India and Pakistan.* Bombay: Bombay Nat. Hist. Soc., 1961.

SERVENTY, D. L., and WHITTELL, H. M. *Birds of Western Australia,* 3rd Ed. Perth, W.A.: Paterson Brokensha Pty. Ltd., 1962.

SMYTHIES, BERTRAM, E. *The Birds of Borneo.* London: Oliver and Boyd, 1960.

VAN MARLE, J. G., and VOOUS, K. H., JR. "The Endemic Sparrow Hawks of Celebes," *Limosa,* 19 (1946): 15–23.

Species References *(Hawk-like Birds)*—Additional Scientific Publications

Accipiter

A. CASTANILIUS

AMADON, DEAN. "Avian Systematics and Evolution in the Gulf of Guinea," *Bull. Amer. Mus.,* 100 (1953):410.

A. CIRRHOCEPHALUS

SYMON, O. S. "A Sparrow-Hawk's Breakfast," *S. Aust. Orn.,* 18 (1948):74.

A. COOPERI

MENG, HEINZ. "Food Habits of Nesting Cooper's Hawks and Goshawks in New York and Pennsylvania," *Wils. Bull.,* 71 (1959):169–74.

A. GENTILIS

GLADKOV, N. A. "Taxonomy of Palaearctic Goshawks," *Auk,* 58 (1941):80–90.

MENG, HEINZ. "Food Habits of Nesting Cooper's Hawks and Goshawks in New York and Pennsylvania," *Wils. Bull.,* 71 (1959):169–74.

A. NISUS

KLAAS, C. "Aus dem Leben eines Frankfurter Sperber-Paares," *Natur. u. Volk,* 73 (1943):260–67.

A. NOVAEHOLLANDIAE

MAYR, E. "Notes on Birds of Northern Melanesia," *Amer. Mus. Nov.,* 1294 (1945):4–12.

RAND, A. L. "Results of the Archbold Expedition. No. 44, Some Notes on Bird Behavior," *Bull. Amer. Mus.,* 79 (1942):432.

SOUTHERN, H. N. and SERVENTY, D. L. "The Two Phases of *Astur* [*Accipiter*] *novaehollandiae,*" *Emu,* 46 (1947):331–47.

A. POLIOGASTER

PARTRIDGE, WILLIAM H. "*Accipiter pectoralis,* a Synonym of *Accipiter poliogaster,*" *Condor,* 63 (1961):505–06.

A. STRIATUS

STORER, ROBERT W. "Variation in the Resident Sharp-shinned Hawks of Mexico," *Condor,* 54 (1952):283–89.

A. TACHIRO

AMADON, DEAN. "Avian Systematics and Evolution

in the Gulf of Guinea," *Bull. Amer. Mus.*, 100 (1953):408–09.

Aegypius

A. MONACHUS

DE. REUVER, H. J. A. [and others]. "Dutch Bird Notes," *Ardea*, 43 (1955):175–83.

Aquila

A. AUDAX

CORKE, DAVID. "Photographing the Wedge-tailed Eagle," *Walkabout*, (May 1st, 1956):15–18.

A. CHRYSAETOS

ARNOLD, L. W. "The Golden Eagle," *Circ. U.S. Fish and Wildlife Serv.*, 27 (1954):1–35.

BROWN, LESLIE H. and WATSON, A. "The Golden Eagle in Relation to Its Food Supply," *Ibis*, 106 (1964):78–100.

GORDON, SETON. *The Golden Eagle*. New York: Citadel, 1955.

JOLLIE, M. "Plumage Changes in the Golden Eagle," *Auk*, 64 (1947):549–76.

LOCKE, J. D. and RATCLIFFE, D. A. "Insecticides and Scottish Golden Eagles," *British Birds*, 57 (1964):89–102.

A. CLANGA

EATES, K. R. "The Distribution and Nidification of the Greater Spotted Eagle in Sind," *J. Bombay Nat. Hist. Soc.*, 39 (1937):403–05.

MOLTONI, D. EDGARDO. "L'alimentazione dell'Aquila anatraia (*Aquila clanga*)," *Riv. Ital. Orn.*, 13 (1943):97–100.

A. POMARINA

WENDLAND, VICTOR. "Der Schreiadler," *Der Falke*, 5 (1958):6–13.

A. VERREAUXII

ROWE, E. G. "The Breeding Biology of Aquila verreauxii," *Ibis*, 89 (1947):387–410; 576–606.

Aviceda

INGLIS, C. M. "The Bazas of the Darjeeling District, Sikkim and the Duars," *J. Bengal Nat. Hist. Soc.*, 14 (1940):83–88.

A. JERDONI

PHILLIPS, W. W. A. "Legge's Baza," *Loris*, 5 (1950):189–93.

A. SUBCRISTATA

MAYR, E. "Notes on Birds of Northern Melanesia," *Amer. Mus. Nov.*, 1294 (1945):4–12.

Buteo

B. ALBICAUDATUS

STEVENSON, J. O., and MEITZEN, L. H. "Behavior and Food Habits of Sennett's White-tailed Hawk," *Wils. Bull.*, 58 (1946):198–203.

B. ALBIGULA

STRESEMANN, E. "*Buteo albigula, Philippi,* ein in Südamerika Weit Verbreiteter Bussard," *J. für Orn.*, 100 (1959):337–40.

B. BRACHYURUS

MOORE, J. C., STIMSON, L. A., and ROBERTSON, W. B., "Observations of the Short-tailed Hawk in Florida," *Auk*, 70 (1953):470–78.

RAND, A. L. "Races of the Short-tailed Hawk, *Buteo brachyurus*," *Auk*, 77 (1960):448–59.

B. BUTEO

TABOR, T. "The Influence of Temperature and Activity on the Rough-legged and Common Buzzard," *Folio Biol.*, 4 (1956):327–30.

B. HARLANI

WOOD, N. A. "Harlan's Hawk," *Wils. Bull.*, 44 (1932):78–87.

B. NITIDA

AMADON, DEAN, and PHILLIPS, A. R. "Notes on the Mexican Goshawk," *Auk*, 56 (1939):183–84.

B. OREOPHILUS

COURTNEY-LATIMER, M. "Breeding of the Mountain Buzzard," *Ostrich*, 12 (1941):20–23.

B. POLYOSOMA

VAURIE, CHARLES. "A Systematic Study of the Red-Backed Hawks of South America," *Condor*, 64 (1962):277–90.

B. REGALIS

SALT, W. R. "Notes on Recoveries of Banded Ferruginous Rough-legged Hawks," *Bird Banding*, 10 (1939):80–84.

B. RUFOFUSCUS

NORGARB, C., and LASBERY, J. "Jackal Buzzards," *Ostrich*, 24 (1953):33–36.

Cathartes

C. AURA

MEHNER, J. F. "Turkey Vultures Attacking Great Blue Heron," *Wils. Bull.*, 64 (1952):242.

C. MELAMBROTUS

WETMORE, ALEXANDER. "A Revision of the American Vultures of the Genus Cathartes," *Smithson. Misc. Coll.*, 146, No. 6 (1964):15–17.

Circaetus

C. GALLICUS

BOUDOINT, Y. "Le Vol du Circaete Jean Le Blanc, Plus Particulièrement dans le Massif Central," *Alauda*, 19 (1951):1–18.

BOUILLAULT, J. and FILAUX, J. C. "Un Mangeur Exclusif de Reptiles, Le Circaete," *Nature Paris*, 3250 (1956):60–62.

Circus

C. AERUGINOSUS

SHARKLAND, M. "The Swamp Harrier as a Migrant," *Emu*, 58 (1958):75–80.

SOPER, M .F. "The Nesting of the Harrier," *Notornis,* 7 (1957):182–84.

WATSON, J. S. "Recovery of Ringed Harriers," *Notornis,* 6 (1954):6–10.

WODZICKI, K. "Display of the Harrier," *New Zealand Bird Notes,* 3 (1949):174.

C. CINEREUS
AMADON, DEAN. "Relationships of the Cinereous Harrier," *Auk,* 78 (1961):256–57.

C. MACROURUS
LUNDEVALL, C. F. and ROSENBERG, E. "Some Aspects of the Behavior and Breeding Biology of the Pallid Harrier," *Internat. Orn. Congr.,* 11 (1954): 599–603.

Coragyps

C. ATRATUS
BROADKORB, PIERCE. "Geographical Variations in the Black Vulture," *Pap. Mich. Acad. Sci.,* 29 (1944): 115–21.

C. ATRATUS
LOVELL, A. B. "Black Vulture Depredations at Kentucky Woodlands," *Wils. Bull.,* 64 (1952):48.

Daptrius

D. AMERICANUS
SKUTCH, ALEXANDER F. "Red-throated Caracara, the Scourge of the Wasps," *Animal Kingdom,* 62 (1959):8–13.

Elanus

PARKES, KENNETH, C. "Specific Relationships in the Genus *Elanus,*" *Condor,* 60 (1958):139–40.

PLOTNICK, R. "Affinidad entre los Generos *Elanus* y *Gampsonyx,*" *Rev. Invest. Agric.,* 10 (1956):313–15.

E. CAERULEUS
GREEN, C. "The Black Shouldered Kite in Masira (Oman)," *Ibis,* 91 (1949):459–64.

E. LEUCURUS
MOORE, ROBERT, and BARR, ARTHUR. "Habits of the White-tailed Kite," *Auk,* 58 (1941):461.

WATSON, F. G. "A Behavior Study of the White-tailed Kite," *Condor,* 42 (1940):295–304.

E. NOTATUS
WHITTELL, H. M. "Black Shouldered Kite in Western Australia," *Emu,* 43 (1944):294–96.

Erythrotriorchis

E. RADIATUS
LORD, E. A. R. "Field Notes on the Red Goshawks," *Emu,* 52 (1952):23–24.

Falco

F. ALBIGULARIS
BEEBE, WILLIAM. "Home Life of the Bat Falcon," *Zoologica,* 35 (1950):69–86.

F. BERIGORA
CONDON, H. T. "Variation in the Brown Hawk," *Emu,* 50 (1951):152–74.

F. COLUMBARIUS
BOND, R. M. "Pigeon Hawk Catching Dragonflies," *Condor,* 53 (1951):256.

F. DICKINSONI
ROBERTS, AUSTIN. "The Birds of South Africa," *Ostrich,* 13 (1942):169–72.

F. ELEONORAE
VAUGHAN, R. *"Falco eleonorae," Ibis,* 103 (1961): 114–28.

F. FASCIINUCHA
BENSON, C. W., and SMITHERS, R. H. N. "The Teita Falcon at Victoria Falls," *Ostrich,* 29 (1958):57–58.

F. LONGIPENNIS
LORD, E. A. R. "The Little Falcon," *Emu,* 48 (1948):164–66.

F. MEXICANUS
MUNRO, D. A. "Prairie Falcon 'Playing,'" *Auk,* 71 (1954):333.

WEBSTER, HAROLD M., JR. "A Survey of the Prairie Falcon in Colorado," *Auk,* 61 (1944):609–16.

F. PELEGRINOIDES
VAURIE, CHARLES. "Systematic Notes on Palearctic Birds, No. 44, Falconidae: The Genus *Falco* (Part I, *Falco peregrinus* and *Falco pelegrinoides*)," *Amer. Mus. Nov.,* 2035 (1961):1–19.

F. PEREGRINUS
CADE, TOM. "A Study of the Peregrine and Gyrfalcon in Alaska," *Univ. Calif. Publ. Zool.,* 63 (1960): 151–290.

FERGUSON-LEES, I. J. "The Rare Birds of Prey, Their Present Status in the British Isles: Peregrine," *British Birds,* 50 (1957):149–55.

GULLION, G. W. "Duck Hawk Predation upon Ring-necked Pheasants," *Condor,* 49 (1947):209.

HYDE, A. S. "The Perceptive Powers of the Duck Hawk," *Condor,* 55 (1953):277.

RATCLIFFE, D. A. "The Status of the Peregrine in Great Britain," *Bird Study,* 10 (1963):56–90.

SPRUNT, ALEXANDER, JR. "Aerial Feeding of the Duck Hawk," *Auk,* 68 (1951):372.

F. RUSTICOLUS
TODD, W. E. C., and FRIEDMANN, H. "A Study of the Gyrfalcons with Particular Reference to North America," *Wils. Bull.,* 59 (1947):143–44.

WAYNE, PHILIP and JOLLY, G. F. "Notes on the Breeding of the Iceland Gyrfalcon," *Brit. Birds,* 51 (1958):285–90.

F. SEVERUS
MAYR, E. "Notes on Bifds of Northern Melanesia," *Amer. Mus. Nov.,* 1294 (1945):4–12.

F. SUBNIGER

Austin, Claude N. "The Black Falcon and Some Other Raptors in Southwest Australia," *Emu,* 53 (1953):77–80.

Shanks, Donald. "Hawks Unusual to the Southwest of Victoria," *Emu,* 52 (1952):102–04.

F. TINNUNCULUS

Davis, T. A. W. "Kestrel Pellets at a Winter Roost," *Brit. Birds,* 53 (1960):281–85.

Ecke, H. "Vanderwege Schlesischer Turmfalken (*Falco tinnunculus tinnunculus*)," *Ber. Ver. Schles. Orn.,* 23 (1938):27–31.

F. VESPERTINUS

Benson, C. W. "A Roosting Site of the Eastern Red-footed Falcon, *Falco amurensis,*" *Ibis,* 93 (1951): 467–68.

Horváth, L. "The Life of the Red-legged Falcon (*Falco vespertinus*) in the Ohat Forest," *Int. Orn. Congr.,* 11 (1954):583–87.

von Transehe, N. and Schiiz, E. "Massendurchzug des Rotfuss Falken (*Falco vespertinus*) in Spätsommer 1939," *Vogelzug,* 11 (1940):31–55.

Gampsonyx

G. SWAINSONII

Friedmann, H. and Smith, Foster D., Jr. "A Contribution to the Ornithology of Northeastern Venezuela," *U.S. Natl. Mus.,* 100 (1950):444–45.

Plotnick, R. "Afinidad entre los Generos *Elanus* y *Gampsonyx,*" *Rev. Invest. Agric.,* 10 (1956):313–15.

Stresemann, V. "Wing Molt and the Systematic Position of the Genus *Gampsonyx,*" *Auk.,* 76 (1959):360.

Geranospiza

G. NIGRA

Sutton, G. M. "The Blackish Crane Hawk," *Wils. Bull.,* 66 (1954):237–42.

Gymnogenys

G. TYPICUS

Davies, J. J. L. "Some Observations on the South African Harrier Hawk, *Polyboroides typus,*" *Ostrich,* 22 (1951):39.

Gymnogyps

G. CALIFORNIANUS

Koford, Carl B. *The California Condor.* New York: National Audubon Society, 1953.

Gypaetus

G. BARBATUS

Ferguson-Lees, I. J. "The Lammergeier," *British Birds,* 53 (1960):25–29.

Fleming, R. L. "Bone-dropping Habit of the Lammergeier," *J. Bombay Nat. Hist. Soc.,* 53 (1955): 953.

G. BARBATUS

Lowther, E. H. N. "The Lammergeier," *J. Bombay Nat. Hist. Soc.,* 46 (1946):501–08.

Stegman, B. "Zur Brutbiologie des Bartgeiers (*Gypaetus barbaetus*) im Tjan Schan. *J. für. Orn.,* (1961):68–74.

Gypohierax

G. ANGOLENSIS

Austen, W. M. "Palm-nut Vultures in Raphia Palms at Mtunzini, Zululand," *Ostrich,* 24 (1953):98–102.

Gyps

G. FULVUS

Valverde, José A. "Moyens d'Expression et Hiérarchie Sociale chez le Vautour Fauve," *Alauda,* 27 (1959):1–15.

Haliaetus

H. LEUCOCEPHALUS

Barnes, I. R. "Persecution or Freedom," *Audubon Magazine,* 53 (1951):282–89.

Broley, C. L. "Migration and Nesting of Florida Bald Eagles," *Wils. Bull.,* 59 (1947):3–20.

Crandall, L. S. "Notes on Plumage Changes in the Bald Eagle," *Zoologica,* 26 (1941)7–8.

Imler, Ralph H., and Kalmbach, E. R. "The Bald Eagle and Its Economic Status," *U.S. Fish and Wildlife Service,* Circular 30 (1955).

H. LEUCOGASTER

Favaloro, Norman. "The White-breasted Sea-Eagle along the Murray Valley," *Emu,* 43 (1944): 233–42.

Green, R. H. "A Tasmanian Nesting Note on the White-breasted Sea Eagle," *Emu,* 59 (1959):215–22.

Somanader, S. V. O. "Ceylon's White-bellied Sea Eagle," *Loris,* 1 (1939):356–59.

H. LEUCORYPHUS

Lewis, N. A. S. "Pallas' Fishing Eagle (*Haliaetus leucoryphus*) Photographed at the Nest, Khulna, 1938–39," *J. Bengal Nat. Hist. Soc.,* 15 (1941): 109–19.

H. PELAGICUS

Belopolski, L. "Age Variations in the Plumage of Steller's Sea Eagle," *Arch. Mus. Zool. Moscou,* 15 (1939):127–34.

Steinbacher, Joachim. "Die Geschichte eines Seeadlers," *Natur und Volk,* 80 (1950):41–44.

Haliastur

H. INDUS

Somanader, S. V. O. "The Brahminy Kite and Its Ways," *Loris,* 2 (1942):316–20.

H. SPHENURUS

Brown, R. F. "Whistling Eagles in Western Bass Strait," *S. Aust. Orn.,* 21 (1955):52.

Hamirostra

H. MELANOSTERNON

STRESEMANN, E. "Der Australische Buzzard Zertrummert Eier durch Steinwurf," *J. für Orn.*, 96 (1955): 215.

Harpagus

AMADON, DEAN. "Relationships of the Falconiform Genus *Harpagus*," *Condor*, 63 (1961):178–79.

H. BIDENTATUS

LAUGHLIN, R. M. "A Nesting of the Double-toothed Kite in Panama," *Condor*, 54 (1952):137–39.

Harpia

H. HARPYJA

FOWLER, JAMES M., and COPE, JAMES B. "Notes on the Harpy Eagle in British Guiana," *Auk*, 81 (1964):257–273.

Harpyhaliaetus

AMADON, DEAN. "Notes on *Harpyhaliaetus*," *Auk*, 66 (1949):53–56.

Herpetotheres

H. CACHINNANS

MARCHANT, S. "The Breeding of Some Southwest Ecuadorian Birds," *Ibis*, 102 (1960):362.

SKUTCH, ALEXANDER F. "The Laughing Reptile Hunter of Tropical America," *Animal Kingdom*, 43 (May-June, 1960):115–19.

WOLFE, L. R. "Nest of the Laughing Falcon," *Condor*, 56 (1954):161.

Heterospizias

H. MERIDIONALIS

FRIEDMANN, H., and SMITH, FOSTER D., JR. "A Contribution to the Ornithology of Northeastern Venezuela," *Proc. U.S. Natl. Mus.*, 100 (1950):411–538.

WETMORE, A. "Observations on the Birds of Argentina, Paraguay, Uruguay, and Chile," *Bull. U.S. Nat. Mus.*, 133 (1926):113–15.

Hieraetus

H. FASCIATUS

RIVOIRE, A., and HUE, F. "L'Aigle de Bonelli," *Oiseau*, 19 (1949):118–49.

H. MORPHNOIDES

CALABY, J. H. "Notes on the Little Eagle," *Emu*, 51 (1951):33–65.

H. PENNATUS

LABITTE, ANDRÉ. "Reproduction de l'Aigle Botte dans le Département de 'a Haute-Marne en 1955," *Alauda*, 23:249–53.

Icthyophaga

I. ICTHYAETUS

LEWIS, W. A. S. "A Note on the White-bellied Sea Eagle and the Large Grey-headed Fishing Eagle," *J. Bengal Nat. Hist. Soc.* 21 (1946):3–6.

Ictinia

SUTTON, G. M. "The Kites of the Genus *Ictinia*," *Wils. Bull.*, 56 (1944):3–6.

I. MISISIPPIENSIS

SUTTON, G. M. "The Mississippi Kite in Spring," *Condor*, 41 (1939):41–53.

I. PLUMBEA

SKUTCH, A. F. "A Nesting of the Plumbeous Kite in Ecuador," *Condor*, 49 (1947):25–31.

Lophaetus

L. OCCIPITALIS

ASTLEY-MABERLEY, C. T. "Notes on the Birds of Northeastern Transvaal," *Ostrich*, 8 (1937):14.

Machaeramphus

M. ALCINUS

BARTELS, H. "Observations on the Bird, the Nest and the Egg," *Limosa*, 25 (1952):93–100.

Melierax

M. METABATES

CLANCEY, P. L. "On the Range of Mechow's Chanting Goshawk in Southeast Africa," *Ostrich*, 26 (1955):164–65.

M. MUSICUS

WHITE, C. M. N. [and others] "Systematic Notes on South African Birds," *Ostrich*, 23 (1952):43–55, 62–64.

Micrastur

M. PLUMBEUS

LEHMANN, F. C. "Hallazgo di *Micrastur plumbeus* en Colombia," *Caldasia*, 3 (1944):225–28.

Milvus

SCHNURRE, O. "Über Einige Strittige Fragen aus dem Leben der Beiden Milanarten," *Vogelvelt*, 77 (1956):65–74.

M. MIGRANS

LUNDBERG, S. "Breeding Records of *Milvus migrans* and *Strix nebulosa* from Northern Sweden," *Vår Fågelv.*, 14 (1955):224–30.

Morphnus

LEHMANN, F. C. "El Genero *Morphnus* [A Review of the Genus *Morphnus*]," *Caldasia*, 2 (1943):165–79.

Oroaetus

O. ISIDORI

AMADON, DEAN. "What Is *Spizaetus devillei?*" *Auk,* 67 (1950):235–36.

LEHMANN, F. C. "Neuvas Observaciones Sobre *Oroaetus isidori* (*Des Murs*)," *Novedades Colombianas,* 1 (Sept. 1, 1959):169–95.

Pandion

P. HALIAEETUS

AMES, PETER L. "A Preliminary Report on a Colony of Ospreys," *Atlantic Naturalist,* (Oct.–Dec., 1961): 26–33.

Pernis

P. APIVORUS

STRESEMANN, E. "Zur Kenntnis de Wespenbussarde," *Arch. Naturgesche,* 9 (1940):137–93.

P. PTILORHYNCUS

PHILLIPS, W. W. A. "The Status and Habits in Ceylon of the Crested Honey Buzzard," *Loris,* 4 (1948):425–29.

VAURIE, CHARLES, and AMADON, DEAN. "Notes on the Honey Buzzards of Eastern Asia," *Amer. Mus. Nov.,* 2111 (1962).

Phalcoboenus

P. MEGALOPTERUS

HOUSSE, P. R. "El Tiuque Cordillerano, *Phalcobenus megalopterus,*" *Rev. Chil. Nat. Hist.,* 41 (1937): 131–34.

Polemaetus

P. BELLICOSUS

SIMPSON, J. M. "A Visit to a Martial Eagle's Nest," *Ostrich,* 9 (1938):101–04.

Rostrhamus

R. HAMATUS

HAVERSCHMIDT, F. "Notes on *Helicolestes hamatus* in Surinam," *Auk,* 76 (1959):32–36.

R. SOCIABILIS

BARBOUR, T. "Birds of Cuba," *Mem. Nuttall Ornith. Club,* No. IV (1923):48.

Sagittarius

S. SERPENTARIUS

KNIGHT, C. W. R. "Snake Killer of Africa," *Nat. Hist.,* 47 (1941):265–67.

Spilornis

S. CHEELA

STRESEMANN, E. "Die Gliederung der Schlangenadler —Gattung *Spilornis,*" *Vjschr. Naturf. Ges.,* 104 (1959):208–13.

Spizaetus

AMADON, DEAN. "Remarks on the Asiatic Hawk-eagles of the Genus Spizaetus," *Ibis,* 95 (1953):492–500.

S. NIPALENSIS

SPITTEL, R. L. "The Devil Bird," *Loris,* 6 (1953): 90–96.

S. ORNATUS

SUTTON, G. M. and PETTINGILL, OLIN S., JR. "Birds of the Gomez Farias Region, Southwest Tamaulipas," *Auk,* 59 (1942):9.

Spizastur

S. MELANOLEUCUS

CARRIKER, M. A., JR. "An Annotated List of the Birds of Costa Rica, Including Cocos Island," *Ann. Carnegie Mus.,* 6 (1910):465.

Stephanoaetus

S. CORONATUS

BAYLY, P. N. and SPHERIS, N. "The Crowned Hawk-eagle, [Natal]," *Afr. Wild.,* 10 (June, 1956):115–19.

CHAPIN, JAMES P. "The Crowned Eagle, Ogre of Africa's Monkeys," *Natural History,* 25 (1925): 459–69.

HADDOW, A. J. "Field and Laboratory Studies on an African Monkey, *Cercopithecus ascanius schmidti,* (Including Notes on the Habits of Its Chief Predator, the Crowned Hawk-eagle)," *Proc. Zool. Soc. of London,* 122 (1952):370–72.

HOLCROFT, R. B. "The Crowned Hawk-eagle [South Africa]," *Afr. Wild.,* 5 (1951):107–09.

Terathopius

T. ECAUDATUS

MOREAU, R. E. "On the Bateleur, Especially at the Nest," *Ibis,* 87 (1945):224-49.

Vultur

V. GRYPHUS

HOUSSE, E. "El Condor (*Vultur gryphus Linne*)," *Bol. Mus. Hist. Nat.,* Lima, 3 (1940):233–42.

WIGGINS, I. L. "Observations of the South American Condor," *Condor,* 47 (1945):167–68.

Species Reference *(Owls)*

Aegolius

A. ACADICUS

AUSTING, G. R. "The Saw-whet Owl," *Nat. Hist.,* 66 (1957):154–58.

MILLER, A. H. "Notes on the Saw-whet Owl," *Condor,* 39 (1937):130–31.

MUMFORD, R. E. "Notes on Movements, Territory and Habitat of Wintering Saw-whet Owls," *Wils. Bull.,* 70 (1958):188–91.

A. FUNEREUS

KUHK, R. "Lautäusserungen und Jahreszeitliche Gesangstätigkeit des Rauhfusskauzes, *Aegolius funereus,*" *J. für Orn.*, 94 (1953):83–93.

———. "Ehemalige Bruten des Rauhfusskauses, *Aegolius funereus,* in Thüringen, Württenberg, und der Schweiz," *Beitr. Vogelk.*, 6 (1959):358–59.

Asio

A. CAPENSIS

ATTWOOD, L. and M. "March Owl Under Observation," *Afr. Wild Life,* 2 (1949):62–66.

A. FLAMMEUS

FISLER, G. F. "Changes in Food Habits of Short-eared Owls Feeding in a Salt Marsh," *Condor,* 62 (1960):486–87.

JOHNSTON, R. F. "Predation by Short-eared Owls on a Salicornia Marsh," *Wil. Bull.*, 68 (1956):91–102.

LOCKIE, J. D. "The Breeding Habits of Short-eared Owls after a Vole Plague," *Bird Study,* 2 (1955):53–69.

PITELKA, F. A., TOMICH, Q. F., and TREICHEL, G. E., "Breeding Behavior of Jaegers and Owls near Barrow, Alaska," *Condor,* 57 (1955):3–18.

URNER, C. A. "Notes on the Short-eared Owl," *Auk,* 40 (1923):31–36.

A. OTUS

ARMSTRONG, W. H. "Nesting and Food Habits of the Long-eared Owl in Miehigan," *Mich. St. Univ. Biol. Ser.*, 1 (1958):63–96.

GETZ, L. L. "Hunting Areas of the Long-eared Owl," *Wils. Bull.*, 73 (1961):79–82.

RÄBER, H. "Das Verkalten von Gefangener Waldohreulen (*Asio otus*) und Waldkauze (*Strix aluco*) zur Beute," *Behavior,* 2 (1949):1–95.

WENDLAND, V. "Ergänzende Feststellungen Über Brutbiologie und Verhalten der Waldohreule," *J. für Orn.*, 99 (1958):23–31.

A. STYGIUS

BOND, J. "Notes on the Devil Owl," *Auk,* 59 (1942):308–09.

Athene

VAURIE, CHARLES. "The Genus Athene," *Amer. Mus. Nov.*, 2015 (1960):1–21.

A. BRAMA

HALL, B. P. "Taxonomic Notes on the Spotted Owl," *Bull. Br. Orn. Cl.*, 77 (1957):44–46.

A. NOCTUA

HIBBERT-WARE, A. "Report of the Little Owl Enquiry, 1936–37," *Brit. Birds,* 31 (1938):249–64.

MARPLES, B. J. "A Study of The Little Owl (*Athene noctua*) in New Zealand," *Trans. Proc. Roy. Soc. N.Z.*, 72 (1942):237–52.

MAYKNECKE, J. "Farbensehen und Helligkeitsuntersheidung beim Steinkauz," *Ardea,* 30 (1941):129–74.

Bubo

VAURIE, CHARLES. "Systematic Notes on Palearctic Birds. No. 41, Strigidae: The Genus *Bubo,*" *Amer. Mus. Nov.*, 2000 (1960):1–13.

B. AFRICANUS

AURELIAN, F. "*Bubo africanus Temminck,*" *Zooleo.*, 37 (1957):231–34.

MURRAY, C. "An Unusual Item in the Diet of *Bubo africanus,*" *Ostrich,* 22 (1951):121.

B. BUBO

GUICHARD, G. "Notes sur la Biologie du Grand-duc, *Bubo bubo,*" *Oiseau,* 26 (1956):126–34.

LUND, H. M. K. "Eagle Owl (*Bubo bubo*) Breeding in 69° N. Lat. in Norway," *Dansk. Orn. Foren. Tidsskr.*, 49 (1955):12–15.

MÄRZ, R. "Neues Material zur Ernahrung des Uhus," *Vogelwelt,* 75 (1954):181–88.

MEBS, T. "Der Uhu (*Bubo bubo*) im Fränkischen Jura," *Anz. Orn. Ges.*, 4 (1953):67–69.

B. CAPENSIS

LEAKEY, L. S. B. "Mackinder's Owl, *Bubo capensis mackienderi,*" *J. E. Afr. Nat. Hist. Soc.*, 17 (1943):284.

B. LEUCOSTICTUS

JELLICOE, M. "The Akun Eagle Owl," Sierra Leone Studies, (1954):154–67.

B. VIRGINIANUS

GULLION, G. W. "Great Horned Owl Preys on Cooper's Hawk," *Condor,* 49 (1947):244.

BURNS, B. J. "Food of a Family of Great Horned Owls in Florida," *Auk,* 69 (1952):86–87.

CUNNINGHAM, J. D. "Food Habits of the Horned and Barn Owls," *Condor,* 62 (1960):222.

HOWARD, W. E. "Food Intake and Pellet Formation of a Horned Owl," *Wils. Bull.*, 70 (1958):145–50.

Ciccaba

C. HUHULA

PARTRIDGE, W. M. "Variaciones Geográficas en la Lechuza Negra, *Ciccaba huhula,*" *Hornero,* 10 (1956):143–46.

C. WOODFORDII

MARCHANT, S. "The West African Wood Owl," *Nigerian Field,* 13 (1948):16–20.

MARTIN, J. "Nest of South African Wood Owl," *Ostrich,* 27 (1956):149–50.

BLAKER, D. "Breeding of Wood Owl, *Ciccaba woodfordii,*" *Ostrich,* 30 (1959):139.

Glaucidium

G. BRASILIANUM

STILLWELL, JERRY AND NORMA. "Notes on the Call of a Ferruginous Pigmy Owl," *Wils. Bull.*, 66 (1954):152.

G. CUCULOIDES

RIPLEY, S. D. "Notes on Indian Birds," *Zoologica,* 33 (1948):199–202.

G. PASSERINUM

SCHÜZ, E. "Sperlingskauz als Zuggast am Kurischen Haff," *Orn. Montasb.*, 51 (1943):101–03.

LAFERRERE, M. "Chant Nocturne de la Chouette Chevêchette en Haute-Savoie," *Alauda,* 20 (1952): 181–88.

G. PERLATUM

RAND, A. L. "Geographical Variation in the Pearl-Spotted Owlet," *Nat. Hist. Misc.,* Chicago, 86 (1951):1–6.

G. SJOSTEDTI

SCHOUTENDEN, H. "Quelques Strigides Congolais," *Rev. Zool. Bot. Afr.* 47 (1953):400.

Micrathene

M. WHITNEYI

PHILLIPS, A. R. "Notes on the Migrations of the Elf and Flammulated Screech Owls," *Wils. Bull.,* 54 (1942):132–37.

WALKER, L. W. "Nocturnal Observations of Elf Owls," *Condor,* 45 (1943):165–67.

Ninox

N. CONNIVENS

FLEAY, D. "The Barking Owl Mystery," *Vict. Nat.,* 57 (1940):71–95.

———. "Barking Owl (Rather Than Winking Owl), Record of Nesting Habits," *Emu,* 42 (1942):25–30.

———. "The 'Screaming Woman' Identified," *Nat. Hist.,* 61 (1952):354–58.

N. NOVAESEELANDIAE

BRYANT, C. E. "Notes on Boobook Owl Nestlings," *Emu,* 41 (1941):97–100.

CUNNINGHAM, J. M. "Food of a Morepork," *N. Zeal. Bird Notes,* 1 (1948–49):22–24.

MAYR, E. "Ninox novaeseelandiae, Revision of Australasian Races," *Emu,* 43 (1943):12–16.

N. PHILIPPENSIS

MAYR, E. "The Races of Ninox philippensis," *Zoologica,* 30 (1945):46.

N. STRENUA

FLEAY, D. "Watching the Powerful Owl," *Emu,* 44 (1944):97–112.

LEARMOUTH, N. F. "Powerful Owls in Southwestern Victoria," *Emu,* 50 (1951):178.

Nyctea

N. SCANDIACA

CHITTY, D. and H. "Nyctea in Canada, Canadian Wildlife Enquiry, 1939–40," *J. Animal Ecol.,* 10 (1941):184–203.

GROSS, A. O. "Cyclic Invasions of the Snowy Owl and the Migration of 1945–1946," *Auk,* 64 (1947): 584–601.

PITELKA, F. A., TOMICH, Q. P., and TREICHEL, G. E. "Breeding Behavior of Jaegers and Owls near Barrow, Alaska," *Condor,* 57 (1955):3–18.

SHELFORD, V. E. "The Relation of Snowy Owl Migration to the Abundance of the Collared Lemming," *Auk,* 62 (1945):592–96.

SNYDER, L. L. "The Snowy Owl Migration of 1946–47," *Wils. Bull.,* 61 (1949):99–102.

WATSON, A. "The Behavior, Breeding and Food Ecology of the Snowy Owl, *Nyctea scandiaca,*" *Ibis,* 99 (1957):419–62.

Otus

MOORE, R. and PETERS, J. "The Genus Otus of Mexico and Central America," *Auk,* 56 (1939):38–56.

O. ASIO

KELSO, LEON. "The Post Juvenal Molt of the Northeastern Screech Owl," *Biological Leaflet,* No. 50 (August 10, 1950):1–3.

HRUBAUT, H. E. "An Analysis of the Color Phases of the Eastern Screech Owl, *Otus asio,* by the Gene Frequency Method," *Amer. Nat.,* 89 (1955):223–39.

MILLER, ALDEN H. "Geographical Variations of the Screech Owls of the Deserts of Western North America," *Condor,* 53 (1951):161–77.

O. BAKKAMOENA

DEIGNAN, H. G. "Review of *Otus bakkamoena* races," *Auk,* 67 (1950):189–201.

———. "A Trio of New Birds from Tropical Asia," *Proc. Biol. Soc. Wash.,* 70 (1957):43–44.

O. BECCARII

MAYR, E., and DE SCHAUENSEE, R. M. "Birds of the Island of Biak," *Proc. Acad. Nat. Sci. Phila.,* 91 (1939):1–37.

O. FLAMMEOLUS

MARSHALL, JOE T., JR. "Territorial Behavior of the Flammulated Screech Owl," *Condor,* 41 (1939):71–78.

MILLER, ALDEN H. "The Structural Basis of the Voice of the Flammulated Owl," *Auk,* 64 (1947): 133–35.

PHILLIPS, A. R. "Notes on the Migrations of the Elf and Flammulated Screech Owls," *Wils. Bull.,* 54 (1942):132–37.

O. LEUCOTIS

PRIEST, C. D. "The Southern White-faced Scops Owl," *Ostrich,* 10 (1939):51–53.

O. SCOPS

DELACOUR, J. "On the Species of *Otus scops,*" *Zoologica,* 26 (1941):133–42.

O. UMBRA

RICHMOND, CHARLES W. "Birds Collected by Dr. W. L. Abbott on the Coast and Islands of Northwest Sumatra," *Proc. U.S. Natl. Mus.,* 26 (1903): 494.

Phodilus

P. BADIUS

INGLIS, C. M. "The Northern Bay Owl," *J. Bengal Nat. Hist. Soc.,* 19 (1945):93–96.

P. PRIGOGINEI
SCHOUTENDEN, H. "Un Strigide Nouveau d'Afrique Noire," *Rev. Zool. Bot. Afr.*, 46 (1952):423–28.

Pulsatrix

KELSO, L. "A Study of the Spectacled Owls, Genus *Pulsatrix*," *Biol. Leaflet, No.* 33 (1946):1–13.

Rhinoptynx

R. CLAMATOR
HARTMAN, F. A. "A Nest of the Striped Horned Owl," *Condor*, 58 (1956):73.

Strix

S. ALUCO
GURSTON, D. "Little Owl as Prey of Tawny Owls," *Brit. Birds*, 41 (1948):388.

RÄBER, H. "Das Verkalten von Gefangener Waldohreulen (*Asio otus*) und Waldkauze (*Strix aluco*) zur Beute," *Behavior*, 2 (1949):1–95.

SOUTHERN, H. N. "Tawny Owls and Their Prey," *Ibis*, 96 (1954):384–410.

SOUTHERN, H. N. VAUGHAN, R., and MUIR, R. C. "The Behavior of Young Tawny Owls after Fledging," *Bird Study*, 1 (1954):101–10.

S. NEBULOSA
LUNDBERG, S. "Breeding Records of *Milvus migrans* and *Strix nebulosa* from Northern Sweden," *Vår Fågelv.*, 14 (1955):224–30.

S. OCCIDENTALIS
MARSHALL, JOE T. "Food and Habitat of Spotted Owl," *Condor*, 44 (1942):66–67.

S. RUFIPES
PHILIPPI, R. A. "Notas Ornithologicas," *Rev. Chil. Hist. Nat.*, 44 (1940):147–52.

S. VARIA
ROBERTSON, W. B. "Barred Owl Nesting on the Ground," *Auk*, 76 (1959):227–30.

Surnia

S. ULULA
EDBERG, R. "The Eruption of Hawk Owls in Northwestern Europe 1950–51," *Vår Fågelv.*, 14 (1955): 10–21.

HAGEN, Y. "Eruption of Hawk Owls in Fenoscandia 1950–51," *Sterna*, 24 (1956):1–22.

Tyto

T. ALBA
CUNNINGHAM, J. D. "Food Habits of the Horned and Barn Owls," *Condor*, 62 (1960):222.

EVANS, F. C., and EMLEN, J. T., JR. "Ecological Notes on the Prey Selected by a Barn Owl," *Condor*, 49 (1947):3–9.

GILLIARD, E. T. *"Tyto alba," Nat. Hist.*, 67 (1958): 239–45.

MOREJOHN, G. VICTOR. "Barn Owls with Two Broods of Young," *Auk*, 72 (1955):208.

PAYNE, ROGER A. and DRURY, WILLIAM H., JR. "Marksman of the Darkness," *Nat. Hist.*, 67 (1958): 316–23.

STEWART, P. A. "Dispersal, Breeding and Longevity of Banded Barn Owls in North America," *Auk*, 69 (1952):227–45.

T. CAPENSIS
AMADON, DEAN and JEWETT, STANLEY, G., JR. "Notes on Philippine Birds," *Auk*, 63 (1946):551–58.

T. NOVAEHOLLANDIAE
FLEAY, D. "The Tasmanian Masked Owl," *Emu*, 48 (1949):169–76.

HILL, L. H. "Notes on the Habits and Breeding of the Tasmanian Masked Owl," *Emu*, 55 (1955):203–10.

SKEMP, J. R. "Size and Colour Discrepancy in Tasmanian Masked Owls," *Emu*, 55 (1955):210–11.

T. SOUMAGNEI
ALLEN, G. M. and GREENWAY, JAMES C., JR. "A Specimen of *Tyto* (*Heliodilus*) *soumangii*," *Auk*, 52 (1935):414–17.

INDEX

Italic figures denote illustrations.